THE NORTON
INTRODUCTION TO
LITERATURE

Shorter Fourth Edition

Carl E. Bain
Jerome Beaty
J. Paul Hunter

THE NORTON
INTRODUCTION TO
LITERATURE

Shorter Fourth Edition

W · W · NORTON & COMPANY · NEW YORK · LONDON

Library of Congress Cataloging-in-Publication Data

The Norton introduction to literature.

Includes index.
1. Literature—Collections.   I. Bain, Carl E.
II. Beaty, Jerome, 1924-   .   III. Hunter J. Paul,
1934-
PN6014.N67   1986b   808.8   86-8407

ISBN 0-393-95532-X

W. W. Norton & Company, Inc., 500 Fifth Avenue, New York, N. Y. 10110
W. W. Norton & Company Ltd., 37 Great Russell Street, London WC1B 3NU

2 3 4 5 6 7 8 9 0

Contents

Foreword
Acknowledgments

FICTION

v

POETRY

6   FIGURATIVE LANGUAGE   434

Metaphor and Simile

Symbol

7   SOUND AND SIGHT   451

The Sounds of Poetry

8   STANZAS AND VERSE FORMS   470

POEMS FOR FURTHER READING   479

DRAMA

WRITING ABOUT LITERATURE

FOREWORD TO THE SHORTER FOURTH EDITION

This briefer version of *The Norton Introduction to Literature* offers in one handy volume a complete course in reading and writing about literature. Instructors teaching both literature and composition in a single term or those wanting to linger over a comparatively few works will, we hope, find here the brevity they seek without losing the richness they demand from a Norton anthology.

The Shorter Fourth Edition includes 30 stories, 8 of which are new; 172 poems, 48 of which are new; and 10 plays, 5 of which are new.

The drama section, especially, has been reinvigorated. New selections include Harold Pinter's sketch *The Black and White* and Anton Chekhov's one-act play *The Brute;* Arthur Miller's *Death of a Salesman;* Samuel Beckett's *Krapp's Last Tape;* and Marsha Norman's *Third and Oak: The Laundromat.*

In fiction, we have added William Faulkner's widely taught classics *A Rose for Emily* and *Barn Burning* as well as stories by Henry James, Bobbie Ann Mason, Guy de Maupassant, Katherine Anne Porter, Leo Tolstoy, and William Trevor.

The poetry section has been similarly infused with selections familiar and fresh, with newly included works by Margaret Atwood, Robert Creeley, Emily Dickinson, Alan Dugan, T. S. Eliot, Robert Frost, Thomas Hardy, Robert Hayden, Seamus Heaney, John Hollander, Gerard Manley Hopkins, Langston Hughes, Richard Hugo, Ben Jonson, Galway Kinnell, Philip Larkin, D. H. Lawrence, James Merrill, Marianne Moore, Ogden Nash, Howard Nemerov, Gabriel Okara, Sharon Olds, Dorothy Parker, Marge Piercy, Sylvia Plath, Theodore Roethke, William Shakespeare, Stephen Spender, William Stafford, Wallace Stevens, Alfred, Lord Tennyson, Dylan Thomas, Edward Thomas, Edmund Waller, Tom Wayman, Richard Wilbur, and William Carlos Williams.

But *The Norton Introduction to Literature* remains more than a grab-bag of good things to read. The works are not only selected but arranged in order to introduce a reader to the serious study of literature. Each genre is introduced by a chapter which treats the purpose and nature of the genre and the reading experience generally. This is followed by chapters concentrating on questions of craft, the so-called elements of fiction, poetry, and drama. There follows a group of works "for further reading," a reservoir of additional examples, for independent study or a different approach.

An extensive section called "Writing about Literature" deals both with the writing process as applied to literary works—choosing a topic, gathering evidence, developing an argument, and so forth—and with the varieties of a reader's written responses—from copying and paraphrase to analysis and interpretation: we explore not merely the *hows*, but the *whats* and *whys* as well.

Certain editorial procedures that proved their usefulness in earlier editions have been retained. First of all, the works are annotated, as is customary in Norton anthologies; the notes are informational and not interpretative, for the aim is to help readers understand and appreciate the work, not to dictate a meaning or a response. To offer the texts in the form most immediately available to their particular audience, we have normalized spelling according to modern American usage. In order to avoid giving the impression that all literature was written at the same time, we have noted for each selection the date of first book publication (or, when preceded by a *p*, first periodical publication).

In all our work on this edition we have been guided by teachers in other English departments and in our own, and by students who wrote us as the authors of the textbook they were using and by those who were able to approach us after class as their teachers: we hope that with such help we have been able to offer you a solid and stimulating introduction to the experience fo literature.

J.B., J.P.H.

ACKNOWLEDGMENTS

We would like to thank our teachers, for their example in the love of literature and in the art of sharing that love; our students, for their patience as we are learning from them to be better teachers of literature; our wives and children, for their understanding when the work of preparing this text made us seem less than perfectly loving husbands and fathers.

We would also like to thank our colleagues, many of whom have taught our book and evaluated our efforts, for their constant encouragement and enlightenment. Of our colleagues at Emory University, we would like especially to thank Michaelyn Burnette, Lore Metzger, Lee Pederson, Harry Rusche, Ronald Schuchard, Floyd C. Watkins, and Sally Wolff. And we thank also Paula R. Backscheider (University of Rochester); T. E. Blom (University of British Columbia); Patricia Brocker; Thomas R. Carper (University of Maine); Frank W. Childrey (Northwest Mississippi Junior College); Randy R. Conine (El Centro College); Michael P. Dean (University of Mississippi); Stephen F. Evans (University of Kansas); Norman Feltes (York University); Lila F. Fink (Pepperdine University); Frederick Goldberg (Clayton Junior College); Larry Gray (Southeastern Louisiana University); Alan Grob (Rice University); Christopher Hudgins (University of Nevada); Kristin Hunter (University of Pennsylvania); Lisa Hunter; Elizabeth Lunz; William Morgan (Illinois State University); Nils Peterson (San Jose State University); Ellanor Pruitt (Oxford College); Richard Quaintance (Douglass College); Joseph N. Riddell (University of California at Los Angeles); Ronald Schleifer (University of Oklahoma); John Shaw (Florida State University); John R. Shriver (Wayne State University); Irwin Simpkins (DeKalb College); Frederick Stocking (Williams College); Kristina Straub (Miami University, Ohio); Rae Thompson (University of Guelph); Dennis Todd (Georgetown University); Richard Turner (Indiana University-Purdue University at Indianapolis); Patricia Vicari (Scarborough College of the University of Toronto); Melissa Walker (Mercer University); Arthur Williams (Louisiana School for Math, Science, and the Arts); Dorothy A. Winsor (Wayne State University); and Curt R. Zimansky (University of Colorado).

On several occasions during the preparation of this work a retreat from everyday was needed. The Ossabaw Island Project provided it, and we wish to thank the Ossabaw Island Foundation and particularly Eleanor West for the provision and for the grace with which it was offered.

We would also like to thank our friends at W. W. Norton & Company, especially John Benedict, Fred McFarland, Diane O'Connor, Roy Tedoff, Victoria Thys, and Barry Wade.

J.B., J.P.H.

THE NORTON
INTRODUCTION TO
LITERATURE

Shorter Fourth Edition

FICTION

1   EXPERIENCING FICTION

SPENCER HOLST

The Zebra Storyteller

Once upon a time there was a Siamese cat who pretended to be a lion and spoke inappropriate Zebraic.

That language is whinnied by the race of striped horses in Africa.

Here now: An innocent zebra is walking in a jungle and approaching from another direction is the little cat; they meet.

"Hello there!" says the Siamese cat in perfectly pronounced Zebraic. "It certainly is a pleasant day, isn't it? The sun is shining, the birds are singing, isn't the world a lovely place to live today!"

The zebra is so astonished at hearing a Siamese cat speaking like a zebra, why—he's just fit to be tied.

So the little cat quickly ties him up, kills him, and drags the better parts of the carcass back to his den.

The cat successfully hunted zebras many months in this manner, dining on filet mignon of zebra every night, and from the better hides he made bow neckties and wide belts after the fashion of the decadent princes of the Old Siamese court.

He began boasting to his friends he was a lion, and he gave them as proof the fact that he hunted zebras.

The delicate noses of the zebras told them there was really no lion in the neighborhood. The zebra deaths caused many to avoid the region. Superstitious, they decided the woods were haunted by the ghost of a lion.

One day the storyteller of the zebras was ambling, and through his mind ran plots for stories to amuse the other zebras, when suddenly his eyes brightened, and he said, "That's it! I'll tell a story about a Siamese cat who learns to speak our language! What an idea! That'll make 'em laugh!"

Just then the Siamese cat appeared before him, and said, "Hello there! Pleasant day today, isn't it!"

The zebra storyteller wasn't fit to be tied at hearing a cat speaking his language, because he'd been thinking about that very thing.

He took a good look at the cat, and he didn't know why, but there was something about his looks he didn't like, so he kicked him with a hoof and killed him.

That is the function of the storyteller.

1971

The Zebra Storyteller suggests that the purpose of stories is to prepare us for the unexpected. Though the storyteller thinks he is just spinning stories out of his own imagination, in order to amuse, his stories prove to be practical. When the extraordinary, the unheard-of occurs—like a Siamese cat speaking Zebraic—he is prepared because he has already imagined it, and he alone is able to protect his tribe against the unusual.

Other storytellers make the function of fiction less extraordinary. According to them, fiction enables readers to avoid projecting false hopes and fears (such as the zebras' superstitious belief that they are being preyed on by the ghost of a lion) and shows them what they can actually expect in their everyday lives, so that they can prepare themselves. In George Eliot's novel *Adam Bede*, Hetty Sorrel is being paid admiring attention by the young squire, and she dreams of elopement, marriage, all sorts of vague pleasures. She does not dream that she will be seduced, made pregnant, abandoned. Her imagination has not been trained to project any "narrative" other than her dreams: "Hetty had never read a novel," George Eliot tells us, "[so] how could she find a shape for her expectations?"

We are all storytellers, then, of one stripe or another. Whenever we plan the future or ponder a decision, we are telling stories—projecting expectations through narrative. Whenever we tell stories or read them, we are educating our imaginations, either extending our mental experience in the actual, as Hetty might have done by reading novels, or preparing ourselves for the extraordinary and unexpected, like the zebra storyteller.

The actual and the extraordinary suggest two different uses readers make of fiction. Sometimes we want to read about people like ourselves, or about places, things, experiences, and ideas that are familiar and agreeable. Most of us initially prefer American literature and twentieth-century literature to literature remote in time or place. Indeed, stories must somehow be related to our own lives before we can find them intellectually or emotionally meaningful. No matter what our literary experience and taste, most of us relate in a special way to stories about people like us, experiences like our own, and especially to a story that mentions our hometown or neighborhood or the name of the street that we used to walk along on our way to school. Whether we call this reading for identification or for relevance, no one would deny that one of the many things that fiction may be "for" is learning about ourselves and the world around us.

But at other times the last thing we want is a story about people like ourselves, experiences like those of our everyday lives, and places and times like here and now. At such times we want (or are accused of wanting) to escape. If fiction must be relevant enough to relate meaningfully to us, it must also be "irrelevant," different, other, strange—as strange, perhaps, as a Siamese cat speaking Zebraic. It must take us out of ourselves, out of the confining vision of our own eyes, conditioned by our own background and experience, and show us that there are ways of looking at the world other than our own. So, in addition to many stories about approximately our own time and place, this collection includes a sprinkling of stories written in the last century, a few written in vastly different cultures, and a fair number written about worlds that have not existed or do not (yet) exist.

portable

What a story shows us or teaches us we may call its **message**—an objective, universal truth that we were unaware of before reading the story. We gradually learn, however, that stories tell us not so much what life means as what it's like. Rather than abstract or "objective" truths, stories deal with perceptions. These perceptions may be translated into messages, but we soon discover that the messages boil down to things like "There's good and bad in everybody," "Hurting people is wrong," and "Everything is not what it seems"—messages that Western Union, much less Western literature, might not find too urgent or startlingly illuminating. Indeed, we do not have to agree with what a story says or shows so long as we are convinced that if we had *those* eyes and were *there*, this is what we might see.

Whenever we can say yes, we are convinced, then we have been able to go beyond the limitations of our own vision, our own past and conditions, and we are able to see a new world, or the same old world in a new way. And by recognizing that we can see things differently, we realize that things we used to think were fixed, objective entities "out there" were fixed only in our perceptions. Or, as is too often the case, we realize that we have been accepting things at face value; we have been perceiving what habit and convention have told us is "really there." This, then, may awaken us to look at things for ourselves rather than accept them at conventional face value. For example, we "know" a table top is square, but in a story we are told it is diamond-shaped. We understand that if we were to look at the table top from a certain angle it would look diamond-shaped. But doesn't that imply that the table top is square only when we look from a certain angle? And are we looking at it from that angle? We look again, and we recognize that though we've always *known* it's a square, we've never really *seen* it as one. The story has not only allowed us to see reality from another angle, but it has helped us to sharpen our own vision, our own experience.

Reading fiction may ultimately contribute significantly to the way we understand and experience our own lives, but what kind of an experience is reading fiction itself? What is going on inside us while we are reading? What are we thinking? What are we feeling?

One way to find out is by an act of mental contortion: try looking over your own shoulder while you read. Try it with this next story, Guy de Maupassant's *The Jewelry*, paying more attention than you usually do not just to the story but to your own thoughts and responses while you are reading it. You may want to pause a few extra heartbeats after each sentence, fifteen to thirty extra seconds after each paragraph, and two or three minutes after you finish reading the whole thing.

Consider the title first. *The Jewelry*—Will it be lost? Will it be stolen? Inherited? Something else? What will happen? What kind of story will it be? Read the one-sentence first paragraph: nothing about jewelry! But we have a young man and a young woman and love. M. Lantin is "enveloped in love as in a net." This does not sound very promising, does it? What are these people like? What is their situation? As you read along how do your expectations change? How does your view of the characters deepen? change? As you get into the story notice what you remember of the early portions and any details in mid-story that remind you of earlier ones. There are other questions, but perhaps some of them can wait until after you have watched yourself read the story.

GUY DE MAUPASSANT

The Jewelry°

Having met the girl one evening, at the house of the office-superinten-dent, M. Lantin became enveloped in love as in a net.

She was the daughter of a country-tutor, who had been dead for several years. Afterward she had come to Paris with her mother, who made regular visits to several bourgeois families of the neighborhood, in hopes of being able to get her daughter married. They were poor and respectable, quiet and gentle. The young girl seemed to be the very ideal of that pure good woman to whom every young man dreams of entrusting his future. Her modest beauty had a charm of angelic shyness; and the slight smile that always dwelt about her lips seemed a reflection of her heart.

Everybody sang her praises; all who knew her kept saying: "The man who gets her will be lucky. No one could find a nicer girl than that."

M. Lantin, who was then chief clerk in the office of the Minister of the Interior, with a salary of 3,500 francs[1] a year, demanded her hand, and married her.

He was unutterably happy with her. She ruled his home with an economy so adroit that they really seemed to live in luxury. It would be impossible to conceive of any attentions, tendernesses, playful caresses which she did not lavish upon her husband; and such was the charm of her person that, six years after he married her, he loved her even more than he did the first day.

There were only two points upon which he ever found fault with her—her love of the theater, and her passion for false jewelry.

Her lady-friends (she was acquainted with the wives of several small office holders) were always bringing her tickets for the theaters; whenever there was a performance that made a sensation, she always had her *loge* secured, even for first performances; and she would drag her husband with her to all these entertainments, which used to tire him horribly after his day's work. So at last he begged her to go to the theater with some lady-acquaintances who would consent to see her

---

° Translated by Lafcadio Hearn.

1. The rate of exchange was five francs to the dollar, but in purchasing power those francs would now be worth about five dollars or more.

home afterward. She refused for quite a while—thinking it would not look very well to go out thus unaccompanied by her husband. But finally she yielded, just to please him; and he felt infinitely grateful to her therefor.

Now this passion for the theater at last evoked in her the desire of dress. It was true that her toilette remained simple, always in good taste, but modest; and her sweet grace, her irresistible grace, ever smiling and shy, seemed to take fresh charm from the simplicity of her robes. But she got into the habit of suspending in her pretty ears two big cut pebbles, fashioned in imitation of diamonds; and she wore necklaces of false pearls, bracelets of false gold, and haircombs studded with paste-imitations of precious stones.

Her husband who felt shocked by this love of tinsel and show, would often say—"My dear, when one has not the means to afford real jewelry, one should appear adorned with one's natural beauty and grace only—and these gifts are the rarest of jewels."

But she would smile sweetly and answer: "What does it matter? I like those things—that is my little whim. I know you are right; but one can't make oneself over again. I've always loved jewelry so much!"

And then she would roll the pearls of the necklaces between her fingers, and make the facets of the cut crystals flash in the light, repeating: "Now look at them—see how well the work is done. You would swear it was real jewelry."

He would then smile in his turn, and declare to her: "You have the tastes of a regular Gypsy."

Sometimes, in the evening, when they were having a chat by the fire, she would rise and fetch the morocco box in which she kept her "stock" (as M. Lantin called it)—would put it on the tea-table, and begin to examine the false jewelry with passionate delight, as if she experienced some secret and mysterious sensations of pleasure in their contemplation; and she would insist on putting one of the necklaces round her husband's neck, and laugh till she couldn't laugh any more, crying out: "Oh! how funny you look!" Then she would rush into his arms, and kiss him furiously.

One winter's night, after she had been to the Opera, she came home chilled through, and trembling. Next day she had a bad cough. Eight days after that, she died of pneumonia.

Lantin was very nearly following her into the tomb. His despair was so frightful that in one single month his hair turned white. He wept from morning till night, feeling his heart torn by inexpressible suffering—ever haunted by the memory of her, by the smile, by the voice, by all the charm of the dead woman.

Time did not assuage his grief. Often during office hours his fellow-clerks went off to a corner to chat about this or that topic of the day—his cheeks might have been seen to swell up all of a sudden, his nose wrinkle, his eyes fill with water—he would pull a frightful face, and begin to sob.

He had kept his dead companion's room just in the order she had left it, and he used to lock himself up in it every evening to think about her—all the furniture, and even all her dresses, remained in the same place they had been on the last day of her life.

But life became hard for him. His salary, which, in his wife's hands, had amply sufficed for all household needs, now proved scarcely sufficient to supply his own few wants. And he asked himself in astonishment how she had managed always to furnish him with excellent wines and with delicate eating which he could not now afford at all with his scanty means.

He got a little into debt, like men obliged to live by their wits. At last one morning that he happened to find himself without a cent in his pocket, and a whole week to wait before he could draw his monthly salary, he thought of selling something; and almost immediately it occurred to him to sell his wife's "stock"—for he had always borne a secret grudge against the flash-jewelry that used to annoy him so much in former days. The mere sight of it, day after day, somewhat spoiled the sad pleasure of thinking of his darling.

He tried a long time to make a choice among the heap of trinkets she had left behind her—for up to the very last day of her life she had kept obstinately buying them, bringing home some new thing almost every night—and finally he resolved to take the big pearl necklace which she used to like the best of all, and which he thought ought certainly to be worth six or eight francs, as it was really very nicely mounted for an imitation necklace.

He put it in his pocket, and walked toward the office, following the boulevards, and looking for some jewelry-store on the way, where he could enter with confidence.

Finally he saw a place and went in; feeling a little ashamed of thus exposing his misery, and of trying to sell such a trifling object.

"Sir," he said to the jeweler, "please tell me what this is worth."

The jeweler took the necklace, examined it, weighed it, took up a magnifying glass, called his clerk, talked to him in whispers, put down the necklace on the counter, and drew back a little bit to judge of its effect at a distance.

M. Lantin, feeling very much embarrassed by all these ceremonies, opened his mouth and began to declare—"Oh! I know it can't be worth much" . . . when the jeweler interrupted him saying:

"Well, sir, that is worth between twelve and fifteen thousand francs; but I cannot buy it unless you can let me know exactly how you came by it."

The widower's eyes opened enormously, and he stood gaping—unable to understand. Then after a while he stammered out: "You said? . . . Are you sure?" The jeweler, misconstruing the cause of this astonishment, replied in a dry tone—"Go elsewhere if you like, and see if you can get any more for it. The very most I would give for it is fifteen thousand. Come back and see me again, if you can't do better."

M. Lantin, feeling perfectly idiotic, took his necklace and departed; obeying a confused desire to find himself alone and to get a chance to think.

But the moment he found himself in the street again, he began to laugh, and he muttered to himself: "The fool!—oh! what a fool; If I had only taken him at his word. Well, well!—a jeweler who can't tell paste from real jewelry!"

And he entered another jewelry-store, at the corner of the Rue de la Paix. The moment the jeweler set eyes on the necklace, he exclaimed —"Hello! I know that necklace well—it was sold here!"

M. Lantin, very nervous, asked:

"What's it worth?"

"Sir, I sold it for twenty-five thousand francs. I am willing to buy it back again for eighteen thousand—if you can prove to me satisfactorily, according to legal prescriptions, how you came into possession of it"—This time, M. Lantin was simply paralyzed with astonishment. He said: "Well . . . but please look at it again, sir. I always thought until now that it was . . . was false."

The jeweler said:

"Will you give me your name, sir?"

"Certainly. My name is Lantin; I am employed at the office of the Minister of the Interior. I live at No. 16, Rue des Martyrs."

The merchant opened the register, looked, and said: "Yes; this necklace was sent to the address of Madame Lantin, 16 Rue des Martyrs, on July 20th, 1876."

And the two men looked into each other's eyes—the clerk wild with surprise; the jeweler suspecting he had a thief before him.

The jeweler resumed:

"Will you be kind enough to leave this article here for twenty-four hours only—I'll give you a receipt."

M. Lantin stuttered: "Yes—ah! certainly." And he went out, folding up the receipt, which he put in his pocket.

Then he crossed the street, went the wrong way, found out his mistake, returned by way of the Tuileries, crossed the Seine, found out he had taken the wrong road again, and went back to the Champs-Elysées without being able to get one clear idea into his head. He tried to reason, to understand. His wife could never have bought so valuable an object as that. Certainly not. But then, it must have been a present! . . . A present from whom? What for?

He stopped and stood stock-still in the middle of the avenue.

A horrible suspicion swept across his mind. . . . She? . . . But then all those other pieces of jewelry must have been presents also! . . . Then it seemed to him that the ground was heaving under his feet; that a tree, right in front of him, was falling toward him; he thrust out his arms instinctively, and fell senseless.

He recovered his consciousness again in a drug-store to which some bystanders had carried him. He had them lead him home, and he locked himself into his room.

Until nightfall he cried without stopping, biting his handkerchief to keep himself from screaming out. Then, completely worn out with grief and fatigue, he went to bed, and slept a leaden sleep.

A ray of sunshine awakened him, and he rose and dressed himself slowly to go to the office. It was hard to have to work after such a shock. Then he reflected that he might be able to excuse himself to the superintendent, and he wrote to him. Then he remembered he would have to go back to the jeweler's; and shame made his face purple. He remained thinking a long time. Still he could not leave the necklace there; he put on his coat and went out.

It was a fine day; the sky extended all blue over the city, and seemed to make it smile. Strollers were walking aimlessly about, with their hands in their pockets.

Lantin thought as he watched them passing: "How lucky the men are who have fortunes! With money a man can even shake off grief—you can go where you please—travel—amuse yourself! Oh! if I were only rich!"

He suddenly discovered he was hungry—not having eaten anything since the evening before. But his pockets were empty; and he remembered the necklace. Eighteen thousand francs! Eighteen thousand francs!—that was a sum—that was!

He made his way to the Rue de la Paix and began to walk backward and forward on the sidewalk in front of the store. Eighteen thousand francs! Twenty times he started to go in; but shame always kept him back.

Still he was hungry—very hungry—and had not a cent. He made one brusque resolve, and crossed the street almost at a run, so as not to let himself have time to think over the matter; and he rushed into the jeweler's.

As soon as he saw him, the merchant hurried forward, and offered him a chair with smiling politeness. Even the clerks came forward to stare at Lantin, with gaiety in their eyes and smiles about their lips.

The jeweler said: "Sir, I made inquiries; and if you are still so disposed, I am ready to pay you down the price I offered you."

The clerk stammered: "Why, yes—sir, certainly."

The jeweler took from a drawer eighteen big bills,[2] counted them, and held them out to Lantin, who signed a little receipt, and thrust the money feverishly into his pocket.

Then, as he was on the point of leaving, he turned to the ever-smiling merchant, and said, lowering his eyes: "I have some—I have some other jewelry, which came to me in the same—from the same inheritance. Would you purchase them also from me?"

The merchant bowed, and answered: "Why, certainly, sir—certainly. . . ." One of the clerks rushed out to laugh at his ease; another kept blowing his nose as hard as he could.

Lantin, impassive, flushed and serious, said: "I will bring them to you."

And he hired a cab to get the jewelry.

When he returned to the store, an hour later, he had not yet breakfasted. They examined the jewelry—piece by piece—putting a value on each. Nearly all had been purchased from that very house.

Lantin, now, disputed estimates made, got angry, insisted on seeing the books, and talked louder and louder the higher the estimates grew.

The big diamond earrings were worth 20,000 francs; the bracelets, 35,000; the brooches, rings, and medallions, 16,000; a set of emeralds and sapphires, 14,000; solitaire, suspended to a gold neckchain, 40,000; the total value being estimated at 196,000 francs.

2. French paper money varies in size, the larger the bill the larger the denomination.

The merchant observed with mischievous good nature: "The person who owned these must have put all her savings into jewelry."

Lantin answered with gravity: "Perhaps that is as good a way of saving money as any other." And he went off, after having agreed with the merchant that an expert should make a counter-estimate for him the next day.

When he found himself in the street again, he looked at the Column Vendôme[3] with the desire to climb it, as if it were a May pole. He felt jolly enough to play leapfrog over the Emperor's head—up there in the blue sky.

He breakfasted at Voisin's[4] restaurant, and ordered wine at 20 francs a bottle.

Then he hired a cab and drove out to the Bois.[5] He looked at the carriages passing with a sort of contempt, and a wild desire to yell out to the passers-by: "I am rich, too—I am! I have 200,000 francs!"

The recollection of the office suddenly came back to him. He drove there, walked right into the superintendent's private room, and said: "Sir, I come to give you my resignation. I have just come into a fortune of *three* hundred thousand francs." Then he shook hands all round with his fellow-clerks; and told them all about his plans for a new career. Then he went to dinner at the Café Anglais.

Finding himself seated at the same table with a man who seemed to him quite genteel, he could not resist the itching desire to tell him, with a certain air of coquetry, that he had just inherited a fortune of *four* hundred thousand francs.

For the first time in his life he went to the theater without feeling bored by the performance; and he passed the night in revelry and debauch.

Six months after he married again. His second wife was the most upright of spouses, but had a terrible temper. She made his life very miserable.

irony apparent

1883

Did you notice the "seemed" in the second paragraph? If you did, it probably alerted you to the fact that the girl may not have been what she appeared to be. Were you surprised by the "boy-gets-girl" phase ending so abruptly with the one-sentence fourth paragraph? Surely most readers have some expectations of a typical, drawn-out love story, full of difficulties. In the fifth paragraph—a little longer, three sentences, one of them longish—six years pass and all is going well. You've probably read enough stories to know that this cannot go on; something has to interrupt their perfect happiness. So you are prepared for the turn in the next paragraph—she has faults. But such

3. Famous column with statue of Napoleon at the top.

4. Like the Café Anglais below, a well-known and high-priced restaurant. When, at Christmas 1870, Paris was under siege and thousands were starving, Voisin's served elephant soup, stuffed head of donkey, jugged kangaroo, roast camel, and cat dressed with rats—some, but obviously not all, the delicacies from the zoo.

5. Large Parisian park where the rich took their outings.

little faults. Why are such little faults dwelt on for a page when it took less space than that for M. Lantin to fall in love, marry, and have six years of bliss? Then, all of a sudden—we're scarcely a third of the way into the story—she dies, as abruptly and with as little fuss as she was married. Where do we go from here?

Did you notice that the wife's first name is never mentioned? What do we know about her? How do we learn it? What kind of a person is she? How do our early opinions or suppositions fare as we read the story to the end?

What we know of her is limited by the fact that we see and know of her only what M. Lantin knows and sees, and we learn what we learn only as he learns it. We do not know much more about him, however, for though we follow him and his experiences through the story we rarely get into his mind and never get in very deeply. Of course if we knew all there was to know, what Lantin did not know, there would not be much of a story.

How much of a story is there, in fact? What does it amount to? Well, it is about a woman who is not exactly what she seems to be, and it is called *The Jewelry*, and the jewelry is not exactly what it seems to be either. That's how we learn that she was not what she seemed to be, so the title and the jewelry itself offer an insight into what the story is all about.

If someone told you about a story in which jewels were not what they seemed, you would more than likely expect the story to be about fake jewelry that was supposed to be real (and indeed de Maupassant did write another story in which that is the case). The idea would still be the same—things are not always what they seem to be. We would be readier for that kind of switch, however: that people are greedy and some will try to substitute worthless things for those of real value may be disappointing but not surprising. But vice versa? Who ever substitutes real money for counterfeit or tries to pass off an original composition as a plagiarism?

Is the twist just a gimmick? It certainly is a flouting of expectations. So is tossing off the marriage and the death of M. Lantin's wife in a sentence or two, without a dramatized scene. And how about the ending? Though upset at his discovery and ashamed at first, it takes Lantin less than a day to recognize how rich he is and what such riches mean. Not many of us, I should think, expected him to shrug off his shame so quickly and debauch so rapidly and deeply. Was his earlier morality destroyed when he recognized his wife's deception, or was it too superficial, "fake," based upon his own modest means and lack of opportunity? So the flouting of narrative convention, the twists on the expected, are echoed in the story's flouting of moral conventions, its cynicism: things are not what they seem, and those "things" include human values, moral precepts, as well as jewels—and wives.

The final twist, the almost gratuitous last short paragraph would seem to confirm this cynicism: Lantin's upright wife made his life miserable. Or does it? We are so used to twisting by now we might find de Maupassant doing it again: although the story seems to suggest the ironical view that Lantin was better off with his "fake jewel" of a first wife than with his truly upright second wife, in terms of Lantin's conduct he got what he deserved in very conventional terms. *He* married his first wife for love; *he* led a decent life; *he* was happy. Then *he* grew cynical and debauched; and now *he* is miserable.

We have read of Lantin's love and of his grief, of his shock and shame, his exhilaration, revelry, and misery. We have imagined what such experiences were like and, to a degree, shared them with him, but we have also had other responses as well—surprise; a different kind of shock; disgust perhaps, perhaps a wrenching feeling of the cruelty, injustice, meaninglessness of life as seen from a certain cynical angle. Each of the elements of the story has contributed to our intellectual and emotional experience of it. We will now look more closely at each of these elements of fiction in turn, and see how they work in other stories. And we will then broaden our perspectives, looking at stories in biographical, cultural, and literary contexts. Our aim will be to learn to read in a more informed, sensitive, receptive, and perceptive way, getting more enjoyment and insight out of each story.

2   PLOT

In *The Zebra Storyteller* you can see the skeleton of the typical short story **plot** or **plot structure**. Plot simply means the arrangement of the action, an imagined event or a series of such events.

Action usually involves **conflict**, a struggle between opposing forces, and it often falls into something like the same five parts that we find in a play: exposition, rising action, turning point (or climax), falling action, conclusion (or catastrophe). The conflict in this little tale is between the Siamese cat and the zebras, especially the zebra storyteller. The first part of the action, called the **exposition**, introduces characters, situation, and, usually, time and place. The exposition here is achieved in three sentences: the time is "once upon a," the place Africa, the characters a Siamese cat who speaks Zebraic and an innocent zebra, and the situation their meeting. We then enter the second part of the plot, the **rising action**: events that complicate the situation and intensify or complicate the conflict or introduce new ones. The first event here is the meeting between an innocent zebra and the Zebraic-speaking cat. That initial conflict of zebra and cat is over in a hurry—the zebra who is "fit to be tied" is tied up and eaten. Complications build with the cat's continuing success in killing zebras, and the zebras' growing fears and consequent superstitious belief that the ghost of a lion haunts the region preying on zebras. The **turning point** or **climax** of the action is the third part of the story, the appearance of the zebra storyteller: until now the cat has had it all going his way, but his luck is about to change. From this point on the complications that grew in the first part of the story are untangled—the zebra storyteller, for example, is not surprised when he meets a Siamese cat speaking Zebraic, "because he'd been thinking about that very thing" —this is the fourth part of the story, the reverse movement or **falling action**. The story ends at the fifth part, the **conclusion** or **catastrophe**: the point at which the situation that was destabilized at the beginning of the story (when the Zebraic-speaking cat appears) becomes stable once more: Africa is once again free of cats speaking the language of zebras.

Before the parts of the action can be arranged, of course, they must be selected. The opening passages of the first two stories in this chapter may show some of the issues involved in **selection.**

"The thousand injuries of Fortunato I had borne as I best could, but when he ventured upon insult I vowed revenge." So begins Edgar Allan Poe's *The Cask of Amontillado*. What kinds of injuries? Were there actually that many? Were they real injuries or imaginary? What was the insult? Why was the insult worse than all the injuries? Poe

14

could have invented answers for these questions, but he chose not to.

The first scene of Richard Connell's *The Most Dangerous Game* provides some information—the general location of the yacht, the superstition about the island, the fact that Rainsford is an expert hunter—but it is a rather full scene for one that, on first reading at least, seems to have no essential connection with the exciting events that follow. And Whitney, who appears to be a major character here, we see no more. Why does Connell include this scene and this character?

Authors leave out some things that seem at first to be important to the story and include some things that do not seem very important. Selection of events is a significant element of storytelling.

But what do we mean when we say an author selects events? Selects from where? It's not as if these events exist somewhere, as historical events do. Like scientists with their hypotheses and philosophers with their premises, many of us who talk or write about fiction begin with a fiction: we speak as if the people and places exist and the events of a story take place in a world of the author's imagination, a world from which he or she chooses the story elements, a world we can understand and almost re-create in terms of our own. We call this world the **history** behind the story.

A R Richard

Once events have been selected, they must be connected. In the history, events take place in simple chronological sequence: "The king died and then the queen died," to use one critic's example. This sequential narrative of events, the critic says, is not a plot. But if we connect the events, if we structure the history—"The king died and then the queen died of grief"—we have a plot.

Many of us are used to thinking of cause and effect as a natural part of an event, as somehow *in* the event, rather than as an interpretation of a relationship between two events. Often authors, bent on getting us to accept the fiction as a kind of truth, try to hide their structuring of that history from us. Montresor's scheme of revenge against Fortunato in *The Cask of Amontillado* is not the author's plot, Poe leads us to believe, but Montresor's; and, while reading, we probably accept that it is Montresor who, interpreting Fortunato's insult as cause for revenge, generates the events that follow. Only later, putting the story down, do we bother to think that it was Poe who invented and arranged the events, created the plot.

Sometimes, when the characters do not make the connections that turn history to plot, the author makes the reader do it. Hemingway, for example, is very reluctant to structure his stories by connecting events or other details. He just puts down one after another, as if they came into the story that way directly from the history. He uses few connectives, and most of these are neutral, noninterpretive *ands*. In the eleventh paragraph of *The Short Happy Life of Francis Macomber*, for example, an *and* appears where many of us would expect (and perhaps silently insert) a *so*: Macomber is waiting for his wife to enter their tent: "She did not speak to him when she came in *and* he left the tent at once. . . . ." Poe's characters make the connections; Hemingway's reader must make them.

In the history, events exist in chronological sequence, and they can be reported that way in the story: "The king died and then the queen died." But the story can be ordered differently: "The queen died after the king died" recounts the same history, but the sequence of events has been changed. The history has been structured. The reader of the first sentence focuses on the king first, the reader of the second sentence on the queen. The difference in emphasis can be significant.

In some stories, such as *The Most Dangerous Game*, the events seem to come unstructured from the history: Rainsford speaks with Whitney aboard the yacht; Whitney goes below; Rainsford falls overboard. . . . The events are presented one after another in the same sequence as in the history. The reader reads along finding out what happens next. In a detective story, on the other hand, the major action (the crime) has taken place before the story begins, and the forward action of the story is the detective's attempt to re-create the past and figure out what happened. The reader does not ask *What will happen?* but *What has happened?* In some other stories, like Faulkner's *A Rose for Emily* in the next chapter, readers may not feel compelled to ask themselves *What happened?* until the end of the story, when a sudden revelation from the fictional past forces them to reconsider all that has gone before. In such stories it is obvious that the author is creating a plot, ordering the events in the story in a sequence different from that in which they occurred, but just as Poe disguised his plot as his narrator's, so Faulkner disguises his reordering of events as the order of the recollections of his narrator followed by that narrator's learning a new fact about the past at the end of the story.

Though the sequence of events in the detective story is reordered in terms of the reader's knowledge of the events—we learn who done it in the past only long after the story begins—the past is not usually replayed. We do not see the crime reenacted before us (although the detective may describe the crime when he gives his solution). The story simply begins in the middle of the history—after the crime—and moves forward as the detective figures out what happened. In *The Short Happy Life of Francis Macomber*, however, there is a replay or flashback. As in a detective story, *Macomber* begins in the middle of the history, which is made up essentially of two hunting episodes. The story begins not with the first but between the two. The first sentence of the story ends, "pretending that nothing had happened," clearly suggesting that, as in a detective story, something significant *had* happened. The reader asks what it was, with curiosity and interest aroused. There are some clues in the first few pages, but neither a detective nor the reader has to reconstruct the past episode from clues. That episode is brought forward into the fictional present and re-presented. About six pages into the story we are told, "It had started the night before," and the following paragraph begins a scene that took place earlier.

One reason for structuring the history into plot is to engage the reader's attention, to make the reader read on. The story of a crime can be written chronologically, so that we know who done it from the beginning and are just reading on to discover if or when or how the criminal is caught; Dostoevsky tells the story of *Crime and Punishment* this way. Such stories are not, strictly speaking, detective stories: they do not play so much on **curiosity**—the desire to know what is happening or has happened. It is the sheer power of curiosity that keeps us reading intensely when we know as little as Watson or Sherlock Holmes himself at the beginning. Nor is it only the detective story that plays upon our curiosity. We have already seen how the phrase "pretending that nothing had happened" at the end of the first sentence of *Macomber* sets us to wondering just what had happened; by the time we find out, six pages later, we are already deep into the characters and situation—we're hooked. Even titles, such as *A Very Old Man with Enormous Wings* or *The Rocking-Horse Winner*, can make us pick up a story; after that, it's up to the story to keep us engaged.

Perhaps stronger than curiosity, or interest in what *is* happening, is **suspense**, the expectation of and doubt about what is *going* to happen next, as in the lion hunt in *Macomber*. The very title of *The Most Dangerous Game* arouses suspense. What *is* the most dangerous game? Russian roulette, perhaps? Within the first fifty words we run across such terms as *mystery, suggestive, curious dread, superstition,* and we may begin to think of the supernatural (but what kind of "game" does that suggest?). In the same passage is *Ship-Trap Island,* and another possible meaning for game, another direction for our anticipation, opens up: hunting and trapping game. This is reinforced in the next twenty-five lines by the talk of hunting. The game must be some exceedingly fierce animal. All sorts of expectations build: supernatural animals, monsters, prehistoric animals, cannibals, Satan himself—worse! By the time Whitney says good night and we come to the first break in the story, our expectations are at a pretty high pitch. There's a good deal of suspense, and our minds are actively scanning four, five, maybe six possibilities of what kinds of things might happen next.

Try reading another couple of pages—say, down to Rainsford's introducing himself ("I'm Sanger Rainsford of New York")—watching yourself anticipate and put together details or clues. What kind of reinforcement do those early references to mystery and superstition get from the unexpected, mirage-like appearance of a palatial chateau, a tall spiked iron gate, a gargoyle on the door knocker, and a gigantic man opening the door? Don't you find yourself trying to fit these things into a pattern? Sooner or later some possibilities are eliminated and one pattern dominates; the story may at some point simply tell you what possibility will be pursued. It is not too long before you learn for sure what the game is. But by that time there are new reasons for suspense—how will it come out? You get to another layer of suspense following Rainsford through a **serial ordeal**, a series of dangerous episodes.

Stories are not all fun and games, no matter how dangerous. Many of them seek to give you new insights into human perception, experience, meaning. They strive to tell truths—new, subjective truths, but truths—even though they "lie" about the actuality of the people and events represented. But first they have to get your attention, and one way is by arousing your curiosity and exciting your anticipation; that's what plot is primarily for. In order to keep you engaged and alert, a story must make you ask questions about what will happen or what will be revealed next. To respond fully to a story you must be alert to the signals and guess along with the author. At least in one aspect, fiction is a guessing game.

Like all guessing games, from quiz shows to philosophy, the plot game in fiction has certain guidelines. A well-structured plot will play fair with you, offering at appropriate points all the necessary indicators or clues to what will happen next, not just springing new and essential information on you at the last minute ("Meanwhile, unknown to our hero, the Marines were just on the other side of the hill . . ."). It is this playing fair that makes the ending of a well-structured story satisfying or, when you look back on it, inevitable. Most stories also offer a number of reasonable but false signals (red herrings) to get you off the scent, so that in a well-structured story the ending, though inevitable, is also surprising. And though there is usually an overarching action from beginning to end, in many stories there are layers of expectation or suspense, so that as soon as one question is answered another comes forth to replace it, keeping you in doubt and suspense as to the final outcome.

Unlike most guessing games, however, the reward is not for the right guess—anticipating the outcome before the final paragraph—but for the number of guesses, right *and* wrong, that you make, the number of signals you respond to. If you are misled by none of the false signals in the early pages of *The Most Dangerous Game*, you may be closer to being "right," but you may have missed many of the implications of the story. But, more important, you have missed the pleasure of learning the "truth" offered by the story for yourself, and you know how much less meaningful it is to be told something than it is to learn it for yourself, through your own experience. Fiction is a way of transmitting not just perception but experience.

How do you react, in *The Cask of Amontillado*, to Montresor's concern for Fortunato's coughing? What do you anticipate? What is it that you later discover? Alertness to signals, anticipating what is to come next, and remembering what has been said and signaled earlier are essential to fully appreciating and understanding stories. By the time you finish the Connell story, you should be able to figure out why he structured it so, why the first scene was there. You might have some idea—though not necessarily a firm and simple answer—as to why, in addition to arousing suspense, Hemingway wanted *The Short Happy Life of Francis Macomber* to begin in the middle of the history and later flash back to the beginning. You may know why insult is more important to Montresor than injury; you may even be able to suggest why Poe did not recount the thousand injuries or the fatal insult.

EDGAR ALLAN POE

The Cask of Amontillado

add insult to injury — intentional

The thousand injuries of Fortunato I had borne as I best could, but when he ventured upon insult I vowed revenge. You, who so well know the nature of my soul, will not suppose, however, that I gave utterance to a threat. *At length* I would be avenged; this was a point definitely settled—but the very definitiveness with which it was resolved precluded the idea of risk. I must not only punish but punish with impunity. A wrong is unredressed when retribution overtakes its redresser. It is equally unredressed when the avenger fails to make himself felt as such to him who has done the wrong.

It must be understood that neither by word nor deed had I given Fortunato cause to doubt my good will. I continued, as was my wont, to smile in his face, and he did not perceive that my smile *now* was at the thought of his immolation.

He had a weak point—this Fortunato—although in other regards he was a man to be respected and even feared. He prided himself on his connoisseurship in wine. Few Italians have the true virtuoso spirit. For the most part their enthusiasm is adopted to suit the time and opportunity, to practice imposture upon the British and Austrian millionaires. In painting and gemmary, Fortunato, like his countrymen, was a quack, but in the matter of old wines he was sincere. In this respect I did not differ from him materially;—I was skilful in the Italian vintages myself, and bought largely whenever I could.

It was about dusk, one evening during the supreme madness of the carnival season, that I encountered my friend. He accosted me with excessive warmth, for he had been drinking much. The man wore motley. He had on a tight-fitting parti-striped dress, and his head was surmounted by the conical cap and bells. I was so pleased to see him that I thought I should never have done wringing his hand.

I said to him—"My dear Fortunato, you are luckily met. How remarkably well you are looking to-day. But I have received a pipe[1] of what passes for Amontillado, and I have my doubts."

"How?" said he. "Amontillado? A pipe? Impossible! And in the middle of the carnival!"

"I have my doubts," I replied; "and I was silly enough to pay the full Amontillado price without consulting you in the matter. You were not to be found, and I was fearful of losing a bargain."

"Amontillado!"

"I have my doubts."

"Amontillado!"

"And I must satisfy them."

"Amontillado!"

repetition rhythm

"As you are engaged, I am on my way to Luchresi. If any one has a critical turn, it is he. He will tell me——"

1. A cask holding 126 gallons. *" Don't read this "*

"Luchresi cannot tell Amontillado from Sherry."

"And yet some fools will have it that his taste is a match for your own."

"Come, let us go."

"Whither?"

"To your vaults."

"My friend, no; I will not impose upon your good nature. I perceive you have an engagement. Luchresi——"

"I have no engagement;—come."

"My friend, no. It is not the engagement, but the severe cold with which I perceive you are afflicted. The vaults are insufferably damp. They are encrusted with niter."

"Let us go, nevertheless. The cold is merely nothing. Amontillado! You have been imposed upon. And as for Luchresi, he cannot distinguish Sherry from Amontillado."

Thus speaking, Fortunato possessed himself of my arm; and putting on a mask of black silk and drawing a *roquelaire*[2] closely about my person, I suffered him to hurry me to my palazzo.

There were no attendants at home; they had absconded to make merry in honor of the time. I had told them that I should not return until the morning, and had given them explicit orders not to stir from the house. These orders were sufficient, I well knew, to insure their immediate disappearance, one and all, as soon as my back was turned.

I took from their sconces two flambeaux, and giving one to Fortunato, bowed him through several suites of rooms to the archway that led into the vaults. I passed down a long and winding staircase, requesting him to be cautious as he followed. We came at length to the foot of the descent, and stood together on the damp ground of the catacombs of the Montresors.

The gait of my friend was unsteady, and the bells upon his cap jingled as he strode.

"The pipe?" said he.

"It is farther on," said I; "but observe the white web-work which gleams from these cavern walls."

He turned towards me, and looked into my eyes with two filmy orbs that distilled the rheum of intoxication.

"Niter?" he asked, at length.

"Niter," I replied. "How long have you had that cough?"

"Ugh! ugh! ugh!—ugh! ugh! ugh!—ugh! ugh! ugh! ugh! ugh! ugh!—ugh! ugh! ugh!"

My poor friend found it impossible to reply for many minutes.

"It is nothing," he said, at last.

"Come," I said, with decision, "we will go back; your health is precious. You are rich, respected, admired, beloved; you are happy, as once I was. You are a man to be missed. For me it is no matter. We will go back; you will be ill, and I cannot be responsible. Besides, there is Luchresi——"

2. Roquelaure, man's heavy, knee-length cloak, usually trimmed in fur and silk-lined, 18th century.

"Enough," he said; "the cough is a mere nothing; it will not kill me. I shall not die of a cough."

"True—true," I replied; "and, indeed, I had no intention of alarming you unnecessarily—but you should use all proper caution. A draft of this Medoc will defend us from the damps."

Here I knocked off the neck of a bottle which I drew from a long row of its fellows that lay upon the mold.

"Drink," I said, presenting him the wine.

He raised it to his lips with a leer. He paused and nodded to me familiarly, while his bells jingled.

"I drink," he said, "to the buried that repose around us."

"And I to your long life."

He again took my arm, and we proceeded.

"These vaults," he said, "are extensive."

"The Montresors," I replied, "were a great and numerous family."

"I forget your arms."

"A huge human foot d'or,[3] in a field azure; the foot crushes a serpent rampant whose fangs are imbedded in the heel."

"And the motto?"

"*Nemo me impune lacessit.*"[4]

"Good!" he said.

The wine sparkled in his eyes and the bells jingled. My own fancy grew warm with the Medoc. We had passed through long walls of piled skeletons, with casks and puncheons intermingling, into the inmost recesses of the catacombs. I paused again, and this time I made bold to seize Fortunato by an arm above the elbow.

"The niter!" I said; "see, it increases. It hangs like moss upon the vaults. We are below the river's bed. The drops of moisture trickle among the bones. Come, we will go back ere it is too late. Your cough——"

"It is nothing," he said; "let us go on. But first, another draft of the Medoc."

I broke and reached him a flagon of De Grâve.[5] He emptied it at a breath. His eyes flashed with a fierce light. He laughed and threw the bottle upward with a gesticulation I did not understand.

I looked at him in surprise. He repeated the movement—a grotesque one.

"You do not comprehend?" he said.

"Not I," I replied.

"Then you are not of the brotherhood."

"How?"

"You are not of the masons."[6]

"Yes, yes," I said; "yes, yes."

"You? Impossible! A mason?"

"A mason," I replied.

---

3. Of gold.
' 4. No one provokes me with impunity.
5. Like Médoc, a French wine.
6. Masons or Freemasons, an interna-tional secret society condemned by the Catholic church. Montresor means by mason one who builds with stone, brick, etc.

"A sign," he said, "a sign."

"It is this," I answered, producing from beneath the folds of my *roquelaire* a trowel.

"You jest," he exclaimed, recoiling a few paces. "But let us proceed to the Amontillado."

"Be it so," I said, replacing the tool beneath the cloak and again offering him my arm. He leaned upon it heavily. We continued our route in search of the Amontillado. We passed through a range of low arches, descended, passed on, and descending again, arrived at a deep crypt, in which the foulness of the air caused our flambeaux rather to glow than flame.

At the most remote end of the crypt there appeared another less spacious. Its walls had been lined with human remains, piled to the vault overhead, in the fashion of the great catacombs of Paris. Three sides of this interior crypt were still ornamented in this manner. From the fourth the bones had been thrown down, and lay promiscuously upon the earth, forming at one point a mound of some size. Within the wall thus exposed by the displacing of the bones, we perceived a still interior crypt or recess, in depth about four feet, in width three, in height six or seven. It seemed to have been constructed for no especial use within itself, but formed merely the interval between two of the colossal supports of the roof of the catacombs, and was backed by one of their circumscribing walls of solid granite.

It was in vain that Fortunato, uplifting his dull torch, endeavored to pry into the depth of the recess. Its termination the feeble light did not enable us to see.

"Proceed," I said; "herein is the Amontillado. As for Luchresi——"

"He is an ignoramus," interrupted my friend, as he stepped unsteadily forward, while I followed immediately at his heels. In an instant he had reached the extremity of the niche, and finding his progress arrested by the rock, stood stupidly bewildered. A moment more and I had fettered him to the granite. In its surface were two iron staples, distant from each other about two feet, horizontally. From one of these depended a short chain, from the other a padlock. Throwing the links about his waist, it was but the work of a few seconds to secure it. He was too much astounded to resist. Withdrawing the key I stepped back from the recess.

"Pass your hand," I said, "over the wall; you cannot help feeling the niter. Indeed it is *very* damp. Once more let me *implore* you to return. No? Then I must positively leave you. But I must first render you all the little attentions in my power."

"The Amontillado!" ejaculated my friend, not yet recovered from his astonishment.

"True," I replied; "the Amontillado."

As I said these words I busied myself among the pile of bones of which I have before spoken. Throwing them aside, I soon uncovered a quantity of building stone and mortar. With these materials and with the aid of my trowel, I began vigorously to wall up the entrance of the niche.

I had scarcely laid the first tier of the masonry when I discovered that the intoxication of Fortunato had in a great measure worn off. The earliest indication I had of this was a low moaning cry from the depth of the recess. It was *not* the cry of a drunken man. There was then a long and obstinate silence. I laid the second tier, and the third, and the fourth; and then I heard the furious vibrations of the chain. The noise lasted for several minutes, during which, that I might hearken to it with the more satisfaction, I ceased my labors and sat down upon the bones. When at last the clanking subsided, I resumed the trowel, and finished without interruption the fifth, the sixth, and the seventh tier. The wall was now nearly upon a level with my breast. I again paused, and holding the flambeaux over the mason-work, threw a few feeble rays upon the figure within.

A succession of loud and shrill screams, bursting suddenly from the throat of the chained form, seemed to thrust me violently back. For a brief moment I hesitated, I trembled. Unsheathing my rapier, I began to grope with it about the recess; but the thought of an instant reassured me. I placed my hand upon the solid fabric of the catacombs, and felt satisfied. I reapproached the wall. I replied to the yells of him who clamored. I reechoed, I aided, I surpassed them in volume and in strength. I did this, and the clamorer grew still.

It was now midnight, and my task was drawing to a close. I had completed the eighth, the ninth and the tenth tier. I had finished a portion of the last and the eleventh; there remained but a single stone to be fitted and plastered in. I struggled with its weight; I placed it partially in its destined position. But now there came from out the niche a low laugh that erected the hairs upon my head. It was succeeded by a sad voice, which I had difficulty in recognizing as that of the noble Fortunato. The voice said—

"Ha! ha! ha!—he! he! he!—a very good joke, indeed—an excellent jest. We will have many a rich laugh about it at the palazzo[7]—he! he! he!—over our wine—he! he! he!"

"The Amontillado!" I said.

"He! he! he!—he! he! he!—yes, the Amontillado. But is it not getting late? Will not they be awaiting us at the palazzo, the Lady Fortunato and the rest? Let us be gone."

"Yes," I said, "let us be gone."

"*For the love of God, Montresor!*"

"Yes," I said, "for the love of God!"

But to these words I hearkened in vain for a reply. I grew impatient. I called aloud—

"Fortunato!"

No answer. I called again—

"Fortunato!"

No answer still. I thrust a torch through the remaining aperture and let it fall within. There came forth in return only a jingling of the bells. My heart grew sick; it was the dampness of the catacombs

7. Palace.

that made it so. I hastened to make an end of my labor. I forced the
last stone into its position; I plastered it up. Against the new masonry
I re-erected the old rampart of bones. For the half of a century no
mortal has disturbed them. *In pace requiescat!*[8]

RICHARD CONNELL

The Most Dangerous Game

"Off there to the right—somewhere—is a large island," said Whitney.
"It's rather a mystery—"

"What island is it?" Rainsford asked.

"The old charts call it 'Ship-Trap Island,'" Whitney replied. "A
suggestive name, isn't it? Sailors have a curious dread of the place.
I don't know why. Some superstition—"

"Can't see it," remarked Rainsford, trying to peer through the
dank tropical night that was palpable as it pressed its thick warm
blackness in upon the yacht.

"You've good eyes," said Whitney, with a laugh, "and I've seen you
pick off a moose moving in the brown fall bush at four hundred yards,
but even you can't see four miles or so through a moonless Caribbean
night."

"Nor four yards," admitted Rainsford. "Ugh! It's like moist black
velvet."

"It will be light in Rio," promised Whitney. "We should make it
in a few days. I hope the jaguar guns have come from Purdey's. We
should have some good hunting up the Amazon. Great sport, hunting."

"The best sport in the world," agreed Rainsford.

"For the hunter," amended Whitney. "Not for the jaguar."

"Don't talk rot, Whitney," said Rainsford. "You're a big-game
hunter, not a philosopher. Who cares how a jaguar feels?"

"Perhaps the jaguar does," observed Whitney.

"Bah! They've no understanding."

"Even so, I rather think they understand one thing—fear. The fear
of pain and the fear of death."

"Nonsense," laughed Rainsford. "This hot weather is making you
soft, Whitney. Be a realist. The world is made up of two classes—the
hunters and the huntees. Luckily, you and I are hunters. Do you think
we've passed that island yet?"

"I can't tell in the dark. I hope so."

"Why?" asked Rainsford.

"The place has a reputation—a bad one."

"Cannibals?" suggested Rainsford.

"Hardly. Even cannibals wouldn't live in such a God-forsaken place.

8. May he rest in peace.

But it's gotten into sailor lore, somehow. Didn't you notice that the crew's nerves seemed a bit jumpy today?"

"They were a bit strange, now you mention it. Even Captain Nielsen—"

"Yes, even that tough-minded old Swede, who'd go up to the devil himself and ask him for a light. Those fishy blue eyes held a look I never saw there before. All I could get out of him was: 'This place has an evil name among sea-faring men, sir.' Then he said to me, very gravely: 'Don't you feel anything?'—as if the air about us was actually poisonous. Now, you mustn't laugh when I tell you this—I did feel something like a sudden chill.

"There was no breeze. The sea was as flat as a plate-glass window. We were drawing near the island then. What I felt was a—a mental chill; a sort of sudden dread."

"Pure imagination," said Rainsford. "One superstitious sailor can taint the whole ship's company with his fear."

"Maybe. But sometimes I think sailors have an extra sense that tells them when they are in danger. Sometimes I think evil is a tangible thing—with wave lengths, just as sound and light have. An evil place can, so to speak, broadcast vibrations of evil. Anyhow, I'm glad we're getting out of this zone. Well, I think I'll turn in now, Rainsford."

"I'm not sleepy," said Rainsford. "I'm going to smoke another pipe up on the after deck."

"Good night, then, Rainsford. See you at breakfast."

"Right. Good night, Whitney."

There was no sound in the night as Rainsford sat there, but the muffled throb of the engine that drove the yacht swiftly through the darkness, and the swish and ripple of the wash of the propeller.

Rainsford, reclining in a steamer chair, indolently puffed on his favorite brier. The sensuous drowsiness of the night was on him. "It's so dark," he thought, "that I could sleep without closing my eyes; the night would be my eyelids—"

An abrupt sound startled him. Off to the right he heard it, and his ears, expert in such matters, could not be mistaken. Again he heard the sound, and again. Somewhere, off in the blackness, some one had fired a gun three times.

Rainsford sprang up and moved quickly to the rail, mystified. He strained his eyes in the direction from which the reports had come, but it was like trying to see through a blanket. He leaped upon the rail and balanced himself there, to get greater elevation; his pipe, striking a rope, was knocked from his mouth. He lunged for it; a short, hoarse cry came from his lips as he realized he had reached too far and had lost his balance. The cry was pinched off short as the blood-warm waters of the Caribbean Sea closed over his head.

He struggled up to the surface and tried to cry out, but the wash from the speeding yacht slapped him in the face and the salt water in his open mouth made him gag and strangle. Desperately he struck out with strong strokes after the receding lights of the yacht, but he stopped before he had swum fifty feet. A certain cool-headedness had come to him; it was not the first time he had been in a tight place. There was a chance that his cries could be heard by some one aboard the yacht, but that chance was slender, and grew more slender as the yacht raced on. He wrestled himself out of his clothes, and shouted with all his power. The lights of the yacht became faint and ever-vanishing fireflies; then they were blotted out entirely by the night.

Rainsford remembered the shots. They had come from the right, and doggedly he swam in that direction, swimming with slow, deliberate strokes, conserving his strength. For a seemingly endless time he fought the sea. He began to count his strokes; he could do possibly a hundred more and then—

Rainsford heard a sound. It came out of the darkness, a high scream-ing sound, the sound of an animal in an extremity of anguish and terror.

He did not recognize the animal that made the sound; he did not try to; with fresh vitality he swam toward the sound. He heard it again; then it was cut short by another noise, crisp, staccato.

"Pistol shot," muttered Rainsford, swimming on.

Ten minutes of determined effort brought another sound to his ears —the most welcome he had ever heard—the muttering and growling of the sea breaking on a rocky shore. He was almost on the rocks before he saw them; on a night less calm he would have been shattered against them. With his remaining strength he dragged himself from the swirling waters. Jagged crags appeared to jut into the opaqueness; he forced himself upward, hand over hand. Gasping, his hands raw, he reached a flat place at the top. Dense jungle came down to the very edge of the cliffs. What perils that tangle of trees and under-brush might hold for him did not concern Rainsford just then. All he knew was that he was safe from his enemy, the sea, and that utter weariness was on him. He flung himself down at the jungle edge and tumbled headlong into the deepest sleep of his life.

When he opened his eyes he knew from the position of the sun that it was late in the afternoon. Sleep had given him new vigor; a sharp hunger was picking at him. He looked about him, almost cheerfully.

"Where there are pistol shots, there are men. Where there are men, there is food," he thought. But what kind of men, he wondered, in so forbidding a place? An unbroken front of snarled and ragged jungle fringed the shore.

He saw no sign of a trail through the closely knit web of weeds and trees; it was easier to go along the shore, and Rainsford floundered along by the water. Not far from where he had landed, he stopped.

Some wounded thing, by the evidence a large animal, had thrashed about in the underbrush; the jungle weeds were crushed down and the moss was lacerated; one patch of weeds was stained crimson. A small, glittering object not far away caught Rainsford's eye and he picked it up. It was an empty cartridge.

"A twenty-two," he remarked. "That's odd. It must have been a fairly large animal too. The hunter had his nerve with him to tackle it with a light gun. It's clear that the brute put up a fight. I suppose the first three shots I heard was when the hunter flushed his quarry and wounded it. The last shot was when he trailed it here and finished it."

He examined the ground closely and found what he had hoped to find—the print of hunting boots. They pointed along the cliff in the direction he had been going. Eagerly he hurried along, now slipping on a rotten log or a loose stone, but making headway; night was beginning to settle down on the island.

Bleak darkness was blacking out the sea and jungle when Rainsford sighted the lights. He came upon them as he turned a crook in the coast line, and his first thought was that he had come upon a village, for there were many lights. But as he forged along he saw to his great astonishment that all the lights were in one enormous building—a lofty structure with pointed towers plunging upward into the gloom. His eyes made out the shadowy outlines of a palatial château; it was set on a high bluff, and on three sides of it cliffs dived down to where the sea licked greedy lips in the shadows.

"Mirage," thought Rainsford. But it was no mirage, he found, when he opened the tall spiked iron gate. The stone steps were real enough; the massive door with a leering gargoyle for a knocker was real enough; yet about it all hung an air of unreality.

He lifted the knocker, and it creaked up stiffly, as if it had never before been used. He let it fall, and it startled him with its booming loudness. He thought he heard steps within; the door remained closed. Again Rainsford lifted the heavy knocker, and let it fall. The door opened then, opened as suddenly as if it were on a spring, and Rainsford stood blinking in the river of glaring gold light that poured out. The first thing Rainsford's eyes discerned was the largest man Rainsford had ever seen—a gigantic creature, solidly made and black-bearded to the waist. In his hand the man held a long-barreled revolver, and he was pointing it straight at Rainsford's heart.

Out of the snarl of beard two small eyes regarded Rainsford.

"Don't be alarmed," said Rainsford, with a smile which he hoped was disarming. "I'm no robber. I fell off a yacht. My name is Sanger Rainsford of New York City."

The menacing look in the eyes did not change. The revolver pointed as rigidly as if the giant were a statue. He gave no sign that he understood Rainsford's words, or that he had even heard them. He was dressed in uniform, a black uniform trimmed with gray astrakhan.

"I'm Sanger Rainsford of New York," Rainsford began again. "I fell off a yacht. I am hungry."

The man's only answer was to raise with his thumb the hammer of his revolver. Then Rainsford saw the man's free hand go to his forehead in a military salute, and he saw him click his heels together and stand at attention. Another man was coming down the broad marble steps, an erect, slender man in evening clothes. He advanced to Rainsford and held out his hand.

In a cultivated voice marked by a slight accent that gave it added precision and deliberateness, he said: "It is a very great pleasure and honor to welcome Mr. Sanger Rainsford, the celebrated hunter, to my home."

Automatically Rainsford shook the man's hand.

"I've read your book about hunting snow leopards[1] in Tibet, you see," explained the man. "I am General Zaroff."

Rainsford's first impression was that the man was singularly handsome; his second was that there was an original, almost bizarre quality about the general's face. He was a tall man past middle age, for his hair was a vivid white; but his thick eyebrows and pointed military mustache were as black as the night from which Rainsford had come. His eyes, too, were black and very bright. He had high cheek bones, a sharp-cut nose, a spare, dark face, the face of a man used to giving orders, the face of an aristocrat. Turning to the giant in uniform, the general made a sign. The giant put away his pistol, saluted, withdrew.

"Ivan is an incredibly strong fellow," remarked the general, "but he has the misfortune to be deaf and dumb. A simple fellow, but, I'm afraid, like all his race, a bit of a savage."

"Is he Russian?"

"He is a Cossack,"[2] said the general, and his smile showed red lips and pointed teeth. "So am I."

"Come," he said, "we shouldn't be chatting here. We can talk later. Now you want clothes, food, rest. You shall have them. This is a most restful spot."

Ivan had reappeared, and the general spoke to him with lips that moved but gave forth no sound.

"Follow Ivan, if you please, Mr. Rainsford," said the general. "I was about to have my dinner when you came. I'll wait for you. You'll find that my clothes will fit you, I think."

It was to a huge, beam-ceilinged bedroom with a canopied bed big enough for six men that Rainsford followed the silent giant. Ivan laid out an evening suit, and Rainsford, as he put it on, noticed that it came from a London tailor who ordinarily cut and sewed for none below the rank of duke.

The dining room to which Ivan conducted him was in many ways remarkable. There was a medieval magnificence about it; it suggested a baronial hall of feudal times with its oaken panels, its high ceiling, its vast refectory table where twoscore men could sit down to eat. About the hall were the mounted heads of many animals—lions, tigers, elephants, moose, bears; larger or more perfect specimens Rainsford had never seen. At the great table the general was sitting, alone.

"You'll have a cocktail, Mr. Rainsford," he suggested. The cocktail was surpassingly good; and, Rainsford noted, the table appointments were of the finest—the linen, the crystal, the silver, the china.

They were eating *borsch*, the rich, red soup with whipped cream so dear to Russian palates. Half apologetically General Zaroff said: "We do our best to preserve the amenities of civilization here. Please forgive any lapses. We are well off the beaten track, you know. Do you think the champagne has suffered from its long ocean trip?"

---

1. The ounce, native to the Himalayas, and quite rare.

2. From the southern part of European Russia, the Cossacks were known as exceptionally fine horsemen and light cavalrymen and, under the Czars, were feared for their ruthless raids.

"Not in the least," declared Rainsford. He was finding the general a most thoughtful and affable host, a true cosmopolite. But there was one small trait of the general's that made Rainsford uncomfortable. Whenever he looked up from his plate he found the general studying him, appraising him narrowly.

"Perhaps," said General Zaroff, "you were surprised that I recognized your name. You see, I read all books on hunting published in English, French, and Russian. I have but one passion in my life, Mr. Rainsford, and it is the hunt."

"You have some wonderful heads here," said Rainsford as he ate a particularly well cooked filet mignon. "That Cape buffalo[3] is the largest I ever saw."

"Oh, that fellow. Yes, he was a monster."

"Did he charge you?"

"Hurled me against a tree," said the general. "Fractured my skull. But I got the brute."

"I've always thought," said Rainsford, "that the Cape buffalo is the most dangerous of all big game."

For a moment the general did not reply; he was smiling his curious red-lipped smile. Then he said slowly: "No. You are wrong, sir. The Cape buffalo is not the most dangerous big game." He sipped his wine. "Here in my preserve on this island," he said in the same slow tone, "I hunt more dangerous game."

Rainsford expressed his surprise. "Is there big game on this island?"

The general nodded. "The biggest."

"Really?"

"Oh, it isn't here naturally, of course. I have to stock the island."

"What have you imported, general?" Rainsford asked. "Tigers?"

The general smiled. "No," he said. "Hunting tigers ceased to interest me some years ago. I exhausted their possibilities, you see. No thrill left in tigers, no real danger. I live for danger, Mr. Rainsford."

The general took from his pocket a gold cigarette case and offered his guest a long black cigarette with a silver tip; it was perfumed and gave off a smell like incense.

"We will have some capital hunting, you and I," said the general. "I shall be most glad to have your society."

"But what game——" began Rainsford.

"I'll tell you," said the general. "You will be amused, I know. I think I may say, in all modesty, that I have done a rare thing. I have invented a new sensation. May I pour you another glass of port, Mr. Rainsford?"

"Thank you, general."

The general filled both glasses, and said: "God makes some men poets. Some He makes kings, some beggars. Me He made a hunter. My hand was made for the trigger, my father said. He was a very rich man with a quarter of a million acres in the Crimea, and he was an ardent sportsman. When I was only five years old he gave me a little gun, specially made in Moscow for me, to shoot sparrows with. When I shot some of his prize turkeys with it, he did not punish me; he

---

3. Big, quick, intelligent, when separated from the herd ("rogue"), one of the most dangerous of African game animals.

complimented me on my marksmanship. I killed my first bear in the Caucasus when I was ten. My whole life has been one prolonged hunt. I went into the army—it was expected of noblemen's sons—and for a time commanded a division of Cossack cavalry, but my real interest was always the hunt. I have hunted every kind of game in every land. It would be impossible for me to tell you how many animals I have killed."

The general puffed at his cigarette.

"After the debacle in Russia[4] I left the country, for it was imprudent for an officer of the Czar to stay there. Many noble Russians lost everything. I, luckily, had invested heavily in American securities, so I shall never have to open a tea room in Monte Carlo or drive a taxi in Paris. Naturally, I continued to hunt—grizzlies in your Rockies, crocodiles in the Ganges, rhinoceroses in East Africa. It was in Africa that the Cape buffalo hit me and laid me up for six months. As soon as I recovered I started for the Amazon to hunt jaguars, for I had heard they were unusually cunning. They weren't." The Cossack sighed. "They were no match at all for a hunter with his wits about him, and a high-powered rifle. I was bitterly disappointed. I was lying in my tent with a splitting headache one night when a terrible thought pushed its way into my mind. Hunting was beginning to bore me! And hunting, remember, had been my life. I have heard that in America business men often go to pieces when they give up the business that has been their life."

"Yes, that's so," said Rainsford.

The general smiled. "I had no wish to go to pieces," he said. "I must do something. Now, mine is an analytical mind, Mr. Rainsford. Doubtless that is why I enjoy the problems of the chase."

"No doubt, General Zaroff."

"So," continued the general, "I asked myself why the hunt no longer fascinated me. You are much younger than I am, Mr. Rainsford, and have not hunted as much, but you perhaps can guess the answer."

"What was it?"

"Simply this: hunting had ceased to be what you call 'a sporting proposition.' It had become too easy. I always got my quarry. Always. There is no greater bore than perfection."

The general lit a fresh cigarette.

"No animal had a chance with me any more. That is no boast; it is a mathematical certainty. The animal had nothing but his legs and his instinct. Instinct is no match for reason. When I thought of this it was a tragic moment for me, I can tell you."

Rainsford leaned across the table, absorbed in what his host was saying.

"It came to me as an inspiration what I must do," the general went on.

"And that was?"

The general smiled the quiet smile of one who had faced an obstacle and surmounted it with success. "I had to invent a new animal to hunt," he said.

"A new animal? You're joking."

4. **The Revolution of 1917** which overthrew the Czar and prepared the way for Communist rule.

"Not at all," said the general. "I never joke about hunting. I needed a new animal. I found one. So I bought this island, built this house, and here I do my hunting. The island is perfect for my purposes—there are jungles with a maze of trails in them, hills, swamps—"

"But the animal, General Zaroff?"

"Oh," said the general, "it supplies me with the most exciting hunting in the world. No other hunting compares with it for an instant. Every day I hunt, and I never grow bored now, for I have a quarry with which I can match my wits."

Rainsford's bewilderment showed in his face.

"I wanted the ideal animal to hunt," explained the general. "So I said: 'What are the attributes of an ideal quarry?' And the answer was, of course: 'It must have courage, cunning, and, above all, it must be able to reason.'"

"But no animal can reason," objected Rainsford.

"My dear fellow," said the general, "there is one that can."

"But you can't mean—" gasped Rainsford.

"And why not?"

"I can't believe you are serious, General Zaroff. This is a grisly joke."

"Why should I not be serious? I am speaking of hunting."

"Hunting? Good God, General Zaroff, what you speak of is murder."

The general laughed with entire good nature. He regarded Rainsford quizzically. "I refuse to believe that so modern and civilized a young man as you seem to be harbors romantic ideas about the value of human life. Surely your experiences in the war—"

"Did not make me condone cold-blooded murder," finished Rainsford stiffly.

Laughter shook the general. "How extraordinarily droll you are!" he said. "One does not expect nowadays to find a young man of the educated class, even in America, with such a naïve, and, if I may say so, mid-Victorian point of view. It's like finding a snuff-box in a limousine. Ah, well, doubtless you had Puritan ancestors. So many Americans appear to have had. I'll wager you'll forget your notions when you go hunting with me. You've a genuine new thrill in store for you, Mr. Rainsford."

"Thank you, I'm a hunter, not a murderer."

"Dear me," said the general, quite unruffled, "again that unpleasant word. But I think I can show you that your scruples are quite ill founded."

"Yes?"

"Life is for the strong, to be lived by the strong, and, if need be, taken by the strong. The weak of the world were put here to give the strong pleasure. I am strong. Why should I not use my gift? If I wish to hunt, why should I not? I hunt the scum of the earth—sailors from tramp ships—lascars, blacks, Chinese, whites, mongrels—a thoroughbred horse or hound is worth more than a score of them."

"But they are men," said Rainsford hotly.

"Precisely," said the general. "That is why I use them. It gives me pleasure. They can reason, after a fashion. So they are dangerous."

"But where do you get them?"

The general's left eyelid fluttered down in a wink. "This island is called Ship-Trap," he answered. "Sometimes an angry god of the high seas sends them to me. Sometimes, when Providence is not so kind, I help Providence a bit. Come to the window with me."

Rainsford went to the window and looked out toward the sea.

"Watch! Out there!" exclaimed the general, pointing into the night. Rainsford's eyes saw only blackness, and then, as the general pressed a button, far out to sea Rainsford saw the flash of lights.

The general chuckled. "They indicate a channel," he said, "where there's none: giant rocks with razor edges crouch like a sea monster with wide-open jaws. They can crush a ship as easily as I crush this nut." He dropped a walnut on the hardwood floor and brought his heel grinding down on it. "Oh, yes," he said, casually, as if in answer to a question, "I have electricity. We try to be civilized here."

"Civilized? And you shoot down men?"

A trace of anger was in the general's black eyes, but it was there for but a second, and he said, in his most pleasant manner: "Dear me, what a righteous young man you are! I assure you I do not do the thing you suggest. That would be barbarous. I treat these visitors with every consideration. They get plenty of good food and exercise. They get into splendid physical condition. You shall see for yourself tomorrow."

"What do you mean?"

"We'll visit my training school," smiled the general. "It's in the cellar. I have about a dozen pupils down there now. They're from the Spanish bark San Lucar that had the bad luck to go on the rocks out there. A very inferior lot, I regret to say. Poor specimens and more accustomed to the deck than to the jungle."

He raised his hand, and Ivan, who served as waiter, brought thick Turkish coffee. Rainsford, with an effort, held his tongue in check.

"It's a game, you see," pursued the general blandly. "I suggest to one of them that we go hunting. I give him a supply of food and an excellent hunting knife. I give him three hours' start. I am to follow, armed only with a pistol of the smallest caliber and range. If my quarry eludes me for three whole days, he wins the game. If I find him"—the general smiled—"he loses."

"Suppose he refuses to be hunted?"

"Oh," said the general, "I give him his option, of course. He need not play that game if he doesn't wish to. If he does not wish to hunt, I turn him over to Ivan. Ivan once had the honor of serving as official knouter[5] to the Great White Czar,[6] and he has his own ideas of sport. Invariably, Mr. Rainsford, invariably they choose the hunt."

"And if they win?"

The smile on the general's face widened. "To date I have not lost," he said.

Then he added, hastily: "I don't wish you to think me a braggart, Mr. Rainsford. Many of them afford only the most elementary sort of problem. Occasionally I strike a tartar. One almost did win. I eventually had to use the dogs."

"The dogs?"

5. In Czarist Russia the official flogger of criminals.
6. Probably Nicholas II (1868–1918) who was overthrown by the Revolution and executed; "White" designates those opposed to the Communists, or "Reds."

"This way, please. I'll show you."

The general steered Rainsford to a window. The lights from the windows sent a flickering illumination that made grotesque patterns on the courtyard below, and Rainsford could see moving about there a dozen or so huge black shapes; as they turned toward him, their eyes glittered greenly.

"A rather good lot, I think," observed the general. "They are let out at seven every night. If anyone should try to get into my house—or out of it—something extremely regrettable would occur to him." He hummed a snatch of song from the Folies Bergère.[7]

"And now," said the general, "I want to show you my new collection of heads. Will you come with me to the library?"

"I hope," said Rainsford, "that you will excuse me tonight, General Zaroff. I'm really not feeling at all well."

"Ah, indeed?" the general inquired solicitously. "Well, I suppose that's only natural, after your long swim. You need a good, restful night's sleep. Tomorrow you'll feel like a new man, I'll wager. Then we'll hunt, eh? I've one rather promising prospect—"

Rainsford was hurrying from the room.

"Sorry you can't go with me tonight," called the general. "I expect rather fair sport—a big, strong black. He looks resourceful—Well, good night, Mr. Rainsford; I hope you have a good night's rest."

The bed was good, and the pajamas of the softest silk, and he was tired in every fiber of his being, but nevertheless Rainsford could not quiet his brain with the opiate of sleep. He lay, eyes wide open. Once he thought he heard stealthy steps in the corridor outside his room. He sought to throw open the door; it would not open. He went to the window and looked out. His room was high up in one of the towers. The lights of the château were out now; and it was dark and silent, but there was a fragment of sallow moon, and by its wan light he could see, dimly, the courtyard; there, weaving in and out in the pattern of shadow, were black, noiseless forms; the hounds heard him at the window and looked up, expectantly, with their green eyes. Rainsford went back to bed and lay down. By many methods he tried to put himself to sleep. He had achieved a doze when, just as morning began to come, he heard, far off in the jungle, the faint report of a pistol.

General Zaroff did not appear until luncheon. He was dressed faultlessly in the tweeds of a country squire. He was solicitous about the state of Rainsford's health.

"As for me," sighed the general, "I do not feel so well. I am worried, Mr. Rainsford. Last night I detected traces of my old complaint."

To Rainsford's questioning glance the general said: "Ennui. Boredom."

Then, taking a second helping of *crêpes suzette*, the general explained: "The hunting was not good last night. The fellow lost his head. He made a straight trail that offered no problems at all. That's the trouble with these sailors; they have dull brains to begin with, and they do not know how to get about in the woods. They do excessively stupid and obvious things. It's most annoying. Will you have another

---

7. Paris theater and music hall which in 1918 reestablished itself as the scene for revues, spectaculars, etc.

glass of Chablis, Mr. Rainsford?"

"General," said Rainsford firmly, "I wish to leave this island at once."

The general raised his thickets of eyebrows; he seemed hurt. "But, my dear fellow," the general protested, "you've only just come. You've had no hunting—"

"I wish to go today," said Rainsford. He saw the dead black eyes of the general on him, studying him. General Zaroff's face suddenly brightened.

He filled Rainsford's glass with venerable Chablis from a dusty bottle.

"Tonight," said the general, "we will hunt—you and I."

Rainsford shook his head. "No, general," he said, "I will not hunt."

The general shrugged his shoulders and delicately ate a hothouse grape. "As you wish, my friend," he said. "The choice rests entirely with you. But may I not venture to suggest that you will find my idea of sport more diverting than Ivan's?"

He nodded toward the corner to where the giant stood, scowling, his thick arms crossed on his hogshead of a chest.

"You don't mean—" cried Rainsford.

"My dear fellow," said the general, "have I not told you I always mean what I say about hunting? This is really an inspiration. I drink to a foeman worthy of my steel—at last."

The general raised his glass, but Rainsford sat staring at him.

"You'll find this game worth playing," the general said enthusiastically. "Your brain against mine. Your woodcraft against mine. Your strength and stamina against mine. Outdoor chess! And the stake is not without value, eh?"

"And if I win—" began Rainsford huskily.

"I'll cheerfully acknowledge myself defeated if I do not find you by midnight of the third day," said General Zaroff. "My sloop will place you on the mainland near a town."

The general read what Rainsford was thinking.

"Oh, you can trust me," said the Cossack. "I will give you my word as a gentleman and a sportsman. Of course you, in turn, must agree to say nothing of your visit here."

"I'll agree to nothing of the kind," said Rainsford.

"Oh," said the general, "in that case—But why discuss that now? Three days hence we can discuss it over a bottle of Veuve Cliquot,[8] unless—"

The general sipped his wine.

Then a businesslike air animated him. "Ivan," he said to Rainsford, "will supply you with hunting clothes, food, a knife. I suggest you wear moccasins; they leave a poorer trail. I suggest too that you avoid the big swamp in the southeast corner of the island. We call it Death Swamp. There's quicksand there. One foolish fellow tried it. The deplorable part of it was that Lazarus followed him. You can imagine my feelings, Mr. Rainsford. I loved Lazarus; he was the finest hound in my pack. Well, I must beg you to excuse me now. I always take a siesta after lunch. You'll hardly have time for a nap, I fear. You'll want to start, no doubt. I shall not follow till dusk. Hunting at night is so

---

8. A fine champagne; Chablis, above, is a very dry white Burgundy table wine; Chambertin, later, is a highly esteemed red Burgundy wine.

much more exciting than by day, don't you think? Au revoir, Mr. Rainsford, au revoir."

General Zaroff, with a deep, courtly bow, strolled from the room.

From another door came Ivan. Under one arm he carried khaki hunting clothes, a haversack of food, a leather sheath containing a long-bladed hunting knife; his right hand rested on a cocked revolver thrust in the crimson sash about his waist. . . .

Rainsford had fought his way through the bush for two hours. "I must keep my nerve. I must keep my nerve," he said through tight teeth.

He had not been entirely clear-headed when the château gates snapped shut behind him. His whole idea at first was to put distance between himself and General Zaroff, and, to this end, he had plunged along, spurred on by the sharp rowels of something very like panic. Now he had got a grip on himself, had stopped, and was taking stock of himself and the situation.

He saw that straight flight was futile; inevitably it would bring him face to face with the sea. He was in a picture with a frame of water, and his operations, clearly, must take place within that frame.

"I'll give him a trail to follow," muttered Rainsford, and he struck off from the rude paths he had been following into the trackless wilderness. He executed a series of intricate loops; he doubled on his trail again and again, recalling all the lore of the fox hunt, and all the dodges of the fox. Night found him leg-weary, with hands and face lashed by the branches, on a thickly wooded ridge. He knew it would be insane to blunder on through the dark, even if he had the strength. His need for rest was imperative and he thought: "I have played the fox, now I must play the cat of the fable."[9] A big tree with a thick trunk and outspread branches was nearby, and, taking care to leave not the slightest mark, he climbed up into the crotch, and stretching out on one of the broad limbs, after a fashion, rested. Rest brought him new confidence and almost a feeling of security. Even so zealous a hunter as General Zaroff could not trace him there, he told himself; only the devil himself could follow that complicated trail through the jungle after dark. But, perhaps, the general was a devil—

An apprehensive night crawled slowly by like a wounded snake, and sleep did not visit Rainsford, although the silence of a dead world was on the jungle. Toward morning when a dingy gray was varnishing the sky, the cry of some startled bird focused Rainsford's attention in that direction. Something was coming through the bush, coming slowly, carefully, coming by the same winding way Rainsford had come. He flattened himself down on the limb, and through a screen of leaves almost as thick as tapestry, he watched. The thing that was approaching was a man.

It was General Zaroff. He made his way along with his eyes fixed in utmost concentration on the ground before him. He paused, almost beneath the tree, dropped to his knees and studied the ground. Rainsford's impulse was to hurl himself down like a panther, but he saw

9. The fox boasts of his many tricks to elude the hounds; the cat responds he knows only one—to climb the nearest tree—but that this is worth more than all the fox's tricks.

that the general's right hand held something metallic—a small automatic pistol.

The hunter shook his head several times, as if he were puzzled. Then he straightened up and took from his case one of his black cigarettes; its pungent incense-like smoke floated up to Rainsford's nostrils.

Rainsford held his breath. The general's eyes had left the ground and were traveling inch by inch up the tree. Rainsford froze there, every muscle tensed for a spring. But the sharp eyes of the hunter stopped before they reached the limb where Rainsford lay; a smile spread over his brown face. Very deliberately he blew a smoke ring into the air; then he turned his back on the tree and walked carelessly away, back along the trail he had come. The swish of the underbrush against his hunting boots grew fainter and fainter.

The pent-up air burst hotly from Rainsford's lungs. His first thought made him feel sick and numb. The general could follow a trail through the woods at night; he could follow an extremely difficult trail; he must have uncanny powers; only by the merest chance had the Cossack failed to see his quarry.

Rainsford's second thought was even more terrible. It sent a shudder of cold horror through his whole being. Why had the general smiled? Why had he turned back?

Rainsford did not want to believe what his reason told him was true, but the truth was as evident as the sun that had by now pushed through the morning mists. The general was playing with him! The general was saving him for another day's sport! The Cossack was the cat; he was the mouse.[1] Then it was that Rainsford knew the full meaning of terror.

"I will not lose my nerve. I will not."

He slid down from the tree, and struck off again into the woods. His face was set and he forced the machinery of his mind to function. Three hundred yards from his hiding place he stopped where a huge dead tree leaned precariously on a smaller, living one. Throwing off his sack of food, Rainsford took his knife from its sheath and began to work with all his energy.

The job was finished at last, and he threw himself down behind a fallen log a hundred feet away. He did not have to wait long. The cat was coming again to play with the mouse.

Following the trail with the sureness of a bloodhound, came General Zaroff. Nothing escaped those searching black eyes, no crushed blade of grass, no bent twig, no mark, no matter how faint, in the moss. So intent was the Cossack on his stalking that he was upon the thing Rainsford had made before he saw it. His foot touched the protruding bough that was the trigger. Even as he touched it, the general sensed his danger and leaped back with the agility of an ape. But he was not quite quick enough; the dead tree, delicately adjusted to rest on the cut living one, crashed down and struck the general a glacing blow on the shoulder as it fell; but for his alertness, he must have been smashed beneath it. He staggered, but he did not fall; nor did he drop his revolver. He stood there, rubbing his injured shoulder, and Rainsford,

---

1. A cat, sure of his prey, plays with a mouse before killing him.

with fear again gripping his heart, heard the general's mocking laugh ring through the jungle.

"Rainsford," called the general, "if you are within sound of my voice, as I suppose you are, let me congratulate you. Not many men know how to make a Malay man-catcher. Luckily, for me, I too have hunted in Malacca. You are proving interesting, Mr. Rainsford. I am going now to have my wound dressed; it's only a slight one. But I shall be back. I shall be back."

When the general, nursing his bruised shoulder, had gone, Rainsford took up his flight again. It was flight now, a desperate, hopeless flight, that carried him on for some hours. Dusk came, then darkness, and still he pressed on. The ground grew softer under his moccasins; the vegetation grew ranker, denser; insects bit him savagely. Then, as he stepped forward, his foot sank into the ooze. He tried to wrench it back, but the muck sucked viciously at his foot as if it were a giant leech. With a violent effort, he tore his foot loose. He knew where he was now. Death Swamp and its quicksand.

His hands were tight closed as if his nerve were something tangible that someone in the darkness was trying to tear from his grip. The softness of the earth had given him an idea. He stepped back from the quicksand a dozen feet or so and, like some huge prehistoric beaver, he began to dig.

Rainsford had dug himself in in France[2] when a second's delay meant death. That had been a placid pastime compared to his digging now. The pit grew deeper; when it was above his shoulders, he climbed out and from some hard saplings cut stakes and sharpened them to a fine point. These stakes he planted in the bottom of the pit with the points sticking up. With flying fingers he wove a rough carpet of weeds and branches and with it he covered the mouth of the pit. Then, wet with sweat and aching with tiredness, he crouched behind the stump of a lightning-charred tree.

He knew his pursuer was coming; he heard the padding sound of feet on the soft earth, and the night breeze brought him the perfume of the general's cigarette. It seemed to Rainsford that the general was coming with unusual swiftness; he was not feeling his way along, foot by foot. Rainsford, crouching there, could not see the general, nor could he see the pit. He lived a year in a minute. Then he felt an impulse to cry aloud with joy, for he heard the sharp crackle of the breaking branches as the cover of the pit gave way; he heard the sharp scream of pain as the pointed stakes found their mark. He leaped up from his place of concealment. Then he cowered back. Three feet from the pit a man was standing, with an electric torch in his hand.

"You've done well, Rainsford," the voice of the general called. "Your Burmese tiger pit has claimed one of my best dogs. Again you score. I think, Mr. Rainsford, I'll see what you can do against my whole pack. I'm going home for a rest now. Thank you for a most amusing evening."

At daybreak Rainsford, lying near the swamp, was awakened by a sound that made him know that he had new things to learn about

2. During World War I he had quickly dug a hole or trench to shelter himself from exploding shells, bullets, etc.

fear. It was a distant sound, faint and wavering, but he knew it. It was the baying of a pack of hounds.

Rainsford knew he could do one of two things. He could stay where he was and wait. That was suicide. He could flee. That was postponing the inevitable. For a moment he stood there, thinking. An idea that held a wild chance came to him, and, tightening his belt, he headed away from the swamp.

The baying of the hounds drew nearer, then still nearer, nearer, ever nearer. On a ridge Rainsford climbed a tree. Down a watercourse, not a quarter of a mile away, he could see the bush moving. Straining his eyes, he saw the lean figure of General Zaroff; just ahead of him Rainsford made out another figure whose wide shoulders surged through the tall jungle weeds; it was the giant Ivan, and he seemed pulled forward by some unseen force; Rainsford knew that Ivan must be holding the pack in leash.

They would be on him any minute now. His mind worked frantically. He thought of a native trick he had learned in Uganda. He slid down the tree. He caught hold of a springy young sapling and to it he fastened his hunting knife, with the blade pointing down the trail; with a bit of wild grapevine he tied back the sapling. Then he ran for his life. The hounds raised their voices as they hit the fresh scent. Rainsford knew now how an animal at bay feels.

He had to stop to get his breath. The baying of the hounds stopped abruptly, and Rainsford's heart stopped too. They must have reached the knife.

He shinned excitedly up a tree and looked back. His pursuers had stopped. But the hope that was in Rainsford's brain when he climbed died, for he saw in the shallow valley that General Zaroff was still on his feet. But Ivan was not. The knife, driven by the recoil of the springing tree, had not wholly failed.

Rainsford had hardly tumbled to the ground when the pack took up the cry again.

"Nerve, nerve, nerve!" he panted, as he dashed along. A blue gap showed between the trees dead ahead. Ever nearer drew the hounds. Rainsford forced himself on toward that gap. He reached it. It was the shore of the sea. Across a cove he could see the gloomy gray stone of the château. Twenty feet below him the sea rumbled and hissed. Rainsford hesitated. He heard the hounds. Then he leaped far out into the sea. . . .

When the general and his pack reached the place by the sea, the Cossack stopped. For some minutes he stood regarding the blue-green expanse of water. He shrugged his shoulders. Then he sat down, took a drink of brandy from a silver flask, lit a perfumed cigarette, and hummed a bit from "Madame Butterfly."

General Zaroff had an exceedingly good dinner in his great paneled dining hall that evening. With it he had a bottle of Pol Roger and half a bottle of Chambertin. Two slight annoyances kept him from perfect enjoyment. One was the thought that it would be difficult to replace Ivan; the other was that his quarry had escaped him; of course the American hadn't played the game—so thought the general as he tasted his after-dinner liqueur. In his library he read, to soothe himself, from the works of Marcus Aurelius.[3] At ten he went up to his bedroom. He was deliciously tired, he said to himself, as he locked himself in. There was a little moonlight, so, before turning on his light, he went to the window and looked down at the courtyard. He could see the great hounds, and he called: "Better luck another time," to them. Then he switched on the light.

A man, who had been hiding in the curtains of the bed, was standing there.

"Rainsford!" screamed the general. "How in God's name did you get here?"

"Swam," said Rainsford. "I found it quicker than walking through the jungle."

The general sucked in his breath and smiled. "I congratulate you," he said. "You have won the game."

Rainsford did not smile. "I am still a beast at bay," he said, in a low, hoarse voice. "Get ready, General Zaroff."

The general made one of his deepest bows. "I see," he said. "Splendid! One of us is to furnish a repast for the hounds. The other will sleep in this very excellent bed. On guard, Rainsford. . . ."

He had never slept in a better bed, Rainsford decided.

1924

ERNEST HEMINGWAY

The Short Happy Life of Francis Macomber

It was now lunch time and they were all sitting under the double green fly of the dining tent pretending that nothing had happened.

"Will you have lime juice or lemon squash?" Macomber asked.

"I'll have a gimlet,"[1] Robert Wilson told him.

"I'll have a gimlet too. I need something," Macomber's wife said.

"I suppose it's the thing to do," Macomber agreed. "Tell him to make three gimlets."

The mess boy had started them already, lifting the bottles out of the canvas cooling bags that sweated wet in the wind that blew through the trees that shaded the tents.

"What had I ought to give them?" Macomber asked.

"A quid[2] would be plenty," Wilson told him. "You don't want to spoil them."

"Will the headman distribute it?"

"Absolutely."

---

3. Roman Emperor (A.D. 161–180), Stoic philosopher, writer, and humanitarian, who, though good to the poor and opposed to the cruelty of gladiatorial shows, persecuted early Christians.

1. Drink of lime juice, gin, and soda or water.

2. Slang for a British pound.

Francis Macomber had, half an hour before, been carried to his tent from the edge of the camp in triumph on the arms and shoulders of the cook, the personal boys, the skinner and the porters. The gun-bearers had taken no part in the demonstration. When the native boys put him down at the door of his tent, he had shaken all their hands, received their congratulations, and then gone into the tent and sat on the bed until his wife came in. She did not speak to him when she came in and he left the tent at once to wash his face and hands in the portable wash basin outside and go over to the dining tent to sit in a comfortable canvas chair in the breeze and the shade.

"You've got your lion," Robert Wilson said to him, "and a damned fine one too."

Mrs. Macomber looked at Wilson quickly. She was an extremely handsome and well-kept woman of the beauty and social position which had, five years before, commanded five thousand dollars as the price of endorsing, with photographs, a beauty product which she had never used. She had been married to Francis Macomber for eleven years.

"He is a good lion, isn't he?" Macomber said. His wife looked at him now. She looked at both these men as though she had never seen them before.

One, Wilson, the white hunter, she knew she had never truly seen before. He was about middle height with sandy hair, a stubby mustache, a very red face and extremely cold blue eyes with faint white wrinkles at the corners that grooved merrily when he smiled. He smiled at her now and she looked away from his face at the way his shoulders sloped in the loose tunic he wore with the four big cartridges held in loops where the left breast pocket should have been, at his big brown hands, his old slacks, his very dirty boots and back to his red face again. She noticed where the baked red of his face stopped in a white line that marked the circle left by his Stetson hat[3] that hung now from one of the pegs of the tent pole.

"Well, here's to the lion," Robert Wilson said. He smiled at her again and, not smiling, she looked curiously at her husband.

Francis Macomber was very tall, very well built if you did not mind that length of bone, dark, his hair cropped like an oarsman, rather thin-lipped, and was considered handsome. He was dressed in the same sort of safari clothes that Wilson wore except that his were new, he was thirty-five years old, kept himself very fit, was good at court games, had a number of big-game fishing records, and had just shown himself, very publicly, to be a coward.

"Here's to the lion," he said. "I can't ever thank you for what you did."

Margaret, his wife, looked away from him and back to Wilson.

"Let's not talk about the lion," she said.

Wilson looked over at her without smiling and now she smiled at him.

"It's been a very strange day," she said. "Hadn't you ought to

---

3. Cowboy-type hat.

put your hat on even under the canvas at noon? You told me that, you know."

"Might put it on," said Wilson.

"You know you have a very red face, Mr. Wilson," she told him and smiled again.

"Drink," said Wilson.

"I don't think so," she said. "Francis drinks a great deal, but his face is never red."

"It's red today," Macomber tried a joke.

"No," said Margaret. "It's mine that's red today. But Mr. Wilson's is always red."

"Must be racial," said Wilson. "I say, you wouldn't like to drop my beauty as a topic, would you?"

"I've just started on it."

"Let's chuck it," said Wilson.

"Conversation is going to be so difficult," Margaret said.

"Don't be silly, Margot," her husband said.

"No difficulty," Wilson said. "Got a damn fine lion."

Margot looked at them both and they both saw that she was going to cry. Wilson had seen it coming for a long time and he dreaded it. Macomber was past dreading it.

"I wish it hadn't happened. Oh, I wish it hadn't happened," she said and started for her tent. She made no noise of crying but they could see that her shoulders were shaking under the rose-colored, sun-proofed shirt she wore.

"Women upset," said Wilson to the tall man. "Amounts to nothing. Strain on the nerves and one thing'n another."

"No," said Macomber. "I suppose that I rate that for the rest of my life now."

"Nonsense. Let's have a spot of the giant killer," said Wilson. "Forget the whole thing. Nothing to it anyway."

"We might try," said Macomber. "I won't forget what you did for me though."

"Nothing," said Wilson. "All nonsense."

So they sat there in the shade where the camp was pitched under some wide-topped acacia trees with a boulder-strewn cliff behind them, and a stretch of grass that ran to the bank of a boulder-filled stream in front with forest beyond it, and drank their just-cool lime drinks and avoided one another's eyes while the boys set the table for lunch. Wilson could tell that the boys all knew about it now and when he saw Macomber's personal boy looking curiously at his master while he was putting dishes on the table he snapped at him in Swahili. The boy turned away with his face blank.

"What were you telling him?" Macomber asked.

"Nothing. Told him to look alive or I'd see he got about fifteen of the best."

"What's that? Lashes?"

"It's quite illegal," Wilson said. "You're supposed to fine them."

"Do you still have them whipped?"

"Oh, yes. They could raise a row if they chose to complain. But they don't. They prefer it to the fines."

"How strange!" said Macomber.

"Not strange, really," Wilson said. "Which would you rather do? Take a good birching or lose your pay?"

Then he felt embarrassed at asking it and before Macomber could answer he went on, "We all take a beating every day, you know, one way or another."

This was no better. "Good God," he thought. "I am a diplomat, aren't I?"

"Yes, we take a beating," said Macomber, still not looking at him. "I'm awfully sorry about that lion business. It doesn't have to go any further, does it? I mean no one will hear about it, will they?"

"You mean will I tell it at the Mathaiga Club?" Wilson looked at him now coldly. He had not expected this. So he's a bloody four-letter man as well as a bloody coward, he thought. I rather liked him too until today. But how is one to know about an American?

"No," said Wilson. "I'm a professional hunter. We never talk about our clients. You can be quite easy on that. It's supposed to be bad form to ask us not to talk though."

He had decided now that to break would be much easier. He would eat, then, by himself and could read a book with his meals. They would eat by themselves. He would see them through the safari on a very formal basis—what was it the French called it? Distinguished consideration[4]—and it would be a damn sight easier than having to go through this emotional trash. He'd insult him and make a good clean break. Then he could read a book with his meals and he'd still be drinking their whisky. That was the phrase for it when a safari went bad. You ran into another white hunter and you asked, "How is everything going?" and he answered, "Oh, I'm still drinking their whisky," and you knew everything had gone to pot.

"I'm sorry," Macomber said and looked at him with his American face that would stay adolescent until it became middle-aged, and Wilson noted his crew-cropped hair, fine eyes only faintly shifty, good nose, thin lips and handsome jaw. "I'm sorry I didn't realize that. There are lots of things I don't know."

So what could he do, Wilson thought. He was all ready to break it off quickly and neatly and here the beggar was apologizing after he had just insulted him. He made one more attempt. "Don't worry about me talking," he said. "I have a living to make. You know in Africa no woman ever misses her lion and no white man ever bolts."

"I bolted like a rabbit," Macomber said.

Now what in hell were you going to do about a man who talked like that, Wilson wondered.

Wilson looked at Macomber with his flat, blue, machine-gunner's eyes and the other smiled back at him. He had a pleasant smile if you did not notice how his eyes showed when he was hurt.

"Maybe I can fix it up on buffalo," he said. "We're after them next, aren't we?"

"In the morning if you like," Wilson told him. Perhaps he had been wrong. This was certainly the way to take it. You most cer-

4. Highest regard.

tainly could not tell a damned thing about an American. He was all for Macomber again. If you could forget the morning. But, of course, you couldn't. The morning had been about as bad as they come.

"Here comes the Memsahib," he said. She was walking over from her tent looking refreshed and cheerful and quite lovely. She had a very perfect oval face, so perfect that you expected her to be stupid. But she wasn't stupid, Wilson thought, no, not stupid.

"How is the beautiful red-faced Mr. Wilson? Are you feeling better, Francis, my pearl?"

"Oh, much," said Macomber.

"I've dropped the whole thing," she said, sitting down at the table. "What importance is there to whether Francis is any good at killing lions? That's not his trade. That's Mr. Wilson's trade. Mr. Wilson is really very impressive killing anything. You do kill anything, don't you?"

"Oh, anything," said Wilson. "Simply anything." They are, he thought, the hardest in the world; the hardest, the cruelest, the most predatory and the most attractive and their men have softened or gone to pieces nervously as they have hardened. Or is it that they pick men they can handle? They can't know that much at the age they marry, he thought. He was grateful that he had gone through his education on American women before now because this was a very attractive one.

"We're going after buff in the morning," he told her.

"I'm coming," she said.

"No, you're not."

"Oh, yes, I am. Mayn't I, Francis?"

"Why not stay in camp?"

"Not for anything," she said. "I wouldn't miss something like today for anything."

When she left, Wilson was thinking, when she went off to cry, she seemed a hell of a fine woman. She seemed to understand, to realize, to be hurt for him and for herself and to know how things really stood. She is away for twenty minutes and now she is back, simply enamelled in that American female cruelty. They are the damnedest women. Really the damnedest.

"We'll put on another show for you tomorrow," Francis Macomber said.

"You're not coming," Wilson said.

"You're very mistaken," she told him. "And I want *so* to see you perform again. You were lovely this morning. That is if blowing things' heads off is lovely."

"Here's the lunch," said Wilson. "You're very merry, aren't you?"

"Why not? I didn't come out here to be dull."

"Well, it hasn't been dull," Wilson said. He could see the boulders in the river and the high bank beyond with the trees and he remembered the morning.

"Oh, no," she said. "It's been charming. And tomorrow. You don't know how I look forward to tomorrow."

"That's eland he's offering you," Wilson said.

"They're the big cowy things that jump like hares, aren't they?"

"I suppose that describes them," Wilson said.

"It's very good meat," Macomber said.

"Didn't you shoot it, Francis?" she asked.

"Yes."

"They're not dangerous, are they?"

"Only if they fall on you," Wilson told her.

"I'm so glad."

"Why not let up on the bitchery just a little, Margot," Macomber said, cutting the eland steak and putting some mashed potato, gravy and carrot on the down-turned fork that tined through the piece of meat.

"I suppose I could," she said, "since you put it so prettily."

"Tonight we'll have champagne for the lion," Wilson said. "It's a bit too hot at noon."

"Oh, the lion," Margot said. "I'd forgotten the lion!"

So, Robert Wilson thought to himself, she *is* giving him a ride, isn't she? Or do you suppose that's her idea of putting up a good show? How should a woman act when she discovers her husband is a bloody coward? She's damn cruel but they're all cruel. They govern, of course, and to govern one has to be cruel sometimes. Still, I've seen enough of their damn terrorism.

"Have some more eland," he said to her politely.

That afternoon, late, Wilson and Macomber went out in the motor car with the native driver and the two gun-bearers. Mrs. Macomber stayed in the camp. It was too hot to go out, she said, and she was going with them in the early morning. As they drove off Wilson saw her standing under the big tree, looking pretty rather than beautiful in her faintly rosy khaki, her dark hair drawn back off her forehead and gathered in a knot low on her neck, her face as fresh, he thought, as though she were in England. She waved to them as the car went off through the swale of high grass and curved around through the trees into the small hills of orchard bush.

In the orchard bush they found a herd of impala,[5] and leaving the car they stalked one old ram with long, wide-spread horns and Macomber killed it with a very creditable shot that knocked the buck down at a good two hundred yards and sent the herd off bounding wildly and leaping over one another's backs in long, leg-drawn-up leaps as unbelievable and as floating as those one makes sometimes in dreams.

"That was a good shot," Wilson said. "They're a small target."

"Is it a worthwhile head?" Macomber asked.

"It's excellent," Wilson told him. "You shoot like that and you'll have no trouble."

"Do you think we'll find buffalo tomorrow?"

"There's a good chance of it. They feed out early in the morning and with luck we may catch them in the open."

"I'd like to clear away that lion business," Macomber said. "It's not very pleasant to have your wife see you do something like that."

5. Antelope of bush country of east and south Africa with lyre-shaped horns.

I should think it would be even more unpleasant to do it, Wilson thought, wife or no wife, or to talk about it having done it. But he said, "I wouldn't think about that any more. Anyone could be upset by his first lion. That's all over."

But that night after dinner and a whisky and soda by the fire before going to bed, as Francis Macomber lay on his cot with the mosquito bar over him and listened to the night noises, it was not all over. It was neither all over nor was it beginning. It was there exactly as it happened with some parts of it indelibly emphasized and he was miserably ashamed at it. But more than shame he felt cold, hollow fear in him. The fear was still there like a cold slimy hollow in all the emptiness where once his confidence had been and it made him feel sick. It was still there with him now.

It had started the night before when he had wakened and heard the lion roaring somewhere up along the river. It was a deep sound and at the end there were sort of coughing grunts that made him seem just outside the tent, and when Francis Macomber woke in the night to hear it he was afraid. He could hear his wife breathing quietly, asleep. There was no one to tell he was afraid, nor to be afraid with him, and, lying alone, he did not know the Somali proverb that says a brave man is always frightened three times by a lion; when he first sees his track, when he first hears him roar and when he first confronts him. Then while they were eating breakfast by lantern light out in the dining tent, before the sun was up, the lion roared again and Francis thought he was just at the edge of camp.

"Sounds like an old-timer," Robert Wilson said, looking up from his kippers and coffee. "Listen to him cough."

"Is he very close?"

"A mile or so up the stream."

"Will we see him?"

"We'll have a look."

"Does his roaring carry that far? It sounds as though he were right in camp."

"Carries a hell of a long way," said Robert Wilson. "It's strange the way it carries. Hope he's a shootable cat. The boys said there was a very big one about here."

"If I get a shot, where should I hit him," Macomber asked, "to stop him?"

"In the shoulders," Wilson said. "In the neck if you can make it. Shoot for bone. Break him down."

"I hope I can place it properly," Macomber said.

"You shoot very well," Wilson told him. "Take your time. Make sure of him. The first one in is the one that counts."

"What range will it be?"

"Can't tell. Lion has something to say about that. Won't shoot unless it's close enough so you can make sure."

"At under a hundred yards?" Macomber asked.

Wilson looked at him quickly.

"Hundred's about right. Might have to take him a bit under. Shouldn't chance a shot at much over that. A hundred's a decent range. You can hit him wherever you want at that. Here comes the Memsahib."

"Good morning," she said. "Are we going after that lion?"

"As soon as you deal with your breakfast," Wilson said. "How are you feeling?"

"Marvellous," she said. "I'm very excited."

"I'll just go and see that everything is ready," Wilson went off. As he left the lion roared again.

"Noisy beggar," Wilson said. "We'll put a stop to that."

"What's the matter, Francis?" his wife asked him.

"Nothing," Macomber said.

"Yes, there is," she said. "What are you upset about?"

"Nothing," he said.

"Tell me," she looked at him. "Don't you feel well?"

"It's that damned roaring," he said. "It's been going on all night, you know."

"Why didn't you wake me," she said. "I'd love to have heard it."

"I've got to kill the damned thing," Macomber said, miserably.

"Well, that's what you're out here for, isn't it?"

"Yes. But I'm nervous. Hearing the thing roar gets on my nerves."

"Well then, as Wilson said, kill him and stop his roaring."

"Yes, darling," said Francis Macomber. "It sounds easy, doesn't it?"

"You're not afraid, are you?"

"Of course not. But I'm nervous from hearing him roar all night."

"You'll kill him marvellously," she said. "I know you will. I'm awfully anxious to see it."

"Finish your breakfast and we'll be starting."

"It's not light yet," she said. "This is a ridiculous hour."

Just then the lion roared in a deep-chested moaning, suddenly guttural, ascending vibration that seemed to shake the air and ended in a sigh and a heavy, deep-chested grunt.

"He sounds almost here," Macomber's wife said.

"My God," said Macomber. "I hate that damned noise."

"It's very impressive."

"Impressive. It's frightful."

Robert Wilson came up then carrying his short, ugly, shockingly big-bored .505 Gibbs and grinning.

"Come on," he said. "Your gun-bearer has your Springfield and the big gun. Everything's in the car. Have you solids?"[6]

"Yes."

"I'm ready," Mrs. Macomber said.

"Must make him stop that racket," Wilson said. "You get in front. The Memsahib can sit back here with me."

They climbed into the motor car and, in the gray first daylight, moved off up the river through the trees. Macomber opened the breech of his rifle and saw he had metal-cased bullets, shut the bolt and put the rifle on safety. He saw his hand was trembling. He felt in his pocket for more cartridges and moved his fingers over the cartridges in the loops of his tunic front. He turned back to where

---

6. They are using jacketed bullets for quick, clean kill; the Springfield is a thirty-caliber rifle as opposed to Wilson's fifty-caliber Gibbs.

Wilson sat in the rear seat of the doorless, box-bodied motor car beside his wife, them both grinning with excitement, and Wilson leaned forward and whispered,

"See the birds dropping. Means the old boy has left his kill."

On the far bank of the stream Macomber could see, above the trees, vultures circling and plummeting down.

"Chances are he'll come to drink along here," Wilson whispered. "Before he goes to lay up. Keep an eye out."

They were driving slowly along the high bank of the stream which here cut deeply to its boulder-filled bed, and they wound in and out through big trees as they drove. Macomber was watching the opposite bank when he felt Wilson take hold of his arm. The car stopped.

"There he is," he heard the whisper. "Ahead and to the right. Get out and take him. He's a marvellous lion."

Macomber saw the lion now. He was standing almost broadside, his great head up and turned toward them. The early morning breeze that blew toward them was just stirring his dark mane, and the lion looked huge, silhouetted on the rise of bank in the gray morning light, his shoulders heavy, his barrel of a body bulking smoothly.

"How far is he?" asked Macomber, raising his rifle.

"About seventy-five. Get out and take him."

"Why not shoot from where I am?"

"You don't shoot them from cars," he heard Wilson saying in his ear. "Get out. He's not going to stay there all day."

Macomber stepped out of the curved opening at the side of the front seat, onto the step and down onto the ground. The lion still stood looking majestically and coolly toward this object that his eyes only showed in silhouette, bulking like some super-rhino. There was no man smell carried toward him and he watched the object, moving his great head a little from side to side. Then watching the object, not afraid, but hesitating before going down the bank to drink with such a thing opposite him, he saw a man figure detach itself from it and he turned his heavy head and swung away toward the cover of the trees as he heard a cracking crash and felt the slam of a .30–06 220-grain solid bullet that bit his flank and ripped in sudden hot scalding nausea through his stomach. He trotted, heavy, big-footed, swinging wounded full-bellied, through the trees toward the tall grass and cover, and the crash came again to go past him ripping the air apart. Then it crashed again and he felt the blow as it hit his lower ribs and ripped on through, blood sudden hot and frothy in his mouth, and he galloped toward the high grass where he could crouch and not be seen and make them bring the crashing thing close enough so he could make a rush and get the man that held it.

Macomber had not thought how the lion felt as he got out of the car. He only knew his hands were shaking and as he walked away from the car it was almost impossible for him to make his legs move. They were stiff in the thighs, but he could feel the muscles fluttering. He raised the rifle, sighted on the junction of the lion's head and shoulders and pulled the trigger. Nothing happened though he pulled until he thought his finger would break. Then he knew he had the safety on and as he lowered the rifle to move the safety over he moved another frozen pace forward, and the lion seeing his silhouette now clear of the silhouette of the car, turned and started off at a trot, and, as Macomber fired, he heard a whunk that meant that the bullet was home; but the lion kept on going. Macomber shot again and everyone saw the bullet throw a spout of dirt beyond the trotting lion. He shot again, remembering to lower his aim, and they all heard the bullet hit, and the lion went into a gallop and was in the tall grass before he had the bolt pushed forward.

Macomber stood there feeling sick at his stomach, his hands that held the Springfield still cocked, shaking, and his wife and Robert Wilson were standing by him. Beside him too were the two gun-bearers chattering in Wakamba.[7]

"I hit him," Macomber said. "I hit him twice."

"You gut-shot him and you hit him somewhere forward," Wilson said without enthusiasm. The gun-bearers looked very grave. They were silent now.

"You may have killed him," Wilson went on. "We'll have to wait a while before we go in to find out."

"What do you mean?"

"Let him get sick before we follow him up."

"Oh," said Macomber.

"He's a hell of a fine lion," Wilson said cheerfully. "He's gotten into a bad place though."

"Why is it bad?"

"Can't see him until you're on him."

"Oh," said Macomber.

"Come on," said Wilson. "The Memsahib can stay here in the car. We'll go to have a look at the blood spoor."

"Stay here, Margot," Macomber said to his wife. His mouth was very dry and it was hard for him to talk.

"Why?" she asked.

"Wilson says to."

"We're going to have a look," Wilson said. "You stay here. You can see even better from here."

"All right."

Wilson spoke in Swahili to the driver. He nodded and said, "Yes, Bwana."

Then they went down the steep bank and across the stream, climbing over and around the boulders and up the other bank, pulling up by some projecting roots, and along it until they found where the lion had been trotting when Macomber first shot. There was dark blood on the short grass that the gun-bearers pointed out with grass stems, and that ran away behind the river bank trees.

"What do we do?" asked Macomber.

"Not much choice," said Wilson. "We can't bring the car over. Bank's too steep. We'll let him stiffen up a bit and then you and

7. A Bantu dialect spoken in Kenya.

I'll go in and have a look for him."

"Can't we set the grass on fire?" Macomber asked.

"Too green."

"Can't we send beaters?"

Wilson looked at him appraisingly. "Of course we can," he said. "But it's just a touch murderous. You see we know the lion's wounded. You can drive an unwounded lion—he'll move on ahead of a noise— but a wounded lion's going to charge. You can't see him until you're right on him. He'll make himself perfectly flat in cover you wouldn't think would hide a hare. You can't very well send boys in there to that sort of a show. Somebody bound to get mauled."

"What about the gun-bearers?"

"Oh, they'll go with us. It's their *shauri*.[8] You see, they signed on for it. They don't look too happy though, do they?"

"I don't want to go in there," said Macomber. It was out before he knew he'd said it.

"Neither do I," said Wilson very cheerily. "Really no choice though." Then, as an afterthought, he glanced at Macomber and saw suddenly how he was trembling and the pitiful look on his face.

"You don't have to go in, of course," he said. "That's what I'm hired for, you know. That's why I'm so expensive."

"You mean you'd go in by yourself? Why not leave him there?"

Robert Wilson, whose entire occupation had been with the lion and the problem he presented, and who had not been thinking about Macomber except to note that he was rather windy, suddenly felt as though he had opened the wrong door in a hotel and seen something shameful.

"What do you mean?"

"Why not just leave him?"

"You mean pretend to ourselves he hasn't been hit?"

"No. Just drop it."

"It isn't done."

"Why not?"

"For one thing, he's certain to be suffering. For another, some one else might run onto him."

"I see."

"But you don't have to have anything to do with it."

"I'd like to," Macomber said. "I'm just scared, you know."

"I'll go ahead when we go in," Wilson said, "with Kongoni tracking. You keep behind me and a little to one side. Chances are we'll hear him growl. If we see him we'll both shoot. Don't worry about anything. I'll keep you backed up. As a matter of fact, you know, perhaps you'd better not go. It might be much better. Why don't you go over and join the Memsahib while I just get it over with?"

"No, I want to go."

"All right," said Wilson. "But don't go in if you don't want to. This is my *shauri* now, you know."

"I want to go," said Macomber.

They sat under a tree and smoked.

8. Problem (a Swahili word).

"Want to go back and speak to the Memsahib while we're waiting?" Wilson asked.

"No."

"I'll just step back and tell her to be patient."

"Good," said Macomber. He sat there, sweating under his arms, his mouth dry, his stomach hollow feeling, wanting to find courage to tell Wilson to go on and finish off the lion without him. He could not know that Wilson was furious because he had not noticed the state he was in earlier and sent him back to his wife. While he sat there Wilson came up. "I have your big gun," he said. "Take it. We've given him time, I think. Come on."

Macomber took the big gun and Wilson said:

"Keep behind me and about five yards to the right and do exactly as I tell you." Then he spoke in Swahili to the two gun-bearers, who looked the picture of gloom.

"Let's go," he said.

"Could I have a drink of water?" Macomber asked. Wilson spoke to the older gun-bearer, who wore a canteen on his belt, and the man unbuckled it, unscrewed the top and handed it to Macomber, who took it noticing how heavy it seemed and how hairy and shoddy the felt covering was in his hand. He raised it to drink and looked ahead at the high grass with the flat-topped trees behind it. A breeze was blowing toward them and the grass rippled gently in the wind. He looked at the gun-bearer and he could see the gun-bearer was suffering too with fear.

Thirty-five yards into the grass the big lion lay flattened out along the ground. His ears were back and his only movement was a slight twitching up and down of his long, black-tufted tail. He had turned at bay as soon as he had reached this cover and he was sick with the wound through his full belly, and weakening with the wound through his lungs that brought a thin foamy red to his mouth each time he breathed. His flanks were wet and hot and flies were on the little openings the solid bullets had made in his tawny hide, and his big yellow eyes, narrowed with hate, looked straight ahead, only blinking when the pain came as he breathed, and his claws dug in the soft baked earth. All of him, pain, sickness, hatred and all of his remaining strength, was tightening into an absolute concentration for a rush. He could hear the men talking and he waited, gathering all of himself into this preparation for a charge as soon as the men would come into the grass. As he heard their voices his tail stiffened to twitch up and down, and, as they came into the edge of the grass, he made a coughing grunt and charged.

Kongoni, the old gun-bearer, in the lead watching the blood spoor, Wilson watching the grass for any movement, his big gun ready, the second gun-bearer looking ahead and listening, Macomber close to Wilson, his rifle cocked, they had just moved into the grass when Macomber heard the blood-choked coughing grunt, and saw the swishing rush in the grass. The next thing he knew he was running; running wildly, in panic in the open, running toward the stream.

He heard the *ca-ra-wong!* of Wilson's big rifle, and again in a second crashing *carawong!* and turning saw the lion, horrible-looking now, with half his head seeming to be gone, crawling toward Wilson in the edge of the tall grass while the red-faced man worked the bolt on the short ugly rifle and aimed carefully as another blasting *carawong!* came from the muzzle, and the crawling, heavy, yellow bulk of the lion stiffened and the huge, mutilated head slid forward and Macomber, standing by himself in the clearing where he had run, holding a loaded rifle, while two black men and a white man looked back at him in contempt, knew the lion was dead. He came toward Wilson, his tallness all seeming a naked reproach, and Wilson looked at him and said:

"Want to take pictures?"

"No," he said.

That was all any one had said until they reached the motor car. Then Wilson had said:

"Hell of a fine lion. Boys will skin him out. We might as well stay here in the shade."

Macomber's wife had not looked at him nor he at her and he had sat by her in the back seat with Wilson sitting in the front seat. Once he had reached over and taken his wife's hand without looking at her and she had removed her hand from his. Looking across the stream to where the gun-bearers were skinning out the lion he could see that she had been able to see the whole thing. While they sat there his wife had reached forward and put her hand on Wilson's shoulder. He turned and she had leaned forward over the low seat and kissed him on the mouth.

"Oh, I say," said Wilson, going redder than his natural baked color.

"Mr. Robert Wilson," she said. "The beautiful red-faced Mr. Robert Wilson."

Then she sat down beside Macomber again and looked away across the stream to where the lion lay, with uplifted, white-muscled, tendon-marked naked forearms, and white bloating belly, as the black men fleshed away the skin. Finally the gun-bearers brought the skin over, wet and heavy, and climbed in behind with it, rolling it up before they got in, and the motor car started. No one had said anything more until they were back in camp.

That was the story of the lion. Macomber did not know how the lion had felt before he started his rush, nor during it when the unbelievable smash of the .505 with a muzzle velocity of two tons had hit him in the mouth, nor what kept him coming after that, when the second ripping crash had smashed his hind quarters and he had come crawling on toward the crashing, blasting thing that had destroyed him. Wilson knew something about it and only expressed it by saying, "Damned fine lion," but Macomber did not know how Wilson felt about things either. He did not know how his wife felt except that she was through with him.

His wife had been through with him before but it never lasted. He was very wealthy, and would be much wealthier, and he knew she would not leave him ever now. That was one of the few things that he really knew. He knew about that, about motorcycles—that was earliest—about motor cars, about duck-shooting, about fishing,

trout, salmon and big-sea, about sex in books, many books, too many
books, about all court games, about dogs, not much about horses,
about hanging on to his money, about most of the other things his
world dealt in, and about his wife not leaving him. His wife had been
a great beauty and she was still a great beauty in Africa, but she was
not a great enough beauty any more at home to be able to leave him
and better herself and she knew it and he knew it. She had missed
the chance to leave him and he knew it. If he had been better with
women she would probably have started to worry about him getting
another new, beautiful wife; but she knew too much about him to
worry about him either. Also, he had always had a great tolerance
which seemed the nicest thing about him if it were not the most
sinister.

All in all they were known as a comparatively happily married
couple, one of those whose disruption is often rumored but never
occurs, and as the society columnist put it, they were adding more
than a spice of *adventure* to their much envied and ever-enduring
Romance by a *Safari* in what was known as *Darkest Africa* until the
Martin Johnsons lighted it on so many silver screens where they were
pursuing *Old Simba* the lion, the buffalo, *Tembo* the elephant and
as well collecting specimens for the Museum of Natural History.[9]
This same columnist had reported them *on the verge* at least three
times in the past and they had been. But they always made it up.
They had a sound basis of union. Margot was too beautiful for
Macomber to divorce her and Macomber had too much money for
Margot ever to leave him.

It was now about three o'clock in the morning and Francis Macomber, who had been asleep a little while after he had stopped
thinking about the lion, wakened and then slept again, woke suddenly, frightened in a dream of the bloody-headed lion standing over
him, and listening while his heart pounded, he realized that his wife
was not in the other cot in the tent. He lay awake with that knowledge for two hours.

At the end of that time his wife came into the tent, lifted her
mosquito bar and crawled cozily into bed.

"Where have you been?" Macomber asked in the darkness.

"Hello," she said. "Are you awake?"

"Where have you been?"

"I just went out to get a breath of air."

"You did, like hell."

"What do you want me to say, darling?"

"Where have you been?"

"Out to get a breath of air."

"That's a new name for it. You *are* a bitch."

"Well, you're a coward."

"All right," he said. "What of it?"

"Nothing as far as I'm concerned. But please let's not talk, darling,
because I'm very sleepy."

"You think that I'll take anything."

9. Martin and Osa Johnson from 1921 to 1936 made nature films in Africa.

"I know you will, sweet."

"Well, I won't."

"Please, darling, let's not talk. I'm so very sleepy."

"There wasn't going to be any of that. You promised there wouldn't be."

"Well, there is now," she said sweetly.

"You said if we made this trip that there would be none of that. You promised."

"Yes, darling. That's the way I meant it to be. But the trip was spoiled yesterday. We don't have to talk about it, do we?"

"You don't wait long when you have an advantage, do you?"

"Please let's not talk. I'm so sleepy, darling."

"I'm going to talk."

"Don't mind me then, because I'm going to sleep." And she did.

At breakfast they were all three at the table before daylight and Francis Macomber found that, of all the many men that he had hated, he hated Robert Wilson the most.

"Sleep well?" Wilson asked in his throaty voice, filling a pipe.

"Did you?"

"Topping," the white hunter told him.

You bastard, thought Macomber, you insolent bastard.

So she woke him when she came in, Wilson thought, looking at them both with his flat, cold eyes. Well, why doesn't he keep his wife where she belongs? What does he think I am, a bloody plaster saint? Let him keep her where she belongs. It's his own fault.

"Do you think we'll find buffalo?" Margot asked, pushing away a dish of apricots.

"Chance of it," Wilson said and smiled at her. "Why don't you stay in camp?"

"Not for anything," she told him.

"Why not order her to stay in camp?" Wilson said to Macomber.

"You order her," said Macomber coldly.

"Let's not have any ordering, nor," turning to Macomber, "any silliness, Francis," Margot said quite pleasantly.

"Are you ready to start?" Macomber asked.

"Any time," Wilson told him. "Do you want the Memsahib to go?"

"Does it make any difference whether I do or not?"

The hell with it, thought Robert Wilson. The utter complete hell with it. So this is what it's going to be like. Well, this is what it's going to be like, then.

"Makes no difference," he said.

"You're sure you wouldn't like to stay in camp with her yourself and let me go out and hunt the buffalo?" Macomber asked.

"Can't do that," said Wilson. "Wouldn't talk rot if I were you."

"I'm not talking rot. I'm disgusted."

"Bad word, disgusted."

"Francis, will you please try to speak sensibly?" his wife said.

"I speak too damned sensibly," Macomber said. "Did you ever eat such filthy food?"

"Something wrong with the food?" asked Wilson quietly.

"No more than with everything else."

"I'd pull yourself together, laddybuck," Wilson said very quietly. "There's a boy waits at table that understands a little English."

"The hell with him."

Wilson stood up and puffing on his pipe strolled away, speaking a few words in Swahili to one of the gun-bearers who was standing waiting for him. Macomber and his wife sat on at the table. He was staring at his coffee cup.

"If you make a scene I'll leave you, darling," Margot said quietly.

"No, you won't."

"You can try it and see."

"You won't leave me."

"No," she said. "I won't leave you and you'll behave yourself."

"Behave myself? That's a way to talk. Behave myself."

"Yes. Behave yourself."

"Why don't *you* try behaving?"

"I've tried it so long. So very long."

"I hate that red-faced swine," Macomber said. "I loathe the sight of him."

"He's really *very* nice."

"Oh, *shut up*," Macomber almost shouted. Just then the car came up and stopped in front of the dining tent and the driver and the two gun-bearers got out. Wilson walked over and looked at the husband and wife sitting there at the table.

"Going shooting?" he asked.

"Yes," said Macomber, standing up. "Yes."

"Better bring a woolly. It will be cool in the car," Wilson said.

"I'll get my leather jacket," Margot said.

"The boy has it," Wilson told her. He climbed into the front with the driver and Francis Macomber and his wife sat, not speaking, in the back seat.

Hope the silly beggar doesn't take a notion to blow the back of my head off, Wilson thought to himself. Women *are* a nuisance on safari.

The car was grinding down to cross the river at a pebbly ford in the gray daylight and then climbed, angling up the steep bank, where Wilson had ordered a way shovelled out the day before so they could reach the parklike wooded rolling country on the far side.

It was a good morning, Wilson thought. There was a heavy dew and as the wheels went through the grass and low bushes he could smell the odor of the crushed fronds. It was an odor like verbena and he liked this early morning smell of the dew, the crushed bracken and the look of the tree trunks showing black through the early morning mist, as the car made its way through the untracked, parklike country. He had put the two in the back seat out of his mind now and was thinking about buffalo. The buffalo that he was after stayed in the daytime in a thick swamp where it was impossible to get a shot, but in the night they fed out into an open stretch of country and if he could come between them and their swamp with the car, Macomber would have a good chance at them in the open. He did not want to hunt buff with Macomber in thick cover. He did not want to hunt buff or anything else with Macomber at all, but he was a professional hunter and he had hunted with some rare ones in his time. If they got buff today there would only be rhino to come and the poor man would have gone through his dangerous game and things might pick up. He'd have nothing more to do with the woman and Macomber would get over that too. He must have gone through plenty of that before by the look of things. Poor beggar. He must have a way of getting over it. Well, it was the poor sod's[1] own bloody fault.

He, Robert Wilson, carried a double size cot on safari to accommodate any windfalls he might receive. He had hunted for a certain clientele, the international, fast, sporting set, where the women did not feel they were getting their money's worth unless they had shared that cot with the white hunter. He despised them when he was away from them although he liked some of them well enough at the time, but he made his living by them; and their standards were his standards as long as they were hiring him.

They were his standards in all except the shooting. He had his own standards about the killing and they could live up to them or get some one else to hunt them. He knew, too, that they all respected him for this. This Macomber was an odd one though. Damned if he wasn't. Now the wife. Well, the wife. Yes, the wife. Hm, the wife. Well he'd dropped all that. He looked around at them. Macomber sat grim and furious. Margot smiled at him. She looked younger today, more innocent and fresher and not so professionally beautiful. What's in her heart God knows, Wilson thought. She hadn't talked much last night. At that it was a pleasure to see her.

The motor car climbed up a slight rise and went on through the trees and then out into a grassy prairie-like opening and kept in the shelter of the trees along the edge, the driver going slowly and Wilson looking carefully out across the prairie and all along its far side. He stopped the car and studied the opening with his field glasses. Then he motioned to the driver to go on and the car moved slowly along, the driver avoiding wart-hog holes and driving around the mud castles ants had built. Then, looking across the opening, Wilson suddenly turned and said,

"By God, there they are!"

And looking where he pointed, while the car jumped forward and Wilson spoke in rapid Swahili to the driver, Macomber saw three huge, black animals looking almost cylindrical in their long heaviness, like big black tank cars, moving at a gallop across the far edge of the open prairie. They moved at a stiff-necked, stiff bodied gallop and he could see the upswept wide black horns on their heads as they galloped heads out; the heads not moving.

"They're three old bulls," Wilson said. "We'll cut them off before they get to the swamp."

The car was going a wild forty-five miles an hour across the open and as Macomber watched, the buffalo got bigger and bigger until he could see the gray, hairless, scabby look of one huge bull and how his neck was a part of his shoulders and the shiny black of his

---

1. Chap or fellow, now nonpejorative but originally "sodomite" (cp. "bugger").

horns as he galloped a little behind the others that were strung out
in that steady plunging gait; and then, the car swaying as though
it had just jumped a road, they drew up close and he could see
the plunging hugeness of the bull, and the dust in his sparsely haired
hide, the side boss of horn and his outstretched, wide-nostrilled
muzzle, and he was raising his rifle when Wilson shouted, "Not from
the car, you fool!" and he had no fear, only hatred of Wilson, while
the brakes clamped on and the car skidded, plowing sideways to
an almost stop and Wilson was out on one side and he on the other,
stumbling as his feet hit the still speeding-by of the earth, and then
he was shooting at the bull as he moved away, hearing the bullets
whunk into him, emptying his rifle at him as he moved steadily away,
finally remembering to get his shots forward into the shoulder, and
as he fumbled to re-load, he saw the bull was down. Down on his
knees, his big head tossing, and seeing the other two still galloping
he shot at the leader and hit him. He shot again and missed and
he heard the *carawonging* roar as Wilson shot and saw the leading
bull slide forward onto his nose.

"Get that other," Wilson said. "Now you're shooting!"

But the other bull was moving steadily at the same gallop and he
missed, throwing a spout of dirt, and Wilson missed and the dust
rose in a cloud and Wilson shouted, "Come on. He's too far!" and
grabbed his arm and they were in the car again, Macomber and
Wilson hanging on the sides and rocketing swayingly over the un-
even ground, drawing up on the steady, plunging, heavy-necked,
straight-moving gallop of the bull.

They were behind him and Macomber was filling his rifle, dropping
shells onto the ground, jamming it, clearing the jam, then they were
almost up with the bull when Wilson yelled "Stop," and the car
skidded so that it almost swung over and Macomber fell forward
onto his feet, slammed his bolt forward and fired as far forward
as he could aim into the galloping, rounded black back, aimed and
shot again, then again, then again, and the bullets, all of them hitting,
had no effect on the buffalo that he could see. Then Wilson shot,
the roar deafening him, and he could see the bull stagger. Macomber
shot again, aiming carefully, and down he came, onto his knees.

"All right," Wilson said. "Nice work. That's the three."

Macomber felt a drunken elation.

"How many times did you shoot?" he asked.

"Just three," Wilson said. "You killed the first bull. The biggest one.
I helped you finish the other two. Afraid they might have got into
cover. You had them killed. I was just mopping up a little. You
shot damn well."

"Let's go to the car," said Macomber. "I want a drink."

"Got to finish off that buff first," Wilson told him. The buffalo was
on his knees and he jerked his head furiously and bellowed in pig-
eyed, roaring rage as they came toward him.

"Watch he doesn't get up," Wilson said. Then, "Get a little broadside and take him in the neck just behind the ear."

Macomber aimed carefully at the center of the huge, jerking, rage-
driven neck and shot. At the shot the head dropped forward.

"That does it," said Wilson. "Got the spine. They're a hell of a looking thing, aren't they?"

"Let's get the drink," said Macomber. In his life he had never felt so good.

In the car Macomber's wife sat very white faced. "You were marvellous, darling," she said to Macomber. "What a ride."

"Was it rough?" Wilson asked.

"It was frightful. I've never been more frightened in my life."

"Let's all have a drink," Macomber said.

"By all means," said Wilson. "Give it to the Memsahib." She drank the neat whisky from the flask and shuddered a little when she swallowed. She handed the flask to Macomber who handed it to Wilson.

"It was frightfully exciting," she said. "It's given me a dreadful headache. I didn't know you were allowed to shoot them from cars though."

"No one shot from cars," said Wilson coldly.

"I mean chase them from cars."

"Wouldn't ordinarily," Wilson said. "Seemed sporting enough to me though while we were doing it. Taking more chance driving that way across the plain full of holes and one thing and another than hunting on foot. Buffalo could have charged us each time we shot if he liked. Gave him every chance. Wouldn't mention it to any one though. It's illegal if that's what you mean."

"It seemed very unfair to me," Margot said, "chasing those big helpless things in a motor car."

"Did it?" said Wilson.

"What would happen if they heard about it in Nairobi?"

"I'd lose my license for one thing. Other unpleasantnesses," Wilson said, taking a drink from the flask. "I'd be out of business."

"Really?"

"Yes, really."

"Well," said Macomber, and he smiled for the first time all day. "Now she has something on you."

"You have such a pretty way of putting things, Francis," Margot Macomber said. Wilson looked at them both. If a four-letter man marries a five-letter woman, he was thinking, what number of letters would their children be? What he said was, "We lost a gun-bearer. Did you notice it?"

"My God, no," Macomber said.

"Here he comes," Wilson said. "He's all right. He must have fallen off when we left the first bull."

Approaching them was the middle-aged gun-bearer, limping along in his knitted cap, khaki tunic, shorts and rubber sandals, gloomy-faced and disgusted looking. As he came up he called out to Wilson in Swahili and they all saw the change in the white hunter's face.

"What does he say?" asked Margot.

"He says the first bull got up and went into the bush," Wilson said with no expression in his voice.

"Oh," said Macomber blankly.

"Then it's going to be just like the lion," said Margot, full of anticipation.

"It's not going to be a damned bit like the lion," Wilson told her.

"Did you want another drink, Macomber?"

"Thanks, yes," Macomber said. He expected the feeling he had had about the lion to come back but it did not. For the first time in his life he really felt wholly without fear. Instead of fear he had a feeling of definite elation.

"We'll go and have a look at the second bull," Wilson said. "I'll tell the driver to put the car in the shade."

"What are you going to do?" asked Margaret Macomber.

"Take a look at the buff," Wilson said.

"I'll come."

"Come along."

The three of them walked over to where the second buffalo bulked blackly in the open, head forward on the grass, the massive horns swung wide.

"He's a very good head," Wilson said. "That's close to a fifty-inch spread."

Macomber was looking at him with delight.

"He's hateful looking," said Margot. "Can't we go into the shade?"

"Of course," Wilson said. "Look," he said to Macomber, and pointed. "See that patch of bush?"

"Yes."

"That's where the first bull went in. The gun-bearer said when he fell off the bull was down. He was watching us helling along and the other two buff galloping. When he looked up there was the bull up and looking at him. Gun-bearer ran like hell and the bull went off slowly into that bush."

"Can we go in after him now?" asked Macomber eagerly.

Wilson looked at him appraisingly. Damned if this isn't a strange one, he thought. Yesterday he's scared sick and today he's a ruddy[2] fire eater.

"No, we'll give him a while."

"Let's please go into the shade," Margot said. Her face was white and she looked ill.

They made their way to the car where it stood under a single, wide-spreading tree and all climbed in.

"Chances are he's dead in there," Wilson remarked. "After a little we'll have a look."

Macomber felt a wild unreasonable happiness that he had never known before.

"By God, that was a chase," he said. "I've never felt any such feeling. Wasn't it marvellous, Margot?"

"I hated it."

"Why?"

"I hated it," she said bitterly. "I loathed it."

"You know I don't think I'd ever be afraid of anything again," Macomber said to Wilson. "Something happened in me after we first saw the buff and started after him. Like a dam bursting. It was pure excitement."

"Cleans out your liver," said Wilson. "Damn funny things happen to people."

2. Euphemism for the stronger "bloody."

Cowards die many times before their death
The Short Happy Life of Francis Macomber 59
The valiant never taste of death but once—

Macomber's face was shining. "You know something did happen to me," he said. "I feel absolutely different."

His wife said nothing and eyed him strangely. She was sitting far back in the seat and Macomber was sitting forward talking to Wilson who turned sideways talking over the back of the front seat.

"You know, I'd like to try another lion," Macomber said. "I'm really not afraid of them now. After all, what can they do to you?"

"That's it," said Wilson. "Worst one can do is kill you. How does it go? Shakespeare. Damned good. See if I can remember. Oh, damned good. Used to quote it to myself at one time. Let's see. 'By my troth, I care not; a man can die but once; we owe God a death and let it go which way it will he that dies this year is quit for the next.'[3] Damned fine, eh?"

He was very embarrassed, having brought out this thing he had lived by, but he had seen men come of age before and it always moved him. It was not a matter of their twenty-first birthday.

It had taken a strange chance of hunting, a sudden precipitation into action without opportunity for worrying beforehand, to bring this about with Macomber, but regardless of how it had happened it had most certainly happened. Look at the beggar now, Wilson thought. It's that some of them stay little boys so long, Wilson thought. Sometimes all their lives. Their figures stay boyish when they're fifty. The great American boy-men. Damned strange people. But he liked this Macomber now. Damned strange fellow. Probably meant the end of cuckoldry too. Well, that would be a damned good thing. Damned good thing. Beggar had probably been afraid all his life. Don't know what started it. But over now. Hadn't had time to be afraid with the buff. That and being angry too. Motor car too. Motor cars made it familiar. Be a damn fire eater now. He'd seen it in the war work the same way. More of a change than any loss of virginity. Fear gone like an operation. Something else grew in its place. Main thing a man had. Made him into a man. Women knew it too. No bloody fear.

From the far corner of the seat Margaret Macomber looked at the two of them. There was no change in Wilson. She saw Wilson as she had seen him the day before when she had first realized what his great talent was. But she saw the change in Francis Macomber now.

"Do you have that feeling of happiness about what's going to happen?" Macomber asked, still exploring his new wealth.

"You're not supposed to mention it," Wilson said, looking in the other's face. "Much more fashionable to say you're scared. Mind you, you'll be scared too, plenty of times."

"But you *have* a feeling of happiness about action to come?"

"Yes," said Wilson. "There's that. Doesn't do to talk too much about all this. Talk the whole thing away. No pleasure in anything if you mouth it up too much."

"You're both talking rot," said Margot. "Just because you've chased

---

3. Shakespeare, *Henry IV Part 2*, III, 2, 250–55. There are some differences in punctuation, and after "owe God a death," the following is omitted: "I'll ne'er bear a base mind. An't be my destiny, so; an't be not, so. No man's too good to serve's prince."

some helpless animals in a motor car you talk like heroes."

"Sorry," said Wilson. "I have been gassing too much." She's worried about it already, he thought.

"If you don't know what we're talking about why not keep out of it?" Macomber asked his wife.

"You've gotten awfully brave, awfully suddenly," his wife said contemptuously, but her contempt was not secure. She was very afraid of something.

Macomber laughed, a very natural hearty laugh. "You know I *have*," he said. "I really have."

"Isn't it sort of late?" Margot said bitterly. Because she had done the best she could for many years back and the way they were together now was no one person's fault.

"Not for me," said Macomber.

Margot said nothing but sat back in the corner of the seat.

"Do you think we've given him time enough?" Macomber asked Wilson cheerfully.

"We might have a look," Wilson said. "Have you any solids left?"

"The gun-bearer has some."

Wilson called in Swahili and the older gun-bearer, who was skinning out one of the heads, straightened up, pulled a box of solids out of his pocket and brought them over to Macomber, who filled his magazine and put the remaining shells in his pocket.

"You might as well shoot the Springfield," Wilson said. "You're used to it. We'll leave the Mannlicher in the car with the Memsahib. Your gun-bearer can carry your heavy gun. I've this damned cannon. Now let me tell you about them." He had saved this until the last because he did not want to worry Macomber. "When a buff comes he comes with his head high and thrust straight out. The boss of the horns covers any sort of a brain shot. The only shot is straight into the nose. The only other shot is into his chest or, if you're to one side, into the neck or the shoulders. After they've been hit once they take a hell of a lot of killing. Don't try anything fancy. Take the easiest shot there is. They've finished skinning out that head now. Should we get started."

He called to the gun-bearers, who came up wiping their hands, and the older one got into the back.

"I'll only take Kongoni," Wilson said. "The other can watch to keep the birds away."

As the car moved slowly across the open space toward the island of brushy trees that ran in a tongue of foliage along a dry water course that cut the open swale, Macomber felt his heart pounding and his mouth was dry again, but it was excitement, not fear.

"Here's where he went in," Wilson said. Then to the gun-bearer in Swahili, "Take the blood spoor."

The car was parallel to the patch of bush. Macomber, Wilson and the gun-bearer got down. Macomber, looking back, saw his wife, with the rifle by her side, looking at him. He waved to her and she did not wave back.

The brush was very thick ahead and the ground was dry. The middle-aged gun-bearer was sweating heavily and Wilson had his hat down over his eyes and his red neck showed just ahead of Macomber. Suddenly the gun-bearer said something in Swahili to Wilson and ran forward.

"He's dead in there," Wilson said. "Good work," and he turned to grip Macomber's hand and as they shook hands, grinning at each other, the gun-bearer shouted wildly and they saw him coming out of the brush sideways, fast as a crab, and the bull coming, nose out, mouth tight closed, blood dripping, massive head straight out, coming in a charge, his little pig eyes bloodshot as he looked at them. Wilson, who was ahead was kneeling shooting, and Macomber, as he fired, unhearing his shot in the roaring of Wilson's gun, saw fragments like slate burst from the huge boss of the horns, and the head jerked, he shot again at the wide nostrils and saw the horns jolt again and fragments fly, and he did not see Wilson now and, aiming carefully, shot again with the buffalo's huge bulk almost on him and his rifle almost level with the on-coming head, nose out, and he could see the little wicked eyes and the head started to lower and he felt a sudden white-hot, blinding flash explode inside his head and that was all he ever felt.

Wilson had ducked to one side to get in a shoulder shot. Macomber had stood solid and shot for the nose, shooting a touch high each time and hitting the heavy horns, splintering and chipping them like hitting a slate roof, and Mrs. Macomber, in the car, had shot at the buffalo with the 6.5 Mannlicher as it seemed about to gore Macomber and had hit her husband about two inches up and a little to one side of the base of his skull.

Francis Macomber lay now, face down, not two yards from where the buffalo lay on his side and his wife knelt over him with Wilson beside her.

"I wouldn't turn him over," Wilson said.

The woman was crying hysterically.

"I'd get back in the car," Wilson said. "Where's the rifle?"

She shook her head, her face contorted. The gun-bearer picked up the rifle.

"Leave it as it is," said Wilson. Then, "Go get Abdulla so that he may witness the manner of the accident."

He knelt down, took a handkerchief from his pocket, and spread it over Francis Macomber's crew-cropped head where it lay. The blood sank into the dry, loose earth.

Wilson stood up and saw the buffalo on his side, his legs out, his thinly-haired belly crawling with ticks. "Hell of a good bull," his brain registered automatically. "A good fifty inches, or better. Better." He called to the driver and told him to spread a blanket over the body and stay by it. Then he walked over to the motor car where the woman sat crying in the corner.

"That was a pretty thing to do," he said in a toneless voice. "He *would* have left you too."

"Stop it," she said.

"Of course it's an accident," he said. "I know that."

"Stop it," she said.

"Don't worry," he said. "There will be a certain amount of unpleasantness but I will have some photographs taken that will be very useful at the inquest. There's the testimony of the gun-bearers and the driver too. You're perfectly all right."

"Stop it," she said.

"There's a hell of a lot to be done," he said. "And I'll have to send a truck off to the lake to wireless for a plane to take the three of us into Nairobi. Why didn't you poison him? That's what they do in England."

"Stop it. Stop it. Stop it," the woman cried.

Wilson looked at her with his flat blue eyes.

"I'm through now," he said. "I was a little angry. I'd begun to like your husband."

"Oh, please stop it," she said. "Please, please stop it."

"That's better," Wilson said. "Please is much better. Now I'll stop."

p. 1936

3   FOCUS AND VOICE

Who is telling us the story—whose words are we reading? Where does this person stand in relation to what is going on in the story? In narrative someone is always between us and the events—a viewer, a speaker, or both; narrative, unlike drama, is always mediated. The way a story is mediated is a key element in fictional structure. This mediation involves both the angle of vision, the point from which the people, events, and other details are viewed, and also the words of the story lying between us and the history. The viewing aspect is called the focus or point of view, and the verbal aspect the voice.

Focus acts much as a movie camera does, choosing what we can look at and the angle at which we can view it, framing, proportioning, emphasizing—even distorting. Plot is a structure that places us in a time relationship to the history; focus places us in a spatial relationship.

We must pay careful attention to the focus at any given point in a story. Is it fixed or mobile? Does it stay at more or less the same angle to, and at the same distance from, the characters and action, or does it move around or in and out? In the first three and a half paragraphs of *An Occurrence at Owl Creek Bridge,* for example, we seem to be seeing through the lens of a camera that can swing left or right, up or down, but that stays pretty much at the same angle and distance from the bridge. By the middle of the fourth paragraph, however, we're inside the mind of the man who's about to be hanged: "The arrangement commended itself to his judgment. . . . He looked a moment. . . . A piece of dancing driftwood caught his attention. . . . How slowly it appeared to move!" From now on we are inside the condemned man's head. The focus is more limited in scope—for almost all the rest of the story we can see and hear only what he sees and hears. But because the focus is internal as well as limited, we can also know what he thinks. This limited, internal focus, used here as well as in *The Most Dangerous Game*, is usually called the **centered** or **central con- sciousness.**

The centered consciousness has been perhaps the most popular focus in fiction for the past hundred years—through most of the history of the modern short story, in fact—and its tightly controlled range and concentration on a single individual seem particularly suited for the short form. During much of this period, fiction, both long and short, has been in one sense realistic—that is, treating the everyday and the natural. It has become increasingly clear, however, that the apparently real is not necessarily what "is" but what is *perceived* by the senses and mind of the individual. (This is sometimes called **psy- chological realism**.) The centered consciousness, in which things, people, and events are narrated as if they have been perceived through the filter of an individual character's consciousness, has therefore seemed the more realistic way to tell a story. It is a comfortable focus for readers, too. On the one hand, they can identify with someone whose thoughts and perception they share, even if the character is fallible, like Rainsford in *The Most Dangerous Game*, or reprehen- sible, like the womanizing Gurov at the beginning of Chekhov's *The Lady with the Dog*. We can identify with the focus in a story told in the first person ("I"), too, but we are too close at times. We cannot escape. The camera cannot pull back as it can in a third-person story.

First-person stories, like *The Summer My Grandmother Was Sup- posed to Die*, are always limited too, and almost all the time are internal as well (though Montresor, in *The Cask of Amontillado*, hides his plans from us). While they cannot retract spatially from the narrator, they almost always are withdrawn temporally: that is, the "I" telling the story is older than the "I" experiencing the events of the story.

The psychological realism gained by having a limited narrator ex- acts a price from the reader. If we don't hold the author (or the story) responsible for the absolute truth, validity, accuracy, and opinions of the focal character—if he or she is just telling us what he or she thinks, feels, sees—we must accept the possibility that the narrator's vision may be **unreliable.** At a significant point in *Owl Creek Bridge*, for example, you will find that the camera pulls back from Peyton Farquhar and we are made to recognize to what extent his conscious- ness is a reliable witness to what has been going on. The history here is only an occurrence; the limited focus structures the mere occur- rence into a story.

When the focus is limited, whether to a first-person narrator or to a centered consciousness, it is tied to that individual. When he or she leaves the room, the camera must go too, and if we are to know what happens in the room when the focal character is gone, some means of bringing the information to that character must be devised, such as a letter or a report by another character. The camera may pull back out of the character's mind or even, as in *Owl Creek Bridge,* above and away from the character, but it does not generally jump around. The somewhat unusual first-person plural focus of *A Rose for Emily* is not limited to a single individual; anything the town of Jefferson in general can know of past or present, the narrative can know. But neither is it an unlimited focus; "we" could not get into Emily's house before she died and could never get into her mind.

An **unlimited focus** permits such freedom. In *The Short Happy Life of Francis Macomber* we enter the minds of each of the main characters periodically throughout the story. We get inside Margot Macomber's consciousness on the first page as she looks at Wilson and knows she hasn't seen him before, and on another page Macomber and Robert Wilson "both saw that she was going to cry. Wilson had seen it coming for a long time and he dreaded it. Macomber was past dreading it." Throughout, the story seems free to dip inside one consciousness or another, and can move with any of the characters. This unlimited, internal/external focus is called **omniscient** and the all-knowing narrator is the **omniscient observer.**

There are no laws governing focus in fiction, but there is a general feeling that once a focus is chosen that ought to be the law for that story. Do you feel manipulated when the focus, which has been on Rainsford for the entire length of *The Most Dangerous Game,* shifts, very near the end, from him to the general, apparently just to heighten our suspense? Do you feel betrayed by the fact that we are not allowed to enter Margot Macomber's mind at one crucial moment, even though the focus has shifted freely at less crucial times?

Focus and voice often coincide. There is no discrepancy that I can see (or hear) between the viewing and the telling in *The Cask of Amontillado,* for example. But in *The Summer My Grandmother Was Supposed to Die,* the "I" telling the story is older than the "I" experiencing the events of the story. Notice how many phrases there are like "years later I was shown the telegram" and "In those days . . ." So, too, the language of the story is clearly not that of a young boy: "She arrived punctually at noon"; "I've been told that to study Talmud with him had been a rare pleasure"; "lots of slender volumes of sermons, chassidic tales, and rabbinical commentaries." Such expressions may deal with incidents and information within the boy's perception, but the language in which they are expressed is clearly beyond him.

Like the focus, the voice in *Owl Creek Bridge* at the beginning of the story is not centered in Peyton Farquhar, but even when the focus narrows on him the voice telling the story is not his; note, for example, "As these thoughts, *which have here to be set down in words,* were flashed into the doomed man's brain" (emphasis added). The discrepancy may prepare a careful reader for later developments in the story.

I have used the common term **narrator** in the usual way—to mean the person who tells the story. You will have noticed that often the narrator really is a person in the story, like Muttel, the narrator in *The Summer My Grandmother Was Supposed to Die.* But how about the

dramatic → simple description

narrator in *Owl Creek Bridge* or in *Macomber*? Who is it who sets down Farquhar's words and can say things like this: "Death is a dignitary who when he comes announced is to be received with formal manifestations of respect, even by those most familiar with him. In the code of military etiquette silence and fixity are forms of deference." Where is he or she standing? What kind of person is this narrator? We might ask the same question of the elusive, unnamed spokesman for the town of Jefferson in *A Rose for Emily*. Close attention to the language and chronology of the story, to the references to race and gender, to the use of "they" and "we" reveals that the narrator is an educated white male who at the time of Emily's death is probably a boy or very young man.

Is he Faulkner? Where the narrator plays some role in the story we are less likely to routinely identify him with the author, though we sometimes thoughtlessly do. Where the narrator is more of a disembodied voice and there is no indication to the contrary we often do tend to identify him or her with the author. We call the narrator of *Owl Creek Bridge* "Bierce," of *Macomber* "Hemingway." This is not necessarily wrong, but it can be misleading. We can dig up a few facts about the author's life and read them into the story, or, worse, read the character or detail of the story into the author's life. It is more prudent, therefore, especially on the basis of a single story, not to speak of the author but of the author's persona, the voice or figure of the author who tells and structures the story, who may or may not resemble in nature or values the actual person of the author. Mary Anne Evans wrote novels under the name of George Eliot; her first-person narrator speaks of "himself." That male narrator may be a good example of the persona or representative that most authors construct to "write" their stories.

We say *write* the stories. The narrator of *Owl Creek Bridge* has to "set down in words" what Farquhar is thinking. But, just as poets write of singing their songs (poems), so we often speak of telling a story, and we speak of a narrator, which means a teller. There are stories, usually with first-person narrators, that make much of the convention of oral storytelling: *My Man Bovanne*, for example, or *Spotted Horses*. Often these stories not only have an "oral" taleteller but imply a certain audience. Sometimes, as in *The Celebrated Jumping Frog of Calaveras County*, there is a narrator who tells the story within the story to someone else who retells it or writes it down, and the nature and response of this **auditor** can be a significant part of the meaning and effect of the story.

We are used to thinking of a story in terms of its plot, so that to summarize a story usually means giving a plot summary. But if you shift focus and voice you will often find that though the history has not changed, the story has. You might want to test this out by rewriting *Macomber* with any one character as the focus, or *The Summer My Grandmother Was Supposed to Die* with the focus and perhaps with the voice of Muttel's mother. An element is a basic, irreducible part of something; in fiction, focus and voice are elementary.

AMBROSE BIERCE

An Occurrence at Owl Creek Bridge

I

A man stood upon a railroad bridge in northern Alabama, looking down into the swift water twenty feet below. The man's hands were behind his back, the wrists bound with a cord. A rope closely encircled his neck. It was attached to a stout cross-timber above his head and the slack fell to the level of his knees. Some loose boards laid upon the sleepers[1] supporting the metals of the railway supplied a footing for him and his executioners—two private soldiers of the Federal army, directed by a sergeant who in civil life may have been a deputy sheriff. At a short remove upon the same temporary platform was an officer in the uniform of his rank, armed. He was a captain. A sentinel at each end of the bridge stood with his rifle in the position known as "support," that is to say, vertical in front of the left shoulder, the hammer resting on the forearm thrown straight across the chest—a formal and unnatural position, enforcing an erect carriage of the body. It did not appear to be the duty of these two men to know what was occurring at the center of the bridge; they merely blockaded the two ends of the foot planking that traversed it.

Beyond one of the sentinels nobody was in sight; the railroad ran straight away into a forest for a hundred yards, then, curving, was lost to view. Doubtless there was an outpost farther along. The other bank of the stream was open ground—a gentle acclivity topped with a stockade of vertical tree trunks, loopholed for rifles, with a single embrasure through which protruded the muzzle of a brass cannon commanding the bridge. Midway of the slope between bridge and fort were the spectators—a single company of infantry in line, at "parade rest," the butts of the rifles on the ground, the barrels inclining slightly backward against the right shoulder, the hands crossed upon the stock. A lieutenant stood at the right of the line, the point of his sword upon the ground, his left hand resting upon his right. Excepting the group of four at the center of the bridge, not a man moved. The company faced the bridge, staring stonily, motionless. The sentinels, facing the banks of the stream, might have been statues to adorn the bridge. The captain stood with folded arms, silent, observing the work of his subordinates, but making no sign. Death is a dignitary who when he comes announced is to be received with formal manifestations of respect, even by those most familiar with him. In the code of military etiquette silence and fixity are forms of deference.

The man who was engaged in being hanged was apparently about thirty-five years of age. He was a civilian, if one might judge from his habit, which was that of a planter. His features were good—a straight nose, firm mouth, broad forehead, from which his long, dark hair was combed straight back, falling behind his ears to the collar of his well-

---

1. Crossties that support railroad track.

fitting frock coat. He wore a mustache and pointed beard, but no whiskers; his eyes were large and dark gray, and had a kindly expression which one would hardly have expected in one whose neck was in the hemp. Evidently this was no vulgar assassin. The liberal military code makes provision for hanging many kinds of persons, and gentlemen are not excluded.

The preparations being complete, the two private soldiers stepped aside and each drew away the plank upon which he had been standing. The sergeant turned to the captain, saluted and placed himself immediately behind that officer, who in turn moved apart one pace. These movements left the condemned man and the sergeant standing on the two ends of the same plank, which spanned three of the crossties of the bridge. The end upon which the civilian stood almost, but not quite, reached a fourth. This plank had been held in place by the weight of the captain; it was now held by that of the sergeant. At a signal from the former the latter would step aside, the plank would tilt and the condemned man go down between two ties. The arrangement commended itself to his judgment as simple and effective. His face had not been covered nor his eyes bandaged. He looked a moment at his "unsteadfast footing," then let his gaze wander to the swirling water of the stream racing madly beneath his feet. A piece of dancing driftwood caught his attention and his eyes followed it down the current. How slowly it appeared to move! What a sluggish stream!

He closed his eyes in order to fix his last thoughts upon his wife and children. The water, touched to gold by the early sun, the brooding mists under the banks at some distance down the stream, the fort, the soldiers, the piece of drift—all had distracted him. And now he became conscious of a new disturbance. Striking through the thought of his dear ones was a sound which he could neither ignore nor understand, a sharp, distinct, metallic percussion like the stroke of a blacksmith's hammer upon the anvil; it had the same ringing quality. He wondered what it was, and whether immeasurably distant or near by—it seemed both. Its recurrence was regular, but as slow as the tolling of a death knell. He awaited each stroke with impatience and—he knew not why —apprehension. The intervals of silence grew progressively longer; the delays became maddening. With their greater infrequency the sounds increased in strength and sharpness. They hurt his ear like the thrust of a knife; he feared he would shriek. What he heard was the ticking of his watch.

He unclosed his eyes and saw again the water below him. "If I could free my hands," he thought, "I might throw off the noose and spring into the stream. By diving I could evade the bullets and, swimming vigorously, reach the bank, take to the woods and get away home. My home, thank God, is as yet outside their lines; my wife and little ones are still beyond the invader's farthest advance."

As these thoughts, which have here to be set down in words, were flashed into the doomed man's brain rather than evolved from it the captain nodded to the sergeant. The sergeant stepped aside.

II

Peyton Farquhar was a well-to-do planter, of an old and highly respected Alabama family. Being a slave owner and like other slave owners a politician he was naturally an original secessionist and ardently devoted to the Southern cause. Circumstances of an imperious nature, which it is unnecessary to relate here, had prevented him from taking service with the gallant army that had fought the disastrous campaigns ending with the fall of Corinth,[2] and he chafed under the inglorious restraint, longing for the release of his energies, the larger life of the soldier, the opportunity for distinction. That opportunity, he felt, would come, as it comes to all in war time. Meanwhile he did what he could. No service was too humble for him to perform in aid of the South, no adventure too perilous for him to undertake if consistent with the character of a civilian who was at heart a soldier, and who in good faith and without too much qualification assented to at least a part of the frankly villainous dictum that all is fair in love and war.

One evening while Farquhar and his wife were sitting on a rustic bench near the entrance to his grounds, a gray-clad soldier rode up to the gate and asked for a drink of water. Mrs. Farquhar was only too happy to serve him with her own white hands. While she was fetching the water her husband approached the dusty horseman and inquired eagerly for news from the front.

"The Yanks are repairing the railroads," said the man, "and are getting ready for another advance. They have reached the Owl Creek bridge, put it in order and built a stockade on the north bank. The commandant has issued an order, which is posted everywhere, declaring that any civilian caught interfering with the railroad, its bridges, tunnels or trains will be summarily hanged. I saw the order."

"How far is it to the Owl Creek bridge?" Farquhar asked.

"About thirty miles."

"Is there no force on this side the creek?"

"Only a picket post half a mile out, on the railroad, and a single sentinel at this end of the bridge."

"Suppose a man—a civilian and student of hanging—should elude the picket post and perhaps get the better of the sentinel," said Farquhar, smiling, "what could he accomplish?"

The soldier reflected. "I was there a month ago," he replied. "I observed that the flood of last winter had lodged a great quantity of driftwood against the wooden pier at this end of the bridge. It is now dry and would burn like tow."

The lady had now brought the water, which the soldier drank. He thanked her ceremoniously, bowed to her husband and rode away. An hour later, after nightfall, he repassed the plantation, going northward in the direction from which he had come. He was a Federal scout.

---

2. Corinth, Mississippi, captured by General Grant in April 1862.

III

As Peyton Farquhar fell straight downward through the bridge he lost consciousness and was as one already dead. From this state he was awakened—ages later, it seemed to him—by the pain of a sharp pressure upon his throat, followed by a sense of suffocation. Keen, poignant agonies seemed to shoot from his neck downward through every fiber of his body and limbs. These pains appeared to flash along well-defined lines of ramification and to beat with an inconceivably rapid periodicity. They seemed like streams of pulsating fire heating him to an intolerable temperature. As to his head, he was conscious of nothing but a feeling of fulness—of congestion. These sensations were unaccompanied by thought. The intellectual part of his nature was already effaced; he had power only to feel, and feeling was torment. He was conscious of motion. Encompassed in a luminous cloud, of which he was now merely the fiery heart, without material substance, he swung through unthinkable arcs of oscillation, like a vast pendulum. Then all at once, with terrible suddenness, the light about him shot upward with the noise of a loud plash; a frightful roaring was in his ears, and all was cold and dark. The power of thought was restored; he knew that the rope had broken and he had fallen into the stream. There was no additional strangulation; the noose about his neck was already suffocating him and kept the water from his lungs. To die of hanging at the bottom of a river!—the idea seemed to him ludicrous. He opened his eyes in the darkness and saw above him a gleam of light, but how distant, how inaccessible! He was still sinking, for the light became fainter and fainter until it was a mere glimmer. Then it began to grow and brighten, and he knew that he was rising toward the surface—knew it with reluctance, for he was now very comfortable. "To be hanged and drowned," he thought, "that is not so bad; but I do not wish to be shot. No; I will not be shot; that is not fair."

He was not conscious of an effort, but a sharp pain in his wrist appraised him that he was trying to free his hands. He gave the struggle his attention, as an idler might observe the feat of a juggler, without interest in the outcome. What splendid effort!—what magnificent, what superhuman strength! Ah, that was a fine endeavor! Bravo! The cord fell away; his arms parted and floated upward, the hands dimly seen on each side in the growing light. He watched them with a new interest as first one and then the other pounced upon the noose at his neck. They tore it away and thrust it fiercely aside, its undulations resembling those of a water snake. "Put it back, put it back!" He thought he shouted these words to his hands, for the undoing of the noose had been succeeded by the direct pang that he had yet experienced. His neck ached horribly; his brain was on fire; his heart, which had been fluttering faintly, gave a great leap, trying to force itself out at his mouth. His whole body was racked and wrenched with an insupportable anguish! But his disobedient hands gave no heed to the command. They beat the water vigorously with quick, downward strokes, forcing him to the surface. He felt his head emerge; his eyes were blinded by the sunlight; his chest expanded convulsively, and with a supreme and crowning agony his lungs engulfed a great draught of air, which instantly he expelled in a shriek!

He was now in full possession of his physical senses. They were, indeed, preternaturally keen and alert. Something in the awful disturbance of his organic system had so exalted and refined them that they made record of things never before perceived. He felt the ripples upon his face and heard their separate sounds as they struck. He looked at the forest on the bank of the stream, saw the individual trees, the leaves and the veining of each leaf—saw the very insects upon them: the locusts, the brilliant-bodied flies, the gray spiders stretching their webs from twig to twig. He noted the prismatic colors in all the dewdrops upon a million blades of grass. The humming of the gnats that danced above the eddies of the stream, the beating of the dragonflies' wings, the strokes of the waterspiders' legs, like oars which had lifted their boat—all these made audible music. A fish slid along beneath his eyes and he heard the rush of its body parting the water.

He had come to the surface facing down the stream; in a moment the visible world seemed to wheel slowly round, himself the pivotal point, and he saw the bridge, the fort, the soldiers upon the bridge, the captain, the sergeant, the two privates, his executioners. They were in silhouette against the blue sky. They shouted and gesticulated, pointing at him. The captain had drawn his pistol, but did not fire; the others were unarmed. Their movements were grotesque and horrible, their forms gigantic.

Suddenly he heard a sharp report and something struck the water smartly within a few inches of his head, spattering his face with spray. He heard a second report, and saw one of the sentinels with his rifle at his shoulder, a light cloud of blue smoke rising from the muzzle. The man in the water saw the eye of the man on the bridge gazing into his own through the sights of the rifle. He observed that it was a gray eye and remembered having read that gray eyes were keenest, and that all famous marksmen had them. Nevertheless, this one had missed.

A counter-swirl had caught Farquhar and turned him half round; he was again looking into the forest on the bank opposite the fort. The sound of a clear, high voice in a monotonous singsong now rang out behind him and came across the water with a distinctness that pierced and subdued all other sounds, even the beating of the ripples in his ears. Although no soldier, he had frequented camps enough to know the dread significance of that deliberate, drawling, aspirated chant; the lieutenant on shore was taking a part in the morning's work. How coldly and pitilessly—with what an even, calm intonation, presaging, and enforcing tranquility in the men—with what accurately measured intervals fell those cruel words:

"Attention, company! . . . Shoulder arms! . . . Ready! . . . Aim! . . . Fire!"

Farquhar dived—dived as deeply as he could. The water roared in his ears like the voice of Niagara, yet he heard the dulled thunder of the volley and, rising again toward the surface, met shining bits of metal, singularly flattened, oscillating slowly downward. Some of them touched him on the face and hands, then fell away, continuing their descent. One lodged between his collar and neck; it was uncomfortably warm and he snatched it out.

As he rose to the surface, gasping for breath, he saw that he had been a long time under water; he was perceptibly farther downstream —nearer to safety. The soldiers had almost finished reloading; the metal ramrods flashed all at once in the sunshine as they were drawn from the barrels, turned in the air, and thrust into their sockets. The two sentinels fired again, independently and ineffectually.

The hunted man saw all this over his shoulder; he was now swimming vigorously with the current. His brain was as energetic as his arms and legs; he thought with the rapidity of lightning.

"The officer," he reasoned, "will not make that martinet's error a second time. It is as easy to dodge a volley as a single shot. He has probably already given the command to fire at will. God help me, I cannot dodge them all!"

An appalling plash within two yards of him was followed by a loud, rushing sound, *diminuendo*, which seemed to travel back through the air to the fort and died in an explosion which stirred the very river to its deeps! A rising sheet of water curved over him, fell down upon him, blinded him, strangled him! The cannon had taken a hand in the game. As he shook his head free from the commotion of the smitten water he heard the deflected shot humming through the air ahead, and in an instant it was cracking and smashing the branches in the forest beyond.

"They will not do that again," he thought; "the next time they will use a charge of grape.[3] I must keep my eye upon the gun; the smoke will apprise me—the report arrives too late; it lags behind the missile. That is a good gun."

Suddenly he felt himself whirled round and round—spinning like a top. The water, the banks, the forests, the now distant bridge, fort and men—all were commingled and blurred. Objects were represented by their colors only; circular horizontal streaks of color—that was all he saw. He had been caught in a vortex and was being whirled on with a velocity of advance and gyration that made him giddy and sick. In a few moments he was flung upon the gravel at the foot of the left bank of the stream—the southern bank—and behind a projecting point which concealed him from his enemies. The sudden arrest of his motion, the abrasion of one of his hands on the gravel, restored him, and he wept with delight. He dug his fingers into the sand, threw it over himself in handfuls and audibly blessed it. It looked like diamonds, rubies, emeralds; he could think of nothing beautiful which it did not resemble. The trees upon the bank were giant garden plants; he noted a definite order in their arrangement, inhaled the fragrance of their blooms. A strange, roseate light shone through the spaces among their trunks and the wind made in their branches the music of aeolian harps. He had no wish to perfect his escape—was

---

3. Grapeshot, a cluster of small iron balls that scatter when fired from cannon.

content to remain in that enchanting spot until retaken.

A whiz and rattle of grapeshot among the branches high above his head roused him from his dream. The baffled cannoneer had fired him a random farewell. He sprang to his feet, rushed up the sloping bank, and plunged into the forest.

All that day he traveled, laying his course by the rounding sun. The forest seemed interminable; nowhere did he discover a break in it, not even a woodman's road. He had not known that he lived in so wild a region. There was something uncanny in the revelation.

By nightfall he was fatigued, footsore, famishing. The thought of his wife and children urged him on. At last he found a road which led him in what he knew to be the right direction. It was as wide and straight as a city street, yet it seemed untraveled. No fields bordered it, no dwelling anywhere. Not so much as the barking of a dog suggested human habitation. The black bodies of the trees formed a straight wall on both sides, terminating on the horizon in a point, like a diagram in a lesson in perspective. Overhead, as he looked up through this rift in the wood, shone great golden stars looking unfamiliar and grouped in strange constellations. He was sure they were arranged in some order which had a secret and malign significance. The wood on either side was full of singular noises, among which— once, twice, and again—he distinctly heard whispers in an unknown tongue.

His neck was in pain and lifting his hand to it he found it horribly swollen. He knew that it had a circle of black where the rope had bruised it. His eyes felt congested; he could no longer close them. His tongue was swollen with thirst; he relieved its fever by thrusting it forward from between his teeth into the cold air. How softly the turf had carpeted the untraveled avenue—he could no longer feel the roadway beneath his feet!

Doubtless, despite his suffering, he had fallen asleep while walking, for now he sees another scene—perhaps he has merely recovered from a delirium. He stands at the gate of his own home. All is as he left it, and all bright and beautiful in the morning sunshine. He must have traveled the entire night. As he pushes upon the gate and passes up the wide white walk, he sees a flutter of female garments; his wife, looking fresh and cool and sweet, steps down from the veranda to meet him. At the bottom of the steps she stands waiting, with a smile of ineffable joy, an attitude of matchless grace and dignity. Ah, how beautiful she is! He springs forward with extended arms. As he is about to clasp her he feels a stunning blow upon the back of the neck; a blinding white light blazes all about him with a sound like the shock of a cannon—then all is darkness and silence!

Peyton Farquhar was dead; his body, with a broken neck, swung gently from side to side beneath the timbers of the Owl Creek bridge.

1891

WILLIAM FAULKNER

A Rose for Emily

I

When Miss Emily Grierson died, our whole town went to her funeral: the men through a sort of respectful affection for a fallen monument, the women mostly out of curiosity to see the inside of her house, which no one save an old manservant—a combined gardener and cook—had seen in at least ten years.

It was a big, squarish frame house that had once been white, decorated with cupolas and spires and scrolled balconies in the heavily lightsome style of the seventies, set on what had once been our most select street. But garages and cotton gins had encroached and obliterated even the august names of that neighborhood; only Miss Emily's house was left, lifting its stubborn and coquettish decay above the cotton wagons and the gasoline pumps—an eyesore among eyesores. And now Miss Emily had gone to join the representatives of those august names where they lay in the cedar-bemused cemetery among the ranked and anonymous graves of Union and Confederate soldiers who fell at the battle of Jefferson.

Alive, Miss Emily had been a tradition, a duty, and a care; a sort of hereditary obligation upon the town, dating from that day in 1894 when Colonel Sartoris, the mayor—he who fathered the edict that no Negro woman should appear on the streets without an apron—remitted her taxes, the dispensation dating from the death of her father on into perpetuity. Not that Miss Emily would have accepted charity. Colonel Sartoris invented an involved tale to the effect that Miss Emily's father had loaned money to the town, which the town, as a matter of business, preferred this way of repaying. Only a man of Colonel Sartoris' generation and thought could have invented it, and only a woman could have believed it.

When the next generation, with its more modern ideas, became mayors and aldermen, this arrangement created some little dissatisfaction. On the first of the year they mailed her a tax notice. February came, and there was no reply. They wrote her a formal letter, asking her to call at the sheriff's office at her convenience. A week later the mayor wrote her himself, offering to call or to send his car for her, and received in reply a note on paper of an archaic shape, in a thin, flowing calligraphy in faded ink, to the effect that she no longer went out at all. The tax notice was also enclosed, without comment.

They called a special meeting of the Board of Aldermen. A deputation waited upon her, knocked at the door through which no visitor had passed since she ceased giving china-painting lessons eight or ten years earlier. They were admitted by the old Negro into a dim hall from which a stairway mounted into still more shadow. It smelled of dust and disuse—a close, dank smell. The Negro led them into the parlor. It was furnished in heavy, leather-covered furniture. When the Negro opened the blinds of one window, they could see that the leather was cracked; and when they sat down, a faint dust rose sluggishly about their thighs, spinning with slow motes in the single sun-ray. On a tarnished gilt easel before the fireplace stood a crayon portrait of Miss Emily's father.

They rose when she entered—a small, fat woman in black, with a thin gold chain descending to her waist and vanishing into her belt, leaning on an ebony cane with a tarnished gold head. Her skeleton was small and spare; perhaps that was why what would have been merely plumpness in another was obesity in her. She looked bloated, like a body long submerged in motionless water, and of that pallid hue. Her eyes, lost in the fatty ridges of her face, looked like two small pieces of coal pressed into a lump of dough as they moved from one face to another while the visitors stated their errand.

She did not ask them to sit. She just stood in the door and listened quietly until the spokesman came to a stumbling halt. Then they could hear the invisible watch ticking at the end of the gold chain.

Her voice was dry and cold. "I have no taxes in Jefferson. Colonel Sartoris explained it to me. Perhaps one of you can gain access to the city records and satisfy yourselves."

"But we have. We are the city authorities, Miss Emily. Didn't you get a notice from the sheriff, signed by him?"

"I received a paper, yes," Miss Emily said. "Perhaps he considers himself the sheriff . . . I have no taxes in Jefferson."

"But there is nothing on the books to show that, you see. We must go by the—"

"See Colonel Sartoris. I have no taxes in Jefferson."

"But, Miss Emily—"

"See Colonel Sartoris." (Colonel Sartoris had been dead almost ten years.) "I have no taxes in Jefferson. Tobe!" The Negro appeared. "Show these gentlemen out."

II

So she vanquished them, horse and foot, just as she had vanquished their fathers thirty years before about the smell. That was two years after her father's death and a short time after her sweetheart—the one we believed would marry her—had deserted her. After her father's death she went out very little; after her sweetheart went away, people hardly saw her at all. A few of the ladies had the temerity to call, but were not received, and the only sign of life about the place was the Negro man—a young man then—going in and out with a market basket.

"Just as if a man—any man—could keep a kitchen properly," the ladies said; so they were not surprised when the smell developed. It was another link between the gross, teeming world and the high and mighty Griersons.

A neighbor, a woman, complained to the mayor, Judge Stevens, eighty years old.

"But what will you have me do about it, madam?" he said.

"Why, send her word to stop it," the woman said. "Isn't there a law?"

"I'm sure that won't be necessary," Judge Stevens said. "It's prob-

ably just a snake or a rat that nigger of hers killed in the yard. I'll speak to him about it."

The next day he received two more complaints, one from a man who came in diffident deprecation. "We really must do something about it, Judge. I'd be the last one in the world to bother Miss Emily, but we've got to do something." That night the Board of Aldermen met—three graybeards and one younger man, a member of the rising generation.

"It's simple enough," he said. "Send her word to have her place cleaned up. Give her a certain time to do it in, and if she don't . . ."

"Dammit, sir," Judge Stevens said, "will you accuse a lady to her face of smelling bad?"

So the next night, after midnight, four men crossed Miss Emily's lawn and slunk about the house like burglars, sniffing along the base of the brickwork and at the cellar openings while one of them performed a regular sowing motion with his hand out of a sack slung from his shoulder. They broke open the cellar door and sprinkled lime there, and in all the outbuildings. As they recrossed the lawn, a window that had been dark was lighted and Miss Emily sat in it, the light behind her, and her upright torso motionless as that of an idol. They crept quietly across the lawn and into the shadow of the locusts that lined the street. After a week or two the smell went away.

That was when people had begun to feel really sorry for her. People in our town, remembering how old lady Wyatt, her great-aunt, had gone completely crazy at last, believed that the Griersons held themselves a little too high for what they really were. None of the young men were quite good enough for Miss Emily and such. We had long thought of them as a tableau, Miss Emily a slender figure in white in the background, her father a spraddled silhouette in the foreground, his back to her and clutching a horsewhip, the two of them framed by the back-flung front door. So when she got to be thirty and was still single, we were not pleased exactly, but vindicated; even with insanity in the family she wouldn't have turned down all of her chances if they had really materialized.

When her father died, it got about that the house was all that was left to her; and in a way, people were glad. At last they could pity Miss Emily. Being left alone, and a pauper, she had become humanized. Now she too would know the old thrill and the old despair of a penny more or less.

The day after his death all the ladies prepared to call at the house and offer condolence and aid, as is our custom. Miss Emily met them at the door, dressed as usual and with no trace of grief on her face. She told them that her father was not dead. She did that for three days, with the ministers calling on her, and the doctors, trying to persuade her to let them dispose of the body. Just as they were about to resort to law and force, she broke down, and they buried her father quickly.

We did not say she was crazy then. We believed she had to do that. We remembered all the young men her father had driven away, and we knew that with nothing left, she would have to cling to that which had robbed her, as people will.

III

She was sick for a long time. When we saw her again, her hair was cut short, making her look like a girl, with a vague resemblance to those angels in colored church windows—sort of tragic and serene.

The town had just let the contracts for paving the sidewalks, and in the summer after her father's death they began the work. The construction company came with niggers and mules and machinery, and a foreman named Homer Barron, a Yankee—a big, dark, ready man, with a big voice and eyes lighter than his face. The little boys would follow in groups to hear him cuss the niggers, and the niggers singing in time to the rise and fall of picks. Pretty soon he knew everybody in town. Whenever you heard a lot of laughing anywhere about the square, Homer Barron would be in the center of the group. Presently we began to see him and Miss Emily on Sunday afternoons driving in the yellow-wheeled buggy and the matched team of bays from the livery stable.

At first we were glad that Miss Emily would have an interest, because the ladies all said, "Of course a Grierson would not think seriously of a Northerner, a day laborer." But there were still others, older people, who said that even grief could not cause a real lady to forget *noblesse oblige*—without calling it *noblesse oblige*. They just said, "Poor Emily. Her kinsfolk should come to her." She had some kin in Alabama; but years ago her father had fallen out with them over the estate of old lady Wyatt, the crazy woman, and there was no communication between the two families. They had not even been represented at the funeral.

And as soon as the old people said, "Poor Emily," the whispering began. "Do you suppose it's really so?" they said to one another. "Of course it is. What else could . . ." This behind their hands; rustling of craned silk and satin behind jalousies closed upon the sun of Sunday afternoon as the thin, swift clop-clop-clop of the matched team passed: "Poor Emily."

She carried her head high enough—even when we believed that she was fallen. It was as if she demanded more than ever the recognition of her dignity as the last Grierson; as if it had wanted that touch of earthiness to reaffirm her imperviousness. Like when she bought the rat poison, the arsenic. That was over a year after they had begun to say "Poor Emily," and while the two female cousins were visiting her.

"I want some poison," she said to the druggist. She was over thirty then, still a slight woman, though thinner than usual, with cold, haughty black eyes in a face the flesh of which was strained across the temples and about the eye-sockets as you imagine a lighthouse-keeper's face ought to look. "I want some poison," she said.

"Yes, Miss Emily. What kind? For rats and such? I'd recom—"

"I want the best you have. I don't care what kind."

The druggist named several. "They'll kill anything up to an elephant. But what you want is—"

"Arsenic," Miss Emily said. "Is that a good one?"

"Is . . . arsenic? Yes, ma'am. But what you want—"

"I want arsenic."

The druggist looked down at her. She looked back at him, erect, her face like a strained flag. "Why, of course," the druggist said. "If that's what you want. But the law requires you to tell what you are going to use it for."

Miss Emily just stared at him, her head tilted back in order to look him eye for eye, until he looked away and went and got the arsenic and wrapped it up. The Negro delivery boy brought her the package; the druggist didn't come back. When she opened the package at home there was written on the box, under the skull and bones: "For rats."

IV

So the next day we all said, "She will kill herself"; and we said it would be the best thing. When she had first begun to be seen with Homer Barron, we had said, "She will marry him." Then we said, "She will persuade him yet," because Homer himself had remarked— he liked men, and it was known that he drank with the younger men in the Elks' Club—that he was not a marrying man. Later we said, "Poor Emily" behind the jalousies as they passed on Sunday afternoon in the glittering buggy, Miss Emily with her head high and Homer Barron with his hat cocked and a cigar in his teeth, reins and whip in a yellow glove.

Then some of the ladies began to say that it was a disgrace to the town and a bad example to the young people. The men did not want to interfere, but at last the ladies forced the Baptist minister—Miss Emily's people were Episcopal—to call upon her. He would never divulge what happened during that interview, but he refused to go back again. The next Sunday they again drove about the streets, and the following day the minister's wife wrote to Miss Emily's relations in Alabama.

So she had blood-kin under her roof again and we sat back to watch developments. At first nothing happened. Then we were sure that they were to be married. We learned that Miss Emily had been to the jeweler's and ordered a man's toilet set in silver, with the letters H. B. on each piece. Two days later we learned that she had bought a complete outfit of men's clothing, including a nightshirt, and we said, "They are married." We were really glad. We were glad because the two female cousins were even more Grierson than Miss Emily had ever been.

So we were not surprised when Homer Barron—the streets had been finished some time since—was gone. We were a little disappointed that there was not a public blowing-off, but we believed that he had gone on to prepare for Miss Emily's coming, or to give her a chance to get rid of the cousins. (By that time it was a cabal, and we were all Miss Emily's allies to help circumvent the cousins.) Sure enough, after another week they departed. And, as we had expected all along, within three days Homer Barron was back in town. A neighbor saw the Negro man admit him at the kitchen door at dusk one evening.

And that was the last we saw of Homer Barron. And of Miss Emily for some time. The Negro man went in and out with the market basket, but the front door remained closed. Now and then we would see her at a window for a moment, as the men did that night when they sprinkled the lime, but for almost six months she did not appear on the streets. Then we knew that this was to be expected too; as if that quality of her father which had thwarted her woman's life so many times had been too virulent and too furious to die.

When we next saw Miss Emily, she had grown fat and her hair was turning gray. During the next few years it grew grayer and grayer until it attained an even pepper-and-salt iron-gray, when it ceased turning. Up to the day of her death at seventy-four it was still that vigorous iron-gray, like the hair of an active man.

From that time on her front door remained closed, save for a period of six or seven years, when she was about forty, during which she gave lessons in china-painting. She fitted up a studio in one of the downstairs rooms, where the daughters and granddaughters of Colonel Sartoris' contemporaries were sent to her with the same regularity and in the same spirit that they were sent to church on Sundays with a twenty-five-cent piece for the collection plate. Meanwhile her taxes had been remitted.

Then the newer generation became the backbone and the spirit of the town, and the painting pupils grew up and fell away and did not send their children to her with boxes of color and tedious brushes and pictures cut from the ladies' magazines. The front door closed upon the last one and remained closed for good. When the town got free postal delivery, Miss Emily alone refused to let them fasten the metal numbers above her door and attach a mailbox to it. She would not listen to them.

Daily, monthly, yearly we watched the Negro grow grayer and more stooped, going in and out with the market basket. Each December we sent her a tax notice, which would be returned by the post office a week later, unclaimed. Now and then we would see her in one of the downstairs windows—she had evidently shut up the top floor of the house—like the carven torso of an idol in a niche, looking or not looking at us, we could never tell which. Thus she passed from generation to generation—dear, inescapable, impervious, tranquil, and perverse.

And so she died. Fell ill in the house filled with dust and shadows, with only a doddering Negro man to wait on her. We did not even know she was sick; we had long since given up trying to get any information from the Negro. He talked to no one, probably not even to her, for his voice had grown harsh and rusty, as if from disuse.

She died in one of the downstairs rooms, in a heavy walnut bed with a curtain, her gray head propped on a pillow yellow and moldy with age and lack of sunlight.

V

The Negro met the first of the ladies at the front door and let them in, with their hushed, sibilant voices and their quick, curious glances, and then he disappeared. He walked right through the house and out the back and was not seen again.

The two female cousins came at once. They held the funeral on the second day, with the town coming to look at Miss Emily beneath a mass of bought flowers, with the crayon face of her father musing profoundly above the bier and the ladies sibilant and macabre; and the very old men—some in their brushed Confederate uniforms—on the porch and the lawn, talking of Miss Emily as if she had been a contemporary of theirs, believing that they had danced with her and courted her perhaps, confusing time with its mathematical progression, as the old do, to whom all the past is not a diminishing road but, instead, a huge meadow which no winter ever quite touches, divided from them now by the narrow bottle-neck of the most recent decade of years.

Already we knew that there was one room in that region above stairs which no one had seen in forty years, and which would have to be forced. They waited until Miss Emily was decently in the ground before they opened it.

The violence of breaking down the door seemed to fill this room with pervading dust. A thin, acrid pall as of the tomb seemed to lie everywhere upon this room decked and furnished as for a bridal: upon the valance curtains of faded rose color, upon the rose-shaded lights, upon the dressing table, upon the delicate array of crystal and the man's toilet things backed with tarnished silver, silver so tarnished that the monogram was obscured. Among them lay a collar and tie, as if they had just been removed, which, lifted, left upon the surface a pale crescent in the dust. Upon a chair hung the suit, carefully folded; beneath it the two mute shoes and the discarded socks.

The man himself lay in the bed.

For a long while we just stood there, looking down at the profound and fleshless grin. The body had apparently once lain in the attitude of an embrace, but now the long sleep that outlasts love, that conquers even the grimace of love, had cuckolded him. What was left of him, rotted beneath what was left of the nightshirt, had become inextricable from the bed in which he lay; and upon him and upon the pillow beside him lay that even coating of the patient and biding dust.

Then we noticed that in the second pillow was the indentation of a head. One of us lifted something from it, and leaning forward, that faint and invisible dust dry and acrid in the nostrils, we saw a long strand of iron-gray hair.

1931

MORDECAI RICHLER

The Summer My Grandmother Was Supposed to Die

Dr. Katzman discovered the gangrene on one of his monthly visits. "She won't last a month," he said.

He repeated that the second month, the third, and the fourth, and now she lay dying in the heat of the back bedroom.

"If only she'd die," my mother said. "Oh, God, why doesn't she die? God in heaven, what's she holding on for?"

The summer my grandmother was supposed to die we did not chip in with the Breenbaums to take a cottage in the Laurentians.[1] It wouldn't have been practical. The old lady couldn't be moved, the nurse came daily and the doctor twice a week, and so it seemed best to stay in the city and wait for her to die or, as my mother said, pass away. It was a hot summer, her bedroom was just behind the kitchen, and when we sat down to eat we could smell her. The dressings on my grandmother's left leg had to be changed several times a day and, according to Dr. Katzman, her condition was hopeless. "It's in the hands of the Almighty," he said.

"It won't be long now," my father said, "and she'll be better off, if you know what I mean."

"Please," my mother said.

A nurse came every day from the Royal Victorian Order.[2] She arrived punctually at noon and at five to twelve I'd join the rest of the boys under the outside staircase to look up her dress as she climbed to our second-story flat. Miss Monohan favored lacy pink panties and that was better than waiting under the stairs for Cousin Bessie, for instance. She wore enormous cotton bloomers, rain or shine.

I was sent out to play as often as possible, because my mother felt it was not good for me to see somebody dying. Usually I'd just roam the scorched streets shooting the breeze. There was Arty, Gas sometimes, Hershey, Stan, and me. We talked about everything from A to Z.

"Why is it," Arty wanted to know, "that Tarzan never shits?"

"Dick Tracy too."

"Or Wonder Woman."

"She's a dame."

"So?"

"Jees, wouldn't it be something if Superman crapped in the sky? He could just be flying over Waverly Street when, whamo, Mr. Rabinovitch catches it right in the kisser."

Mr. Rabinovitch was our Hebrew teacher.

"But there's Tarzan," Arty insisted, "in the jungle, week in and week out, and never once does he need to go to the toilet. It's not real, that's all."

Arty told me, "Before your grandma dies she's going to roll her eyes and gurgle. That's what they call the death-rattle."

"Aw, you know everything. Big shot."

"I *read* it, you jerk," Arty said, whacking me one, "in Perry Mason."

Home again I'd find my mother weeping.

"She's dying by inches," she said to my father one stifling night, "and none of them even come to see her. Oh, such children! They should only rot in hell."

1. Mountains in eastern Canada between Hudson Bay and the St. Lawrence River.

2. The Victorian Order of Nurses for Canada.

"They're not behaving right. It's certainly not according to Hoyle," my father said.

"When I think of all the money and effort that went into making a rabbi out of Israel—the way Mother doted on him—and for what? Oh, what's the world coming to? God."

"It's not right."

Dr. Kaztman was amazed. "I never believed she'd last this long. Really, it must be will-power alone that keeps her going. And your excellent care."

"I want her to die, Doctor. That's not my mother in the back room. It's an animal. I want her to please please die."

"Hush. You don't mean it. You're tired." And Dr. Katzman gave my father some pills for my mother to take. "A remarkable woman," he said. "A born nurse."

At night in bed my brother Harvey and I used to talk about our grandmother. "After she dies," I said, "her hair will go on growing for another twenty-four hours."

"Sez who?"

"Arty. It's a scientific fact. Do you think Uncle Lou will come from New York for the funeral?"

"Sure."

"Boy, that means another fiver for me. You too."

"You shouldn't say things like that, kiddo, or *her ghost will come back to haunt you.*"

"Well," I said, "I'll be able to go to her funeral, anyway. I'm not too young any more."

I was only six years old when my grandfather died, and I wasn't allowed to go to his funeral.

I have only one memory of my grandfather. Once he called me into his study, set me down on his lap, and made a drawing of a horse for me. On the horse he drew a rider. While I watched and giggled he gave the rider a beard and the round fur-trimmed cap of a rabbi.

My grandfather was a Zaddik,[3] one of the Righteous, and I've been told that to study Talmud with him had been a rare pleasure. I wasn't allowed to go to his funeral, but years after I was shown the telegram of condolence that had come from Eire and Poland and Israel and even Japan. My grandfather had written many books: a translation of the Zohar[4] into modern Hebrew—some twenty years' work—and lots of slender volumes of sermons, chassidic tales, and rabbinical commentaries. His books had been published in Warsaw and later in New York. He had been famous.

"At the funeral," my mother told me, "they had to have six motorcycle policemen to control the crowds. It was such a heat that twelve women fainted—and I'm *not* counting Mrs. Waxman from upstairs. With her, you know, *anything* to fall into a man's arms. Even Pinsky's. And did I tell you that there was even a French-Canadian priest there?"

3. "Righteous man" in Hebrew.
4. "The Book of Splendor," the central part of the Kabbalah, the esoteric teach-   ings of Judaism and the source of Jewish mysticism.

"No kidding?"

"The priest was a real big *knacker*.[5] A bishop maybe. He used to study with the *zeyda*.[6] The *zeyda* was some personality, you know. Spiritual and wordly-wise at the same time. Such personalities they don't make any more. Today, rabbis and peanuts are the same size."

But, according to my father, the *zeyda* (his father-in-law) hadn't been as famous as all that. "There are things I could say," he told me. "There was another side to him."

My grandfather had come from generations and generations of rabbis, his youngest son was a rabbi, but none of his grandchildren would be one. My brother Harvey was going to be a dentist and at the time, 1937, I was interested in flying and my cousin Jerry was already a communist. I once heard Jerry say, "Our grandpappy wasn't all he was cracked up to be." When the men at the kosher bakeries went out on strike he spoke up against them on the streets where they were picketing and in the *shule*.[7] It was of no consequence to him that they were grossly underpaid. His superstitious followers had to have bread. "Grandpappy," Jerry said, "was a prize reactionary."

A week after my grandfather died my grandmother suffered a stroke. Her right side was completely paralyzed. She couldn't speak. At first, it's true, my grandmother could say a few words and move her right hand enough to write her name in Hebrew. Her name was Malka. But her condition soon began to deteriorate.

My grandmother had six children and seven stepchildren, for my grandfather had been married before. His first wife had died in the old country. Two years later he had married my grandmother, the only daughter of the richest man in the village, and their marriage had been a singularly happy one. My grandmother had been a beautiful girl. She had also been a wise, resourceful, and patient wife. Qualities, I fear, indispensable to life with a Zaddik. For the synagogue had paid my grandfather no stipulated salary and much of the money he had picked up here and there he had habitually distributed among rabbinical students, needy immigrants, and widows. A vice, and such it was to his hard-pressed family, which made him as unreliable a provider as a drunkard. And indeed, to carry the analogy further, my grandmother had had to make many hurried trips to the pawnbroker with her jewelry. Not all of it had been redeemed, either. But her children had been looked after. The youngest, her favorite, was a rabbi in Boston, the eldest was the actor-manager of a Yiddish theater in New York, and another was a lawyer. One daughter lived in Toronto, two in Montreal. My mother was the youngest daughter, and when my grandmother had her stroke there was a family meeting and it was decided that my mother would take care of her. This was my father's fault. All the other husbands spoke up—they protested their wives had too much work, they could never manage it—but my father detested quarrels, and he was silent. So my grandmother came to stay with us.

Her bedroom, the back bedroom, had actually been promised to me for my seventh birthday. But all that was forgotten now, and I had to go on sharing a bedroom with my brother Harvey. So naturally I was resentful when each morning before I left for school my mother said, "Go in and kiss the *baba*[8] good-bye."

All the same I'd go into the bedroom and kiss my grandmother hastily. She'd say "Bouyo-bouyo," for that was the only sound she could make. And after school it was, "Go in and tell the *baba* you're home."

"I'm home, *baba*."

"Bouyo-bouyo."

During those first hopeful months—"Twenty years ago who would have thought there'd be a cure for diabetes?" my father asked; "where there's life there's hope, you know"—she'd smile at me and try to speak, her eyes charged with effort. And even later there were times when she pressed my head urgently to her bosom with her surprisingly strong left arm. But as her illness dragged on and on and she became a condition in the house, something beyond hope or reproach, like the leaky icebox, there was less recognition and more ritual in those kisses. I came to dread her room. A clutter of sticky medicine bottles and the cracked toilet chair beside the bed; glazed but imploring eyes and a feeble smile, the wet slap of her lips against my cheeks. I flinched from her touch. After two years of it I protested to my mother. "Look, what's the use of telling her I'm going or I'm here. She doesn't even recognize me any more."

"Don't be fresh. She's your grandmother."

My uncle who was in the theater in New York sent money regularly to help support my grandmother and, for the first few months, so did the other children. But once the initial and sustaining excitement had passed and it became likely that my grandmother might linger in her invalid condition for two or maybe even three more years, the checks began to drop off, and the children seldom came to our house any more. Anxious weekly visits—"and how is she today, poor lamb?"—quickly dwindled to a dutiful monthly looking in, then a semi-annual visit, and these always on the way to somewhere.

"The way they act," my father said, "you'd think that if they stayed long enough to take off their coats we'd make them take the *baba* home with them."

When the children did come to visit, my mother made it difficult for them.

"It's killing me," she said. "I have to lift her onto that chair three times a day maybe. Have you any idea how heavy she is? And what makes you think I always catch her in time? Sometimes I have to change her bed twice a day. That's a job I'd like to see your wife do," she said to my uncle, the rabbi.

"We could send her to the Old People's Home," the rabbi said.

"Now there's an idea," my father said.

But my mother began to sob. "Not as long as I'm alive," she said. And she gave my father a stony look. "Say something."

8. Grandma.

"It wouldn't be according to Hoyle."

"You want to be able to complain to everybody in town about all the other children," the rabbi said. "You've got a martyr complex."

"Everybody has a point of view, you know. You know what I mean?" my father said. "So what's the use of fighting?"

Meanwhile, Dr. Katzman came once a month to examine my grandmother. "It's remarkable, astonishing," he'd say each time. "She's as strong as a horse."

"Some life for a person," my father said. "She can't speak—she doesn't recognize anybody—what is there for her?"

The doctor was a cultivated man; he spoke often for women's clubs, sometimes on Yiddish literature and other times, his rubicund face hot with impatience, the voice taking on a doomsday tone, on the cancer threat.

"Who are we to judge?" he asked.

Every evening, during the first months of my grandmother's illness, my mother read her a story by Sholem Aleichem.[9] "Tonight she smiled," my mother would say. "She understood. I can tell." And my father, my brother, and I would not comment. Once a week my mother used to give the old lady a manicure. Sunny afternoons she'd lift her into a wheelchair and put her out in the sun. Somebody always had to stay in the house in case my grandmother called. Often, during the night, she would begin to wail unaccountably, and my mother would get up and rock the old lady in her arms for hours. But in the fourth year of my grandmother's illness the strain and fatigue began to tell on my mother. Besides looking after my grandmother—"and believe you me," the doctor assured her with a clap on the back, "it would be a full-time job for a professional nurse"—she had to keep house for a husband and two sons. She began to quarrel with my father and she became sharp with Harvey and me. My father started to spend his evenings playing pinochle at Tansky's Cigar & Soda. Weekends he took Harvey and me to visit his brothers and sisters. And everywhere he went people had little bits of advice for him.

"Sam, you might as well be a bachelor. You're just going to have to put your foot down for once."

"Yeah, in your face maybe."

My cousin Libby, who was at McGill,[1] said, "This could have a very damaging effect on the development of your boys. These are their formative years, Uncle Samuel, and the omnipresence of death in the house . . ."

"What you need," my father said, "is a boy friend. *And how.*"

At Tansky's Cigar & Soda it was, "Come clean, Sam. It's no hardship. If I know you, the old lady's got a big insurance policy and when the time comes . . ."

My mother lost lots of weight. After dinner she'd fall asleep in her chair in the middle of Lux Radio Theater.[2] One minute she'd be sewing a patch on my breeches or be making a list of girls to call

---

9. "Peace be with you," pen name of Yiddish author and humorist Shalom Rabinovitz (1859–1916).

1. University in Montreal.
2. Radio weekly drama sponsored by Lux soap.

for a bingo party (proceeds for the Talmud Torah),[3] and the next she'd be snoring. Then, one morning, she just couldn't get out of bed, and Dr. Katzman came round a week before his regular visit. "Well, well, this won't do, will it?" He sat in the kitchen with my father and the two men drank apricot brandy out of small glasses.

"Your wife is a remarkable woman," Dr. Katzman said.

"You don't say?"

"She's got a gallstone condition."

My father shrugged. "Have another one for the road," he said.

"Thank you, but I have several more calls to make." Dr. Katzman rose, sighing. "There she lies in that back room, poor old woman," he said, "hanging desperately onto life. There's food for thought there."

My grandmother's children met again, and the five of them sat around my mother's bed embarrassed, irritated, and quick to take insult. All except my uncle who was in the theater. He sucked a cigar and drank whisky. He teased my mother, the rabbi, and my aunts, and if not for him I think they would have been at each other's throats. It was decided, over my mother's protests, to send my grandmother to the Old People's Home on Esplanade Street. An ambulance came to take my grandmother away and Dr. Katzman said, "It's for the best." But my father had been in the back bedroom when the old lady had held on tenaciously to the bedpost, not wanting to be moved by the two men in white—"Easy does it, granny," the younger one had said—and afterwards he could not go in to see my mother. He went out for a walk.

"She looked at me with such a funny expression," he told my brother. "Is it my fault?"

My mother stayed in bed for another two weeks. My father cooked for us and we hired a woman to do the housework. My mother put on weight quickly, her cheeks regained their normal pinkish hue and, for the first time in months, she actually joked with Harvey and me. She became increasingly curious about our schools and whether or not we shined our shoes regularly. She began to cook again, special dishes for my father, and she resumed old friendships with women on the parochial school board. The change reflected on my father. Not only did his temper improve, but he stopped going to Tansky's every other night, and began to come home early from work. Life at home had never been so rich. But my grandmother's name was never mentioned. The back bedroom remained empty and I continued to share a room with Harvey. I couldn't see the point and so one evening I said, "Look, why don't I move into the back bedroom?"

My father glared at me across the table.

"But it's empty like."

My mother left the table. And the next afternoon she put on her best dress and coat and new spring hat.

"Where are you going?" my father asked.

"To see my mother."

"Don't go looking for trouble."

"It's been a month. Maybe they're not treating her right."

---

3. Orthodox Jewish school for boys.

"They're experts."

"Did you think I was never going to visit her? I'm not inhuman, you know."

"All right, go," he said.

But after she'd gone my father went to the window and said, "Son-of-a-bitch."

Harvey and I sat outside on the steps watching the cars go by. My father sat on the balcony above, cracking peanuts. It was six o'clock, maybe later, when the ambulance turned the corner, slowed down, and parked right in front of the house.

"Son-of-a-bitch," my father said. "I knew it."

My mother got out first, her eyes red and swollen, and hurried up-stairs to make my grandmother's bed.

"I'm sorry, Sam, I had to do it."

"You'll get sick again, that's what."

"You think she doesn't recognize people. From the moment she saw me she cried and cried. Oh, it was terrible."

"They're experts there. They know how to handle her better than you do."

"Experts? Expert murderers you mean. She's got bedsores, Sam. Those dirty little Irish nurses they don't change her linen often enough, they hate her. She must have lost twenty pounds there."

"Another month and you'll be flat on your back again."

"Sam, what could I do? Please Sam."

"She'll outlive all of us. Even Muttel.[4] I'm going out for a walk."

She was back and I was to blame.

My father became a regular at Tansky's Cigar & Soda again and every morning I had to go in and kiss my grandmother. She began to look like a man. Little hairs had sprouted on her chin, she had a spiky gray mustache and, of course, she was practically bald. This near-baldness, I guess, sprang from the fact that she had been shaving her head ever since she had married my grandfather the rabbi.[5] My grandmother had four different wigs, but she had not worn one since the first year of her illness. She wore a little pink cap instead. And so, as before, she said, "bouyo-bouyo," to everything.

Once more uncles and aunts sent five-dollar bills, though erratically, to help pay for my grandmother's support. Elderly people, former followers of my grandfather, came to inquire after the old lady's health. They sat in the back bedroom with her for hours, leaning on their canes, talking to themselves, rocking, always rocking to and fro. "The Holy Shakers," my father called them, and Harvey and I avoided them, because they always wanted to pinch our cheeks, give us a dash of snuff and laugh when we sneezed, or offer us a sticky old candy from a little brown bag with innumerable creases in it. When the visit was done the old people would unfailingly sit in the kitchen with my mother for another hour, watching her make lock-shen[6] or bake bread. My mother always served them lemon tea and

4. The narrator's Yiddish name; could be the equivalent of Mordecai.
5. Married Orthodox Jewish women
customarily either shave their heads or cover their hair.
6. Noodles.

they would talk about my grandfather, recalling his books, his sayings, and his charitable deeds.

And so another two years passed, with no significant change in my grandmother's condition. But fatigue, bad temper, and even morbidity enveloped my mother again. She fought with her brothers and sisters and once, when I stepped into the living room, I found her sitting with her head in her hands, and she looked up at me with such anguish that I was frightened.

"What did I do now?" I asked.

"If, God forbid, I had a stroke, would you send me to the Old People's Home?"

"Don't be a joke. Of course not."

"I hope that never in my life do I have to count on my children for anything."

The summer my grandmother was supposed to die, the seventh year of her illness, my brother took a job as a shipper and he kept me awake at night with stories about the factory. "What we do, see, is clear out the middle of a huge pile of lengths of material. That makes for a kind of secret cave. A hideout. Well, then you coax one of the *shiksas*[7] inside and hi-diddle-diddle."

One night Harvey waited until I had fallen asleep and then he wrapped himself in a white sheet, crept up to my bed, and shouted, "Bouyo-bouyo."

I hit him. He shouted.

"Children. Children, please," my mother called. "I must get some rest."

As my grandmother's condition worsened—from day to day we didn't know when she'd die—I was often sent out to eat at my aunt's or at my other grandmother's house. I was hardly ever at home. On Saturday mornings I'd get together with the other guys and we'd walk all the way past the mountain to Eaton's, which was our favorite department store for riding up and down escalators and stealing.

In those days they let boys into the left-field bleachers free during the week and we spent many an afternoon at the ball park. The Montreal Royals, part of the Dodger farm system, was some ball club too. There was Jackie Robinson and Roy Campanella, Honest John Gabbard, Chuck Connors, and Kermit Kitman was our hero. It used to kill us to see that crafty little hebe[8] running around there with all those tall dumb *goyim*.[9] "Hey, Kitman," we'd yell. "Hey, hey, sho-head,[1] if your father knew you played ball on *shabus*—"[2] Kitman, unfortunately, was all field and no hit. He never made the majors. "There goes Kermit Kitman," we'd yell, after he'd gone down swinging again, "the first Jewish strike-out king of the International League." This we usually followed up by bellowing some choice imprecations in Yiddish.

7. Gentile girls.
8. Hebrew, Jew.
9. Gentiles.
1. Possibly *shorn-head* (?), referring to

short hair or crew cut of athlete, in contrast to traditional long locks of Orthodox Jews (?).
2. Sabbath.

It was after one of these games, on a Friday afternoon, that I came home to find a small crowd gathered in front of the house.

"That's the grandson."

"Poor kid."

Old people stood silent and expressionless across the street staring at our front door. A taxi pulled up and my aunt hurried out, hiding her face in her hands.

"After so many years," somebody said.

"And probably next year they'll discover a cure. Isn't that *always* the case?"

I took the stairs two at a time. The flat was full. Uncles and aunts from my father's side of the family, odd old people, Dr. Katzman, Harvey, neighbors, were all standing around and talking in hushed voices in the living room. I found my father in the kitchen, getting out the apricot brandy. "Your grandmother's dead," he said.

"She didn't suffer," somebody said. "She passed away in her sleep."

"A merciful death."

"Where's Maw?"

"In the bedroom with . . . you'd better not go in," my father said.

"I want to see her."

My mother's face was long with grief. She wore a black shawl, and glared down at a knot of handkerchief clutched in a fist that had been cracked by washing soda. "Don't come in here," she said.

Several bearded, round-shouldered men in black shiny coats stood round the bed. I couldn't see my grandmother.

"Your grandmother's dead."

"Daddy told me."

"Go and wash your face and comb your hair. You'll have to get your own supper."

"O.K."

"One minute. The *baba* left some jewelry. The ring is for Harvey's wife and the necklace is for yours."

"Who's getting married?"

"Better go and wash your face. And remember behind the ears, Muttel."

Telegrams were sent, long-distance calls were made, and all through the evening relatives and neighbors came and went like swarms of fish when crumbs have been dropped into the water.

"When my father died," my mother said, "they had to have *six* motorcycle policemen to control the crowds. Twelve people fainted, such a heat . . ."

The man from the funeral parlor came.

"There goes the only Jewish businessman in town," my Uncle Harry said, "who wishes all his customers were Germans."

"This is no time for jokes."

"Listen, life goes on."

My cousin Jerry had begun to use a cigarette holder. "Everyone's going to be sickeningly sentimental," he said. "Soon the religious mumbo-jumbo starts. I can hardly wait."

Tomorrow was the Sabbath and so, according to the law, my grandmother couldn't be buried until Sunday. She would have to lie on the floor all night. Two old grizzly women in white came to move and wash the body and a professional mourner arrived to sit up and pray for her.

"I don't trust his face," my mother said. "He'll fall asleep. You watch him, Sam."

"A fat lot of good prayers will do her now."

"Will you just watch him, please."

"I'll watch him, I'll watch him." My father was livid about my Uncle Harry. "The way he's gone after that apricot brandy you'd think that guy never saw a bottle in his life before."

Harvey and I were sent to bed, but we couldn't sleep. My aunt was sobbing over the body in the living room—"That dirty hypocrite," my mother said—there was the old man praying, coughing, and spitting into his handkerchief each time he woke; and hushed voices and whimpering from the kitchen, where my father and mother sat. Harvey was in a good mood, he let me have a few puffs of his cigarette.

"Well, kiddo, this is our last night together. Tomorrow you can take over the back bedroom."

"*Are you crazy?*"

"You always wanted it for yourself."

"She died in there, but. You think I'm going to sleep in there?"

"Good night. Happy dreams, kiddo."

"Hey, let's talk some more."

Harvey told me a ghost story. "Did you know that when they hang a man," he said, "the last thing that happens is that he has an orgasm?"

"A what?"

"Forget it. I forgot you were still in kindergarten."

"I know plenty. Don't worry."

"At the funeral they're going to open her coffin to throw dirt in her face. It's supposed to be earth from Eretz.[3] They open it and you're going to have to look." Harvey stood up on his bed, holding his hands over his head like claws. He made a hideous face. "Bouyo-bouyo. Who's that sleeping in my bed? Woo-woo."

My uncle who was in the theater, the rabbi, and my aunt from Toronto, all came to Montreal for the funeral. Dr. Katzman came too.

"As long as she was alive," my mother said, "he couldn't even send five dollars a month. Some son! What a rabbi! I don't want him in my house, Sam. I can't bear the sight of him."

"You don't mean a word of that and you know it," Dr. Katzman said.

"Maybe you'd better give her a sedative," the rabbi said.

"Sam. Sam, will you say something, please."

My father stepped up to the rabbi, his face flushed. "I'll tell you this straight to your face, Israel," he said. "You've gone down in my estimation."

"Really," the rabbi said, smiling a little.

3. **Eretz Yisrael**, the Land of Israel.

My father's face burned a deeper red. "Year by year," he said, "your stock has gone down with me."

And my mother began to weep bitterly, helplessly, without control. She was led unwillingly to bed. While my father tried his best to comfort her, as he said consoling things, Dr. Katzman plunged a needle into her arm. "There we are," he said.

I went to sit in the sun on the outside stairs with Arty. "I'm going to the funeral," I said.

"I couldn't go anyway."

Arty was descended from the tribe of high priests and so was not allowed to be in the presence of a dead body. I was descended from the Yisroelis.[4]

"The lowest of the low," Arty said.

"Aw."

My uncle, the rabbi, and Dr. Katzman stepped into the sun to light cigarettes.

"It's remarkable that she held out for so long," Dr. Katzman said.

"Remarkable?" my uncle said. "It's written that if a man has been married twice he will spend as much time with his first wife in heaven as he did on earth. My father, may he rest in peace, was married to his first wife for seven years and my mother, may she rest in peace, has managed to keep alive for seven years. Today in heaven she will be able to join my father, may he rest in peace."

Dr. Katzman shook his head, he pursed his lips. "It's amazing," he said. "The mysteries of the human heart. Astonishing."

My father hurried outside. "Dr. Katzman, please. It's my wife. Maybe the injection wasn't strong enough? She just doesn't stop crying. It's like a tap. Could you come please?"

"Excuse me," Dr. Katzman said to my uncle.

"Of course."

My uncle approached Arty and me.

"Well, boys," he said, "what would you like to be when you grow up?"

1961

4   CHARACTERIZATION

In a good many stories the narrator is a disembodied offstage voice, without an identity or a personal history, without influence on the action, without qualities other than those that a voice and style may suggest. So it is in most of the earlier stories in this volume—*The Most Dangerous Game, Macomber, Owl Creek Bridge.* Poe's narrator, however, not only tells us the story but acts out the action; without him we not only would not know the story, there just would not be any. Richler's narrator looks back into his past; he is there *in* the

---

4. The lowest of the three categories into which the Jewish people are traditionally divided.

story, speaking, listening, reacting. In addition to being the narrator, he is a **character:** someone who acts, appears, or is referred to in a work.

The most common term for the character with the leading male role is **hero,** the "good guy" who opposes the **villain,** or "bad guy." The leading female character is the **heroine.** Heroes are usually larger than life, stronger or better than most human beings, almost godlike (and there's even a brand of heroes nowadays so close to being godlike that they are called superheroes). In most modern fiction, however, the leading character is much more ordinary, more like the rest of us. Such a character is called the **antihero,** not because he opposes the hero but because he is not like a hero in stature or perfection. An older and more neutral term than *hero* for the leading character, a term that does not imply either the presence or absence of outstanding virtue (and with the added advantage of referring equally to male and female), is **protagonist,** whose opponent is the **antagonist.** You might get into long and pointless arguments by calling Montresor or Macomber a hero, but either is his story's protagonist.

The major characters are those we see more of over a longer period of time; we learn more about them, and we think of them as more complex and frequently therefore more "realistic" than the minor characters, the figures who fill out the story. These major characters can grow and change, as Macomber does and as Judith does in Doris Lessing's *Our Friend Judith;* by the end of these stories both protagonists have acted in a way not predictable from what we learned about them and their past actions earlier in the story. Characters who can thus "surprise convincingly," an influential critic says, are **round characters.** Poe's and Connell's characters are not very complex and they do not change in surprising ways; they are therefore called **flat.** But we must be careful not to let terms like *flat* and *round* turn into value judgments. Because flat characters are less complex than round ones it is easy to assume they are artistically inferior; we need only to think of the characters of Charles Dickens, almost all of whom are flat, to realize that this is not always true. *Caricature*

The terms *flat* and *round,* like the terms *hero* and *antihero,* are not absolute or precise. They designate extremes or tendencies, not pigeonholes. Is Poe's Montresor entirely flat? Is Shakespeare's Iago? Falstaff? Charlie Chaplin's Little Tramp? Little Orphan Annie? Archie Bunker? Are all these characters equally flat? We will probably agree that Francis Macomber is a round character, for he is complex and changes before our eyes, but what about the hunter Wilson in the same story? Is he more or less flat than the hunter Rainsford in *The Most Dangerous Game?* Our answers are less important than our looking carefully at these characters to see what we know about each of them, to what degree they can be summed up in a phrase or a sentence; to discover how we learned what we know about them and how our judgment has been controlled by the story; to think about and perhaps judge the assumptions about human motivation, behavior, and nature that underlie the character and his or her characterization. Flat and round are useful as categories but are even more useful as tools of investigation, ways of focusing our attention and sharpening our perception.

Though most of Dickens's flat characters are highly individualized, not to say unique, some, like Fagin, the avaricious Jewish money-lender, are stereotypes: characters based on conscious or unconscious cultural assumptions that sex, age, ethnic or national identification, occupation, marital status, and so on are predictably accompanied by certain character traits, actions, even values.

The stereotype may be very useful in creating a round character, one who can surprise convincingly: Macomber is a spoiled, rich American; Judith, according to a Canadian woman, "one of your typical English spinsters." Both Macomber and Judith, however, act in ways that deny the limitations of the stereotype. A stereotype is, after all, only a quick—and somewhat superficial—form of classification, and classification is a common first step in definitions. One of the chief ways we have of describing or defining is by placing the thing to be defined in a category or class and then distinguishing it from the other members of that class. A good deal of **characterization**—the art, craft, method of presentation, or creation of fictional personages—involves a similar process. Characters are almost inevitably identified by category —by sex, age, nationality, occupation, etc. We soon learn that the narrator of *My Man Bovanne* is a middle-aged urban black woman, that Major Monarch is a middle-aged English gentleman, and, as we have seen, that Judith is an English spinster.

You may have noticed something that may seem odd at first: putting a character in more than one general group does not make that character more generalized or stereotyped, but more individual. The category *middle-aged* includes the narrator of *Bovanne*, Major and Mrs. Monarch, and Judith. That Major Monarch is male separates him from the other three; that the narrator of *Bovanne* is American and black separates her from the others, though she is, like Mrs. Monarch and Judith, a woman. So Hazel is to some degree particularized by being identified as a member of three general categories.

Not all generalizations involve cultural stereotypes, of course. Some may involve generalized character traits that the story or narrator defines for us (and that we must accept unless events in the story prove otherwise). Bovanne is said to be "just a nice old gent from the block," the kind of man whose conversation is "Comfy and cheery." Physical characteristics also serve as categories. Bovanne is blind. Before we are introduced to him, we are told that blind people hum, and that a blind man call Shakey Bee hums. Only then are we told that there is a blind man named Bovanne who also has the habit of humming. As physical characteristics are multiplied, the result is more and more particularizing or individualizing. The detailed physical description of Judith makes it possible to visualize her rather fully, almost to recognize her as an individual:

Judith is tall, small-breasted, slender. Her light brown hair is parted in the center and cut straight around her neck. A high straight forehead, straight nose, a full grave mouth are setting for her eyes, which are green, large and prominent. Her lids are very white, fringed with gold, and molded close over the eyeball. . . .

There are many other ways in which a character is characterized and individualized besides stereotyping and "de-stereotyping," and besides classifying and particularizing by physical description. In most cases we see what characters do and hear what they say; we sometimes learn what they think, and what other people think or say about them; we often know what kind of clothes they wear, what and how much they own, treasure, or covet; we may be told about their childhood, parents, or some parts of their past. We learn a bit about Hazel, the narrator of *Bovanne*, from her age, sex, and ethnic identification. We learn a great deal more from the way she talks to her children and they to her, from the fact that men call her "long distance and in the middle of the night for a little Mama comfort," the fact that she carried her baby daughter strapped to her chest until the baby was nearly two years old, and from her short, low-cut dress. We even know what she is thinking.

No matter how many methods of characterization are employed, however, at some point the particularization of the individual stops. No matter how individualized the character may be, he or she remains a member of a number of groups, and we make certain assumptions about the character based on our fixed or stereotyped notions of the groups. To destroy a stereotype, a story must introduce a stereotype to destroy. And somehow the de-stereotyped character, no matter how particularized, remains to some degree representative. If Judith turns out to be not as prudish and prissy as the stereotype of the English spinster has led us to believe, we may well conclude that the stereotype is false and Judith is more representative of the real English spinster than the stereotype is. Indeed, this tendency to generalize from the particulars of a story extends beyond cultural groups, sometimes to human character at large: if Francis Macomber can change his ways after years of habitual conduct, then human character, the story might seem to say, is not permanently fixed at birth, in infancy, childhood, ever.

One of the reasons it is so difficult to discuss character is precisely that the principles of definition and evaluation of fictional characters (not of their characterization, the way they are presented) are the same as those we use for real people, an area of violent controversy and confusion. The very term *character* itself, when it refers not to a fictional personage but to a combination of qualities in a human being, is somewhat ambiguous. It usually has moral overtones, often favorable (a man of character); it is sometimes neutral but evaluative (character reference). Judgment about character (not characterization, remember) usually involves moral terms like *good* and *bad* and *strong* and *weak*. *Personality* usually implies that which distinguishes or individualizes a person, and the judgment called for is not so much moral as social—*pleasing* or *displeasing*. An older term, *nature* (it is his nature to be so or do such), usually implies something inherent or inborn, something fixed and thus predictable. The **existential character** implies the opposite; that is, whatever our past, our conditioning, our pattern or previous behavior, we can, by an act of will, change all that right this minute, as Macomber does.

Fictional characters thus frequently seem to be part of the history that lies behind the story or beyond the story as part of our own world, to exist in a reality that is detachable from the words and events of the story in which they appear. We feel we might recognize Tom Jones, Jane Eyre, or Sherlock Holmes on the street, and we might be able to anticipate what they might say or do in *our* world, outside the story. Fictional characters are neither real nor detachable, of course, and they exist only in the words of the works in which they are presented. We must not forget the distinction between the character and the characterization, the method by which he or she is presented; so we must be careful to distinguish the *good character*, meaning someone whom, if real, we would consider virtuous, and the *good characterization*, meaning a fictional person who, no matter what his or her morality or behavior, is well presented.

Henry James's story *The Real Thing* is about the difference between reality and art, character and characterization. Major Monarch is described as a "gentleman, a man of fifty, very high and very straight, with a mustache slightly grizzled and a dark gray walking-coat admirably fitted, . . ." He looks like the stereotype of a celebrity. The painter-narrator of *The Real Thing*, however, immediately recognizes that, because of a "paradoxical law," Major Monarch's appearance means that he is *not* a celebrity: celebrities are not often so "striking." It does not take the narrator long to recognize the Major's real type. Just by the Major's appearance, the painter can "see" the Major's whole gentlemanly life: his hunting, his clothes, his umbrellas, his luggage, his servants, and he can see as well Mrs. Monarch's lady's life, clothes, etc. They are "the real thing," a real gentleman and a real lady. They are therefore useless as models for the artist. Not only are they so much *one* real thing that they can pose only for that type and no other, but even as a lady or gentleman they are so stereotypical they are useful only for illustrations of bad, stereotyped novels. James seems to be distinguishing *character* and *characterization*: the first is "the real thing" which will not do for art or the *representation* of the real; the second, "the alchemy of art," offers not a copy of reality but an *illusion* of reality, an illusion that seems more real in its representation than the real thing would.

Even if we entirely agree with Henry James—and not all readers do—his distinction between reality and its representation does not mean that we cannot learn from one about the other. We must recognize that characters are not finally detachable—that they have roles, functions, limitations, and their very existence in the context of other elements in the story; we must not confuse fictional characters with real people, or character with characterization. This is not to say, however, that we may not learn about real people from characters in fiction or learn to understand fictional characters in part from what we know about real people. For real people too exist in a context of other people and other elements, their history and geography and their "narrator," the one who is representing them—that is, *you*. Indeed, it may be worth paying particular attention to how stories create the images of people and what those images assume about human character precisely because this process and these assumptions are so similar to the way we get to know and understand real people. For we are all artists representing reality to ourselves. If we study the art of characterization we may become better artists, able to enrich both our reading and our lives.

TONI CADE BAMBARA

My Man Bovanne

Blind people got a hummin jones[1] if you notice. Which is understandable completely once you been around one and notice what no eyes will force you into to see people, and you get past the first time, which seems to come out of nowhere, and it's like you in church again with fat-chest ladies and old gents gruntin a hum low in the throat to whatever the preacher be saying. Shakey Bee bottom lip all swole up with Sweet Peach[2] and me explainin how come the sweet-potato bread was a dollar-quarter this time stead of dollar regular and he say uh hunh he understand, then he break into this *thizzin* kind of hum which is quiet, but fiercesome just the same, if you ain't ready for it. Which I wasn't. But I got used to it and the onliest time I had to say somethin bout it was when he was playin checkers on the stoop one time and he commenst to hummin quite churchy seem to me. So I says, "Look here Shakey Bee, I can't beat you and Jesus too." He stop.

So that's how come I asked My Man Bovanne to dance. He ain't my man mind you, just a nice ole gent from the block that we all know cause he fixes things and the kids like him. Or used to fore Black Power got hold their minds and mess em around till they can't be civil to ole folks. So we at this benefit for my niece's cousin who's runnin for somethin with this Black party somethin or other behind her. And I press up close to dance with Bovanne who blind and I'm hummin and he hummin, chest to chest like talkin. Not jammin my breasts into the man. Wasn't bout tits. Was bout vibrations. And he dug it and asked me what color dress I had on and how my hair was fixed and how I was doin without a man, not nosy but nice-like, and who was at this affair and was the canapés daintystingy or healthy enough to get hold of proper. Comfy and cheery is what I'm tryin to get across. Touch talkin like the heel of the hand on the tambourine or on a drum.

But right away Joe Lee come up on us and frown for dancin so close to the man. My own son who knows what kind of warm I am about; and don't grown men all call me long distance and in the

---

1. A compelling need.   2. A brand of dipping snuff.

middle of the night for a little Mama comfort? But he frown. Which ain't right since Bovanne can't see and defend himself. Just a nice old man who fixes toasters and busted irons and bicycles and things and changes the lock on my door when my men friends get messy. Nice man. Which is not why they invited him. Grass roots you see. Me and Sister Taylor and the woman who does heads at Mamies and the man from the barber shop, we all there on account of we grass roots. And I ain't never been souther than Brooklyn Battery and no more country than the window box on my fire escape. And just yesterday my kids tellin me to take them countrified rags off my head and be cool. And now can't get Black enough to suit em. So everybody passin sayin My Man Bovanne. Big deal, keep steppin and don't even stop a minute to get the man a drink or one of them cute sandwiches or tell him what's goin on. And him standin there with a smile ready case someone do speak he want to be ready. So that's how come I pull him on the dance floor and we dance squeezin past the tables and chairs and all them coats and people standin round up in each other face talkin bout this and that but got no use for this blind man who mostly fixed skates and skooters for all these folks when they was just kids. So I'm pressed up close and we touch talkin with the hum. And here come my daughter cuttin her eye[3] at me like she do when she tell me about my "apolitical" self like I got hoof and mouf disease and there ain't no hope at all. And I don't pay her no mind and just look up in Bovanne shadow face and tell him his stomach like a drum and he laugh. Laugh real loud. And here come my youngest, Task, with a tap on my elbow like he the third grade monitor and I'm cuttin up on the line to assembly.

"I was just talkin on the drums," I explained when they hauled me into the kitchen. I figured drums was my best defense. They can get ready for drums what with all this heritage business. And Bovanne stomach just like that drum Task give me when he come back from Africa. You just touch it and it hum thizzm, thizzm. So I stuck to the drum story. "Just drummin that's all."

"Mama, what are you talkin about?"

"She had too much to drink," say Elo to Task cause she don't hardly say nuthin to me direct no more since that ugly argument about my wigs.

"Look here Mama," say Task, the gentle one. "We just tryin to pull your coat. You were makin a spectacle of yourself out there dancing like that."

"Dancin like what?"

Task run a hand over his left ear like his father for the world and his father before that.

"Like a bitch in heat," say Elo.

"Well uhh, I was goin to say like one of them sex-starved ladies gettin on in years and not too discriminating. Know what I mean?"

I don't answer cause I'll cry. Terrible thing when your own children talk to you like that. Pullin me out the party and hustlin me into some

3. Giving a sharp look.

stranger's kitchen in the back of a bar just like the damn police. And ain't like I'm old old. I can still wear me some sleeveless dresses without the meat hangin off my arm. And I keep up with some thangs through my kids. Who ain't kids no more. To hear them tell it. So I don't say nuthin.

"Dancin with that tom," say Elo to Joe Lee, who leanin on the folks' freezer. "His feet can smell a cracker a mile away and go into their shuffle number post haste. And them eyes. He could be a little considerate and put on some shades. Who wants to look into them blown-out fuses that—"

"Is this what they call the generation gap?" I say.

"Generation gap," spits Elo, like I suggested castor oil and fricassee possum in the milk-shakes or somethin. "That's a white concept for a white phenomenon. There's no generation gap among Black people. We are a col—"

"Yeh, well never mind," says Joe Lee. "The point is Mama . . . well, it's pride. You embarrass yourself and us too dancin like that."

"I wasn't shame." Then nobody say nuthin. Them standin there in they pretty clothes with drinks in they hands and gangin up on me, and me in the third-degree chair and nary a olive to my name. Felt just like the police got hold to me.

"First of all," Task say, holdin up his hand and tickin off the offenses, "the dress. Now that dress is too short, Mama, and too low-cut for a woman your age. And Tamu's going to make a speech tonight to kick off the campaign and will be introducin you and expecting you to organize the council of elders—"

"Me? Didn nobody ask me nuthin. You mean Nisi? She change her name?"

"Well, Norton was supposed to tell you about it. Nisi wants to introduce you and then encourage the older folks to form a Council of the Elders to act as an advisory—"

"And you going to be standing there with your boobs out and that wig on your head and that hem up to your ass. And people'll say, 'Ain't that the horny bitch that was grindin with the blind dude?' "

"Elo, be cool a minute," say Task, gettin to the next finger. "And then there's the drinkin. Mama, you know you can't drink cause next thing you know you be laughin loud and carryin on," and he grab another finger for the loudness. "And then there's the dancin. You been tattooed on the man for four records straight and slow draggin even on the fast numbers. How you think that look for a woman your age?"

"What's my age?"

"What?"

"I'm axin you all a simple question. You keep talkin bout what's proper for a woman my age. How old am I anyhow?" And Joe Lee slams his eyes shut and squinches up his face to figure. And Task run a hand over his ear and stare into his glass like the ice cubes goin calculate for him. And Elo just starin at the top of my head like she goin rip the wig off any minute now.

"Is your hair braided up under that thing? If so, why don't you take it off? You always did do a neat cornroll."[4]

"Uh huh," cause I'm thinkin how she couldn't undo her hair fast enough talking bout cornroll so countrified. None of which was the subject. "How old, I say?"

"Sixtee-one or—"

"You a damn lie Joe Lee Peoples."

"And that's another thing," say Task on the fingers.

"You know what you all can kiss," I say, gettin up and brushin the wrinkles out my lap.

"Oh, Mama," Elo say, puttin a hand on my shoulder like she hasn't done since she left home and the hand landin light and not sure it supposed to be there. Which hurt me to my heart. Cause this was the child in our happiness fore Mr. Peoples die. And I carried that child strapped to my chest till she was nearly two. We was close is what I'm tryin to tell you. Cause it was more me in the child than the others. And even after Task it was the girlchild I covered in the night and wept over for no reason at all less it was she was a chub-chub like me and not very pretty, but a warm child. And how did things get to this, that she can't put a sure hand on me and say Mama we love you and care about you and you entitled to enjoy yourself cause you a good woman?

"And then there's Reverend Trent," say Task, glancin from left to right like they hatchin a plot and just now lettin me in on it. "You were suppose to be talking with him tonight, Mama, about giving us his basement for campaign headquarters and—"

"Didn nobody tell me nuthin. If grass roots mean you kept in the dark I can't use it. I really can't. And Reven Trent a fool anyway the way he tore into the widow man up there on Edgecomb cause he wouldn't take in three of them foster children and the woman not even comfy in the ground yet and the man's mind messed up and—"

"Look here," say Task. "What we need is a family conference so we can get all this stuff cleared up and laid out on the table. In the meantime I think we better get back into the other room and tend to business. And in the meantime, Mama, see if you can't get to Reverend Trent and—"

"You want me to belly rub with the Reven, that it?"

"Oh damn," Elo say and go through the swingin door.

"We'll talk about all this at dinner. How's tomorrow night, Joe Lee?" While Joe Lee being self-important I'm wonderin who's doin the cookin and how come no body ax me if I'm free and do I get a corsage and things like that. Then Joe nod that it's O.K. and he go through the swingin door and just a little hubbub come through from the other room. Then Task smile his smile, lookin just like his daddy, and he leave. And it just me in this stranger's kitchen, which was a mess I wouldn't never let my kitchen look like. Poison you just to look at the pots. Then the door swing the other way and it's My Man Bo-vanne standin there sayin Miss Hazel but lookin at the deep fry and

4. Cornrow, a hairstyle in which all the hair is interwoven from the scalp into small braids.

then at the steam table, and most surprised when I come up on him from the other direction and take him on out of there. Pass the folks pushin up towards the stage where Nisi and some other people settin and ready to talk, and folks gettin to the last of the sandwiches and the booze fore they settle down in one spot and listen serious. And I'm thinkin bout tellin Bovanne what a lovely long dress Nisi got on and the earrings and her hair piled up in a cone and the people bout to hear how we all gettin screwed and gotta form our own party and everybody there listenin and lookin. But instead I just haul the man on out of there, and Joe Lee and his wife look at me like I'm terrible, but they ain't said boo to the man yet. Cause he blind and old and don't nobody there need him since they grown up and don't need they skates fixed no more.

"Where we goin, Miss Hazel?" Him knowin all the time.

"First we gonna buy you some dark sunglasses. Then you comin with me to the supermarket so I can pick up tomorrow's dinner, which is goin to be a grand thing proper and you invited. Then we goin to my house."

"That be fine. I surely would like to rest my feet." Bein cute, but you got to let men play out they little show, blind or not. So he chat on bout how tired he is and how he appreciate me takin him in hand this way. And I'm thinkin I'll have him change the lock on my door first thing. Then I'll give the man a nice warm bath with jasmine leaves in the water and a little Epsom salt on the sponge to do his back. And then a good rubdown with rose water and olive oil. Then a cup of lemon tea with a taste in it. And a little talcum, some of that fancy stuff Nisi mother sent over last Christmas. And then a massage, a good face massage round the forehead which is the worryin part. Cause you gots to take care of the older folks. And let them know they still needed to run the mimeo machine and keep the spark plugs clean and fix the mailboxes for folks who might help us get the breakfast program goin, and the school for the little kids and the campaign and all. Cause old folks in the nation. That what Nisi was sayin and I mean to do my part.

"I imagine you are a very pretty woman, Miss Hazel."

"I surely am," I say just like the hussy my daughter always say I was.

1972

HENRY JAMES

The Real Thing

I

When the porter's wife, who used to answer the house-bell, announced "A gentleman and a lady, sir," I had, as I often had in those days—the wish being father to the thought—an immediate vision of sitters. Sitters my visitors in this case proved to be; but not in the sense I should have preferred. There was nothing at first however to indicate that they mightn't have come for a portrait. The gentleman, a man of fifty, very high and very straight, with a mustache slightly grizzled and a dark gray walking-coat admirably fitted, both of which I noted professionally—I don't mean as a barber or yet as a tailor—would have struck me as a celebrity if celebrities often were striking. It was a truth of which I had for some time been conscious that a figure with a good deal of frontage was, as one might say, almost never a public institution. A glance at the lady helped to remind me of this paradoxical law: she also looked too distinguished to be a "personality." Moreover one would scarcely come across two variations together.

Neither of the pair immediately spoke—they only prolonged the preliminary gaze suggesting that each wished to give the other a chance. They were visibly shy; they stood there letting me take them in—which, as I afterwards perceived, was the most practical thing they could have done. In this way their embarrassment served their cause. I had seen people painfully reluctant to mention that they desired anything so gross as to be represented on canvas; but the scruples of my new friends appeared almost insurmountable. Yet the gentleman might have said "I should like a portrait of my wife," and the lady might have said "I should like a portrait of my husband." Perhaps they weren't husband and wife—this naturally would make the matter more delicate. Perhaps they wished to be done together—in which case they ought to have brought a third person to break the news.

"We come from Mr. Rivet," the lady finally said with a dim smile that had the effect of a moist sponge passed over a "sunk" piece of painting, as well as of a vague allusion to vanished beauty. She was as tall and straight, in her degree, as her companion, and with ten years less to carry. She looked as sad as a woman could look whose face was not charged with expression; that is her tinted oval mask showed waste as an exposed surface shows friction. The hand of time had played over her freely, but to an effect of elimination. She was slim and stiff, and so well-dressed, in dark blue cloth, with lappets and pockets and buttons, that it was clear she employed the same tailor as her husband. The couple had an indefinable air of prosperous thrift—they evidently got a good deal of luxury for their money. If I was to be one of their luxuries it would behove me to consider my terms.

"Ah Claude Rivet recommended me?" I echoed; and I added that it was very kind of him, though I could reflect that, as he only painted landscape, this wasn't a sacrifice.

The lady looked very hard at the gentleman, and the gentleman looked round the room. Then staring at the floor a moment and stroking his mustache, he rested his pleasant eyes on me with the remark: "He said you were the right one."

"I try to be, when people want to sit."

"Yes, we should like to," said the lady anxiously.

"Do you mean together?"

My visitors exchanged a glance. "If you could do anything with *me* I suppose it would be double," the gentleman stammered.

"Oh yes, there's naturally a higher charge for two figures than for one."

"We should like to make it pay," the husband confessed.

"That's very good of you," I returned, appreciating so unwonted a sympathy—for I supposed he meant pay the artist.

A sense of strangeness seemed to dawn on the lady. "We mean for the illustrations—Mr. Rivet said you might put one in."

"Put in—an illustration?" I was equally confused.

"Sketch her off, you know" said the gentleman, coloring.

It was only then that I understood the service Claude Rivet had rendered me; he had told them how I worked in black-and-white, for magazines, for storybooks, for sketches of contemporary life, and consequently had copious employment for models. These things were true, but it was not less true—I may confess it now; whether because the aspiration was to lead to everything or to nothing I leave the reader to guess—that I couldn't get the honors, to say nothing of the emoluments, of a great painter of portraits out of my head. My "illustrations" were my pot-boilers; I looked to a different branch of art—far and away the most interesting it had always seemed to me— to perpetuate my fame. There was no shame in looking to it also to make my fortune; but that fortune was by so much further from being made from the moment my visitors wished to be "done" for nothing. I was disappointed; for in the pictorial sense I had immediately *seen* them. I had seized their type—I had already settled what I would do with it. Something that wouldn't absolutely have pleased them, I afterwards reflected.

"Ah you're—you're—a—?" I began as soon as I had mastered my surprise. I couldn't bring out the dingy word "models": it seemed so little to fit the case.

"We haven't had much practice," said the lady.

"We've got to *do* something, and we've thought that an artist in your line might perhaps make something of us," her husband threw off. He further mentioned that they didn't know many artists and that they had gone first, on the off-chance—he painted views of course, but sometimes put in figures; perhaps I remembered—to Mr. Rivet, whom they had met a few years before at a place in Norfolk where he was sketching.

"We used to sketch a little ourselves," the lady hinted.

"It's very awkward, but we absolutely *must* do something," her husband went on.

"Of course we're not so *very* young," she admitted with a wan smile.

With the remark that I might as well know something more about them the husband had handed me a card extracted from a neat new pocket-book—their appurtenances were all of the freshest—and inscribed with the words "Major Monarch." Impressive as these words were they didn't carry my knowledge much further; but my visitor presently added: "I've left the army and we've had the misfortune to lose our money. In fact our means are dreadfully small."

"It's awfully trying—a regular strain," said Mrs. Monarch.

They evidently wished to be discreet—to take care not to swagger because they were gentlefolk. I felt them willing to recognize this as something of a drawback, at the same time that I guessed at an underlying sense—their consolation in adversity—that they *had* their points. They certainly had; but these advantages struck me as preponderantly social; such for instance as would help to make a drawing-room look well. However, a drawing-room was always, or ought to be, a picture.

In consequence of his wife's allusion to their age Major Monarch observed: "Naturally it's more for the figure that we thought of going in. We can still hold ourselves up." On the instant I saw that the figure was indeed their strong point. His "naturally" didn't sound vain, but it lighted up the question. "*She* has the best one," he continued, nodding at his wife with a pleasant after-dinner absence of circumlocution. I could only reply, as if we were in fact sitting over our wine, that this didn't prevent his own from being very good; which led him in turn to make answer: "We thought that if you ever have to do people like us we might be something like it. *She* particularly—for a lady in a book, you know."

I was so amused by them that, to get more of it, I did my best to take their point of view; and though it was an embarrassment to find myself appraising physically, as if they were animals on hire or useful blacks, a pair whom I should have expected to meet only in one of the relations in which criticism is tacit, I looked at Mrs. Monarch judicially enough to be able to exclaim after a moment with conviction: "Oh yes, a lady in a book!" She was singularly like a bad illustration.

"We'll stand up, if you like," said the Major; and he raised himself before me with a really grand air.

I could take his measure at a glance—he was six feet two and a perfect gentleman. It would have paid any club in process of formation and in want of a stamp to engage him at a salary to stand in the principal window. What struck me at once was that in coming to me they had rather missed their vocation; they could surely have been turned to better account for advertising purposes. I couldn't of course see the thing in detail, but I could see them make somebody's fortune —I don't mean their own. There was something in them for a waistcoat-maker, a hotel-keeper or a soap-vendor. I could imagine "We always use it" pinned on their bosoms with the greatest effect; I had a vision of the brilliancy with which they would launch a table d'hôte.

Mrs. Monarch sat still, not from pride but from shyness, and presently her husband said to her: "Get up, my dear, and show how smart you are." She obeyed, but she had no need to get up to show it. She walked to the end of the studio and then came back blushing, her fluttered eyes on the partner of her appeal. I was reminded of an incident I had accidentally had a glimpse of in Paris—being with a friend there, a dramatist about to produce a play, when an actress came to him to ask to be entrusted with a part. She went through her paces before him, walked up and down as Mrs. Monarch was doing. Mrs. Monarch did it quite as well, but I abstained from applauding. It was very odd to see such people apply for such poor pay. She looked as if she had ten thousand a year. Her husband had used the word that described her: she was in the London current jargon essentially and typically "smart." Her figure was, in the same order of ideas, conspicuously and irreproachably "good." For a woman of her age her waist was surprisingly small; her elbow moreover had the orthodox crook. She held her head at the conventional angle, but why did she come to *me*? She ought to have tried on jackets at a big shop. I feared my visitors were not only destitute but "artistic"—which would be a great complication. When she sat down again I thanked her, observing that what a draftsman most valued in his model was the faculty of keeping quiet.

"Oh *she* can keep quiet," said Major Monarch. Then he added jocosely: "I've always kept her quiet."

"I'm not a nasty fidget, am I?" It was going to wring tears from me, I felt, the way she hid her head, ostrich-like, in the other broad bosom.

The owner of this expanse addressed his answer to me. "Perhaps it isn't out of place to mention—because we ought to be quite business-like, oughtn't we?—that when I married her she was known as the Beautiful Statue."

"Oh dear!" said Mrs. Monarch ruefully.

"Of course I should want a certain amount of expression," I rejoined.

"Of *course!*"—and I had never heard such unanimity.

"And then I suppose you know that you'll get awfully tired."

"Oh we *never* get tired!" they eagerly cried.

"Have you had any kind of practice?"

They hesitated—they looked at each other. "We've been photographed—*immensely*," said Mrs. Monarch.

"She means the fellows have asked us themselves," added the Major.

"I see—because you're so good-looking."

"I don't know what they thought, but they were always after us."

"We always got our photographs for nothing," smiled Mrs. Monarch.

"We might have brought some, my dear," her husband remarked.

"I'm not sure we have any left. We've given quantities away," she explained to me.

"With our autographs and that sort of thing," said the Major.

"Are they to be got in the shops?" I enquired as a harmless pleasantry.

"Oh yes, *hers*—they used to be."

"Not now," said Mrs. Monarch with her eyes on the floor.

II

I could fancy the "sort of thing" they put on the presentation copies of their photographs, and I was sure they wrote a beautiful hand. It was odd how quickly I was sure of everything that concerned them. If they were now so poor as to have to earn shillings and pence they could never have had much of a margin. Their good looks had been their capital, and they had good-humoredly made the most of the career that this resource marked out for them. It was in their faces, the blankness, the deep intellectual repose of the twenty years of country-house visiting that had given them pleasant intonations. I could see the sunny drawing-rooms, sprinkled with periodicals she didn't read, in which Mrs. Monarch had continuously sat; I could see the wet shrubberies in which she had walked, equipped to admiration for either exercise. I could see the rich covers[1] the Major had helped to shoot and the wonderful garments in which, late at night, he repaired to the smoking-room to talk about them. I could imagine their leggings and waterproofs, their knowing tweeds and rugs, their rolls of sticks and cases of tackle and neat umbrellas; and I could evoke the exact appearance of their servants and the compact variety of their luggage on the platforms of country stations.

They gave small tips, but they were liked; they didn't do anything themselves, but they were welcome. They looked so well everywhere; they gratified the general relish for stature, complexion and "form." They knew it without fatuity or vulgarity, and they respected themselves in consequence. They weren't superficial; they were thorough and kept themselves up—it had been their line. People with such a taste for activity had to have some line. I could feel how even in a dull house they could have been counted on for the joy of life. At present something had happened—it didn't matter what, their little income had grown less, it had grown least—and they had to do something for pocket-money. Their friends could like them, I made out, without liking to support them. There was something about them that represented credit—their clothes, their manners, their type; but if credit is a large empty pocket in which an occasional chink reverberates, the chink at least must be audible. What they wanted of me was to help to make it so. Fortunately they had no children—I soon divined that. They would also perhaps wish our relations to be kept secret: this was why it was "for the figure"—the reproduction of the face would betray them.

I liked them—I felt, quite as their friends must have done—they were so simple; and I had no objection to them if they would suit. But somehow with all their perfections I didn't easily believe in them. After all they were amateurs, and the ruling passion of my life was the detestation of the amateur. Combined with this was another perversity —an innate preference for the represented subject over the real one: the defect of the real one was so apt to be a lack of representation. I liked things that appeared; then one was sure. Whether they *were* or not was a subordinate and almost always a profitless question. There were other considerations, the first of which was that I already had two or three recruits in use, notably a young person with big feet, in alpaca, from Kilburn, who for a couple of years had come to me regularly for my illustrations and with whom I was still—perhaps ignobly—satisfied. I frankly explained to my visitors how the case stood, but they had taken more precautions than I supposed. They had reasoned out their opportunity, for Claude Rivet had told them of the

1. Flocks of game birds.

projected *édition de luxe* of one of the writers of our day—the rarest of the novelists—who, long neglected by the multitudinous vulgar and dearly prized by the attentive (need I mention Philip Vincent?), had had the happy fortune of seeing, late in life, the dawn and then the full light of a higher criticism; an estimate in which on the part of the public there was something really of expiation. The edition preparing, planned by a publisher of taste, was practically an act of high reparation; the wood-cuts with which it was to be enriched were the homage of English art to one of the most independent representatives of English letters. Major and Mrs. Monarch confessed to me they had hoped I might be able to work *them* into my branch of the enterprise. They knew I was to do the first of the books, "Rutland Ramsay," but I had to make clear to them that my participation in the rest of the affair—this first book was to be a test—must depend on the satisfaction I should give. If this should be limited my employers would drop me with scarce common forms. It was therefore a crisis for me, and naturally I was making special preparations, looking about for new people, should they be necessary and securing the best types. I admitted however that I should like to settle down to two or three good models who would do for everything.

"Should we have often to—a—put on special clothes?" Mrs. Monarch timidly demanded.

"Dear yes—that's half the business."

"And should we be expected to supply our own costumes?"

"Oh no; I've got a lot of things. A painter's models put on—or put off—anything he likes."

"And you mean—a—the same?"

"The same?"

Mrs. Monarch looked at her husband again.

"Oh she was just wondering," he explained, "if the costumes are in *general* use." I had to confess that they were, and I mentioned further that some of them—I had a lot of genuine greasy last-century things—had served their time, a hundred years ago, on living world-stained men and women; on figures not perhaps so far removed, in that vanished world, from *their* type, the Monarchs', *quoi!*[2] of a breeched and bewigged age. "We'll put on anything that *fits*," said the Major.

"Oh I arrange that—they fit in the pictures."

"I'm afraid I should do better for the modern books. I'd come as you like," said Mrs. Monarch.

"She has got a lot of clothes at home: they might do for contemporary life," her husband continued.

"Oh I can fancy scenes in which you'd be quite natural." And indeed I could see the slipshod rearrangements of stale properties—the stories I tried to produce pictures for without the exasperation of reading them—whose sandy tracts the good lady might help to people. But I had to return to the fact that for this sort of work—the daily mechanical grind—I was already equipped: the people I was working with were fully adequate.

"We only thought we might be more like *some* characters," said

2. What!

Mrs. Monarch mildly, getting up.

Her husband also rose; he stood looking at me with a dim wistfulness that was touching in so fine a man. "Wouldn't it be rather a pull sometimes to have—a—to have—?" He hung fire; he wanted me to help him by phrasing what he meant. But I couldn't—I didn't know. So he brought it out awkwardly: "The *real* thing; a gentleman, you know, or a lady." I was quite ready to give a general assent—I admitted that there was a great deal in that. This encouraged Major Monarch to say, following up his appeal with an unacted gulp: "It's awfully hard—we've tried everything." The gulp was communicative; it proved too much for his wife. Before I knew it Mrs. Monarch had dropped again upon a divan and burst into tears. Her husband sat down beside her, holding one of her hands; whereupon she quickly dried her eyes with the other, while I felt embarrassed as she looked up at me. "There isn't a confounded job I haven't applied for—waited for—prayed for. You can fancy we'd be pretty bad first. Secretaryships and that sort of thing? You might as well ask for a peerage. I'd be *anything*—I'm strong; a messenger or a coalheaver. I'd put on a gold-laced cap and open carriage-doors in front of the haberdasher's; I'd hang about a station to carry portmanteaux; I'd be a postman. But they won't *look* at you; there are thousands as good as yourself already on the ground. *Gentlemen*, poor beggars, who've drunk their wine, who've kept their hunters!"

I was as reassuring as I knew how to be, and my visitors were presently on their feet again while, for the experiment, we agreed on an hour. We were discussing it when the door opened and Miss Churm came in with a wet umbrella. Miss Churm had to take the omnibus to Maida Vale and then walk half a mile. She looked a trifle blowzy and slightly splashed. I scarcely ever saw her come in without thinking afresh how odd it was that, being so little in herself, she should yet be so much in others. She was a meager little Miss Churm, but was such an ample heroine of romance. She was only a freckled cockney, but she could represent everything, from a fine lady to a shepherdess; she had the faculty as she might have had a fine voice or long hair. She couldn't spell and she loved beer, but she had two or three "points," and practice, and a knack, and mother-wit, and a whimsical sensibility, and a love of the theater, and seven sisters, and not an ounce of respect, especially for the *h*.[3] The first thing my visitors saw was that her umbrella was wet, and in their spotless perfection they visibly winced at it. The rain had come on since their arrival.

"I'm all in a soak; there *was* a mess of people in the 'bus. I wish you lived near a styion," said Miss Churm. I requested her to get ready as quickly as possible, and she passed into the room in which she always changed her dress. But before going out she asked me what she was to get into this time.

"It's the Russian princess, don't you know?" I answered; "the one with the 'golden eyes,' in black velvet, for the long thing in the *Cheapside*."

3. Working-class Londoners, especially in the East End (cockneys), drop *h*'s 'orribly.

"Golden eyes? I *say!*" cried Miss Churm, while my companions watched her with intensity as she withdrew. She always arranged herself, when she was late, before I could turn round; and I kept my visitors a little on purpose, so that they might get an idea, from seeing her, what would be expected of themselves. I mentioned that she was quite my notion of an excellent model—she was really very clever.

"Do you think she looks like a Russian princess?" Major Monarch asked with lurking alarm.

"When I make her, yes."

"Oh if you have to *make* her—!" he reasoned, not without point.

"That's the most you can ask. There are so many who are not makeable."

"Well now, *here's* a lady"—and with a persuasive smile he passed his arm into his wife's—"who's already made!"

"Oh I'm not a Russian princess," Mrs. Monarch protested a little coldly. I could see she had known some and didn't like them. There at once was a complication of a kind I never had to fear with Miss Churm.

This young lady came back in black velvet—the gown was rather rusty and very low on her lean shoulders—and with a Japanese fan in her red hands. I reminded her that in the scene I was doing she had to look over someone's head. "I forgot whose it is; but it doesn't matter. Just look over a head."

"I'd rather look over a stove," said Miss Churm; and she took her station near the fire. She fell into position, settled herself into a tall attitude, gave a certain backward inclination to her head and a certain forward droop to her fan, and looked, at least to my prejudiced sense, distinguished and charming, foreign and dangerous. We left her looking so while I went downstairs with Major and Mrs. Monarch.

"I believe I could come about as near it as that," said Mrs. Monarch.

"Oh you think she's shabby, but you must allow for the alchemy of art."

However, they went off with an evident increase of comfort founded on their demonstrable advantage in being the real thing. I could fancy them shuddering over Miss Churm. She was very droll about them when I went back, for I told her what they wanted.

"Well, if *she* can sit I'll tyke to bookkeeping," said my model.

"She's very ladylike," I replied as an innocent form of aggravation.

"So much the worse for *you*. That means she can't turn round."

"She'll do for the fashionable novels."

"Oh yes, she'll *do* for them!" my model humorously declared. "Ain't they bad enough without her?" I had often sociably denounced them to Miss Churm.

III

It was for the elucidation of a mystery in one of these works that I first tried Mrs. Monarch. Her husband came with her, to be useful if necessary—it was sufficiently clear that as a general thing he would prefer to come with her. At first I wondered if this were for "propriety's" sake—if he were going to be jealous and meddling. The idea was too tiresome, and if it had been confirmed it would speedily have brought our acquaintance to a close. But I soon saw there was nothing in it and that if he accompanied Mrs. Monarch it was—in addition to the chance of being wanted—simply because he had nothing else to do. When they were separate his occupation was gone and they never *had* been separate. I judged rightly that in their awkward situation their close union was their main comfort and that this union had no weak spot. It was a real marriage, an encouragement to the hesitating, a nut for pessimists to crack. Their address was humble—I remember afterwards thinking it had been the only thing about them that was really professional—and I could fancy the lamentable lodgings in which the Major would have been left alone. He could sit there more or less grimly with his wife—he couldn't sit there anyhow without her.

He had too much tact to try and make himself agreeable when he couldn't be useful; so when I was too absorbed in my work to talk he simply sat and waited. But I liked to hear him talk—it made my work, when not interrupting it, less mechanical, less special. To listen to him was to combine the excitement of going out with the economy of staying at home. There was only one hindrance—that I seemed not to know any of the people this brilliant couple had known. I think he wondered extremely, during the term of our intercourse, whom the deuce I *did* know. He hadn't a stray sixpence[4] of an idea to fumble for, so we didn't spin it very fine; we confined ourselves to questions of leather and even of liquor—saddlers and breeches-makers and how to get excellent claret cheap—and matters like "good trains" and the habits of small game. His lore on these last subjects was astonishing—he managed to interweave the station-master with the ornithologist. When he couldn't talk about greater things he could talk cheerfully about smaller, and since I couldn't accompany him into reminiscences of the fashionable world he could lower the conversation without a visible effort to my level.

So earnest a desire to please was touching in a man who could so easily have knocked one down. He looked after the fire and had an opinion on the draft of the stove without my asking him, and I could see that he thought many of my arrangements not half knowing. I remember telling him that if I were only rich I'd offer him a salary to come and teach me how to live. Sometimes he gave a random sigh of which the essence might have been: "Give me even such a bare old barrack as *this*, and I'd do something with it!" When I wanted to use him he came alone; which was an illustration of the superior courage of women. His wife could bear her solitary second floor, and she was in general more discreet; showing by various small reserves that she was alive to the propriety of keeping our relations markedly professional—not letting them slide into sociability. She wished it to remain clear that she and the Major were employed, not cultivated, and if she approved of me as a superior, who could be kept in his place, she never thought me quite good enough for an equal.

She sat with great intensity, giving the whole of her mind to it, and was capable of remaining for an hour almost as motionless as before a photographer's lens. I could see she had been photographed often, but

---

4. Roughly, "a dime's worth."

somehow the very habit that made her good for that purpose unfitted her for mine. At first I was extremely pleased with her ladylike air, and it was a satisfaction, on coming to follow her lines, to see how good they were and how far they could lead the pencil. But after a little skirmishing I began to find her too insurmountably stiff; do what I would with it my drawing looked like a photograph or a copy of a photograph. Her figure had no variety of expression—she herself had no sense of variety. You may say that this was my business and was only a question of placing her. Yet I placed her in every conceivable position and she managed to obliterate their differences. She was always a lady certainly, and into the bargain was always the same lady. She was the real thing, but always the same thing. There were moments when I rather writhed under the serenity of her confidence that she *was* the real thing. All her dealings with me and all her husband's were an implication that this was lucky for *me*. Meanwhile I found myself trying to invent types that approached her own, instead of making her own transform itself—in the clever way that was not impossible for instance to poor Miss Churm. Arrange as I would and take the precautions I would, she always came out, in my pictures, too tall—landing me in the dilemma of having represented a fascinating woman as seven feet high, which (out of respect perhaps to my own very much scantier inches) was far from my idea of such a personage.

The case was worse with the Major—nothing I could do would keep *him* down, so that he became useful only for the representation of brawny giants. I adored variety and range, I cherished human accidents, the illustrative note; I wanted to characterize closely, and the thing in the world I most hated was the danger of being ridden by a type. I had quarreled with some of my friends about it; I had parted company with them for maintaining that one *had* to be, and that if the type was beautiful—witness Raphael and Leonardo[5]—the servitude was only a gain. I was neither Leonardo nor Raphael—I might only be a presumptuous young modern searcher; but I held that everything was to be sacrificed sooner than character. When they claimed that the obsessional form could easily *be* character I retorted, perhaps superficially, "Whose?" It couldn't be everybody's—it might end in being nobody's.

After I had drawn Mrs. Monarch a dozen times I felt surer even than before that the value of such a model as Miss Churm resided precisely in the fact that she had no positive stamp, combined of course with the other fact that what she did have was a curious and inexplicable talent for imitation. Her usual appearance was like a curtain which she could draw up at request for a capital performance. This performance was simply suggestive; but it was a word to the wise—it was vivid and pretty. Sometimes even I thought it, though she was plain herself, too insipidly pretty; I made it a reproach to her that the figures drawn from her were monotonously (*bêtement*,[6] as we used to say) graceful. Nothing made her more angry; it was so much

5. Raffaello Sanzio (1483–1520), Leonardo, da Vinci (1452–1519), famous Italian Renaissance painters. Leonardo, of course, was also an inventor, military engineer, architect, sculptor, anatomist, etc.

6. Foolishly.

her pride to feel she could sit for characters that had nothing in common with each other. She would accuse me at such moments of taking away her "reputytion."

It suffered a certain shrinkage, this queer quantity, from the repeated visits of my new friends. Miss Churm was greatly in demand, never in want of employment, so I had no scruple in putting her off occasionally, to try them more at my ease. It was certainly amusing at first to do the real thing—it was amusing to do Major Monarch's trousers. They *were* the real thing, even if he did come out colossal. It was amusing to do his wife's back hair—it was so mathematically neat—and the particular "smart" tension of her tight stays. She lent herself especially to positions in which the face was somewhat averted or blurred; she abounded in ladylike back views and *profils perdus.*[7] When she stood erect she took naturally one of the attitudes in which court-painters represent queens and princesses; so that I found myself wondering whether, to draw out this accomplishment, I couldn't get the editor of the *Cheapside* to publish a really royal romance, "A Tale of Buckingham Palace." Sometimes however the real thing and the make-believe came into contact; by which I mean that Miss Churm, keeping an appointment or coming to make one on days when I had much work in hand, encountered her invidious rivals. The encounter was not on their part, for they noticed her no more than if she had been the housemaid; not from intentional loftiness, but simply because as yet, professionally, they didn't know how to fraternize, as I could imagine they would have liked—or at least that the Major would. They couldn't talk about the omnibus—they always walked; and they didn't know what else to try—she wasn't interested in good trains or cheap claret. Besides, they must have felt—in the air—that she was amused at them, secretly derisive of their ever knowing how. She wasn't a person to conceal the limits of her faith if she had had a chance to show them. On the other hand Mrs. Monarch didn't think her tidy; for why else did she take pains to say to me—it was going out of the way, for Mrs. Monarch—that she didn't like dirty women?

One day when my young lady happened to be present with my other sitters—she even dropped in, when it was convenient, for a chat—I asked her to be so good as to lend a hand in getting tea, a service with which she was familiar and which was one of a class that, living as I did in a small way, with slender domestic resources, I often appealed to my models to render. They liked to lay hands on my property, to break the sitting, and sometimes the china—it made them feel Bohemian. The next time I saw Miss Churm after this incident she surprised me greatly by making a scene about it—she accused me of having wished to humiliate her. She hadn't resented the outrage at the time, but had seemed obliging and amused, enjoying the comedy of asking Mrs. Monarch, who sat vague and silent, whether she would have cream and sugar, and putting an exaggerated simper into the question. She had tried intonations—as if she too wished to pass for the real thing—till I was afraid my other visitors would take offense. Oh they were determined not to do this, and their touching patience

---

7. Incomplete profile, showing more of the back of the head and less of the face.

was the measure of their great need. They would sit by the hour, uncomplaining, till I was ready to use them; they would come back on the chance of being wanted and would walk away cheerfully if it failed. I used to go to the door with them to see in what magnificent order they retreated. I tried to find other employment for them—I introduced them to several artists. But they didn't "take," for reasons I could appreciate, and I became rather anxiously aware that after such disappointments they fell back upon me with a heavier weight. They did me the honor to think me most *their* form. They weren't romantic enough for the painters, and in those days there were few serious workers in black-and-white. Besides, they had an eye to the great job I had mentioned to them—they had secretly set their hearts on supplying the right essence for my pictorial vindication of our fine novelist. They knew that for this undertaking I should want no costume-effects, none of the frippery of past ages—that it was a case in which everything would be contemporary and satirical and presumably genteel. If I could work them into it their future would be assured, for the labor would of course be long and the occupation steady.

One day Mrs. Monarch came without her husband—she explained his absence by his having had to go to the City.[8] While she sat there in her usual relaxed majesty there came at the door a knock which I immediately recognized as the subdued appeal of a model out of work. It was followed by the entrance of a young man whom I at once saw to be a foreigner and who proved in fact an Italian acquainted with no English word but my name, which he uttered in a way that made it seem to include all others. I hadn't then visited his country, nor was I proficient in his tongue; but as he was not so meanly constituted—what Italian is?—as to depend only on that member for expression he conveyed to me, in familiar but graceful mimicry, that he was in search of exactly the employment in which the lady before me was engaged. I was not struck with him at first, and while I continued to draw I dropped few signs of interest or encouragement. He stood his ground however—not importunately, but with a dumb dog-like fidelity in his eyes that amounted to innocent impudence, the manner of a devoted servant—he might have been in the house for years—unjustly suspected. Suddenly it struck me that this very attitude and expression made a picture; whereupon I told him to sit down and wait till I should be free. There was another picture in the way he obeyed me, and I observed as I worked that there were others still in the way he looked wonderingly, with his head thrown back, about the high studio. He might have been crossing himself in Saint Peter's. Before I finished I said to myself "The fellow's a bankrupt orange-monger, but a treasure."

When Mrs. Monarch withdrew he passed across the room like a flash to open the door for her, standing there with the rapt pure gaze of the young Dante spellbound by the young Beatrice.[9] As I never

---

8. Financial and legal center of London.

9. Dante Alighieri (1265–1321), Italian poet, author of *The Divine Comedy*, was inspired for his whole lifetime poetically and spiritually by Beatrice Fortinari whom he first saw when they were children and saw only infrequently thereafter.

insisted, in such situations, on the blankness of the British domestic, I reflected that he had the making of a servant—and I needed one, but couldn't pay him to be only that—as well as of a model; in short I resolved to adopt my bright adventurer if he would agree to officiate in the double capacity. He jumped at my offer, and in the event my rashness—for I had really known nothing about him—wasn't brought home to me. He proved a sympathetic though a desultory ministrant, and had in a wonderful degree the *sentiment de la pose*.[1] It was uncultivated, instinctive, a part of the happy instinct that had guided him to my door and helped him to spell out my name on the card nailed to it. He had had no other introduction to me than a guess, from the shape of my high north window, seen outside, that my place was a studio and that as a studio it would contain an artist. He had wandered to England in search of fortune, like other itinerants, and had embarked, with a partner and a small green hand-cart, on the sale of penny ices. The ices had melted away and the partner had dissolved in their train. My young man wore tight yellow trousers with reddish stripes and his name was Oronte. He was sallow but fair, and when I put him into some old clothes of my own he looked like an Englishman. He was as good as Miss Churm, who could look, when requested, like an Italian.

IV

I thought Mrs. Monarch's face slightly convulsed when, on her coming back with her husband, she found Oronte installed. It was strange to have to recognize in a scrap of a lazzarone[2] a competitor to her magnificent Major. It was she who scented danger first, for the Major was anecdotically unconscious. But Oronte gave us tea, with a hundred eager confusions—he had never been concerned in so queer a process—and I think she thought better of me for having at last an "establishment." They saw a couple of drawings that I had made of the establishment, and Mrs. Monarch hinted that it never would have struck her he had sat for them. "Now the drawings you make from *us*, they look exactly like us," she reminded me, smiling in triumph; and I recognized that this was indeed just their defect. When I drew the Monarchs I couldn't anyhow get away from them—get into the character I wanted to represent; and I hadn't the least desire my model should be discoverable in my picture. Miss Churm never was, and Mrs. Monarch thought I hid her, very properly, because she was vulgar; whereas if she was lost it was only as the dead who go to heaven are lost—in the gain of an angel the more.

By this time I had got a certain start with "Rutland Ramsay," the first novel in the great projected series; that is I had produced a dozen drawings, several with the help of the Major and his wife, and I had sent them in for approval. My understanding with the publishers, as I have already hinted, had been that I was to be left to do my work, in this particular case, as I liked, with the whole book committed to me; but my connection with the rest of the series was only contingent. There were moments when, frankly, it *was* a comfort to have the real

---

1. Instinct for striking poses.   2. Street-person.

thing under one's hand; for there were characters in "Rutland Ramsay" that were very much like it. There were people presumably as erect as the Major and women of as good a fashion as Mrs. Monarch. There was a great deal of country-house life—treated, it is true, in a fine fanciful ironical generalized way—and there was a considerable implication of knickerbockers and kilts.[3] There were certain things I had to settle at the outset; such things for instance as the exact appearance of the hero and the particular bloom and figure of the heroine. The author of course gave me a lead, but there was a margin for interpretation. I took the Monarchs into my confidence, I told them frankly what I was about, I mentioned my embarrassments and alternatives. "Oh take *him!*" Mrs. Monarch murmured sweetly, looking at her husband; and "What could you want better than my wife?" the Major inquired with the comfortable candor that now prevailed between us.

I wasn't obliged to answer these remarks—I was only obliged to place my sitters. I wasn't easy in mind, and I postponed a little timidly perhaps the solving of my question. The book was a large canvas, the other figures were numerous, and I worked off at first some of the episodes in which the hero and the heroine were not concerned. When once I had set *them* up I should have to stick to them—I couldn't make my young man seven feet high in one place and five feet nine in another. I inclined on the whole to the latter measurement, though the Major more than once reminded me that *he* looked about as young as anyone. It was indeed quite possible to arrange him, for the figure, so that it would have been difficult to detect his age. After the spontaneous Oronte had been with me a month, and after I had given him to understand several times over that his native exuberance would presently constitute an insurmountable barrier to our further intercourse, I waked to a sense of his heroic capacity. He was only five feet seven, but the remaining inches were latent. I tried him almost secretly at first, for I was really rather afraid of the judgment my other models would pass on such a choice. If they regarded Miss Churm as little better than a snare what would they think of the representation by a person so little the real thing as an Italian street-vendor of a protagonist formed by a public school?

If I went a little in fear of them it wasn't because they bullied me, because they had got an oppressive foothold, but because in their really pathetic decorum and mysteriously permanent newness they counted on me so intensely. I was therefore very glad when Jack Hawley came home: he was always of such good counsel. He painted badly himself, but there was no one like him for putting his finger on the place. He had been absent from England for a year; he had been somewhere—I don't remember where—to get a fresh eye. I was in a good deal of dread of any such organ, but we were old friends; he had been away for months and a sense of emptiness was creeping into my life. I hadn't dodged a missile for a year.

He came back with a fresh eye, but with the same old black velvet blouse, and the first evening he spent in my studio we smoked ciga-

3. Country-house-type outdoor clothing.

rettes till the small hours. He had done no work himself, he had only got the eye; so the field was clear for the production of my little things. He wanted to see what I had produced for the *Cheapside*, but he was disappointed in the exhibition. That at least seemed the meaning of two or three comprehensive groans which, as he lounged on my big divan, his leg folded under him, looking at my latest drawings, issued from his lips with the smoke of the cigarette.

"What's the matter with you?" I asked.

"What's the matter with *you?*"

"Nothing save that I'm mystified."

"You are indeed. You're quite off the hinge. What's the meaning of this new fad?" And he tossed me, with visible irreverence, a drawing in which I happened to have depicted both my elegant models. I asked if he didn't think it good, and he replied that it struck him as execrable, given the sort of thing I had always represented myself to him as wishing to arrive at; but I let that pass—I was so anxious to see exactly what he meant. The two figures in the picture looked colossal, but I supposed this was *not* what he meant, inasmuch as, for aught he knew to the contrary, I might have been trying for some such effect. I maintained that I was working exactly in the same way as when he last had done me the honor to tell me I might do something some day. "Well, there's a screw loose somewhere," he answered, "wait a bit and I'll discover it." I depended upon him to do so: where else was the fresh eye? But he produced at last nothing more luminous than "I don't know—I don't like your types." This was lame for a critic who had never consented to discuss with me anything but the question of execution, the direction of strokes and the mystery of values.

"In the drawings you've been looking at I think my types are very handsome."

"Oh they won't do!"

"I've been working with new models."

"I see you have. *They* won't do."

"Are you very sure of that?"

"Absolutely—they're stupid."

"You mean *I* am—for I ought to get round that."

"You *can't*—with such people. Who are they?"

I told him, so far as was necessary, and he concluded heartlessly: "Ce sort des gens qu'il faut mettre à la porte."[4]

"You've never seen them; they're awfully good"—I flew to their defense.

"Not seen them? Why all this recent work of yours drops to pieces with them. It's all I want to see of them."

"No one else has said anything against it—the *Cheapside* people are pleased."

"Every one else is an ass, and the *Cheapside* people the biggest asses of all. Come, don't pretend at this time of day to have pretty illusions about the public, especially about publishers and editors. It's not for *such* animals you work—it's for those who know, *coloro che sanno*;[5]

4. That kind of person should be shown the door.

5. Dante, *The Divine Comedy*, "The Inferno," 4:131: actually, *color che sanno* —"those who know."

so keep straight for *me* if you can't keep straight for yourself. There was a certain sort of thing you used to try for—and a very good thing it was. But this twaddle isn't *in* it." When I talked with Hawley later about "Rutland Ramsay" and its possible successors he declared that I must get back into my boat again or I should go to the bottom. His voice in short was the voice of warning.

I noted the warning, but I didn't turn my friends out of doors. They bored me a good deal; but the very fact that they bored me admonished me not to sacrifice them—if there was anything to be done with them—simply to irritation. As I look back at this phase they seem to me to have pervaded my life not a little. I have a vision of them as most of the time in my studio, seated against the wall on an old velvet bench to be out of the way, and resembling the while a pair of patient courtiers in a royal ante-chamber. I'm convinced that during the coldest weeks of the winter they held their ground because it saved them fire. Their newness was losing its gloss, and it was impossible not to feel them objects of charity. Whenever Miss Churm arrived they went away, and after I was fairly launched in "Rutland Ramsay" Miss Churm arrived pretty often. They managed to express to me tacitly that they supposed I wanted her for the low life of the book, and I let them suppose it, since they had attempted to study the work—it was lying about the studio—without discovering that it dealt only with the highest circles. They had dipped into the most brilliant of our novelists without deciphering many passages. I still took an hour from them, now and again, in spite of Jack Hawley's warning: it would be time enough to dismiss them, if dismissal should be necessary, when the rigor of the season was over. Hawley had made their acquaintance— he had met them at my fireside—and thought them a ridiculous pair. Learning that he was a painter they tried to approach him, to show him too that they were the real thing; but he looked at them, across the big room, as if they were miles away: they were a compendium of everything he most objected to in the social system of his country. Such people as that, all convention and patent-leather, with ejaculations that stopped conversation, had no business in a studio. A studio was a place to learn to see, and how could you see through a pair of feather-beds?

The main inconvenience I suffered at their hands was that at first I was shy of letting it break upon them that my artful little servant had begun to sit to me for "Rutland Ramsay." They knew I had been odd enough—they were prepared by this time to allow oddity to artists—to pick a foreign vagabond out of the streets when I might have had a person with whiskers and credentials; but it was some time before they learned how high I rated his accomplishments. They found him in an attitude more than once, but they never doubted I was doing him as an organ-grinder. There were several things they never guessed, and one of them was that for a striking scene in the novel, in which a footman briefly figured, it occurred to me to make use of Major Monarch as the menial. I kept putting this off, I didn't like to ask him to don the livery—besides the difficulty of finding a livery to fit him. At last, one day late in the winter, when I was at work on the despised Oronte, who caught one's idea on the wing, and was in the glow of feeling myself go very straight, they came in, the Major and his wife, with their society laugh about nothing (there was less and less to laugh at); came in like country-callers—they always reminded me of that— who have walked across the park after church and are presently persuaded to stay to luncehon. Luncheon was over, but they could stay to tea—I knew they wanted it. The fit was on me, however, and I couldn't let my ardor cool and my work wait, with the fading daylight, while my model prepared it. So I asked Mrs. Monarch if she would mind laying it out—a request which for an instant brought all the blood to her face. Her eyes were on her husband's for a second, and some mute telegraphy passed between them. Their folly was over the next instant; his cheerful shrewdness put an end to it. So far from pitying their wounded pride, I must add, I was moved to give it as complete a lesson as I could. They bustled about together and got out the cups and saucers and made the kettle boil. I know they felt as if they were waiting on my servant, and when the tea was prepared I said: "He'll have a cup, please—he's tired." Mrs. Monarch brought him one where he stood, and he took it from her as if he had been a gentleman at a party squeezing a crush-hat with an elbow.

Then it came over me that she had made a great effort for me— made it with a kind of nobleness—and that I owed her a compensation. Each time I saw her after this I wondered what the compensation could be. I couldn't go on doing the wrong thing to oblige them. Oh it *was* the wrong thing, the stamp of the work for which they sat— Hawley was not the only person to say it now. I sent in a large number of the drawings I had made for "Rutland Ramsay," and I received a warning that was more to the point than Hawley's. The artistic adviser of the house for which I was working was of opinion that many of my illustrations were not what had been looked for. Most of these illustrations were the subjects in which the Monarchs had figured. Without going into the question of what *had* been looked for, I had to face the fact that at this rate I shouldn't get the other books to do. I hurled myself in despair on Miss Churm—I put her through all her paces. I not only adopted Oronte publicly as my hero, but one morning when the Major looked in to see if I didn't require him to finish a *Cheapside* figure for which he had begun to sit the week before, I told him I had changed my mind—I'd do the drawing from my man. At this my visitor turned pale and stood looking at me. "Is *he* your idea of an English gentleman?" he asked.

I was disappointed, I was nervous, I wanted to get on with my work; so I replied with irritation: "Oh my dear Major—I can't be ruined for *you!*"

It was a horrid speech, but he stood another moment—after which, without a word, he quitted the studio. I drew a long breath, for I said to myself that I shouldn't see him again. I hadn't told him definitely that I was in danger of having my work rejected, but I was vexed at his not having felt the catastrophe in the air, read with me the moral of our fruitless collaboration, the lesson that in the deceptive atmosphere of art even the highest respectability may fail of being plastic.

I didn't owe my friends money, but I did see them again. They reappeared together three days later, and, given all the other facts, there was something tragic in that one. It was a clear proof they could find nothing else in life to do. They had threshed the matter out in a dismal conference—they had digested the bad news that they were not in for the series. If they weren't useful to me even for the *Cheapside* their function seemed difficult to determine, and I could only judge at first that they had come, forgivingly, decorously, to take a last leave. This made me rejoice in secret that I had little leisure for a scene; for I had placed both my other models in position together and I was pegging at a drawing from which I hoped to derive glory. It had been suggested by the passage in which Rutland Ramsay, drawing up a chair to Artemisia's piano-stool, says extraordinary things to her while she ostensibly fingers out a difficult piece of music. I had done Miss Churm at the piano before—it was an attitude in which she knew how to take on an absolutely poetic grace. I wished the two figures to "compose" together with intensity, and my little Italian had entered perfectly into my conception. The pair were vividly before me, the piano had been pulled out; it was a charming show of blended youth and murmured love, which I had only to catch and keep. My visitors stood and looked at it, and I was friendly to them over my shoulder.

They made no response, but I was used to silent company and went on with my work, only a little disconcerted—even though exhilarated by the sense that *this* was at least the ideal thing—at not having got rid of them after all. Presently I heard Mrs. Monarch's sweet voice beside or rather above me: "I wish her hair were a little better done." I looked up and she was staring with a strange fixedness at Miss Churm, whose back was turned to her. "Do you mind my just touching it?" she went on—a question which made me spring up for an instant as with the instinctive fear that she might do the young lady a harm. But she quieted me with a glance I shall never forget—I confess I should like to have been able to paint *that*—and went for a moment to my model. She spoke to her softly, laying a hand on her shoulder and bending over her; and as the girl, understanding, gratefully assented, she disposed her rough curls, with a few quick passes, in such a way as to make Miss Churm's head twice as charming. It was one of the most heroic personal services I've ever seen rendered. Then Mrs. Monarch turned away with a low sigh and, looking about her as if for something to do, stooped to the floor with a noble humility and picked up a dirty rag that had dropped out of my paint-box.

The Major meanwhile had also been looking for something to do, and, wandering to the other end of the studio, saw before him my breakfast-things neglected, unremoved. "I say, can't I be useful *here*?" he called out to me with an irrepressible quaver. I assented with a laugh that I fear was awkward, and for the next ten minutes, while I worked, I heard the light clatter of china and the tinkle of spoons and glass. Mrs. Monarch assisted her husband—they washed up my crockery, they put it away. They wandered off into my little scullery, and I afterwards found that they had cleaned my knives and that my slender stock of plate had an unprecedented surface. When it came over me, the latent eloquence of what they were doing, I confess that my drawing was blurred for a moment—the picture swam. They had accepted their failure, but they couldn't accept their fate. They had bowed their heads in bewilderment to the perverse and cruel law in virtue of which the real thing could be so much less precious than the unreal; but they didn't want to starve. If my servants were my models, then my models might be my servants. They would reverse the parts— the others would sit for the ladies and gentlemen and *they* would do the work. They would still be in the studio—it was an intense dumb appeal to me not to turn them out. "Take us on," they wanted to say—"we'll do *anything*."

My pencil dropped from my hand; my sitting was spoiled and I got rid of my sitters, who were also evidently rather mystified and awe- struck. Then, alone with the Major and his wife I had a most uncom- fortable moment. He put their prayer into a single sentence: "I say, you know—just let *us* do for you, can't you?" I couldn't—it was dreadful to see them emptying my slops; but I pretended I could, to oblige them, for about a week. Then I gave them a sum of money to go away, and I never saw them again. I obtained the remaining books, but my friend Hawley repeats that Major and Mrs. Monarch did me a permanent harm, got me into false ways. If it be true I'm content to have paid the price—for the memory.

1893

DORIS LESSING

Our Friend Judith

I stopped inviting Judith to meet people when a Canadian woman remarked, with the satisfied fervor of one who has at last pinned a label on a rare specimen: "She is, of course, one of your typical English spinsters."

This was a few weeks after an American sociologist, having elicited from Judith the facts that she was fortyish, unmarried, and living alone, had inquired of me: "I suppose she has given up?" "Given up what?" I asked; and the subsequent discussion was unrewarding.

Judith did not easily come to parties. She would come after pres- sure, not so much—one felt—to do one a favor, but in order to correct what she believed to be a defect in her character. "I really ought to enjoy meeting new people more than I do," she said once. We re- verted to an earlier pattern of our friendship: odd evenings together, an occasional visit to the cinema, or she would telephone to say: "I'm on my way past you to the British Museum. Would you care for a cup of coffee with me? I have twenty minutes to spare."

It is characteristic of Judith that the word "spinster," used of her, provoked fascinated speculation about other people. There are my aunts, for instance: aged seventy-odd, both unmarried, one an ex- missionary from China, one a retired matron of a famous London hos- pital. These two old ladies live together under the shadow of the cathedral in a country town. They devote much time to the Church, to good causes, to letter writing with friends all over the world, to the grandchildren and the great-grandchildren of relatives. It would be a mistake, however, on entering a house in which nothing has been moved for fifty years, to diagnose a condition of fossilized late-Victorian integrity. They read every book reviewed in the *Observer* or the *Times*,[1] so that I recently got a letter from Aunt Rose inquiring whether I did not think that the author of *On the Road*[2] was not—perhaps?—exaggerating his difficulties. They know a good deal about music, and write letters of encouragement to young composers they feel are being neglected—"You must understand that anything new and original takes time to be understood." Well-informed and critical Tories, they are as likely to dispatch telegrams of protest to the Home Secretary[3] as letters of support. These ladies, my aunts Emily and Rose, are surely what is meant by the phrase "English spinster." And yet, once the connection has been pointed out, there is no doubt that Judith and they are spiritual cousins, if not sisters. Therefore it follows that one's pitying admiration for women who have supported manless and uncomforted lives needs a certain modification?

One will, of course, never know; and I feel now that it is entirely my fault that I shall never know. I had been Judith's friend for upwards of five years before the incident occurred which I involuntarily thought of—stupidly enough—as the first time Judith's mask slipped.

A mutual friend, Betty, had been given a cast-off Dior[4] dress. She was too short for it. Also she said: "It's not a dress for a married woman with three children and a talent for cooking. I don't know why not, but it isn't." Judith was the right build. Therefore one evening the three of us met by appointment in Judith's bedroom, with the dress. Neither Betty nor I was surprised at the renewed discovery that Judith was beautiful. We had both often caught each other, and ourselves, in moments of envy when Judith's calm and severe face, her undemonstratively perfect body, succeeded in making everyone else in a room or a street look cheap.

Judith is tall, small-breasted, slender. Her light brown hair is parted in the center and cut straight around her neck. A high straight forehead, straight nose, a full grave mouth are setting for her eyes, which are green, large and prominent. Her lids are very white, fringed with gold, and molded close over the eyeball, so that in profile she has the look of a staring gilded mask. The dress was of dark green glistening stuff, cut straight, with a sort of loose tunic. It opened simply at the throat. In it Judith could of course evoke nothing but classical images. Diana, perhaps, back from the hunt, in a relaxed moment? A rather intellectual wood nymph who had opted for an afternoon in the British Museum Reading Room? Something like that. Neither Betty nor I said a word, since Judith was examining herself in a long mirror, and must know she looked magnificent.

1. Prestigious London newspapers representing roughly the younger more liberal establishment and the Establishment proper.

2. Jack Kerouac (1922–69), leader of the beatniks, 1950s forerunners of the hippies. Kerouac heroes felt themselves completely cut off from and victimized by American society.

3. Head of the British government department responsible for domestic matters.

4. Famous French designer of high fashions.

Slowly she drew off the dress and laid it aside. Slowly she put on the old cord skirt and woolen blouse she had taken off. She must have surprised a resigned glance between us, for she then remarked, with the smallest of mocking smiles: "One surely ought to stay in character, wouldn't you say?" She added, reading the words out of some invisible book, written not by her, since it was a very vulgar book, but perhaps by one of us: "It does everything *for* me, I must admit."

"After seeing you in it," Betty cried out, defying her, "I can't bear for anyone else to have it. I shall simply put it away." Judith shrugged, rather irritated. In the shapeless skirt and blouse, and without makeup, she stood smiling at us, a woman at whom forty-nine out of fifty people would not look twice.

A second revelatory incident occurred soon after. Betty telephoned me to say that Judith had a kitten. Did I know that Judith adored cats? "No, but of course she would," I said.

Betty lived in the same street as Judith and saw more of her than I did. I was kept posted about the growth and habits of the cat and its effect on Judith's life. She remarked for instance that she felt it was good for her to have a tie and some responsibility. But no sooner was the cat out of kittenhood than all the neighbors complained. It was a tomcat, ungelded, and making every night hideous. Finally the landlord said that either the cat or Judith must go, unless she was prepared to have the cat "fixed."[5] Judith wore herself out trying to find some person, anywhere in Britain, who would be prepared to take the cat. This person would, however, have to sign a written statement not to have the cat "fixed." When Judith took the cat to the vet to be killed, Betty told me she cried for twenty-four hours.

"She didn't think of compromising? After all, perhaps the cat might have preferred to live, if given the choice?"

"Is it likely I'd have the nerve to say anything so sloppy to Judith? It's the nature of a male cat to rampage lustfully about, and therefore it would be morally wrong for Judith to have the cat fixed, simply to suit her own convenience."

"She said that?"

"She wouldn't have to *say* it, surely?"

A third incident was when she allowed a visiting young American, living in Paris, the friend of a friend and scarcely known to her, to use her flat while she visited her parents over Christmas. The young man and his friends lived it up for ten days of alcohol and sex and marijuana, and when Judith came back it took a week to get the place clean again and the furniture mended. She telephoned twice to Paris, the first time to say that he was a disgusting young thug and if he knew what was good for him he would keep out of her way in the future; the second time to apologize for losing her temper. "I had a choice either to let someone use my flat, or to leave it empty. But having chosen that you should have it, it was clearly an unwarrantable infringement of your liberty to make any conditions at all.

5. Gelded, castrated.

I do most sincerely ask your pardon." The moral aspects of the matter having been made clear, she was irritated rather than not to receive letters of apology from him—fulsome, embarrassed, but above all, baffled.

It was the note of curiosity in the letters—he even suggested coming over to get to know her better—that irritated her most. "What do you suppose he means?" she said to me. "He lived in my flat for ten days. One would have thought that should be enough, wouldn't you?"

The facts about Judith, then, are all in the open, unconcealed, and plain to anyone who cares to study them; or, as it became plain she feels, to anyone with the intelligence to interpret them.

She has lived for the last twenty years in a small two-room flat high over a busy West London street. The flat is shabby and badly heated. The furniture is old, was never anything but ugly, is now frankly rickety and fraying. She has an income of two hundred pounds[6] a year from a dead uncle. She lives on this and what she earns from her poetry, and from lecturing on poetry to night classes and extramural university classes.

She does not smoke or drink, and eats very little, from preference, not self-discipline.

She studied poetry and biology at Oxford, with distinction.

She is a Castlewell. That is, she is a member of one of the academic upper-middle-class families, which have been producing for centuries a steady supply of brilliant but sound men and women who are the backbone of the arts and sciences in Britain. She is on cool good terms with her family, who respect her and leave her alone.

She goes on long walking tours, by herself, in such places as Exmoor[7] or West Scotland.

Every three or four years she publishes a volume of poems.

The walls of her flat are completely lined with books. They are scientific, classical and historical; there is a great deal of poetry and some drama. There is not one novel. When Judith says: "Of course I don't read novels," this does not mean that novels have no place, or a small place, in literature; or that people should not read novels; but that it must be obvious she can't be expected to read novels.

I had been visiting her flat for years before I noticed two long shelves of books, under a window, each shelf filled with the works of a single writer. The two writers are not, to put it at the mildest, the kind one would associate with Judith. They are mild, reminiscent, vague and whimsical. Typical English *belles-lettres*, in fact, and by definition abhorrent to her. Not one of the books in the two shelves has been read; some of the pages are still uncut. Yet each book is inscribed or dedicated to her: gratefully, admiringly, sentimentally and, more than once, amorously. In short, it is open to anyone who cares to examine these two shelves, and to work out dates, to conclude that Judith from the age of fifteen to twenty-five had been the

6. About $500–$550 at the time of the story, but probably close to one-third or even one-half of a subsistence income.

7. Swampy or heathery wastelands in western Britain, from southwestern coast to north of England.

beloved young companion of one elderly literary gentleman, and from twenty-five to thirty-five the inspiration of another.

During all that time she had produced her own poetry, and the sort of poetry, it is quite safe to deduce, not at all likely to be admired by her two admirers. Her poems are always cool and intellectual; that is their form, which is contradicted or supported by a gravely sensuous texture. They are poems to read often; one has to, to understand them.

I did not ask Judith a direct question about these two eminent but rather fusty lovers. Not because she would not have answered, or because she would have found the question impertinent, but because such questions are clearly unnecessary. Having those two shelves of books where they are, and books she could not conceivably care for, for their own sake, is publicly giving credit where credit is due. I can imagine her thinking the thing over, and deciding it was only fair, or perhaps honest, to place the books there; and this despite the fact that she would not care at all for the same attention to be paid to her. There is something almost contemptuous in it. For she certainly despises people who feel they need attention.

For instance, more than once a new emerging wave of "modern" young poets have discovered her as the only "modern" poet among their despised and well-credited elders. This is because, since she began writing at fifteen, her poems have been full of scientific, mechanical and chemical imagery. This is how she thinks, or feels.

More than once has a young poet hastened to her flat, to claim her as an ally, only to find her totally and by instinct unmoved by words like "modern," "new," "contemporary." He has been outraged and wounded by her principle, so deeply rooted as to be unconscious, and to need no expression but a contemptuous shrug of the shoulders, that publicly seeking or to want critical attention is despicable. It goes without saying that there is perhaps one critic in the world she has any time for. He has sulked off, leaving her on her shelf, which she takes it for granted is her proper place, to be read by an appreciative minority.

Meanwhile she gives her lectures, walks alone through London, writes her poems, and is seen sometimes at a concert or a play with a middle-aged professor of Greek, who has a wife and two children.

Betty and I had speculated about this professor, with such remarks as: Surely she must sometimes be lonely? Hasn't she ever wanted to marry? What about that awful moment when one comes in from somewhere at night to an empty flat?

It happened recently that Betty's husband was on a business trip, her children visiting, and she was unable to stand the empty house. She asked Judith for a refuge until her own home filled again.

Afterwards Betty rang me up to report: "Four of the five nights Professor Adams came in about ten or so."

"Was Judith embarrassed?"

"Would you expect her to be?"

"Well, if not embarrassed, at least conscious there was a situation?"

"No, not at all. But I must say I don't think he's good enough for her. He can't possibly understand her. He calls her Judy."

"Good God."

"Yes. But I was wondering. Suppose the other two called her Judy '—little Judy'—imagine it! Isn't it awful? But it does rather throw a light on Judith?"

"It's rather touching."

"I suppose it's touching. But *I* was embarrassed—oh, not because of the situation. Because of how she was, with him. 'Judy, is there another cup of tea in that pot?' And she, rather daughterly and demure, pouring him one."

"Three of the nights he went to her bedroom with her—very casual about it, because she was being. But he was not there in the mornings. So I asked her. You know how it is when you ask her a question. As if you've been having long conversations on that very subject for years and years, and she is merely continuing where you left off last. So when she says something surprising, one feels such a fool to be surprised?"

"Yes. And then?"

"I asked her if she was sorry not to have children. She said yes, but one couldn't have everything."

"One can't have everything, she said?"

"Quite clearly feeling she *has* nearly everything. She said she thought it was a pity, because she would have brought up children very well."

"When you come to think of it, she would, too."

"I asked about marriage, but she said on the whole the role of a mistress suited her better."

"She used the word 'mistress'?"

"You must admit it's the accurate word."

"I suppose so."

"And then she said that while she liked intimacy and sex and everything, she enjoyed waking up in the morning alone and *her own person.*"

"Yes, *of course.*"

"Of course. but now she's bothered because the professor would like to marry her. Or he feels he ought. At least, he's getting all guilty and obsessive about it. She says she doesn't see the point of divorce, and anyway, surely it would be very hard on his poor old wife after all these years, particularly after bringing up two children so satisfactorily. She talks about his wife as if she's a kind of nice old charwoman, and it wouldn't be *fair* to sack her, you know. Anyway. What with one thing and another. Judith's going off to Italy soon in order *to collect herself.*"

"But how's she going to pay for it?"

"Luckily the Third Program's[8] commissioning her to do some arty programs. They offered her a choice of The Cid—El Thid,[9] you know

---

8. British Broadcasting Corporation public radio service (and now also television channel) specializing in classical music, literature and plays, lectures, etc.

9. Castilian, standard Spanish, pronunciation of El Cid, the title of an eleventh-century soldier-hero and hero of many works of literature.

—and the Borgias. Well, the Borghese, then. And Judith settled for the Borgias."

"The Borgias," I said, "*Judith?*"

"Yes, quite. I said that too, in that tone of voice. She saw my point. She says the epic is right up her street, whereas the Renaissance has never been on her wave length. Obviously it couldn't be, all the magnificence and cruelty and *dirt*. But of course chivalry and a high moral code and all those idiotically noble goings-on are right on her wave length."

"Is the money the same?"

"Yes. But is it likely Judith would let money decide? No, she said that one should always choose something new, that isn't up one's street. Well, because it's better for her character, and so on, to get herself unsettled by the Renaissance. She didn't say *that*, of course."

"Of course not."

Judith went to Florence; and for some months postcards informed us tersely of her doings. Then Betty decided she must go by herself for a holiday. She had been appalled by the discovery that if her husband was away for a night she couldn't sleep; and when he went to Australia for three weeks, she stopped living until he came back. She had discussed this with him, and he had agreed that if she really felt the situation to be serious, he would dispatch her by air, to Italy, in order to recover her self-respect. As she put it.

I got this letter from her: "It's no use, I'm coming home. I might have known. Better face it, once you're really married you're not fit for man nor beast. And if you remember what I used to be like! *Well!* I moped around Milan. I sunbathed in Venice, then I thought my tan was surely worth something, so I was on the point of starting an affair with another lonely soul, but I lost heart, and went to Florence to see Judith. She wasn't there. She'd gone to the Italian Riviera. I had nothing better to do, so I followed her. When I saw the place I wanted to laugh, it's so much not Judith, you know, all those palms and umbrellas and gaiety at all costs and ever such an ornamental blue sea. Judith is in an enormous stone room up on the hillside above the sea, with grape vines all over the place. You should see her, she's got beautiful. It seems for the last fifteen years she's been going to Soho[1] every Saturday morning to buy food at an Italian shop. I must have looked surprised, because she explained she liked Soho. I suppose because all that dreary vice and nudes and prostitutes and everything prove how right she is to be as she is? She told the people in the shop she was going to Italy, and the *signora*[2] said, what a coincidence, she was going back to Italy too, and she did hope an old friend like Miss Castlewell would visit her there. Judith said to me: 'I felt lacking, when she used the word friend. Our relations have always been formal. Can you understand it?' she said to me. 'For fifteen years,' I said to her. She said: 'I think I must feel it's a kind of imposition, don't you know, expecting people to feel friendship for

1. A section of London roughly equivalent to Greenwich Village in New York—foreign restaurants and groceries, haunt of writers, painters, etc.—but in recent years increasingly known for prostitutes and pornography.
2. Proprietress.

one.' *Well.* I said: 'You ought to understand it, because you're like that yourself.' 'Am I?' she said. 'Well, think about it,' I said. But I could see she didn't want to think about it. Anyway, she's here, and I've spent a week with her. The widow Maria Rineiri inherited her mother's house, so she came home, from Soho. On the ground floor is a tatty little *rosticceria*[3] patronized by the neighbors. They are all working people. This isn't tourist country, up on the hill. The widow lives above the shop with her little boy, a nasty little brat of about ten. Say what you like, the English are the only people who know how to bring up children, I don't care if that's insular. Judith's room is at the back, with a balcony. Underneath her room is the barber's shop, and the barber is Luigi Rineiri, the widow's younger brother. Yes, I was keeping him until the last. He is about forty, tall dark handsome, a great *bull*, but rather a sweet fatherly bull. He has cut Judith's hair and made it lighter. Now it looks like a sort of gold helmet. Judith is all brown. The widow Rineiri has made her a white dress and a green dress. They fit, for a change. When Judith walks down the street to the lower town, all the Italian males take one look at the golden girl and melt in their own oil like ice cream. Judith takes all this in her stride. She sort of acknowledges the homage. Then she strolls into the sea and vanishes into the foam. She swims five miles every day. *Naturally.* I haven't asked Judith whether she has collected herself, because you can see she hasn't. The widow Rineiri is matchmaking. When I noticed this I wanted to laugh, but luckily I didn't because Judith asked me, really wanting to know: 'Can you see me married to an Italian barber?' (Not being snobbish, but stating the position, so to speak.) 'Well yes,' I said, 'you're the only woman I know who I can see married to an Italian barber.' Because it wouldn't matter who she married, she'd always be her *own person.* 'At any rate, for a time,' I said. At which she said, asperously:[4] 'You can use phrases like *for a time* in England but not in Italy.' Did you ever see England, at least London, as the home of license, liberty and free love? No, neither did I, but of course she's right. Married to Luigi it would be the family, the neighbors, the church and the *bambini.*[5] All the same she's thinking about it, believe it or not. Here she's quite different, all relaxed and free. She's melting in the attention she gets. The widow mothers her and makes her coffee all the time, and listens to a lot of good advice about how to bring up that nasty brat of hers. Unluckily she doesn't take it. Luigi is crazy for her. At mealtimes she goes to the *trattoria*[6] in the upper square and all the workmen treat her like a goddess. Well, a film star then. I said to her, you're mad to come home. For one thing her rent is ten bob[7] a week, and you eat *pasta* and drink red wine till you bust for about one and sixpence. No, she said, it would be nothing but self-indulgence to stay. Why? I said. She said, she's got nothing to stay for. (Ho ho.) And besides, she's done her research on the Borghese, though so far she can't see her way to an honest presentation of the facts. What made these people

3. Grill.
4. Sharply, harshly.
5. Children.
6. Restaurant.
7. Shillings. There are twenty shillings to the pound; *one and sixpence* below is one and a half shillings. Living in Italy at the time was very inexpensive by British standards.

tick? she wants to know. And so she's only staying because of the cat. I forgot to mention the cat. This is a town of cats. The Italians here love their cats. I wanted to feed a stray cat at the table, but the waiter said no; and after lunch, all the waiters came with trays crammed with leftover food and stray cats came from everywhere to eat. And at dark when the tourists go in to feed and the beach is empty—you know how empty and forlorn a beach is at dusk?—well cats appear from everywhere. The beach seems to move, then you see it's cats. They go stalking along the thin inch of gray water at the edge of the sea, shaking their paws crossly at each step, snatching at the dead little fish, and throwing them with their mouths up onto the dry sand. Then they scamper after them. You've never seen such a snarling and fighting. At dawn when the fishing boats come in to the empty beach, the cats are there in dozens. The fishermen throw them bits of fish. The cats snarl and fight over it. Judith gets up early and goes down to watch. Sometimes Luigi goes too, being tolerant. Because what he really likes is to join the evening promenade with Judith on his arm around and around the square of the upper town. Showing her off. Can you *see* Judith? But she does it. Being tolerant. But she smiles and enjoys the attention she gets, there's no doubt of it.

"She has a cat in her room. It's a kitten really, but it's pregnant. Judith says she can't leave until the kittens are born. The cat is too young to have kittens. Imagine Judith. She sits on her bed in that great stone room, with her bare feet on the stone floor, and watches the cat, and tries to work out why a healthy uninhibited Italian cat always fed on the best from the *rosticceria* should be neurotic. Because it is. When it sees Judith watching it gets nervous and starts licking at the roots of its tail. But Judith goes on watching, and says about Italy that the reason why the English love the Italians is because the Italians make the English feel superior. They have no discipline. And that's a despicable reason for one nation to love another. Then she talks about Luigi and says he has no sense of guilt, but a sense of sin; whereas she has no sense of sin but she has guilt. I haven't asked her if this has been an insuperable barrier, because judging from how she looks, it hasn't. She says she would rather have a sense of sin, because sin can be attoned for, and if she understood sin, perhaps she would be more at home with the Renaissance. Luigi is very healthy, she says, and not neurotic. He is a Catholic of course. He doesn't mind that she's an atheist. His mother has explained to him that the English are all pagans, but good people at heart. I suppose he thinks a few smart sessions with the local priest would set Judith on the right path for good and all. Meanwhile the cat walks nervously around the room, stopping to lick, and when it can't stand Judith watching it another second, it rolls over on the floor, with its paws tucked up, and rolls up its eyes, and Judith scratches its lumpy pregnant stomach and tells it to relax. It makes *me* nervous to see her, it's not like her. I don't know why. Then Luigi shouts up from the barber's shop, then he comes up and stands at the door laughing, and Judith laughs, and the widow says: Children, enjoy yourselves. And off they go, walking down to the town eating ice cream. The cat follows them. It won't let Judith out of its sight, like a dog. When she swims miles out to sea, the cat hides under a beach hut until she comes back. Then she carries it back up the hill, because that nasty little boy chases it. *Well.* I'm coming home tomorrow thank God, to my dear old Billy, I was mad ever to leave him. There is something about Judith and Italy that has upset me, I don't know what. The point is, what on earth can Judith and Luigi *talk* about? Nothing. How can they? And of course it doesn't matter. So I turn out to be a prude as well. See you next week."

It was my turn for a dose of the sun, so I didn't see Betty. On my way back from Rome I stopped off in Judith's resort and walked up through narrow streets to the upper town, where, in the square with the vine-covered *trattoria* at the corner, was a house with ROSTICCERIA written in black paint on a cracked wooden board over a low door. There was a door curtain of red beads, and flies settled on the beads. I opened the beads with my hands and looked into a small dark room with a stone counter. Loops of salami hung from metal hooks. A glass bell covered some plates of cooked meats. There were flies on the salami and on the glass bell. A few tins on the wooden shelves, a couple of pale loaves, some wine casks and an open case of sticky pale green grapes covered with fruit flies seemed to be the only stock. A single wooden table with two chairs stood in a corner, and two workmen sat there, eating lumps of sausage and bread. Through another bead curtain at the back came a short, smoothly fat, slender-limbed woman with graying hair. I asked for Miss Castlewell, and her face changed. She said in an offended, offhand way: "Miss Castlewell left last week." She took a white cloth from under the counter, and flicked at the flies on the glass bell. "I'm a friend of hers," I said, and she said: "*Si*,"[8] and put her hands palm down on the counter and looked at me, expressionless. The workmen got up, gulped down the last of their wine, nodded and went. She *ciao*'d[9] them; and looked back at me. Then, since I didn't go, she called: "Luigi!" A shout came from the back room, there was a rattle of beads, and in came first a wiry sharp-faced boy, and then Luigi. He was tall, heavy-shouldered, and his black rough hair was like a cap, pulled low over his brows. He looked good-natured, but at the moment uneasy. His sister said something, and he stood beside her, an ally, and confirmed: "Miss Castlewell went away." I was on the point of giving up, when through the bead curtain that screened off a dazzling light eased a thin tabby cat. It was ugly and it walked uncomfortably, with its back quarters bunched up. The child suddenly let out a "Sssss" through his teeth, and the cat froze. Luigi said something sharp to the child, and something encouraging to the cat, which sat down, looked straight in front of it, then began frantically licking at its flanks. "Miss Castlewell was offended with us," said Mrs. Rineiri suddenly, and with dignity. "She left early one morning. We did not expect her to go." I said: "Perhaps she had to go home and finish some work."

---

8. "Yes." 9. Said good-bye to.

Mrs. Rineiri shrugged, then sighed. Then she exchanged a hard look with her brother. Clearly the subject had been discussed, and closed forever.

"I've known Judith a long time," I said, trying to find the right note. "She's a remarkable woman. She's a poet." But there was no response to this at all. Meanwhile the child, with a fixed bared-teeth grin, was staring at the cat, narrowing his eyes. Suddenly he let out another "Sssssss" and added a short high yelp. The cat shot backwards, hit the wall, tried desperately to claw its way up the wall, came to its senses and again sat down and began its urgent, undirected licking at its fur. This time Luigi cuffed the child, who yelped in earnest, and then ran out into the street past the cat. Now that the way was clear the cat shot across the floor, up onto the counter, and bounded past Luigi's shoulder and straight through the bead curtain into the barber's shop, where it landed with a thud.

"Judith was sorry when she left us," said Mrs. Rineiri uncertainly. "She was crying."

"I'm sure she was."

"And so," said Mrs. Rineiri, with finality, laying her hands down again, and looking past me at the bead curtain. That was the end. Luigi nodded brusquely at me, and went into the back. I said goodbye to Mrs. Rineiri and walked back to the lower town. In the square I saw the child, sitting on the running board of a lorry[1] parked outside the *trattoria,* drawing in the dust with his bare toes, and directing in front of him a blank, unhappy stare.

I had to go through Florence, so I went to the address Judith had been at. No, Miss Castlewell had not been back. Her papers and books were still here. Would I take them back with me to England? I made a great parcel and brought them back to England.

I telephoned Judith and she said she had already written for the papers to be sent, but it was kind of me to bring them. There had seemed to be no point, she said, in returning to Florence.

"Shall I bring them over?"

"I would be very grateful, of course."

Judith's flat was chilly, and she wore a bunchy sage-green woolen dress. Her hair was still a soft gold helmet, but she looked pale and rather pinched. She stood with her back to a single bar of electric fire—lit because I demanded it—with her legs apart and her arms folded. She contemplated me.

"I went to the Rineiris' house."

"Oh. Did you?"

"They seemed to miss you."

She said nothing.

"I saw the cat too."

"Oh. Oh, I suppose you and Betty discussed it?" This was with a small unfriendly smile.

"Well, Judith, you must see we were likely to?"

She gave this her consideration and said: "I don't understand why people discuss other people. Oh—I'm not criticizing you. But I

_____
1. Truck.

don't see why you are so interested. I don't understand human behavior and I'm not particularly interested."

"I think you should write to the Rineiris."

"I wrote and thanked them, of course."

"I don't mean that."

"You and Betty have worked it out?"

"Yes, we talked about it. We thought we should talk to you, so you
should write to the Rineiris."

"Why?"

"For one thing, they are both very fond of you."

"Fond," she said smiling.

"Judith, I've never in my life felt such an atmosphere of being let
down."

Judith considered this. "When something happens that shows one
there is really a complete gulf in understanding, what is there to say?"

"It could scarcely have been a complete gulf in understanding. I
suppose you are going to say we are being interfering?"

Judith showed distaste. "That is a very stupid word. And it's a
stupid idea. No one can interfere with me if I don't let them. No, it's
that I don't understand people. I don't understand why you or Betty
should care. Or why the Rineiris should, for that matter," she added
with the small tight smile.

"Judith!"

"If you've behaved stupidly, there's no point in going on. You put
an end to it."

"What happened? Was it the cat?"

"Yes, I suppose so. But it's not important." She looked at me, saw
my ironical face, and said: "The cat was too young to have kittens.
That is all there was to it."

"Have it your way. But that is obviously not all there is to it."

"What upsets me is that I don't understand at all why I was so
upset then."

"What happened? Or don't you want to talk about it?"

"I don't give a damn whether I talk about it or not. You really do
say the most extraordinary things, you and Betty. If you want to
know, I'll tell you. What does it matter?"

"I would like to know, of course."

"*Of course!*" she said. "In your place I wouldn't care. Well, I think
the essence of the thing was that I must have had the wrong attitude
to that cat. Cats are supposed to be independent. They are supposed
to go off by themselves to have their kittens. This one didn't. It was
climbing up on to my bed all one night and crying for attention. I
don't like cats on my bed. In the morning I saw she was in pain. I
stayed with her all that day. Then Luigi—he's the brother, you know."

"Yes."

"Did Betty mention him? Luigi came up to say it was time I went
for a swim. He said the cat should look after itself. I blame myself
very much. That's what happens when you submerge yourself in
somebody else."

Her look at me was now defiant; and her body showed both
defensiveness and aggression. "Yes. It's true. I've always been afraid

of it. And in the last few weeks I've behaved badly. It's because I let it happen."

"Well, go on."

"I left the cat and swam. It was late, so it was only for a few minutes. When I came out of the sea the cat had followed me and had had a kitten on the beach. That little beast Michele—the son, you know?—well, he always teased the poor thing, and now he had frightened her off the kitten. It was dead, though. He held it up by the tail and waved it at me as I came out of the sea. I told him to bury it. He scooped two inches of sand away and pushed the kitten in— on the beach, where people are all day. So I buried it properly. He had run off. He was chasing the poor cat. She was terrified and running up the town. I ran too. I caught Michele and I was so angry I hit him. I don't believe in hitting children. I've been feeling beastly about it ever since."

"You were angry."

"It's no excuse. I would never have believed myself capable of hitting a child. I hit him very hard. He went off, crying. The poor cat had got under a big lorry parked in the square. Then she screamed. And then a most remarkable thing happened. She screamed just once, and all at once cats just materialized. One minute there was just one cat, lying under a lorry, and the next, dozens of cats. They sat in a big circle around the lorry, all quite still, and watched my poor cat."

"Rather moving," I said.

"Why?"

"There is no evidence one way or the other," I said in inverted commas, "that the cats were there out of concern for a friend in trouble."

"No," she said energetically. "There isn't. It might have been curiosity. Or anything. How do we know? However, I crawled under the lorry. There were two paws sticking out of the cat's back end. The kitten was the wrong way round. It was stuck. I held the cat down with one hand and I pulled the kitten out with the other." She held out her long white hands. They were still covered with fading scars and scratches. "She bit and yelled, but the kitten was alive. She left the kitten and crawled across the square into the house. Then all the cats got up and walked away. It was the most extraordinary thing I've ever seen. They vanished again. One minute they were all there, and then they had vanished. I went after the cat, with the kitten. Poor little thing, it was covered with dust—being wet, don't you know. The cat was on my bed. There was another kitten coming, but it got stuck too. So when she screamed and screamed I just pulled it out. The kittens began to suck. One kitten was very big. It was a nice fat black kitten. It must have hurt her. But she suddenly bit out—snapped, don't you know, like a reflex action, at the back of the kitten's head. It died, just like that. Extraordinary, isn't it?" she said, blinking hard, her lips quivering. "She was its mother, but she killed it. Then she ran off the bed and went downstairs into the shop under the counter. I called to Luigi. You know, he's Mrs. Rineiri's brother."

"Yes, I know."

"He said she was too young, and she was badly frightened and very hurt. He took the alive kitten to her but she got up and walked away. She didn't want it. Then Luigi told me not to look. But I followed him. He held the kitten by the tail and he banged it against the wall twice. Then he dropped it into the rubbish heap. He moved aside some rubbish with his toe, and put the kitten there and pushed rubbish over it. Then Luigi said the cat should be destroyed. He said she was badly hurt and it would always hurt her to have kittens."

"He hasn't destroyed her. She's still alive. But it looks to me as if he were right."

"Yes, I expect he was."

"What upset you—that he killed the kitten?"

"Oh no, I expect the cat would if he hadn't. But that isn't the point, is it?"

"What is the point?"

"I don't think I really know." She had been speaking breathlessly, and fast. Now she said slowly: "It's not a question of right or wrong, is it? Why should it be? It's a question of what one is. That night Luigi wanted to go promenading with me. For him, that was *that*. Something had to be done, and he'd done it. But I felt ill. He was very nice to me. He's a very good person," she said, defiantly.

"Yes, he looks it."

"That night I couldn't sleep. I was blaming myself. I should never have left the cat to go swimming. Well, and then I decided to leave the next day. And I did. And that's all. The whole thing was a mistake from start to finish."

"Going to Italy at all?"

"Oh, to go for a holiday would have been all right."

"You've done all that work for nothing? You mean you aren't going to make use of all that research?"

"No. It was a mistake."

"Why don't you leave it a few weeks and see how things are then?"

"Why?"

"You might feel differently about it."

"What an extraordinary thing to say. Why should I? Oh, you mean, time passing, healing wounds—that sort of thing? What an extraordinary idea. It's always seemed to me an extraordinary idea. No, right from the beginning I've felt ill at ease with the whole business, not myself at all."

"Rather irrationally, I should have said."

Judith considered this, very seriously. She frowned while she thought it over. Then she said: "But if one cannot rely on what one feels, what can one rely on?"

"On what one thinks, I should have expected you to say."

"Should you? Why? Really, you people are all very strange. I don't understand you." She turned off the electric fire, and her face closed up. She smiled, friendly and distant, and said: "I don't really see any point at all in discussing it."

1963

5   SYMBOLS

One of the chief devices for bridging the gap between the writer's vision and the reader's is the **symbol,** commonly defined as something that stands for something else: a flower, for example, may be seen as a symbol of a particular state. But notice that symbols are generally **figurative;** that is, they compare or put together two unlike things. A senator may represent a state, but he represents it *literally*: the state is a governmental unit, and the senator is a member of the government. But the flower has little to do with governing the state, and so represents it only figuratively.

But why speak of anything in terms of something else? Is there no nonarbitrary reason why snakes are commonly symbolic of evil? Sure, some snakes are poisonous, but for some people so are bees, and a lot of snakes are not only harmless but actually helpful ecologically. (In Kipling's *The Jungle Book* the python Ka, while frightening, is on the side of Law and Order.) Through repeated use over the centuries, the snake has become a traditional symbol of Evil—not just danger, sneakiness, repulsiveness, but theological, absolute Evil. Had Macomber been startled by a snake during the lion hunt, we would not necessarily have said, "Aha—snake, symbol of Evil," though that potential meaning might have hovered around the incident and sent us looking backward and forward in the story for supporting evidence that this snake was indeed being used symbolically. However, when we discover that the stranger in *Young Goodman Brown* has a walking stick upon which is carved the image of a snake, we are much more likely to find it such a symbol because of other, related potential symbols or meanings in the context: the term *Goodman* in the title of the story sets up the distinct possibility that Brown (how common a name) stands for more than a "mere" individual young man. Brown's bride is named Faith—a common name among the early Puritans, but, together with Goodman, suggesting symbolic possibilities. Then, just before the stranger with the walking stick appears, Brown says, "What if the devil himself should be at my very elbow!"

A single item, even something as traditionally fraught with meaning as a snake or a rose, becomes a symbol only when its potentially symbolic meaning is confirmed by something else in the story, just as a point needs a second point to define a line. Multiple symbols, potential symbols, direct and indirect hints, such as Brown's mention of the devil: these are among the ways in which details may be identified as symbols (for interpreting symbols is relatively easy once you know what is and what is probably not a symbol).

One form of what may be called an indirect hint is repetition. That an "old maid" like Judith should have a cat seems so ordinary it borders on the trite. But when she chooses to have her male cat put to death rather than neutered, it makes us sit up and take notice, doesn't it? This choice may suggest something about the unconventional in her character, but we probably don't think of the cat in itself representing anything. What happens, though, when there appears another cat, a female this time, whose sex life calls forth strange behavior on

Judith's part? And when the killing of a kitten interrupts Judith's affair with Luigi? It is difficult to say when or if the literal cats shade off into symbols, for they remain so solidly cats in the story. All we can say for sure is that cats become more important in reading and understanding this story than, say, the cask of Amontillado does in the Poe story. The cask remains a thing pure and simple. Repetition, then, calls attention to details and may alert us to potential symbolic overtones, but it does not necessarily turn a thing into a symbol; so long as we get the suggestions of significance, however, agreeing on exactly what—or when—something can be called a symbol is not important.

Direct hints may take the form of explicit statements. (Authors are not so anxious to hide their meanings as some readers are prone to believe.) We also may be alerted to the fact that something is standing for something else when the something does not seem to make literal sense in itself. It does not take us long to realize that *Young Goodman Brown* is not entirely as realistic a story as *Bovanne* or *Macomber*. When things do not seem explicable in terms of everyday reality, we often look beyond them for some meaning, as we do in *The Lottery*. Roses are real enough, but neither Faulkner's narrator nor anyone else in the story gives Emily a real rose. What, then, does the rose in the title *A Rose for Emily* suggest?

We must remember, however, that symbols do not exist solely for the transmission of a meaning we can paraphrase; they do not disappear from the story, our memory, or our response once their "meaning" has been sucked out of them, any more than Francis Macomber ceases to exist as an individual after we recognize his representative or universal nature. Faith's pink ribbons and Judith's cats are objects in their stories, whatever meanings or suggestions of meanings they have given rise to.

As I've often implied and occasionally said, few symbols can be exhausted, translated into an abstract phrase or equivalent: the "something else" that the "something" stands for is ultimately elusive. When you get to the scene in *The Artificial Nigger* in which Nelson and his grandfather are brought back together by their puzzlement over the function of the statue of a little black jockey, a once-common and now unlamentably rare suburban lawn decoration, try to paraphrase exactly what the "artificial nigger" stands for. Or explain with certainty what Faith's pink ribbon symbolizes. It is not that the statue and the ribbon mean nothing but that they mean so many things that no one equivalence will do; even an abstract statement seems to reduce rather than fully explain the significance for the reader. Yes, the "artificial nigger" is a mystery that unites the boy and his grandfather in their ignorance, but is that the whole meaning of the story's description of the statue as "some monument to another's victory that brought them together in their common defeat"? Do any other incidents involving blacks in the story—on the train, on the city streets— relate to the statue? How does "artificial" fit in? And how about the tone? The phrase is offensive and suggests prejudice and ignorance; but the incident and ignorance are a little funny, too, and pathetic. Are this incident and this symbol representative of the tone of the story as a whole? Or disruptive of it? It seems to me the statue appropriately encapsulates the unsettling, frightening, and revealing experiences of grandfather and grandson in the city, but I'm not sure I could say everything I think the "artificial nigger" means or all the feelings it generates.

When a figure is expressed as an explicit comparison, often signaled by *like* or *as*, it is called a **simile**: "eyes as blue as the sky"; "the baby brother I'd never known looked out from the depths of his private life, like an animal waiting to be coaxed into the light" (*Sonny's Blues*). An implicit comparison or identification of one thing with another unlike itself, without a verbal signal but just seeming to say "A *is* B," is called a **metaphor**: "The sea was a sheet of glass"; "the grass was a green carpet"; "there was a boiling wave of dogs about them" (*The Old People*). Sometimes all figures are loosely referred to as metaphors. There is another figure of speech, which seems to border on the one hand on representation and on the other on symbol —the **synechdoche**, a figure in which the part stands for the whole, as when a whole creature of terror is called up by the word "Jaws."

An **allegory** is like a metaphor in that one thing (usually non-rational, abstract, religious) is implicitly spoken of in terms of something that is concrete and usually sensuous (perceptible by the senses), but the comparison in allegory is extended to include a whole work or a large portion of a work. *The Pilgrim's Progress* is probably the most famous prose allegory in English; its central character is named Christian; he was born in the City of Destruction and sets out for the Celestial City, passes through the Slough of Despond and Vanity Fair, meets men named Pliable and Obstinate, and so on.

When an entire story, like *The Lottery*, is symbolic, it is sometimes called a **myth**. *Myth* originally meant a story of communal origin that provided an explanation or religious interpretation of man, nature, the universe, and the relation between them. From the vantage point of another culture or set of beliefs, the word usually implied that the story was false: we speak of classical myths, but Christians do not speak of Christian myth. We also apply the term *myth* now to stories by individuals, sophisticated authors, but often there is still the implication that the mythic story relates to a communal or group experience, whereas a symbolic story may be more personal or private. It is hard to draw the line firmly: *The Lottery* seems to have clearly national, American implications, while *The Rocking-Horse Winner* may be a private Lawrencian symbol or a myth of modern bourgeois society. A plot or character element that recurs in cultural or cross-cultural myths, such as images of the devil, as in *Young Goodman Brown*, is now widely called an **archetype**.

A symbol can be as brief and local as a metaphor or as extended as an allegory, and like an allegory usually speaks in concrete terms of the non- or super-rational, the abstract, that which is not immediately perceived by the senses. Though some allegories can be complex, with many layers or levels of equivalence, and some symbols can be very simple, with paraphrasable equivalences, allegory usually refers to a one-to-one relationhip (as the names from *The Pilgrim's Progress* imply), and literary symbols usually have highly complex or even inexpressible equivalences. *The Lottery* may be considered a symbolic story, but precisely what it "stands for" is extremely difficult to express briefly and satisfactorily—New England Puritanism? Man's cruelty to man? Original Sin? The dulling of human sensibility by ritualistic actions? The use of a scapegoat to suffer for the sins of the community? The operation of chance rather than justice or morality in the universe? It seems to partake of all these meanings but to limit itself to none. It creates a new meaning which seems to stand for a kind of human communal activity for which there is no other satisfactory name. That is what we mean by a symbol—something that cannot be paraphrased, something that has areas of meaning or implication that cannot be wholly rendered in other terms or conveniently separated from the particulars of the work. The unparaphrasable nature of symbolic images or stories is not vagueness but richness, not disorder but complexity.

NATHANIEL HAWTHORNE

Young Goodman Brown

Young Goodman Brown came forth, at sunset, into the street of Salem village,[1] but put his head back, after crossing the threshold, to exchange a parting kiss with his young wife. And Faith, as the wife was aptly named, thrust her own pretty head into the street, letting the wind play with the pink ribbons of her cap, while she called to Goodman Brown.

"Dearest heart," whispered she, softly and rather sadly, when her lips were close to his ear, "pr'y thee, put off your journey until sunrise, and sleep in your own bed tonight. A lone woman is troubled with such dreams and such thoughts, that she's afeard of herself, sometimes. Pray, tarry with me this night, dear husband, of all nights in the year!"

"My love and my Faith," replied young Goodman Brown, "of all nights in the year, this one night must I tarry away from thee. My journey, as thou callest it, forth and back again, must needs be done 'twixt now and sunrise. What, my sweet, pretty wife, dost thou doubt me already, and we but three months married!"

"Then, God bless you!" said Faith, with the pink ribbons, "and may you find all well, when you come back."

"Amen!" cried Goodman Brown. "Say thy prayers, dear Faith, and go to bed at dusk, and no harm will come to thee."

So they parted; and the young man pursued his way, until, being about to turn the corner by the meeting-house, he looked back, and saw the head of Faith still peeping after him, with a melancholy air, in spite of her pink ribbons.

"Poor little Faith!" thought he, for his heart smote him. "What a

1. Salem, Massachusetts, Hawthorne's birthplace (1804) was the scene of the famous witch trials of 1692; *Goodman:* husband, master of household.

wretch am I, to leave her on such an errand! She talks of dreams, too. Methought, as she spoke, there was trouble in her face, as if a dream had warned her what work is to be done tonight. But, no, no! 'twould kill her to think it. Well; she's a blessed angel on earth; and after this one night, I'll cling to her skirts and follow her to Heaven."

With this excellent resolve for the future, Goodman Brown felt himself justfiied in making more haste on his present evil purpose. He had taken a dreary road, darkened by all the gloomiest trees of the forest, which barely stood aside to let the narrow path creep through, and closed immediately behind. It was all as lonely as could be; and there is this peculiarity in such a solitude, that the traveler knows not who may be concealed by the innumerable trunks and the thick boughs overhead; so that, with lonely footsteps, he may yet be passing through an unseen multitude.

"There may be a devilish Indian behind every tree," said Goodman Brown, to himself; and he glanced fearfully behind him, as he added, "What if the devil himself should be at my very elbow!"

His head being turned back, he passed a crook of the road, and looking forward again, beheld the figure of a man, in grave and decent attire, seated at the foot of an old tree. He arose, at Goodman Brown's approach, and walked onward, side by side with him.

"You are late, Goodman Brown," said he. "The clock of the Old South[2] was striking as I came through Boston; and that is full fifteen minutes agone."

"Faith kept me back awhile," replied the young man, with a tremor in his voice, caused by the sudden appearance of his companion, though not wholly unexpected.

It was now deep dusk in the forest, and deepest in that part of it where these two were journeying. As nearly as could be discerned, the second traveler was about fifty years old, apparently in the same rank of life as Goodman Brown, and bearing a considerable resemblance to him, though perhaps more in expression than features. Still, they might have been taken for father and son. And yet, though the elder person was as simply clad as the younger, and as simple in manner too, he had an indescribable air of one who knew the world, and would not have felt abashed at the governor's dinner table, or in King William's[3] court, were it possible that his affairs should call him thither. But the only thing about him, that could be fixed upon as remarkable, was his staff, which bore the likeness of a great black snake, so curiously wrought, that it might almost be seen to twist and wriggle itself, like a living serpent. This, of course, must have been an ocular deception, assisted by the uncertain light.

"Come, Goodman Brown!" cried his fellow-traveler, "this is a dull pace for the beginning of a journey. Take my staff, if you are so soon weary."

"Friend," said the other, exchanging his slow pace for a full stop, "having kept covenant by meeting thee here, it is my purpose now

---

2. The Third Church of Boston, established in 1669 in opposition to the requirement of church membership for political rights and thus a landmark of religious freedom.

3. William III—William of Orange—1650-1702, ruled England from 1689 to 1702, until 1694 jointly with his wife, Mary II.

to return whence I came. I have scruples, touching the matter thou wot'st of."

"Sayest thou so?" replied he of the serpent, smiling apart. "Let us walk on, nevertheless, reasoning as we go, and if I convince thee not, thou shalt turn back. We are but a little way in the forest, yet."

"Too far, too far!" exclaimed the goodman, unconsciously resuming his walk. "My father never went into the woods on such an errand, nor his father before him. We have been a race of honest men and good Christians, since the days of the martyrs. And shall I be the first of the name of Brown, that ever took this path, and kept—"

"Such company, thou wouldst say," observed the elder person, interpreting his pause. "Well said, Goodman Brown! I have been as well acquainted with your family as with ever a one among the Puritans; and that's no trifle to say. I helped your grandfather, the constable, when he lashed the Quaker woman so smartly through the streets of Salem. And it was I that brought your father a pitch-pine knot, kindled at my own hearth, to set fire to an Indian village, in King Philip's war.[4] They were my good friends, both; and many a pleasant walk have we had along this path, and returned merrily after midnight. I would fain be friends with you, for their sake."

"If it be as thou sayest," replied Goodman Brown, "I marvel they never spoke of these matters. Or, verily, I marvel not, seeing that the least rumor of the sort would have driven them from New England. We are a people of prayer, and good works, to boot, and abide no such wickedness."

"Wickedness or not," said the traveler with the twisted staff, "I have a very general acquaintance here in New England. The deacons of many a church have drunk the communion wine with me; the selectmen, of divers towns, make me their chairman; and a majority of the Great and General Court are firm supporters of my interest. The governor and I, too—but these are state secrets."

"Can this be so!" cried Goodman Brown, with a stare of amazement at his undisturbed companion. "Howbeit, I have nothing to do with the governor and council; they have their own ways, and are no rule for a simple husbandman, like me. But, were I to go on with thee, how should I meet the eye of that good old man, our minister, at Salem village? Oh, his voice would make me tremble, both Sabbath-day and lecture-day!"[5]

Thus far, the elder traveler had listened with due gravity, but now burst into a fit of irrepressible mirth, shaking himself so violently, that his snake-like staff actually seemed to wriggle in sympathy.

"Ha! ha! ha!" shouted he, again and again; then composing himself, "Well, go on, Goodman Brown, go on; but pr'y thee, don't kill me with laughing!"

"Well, then, to end the matter at once," said Goodman Brown, considerably nettled, "there is my wife, Faith. It would break her

---

4. Metacom or Metacomet, chief of the Wampanoag Indians, known as King Philip, led a war against the New England colonists in 1675–76 which devastated many frontier communities.

5. The day—in the New England colonies usually a Thursday—appointed for a periodical lecture, the lecture being less formal than a sermon or delivered on a different occasion.

dear little heart; and I'd rather break my own!"

"Nay, if that be the case," answered the other, "e'en[6] go thy ways, Goodman Brown. I would not, for twenty old women like the one hobbling before us, that Faith should come to any harm."

As he spoke, he pointed his staff at a female figure on the path, in whom Goodman Brown recognized a very pious and exemplary dame, who had taught him his catechism, in youth, and was still his moral and spiritual adviser, jointly with the minister and Deacon Gookin.

"A marvel, truly, that Goody[7] Cloyse should be so far in the wilderness, at nightfall!" said he. "But, with your leave, friend, I shall take a cut through the woods, until we have left this Christian woman behind. Being a stranger to you, she might ask whom I was consorting with, and whither I was going."

"Be it so," said his fellow-traveler. "Betake you to the woods, and let me keep the path."

Accordingly, the young man turned aside, but took care to watch his companion, who advanced softly along the road, until he had come within a staff's length of the old dame. She, meanwhile, was making the best of her way, with singular speed for so aged a woman, and mumbling some indistinct words, a prayer, doubtless, as she went. The traveler put forth his staff, and touched her withered neck with what seemed the serpent's tail.

"The devil!" screamed the pious old lady.

"Then Goody Cloyse knows her old friend?" observed the traveler, confronting her, and leaning on his writhing stick.

"Ah, forsooth, and is it your worship, indeed?" cried the good dame. "Yea, truly is it, and in the very image of my old gossip, Goodman Brown, the grandfather of the silly fellow that now is. But—would your worship believe it?—my broomstick hath strangely disappeared, stolen, as I suspect, by that unhanged witch, Goody Cory, and that, too, when I was all anointed with the juice of smallage and cinque-foil and wolf's-bane—"

"Mingled with fine wheat and the fat of a new-born babe," said the shape of old Goodman Brown.

"Ah, your worship knows the receipt," cried the old lady, cackling aloud. "So, as I was saying, being all ready for the meeting, and no horse to ride on, I made up my mind to foot it; for they tell me, there is a nice young man to be taken into communion tonight. But now your good worship will lend me your arm, and we shall be there in a twinkling."

"That can hardly be," answered her friend. "I may not spare you my arm, Goody Cloyse, but here is my staff, if you will."

So saying, he threw it down at her feet, where, perhaps, it assumed life, being one of the rods which its owner had formerly lent to the Egyptian Magi.[8] Of this fact, however, Goodman Brown could not

---

6. Just.
7. Short for "goodwife" or housewife.
8. *Exodus* 7:9-12. The Lord instructs Moses to have his prophet Aaron throw down his rod before the Pharaoh, whereupon it will be turned into a serpent, and by which miracle the Pharaoh will be persuaded to let the Jews go into the wilderness to sacrifice to God. The Pharaoh has his magicians (Magi) do likewise, "but Aaron's rod swallowed up their rods."

take cognizance. He had cast up his eyes in astonishment, and looking down again, beheld neither Goody Cloyse nor the serpentine staff,
but his fellow-traveler alone, who waited for him as calmly as if
nothing had happened.

"That old woman taught me my catechism!" said the young man;
and there was a world of meaning in this simple comment.

They continued to walk onward, while the elder traveler exhorted
his companion to make good speed and persevere in the path, dis-
coursing so aptly, that his arguments seemed rather to spring up in *self*
the bosom of his auditor, than to be suggested by himself. As they
went, he plucked a branch of maple, to serve for a walking stick,
and began to strip it of the twigs and little boughs, which were wet
with evening dew. The moment his fingers touched them, they became strangely withered and dried up, as with a week's sunshine.
Thus the pair proceeded, at a good free pace, until suddenly, in a
gloomy hollow of the road, Goodman Brown sat himself down on the
stump of a tree, and refused to go any farther.

"Friend," said he, stubbornly, "my mind is made up. Not another
step will I budge on this errand. What if a wretched old woman do
choose to go to the devil, when I thought she was going to Heaven!
Is that any reason why I should quit my dear Faith, and go after her?"

"You will think better of this, by-and-by," said his acquaintance,
composedly. "Sit here and rest yourself awhile; and when you feel
like moving again, there is my staff to help you along."

Without more words, he threw his companion the maple stick, and
was as speedily out of sight, as if he had vanished into the deepen-
ing gloom. The young man sat a few moments, by the roadside,
applauding himself greatly, and thinking with how clear a conscience
he should meet the minister, in his morning walk, nor shrink from
the eye of good old Deacon Gookin. And what calm sleep would be
his, that very night, which was to have been spent so wickedly, but
purely and sweetly now, in the arms of Faith! Amidst these pleasant
and praiseworthy meditations, Goodman Brown heard the tramp of
horses along the road, and deemed it advisable to conceal himself
within the verge of the forest, conscious of the guilty purpose that
had brought him thither, though now so happily turned from it.

On came the hoof-tramps and the voices of the riders, two grave
old voices, conversing soberly as they drew near. These mingled
sounds appeared to pass along the road, within a few yards of the
young man's hiding-place; but owing, doubtless, to the depth of the
gloom, at that particular spot, neither the travelers nor their steeds
were visible. Though their figures brushed the small boughs by the
wayside, it could not be seen that they intercepted, even for a
moment, the faint gleam from the strip of bright sky, athwart which
they must have passed. Goodman Brown alternately crouched and
stood on tiptoe, pulling aside the branches, and thrusting forth
his head as far as he durst, without discerning so much as a
shadow. It vexed him the more, because he could have sworn,
were such a thing possible, that he recognized the voices of the
minister and Deacon Gookin, jogging along quietly, as they were
wont to do, when bound to some ordination or ecclesiastical coun-

cil. While yet within hearing, one of the riders stopped to pluck a switch.

"Of the two, reverend Sir," said the voice like the deacon's, "I had rather miss an ordination-dinner than tonight's meeting. They tell me that some of our community are to be here from Falmouth[9] and beyond, and others from Connecticut and Rhode Island; besides several of the Indian powows, who, after their fashion, know almost as much deviltry as the best of us. Moreover, there is a goodly young woman to be taken into communion."

"Mighty well, Deacon Gookin!" replied the solemn old tones of the minister. "Spur up, or we shall be late. Nothing can be done, you know, until I get on the ground."

The hoofs clattered again, and the voices, talking so strangely in the empty air, passed on through the forest, where no church had ever been gathered, nor solitary Christian prayed. Whither, then, could these holy men be journeying, so deep into the heathen wilderness? Young Goodman Brown caught hold of a tree, for support, being ready to sink down on the ground, faint and overburdened with the heavy sickness of his heart. He looked up to the sky, doubting whether there really was a Heaven above him. Yet there was the blue arch, and the stars brightening in it.

"With Heaven above, and Faith below, I will yet stand firm against the devil!" cried Goodman Brown.

While he still gazed upward, into the deep arch of the firmament, and had lifted his hands to pray, a cloud, though no wind was stirring, hurried across the zenith, and hid the brightening stars. The blue sky was still visible, except directly overhead, where this black mass of cloud was sweeping swiftly northward. Aloft in the air, as if from the depths of the cloud, came a confused and doubtful sound of voices. Once, the listener fancied that he could distinguish the accents of townspeople of his own, men and women, both pious and ungodly, many of whom he had met at the communion-table, and had seen others rioting at the tavern. The next moment, so indistinct were the sounds, he doubted whether he had heard aught but the murmur of the old forest, whispering without a wind. Then came a stronger swell of those familiar tones, heard daily in the sunshine, at Salem village, but never, until now, from a cloud of night. There was one voice, of a young woman, uttering lamentations, yet with an uncertain sorrow, and entreating for some favor, which, perhaps, it would grieve her to obtain. And all the unseen multitude, both saints and sinners, seemed to encourage her onward.

"Faith!" shouted Goodman Brown, in a voice of agony and desperation; and the echoes of the forest mocked him, crying—"Faith! Faith!" as if bewildered wretches were seeking her, all through the wilderness.

The cry of grief, rage, and terror, was yet piercing the night, when the unhappy husband held his breath for a response. There was a scream, drowned immediately in a louder murmur of voices, fading into far-off laughter, as the dark cloud swept away, leaving

9. A port in extreme southern Massachusetts; Salem is in northern Massachusetts.

the clear and silent sky above Goodman Brown. But something fluttered lightly down through the air, and caught on the branch of a tree. The young man seized it, and beheld a pink ribbon.

"My Faith is gone!" cried he, after one stupefied moment. "There is no good on earth; and sin is but a name. Come, devil! for to thee is this world given."

And maddened with despair, so that he laughed loud and long, did Goodman Brown grasp his staff and set forth again, at such a rate, that he seemed to fly along the forest path, rather than to walk or run. The road grew wilder and drearier, and more faintly traced, and vanished at length, leaving him in the heart of the dark wilderness, still rushing onward, with the instinct that guides mortal man to evil. The whole forest was peopled with frightful sounds; the creaking of the trees, the howling of wild beasts, and the yell of Indians; while, sometimes, the wind tolled like a distant church bell, and sometimes gave a broad roar around the traveler, as if all Nature were laughing him to scorn. But he was himself the chief horror of the scene, and shrank not from its other horrors.

"Ha! ha! ha!" roared Goodman Brown, when the wind laughed at him. "Let us hear which will laugh loudest! Think not to frighten me with your deviltry! Come witch, come wizard, come Indian powow, come devil himself! and here comes Goodman Brown. You may as well fear him as he fear you!"

In truth, all through the haunted forest, there could be nothing more frightful than the figure of Goodman Brown. On he flew, among the black pines, brandishing his staff with frenzied gestures, now giving vent to an inspiration of horrid blasphemy, and now shouting forth such laughter, as set all the echoes of the forest laughing like demons around him. The fiend in his own shape is less hideous, than when he rages in the breast of man. Thus sped the demoniac on his course, until, quivering among the trees, he saw a red light before him, as when the felled trunks and branches of a clearing have been set on fire, and throw up their lurid blaze against the sky, at the hour of midnight. He paused, in a lull of the tempest that had driven him onward, and heard the swell of what seemed a hymn, rolling solemnly from a distance, with the weight of many voices. He knew the tune: it was a familiar one in the choir of the village meeting-house. The verse died heavily away, and was lengthened by a chorus, not of human voices, but of all the sounds of the benighted wilderness, pealing in awful harmony together. Goodman Brown cried out; and his cry was lost to his own ear, by its unison with the cry of the desert.

In the interval of silence, he stole forward, until the light glared full upon his eyes. At one extremity of an open space, hemmed in by the dark wall of the forest, arose a rock, bearing some rude, natural resemblance either to an altar or a pulpit, and surrounded by four blazing pines, their tops aflame, their stems untouched, like candles at an evening meeting. The mass of foliage, that had overgrown the summit of the rock, was all on fire, blazing high into the night, and fitfully illuminating the whole field. Each pendent twig and leafy festoon was in a blaze. As the red light arose and fell, a numerous congregation alternately shone forth, then disappeared in shadow, and again grew, as it were, out of the darkness, peopling the heart of the solitary woods at once.

"A grave and dark-clad company!" quoth Goodman Brown.

In truth, they were such. Among them, quivering to-and-fro, between gloom and splendor, appeared faces that would be seen, next day, at the council-board of the province, and others which, Sabbath after Sabbath, looked devoutly heavenward, and benignantly over the crowded pews, from the holiest pulpits in the land. Some affirm, that the lady of the governor was there. At least, there were high dames well known to her, and wives of honored husbands, and widows, a great multitude, and ancient maidens, all of excellent repute, and fair young girls, who trembled, lest their mothers should espy them. Either the sudden gleams of light, flashing over the obscure field, bedazzled Goodman Brown, or he recognized a score of the church-members of Salem village, famous for their especial sanctity. Good old Deacon Gookin had arrived, and waited at the skirts of that venerable saint, his revered pastor. But, irreverently consorting with these grave, reputable, and pious people, these elders of the church, these chaste dames and dewy virgins, there were men of dissolute lives and women of spotted fame, wretches given over to all mean and filthy vice, and suspected even of horrid crimes. It was strange to see, that the good shrank not from the wicked, nor were the sinners abashed by the saints. Scattered, also, among their pale-faced enemies, were the Indian priests, or powows, who had often scared their native forest with more hideous incantations than any known to English witchcraft.

"But, where is Faith?" thought Goodman Brown; and, as hope came into his heart, he trembled.

Another verse of the hymn arose, a slow and mournful strain, such as the pious love, but joined to words which expressed all that our nature can conceive of sin, and darkly hinted at far more. Unfathomable to mere mortals is the lore of fiends. Verse after verse was sung, and still the chorus of the desert swelled between, like the deepest tone of a mighty organ. And, with the final peal of that dreadful anthem, there came a sound, as if the roaring wind, the rushing streams, the howling beasts, and every other voice of the unconverted wilderness, were mingling and according with the voice of guilty man, in homage to the prince of all. The four blazing pines threw up a loftier flame, and obscurely discovered shapes and visages of horror on the smoke-wreaths, above the impious assembly. At the same moment, the fire on the rock shot redly forth, and formed a glowing arch above its base, where now appeared a figure. With reverence be it spoken, the figure bore no slight similitude, both in garb and manner, to some grave divine of the New England churches.

"Bring forth the converts!" cried a voice, that echoed through the field and rolled into the forest.

At the word, Goodman Brown stepped forth from the shadow of the trees, and approached the congregation, with whom he felt a loathful brotherhood, by the sympathy of all that was wicked in his heart. He could have well nigh sworn, that the shape of his own dead father beckoned him to advance, looking downward from a smoke-wreath, while a woman, with dim features of despair, threw out her hand to warn him back. Was it his mother? But he had no power to retreat one step, nor to resist, even in thought, when the minister and good old Deacon Gookin seized his arms, and led him to the blazing rock. Thither came also the slender form of a veiled female, led between Goody Cloyse, that pious teacher of the catechism, and Martha Carrier, who had received the devil's promise to be queen of hell. A rampant hag was she! And there stood the proselytes, beneath the canopy of fire.

"Welcome, my children," said the dark figure, "to the communion of your race! Ye have found, thus young, your nature and your destiny. My children, look behind you!"

They turned; and flashing forth, as it were, in a sheet of flame, the fiend-worshippers were seen; the smile of welcome gleamed darkly on every visage.

"There," resumed the sable form, "are all whom ye have reverenced from youth. Ye deemed them holier than yourselves, and shrank from your own sin, contrasting it with their lives of righteousness, and prayerful aspirations heavenward. Yet, here are they all, in my worshipping assembly! This night it shall be granted you to know their secret deeds; how hoary-bearded elders of the church have whispered wanton words to the young maids of their households; how many a woman, eager for widow's weeds, has given her husband a drink at bedtime, and let him sleep his last sleep in her bosom; how beardless youths have made haste to inherit their fathers' wealth; and how fair damsels—blush not, sweet ones!—have dug little graves in the garden, and bidden me, the sole guest, to an infant's funeral. By the sympathy of your human hearts for sin, ye shall scent out all the places—whether in church, bedchamber, street, field, or forest—where crime has been committed, and shall exult to behold the whole earth one stain of guilt, one mighty bloodspot. Far more than this! It shall be yours to penetrate, in every bosom, the deep mystery of sin, the fountain of all wicked arts, and which inexhaustibly supplies more evil impulses than human power—than my power, at its utmost!—can make manifest in deeds. And now, my children, look upon each other."

They did so; and, by the blaze of the hell-kindled torches, the wretched man beheld his Faith, and the wife her husband, trembling before that unhallowed altar.

"Lo! there ye stand, my children," said the figure, in a deep and solemn tone, almost sad, with its despairing awfulness, as if his once angelic nature could yet mourn for our miserable race. "Depending upon one another's hearts, ye had still hoped, that virtue were not all a dream. Now are ye undeceived! Evil is the nature of mankind. Evil must be your only happiness. Welcome, again, my children, to the communion of your race!"

"Welcome!" repeated the fiend-worshippers, in one cry of despair and triumph.

And there they stood, the only pair, as it seemed, who were yet hesitating on the verge of wickedness, in this dark world. A basin was hollowed, naturally, in the rock. Did it contain water, reddened by the lurid light? or was it blood? or, perchance, a liquid flame? Herein did the Shape of Evil dip his hand, and prepare to lay the mark of baptism upon their foreheads, that they might be partakers of the mystery of sin, more conscious of the secret guilt of others, both in deed and thought, than they could now be of their own. The husband cast one look at his pale wife, and Faith at him. What polluted wretches would the next glance shew them to each other, shuddering alike at what they disclosed and what they saw!

"Faith! Faith!" cried the husband. "Look up to Heaven, and resist the Wicked One!"

Whether Faith obeyed, he knew not. Hardly had he spoken, when he found himself amid calm night and solitude, listening to a roar of the wind, which died heavily away through the forest. He staggered against the rock and felt it chill and damp, while a hanging twig, that had been on fire, besprinkled his cheek with the coldest dew.

The next morning, young Goodman Brown came slowly into the street of Salem village, staring around him like a bewildered man. The good old minister was taking a walk along the graveyard, to get an appetite for breakfast and meditate his sermon, and bestowed a blessing, as he passed, on Goodman Brown. He shrank from the venerable saint, as if to avoid an anathema. Old Deacon Gookin was at domestic worship, and the holy words of his prayer were heard though the open window. "What God doth the wizard pray to?" quoth Goodman Brown. Goody Cloyse, that excellent old Christian, stood in the early sunshine, at her own lattice, catechizing a little girl, who had brought her a pint of morning's milk. Goodman Brown snatched away the child, as from the grasp of the fiend himself. Turning the corner by the meeting-house, he spied the head of Faith, with the pink ribbons, gazing anxiously forth, and bursting into such joy at sight of him, that she skipped along the street, and almost kissed her husband before the whole village. But, Goodman Brown looked sternly and sadly into her face, and passed on without a greeting.

Had Goodman Brown fallen asleep in the forest, and only dreamed a wild dream of a witch-meeting?

Be it so, if you will. But, alas! it was a dream of evil omen for young Goodman Brown. A stern, a sad, a darkly meditative, a distrustful, if not a desperate man, did he become, from the night of that fearful dream. On the Sabbath day, when the congregation were singing a holy psalm, he could not listen, because an anthem of sin rushed loudly upon his ear, and drowned all the blessed strain. When the minister spoke from the pulpit, with power and fervid eloquence, and, with his hand on the open Bible, of the sacred truths of our religion, and of saint-like lives and triumphant deaths, and of future bliss or misery unutterable, then did Goodman Brown turn pale, dreading, lest the roof should thunder down upon the gray blasphemer and his hearers. Often, awakening suddenly at midnight, he shrank from the bosom of Faith, and at morning or eventide, when the family knelt down at prayer, he scowled, and muttered to himself, and gazed sternly at his wife, and turned away. And when he had lived long, and was borne to his grave, a hoary corpse, followed by Faith, an aged woman, and children and grandchildren, a goodly procession, besides neighbors, not a few, they carved no hopeful verse upon his tombstone; for his dying hour was gloom.

1846

SHIRLEY JACKSON

fanturi

The Lottery

The morning of June 27th was clear and sunny, with the fresh warmth of a full-summer day; the flowers were blossoming profusely and the grass was richly green. The people of the village began to gather in the square, between the post office and the bank, around ten o'clock; in some towns there were so many people that the lottery took two days and had to be started on June 26th, but in this village, where there were only about three hundred people, the whole lottery took less than two hours, so it could begin at ten o'clock in the morning and still be through in time to allow the villagers to get home for noon dinner.

The children assembled first, of course. School was recently over for the summer, and the feeling of liberty sat uneasily on most of them; they tended to gather together quietly for a while before they broke into boisterous play, and their talk was still of the classroom and the teacher, of books and reprimands. Bobby Martin had already stuffed his pockets full of stones, and the other boys soon followed his example, selecting the smoothest and roundest stones; Bobby and Harry Jones and Dickie Delacroix—the villagers pronounced this name "Dellacroy" —eventually made a great pile of stones in one corner of the square and guarded it against the raids of the other boys. The girls stood aside, talking among themselves, looking over their shoulders at the boys, and the very small children rolled in the dust or clung to the hands of their older brothers or sisters. *neutral*

Soon the men began to gather, surveying their own children, speaking of planting and rain, tractors and taxes. They stood together, away from the pile of stones in the corner, and their jokes were quiet and they smiled rather than laughed. The women, wearing faded house dresses and sweaters, came shortly after their menfolk. They greeted one another and exchanged bits of gossip as they went to join their husbands. Soon the women, standing by their husbands, began to call to their children, and the chidren came reluctantly, having to be called four or five times. Bobby Martin ducked under his mother's grasping hand and ran, laughing, back to the pile of stones. His father spoke up sharply, and Bobby came quickly and took his place between his father and his oldest brother.

The lottery was conducted—as were the square dances, the teenage club, the Halloween program—by Mr. Summers, who had time and energy to devote to civic activities. He was a round-faced, jovial man and he ran the coal business, and people were sorry for him, because

or dreary

he had no children and his wife was a scold. When he arrived in the square, carrying the black wooden box, there was a murmur of conversation among the villagers, and he waved and called, "Little late today, folks." The postmaster, Mr. Graves, followed him, carrying a three-legged stool, and the stool was put in the center of the square and Mr. Summers set the black box down on it. The villagers kept their distance, leaving a space between themselves and the stool, and when Mr. Summers said, "Some of you fellows want to give me a hand?" there was a hesitation before two men, Mr. Martin and his oldest son, Baxter, came forward to hold the box steady on the stool while Mr. Summers stirred up the papers inside it.

The original paraphernalia for the lottery had been lost long ago, and the black box now resting on the stool had been put into use even before Old Man Warner, the oldest man in town, was born. Mr. Summers spoke frequently to the villagers about making a new box, but no one liked to upset even as much tradition as was represented by the black box. There was a story that the present box had been made with some pieces of the box that had preceded it, the one that had been constructed when the first people settled down to make a village here. Every year, after the lottery, Mr. Summers began talking again about a new box, but every year the subject was allowed to fade off without anything's being done. The black box grew shabbier each year; by now it was no longer completely black but splintered badly along one side to show the original wood color, and in some places faded or stained.

Mr. Martin and his oldest son, Baxter, held the black box securely on the stool until Mr. Summers had stirred the papers thoroughly with his hand. Because so much of the ritual had been forgotten or discarded, Mr. Summers had been successful in having slips of paper substituted for the chips of wood that had been used for generations. Chips of wood, Mr. Summers had argued, had been all very well when the village was tiny, but now that the population was more than three hundred and likely to keep on growing, it was necessary to use something that would fit more easily into the black box. The night before the lottery, Mr. Summers and Mr. Graves made up the slips of paper and put them in the box, and it was then taken to the safe of Mr. Summers' coal company and locked up until Mr. Summers was ready to take it to the square next morning. The rest of the year, the box was put away, sometimes one place, sometimes another; it had spent one year in Mr. Graves's barn and another year underfoot in the post office, and sometimes it was set on a shelf in the Martin grocery and left there.

There was a great deal of fussing to be done before Mr. Summers declared the lottery open. There were the lists to make up—of heads of families, heads of households in each family, members of each household in each family. There was the proper swearing-in of Mr. Summers by the postmaster, as the official of the lottery; at one time, some people remembered, there had been a recital of some sort, performed by the official of the lottery, a perfunctory, tuneless chant that had been rattled off duly each year; some people believed that the official of the lottery used to stand just so when he said or sang it, others believed that he was supposed to walk among the people, but years and years ago this part of the ritual had been allowed to lapse. There had been, also, a ritual salute, which the official of the lottery had had to use in addressing each person who came up to draw from the box, but this also had changed with time, until now it was felt necessary only for the official to speak to each person approaching. Mr. Summers was very good at all this; in his clean white shirt and blue jeans, with one hand resting carelessly on the black box, he seemed very proper and important as he talked interminably to Mr. Graves and the Martins.

Just as Mr. Summers finally left off talking and turned to the assembled villagers, Mrs. Hutchinson came hurriedly along the path to the square, her sweater thrown over her shoulders, and slid into place in the back of the crowd. "Clean forgot what day it was," she said to Mrs. Delacroix, who stood next to her, and they both laughed softly. "Thought my old man was out back stacking wood," Mrs. Hutchinson went on, "and then I looked out the window and the kids was gone, and then I remembered it was the twenty-seventh and came a-running." She dried her hands on her apron, and Mrs. Delacroix said, "You're in time, though. They're still talking away up there."

Mrs. Hutchinson craned her neck to see through the crowd and found her husband and children standing near the front. She tapped Mrs. Delacroix on the arm as a farewell and began to make her way through the crowd. The people separated good-humoredly to let her through; two or three people said, in voices just loud enough to be heard across the crowd, "Here comes your Missus, Hutchinson," and "Bill, she made it after all." Mrs. Hutchinson reached her husband, and Mr. Summers, who had been waiting, said cheerfully, "Thought we were going to have to get on without you, Tessie." Mrs. Hutchinson said, grinning, "Wouldn't have me leave m'dishes in the sink, now, would you, Joe?," and soft laughter ran through the crowd as the people stirred back into position after Mrs. Hutchinson's arrival.

"Well, now," Mr. Summers said soberly, "guess we better get started, get this over with, so's we can go back to work. Anybody ain't here?"

"Dunbar," several people said. "Dunbar, Dunbar."

Mr. Summers consulted his list. "Clyde Dunbar," he said. "That's right. He's broke his leg, hasn't he? Who's drawing for him?"

"Me, I guess," a woman said, and Mr. Summers turned to look at her. "Wife draws for her husband," Mr. Summers said. "Don't you have a grown boy to do it for you, Janey?" Although Mr. Summers and everyone else in the village knew the answer perfectly well, it was the business of the official of the lottery to ask such questions formally. Mr. Summers waited with an expression of polite interest while Mrs. Dunbar answered.

"Horace's not but sixteen yet," Mrs. Dunbar said regretfully. "Guess I gotta fill in for the old man this year."

"Right," Mr. Summers said. He made a note on the list he was holding. Then he asked, "Watson boy drawing this year?"

A tall boy in the crowd raised his hand. "Here," he said. "I'm drawing for m'mother and me." He blinked his eyes nervously and ducked his head as several voices in the crowd said things like "Good fellow, Jack," and "Glad to see your mother's got a man to do it."

"Well," Mr. Summers said, "guess that's everyone. Old Man Warner make it?"

"Here," a voice said, and Mr. Summers nodded.

A sudden hush fell on the crowd as Mr. Summers cleared his throat and looked at the list. "All ready?" he called. "Now, I'll read the names —heads of families first—and the men come up and take a paper out of the box. Keep the paper folded in your hand without looking at it until everyone has had a turn. Everything clear?"

The people had done it so many times that they only half listened to the directions; most of them were quiet, wetting their lips, not looking around. Then Mr. Summers raised one hand high and said, "Adams." A man disengaged himself from the crowd and came forward. "Hi, Steve," Mr. Summers said, and Mr. Adams said, "Hi, Joe." They grinned at one another humorlessly and nervously. Then Mr. Adams reached into the black box and took out a folded paper. He held it firmly by one corner as he turned and went hastily back to his place in the crowd, where he stood a little apart from his family, not looking down at his hand.

"Allen," Mr. Summers said. "Anderson. . . . Bentham."

"Seems like there's no time at all between lotteries any more," Mrs. Delacroix said to Mrs. Graves in the back row. "Seems like we got through with the last one only last week."

"Time sure goes fast," Mrs. Graves said.

"Clark. . . . Delacroix."

"There goes my old man," Mrs. Delacroix said. She held her breath while her husband went forward.

"Dunbar," Mr. Summers said, and Mrs. Dunbar went steadily to the box while one of the women said, "Go on, Janey," and another said, "There she goes."

"We're next," Mrs. Graves said. She watched while Mr. Graves came around from the side of the box, greeted Mr. Summers gravely, and selected a slip of paper from the box. By now, all through the crowd there were men holding the small folded papers in their large hands, turning them over and over nervously. Mrs. Dunbar and her two sons stood together, Mrs. Dunbar holding the slip of paper.

"Harburt. . . . Hutchinson."

"Get up there, Bill," Mrs. Hutchinson said, and the people near her laughed.

"Jones."

"They do say," Mr. Adams said to Old Man Warner, who stood next to him, "that over in the north village they're talking of giving up the lottery."

Old Man Warner snorted. "Pack of crazy fools," he said. "Listening to the young folks, nothing's good enough for *them*. Next thing you know, they'll be wanting to go back to living in caves, nobody work any more, live *that* way for a while. Used to be a saying about 'Lottery in June, corn be heavy soon.' First thing you know, we'd all be eating stewed chickweed and acorns. There's *always* been a lottery," he added petulantly. "Bad enough to see young Joe Summers up there joking with everybody."

"Some places have already quit lotteries," Mrs. Adams said.

"Nothing but trouble in *that*," Old Man Warner said stoutly. "Pack of young fools."

"Martin." And Bobby Martin watched his father go forward. "Over-dyke. . . . Percy."

"I wish they'd hurry," Mrs. Dunbar said to her older son. "I wish they'd hurry."

"They're almost through," her son said.

"You get ready to run tell Dad," Mrs. Dunbar said.

Mr. Summers called his own name and then stepped forward precisely and selected a slip from the box. Then he called, "Warner."

"Seventy-seventh year I been in the lottery," Old Man Warner said as he went through the crowd. "Seventy-seventh time."

"Watson." The tall boy came awkwardly through the crowd. Someone said, "Don't be nervous, Jack," and Mr. Summers said, "Take your time, son."

"Zanini."

After that, there was a long pause, a breathless pause, until Mr. Summers, holding his slip of paper in the air, said, "All right, fellows." For a minute, no one moved, and then all the slips of paper were opened. Suddenly, all the women began to speak at once, saying, "Who is it?," "Who's got it?," "Is it the Dunbars?," "Is it the Watsons?" Then the voices began to say, "It's Hutchinson. It's Bill," "Bill Hutchinson's got it."

"Go tell your father," Mrs. Dunbar said to her older son.

People began to look around to see the Hutchinsons. Bill Hutchinson was standing quiet staring down at the paper in his hand. Suddenly, Tessie Hutchinson shouted to Mr. Summers, "You didn't give him time enough to take any paper he wanted. I saw you. It wasn't fair."

"Be a good sport, Tessie," Mrs. Delacroix called, and Mrs. Graves said, "All of us took the same chance."

"Shut up, Tessie," Bill Hutchinson said.

"Well, everyone," Mr. Summers said, "that was done pretty fast, and now we've got to be hurrying a little more to get done in time." He consulted his next list. "Bill," he said, "you draw for the Hutchinson family. You got any other households in the Hutchinsons?"

"There's Don and Eva," Mrs. Hutchinson yelled. "Make *them* take their chance!"

"Daughters draw with their husbands' families, Tessie," Mr. Summers said gently. "You know that as well as anyone else."

"It wasn't *fair*," Tessie said.

"I guess not, Joe," Bill Hutchinson said regretfully. "My daughter draws with her husband's family, that's only fair. And I've got no other family except the kids."

"Then, as far as drawing for families is concerned, it's you," Mr. Summers said in explanation, "and as far as drawing for households is concerned, that's you, too. Right?"

"Right," Bill Hutchinson said.

"How many kids, Bill?" Mr. Summers asked formally.

"Three," Bill Hutchinson said. "There's Bill, Jr., and Nancy, and little Dave. And Tessie and me."

"All right, then," Mr. Summers said. "Harry, you got their tickets back?"

Mr. Graves nodded and held up the slips of paper. "Put them in the box, then," Mr. Summers directed. "Take Bill's and put it in."

"I think we ought to start over," Mrs. Hutchinson said, as quietly as she could. "I tell you it wasn't *fair.* You didn't give him time enough to choose. *Every*body saw that."

Mr. Graves had selected the five slips and put them in the box, and he dropped all the papers but those onto the ground, where the breeze caught them and lifted them off.

"Listen, everybody," Mrs. Hutchinson was saying to the people around her.

"Ready, Bill?" Mr. Summers asked, and Bill Hutchinson, with one quick glance around at his wife and children, nodded.

"Remember," Mr. Summers said, "take the slips and keep them folded until each person has taken one. Harry, you help little Dave." Mr. Graves took the hand of the little boy, who came willingly with him up to the box. "Take a paper out of the box, Davy," Mr. Summers said. Davy put his hand into the box and laughed. "Take just *one* paper." Mr. Summers said. "Harry, you hold it for him." Mr. Graves took the child's hand and removed the folded paper from the tight fist and held it while little Dave stood next to him and looked up at him wonderingly.

"Nancy next," Mr. Summers said. Nancy was twelve, and her school friends breathed heavily as she went forward, switching her skirt, and took a slip daintily from the box. "Bill, Jr.," Mr. Summers said, and Billy, his face red and his feet over-large, nearly knocked the box over as he got a paper out. "Tessie," Mr. Summers said. She hesitated for a minute, looking around defiantly, and then set her lips and went up to the box. She snatched a paper out and held it behind her.

"Bill," Mr. Summers said, and Bill Hutchinson reached into the box and felt around, bringing his hand out at last with the slip of paper in it.

The crowd was quiet. A girl whispered, "I hope it's not Nancy," and the sound of the whisper reached the edges of the crowd.

"It's not the way it used to be," Old Man Warner said clearly. "People ain't the way they used to be."

"All right," Mr. Summers said. "Open the papers. Harry, you open little Dave's."

Mr. Graves opened the slip of paper and there was a general sigh through the crowd as he held it up and everyone could see that it was blank. Nancy and Bill, Jr., opened theirs at the same time, and both beamed and laughed, turning around to the crowd and holding their slips of paper above their heads.

"Tessie," Mr. Summers said. There was a pause, and then Mr. Summers looked at Bill Hutchinson, and Bill unfolded his paper and showed it. It was blank.

"It's Tessie," Mr. Summers said, and his voice was hushed. "Show us her paper, Bill."

Bill Hutchinson went over to his wife and forced the slip of paper out of her hand. It had a black spot on it, the black spot Mr. Summers had made the night before with the heavy pencil in the coal-company office. Bill Hutchinson held it up, and there was a stir in the crowd.

"All right, folks," Mr. Summers said. "Let's finish quickly."

Although the villagers had forgotten the ritual and lost the original black box, they still remembered to use stones. The pile of stones the boys had made earlier was ready; there were stones on the ground with the blowing scraps of paper that had come out of the box. Mrs. Delacroix selected a stone so large she had to pick it up with both hands and turned to Mrs. Dunbar. "Come on," she said. "Hurry up."

Mrs. Dunbar had small stones in both hands, and she said, gasping for breath, "I can't run at all. You'll have to go ahead and I'll catch up with you."

The children had stones already, and someone gave little Davy Hutchinson a few pebbles.

Tessie Hutchinson was in the center of a cleared space by now, and she held her hands out desperately as the villagers moved in on her. "It isn't fair," she said. A stone hit her on the side of the head.

Old Man Warner was saying, "Come on, come on, everyone." Steve Adams was in the front of the crowd of villagers, with Mrs. Graves beside him.

"It isn't fair, it isn't right," Mrs. Hutchinson screamed, and then they were upon her.

1948

FLANNERY O'CONNOR

The Artificial Nigger

Mr. Head awakened to discover that the room was full of moonlight. He sat up and stared at the floor boards—the color of silver—and then at the ticking on his pillow, which might have been brocade, and after a second, he saw half of the moon five feet away in his shaving mirror, paused as if it were waiting for his permission to enter. It rolled forward and cast a dignifying light on everything. The straight chair against the wall looked stiff and attentive as if it were awaiting an order and Mr. Head's trousers, hanging to the back of it, had an almost noble air, like the garment some great man had just flung to his servant; but the face on the moon was a grave one. It gazed across the room and out the window where it floated over the horse stall and appeared to contemplate itself with the look of a young man who sees his old age before him.

Mr. Head could have said to it that age was a choice blessing and that only with years does a man enter into that calm understanding of life that makes him a suitable guide for the young. This, at least, had been his own experience.

He sat up and grasped the iron posts at the foot of his bed and raised himself until he could see the face on the alarm clock which sat on an overturned bucket beside the chair. The hour was two in the morning. The alarm on the clock did not work but he was not dependent on any mechanical means to awaken him. Sixty years had not dulled his responses; his physical reactions, like his moral ones, were guided by his will and strong character, and these could be seen plainly in his features. He had a long tube-like face with a long rounded open jaw and a long depressed nose. His eyes were alert but quiet, and in the miraculous moonlight they had a look of composure and of ancient wisdom as if they belonged to one of the great guides of men. He might have been Vergil summoned in the middle of the night to go to Dante, or better, Raphael, awakened by a blast of God's light to fly to the side of Tobias.[1] The only dark spot in the room was Nelson's pallet, underneath the shadow of the window.

Nelson was hunched over on his side, his knees under his chin and his heels under his bottom. His new suit and hat were in the boxes that they had been sent in and these were on the floor at the foot of the pallet where he could get his hands on them as soon as he woke up. The slop jar, out of the shadow and made snow-white in the moonlight, appeared to stand guard over him like a small personal angel. Mr. Head lay back down, feeling entirely confident that he could carry out the moral mission of the coming day. He meant to be up before Nelson and to have the breakfast cooking by the time he awakened. The boy was always irked when Mr. Head was the first up. They would have to leave the house at four to get to the railroad junction by five-thirty. The train was to stop for them at five forty-five and they had to be there on time for this train was stopping merely to accommodate them.

This would be the boy's first trip to the city though he claimed it would be his second because he had been born there. Mr. Head had tried to point out to him that when he was born he didn't have the intelligence to determine his whereabouts but this had made no impression on the child at all and he continued to insist that this was to be his second trip. It would be Mr. Head's third trip. Nelson had said, "I will've already been there twict and I ain't but ten."

Mr. Head had contradicted him.

"If you ain't been there in fifteen years, how you know you'll be able to find your way about?" Nelson had asked. "How you know it hasn't changed some?"

"Have you ever," Mr. Head had asked, "seen me lost?"

Nelson certainly had not but he was a child who was never satisfied until he had given an impudent answer and he replied, "It's nowhere around here to get lost at."

"The day is going to come," Mr. Head prophesied, "when you'll find you ain't as smart as you think you are." He had been thinking about this trip for several months but it was for the most part in moral terms that he conceived it. It was to be a lesson that the boy would never forget. He was to find out from it that he had no cause for pride merely because he had been born in a city. He was to find out that the city is not a great place. Mr. Head meant him to see everything there

---

1. Vergil, Publius Vergilius Maro (70–19 B.C.), author of the *Aeneid*, in *The Divine Comedy* of Dante Alighieri (1265–1321), is summoned by Beatrice (*Inferno*, II, 49–70) to assist Dante and serves as his guide through Hell and Purgatory; the angel Raphael in the Book of Tobit in the *Apocrypha* serves as Tobias's instructor and companion in the overcoming of the demon Asmodeus.

is to see in a city so that he would be content to stay at home for the rest of his life. He fell asleep thinking how the boy would at last find out that he was not as smart as he thought he was.

He was awakened at three-thirty by the smell of fatback frying and he leaped off his cot. The pallet was empty and the clothes boxes had been thrown open. He put on his trousers and ran into the other room. The boy had a corn pone on cooking and had fried the meat. He was sitting in the half-dark at the table, drinking cold coffee out of a can. He had on his new suit and his new gray hat pulled low over his eyes. It was too big for him but they had ordered it a size large because they expected his head to grow. He didn't say anything but his entire figure suggested satisfaction at having arisen before Mr. Head.

Mr. Head went to the stove and brought the meat to the table in the skillet. "It's no hurry," he said. "You'll get there soon enough and it's no guarantee you'll like it when you do neither," and he sat down across from the boy whose hat teetered back slowly to reveal a fiercely expressionless face, very much the same shape as the old man's. They were grandfather and grandson but they looked enough alike to be brothers and brothers not too far apart in age, for Mr. Head had a youthful expression by daylight, while the boy's look was ancient, as if he knew everything already and would be pleased to forget it.

Mr. Head had once had a wife and daughter and when the wife died, the daughter ran away and returned after an interval with Nelson. Then one morning, without getting out of bed, she died and left Mr. Head with sole care of the year-old child. He had made the mistake of telling Nelson that he had been born in Atlanta. If he hadn't told him that, Nelson couldn't have insisted that this was going to be his second trip.

"You may not like it a bit," Mr. Head continued. "It'll be full of niggers."

The boy made a face as if he could handle a nigger.

"All right," Mr. Head said. "You ain't ever seen a nigger."

"You wasn't up very early," Nelson said.

"You ain't ever seen a nigger," Mr. Head repeated. "There hasn't been a nigger in this county since we run that one out twelve years ago and that was before you were born." He looked at the boy as if he were daring him to say he had ever seen a Negro.

"How you know I never saw a nigger when I lived there before?" Nelson asked. "I probably saw a lot of niggers."

"If you seen one you didn't know what he was," Mr. Head said, completely exasperated. "A six-month-old child don't know a nigger from anybody else."

"I reckon I'll know a nigger if I see one," the boy said and got up and straightened his slick sharply creased gray hat and went outside to the privy.

They reached the junction some time before the train was due to arrive and stood about two feet from the first set of tracks. Mr. Head carried a paper sack with some biscuits and a can of sardines in it for their lunch. A coarse-looking orange-colored sun coming up behind the east range of mountains was making the sky a dull red behind them, but in front of them it was still gray and they faced a gray transparent moon, hardly stronger than a thumbprint and completely without light. A small tin switch box and a black fuel tank were all there was to mark the place as a junction; the tracks were double and did not converge again until they were hidden behind the bends at either end of the clearing. Trains passing appeared to emerge from a tunnel of trees and, hit for a second by the cold sky, vanish terrified into the woods again. Mr. Head had had to make special arrangements with the ticket agent to have this train stop and he was secretly afraid it would not, in which case, he knew Nelson would say, "I never thought no train was going to stop for you." Under the useless morning moon the tracks looked white and fragile. Both the old man and the child stared ahead as if they were awaiting an apparition.

Then suddenly, before Mr. Head could make up his mind to turn back, there was a deep warning bleat and the train appeared, gliding very slowly, almost silently around the bend of trees about two hundred yards down the track, with one yellow front light shining. Mr. Head was still not certain it would stop and he felt it would make an even bigger idiot of him if it went by slowly. But he and Nelson, however, were prepared to ignore the train if it passed them.

The engine charged by, filling their noses with the smell of hot metal and then the second coach came to a stop exactly where they were standing. A conductor with the face of an ancient bloated bulldog was on the step as if he expected them, though he did not look as if it mattered one way or the other to him if they got on or not. "To the right," he said.

Their entry took only a fraction of a second and the train was already speeding on as they entered the quiet car. Most of the travelers were still sleeping, some with their heads hanging off the chair arms, some stretched across two seats, and some sprawled out with their feet in the aisle. Mr. Head saw two unoccupied seats and pushed Nelson toward them. "Get in there by the winder," he said in his normal voice which was very loud at this hour of the morning. "Nobody cares if you set there because it's nobody in it. Sit right there."

"I heard you," the boy muttered. "It's no use in you yelling," and he sat down and turned his head to the glass. There he saw a pale ghost-like face scowling at him beneath the brim of a pale ghost-like hat. His grandfather, looking quickly too, saw a different ghost, pale but grinning, under a black hat.

Mr. Head sat down and settled himself and took out his ticket and started reading aloud everything that was printed on it. People began to stir. Several woke up and stared at him. "Take off your hat," he said to Nelson and took off his own and put it on his knee. He had a small amount of white hair that had turned tobacco-colored over the years and this lay flat across the back of his head. The front of his head was bald and creased. Nelson took off his hat and put it on his knee and they waited for the conductor to come ask for their tickets.

The man across the aisle from them was spread out over two seats, his feet propped on the window and his head jutting into the aisle. He had on a light blue suit and a yellow shirt unbuttoned at the neck. His eyes had just opened and Mr. Head was ready to introduce himself when the conductor came up from behind and growled, "Tickets."

When the conductor had gone, Mr. Head gave Nelson the return half of his ticket and said, "Now put that in your pocket and don't lose it or you'll have to stay in the city."

"Maybe I will," Nelson said as if this were a reasonable suggestion.

Mr. Head ignored him. "First time this boy has ever been on a train," he explained to the man across the aisle, who was sitting up now on the edge of his seat with both feet on the floor.

Nelson jerked his hat on again and turned angrily to the window.

"He's never seen anything before," Mr. Head continued. "Ignorant as the day he was born, but I mean for him to get his fill once and for all."

The boy leaned forward, across his grandfather and toward the stranger. "I was born in the city," he said. "I was born there. This is my second trip." He said it in a high positive voice but the man across the aisle didn't look as if he understood. There were heavy purple circles under his eyes.

Mr. Head reached across the aisle and tapped him on the arm. "The thing to do with a boy," he said sagely, "is to show him all it is to show. Don't hold nothing back."

"Yeah," the man said. He gazed down at his swollen feet and lifted the left one about ten inches from the floor. After a minute he put it down and lifted the other. All through the car people began to get up and move about and yawn and stretch. Separate voices could be heard here and there and then a general hum. Suddenly Mr. Head's serene expression changed. His mouth almost closed and a light, fierce and cautious both, came into his eyes. He was looking down the length of the car. Without turning, he caught Nelson by the arm and pulled him forward. "Look," he said.

A huge coffee-colored man was coming slowly forward. He had on a light suit and a yellow satin tie with a ruby pin in it. One of his hands rested on his stomach which rode majestically under his buttoned coat, and in the other he held the head of a black walking stick that he picked up and set down with a deliberate outward motion each time he took a step. He was proceeding very slowly, his large brown eyes gazing over the heads of the passengers. He had a small white mustache and white crinkly hair. Behind him there were two young women, both coffee-colored, one in a yellow dress and one in a green. Their progress was kept at the rate of his and they chatted in low throaty voices as they followed him.

Mr. Head's grip was tightening insistently on Nelson's arm. As the procession passed them, the light from a sapphire ring on the brown hand that picked up the cane reflected in Mr. Head's eye, but he did not look up nor did the tremendous man look at him. The group proceeded up the rest of the aisle and out of the car. Mr. Head's grip on Nelson's arm loosened. "What was that?" he asked.

"A man," the boy said and gave him an indignant look as if he were tired of having his intelligence insulted.

"What kind of a man?" Mr. Head persisted, his voice expressionless.

"A fat man," Nelson said. He was beginning to feel that he had better be cautious.

"You don't know what kind?" Mr. Head said in a final tone.

"An old man," the boy said and had a sudden foreboding that he was not going to enjoy the day.

"That was a nigger," Mr. Head said and sat back.

Nelson jumped up on the seat and stood looking backward to the end of the car but the Negro had gone.

"I'd of thought you'd know a nigger since you seen so many when you was in the city on your first visit," Mr. Head continued. "That's his first nigger," he said to the man across the aisle.

The boy slid down into the seat. "You said they were black," he said in an angry voice. "You never said they were tan. How do you expect me to know anything when you don't tell me right?"

"You're just ignorant is all," Mr. Head said and he got up and moved over in the vacant seat by the man across the aisle.

Nelson turned backward again and looked where the Negro had disappeared. He felt that the Negro had deliberately walked down the aisle in order to make a fool of him and he hated him with a fierce raw fresh hate; and also, he understood now why his grandfather disliked them. He looked toward the window and the face there seemed to suggest that he might be inadequate to the day's exactions. He wondered if he would even recognize the city when they came to it.

After he had told several stories, Mr. Head realized that the man he was talking to was asleep and he got up and suggested to Nelson that they walk over the train and see the parts of it. He particularly wanted the boy to see the toilet so they went first to the men's room and examined the plumbing. Mr. Head demonstrated the ice-water cooler as if he had invented it and showed Nelson the bowl with the single spigot where the travelers brushed their teeth. They went through several cars and came to the diner.

This was the most elegant car in the train. It was painted a rich egg-yellow and had a wine-colored carpet on the floor. There were wide windows over the tables and great spaces of the rolling view were caught in miniature in the sides of the coffee pots and in the glasses. Three very black Negroes in white suits and aprons were running up and down the aisle, swinging trays and bowing and bending over the travelers eating breakfast. One of them rushed up to Mr. Head and Nelson and said, holding up two fingers, "Space for two!" but Head replied in a loud voice, "We eaten before we left!"

The waiter wore large brown spectacles that increased the size of his eye whites. "Stan' aside then please," he said with an airy wave of the arm as if he were brushing aside flies.

Neither Nelson nor Mr. Head moved a fraction of an inch. "Look," Mr. Head said.

The near corner of the diner, containing two tables, was set off from the rest by a saffron-colored curtain. One table was set but empty but at the other, facing them, his back to the drape, sat the tremendous Negro. He was speaking in a soft voice to the two women while he buttered a muffin. He had a heavy sad face and his neck bulged over his white collar on either side. "They rope them off," Mr. Head explained. Then he said, "Let's go see the kitchen," and they walked the length of the diner but the black waiter was coming fast behind them.

"Passengers are not allowed in the kitchen!" he said in a haughty voice. "Passengers are NOT allowed in the kitchen!"

Mr. Head stopped where he was and turned. "And there's good reason for that," he shouted into the Negro's chest, "because the cockroaches would run the passengers out!"

All the travelers laughed and Mr. Head and Nelson walked out, grinning. Mr. Head was known at home for his quick wit and Nelson felt a sudden keen pride in him. He realized the old man would be his only support in the strange place they were approaching. He would be entirely alone in the world if he were ever lost from his grandfather. A terrible excitement shook him and he wanted to take hold of Mr. Head's coat and hold on like a child.

As they went back to their seats they could see through the passing windows that the countryside was becoming speckled with small houses and shacks and that a highway ran alongside the train. Cars sped by on it, very small and fast. Nelson felt that there was less breath in the air than there had been thirty minutes ago. The man across the aisle had left and there was no one near for Mr. Head to hold a conversation with so he looked out the window, through his own reflection, and read aloud the names of the buildings they were passing. "The Dixie Chemical Corp!" he announced. "Southern Maid Flour! Dixie Doors! Southern Belle Cotton Products! Patty's Peanut Butter! Southern Mammy Cane Syrup!"

"Hush up!" Nelson hissed.

All over the car people were beginning to get up and take their luggage off the overhead racks. Women were putting on their coats and hats. The conductor stuck his head in the car and snarled, "Firstop-ppppmry,"[2] and Nelson lunged out of his sitting position, trembling. Mr. Head pushed him down by the shoulder.

"Keep your seat," he said in dignified tones. "The first stop is on the edge of town. The second stop is at the main railroad station." (He had come by this knowledge on his first trip when he had got off at the first stop and had had to pay a man fifteen cents to take him into the heart of town.) Nelson sat back down, very pale. For the first time in his life, he understood that his grandfather was indispensable to him.

The train stopped and let off a few passengers and glided on as if it had never ceased moving. Outside, behind rows of brown rickety houses, a line of blue buildings stood up, and beyond them a pale rose-gray sky faded away to nothing. The train moved into the railroad yard. Looking down, Nelson saw lines and lines of silver tracks multiplying and criss-crossing. Then before he could start counting them, the face in the window stared out at him, gray but distinct, and he looked the other way. The train was in the station. Both he and Mr. Head jumped up and ran to the door. Neither noticed that they had left the paper sack with the lunch in it on the seat.

They walked stiffly through the small station and came out of a heavy door into the squall of traffic. Crowds were hurrying to work. Nelson didn't know where to look. Mr. Head leaned against the side

---

2. "First stop, Emory," station in suburban Atlanta.

of the building and glared in front of him.

Finally Nelson said, "Well, how do you see what all it is to see?"

Mr. Head didn't answer. Then as if the sight of people passing had given him the clue, he said, "You walk," and started off down the street. Nelson followed, steadying his hat. So many sights and sounds were flooding in on him that for the first block he hardly knew what he was seeing. At the second corner, Mr. Head turned and looked behind him at the station they had left, a putty-colored terminal with a concrete dome on top. He thought that if he could keep the dome always in sight, he would be able to get back in the afternoon to catch the train again.

As they walked along, Nelson began to distinguish details and take note of the store windows, jammed with every kind of equipment—hardware, drygoods, chicken feed, liquor. They passed one that Mr. Head called his particular attention to where you walked in and sat on a chair with your feet upon two rests and let a Negro polish your shoes. They walked slowly and stopped and stood at the entrances so he could see what went on in each place but they did not go into any of them. Mr. Head was determined not to go into any city store because on his first trip here, he had got lost in a large one and had found his way out only after many people had insulted him.

They came in the middle of the next block to a store that had a weighing machine in front of it and they both in turn stepped up on it and put in a penny and received a ticket. Mr. Head's ticket said, "You weigh 120 pounds. You are upright and brave and all your friends admire you." He put the ticket in his pocket, surprised that the machine should have got his character correct but his weight wrong, for he had weighed on a grain scale not long before and knew he weighed 110. Nelson's ticket said, "You weigh 98 pounds. You have a great destiny ahead of you but beware of dark women." Nelson did not know any women and he weighed only 68 pounds but Mr. Head pointed out that the machine had probably printed the number upsidedown, meaning the 9 for a 6.

They walked on and at the end of five blocks the dome of the terminal sank out of sight and Mr. Head turned to the left. Nelson could have stood in front of every store window for an hour if there had not been another more interesting one next to it. Suddenly he said, "I was born here!" Mr. Head turned and looked at him with horror. There was a sweaty brightness about his face. "This is where I come from!" he said.

Mr. Head was appalled. He saw the moment had come for drastic action. "Lemme show you one thing you ain't seen yet," he said and took him to the corner where there was a sewer entrance. "Squat down," he said, "and stick you head in there," and he held the back of the boy's coat while he got down and put his head in the sewer. He drew it back quickly, hearing a gurgling in the depths under the sidewalk. Then Mr. Head explained the sewer system, how the entire city was underlined with it, how it contained all the drainage and was full of rats and how a man could slide into it and be sucked along down endless pitchblack tunnels. At any minute any man in the city might be sucked into the sewer and never heard from again. He described it so well that Nelson was for some seconds shaken. He connected the sewer passages with the entrance to hell and understood for the first time how the world was put together in its lower parts. He drew away from the curb.

Then he said, "Yes, but you can stay away from the holes," and his face took on that stubborn look that was so exasperating to his grandfather. "This is where I come from!" he said.

Mr. Head was dismayed but he only muttered, "You'll get your fill," and they walked on. At the end of two more blocks he turned to the left, feeling that he was circling the dome; and he was correct for in a half-hour they passed in front of the railroad station again. At first Nelson did not notice that he was seeing the same stores twice but when they passed the one where you put your feet on the rests while the Negro polished your shoes, he perceived that they were walking in a circle.

"We done been here!" he shouted. "I don't believe you know where you're at!"

"The direction just slipped my mind for a minute," Mr. Head said and they turned down a different street. He still did not intend to let the dome get too far away and after two blocks in their new direction, he turned to the left. This street contained two- and three-story wooden dwellings. Anyone passing on the sidewalk could see into the rooms and Mr. Head, glancing through one window, saw a woman lying on an iron bed, looking out, with a sheet pulled over her. Her knowing expression shook him. A fierce-looking boy on a bicycle came driving down out of nowhere and he had to jump to the side to keep from being hit. "It's nothing to them if they knock you down," he said. "You better keep closer to me."

They walked on for some time on streets like this before he remembered to turn again. The houses they were passing now were all unpainted and the wood in them looked rotten; the street between was narrower. Nelson saw a colored man. Then another. Then another. "Niggers live in these houses," he observed.

"Well come on and we'll go somewhere else," Mr. Head said. "We didn't come to look at niggers," and they turned down another street but they continued to see Negroes everywhere. Nelson's skin began to prickle and they stepped along at a faster pace in order to leave the neighborhood as soon as possible. There were colored men in their undershirts standing in the doors and colored women rocking on the sagging porches. Colored children played in the gutters and stopped what they were doing to look at them. Before long they began to pass rows of stores with colored customers in them but they didn't pause at the entrances of these. Black eyes in black faces were watching them from every direction. "Yes," Mr. Head said, "this is where you were born—right here with all these niggers."

Nelson scowled. "I think you done got us lost," he said.

Mr. Head swung around sharply and looked for the dome. It was nowhere in sight. "I ain't got us lost either," he said. "You're just tired of walking."

"I ain't tired, I'm hungry," Nelson said. "Give me a biscuit."

They discovered then that they had lost the lunch.

"You were the one holding the sack," Nelson said. "I would have kepaholt of it."

"If you want to direct this trip, I'll go on by myself and leave you right here," Mr. Head said and was pleased to see the boy turn white. However, he realized they were lost and drifting farther every minute from the station. He was hungry himself and beginning to be thirsty and since they had been in the colored neighborhood, they had both begun to sweat. Nelson had on his shoes and he was unaccustomed to them. The concrete sidewalks were very hard. They both wanted to find a place to sit down but this was impossible and they kept on walking, the boy muttering under his breath, "First you lost the sack and then you lost the way," and Mr. Head growling from time to time, "Anybody wants to be from this nigger heaven can be from it!"

By now the sun was well forward in the sky. The odor of dinners cooking drifted out to them. The Negroes were all at their doors to see them pass. "Whyn't you ast one of these niggers the way?" Nelson said. "You got us lost."

"This is where you were born," Mr. Head said. "You can ast one yourself if you want to."

Nelson was afraid of the colored men and he didn't want to be laughed at by the colored children. Up ahead he saw a large colored woman leaning in a doorway that opened onto the sidewalk. Her hair stood straight out from her head for about four inches all around and she was resting on bare brown feet that turned pink at the sides. She had on a pink dress that showed her exact shape. As they came abreast of her, she lazily lifted one hand to her head and her fingers disappeared into her hair.

Nelson stopped. He felt his breath drawn up by the woman's dark eyes. "How do you get back to town?" he said in a voice that did not sound like his own.

After a minute she said, "You in town now," in a rich low tone that made Nelson feel as if a cool spray had been turned on him.

"How do you get back to the train?" he said in the same reed-like voice.

"You can catch you a car," she said.

He understood she was making fun of him but he was too paralyzed even to scowl. He stood drinking in every detail of her. His eyes traveled up from her great knees to her forehead and then made a triangular path from the glistening sweat on her neck down and across her tremendous bosom and over her bare arm back to where her fingers lay hidden in her hair. He suddenly wanted her to reach down and pick him up and draw him against her and then he wanted to feel her breath on his face. He wanted to look down and down into her eyes while she held him tighter and tighter. He had never had such a feeling before. He felt as if he were reeling down through a pitchblack tunnel.

"You can go a block down yonder and catch you a car take you to the railroad station, Sugarpie," she said.

Nelson would have collapsed at her feet if Mr. Head had not pulled him roughly away. "You act like you don't have any sense!" the old man growled.

They hurried down the street and Nelson did not look back at the woman. He pushed his hat sharply forward over his face which was already burning with shame. The sneering ghost he had seen in the train window and all the foreboding feelings he had on the way returned to him and he remembered that his ticket from the scale had said to beware of dark women and that his grandfather's had said he was upright and brave. He took hold of the old man's hand, a sign of dependence that he seldom showed.

They headed down the street toward the car tracks where a long yellow rattling trolley was coming. Mr. Head had never boarded a streetcar and he let that one pass. Nelson was silent. From time to time his mouth trembled slightly but his grandfather, occupied with his own problems, paid him no attention. They stood on the corner and neither looked at the Negroes who were passing, going about their business just as if they had been white, except that most of them stopped and eyed Mr. Head and Nelson. It occurred to Mr. Head that since the streetcar ran on tracks, they could simply follow the tracks. He gave Nelson a slight push and explained that they would follow the tracks on into the railroad station, walking, and they set off.

Presently to their great relief they began to see white people again and Nelson sat down on the sidewalk against the wall of a building. "I got to rest myself some," he said. "You lost the sack and the direction. You can just wait on me to rest myself."

"There's the tracks in front of us," Mr. Head said. "All we got to do is keep them in sight and you could have remembered the sack as good as me. This is where you were born. This is your old home town. This is your second trip. You ought to know how to do," and he squatted down and continued in this vein but the boy, easing his burning feet out of his shoes, did not answer.

"And standing there grinning like a chim-pan-zee while a nigger woman gives you directions. Great Gawd!" Mr. Head said.

"I never said I was nothing but born here," the boy said in a shaky voice. "I never said I would or wouldn't like it. I never said I wanted to come. I only said I was born here and I never had nothing to do with that. I want to go home. I never wanted to come in the first place. It was all your big idea. How you know you ain't following the tracks in the wrong direction?"

This last had occurred to Mr. Head too. "All these people are white," he said.

"We ain't passed here before," Nelson said. This was a neighborhood of brick buildings that might have been lived in or might not. A few empty automobiles were parked along the curb and there was an occasional passer-by. The heat of the pavement came up through Nelson's thin suit. His eyelids began to droop, and after a few minutes his head tilted forward. His shoulders twitched once or twice and then he fell over on his side and lay sprawled in an exhausted fit of sleep.

Mr. Head watched him silently. He was very tired himself but they could not both sleep at the same time and he could not have slept anyway because he did not know where he was. In a few minutes Nelson would wake up, refreshed by his sleep and very cocky, and would begin complaining that he had lost the sack and the way. You'd have a mighty sorry time if I wasn't here, Mr. Head thought; and then another idea occurred to him. He looked at the sprawled figure for several minutes; presently he stood up. He justified what he was going to do on the grounds that it is sometimes necessary to teach a child a lesson he won't forget, particularly when the child is always reasserting his position with some new impudence. He walked without a sound to the corner about twenty feet away and sat down on a covered garbage can in the alley where he could look out and watch Nelson wake up alone.

The boy was dozing fitfully, half conscious of vague noises and black forms moving up from some dark part of him into the light. His face worked in his sleep and he had pulled his knees up under his chin. The sun shed a dull dry light on the narrow street; everything looked like exactly what it was. After a while Mr. Head, hunched like an old monkey on the garbage can lid, decided that if Nelson didn't wake up soon, he would make a loud noise by bamming his foot against the can. He looked at his watch and discovered that it was two o'clock. Their train left at six and the possibility of missing it was too awful for him to think of. He kicked his foot backwards on the can and a hollow boom reverberated in the alley.

Nelson shot up onto his feet with a shout. He looked where his grandfather should have been and stared. He seemed to whirl several times and then, picking up his feet and throwing his head back, he dashed down the street like a wild maddened pony. Mr. Head jumped off the can and galloped after but the child was almost out of sight. He saw a streak of gray disappearing diagonally a block ahead. He ran as fast as he could, looking both ways down every intersection, but without sight of him again. Then as he passed the third intersection completely winded, he saw about half a block down the street a scene that stopped him altogether. He crouched behind a trash box to watch and get his bearings.

Nelson was sitting with both legs spread out and by his side lay an elderly woman, screaming. Groceries were scattered about the sidewalk. A crowd of women had already gathered to see justice done and Mr. Head distinctly heard the old woman on the pavement shout, "You've broken my ankle and your daddy'll pay for it! Every nickel! Police! Police!" Several of the women were plucking at Nelson's shoulder but the boy seemed too dazed to get up.

Something forced Mr. Head from behind the trash box and forward, but only at a creeping pace. He had never in his life been accosted by a policeman. The women were milling around Nelson as if they might suddenly all dive on him at once and tear him to pieces, and the old woman continued to scream that her ankle was broken and to call for an officer. Mr. Head came on so slowly that he could have been taking a backward step after each forward one, but when he was about ten feet away, Nelson saw him and sprang. The child caught him around the hips and clung panting against him.

The women all turned on Mr. Head. The injured one sat up and shouted, "You sir! You'll pay every penny of my doctor's bill that your boy has caused. He's a juve-nile delinquent! Where is an officer? Somebody take this man's name and address!"

Mr. Head was trying to detach Nelson's fingers from the flesh in the back of his legs. The old man's head had lowered itself into his collar like a turtle; his eyes were glazed with fear and caution.

"Your boy has broken my ankle!" the old woman shouted. "Police!"

Mr. Head sensed the approach of the policeman from behind. He stared straight ahead at the women who were massed in their fury like a solid wall to block his escape. "This is not my boy," he said. "I never seen him before."

betrayal

He felt Nelson's fingers fall out of his flesh.

The women dropped back, staring at him with horror, as if they were so repulsed by a man who could deny his own image and likeness that they could not bear to lay hands on him. Mr. Head walked on, through a space they silently cleared, and left Nelson behind. Ahead of him he saw nothing but a hollow tunnel that had once been the street.

The boy remained standing where he was, his neck craned forward and his hands hanging by his sides. His hat was jammed on his head so that there were no longer any creases in it. The injured woman got up and shook her fist at him and the others gave him pitying looks, but he didn't notice any of them. There was no policeman in sight.

In a minute he began to move mechanically, making no effort to catch up with his grandfather but merely following at about twenty paces. They walked on for five blocks in this way. Mr. Head's shoulders were sagging and his neck hung forward at such an angle that it was not visible from behind. He was afraid to turn his head. Finally he cut a short hopeful glance over his shoulder. Twenty feet behind him, he saw two small eyes piercing into his back like pitchfork prongs.

The boy was not of a forgiving nature but this was the first time he had ever had anything to forgive. Mr. Head had never disgraced himself before. After two more blocks, he turned and called over his shoulder in a high desperately gay voice, "Let's us go get a Co' Cola somewheres!"

Nelson, with a dignity he had never shown before, turned and stood with his back to his grandfather.

Mr. Head began to feel the depth of his denial. His face as they walked on became all hollows and bare ridges. He saw nothing they were passing but he perceived that they had lost the car tracks. There was no dome to be seen anywhere and the afternoon was advancing. He knew that if dark overtook them in the city, they would be beaten and robbed. The speed of God's justice was only what he expected for himself, but he could not stand to think that his sins would be visited upon Nelson and that even now, he was leading the boy to his doom.

They continued to walk on block after block through an endless section of small brick houses until Mr. Head almost fell over a water spigot sticking up about six inches off the edge of a grass plot. He had not had a drink of water since early morning but he felt he did not deserve it now. Then he thought that Nelson would be thirsty and they would both drink and be brought together. He squatted down and put his mouth to the nozzle and turned a cold stream of water into his throat. Then he called out in the high desperate voice, "Come on and getcher some water!"

This time the child stared through him for nearly sixty seconds. Mr. Head got up and walked on as if he had drunk poison. Nelson, though he had not had water since some he had drunk out of a paper cup on the train, passed by the spigot, disdaining to drink where his grandfather had. When Mr. Head realized this, he lost all hope. His face in the waning afternoon light looked ravaged and abandoned. He could feel the boy's steady hate, traveling at an even pace behind him and he knew that (if by some miracle they escaped being murdered in the city) it would continue just that way for the rest of his life. He knew that now he was wandering into a black strange place where nothing was like it had even been before, a long old age without respect and an end that would be welcome because it would be the end.

As for Nelson, his mind had frozen around his grandfather's treachery as if he were trying to preserve it intact to present at the final judgment. He walked without looking to one side or the other, but every now and then his mouth would twitch and this was when he felt, from some remote place inside himself, a black mysterious form reach up as if it would melt his frozen vision in one hot grasp.

The sun dropped down behind a row of houses and hardly noticing, they passed into an elegant suburban section where mansions were set back from the road by lawns with birdbaths on them. Here everything was entirely deserted. For blocks they didn't pass even a dog. The big white houses were like partially submerged icebergs in the distance. There were no sidewalks, only drives and these wound around and around in endless ridiculous circles. Nelson made no move to come nearer to Mr. Head. The old man felt that if he saw a sewer entrance he would drop down into it and let himself be carried away; and he could imagine the boy standing by, watching with only a slight interest, while he disappeared.

A loud bark jarred him to attention and he looked up to see a fat man approaching with two bulldogs. He waved both arms like someone shipwrecked on a desert island. "I'm lost!" he called. "I'm lost and can't find my way and me and this boy have got to catch this train and I can't find the station. Oh Gawd I'm lost! Oh hep me Gawd I'm lost!"

The man, who was bald-headed and had on golf knickers, asked him what train he was trying to catch and Mr. Head began to get out his tickets, trembling so violently he could hardly hold them. Nelson had come up to within fifteen feet and stood watching.

"Well," the fat man said, giving him back the tickets, "you won't have time to get back to town to make this but you can catch it at the suburb stop. That's three blocks from here," and he began explaining how to get there.

Mr. Head stared as if he were slowly returning from the dead and when the man had finished and gone off with the dogs jumping at his heels, he turned to Nelson and said breathlessly, "We're going to get home!"

The child was standing about ten feet away, his face bloodless under the gray hat. His eyes were triumphantly cold. There was no light in them, no feeling, no interest. He was merely there, a small figure, waiting. Home was nothing to him.

Mr. Head turned slowly. He felt he knew now what time would be like without seasons and what heat would be like without light and what man would be like without salvation. He didn't care if he never made the train and if it had not been for what suddenly caught his attention, like a cry out of the gathering dusk, he might have forgotten there was a station to go to.

He had not walked five hundred yards down the road when he saw, within reach of him, the plaster figure of a Negro sitting bent over on a low yellow brick fence that curved around a wide lawn. The Negro was about Nelson's size and he was pitched forward at an unsteady angle because the putty that held him to the wall had cracked. One of his eyes was entirely white and he held a piece of brown watermelon.

Mr. Head stood looking at him silently until Nelson stopped at a little distance. Then as the two of them stood there, Mr. Head breathed, "An artificial nigger!"

It was not possible to tell if the artificial Negro were meant to be young or old; he looked too miserable to be either. He was meant to look happy because his mouth was stretched up at the corners but the chipped eye and the angle he was cocked at gave him a wild look of misery instead.

"An artificial nigger!" Nelson repeated in Mr. Head's exact tone.

The two of them stood there with their necks forward at almost the same angle and their shoulders curved in almost exactly the same way and their hands trembling identically in their pockets. Mr. Head looked like an ancient child and Nelson like a miniature old man. They stood gazing at the artificial Negro as if they were faced with some great mystery, some monument to another's victory that brought them together in their common defeat. They could both feel it dissolving their differences like an action of mercy. Mr. Head had never known before what mercy felt like because he had been too good to deserve any, but he felt he knew now. He looked at Nelson and understood that he must say something to the child to show that he was still wise and in the look the boy returned he saw a hungry need for that assurance. Nelson's eyes seemed to implore him to explain once and for all the mystery of existence.

Mr. Head opened his lips to make a lofty statement and heard himself say, "They ain't got enough real ones here. They got to have an artificial one."

After a second, the boy nodded with a strange shivering about his mouth, and said, "Let's go home before we get ourselves lost again."

Their train glided into the suburb stop just as they reached the station and they boarded it together, and ten minutes before it was due to arrive at the junction, they went to the door and stood ready to jump off if it did not stop; but it did, just as the moon, restored to its full splendor, sprang from a cloud and flooded the clearing with light. As they stepped off, the sage grass was shivering gently in shades of silver and the clinkers under their feet glittered with a fresh black light. The treetops, fencing the junction like the protecting walls of a garden, were darker than the sky which was hung with gigantic white clouds illuminated like lanterns.

Mr. Head stood very still and felt the action of mercy touch him again but this time he knew that there were no words in the world that could name it. He understood that it grew out of agony, which is not denied to any man and which is given in strange ways to children. He understood it was all a man could carry into death to give his Maker and he suddenly burned with shame that he had so little of it to take with him. He stood appalled, judging himself with the thoroughness of God, while the action of mercy covered his pride like a flame and consumed it. He had never thought himself a great sinner before but he saw now that his true depravity had been hidden from him lest it cause him despair. He realized that he was forgiven for sins from the beginning of time, when he had conceived in his own heart the sin of Adam, until the present, when he had denied poor Nelson. He saw that no sin was too monstrous for him to claim as his own, and since God loved in proportion as He forgave, he felt ready at that instant to enter Paradise.

Nelson, composing his expression under the shadow of his hat brim, watched him with a mixture of fatigue and suspicion, but as the train glided past them and disappeared like a frightened serpent into the woods, even his face lightened and he muttered, "I'm glad I've went once, but I'll never go back again!"

1955

6   THEME

If you ask what a story is "about," an author is likely to answer by telling you the subject. Indeed, many authors tell you the subject in their titles: *An Occurrence at Owl Creek Bridge, The Lottery, Our Friend Judith, Her First Ball*. Though a subject is always concrete, it may be stated at somewhat greater length than the few words of a title: "a man's thoughts as he faces execution for spying during the Civil War" (*Owl Creek Bridge*); "a young girl's excitement at her first grown-up dance and an incident that temporarily depresses her" (*Her First Ball*).

A friend might be more likely to tell you what a story is about by giving you a summary of the action: "This guy shoots a lion but is too chicken to go in and put it out of its misery, so his wife. . . ." (We sometimes call this a **plot summary,** but you will notice that this summary is of the history, of the events in more or less chronological order, while the plot is an arrangement or structuring of that history; in *Macomber*, remember, the lion incident is not told to us first, thought it did happen first.)

Your teacher may well tell you what a story is about by summarizing its **theme.** Some refer to the central idea, the thesis, or even the

portable abstraction

message of a story, and that is roughly what we mean by theme: a generalization or abstraction from the story.

The subject of *Young Goodman Brown* may be said to be a coven (witches' meeting) or, more fully, "a young colonial New England husband is driven mad by finding everyone he thought good and pure attending a witches' meeting." The theme may be "everyone partakes of evil," or, more succinctly, "the Fall." There are, as you can see, degrees of generalization and abstraction; subject (a young man finds that everyone is evil) shades off into theme, which itself can be more or less general and abstract.

Discussions of literature in or out of class sometimes seem to suggest that stories exist for their themes, that we read only to get the "point" or message. But most themes, you must admit, are somewhat less than earth-shattering. That all men and women are evil may be debatable, but it certainly isn't news. That living beings, human and otherwise, should not be divided into exploiters (hunters) and exploited (hunted)—the apparent theme of *The Most Dangerous Game* —is pretty obvious, something we don't need to read fifteen pages of fiction to find out. No wonder, then, that some of our more skeptical friends contend that stories are only elaborate ways of "saying something simple," that literature is a game in which authors hide their meanings under shells of words.

Of course, reading fifteen pages of a story like *The Most Dangerous Game* can be fun. Could it be that we really read fiction for the fun, and all our talk about themes is just hiding from our Puritan natures the fact that we are goofing off?

I don't believe that articulating the theme of a story is either the purpose of or the excuse for reading fiction, or that authors hide their meanings like Easter eggs. In order to relate his or her unique vision of reality to an absent and unknown reader, a writer must find a way of communicating—some common ground on which to meet the various unique individuals who will read the story. Common experiences, common assumptions, common language, and commonplaces offer such ground. Readers reach out from their own subjective worlds toward that new and different vision of the author with the help of the common elements (the general), and especially through the commonplaces of theme, bringing back the particulars and generalizations of the story to their own reading and living experience. The reader sees a spoiled Easterner on safari in Africa overcome his cowardice in an attempt to put a dangerous animal out of its misery. Generalizing, the reader may conclude that what the story says (its theme) is that life (or happy life) is more than survival, that honor is more important than existence, and that when one's values change one's behavior can be changed. Not planning to go on safari in the very near future, the reader may test out the experience of the story by translating it through its theme to his or her own experience: does this mean that I can change long-standing patterns of behavior that I know are wrong? Do I have any ideals I believe greater than life itself?

We should not confuse these questions with the story, but the significance of any story is modified to some extent by the reader's experience of books and life. This does not imply that you are to reduce every story to the dimensions of what you already know and feel, but rather that you reach out to the story and bring it back to your own experience as an addition and modification. If you're going to make a story yours, and if you are going to make it more than a yarn about a guy who drinks a lot, has an unfaithful wife, and hunts lions and water buffaloes, you will translate it somehow into terms that, while not necessarily psychological or moral precepts, alter or broaden to some degree your own vision of yourself, others, life in general.

When I discussed symbols, I said that, even while a symbol suggests a meaning beyond the particulars of the fiction it remains a detail in the fictional world—the snakelike staff of the stranger in *Young Goodman Brown* remains a staff, Judith's cats remain cats. Some critics would say that this is true also of theme and that theme is related to the story as integrally as symbolic meaning is to detail; that is, rather than *Young Goodman Brown* telling us something we did not know before, its theme and its story modify each other. The theme as I've stated it relates to spiritual evil, the kind of evil suggested by the snake and Satan figures. But this theme is not entirely portable—it cannot be taken out of the story and used as substitute for what the story "means"—nor can it, without qualification, be used to explain all the significant details in the story—the facts that Brown is a newly-wed, that Faith wears pink (coquettish?) ribbons, and that she, whom Brown thought so pure and innocent, shows up at the meeting of witches and sinners suggest a more specific kind of evil than the spiritual or theological evil suggested by the snake and Satan: moral or, even more specifically, sexual evil. This means we must modify our definition of the theme. But how? What does the story imply about the relationship of sex and evil? Is all sex evil? Is original sin sexual? Some details—the snake, the Satanic guide—suggest a theme, other details modify it; still others—Brown's behavior after the night of the witches' meeting—may modify it still further, so that the theme, though an approximate version of it may be abstracted from the story, remains embedded in it, ultimately inseparable from the details of plot, character, setting, and symbol.

A statement that can do justice to all the complexity and all the particulars of the story is not likely to take the simple form of a message. Indeed, it is the complex particularity of literature, its ultimate irreducibility, that makes critics and teachers reject *message* (which suggests a simple packaged statement) as a suitable term even for the paraphrasable thematic content of a story.

Young Goodman Brown is an allegorical story whose details do function as symbols with paraphrasable meanings, yet even its theme refuses to be reduced to a simple statement. *How Much Land Does a Man Need?* is a **parable**, a short fiction that illustrates an explicit moral lesson. That lesson, the theme, is implied in the title. (And here the devil appears not only, at times, in disguise, but also in his proper person.) Even so, Tolstoy's story is not without complexity. How do you account for the first section of the story? Does your paraphrase of the theme accommodate the conversation between the sisters there?

Her First Ball is not allegorical and neither is it parabolic. Though realistic, however, it is a short, rather simple story that seems to have a simple theme overtly enunciated by one of the characters: Leila's elderly partner suggests that her first ball is "only the beginning of her last ball." That youth and life itself are fleeting (scarcely a new truth, but one that we must be reminded of from time to time, no doubt) would seem to be the simple theme of this story. But the scene with the elderly partner is not the end of the story. Leila goes on to dance with a young partner, doesn't recognize her former partner, has fun, and seems to have completely forgotten the man's "message." What is the story "saying"? Is her forgetting "bad"? Or "sad"? Or "good"? Does the theme suggest the thoughtlessness of youth, the incommunicability of experience, trapping us in inescapable patterns, dooming us to repeat the experiences of our predecessors? Or is it better for Leila to live while she's young, to make the most of life, rather than dwelling on life's brevity? The specifics of the story modify and enrich all the generalizations we can abstract from it, while these themes and questions, if we recognize them, modify and enrich our reading, our experience of the story.

I realize I have been talking as if a theme or themes spring out at the reader, while to some of you my inference of themes may seem more like pulling rabbits out of hats. *How Much Land Does a Man Need?* does not involve much of a trick: the title asks the question that, once answered, suggests the theme. But there isn't even too much conjuring with *Young Goodman Brown*: I derived the theme of theological evil from the symbols (the snake-staff, Satan figure, names) and I tested physical details—like pink ribbons and the narrative situation (the three-month marriage)—which had sexual implications against the theme to see if I would have to modify my paraphrase. In *Her First Ball* a character raises a general issue that is tested by subsequent events in the story and modified by them. In *The Most Dangerous Game* the opening conversation raises thematic issues (the morality of hunting) that are dramatically reinforced by the subsequent action of the story (Rainsford now the hunted rather than hunter). The title *Beyond the Pale* hints at a theme but too faintly and obliquely to signify until it comes to the surface toward the end of the story. The story itself seems almost to break in half, the first part treating the superficial lives and relationships of four upper-middle-class Britons vacationing in Northern Ireland, the second half threatening to become a political tract about the troubled past and present of Ireland. But Cynthia Strafe, one of the four British vacationers, connects their attitudes towards the strife in Ireland and towards their own lives and conduct in a way that profoundly illuminates the title and theme of the story.

There are, of course, other means by which details suggest generalizations or meaning or by which meaning may be abstracted from detail. You no doubt noticed in *The Most Dangerous Game* the historical allusions—references outside the story, in this case to history but sometimes to literature, the Bible, and so on. Zaroff is a White Russian general, Ivan a Cossack flogger. The time is not long after the

First World War and the Russian Revolution. The theme of hunter and hunted expands into the historical context as exploiter and exploited and the theme seems to support the weak, the underdog, and predict the overthrow of tyrants like Zaroff or the Czar (-ov or -off is a Russian suffix meaning "son of," so Zaroff implies "son" or product of the Czar). So allusion as well as symbols, plot, focus and voice, and character are elements that contribute to and must be accounted for in paraphrasing a theme. That is why theme is important, and why it comes last in a dicussion of the elements of fiction.

But remember, the theme is an inadequate abstraction from the story; the story and its details do not disappear or lose significance once distilled into theme, nor could you reconstruct a story merely from its paraphrased theme. Indeed, theme and story, history and structure, do not so much interact, are not so much interrelated, as they are fused, inseparable.

Is the connection between the private lives of the vacationing Englishmen in *Beyond the Pale* and the Irish "troubles" part of the plot or part of the theme of that story? Is Pahóm's greed a constituent of character or of theme in *How Much Land Does a Man Need*?

Though they are useful, may be necessary, and seem reasonable or even obvious, constructs, the elements of fiction—plot, focus and voice, character, symbol, and theme—do not, in a sense, really exist. They are convenient ways for us to extricate inextricable threads from the fabric of fiction. As the Old Master Henry James said a hundred years ago:

> A novel is a living thing, all one and continuous, like any other organism, and in proportion as it lives will it be found . . . that in each of its parts there is something of each of the other parts. The critic who over the close texture of a finished work shall pretend to trace a geography of items will mark some frontiers as artificial, I fear, as any that have been known to history. . . . What is character but the determination of incident? What is incident but the illustration of character?

LEO TOLSTOY

How Much Land Does a Man Need?*

I

An elder sister came to visit her younger sister in the country. The elder was married to a tradesman in town, the younger to a peasant in the village. As the sisters sat over their tea talking, the elder began to boast of the advantages of town life: saying how comfortably they lived there, how well they dressed, what fine clothes her children wore, what good things they ate and drank, and how she went to the theater, promenades, and entertainments.

---

* Translated by Louise and Aylmer Maude.

The younger sister was piqued, and in turn disparaged the life of a tradesman, and stood up for that of a peasant.

"I would not change my way of life for yours," said she. "We may live roughly, but at least we are free from anxiety. You live in better style than we do, but though you often earn more than you need, you are very likely to lose all you have. You know the proverb, 'Loss and gain are brothers twain.' It often happens that people who are wealthy one day are begging their bread the next. Our way is safer. Though a peasant's life is not a fat one, it is a long one. We shall never grow rich, but we shall always have enough to eat."

The elder sister said sneeringly:

"Enough? Yes, if you like to share with the pigs and the calves! What do you know of elegance or manners! However much your goodman may slave, you will die as you are living—on a dung heap— and your children the same."

"Well, what of that?" replied the younger. "Of course our work is rough and coarse. But, on the other hand, it is sure, and we need not bow to anyone. But you, in your towns, are surrounded by temptations; to-day all may be right, but to-morrow the Evil One may tempt your husband with cards, wine, or women, and all will go to ruin. Don't such things happen often enough?"

Pahóm, the master of the house, was lying on the top of the stove and he listened to the women's chatter.

"It is perfectly true," thought he. "Busy as we are from childhood tilling mother earth, we peasants have no time to let any nonsense settle in our heads. Our only trouble is that we haven't land enough. If I had plenty of land, I shouldn't fear the Devil himself!"

The women finished their tea, chatted a while about dress, and then cleared away the tea-things and lay down to sleep.

But the Devil had been sitting behind the stove, and had heard all that was said. He was pleased that the peasant's wife had led her husband into boasting, and that he had said that if he had plenty of land he would not fear the Devil himself.

"All right," thought the Devil. "We will have a tussle. I'll give you land enough; and by means of that land I will get you into my power."

II

Close to the village there lived a lady, a small land-owner who had an estate of about three hundred acres.[1] She had always lived on good terms with the peasants until she engaged as her steward an old soldier, who took to burdening the people with fines. However careful Pahóm tried to be, it happened again and again that now a horse of his got among the lady's oats, now a cow strayed into her garden, now his calves found their way into her meadows—and he always had to pay a fine.

Pahóm paid up, but grumbled, and going home in a temper, was rough with his family. All through that summer, Pahóm had much

---

1. 120 *desyatíns.* The *desyatína* is properly 2.7 acres but in this story round   numbers are used [Maude note].

trouble because of this steward, and he was even glad when winter came and the cattle had to be stabled. Though he grudged the fodder when they could no longer graze on the pasture-land, at least he was free from anxiety about them.

In the winter the news got about that the lady was going to sell her land and that the keeper of the inn on the high road was bargaining for it. When the peasants heard this they were very much alarmed.

"Well," thought they, "if the innkeeper gets the land, he will worry us with fines worse than the lady's steward. We all depend on that estate."

So the peasants went on behalf of their Commune, and asked the lady not to sell the land to the innkeeper, offering her a better price for it themselves. The lady agreed to let them have it. Then the peasants tried to arrange for the Commune to buy the whole estate, so that it might be held by them all in common. They met twice to discuss it, but could not settle the matter; the Evil One sowed discord among them and they could not agree. So they decided to buy the land individually, each according to his means; and the lady agreed to this plan as she had to the other.

Presently Pahóm heard that a neighbor of his was buying fifty acres, and that the lady had consented to accept one half in cash and to wait a year for the other half. Pahóm felt envious.

"Look at that," thought he, "the land is all being sold, and I shall get none of it." So he spoke to his wife.

"Other people are buying," said he, "and we must also buy twenty acres or so. Life is becoming impossible. That steward is simply crushing us with his fines."

So they put their heads together and considered how they could manage to buy it. They had one hundred rúbles[2] laid by. They sold a colt and one half of their bees, hired out one of their sons as a laborer and took his wages in advance; borrowed the rest from a brother-in-law, and so scraped together half the purchase money.

Having done this, Pahóm chose out a farm of forty acres, some of it wooded, and went to the lady to bargain for it. They came to an agreement, and he shook hands with her upon it and paid her a deposit in advance. Then they went to town and signed the deeds; he paying half the price down, and undertaking to pay the remainder within two years.

So now Pahóm had land of his own. He borrowed seed, and sowed it on the land he had bought. The harvest was a good one, and within a year he had managed to pay off his debts both to the lady and to his brother-in-law. So he became a landowner, plowing and sowing his own land, making hay on his own land, cutting his own trees, and feeding his cattle on his own pasture. When he went out to plow his fields, or to look at his growing corn, or at his grass-meadows, his heart would fill with joy. The grass that grew and the flowers that bloomed there seemed to him unlike any that grew elsewhere. Formerly, when he had passed by that land, it had appeared the same as any other land, but now it seemed quite different.

2. That is, about fifty dollars.

III

So Pahóm was well-contented, and everything would have been right if the neighboring peasants would only not have trespassed on his corn-fields and meadows. He appealed to them most civilly, but they still went on: now the Communal herdsmen would let the village cows stray into his meadows, then horses from the night pasture would get among his corn. Pahóm turned them out again and again, and forgave their owners, and for a long time he forbore to prosecute anyone. But at last he lost patience and complained to the District Court. He knew it was the peasants' want of land, and no evil intent on their part, that caused the trouble, but he thought:

"I cannot go on overlooking it or they will destroy all I have. They must be taught a lesson."

So he had them up, gave them one lesson, and then another, and two or three of the peasants were fined. After a time Pahóm's neighbors began to bear him a grudge for this, and would now and then let their cattle on to his land on purpose. One peasant even got into Pahóm's wood at night and cut down five young lime trees for their bark. Pahóm passing through the wood one day noticed something white. He came nearer and saw the stripped trunks lying on the ground, and close by stood the stumps where the trees had been. Pahóm was furious.

"If he had only cut one here and there it would have been bad enough," thought Pahóm, "but the rascal has actually cut down a whole clump. If I could only find out who did this, I would pay him out."

He racked his brains as to who it could be. Finally he decided: "It must be Simon—no one else could have done it." So he went to Simon's homestead to have a look round, but he found nothing, and only had an angry scene. However, he now felt more certain than ever that Simon had done it, and he lodged a complaint. Simon was summoned. The case was tried, and retried, and at the end of it all Simon was acquitted, there being no evidence against him. Pahóm felt still more aggrieved, and let his anger loose upon the Elder and the Judges.

"You let thieves grease your palms," said he. "If you were honest folk yourselves you would not let a thief go free."

So Pahóm quarreled with the Judges and with his neighbors. Threats to burn his building began to be uttered. So though Pahóm had more land, his place in the Commune was much worse than before.

About this time a rumor got about that many people were moving to new parts.

"There's no need for me to leave my land," thought Pahóm. "But some of the others might leave our village and then there would be more room for us. I would take over their land myself and make my estate a bit bigger. I could then live more at ease. As it is, I am still too cramped to be comfortable."

One day Pahóm was sitting at home when a peasant, passing through the village, happened to call in. He was allowed to stay the night, and supper was given him. Pahóm had a talk with this peasant and asked him where he came from. The stranger answered that he came from beyond the Vólga, where he had been working. One word led to another, and the man went on to say that many people were settling in those parts. He told how some people from his village had settled there. They had joined the Commune, and had had twenty-five acres per man granted them. The land was so good, he said, that the rye sown on it grew as high as a horse, and so thick that five cuts of a sickle made a sheaf. One peasant, he said, had brought nothing with him but his bare hands, and now he had six horses and two cows of his own.

Pahóm's heart kindled with desire. He thought:

"Why should I suffer in this narrow hole, if one can live so well elsewhere? I will sell my land and my homestead here, and with the money I will start afresh over there and get everything new. In this crowded place one is always having trouble. But I must first go and find out all about it myself."

Towards summer he got ready and started. He went down the Vólga on a steamer to Samára, then walked another three hundred miles on foot, and at last reached the place. It was just as the stranger had said. The peasants had plenty of land: every man had twenty-five acres of Communal land given him for his use, and any one who had money could buy, besides, at two shillings an acre[3] as much good freehold land as he wanted.

Having found out all he wished to know, Pahóm returned home as autumn came on, and began selling off his belongings. He sold his land at a profit, sold his homestead and all his cattle, and withdrew from membership of the Commune. He only waited till the spring, and then started with his family for the new settlement.

IV

As soon as Pahóm and his family reached their new abode, he applied for admission into the Commune of a large village. He stood treat to the Elders and obtained the necessary documents. Five shares of Communal land were given him for his own and his sons' use: that is to say—125 acres (not all together, but in different fields) besides the use of the Communal pasture. Pahóm put up the buildings he needed, and bought cattle. Of the Communal land alone he had three times as much as at his former home, and the land was good corn-land. He was ten times better off than he had been. He had plenty of arable land and pasturage, and could keep as many head of cattle as he liked.

At first, in the bustle of building and settling down, Pahóm was pleased with it all, but when he got used to it he began to think that even here he had not enough land. The first year, he sowed wheat on his share of the Communal land and had a good crop. He wanted to go on sowing wheat, but had not enough Communal land for the purpose, and what he had already used was not available; for in those parts wheat is only sown on virgin soil or on fallow land. It is sown for one or two years, and then the land lies fallow till it is again overgrown with prairie grass. There were many who wanted such land and there was not enough for all; so that people quarreled about it.

---

3. Three rubles per *desyatína* [Maude note]; that is, about a half-dollar an acre.

Those who were better off wanted it for growing wheat, and those who were poor wanted it to let to dealers, so that they might raise money to pay their taxes. Pahóm wanted to sow more wheat, so he rented land from a dealer for a year. He sowed much wheat and had a fine crop, but the land was too far from the village—the wheat had to be carted more than ten miles. After a time Pahóm noticed that some peasant-dealers were living on separate farms and were growing wealthy; and he thought:

"If I were to buy some freehold land and have a homestead on it, it would be a different thing altogether. Then it would all be nice and compact."

The question of buying freehold land recurred to him again and again.

He went on in the same way for three years, renting land and sowing wheat. The seasons turned out well and the crops were good, so that he began to lay money by. He might have gone on living contentedly, but he grew tired of having to rent other people's land every year, and having to scramble for it. Wherever there was good land to be had, the peasants would rush for it and it was taken up at once, so that unless you were sharp about it you got none. It happened in the third year that he and a dealer together rented a piece of pasture land from some peasants; and they had already plowed it up, when there was some dispute and the peasants went to law about it, and things fell out so that the labor was all lost.

"If it were my own land," thought Pahóm, "I should be independent, and there would not be all this unpleasantness."

So Pahóm began looking out for land which he could buy; and he came across a peasant who had bought thirteen hundred acres, but having got into difficulties was willing to sell again cheap. Pahóm bargained and haggled with him, and at last they settled the price at 1,500 rúbles, part in cash and part to be paid later. They had all but clinched the matter when a passing dealer happened to stop at Pahóm's one day to get a feed for his horses. He drank tea with Pahóm and they had a talk. The dealer said that he was just returning from the land of the Baskírs,[4] far away, where he had bought thirteen thousand acres of land, all for 1,000 rúbles. Pahóm questioned him further, and the tradesman said:

"All one need do is to make friends with the chiefs. I gave away about one hundred rúbles' worth of silk robes and carpets, besides a case of tea, and I gave wine to those who would drink it; and I got the land for less than a penny an acre."[5] And he showed Pahóm the title-deeds, saying:

"The land lies near a river, and the whole prairie is virgin soil."

Pahóm plied him with questions, and the tradesman said:

"There is more land there than you could cover if you walked a year, and it all belongs to the Bashkírs. They are as simple as sheep, and land can be got almost for nothing."

4. Extreme eastern European Russia, extending southwest from the Ural mountains; the land is chiefly steppes with fertile meadows in the valleys.

5. Five *kopeks* for a *desyatina* [Maude note]. There are 100 *kopeks* to the *rúble*. The English penny (240 to the pound) was roughly equal to two American cents.

"There now," thought Pahóm, "with my one thousand rúbles, why should I get only thirteen hundred acres, and saddle myself with a debt besides? If I take it out there, I can get more than ten times as much for the money."

V

Pahóm inquired how to get to the place, and as soon as the tradesman had left him, he prepared to go there himself. He left his wife to look after the homestead, and started on his journey taking his man with him. They stopped at a town on their way and bought a case of tea, some wine, and other presents, as the tradesman had advised. On and on they went until they had gone more than three hundred miles, and on the seventh day they came to a place where the Bashkírs had pitched their tents. It was all just as the tradesman had said. The people lived on the steppes, by a river, in felt-covered tents. They neither tilled the ground, nor ate bread. Their cattle and horses grazed in herds on the steppe. The colts were tethered behind the tents, and the mares were driven to them twice a day. The mares were milked, and from the milk kumiss was made. It was the women who prepared kumiss, and they also made cheese. As far as the men were concerned, drinking kumiss and tea, eating mutton, and playing on their pipes was all they cared about. They were all stout and merry, and all the summer long they never thought of doing any work. They were quite ignorant, and knew no Russian, but were good-natured enough.

As soon as they saw Pahóm, they came out of their tents and gathered round their visitor. An interpreter was found, and Pahóm told them he had come about some land. The Bashkírs seemed very glad; they took Pahóm and led him into one of the best tents, where they made him sit on some down cushions placed on a carpet, while they sat round him. They gave him some tea and kumiss, and had a sheep killed, and gave him mutton to eat. Pahóm took presents out of his cart and distributed them among the Bashkírs, and divided the tea amongst them. The Bashkírs were delighted. They talked a great deal among themselves, and then told the interpreter to translate.

"They wish to tell you," said the interpreter, "that they like you, and that it is our custom to do all we can to please a guest and to repay him for his gifts. You have given us presents, now tell us which of the things we possess please you best, that we may present them to you."

"What pleases me best here," answered Pahóm, "is your land. Our land is crowded and the soil is exhausted; but you have plenty of land and it is good land. I never saw the like of it."

The interpreter translated. The Bashkírs talked among themselves for a while. Pahóm could not understand what they were saying, but saw that they were much amused and that they shouted and laughed. Then they were silent and looked at Pahóm while the interpreter said:

"They wish me to tell you that in return for your presents they will gladly give you as much land as you want. You have only to point it out with your hand and it is yours."

The Bashkírs talked again for a while and began to dispute. Pahóm asked what they were disputing about, and the interpreter told him that some of them thought they ought to ask their Chief about the land and not act in his absence, while others thought there was no need to wait for his return.

VI

While the Bashkírs were disputing, a man in a large fox-fur cap appeared on the scene. They all became silent and rose to their feet. The interpreter said, "This is our Chief himself."

Pahóm immediately fetched the best dressing-gown and five pounds of tea, and offered these to the Chief. The Chief accepted them, and seated himself in the place of honor. The Bashkírs at once began telling him something. The Chief listened for a while, then made a sign with his head for them to be silent, and addressing himself to Pahóm, said in Russian:

"Well, let it be so. Choose whatever piece of land you like; we have plenty of it."

"How can I take as much as I like?" thought Pahóm. "I must get a deed to make it secure, or else they may say, 'It is yours,' and afterwards may take it away again."

"Thank you for your kind words," he said aloud. "You have much land, and I only want a little. But I should like to be sure which bit is mine. Could it not be measured and made over to me? Life and death are in God's hands. You good people give it to me, but your children might wish to take it away again."

"You are quite right," said the Chief. "We will make it over to you."

"I heard that a dealer had been here," continued Pahóm, "and that you gave him a little land, too, and signed title-deeds to that effect. I should like to have it done in the same way."

The Chief understood.

"Yes," replied he, "that can be done quite easily. We have a scribe, and we will go to town with you and have the deed properly sealed."

"And what will be the price?" asked Pahóm.

'Our price is always the same: one thousand rúbles a day."

Pahóm did not understand.

"A day? What measure is that? How many acres would that be?"

"We do not know how to reckon it out," said the Chief. "We sell it by the day. As much as you can go round on your feet in a day is yours, and the price is one thousand rúbles a day."

Pahóm was surprised.

"But in a day you can get round a large tract of land," he said.

The Chief laughed.

"It will all be yours!" said he. "But there is one condition: If you don't return on the same day to the spot whence you started, your money is lost."

"But how am I to mark the way that I have gone?"

"Why, we shall go to any spot you like, and stay there. You must start from that spot and make your round, taking a spade with you.

Wherever you think necessary, make a mark. At every turning, dig a hole and pile up the turf; then afterwards we will go round with a plow from hole to hole. You may make as large a circuit as you please, but before the sun sets you must return to the place you started from. All the land you cover will be yours."

Pahóm was delighted. It was decided to start early next morning. They talked a while, and after drinking some more kumiss and eating some more mutton, they had tea again, and then the night came on. They gave Pahóm a feather-bed to sleep on, and the Bashkírs dispersed for the night, promising to assemble the next morning at daybreak and ride out before sunrise to the appointed spot.

VII

Pahóm lay on the feather-bed, but could not sleep. He kept thinking about the land.

"What a large tract I will mark off!" thought he. "I can easily do thirty-five miles in a day. The days are long now, and within a circuit of thirty-five miles what a lot of land there will be! I will sell the poorer land, or let it to peasants, but I'll pick out the best and farm it. I will buy two ox-teams, and hire two more laborers. About a hundred and fifty acres shall be plow-land, and I will pasture cattle on the rest."

Pahóm lay awake all night, and dozed off only just before dawn. Hardly were his eyes closed when he had a dream. He thought he was lying in that same tent and heard somebody chuckling outside. He wondered who it could be, and rose and went out, and he saw the Bashkír Chief sitting in front of the tent holding his sides and rolling about with laughter. Going nearer to the Chief, Pahóm asked: "What are you laughing at?" But he saw that it was no longer the Chief, but the dealer who had recently stopped at his house and had told him about the land. Just as Pahóm was going to ask, "Have you been here long?" he saw that it was not the dealer, but the peasant who had come up from the Vólga, long ago, to Pahóm's old home. Then he saw that it was not the peasant either, but the Devil himself with hoofs and horns, sitting there and chuckling, and before him lay a man barefoot, prostrate on the ground, with only trousers and a shirt on. And Pahóm dreamt that he looked more attentively to see what sort of a man it was that was lying there, and he saw that the man was dead, and that it was himself! He awoke horror-struck.

"What things one does dream," thought he.

Looking round he saw through the open door that the dawn was breaking.

"It's time to wake them up," thought he. "We ought to be starting."

He got up, roused his man (who was sleeping in his cart), bade him harness; and went to call the Bashkírs.

"It's time to go to the steppe to measure the land," he said.

The Bashkírs rose and assembled, and the Chief came too. Then they began drinking kumiss again, and offered Pahóm some tea, but he would not wait.

"If we are to go, let us go. It is high time," said he.

VIII

The Bashkírs got ready and they all started: some mounted on horses, and some in carts. Pahóm drove in his own small cart with his servant and took a spade with him. When they reached the steppe, the morning red was beginning to kindle. They ascended a hillock (called by the Bashkírs a *shikhan*) and dismounting from their carts and their horses, gathered in one spot. The Chief came up to Pahóm and stretching out his arm towards the plain:

"See," said he, "all this, as far as your eye can reach, is ours. You may have any part of it you like."

Pahóm's eyes glistened: it was all virgin soil, as flat as the palm of your hand, as black as the seed of a poppy, and in the hollows different kinds of grasses grew breast high.

The Chief took off his fox-fur cap, placed it on the ground and said:

"This will be the mark. Start from here, and return here again. All the land you go round shall be yours."

Pahóm took out his money and put it on the cap. Then he took off his outer coat, remaining in his sleeveless under-coat. He unfastened his girdle and tied it tight below his stomach, put a little bag of bread into the breast of his coat, and tying a flask of water to his girdle, he drew up the tops of his boots, took the spade from his man, and stood ready to start. He considered for some moments which way he had better go—it was tempting everywhere.

"No matter," he concluded, "I will go towards the rising sun."

He turned his face to the east, stretched himself, and waited for the sun to appear above the rim.

"I must lose no time," he thought, "and it is easier walking while it is still cool."

The sun's rays had hardly flashed above the horizon, before Pahóm, carrying the spade over his shoulder, went down into the steppe.

Pahóm started walking neither slowly nor quickly. After having gone a thousand yards he stopped, dug a hole, and placed pieces of turf one on another to make it more visible. Then he went on; and now that he had walked off his stiffness he quickened his pace. After a while he dug another hole.

Pahóm looked back. The hillock could be distinctly seen in the sunlight, with the people on it, and the glittering tires of the cart-wheels. At a rough guess Pahóm concluded that he had walked three miles. It was growing warmer; he took off his under-coat, flung it across his shoulder, and went on again. It had grown quite warm now; he looked at the sun, it was time to think of breakfast.

"The first shift is done, but there are four in a day, and it is too soon yet to turn. But I will just take off my boots," said he to himself.

He sat down, took off his boots, stuck them into his girdle, and went on. It was easy walking now.

"I will go on for another three miles," thought he, "and then turn to the left. This spot is so fine, that it would be a pity to lose it. The further one goes, the better the land seems."

He went straight on for a while, and when he looked round, the hillock was scarcely visible and the people on it looked like black ants, and he could just see something glistening there in the sun.

"Ah," thought Pahóm, "I have gone far enough in this direction, it is time to turn. Besides I am in a regular sweat, and very thirsty."

He stopped, dug a large hole, and heaped up pieces of turf. Next he untied his flask, had a drink, and then turned sharply to the left. He went on and on; the grass was high, and it was very hot.

Pahóm began to grow tired: he looked at the sun and saw that it was noon.

"Well," he thought, "I must have a rest."

He sat down, and ate some bread and drank some water; but he did not lie down, thinking that if he did he might fall asleep. After sitting a little while, he went on again. At first he walked easily: the food had strengthened him; but it had become terribly hot and he felt sleepy, still he went on, thinking: "An hour to suffer, a life-time to live."

He went a long way in this direction also, and was about to turn to the left again, when he perceived a damp hollow: "It would be a pity to leave that out," he thought. "Flax would do well there." So he went on past the hollow, and dug a hole on the other side of it before he turned the corner. Pahóm looked towards the hillock. The heat made the air hazy: it seemed to be quivering, and through the haze the people on the hillock could scarcely be seen.

"Ah!" thought Pahóm, "I have made the sides too long; I must make this one shorter." And he went along the third side, stepping faster. He looked at the sun: it was nearly half-way to the horizon, and he had not yet done two miles of the third side of the square. He was still ten miles from the goal.

"No," he thought, "though it will make my land lop-sided, I must hurry back in a straight line now. I might go too far, and as it is I have a great deal of land."

So Pahóm hurriedly dug a hole, and turned straight towards the hillock.

IX

Pahóm went straight towards the hillock, but he now walked with difficulty. He was done up with the heat, his bare feet were cut and bruised, and his legs began to fail. He longed to rest, but it was impossible if he meant to get back before sunset. The sun waits for no man, and it was sinking lower and lower.

"Oh dear," he thought, "if only I have not blundered trying for too much! What if I am too late?"

He looked towards the hillock and at the sun. He was still far from his goal, and the sun was already near the rim.

Pahóm walked on and on; it was very hard walking but he went quicker and quicker. He pressed on, but was still far from the place. He began running, threw away his coat, his boots, his flask, and his cap, and kept only the spade which he used as a support.

"What shall I do," he thought again, "I have grasped too much and ruined the whole affair. I can't get there before the sun sets."

And this fear made him still more breathless. Pahóm went on running, his soaking shirt and trousers stuck to him and his mouth was parched. His breast was working like a blacksmith's bellows, his heart was beating like a hammer, and his legs were giving way as if they did not belong to him. Pahóm was seized with terror lest he should die of the strain.

Though afraid of death, he could not stop. "After having run all that way they will call me a fool if I stop now," thought he. And he ran on and on, and drew near and heard the Bashkírs yelling and shouting to him, and their cries inflamed his heart still more. He gathered his last strength and ran on.

The sun was close to the rim, and cloaked in mist looked large, and red as blood. Now, yes now, it was about to set! The sun was quite low, but he was also quite near his aim. Pahóm could already see the people on the hillock waving their arms to hurry up. He could see the fox-fur cap on the ground and the money on it, and the Chief sitting on the ground holding his sides. And Pahóm remembered his dream.

"There is plenty of land," thought he, "but will God let me live on it? I have lost my life, I have lost my life! I shall never reach that spot!"

Pahóm looked at the sun, which had reached the earth: one side of it had already disappeared. With all his remaining strength he rushed on, bending his body forward so that his legs could hardly follow fast enough to keep him from falling. Just as he reached the hillock it suddenly grew dark. He looked up—the sun had already set! He gave a cry: "All my labor has been in vain," thought he, and was about to stop, but he heard the Bashkírs still shouting, and remembered that though to him, from below, the sun seemed to have set, they on the hillock could still see it. He took a long breath and ran up the hillock. It was still light there. He reached the top and saw the cap. Before it sat the Chief laughing and holding his sides. Again Pahóm remembered his dream, and he uttered a cry: his legs gave way beneath him, he fell forward and reached the cap with his hands.

"Ah, that's a fine fellow!" exclaimed the Chief. "He has gained much land!"

Pahóm's servant came running up and tried to raise him, but he saw that blood was flowing from his mouth. Pahóm was dead!

The Bashkírs clicked their tongues to show their pity.

His servant picked up the spade and dug a grave long enough for Pahóm to lie in, and buried him in it. Six feet from his head to his heels was all he needed.

1886

KATHERINE MANSFIELD

Her First Ball

Exactly when the ball began Leila would have found it hard to say. Perhaps her first real partner was the cab. It did not matter that she shared the cab with the Sheridan girls and their brother. She sat back in her own little corner of it, and the bolster on which her hand rested felt like the sleeve of an unknown young man's dress suit; and away they bowled, past waltzing lampposts and houses and fences and trees.

"Have you really never been to a ball before, Leila? But, my child, how too weird—" cried the Sheridan girls.

"Our nearest neighbor was fifteen miles," said Leila softly, gently opening and shutting her fan.

Oh, dear, how hard it was to be indifferent like the others! She tried not to smile too much; she tried not to care. But every single thing was so new and exciting . . . Meg's tuberoses, Jose's long loop of amber, Laura's little dark head, pushing above her white fur like a flower through snow. She would remember for ever. It even gave her a pang to see her cousin Laurie throw away the wisps of tissue paper he pulled from the fastenings of his new gloves. She would like to have kept those wisps as a keepsake, as a remembrance. Laurie leaned forward and put his hand on Laura's knee.

"Look here, darling," he said. "The third and the ninth as usual. Twig?"

Oh, how marvellous to have a brother! In her excitement Leila felt that if there had been time, if it hadn't been impossible, she couldn't have helped crying because she was an only child, and no brother had ever said "Twig?" to her; no sister would ever say, as Meg said to Jose that moment, "I've never known your hair go up more successfully than it has tonight!"

But, of course, there was no time. They were at the drill hall already; there were cabs in front of them and cabs behind. The road was bright on either side with moving fan-like lights, and on the pavement gay couples seemed to float through the air; little satin shoes chased each other like birds.

"Hold on to me, Leila; you'll get lost," said Laura.

"Come on, girls, let's make a dash for it," said Laurie.

Leila put two fingers on Laura's pink velvet cloak, and they were somehow lifted past the big golden lantern, carried along the passage, and pushed into the little room marked "Ladies." Here the crowd was so great there was hardly space to take off their things; the noise was deafening. Two benches on either side were stacked high with wraps. Two old women in white aprons ran up and down tossing fresh armfuls. And everybody was pressing forward trying to get at the little dressing table and mirror at the far end.

A great quivering jet of gas lighted the ladies' room. It couldn't wait; it was dancing already. When the door opened again and there came a burst of tuning from the drill hall, it leaped almost to the ceiling.

Dark girls, fair girls were patting their hair, tying ribbons again, tucking handkerchiefs down the fronts of their bodices, smoothing marble-white gloves. And because they were all laughing it seemed to Leila that they were all lovely.

"Aren't there any invisible hairpins?" cried a voice. "How most extraordinary! I can't see a single invisible hairpin."

"Powder my back, there's a darling," cried some one else.

"But I must have a needle and cotton. I've torn simply miles and miles of the frill," wailed a third.

Then, "Pass them along, pass them along!" The straw basket of programs was tossed from arm to arm. Darling little pink-and-silver programs, with pink pencils and fluffy tassels. Leila's fingers shook as she took one out of the basket. She wanted to ask someone, "Am I meant to have one too?" but she had just time to read: "Waltz 3. *Two, Two in a Canoe*. Polka 4. *Making the Feathers Fly*," when Meg cried, "Ready, Leila?" and they pressed their way through the crush in the passage towards the big double doors of the drill hall.

Dancing had not begun yet, but the band had stopped tuning, and the noise was so great it seemed that when it did begin to play it would never be heard. Leila, pressing close to Meg, looking over Meg's shoulder, felt that even the little quivering colored flags strung across the ceiling were talking. She quite forgot to be shy; she forgot how in the middle of dressing she had sat down on the bed with one shoe off and one shoe on and begged her mother to ring up her cousins and say she couldn't go after all. And the rush of longing she had had to be sitting on the veranda of their forsaken upcountry home, listening to the baby owls crying "More pork" in the moonlight, was changed to a rush of joy so sweet that it was hard to bear alone. She clutched her fan, and, gazing at the gleaming, golden floor, the azaleas, the lanterns, the stage at one end with its red carpet and gilt chairs and the band in a corner, she thought breathlessly, "How heavenly; how simply heavenly!"

All the girls stood grouped together at one side of the doors, the men at the other, and the chaperones in dark dresses, smiling rather foolishly, walked with little careful steps over the polished floor towards the stage.

"This is my little country cousin Leila. Be nice to her. Find her partners; she's under my wing," said Meg, going up to one girl after another.

Strange faces smiled at Leila—sweetly, vaguely. Strange voices answered, "Of course, my dear." But Leila felt the girls didn't really see her. They were looking towards the men. Why didn't the men begin? What were they waiting for? There they stood, smoothing their gloves, patting their glossy hair and smiling among themselves. Then, quite suddenly, as if they had only just made up their minds that that was what they had to do, the men came gliding over the parquet. There was a joyful flutter among the girls. A tall, fair man flew up to Meg, seized her program, scribbled something; Meg passed him on to Leila. "May I have the pleasure?" He ducked and smiled. There came a dark man wearing an eyeglass, then cousin Laurie with a friend, and Laura with a little freckled fellow whose tie was crooked. Then quite an old man—fat, with a big bald patch on his head—took her program and murmured, "Let me see, let me see!" And he was a long time comparing his program, which looked black with names, with hers. It seemed to give him so much trouble that Leila was ashamed. "Oh, please don't bother," she said eagerly. But instead of replying the fat man wrote something, glanced at her again. "Do I remember this bright little face?" he said softly. "Is it known to me of yore?" At that moment the band began playing; the fat man disappeared. He was tossed away on a great wave of music that came flying over the gleaming floor, breaking the groups up into couples, scattering them, sending them spinning. . . .

Leila had learned to dance at boarding school. Every Saturday afternoon the boarders were hurried off to a little corrugated iron mission hall where Miss Eccles (of London) held her "select" classes. But the difference between that dusty-smelling hall—with calico texts on the walls, the poor terrified little woman in a brown velvet toque with rabbit's ears thumping the cold piano, Miss Eccles poking the girls' feet with her long white wand—and this was so tremendous that Leila was sure if her partner didn't come and she had to listen to that marvelous music and to watch the others sliding, gliding over the golden floor, she would die at least, or faint, or lift her arms and fly out of one of those dark windows that showed the stars.

"Ours, I think—" Some one bowed, smiled, and offered her his arm; she hadn't to die after all. Some one's hand pressed her waist, and she floated away like a flower that is tossed into a pool.

"Quite a good floor, isn't it?" drawled a faint voice close to her ear.

"I think it's most beautifully slippery," said Leila.

"Pardon!" The faint voice sounded surprised. Leila said it again. And there was a tiny pause before the voice echoed, "Oh, quite!" and she was swung round again.

He steered so beautifully. That was the great difference between dancing with girls and men, Leila decided. Girls banged into each other, and stamped on each other's feet; the girl who was gentleman always clutched you so.

The azaleas were separate flowers no longer; they were pink and white flags streaming by.

"Were you at the Bells' last week." the voice came again. It sounded tired. Leila wondered whether she ought to ask him if he would like to stop.

"No, this is my first dance," said she.

Her partner gave a little gasping laugh. "Oh, I say," he protested.

"Yes, it is really the first dance I've ever been to." Leila was most fervent. It was such a relief to be able to tell somebody. "You see, I've lived in the country all my life up until now. . . ."

At that moment the music stopped, and they went to sit on two chairs against the wall. Leila tucked her pink satin feet under and fanned herself, while she blissfully watched the other couples passing and disappearing through the swing doors.

"Enjoying yourself, Leila?" asked Jose, nodding her golden head.

Laura passed and gave her the faintest little wink; it made Leila wonder for a moment whether she was quite grown up after all. Certainly her partner did not say very much. He coughed, tucked his handkerchief away, pulled down his waistcoat, took a minute thread off his sleeve. But it didn't matter. Almost immediately the band started, and her second partner seemed to spring from the ceiling.

"Floor's not bad," said the new voice. Did one always begin with the floor? And then, "Were you at the Neaves' on Tuesday?" And again Leila explained. Perhaps it was a little strange that her partners were not more interested. For it was thrilling. Her first ball! She was only at the beginning of everything. It seemed to her that she had never known what the night was like before. Up till now it had been dark, silent, beautiful very often—oh, yes—but mournful somehow. Solemn. And now it would never be like that again—it had opened dazzling bright.

"Care for an ice?" said her partner. And they went through the swing doors, down the passage, to the supper room. Her cheeks burned, she was fearfully thirsty. How sweet the ices looked on little glass plates, and how cold the frosted spoon was, iced too! And when they came back to the hall there was the fat man waiting for her by the door. It gave her quite a shock again to see how old he was; he ought to have been on the stage with the fathers and mothers. And when Leila compared him with her other partners he looked shabby. His waistcoat was creased, there was a button off his glove, his coat looked as if it was dusty with French chalk.

'Come along, little lady," said the fat man. He scarcely troubled to clasp her, and they moved away so gently, it was more like walking than dancing. But he said not a word about the floor. "Your first dance, isn't it?" he murmured.

"How *did* you know?"

"Ah," said the fat man, "that's what it is to be old!" He wheezed faintly as he steered her past an awkward couple. "You see, I've been doing this kind of thing for the last thirty years."

"Thirty years?" cried Leila. Twelve years before she was born!

"It hardly bears thinking about, does it?" said the fat man gloomily. Leila looked at his bald head, and she felt quite sorry for him.

"I think it's marvelous to be still going on," she said kindly.

"Kind little lady," said the fat man, and he pressed her a little closer, and hummed a bar of the waltz. "Of course," he said, "you can't hope to last anything like as long as that. No-o," said the fat man, "long before that you'll be sitting up there on the stage, looking on, in your nice black velvet. And these pretty arms will have turned into little short fat ones, and you'll beat time with such a different kind of fan—a black bony one." The fat man seemed to shudder. "And you'll smile away like the poor old dears up there, and point to your daughter, and tell the elderly lady next to you how some dreadful man tried to kiss her at the club ball. And your heart will ache, ache"—the fat man squeezed her closer still, as if he really was sorry for that poor heart—"because no one wants to kiss you now. And you'll say how unpleasant these polished floors are to walk on, how dangerous they are. Eh, Mademoiselle Twinkletoes?" said the fat man softly.

Leila gave a light little laugh, but she did not feel like laughing. Was it—could it all be true? It sounded terribly true. Was this first ball only the beginning of her last ball after all? At that the music seemed to change; it sounded sad, sad it rose upon a great sigh. Oh, how quickly things changed! Why didn't happiness last for ever? For ever wasn't a bit too long.

"I want to stop," she said in a breathless voice. The fat man led her to the door.

"No," she said, "I won't go outside. I won't sit down. I'll just stand here, thank you." She leaned against the wall, tapping with her foot, pulling up her gloves and trying to smile. But deep inside her a little girl threw her pinafore over her head and sobbed. Why had he spoiled it all?

"I say, you know," said the fat man, "you mustn't take me seriously, little lady."

"As if I should!" said Leila, tossing her small dark head and sucking her underlip. . . .

Again the couples paraded. The swing doors opened and shut. Now new music was given out by the bandmaster. But Leila didn't want to dance any more. She wanted to be home, or sitting on the veranda listening to those baby owls. When she looked through the dark windows at the stars, they had long beams like wings. . . .

But presently a soft, melting, ravishing tune began, and a young man with curly hair bowed before her. She would have to dance, out of politeness, until she could find Meg. Very stiffly she walked into the middle; very haughtily she put her hand on his sleeve. But in one minute, in one turn, her feet glided, glided. The lights, the azaleas, the dresses, the pink faces, the velvet chairs, all became one beautiful flying wheel. And when her next partner bumped her into the fat man and he said, "Par*don*," she smiled at him more radiantly than ever. She didn't even recognize him again.

1922

WILLIAM TREVOR

Beyond the Pale

We always went to Ireland in June.

Ever since the four of us began to go on holidays together, in 1965 it must have been, we had spent the first fortnight of the month at Glencorn Lodge in Co. Antrim.[1] Perfection, as Dekko put it once, and none of us disagreed. It's a Georgian house by the sea, not far

---

1. County in Northern Ireland containing the national capital, Belfast.

from the village of Ardbeag. It's quite majestic in its rather elegant way, a garden running to the very edge of a cliff, its long rhododendron drive—or avenue, as they say in Ireland. The English couple who bought the house in the early sixties, the Malseeds, have had to build on quite a bit but it's all been discreetly done, the Georgian style preserved throughout. Figs grow in the sheltered gardens, and apricots, and peaches in the greenhouses which old Mr. Saxton presides over. He's Mrs. Malseed's father actually. They brought him with them from Surrey, and their Dalmatians, Charger and Snooze.

It was Strafe who found Glencorn for us. He'd come across an advertisement in the *Lady* in the days when the Malseeds still felt the need to advertise. "How about this?" he said one evening at the end of the second rubber, and then read out the details. We had gone away together the summer before, to a hotel that had been recommended on the Costa del Sol, but it hadn't been a success because the food was so appalling. "We could try this Irish one," Dekko suggested cautiously, which is what eventually we did.

The four of us have been playing bridge together for ages, Dekko, Strafe, Cynthia and myself. They call me Milly, though strictly speaking my name is Dorothy Milson. Dekko picked up his nickname at school, Dekko Deakin sounding rather good, I dare say. He and Strafe were in fact at school together, which must be why we all call Strafe by his surname: Major R. B. Strafe he is, the initials standing for Robert Buchanan. We're of an age, the four of us, all in the early fifties: the prime of life, so Dekko insists. We live quite close to Leatherhead, where the Malseeds were before they decided to make the change from Surrey to Co. Antrim. Quite a coincidence, we always think.

"How *very* nice," Mrs. Malseed said, smiling her welcome again this year. Some instinct seems to tell her when guests are about to arrive, for she's rarely not waiting in the large low-ceilinged hall that always smells of flowers. She dresses beautifully, differently every day, and changing of course in the evening. Her blouse on this occasion was scarlet and silver, in stripes, her skirt black. This choice gave her a brisk look, which was fitting because being so busy she often has to be a little on the brisk side. She has smooth gray hair which she once told me she entirely looks after herself, and she almost always wears a black velvet band in it. Her face is well made up, and for one who arranges so many vases of flowers and otherwise has to use her hands she manages to keep them marvelously in condition. Her fingernails are varnished a soft pink, and a small gold bangle always adorns her right wrist, a wedding present from her husband.

"Arthur, take the party's luggage," she commanded the old porter, who doubles as odd-job man. "Rose, Geranium, Hydrangea, Fuchsia." She referred to the titles of the rooms reserved for us: in winter, when no one much comes to Glencorn Lodge, pleasant little details like that are seen to. Mrs. Malseed herself painted the flower-plaques that are attached to the doors of the hotel instead of numbers; her husband sees to redecoration and repairs.

"Well, well, well," Mr. Malseed said now, entering the hall through the door that leads to the kitchen regions. "A hundred thousand welcomes," he greeted us in the Irish manner. He's rather shorter than Mrs. Malseed, who's handsomely tall. He wears Donegal[2] tweed suits and is brown as a berry, including his head, which is bald. His dark brown eyes twinkle at you, making you feel rather more than just another hotel guest. They run the place like a country house, really.

"Good trip?" Mr. Malseed inquired.

"Super," Dekko said. "Not a worry all the way."

"Splendid."

"The wretched boat sailed an hour early one day last week," Mrs. Malseed said. "Quite a little band were left stranded at Stranraer."

Strafe laughed. Typical of that steamship company, he said. "Catching the tide, I dare say?"

"They caught a rocket from me," Mrs. Malseed replied good-humoredly. "A couple of old dears were due with us on Tuesday and had to spend the night in some awful Scottish lodging-house. It nearly finished them."

Everyone laughed, and I could feel the others thinking that our holiday had truly begun. Nothing had changed at Glencorn Lodge, all was well with its Irish world. Kitty from the dining-room came out to greet us, spotless in her uniform. "Ach, you're looking younger," she said, paying the compliment to all four of us, causing everyone in the hall to laugh again. Kitty's a bit of a card.

Arthur led the way to the rooms called Rose, Geranium, Hydrangea and Fuchsia, carrying as much of our luggage as he could manage and returning for the remainder. Arthur has a beaten, fisherman's face and short gray hair. He wears a green baize apron, and a white shirt with an imitation-silk scarf tucked into it at the neck. The scarf, in different swirling greens which blend nicely with the green of his apron, is an idea of Mrs. Malseed's and one appreciates the effort, if not at a uniform, at least at tidiness.

"Thank you very much," I said to Arthur in my room, smiling and finding him a coin.

We played a couple of rubbers after dinner as usual, but not of course going on for as long as we might have because we were still quite tired after the journey. In the lounge there was a French family, two girls and their parents, and a honeymoon couple—or so we had speculated during dinner—and a man on his own. There had been other people at dinner of course, because in June Glencorn Lodge is always full: from where we sat in the window we could see some of them strolling about the lawns, a few taking the cliff path down to the seashore. In the morning we'd do the same: we'd walk along the sands to Ardbeag and have coffee in the hotel there, back in time for lunch. In the afternoon we'd drive somewhere.

I knew all that because over the years this kind of pattern had developed. We had our walks and our drives, tweed to buy in Cushendall, Strafe's and Dekko's fishing day when Cynthia and I just sat on

---

2. County in the northern portion of the Irish Republic.

the beach, our visit to the Giant's Causeway[3] and one to Donegal perhaps, though that meant an early start and taking pot-luck for dinner somewhere. We'd come to adore Co. Antrim, its glens and coastline, Rathlin Island and Tievebulliag. Since first we got to know it, in 1965, we'd all four fallen hopelessly in love with every variation of this remarkable landscape. People in England thought us mad of course: they see so much of the troubles on television that it's naturally difficult for them to realize that most places are just as they've always been. Yet coming as we did, taking the road along the coast, dawdling through Ballygally, it was impossible to believe that somewhere else the unpleasantness was going on. We'd never seen a thing, nor even heard people talking about incidents that might have taken place. It's true that after a particularly nasty carry-on a few winters ago we did consider finding somewhere else, in Scotland perhaps, or Wales. But as Strafe put it at the time, we felt we owed a certain loyalty to the Malseeds and indeed to everyone we'd come to know round about, people who'd always been glad to welcome us back. It seemed silly to lose our heads, and when we returned the following summer we knew immediately we'd been right. Dekko said that nothing could be further away from all the violence than Glencorn Lodge, and though his remark could hardly be taken literally I think we all knew what he meant.

"Cynthia's tired," I said because she'd been stifling yawns. "I think we should call it a day."

"Oh, not at all," Cynthia protested. "No, please."

But Dekko agreed with me that she was tired, and Strafe said he didn't mind stopping now. He suggested a nightcap, as he always does, and as we always do also, Cynthia and I declined. Dekko said he'd like a Cointreau.

The conversation drifted about. Dekko told us an Irish joke about a drunk who couldn't find his way out of a telephone box, and then Strafe remembered an incident at school concerning his and Dekko's housemaster, A. D. Cowley-Stubbs, and the house wag, Thrive Major. A. D. Cowley-Stubbs had been known as Cows and often featured in our after-bridge reminiscing. So did Thrive Major.

"Perhaps I *am* sleepy," Cynthia said. "I don't think I closed my eyes once last night."

She never does on a sea crossing. Personally I'm out like a light the moment my head touches the pillow; I often think it must be the salt in the air because normally I'm an uneasy sleeper at the best of times.

"You run along, old girl," Strafe advised.

"Brekky at nine," Dekko said.

Cynthia said good-night and went, and we didn't remark on her tiredness because as a kind of unwritten rule we never comment on one another. We're four people who play bridge. The companionship it offers, and the holidays we have together, are all part of that. We share everything: the cost of petrol, the cups of coffee or drinks we

3. A formation of basalt cliffs projecting several hundred feet into the sea on the north coast of Antrim.

have; we even each make a contribution towards the use of Strafe's car because it's always his we go on holiday in, a Rover it was on this occasion.

"Funny, being here on your own," Strafe said, glancing across what the Malseeds call the After-Dinner Lounge at the man who didn't have a companion. He was a red-haired man of about thirty, not wearing a tie, his collar open at the neck and folded back over the jacket of his blue serge suit. He was uncouth-looking, though it's a hard thing to say, not at all the kind of person one usually sees at Glencorn Lodge. He sat in the After-Dinner Lounge as he had in the dining-room, lost in some concentration of his own, as if calculating sums in his mind. There had been a folded newspaper on his table in the dining-room. It now reposed tidily on the arm of his chair, still unopened.

"Commercial gent," Dekko said. "Fertilizers."

"Good heavens, never. You wouldn't get a rep in here."

I took no part in the argument. The lone man didn't much interest me, but I felt that Strafe was probably right: if there was anything dubious about the man's credentials he might have found it difficult to secure a room. In the hall of Glencorn Lodge there's a notice which reads: *We prefer not to feature in hotel guides, and we would be grateful to our guests if they did not seek to include Glencorn Lodge in the Good Food Guide, the Good Hotel Guide, the Michelin, Egon Ronay or any others. We have not advertized Glencorn since our early days, and prefer our recommendations to be by word of mouth.*

"Ah, thank you," Strafe said when Kitty brought his whisky and Dekko's Cointreau. "Sure you won't have something?" he said to me, although he knew I never did.

Strafe is on the stout side, I suppose you could say, with a gingery moustache and gingery hair, hardly touched at all by gray. He left the Army years ago, I suppose because of me in a sense, because he didn't want to be posted abroad again. He's in the Ministry of Defense now.

I'm still quite pretty in my way, though nothing like as striking as Mrs. Malseed, for I've never been that kind of woman. I've put on weight, and wouldn't have allowed myself to do so if Strafe hadn't kept saying he can't stand a bag of bones. I'm careful about my hair and, unlike Mrs. Malseed, I have it very regularly seen to because if I don't it gets a salt and pepper look, which I hate. My husband, Ralph, who died of food-poisoning when we were still quite young, used to say I wouldn't lose a single look in middle age, and to some extent that's true. We were still putting off having children when he died, which is why I haven't any. Then I met Strafe, which meant I didn't marry again.

Strafe is married himself, to Cynthia. She's small and ineffectual, I suppose you'd say without being untruthful or unkind. Not that Cynthia and I don't get on or anything like that, in fact we get on extremely well. It's Strafe and Cynthia who don't seem quite to hit it off, and I often think how much happier all round it would have been if Cynthia had married someone completely different, someone like Dekko in a way, except that that mightn't quite have worked out either. The Strafes have two sons, both very like their father, both of them in the Army. And the very sad thing is they think nothing of poor Cynthia.

"Who's that chap?" Dekko asked Mr. Malseed, who'd come over to wish us good-night.

"Awfully sorry about that, Mr. Deakin. My fault entirely, a booking that came over the phone."

"Good heavens, not at all," Strafe protested, and Dekko looked horrified in case it should be thought he was objecting to the locals. "Splendid-looking fellow," he said, overdoing it.

Mr. Malseed murmured that the man had only booked in for a single night, and I smiled the whole thing away, reassuring him with a nod. It's one of the pleasantest of the traditions at Glencorn Lodge that every evening Mr. Malseed makes the rounds of his guests just to say good-night. It's because of little touches like that that I, too, wished Dekko hadn't questioned Mr. Malseed about the man because it's the kind of thing one doesn't do at Glencorn Lodge. But Dekko is a law unto himself, very tall and gangling, always immaculately suited, a beaky face beneath mousy hair in which flecks of gray add a certain distinction. Dekko has money of his own and though he takes out girls who are half his age he has never managed to get around to marriage. The uncharitable might say he has a rather gormless laugh; certainly it's sometimes on the loud side.

We watched while Mr. Malseed bade the lone man good-night. The man didn't respond, but just sat gazing. It was ill-mannered, but this lack of courtesy didn't appear to be intentional: the man was clearly in a mood of some kind, miles away.

"Well, I'll go up," I said. "Good-night, you two."

"Cheery-bye, Milly," Dekko said. "Brekky at nine, remember."

"Good-night, Milly," Strafe said.

The Strafes always occupy different rooms on holidays, and at home also. This time he was in Geranium and she in Fuchsia. I was in Rose, and in a little while Strafe would come to see me. He stays with her out of kindness, because he fears for her on her own. He's a sentimental, good-hearted man, easily moved to tears: he simply cannot bear the thought of Cynthia with no one to talk to in the evenings, with no one to make her life around. "And besides," he often says when he's being jocular, "it would break up our bridge four." Naturally we never discuss her shortcomings or in any way analyze the marriage. The unwritten rule that exists among the four of us seems to extend as far as that.

He slipped into my room after he'd had another drink or two, and I was waiting for him as he likes me to wait, in bed not quite undressed. He has never said so, but I know that that is something Cynthia would not understand in him, or ever attempt to comply with. Ralph, of course, would not have understood either; poor old Ralph would have been shocked. Actually it's all rather sweet, Strafe and his little ways.

"I love you, dear," I whispered to him in the darkness, but just then he didn't wish to speak of love and referred instead to my body.

If Cynthia hadn't decided to remain in the hotel the next morning instead of accompanying us on our walk to Ardbeag everything might have been different. As it happened, when she said at breakfast she thought she'd just potter about the garden and sit with her book out of the wind somewhere, I can't say I was displeased. For a moment I hoped Dekko might say he'd stay with her, allowing Strafe and myself to go off on our own, but Dekko—who doesn't go in for saying what you want him to say—didn't. "Poor old sausage,"[4] he said instead, examining Cynthia with a solicitude that suggested she was close to the grave, rather than just a little lowered by the change of life or whatever it was.

"I'll be perfectly all right," Cynthia assured him. "Honestly."

"Cynthia likes to mooch,[5] you know," Strafe pointed out, which of course is only the truth. She reads too much, I always think. You often see her putting down a book with the most melancholy look in her eyes, which can't be good for her. She's an imaginative woman, I suppose you would say, and of course her habit of reading so much is often useful on our holidays: over the years she has read her way through dozen of Irish guide-books. "That's where the garrison pushed the natives over the cliffs," she once remarked on a drive. "Those rocks are known as the Maidens," she remarked on another occasion. She has led us to places of interest which we had no idea existed: Garron Tower on Garron Point, the mausoleum at Bonamargy, the Devil's Backbone.[6] As well as which, Cynthia is extremely knowledgeable about all matters relating to Irish history. Again she has read endlessly: biographies and autobiographies, long accounts of the centuries of battling and politics there've been. There's hardly a town or village we ever pass through that hasn't some significance for Cynthia, although I'm afraid her impressive fund of information doesn't always receive the attention it deserves. Not that Cynthia ever minds; it doesn't seem to worry her when no one listens. My own opinion is that she'd have made a much better job of her relationship with Strafe and her sons if she could have somehow developed a bit more character.

We left her in the garden and proceeded down the cliff path to the shingle beneath. I was wearing slacks and a blouse, with the arms of a cardigan looped round my neck in case it turned chilly: the outfit was new, specially bought for the holiday, in shades of tangerine. Strafe never cares how he dresses and of course she doesn't keep him up to the mark: that morning, as far as I remember, he wore rather shapeless corduroy trousers, the kind men sometimes garden in, and a navy-blue fisherman's jersey. Dekko as usual was a fashion plate: a plane green linen suit with pleated jacket pockets, a maroon shirt open at the neck, revealing a medallion on a fine gold chain. We didn't converse as we crossed the rather difficult shingle, but when we reached the sand Dekko began to talk about some girl or other,

4. Soul.   (Cockney   rhyming   slang: "sausage [roll]" = soul.)
5. Wander about.
6. The Tower, now a hotel, was formerly a government center; the mausoleum is in the ruins of a monastery near Ballygalley Castle; the Backbone (Knockalla Mountain) is to the west of Lough Swelly in Donegal.

someone called Juliet who had apparently proposed marriage to him just before we'd left Surrey. He'd told her, so he said, that he'd think about it while on holiday and he wondered now about dispatching a telegram from Ardbeag saying, *Still thinking*. Strafe, who has a simple sense of humor, considered this hugely funny and spent most of the walk persuading Dekko that the telegram must certainly be sent, and other telegrams later on, all with the same message. Dekko kept laughing, throwing his head back in a way that always reminds me of an Australian bird I once saw in a nature film on television. I could see this was going to become one of those jokes that would accompany us all through the holiday, a man's thing really, but of course I didn't mind. The girl called Juliet was nearly thirty years younger than Dekko. I supposed she knew what she was doing.

Since the subject of telegrams had come up, Strafe recalled the occasion when Thrive Major had sent one to A. D. Cowley-Stubbs: *Darling regret three months gone love Rowena*. Carefully timed, it had arrived during one of Cows' Thursday evening coffee sessions. Rowena was a maid, known as the Bicycle, who had been sacked the previous term, and old Cows had something of a reputation as a misogynist. When he read the message he apparently went white and collapsed into an armchair. Warrington P. J. managed to read it too, and after that the fat was in the fire. The consequences went on rather, but I never minded listening when Strafe and Dekko drifted back to their schooldays. I just wish I'd known Strafe then, before either of us had gone and got married.

We had our coffee at Ardbeag, the telegram was sent off, and then Strafe and Dekko wanted to see a man called Henry O'Reilly whom we'd met on previous holidays, who organizes mackerel-fishing trips. I waited on my own, picking out postcards in the village shop that sells almost everything, and then I wandered down towards the shore. I knew that they would be having a drink with the boatman because a year had passed since they'd seen him last. They joined me after about twenty minutes, Dekko apologizing but Strafe not seeming to be aware that I'd had to wait because Strafe is not a man who notices little things. It was almost one o'clock when we reached Glencorn Lodge and were told by Mr. Malseed that Cynthia needed looking after.

The hotel, in fact, was in a turmoil. I have never seen anyone as ashen-faced as Mr. Malseed; his wife, in a forget-me-not[7] dress, was limp. It wasn't explained to us immediately what had happened, because in the middle of telling us that Cynthia needed looking after Mr. Malseed was summoned to the telephone. I could see through the half-open door of their little office a glass of whisky or brandy on the desk and Mrs. Malseed's bangled arm reaching out for it. Not for ages did we realize that it all had to do with the lone man whom we'd speculated about the night before.

"He just wanted to talk to me," Cynthia kept repeating hysterically in the hall. "He sat with me by the magnolias."

I made her lie down. Strafe and I stood on either side of her bed as

7. Blue.

she lay there with her shoes off, her rather unattractively cut plain pink dress crumpled and actually damp from her tears. I wanted to make her take it off and to slip under the bed-clothes in her petticoat but somehow it seemed all wrong, in the circumstances, for Strafe's wife to do anything so intimate in my presence.

"I couldn't stop him," Cynthia said, the rims of her eyes crimson by now, her nose beginning to run again. "From half past ten till well after twelve. He had to talk to someone, he said."

I could sense that Strafe was thinking precisely the same as I was: that the red-haired man had insinuated himself into Cynthia's company by talking about himself and had then put a hand on her knee. Instead of simply standing up and going away Cynthia would have stayed where she was, embarrassed or tongue-tied, at any rate unable to cope. And when the moment came she would have turned hysterical. I could picture her screaming in the garden, running across the lawn to the hotel, and then the pandemonium in the hall. I could sense Strafe picturing that also.

"My God, it's terrible," Cynthia said.

"I think she should sleep," I said quietly to Strafe. "Try to sleep, dear," I said to her, but she shook her head, tossing her jumble of hair about on the pillow.

"Milly's right," Strafe urged. "You'll feel much better after a little rest. We'll bring you a cup of tea later on."

"My God!" she cried again. "My God, how could I sleep?"

I went away to borrow a couple of mild sleeping pills from Dekko, who is never without them, relying on the things too much in my opinion. He was tidying himself in his room, but found the pills immediately. Strangely enough, Dekko's always sound in a crisis.

I gave them to her with water and she took them without asking what they were. She was in a kind of daze, one moment making a fuss and weeping, the next just peering ahead of her, as if frightened. In a way she was like someone who'd just had a bad nightmare and hadn't yet completely returned to reality. I remarked as much to Strafe while we made our way down to lunch, and he said he quite agreed.

"Poor old Cynth!" Dekko said when we'd all ordered lobster bisque and entrecôte[8] béarnaise. "Poor old sausage."

You could see that the little waitress, a new girl this year, was bubbling over with excitement; but Kitty, serving the other half of the dining-room, was grim, which was most unusual. Everyone was talking in hushed tones and when Dekko said, "Poor old Cynth!" a couple of heads were turned in our direction because he can never keep his voice down. The little vases of roses with which Mrs. Malseed must have decorated each table before the fracas had occurred seemed strangely out of place in the atmosphere which had developed.

The waitress had just taken away our soup-plates when Mr. Malseed hurried into the dining-room and came straight to our table. The lobster bisque surprisingly hadn't been quite up to scratch, and in passing I couldn't help wondering if the fuss had caused the kitchen to go to pieces also.

8. Steak cut from between ribs.

"I wonder if I might have a word, Major Strafe," Mr. Malseed said, and Strafe rose at once and accompanied him from the dining-room. A total silence had fallen, everyone in the dining-room pretending to be intent on eating. I had an odd feeling that we had perhaps got it all wrong, that because we'd been out for our walk when it had happened all the other guests knew more of the details than Strafe and Dekko and I did. I began to wonder if poor Cynthia had been raped.

Afterwards Strafe told us what occurred in the Malseeds' office, how Mrs. Malseed had been sitting there, slumped, as he put it, and how two policemen had questioned him. "Look, what on earth's all this about?" he had demanded rather sharply.

"It concerns this incident that's taken place, sir," one of the policemen explained in an unhurried voice. "On account of your wife—"

"My wife's lying down. She must not be questioned or in any way disturbed."

"Ach, we'd never do that, sir."

Strafe does a good Co. Antrim brogue and in relating all this to us he couldn't resist making full use of it. The two policemen were in uniform and their natural slowness of intellect was rendered more noticeable by the lugubrious air the tragedy had inspired in the hotel. For tragedy was what it was; after talking to Cynthia for nearly two hours the lone man had walked down to the rocks and been drowned.

When Strafe finished speaking I placed my knife and fork together on my plate, unable to eat another mouthful. The facts appeared to be that the man, having left Cynthia by the magnolias, had clambered down the cliff to a place no one ever went to, on the other side of the hotel from the sands we had walked along to Ardbeag. No one had seen him except Cynthia, who from the cliff-top had apparently witnessed his battering by the treacherous waves. The tide had been coming in, but by the time old Arthur and Mr. Malseed reached the rocks it had begun to turn, leaving behind it the fully dressed corpse. Mr. Malseed's impression was that the man had lost his footing on the seaweed and accidentally stumbled into the depths, for the rocks were so slippery it was difficult to carry the corpse more than a matter of yards. But at least it had been placed out of view, while Mr. Malseed hurried back to the hotel to telephone for assistance. He told Strafe that Cynthia had been most confused, insisting that the man had walked out among the rocks and then into the sea, knowing what he was doing.

Listening to it all, I no longer felt sory for Cynthia. It was typical of her that she should so sillily have involved us in all this. Why on earth had she sat in the garden with a man of that kind instead of standing up and making a fuss the moment he'd begun to paw her? If she'd acted intelligently the whole unfortunate episode could clearly have been avoided. Since it hadn't, there was no point whatsoever in insisting that the man had committed suicide when at that distance no one could possibly be sure.

"It really does astonish me," I said at the lunch table, unable to prevent myself from breaking our unwritten rule. "Whatever came over her?"

"It can't be good for the hotel," Dekko commented, and I was glad to see Strafe giving him a little glance of irritation.

"It's hardly the point," I said coolly.

"What I meant was, hotels occasionally hush things like this up."

"Well, they haven't this time." It seemed an age since I had waited for them in Ardbeag, since we had been so happily laughing over the effect of Dekko's telegram. He'd included his address in it so that the girl could send a message back, and as we'd returned to the hotel along the seashore there's been much speculation between the two men about the form this would take.

"I suppose what Cynthia's thinking," Strafe said, "is that after he'd tried something on with her he became depressed."

"Oh, but he could just as easily have lost his footing. He'd have been on edge anyway, worried in case she reported him."

"Dreadful kind of death," Dekko said. His tone suggested that that was that, that the subject should now be closed, and so it was.

After lunch we went to our rooms, as we always do at Glencorn Lodge, to rest for an hour. I took my slacks and blouse off, hoping that Strafe would knock on my door, but he didn't and of course, that was understandable. Oddly enough I found myself thinking of Dekko, picturing his long form stretched out in the room called Hydrangea, his beaky face in profile on his pillow. The precise nature of Dekko's relationship with these girls he picks up has always privately intrigued me: was it really possible that somewhere in London there was a girl called Juliet who was prepared to marry him for his not inconsiderable money?

I slept and briefly dreamed. Thrive Major and Warrington P. J. were running the post office in Ardbeag, sending telegrams to everyone they could think of, including Dekko's friend Juliet. Cynthia had been found dead beside the magnolias and people were waiting for Hercule Poirot[9] to arrive. "Promise me you didn't do it," I whispered to Strafe, but when Strafe replied it was to say that Cynthia's body reminded him of a bag of old chicken bones.

Strafe and Dekko and I met for tea in the tea-lounge. Strafe had looked in to see if Cynthia had woken, but apparently she hadn't. The police officers had left the hotel, Dekko said, because he'd noticed their car wasn't parked at the front anymore. None of the three of us said, but I think we presumed, that the man's body had been removed from the rocks during the quietness of the afternoon. From where we sat I caught a glimpse of Mrs. Malseed passing quite briskly through the hall, seeming almost herself again. Certainly our holiday would be affected, but it might not be totally ruined. All that remained to hope for was Cynthia's recovery, and then everyone could set about forgetting the unpleasantness. The nicest thing would be if a jolly young couple turned up and occupied the man's room, exorcising the incident, as newcomers would.

The family from France—the two little girls and their parents— were chattering away in the tea-lounge, and an elderly trio who'd

---

9. Detective in many of Agatha Christie's murder mysteries.

arrived that morning were speaking in American accents. The honeymoon couple appeared, looking rather shy, and began to whisper and giggle in a corner. People who occupied the table next to ours in the dining-room, a Wing-Commander Orfell and his wife, from Guildford,[1] nodded and smiled as they passed. Everyone was making an effort, and I knew it would help matters further if Cynthia felt up to a rubber or two before dinner. That life should continue as normally as possible was essential for Glencorn Lodge, the example already set by Mrs. Malseed.

Because of our interrupted lunch I felt quite hungry, and the Malseeds pride themselves on their teas. The chef, Mr. McBride, whom of course we've met, has the lightest touch I know with sponge cakes and little curranty scones. I was, in fact, buttering a scone when Strafe said:

"Here she is."

And there indeed she was. By the look of her she had simply pushed herself off her bed and come straight down. Her pink dress was even more crumpled than it had been. She hadn't so much as run a comb through her hair, her face was puffy and unpowdered. For a moment I really thought she was walking in her sleep.

Strafe and Dekko stood up. "Feeling better, dear?" Strafe said, but she didn't answer.

"Sit down, Cynth," Dekko urged, pushing back a chair to make room for her.

"He told me a story I can never forget. I've dreamed about it all over again." Cynthia swayed in front of us, not even attempting to sit down. To tell the truth, she sounded inane.

"Story, dear?" Strafe inquired, humoring her.

She said it was the story of two children who had apparently ridden bicycles through the streets of Belfast, out into Co. Antrim. The bicycles were dilapidated, she said; she didn't know if they were stolen or not. She didn't know about the children's home because the man hadn't spoken of them, but she claimed to know instinctively that they had ridden away from poverty and unhappiness. "From the clatter and the quarreling," Cynthia said. "Two children who later fell in love."

"Horrid old dream," Strafe said. "Horrid for you, dear."

She shook her head, and then sat down. I poured another cup of tea. "I had the oddest dream myself," I said. "Thrive Major was running the post office in Ardbeag."

Strafe smiled and Dekko gave his laugh, but Cynthia didn't in any way acknowledge what I'd said.

"A fragile thing the girl was, with depths of mystery in her wide brown eyes. Red-haired of course he was himself, thin as a rake in those days. Glencorn Lodge was derelict then."

"You've had a bit of a shock, old thing," Dekko said.

Strafe agreed, kindly adding, "Look dear, if the chap actually interfered with you—"

"Why on earth should he do that?" Her voice was shrill in the tea-lounge, edged with a note of hysteria. I glanced at Strafe, who was

---

1. In Surrey, southern England.

frowning into his tea-cup. Dekko began to say something, but broke off before his meaning emerged. Rather more calmly Cynthia said:

"It was summer when they came here. Honeysuckle he described. And mother of thyme.[2] He didn't know the name of either."

No one attempted any kind of reply, not that it was necessary, for Cynthia just continued.

"At school there were the facts of geography and arithmetic. And the legends of scholars and of heroes, of Queen Maeve and Finn MacCool. There was the coming of St. Patrick[3] to a heathen people. History was full of kings and high-kings, and Silken Thomas and Wolfe Tone, the Flight of the Earls, the Siege of Limerick."[4]

When Cynthia said that, it was impossible not to believe that the unfortunate events of the morning had touched her with some kind of madness. It seemed astonishing that she had walked into the tea-lounge without having combed her hair, and that she'd stood there swaying before sitting down, that out of the blue she had started on about two children. None of it made an iota of sense, and surely she could see that the nasty experience she'd suffered should not be dwelt upon? I offered her the plate of scones, hoping that if she began to eat she would stop talking, but she took no notice of my gesture.

"Look, dear," Strafe said, "there's not one of us who knows what you're talking about."

"I'm talking about a children's story, I'm talking about a girl and a boy who visited this place we visit also. He hadn't been here for years, but he returned last night, making one final effort to understand. And then he walked out into the sea."

She had taken a piece of her dress and was agitatedly crumpling it between the finger and thumb of her left hand. It was dreadful really, having her so grubby-looking. For some odd reason I suddenly thought of her cooking, how she wasn't in the least interested in it or in anything about the house. She certainly hadn't succeeded in making a home for Strafe.

"They rode those worn-out bicycles through a hot afternoon. Can you feel all that? A newly surfaced road, the snap of chippings beneath their tires, the smell of tar? Dust from a passing car, the city they left behind?"

"Cynthia dear," I said, "drink your tea, and why not have a scone?"

"They swam and sunbathed on the beach you walked along today. They went to a spring for water. There were no magnolias then. There was no garden, no neat little cliff paths to the beach. Surely you can

---

2. A low-growing, wide-spreading variety of the aromatic thyme.

3. Maeve, first-century (A.D.) ruler of Connaught who reputedly invaded Ulster and in folk tradition is queen of the fairies; Finn MacCumhaill, third-century chieftain who reputedly possessed gifts of poetry, second sight, and healing; Patrick converted the Irish to Catholicism and reputedly freed Ireland of snakes.

4. Thomas Fitzgerald, tenth Earl of Kildare, rebelled against Henry VIII when he heard his father had been executed and adorned his helmet and those of his supporters with silken fringe; Theobald Wolfe Tone, a founder and leader of the United Irishmen, supported religious toleration, separation from England, and the French Revolution, and was sentenced to death as a traitor. In 1607 almost a hundred leaders ("Earls") of the North fled rather than serve England and James I, a flight that some believe permanently damaged the Celtic cause; the town of Limerick in southwest Ireland was, in 1791, besieged by troops of King William, and the Irish Army, loyal to the Catholic James II who had been forced off the British throne, was defeated.

see it clearly?"

"No," Strafe said. "No, we really cannot, dear."

"This place that is an idyll for us was an idyll for them too: the trees, the ferns, the wild rose near the water spring, the very sea and sun they shared. There was a cottage lost in the middle of the woods: they sometimes looked for that. They played a game, a kind of hide and seek. People in a white farmhouse gave them milk."

For the second time I offered Cynthia the plate of scones and for the second time she pointedly ignored me. Her cup of tea hadn't been touched. Dekko took a scone and cheerfully said:

"All's well that's over."

But Cynthia appeared to have drifted back into a daze, and I wondered again if it could really be possible that the experience had unhinged her. Unable to help myself, I saw her being led away from the hotel, helped into the back of a blue van, something like an ambulance. She was talking about the children again, how they had planned to marry and keep a sweetshop.

"Take it easy, dear," Strafe said, which I followed up by suggesting for the second time that she should make an effort to drink her tea.

"Has it to do with the streets they came from? Or the history they learnt, he from his Christian Brothers, she from her nuns? History is unfinished in this island; long since it has come to a stop in Surrey."

Dekko said, and I really had to hand it to him:

"Cynth, we have to put it behind us."

It didn't do any good. Cynthia just went rambling on, speaking again of the girl being taught by nuns, and the boy by Christian Brothers. She began to recite the history they might have learnt, the way she sometimes did when we were driving through an area that had historical connections. "Can you imagine," she embarrassingly asked, "our very favorite places bitter with disaffection, with plotting and revenge? Can you imagine the treacherous murder of Shane O'Neill the Proud?"[5]

Dekko made a little sideways gesture of his head, politely marveling. Strafe seemed about to say something, but changed his mind. Confusion ran through Irish history, Cynthia said, like convolvulus in a hedgerow. On May 24th, 1487, a boy of ten called Lambert Simnel, brought to Dublin by a priest from Oxford, was declared Edward VI of all England and Ireland, crowned with a golden circlet taken from a statue of the Virgin Mary. On May 24th, 1798, here in Antrim, Presbyterian farmers fought for a common cause with their Catholic laborers.[6] She paused and looked at Strafe. Chaos and contradiction, she informed him, were hidden everywhere beneath nice-sounding names. "The Battle of the Yellow Ford," she suddenly chanted in a sing-song way that sounded thoroughly peculiar, "the Statues of

5. Sixteenth-century leader who tried to take control of Ulster from England (Elizabeth); when the O'Donnells, egged on by the government, defeated Shane (1567), he fled to Scotland, where, though received peacefully, he was mur- dered.

6. "Edward VI's" rebel forces were defeated by Henry VII and he and the priest were jailed; Antrim was one of the sites of the uprising of the United Irishmen.

Kilkenny. The Battle of Glenmama, the Convention of Drumceat.[7] The Act of Settlement, the Renunciation Act. The Act of Union, the Toleration Act.[8] Just so much history it sounds like now, yet people starved or died while other people watched. A language was lost, a faith forbidden. Famine followed revolt, plantation followed that. But it was people who were struck into the soil of other people's land, not forests of new trees; and it was greed and treachery that spread as a disease among them all. No wonder unease clings to these shreds of history and shots ring out in answer to the mockery of drums. No wonder the air is nervy with suspicion."

There was an extremely awkward silence when she ceased to speak. Dekko nodded, doing his best to be companionable. Strafe nodded also. I simply examined the pattern of roses on our tea-time china, not knowing what else to do. Eventually Dekko said:

"What an awful lot you know, Cynth!"

"Cynthia's always been interested," Strafe said. "Always had a first-rate memory."

"Those children of the streets are part of the battles and the Acts," she went on, seeming quite unaware that her talk was literally almost crazy. "They're part of the blood that flowed around those nice-sounding names." She paused, and for a moment seemed disinclined to continue. Then she said:

"The second time they came here the house was being built. There were concrete-mixers, and lorries drawn up on the grass, noise and scaffolding everywhere. They watched all through another afternoon and then they went their different ways: their childhood was over, lost with their idyll. He became a dockyard clerk. She went to London, to work in a betting shop."

"My dear," Strafe said very gently, "it's interesting, everything you say, but it really hardly concerns us."

"No, of course not." Quite emphatically Cynthia shook her head, appearing wholly to agree. "They were degenerate, awful creatures. They must have been."

"No one's saying that, my dear."

"Their story should have ended there, he in the docklands of Belfast, she recording bets. Their complicated childhood love should just have dissipated, as such love often does. But somehow nothing was as neat as that."

Dekko, in an effort to lighten the conversation, mentioned a boy called Gollsol who'd been at school with Strafe and himself, who'd

---

7. At the Battle of Yellow Ford, 1598, Hugh O'Neill, nephw of Shane, Earl of Tyrone, in his struggle to prevent anglicization of Ireland, defeated the English. The statutes, 1366, ordered English (Norman) settlers not to intermarry with Irish, speak their language, or adopt their customs. At Glenmama, near Dublin, in 999, the Irish defeated the Danes. Dalriada was a kingdom, partly in northeastern Ireland, partly in southwestern Scotland, and in 590 a convention was called at Drumceat County, Londonderry, to see if Scots should give allegiance to the Irish "high king."

8. Under the Settlement of 1652, those not friendly to Cromwell's Puritan English government could forfeit part or all of their property. In 1783 the English Parliament recognized Irish independence, rights of Irish courts, and as valid for Ireland only those laws enacted by English king *and* Irish Parliament. Not much later, 1800, the Act of Union united the parliament and kingdoms (thus the United Kingdom or U.K.). Earlier, 1719, the Toleration Act, forced on the Irish Parliament, allowed the Irish freedom to worship and to serve in parish offices if they would swear civil allegiance and renounce "popish" doctrines.

formed a romantic attachment for the daughter of one of the grounds-
men and had later actually married her. There was a silence for a
moment, then Cynthia, without emotion, said:

"You none of you care. You sit there not caring that two people are
dead."

"Two people, Cynthia?" I said.

"For God's sake, I'm telling you!" she cried. "That girl was murdered in a room in Maida Vale."[9]

Although there is something between Strafe and myself, I do try my
best to be at peace about it. I go to church and take communion, and I
know Strafe occasionally does too, though not as often as perhaps he
might. Cynthia has no interest in that side of life, and it rankled with
me now to hear her blaspheming so casually, and so casually speaking
about death in Maida Vale on top of all this stuff about history and
children. Strafe was shaking his head, clearly believing that Cynthia
didn't know what she was talking about.

"Cynthia dear," I began, "are you sure you're not muddling something up here? You've been upset, you've had a nightmare: don't you
think your imagination, or something you've been reading—"

"Bombs don't go off on their own. Death doesn't just happen to
occur in Derry and Belfast, in London and Amsterdam and Dublin, in
Berlin and Jerusalem. There are people who are murderers: that is
what this children's story is about."

A silence fell, no one knowing what to say. It didn't matter of
course because without any prompting Cynthia continued.

"We drink our gin with Angostura bitters, there's lamb or chicken
Kiev. Old Kitty's kind to us in the dining-room and old Arthur in the
hall. Flowers are everywhere, we have our special table."

"Please let us take you to your room now," Strafe begged, and as he
spoke I reached out a hand in friendship and placed it on her arm.
"Come on, old thing," Dekko said.

"The limbless are left on the streets, blood spatters the car-parks.
Brits Out it says on a rockface, but we know it doesn't mean us."

I spoke quietly then, measuring my words, measuring the pause
between each so that its effect might be registered. I felt the statement
had to be made, whether it was my place to make it or not. I said:

"You are very confused, Cynthia."

The French family left the tea-lounge. The two Dalmatians,
Charger and Snooze, ambled in and sniffed and went away again.
Kitty came to clear the French family's tea things. I could hear her
speaking to the honeymoon couple, saying the weather forecast was
good.

"Cynthia," Strafe said, standing up, "we've been very patient with
you but this is now becoming silly."

I nodded just a little. "I really think," I softly said, but Cynthia
didn't permit me to go on.

"Someone told him about her. Someone mentioned her name, and
he couldn't believe it. She sat alone in Maida Vale, putting together
the mechanisms of her bombs: this girl who had laughed on the

9. Section of London with many foreign transients and rooming houses.

seashore, whom he had loved."

"Cynthia," Strafe began, but he wasn't permitted to continue either. Hopelessly, he just sat down again.

"Whenever he heard of bombs exploding he thought of her, and couldn't understand. He wept when he said that; her violence haunted him, he said. He couldn't work, he couldn't sleep at night. His mind filled up with images of her, their awkward childhood kisses, her fingers working neatly now. He saw her with a carrier-bag, hurrying it through a crowd, leaving it where it could cause most death. In front of the moldering old house that had once been Glencorn Lodge they'd made a fire and cooked their food. They'd lain for ages on the grass. They'd cycled home to their city streets."

It suddenly dawned on me that Cynthia was knitting this whole fantasy out of nothing. It all worked backwards from the moment when she'd had the misfortune to witness the man's death in the sea. A few minutes before he'd been chatting quite normally to her, he'd probably even mentioned a holiday in his childhood and some girl there'd been: all of it would have been natural in the circumstances, possibly even the holiday had taken place at Glencorn. He'd said good-bye and then unfortunately he'd had his accident. As she watched from the cliff edge, something had cracked in poor Cynthia's brain, she having always been a prey to melancholy. I suppose it must be hard having two sons who don't think much of you, and a marriage not offering you a great deal, bridge and holidays probably the best part of it. For some odd reason of her own she'd created her fantasy about a child turning into a terrorist. The violence of the man's death had clearly filled her imagination with Irish violence, so regularly seen on television. If we'd been on holiday in Suffolk I wondered how it would have seemed to the poor creature.

I could feel Strafe and Dekko beginning to put all that together also, beginning to realize that the whole story of the red-haired man and the girl was clearly Cynthia's invention. "Poor creature," I wanted to say, but did not do so.

"For months he searched for her, pushing his way among the people of London, the people who were her victims. When he found her she just looked at him, as if the past hadn't even existed. She didn't smile, as if incapable of smiling. He wanted to take her away, back to where they came from, but she didn't reply when he suggested that. Bitterness was like a disease in her, and when he left her he felt the bitterness in himself."

Again Strafe and Dekko nodded, and I could feel Strafe thinking that there really was no point in protesting further. All we could hope for was that the end of the saga was in sight.

"He remained in London, working on the railways. But in the same way as before he was haunted by the person she'd become, and the haunting was more awful now. He bought a gun from a man he'd been told about and kept it hidden in a shoe-box in his rented room. Now and again he took it out and looked at it, then put it back. He hated the violence that possessed her, yet he was full of it himself: he knew he couldn't betray her with anything but death. Humanity had left both of them when he visited her again in Maida Vale."

To my enormous relief and, I could feel, to Strafe's and Dekko's too, Mr. and Mrs. Malseed appeared beside us. Like his wife, Mr. Malseed had considerably recovered. He spoke in an even voice, clearly wishing to dispose of the matter. It was just the diversion we needed.

"I must apologize, Mr. Strafe," he said. "I cannot say how sorry we are that you were bothered by that man."

"My wife is still a little dicky,"[1] Strafe explained, "but after a decent night's rest I think we can say she'll be as right as rain again."

"I only wish, Mrs. Strafe, you had made contact with my wife, or myself when he first approached you." There was a spark of irritation in Mr. Malseed's eyes, but his voice was still controlled. "I mean, the unpleasantness you suffered might just have been averted."

"Nothing would have been averted, Mr. Malseed, and certainly not the horror we are left with. Can you see her as the girl she became, seated at a chipped white table, her wires and fuses spread around her? What were her thoughts in that room, Mr. Malseed? What happens in the mind of anyone who wishes to destroy? In a back street he bought his gun for too much money. When did it first occur to him to kill her?"

"We really are a bit at sea," Mr. Malseed replied without the slightest hesitation. He humored Cynthia by displaying no surprise, by speaking very quietly.

"All I am saying, Mr. Malseed, is that we should root our heads out of the sand and wonder about two people who are beyond the pale."

"My dear," Strafe said, "Mr. Malseed is a busy man."

Still quietly, still perfectly in control of every intonation, without a single glance around the tea-lounge to ascertain where his guests' attention was, Mr. Malseed said:

"There is unrest here, Mrs. Strafe, but we do our best to live with it."

"All I am saying is that perhaps there can be regret when two children end like this."

Mr. Malseed did not reply. His wife did her best to smile away the awkwardness. Strafe murmured privately to Cynthia, no doubt beseeching her to come to her senses. Again I imagined a blue van drawn up in front of Glencorn Lodge, for it was quite understandable now that an imaginative woman should go mad, affected by the ugliness of death. The garbled speculation about the man and the girl, the jumble in the poor thing's mind—a children's story as she called it—all somehow hung together when you realized they didn't have to make any sense whatsoever.

"Murderers are beyond the pale, Mr. Malseed, and England has always had its pales. The one in Ireland began in 1395."[2]

"Dear," I said, "what has happened has nothing whatsoever to do with calling people murderers and placing them beyond some pale or other. You witnessed a most unpleasant accident, dear, and it's only to

---

1. Shaky.
2. Richard II visited Ireland 1394–95 to bolster royal authority and (unsuccess-fully) to extend English control over lands.

be expected that you've become just a little lost. The man had a chat with you when you were sitting by the magnolias and then the shock of seeing him slip on the seaweed—"

"He didn't slip on the seaweed," she suddenly screamed. "My God, he didn't slip on the seaweed."

Strafe closed his eyes. The other guests in the tea-lounge had fallen silent ages ago, openly listening. Arthur was standing near the door and was listening also. Kitty was waiting to clear away our tea things, but didn't like to because of what was happening.

"I must request you to take Mrs. Strafe to her room, Major," Mr. Malseed said. "And I must make it clear that we cannot tolerate further upset in Glencorn Lodge."

Strafe reached for her arm, but Cynthia took no notice.

"An Irish joke," she said, and then she stared at Mr. and Mrs. Malseed, her eyes passing over each feature of their faces. She stared at Dekko and Strafe, and last of all at me. She said eventually:

"An Irish joke, an unbecoming tale: of course it can't be true. Ridiculous, that a man returned here. Ridiculous, that he walked again by the seashore and through the woods, hoping to understand where a woman's cruelty had come from."

"This talk is most offensive," Mr. Malseed protested, his calmness slipping just a little. The ashen look that had earlier been in his face returned. I could see he was beside himself with rage. "You are trying to bring something to our doorstep which most certainly does not belong there."

"On your doorstep they talked about a sweetshop: Cadbury's bars and different-flavored creams, nut-milk toffee, Aero and Crunchie."

"For God's sake pull yourself together," I clearly heard Strafe whispering, and Mrs. Malseed attempted to smile. "Come along now, Mrs. Strafe," she said, making a gesture. "Just to please us, dear. Kitty wants to clear away the dishes. Kitty!" she called out, endeavoring to bring matters down to earth.

Kitty crossed the lounge with her tray and gathered up the cups and saucers. The Malseeds, naturally still anxious, hovered. No one was surprised when Cynthia began all over again, by crazily asking Kitty what she thought of us.

"I think, dear," Mrs. Malseed began, "Kitty's quite busy really."

"Stop this at once," Strafe quietly ordered.

"For fourteen years, Kitty, you've served us with food and cleared away the tea-cups we've drunk from. For fourteen years we've played our bridge and walked about the garden. We've gone for drives, we've bought our tweed, we've bathed as those children did."

"Stop it," Strafe said again, a little louder. Bewildered and getting red in the face, Kitty hastily bundled china on to her tray. I made a sign at Strafe because for some reason I felt that the end was really in sight. I wanted him to retain his patience, but what Cynthia said next was almost unbelievable.

"In Surrey we while away the time, we clip our hedges. On a bridge night there's coffee at nine o'clock, with macaroons or *petits fours*. Last thing of all we watch the late-night News, packing away our

cards and scoring-pads, our sharpened pencils. There's been an incident in Armagh, one soldier's had his head shot off, another's run
amok. Our lovely Glens of Antrim, we all four think, our coastal
drives: we hope that nothing disturbs the peace. We think of Mr.
Malseed, still busy in Glencorn Lodge, and Mrs. Malseed finishing her
flower-plaques for the rooms of the completed annex."

"Will you for God's sake shut up?" Strafe suddenly shouted. I could
see him struggling with himself, but it didn't do any good. He called
Cynthia a bloody spectacle, sitting there talking rubbish. I don't believe she even heard him.

"Through honey-tinted glasses we love you and we love your island,
Kitty. We love the lilt of your racy history, we love your earls and
heroes. Yet we made a sensible pale here once, as civilized people
create a garden, pretty as a picture."

Strafe's outburst had been quite noisy and I could sense him being
ashamed of it. He muttered that he was sorry, but Cynthia simply took
advantage of his generosity, continuing about a pale.

"Beyond it lie the bleak untouchables, best kept as dots on the
horizon, too terrible to contemplate. How can we be blamed if we
make neither head nor tail of anything, Kitty, your past and your
present, those battles and Acts of Parliament? We people of Surrey:
how can we know? Yet I stupidly thought, you see, that the tragedy of
two children could at least be understood. He didn't discover where
her cruelty had come from because perhaps you never can: evil breeds
evil in a mysterious way. That's the story the red-haired stranger
passed on to me, the story you huddle away from."

Poor Strafe was pulling at Cynthia, pleading with her, still saying he
was sorry.

"Mrs. Strafe," Mr. Malseed tried to say, but got no further. To my
horror Cynthia abruptly pointed at me.

"That woman," she said, "is my husband's mistress, a fact I am
supposed to be unaware of, Kitty."

"My God!" Strafe said.

"My husband is perverted in his sexual desires. His friend, who
shared his schooldays, has never quite recovered from that time. I
myself am a pathetic creature who has closed her eyes to a husband's
infidelity and his mistress's viciousness. I am dragged into the days of
Thrive Major and A. D. Cowley-Stubbs: mechanically I smile. I
hardly exist, Kitty."

There was a most unpleasant silence, and then Strafe said:

"None of that's true. For God's sake, Cynthia," he suddenly
shouted, "go and rest yourself."

Cynthia shook her head and continued to address the waitress.
She'd had a rest, she told her. "But it didn't do any good, Kitty,
because hell has invaded the paradise of Glencorn, as so often it has
invaded your island. And we, who have so often brought it, pretend it
isn't there. Who cares about children made into murderers?"

Strafe shouted again. "You fleshless ugly bitch!" he cried. "You
bloody old fool!" He was on his feet, trying to get her to hers. The
blood was thumping in his bronzed face, his eyes had a fury in them

I'd never seen before. "Fleshless!" he shouted at her, not caring that
so many people were listening. He closed his eyes in misery and in
shame again, and I wanted to reach out and take his hand but of
course I could not. You could see the Malseeds didn't blame him, you
could see them thinking that everything was ruined for us. I wanted to
shout at Cynthia too, to batter the silliness out of her, but of course I
could not do that. I feel the tears behind my eyes, and I couldn't help
noticing that Dekko's hands were shaking. He's quite sensitive behind
his joky manner, and had quite obviously taken to heart her statement
that he had never recovered from his schooldays. Nor had it been
pleasant, hearing myself described as vicious.

"No one cares," Cynthia said in the same unbalanced way, as if she
hadn't just been called ugly and a bitch. "No one cares, and on our
journey home we shall all four be silent. Yet is the truth about ourselves at least a beginning? Will we wonder in the end about the hell
that frightens us?"

Strafe still looked wretched, his face deliberately turned away from
us. Mrs. Malseed gave a little sigh and raised the fingers of her left
hand to her cheek, as if something tickled it. Her husband breathed
heavily. Dekko seemed on the point of tears.

Cynthia stumbled off, leaving a silence behind her. Before it was
broken I knew she was right when she said we would just go home,
away from this country we had come to love. And I knew as well that
neither here nor at home would she be led to a blue van that was not
quite an ambulance. Strafe would stay with her because Strafe is made
like that, honorable in his own particular way. I felt a pain where
perhaps my heart is, and again I wanted to cry. Why couldn't it have
been she who had gone down to the rocks and slipped on the seaweed
or just walked into the sea, it didn't matter which? Her awful rig-
marole hung about us as the last of the tea things were gathered
up—the earls who'd fled, the famine and the people planted. The
children were there too, grown up into murdering riff-raff.

1981

Stories for Further Reading

KATE CHOPIN

Beyond the Bayou

The bayou curved like a crescent around the point of land on which La Folle's cabin stood. Between the stream and the hut lay a big abandoned field, where cattle were pastured when the bayou supplied them with water enough. Through the woods that spread back into unknown regions the woman had drawn an imaginary line, and past this circle she never stepped. This was the form of her only mania.

She was now a large, gaunt black woman, past thirty-five. Her real name was Jacqueline, but everyone on the plantation called her La Folle,[1] because in childhood she had been frightened literally "out of her senses," and had never wholly regained them.

It was when there had been skirmishing and sharpshooting all day in the woods. Evening was near when P'tit Maître,[2] black with powder and crimson with blood, had staggered into the cabin of Jacqueline's mother, his pursuers close at his heels. The sight had stunned her childish reason.

She dwelt alone in her solitary cabin, for the rest of the quarters had long since been removed beyond her sight and knowledge. She had more physical strength than most men, and made her patch of cotton and corn and tobacco like the best of them. But of the world beyond the bayou she had long known nothing, save what her morbid fancy conceived.

People at Bellissime had grown used to her and her way, and they thought nothing of it. Even when "Old Mis'" died, they did not wonder that La Folle had not crossed the bayou, but had stood upon her side of it, wailing and lamenting.

P'tit Maître was now the owner of Bellissime. He was a middle-aged man, with a family of beautiful daughters about him, and a little son whom La Folle loved as if he had been her own. She called him Chéri,[3] and so did every one else because she did.

None of the girls had ever been to her what Chéri was. They had each and all loved to be with her, and to listen to her wondrous stories of things that always happened "yonda, beyon' de bayou."

But none of them had stroked her black hand quite as Chéri did, nor rested their heads against her knee so confidingly, nor fallen asleep in her arms as he used to do. For Chéri hardly did such things

1. The crazy woman.   2. Little Master.   3. Darling.

now, since he had become the proud possessor of a gun, and had had his black curls cut off.

That summer—the summer Chéri gave La Folle two black curls tied with a knot of red ribbon—the water ran so low in the bayou that even the little children at Bellissime were able to cross it on foot, and the cattle were sent to pasture down by the river. La Folle was sorry whan they were gone, for she loved these dumb companions well, and liked to feel that they were there, and to hear them browsing by night up to her own enclosure.

It was Saturday afternoon, when the fields were deserted. The men had flocked to a neighboring village to do their week's trading, and the women were occupied with household affairs—La Folle as well as the others. It was then she mended and washed her handful of clothes, scoured her house, and did her baking.

In this last employment she never forgot Chéri. Today she had fashioned croquignoles[4] of the most fantastic and alluring shapes for him. So when she saw the boy come trudging across the old field with his gleaming little new rifle on his shoulder, she called out gaily to him, "Chéri! Chéri!"

But Chéri did not need the summons, for he was coming straight to her. His pockets all bulged out with almonds and raisins and an orange that he had secured for her from the very fine dinner which had been given that day up at his father's house.

He was a sunny-faced youngster of ten. When he had emptied his pockets, La Folle patted his round red cheek, wiped his soiled hands on her apron, and smoothed his hair. Then she watched him as, with his cakes in his hand, he crossed her strip of cotton back of the cabin, and disappeared into the wood.

He had boasted of the things he was going to do with his gun out there.

"You think they got plenty deer in the wood, La Folle?" he had inquired, with the calculating air of an experienced hunter.

"*Non, non!*" the woman laughed. "Don't you look fo' no deer, Chéri. Dat 's too big. But you bring La Folle one good fat squirrel fo' her dinner to-morrow, an' she goin' be satisfi'."

"One squirrel ain't a bit. I'll bring you mo' 'an one, La Folle," he had boasted pompously as he went away.

When the woman, an hour later, heard the report of the boy's rifle close to the wood's edge, she would have thought nothing of it if a sharp cry of distress had not followed the sound.

She withdrew her arms from the tub of suds in which they had been plunged, dried them upon her apron, and as quickly as her trembling limbs would bear her, hurried to the spot whence the ominous report had come.

It was as she feared. There she found Chéri stretched upon the ground, with his rifle beside him. He moaned piteously:

"I'm dead, La Folle! I'm dead! I'm gone!"

"*Non, non!*" she exclaimed resolutely, as she knelt beside him. "Put you' arm 'roun' La Folle's nake, Chéri. Dat's nuttin'; dat goin' be

4. Biscuits.

nuttin'." She lifted him in her powerful arms.

Chéri had carried his gun muzzle-downward. He had stumbled, he did not know how. He only knew that he had a ball lodged somewhere in his leg, and he thought that his end was at hand. Now, with his head upon the woman's shoulder, he moaned and wept with pain and fright.

"Oh, La Folle! La Folle! it hurt so bad! I can' stan' it, La Folle!"

"Don't cry, *mon bébé,*[5] *mon bébé, mon Chéri!*" the woman spoke soothingly as she covered the ground with long strides. "La Folle goin' mine you; Doctor Bonfils goin' come make *mon Chéri* well agin."

She had reached the abandoned field. As she crossed it with her precious burden, she looked constantly and restlessly from side to side. A terrible fear was upon her—the fear of the world beyond the bayou, the morbid and insane dread she had been under since childhood.

When she was at the bayou's edge she stood there, and shouted for help as if a life depended upon it:

"Oh, P'tit Maître! P'tit Maître! *Venez donc! Au secours! Au secours!*" [6]

No voice responded. Chéri's hot tears were scalding her neck. She called for each and every one upon the place, and still no answer came.

She shouted, she wailed; but whether her voice remained unheard or unheeded, no reply came to her frenzied cries. And all the while Chéri moaned and wept and entreated to be taken home to his mother.

La Folle gave a last despairing look around her. Extreme terror was upon her. She clasped the child close against her breast, where he could feel her heart beat like a muffled hammer. Then shutting her eyes, she ran suddenly down the shallow bank of the bayou, and never stopped till she had climbed the opposite shore.

She stood there quivering an instant as she opened her eyes. Then she plunged into the footpath through the trees.

She spoke no more to Chéri, but muttered constantly, "*Bon Dieu, ayez pitié La Folle! Bon Dieu, ayez pitié moi!*"[7]

Instinct seemed to guide her. When the pathway spread clear and smooth enough before her, she again closed her eyes tightly against the sight of that unknown and terrifying world.

A child, playing in some weeds, caught sight of her as she neared the quarters. The little one uttered a cry of dismay.

"La Folle!" she screamed, in her piercing treble. "La Folle done cross de bayer!"

Quickly the cry passed down the line of cabins.

"Yonda, La Folle done cross de bayou!"

Children, old men, old women, young ones with infants in their arms, flocked to doors and windows to see this awe-inspiring spectacle. Most of them shuddered with superstitious dread of what it might portend. "She totin' Chéri!" some of them shouted.

Some of the more daring gathered about her, and followed at her heels, only to fall back with new terror when she turned her distorted

---

5. My baby.
6. Come here! Help! Help!

7. Good Lord, have pity on La Folle! Good Lord, have pity on me!

face upon them. Her eyes were bloodshot and the saliva had gathered in a white foam on her black lips.

Some one had run ahead of her to where P'tit Maître sat with his family and guests upon the gallery.

"P'tit Maître! La Folle done cross de bayou! Look her! Look her yonda totin' Chéri!" This startling intimation was the first which they had of the woman's approach.

She was now near at hand. She walked with long strides. Her eyes were fixed desperately before her, and she breathed heavily, as a tired ox.

At the foot of the stairway, which she could not have mounted, she laid the boy in his father's arms. Then the world that had looked red to La Folle suddenly turned black—like that day she had seen powder and blood.

She reeled for an instant. Before a sustaining arm could reach her, she fell heavily to the ground.

When La Folle regained consciousness, she was at home again, in her own cabin and upon her own bed. The moon rays, streaming in through the open door and windows, gave what light was needed to the old black mammy who stood at the table concocting a tisane of fragrant herbs. It was very late.

Others who had come, and found that the stupor clung to her, had gone again. P'tit Maître had been there, and with him Doctor Bonfils, who said that La Folle might die.

But death had passed her by. The voice was very clear and steady with which she spoke to Tante[8] Lizette, brewing her tisane there in a corner.

"Ef you will give me one good drink tisane, Tante Lizette, I b'lieve I'm goin' sleep, me."

And she did sleep; so soundly, so healthfully, that old Lizette without compunction stole softly away to creep back through the moonlit fields to her own cabin in the new quarters.

The first touch of the cool gray morning awoke La Folle. She arose, calmly, as if no tempest had shaken and threatened her existence but yesterday.

She donned her new blue cottonade[9] and white apron, for she remembered that this was Sunday. When she had made for herself a cup of strong black coffee, and drunk it with relish, she quitted the cabin and walked across the old familiar field to the bayou's edge again.

She did not stop there as she had always done before, but crossed with a long, steady stride as if she had done this all her life.

When she had made her way through the brush and scrub cottonwood-trees that lined the opposite bank, she found herself upon the border of a field where the white, bursting cotton, with the dew upon it, gleamed for acres and acres like frosted silver in the early dawn.

La Folle drew a long, deep breath as she gazed across the country. She walked slowly and uncertainly, like one who hardly knows how, looking about her as she went.

8. Aunt.   9. Cotton fabric made to resemble wool.

The cabins, that yesterday had sent a clamor of voices to pursue her, were quiet now. No one was yet astir at Bellissime. Only the birds that darted here and there from hedges were awake, and singing their matins.

When La Folle came to the broad stretch of velvety lawn that surrounded the house, she moved slowly and with delight over the springy turf, that was delicious beneath her tread.

She stopped to find whence came those perfumes that were assailing her senses with memories from a time far gone.

There they were, stealing up to her from the thousand blue violets that peeped out from green, luxuriant beds. There they were, showering down from the big waxen bells of the magnolias far above her head, and from the jessamine clumps around her.

There were roses, too, without number. To right and left palms spread in broad and graceful curves. It all looked like enchantment beneath the sparkling sheen of dew.

When La Folle had slowly and cautiously mounted the many steps that led up to the veranda, she turned to look back at the perilous ascent she had made. Then she caught sight of the river, bending like a silver bow at the foot of Bellissime. Exultation possessed her soul.

La Folle rapped softly upon a door near at hand. Chéri's mother soon cautiously opened it. Quickly and cleverly she dissembled the astonishment she felt at seeing La Folle.

"Ah, La Folle? Is it you, so early?"

"*Oui*,[1] madame. I come ax how my po' li'le Chéri to, 's mo'nin'."

"He is feeling easier, thank you, La Folle. Dr. Bonfils says it will be nothing serious. He's sleeping now. Will you come back when he awakes?"

"*Non*, madame. I'm goin' wait yair tell Chéri wake up." La Folle seated herself upon the topmost step of the veranda.

A look of wonder and deep content crept into her face as she watched for the first time the sun rise upon the new, the beautiful world beyond the bayou.

1894

1. Yes.

The Secret Sharer

1

On my right hand there were lines of fishing-stakes resembling a mysterious system of half-submerged bamboo fences, incomprehensible in its division of the domain of tropical fishes, and crazy[1] of aspect as if abandoned for ever by some nomad tribe of fishermen now gone to the other end of the ocean; for there was no sign of human habitation as far as the eye could reach. To the left a group of barren islets, suggesting ruins of stone walls, towers, and block-houses, had its foundations set in a blue sea that itself looked solid, so still and stable did it lie below my feet; even the track of light from the westering sun shone smoothly, without that animated glitter which tells of an imperceptible ripple. And when I turned my head to take a parting glance at the tug which had just left us anchored outside the bar, I saw the straight line of the flat shore joined to the stable sea, edge to edge, with a perfect and unmarked closeness, in one leveled floor half brown, half blue under the enormous dome of the sky. Corresponding in their insignificance to the islets of the sea, two small clumps of trees, one on each side of the only fault in the impeccable joint, marked the mouth of the river Meinam[2] we had just left on the first preparatory stage of our homeward journey; and, far back on the inland level, a larger and loftier mass, the grove surrounding the great Paknam pagoda, was the only thing on which the eye could rest from the vain task of exploring the monotonous sweep of the horizon. Here and there gleams as of a few scattered pieces of silver marked the windings of the great river; and on the nearest of them, just within the bar, the tug steaming right into the land became lost to my sight, hull and funnel and masts, as though the impassive earth had swallowed her up without an effort, without a tremor. My eye followed the light cloud of her smoke, now here, now there, above the plain, according to the devious curves of the stream, but always fainter and farther away, till I lost it at last behind the mitre-shaped hill of the great pagoda. And then I was left alone with my ship, anchored at the head of the Gulf of Siam.

She floated at the starting-point of a long journey, very still in an immense stillness, the shadows of her spars flung far to the eastward by the setting sun. At that moment I was alone on her decks. There

1. Irregular, rickety.
2. The Menan (Chao Phraya) runs through Bangkok into the Gulf of Siam. The Paknam Pagoda (Wat Prachadi Klang-nam) is behind the Fort of Paknam at the mouth of the river. H. Warrington Smyth, in *Five Years in Siam* (1898), describes Bangkok as "a land of myths and terror," and says that when he first crossed the bar of the river his heart sank at the sight: "All around an expanse of dirty mud-brown water . . . stuck here and there with fishing stakes, which gave to the whole scene a disorderly, ragged sort of look. . . ."

was not a sound in her—and around us nothing moved, nothing lived, not a canoe on the water, not a bird in the air, not a cloud in the sky. In this breathless pause at the threshold of a long passage we seemed to be measuring our fitness for a long and arduous enterprise, the appointed task of both our existences to be carried out, far from all human eyes, with only sky and sea for spectators and for judges.

There must have been some glare in the air to interfere with one's sight, because it was only just before the sun left us that my roaming eyes made out beyond the highest ridge of the principal islet of the group something which did away with the solemnity of perfect solitude. The tide of darkness flowed on swiftly; and with tropical suddenness a swarm of stars came out above the shadowy earth, while I lingered yet, my hand resting lightly on my ship's rail as if on the shoulder of a trusted friend. But, with all that multitude of celestial bodies staring down at one, the comfort of quiet communion with her was gone for good. And there were also disturbing sounds by this time—voices, footsteps forward; the steward flitted along the main deck, a busily ministering spirit; a hand-bell tinkled urgently under the poop deck. . . .

I found my two officers waiting for me near the supper table, in the lighted cuddy. We sat down at once, and as I helped the chief mate, I said:

"Are you aware that there is a ship anchored inside the islands? I saw her mast-heads above the ridge as the sun went down."

He raised sharply his simple face, overcharged by a terrible growth of whisker, and emitted his usual ejaculations, "Bless my soul, sir! You don't say so!"

My second mate was a round-cheeked, silent young man, grave beyond his years, I thought; but as our eyes happened to meet I detected a slight quiver on his lips. I looked down at once. It was not my part to encourage sneering on board my ship. It must be said, too, that I knew very little of my officers. In consequence of certain events of no particular significance, except to myself, I had been appointed to the command only a fortnight before. Neither did I know much of the hands forward. All these people had been together for eighteen months or so, and my position was that of the only stranger on board. I mention this because it has some bearing on what is to follow. But what I felt most was my being a stranger to the ship; and if all the truth must be told, I was somewhat of a stranger to myself. The youngest man on board (barring the second mate), and untried as yet by a position of the fullest responsibility, I was willing to take the adequacy of the others for granted. They had simply to be equal to their tasks; but I wondered how far I should turn out faithful to that ideal conception of one's own personality every man sets up for himself secretly.

Meantime the chief mate, with an almost visible effect of collaboration on the part of his round eyes and frightful whiskers, was trying to evolve a theory of the anchored ship. His dominant trait was to take all things into earnest consideration. He was of a painstaking turn of mind. As he used to say, he "liked to account to himself" for practically everything that came in his way, down to a miserable scorpion he had found in his cabin a week before. The why and the wherefore of that scorpion—how it got on board and came to select his room rather than the pantry (which was a dark place and more what a scorpion would be partial to), and how on earth it managed to drown itself in the inkwell of his writing-desk—had exercised him infinitely. The ship within the islands was much more easily accounted for; and just as we were about to rise from table he made his pronouncement. She was, he doubted not, a ship from home lately arrived. Probably she drew too much water to cross the bar except at the top of spring tides. Therefore she went into that natural harbor to wait for a few days in preference to remaining in an open roadstead.

"That's so," confirmed the second mate suddenly, in his slightly hoarse voice. "She draws over twenty feet. She's the Liverpool ship *Sephora*[3] with a cargo of coal. Hundred and twenty-three days from Cardiff."

We looked at him in surprise.

"The tugboat skipper told me when he come on board for your letters, sir," explained the young man. "He expects to take her up the river the day after tomorrow."

After thus overwhelming us with the extent of his information he slipped out of the cabin. The mate observed regretfully that he "could not account for that young fellow's whims." What prevented him telling us all about it at once, he wanted to know.

I detained him as he was making a move. For the last two days the crew had had plenty of hard work, and the night before they had very little sleep. I felt painfully that I—a stranger—was doing something unusual when I directed him to let all hands turn in without setting an anchor-watch.[4] I proposed to keep on deck myself till one o'clock or thereabouts. I would get the second mate to relieve me at that hour.

"He will turn out the cook and the steward at four," I concluded, "and then give you a call. Of course at the slightest sign of any sort of wind we'll have the hands up and make a start at once."

He concealed his astonishment. "Very well, sir." Outside the cuddy he put his head in the second mate's door to inform him of my unheard-of caprice to take a five hours' anchor-watch on myself. I heard the other raise his voice incredulously—"What? The captain himself?" Then a few more murmurs, a door closed, then another. A few moments later I went on deck.

My strangeness, which had made me sleepless, had prompted that unconventional arrangement, as if I had expected in those solitary hours of the night to get on terms with the ship of which I knew

3. See *Leviticus* 23:15–16, for the system of counting days for offerings; *sephor*, to count, refers to a forty-day period during which no marriages can take place.

4. A detachment of seamen kept on deck while the ship lies at anchor.

nothing, manned by men of whom I knew very little more. Fast alongside a wharf, littered like any ship in port with a tangle of unrelated things, invaded by unrelated shore people, I had hardly seen her yet properly. Now, as she lay cleared for sea, the stretch of her main deck seemed to me very fine under the stars. Very fine, very roomy for her size, and very inviting. I descended the poop and paced the waist, my mind picturing to myself the coming passage through the Malay Archipelago, down the Indian Ocean, and up the Atlantic. All its phases were familiar enough to me, every characteristic, all the alternatives which were likely to face me on the high seas—everything! . . . except the novel responsibility of command. But I took heart from the reasonable thought that the ship was like other ships, the men like other men, and that the sea was not likely to keep any special surprises expressly for my discomfiture.

Arrived at that comforting conclusion, I bethought myself of a cigar and went below to get it. All was still down there. Everybody at the after end of the ship was sleeping profoundly. I came out again on the quarter-deck, agreeably at ease in my sleeping suit on that warm, breathless night, barefooted, a glowing cigar in my teeth, and, going forward, I was met by the profound silence of the fore end of the ship. Only as I passed the door of the forecastle I heard a deep, quiet, trustful sigh of some sleeper inside. And suddenly I rejoiced in the great security of the sea as compared with the unrest of the land, in my choice of that untempted life presenting no disquieting problems, invested with an elementary moral beauty by the absolute straightforwardness of its appeal and by the singleness of its purpose.

The riding-light [5] in the fore-rigging burned with a clear, untroubled, as if symbolic, flame, confident and bright in the mysterious shades of the night. Passing on my way aft along the other side of the ship, I observed that the rope side-ladder, put over, no doubt, for the master of the tug when he came to fetch away our letters, had not been hauled in as it should have been. I became annoyed at this, for exactitude in small matters is the very soul of discipline. Then I reflected that I had myself peremptorily dismissed my officers from duty, and by my own act had prevented the anchor-watch being formally set and things properly attended to. I asked myself whether it was wise ever to interfere with the established routine of duties even from the kindest of motives. My action might have made me appear eccentric. Goodness only knew how that absurdly whiskered mate would "account" for my conduct, and what the whole ship thought of that informality of their new captain. I was vexed with myself.

Not from compunction certainly, but, as it were mechanically, I proceeded to get the ladder in myself. Now a side-ladder of that sort is a light affair and comes in easily, yet my vigorous tug, which should have brought it flying on board, merely recoiled upon my

---

5. Special light displayed by ship while ("riding") at anchor.

body in a totally unexpected jerk. What the devil! . . . I was so astounded by the immovableness of that ladder that I remained stock-still, trying to account for it to myself like that imbecile mate of mine. In the end, of course, I put my head over the rail.

The side of the ship made an opaque belt of shadow on the dark-ling glassy shimmer of the sea. But I saw at once something elongated and pale floating very close to the ladder. Before I could form a guess a faint flash of phosphorescent light, which seemed to issue suddenly from the naked body of a man, flickered in the sleeping water with the elusive, silent play of summer lightning in a night sky. With a gasp I saw revealed to my stare a pair of feet, the long legs, a broad livid back immersed right up to the neck in a greenish cadaverous glow. One hand, awash, clutched the bottom rung of the ladder. He was complete but for the head. A headless corpse! The cigar dropped out of my gaping mouth with a tiny plop and a short hiss quite audible in the absolute stillness of all things under heaven. At that I suppose he raised up his face, a dimly pale oval in the shadow of the ship's side. But even then I could only barely make out down there the shape of his black-haired head. However, it was enough for the horrid, frost-bound sensation which had gripped me about the chest to pass off. The moment of vain exclamations was past too. I only climbed on the spare spar and leaned over the rail as far as I could, to bring my eyes nearer to that mystery floating alongside.

As he hung by the ladder, like a resting swimmer, the sea-lightning played about his limbs at every stir; and he appeared in it ghastly, silvery, fish-like. He remained as mute as a fish, too. He made no motion to get out of the water, either. It was inconceivable that he should not attempt to come on board, and strangely troubling to suspect that perhaps he did not want to. And my first words were prompted by just that troubled incertitude.

"What's the matter?" I asked in my ordinary tone, speaking down to the face upturned exactly under mine.

"Cramp," it answered, no louder. Then slightly anxious, "I say, no need to call any one."

"I was not going to," I said.

"Are you alone on deck?"

"Yes."

I had somehow the impression that he was on the point of letting go the ladder to swim away beyond my ken—mysterious as he came. But, for the moment, this being appearing as if he had risen from the bottom of the sea (it was certainly the nearest land to the ship) wanted only to know the time. I told him. And he, down there, tentatively:

"I suppose your captain's turned in?"

"I am sure he isn't," I said.

He seemed to struggle with himself, for I heard something like the low, bitter murmur of doubt. "What's the good?" His next words came out with a hesitating effort.

"Look here, my man. Could you call him out quietly?"

I thought the time had come to declare myself.

"*I* am the captain."

I heard a "By Jove!" whispered at the level of the water. The phosphorescence flashed in the swirl of the water all about his limbs, his other hand seized the ladder.

"My name's Leggatt."

The voice was calm and resolute. A good voice. The self-possession of that man had somehow induced a corresponding state in myself. It was very quietly that I remarked:

"You must be a good swimmer."

"Yes. I've been in the water practically since nine o'clock. The question for me now is whether I am to let go this ladder and go on swimming till I sink from exhaustion or—to come on board here."

I felt this was no mere formula of desperate speech, but a real alternative in the view of a strong soul. I should have gathered from this that he was young; indeed, it is only the young who are ever confronted by such clear issues. But at the time it was pure intuition on my part. A mysterious communication was established already between us two—in the face of that silent, darkened tropical sea. I was young, too; young enough to make no comment. The man in the water began suddenly to climb up the ladder, and I hastened away from the rail to fetch some clothes.

Before entering the cabin I stood still, listening in the lobby at the foot of the stairs. A faint snore came through the closed door of the chief mate's room. The second mate's door was on the hook, but the darkness in there was absolutely soundless. He, too, was young and could sleep like a stone. Remained the steward, but he was not likely to wake up before he was called. I got a sleeping suit out of my room, and, coming back on deck, saw the naked man from the sea sitting on the main-hatch, glimmering white in the darkness, his elbows on his knees and his head in his hands. In a moment he had concealed his damp body in a sleeping suit of the same gray-stripe pattern as the one I was wearing, and followed me like my double on the poop. Together we moved right aft, barefooted, silent.

"What is it?" I asked in a deadened voice, taking the lighted lamp out of the binnacle, and raising it to his face.

"An ugly business."

He had rather regular features; a good mouth; light eyes under somewhat heavy, dark eyebrows; a smooth, square forehead; no growth on his cheeks; a small, brown mustache, and a well-shaped, round chin. His expression was concentrated, meditative, under the inspecting light of the lamp I held up to his face; such as a man thinking hard in solitude might wear. My sleeping suit was just right for his size. A well-knit young fellow of twenty-five at most. He caught his lower lip with the edge of white, even teeth.

"Yes," I said, replacing the lamp in the binnacle. The warm, heavy tropical night closed upon his head again.

"There's a ship over there," he murmured.

"Yes, I know. The *Sephora*. Did you know of us?"

"Hadn't the slightest idea. I am the mate of her—" He paused and corrected himself. "I should say I *was*."

"Aha! Something wrong?"

"Yes. Very wrong indeed. I've killed a man."

"What do you mean? Just now?"

"No, on the passage. Weeks ago. Thirty-nine south. When I say a man—"

"Fit of temper," I suggested confidently.

The shadowy, dark head, like mine, seemed to nod imperceptibly above the ghostly gray of my sleeping suit. It was, in the night, as though I had been faced by my own reflection in the depths of a sombre and immense mirror.

"A pretty thing to have to own up to for a Conway boy," [6] murmured my double distinctly.

"You're a Conway boy?"

"I am," he said, as if startled. Then, slowly . . . "Perhaps you too . . ."

It was so; but being a couple of years older I had left before he joined. After a quick interchange of dates a silence fell; and I thought suddenly of my absurd mate with his terrific whiskers and the "Bless my soul—you don't say so" type of intellect. My double gave me an inkling of his thoughts by saying:

"My father's a parson in Norfolk. Do you see me before a judge and jury on that charge? For myself I can't see the necessity. There are fellows that an angel from heaven—And I am not that. He was one of those creatures that are just simmering all the time with a silly sort of wickedness. Miserable devils that have no business to live at all. He wouldn't do his duty and wouldn't let anybody else do theirs. But what's the good of talking! You know well enough the sort of ill-conditioned snarling cur . . ."

He appealed to me as if our experiences had been as identical as our clothes. And I knew well enough the pestiferous danger of such a character where there are no means of legal repression. And I knew well enough also that my double there was no homicidal ruffian. I did not think of asking him for details, and he told me the story roughly in brusque, disconnected sentences. I needed no more. I saw it all going on as though I were myself inside that other sleeping suit.

"It happened while we were setting a reefed foresail, at dusk. Reefed foresail! You understand the sort of weather. The only sail we had left to keep the ship running; so you may guess what it had been like for days. Anxious sort of job, that. He gave me some of his cursed insolence at the sheet.[7] I tell you I was overdone with this terrific weather that seemed to have no end to it. Terrific, I tell you— and a deep ship. I believe the fellow himself was half crazed with

---

6. The wooden battleship Conway, which was used to train young officers for the Royal Navy and merchant service. She ran aground in the Menai Straits (Wales) in 1953 and burned in 1956.

7. Rope or chain attached to lower corner of sail used for shortening or slackening it.

funk. It was no time for gentlemanly reproof, so I turned round and felled him like an ox. He up and at me. We closed just as an awful sea made for the ship. All hands saw it coming and took to the rigging, but I had him by the throat, and went on shaking him like a rat, the men above us yelling. 'Look out! Look out!' Then a crash as if the sky had fallen on my head. They say that for over ten minutes hardly anything was to be seen of the ship—just the three masts and a bit of the forecastle head and of the poop all awash driving along in a smother of foam. It was a miracle that they found us, jammed together behind the forebits. It's clear that I meant business, because I was holding him by the throat still when they picked us up. He was black in the face. It was too much for them. It seems they rushed us aft together, gripped as we were, screaming 'Murder!' like a lot of lunatics, and broke into the cuddy. And the ship running for her life, touch and go all the time, any minute her last in a sea fit to turn your hair gray only a-looking at it. I understand that the skipper, too, started raving like the rest of them. The man had been deprived of sleep for more than a week, and to have this sprung on him at the height of a furious gale nearly drove him out of his mind. I wonder they didn't fling me overboard after getting the carcass of their precious shipmate out of my fingers. They had rather a job to separate us, I've been told. A sufficiently fierce story to make an old judge and a respectable jury sit up a bit. The first thing I heard when I came to myself was the maddening howling of that endless gale, and on that the voice of the old man. He was hanging on to my bunk, staring into my face out of his sou'wester.

" 'Mr. Leggatt, you have killed a man. You can act no longer as chief mate of this ship.' "

His care to subdue his voice made it sound monotonous. He rested a hand on the end of the skylight to steady himself with, and all that time did not stir a limb, so far as I could see. "Nice little tale for a quiet tea party," he concluded in the same tone.

One of my hands, too, rested on the end of the skylight; neither did I stir a limb, so far as I knew. We stood less than a foot from each other. It occurred to me that if old "Bless my soul—you don't say so" were to put his head up the companion and catch sight of us, he would think he was seeing double, or imagine himself come upon a scene of weird witchcraft: the strange captain having a quiet confabulation by the wheel with his own gray ghost. I became very much concerned to prevent anything of the sort. I heard the other's soothing undertone:

"My father's a parson in Norfolk," it said. Evidently he had forgotten he had told me this important fact before. Truly a nice little tale.

"You had better slip down into my stateroom now," I said, moving off stealthily. My double followed my movements; our bare feet made no sound; I let him in, closed the door with care, and, after giving a call to the second mate, returned on deck for my relief.

"Not much sign of any wind yet," I remarked when he approached.

"No, sir. Not much," he assented sleepily in his hoarse voice, with just enough deference, no more, and barely suppressing a yawn.

"Well, that's all you have to look out for. You have got your orders."

"Yes, sir."

I paced a turn or two on the poop and saw him take up his position face forward with his elbow in the ratlines of the mizzen-rigging before I went below. The mate's faint snoring was still going on peacefully. The cuddy lamp was burning over the table on which stood a vase with flowers, a polite attention from the ship's provision merchant—the last flowers we should see for the next three months at the very least. Two bunches of bananas hung from the beam symmetrically, one on each side of the rudder-casing. Everything was as before in the ship—except that two of her captain's sleeping suits were simultaneously in use, one motionless in the cuddy, the other keeping very still in the captain's stateroom.

It must be explained here that my cabin had the form of the capital letter L, the door being within the angle and opening into the short part of the letter. A couch was to the left, the bedplace to the right; my writing-desk and the chronometers' table faced the door. But any one opening it, unless he stepped right inside, had no view of what I call the long (or vertical) part of the letter. It contained some lockers surmounted by a bookcase; and a few clothes, a thick jacket or two, caps, oilskin coat, and such-like, hung on hooks. There was at the bottom of that part a door opening into my bathroom, which could be entered also directly from the saloon. But that way was never used.

The mysterious arrival had discovered the advantage of this particular shape. Entering my room, lighted strongly by a big bulkhead lamp swung on gimbals above my writing-desk, I did not see him anywhere till he stepped out quietly from behind the coats hung in the recessed part.

"I heard somebody moving about, and went in there at once," he whispered.

I, too, spoke under my breath.

"Nobody is likely to come in here without knocking and getting permission."

He nodded. His face was thin and the sunburn faded, as though he had been ill. And no wonder. He had been, I heard presently, kept under arrest in his cabin for nearly nine weeks. But there was nothing sickly in his eyes or in his expression. He was not a bit like me, really; yet, as we stood leaning over my bedplace, whispering side by side, with our dark heads together and our backs to the door, anybody bold enough to open it stealthily would have been treated to the uncanny sight of a double captain busy talking in whispers with his other self.

"But all this doesn't tell me how you came to hang on to our side-ladder," I inquired, in the hardly audible murmurs we used, after he had told me something more of the proceedings on board the *Sephora* once the bad weather was over.

"When we sighted Java Head⁸ I had had time to think all those matters out several times over. I had six weeks of doing nothing else, and with only an hour or so every evening for a tramp on the quarterdeck."

He whispered, his arms folded on the side of my bedplace, staring through the open port. And I could imagine perfectly the manner of this thinking out—a stubborn if not a steadfast operation; something of which I should have been perfectly incapable.

"I reckoned it would be dark before we closed with the land," he continued, so low that I had to strain my hearing, near as we were to each other, shoulder touching shoulder almost. "So I asked to speak to the old man. He always seemed very sick when he came to see me—as if he could not look me in the face. You know, that foresail saved the ship. She was too deep to have run long under bare poles. And it was I that managed to set it for him. Anyway, he came. When I had him in my cabin—he stood by the door looking at me as if I had the halter round my neck already—I asked him right away to leave my cabin door unlocked at night while the ship was going through Sunda Straits. There would be the Java coast within two or three miles, off Anjer Point. I wanted nothing more. I've had a prize for swimming my second year in the Conway."

"I can believe it," I breathed out.

"God only knows why they locked me in every night. To see some of their faces you'd have thought they were afraid I'd go about at night strangling people. Am I a murdering brute? Do I look it? By Jove! if I had been he wouldn't have trusted himself like that into my room. You'll say I might have chucked him aside and bolted out, there and then—it was dark already. Well, no. And for the same reason I wouldn't think of trying to smash the door. There would have been a rush to stop me at the noise, and I did not mean to get into a confounded scrimmage. Somebody else might have got killed—for I would not have broken out only to get chucked back, and I did not want any more of that work. He refused, looking more sick than ever. He was afraid of the men, and also of that old second mate of his who had been sailing with him for years—a gray-headed old humbug; and his steward, too, had been with him devil knows how long—seventeen years or more—a dogmatic sort of loafer who hated me like poison, just because I was the chief mate. No chief mate ever made more than one voyage in the *Sephora*, you know. Those two old chaps ran the ship. Devil only knows what the skipper wasn't afraid of (all his nerve went to pieces altogether in that hellish spell of bad weather we had)—of what the law would do to him—of his wife, perhaps. Oh yes! she's on board. Though I don't think she would have meddled. She would have been only too glad to have me out of the ship in any way. The 'brand of Cain' business, don't you see? That's all right. I was ready enough to go off wandering on the face of the earth—and that was price enough to pay

---

8. A famous landmark for clipper ships engaged in the China trade on the western end of Java, the southern entrance to the Sunda Straits mentioned below; the Leggatt incident thus took place some 1,500 miles south of the present scene.

for an Abel[9] of that sort. Anyhow, he wouldn't listen to me. 'This thing must take its course. I represent the law here.' He was shaking like a leaf. 'So you won't?' 'No!' 'Then I hope you will be able to sleep on that," I said, and turned my back on him. 'I wonder that *you* can,' cries he, and locks the door.

"Well, after that, I couldn't. Not very well. That was three weeks ago. We have had a slow passage through the Java Sea; drifted about Carimata[1] for ten days. When we anchored here they thought, I suppose, it was all right. The nearest land (and that's five miles) is the ship's destination; the consul would soon set about catching me; and there would have been no object in bolting to these islets there. I don't suppose there's a drop of water on them. I don't know how it was, but tonight that steward, after bringing me my supper, went out to let me eat it, and left the door unlocked. And I ate it—all there was, too. After I had finished I strolled out on the quarter-deck. I don't know that I meant to do anything. A breath of fresh air was all I wanted, I believe. Then a sudden temptation came over me. I kicked off my slippers and was in the water before I had made up my mind fairly. Somebody heard the splash and they raised an awful hullabaloo. 'He's gone! Lower the boats! He's committed suicide! No, he's swimming.' Certainly I was swimming. It's not easy for a swimmer like me to commit suicide by drowning. I landed on the nearest islet before the boat left the ship's side. I heard them pulling about in the dark, hailing, and so on, but after a bit they gave up. Everything quieted down and the anchorage became as still as death. I sat down on a stone and began to think. I felt certain they would start searching for me at daylight. There was no place to hide on those stony things—and if there had been, what would have been the good? But now I was clear of that ship, I was not going back. So after a while I took off all my clothes, tied them up in a bundle with a stone inside, and dropped them in the deep water on the outer side of that islet. That was suicide enough for me. Let them think what they liked, but I didn't mean to drown myself. I meant to swim till I sank—but that's not the same thing. I struck out for another of these little islands, and it was from that one that I first saw your riding-light. Something to swim for. I went on easily, and on the way I came upon a flat rock a foot or two above water. In the daytime, I dare say, you might make it out with a glass from your poop. I scrambled up on it and rested myself for a bit. Then I made another start. That last spell must have been over a mile."

His whisper was getting fainter and fainter, and all the time he stared straight out through the porthole, in which there was not even a star to be seen. I had not interrupted him. There was something that made comment impossible, in his narrative, or perhaps in himself; a sort of feeling, a quality, which I can't find a name for. And when

9. In *Genesis* (4:14-15) Cain says to the Lord, "Behold, though hast driven me out this day from the face of the earth; and from thy face shall I be hid; and I shall be a fugitive and a vagabond in the earth; and it shall come to pass, that every one that findeth me shall slay me. And the Lord said unto him, Therefore whosoever slayeth Cain, vengeance shall be taken on him sevenfold. And the Lord set a mark upon Cain, lest any finding him should kill him."

1. The Karimata Islands in the straits between Borneo and Sumatra, some three hundred miles northeast of the Sunda Straits.

he ceased, all I found was a futile whisper, "So you swam for our light?"

"Yes—straight for it. It was something to swim for. I couldn't see any stars low down because the coast was in the way, and I couldn't see the land, either. The water was like glass. One might have been swimming in a confounded thousand feet deep cistern with no place for scrambling out anywhere; but what I didn't like was the notion of swimming round and round like a crazed bullock before I gave out; and as I didn't mean to go back . . . No. Do you see me being hauled back, stark naked, off one of these little islands by the scruff of the neck and fighting like a wild beast? Somebody would have got killed for certain, and I did not want any of that. So I went on. Then your ladder—"

"Why didn't you hail the ship?" I asked, a little louder.

He touched my shoulder lightly. Lazy footsteps came right over our heads and stopped. The second mate had crossed from the other side of the poop and might have been hanging over the rail, for all we knew.

"He couldn't hear us talking—could he?" My double breathed into my very ear anxiously.

His anxiety was an answer, a sufficient answer, to the question I had put to him. An answer containing all the difficulty of that situation. I closed the porthole quietly, to make sure. A louder word might have been overheard.

"Who's that?" he whispered then.

"My second mate. But I don't know much more of the fellow than you do."

And I told him a little about myself. I had been appointed to take charge while I least expected anything of the sort, not quite a fortnight ago. I didn't know either the ship or the people. Hadn't had the time in port to look about me or size anybody up. And as to the crew, all they knew was that I was appointed to take the ship home. For the rest, I was almost as much of a stranger on board as himself, I said. And at the moment I felt it most acutely. I felt that it would take very little to make me a suspect person in the eyes of the ship's company.

He had turned about meantime; and we, the two strangers in the ship, faced each other in identical attitudes.

"Your ladder—" he murmured, after a silence. "Who'd have thought of finding a ladder hanging over at night in a ship anchored out here! I felt just then a very unpleasant faintness. After the life I've been leading for nine weeks, anybody would have got out of condition. I wasn't capable of swimming round as far as your rudder-chains. And, lo and behold! there was a ladder to get hold of. After I gripped it I said to myself, 'What's the good?' When I saw a man's head looking over I thought I would swim away presently and leave him shouting—in whatever language it was. I didn't mind being looked at. I—I liked it. And then you speaking to me so quietly—as if you had expected me—made me hold on a little longer. It had been a confounded lonely time—I don't mean while swimming. I was glad to talk a little to somebody that didn't belong to the *Sephora*. As to asking for the captain, that was a mere impulse. It could have been no use, with all the ship knowing about me and the other people pretty certain to be round here in the morning. I don't know—I wanted to be seen, to talk with somebody, before I went on. I don't know what I would have said. . . . 'Fine night, isn't it?' or something of the sort."

"Do you think they will be round here presently?" I asked, with some incredulity.

"Quite likely," he said faintly.

He looked extremely haggard all of a sudden. His head rolled on his shoulders.

"H'm. We shall see then. Meantime get into that bed," I whispered. "Want help? There."

It was a rather high bedplace with a set of drawers underneath. This amazing swimmer really needed the lift I gave him by seizing his leg. He tumbled in, rolled over on his back, and flung one arm across his eyes. And then, with his face nearly hidden, he must have looked exactly as I used to look in that bed. I gazed upon my other self for a while before drawing across carefully the two green serge curtains which ran on a brass rod. I thought for a moment of pinning them together for greater safety, but I sat down on the couch, and once there I felt unwilling to rise and hunt for a pin. I would do it in a moment. I was extremely tired, in a peculiarly intimate way, by the strain of stealthiness, by the effort of whispering, and the general secrecy of this excitement. It was three o'clock by now, and I had been on my feet since nine, but I was not sleepy; I could not have gone to sleep. I sat there, fagged out, looking at the curtains, trying to clear my mind of the confused sensation of being in two places at once, and greatly bothered by an exasperating knocking in my head. It was a relief to discover suddenly that it was not in my head at all, but on the outside of the door. Before I could collect myself, the words "Come in" were out of my mouth, and the steward entered with a tray, bringing in my morning coffee. I had slept, after all, and I was so frightened that I shouted, "This way! I am here, steward," as though he had been miles away. He put down the tray on the table next the couch and only then said, very quietly, "I can see you are here, sir." I felt him give me a keen look, but I dared not meet his eyes just then. He must have wondered why I had drawn the curtains of my bed before going to sleep on the couch. He went out, hooking the door open as usual.

I heard the crew washing decks above me. I knew I would have been told at once if there had been any wind. Calm, I thought, and I was doubly vexed. Indeed, I felt dual more than ever. The steward reappeared suddenly in the doorway. I jumped up from the couch so quickly that he gave a start.

"What do you want here?"

"Close your port, sir—they are washing decks."

"It is closed," I said, reddening.

"Very well, sir." But he did not move from the doorway and returned my stare in an extraordinary, equivocal manner for a time. Then his eyes wavered, all his expression changed, and in a voice unusually gentle, almost coaxingly.

"May I come in to take the empty cup away, sir?"

"Of course!" I turned my back on him while he popped in and out. Then I unhooked and closed the door and even pushed the bolt. This sort of thing could not go on very long. The cabin was as hot as an oven, too. I took a peep at my double, and discovered that he had not moved; his arm was still over his eyes; but his chest heaved, his hair was wet, his chin glistened with perspiration. I reached over him and opened the port.

"I must show myself on deck," I reflected.

Of course, theoretically, I could do what I liked, with no one to say nay to me within the whole circle of the horizon; but to lock my cabin door and take the key away I did not dare. Directly I put my head out of the companion I saw the group of my two officers, the second mate barefooted, the chief mate in long india-rubber boots, near the break of the poop, and the steward half-way down the poop ladder talking to them eagerly. He happened to catch sight of me and dived, the second ran down on the main deck shouting some order or other, and the chief mate came to meet me, touching his cap.

There was a sort of curiosity in his eye that I did not like. I don't know whether the steward had told them that I was "queer" only, or downright drunk, but I know the man meant to have a good look at me. I watched him coming with a smile which, as he got into point-blank range, took effect and froze his very whiskers. I did not give him time to open his lips.

"Square the yards by lifts and braces before the hands go to breakfast."

It was the first particular order I had given on board that ship; and I stayed on deck to see it executed too. I had felt the need of asserting myself without loss of time. That sneering young cub got taken down a peg or two on that occasion, and I also seized the opportunity of having a good look at the face of every foremast man as they filed past me to go to the after braces. At breakfast time, eating nothing myself, I presided with such frigid dignity that the two mates were only too glad to escape from the cabin as soon as decency permitted; and all the time the dual working of my mind distracted me almost to the point of insanity. I was constantly watching myself, my secret self, as dependent on my actions as my own personality, sleeping in that bed, behind that door which faced me as I sat at the head of the table. It was very much like being mad, only it was worse, because one was aware of it.

I had to shake him for a solid minute, but when at last he opened his eyes it was in the full possession of his senses, with an inquiring look.

"All's well so far," I whispered. "Now you must vanish into the bathroom."

He did so, as noiseless as a ghost, and I then rang for the steward, and facing him boldly, directed him to tidy up my stateroom while I was having my bath—"and be quick about it." As my tone admitted of no excuses, he said, "Yes, sir," and ran off to fetch his dustpan and brushes. I took a bath and did most of my dressing, splashing, and whistling softly for the steward's edification, while the secret sharer of my life stood drawn bolt upright in that little space, his face looking very sunken in daylight, his eyelids lowered under the stern, dark line of his eyebrows drawn together by a slight frown.

When I left him there to go back to my room the steward was finishing dusting. I sent for the mate and engaged him in some insignificant conversation. It was, as it were, trifling with the terrific character of his whiskers; but my object was to give him an opportunity for a good look at my cabin. And then I could at last shut, with a clear conscience, the door of my stateroom and get my double back into the recessed part. There was nothing else for it. He had to sit still on a small folding stool, half smothered by the heavy coats hanging there. We listened to the steward going into the bathroom out of the saloon, filling the water-bottles there, scrubbing the bath, setting things to rights, whisk, bang, clatter—out again into the saloon —turn the key—click. Such was my scheme for keeping my second self invisible. Nothing better could be contrived under the circumstances. And there we sat: I at my writing-desk ready to appear busy with some papers, he behind me, out of sight of the door. It would not have been prudent to talk in daytime; and I could not have stood the excitement of that queer sense of whispering to myself. Now and then, glancing over my shoulder, I saw him far back there, sitting rigidly on the low stool, his bare feet close together, his arms folded, his head hanging on his breast—and perfectly still. Anybody would have taken him for me.

I was fascinated by it myself. Every moment I had to glance over my shoulder. I was looking at him when a voice outside the door said: "Beg pardon, sir."

"Well!" . . . I kept my eyes on him, and so when the voice outside the door announced, "There's a ship's boat coming our way, sir," I saw him give a start—the first movement he had made for hours. But he did not raise his bowed head.

"All right. Get the ladder over."

I hesitated. Should I whisper something to him? But what? His immobility seemed to have been never disturbed. What could I tell him he did not know already? . . . Finally I went on deck.

2

The skipper of the *Sephora* had a thin, red whisker all round his face, and the sort of complexion that goes with hair of that color; also the particular, rather smeary shade of blue in the eyes. He was not exactly a showy figure; his shoulders were high, his stature but middling—one leg slightly more bandy than the other. He shook hands, looking vaguely around. A spiritless tenacity was his main characteristic, I judged. I behaved with a politeness which seemed to disconcert him. Perhaps he was shy. He mumbled to me as if he were ashamed of what he was saying; gave his name (it was something like Archbold—but at this distance of years I hardly am sure), his ship's name, and a few other particulars of that sort, in the manner of a criminal making a reluctant and doleful confession. He had had terrible weather on the passage out—terrible—terrible—wife aboard, too.

By this time we were seated in the cabin and the steward brought in a tray with a bottle and glasses. "Thanks! No." Never took liquor. Would have some water, though. He drank two tumblerfuls. Terrible thirsty work. Ever since daylight had been exploring the islands round his ship.

"What was that for—fun?" I asked with an appearance of polite interest.

"No!" He sighed. "Painful duty."

As he persisted in his mumbling and I wanted my double to hear every word, I hit upon the notion of informing him that I regretted to say I was hard of hearing.

"Such a young man too!" he nodded, keeping his smeary, blue, unintelligent eyes fastened upon me. "What was the cause of it—some disease?" he inquired, without the least sympathy and as if he thought that, if so, I'd got no more than I deserved.

"Yes; disease," I admitted in a cheerful tone which seemed to shock him. But my point was gained, because he had to raise his voice to give me his tale. It is not worth while to record that version. It was just over two months since all this had happened, and he had thought so much about it that he seemed completely muddled as to its bearings, but still immensely impressed.

"What would you think of such a thing happening on board your own ship? I've had the *Sephora* for these fifteen years. I am a well-known shipmaster."

He was densely distressed—and perhaps I should have sympathized with him if I had been able to detach my mental vision from the unsuspected sharer of my cabin as though he were my second self. There he was on the other side of the bulkhead, four or five feet from us, no more, as we sat in the saloon. I looked politely at Captain Archbold (if that was his name), but it was the other I saw, in a gray sleeping suit, seated on a low stool, his bare feet close together, his arms folded, and every word said between us falling into the ears of his dark head bowed on his chest.

"I have been at sea now, man and boy, for seven and thirty years, and I've never heard of such a thing happening in an English ship. And that it should be my ship. Wife on board, too."

I was hardly listening to him.

"Don't you think," I said, "that the heavy sea which, you told me, came aboard just then might have killed the man? I have seen the sheer weight of a sea kill a man very neatly, by simply breaking his neck."

"Good God!" he uttered impressively, fixing his smeary blue eyes on me. "The sea! No man killed by the sea ever looked like that." He seemed positively scandalized at my suggestion. And as I gazed at him, certainly not prepared for anything original on his part, he advanced his head close to mine and thrust his tongue out at me so suddenly that I couldn't help starting back.

After scoring over my calmness in this graphic way he nodded wisely. If I had seen the sight, he assured me, I would never forget it as long as I lived. The weather was too bad to give the corpse a proper sea burial. So next day at dawn they took it up on the poop, covering its face with a bit of bunting; he read a short prayer, and then, just as it was, in its oilskins and long boots, they launched it amongst those mountainous seas that seemed ready every moment to swallow up the ship herself and the terrified lives on board of her.

"That reefed foresail saved you," I threw in.

"Under God—it did," he exclaimed fervently. "It was by a special mercy, I firmly believe, that it stood some of those hurricane squalls."

"It was the setting of that sail which—" I began.

"God's own hand in it," he interrupted me. "Nothing less could have done it. I don't mind telling you that I hardly dared give the order. It seemed impossible that we could touch anything without losing it, and then our last hope would have been gone."

The terror of that gale was on him yet. I let him go on for a bit, then said casually—as if returning to a minor subject:

"You were very anxious to give up your mate to the shore people, I believe?"

He was. To the law. His obscure tenacity on that point had in it something incomprehensible and a little awful; something, as it were, mystical, quite apart from his anxiety that he should not be suspected of "countenancing any doings of that sort." Seven and thirty virtuous years at sea, of which over twenty of immaculate command, and the last fifteen in the *Sephora*, seemed to have laid him under some pitiless obligation.

"And you know," he went on, groping shamefacedly amongst his feelings, "I did not engage that young fellow. His people had some interest with my owners. I was in a way forced to take him on. He looked very smart, very gentlemanly, and all that. But do you know—I never liked him, somehow. I am a plain man. You see, he wasn't exactly the sort for the chief mate of a ship like the *Sephora*."

I had become so connected in thoughts and impressions with the secret sharer of my cabin that I felt as if I, personally, were being given to understand that I, too, was not the sort that would have done for the chief mate of a ship like the *Sephora*. I had no doubt of it in my mind.

"Not at all the style of man. You understand," he insisted superfluously, looking hard at me.

I smiled urbanely. He seemed at a loss for a while.

"I suppose I must report a suicide."

"Beg pardon?"

"Sui-cide! That's what I'll have to write to my owners directly I get in."

"Unless you manage to recover him before tomorrow," I assented dispassionately. . . . "I mean, alive."

He mumbled something which I really did not catch, and I turned my ear to him in a puzzled manner. He fairly bawled:

"The land—I say, the mainland is at least seven miles off my anchorage."

"About that."

My lack of excitement, of curiosity, of surprise, of any sort of pronounced interest, began to arouse his distrust. But except for the felicitous pretense of deafness I had not tried to pretend anything. I had felt utterly incapable of playing the part of ignorance properly, and therefore was afraid to try. It is also certain that he had brought some ready-made suspicions with him, and that he viewed my politeness as a strange and unnatural phenomenon. And yet how else could I have received him? Not heartily! That was impossible for psychological reasons, which I need not state here. My only object was to keep off his inquiries. Surlily? Yes, but surliness might have provoked a point-blank question. From its novelty to him and from its nature, punctilious courtesy was the manner best calculated to restrain the man. But there was the danger of his breaking through my defense bluntly. I could not, I think, have met him by a direct lie, also for psychological (not moral) reasons. If he had only known how afraid I was of his putting my feeling of identity with the other to the test! But, strangely enough (I thought of it only afterward), I believe that he was not a little disconcerted by the reverse side of that weird situation, by something in me that reminded him of the man he was seeking—suggested a mysterious similitude to the young fellow he had distrusted and disliked from the first.

However that might have been, the silence was not very prolonged. He took another oblique step.

"I reckon I had no more than a two-mile pull to your ship. Not a bit more."

"And quite enough, too, in this awful heat," I said.

Another pause full of mistrust followed. Necessity, they say, is mother of invention, but fear, too, is not barren of ingenious suggestions. And I was afraid he would ask me point-blank for news of my other self.

"Nice little saloon, isn't it?" I remarked, as if noticing for the first time the way his eyes roamed from one closed door to the other. "And very well fitted out, too. Here, for instance," I continued, reaching over the back of my seat negligently and flinging the door open, "is my bathroom."

He made an eager movement, but hardly gave it a glance. I got up, shut the door of the bathroom, and invited him to have a look round, as if I were very proud of my accommodation. He had to rise and be shown round, but he went through the business without any raptures whatever.

"And now we'll have a look at my stateroom," I declared, in a voice as loud as I dared to make it, crossing the cabin to the starboard side with purposely heavy steps.

He followed me in and gazed around. My intelligent double had vanished. I played my part.

"Very convenient—isn't it?"

"Very nice. Very comf . . ." He didn't finish, and went out brusquely as if to escape from some unrighteous wiles of mine. But it was not to be. I had been too frightened not to feel vengeful; I felt I had him on the run, and I meant to keep him on the run. My polite insistence must have had something menacing in it, because he gave in suddenly. And I did not let him off a single item: mates' rooms, pantry, storerooms, the very sail-locker, which was also under the poop—he had to look into them all. When at last I showed him out on the quarter-deck he drew a long, spiritless sigh, and mumbled dismally that he must really be going back to his ship now. I desired my mate, who had joined us, to see to the captain's boat.

The man of whiskers gave a blast on the whistle which he used to wear hanging round his neck, and yelled, "*Sephora's* away!" My double down there in my cabin must have heard, and certainly could not feel more relieved than I. Four fellows came running out from somewhere forward and went over the side, while my own men, appearing on deck too, lined the rail. I escorted my visitor to the gangway ceremoniously, and nearly overdid it. He was a tenacious beast. On the very ladder he lingered, and in that unique, guiltily conscientious manner of sticking to the point:

"I say . . . you . . . you don't think that—"

I covered his voice loudly.

"Certainly not. . . . I am delighted. Goodbye."

I had an idea of what he meant to say, and just saved myself by the privilege of defective hearing. He was too shaken generally to insist, but my mate, close witness of that parting, looked mystified and his face took on a thoughtful cast. As I did not want to appear as if I wished to avoid all communication with my officers, he had the opportunity to address me.

"Seems a very nice man. His boat's crew told our chaps a very extraordinary story, if what I am told by the steward is true. I suppose you had it from the captain, sir?"

"Yes. I had a story from the captain."

"A very horrible affair—isn't it, sir?"

"It is."

"Beats all these tales we hear about murders in Yankee ships."

"I don't think it beats them. I don't think it resembles them in the least."

"Bless my soul—you don't say so! But of course I've no acquaintance whatever with American ships, not I, so I couldn't go against your knowledge. It's horrible enough for me. . . . But the queerest part is that those fellows seemed to have some idea the man was hidden aboard here. They had really. Did you ever hear of such a thing?"

"Preposterous—isn't it?"

We were walking to and fro athwart the quarter-deck. No one of the crew forward could be seen (the day was Sunday), and the mate pursued:

"There was some little dispute about it. Our chaps took offense. 'As if we would harbor a thing like that,' they said. 'Wouldn't you like to look for him in our coal-hole?' Quite a tiff. But they made it up in the end. I suppose he did drown himself. Don't you, sir?"

"I don't suppose anything."

"You have no doubt in the matter, sir?"

"None whatever."

I left him suddenly. I felt I was producing a bad impression, but with my double down there it was most trying to be on deck. And it was almost as trying to be below. Altogether a nerve-trying situation. But on the whole I felt less torn in two when I was with him. There was no one in the whole ship whom I dared take into my confidence. Since the hands had got to know his story, it would have been impossible to pass him off for any one else, and an accidental discovery was to be dreaded now more than ever. . . .

The steward being engaged in laying the table for dinner, we could talk only with our eyes when I first went down. Later in the afternoon we had a cautious try at whispering. The Sunday quietness of the ship was against us; the stillness of air and water around her was against us; the elements, the men were against us—everything was against us in our secret partnership; time itself—for this could not go on for ever. The very trust in Providence was, I supposed, denied to his guilt. Shall I confess that this thought cast me down very much? And as to the chapter of accidents which counts for so much in the book of success, I could only hope that it was closed. For what favorable accident could be expected?

"Did you hear everything?" were my first words as soon as we took up our position side by side, leaning over my bedplace.

He had. And the proof of it was his earnest whisper, "The man told you he hardly dared to give the order."

I understood the reference to be to that saving foresail.

"Yes. He was afraid of it being lost in the setting."

"I assure you he never gave the order. He may think he did, but he never gave it. He stood there with me on the break of the poop after the maintopsail blew away, and whimpered about our last hope —positively whimpered about it and nothing else—and the night coming on! To hear one's skipper go on like that in such weather was enough to drive any fellow out of his mind. It worked me up into a sort of desperation. I just took it into my own hands and went away from him, boiling, and—But what's the use telling you? *You* know! . . . Do you think that if I had not been pretty fierce with them I should have got the men to do anything? Not it! The boss'en[2] perhaps? Perhaps! It wasn't a heavy sea—it was a sea gone mad! I suppose the end of the world will be something like that; and a man may have the heart to see it coming once and be done with it—but to have to face it day after day . . . I don't blame anybody. I was precious little better than the rest. Only—I was an officer of that old coal-wagon, anyhow. . . ."

"I quite understand," I conveyed that sincere assurance into his ear. He was out of breath with whispering; I could hear him pant slightly. It was all very simple. The same strung-up force which had given twenty-four men a chance, at least, for their lives had, in a sort of recoil, crushed an unworthy mutinous existence.

2. *Bosun* or *boatswain,* petty officer in charge of deck crew and of rigging.

But I had no leisure to weigh the merits of the matter—footsteps in the saloon, a heavy knock. "There's enough wind to get under way with, sir." Here was the call of a new claim upon my thoughts and even upon my feelings.

"Turn the hands up," I cried through the door. "I'll be on deck directly."

I was going out to make the acquaintance of my ship. Before I left the cabin our eyes met—the eyes of the only two strangers on board. I pointed to the recessed part where the little camp-stool awaited him and laid my finger on my lips. He made a gesture—somewhat vague—a little mysterious, accompanied by a faint smile, as if of regret.

This is not the place to enlarge upon the sensations of a man who feels for the first time a ship move under his feet to his own independent word. In my case they were not unalloyed. I was not wholly alone with my command; for there was that stranger in my cabin. Or, rather, I was not completely and wholly with her. Part of me was absent. That mental feeling of being in two places at once affected me physically as if the mood of secrecy had penetrated my very soul. Before an hour had elapsed since the ship had begun to move, having occasion to ask the mate (he stood by my side) to take a compass bearing of the Pagoda, I caught myself reaching up to his ear in whispers. I say I caught myself, but enough had escaped to startle the man. I can't describe it otherwise than by saying that he shied. A grave, preoccupied manner, as though he were in possession of some perplexing intelligence, did not leave him henceforth. A little later I moved away from the rail to look at the compass with such a stealthy gait that the helmsman noticed it—and I could not help noticing the unusual roundness of his eyes. These are trifling instances, though it's to no commander's advantage to be suspected of ludicrous eccentricities. But I was also more seriously affected. There are to a seaman certain words, gestures, that should in given conditions come as naturally, as instinctively, as the winking of a menaced eye. A certain order should spring on to his lips without thinking; a certain sign should get itself made, so to speak, without reflection. But all unconscious alertness had abandoned me. I had to make an effort of will to recall myself back (from the cabin) to the conditions of the moment. I felt that I was appearing an irresolute commander to those people who were watching me more or less critically.

And, besides, there were the scares. On the second day out, for instance, coming off the deck in the afternoon (I had straw slippers on my bare feet) I stopped at the open pantry door and spoke to the steward. He was doing something there with his back to me. At the sound of my voice he nearly jumped out of his skin, as the saying is, and incidentally broke a cup.

"What on earth's the matter with you?" I asked, astonished.

He was extremely confused. "Beg your pardon, sir. I made sure you were in your cabin."

"You see I wasn't."

"No, sir. I could have sworn I had heard you moving in there not a moment ago. It's most extraordinary . . . very sorry, sir."

I passed on with an inward shudder. I was so identified with my secret double that I did not even mention the fact in those scanty, fearful whispers we exchanged. I suppose he had made some slight noise of some kind or other. It would have been miraculous if he hadn't at one time or another. And yet, haggard as he appeared, he looked always perfectly self-controled, more than calm—almost invulnerable. On my suggestion he remained almost entirely in the bathroom, which, upon the whole, was the safest place. There could be really no shadow of an excuse for any one ever wanting to go in there, once the steward had done with it. It was a very tiny place. Sometimes he reclined on the floor, his legs bent, his head sustained on one elbow. At others I would find him on the camp-stool, sitting in his gray sleeping suit and with his cropped dark hair like a patient, unmoved convict. At night I would smuggle him into my bedplace, and we would whisper together, with the regular footfalls of the officer of the watch passing and repassing over our heads. It was an infinitely miserable time. It was lucky that some tins of fine preserves were stowed in a locker in my stateroom; hard bread I could always get hold of; and so he lived on stewed chicken, pâté de foie gras, asparagus, cooked oysters, sardines—on all sorts of abominable sham-delicacies out of tins. My early morning coffee he always drank; and it was all I dared do for him in that respect.

Every day there was the horrible maneuvering to go through so that my room and then the bathroom should be done in the usual way. I came to hate the sight of the steward, to abhor the voice of that harmless man. I felt that it was he who would bring on the disaster of discovery. It hung like a sword over our heads.

The fourth day out, I think (we were then working down the east side of the Gulf of Siam, tack for tack,[3] in light winds and smooth water)—the fourth day, I say, of this miserable juggling with the unavoidable, as we sat at our evening meal, that man, whose slightest movement I dreaded, after putting down the dishes ran up on deck busily. This could not be dangerous. Presently he came down again; and then it appeared that he had remembered a coat of mine which I had thrown over a rail to dry after having been wetted in a shower which had passed over the ship in the afternoon. Sitting stolidly at the head of the table I became terrified at the sight of the garment on his arm. Of course he made for my door. There was no time to lose.

"Steward!" I thundered. My nerves were so shaken that I could not govern my voice and conceal my agitation. This was the sort of thing that made my terrifically whiskered mate tap his forehead with his forefinger. I had detected him using that gesture while talking on deck with a confidential air to the carpenter. It was too far to hear a word, but I had no doubt that this pantomime could only refer to the strange new captain.

"Yes, sir," the pale-faced steward turned resignedly to me. It was this maddening course of being shouted at, checked without rhyme or reason, arbitrarily chased out of my cabin, suddenly called into it, sent flying out of his pantry on incomprehensible errands, that ac-

3. By a series of shiftings back and forth of sails.

counted for the growing wretchedness of his expression.

"Where are you going with that coat?"

"To your room, sir."

"Is there another shower coming?"

"I'm sure I don't know, sir. Shall I go up again and see, sir?"

"No! never mind."

My object was attained, as of course my other self in there would have heard everything that passed. During this interlude my two officers never raised their eyes off their respective plates; but the lip of that confounded cub, the second mate, quivered visibly.

I expected the steward to hook my coat on and come out at once. He was very slow about it; but I dominated my nervousness sufficiently not to shout after him. Suddenly I became aware (it could be heard plainly enough) that the fellow for some reason or other was opening the door of the bathroom. It was the end. The place was literally not big enough to swing a cat in. My voice died in my throat and I went stony all over. I expected to hear a yell of surprise and terror, and made a movement, but had not the strength to get on my legs. Everything remained still. Had my second self taken the poor wretch by the throat? I don't know what I could have done next moment if I had not seen the steward come out of my room, close the door, and then stand quietly by the sideboard.

"Saved," I thought. "But, no! Lost! Gone! He was gone!"

I laid my knife and fork down and leaned back in my chair. My head swam. After a while, when sufficiently recovered to speak in a steady voice, I instructed my mate to put the ship round at eight o'clock himself.

"I won't come on deck," I went on. "I think I'll turn in, and unless the wind shifts I don't want to be disturbed before midnight. I feel a bit seedy."

"You did look middling bad a little while ago," the chief mate remarked without showing any great concern.

They both went out, and I stared at the steward clearing the table. There was nothing to be read on that wretched man's face. But why did he avoid my eyes? I asked myself. Then I thought I should like to hear the sound of his voice.

"Steward!"

"Sir!" Startled as usual.

"Where did you hang up that coat?"

"In the bathroom, sir." The usual anxious tone. "It's not quite dry yet, sir."

For some time longer I sat in the cuddy. Had my double vanished as he had come? But of his coming there was an explanation, whereas his disappearance would be inexplicable. . . . I went slowly into my dark room, shut the door, lighted the lamp, and for a time dared not turn round. When at last I did I saw him standing bolt upright in the narrow recessed part. It would not be true to say I had a shock, but an irresistible doubt of his bodily existence flitted through my mind. Can it be, I asked myself, that he is not visible to other eyes than mine? It was like being haunted. Motionless, with a grave face, he raised his hands slightly at me in a gesture which meant clearly, "Heavens! what a narrow escape!" Narrow indeed. I think I had come creeping quietly as near insanity as any man who his not actually gone over the border. That gesture restrained me, so to speak.

The mate with the terrific whiskers was now putting the ship on the other tack. In the moment of profound silence which follows upon the hands going to their stations I heard on the poop his raised voice: "Hard alee!"[4] and the distant shout of the order repeated on the main deck. The sails, in that light breeze, made but a faint fluttering noise. It ceased. The ship was coming round slowly; I held my breath in the renewed stillness of expectation; one wouldn't have thought that there was a single living soul on her decks. A sudden brisk shout, "Mainsail haul!" broke the spell, and in the noisy cries and rush overhead of the men running away with the main brace we two, down in my cabin, came together in our usual position by the bedplace.

He did not wait for my question. "I heard him fumbling here and just managed to squat myself down in the bath," he whispered to me. "The fellow only opened the door and put his arm in to hang the coat up. All the same. . . ."

"I never thought of that," I whispered back, even more appalled than before at the closeness of the shave, and marveling at that something unyielding in his character which was carrying him through so finely. There was no agitation in his whisper. Whoever was being driven distracted, it was not he. He was sane. And the proof of his sanity was continued when he took up the whispering again.

"It would never do for me to come to life again."

It was something that a ghost might have said. But what he was alluding to was his old captain's reluctant admission of the theory of suicide. It would obviously serve his turn—if I had understood at all the view which seemed to govern the unalterable purpose of his action.

"You must maroon me as soon as ever you can get amongst these islands off the Cambodje[5] shore," he went on.

"Maroon you! We are not living in a boy's adventure tale," I protested. His scornful whispering took me up.

"We aren't indeed! There's nothing of a boy's tale in this. But there's nothing else for it. I want no more. You don't suppose I am afraid of what can be done to me? Prison or gallows or whatever they may please. But you don't see me coming back to explain such things to an old fellow in a wig and twelve respectable tradesmen, do you? What can they know whether I am guilty or not—or of *what* I am guilty, either? That's my affair. What does the Bible say? 'Driven off the face of the earth.'[6] Very well. I am off the face of the earth now. As I came at night so I shall go."

"Impossible!" I murmured. "You can't."

"Can't? . . . Not naked like a soul on the Day of Judgment. I shall freeze on to this sleeping suit. The Last Day is not yet—and . . . you have understood thoroughly. Didn't you?"

---

4. Put the helm all the way over to the side away from the wind.

5. Cambodian.
6. See note 9 on page 222.

I felt suddenly ashamed of myself. I may say truly that I understood—and my hesitation in letting that man swim away from my ship's side had been a mere sham sentiment, a sort of cowardice.

"It can't be done now till next night," I breathed out. "The ship is on the offshore tack and the wind may fail us."

"As long as I know that you understand," he whispered. "But of course you do. It's a great satisfaction to have got somebody to understand. You seem to have been there on purpose." And in the same whisper, as if we two whenever we talked had to say things to each other which were not fit for the world to hear, he added, "It's very wonderful."

We remained side by side talking in our secret way—but sometimes silent or just exchanging a whispered word or two at long intervals. And as usual he stared through the port. A breath of wind came now and again into our faces. The ship might have been moored in dock, so gently and on an even keel she slipped through the water, that did not murmur even at our passage, shadowy and silent like a phantom sea.

At midnight I went on deck, and to my mate's great surprise put the ship round on the other tack. His terrible whiskers flitted round me in silent criticism. I certainly should not have done it if it had been only a question of getting out of that sleepy gulf as quickly as possible. I believe he told the second mate, who relieved him, that it was a great want of judgment. The other only yawned. That intolerable cub shuffled about so sleepily and lolled against the rails in such a slack, improper fashion that I came down on him sharply.

"Aren't you properly awake yet?"

"Yes, sir! I am awake."

"Well, then, be good enough to hold yourself as if you were. And keep a look out. If there's any current we'll be closing with some islands long before daylight."

The east side of the gulf is fringed with islands, some solitary, others in groups. On the blue background of the high coast they seem to float on silvery patches of calm water, arid and gray, or dark green and rounded like clumps of evergreen bushes, with the larger ones, a mile or two long, showing the outlines of ridges, ribs of gray rock under the dank mantle of matted leafage. Unknown to trade, to travel, almost to geography, the manner of life they harbor is an unsolved secret. There must be villages—settlements of fishermen at least —on the largest of them, and some communication with the world is probably kept up by native craft. But all that forenoon, as we headed for them, fanned along by the faintest of breezes, I saw no sign of man or canoe in the field of the telescope I kept on pointing at the scattered group.

At noon I gave no orders for a change of course, and the mate's whiskers became much concerned and seemed to be offering themselves unduly to my notice. At last I said:

"I am going to stand right in. Quite in—as far as I can take her."

The stare of extreme surprise imparted an air of ferocity also to his eyes, and he looked truly terrific for a moment.

"We're not doing well in the middle of the gulf," I continued casually. "I am going to look for the land breezes tonight."

"Bless my soul! Do you mean, sir, in the dark amongst the lot of all them islands and reefs and shoals?"

"Well, if there are any regular land breezes at all on this coast one must get close inshore to find them—mustn't one?"

"Bless my soul!" he exclaimed again under his breath. All that afternoon he wore a dreamy, comtemplative appearance which in him was a mark of perplexity. After dinner I went into my state-room as if I meant to take some rest. There we two bent our dark heads over a half-unrolled chart lying on my bed.

"There," I said. "It's got to be Koh-ring.[7] I've been looking at it ever since sunrise. It has got two hills and a low point. It must be inhabited. And on the coast opposite there is what looks like the mouth of a biggish river—with some town, no doubt, not far up. It's the best chance for you that I can see."

"Anything. Koh-ring let it be."

He looked thoughtfully at the chart as if surveying chances and distances from a lofty height—and following with his eyes his own figure wandering on the blank land of Cochin-China, and then passing off that piece of paper clean out of sight into uncharted regions. And it was as if the ship had two captains to plan her course for her. I had been so worried and restless running up and down that I had not had the patience to dress that day. I had remained in my sleeping suit, with straw slippers and a soft floppy hat. The closeness of the heat in the gulf had been most oppressive, and the crew were used to see me wandering in that airy attire.

"She will clear the south point as she heads now," I whispered into his ear. "Goodness only knows when, though—but certainly after dark. I'll edge her in to half a mile, as far as I may be able to judge in the dark . . ."

"Be careful," he murmured warningly—and I realized suddenly that all my future, the only future for which I was fit, would perhaps go irretrievably to pieces in any mishap to my first command.

I could not stop a moment longer in the room. I motioned him to get out of sight and made my way on the poop. That unplayful cub had the watch. I walked up and down for a while thinking things out, then beckoned him over."

"Send a couple of hands to open the two quarter-deck ports," I said mildly.

He actually had the impudence, or else so forgot himself in his wonder at such an incomprehensible order, as to repeat:

"Open the quarter-deck ports! What for, sir?"

"The only reason you need concern yourself about is because I tell you to do so. Have them opened wide and fastened properly."

He reddened and went off, but I believe made some jeering re-mark to the carpenter as to the sensible practice of ventilating a ship's quarter-deck. I know he popped into the mate's cabin to impart the

7. *Koh* or *Ko* means *island;* there are a large number of islands with that prefix at the head of the Gulf of Siam, but not, apparently, a Koh-ring.

fact to him, because the whiskers came on deck, as it were by chance, and stole glances at me from below—for signs of lunacy or drunkenness, I suppose.

A little before supper, feeling more restless than ever, I rejoined, for a moment, my second self. And to find him sitting so quietly was surprising, like something against nature, inhuman.

I developed my plan in a hurried whisper.

"I shall stand in as close as I dare and then put her round. I shall presently find means to smuggle you out of here into the sail-locker, which communicates with the lobby. But there is an opening, a sort of square for hauling the sails out, which gives straight on the quarter-deck and which is never closed in fine weather, so as to give air to the sails. When the ship's way is deadened in stays[8] and all the hands are aft at the main braces you shall have a clear road to slip out and get overboard through the open quarter-deck port. I've had them both fastened up. Use a rope's end to lower yourself into the water so as to avoid a splash—you know. It could be heard and cause some beastly complication."

He kept silent for a while, then whispered, "I understand."

"I won't be there to see you go," I began with an effort. "The rest . . . I only hope I have understood too."

"You have. From first to last"—and for the first time there seemed to be a faltering, something strained in his whisper. He caught hold of my arm, but the ringing of the supper bell made me start. He didn't, though; he only released his grip.

After supper I didn't come below again till well past eight o'clock. The faint, steady breeze was loaded with dew; and the wet, darkened sails held all there was of propelling power in it. The night, clear and starry, sparkled darkly, and the opaque, lightless patches shifting slowly amongst the low stars were the drifting islets. On the port bow there was a big one more distant and shadowily imposing by the great space of sky it eclipsed.

On opening the door I had a back view of my very own self looking at a chart. He had come out of the recess and was standing near the table.

"Quite dark enough," I whispered.

He stepped back and leaned against my bed with a level, quiet glance. I sat on the couch. We had nothing to say to each other. Over our heads the officer of the watch moved here and there. Then I heard him move quickly. I knew what that meant. He was making for the companion; and presently his voice was outside my door.

"We are drawing in pretty fast, sir. Land looks rather close."

"Very well," I answered. "I am coming on deck directly."

I waited till he was gone out of the cuddy, then rose. My double moved too. The time had come to exchange our last whispers, for neither of us was ever to hear each other's natural voice.

"Look here!" I opened a drawer and took out three sovereigns. "Take this, anyhow. I've got six and I'd give you the lot, only I

8. When the ship's forward motion is slowed or stopped while its head is being turned toward the wind for the purpose of shifting the sail.

must keep a little money to buy some fruit and vegetables for the crew from native boats as we go through Sunda Straits."

He shook his head.

"Take it," I urged him, whispering desperately. "No one can tell what . . ."

He smiled and slapped meaningly the only pocket of the sleeping jacket. It was not safe, certainly. But I produced a large old silk handkerchief of mine, and tying the three pieces of gold in a corner, pressed it on him. He was touched, I suppose, because he took it at last and tied it quickly round his waist under the jacket, on his bare skin.

Our eyes met; several seconds elapsed, till, our glances still mingled, I extended my hand and turned the lamp out. Then I passed through the cuddy, leaving the door of my room wide open. . . . "Steward!"

He was still lingering in the pantry in the greatness of his zeal, giving a rub-up to a plated cruet stand the last thing before going to bed. Being carful not to wake up the mate, whose room was opposite, I spoke in an undertone.

He looked round anxiously. "Sir!"

"Can you get me a little hot water from the galley?"

"I am afraid, sir, the galley fire's been out for some time now."

"Go and see."

He fled up the stairs.

"Now," I whispered loudly into the saloon—too loudly, perhaps, but I was afraid I couldn't make a sound. He was by my side in an instant—the double captain slipped past the stairs—through a tiny dark passage . . . a sliding door. We were in the sail-locker, scrambling on our knees over the sails. A sudden thought struck me. I saw myself wandering barefooted, bareheaded, the sun beating on my dark poll. I snatched off my floppy hat and tried hurriedly in the dark to ram it on my other self. He dodged and fended off silently. I wonder what he thought had come to me before he understood and suddenly desisted. Our hands met gropingly, lingered united in a steady, motionless clasp for a second. . . . No word was breathed by either of us when they separated.

I was standing quietly by the pantry door when the steward returned.

"Sorry, sir. Kettle barely warm. Shall I light the spirit-lamp?"

"Never mind."

I came out on deck slowly. It was now a matter of conscience to shave the land as close as possible—for now he must go overboard whenever the ship was put in stays. Must! There could be no going back for him. After a moment I walked over to leeward and my heart flew into my mouth at the nearness of the land on the bow. Under any other circumstances I would not have held on a minute longer. The second mate had followed me anxiously.

I looked on till I felt I could command my voice.

"She will weather," I said then in a quiet tone.

"Are you going to try that, sir?" he stammered out incredulously.

I took no notice of him and raised my tone just enough to be heard by the helmsman.

"Keep her good full!"[9]

"Good full, sir."

The wind fanned my cheek, the sails slept, the world was silent. The strain of watching the dark loom of the land grow bigger and denser was too much for me. I had to shut my eyes—because the ship must go closer. She must! The stillness was intolerable. Were we standing still?

When I opened my eyes the second view started my heart with a thump. The black southern hill of Koh-ring seemed to hang right over the ship like a towering fragment of the everlasting night. On that enormous mass of blackness there was not a gleam to be seen, not a sound to be heard. It was gliding irresistibly towards us and yet seemed already within reach of the hand. I saw the vague figures of the watch grouped in the waist, gazing in awed silence.

"Are you going on, sir?" inquired an unsteady voice at my elbow. I ignored it. I had to go on.

"Keep her full. Don't check her way. That won't do now," I said warningly.

"I can't see the sails very well," the helmsman answered me, in strange, quavering tones.

Was she close enough? Already she was, I won't say in the shadow of the land, but in the very blackness of it, already swallowed up as it were, gone too close to be recalled, gone from me altogether.

"Give the mate a call," I said to the young man who stood at my elbow as still as death. "And turn all hands up."

My tone had a borrowed loudness reverberated from the height of the land. Several voices cried out together, "We are all on deck, sir."

Then stillness again, with the great shadow gliding closer, towering higher, without a light, without a sound. Such a hush had fallen on the ship that she might have been a bark of the dead floating in slowly under the very gate of Erebus.

"My God! Where are we?"

It was the mate moaning at my elbow. He was thunderstruck, and as it were deprived of the moral support of his whiskers. He clapped his hands and absolutely cried out, "Lost!"

"Be quiet," I said sternly.

He lowered his tone, but I saw the shadowy gesture of his despair. "What are we doing here?"

"Looking for the land wind."

He made as if to tear his hair, and addressed me recklessly.

"She will never get out. You have done it, sir. I knew it'd end in something like this. She will never weather, and you are too close now to stay. She'll drift ashore before she's round. O my God!"

I caught his arm as he was raising it to batter his poor devoted head, and shook it violently.

---

9. Keep the ship's sails filled with wind.

"She's ashore already," he wailed, trying to tear himself away.

"Is she? . . . Keep good full there!"

"Good full, sir," cried the helmsman in a frightened, thin, childlike voice.

I hadn't let go the mate's arm and went on shaking it. "Ready about,[1] do you hear? You go forward"—shake—"and stop there"—shake —"and hold your noise"—shake—"and see these head-sheets properly overhauled"—shake, shake—shake.

And all the time I dared not look towards the land lest my heart should fail me. I released my grip at last and he ran forward as if fleeing for dear life.

I wondered what my double there in the sail-locker thought of this commotion. He was able to hear everything—and perhaps he was able to understand why, on my conscience, it had to be thus close— no less. My first order "Hard alee!" re-echoed ominously under the towering shadow of Koh-ring as if I had shouted in a mountain gorge. And then I watched the land intently. In that smooth water and light wind it was impossible to feel the ship coming-to.[2] No! I could not feel her. And my second self was making now ready to slip out and lower himself overboard. Perhaps he was gone already . . . ?

The great black mass brooding over our very mast-heads began to pivot away from the ship's side silently. And now I forgot the secret stranger ready to depart, and remembered only that I was a total stranger to the ship. I did not know her. Would she do it? How was she to be handled?

I swung the mainyard and waited helplessly. She was perhaps stopped, and her very fate hung in the balance, with the black mass of Koh-ring like the gate of the everlasting night towering over her taffrail. What would she do now? Had she way on her yet? I stepped to the side swiftly, and on the shadowy water I could see nothing except a faint phosphorescent flash revealing the glassy smoothness of the sleeping surface. It was impossible to tell—and I had not learned yet the feel of my ship. Was she moving? What I needed was something easily seen, a piece of paper, which I could throw overboard and watch. I had nothing on me. To run down for it I didn't dare. There was no time. All at once my strained, yearning stare distinguished a white object floating within a yard of the ship's side— white, on the black water. A phosphorescent flash passed under it. What was that thing? . . . I recognized my own floppy hat. It must have fallen off his head . . . and he didn't bother. Now I had what I wanted—the saving mark for my eyes. But I hardly thought of my other self, now gone from the ship, to be hidden for ever from all friendly faces, to be a fugitive and a vagabond on the earth, with no brand of the curse on his sane forehead to stay a slaying hand . . . too proud to explain.

1. Be ready to shift the sails (tack). The head-sheets, below, are the lines attached to the sails of the forward mast, and to overhaul is to slacken a rope by pulling it in the opposite direction to that used in hoisting a sail and thus loosening the blocks.

2. Coming to a standstill.

And I watched the hat—the expression of my sudden pity for his mere flesh. It had been meant to save his homeless head from the dangers of the sun. And now—behold—it was saving the ship, by serving me for a mark to help out the ignorance of my strangeness. Ha! It was drifting forward, warning me just in time that the ship had gathered sternway.

"Shift the helm," I said in a low voice to the seaman standing still like a statue.

The man's eyes glistened wildly in the binnacle light as he jumped round to the other side and spun round the wheel.

I walked to the break of the poop. On the overshadowed deck all hands stood by the forebraces waiting for my order. The stars ahead seemed to be gliding from right to left. And all was so still in the world that I heard the quiet remark, "She's round," passed in a tone of intense relief between two seamen.

"Let go and haul."

The foreyards ran round with a great noise, amidst cheery cries. And now the frightful whiskers made themselves heard giving various orders. Already the ship was drawing ahead. And I was alone with her. Nothing! no one in the world should stand now between us, throwing a shadow on the way of silent knowledge and mute affection; the perfect communion of a seaman with his first command.

Walking to the taffrail, I was in time to make out, on the very edge of a darkness thrown by a towering black mass like the very gateway of Erebus—yes, I was in time to catch an evanescent glimpse of my white hat left behind to mark the spot where the secret sharer of my cabin and of my thoughts, as though he were my second self, had lowered himself into the water to take his punishment: a free man, a proud swimmer striking out for a new destiny.

1912

ANTON CHEKHOV

The Lady with the Dog

1

People were telling one another that a newcomer had been seen on the promenade—a lady with a dog. Dmitri Dmitrich Gurov had been a fortnight in Yalta, and was accustomed to its ways, and he, too, had begun to take an interest in fresh arrivals. From his seat in Vernet's outdoor café, he caught sight of a young woman in a toque, passing along the promenade; she was fair and not very tall; after her trotted a white pomeranian.

Later he encountered her in the municipal park, and in the square, several times a day. She was always alone, wearing the same toque, and the pomeranian always trotted at her side. Nobody knew who she was, and people referred to her simply as "the lady with the dog."

"If she's here without her husband, and without any friends," thought Gurov, "it wouldn't be a bad idea to make her acquaintance."

He was not yet forty, but had a twelve-year-old daughter and two schoolboy sons. He had been talked into marrying in his second year at college, and his wife now looked nearly twice as old as he was. She was a tall, black-browed woman, erect, dignified, imposing, and, as she said of herself, a "thinker." She was a great reader, omitted the "hard sign"[1] at the end of words in her letters, and called her husband "Dimitri" instead of Dmitri; and though he secretly considered her shallow, narrow-minded, and dowdy, he stood in awe of her, and disliked being at home. It was long since he had first begun deceiving her and he was now constantly unfaithful to her, and this was no doubt why he spoke slightingly of women, to whom he referred as *the lower race*.

He considered that the ample lessons he had received from bitter experience entitled him to call them whatever he liked, but without this "lower race" he could not have existed a single day. He was bored and ill-at-ease in the company of men, with whom he was always cold and reserved, but felt quite at home among women, and knew exactly what to say to them, and how to behave; he could even be silent in their company without feeling the slightest awkwardness. There was an elusive charm in his appearance and disposition which attracted women and caught their sympathies. He knew this and was himself attracted to them by some invisible force.

Repeated and bitter experience had taught him that every fresh intimacy, while at first introducing such pleasant variety into everyday life, and offering itself as a charming, light adventure, inevitably developed, among decent people (especially in Moscow, where they are so irresolute and slow to move), into a problem of excessive complication leading to an intolerably irksome situation. But every time he encountered an attractive woman he forgot all about this experience, the desire for life surged up in him, and everything suddenly seemed simple and amusing.

One evening, then, while he was dining at the restaurant in the park, the lady in the toque came strolling up and took a seat at a neighboring table. Her expression, gait, dress, coiffure, all told him that she was from the upper classes, that she was married, that she was in Yalta for the first time, alone and bored. . . . The accounts of the laxity of morals among visitors to Yalta are greatly exaggerated, and he paid no heed to them, knowing that for the most part they were invented by people who would gladly have transgressed themselves, had they known how to set about it. But when the lady sat down at a neighboring table a few yards away from him, the stories of easy conquests, of excursions to the mountains, came back to him, and the seductive idea of a brisk transitory liaison, an affair with a woman whose very name he did not know, suddenly took possession of his mind.

---

1. Conventional sign that was used following consonants; to omit it was then "progressive," and it has in fact been eliminated in the reformed alphabet adopted by the Soviet government.

He snapped his fingers at the pomeranian, and when it trotted up to him, shook his forefinger at it. The pomeranian growled. Gurov shook his finger again.

The lady glanced at him and instantly lowered her eyes.

"He doesn't bite," she said, and blushed.

"May I give him a bone?" he asked, and on her nod of consent added in friendly tones: "Have you been in Yalta long?"

"About five days."

"And I am dragging out my second week here."

Neither spoke for a few minutes.

"The days pass quickly, and yet one is so bored here," she said, not looking at him.

"It's the thing to say it's boring here. People never complain of boredom in God-forsaken holes like Belyev or Zhizdra, but when they get here it's: 'Oh, the dullness! Oh, the dust!' You'd think they'd come from Granada,[2] to say the least."

She laughed. Then they both went on eating in silence, like complete strangers. But after dinner they left the restaurant together, and embarked upon the light, jesting talk of people free and contented, for whom it is all the same where they go, or what they talk about. They strolled along, remarking on the strange light over the sea. The water was a warm, tender purple, the moonlight lay on its surface in a golden strip. They said how close it was, after the hot day. Gurov told her he was from Moscow, that he was really a philologist,[3] but worked in a bank; that he had at one time trained himself to sing in a private opera company, but had given up the idea; that he owned two houses in Moscow. . . . And from her he learned that she had grown up in Petersburg, but had got married in the town of S., where she had been living two years, that she would stay another month in Yalta, and that perhaps her husband, who also needed a rest, would join her. She was quite unable to explain whether her husband was a member of the gubernia[4] council, or on the board of the Zemstvo,[5] and was greatly amused at herself for this. Further, Gurov learned that her name was Anna Sergeyevna.

Back in his own room he thought about her, and felt sure he would meet her the next day. It was inevitable. As he went to bed he reminded himself that only a very short time ago she had been a schoolgirl, like his own daughter, learning her lessons; he remembered how much there was of shyness and constraint in her laughter, in her way of conversing with a stranger—it was probably the first time in her life that she found herself alone, and in a situation in which men could follow her and watch her, and speak to her, all the time with a secret aim she could not fail to divine. He recalled her slender, delicate neck, her fine gray eyes.

"And yet there's something pathetic about her," he thought to himself as he fell asleep.

---

2. City in southern Spain, site of the Alhambra and once capital of the Moorish kingdom.
3. In the older sense, classical scholar.
4. Czarist province.
5. In Czarist Russia an elective provincial council responsible for local government.

2

A week had passed since the beginning of their acquaintance. It was a holiday. Indoors it was stuffy, but the dust rose in clouds out of doors, and people's hats blew off. It was a thirsty day and Gurov kept going to the outdoor café for fruit-drinks and ices to offer Anna Sergeyevna. The heat was overpowering.

In the evening, when the wind had dropped, they walked to the pier to see the steamer come in. There were a great many people strolling about the landing-place; some, bunches of flowers in their hands, were meeting friends. Two peculiarities of the smart Yalta crowd stood out distinctly—the elderly ladies all tried to dress very young, and there seemed to be an inordinate number of generals about.

Owing to the roughness of the sea the steamer arrived late, after the sun had gone down, and it had to maneuver for some time before it could get alongside the pier. Anna Sergeyevna scanned the steamer and passengers through her lorgnette, as if looking for someone she knew, and when she turned to Gurov her eyes were glistening. She talked a great deal, firing off abrupt questions and forgetting immediately what it was she had wanted to know. Then she lost her lorgnette in the crush.

The smart crowd began dispersing, features could no longer be made out, the wind had quite dropped, and Gurov and Anna Sergeyevna stood there as if waiting for someone else to come off the steamer. Anna Sergeyevna had fallen silent, every now and then smelling her flowers, but not looking at Gurov.

"It's turned out a fine evening," he said. "What shall we do? We might go for a drive."

She made no reply.

He looked steadily at her and suddenly took her in his arms and kissed her lips, and the fragrance and dampness of the flowers closed round him, but the next moment he looked behind him in alarm—had anyone seen them?

"Let's go to your room," he murmured.

And they walked off together, very quickly.

Her room was stuffy and smelled of some scent she had bought in the Japanese shop. Gurov looked at her, thinking to himself: "How full of strange encounters life is!" He could remember carefree, good-natured women who were exhilarated by love-making and grateful to him for the happiness he gave them, however short-lived; and there had been others—his wife among them—whose caresses were insincere, affected, hysterical, mixed up with a great deal of quite unnecessary talk, and whose expression seemed to say that all this was not just love-making or passion, but something much more significant; then there had been two or three beautiful, cold women, over whose features flitted a predatory expression, betraying a determination to wring from life more than it could give, women no longer in their first youth, capricious, irrational, despotic, brainless, and when Gurov had cooled to these, their beauty aroused in him nothing but repulsion, and the lace trimming on their underclothes reminded him of fish-scales.

But here the timidity and awkwardness of youth and inexperience were still apparent; and there was a feeling of embarrassment in the atmosphere, as if someone had just knocked at the door. Anna Sergeyevna, "the lady with the dog," seemed to regard the affair as something very special, very serious, as if she had become a fallen woman, an attitude he found odd and disconcerting. Her features lengthened and drooped, and her long hair hung mournfully on either side of her face. She assumed a pose of dismal meditation, like a repentant sinner in some classical painting.

"It isn't right," she said. "You will never respect me anymore."

On the table was a watermelon. Gurov cut himself a slice from it and began slowly eating it. At least half an hour passed in silence.

Anna Sergeyevna was very touching, revealing the purity of a decent, naïve woman who had seen very little of life. The solitary candle burning on the table scarcely lit up her face, but it was obvious that her heart was heavy.

"Why should I stop respecting you?" asked Gurov. "You don't know what you're saying."

"May God forgive me!" she exclaimed, and her eyes filled with tears. "It's terrible."

"No need to seek to justify yourself."

"How can I justify myself? I'm a wicked, fallen woman, I despise myself and have not the least thought of self-justification. It isn't my husband I have deceived, it's myself. And not only now, I have been deceiving myself for ever so long. My husband is no doubt an honest, worthy man, but he's a flunkey. I don't know what it is he does at his office, but I know he's a flunkey. I was only twenty when I married him, and I was devoured by curiosity, I wanted something higher. I told myself that there must be a different kind of life. I wanted to live, to live. . . . I was burning with curiosity . . . you'll never understand that, but I swear to God I could no longer control myself, nothing could hold me back, I told my husband I was ill, and I came here. . . . And I started going about like one possessed, like a madwoman . . . and now I have become an ordinary, worthless woman, and everyone has the right to despise me."

Gurov listened to her, bored to death. The naïve accents, the remorse, all was so unexpected, so out of place. But for the tears in her eyes, she might have been jesting or play-acting.

"I don't understand," he said gently. "What is it you want?"
She hid her face against his breast and pressed closer to him.

"Do believe me, I implore you to believe me," she said. "I love all that is honest and pure in life, vice is revolting to me, I don't know what I'm doing. The common people say they are snared by the devil. And now I can say that I have been snared by the devil, too."

"Come, come," he murmured.

He gazed into her fixed, terrified eyes, kissed her, and soothed her with gentle affectionate words, and gradually she calmed down and regained her cheerfulness. Soon they were laughing together again.

When, a little later, they went out, there was not a soul on the promenade, the town and its cypresses looked dead, but the sea was still roaring as it dashed against the beach. A solitary fishing-boat tossed on the waves, its lamp blinking sleepily.

They found a droshky[6] and drove to Oreanda.

"I discovered your name in the hall, just now," said Gurov, "written up on the board. Von Diederitz. Is your husband a German?"

"No. His grandfather was, I think, but he belongs to the Orthodox church himself."

When they got out of the droshky at Oreanda they sat down on a bench not far from the church, and looked down at the sea, without talking. Yalta could be dimly discerned through the morning mist, and white clouds rested motionless on the summits of the mountains. Not a leaf stirred, the grasshoppers chirruped, and the monotonous hollow roar of the sea came up to them, speaking of peace, of the eternal sleep lying in wait for us all. The sea had roared like this long before there was any Yalta or Oreanda, it was roaring now, and it would go on roaring, just as indifferently and hollowly, when we have passed away. And it may be that in this continuity, this utter indifference to life and death, lies the secret of our ultimate salvation, of the stream of life on our planet, and of its never-ceasing movement toward perfection.

Side by side with a young woman, who looked so exquisite in the early light, soothed and enchanted by the sight of all this magical beauty—sea, mountains, clouds and the vast expanse of the sky—Gurov told himself that, when you came to think of it, everything in the world is beautiful really, everything but our own thoughts and actions, when we lose sight of the higher aims of life, and of our dignity as human beings.

Someone approached them—a watchman, probably—looked at them and went away. And there was something mysterious and beautiful even in this. The steamer from Feodosia could be seen coming toward the pier, lit up by the dawn, its lamps out.

"There's dew on the grass," said Anna Sergeyevna, breaking the silence.

"Yes. Time to go home."

They went back to the town.

After this they met every day at noon on the promenade, lunching and dining together, going for walks, and admiring the sea. She complained of sleeplessness, of palpitations, asked the same questions over and over again, alternately surrendering to jealousy and the fear that he did not really respect her. And often, when there was nobody in sight in the square or the park, he would draw her to him and kiss her passionately. The utter idleness, these kisses in broad daylight, accompanied by furtive glances and the fear of discovery, the heat, the smell of the sea, and the idle, smart, well-fed people continually crossing their field of vision, seemed to have given him a new lease on life. He told Anna Sergeyevna she was beautiful and seductive, made love to her with impetuous passion, and never left her side, while she was always pensive, always trying to force from him the admission that he did not respect her, that he did not love her a bit, and considered her

6. Horse-drawn, four-wheeled open carriage.

just an ordinary woman. Almost every night they drove out of town, to Oreanda, the waterfall, or some other beauty spot. And these excursions were invariably a success, each contributing fresh impressions of majestic beauty.

All this time they kept expecting her husband to arrive. But a letter came in which he told his wife that he was having trouble with his eyes, and implored her to come home as soon as possible. Anna Sergeyevna made hasty preparations for leaving.

"It's a good thing I'm going," she said to Gurov. "It's the intervention of fate."

She left Yalta in a carriage, and he went with her as far as the railway station. The drive took nearly a whole day. When she got into the express train, after the second bell had been rung, she said:

"Let me have one more look at you. . . . One last look. That's right."

She did not weep, but was mournful, and seemed ill, the muscles of her cheeks twitching.

"I shall think of you . . . I shall think of you all the time," she said. "God bless you! Think kindly of me. We are parting for ever, it must be so, because we ought never to have met. Good-bye—God bless you."

The train steamed rapidly out of the station, its lights soon disappearing, and a minute later even the sound it made was silenced, as if everything were conspiring to bring this sweet oblivion, this madness, to an end as quickly as possible. And Gurov, standing alone on the platform and gazing into the dark distance, listened to the shrilling of the grasshoppers and the humming of the telegraph wires, with a feeling that he had only just waked up. And he told himself that this had been just one more of the many adventures in his life, and that it, too, was over, leaving nothing but a memory. . . . He was moved and sad, and felt a slight remorse. After all, this young woman whom he would never again see had not been really happy with him. He had been friendly and affectionate with her, but in his whole behavior, in the tones of his voice, in his very caresses, there had been a shade of irony, the insulting indulgence of the fortunate male, who was, moreover, almost twice her age. She had insisted in calling him good, remarkable, high-minded. Evidently he had appeared to her different from his real self, in a word he had involuntarily deceived her. . . .

There was an autumnal feeling in the air, and the evening was chilly.

"It's time for me to be going north, too," thought Gurov, as he walked away from the platform. "High time!"

3

When he got back to Moscow it was beginning to look like winter, the stoves were heated every day, and it was still dark when the children got up to go to school and drank their tea, so that the nurse had to light the lamp for a short time. Frost had set in. When the first snow falls, and one goes for one's first sleigh-ride, it is pleasant to see the white ground, the white roofs; one breathes freely and lightly, and remembers the days of one's youth. The ancient lime-trees and birches, white with rime, have a good-natured look, they are closer to the heart than cypresses and palms, and beneath their branches one is no longer haunted by the memory of mountains and the sea.

Gurov had always lived in Moscow, and he returned to Moscow on a fine frosty day, and when he put on his fur-lined overcoat and thick gloves, and sauntered down Petrovka Street, and when, on Saturday evening, he heard the church bells ringing, his recent journey and the places he had visited lost their charm for him. He became gradually immersed in Moscow life, reading with avidity three newspapers a day, while declaring he never read Moscow newspapers on principle. Once more he was caught up in a whirl of restaurants, clubs, banquets, and celebrations, once more glowed with the flattering consciousness that well-known lawyers and actors came to his house, that he played cards in the Medical Club opposite a professor.

He had believed that in a month's time Anna Sergeyevna would be nothing but a vague memory, and that hereafter, with her wistful smile, she would only occasionally appear to him in dreams, like others before her. But the month was now well over and winter was in full swing, and all was as clear in his memory as if he had only parted with Anna Sergeyevna the day before. And his recollections grew ever more insistent. When the voices of his children at their lessons reached him in his study through the evening stillness, when he heard a song, or the sounds of a musical-box in a restaurant, when the wind howled in the chimney, it all came back to him: early morning on the pier, the misty mountains, the steamer from Feodosia, the kisses. He would pace up and down his room for a long time, smiling at his memories, and then memory turned into dreaming, and what had happened mingled in his imagination with what was going to happen. Anna Sergeyevna did not come to him in his dreams, she accompanied him everywhere, like his shadow, following him everywhere he went. When he closed his eyes, she seemed to stand before him in the flesh, still lovelier, younger, tenderer than she had really been, and looking back, he saw himself, too, as better than he had been in Yalta. In the evenings she looked out at him from the bookshelves, the fireplace, the corner; he could hear her breathing, the sweet rustle of her skirts. In the streets he followed women with his eyes, to see if there were any like her. . . .

He began to feel an overwhelming desire to share his memories with someone. But he could not speak of his love at home, and outside his home who was there for him to confide in? Not the tenants living in his house, and certainly not his colleagues at the bank. And what was there to tell? Was it love that he had felt? Had there been anything exquisite, poetic, anything instructive or even amusing about his relations with Anna Sergeyevna? He had to content himself with uttering vague generalizations about love and women, and nobody guessed what he meant, though his wife's dark eyebrows twitched as she said:

"The role of a coxcomb doesn't suit you a bit, Dimitri."

One evening, leaving the Medical Club with one of his card-partners, a government official, he could not refrain from remarking:

"If you only knew what a charming woman I met in Yalta!"

The official got into his sleigh, and just before driving off turned and called out:

"Dmítri Dmítrich!"

"Yes?"

"You were quite right, you know—the sturgeon was just a *leetle* off."

These words, in themselves so commonplace, for some reason infuriated Gurov, seemed to him humiliating, gross. What savage manners, what people! What wasted evenings, what tedious, empty days! Frantic card-playing, gluttony, drunkenness, perpetual talk always about the same thing. The greater part of one's time and energy went on business that was no use to anyone, and on discussing the same thing over and over again, and there was nothing to show for it all but a stunted, earth-bound existence and a round of trivialities, and there was nowhere to escape to, you might as well be in a madhouse or a convict settlement.

Gurov lay awake all night, raging, and went about the whole of the next day with a headache. He slept badly on the succeeding nights, too, sitting up in bed, thinking, or pacing the floor of his room. He was sick of his children, sick of the bank, felt not the slightest desire to go anywhere or talk about anything.

When the Christmas holidays came, he packed his things, telling his wife he had to go to Petersburg in the interests of a certain young man, and set off for the town of S. To what end? He hardly knew himself. He only knew that he must see Anna Sergeyevna, must speak to her, arrange a meeting, if possible.

He arrived at S. in the morning and engaged the best room in the hotel, which had a carpet of gray military frieze, and a dusty ink-pot on the table, surmounted by a headless rider, holding his hat in his raised hand. The hall porter told him what he wanted to know: von Diederitz had a house of his own in Staro-Goncharnaya Street. It wasn't far from the hotel, he lived on a grand scale, luxuriously, kept carriage-horses, the whole town knew him. The hall porter pronounced the name "Drideritz."

Gurov strolled over to Staro-Goncharnaya Street and discovered the house. In front of it was a long gray fence with inverted nails hammered into the tops of the palings.

"A fence like that is enough to make anyone want to run away," thought Gurov, looking at the windows of the house and the fence.

He reasoned that since it was a holiday, her husband would probably be at home. In any case it would be tactless to embarrass her by calling at the house. And a note might fall into the hands of the husband, and bring about catastrophe. The best thing would be to wait about on the chance of seeing her. And he walked up and down the street, hovering in the vicinity of the fence, watching for his chance. A beggar entered the gate, only to be attacked by dogs; then, an hour later, the faint, vague sounds of a piano reached his ears. That would be Anna Sergeyevna playing. Suddenly the front door opened and an old woman came out, followed by a familiar white pomeranian. Gurov tried to call to it, but his heart beat violently, and in his agitation he could not remember its name.

He walked on, hating the gray fence more and more, and now ready to tell himself irately that Anna Sergeyevna had forgotten him, had already, perhaps, found distraction in another—what could be more natural in a young woman who had to look at this accursed fence from morning to night? He went back to his hotel and sat on the sofa in his room for some time, not knowing what to do, then he ordered dinner, and after dinner, had a long sleep.

"What a foolish, restless business," he thought, waking up and looking toward the dark windowpanes. It was evening by now. "Well, I've had my sleep out. And what am I to do in the night?"

He sat up in bed, covered by the cheap gray quilt, which reminded him of a hospital blanket, and in his vexation he fell to taunting himself.

"You and your lady with a dog . . . there's adventure for you! See what you get for your pains."

On his arrival at the station that morning he had noticed a poster announcing in enormous letters the first performance at the local theater of *The Geisha*.[7] Remembering this, he got up and made for the theater.

"It's highly probable that she goes to first-nights," he told himself.

The theater was full. It was a typical provincial theater, with a mist collecting over the chandeliers, and the crowd in the gallery fidgeting noisily. In the first row of the stalls[8] the local dandies stood waiting for the curtain to go up, their hands clasped behind them. There, in the front seat of the Governor's box, sat the Governor's daughter, wearing a boa, the Governor himself hiding modestly behind the drapes, so that only his hands were visible. The curtain stirred, the orchestra took a long time tuning up their instruments. Gurov's eyes roamed eagerly over the audience as they filed in and occupied their seats.

Anna Sergeyevna came in, too. She seated herself in the third row of the stalls and when Gurov's glance fell on her, his heart seemed to stop, and he knew in a flash that the whole world contained no one nearer or dearer to him, no one more important to his happiness. This little woman, lost in the provincial crowd, in no way remarkable, holding a silly lorgnette in her hand, now filled his whole life, was his grief, his joy, all that he desired. Lulled by the sounds coming from the wretched orchestra, with its feeble, amateurish violinists, he thought how beautiful she was . . . thought and dreamed. . . .

Anna Sergeyevna was accompanied by a tall, round-shouldered young man with small whiskers, who nodded at every step before taking the seat beside her and seemed to be continually bowing to someone. This must be her husband, whom, in a fit of bitterness, at Yalta, she had called a "flunkey." And there really was something of the lackey's servility in his lanky figure, his side-whiskers, and the little bald spot on the top of his head. And he smiled sweetly, and the badge of some scientific society gleaming in his buttonhole was like the number on a footman's livery.

The husband went out to smoke in the first interval, and she was left alone in her seat. Gurov, who had taken a seat in the stalls, went up to her and said in a trembling voice, with a forced smile: "How d'you do?"

She glanced up at him and turned pale, then looked at him again in alarm, unable to believe her eyes, squeezing her fan and lorgnette in one hand, evidently struggling to overcome a feeling of faintness.

---

7. Operetta by Sidney Jones (1861–1946) which toured Eastern Europe in 1898–99.

8. Seats at the front of a theater, near the stage and separated from nearby seats by a railing.

Neither of them said a word. She sat there, and he stood beside her, disconcerted by her embarrassment, and not daring to sit down. The violins and flutes sang out as they were tuned, and there was a tense sensation in the atmosphere, as if they were being watched from all the boxes. At last she got up and moved rapidly toward one of the exits. He followed her and they wandered aimlessly along corridors, up and down stairs; figures flashed by in the uniforms of legal officials, high-school teachers, and civil servants, all wearing badges; ladies' coats hanging on pegs, flashed by; there was a sharp draft, bringing with it an odor of cigarette stubs. And Gurov, whose heart was beating violently, thought:

"What on earth are all these people, this orchestra for? . . ."

The next minute he suddenly remembered how, after seeing Anna Sergeyevna off that evening at the station, he had told himself that all was over, and they would never meet again. And how far away the end seemed to be now!

She stopped on a dark narrow staircase over which was a notice bearing the inscription "To the upper circle."

"How you frightened me!" she said, breathing heavily, still pale and half-stunned. "Oh, how you frightened me! I'm almost dead! Why did you come? Oh, why?"

"But, Anna," he said, in low, hasty tones. "But, Anna. . . . Try to understand . . . do try. . . ."

She cast him a glance of fear, entreaty, love, and then gazed at him steadily, as if to fix his features firmly in her memory.

"I've been so unhappy," she continued, taking no notice of his words. "I could think of nothing but you the whole time, I lived on the thoughts of you. I tried to forget—why, oh, why did you come?"

On the landing above them were two schoolboys, smoking and looking down, but Gurov did not care, and, drawing Anna Sergeyevna toward him, began kissing her face, her lips, her hands.

"What are you doing, oh, what are you doing?" she said in horror, drawing back. "We have both gone mad. Go away this very night, this moment. . . . By all that is sacred, I implore you. . . . Somebody is coming."

Someone was ascending the stairs.

"You must go away," went on Anna Sergeyevna in a whisper. "D'you hear me, Dmitri Dmitrich? I'll come to you in Moscow. I have never been happy, I am unhappy now, and I shall never be happy—never! Do not make me suffer still more! I will come to you in Moscow, I swear it! And now we must part! My dear one, my kind one, my darling, we must part."

She pressed his hand and hurried down the stairs, looking back at him continually, and her eyes showed that she was in truth unhappy. Gurov stood where he was for a short time, listening, and when all was quiet went to look for his coat, and left the theater.

4

And Anna Sergeyevna began going to Moscow to see him. Every

two or three months she left the town of S., telling her husband that she was going to consult a specialist on female diseases, and her husband believed her and did not believe her. In Moscow she always stayed at the "Slavyanski Bazaar," sending a man in a red cap to Gurov the moment she arrived. Gurov went to her, and no one in Moscow knew anything about it.

One winter morning he went to see her as usual (the messenger had been to him the evening before, but had not found him at home). His daughter was with him for her school was on the way, and he thought he might as well see her to it.

"It is three degrees above zero,"[9] said Gurov to his daughter, "and yet it is snowing. You see it is only above zero close to the ground, the temperature in the upper layers of the atmosphere is quite different."

"Why doesn't it ever thunder in winter, Papa?"

He explained this, too. As he was speaking, he kept reminding himself that he was going to a rendezvous and that not a living soul knew about it, or, probably, ever would. He led a double life—one in public, in the sight of all whom it concerned, full of conventional truth and conventional deception, exactly like the lives of his friends and acquaintances, and another which flowed in secret. And, owing to some strange, possibly quite accidental chain of circumstances, everything that was important, interesting, essential, everything about which he was sincere and never deceived himself, everything that composed the kernel of his life, went on in secret, while everything that was false in him, everything that composed the husk in which he hid himself and the truth which was in him—his work at the bank, discussions at the club, his "lower race," his attendance at anniversary celebrations with his wife—was on the surface. He began to judge others by himself, no longer believing what he saw, and always assuming that the real, the only interesting life of every individual goes on as under cover of night, secretly. Every individual existence revolves around mystery, and perhaps that is the chief reason that all cultivated individuals insisted so strongly on the respect due to personal secrets.

After leaving his daughter at the door of her school Gurov set off for the "Slavyanski Bazaar." Taking off his overcoat in the lobby, he went upstairs and knocked softly on the door. Anna Sergeyevna, wearing the gray dress he liked most, exhausted by her journey and by suspense, had been expecting him since the evening before. She was pale and looked at him without smiling, but was in his arms almost before he was fairly in the room. Their kiss was lingering, prolonged, as if they had not met for years.

"Well, how are you?" he asked. "Anything new?"

"Wait. I'll tell you in a minute. . . . I can't. . . ."

She could not speak, because she was crying. Turning away, she held her handkerchief to her eyes.

"I'll wait till she's had her cry out," he thought, and sank into a chair.

9. Probably Réaumur thermometer; about 39 degrees Fahrenheit.

He rang for tea, and a little later, while he was drinking it, she was still standing there, her face to the window. She wept from emotion, from her bitter consciousness of the sadness of their life; they could only see one another in secret, hiding from people, as if they were thieves. Was not their life a broken one?

"Don't cry," he said.

It was quite obvious to him that this love of theirs would not soon come to an end, and that no one could say when this end would be. Anna Sergeyevna loved him ever more fondly, worshipped him, and there would have been no point in telling her that one day it must end. Indeed, she would not have believed him.

He moved over and took her by the shoulders, intending to fondle her with light words, but suddenly he caught sight of himself in the looking-glass.

His hair was already beginning to turn gray. It struck him as strange that he should have aged so much in the last few years. The shoulders on which his hands lay were warm and quivering. He felt a pity for this life, still so warm and exquisite, but probably soon to fade and droop like his own. Why did she love him so? Women had always believed him different from what he really was, had loved in him not himself but the man their imagination pictured him, a man they had sought for eagerly all their lives. And afterwards when they discovered their mistake, they went on loving him just the same. And not one of them had ever been happy with him. Time had passed, he had met one woman after another, become intimate with each, parted with each, but had never loved. There had been all sorts of things between them, but never love.

And only now, when he was gray-haired, had he fallen in love properly, thoroughly, for the first time in his life.

He and Anna Sergeyevna loved one another as people who are very close and intimate, as husband and wife, as dear friends love one another. It seemed to them that fate had intended them for one another, and they could not understand why she should have a husband, and he a wife. They were like two migrating birds, the male and the female, who had been caught and put into separate cages. They forgave one another all that they were ashamed of in the past, in their present, and felt that this love of theirs had changed them both.

Formerly, in moments of melancholy, he had consoled himself by the first argument that came into his head, but now arguments were nothing to him, he felt profound pity, desired to be sincere, tender.

"Stop crying, my dearest," he said. "You've had your cry, now stop. . . . Now let us have a talk, let us try and think what we are to do."

Then they discussed their situation for a long time, trying to think how they could get rid of the necessity for hiding, deception, living in different towns, being so long without meeting. How were they to shake off these intolerable fetters?

"How? How?" he repeated, clutching his head. "How?"

And it seemed to them that they were within an inch of arriving at a decision, and that then a new, beautiful life would begin. And they both realized that the end was still far, far away, and that the hardest, the most complicated part was only just beginning.

1899

JAMES JOYCE

Araby

North Richmond Street, being blind,[1] was a quiet street except at the hour when the Christian Brothers'[2] School set the boys free. An uninhabited house of two stories stood at the blind end, detached from its neighbors in a square ground. The other houses of the street, conscious of decent lives within them, gazed at one another with brown imperturbable faces.

The former tenant of our house, a priest, had died in the back drawing room. Air, musty from having been long enclosed, hung in all the rooms, and the waste room behind the kitchen was littered with old useless papers. Among these I found a few paper-covered books, the pages of which were curled and damp: *The Abbot*, by Walter Scott, *The Devout Communicant* and *The Memoirs of Vidocq*.[3] I liked the last best because its leaves were yellow. The wild garden behind the house contained a central apple tree and a few straggling bushes under one of which I found the late tenant's rusty bicycle pump. He had been a very charitable priest; in his will he had left all his money to institutions and the furniture of his house to his sister.

When the short days of winter came dusk fell before we had well eaten our dinners. When we met in the street the houses had grown somber. The space of sky above us was the color of ever-changing violet and towards it the lamps of the street lifted their feeble lanterns. The cold air stung us and we played till our bodies glowed. Our shouts echoed in the silent street. The career of our play brought us through the dark muddy lanes behind the houses where we ran the gantlet of the rough tribes from the cottages, to the back doors of the dark dripping gardens where odors arose from the ashpits,[4] to the dark odorous stables where a coachman smoothed and combed the horse or shook music from the buckled harness. When we returned to the street light from the kitchen windows had filled the areas. If my uncle was seen turning the corner we hid in the shadow until we had seen him safely housed. Or if Mangan's sister came out on the doorstep to call her brother in to his tea we watched her from

1. Dead-end street. The story takes place in Dublin.
2. Conservative Irish lay order.
3. The 1820 novel by Sir Walter Scott (1771–1834) is a romance about the Catholic Mary Queen of Scots (1542–87), who was beheaded; a Catholic religious tract: *The Devout Communicant: or Pious Meditations and Aspirations for the Three Days Before and Three Days After Receiving the Holy Eucharist* (1813); François Vidocq (1775–1857), a French criminal who became chief of detectives, who died poor and disgraced for his part in a crime that he solved, and who probably did not write the book called his memoirs.
4. Where fireplace ashes were dumped.

our shadow peer up and down the street. We waited to see whether she would remain or go in and, if she remained, we left our shadow and walked up to Mangan's steps resignedly. She was waiting for us, her figure defined by the light from the half-opened door. Her brother always teased her before he obeyed and I stood by the railings looking at her. Her dress swung as she moved her body and the soft rope of her hair tossed from side to side.

Every morning I lay on the floor in the front parlor watching her door. The blind was pulled down to within an inch of the sash so that I could not be seen. When she came out on the doorstep my heart leaped. I ran to the hall, seized my books and followed her. I kept her brown figure always in my eye and, when we came near the point at which our ways diverged, I quickened my pace and passed her. This happened morning after morning. I had never spoken to her, except for a few casual words, and yet her name was like a summons to all my foolish blood.

Her image accompanied me even in places the most hostile to romance. On Saturday evenings when my aunt went marketing I had to go to carry some of the parcels. We walked through the flaring streets, jostled by drunken men and bargaining women, amid the curses of laborers, the shrill litanies of shop-boys who stood on guard by the barrels of pigs' cheeks, the nasal chanting of street-singers, who sang a *come-all-you* about O'Donovan Rossa,[5] or a ballad about the troubles in our native land. These noises converged in a single sensation of life for me: I imagined that I bore my chalice safely through a throng of foes. Her name sprang to my lips at moments in strange prayers and praises which I myself did not understand. My eyes were often full of tears (I could not tell why) and at times a flood from my heart seemed to pour itself out into my bosom. I thought little of the future. I did not know whether I would ever speak to her or not or, if I spoke to her, how I could tell her of my confused adoration. But my body was like a harp and her words and gestures were like fingers running upon the wires.

One evening I went into the back drawing room in which the priest had died. It was a dark rainy evening and there was no sound in the house. Through one of the broken panes I heard the rain impinge upon the earth, the fine incessant needles of water playing in the sodden beds. Some distant lamp or lighted window gleamed below me. I was thankful that I could see so little. All my senses seemed to desire to veil themselves and, feeling that I was about to slip from them, I pressed the palms of my hands together until they trembled, murmuring: *O love! O love!* many times.

At last she spoke to me. When she addressed the first words to me I was so confused that I did not know what to answer. She asked me was I going to *Araby.*[6] I forget whether I answered yes or no. It would be a splendid bazaar, she said; she would love to go.

---

5. A song, of which there were many, which began "Come, all you Irishmen." Jeremiah ("Dynamite Rossa") O'Donovan (1831–1915) was a militant Irish nationalist who fought on despite terms in prison and banishment.

6. A bazaar billed as a "Grand Oriental Fête," Dublin, May 1894.

—And why can't you? I asked.

While she spoke she turned a silver bracelet round and round her
wrist. She could not go, she said, because there would be a retreat
that week in her convent. Her brother and two other boys were
fighting for their caps and I was alone at the railings. She held one
of the spikes, bowing her head towards me. The light from the lamp
opposite our door caught the white curve of her neck, lit up her
hair that rested there and, falling, lit up the hand upon the railing.
It fell over one side of her dress and caught the white border of a
petticoat, just visible as she stood at ease.

—It's well for you, she said.

—If I go, I said, I will bring you something.   *distraction*

What innumerable follies laid waste my waking and sleeping
thoughts after that evening! I wished to annihilate the tedious intervening days. I chafed against the work of school. At night in my bedroom and by day in the classroom her image came between me and
the page I strove to read. The syllables of the word *Araby* were
called to me through the silence in which my soul luxuriated and
cast an Eastern enchantment over me. I asked for leave to go to the
bazaar on Saturday night. My aunt was surprised and hoped it was
not some Freemason[7] affair. I answered few questions in class. I
watched my master's face pass from amiability to sternness; he hoped
I was not beginning to idle. I could not call my wandering thoughts
together. I had hardly any patience with the serious work of life
which, now that it stood between me and my desire, seemed to me
child's play, ugly monotonous child's play.

On Saturday morning I reminded my uncle that I wished to go to
the bazaar in the evening. He was fussing at the hallstand, looking
for the hat brush, and answered me curtly:

—Yes, boy, I know.

As he was in the hall I could not go into the front parlor and lie
at the window. I left the house in bad humor and walked slowly
towards the school. The air was pitilessly raw and already my heart
misgave me.

When I came home to dinner my uncle had not yet been home.
Still it was early. I sat staring at the clock for some time and, when
its ticking began to irritate me, I left the room. I mounted the staircase
and gained the upper part of the house. The high cold empty gloomy
rooms liberated me and I went from room to room singing. From the
front window I saw my companions playing below in the street.
Their cries reached me weakened and indistinct and, leaning my
forehead against the cool glass, I looked over at the dark house
where she lived. I may have stood there for an hour, seeing nothing
but the brown-clad figure cast by my imagination, touched discreetly
by the lamplight at the curved neck, at the hand upon the railings
and at the border below the dress.

When I came downstairs again I found Mrs. Mercer sitting at the
fire. She was an old garrulous woman, a pawnbroker's widow, who

---

7. The Masons, or Freemasons, were considered enemies of the Catholics.

collected used stamps for some pious purpose. I had to endure the gossip of the tea-table. The meal was prolonged beyond an hour and still my uncle did not come. Mrs. Mercer stood up to go: she was sorry she couldn't wait any longer, but it was after eight o'clock and she did not like to be out late, as the night air was bad for her. When she had gone I began to walk up and down the room, clenching my fists. My aunt said:

—I'm afraid you may put off your bazaar for this night of Our Lord.

At nine o'clock I heard my uncle's latchkey in the hall door. I heard him talking to himself and heard the hall stand rocking when it had received the weight of his overcoat. I could interpret these signs. When he was midway through his dinner I asked him to give me the money to go to the bazaar. He had forgotten.

—The people are in bed and after their first sleep now, he said.

I did not smile. My aunt said to him energetically:

—Can't you give him the money and let him go? You've kept him late enough as it is.

My uncle said he was very sorry he had forgotten. He said he believed in the old saying: *All work and no play makes Jack a dull boy.* He asked me where I was going and, when I had told him a second time he asked me did I know *The Arab's Farewell to His Steed.*[8] When I left the kitchen he was about to recite the opening lines of the piece to my aunt.

I held a florin[9] tightly in my hand as I strode down Buckingham Street towards the station. The sight of the streets thronged with buyers and glaring with gas recalled to me the purpose of my journey. I took my seat in a third-class carriage of a deserted train. After an intolerable delay the train moved out of the station slowly. It crept onward among ruinous houses and over the twinkling river. At Westland Row Station a crowd of people pressed to the carriage doors; but the porters moved them back, saying that it was a special train for the bazaar. I remained alone in the bare carriage. In a few minutes the train drew up beside an improvised wooden platform. I passed out on to the road and saw by the lighted dial of a clock that it was ten minutes to ten. In front of me was a large building which displayed the magical name.

I could not find any sixpenny entrance and, fearing that the bazaar would be closed, I passed in quickly through a turnstile, handing a shilling to a weary-looking man. I found myself in a big hall girdled at half its height by a gallery. Nearly all the stalls were closed and the greater part of the hall was in darkness. I recognized a silence like that which pervades a church after a service. I walked into the center of the bazaar timidly. A few people were gathered about the stalls which were still open. Before a curtain, over which the words *Café Chantant*[1] were written in colored lamps, two men were counting money on a salver. I listened to the fall of the coins.

8. Or *The Arab's Farewell to His Horse*, sentimental nineteenth-century poem by Caroline Norton. The speaker has sold the horse.

9. Two-shilling piece; thus four times the "sixpenny entrance" fee.
1. Café with music.

Remembering with difficulty why I had come, I went over to one of the stalls and examined porcelain vases and flowered tea-sets. At the door of the stall a young lady was talking and laughing with two young gentlemen. I remarked their English accents[2] and listened vaguely to their conversation.

desecrate holy place

—O, I never said such a thing!

—O, but you did!

—O, but I didn't!

—Didn't she say that?

—Yes. I heard her.

—O, there's a . . . fib!

Observing me the young lady came over and asked me did I wish to buy anything. The tone of her voice was not encouraging; she seemed to have spoken to me out of a sense of duty. I looked humbly at the great jars that stood like eastern guards at either side of the dark entrance to the stall and murmured:

—No, thank you.

The young lady changed the position of one of the vases and went back to the two young men. They began to talk of the same subject. Once or twice the young lady glanced at me over her shoulder.

I lingered before her stall, though I knew my stay was useless, to make my interest in her wares seem the more real. Then I turned away slowly and walked down the middle of the bazaar. I allowed the two pennies to fall against the sixpence in my pocket. I heard a voice call from one end of the gallery that the light was out. The upper part of the hall was now completely dark.

Gazing up into the darkness I saw myself as a creature driven and derided by vanity; and my eyes burned with anguish and anger.

1914

FRANZ KAFKA

A Hunger Artist *

During these last decades the interest in professional fasting has markedly diminished. It used to pay very well to stage such great performances under one's own management, but today that is quite impossible. We live in a different world now. At one time the whole town took a lively interest in the hunger artist; from day to day of his fast the excitement mounted; everybody wanted to see him at least once a day; there were people who bought season tickets for the last few days and sat from morning till night in front of his small barred cage; even in the nighttime there were visiting hours, when the whole effect was heightened by torch flares; on fine days the cage was set out in the open air, and then it was the children's special treat to see the hunger

2. Remember, the story is set in Ireland.   * Translated by Willa and Edwin Muir.

artist; for their elders he was often just a joke that happened to be in fashion, but the children stood open-mouthed, holding each other's hands for greater security, marveling at him as he sat there pallid in black tights, with his ribs sticking out so prominently, not even on a seat but down among straw on the ground, sometimes giving a courteous nod, answering questions with a constrained smile, or perhaps stretching an arm through the bars so that one might feel how thin it was, and then again withdrawing deep into himself, paying no attention to anyone or anything, not even to the all-important striking of the clock that was the only piece of furniture in his cage, but merely staring into vacancy with half-shut eyes, now and then taking a sip from a tiny glass of water to moisten his lips.

Besides casual onlookers there were also relays of permanent watchers selected by the public, usually butchers, strangely enough, and it was their task to watch the hunger artist day and night, three of them at a time, in case he should have some secret recourse to nourishment. This was nothing but a formality, instituted to reassure the masses, for the initiates knew well enough that during his fast the artist would never in any circumstances, not even under forcible compulsion, swallow the smallest morsel of food; the honor of his profession forbade it. Not every watcher, of course, was capable of understanding this, there were often groups of night watchers who were very lax in carrying out their duties and deliberately huddled together in a retired corner to play cards with great absorption, obviously intending to give the hunger artist the chance of a little refreshment, which they supposed he could draw from some private hoard. Nothing annoyed the artist more than such watchers; they made him miserable; they made his fast seem unendurable; sometimes he mastered his feebleness sufficiently to sing during their watch for as long as he could keep going, to show them how unjust their suspicions were. But that was of little use; they only wondered at his cleverness in being able to fill his mouth even while singing. Much more to his taste were the watchers who sat close up to the bars, who were not content with the dim night lighting of the hall but focused him in the full glare of the electric pocket torch given them by the impresario. The harsh light did not trouble him at all. In any case he could never sleep properly, and he could always drowse a little, whatever the light, at any hour, even when the hall was thronged with noisy onlookers. He was quite happy at the prospect of spending a sleepless night with such watchers; he was ready to exchange jokes with them, to tell them stories out of his nomadic life, anything at all to keep them awake and demonstrate to them again that he had no eatables in his cage and that he was fasting as not one of them could fast. But his happiest moment was when the morning came and an enormous breakfast was brought them, at his expense, on which they flung themselves with the keen appetite of healthy men after a weary night of wakefulness. Of course there were people who argued that this breakfast was an unfair attempt to bribe the watchers, but that was going rather too far, and when they were invited to take on a night's vigil without a breakfast, merely for the sake of the cause, they made themselves scarce, although they stuck stubbornly to their suspicions.

Such suspicions, anyhow, were a necessary accompaniment to the profession of fasting. No one could possibly watch the hunger artist continuously, day and night, and so no one could produce first-hand evidence that the fast had really been rigorous and continuous; only the artist himself could know that; he was therefore bound to be the sole completely satisfied spectator of his own fast. Yet for other reasons he was never satisfied; it was not perhaps mere fasting that had brought him to such skeleton thinness that many people had regretfully to keep away from his exhibitions, because the sight of him was too much for them, perhaps it was dissatisfaction with himself that had worn him down. For he alone knew, what no other initiate knew, how easy it was to fast. It was the easiest thing in the world. He made no secret of this, yet people did not believe him; at the best they set him down as modest; most of them, however, thought he was out for publicity or else was some kind of cheat who found it easy to fast because he had discovered a way of making it easy, and then had the impudence to admit the fact, more or less. He had to put up with all that, and in the course of time had got used to it, but his inner dissatisfaction always rankled, and never yet, after any term of fasting—this must be granted to his credit—had he left the cage of his own free will. The longest period of fasting was fixed by his impresario at forty days, beyond that term he was not allowed to go, not even in great cities, and there was good reason for it, too. Experience had proved that for about forty days the interest of the public could be stimulated by a steadily increasing pressure of advertisement, but after that the town began to lose interest, sympathetic support began notably to fall off; there were of course local variations as between one town and another or one country and another, but as a general rule forty days marked the limit. So on the fortieth day the flower-bedecked cage was opened, enthusiastic spectators filled the hall, a military band played, two doctors entered the cage to measure the results of the fast, which were announced through a megaphone, and finally two young ladies appeared, blissful at having been selected for the honor, to help the hunger artist down the few steps leading to a small table on which was spread a carefully chosen invalid repast. And at this very moment the artist always turned stubborn. True, he would entrust his bony arms to the outstretched helping hands of the ladies bending over him, but stand up he would not. Why stop fasting at this particular moment, after forty days of it? He had held out for a long time, an illimitably long time; why stop now, when he was in his best fasting form, or rather, not yet quite in his best fasting form? Why should he be cheated of the fame he would get for fasting longer, for being not only the record hunger artist of all time, which presumably he was already, but for beating his own record by a performance beyond human imagination, since he felt that there were no limits to his capacity for fasting? His public pretended to admire him so much, why should it have so little patience with him; if he could endure fasting longer, why shouldn't the public endure it? Besides, he was tired, he was comfortable sitting in the straw, and now he was supposed to lift himself to his full height and go down to a meal the very thought of which gave him a nausea that only the presence of the ladies kept him from betraying, and even that with an effort. And he looked up into the eyes of the ladies who were apparently so friendly and in reality so cruel, and shook his head, which felt too heavy on its strengthless neck. But then there happened yet again what always happened. The impresario came forward, without a word—for the band made speech impossible—lifted his arms in the air above the artist, as if inviting Heaven to look down upon its creature here in the straw, this suffering martyr, which indeed he was, although in quite another sense; grasped him round the emaciated waist, with exaggerated caution, so that the frail condition he was in might be appreciated; and committed him to the care of the blenching ladies, not without secretly giving him a shaking so that his legs and body tottered and swayed. The artist now submitted completely; his head lolled on his breast as if it had landed there by chance; his body was hollowed out; his legs in a spasm of self-preservation clung close to each other at the knees, yet scraped on the ground as if it were not really solid ground, as if they were only trying to find solid ground; and the whole weight of his body, a featherweight after all, relapsed onto one of the ladies, who, looking round for help and panting a little —this post of honor was not at all what she had expected it to be— first stretched her neck as far as she could to keep her face at least free from contact with the artist, then finding this impossible, and her more fortunate companion not coming to her aid but merely holding extended on her own trembling hand the little bunch of knucklebones that was the artist's, to the great delight of the spectators burst into tears and had to be replaced by an attendant who had long been stationed in readiness. Then came the food, a little of which the impresario managed to get between the artist's lips, while he sat in a kind of half-fainting trance, to the accompaniment of cheerful patter designed to distract the public's attention from the artist's condition; after that, a toast was drunk to the public, supposedly prompted by a whisper from the artist in the impresario's ear; the band confirmed it with a mighty flourish, the spectators melted away, and no one had any cause to be dissatisfied with the proceedings, no one except the hunger artist himself, he only, as always.

So he lived for many years, with small regular intervals of recuperation, in visible glory, honored by the world, yet in spite of that troubled in spirit, and all the more troubled because no one would take his trouble seriously. What comfort could he possibly need? What more could he possibly wish for? And if some good-natured person, feeling sorry for him, tried to console him by pointing out that his melancholy was probably caused by fasting, it could happen, especially when he had been fasting for some time, that he reacted with an outburst of fury and to the general alarm began to shake the bars of his cage like a wild animal. Yet the impresario had a way of punishing these outbreaks which he rather enjoyed putting into operation. He would apologize publicly for the artist's behavior, which was only to be excused, he admitted, because of the irritability caused by fasting;

a condition hardly to be understood by well-fed people; then by natural transition he went on to mention the artist's equally incomprehensible boast that he could fast for much longer than he was doing; he praised the high ambition, the good will, the great self-denial undoubtedly implicit in such a statement; and then quite simply countered it by bringing out photographs, which were also on sale to the public, showing the artist on the fortieth day of a fast lying in bed almost dead from exhaustion. This perversion of the truth, familiar to the artist though it was, always unnerved him afresh and proved too much for him. What was a consequence of the premature ending of his fast was here presented as the cause of it! To fight against this lack of understanding, against a whole world of non-understanding, was impossible. Time and again in good faith he stood by the bars listening to the impresario, but as soon as the photographs appeared he always let go and sank with a groan back on to his straw, and the reassured public could once more come close and gaze at him. *unfinished*

A few years later when the witnesses of such scenes called them to mind, they often failed to understand themselves at all. For meanwhile the aforementioned change in public interest had set in; it seemed to happen almost overnight; there may have been profound causes for it, but who was going to bother about that; at any rate the pampered hunger artist suddenly found himself deserted one fine day by the amusement seekers, who went streaming past him to other more favored attractions. For the last time the impresario hurried him over half Europe to discover whether the old interest might still survive here and there; all in vain; everywhere, as if by secret agreement, a positive revulsion from professional fasting was in evidence. Of course it could not really have sprung up so suddenly as all that, and many premonitory symptoms which had not been sufficiently remarked or suppressed during the rush and glitter of success now came retrospectively to mind, but it was now too late to take any countermeasures. Fasting would surely come into fashion again at some future date, yet that was no comfort for those living in the present. What, then, was the hunger artist to do? He had been applauded by thousands in his time and could hardly come down to showing himself in a street booth at village fairs, and as for adopting another profession, he was not only too old for that but too fanatically devoted to fasting. So he took leave of the impresario, his partner in an unparalleled career, and hired himself to a large circus; in order to spare his own feelings he avoided reading the conditions of his contract.

A large circus with its enormous traffic in replacing and recruiting men, animals and apparatus can always find a use for people at any time, even for a hunger artist, provided of course that he does not ask too much, and in this particular case anyhow it was not only the artist who was taken on but his famous and long-known name as well; indeed considering the peculiar nature of his performance, which was not impared by advancing age, it could not be objected that here was an artist past his prime, no longer at the height of his professional skill, seeking a refuge in some quiet corner of a circus; on the contrary, the hunger artist averred that he could fast as well as ever, which was entirely credible; he even alleged that if he were allowed to fast as he liked, and this was at once promised him without more ado, he could astound the world by establishing a record never yet achieved, a statement which certainly provoked a smile among the other professionals, since it left out of account the change in public opinion, which the hunger artist in his zeal conveniently forgot.

He had not, however, actually lost his sense of the real situation and took it as a matter of course that he and his cage should be stationed, not in the middle of the ring as a main attraction, but outside, near the animal cages, on a site that was after all easily accessible. Large and gaily painted placards made a frame for the cage and announced what was to be seen inside it. When the public came thronging out in the intervals to see the animals, they could hardly avoid passing the hunger artist's cage and stopping there for a moment; perhaps they might even have stayed longer had not those pressing behind them in the narrow gangway, who did not understand why they should be held up on their way towards the excitements of the menagerie, made it impossible for anyone to stand gazing quietly for any length of time. And that was the reason why the hunger artist, who had of course been looking forward to these visiting hours as the main achievement of his life, began instead to shrink from them. At first he could hardly wait for the intervals; it was exhilarating to watch the crowds come streaming his way, until only too soon—not even the most obstinate self-deception, clung to almost consciously, could hold out against the fact —the conviction was borne in upon him that these people, most of them, to judge from their actions, again and again, without exception, were all on their way to the menagerie. And the first sight of them from the distance remained the best. For when they reached his cage he was at once deafened by the storm of shouting and abuse that arose from the two contending factions, which renewed themselves continuously, of those who wanted to stop and stare at him—he soon began to dislike them more than the others—not out of real interest but only out of obstinate self-assertiveness, and those who wanted to go straight on to the animals. When the first great rush was past, the stragglers came along, and these, whom nothing could have prevented from stopping to look at him as long as they had breath, raced past with long strides, hardly even glancing at him, in their haste to get to the menagerie in time. And all too rarely did it happen that he had a stroke of luck, when some father of a family fetched up before him with his children, pointed a finger at the hunger artist and explained at length what the phenomenon meant, telling stories of earlier years when he himself had watched similar but much more thrilling performances, and the children, still rather uncomprehending, since neither inside nor outside school had they been sufficiently prepared for this lesson—what did they care about fasting?—yet showed by the brightness of their intent eyes that new and better times might be coming. Perhaps, said the hunger artist to himself many a time, things would be a little better if his cage were set not quite so near the menagerie. That made it too easy for people to make their choice, to say nothing of what he suffered from the stench of the menagerie, the animals' restlessness by night, the carrying past of raw lumps of flesh for the beasts of prey, the roaring at feeding times, which depressed him continually. But he did not dare to lodge a complaint with the management; after all, he had the animals to thank for the troops of people who passed his cage, among whom there might always be one here and there to take an interest in him, and who could tell where they might seclude him if he called attention to his existence and thereby to the fact that, strictly speaking, he was only an impediment on the way to the menagerie.

A small impediment, to be sure, one that grew steadily less. People grew familiar with the strange idea that they could be expected, in times like these, to take an interest in a hunger artist, and with this familiarity the verdict went out against him He might fast as much as he could, and he did so; but nothing could save him now, people passed him by. Just try to explain to anyone the art of fasting! Anyone who has no feeling for it cannot be made to understand it. The fine placards grew dirty and illegible, they were torn down; the little notice board telling the number of fast days achieved, which at first was changed carefully every day, had long stayed at the same figure, for after the first few weeks even this small task seemed pointless to the staff; and so the artist simply fasted on and on, as he had once dreamed of doing, and it was no trouble to him, just as he had always foretold, but no one counted the days, no one, not even the artist himself, knew what records he was already breaking, and his heart grew heavy. And when once in a time some leisurely passer-by stopped, made merry over the old figure on the board and spoke of swindling, that was in its way the stupidest lie ever invented by indifference and inborn malice, since it was not the hunger artist who was cheating; he was working honestly, but the world was cheating him of his reward.

Many more days went by, however, and that too came to an end. An overseer's eye fell on the cage one day and he asked the attendants why this perfectly good cage should be left standing there unused with dirty straw inside it; nobody knew, until one man, helped out by the notice board, remembered about the hunger artist. They poked into the straw with sticks and found him in it. "Are you still fasting?" asked the overseer. "When on earth do you mean to stop?" "Forgive me, everybody," whispered the hunger artist; only the overseer, who had his ear to the bars, understood him. "Of course," said the overseer, and tapped his forehead with a finger to let the attendants know what state the man was in, "we forgive you." "I always wanted you to admire my fasting," said the hunger artist. "We do admire it," said the overseer, affably. "But you shouldn't admire it," said the hunger artist. "Well, then we don't admire it," said the overseer, "but why shouldn't we admire it?" "Because I have to fast, I can't help it," said the hunger artist. "What a fellow you are," said the overseer, "and why can't you help it?" "Because," said the hunger artist, lifting his head a little and speaking, with his lips pursed, as if for a kiss, right into the overseer's ear, so that no syllable might be lost, "because I couldn't find the food I liked. If I had found it, believe me, I should have made no fuss and stuffed myself like you or anyone else." These were his last words, but in his dimming eyes remained the firm though no longer proud persuasion that he was still continuing to fast.

"Well, clear this out now!" said the overseer, and they buried the hunger artist, straw and all. Into the cage they put a young panther. Even the most insensitive felt it refreshing to see this wild creature leaping around the cage that had so long been dreary. The panther was all right. The food he liked was brought him without hesitation by the attendants; he seemed not even to miss his freedom; his noble body, furnished almost to the bursting point with all that it needed, seemed to carry freedom around with it too; somewhere in his jaws it seemed to lurk; and the joy of life streamed with such ardent passion from his throat that for the onlookers it was not easy to stand the shock of it. But they braced themselves, crowded round the cage, and did not want ever to move away.

1924

D. H. LAWRENCE

The Rocking-Horse Winner

There was a woman who was beautiful, who started with all the advantages, yet she had no luck. She married for love, and the love turned to dust. She had bonny children, yet she felt they had been thrust upon her, and she could not love them. They looked at her coldly, as if they were finding fault with her. And hurriedly she felt she must cover up some fault in herself. Yet what it was that she must cover up she never knew. Nevertheless, when her children were present, she always felt the center of her heart go hard. This troubled her, and in her manner she was all the more gentle and anxious for her children, as if she loved them very much. Only she herself knew that at the center of her heart was a hard little place that could not feel love, no, not for anybody. Everybody else said of her: "She is such a good mother. She adores her children." Only she herself, and her children themselves, knew it was not so. They read it in each other's eyes.

There were a boy and two little girls. They lived in a pleasant house, with a garden, and they had discreet servants, and felt themselves superior to anyone in the neighborhood.

Although they lived in style, they felt always an anxiety in the house. There was never enough money. The mother had a small income, and the father had a small income, but not nearly enough for the social position which they had to keep up. The father went into town to some office. But though he had good prospects, these prospects never materialized. There was always the grinding sense of the shortage of money, though the style was always kept up.

At last the mother said: "I will see if *I* can't make something." But she did not know where to begin. She racked her brains, and tried this thing and the other, but could not find anything successful. The failure made deep lines come into her face. Her children were growing up, they would have to go to school. There must be more money, there must be more money. The father, who was always very handsome and expensive in his tastes, seemed as if he never *would* be able to do anything worth doing. And the mother, who had a great belief in herself, did not succeed any better, and her tastes were just as expensive.

And so the house came to be haunted by the unspoken phrase: *There must be more money! There must be more money!* The children could hear it all the time, though nobody said it aloud. They heard it at Christmas, when the expensive and splendid toys filled the nursery. Behind the shining modern rocking-horse, behind the smart doll's house, a voice would start whispering: "There *must* be more money! There *must* be more money!" And the children would stop playing, to listen for a moment. They would look into each other's eyes, to see if they had all heard. And each one saw in the eyes of the other two that they too had heard. "There *must* be more money! There *must* be more money!"

It came whispering from the springs of the still-swaying rocking-horse, and even the horse, bending his wooden, champing head, heard it. The big doll, sitting so pink and smirking in her new pram,[1] could hear it quite plainly, and seemed to be smirking all the more self-consciously because of it. The foolish puppy, too, that took the place of the teddy bear, he was looking so extraordinarily foolish for no other reason but that he heard the secret whisper all over the house: "There *must* be more money!"

Yet nobody ever said it aloud. The whisper was everywhere, and therefore no one spoke it. Just as no one ever says: "We are breathing!" in spite of the fact that breath is coming and going all the time.

"Mother," said the boy Paul one day, "why don't we keep a car of our own? Why do we always use uncle's, or else a taxi?"

"Because we're the poor members of the family," said the mother.

"But why *are* we, mother?"

"Well—I suppose," she said slowly and bitterly, "it's because your father has no luck."

The boy was silent for some time.

"Is luck money, mother?" he asked, rather timidly.

"No, Paul. Not quite. It's what causes you to have money."

"Oh!" said Paul vaguely. "I thought when Uncle Oscar said *filthy lucker,* it meant money."

"*Filthy lucre* does mean money," said the mother. "But it's lucre, not luck."

"Oh!" said the boy. "Then what *is* luck, mother?"

"It's what causes you to have money. If you're lucky you have money. That's why it's better to be born lucky than rich. If you're rich, you may lose your money. But if you're lucky, you will always get more money."

"Oh! Will you? And is father not lucky?"

1. Baby carriage.

"Very unlucky, I should say," she said bitterly.

The boy watched her with unsure eyes.

"Why?" he asked.

"I don't know. Nobody ever knows why one person is lucky and another unlucky."

"Don't they? Nobody at all? Does *nobody* know?"

"Perhaps God. But He never tells."

"He ought to, then. And aren't you lucky either, mother?"

"I can't be, if I married an unlucky husband."

"But by yourself, aren't you?"

"I used to think I was, before I married. Now I think I am very unlucky indeed."

"Why?"

"Well—never mind! Perhaps I'm not really," she said.

The child looked at her to see if she meant it. But he saw, by the lines of her mouth, that she was only trying to hide something from him.

"Well, anyhow," he said stoutly, "I'm a lucky person."

"Why?" said his mother, with a sudden laugh.

He stared at her. He didn't even know why he had said it.

"God told me," he asserted, brazening it out.

"I hope He did, dear!" she said, again with a laugh, but rather bitter.

"He did, mother!"

"Excellent!" said the mother, using one of her husband's exclamations.

The boy saw she did not believe him; or rather, that she paid no attention to his assertion. This angered him somewhat, and made him want to compel her attention.

He went off by himself, vaguely, in a childish way, seeking for the clue to "luck." Absorbed, taking no heed of other people, he went about with a sort of stealth, seeking inwardly for luck. He wanted luck, he wanted it, he wanted it. When the two girls were playing dolls in the nursery, he would sit on his big rocking-horse, charging madly into space, with a frenzy that made the little girls peer at him uneasily. Wildly the horse careered, the waving dark hair of the boy tossed, his eyes had a strange glare in them. The little girls dared not speak to him.

When he had ridden to the end of his mad little journey, he climbed down and stood in front of his rocking-horse, staring fixedly into its lowered face. Its red mouth was slightly open, its big eye was wide and glassy-bright.

"Now!" he would silently command the snorting steed. "Now, take me to where there is luck! Now take me!"

And he would slash the horse on the neck with the little whip he had asked Uncle Oscar for. He *knew* the horse could take him to where there was luck, if only he forced it. So he would mount again and start on his furious ride, hoping at last to get there. He knew he could get there.

"You'll break your horse, Paul!" said the nurse.

"He's always riding like that! I wish he'd leave off!" said his elder sister Joan.

But he only glared down on them in silence. Nurse gave him up. She could make nothing of him. Anyhow, he was growing beyond her.

One day his mother and his Uncle Oscar came in when he was on one of his furious rides. He did not speak to them.

"Hallo, you young jockey! Riding a winner?" said his uncle.

"Aren't you growing too big for a rocking-horse? You're not a very little boy any longer, you know," said his mother.

But Paul only gave a blue glare from his big, rather close-set eyes. He would speak to nobody when he was in full tilt. His mother watched him with an anxious expression on her face.

At last he suddenly stopped forcing his horse into the mechanical gallop and slid down.

"Well, I got there!" he announced fiercely, his blue eyes still flaring, and his sturdy long legs straddling apart.

"Where did you get to?" asked his mother.

"Where I wanted to go," he flared back at her.

"That's right, son!" said Uncle Oscar. "Don't you stop till you get there. What's the horse's name?"

"He doesn't have a name," said the boy.

"Gets on without all right?" asked the uncle.

"Well, he has different names. He was called Sansovino last week."

"Sansovino, eh? Won the Ascot. How did you know this name?"

"He always talks about horse-races with Bassett," said Joan.

The uncle was delighted to find that his small nephew was posted with all the racing news. Bassett, the young gardener, who had been wounded in the left foot in the war[2] and had got his present job through Oscar Cresswell, whose batman he had been, was a perfect blade[3] of the "turf." He lived in the racing events, and the small boy lived with him.

Oscar Cresswell got it all from Bassett.

"Master Paul comes and asks me, so I can't do more than tell him, sir," said Bassett, his face terribly serious, as if he were speaking of religious matters.

"And does he ever put anything on a horse he fancies?"

"Well—I don't want to give him away—he's a young sport, a fine sport, sir. Would you mind asking him himself? He sort of takes a pleasure in it, and perhaps he'd feel I was giving him away, sir, if you don't mind."

Bassett was serious as a church.

The uncle went back to his nephew and took him off for a ride in the car.

"Say, Paul, old man, do you ever put anything on a horse?" the uncle asked.

The boy watched the handsome man closely.

"Why, do you think I oughtn't to?" he parried.

2. World War I, 1914–1918.   3. Dashing young man.

"Not a bit of it! I thought perhaps you might give me a tip for the Lincoln."[4]

The car sped on into the country, going down to Uncle Oscar's place in Hampshire.

"Honor bright?" said the nephew.

"Honor bright, son!" said the uncle.

"Well, then, Daffodil."

"Daffodil! I doubt it, sonny. What about Mirza?"

"I only know the winner," said the boy. "That's Daffodil."

"Daffodil, eh?"

There was a pause. Daffodil was an obscure horse comparatively.

"Uncle!"

"Yes, son?"

"You won't let it go any further, will you? I promised Bassett."

"Bassett be damned, old man! What's he got to do with it?"

"We're partners. We've been partners from the first. Uncle, he lent me my first five shillings,[5] which I lost. I promised him, honor bright, it was only between me and him; only you gave me that ten-shilling note I started winning with, so I thought you were lucky. You won't let it go any further, will you?"

The boy gazed at his uncle from those big, hot, blue eyes, set rather close together. The uncle stirred and laughed uneasily.

"Right you are, son! I'll keep your tip private. Daffodil, eh? How much are you putting on him?"

"All except twenty pounds," said the boy. "I keep that in reserve."

The uncle thought it a good joke.

"You keep twenty pounds in reserve, do you, you young romancer? What are you betting, then?"

"I'm betting three hundred," said the boy gravely. "But it's between you and me, Uncle Oscar! Honor bright?"

The uncle burst into a roar of laughter.

"It's between you and me all right, you young Nat Gould,"[6] he said, laughing. "But where's your three hundred?"

"Bassett keeps it for me. We're partners."

"You are, are you! And what is Bassett putting on Daffodil?"

"He won't go quite as high as I do, I expect. Perhaps he'll go a hundred and fifty."

"What, pennies?" laughed the uncle.

"Pounds," said the child, with a surprised look at his uncle. "Bassett keeps a bigger reserve than I do."

Between wonder and amusement Uncle Oscar was silent. He pursued the matter no further, but he determined to take his nephew with him to the Lincoln races.

---

4. Lincolnshire Handicap race then run at Lincoln Downs. Other races mentioned in the story include the St. Leger Stakes (the Leger) run at Doncaster; the Grand National Steeplechase run at Aintree, the most famous steeplechase in the world; the famous Derby, a mile-and-a-half race for three-year-olds run at Epsom Downs, and the Ascot (above) run at the course of that name in Berkshire.

5. Then just over a dollar. The English pound after World War I fluctuated considerably but was generally less than the $4.86 of the pre-War period and more than $4. There are 20 shillings to the pound.

6. Nathaniel Gould (1857–1919) novelist and journalist whose writings in both genres concerned horse-racing.

"Now, son," he said, "I'm putting twenty on Mirza, and I'll put five on for you on any horse you fancy. What's your pick?"

"Daffodil, uncle."

"No, not the fiver on Daffodil!"

"I should if it was my own fiver," said the child.

"Good! Good! Right you are! A fiver for me and a fiver for you on Daffodil."

The child had never been to a race-meeting before, and his eyes were blue fire. He pursed his mouth tight and watched. A Frenchman just in front had put his money on Lancelot. Wild with excitement, he flayed his arms up and down, yelling *"Lancelot! Lancelot!"* in his French accent.

Daffodil came in first, Lancelot second, Mirza third. The child, flushed and with eyes blazing, was curiously serene. His uncle brought him four five-pound notes, four to one.

"What am I to do with these?" he cried, waving them before the boy's eyes.

"I suppose we'll talk to Bassett," said the boy. "I expect I have fifteen hundred now; and twenty in reserve; and this twenty."

His uncle studied him for some moments.

"Look here, son!" he said. "You're not serious about Bassett and that fifteen hundred, are you?"

"Yes, I am. But it's between you and me, uncle. Honor bright?"

"Honor bright all right, son! But I must talk to Bassett."

"If you'd like to be a partner, uncle, with Bassett and me, we could all be partners. Only, you'd have to promise, honor bright, uncle, not to let it go beyond us three. Bassett and I are lucky, and you must be lucky, because it was your ten shillings I started winning with. . . ."

Uncle Oscar took both Bassett and Paul into Richmond Park for an afternoon, and there they talked.

"It's like this, you see, sir," Bassett said. "Master Paul would get me talking about racing events, spinning yarns, you know, sir. And he was always keen on knowing if I'd made or if I'd lost. It's about a year since, now, that I put five shillings on Blush of Dawn for him: and we lost. Then the luck turned, with that ten shillings, he had from you: that we put on Singhalese. And since that time, it's been pretty steady, all things considering. What do you say, Master Paul?"

"We're all right when we're sure," said Paul. "It's when we're not quite sure that we go down."

"Oh, but we're careful then," said Bassett.

"But when are you *sure*?" smiled Uncle Oscar.

"It's Master Paul, sir," said Bassett in a secret, religious voice. "It's as if he had it from heaven. Like Daffodil, now, for the Lincoln. That was as sure as eggs."

"Did you put anything on Daffodil?" asked Oscar Cresswell.

"Yes, sir. I made my bit."

"And my nephew?"

Bassett was obstinately silent, looking at Paul.

"I made twelve hundred, didn't I, Bassett? I told uncle I was putting three hundred on Daffodil."

"That's right," said Bassett, nodding.

"But where's the money?" asked the uncle.

"I keep it safe locked up, sir. Master Paul he can have it any minute he likes to ask for it."

"What, fifteen hundred pounds?"

"And twenty! And *forty*, that is, with the twenty he made on the course."

"It's amazing!" said the uncle.

"If Master Paul offers you to be partners, sir, I would, if I were you: if you'll excuse me," said Bassett.

Oscar Cresswell thought about it.

"I'll see the money," he said.

They drove home again, and, sure enough, Bassett came round to the garden-house with fifteen hundred pounds in notes. The twenty pounds reserve was left with Joe Glee, in the Turf Commission deposit.

"You see, it's all right, uncle, when I'm *sure*! Then we go strong, for all we're worth. Don't we, Bassett?"

"We do that, Master Paul."

"And when are you sure?" said the uncle, laughing.

"Oh, well, sometimes I'm *absolutely* sure, like about Daffodil," said the boy; "and sometimes I have an idea; and sometimes I haven't even an idea, have I, Bassett? Then we're careful, because we mostly go down."

"You do, do you! And when you're sure, like about Daffodil, what makes you sure, sonny?"

"Oh, well, I don't know," said the boy uneasily. "I'm sure, you know, uncle; that's all."

"It's as if he had it from heaven, sir," Bassett reiterated.

"I should say so!" said the uncle.

But he became a partner. And when the Leger was coming on, Paul was "sure" about Lively Spark, which was a quite inconsiderable horse. The boy insisted on putting a thousand on the horse, Bassett went for five hundred, and Oscar Cresswell two hundred. Lively Spark came in first, and the betting had been ten to one against him. Paul had made ten thousand.

"You see," he said, "I was absolutely sure of him."

Even Oscar Cresswell had cleared two thousand.

"Look here, son," he said, "this sort of thing makes me nervous."

"It needn't, uncle! Perhaps I shan't be sure again for a long time."

"But what are you going to do with your money?" asked the uncle.

"Of course," said the boy, "I started it for mother. She said she had no luck, because father is unlucky, so I thought if *I* was lucky, it might stop whispering."

"What might stop whispering?"

"Our house. I *hate* our house for whispering."

"What does it whisper?"

"Why—why"—the boy fidgeted—"why, I don't know. But it's always short of money, you know, uncle."

"I know it, son, I know it."

"You know people send mother writs, don't you, uncle?"

"I'm afraid I do," said the uncle.

"And then the house whispers. like people laughing at you behind your back.. It's awful, that is! I thought if I was lucky—"

"You might stop it," added the uncle.

The boy watched him with big blue eyes, that had an uncanny cold fire in them, and he said never a word.

"Well, then!" said the uncle. "What are we doing?"

"I shouldn't like mother to know I was lucky," said the boy.

"Why not, son?"

"She'd stop me."

"I don't think she would."

"Oh!"—and the boy writhed in an odd way—"I *don't* want her to know, uncle."

"All right, son! We'll manage it without her knowing."

They managed it very easily. Paul, at the other's suggestion, handed over five thousand pounds to his uncle, who deposited it with the family lawyer, who was then to inform Paul's mother that a relative had put five thousand pounds into his hands, which sum was to be paid out a thousand pounds at a time, on the mother's birthday, for the next five years.

"So she'll have a birthday present of a thousand pounds for five successive years," said Uncle Oscar. "I hope it won't make it all the harder for her later."

Paul's mother had her birthday in November. The house had been "whispering" worse than ever lately, and, even in spite of his luck, Paul could not bear up against it. He was very anxious to see the effect of the birthday letter, telling his mother about the thousand pounds.

When there were no visitors, Paul now took his meals with his parents, as he was beyond the nursery control. His mother went into town nearly every day. She had discovered that she had an odd knack of sketching furs and dress materials, so she worked secretly in the studio of a friend who was the chief "artist" for the leading drapers. She drew the figures of ladies in furs and ladies in silk and sequins for the newspaper advertisements. This young woman artist earned several thousand pounds a year, but Paul's mother only made several hundreds, and she was again dissatisfied. She so wanted to be first in something, and she did not succeed, even in making sketches for drapery advertisements.

She was down to breakfast on the morning of her birthday. Paul watched her face as she read her letters. He knew the lawyer's letter. As his mother read it, her face hardened and became more expressionless. Then a cold, determined look came on her mouth. She hid the letter under the pile of others, and said not a word about it.

"Didn't you have anything nice in the post for your birthday, mother?" said Paul.

"Quite moderately nice," she said, her voice cold and absent.

She went away to town without saying more.

But in the afternoon Uncle Oscar appeared. He said Paul's mother had had a long interview with the lawyer, asking if the whole five thousand could not be advanced at once, as she was in debt.

"What do you think, uncle?" said the boy.

"I leave it to you, son."

"Oh, let her have it, then! We can get some more with the other," said the boy.

"A bird in the hand is worth two in the bush, laddie!" said Uncle Oscar.

"But I'm sure to *know* for the Grand National; or the Lincolnshire; or else the Derby. I'm sure to know for one of them," said Paul.

So Uncle Oscar signed the agreement, and Paul's mother touched the whole five thousand. Then something very curious happened. The voices in the house suddenly went mad, like a chorus of frogs on a spring evening. There were certain new furnishings, and Paul had a tutor. He was *really* going to Eton, his father's school, in the following autumn. There were flowers in the winter, and a blossoming of the luxury Paul's mother had been used to. And yet the voices in the house, behind the sprays of mimosa and almond-blossom, and from under the piles of iridescent cushions, simply trilled and screamed in a sort of ecstasy: "There *must* be more money! Oh-h-h; there *must* be more money. Oh, now, now-w! Now-w-w—there *must* be more money! —more than ever! More than ever!"

It frightened Paul terribly. He studied away at his Latin and Greek with his tutor. But his intense hours were spent with Bassett. The Grand National had gone by: he had not "known," and had lost a hundred pounds. Summer was at hand. He was in agony for the Lincoln. But even for the Lincoln he didn't "know," and he lost fifty pounds. He became wild-eyed and strange, as if something were going to explode in him.

"Let it alone, son! Don't you bother about it!" urged Uncle Oscar. But it was as if the boy couldn't really hear what his uncle was saying.

"I've got to know for the Derby! I've got to know for the Derby!" the child reiterated, his big blue eyes blazing with a sort of madness.

His mother noticed how overwrought he was.

"You'd better go to the seaside. Wouldn't you like to go now to the seaside, instead of waiting? I think you'd better," she said, looking down at him anxiously, her heart curiously heavy because of him.

But the child lifted his uncanny blue eyes.

"I couldn't possibly go before the Derby, mother!" he said. "I couldn't possibly!"

"Why not?" she said, her voice becoming heavy when she was opposed. "Why not? You can still go from the seaside to see the Derby with your Uncle Oscar, if that's what you wish. No need for you to wait here. Besides, I think you care too much about these races. It's a bad sign. My family has been a gambling family, and you won't know till you grow up how much damage it has done. But it has done damage. I shall have to send Bassett away, and ask Uncle Oscar not to talk racing to you, unless you promise to be reasonable about it: go away to the seaside and forget it. You're all nerves!"

"I'll do what you like, mother, so long as you don't send me away till after the Derby," the boy said.

"Send you away from where? Just from this house?"

"Yes," he said, gazing at her.

"Why, you curious child, what makes you care about this house so much, suddenly? I never knew you loved it."

He gazed at her without speaking. He had a secret within a secret, something he had not divulged, even to Bassett or to his Uncle Oscar.

But his mother, after standing undecided and a little bit sullen for some moments, said:

"Very well, then! Don't go to the seaside till after the Derby, if you don't wish it. But promise me you won't let your nerves go to pieces. Promise you won't think so much about horse-racing and *events,* as you call them!"

"Oh, no," said the boy casually. "I won't think much about them, mother. You needn't worry. I wouldn't worry, mother, if I were you."

"If you were me and I were you," said his mother, "I wonder what we *should* do!"

"But you know you needn't worry, mother, don't you?" the boy repeated.

"I should be awfully glad to know it," she said wearily.

"Oh, well, you *can,* you know. I mean, you *ought* to know you needn't worry," he insisted.

"Ought I? Then I'll see about it," she said.

Paul's secret of secrets was his wooden horse, that which had no name. Since he was emancipated from a nurse and a nursery-governess, he had had his rocking-horse removed to his own bedroom at the top of the house.

"Surely you're too big for a rocking-horse!" his mother had remonstrated.

"Well, you see, mother, till I can have a *real* horse, I like to have *some* sort of animal about," had been his quaint answer.

"Do you feel he keeps you company?" she laughed.

"Oh, yes! He's very good, he always keeps me company, when I'm there," said Paul.

So the horse, rather shabby, stood in an arrested prance in the boy's bedroom.

The Derby was drawing near, and the boy grew more and more tense. He hardly heard what was spoken to him, he was very frail, and his eyes were really uncanny. His mother had sudden strange seizures of uneasiness about him. Sometimes, for half an hour, she would feel a sudden anxiety about him that was almost anguish. She wanted to rush to him at once, and know he was safe.

Two nights before the Derby, she was at a big party in town, when one of her rushes of anxiety about her boy, her first-born, gripped her heart till she could hardly speak. She fought with the feeling, might and main, for she believed in common sense. But it was too strong. She had to leave the dance and go downstairs to telephone to the country. The children's nursery-governess was terribly surprised and startled at being rung up in the night.

"Are the children all right, Miss Wilmot?"

"Oh, yes, they are quite all right."

"Master Paul? Is he all right?"

"He went to bed as right as a trivet. Shall I run up and look at him?"

"No," said Paul's mother reluctantly. "No! Don't trouble. It's all right. Don't sit up. We shall be home fairly soon." She did not want her son's privacy intruded upon.

"Very good," said the governess.

It was about one o'clock when Paul's mother and father drove up to their house. All was still. Paul's mother went to her room and slipped off her white fur cloak. She had told her maid not to wait up for her. She heard her husband downstairs, mixing a whisky and soda.

And then, because of the strange anxiety at her heart, she stole upstairs to her son's room. Noiselessly she went along the upper corridor. Was there a faint noise? What was it?

She stood, with arrested muscles, outside his door, listening. There was a strange, heavy, and yet not loud noise. Her heart stood still. It was a soundless noise, yet rushing and powerful. Something huge, in violent, hushed motion. What was it? What in God's name was it? She ought to know. She felt that she knew the noise. She knew what it was.

Yet she could not place it. She couldn't say what it was. And on and on it went, like a madness.

Softly, frozen with anxiety and fear, she turned the door-handle.

The room was dark. Yet in the space near the window, she heard and saw something plunging to and fro. She gazed in fear and amazement.

Then suddenly she switched on the light, and saw her son, in his green pajamas, madly surging on the rocking-horse. The blaze of light suddenly lit him up, as he urged the wooden horse, and lit her up, as she stood, blonde, in her dress of pale green and crystal, in the doorway.

"Paul!" she cried. "Whatever are you doing?"

"It's Malabar!" he screamed, in a powerful, strange voice. "It's Malabar!"

His eyes blazed at her for one strange and senseless second, as he ceased urging his wooden horse. Then he fell with a crash to the ground, and she, all her tormented motherhood flooding upon her, rushed to gather him up.

But he was unconscious, and unconscious he remained, with some brain-fever. He talked and tossed, and his mother sat stonily by his side.

"Malabar! It's Malabar! Bassett, Bassett, I *know*! It's Malabar!"

So the child cried, trying to get up and urge the rocking-horse that gave him his inspiration.

"What does he mean by Malabar?" asked the heart-frozen mother.

"I don't know," said the father stonily.

"What does he mean by Malabar?" she asked her brother Oscar.

"It's one of the horses running for the Derby," was the answer.

And, in spite of himself, Oscar Cresswell spoke to Bassett, and himself put a thousand on Malabar: at fourteen to one.

The third day of the illness was critical: they were waiting for a change. The boy, with his rather long, curly hair, was tossing ceaselessly on the pillow. He neither slept nor regained consciousness, and his eyes were like blue stones. His mother sat, feeling her heart had gone, turned actually into a stone.

In the evening, Oscar Cresswell did not come, but Bassett sent a message, saying could he come up for one moment, just one moment? Paul's mother was very angry at the intrusion, but on second thought she agreed. The boy was the same. Perhaps Bassett might bring him to consciousness.

The gardener, a shortish fellow with a little brown moustache and sharp little brown eyes, tiptoed into the room, touched his imaginary cap to Paul's mother, and stole to the bedside, staring with glittering, smallish eyes, at the tossing, dying child.

"Master Paul!" he whispered. "Master Paul! Malabar came in first all right, a clean win. I did as you told me. You've made over seventy thousand pounds, you have; you've got over eighty thousand. Malabar came in all right, Master Paul."

"Malabar! Malabar! Did I say Malabar, mother? Did I say Malabar? Do you think I'm lucky, mother? I knew Malabar, didn't I? Over eighty thousand pounds! I call that lucky, don't you, mother? Over eighty thousand pounds! I knew, didn't I know I knew? Malabar came in all right. If I ride my horse till I'm sure, then I tell you, Bassett, you can go as high as you like. Did you go for all you were worth, Bassett?"

"I went a thousand on it, Master Paul."

"I never told you, mother, that if I can ride my horse, and *get there*, then I'm absolutely sure—oh, absolutely! Mother, did I ever tell you? I *am* lucky!"

"No, you never did," said the mother.

But the boy died in the night.

And even as he lay dead, his mother heard her brother's voice saying to her: "My God, Hester, you're eighty-odd thousand to the good, and a poor devil of a son to the bad. But, poor devil, poor devil, he's best gone out of a life where he rides his rocking-horse to find a winner."

1932

KATHERINE ANNE PORTER

Flowering Judas

Braggioni sits heaped upon the edge of a straight-backed chair much too small for him, and sings to Laura in a furry, mournful voice. Laura has begun to find reasons for avoiding her own house until the latest possible moment, for Braggioni is there almost every night. No matter how late she is, he will be sitting there with a surly, waiting expression, pulling at his kinky yellow hair, thumbing the strings of his guitar, snarling a tune under his breath. Lupe the Indian maid meets Laura at the door, and says with a flicker of a glance towards the upper room, "He waits."

Laura wishes to lie down, she is tired of her hairpins and the feel of her long tight sleeves, but she says to him, "Have you a new song for me this evening?" If he says yes, she asks him to sing it. If he says no, she remembers his favorite one, and asks him to sing it again. Lupe brings her a cup of chocolate and a plate of rice, and Laura eats at the small table under the lamp, first inviting Braggioni, whose answer is always the same: "I have eaten, and besides, chocolate thickens the voice."

Laura says, "Sing, then," and Braggioni heaves himself into song. He scratches the guitar familiarly as though it were a pet animal, and sings passionately off key, taking the high notes in a prolonged painful squeal. Laura, who haunts the markets listening to the ballad singers, and stops every day to hear the blind boy playing his reed-flute in Sixteenth of September Street,[1] listens to Braggioni with pitiless courtesy, because she dares not smile at his miserable performance. Nobody dares to smile at him. Braggioni is cruel to everyone, with a kind of specialized insolence, but he is so vain of his talents, and so sensitive to slights, it would require a cruelty and vanity greater than his own to lay a finger on the vast cureless wound of his self-esteem. It would require courage, too, for it is dangerous to offend him, and nobody has this courage.

Braggioni loves himself with such tenderness and amplitude and eternal charity that his followers—for he is a leader of men, a skilled revolutionist, and his skin has been punctured in honorable warfare— warm themselves in the reflected glow, and say to each other: "He has a real nobility, a love of humanity raised above mere personal affections." The excess of this self-love has flowed out, inconveniently for her, over Laura, who, with so many others, owes her comfortable situation and her salary to him. When he is in a very good humor, he tells her, "I am tempted to forgive you for being a *gringa, gringita!*"[2] and Laura, burning, imagines herself leaning forward suddenly, and with a sound back-handed slap wiping the suety smile from his face. If he notices her eyes at these moments he gives no sign.

She knows what Braggioni would offer her, and she must resist tenaciously without appearing to resist, and if she could avoid it she would not admit even to herself the slow drift of his intention. During these long evenings which have spoiled a long month for her, she sits in her deep chair with an open book on her knees, resting her eyes on the consoling rigidity of the printed page when the sight and sound of Braggioni singing threaten to identify themselves with all her remembered afflictions and to add their weight to her uneasy premonitions of the future. The gluttonous bulk of Braggioni has become a symbol of her many disillusions, for a revolutionist should be lean, animated by heroic faith, a vessel of abstract virtues. This is nonsense, she

1. Street in Mexico City, as are all those streets named later.
2. Fair-haired (American) woman—the regular and the diminutive forms of the word. Like most racial terms, not particularly complimentary.

knows it now and is ashamed of it. Revolution must have leaders, and leadership is a career for energetic men. She is, her comrades tell her, full of romantic error, for what she defines as cynicism in them is merely "a developed sense of reality." She is almost too willing to say, "I am wrong, I suppose I don't really understand the principles," and afterward she makes a secret truce with herself, determined not to surrender her will to such expedient logic. But she cannot help feeling that she has been betrayed irreparably by the disunion between her way of living and her feeling of what life should be, and at times she is almost contented to rest in this sense of grievance as a private store of consolation. Sometimes she wishes to run away, but she stays. Now she longs to fly out of this room, down the narrow stairs, and into the street where the houses lean together like conspirators under a single mottled lamp, and leave Braggioni singing to himself.

Instead she looks at Braggioni, frankly and clearly, like a good child who understands the rules of behavior. Her knees cling together under sound blue serge, and her round white collar is not purposely nun-like. She wears the uniform of an idea, and has renounced vanities. She was born Roman Catholic, and in spite of her fear of being seen by someone who might make a scandal of it, she slips now and again into some crumbling little church, kneels on the chilly stone, and says a Hail Mary on the gold rosary she bought in Tehuantepec.[3] It is no good and she ends by examining the altar with its tinsel flowers and ragged brocades, and feels tender about the battered doll-shape of some male saint whose white, lace-trimmed drawers hang limply around his ankles below the hieratic dignity of his velvet robe. She has encased herself in a set of principles derived from her early training, leaving no detail of gesture or of personal taste untouched, and for this reason she will not wear lace made on machines. This is her private heresy, for in her special group the machine is sacred, and will be the salvation of the workers. She loves fine lace, and there is a tiny edge of fluted cobweb on this collar, which is one of twenty precisely alike, folded in blue tissue paper in the upper drawer of her clothes chest.

Braggioni catches her glance solidly as if he had been waiting for it, leans forward, balancing his paunch between his spread knees, and sings with tremendous emphasis, weighing his words. He has, the song relates, no father and no mother, nor even a friend to console him; lonely as a wave of the sea he comes and goes, lonely as a wave. His mouth opens round and yearns sideways, his balloon cheeks grow oily with the labor of song. He bulges marvelously in his expensive garments. Over his lavender collar, crushed upon a purple necktie, held by a diamond hoop: over his ammunition belt of tooled leather worked in silver, buckled cruelly around his gasping middle: over the tops of his glossy yellow shoes Braggioni swells with ominous ripeness, his mauve silk hose stretched taut, his ankles bound with the stout leather thongs of his shoes.

3. City in southern Mexico.

When he stretches his eyelids at Laura she notes again that his eyes are the true tawny yellow cat's eyes. He is rich, not in money, he tells her, but in power, and this power brings with it the blameless ownership of things, and the right to indulge his love of small luxuries. "I have a taste for the elegant refinements," he said once, flourishing a yellow silk handkerchief before her nose. "Smell that? It is Jockey Club, imported from New York." Nonetheless he is wounded by life. He will say so presently. "It is true everything turns to dust in the hand, to gall on the tongue." He sighs and his leather belt creaks like a saddle girth. "I am disappointed in everything as it comes. Everything." He shakes his head. "You, poor thing, you will be disappointed too. You are born for it. We are more alike than you realize in some things. Wait and see. Some day you will remember what I have told you, you will know that Braggioni was your friend."

Laura feels a slow chill, a purely physical sense of danger, a warning in her blood that violence, mutilation, a shocking death, wait for her with lessening patience. She has translated this fear into something homely, immediate, and sometimes hesitates before crossing the street. "My personal fate is nothing, except as the testimony of a mental attitude," she reminds herself, quoting from some forgotten philosophic primer, and is sensible enough to add, "Anyhow, I shall not be killed by an automobile if I can help it."

"It may be true I am as corrupt, in another way, as Braggioni," she thinks in spite of herself, "as callous, as incomplete," and if this is so, any kind of death seems preferable. Still she sits quietly, she does not run. Where could she go? Uninvited she has promised herself to this place; she can no longer imagine herself as living in another country, and there is no pleasure in remembering her life before she came here.

Precisely what is the nature of this devotion, its true motives, and what are its obligations? Laura cannot say. She spends part of her days in Xochimilco, nearby, teaching Indian children to say in English, "The cat is on the mat." When she appears in the classroom they crowd about her with smiles on their wise, innocent, clay-colored faces; crying, "Good morning, my titcher!" in immaculate voices, and they make of her desk a fresh garden of flowers every day.

During her leisure she goes to union meetings and listens to busy important voices quarreling over tactics, methods, internal politics. She visits the prisoners of her own political faith in their cells, where they entertain themselves with counting cockroaches, repenting of their indiscretions, composing their memoirs, writing out manifestoes and plans for their comrades who are still walking about free, hands in pockets, sniffing fresh air. Laura brings them food and cigarettes and a little money, and she brings messages disguised in equivocal phrases from the men outside who dare not set foot in the prison for fear of disappearing into the cells kept empty for them. If the prisoners confuse night and day, and complain, "Dear little Laura, time doesn't pass in this infernal hole, and I won't know when it is time to sleep unless I have a reminder," she brings them their favorite narcotics, and says in a tone that does not wound them with pity, "Tonight will really be night for you," and though her Spanish amuses them they find her comforting, useful. If they lose patience and all faith, and curse the slowness of their friends in coming to their rescue with money and influence, they trust her not to repeat everything, and if she inquires, "Where do you think we can find money, or influence?" they are certain to answer, "Well, there is Braggioni, why doesn't he do something?"

She smuggles letters from headquarters to men hiding from firing squads in back streets in mildewed houses, where they sit in tumbled beds and talk bitterly as if all Mexico were at their heels, when Laura knows positively they might appear at the band concert in the Alameda[4] on Sunday morning, and no one would notice them. But Braggioni says, "Let them sweat a little. The next time they may be careful. It is very restful to have them out of the way for a while." She is not afraid to knock on any door in any street after midnight, and enter in the darkness, and say to one of these men who is really in danger: "They will be looking for you—seriously—tomorrow morning after six. Here is some money from Vicente. Go to Vera Cruz[5] and wait."

She borrows money from the Roumanian agitator to give to his bitter enemy the Polish agitator. The favor of Braggioni is their disputed territory, and Braggioni holds the balance nicely, for he can use them both. The Polish agitator talks love to her over café tables, hoping to exploit what he believes is her secret sentimental preference for him, and he gives her misinformation which he begs her to repeat as the solemn truth to certain persons. The Roumanian is more adroit. He is generous with his money in all good causes, and lies to her with an air of ingenuous candor, as if he were her good friend and confidant. She never repeats anything they may say. Braggioni never asks questions. He has other ways to discover all that he wishes to know about them.

Nobody touches her, but all praise her gray eyes, and the soft, round under lip which promises gaiety, yet is always grave, nearly always firmly closed: and they cannot understand why she is in Mexico. She walks back and forth on her errands, with puzzled eyebrows, carrying her little folder of drawings and music and school papers. No dancer dances more beautifully than Laura walks, and she inspires some amusing, unexpected ardors, which cause little gossip, because nothing comes of them. A young captain who had been a soldier in Zapata's[6] army attempted, during a horseback ride near Cuernavaca, to express his desire for her with the noble simplicity befitting a rude folk-hero: but gently, because he was gentle. This gentleness was his defeat, for when he alighted, and removed her foot from the stirrup, and essayed to draw her down into his arms, her horse, ordinarily a tame one, shied fiercely, reared and plunged away. The young hero's

---

4. A public square.
5. Mexican port on the Gulf.
6. Emiliano Zapata (1883–1919), Mexican revolutionary leader who, with Pancho Villa, was able, in 1914, to take

Mexico City; but they were forced to withdraw toward Cuernavaca, fifty miles south, in Zapata's native Moralos province. He was known both as an agrarian reformer and as the Attila of the South.

horse careened blindly after his stable-mate, and the hero did not return to the hotel until rather late that evening. At breakfast he came to her table in full charro dress, gray buckskin jacket and trousers with strings of silver buttons down the leg, and he was in a humorous, careless mood. "May I sit with you?" and "You are a wonderful rider. I was terrified that you might be thrown and dragged. I should never have forgiven myself. But I cannot admire you enough for your riding."

"I learned to ride in Arizona," said Laura.

"If you will ride with me again this morning, I promise you a horse that will not shy with you," he said. But Laura remembered that she must return to Mexico City at noon.

Next morning the children made a celebration and spent their playtime writing on the blackboard, "We lov ar titcher," and with tinted chalks they drew wreaths of flowers around the words. The young hero wrote her a letter: "I am a very foolish, wasteful, impulsive man. I should have first said I love you, and then you would not have run away. But you shall see me again." Laura thought, "I must send him a box of colored crayons," but she was trying to forgive herself for having spurred her horse at the wrong moment.

A brown shock-haired youth came and stood in her patio one night and sang like a lost soul for two hours, but Laura could think of nothing to do about it. The moonlight spread a wash of gauzy silver over the clear spaces of the garden, and the shadows were cobalt blue. The scarlet blossoms of the Judas tree[7] were dull purple, and the names of the colors repeated themselves automatically in her mind, while she watched not the boy, but his shadow, fallen like a dark garment across the fountain rim, trailing in the water. Lupe came silently and whispered expert counsel in her ear: "If you will throw him one little flower, he will sing another song or two and go away." Laura threw the flower, and he sang a last song and went away with the flower tucked in the band of his hat. Lupe said, "He is one of the organizers of the Typographers Union, and before that he sold corridos[8] in the Merced market, and before that, he came from Guanajuato, where I was born. I would not trust any man, but I trust least those from Guanajuato."

She did not tell Laura that he would be back again the next day, and the next, nor that he would follow her at a certain fixed distance around the Merced market, through the Zocolo, up Francesco I. Madero Avenue, and so along the Paseo de la Reforma to Chapultepec Park, and into the Philosopher's Footpath, still with that flower withering in his hat, and an indivisible attention in his eyes.

Now Laura is accustomed to him, it means nothing except that he is nineteen years old and is observing a convention with all propriety, as though it were founded on a law of nature, which in the end it might very well prove to be. He is beginning to write poems which he prints on a wooden press, and he leaves them stuck like handbills in her door. She is pleasantly disturbed by the abstract, unhurried watchfulness of his black eyes which will in time turn easily towards another

7. Judas Iscariot, who betrayed Christ, is said to have hanged himself on such a tree.   8. Bullfights tickets.

object. She tells herself that throwing the flower was a mistake, for she is twenty-two years old and knows better; but she refuses to regret it, and persuades herself that her negation of all external events as they occur is a sign that she is gradually perfecting herself in the stoicism she strives to cultivate against that disaster she fears, though she cannot name it.

She is not at home in the world. Every day she teaches children who remain strangers to her, though she loves their tender round hands and their charming opportunistic savagery. She knocks at unfamiliar doors not knowing whether a friend or a stranger shall answer, and even if a known face emerges from the sour gloom of that unknown interior, still it is the face of a stranger. No matter what this stranger says to her, nor what her message to him, the very cells of her flesh reject knowledge and kinship in one monotonous word. No. No. No. She draws her strength from this one holy talismanic word which does not suffer her to be led into evil. Denying everything, she may walk anywhere in safety, she looks at everything without amazement.

No, repeats this firm unchanging voice of her blood; and she looks at Braggioni without amazement. He is a great man, he wishes to impress this simple girl who covers her great round breasts with thick dark cloth, and who hides long, invaluably beautiful legs under a heavy skirt. She is almost thin except for the incomprehensible fullness of her breasts, like a nursing mother's, and Braggioni, who considers himself a judge of women, speculates again on the puzzle of her notorious virginity, and takes the liberty of speech which she permits without a sign of modesty, indeed, without any sort of sign, which is disconcerting.

"You think you are so cold, *gringita*! Wait and see. You will surprise yourself someday! May I be there to advise you!" He stretches his eyelids at her, and his ill-humored cat's eyes waver in a separate glance for the two points of light marking the opposite ends of a smoothly drawn path between the swollen curve of her breasts. He is not put off by that blue serge, nor by her resolutely fixed gaze. There is all the time in the world. His cheeks are bellying with the wind of song. "O girl with the dark eyes," he sings, and reconsiders. "But yours are not dark. I can change all that. O girl with the green eyes, you have stolen my heart away." Then his mind wanders to the song, and Laura feels the weight of his attention being shifted elsewhere. Singing thus, he seems harmless, he is quite harmless, there is nothing to do but sit patiently and say "No," when the moment comes. She draws a full breath, and her mind wanders also, but not far. She dares not wander too far.

Not for nothing has Braggioni taken pains to be a good revolutionist and a professional lover of humanity. He will never die of it. He has the malice, the cleverness, the wickedness, the sharpness of wit, the hardness of heart, stipulated for loving the world profitably. *He will never die of it.* He will live to see himself kicked out from his feeding trough by other hungry world-saviours. Traditionally he must sing in spite of his life which drives him to bloodshed, he tells Laura, for his father was a Tuscany peasant who drifted to Yucatan and married a Maya woman:[9] a woman of race, an aristocrat. They gave him the love and knowledge of music, thus: and under the rip of his thumbnail, the strings of the instrument complain like exposed nerves.

Once he was called Delgadito[1] by all the girls and married women who ran after him; he was so scrawny all his bones showed under his thin cotton clothing, and he could squeeze his emptiness to the very backbone with his two hands. He was a poet and the revolution was only a dream then; too many women loved him and sapped away his youth, and he could never find enough to eat anywhere, anywhere! Now he is a leader of men, crafty men who whisper in his ear, hungry men who wait for hours outside his office for a word with him, emaciated men with wild faces who waylay him at the street gate with a timid, "Comrade, let me tell you . . ." and they blow the foul breath from their empty stomachs in his face.

He is always sympathetic. He gives them handfuls of small coins from his own pockets, he promises them work, there will be demonstrations, they must join the unions and attend the meetings, above all they must be on the watch for spies. They are closer to him than his own brothers, without them he can do nothing—until tomorrow, comrade!

Until tomorrow. "They are stupid, they are lazy, they are treacherous, they would cut my throat for nothing," he says to Laura. He has good food and abundant drink, he hires an automobile and drives in the Paseo on Sunday morning, and enjoys plenty of sleep in a soft bed beside a wife who dares not disturb him; and he sits pampering his bones in easy billows of fat, singing to Laura, who knows and thinks these things about him. When he was fifteen, he tried to drown himself because he loved a girl, his first love, and she laughed at him. "A thousand woman have paid for that," and his tight little mouth turns down at the corners. Now he perfumes his hair with Jockey Club, and confides to Laura: "One woman is really as good as another for me in the dark. I prefer them all."

His wife organizes unions among the girls in the cigarette factories, and walks in picket lines, and even speaks at meetings in the evening. But she cannot be brought to acknowledge the benefits of true liberty. "I tell her I must have my freedom, net.[2] She does not understand my point of view." Laura has heard this many times. Braggioni scratches the guitar and meditates. "She is an instinctively virtuous woman, pure gold, no doubt of that. If she were not, I should lock her up, and she knows it."

His wife, who works so hard for the good of the factory girls, employs part of her leisure lying on the floor weeping because there are so many women in the world, and only one husband for her, and she never knows where nor when to look for him. He told her: "Unless you can learn to cry when I am not here, I must go away for good." That day he went away and took a room at the Hotel Madrid.

---

9. The Mayan Indians had a highly developed civilization from about A.D. 300 to almost 1000. The surviving Mayans live chiefly in Yucatan, a province at the top of the horn of Mexico that juts northward into the Gulf. Tuscany is an Italian region somewhat north and west of Rome.

1. Little skinny one.

2. Clear and final.

It is this month of separation for the sake of higher principles that has been spoiled not only for Mrs. Braggioni, whose sense of reality is beyond criticism, but for Laura, who feels herself bogged in a nightmare. Tonight Laura envies Mrs. Braggioni, who is alone, and free to weep as much as she pleases about a concrete wrong. Laura has just come from a visit to the prison, and she is waiting for tomorrow with a bitter anxiety as if tomorrow may not come, but time may be caught immovably in this hour, with herself transfixed, Braggioni singing on forever, and Eugenio's body not yet discovered by the guard.

Braggioni says: "Are you going to sleep?" Almost before she can shake her head, he begins telling her about the May-day disturbances coming on in Morelia,[3] for the Catholics hold a festival in honor of the Blessed Virgin, and the Socialists celebrate their martyrs on that day. "There will be two independent processions, starting from either end of town, and they will march until they meet, and the rest depends . . ." He asks her to oil and load his pistols. Standing up, he unbuckles his ammunition belt, and spreads it laden across her knees. Laura sits with the shells slipping through the cleaning cloth dipped in oil, and he says again he cannot understand why she works so hard for the revolutionary idea unless she loves some man who is in it. "Are you not in love with someone?" "No," says Laura. "And no one is in love with you?" "No." "Then it is your own fault. No woman need go begging. Why, what is the matter with you? The legless beggar woman in the Alameda has a perfectly faithful lover. Did you know that?"

Laura peers down the pistol barrel and says nothing, but a long, slow faintness rises and subsides in her; Braggioni curves his swollen finger around the throat of the guitar and softly smothers the music out of it, and when she hears him again he seems to have forgotten her, and is speaking in the hypnotic voice he uses when talking in small rooms to a listening, close-gathered crowd. Some day this world, now seemingly so composed and eternal, to the edges of every sea shall be merely a tangle of gaping trenches, of crashing walls and broken bodies. Everything must be torn from its accustomed place where it has rotted for centuries, hurled skyward and distributed, cast down again clean as rain, without separate identity. Nothing shall survive that the stiffened hands of poverty have created for the rich and no one shall be left alive except the elect spirits destined to procreate a new world cleansed of cruelty and injustice, ruled by benevolent anarchy: "Pistols are good, I love them, cannon are even better, but in the end I pin my faith to good dynamite," he concludes, and strokes the pistol lying in her hands. "Once I dreamed of destroying this city, in case it offered resistance to General Ortiz,[4] but it fell into his hands like an overripe pear."

He is made restless by his own words, rises and stands waiting. Laura holds up the belt to him: "Put that on, and go kill somebody in Morelia, and you will be happier," she says softly. The presence of death in the room makes her bold. "Today, I found Eugenio going into a stupor. He refused to allow me to call the prison doctor. He had

3. City about 125 miles west of Mexico City.
4. Pascual Oritiz Rubio (1877–1963),

revolutionary military officer, later diplomat and, in 1930, president of Mexico.

taken all the tablets I brought him yesterday. He said he took them because he was bored."

"He is a fool, and his death is his own business," says Braggioni, fastening his belt carefully.

"I told him if he had waited only a little while longer, you would have got him set free," says Laura. "He said he did not want to wait."

"He is a fool and we are well rid of him," says Braggioni, reaching for his hat.

He goes away. Laura knows his mood has changed, she will not see him anymore for a while. He will send word when he needs her to go on errands into strange streets, to speak to the strange faces that will appear, like clay masks with the power of human speech, to mutter their thanks to Braggioni for his help. Now she is free, and she thinks, I must run while there is time. But she does not go.

Braggioni enters his own house where for a month his wife has spent many hours every night weeping and tangling her hair upon her pillow. She is weeping now, and she weeps more at the sight of him, the cause of all her sorrows. He looks about the room. Nothing is changed, the smells are good and familiar, he is well acquainted with the woman who comes toward him with no reproach except grief on her face. He says to her tenderly: "You are so good, please don't cry anymore, you dear good creature." She says, "Are you tired, my angel? Sit here and I will wash your feet." She brings a bowl of water, and kneeling, unlaces his shoes, and when from her knees she raises her sad eyes under her blackened lids, he is sorry for everything, and bursts into tears. "Ah, yes, I am hungry, I am tired, let us eat something together," he says, between sobs. His wife leans her head on his arm and says, "Forgive me!" and this time he is refreshed by the solemn, endless rain of her tears.

Laura takes off her serge dress and puts on a white linen nightgown and goes to bed. She turns her head a little to one side, and lying still, reminds herself that it is time to sleep. Numbers tick in her brain like little clocks, soundless doors close of themselves around her. If you would sleep, you must not remember anything, the children will say tomorrow, good morning, my teacher, the poor prisoners who come every day bringing flowers to their jailor. 1–2–3–4–5—it is monstrous to confuse love with revolution, night with day, life with death —ah Eugenio!

The tolling of the midnight bell is a signal, but what does it mean? Get up, Laura, and follow me: come out of your sleep, out of your bed, out of this strange house. What are you doing in this house? Without a word, without fear she rose and reached for Eugenio's hand, but he eluded her with a sharp, sly smile and drifted away. This is not all, you shall see—Murderer, he said, follow me, I will show you a new country, but it is far away and we must hurry. No, said Laura, not unless you take my hand, no; and she clung first to the stair rail, and then to the topmost branch of the Judas tree that bent down slowly and set her upon the earth, and then to the rocky ledge of a cliff, and then to the jagged wave of a sea that was not water but a desert of crumbling stone. Where are you taking me? she asked in wonder but without fear. To death, and it is a long way off, and we must hurry, said Eugenio. No, said Laura, not unless you take my hand. Then eat these flowers, poor prisoner, said Eugenio in a voice of pity, take and eat: and from the Judas tree he stripped the warm bleeding flowers, and held them to her lips. She saw that his hand was fleshless, a cluster of small white petrified branches, and his eye sockets were without light, but she ate the flowers greedily for they satisfied both hunger and thirst. Murderer! said Eugenio, and Cannibal! This is my body and my blood.[5] Laura cried No! and at the sound of her own voice, she awoke trembling, and was afraid to sleep again.

1930

WILLIAM FAULKNER

Barn Burning

The store in which the Justice of the Peace's court was sitting smelled of cheese. The boy, crouched on his nail keg at the back of the crowded room, knew he smelled cheese, and more: from where he sat he could see the ranked shelves close-packed with the solid, squat, dynamic shapes of tin cans whose labels his stomach read, not from the lettering which meant nothing to his mind but from the scarlet devils and the silver curve of fish—this, the cheese which he knew he smelled and the hermetic meat which his intestines believed he smelled coming in intermittent gusts momentary and brief between the other constant one, the smell and sense just a little of fear because mostly of despair and grief, the old fierce pull of blood. He could not see the table where the Justic sat and before which his father and his father's enemy (*our enemy* he thought in that despair; *ourn! mine and hisn both! He's my father!*) stood, but he could hear them, the two of them that is, because his father had said no word yet:

"But what proof have you, Mr. Harris?"

"I told you. The hog got into my corn. I caught it up and sent it back to him. He had no fence that would hold it. I told him so, warned him. The next time I put the hog in my pen. When he came to get it. I gave him enough wire to patch up his pen. The next time I put the hog up and kept it. I rode down to his house and saw the wire I gave him still rolled on to the spool in his yard. I told him he could have the hog when he paid me a dollar pound fee. That evening a nigger came with the dollar and got the hog. He was a strange nigger. He said, 'He say to tell you wood and hay kin burn.' I said, 'What?' 'That whut he say to tell you,' the nigger said. 'Wood and

5. Christ's words at the Last Supper— "And he took bread, and gave thanks, and brake it, and gave unto them saying, This is my body which is given for you: this do in remembrance of me. Likewise also the cup after supper, saying, This cup is the new testament in my blood, which is shed for you" (Luke 22:19–20).

hay kin burn.' That night my barn burned. I got the stock out but I lost the barn."

"Where is the nigger? Have you got him?"

"He was a strange nigger, I tell you. I don't know what became of him."

"But that's not proof. Don't you see that's not proof?"

"Get that boy up here. He knows." For a moment the boy thought too that the man meant his older brother until Harris said, "Not him. The little one. The boy," and, crouching, small for his age, small and wiry like his father, in patched and faded jeans even too small for him, with straight, uncombed, brown hair and eyes gray and wild as storm scud, he saw the men between himself and the table part and become a lane of grim faces, at the end of which he saw the Justice, a shabby, collarless, graying man in spectacles, beckoning him. He felt no floor under his bare feet; he seemed to walk beneath the palpable weight of the grim turning faces. His father, stiff in his black Sunday coat donned not for the trial but for the moving, did not even look at him. *He aims for me to lie, he thought,* again with that frantic grief and despair. *And I will have to do hit.*

"What's your name, boy?" the Justice said.

"Colonel Sartoris Snopes," the boy whispered.

"Hey?" the Justice said. "Talk louder. Colonel Sartoris? I reckon anybody named for Colonel Sartoris in this country can't help but tell the truth, can they?" The boy said nothing. *Enemy! Enemy!* he thought; for a moment he could not even see, could not see that the Justice's face was kindly nor discern that his voice was troubled when he spoke to the man named Harris: "Do you want me to question this boy?" But he could hear, and during those subsequent long seconds while there was absolutely no sound in the crowded little room save that of quiet and intent breathing it was as if he had swung outward at the end of a grape vine, over a ravine, and at the top of the swing had been caught in a prolonged instant of mesmerized gravity, weightless in time.

"No!" Harris said violently, explosively. "Damnation! Send him out of here!" Now time, the fluid world, rushed beneath him again, the voices coming to him again through the smell of cheese and sealed meat, the fear and despair and the old grief of blood:

"This case is closed. I can't find against you, Snopes, but I can give you advice. Leave this country and don't come back to it."

His father spoke for the first time, his voice cold and harsh, level, without emphasis: "I aim to. I don't figure to stay in a country among people who . . ." he said something unprintable and vile, addressed to no one.

"That'll do," the Justice said. "Take your wagon and get out of this country before dark. Case dismissed."

His father turned, and he followed the stiff black coat, the wiry figure walking a little stiffly from where a Confederate provost's man's[1] musket ball had taken him in the heel on a stolen horse thirty years ago, followed the two backs now, since his older brother had appeared

---

1. Military policeman.

from somewhere in the crowd, no taller than the father but thicker, chewing tobacco steadily, between the two lines of grim-faced men and out of the store and across the worn gallery and down the sagging steps and among the dogs and half-grown boys in the mild May dust, where as he passed a voice hissed:

"Barn burner!"

Again he could not see, whirling; there was a face in a red haze, moonlike, bigger than the full moon, the owner of it half again his size, he leaping in the red haze toward the face, feeling no blow, feeling no shock when his head struck the earth, scrabbling up and leaping again, feeling no blow this time either and tasting no blood, scrabbling up to see the other boy in full flight and himself already leaping into pursuit as his father's hand jerked him back, the harsh, cold voice speaking above him: "Go get in the wagon."

It stood in a grove of locusts and mulberries across the road. His two hulking sisters in their Sunday dresses and his mother and her sister in calico and sunbonnets were already in it, sitting on and among the sorry residue of the dozen and more movings which even the boy could remember—the battered stove, the broken beds and chairs, the clock inlaid with mother-of-pearl, which would not run, stopped at some fourteen minutes past two o'clock of a dead and forgotten day and time, which had been his mother's dowry. She was crying, though when she saw him she drew her sleeve across her face and began to descend from the wagon. "Get back," the father said.

"He's hurt. I got to get some water and wash his. . . ."

"Get back in the wagon," his father said. He got in too, over the tail-gate. His father mounted to the seat where the older brother already sat and struck the gaunt mules two savage blows with the peeled willow, but without heat. It was not even sadistic; it was exactly that same quality which in later years would cause his descendants to over-run the engine before putting a motor car into motion, striking and reining back in the same movement. The wagon went on, the store with its quiet crowd of grimly watching men dropped behind; a curve in the road hid it. *Forever* he thought. *Maybe he's done satisfied now, now that he has* . . . stopping himself, not to say it aloud even to himself. His mother's hand touched his shoulder.

"Does hit hurt?" she said.

"Naw," he said. "Hit don't hurt. Lemme be."

"Can't you wipe some of the blood off before hit dries?"

"I'll wash to-night," he said. "Lemme be, I tell you."

The wagon went on. He did not know where they were going. None of them ever did or ever asked, because it was always somewhere, always a house of sorts waiting for them a day or two days or even three days away. Likely his father had already arranged to make a crop on another farm before he . . . Again he had to stop himself. He (the father) always did. There was something about his wolflike independence and even courage when the advantage was at least neutral which impressed strangers, as if they got from his latent ravening ferocity not so much a sense of dependability as a feeling that his ferocious conviction in the rightness of his own actions would be of advantage to all whose interest lay with his.

That night they camped, in a grove of oaks and beeches where a spring ran. The nights were still cool and they had a fire against it, of a rail lifted from a nearby fence and cut into lengths—a small fire, neat, niggard almost, a shrewd fire; such fires were his father's habit and custom always, even in freezing weather. Older, the boy might have remarked this and wondered why not a big one; why should not a man who had not only seen the waste and extravagance of war, but who had in his blood an inherent voracious prodigality with material not his own, have burned everything in sight? Then he might have gone a step farther and thought that that was the reason: the niggard blaze was the living fruit of nights passed during those four years in the woods hiding from all men, blue or gray,[2] with his strings of horses (captured horses, he called them). And older still, he might have divined the true reason: that the element of fire spoke to some deep mainspring of his father's being, as the element of steel or of powder spoke to other men, as the one weapon for the preservation of integrity, else breath were not worth the breathing, and hence to be regarded with respect and used with discretion.

But he did not think this now and he had seen those same niggard blazes all his life. He merely ate his supper beside it and was already half asleep over his iron plate when his father called him, and once more he followed the stiff back, the stiff and ruthless limp, up the slope and on to the starlit road where, turning, he could see his father against the stars but without face or depth—a shape black, flat, and bloodless as though cut from tin in the iron folds of the frockcoat which had not been made for him, the voice harsh like tin and without heat like tin:

"You wre fixing to tell them. You would have told them." He didn't answer. His father struck him with the flat of his hand on the side of the head, hard but without heat, exactly as he had struck the two mules at the store, exactly as he would strike either of them with any stick in order to kill a horse fly, his voice still without heat or anger: "You're getting to be a man. You got to learn. You got to learn to stick to your own blood or you ain't going to have any blood to stick to you. Do you think either of them, any man there this morning, would? Don't you know all they wanted was a chance to get at me because they knew I had them beat? Eh?" Later, twenty years later, he was to tell himself, "If I had said they wanted only truth, justice, he would have hit me again." But now he said nothing. He was not crying. He just stood there. "Answer me," his father said.

"Yes," he whispered. His father turned.

"Get on to bed. We'll be there tomorrow."

To-morrow they were there. In the early afternoon the wagon stopped before a paintless two-room house identical almost with the dozen others it had stopped before even in the boy's ten years, and again, as on the other dozen occasions, his mother and aunt got

---

2. In the Civil War (1861–1865), Union soldiers wore blue and Confederate soldiers gray uniforms.

down and began to unload the wagon, although his two sisters and his father and brother had not moved.

"Likely hit ain't fitten for hawgs," one of the sisters said.

"Nevertheless, fit it will and you'll hog it and like it," his father said. "Get out of them chairs and help your Ma unload."

The two sisters got down, big, bovine, in a flutter of cheap ribbons; one of them drew from the jumbled wagon bed a battered lantern, the other a worn broom. His father handed the reins to the older son and began to climb stiffly over the wheel. "When they get unloaded, take the team to the barn and feed them." Then he said, and at first the boy thought he was still speaking to his brother: "Come with me."

"Me?" he said.

"Yes," his father said. "You."

"Abner," his mother said. His father paused and looked back—the harsh level stare beneath the shaggy, graying, irascible brows.

"I reckon I'll have a word with the man that aims to begin tomorrow owning me body and soul for the next eight months."

They went back up the road. A week ago—or before last night, that is—he would have asked where they were going, but not now. His father had struck him before last night but never before had he paused afterward to explain why; it was as if the blow and the following calm, outrageous voice still rang, repercussed, divulging nothing to him save the terrible handicap of being young, the light weight of his few years, just heavy enough to prevent his soaring free of the world as it seemed to be ordered but not heavy enough to keep him footed solid in it, to resist it and try to change the course of its events.

Presently he could see the grove of oaks and cedars and the other flowering trees and shrubs where the house would be, though not the house yet. They walked beside a fence massed with honeysuckle and Chrokee roses and came to a gate swinging open between two brick pillars, and now, beyond a sweep of drive, he saw the house for the first time and at that instant he forgot his father and the terror and despair both, and even when he remembered his father again (who had not stopped) the terror and despair did not return. Because, for all the twelve movings, they had sojourned until now in a poor country, a land of small farms and fields and houses, and he had never seen a house like this before. *Hit's big as a courthouse* he thought quietly, with a surge of peace and joy whose reason he could not have thought into words, being too young for that: *They are safe from him. People whose lives are a part of this peace and dignity are beyond his touch, he no more to them than a buzzing wasp: capable of stinging for a little moment but that's all; the spell of this peace and dignity rendering even the barns and stable and cribs which belong to it impervious to the puny flames he might contrive* . . . this, the peace and joy, ebbing for an instant as he looked again at the stiff black back, the stiff and implacable limp of the figure which was not dwarfed by the house, for the reason that it had never looked big anywhere and which now, against the serene columned backdrop, had more than ever that impervious quality of something cut ruthlessly from tin, depthless, as though, sidewise to the sun, it would cast no shadow. Watching him, the boy remarked the absolutely undeviating course which his father held and saw the stiff foot come squarely down in a pile of fresh droppings where a horse had stood in the drive and which his father could have avoided by a simple change of stride. But it ebbed only for a moment, though he could not have thought this into words either, walking on in the spell of the house, which he could even want but without envy, without sorrow, certainly never with that ravening and jealous rage which unknown to him walked in the ironlike black coat before him: *Maybe he will feel it too. Maybe it will even change him now from what maybe he couldn't help but be.*

They crossed the portico. Now he could hear his father's stiff foot as it came down on the boards with clocklike finality, a sound out of all proportion to the displacement of the body it bore and which was not dwarfed either by the white door before it, as though it had attained to a sort of vicious and ravening minimum not to be dwarfed by anything—the flat, wide, black hat, the formal coat of broadcloth which had once been black but which had now that friction-glazed greenish cast of the bodies of old house flies, the lifted sleeve which was too large, the lifted hand like a curled claw. The door opened so promptly that the boy knew the Negro must have been watching them all the time, an old man with neat grizzled hair, in a linen jacket, who stood barring the door with his body, saying, "Wipe you foots, white man, fo you come in here. Major ain't home nohow."

"Get out of my way, nigger," his father said, without heat too, flinging the door back and the Negro also and entering, his hat still on his head. And now the boy saw the prints of the stiff foot on the doorjamb and saw them appear on the pale rug behind the machine-like deliberation of the foot which seemed to bear (or transmit) twice the weight which the body compassed. The Negro was shouting "Miss Lula! Miss Lula!" somewhere behind them, then the boy, deluged as though by a warm wave by a suave turn of carpeted stair and a pendant glitter of chandeliers and a mute gleam of gold frames, heard the swift feet and saw her too, a lady—perhaps he had never seen her like before either—in a gray, smooth gown with lace at the throat and an apron tied at the waist and the sleeves turned back, wiping cake or biscuit dough from her hands with a towel as she came up the hall, looking not at his father at all but at the tracks on the blond rug with an expression of incredulous amazement.

"I tried," the Negro cried. "I tole him to . . ."

"Will you please go away?" she said in a shaking voice. "Major de Spain is not at home. Will you please go away?"

His father had not spoken again. He did not speak again. He did not even look at her. He just stood stiff in the center of the rug, in his hat, the shaggy iron-gray brows twitching slightly above the pebble-colored eyes as he appeared to examine the house with brief deliberation. Then with the same deliberation he turned; the boy watched him pivot on the good leg and saw the stiff foot drag round the arc of the turning, leaving a final long and fading smear. His father never looked at it, he never once looked down at the rug. The Negro held the door. It closed behind them, upon the hysteric and indistinguishable woman-wail. His father stopped at the top of the steps and scraped his boot clean on the edge of it. At the gate he stopped again. He stood for a moment, planted stiffly on the stiff foot, looking back at the house. "Pretty and white, ain't it?" he said. "That's sweat. Nigger sweat. Maybe it ain't white enough yet to suit him. Maybe he wants to mix some white sweat with it."

Two hours later the boy was chopping wood behind the house within which his mother and aunt and the two sisters (the mother and aunt, not the two girls, he knew that; even at this distance and muffled by walls the flat loud voices of the two girls emanated an incorrigible idle inertia) were setting up the stove to prepare a meal, when he heard the hooves and saw the linen-clad man on a fine sorrel mare, whom he recognized even before he saw the rolled rug in front of the Negro youth following on a fat bay carriage horse—a suffused, angry face vanishing, still at full gallop, beyond the corner of the house where his father and brother were sitting in the two tilted chairs; and a moment later, almost before he could have put the axe down, he heard the hooves again and watched the sorrel mare go back out of the yard, already galloping again. Then his father began to shout one of the sisters' names, who presently emerged backward from the kitchen door dragging the rolled rug along the ground by one end while the other sister walked behind it.

"If you ain't going to tote, go on and set up the wash pot," the first said.

"You, Sarty!" the second shouted. "Set up the wash pot!" His father appeared at the door, framed against that shabbiness, as he had been against that other bland perfection, impervious to either, the mother's anxious face at his shoulder.

"Go on," the father said. "Pick it up." The two sisters stooped, broad, lethargic; stooping, they presented an incredible expanse of pale cloth and a flutter of tawdry ribbons.

"If I thought enough of a rug to have to git hit all the way from France I wouldn't keep hit where folks coming in would have to tromp on it," the first said. They raised the rug.

"Abner," the mother said. "Let me do it."

"You go back and git dinner," his father said. "I'll tend to this."

From the woodpile through the rest of the afternoon the boy watched them, the rug spread flat in the dust beside the bubbling wash-pot, the two sisters stooping over it with that profound and lethargic reluctance, while the father stood over them in turn, implacable and grim, driving them though never raising his voice again. He could smell the harsh homemade lye they were using; he saw his mother come to the door once and look toward them with an expression not anxious now but very like despair; his saw his father turn, and he fell to with the axe and saw from the corner of his eye his father raise from the ground a flattish fragment of field stone and examine it and return to the pot, and this time his mother actually spoke: "Abner. Abner. Please don't. Please, Abner."

Then he was done too. It was dusk; the whippoorwills had already begun. He could smell coffee from the room where they would presently eat the cold food remaining from the mid-afternoon meal, though when he entered the house he realized they were having coffee again probably because there was a fire on the hearth, before which the rug now lay spread over the backs of the two chairs. The tracks of his father's foot were gone. Where they had been were now long, water-cloudy scoriations resembling the sporadic course of a liliputian mowing machine.

It still hung there while they ate the cold food and then went to bed, scattered without order or claim up and down the two rooms, his mother in one bed, where his father would later lie, the older brother in the other, himself, the aunt, and the two sisters on pallets on the floor. But his father was not in bed yet. The last thing the boy remembered was the depthless, harsh silhouette of the hat and coat bending over the rug and it seemed to him that he had not even closed his eyes when the silhouette was standing over him, the fire almost dead behind it, the stiff foot prodding him awake. "Catch up the mule," his father said.

When he returned with the mule his father was standing in the black door, the rolled rug over his shoulder. "Ain't you going to ride?" he said.

"No. Give me your foot."

He bent his knee into his father's hand, the wiry, surprising power flowed smoothly, rising, he rising with it, on to the mule's bare back (they had owned a saddle once; the boy could remember it though not when or where) and with the same effortlessness his father swung the rug up in front of him. Now in the starlight they retraced the afternoon's path, up the dusty road rife with honeysuckle, through the gate and up the black tunnel of the drive to the lightless house, where he sat on the mule and felt the rough warp of the rug drag across his thighs and vanish.

"Don't you want me to help?" he whispered. His father did not answer and now he heard again that stiff foot striking the hollow portico with that wooden and clocklike deliberation, that outrageous overstatement of the weight it carried. The rug, hunched, not flung (the boy could tell that even in the darkness) from his father's shoulder struck the angle of wall and floor with a sound unbelievably loud, thunderous, then the foot again, unhurried and enormous; a light came on in the house and the boy sat, tense, breathing steadily and quietly and just a little fast, though the foot itself did not increase its beat at all, descending the steps now, now the boy could see him.

"Don't you want to ride now?" he whispered. "We kin both ride now," the light within the house altering now, flaring up and sinking. *He's coming down the stairs now,* he thought. He had already ridden the mule up beside the horse block; presently his father was up behind him and he doubled the reins over and slashed the mule across the neck, but before the animal could begin to trot the hard, thin arm came round him, the hard, knotted hand jerking the mule back to a walk.

In the first red rays of the sun they were in the lot, putting plow gear on the mules. This time the sorrel mare was in the lot before he heard it at all, the rider collarless and even bareheaded, trembling, speaking in a shaking voice as the woman in the house had done, his father merely looking up once before stooping again to the hame he was buckling, so that the man on the mare spoke to his stooping back:

"You must realize you have ruined that rug. Wasn't there anybody here, any of your women . . ." he ceased, shaking, the boy watching him, the older brother leaning now in the stable door, chewing, blinking slowly and steadily at nothing apparently. "It cost a hundred dollars. But you never had a hundred dollars. You never will. So I'm going to charge you twenty bushels of corn against your crop. I'll add it in your contract and when you come to the commissary you can sign it. That won't keep Mrs. de Spain quiet but maybe it will teach you to wipe your feet off before you enter her house again."

Then he was gone. The boy looked at his father, who still had not spoken or even looked up again, who was now adjusting the loggerhead in the hame.

"Pap," he said. His father looked at him—the inscrutable face, the shaggy brows beneath which the gray eyes glinted coldly. Suddenly the boy went toward him, fast, stopping as suddenly. "You done the best you could!" he cried. "If he wanted hit done different why didn't he wait and tell you how? He won't git no twenty bushels! He won't git none! We'll gether hit and hide hit! I kin watch . . ."

"Did you put the cutter back in that straight stock like I told you?"

"No, sir," he said.

"Then go do it."

That was Wednesday. During the rest of that week he worked steadily, at what was within his scope and some which was beyond it, with an industry that did not need to be driven nor even commanded twice; he had this from his mother, with the difference that some at least of what he did he liked to do, such as splitting wood with the half-size axe which his mother and aunt had earned, or saved money somehow, to present him with at Christmas. In company with the two older women (and on one afternoon, even one of the sisters), he built pens for the shoat and the cow which were a part of his father's contract with the landlord, and one afternoon, his father being absent, gone somewhere on one of the mules, he went to the field.

They were running a middle buster[3] now, his brother holding the plow straight while he handled the reins, and walking beside the straining mule, the rich black soil shearing cool and damp against his bare ankles, he thought *Maybe this is the end of it. Maybe even that twenty bushels that seems hard to have to pay for just a rug will be a cheap price for him to stop forever and always from being what he used to be;* thinking, dreaming now, so that his brother had to speak sharply to him to mind the mule: *Maybe he even won't collect the twenty bushels. Maybe it will all add up and balance and vanish—corn, rug, fire; the terror and grief, the being pulled two ways like between two teams of horses—gone, done with for ever and ever.*

Then it was Saturday; he looked up from beneath the mule he was

3. A double moldboard plow that throws a ridge of earth both ways.

harnessing and saw his father in the black coat and hat. "Not that," his father said. "The wagon gear." And then, two hours later, sitting in the wagon bed behind his father and brother on the seat, the wagon accomplished a final curve, and he saw the weathered paint-less store with its tattered tobacco- and patent-medicine posters and the tethered wagons and saddle animals below the gallery. He mounted the gnawed steps behind his father and brother, and there again was the lane of quiet, watching faces for the three of them to walk through. He saw the man in spectacles sitting at the plank table and he did not need to be told this was a Justice of the Peace; he sent one glare of fierce, exultant, partisan defiance at the man in collar and cravat now, whom he had seen but twice before in his life, and that on a galloping horse, who now wore on his face an expression not of rage but of amazed unbelief which the boy could not have known was at the incredible circumstance of being sued by one of his own tenants, and came and stood against his father and cried at the Justice: "He ain't done it! He ain't burnt . . ."

"Go back to the wagon," his father said.

"Burnt?" the Justice said. "Do I understand this rug was burned too?"

"Does anybody here claim it was?" his father said. "Go back to the wagon." But he did not, he merely retreated to the rear of the room, crowded as that other had been, but not to sit down this time, instead, to stand pressing among the motionless bodies, listening to the voices:

"And you claim twenty bushels of corn is too high for the damage you did to the rug?"

"He brought the rug to me and said he wanted the tracks washed out of it. I washed the tracks out and took the rug back to him."

"But you didn't carry the rug back to him in the same condition it was in before you made the tracks on it."

His father did not answer, and now for perhaps half a minute there was no sound at all save that of breathing, the faint, steady suspira-tion of complete and intent listening.

"You decline to answer that, Mr. Snopes?" Again his father did not answer. "I'm going to find against you, Mr. Snopes. I'm going to find that you were responsible for the injury to Major de Spain's rug and hold you liable for it. But twenty bushels of corn seems a little high for a man in your circumstances to have to pay. Major de Spain claims it cost a hundred dollars. October corn will be worth about fifty cents. I figure that if Major de Spain can stand a ninety-five dollar loss on something he paid cash for, you can stand a five-dollar loss you haven't earned yet. I hold you in damages to Major de Spain to the amount of ten bushels of corn over and above your contract with him, to be paid to him out of your crop at gathering time. Court adjourned."

It had taken no time hardly, the morning was but half begun. He thought they would return home and perhaps back to the field, since they were late, far behind all other farmers. But instead his father passed on behind the wagon, merely indicating with his hand for the older brother to follow with it, and crossed the road toward the blacksmith shop opposite, pressing on after his father, overtaking him, speaking, whispering up at the harsh, calm face beneath the weathered hat: "He won't git no ten bushels neither. He won't git one. We'll . . ." until his father glanced for an instant down at him, the face absolutely calm, the grizzled eyebrows tangled above the cold eyes, the voice almost pleasant, almost gentle:

"You think so? Well, we'll wait till October anyway."

The matter of the wagon—the setting of a spoke or two and the tightening of the tires—did not take long either, the business of the tires accomplished by driving the wagon into the spring branch behind the shop and letting it stand there, the mules nuzzling into the water from time to time, and the boy on the seat with the idle reins, looking up the slope and through the sooty tunnel of the shed where the slow hammer rang and where his father sat on an upended cypress bolt, easily, either talking or listening, still sitting there when the boy brought the dripping wagon up out of the branch and halted it before the door.

"Take them on to the shade and hitch," his father said. He did so and returned. His father and the smith and a third man squatting on his heels inside the door were talking, about crops and animals; the boy, squatting too in the ammoniac dust and hoof-parings and scales of rust, heard his father tell a long and unhurried story out of the time before the birth of the older brother even when he had been a professional horsetrader. And then his father came up beside him where he stood before a tattered last year's circus poster on the other side of the store, gazing rapt and quiet at the scarlet horses, the incredible poisings and convolutions of tulle and tights and the painted leers of comedians, and said, "It's time to eat."

But not at home. Squatting beside his brother against the front wall, he watched his father emerge from the store and produce from a paper sack a segment of cheese and divide it carefully and deliberately into three with his pocket knife and produce crackers from the same sack. They all three squatted on the gallery and ate, slowly, without talking; then in the store again, they drank from a tin dipper tepid water smelling of the cedar bucket and of living beech trees. And still they did not go home. It was a horse lot this time, a tall rail fence upon and along which men stood and sat and out of which one by one horses were led, to be walked and trotted and then cantered back and forth along the road while the slow swapping and buying went on and the sun began to slant westward, they—the three of them—watching and listening, the older brother with his muddy eyes and his steady, inevitable tobacco, the father commenting now and then on certain of the animals, to no one in particular.

It was after sundown when they reached home. They ate supper by lamplight, then, sitting on the doorstep, the boy watched the night fully accomplish, listening to the whippoorwills and the frogs, when he heard his mother's voice: "Abner! No! No! Oh, God. Oh, God. Abner!" and he rose, whirled, and saw the altered light through the door where a candle stub now burned in a bottle neck on the table and his father, still in the hat and coat, at once formal and burlesque as though dressed carefully for some shabby and ceremonial violence, emptying the reservoir of the lamp back into the five-gallon kerosene can from which it had been filled, while the mother tugged at his arm until he shifted the lamp to the other hand and flung her back, not savagely or viciously, just hard, into the wall, her hands flung out against the wall for balance, her mouth open and in her face the same quality of hopeless despair as had been in her voice. Then his father saw him standing in the door.

"Go to the barn and get that can of oil we were oiling the wagon with," he said. The boy did not move. Then he could speak.

"What . . ." he cried. "What are you . . ."

"Go get that oil," his father said. "Go."

Then he was moving, running, outside the house, toward the stable: this the old habit, the old blood which he had not been permitted to choose for himself, which had been bequeathed him willy nilly and which had run for so long (and who knew where, battening on what of outrage and savagery and lust) before it came to him. *I could keep on,* he thought. *I could run on and on and never look back, never need to see his face again. Only I can't. I can't,* the rusted can in his hand now, the liquid sploshing in it as he ran back to the house and into it, into the sound of his mother's weeping in the next room, and handed the can to his father.

"Ain't you going to even send a nigger?" he cried. "At least you sent a nigger before!"

This time his father didn't strike him. The hand came even faster than the blow had, the same hand which had set the can on the table with almost excruciating care flashing from the can toward him too quick for him to follow it, gripping him by the back of his shirt and on to tiptoe before he had seen it quit the can, the face stooping at him in breathless and frozen ferocity, the cold, dead voice speaking over him to the older brother, who leaned against the table, chewing with that steady, curious, sidewise motion of cows:

"Empty the can into the big one and go on. I'll catch up with you."

"Better tie him up to the bedpost," the brother said.

"Do like I told you," the father said. Then the boy was moving, his bunched shirt and the hard, bony hand between his shoulder-blades, his toes just touching the floor, across the room and into the other one, past the sisters sitting with spread heavy thighs in the two chairs over the cold hearth, and to where his mother and aunt sat side by side on the bed, the aunt's arms about his mother's shoulders.

"Hold him," the father said. The aunt made a startled movement. "Not you," the father said. "Lennie. Take hold of him. You'll hold him better than that. If he gets loose don't you know what he is going to do? He will go up yonder." He jerked his head toward the road. "Maybe I'd better tie him."

"I'll hold him," his mother whispered.

"See you do then." Then his father was gone, the stiff foot heavy and measured upon the boards, ceasing at last.

Then he began to struggle. His mother caught him in both arms, he jerking and wrenching at them. He would be stronger in the end, he knew that. But he had no time to wait for it. "Lemme go!" he cried. "I don't want to have to hit you!"

"Let him go!" the aunt said. "If he don't go, before God, I am going up there myself!"

"Don't you see I can't?" his mother cried. "Sarty! Sarty! No! No! Help me, Lizzie!"

Then he was free. His aunt grasped at him but it was too late. He whirled, running, his mother stumbled forward on to her knees behind him, crying to the nearer sister: "Catch him, Net! Catch him!" But that was too late too, the sister (the sisters were twins, born at the same time, yet either of them now gave the impression of being, encompassing as much living meat and volume and weight as any other two of the family) not yet having begun to rise from the chair, her head, face, alone merely turned, presented to him in the flying instant an astonishing expanse of young female features untroubled by any surprise even, wearing only an expression of bovine interest. Then he was out of the room, out of the house, in the mild dust of the starlit road and the heavy rifeness of honeysuckle, the pale ribbon unspooling with terrific slowness under his running feet, reaching the gate at last and turning in, running, his heart and lungs drumming, on up the drive toward the lighted house, the lighted door. He did not knock, he burst in, sobbing for breath, incapable for the moment of speech; he saw the astonished face of the Negro in the linen jacket without knowing when the Negro had appeared.

"De Spain!" he cried, panted. "Where's . . ." then he saw the white man too emerging from a white door down the hall. "Barn!" he cried. "Barn!"

"What?" the white man said. "Barn?"

"Yes!" the boy cried. "Barn!"

"Catch him!" the white man shouted.

But it was too late this time too. The Negro grasped his shirt, but the entire sleeve, rotten with washing, carried away, and he was out that door too and in the drive again, and had actually never ceased to run even while he was screaming into the white man's face.

Behind him the white man was shouting, "My horse! Fetch my horse!" and he thought for an instant of cutting across the park and climbing the fence into the road, but he did not know the park nor how high the vine-massed fence might be and he dared not risk it. So he ran on down the drive, blood and breath roaring; presently he was in the road again though he could not see it. He could not hear either: the galloping mare was almost upon him before he heard her, and even then he held his course, as if the very urgency of his wild grief and need must in a moment more find his wings, waiting until the ultimate instant to hurl himself aside and into the weed-choked roadside ditch as the horse thundered past and on, for an instant in furious silhouette against the stars, the tranquil early summer night sky which, even before the shape of the horse and rider vanished, stained abruptly and violently upward: a long, swirling roar incredible and soundless, blotting the stars, and he springing up and into the road again, running again, knowing it was too late yet still running even after he heard the shot and, an instant later, two shots, pausing now without knowing he had ceased to run, crying "Pap! Pap!", running again before he knew he had begun to run, stumbling, tripping over something and scrabbling up again without ceasing to run, looking backward over his shoulder at the glare as he got up, running on among the invisible trees, panting, sobbing, "Father! Father!"

At midnight he was sitting on the crest of a hill. He did not know it was midnight and he did not know how far he had come. But there was no glare behind him now and he sat now, his back toward what he had called home for four days anyhow, his face toward the dark woods which he would enter when breath was strong again, small, shaking steadily in the chill darkness, hugging himself into the remainder of his thin, rotten shirt, the grief and despair now no longer terror and fear but just grief and despair. *Father. My father,* he thought. "He was brave!" he cried suddenly, aloud but not loud, no more than a whisper: "He was! He was in the war! He was in Colonel Sartoris' cav'ry!" not knowing that his father had gone to that war a private in the fine old European sense, wearing no uniform, admitting the authority of and giving fidelity to no man or army or flag, going to war as Malbrouck[4] himself did: for booty—it meant nothing and less than nothing to him if it were enemy booty or his own.

The slow constellations wheeled on. It would be dawn and then sun-up after a while and he would be hungry. But that would be tomorrow and now he was only cold, and walking would cure that. His breathing was easier now and he decided to get up and go on, and then he found that he had been asleep because he knew it was almost dawn, the night almost over. He could tell that from the whippoorwills. They were everywhere now among the dark trees below him, constant and inflectioned and ceaseless, so that, as the instant for giving over to the day birds drew nearer and nearer, there was no interval at all between them. He got up. He was a little stiff, but walking would cure that too as it would the cold, and soon there would be the sun. He went on down the hill, toward the dark woods within which the liquid silver voices of the birds called unceasing—the rapid and urgent beating of the urgent and quiring heart of the late spring night. He did not look back.

1939

---

4. The Duke of Marlborough (1650–1722), an English general whose name became distorted as Malbrough and Malbrouch in English and French popular songs celebrating his exploits.

GRACE PALEY

A Conversation with My Father

My father is eighty-six years old and in bed. His heart, that bloody motor, is equally old and will not do certain jobs any more. It still floods his head with brainy light. But it won't let his legs carry the weight of his body around the house. Despite my metaphors, this muscle failure is not due to his old heart, he says, but to a potassium shortage. Sitting on one pillow, leaning on three, he offers last-minute advice and makes a request.

"I would like you to write a simple story just once more," he says, "the kind de Maupassant wrote, or Chekhov,[1] the kind you used to write. Just recognizable people and then write down what happened to them next."

I say, "Yes, why not? That's possible." I want to please him, though I don't remember writing that way. I *would* like to try to tell such a story, if he means the kind that begins: "There was a woman . . ." followed by plot, the absolute line between two points which I've always despised. Not for literary reasons, but because it takes all hope away. Everyone, real or invented, deserves the open destiny of life.

Finally I thought of a story that had been happening for a couple of years right across the street. I wrote it down, then read it aloud. "Pa," I said, "how about this? Do you mean something like this?"

> Once in my time there was a woman and she had a son. They lived nicely, in a small apartment in Manhattan. This boy at about fifteen became a junkie, which is not unusual in our neighborhood. In order to maintain her close friendship with him, she became a junkie too. She said it was part of the youth culture, with which she felt very much at home. After a while, for a number of reasons, the boy gave it all up and left the city and his mother in disgust. Hopeless and alone, she grieved. We all visit her.

"O.K., Pa, that's it," I said, "an unadorned and miserable tale."

"But that's not what I mean," my father said. "You misunderstood me on purpose. You know there's a lot more to it. You know that. You left everything out. Turgenev[2] wouldn't do that. Chekhov wouldn't do that. There are in fact Russian writers you never heard of, you don't have an inkling of, as good as anyone, who can write a plain ordinary story, who would not leave out what you have left out. I object not to facts but to people sitting in trees talking senselessly, voices from who knows where . . ."

"Forget that one, Pa, what have I left out now? In this one?"

"Her looks, for instance."

"Oh. Quite handsome, I think. Yes."

---

1. Guy de Maupassant (1850–93) wrote heavily plotted, ironic stories, Chekhov realistic stories that often had no resolution (see *Lady with the Dog*) and sometimes with little plot.

2. Ivan Sergevich Turgenev (1818–1883) wrote stories and novels deeply embedded in the culture of his time; his best-known novel, *Fathers and Sons*, deals with the conflict between generations.

"Her hair?"

"Dark, with heavy braids, as though she were a girl or a foreigner."

"What were her parents like, her stock? That she became such a person. It's interesting, you know."

"From out of town. Professional people. The first to be divorced in their county. How's that? Enough?" I asked.

"With you, it's all a joke," he said. "What about the boy's father? Why didn't you mention him? Who was he? Or was the boy born out of wedlock?"

"Yes," I said. "He was born out of wedlock."

"For Godsakes, doesn't anyone in your stories get married? Doesn't anyone have the time to run down to City Hall before they jump into bed?"

"No," I said. "In real life, yes. But in my stories, no."

"Why do you answer me like that?"

"Oh, Pa, this is a simple story about a smart woman who came to N.Y.C. full of interest love trust excitement very up to date, and about her son, what a hard time she had in this world. Married or not, it's of small consequence."

"It is of great consequence," he said.

"O.K.," I said.

"O.K. O.K. yourself," he said, "but listen. I believe you that she's good-looking, but I don't think she was so smart."

"That's true," I said. "Actually that's the trouble with stories. People start out fantastic. You think they're extraordinary, but it turns out as the work goes along, they're just average with a good education. Sometimes the other way around, the person's a kind of dumb innocent, but he outwits you and you can't even think of an ending good enough."

"What do you do then?" he asked. He had been a doctor for a couple of decades and then an artist for a couple of decades and he's still interested in details, craft, technique.

"Well, you just have to let the story lie around till some agreement can be reached between you and the stubborn hero."

"Aren't you talking silly, now?" he asked. "Start again," he said. "It so happens I'm not going out this evening. Tell the story again. See what you can do this time."

"O.K.," I said. "But it's not a five-minute job." Second attempt:

Once, across the street from us, there was a fine handsome woman, our neighbor. She had a son whom she loved because she'd known him since birth (in helpless chubby infancy, and in the wrestling, hugging ages, seven to ten, as well as earlier and later). This boy, when he fell into the fist of adolescence, became a junkie. He was not a hopeless one. He was in fact hopeful, an ideologue and successful converter. With his busy brilliance, he wrote persuasive articles for his high-school newspaper. Seeking a wider audience, using important connections, he drummed into Lower Manhattan newsstand distribution a periodical called *Oh! Golden Horse!*

In order to keep him from feeling guilty (because guilt is the stony heart of nine tenths of all clinically diagnosed cancers in America today, she said), and because she had always believed in giving bad habits room at home where one could keep an eye on them, she too became a junkie. Her kitchen was famous for a while—a center for intellectual addicts who knew what they were doing. A few felt artistic like Coleridge and others were scientific and revolutionary like Leary.[3] Although she was often high herself, certain good mothering reflexes remained, and she saw to it that there was lots of orange juice around and honey and milk and vitamin pills. However, she never cooked anything but chili, and that no more than once a week. She explained, when we talked to her, seriously, with neighborly concern, that it was her part in the youth culture and she would rather be with the young, it was an honor, than with her own generation.

One week, while nodding through an Antonioni[4] film, this boy was severely jabbed by the elbow of a stern and proselytizing girl, sitting beside him. She offered immediate apricots and nuts for his sugar level, spoke to him sharply, and took him home.

She had heard of him and his work and she herself published, edited, and wrote a competitive journal called *Man Does Live By Bread Alone*. In the organic heat of her continuous presence he could not help but become interested once more in his muscles, his arteries, and nerve connections. In fact he began to love them, treasure them, praise them with funny little songs in *Man does Live . . .*

> *the fingers of my flesh transcend*
> *my transcendental soul*
> *the tightness in my shoulders end*
> *my teeth have made me whole*

To the mouth of his head (that glory of will and determination) he brought hard apples, nuts, wheat germ, and soybean oil. He said to his old friends, From now on, I guess I'll keep my wits about me. I'm going on the natch. He said he was about to begin a spiritual deep-breathing journey. How about you too, Mom? he asked kindly.

His conversion was so radiant, splendid, that neighborhood kids his age began to say that he had never been a real addict at all, only a journalist along for the smell of the story. The mother tried several times to give up what had become without her son and his friends a lonely habit. This effort only brought it to supportable levels. The boy and his girl took their electronic mimeograph and moved to the bushy edge of another borough. They were very strict. They said they would not see her again until she had been off drugs for sixty days.

---

3. Samuel Taylor Coleridge (1772–1834), English Romantic poet, says he wrote his allegedly unfinished poem *Kubla Khan* in an opium dream. Timothy Leary (b. 1920), American psychologist who promoted the use of psychedelic drugs.

4. Michelangelo Antonioni (b. 1912), Italian director (*Blow-Up, Zabriskie Point*), whose neo-realist, often slow-moving films investigate society.

"Poor woman. Poor girl, to be born in a time of fools, to live among fools. The end. The end. You were right to put that down. The end."

I didn't want to argue, but I had to say, "Well, it is not necessarily the end, Pa."

"Yes," he said, "what a tragedy. The end of a person."

"No, Pa," I begged him. "It doesn't have to be. She's only about forty. She could be a hundred different things in this world as time goes on. A teacher or a social worker. An ex-junkie! Sometimes it's better than having a master's in education."

"Jokes," he said. "As a writer that's your main trouble. You don't want to recognize it. Tragedy! Plain tragedy! Historical tragedy! No hope. The end."

"Oh, Pa," I said. "She could change."

At home alone in the evening, weeping, the mother read and reread the seven issues of *Oh! Golden Horse!* They seemed to her as truthful as ever. We often crossed the street to visit and console. But if we mentioned any of our children who were at college or in the hospital or dropouts at home, she would cry out, My baby! My baby! and burst into terrible, face-scarring, time-consuming tears. The End.

First my father was silent, then he said, "Number One: You have a nice sense of humor. Number Two: I see you can't tell a plain story. So don't waste time." Then he said sadly, "Number Three: I suppose that means she was alone, she was left like that, his mother. Alone. Probably sick?"

I said, "Yes."

"In your own life, too, you have to look it in the face." He took a couple of nitroglycerin.[5] "Turn to five," he said, pointing to the dial on the oxygen tank. He inserted the tubes into his nostrils and breathed deep. He closed his eyes and said, "No."

I had promised the family to always let him have the last word when arguing, but in this case I had a different responsibility. That woman lives across the street. She's my knowledge and my invention. I'm sorry for her. I'm not going to leave her there in that house crying. (Actually neither would Life, which unlike me has no pity.)

Therefore: She did change. Of course her son never came home again. But right now, she's the receptionist in a storefront community clinic in the East Village. Most of the customers are young people, some old friends. The head doctor has said to her, "If we only had three people in this clinic with your experiences . . ."

"The doctor said that?" My father took the oxygen tubes out of his nostrils and said, "Jokes. Jokes again."

"No, Pa, it could really happen that way, it's a funny world nowadays."

"No," he said. "Truth first. She will slide back. A person must have character. She does not."

"No, Pa," I said. "That's it. She's got a job. Forget it. She's in that storefront working."

"How long will it be?" he asked. "Tragedy! You too. When will you look it in the face?"

1974

<hr>

5. Medicine for certain heart conditions.

JAMES BALDWIN

Sonny's Blues

I read about it in the paper, in the subway, on my way to work. I read it, and I couldn't believe it, and I read it again. Then perhaps I just stared at it, at the newsprint spelling out his name, spelling out the story. I stared at it in the swinging lights of the subway car, and in the faces and bodies of the people, and in my own face, trapped in the darkness which roared outside.

It was not to be believed and I kept telling myself that, as I walked from the subway station to the high school. And at the same time I couldn't doubt it. I was scared, scared for Sonny. He became real to me again. A great block of ice got settled in my belly and kept melting there slowly all day long, while I taught my classes algebra. It was a special kind of ice. It kept melting, sending trickles of ice water all up and down my veins, but it never got less. Sometimes it hardened and seemed to expand until I felt my guts were going to come spilling out or that I was going to choke or scream. This would always be at a moment when I was remembering some specific thing Sonny had once said or done.

When he was about as old as the boys in my classes his face had been bright and open, there was a lot of copper in it; and he'd had wonderfully direct brown eyes, and great gentleness and privacy. I wondered what he looked like now. He had been picked up, the evening before, in a raid on an apartment downtown, for peddling and using heroin.

I couldn't believe it: but what I mean by that is that I couldn't find any room for it anywhere inside me. I had kept it outside me for a long time. I hadn't wanted to know. I had had suspicions, but I didn't name them, I kept putting them away. I told myself that Sonny was wild, but he wasn't crazy. And he'd always been a good boy, he hadn't ever turned hard or evil or disrespectful, the way kids can, so quick, so quick, especially in Harlem. I didn't want to believe that I'd ever see my brother going down, coming to nothing, all that light in his face gone out, in the condition I'd already seen so many others. Yet it had happened and here I was, talking about algebra to a lot of boys who might, every one of them for all I knew, be popping off needles every time they went to the head.[1] Maybe it did more for them than algebra could.

I was sure that the first time Sonny had ever had horse,[2] he couldn't have been much older than these boys were now. These boys, now, were living as we'd been living then, they were growing up with a rush and their heads bumped abruptly against the low ceiling of their actual possibilities. They were filled with rage. All they really knew were two darknesses, the darkness of their lives, which was now closing in on them, and the darkness of the movies, which had blinded them to that other darkness, and in which they now, vindictively, dreamed, at once more together than they were at any other time, and more alone.

When the last bell rang, the last class ended, I let out my breath. It seemed I'd been holding it for all that time. My clothes were wet—I may have looked as though I'd been sitting in a steam bath, all dressed

---

1. Lavatory.   2. Heroin.

up, all afternoon. I sat alone in the classroom a long time. I listened to
the boys outside, downstairs, shouting and cursing and laughing. Their
laughter struck me for perhaps the first time. It was not the joyous
laughter which—God knows why—one associates with children. It was
mocking and insular, its intent was to denigrate. It was disenchanted,
and in this, also, lay the authority of their curses. Perhaps I was listening to them because I was thinking about my brother and in them I
heard my brother. And myself.

One boy was whistling a tune, at once very complicated and very
simple, it seemed to be pouring out of him as though he were a bird,
and it sounded very cool and moving through all that harsh, bright air,
only just holding its own through all those other sounds.

I stood up and walked over to the window and looked down into
the courtyard. It was the beginning of the spring and the sap was rising
in the boys. A teacher passed through them every now and again,
quickly, as though he or she couldn't wait to get out of that courtyard,
to get those boys out of their sight and off their minds. I started collecting my stuff. I thought I'd better get home and talk to Isabel.

The courtyard was almost deserted by the time I got downstairs. I
saw this boy standing in the shadow of a doorway, looking just like
Sonny. I almost called his name. Then I saw that it wasn't Sonny, but
somebody we used to know, a boy from around our block. He'd been
Sonny's friend. He'd never been mine, having been too young for me,
and, anyway, I'd never liked him. And now, even though he was a
grown-up man, he still hung around that block, still spent hours on the
street corners, was always high and raggy. I used to run into him from
time to time and he'd often work around to asking me for a quarter or
fifty cents. He always had some real good excuse, too, and I always
gave it to him, I don't know why.

But now, abruptly, I hated him. I couldn't stand the way he looked
at me, partly like a dog, partly like a cunning child. I wanted to ask
him what the hell he was doing in the school courtyard.

He sort of shuffled over to me, and he said, "I see you got the papers.
So you already know about it."

"You mean about Sonny? Yes, I already know about it. How come
they didn't get you?"

He grinned. It made him repulsive and it also brought to mind what
he'd looked like as a kid. "I wasn't there. I stay away from them people."

"Good for you." I offered him a cigarette and I watched him through
the smoke. "You come all the way down here just to tell me about
Sonny?"

"That's right." He was sort of shaking his head and his eyes looked
strange, as though they were about to cross. The bright sun deadened
his damp dark brown skin and it made his eyes look yellow and
showed up the dirt in his kinked hair. He smelled funky.[3] I moved a
little away from him and I said, "Well, thanks. But I already know
about it and I got to get home."

"I'll walk you a little ways," he said. We started walking. There were

3. Obnoxious.

a couple of kids still loitering in the courtyard and one of them said goodnight to me and looked strangely at the boy beside me.

"What're you going to do?" he asked me. "I mean, about Sonny?"

"Look. I haven't seen Sonny for over a year, I'm not sure I'm going to do anything. Anyway, what the hell *can* I do?"

"That's right," he said quickly, "ain't nothing you can do. Can't much help old Sonny no more, I guess."

It was what I was thinking and so it seemed to me he had no right to say it.

"I'm surprised at Sonny, though," he went on—he had a funny way of talking, he looked straight ahead as though he were talking to himself—"I thought Sonny was a smart boy, I thought he was too smart to get hung."

"I guess he thought so too," I said sharply, "and that's how he got hung. And how about you? You're pretty goddamn smart, I bet."

Then he looked directly at me, just for a minute. "I ain't smart," he said. "If I was smart, I'd have reached for a pistol a long time ago."

"Look. Don't tell *me* your sad story, if it was up to me, I'd give you one." Then I felt guilty—guilty, probably, for never having supposed that the poor bastard *had* a story of his own, much less a sad one, and I asked, quickly, "What's going to happen to him now?"

He didn't answer this. He was off by himself some place.

"Funny thing," he said, and from his tone we might have been discussing the quickest way to get to Brooklyn, "when I saw the papers this morning, the first thing I asked myself was if I had anything to do with it. I felt sort of responsible."

I began to listen more carefully. The subway station was on the corner, just before us, and I stopped. He stopped, too. We were in front of a bar and he ducked slightly, peering in, but whoever he was looking for didn't seem to be there. The juke box was blasting away with something black and bouncy and I half watched the barmaid as she danced her way from the juke box to her place behind the bar. And I watched her face as she laughingly responded to something someone said to her, still keeping time to the music. When she smiled one saw the little girl, one sensed the doomed, still-struggling woman beneath the battered face of the semi-whore.

"I never *give* Sonny nothing," the boy said finally, "but a long time ago I come to school high and Sonny asked me how it felt." He paused, I couldn't bear to watch him, I watched the barmaid, and I listened to the music which seemed to be causing the pavement to shake. "I told him it felt great." The music stopped, the barmaid paused and watched the juke box until the music began again. "It did."

All this was carrying me some place I didn't want to go. I certainly didn't want to know how it felt. It filled everything, the people, the houses, the music, the dark, quicksilver barmaid, with menace; and this menace was their reality.

"What's going to happen to him now?" I asked again.

"They'll send him away some place and they'll try to cure him." He shook his head. "Maybe he'll even think he's kicked the habit. Then they'll let him loose"—he gestured, throwing his cigarette into the gutter. "That's all."

"What do you mean, that's *all?*"

But I knew what he meant.

"I *mean*, that's *all*." He turned his head and looked at me, pulling down the corners of his mouth. "Don't you know what I mean?" he asked, softly.

"How the hell *would* I know what you mean?" I almost whispered it, I don't know why.

"That's right," he said to the air, "how would *he* know what I mean?" He turned toward me again, patient and calm, and yet I somehow felt him shaking, shaking as though he were going to fall apart. I felt that ice in my guts again, the dread I'd felt all afternoon; and again I watched the barmaid, moving about the bar, washing glasses, and singing. "Listen. They'll let him out and then it'll just start all over again. That's what I mean."

"You mean—they'll let him out. And then he'll just start working his way back in again. You mean he'll never kick the habit. Is that what you mean?"

"That's right," he said, cheerfully. "*You* see what I mean."

"Tell me," I said at last, "why does he want to die? He must want to die, he's killing himself, why does he want to die?"

He looked at me in surprise. He licked his lips. "He don't want to die. He wants to live. Don't nobody want to die, ever."

Then I wanted to ask him—too many things. He could not have answered, or if he had, I could not have borne the answers. I started walking. "Well, I guess it's none of my business."

"It's going to be rough on old Sonny," he said. We reached the subway station. "This is your station?" he asked. I nodded. I took one step down. "Damn!" he said, suddenly. I looked up at him. He grinned again. "Damn it if I didn't leave all my money home. You ain't got a dollar on you, have you? Just for a couple of days, is all."

All at once something inside gave and threatened to come pouring out of me. I didn't hate him any more. I felt that in another moment I'd start crying like a child.

"Sure," I said. "Don't sweat." I looked in my wallet and didn't have a dollar, I only had a five. "Here," I said. "That hold you?"

He didn't look at it—he didn't want to look at it. A terrible, closed look came over his face, as though he were keeping the number on the bill a secret from him and me. "Thanks," he said, and now he was dying to see me go. "Don't worry about Sonny. Maybe I'll write him or something."

"Sure," I said. "You do that. So long."

"Be seeing you," he said. I went on down the steps.

And I didn't write Sonny or send him anything for a long time. When I finally did, it was just after my little girl died, he wrote me back a letter which made me feel like a bastard.

Here's what he said:

Dear brother,

You don't know how much I needed to hear from you. I wanted to write you many a time but I dug how much I must have hurt you and so I didn't write. But now I feel like a man who's been trying to climb up out of some deep, real deep and funky hole and just saw the sun up there, outside. I got to get outside.

I can't tell you much about how I got here. I mean I don't know how to tell you. I guess I was afraid of something or I was trying to escape from something and you know I have never been very strong in the head (smile). I'm glad Mama and Daddy are dead and can't see what's happened to their son and I swear if I'd known what I was doing I would never have hurt you so, you and a lot of other fine people who were nice to me and who believed in me.

I don't want you to think it had anything to do with me being a musician. It's more than that. Or maybe less than that. I can't get anything straight in my head down here and I try not to think about what's going to happen to me when I get outside again. Sometime I think I'm going to flip and *never* get outside and sometime I think I'll come straight back. I tell you one thing, though, I'd rather blow my brains out than go through this again. But that's what they all say, so they tell me. If I tell you when I'm coming to New York and if you could meet me, I sure would appreciate it. Give my love to Isabel and the kids and I was sure sorry to hear about little Gracie. I wish I could be like Mama and say the Lord's will be done, but I don't know it seems to me that trouble is the one thing that never does get stopped and I don't know what good it does to blame it on the Lord. But maybe it does some good if you believe it.

Your brother,
Sonny

Then I kept in constant touch with him and I sent him whatever I could and I went to meet him when he came back to New York. When I saw him many things I thought I had forgotten came flooding back to me. This was because I had begun, finally, to wonder about Sonny, about the life that Sonny lived inside. This life, whatever it was, had made him older and thinner and it had deepened the distant stillness in which he had always moved. He looked very unlike my baby brother. Yet, when he smiled, when we shook hands, the baby brother I'd never known looked out from the depths of his private life, like an animal waiting to be coaxed into the light.

"How you been keeping?" he asked me.

"All right. And you?"

"Just fine." He was smiling all over his face. "It's good to see you again."

"It's good to see you."

The seven years' difference in our ages lay between us like a chasm: I wondered if these years would ever operate between us as a bridge. I was remembering, and it made it hard to catch my breath, that I had been there when he was born; and I had heard the first words he had ever spoken. When he started to walk, he walked from our mother straight to me. I caught him just before he fell when he took the first steps he ever took in this world.

"How's Isabel?"

"Just fine. She's dying to see you."

"And the boys?"

"They're fine, too. They're anxious to see their uncle."

"Oh, come on. You know they don't remember me."

"Are you kidding? Of course they remember you."

He grinned again. We got into a taxi. We had a lot to say to each other, far too much to know how to begin.

As the taxi began to move, I asked, "You still want to go to India?"

He laughed. "You still remember that. Hell, no. This place is Indian enough for me."

"It used to belong to them," I said.

And he laughed again. "They damn sure knew what they were doing when they got rid of it."

Years ago, when he was around fourteen, he'd been all hipped on the idea of going to India. He read books about people sitting on rocks, naked, in all kinds of weather, but mostly bad, naturally, and walking barefoot through hot coals and arriving at wisdom. I used to say that it sounded to me as though they were getting away from wisdom as fast as they could. I think he sort of looked down on me for that.

"Do you mind," he asked, "if we have the driver drive alongside the park? On the west side—I haven't seen the city in so long."

"Of course not," I said. I was afraid that I might sound as though I were humoring him, but I hoped he wouldn't take it that way.

So we drove along, between the green of the park and the stony, lifeless elegance of hotels and apartment buildings, toward the vivid, killing streets of our childhood. These streets hadn't changed, though housing projects jutted up out of them now like rocks in the middle of a boiling sea. Most of the houses in which we had grown up had vanished, as had the stores from which we had stolen, the basements in which we had first tried sex, the rooftops from which we had hurled tin cans and bricks. But houses exactly like the houses of our past yet dominated the landscape, boys exactly like the boys we once had been found themselves smothering in these houses, came down into the streets for light and air and found themselves encircled by disaster. Some escaped the trap, most didn't. Those who got out always left something of themselves behind, as some animals amputate a leg and leave it in the trap. It might be said, perhaps, that I had escaped, after all, I was a school teacher; or that Sonny had, he hadn't lived in Harlem for years. Yet, as the cab moved uptown through streets which seemed, with a rush, to darken with dark people, and as I covertly studied Sonny's face, it came to me that what we both were seeking through our separate cab windows was that part of ourselves which had been left behind. It's always at the hour of trouble and confrontation that the missing member aches.

We hit 110th Street and started rolling up Lenox Avenue. And I'd known this avenue all my life, but it seemed to me again, as it had seemed on the day I'd first heard about Sonny's trouble, filled with a hidden menace which was its very breath of life.

"We almost there," said Sonny.

"Almost." We were both too nervous to say anything more.

We live in a housing project. It hasn't been up long. A few days after it was up it seemed uninhabitably new, now, of course, it's already rundown. It looks like a parody of the good, clean, faceless life—God knows the people who live in it do their best to make it a parody. The beat-looking grass lying around isn't enough to make their lives green, the hedges will never hold out the streets, and they know it. The big windows fool no one, they aren't big enough to make space out of no space. They don't bother with the windows, they watch the TV screen instead. The playground is most popular with the children who don't play at jacks, or skip rope, or roller skate, or swing, and they can be found in it after dark. We moved in partly because it's not too far from where I teach, and partly for the kids; but it's really just like the houses in which Sonny and I grew up. The same things happen, they'll have the same things to remember. The moment Sonny and I started into the house I had the feeling that I was simply bringing him back into the danger he had almost died trying to escape.

Sonny has never been talkative. So I don't know why I was sure he'd be dying to talk to me when supper was over the first night. Everything went fine, the oldest boy remembered him, and the youngest boy liked him, and Sonny had remembered to bring something for each of them; and Isabel, who is really much nicer than I am, more open and giving, had gone to a lot of trouble about dinner and was genuinely glad to see him. And she's always been able to tease Sonny in a way that I haven't. It was nice to see her face so vivid again and to hear her laugh and watch her make Sonny laugh. She wasn't, or, anyway, she didn't seem to be, at all uneasy or embarrassed. She chatted as though there were no subject which had to be avoided and she got Sonny past his first, faint stiffness. And thank God she was there, for I was filled with that icy dread again. Everything I did seemed awkward to me, and everything I said sounded freighted with hidden meaning. I was trying to remember everything I'd heard about dope addiction and I couldn't help watching Sonny for signs. I wasn't doing it out of malice. I was trying to find out something about my brother. I was dying to hear him tell me he was safe.

"Safe!" my father grunted, whenever Mama suggested trying to move to a neighborhood which might be safer for children. "Safe, hell! Ain't no place safe for kids, nor nobody."

He always went on like this, but he wasn't, ever, really as bad as he sounded, not even on weekends, when he got drunk. As a matter of fact, he was always on the lookout for "something a little better," but he died before he found it. He died suddenly, during a drunken weekend in the middle of the war, when Sonny was fifteen. He and Sonny hadn't ever got on too well. And this was partly because Sonny was the apple of his father's eye. It was because he loved Sonny so much and was frightened for him, that he was always fighting with him. It doesn't do any good to fight with Sonny. Sonny just moves back, inside himself, where he can't be reached. But the principal reason that they never hit it off is that they were so much alike. Daddy was big and rough and loud-talking, just the opposite of Sonny, but they both had—that same privacy.

Mama tried to tell me something about this, just after Daddy died. I was home on leave from the army.

This was the last time I ever saw my mother alive. Just the same, this picture gets all mixed up in my mind with pictures I had of her when she was younger. The way I always see her is the way she used to be on a Sunday afternoon, say, when the old folks were talking after the big Sunday dinner. I always see her wearing pale blue. She'd be sitting on the sofa. And my father would be sitting in the easy chair, not far from her. And the living room would be full of church folks and relatives. There they sit, in chairs all around the living room, and the night is creeping up outside, but nobody knows it yet. You can see the darkness growing against the windowpanes and you hear the street noises every now and again, or maybe the jangling beat of a tambourine from one of the churches close by, but it's real quiet in the room. For a moment nobody's talking, but every face looks darkening, like the sky outside. And my mother rocks a little from the waist, and my father's eyes are closed. Everyone is looking at something a child can't see. For a minute they've forgotten the children. Maybe a kid is lying on the rug, half asleep. Maybe somebody's got a kid in his lap and is absent-mindedly stroking the kid's head. Maybe there's a kid, quiet and big-eyed, curled up in a big chair in the corner. The silence, the darkness coming, and the darkness in the faces frighten the child obscurely. He hopes that the hand which strokes his forehead will never stop—will never die. He hopes that there will never come a time when the old folks won't be sitting around the living room, talking about where they've come from, and what they've seen, and what's happened to them and their kinfolk.

But something deep and watchful in the child knows that this is bound to end, is already ending. In a moment someone will get up and turn on the light. Then the old folks will remember the children and they won't talk any more that day. And when light fills the room, the child is filled with darkness. He knows that every time this happens he's moved just a little closer to that darkness outside. The darkness outside is what the old folks have been talking about. It's what they've come from. It's what they endure. The child knows that they won't talk any more because if he knows too much about what's happened to *them,* he'll know too much too soon, about what's going to happen to *him.*

The last time I talked to my mother, I remember I was restless. I wanted to get out and see Isabel. We weren't married then and we had a lot to straighten out between us.

There Mama sat, in black, by the window. She was humming an old church song, *Lord, you brought me from a long ways off.* Sonny was out somewhere. Mama kept watching the streets.

"I don't know," she said, "if I'll ever see you again, after you go off from here. But I hope you'll remember the things I tried to teach you."

"Don't talk like that," I said, and smiled. "You'll be here a long time yet."

She smiled, too, but she said nothing. She was quiet for a long time. And I said, "Mama, don't you worry about nothing. I'll be writing all the time, and you be getting the checks. . . ."

"I want to talk to you about your brother," she said, suddenly. "If anything happens to me he ain't going to have nobody to look out for him."

"Mama," I said, "ain't nothing going to happen to you *or* Sonny. Sonny's all right. He's a good boy and he's got good sense."

"It ain't a question of his being a good boy," Mama said, "nor of his having good sense. It ain't only the bad ones, nor yet the dumb ones that gets sucked under." She stopped, looking at me. "Your Daddy once had a brother," she said, and she smiled in a way that made me feel she was in pain. "You didn't never know that, did you?"

"No," I said, "I never knew that," and I watched her face.

"Oh, yes," she said, "your Daddy had a brother." She looked out of the window again. "I know you never saw your Daddy cry. But *I* did —many a time, through all these years."

I asked her, "What happened to his brother? How come nobody's ever talked about him?"

This was the first time I ever saw my mother look old.

"His brother got killed," she said, "when he was just a little younger than you are now. I knew him. He was a fine boy. He was maybe a little full of the devil, but he didn't mean nobody no harm."

Then she stopped and the room was silent, exactly as it had sometimes been on those Sunday afternoons. Mama kept looking out into the streets.

"He used to have a job in the mill," she said, "and, like all young folks, he just liked to perform on Saturday nights. Saturday nights, him and your father would drift around to different place, go to dances and things like that, or just sit around with people they knew, and your father's brother would sing, he had a fine voice, and play along with himself on his guitar. Well, this particular Saturday night, him and your father was coming home from some place, and they were both a little drunk and there was a moon that night, it was bright like day. Your father's brother was feeling kind of good, and he was whistling to himself, and he had his guitar slung over his shoulder. They was coming down a hill and beneath them was a road that turned off from the highway. Well, your father's brother, being always kind of frisky, decided to run down this hill, and he did, with that guitar banging and clanging behind him, and he ran across the road, and he was making water behind a tree. And your father was sort of amused at him and he was still coming down the hill, kind of slow. Then he heard a car motor and that same minute his brother stepped from behind the tree, into the road, in the moonlight. And he started to cross the road. And your father started to run down the hill, he says he don't know why. This car was full of white men. They was all drunk, and when they seen your father's brother they let out a great whoop and holler and they aimed the car straight at him. They was having fun, they just wanted to scare him, the way they do sometimes, you know. But they was drunk. And I guess the boy, being drunk, too, and scared, kind of lost his head. By the time he jumped it was too late. Your father says he heard his brother scream when the car rolled over him, and he heard the wood of that guitar when it give, and he heard them strings go flying, and he heard them white men shouting, and the car kept on a-going and it ain't stopped till this day. And, time your father got down the hill, his brother weren't nothing but blood and pulp."

Tears were gleaming on my mother's face. There wasn't anything I could say.

"He never mentioned it," she said, "because I never let him mention it before you children. Your Daddy was like a crazy man that night and for many a night thereafter. He says he never in his life seen anything as dark as that road after the lights of that car had gone away. Weren't nothing, weren't nobody on that road, just your Daddy and his brother and that busted guitar. Oh, yes. Your Daddy never did really get right again. Till the day he died he weren't sure but that every white man he saw was the man that killed his brother."

She stopped and took out her handkerchief and dried her eyes and looked at me.

"I ain't telling you all this," she said, "to make you scared or bitter or to make you hate nobody. I'm telling you this because you got a brother. And the world ain't changed."

I guess I didn't want to believe this. I guess she saw this in my face. She turned away from me, toward the window again, searching those streets.

"But I praise my Redeemer," she said at last, "that He called your Daddy home before me. I ain't saying it to throw no flowers at myself, but, I declare, it keeps me from feeling too cast down to know I helped your father get safely through this world. Your father always acted like he was the roughest, strongest man on earth. And everybody took him to be like that. But if he hadn't had *me* there—to see his tears!"

She was crying again. Still, I couldn't move. I said, "Lord, Lord, Mama, I didn't know it was like that."

"Oh, honey," she said, "there's a lot that you don't know. But you are going to find out." She stood up from the window and came over to me. "You got to hold on to your brother," she said, "and don't let him fall, no matter what it looks like is happening to him and no matter how evil you gets with him. You going to be evil with him many a time. But don't you forget what I told you, you hear?"

"I won't forget," I said. "Don't you worry, I won't forget. I won't let nothing happen to Sonny."

My mother smiled as though she were amused at something she saw in my face. Then, "You may not be able to stop nothing from happening. But you got to let him know you's *there*."

Two days later I was married, and then I was gone. And I had a lot of things on my mind and I pretty well forgot my promise to Mama until I got shipped home on a special furlough for her funeral.

And, after the funeral, with just Sonny and me alone in the empty kitchen, I tried to find out something about him.

"What do you want to do?" I asked him.

"I'm going to be a musician," he said.

For he had graduated, in the time I had been away, from dancing to the juke box to finding out who was playing what, and what they were doing with it, and he had bought himself a set of drums.

"You mean, you want to be a drummer?" I somehow had the feeling that being a drummer might be all right for other people but not for my brother Sonny.

"I don't think," he said, looking at me very gravely, "that I'll ever be a good drummer. But I think I can play a piano."

I frowned. I'd never played the role of the older brother quite so seriously before, had scarcely ever, in fact, *asked* Sonny a damn thing. I sensed myself in the presence of something I didn't really know how to handle, didn't understand. So I made my frown a little deeper as I asked: "What kind of musician do you want to be?"

He grinned. "How many kinds do you think there are?"

"Be *serious*," I said.

He laughed, throwing his head back, and then looked at me. "I *am* serious."

"Well, then, for Christ's sake, stop kidding around and answer a serious question. I mean, do you want to be a concert pianist, you want to play classical music and all that, or—or what?" Long before I finished he was laughing again. "For Christ's *sake*, Sonny!"

He sobered, but with difficulty. "I'm sorry. But you sound so— *scared!*" and he was off again.

"Well, you may think it's funny now, baby, but it's not going to be so funny when you have to make your living at it, let me tell you *that*." I was furious because I knew he was laughing at me and I didn't know why.

"No," he said, very sober now, and afraid, perhaps, that he'd hurt me, "I don't want to be a classical pianist. That isn't what interests me. I mean"—he paused, looking hard at me, as though his eyes would help me to understand, and then gestured helplessly, as though perhaps his hand would help—"I mean, I'll have a lot of studying to do, and I'll have to study *everything*, but, I mean, I want to play *with*—jazz musicians." He stopped. "I want to play jazz," he said.

Well, the word had never before sounded as heavy, as real, as it sounded that afternoon in Sonny's mouth. I just looked at him and I was probably frowning a real frown by this time. I simply couldn't see why on earth he'd want to spend his time hanging around nightclubs, clowning around on bandstands, while people pushed each other around a dance floor. It seemed—beneath him, somehow. I had never thought about it before, had never been forced to, but I suppose I had always put jazz musicians in a class with what Daddy called "good-time people."

"Are you *serious?*"

"Hell, *yes*, I'm serious."

He looked more helpless than ever, and annoyed, and deeply hurt.

I suggested, helpfully: "You mean—like Louis Armstrong?"

His face closed as though I'd struck him. "No. I'm not talking about none of that old-time, down home crap."

"Well, look, Sonny, I'm sorry, don't get mad. I just don't altogether get it, that's all. Name somebody—you know, a jazz musician you admire."

"Bird."

"Who?"

"Bird! Charlie Parker!⁴ Don't they teach you nothing in the goddamn army?"

I lit a cigarette. I was surprised and then a little amused to discover that I was trembling. "I've been out of touch," I said. "You'll have to be patient with me. Now. Who's this Parker character?"

"He's just one of the greatest jazz musicians alive," said Sonny, sullenly, his hands in his pockets, his back to me. "Maybe *the* greatest," he added, bitterly, "that's probably why *you* never heard of him."

"All right," I said, "I'm ignorant. I'm sorry. I'll go out and buy all the cat's records right away, all right?"

"It don't," said Sonny, with dignity, "make any difference to me. I don't care what you listen to. Don't do me no favors."

I was beginning to realize that I'd never seen him so upset before. With another part of my mind I was thinking that this would probably turn out to be one of those things kids go through and that I shouldn't make it seem important by pushing it too hard. Still, I didn't think it would do any harm to ask: "Doesn't all this take a lot of time? Can you make a living at it?"

He turned back to me and half leaned, half sat, on the kitchen table. "Everything takes time," he said, "and—well, yes, sure, I can make a living at it. But what I don't seem to be able to make you understand is that it's the only thing I want to do."

"Well, Sonny," I said, gently, "you know people can't always do exactly what they *want* to do—"

"*No,* I don't know that," said Sonny, surprising me. "I think people *ought* to do what they want to do, what else are they alive for?"

"You getting to be a big boy," I said desperately, "it's time you started thinking about your future."

"I'm thinking about my future," said Sonny, grimly. "I think about it all the time."

I gave up. I decided, if he didn't change his mind, that we could always talk about it later. "In the meantime," I said, "you got to finish school." We had already decided that he'd have to move in with Isabel and her folks. I knew this wasn't the ideal arrangement because Isabel's folks are inclined to be dicty⁵ and they hadn't especially wanted Isabel to marry me. But I didn't know what else to do. "And we have to get you fixed up at Isabel's."

There was a long silence. He moved from the kitchen table to the window. "That's a terrible idea. You know it yourself."

"Do you have a *better* idea?"

---

4. Charlie ("Bird") Parker (1920–1955), for whom Birdland in New York was named, perhaps the greatest saxophonist and innovator of jazz; cofounder, with Dizzy Gillespie, of the new jazz, once called "bebop"; narcotics addict.

5. Snobbish, bossy.

He just walked up and down the kitchen for a minute. He was as tall as I was. He had started to shave. I suddenly had the feeling that I didn't know him at all.

He stopped at the kitchen table and picked up my cigarettes. Looking at me with a kind of mocking, amused defiance, he put one between his lips. "You mind?"

"You smoking already?"

He lit the cigarette and nodded, watching me through the smoke. "I just wanted to see if I'd have the courage to smoke in front of you." He grinned and blew a great cloud of smoke to the ceiling. "It was easy." He looked at my face. "Come on, now. I bet you was smoking at my age, tell the truth."

I didn't say anything but the truth was on my face, and he laughed. But now there was something very strained in his laugh. "Sure. And I bet that ain't all you was doing."

He was frightening me a little. "Cut the crap," I said. "We already decided that you was going to go and live at Isabel's. Now what's got into you all of a sudden?"

"*You* decided it," he pointed out. "*I* didn't decide nothing." He stopped in front of me, leaning against the stove, arms loosely folded. "Look, brother. I don't want to stay in Harlem no more, I really don't." He was very earnest. He looked at me, then over toward the kitchen window. There was something in his eyes I'd never seen before, some thoughtfulness, some worry all his own. He rubbed the muscle of one arm. "It's time I was getting out of here."

"Where do you want to *go*, Sonny?"

"I want to join the army. Or the navy, I don't care. If I say I'm old enough, they'll believe me."

Then I got mad. It was because I was so scared. "You must be crazy. You goddamn fool, what the hell do you want to go and join the *army* for?"

"I just told you. To get out of Harlem."

"Sonny, you haven't even finished *school*. And if you really want to be a musician, how do you expect to study if you're in the *army*?"

He looked at me, trapped, and in anguish. "There's ways. I might be able to work out some kind of deal. Anyway, I'll have the G.I. Bill when I come out."

"*If* you come out." We stared at each other. "Sonny, please. Be reasonable. I know the setup is far from perfect. But we got to do the best we can."

"I ain't learning nothing in school," he said. "Even when I go." He turned away from me and opened the window and threw his cigarette out into the narrow alley. I watched his back. "At least, I ain't learning nothing you'd want me to learn." He slammed the window so hard I thought the glass would fly out, and turned back to me. "And I'm sick of the stink of these garbage cans!"

"Sonny," I said, "I know how you feel. But if you don't finish school now, you're going to be sorry later that you didn't." I grabbed him by the shoulders. "And you only got another year. It ain't so bad. And I'll come back and I swear I'll help you do *whatever* you want to do. Just try to put up with it till I come back. Will you please do that?

For me?"

He didn't answer and he wouldn't look at me.

"Sonny. You hear me?"

He pulled away. "I hear you. But you never hear anything *I* say."

I didn't know what to say to that. He looked out of the window and then back at me. "OK," he said, and sighed. "I'll try."

Then I said, trying to cheer him up a little, "They got a piano at Isabel's. You can practice on it."

And as a matter of fact, it did cheer him up for a minute. "That's right," he said to himself. "I forgot that." His face relaxed a little. But the worry, the thoughtfulness, played on it still, the way shadows play on a face which is staring into the fire.

But I thought I'd never hear the end of that piano. At first, Isabel would write me, saying how nice it was that Sonny was so serious about his music and how, as soon as he came in from school, or wherever he had been when he was supposed to be at school, he went straight to that piano and stayed there until suppertime. And, after supper, he went back to that piano and stayed there until everybody went to bed. He was at the piano all day Saturday and all day Sunday. Then he bought a record player and started playing records. He'd play one record over and over again, all day long sometimes, and he'd improvise along with it on the piano. Or he'd play one section of the record, one chord, one change, one progression, then he'd do it on the piano. Then back to the record. Then back to the piano.

Well, I really don't know how they stood it. Isabel finally confessed that it wasn't like living with a person at all, it was like living with sound. And the sound didn't make any sense to her, didn't make any sense to any of them—naturally. They began, in a way, to be afflicted by this presence that was living in their home. It was as though Sonny were some sort of god, or monster. He moved in an atmosphere which wasn't like theirs at all. They fed him and he ate, he washed himself, he walked in and out of their door; he certainly wasn't nasty or unpleasant or rude, Sonny isn't any of those things; but it was as though he were all wrapped up in some cloud, some fire, some vision all his own; and there wasn't any way to reach him.

At the same time, he wasn't really a man yet, he was still a child, and they had to watch out for him in all kinds of ways. They certainly couldn't throw him out. Neither did they dare to make a great scene about that piano because even they dimly sensed, as I sensed, from so many thousands of miles away, that Sonny was at that piano playing for his life.

But he hadn't been going to school. One day a letter came from the school board and Isabel's mother got it—there had, apparently, been other letters but Sonny had torn them up. This day, when Sonny came in, Isabel's mother showed him the letter and asked where he'd been spending his time. And she finally got it out of him that he'd been down in Greenwich Village, with musicians and other characters, in a white girl's apartment. And this scared her and she started to scream at him and what came up, once she began—though she denies it to this day—was what sacrifices they were making to give Sonny a decent home and how little he appreciated it.

Sonny didn't play the piano that day. By evening, Isabel's mother had calmed down but then there was the old man to deal with, and Isabel herself. Isabel says she did her best to be calm but she broke down and started crying. She says she just watched Sonny's face. She could tell, by watching him, what was happening with him. And what was happening was that they penetrated his cloud, they had reached him. Even if their fingers had been a thousand times more gentle than human fingers ever are, he could hardly help feeling that they had stripped him naked and were spitting on that nakedness. For he also had to see that his presence, that music, which was life or death to him, had been torture for them and that they had endured it, not at all for his sake, but only for mine. And Sonny couldn't take that. He can take it a little better today than he could then but he's still not very good at it and, frankly, I don't know anybody who is.

The silence of the next few days must have been louder than the sound of all the music ever played since time began. One morning, before she went to work, Isabel was in his room for something and she suddenly realized that all of his records were gone. And she knew for certain that he was gone. And he was. He went as far as the navy would carry him. He finally sent me a postcard from some place in Greece and that was the first I knew that Sonny was still alive. I didn't see him any more until we were both back in New York and the war had long been over.

He was a man by then, of course, but I wasn't willing to see it. He came by the house from time to time, but we fought almost every time we met. I didn't like the way he carried himself, loose and dreamlike all the time, and I didn't like his friends, and his music seemed to be merely an excuse for the life he led. It sounded just that weird and disordered.

Then we had a fight, a pretty awful fight, and I didn't see him for months. By and by I looked him up, where he was living, in a furnished room in the Village, and I tried to make it up. But there were lots of other people in the room and Sonny just lay on his bed, and he wouldn't come downstairs with me, and he treated these other people as though they were his family and I weren't. So I got mad and then he got mad, and then I told him that he might just as well be dead as live the way he was living. Then he stood up and he told me not to worry about him any more in life, that he *was* dead as far as I was concerned. Then he pushed me to the door and the other people looked on as though nothing were happening, and he slammed the door behind me. I stood in the hallway, staring at the door. I heard somebody laugh in the room and then the tears came to my eyes. I started down the steps, whistling to keep from crying, I kept whistling to myself, *You going to need me, baby, one of these cold, rainy days.*

I read about Sonny's trouble in the spring. Little Grace died in the fall. She was a beautiful little girl. But she only lived a little over two years. She died of polio and she suffered. She had a slight fever for a couple of days, but it didn't seem like anything and we just kept her in bed. And we would certainly have called the doctor, but the fever dropped, she seemed to be all right. So we thought it had just been a cold. Then, one day, she was up, playing, Isabel was in the kitchen fixing lunch for the two boys when they'd come in from school, and she heard Grace fall down in the living room. When you have a lot of children you don't always start running when one of them falls, unless they start screaming or something. And, this time, Gracie was quiet. Yet, Isabel says that when she heard that *thump* and then that silence, something happened in her to make her afraid. And she ran to the living room and there was little Grace on the floor, all twisted up, and the reason she hadn't screamed was that she couldn't get her breath. And when she did scream, it was the worst sound, Isabel says, that she'd ever heard in all her life, and she still hears it sometimes in her dreams. Isabel will sometimes wake me up with a low, moaning, strangled sound and I have to be quick to awaken her and hold her to me and where Isabel is weeping against me seems a mortal wound.

I think I may have written Sonny the very day that little Grace was buried. I was sitting in the living room in the dark, by myself, and I suddenly thought of Sonny. My trouble made his real.

One Saturday afternoon, when Sonny had been living with us, or anyway, been in our house, for nearly two weeks, I found myself wandering aimlessly about the living room, drinking from a can of beer, and trying to work up courage to search Sonny's room. He was out, he was usually out whenever I was home, and Isabel had taken the children to see their grandparents. Suddenly I was standing still in front of the living room window, watching Seventh Avenue. The idea of searching Sonny's room made me still. I scarcely dared to admit to myself what I'd be searching for. I didn't know what I'd do if I found it. Or if I didn't.

On the sidewalk across from me, near the entrance to a barbecue joint, some people were holding an old-fashioned revival meeting. The barbecue cook, wearing a dirty white apron, his conked[6] hair reddish and metallic in the pale sun, and a cigarette between his lips, stood in the doorway, watching them. Kids and older people paused in their errands and stood there, along with some older men and a couple of very tough-looking women who watched everything that happened on the avenue, as though they owned it, or were maybe owned by it. Well, they were watching this, too. The revival was being carried on by three sisters in black, and a brother. All they had were their voices and their Bibles and a tambourine. The brother was testifying[7] and while he testified two of the sisters stood together, seeming to say, amen, and the third sister walked around with the tambourine outstretched and a couple of people dropped coins into it. Then the brother's testimony ended and the sister who had been taking up the collection dumped the coins into her palm and transferred them to the pocket of her long black robe. Then she raised both hands, striking the tambourine against the air, and then against one hand, and she started to sing. And the two other sisters and the brother joined in.

---

6. Processed: straightened and greased.   7. Publicly professing belief.

It was strange, suddenly, to watch, though I had been seeing these meetings all my life. So, of course, had everybody else down there. Yet, they paused and watched and listened and I stood still at the window. " *'Tis the old ship of Zion*," they sang, and the sister with the tambourine kept a steady, jangling beat, *"it has rescued many a thousand!"* Not a soul under the sound of their voices was hearing this song for the first time, not one of them had been rescued. Nor had they seen much in the way of rescue work being done around them. Neither did they especially believe in the holiness of the three sisters and the brother, they knew too much about them, knew where they lived, and how. The woman with the tambourine, whose voice dominated the air, whose face was bright with joy, was divided by very little from the woman who stood watching her, a cigarette between her heavy, chapped lips, her hair a cuckoo's nest, her face scarred and swollen from many beatings, and her black eyes glittering like coal. Perhaps they both knew this, which was why, when, as rarely, they addressed each other, they addressed each other as Sister. As the singing filled the air the watching, listening faces underwent a change, the eyes focusing on something within; the music seemed to soothe a poison out of them; and time seemed, nearly, to fall away from the sullen, belligerent, battered faces, as though they were fleeing back to their first condition, while dreaming of their last. The barbecue cook half shook his head and smiled, and dropped his cigarette and disappeared into his joint. A man fumbled in his pockets for change and stood holding it in his hand impatiently, as though he had just remembered a pressing appointment further up the avenue. He looked furious. Then I saw Sonny, standing on the edge of the crowd. He was carrying a wide, flat notebook with a green cover, and it made him look, from where I was standing, almost like a schoolboy. The coppery sun brought out the copper in his skin, he was very faintly smiling, standing very still. Then the singing stopped, the tambourine turned into a collection plate again. The furious man dropped in his coins and vanished, so did a couple of the women, and Sonny dropped some change in the plate, looking directly at the woman with a little smile. He started across the avenue, toward the house. He has a slow, loping walk, something like the way Harlem hipsters walk, only he's imposed on this his own half-beat. I had never really noticed it before.

I stayed at the window, both relieved and apprehensive. As Sonny disappeared from my sight, they began singing again. And they were still singing when his key turned in the lock.

"Hey," he said.

"Hey, yourself. You want some beer?"

"No. Well, maybe." But he came up to the window and stood beside me, looking out. "What a warm voice," he said.

They were singing *If I could only hear my mother pray again!*

"Yes," I said, "and she can sure beat that tambourine."

"But what a terrible song," he said, and laughed. He dropped his notebook on the sofa and disappeared into the kitchen. "Where's Isabel and the kids?"

"I think they went to see their grandparents. You hungry?"

"No." He came back into the living room with his can of beer. "You want to come some place with me tonight?"

I sensed, I don't know how, that I couldn't possibly say no. "Sure. Where?"

He sat down on the sofa and picked up his notebook and started leafing through it. "I'm going to sit in with some fellows in a joint in the Village."

"You mean, you're going to play, tonight?"

"That's right." He took a swallow of his beer and moved back to the window. He gave me a sidelong look. "If you can stand it."

"I'll try," I said.

He smiled to himself and we both watched as the meeting across the way broke up. The three sisters and the brother, heads bowed, were singing *God be with you till we meet again*. The faces around them were very quiet. Then the song ended. The small crowd dispersed. We watched the three women and the lone man walk slowly up the avenue.

"When she was singing before," said Sonny, abruptly, "her voice reminded me for a minute of what heroin feels like sometimes—when it's in your veins. It makes you feel sort of warm and cool at the same time. And distant. And—and sure." He sipped his beer, very deliberately not looking at me. I watched his face. "It makes you feel—in control. Sometimes you've got to have that feeling."

"Do you?" I sat down slowly in the easy chair.

"Sometimes." He went to the sofa and picked up his notebook again. "Some people do."

"In order," I asked, "to play?" And my voice was very ugly, full of contempt and anger.

"Well"—he looked at me with great, troubled eyes, as though, in fact, he hoped his eyes would tell me things he could never otherwise say—"they *think* so. And *if* they think so—!"

"And what do *you* think?" I asked.

He sat on the sofa and put his can of beer on the floor. "I don't know," he said, and I couldn't be sure if he were answering my question or pursuing his thoughts. His face didn't tell me. "It's not so much to *play*. It's to *stand* it, to be able to make it at all. On any level." He frowned and smiled: "In order to keep from shaking to pieces."

"But these friends of yours," I said, "they seem to shake themselves to pieces pretty goddamn fast."

"Maybe." He played with the notebook. And something told me that I should curb my tongue, that Sonny was doing his best to talk, that I should listen. "But of course you only know the ones that've gone to pieces. Some don't—or at least they haven't *yet* and that's just about all *any* of us can say." He paused. "And then there are some who just live, really, in hell, and they know it and they see what's happening and they go right on. I don't know." He sighed, dropped the notebook, folded his arms. "Some guys, you can tell from the way they play, they on something *all* the time. And you can see that, well, it makes something real for them. But of course," he picked up his beer from the floor and sipped it and put the can down again, "they *want* to, too, you've got to see that. Even some of them that say they don't—*some*, not all."

"And what about you?" I asked—I couldn't help it. "What about you? Do *you* want to?"

He stood up and walked to the window and I remained silent for a long time. Then he sighed. "Me," he said. Then: "While I was downstairs before, on my way here, listening to that woman sing, it struck me all of a sudden how much suffering she must have had to go through—to sing like that. It's *repulsive* to think you have to suffer that much."

I said: "But there's no way not to suffer—is there, Sonny?"

"I believe not," he said and smiled, "but that's never stopped anyone from trying." He looked at me. "Has it?" I realized, with this mocking look, that there stood between us, forever, beyond the power of time or forgiveness, the fact that I had held silence—so long!—when he had needed human speech to help him. He turned back to the window. "No, there's no way not to suffer. But you try all kinds of ways to keep from drowning in it, to keep on top of it, and to make it seem—well, like *you*. Like you did something, all right, and now you're suffering for it. You know?" I said nothing. "Well you know," he said, impatiently, "why *do* people suffer? Maybe it's better to do something to give it a reason, *any* reason."

"But we just agreed," I said, "that there's no way not to suffer. Isn't it better, then, just to—take it?"

"But nobody just takes it," Sonny cried, "that's what I'm telling you! *Everybody* tries not to. You're just hung up on the *way* some people try—it's not *your* way!"

The hair on my face began to itch, my face felt wet. "That's not true," I said, "that's not true. I don't give a damn what other people do, I don't even care how they suffer. I just care how *you* suffer." And he looked at me. "Please believe me," I said, "I don't want to see you—die—trying not to suffer."

"I won't," he said flatly, "die trying not to suffer. At least, not any faster than anybody else."

"But there's no need," I said, trying to laugh, "is there? in killing yourself."

I wanted to say more, but I couldn't. I wanted to talk about will power and how life could be—well, beautiful. I wanted to say that it was all within; but was it? or, rather, wasn't that exactly the trouble? And I wanted to promise that I would never fail him again. But it would all have sounded—empty words and lies.

So I made the promise to myself and prayed that I would keep it.

"It's terrible sometimes, inside," he said, "that's what's the trouble. You walk these streets, black and funky and cold, and there's not really a living ass to talk to, and there's nothing shaking, and there's no way of getting it out—that storm inside. You can't talk it and you can't make love with it, and when you finally try to get with it and play it, you realize *nobody's* listening. So *you've* got to listen. You got to find a way to listen."

And then he walked away from the window and sat on the sofa

again, as though all the wind had suddenly been knocked out of him. "Sometimes you'll do *anything* to play, even cut your mother's throat." He laughed and looked at me. "Or your brother's." Then he sobered. "Or your own." Then: "Don't worry. I'm all right now and I think I'll *be* all right. But I can't forget—where I've been. I don't mean just the physical place I've been, I mean where I've *been*. And *what* I've been." "What have you been, Sonny?" I asked.

He smiled—but sat sideways on the sofa, his elbow resting on the back, his fingers playing with his mouth and chin, not looking at me. "I've been something I didn't recognize, didn't know I could be. Didn't know anybody could be." He stopped, looking inward, looking helplessly young, looking old. "I'm not talking about it now because I feel *guilty* or anything like that—maybe it would be better if I did, I don't know. Anyway, I can't really talk about it. Not to you, not to anybody," and now he turned and faced me. "Sometimes, you know, and it was actually when I was most *out* of the world, I felt that I was in it, that I was *with* it, really, and I could play or I didn't really have to *play,* it just came out of me, it was there. And I don't know how I played, thinking about it now, but I know I did awful things, those times, sometimes, to people. Or it wasn't that I *did* anything to them—it was that they weren't real." He picked up the beer can; it was empty; he rolled it between his palms: "And other times—well, I needed a fix, I needed to find a place to lean, I needed to clear a space to *listen*—and I couldn't find it, and I—went crazy, I did terrible things to *me,* I was terrible *for* me." He began pressing the beer can between his hands, I watched the metal begin to give. It glittered, as he played with it like a knife, and I was afraid he would cut himself, but I said nothing. "Oh well. I can never tell you. I was all by myself at the bottom of something, stinking and sweating and crying and shaking, and I smelled it, you know? *my* stink, and I thought I'd die if I couldn't get away from it and yet, all the same, I knew that everything I was doing was just locking me in with it. And I didn't know," he paused, still flattening the beer can, "I didn't know, I still *don't* know, something kept telling me that maybe it was good to smell your own stink, but I didn't think that *that* was what I'd been trying to do—and—who can stand it?" and he abruptly dropped the ruined beer can, looking at me with a small, still smile, and then rose, walking to the window as though it were the lodestone rock. I watched his face, he watched the avenue. "I couldn't tell you when Mama died—but the reason I wanted to leave Harlem so bad was to get away from drugs. And then, when I ran away, that's what I was running from—really. When I came back, nothing had changed, *I* hadn't changed, I was just—older." And he stopped, drumming with his fingers on the windowpane. The sun had vanished, soon darkness would fall. I watched his face. "It can come again," he said, almost as though speaking to himself. Then he turned to me. "It can come again," he repeated. "I just want you to know that."

"All right," I said, at last. "So it can come again. All right."

He smiled, but the smile was sorrowful. "I had to try to tell you," he said.

"Yes," I said. "I understand that."

"You're my brother," he said, looking straight at me, and not smiling at all.

"Yes," I repeated, "yes. I understand that."

He turned back to the window, looking out. "All that hatred down there," he said, "all that hatred and misery and love. It's a wonder it doesn't blow the avenue apart."

We went to the only nightclub on a short, dark street, downtown. We squeezed through the narrow, chattering, jampacked bar to the entrance of the big room, where the bandstand was. And we stood there for a moment, for the lights were very dim in this room and we couldn't see. Then, "Hello, boy," said a voice and an enormous black man, much older than Sonny or myself, erupted out of all that atmospheric lighting and put an arm around Sonny's shoulder. "I been sitting right here," he said, "waiting for you."

He had a big voice, too, and heads in the darkness turned toward us.

Sonny grinned and pulled a little away, and said, "Creole, this is my brother. I told you about him."

Creole shook my hand. "I'm glad to meet you, son," he said, and it was clear that he was glad to meet me *there*, for Sonny's sake. And he smiled, "You got a real musician in *your* family," and he took his arm from Sonny's shoulder and slapped him, lightly, affectionately, with the back of his hand.

"Well. Now I've heard it all," said a voice behind us. This was another musician, and a friend of Sonny's, a coal-black, cheerful-looking man, built close to the ground. He immediately began confiding to me, at the top of his lungs, the most terrible things about Sonny, his teeth gleaming like a lighthouse and his laugh coming up out of him like the beginning of an earthquake. And it turned out that everyone at the bar knew Sonny, or almost everyone; some were musicians, working there, or nearby, or not working, some were simply hangers-on, and some were there to hear Sonny play. I was introduced to all of them and they were all very polite to me. Yet, it was clear that, for them, I was only Sonny's brother. Here, I was in Sonny's world. Or, rather: his kingdom. Here, it was not even a question that his veins bore royal blood.

They were going to play soon and Creole installed me, by myself, at a table in a dark corner. Then I watched them, Creole, and the little black man, and Sonny, and the others, while they horsed around, standing just below the bandstand. The light from the bandstand spilled just a little short of them and, watching them laughing and gesturing and moving about, I had the feeling that they, nevertheless, were being most careful not to step into that circle of light too suddenly: that if they moved into the light too suddenly, without thinking, they would perish in flame. Then, while I watched, one of them, the small black man, moved into the light and crossed the bandstand and started fooling around with his drums. Then—being funny and being, also, extremely ceremonious—Creole took Sonny by the arm and led him to the piano. A woman's voice called Sonny's name and a few hands started clapping. And Sonny, also being funny and being ceremonious, and so touched, I think, that he could have cried, but neither hiding it nor showing it, riding it like a man, grinned, and put both hands to his heart and bowed from the waist.

Creole then went to the bass fiddle and a lean, very bright-skinned brown man jumped up on the bandstand and picked up his horn. So there they were, and the atmosphere on the bandstand and in the room began to change and tighten. Someone stepped up to the microphone and announced them. Then there were all kinds of murmurs. Some people at the bar shushed others. The waitress ran around, frantically getting in the last orders, guys and chicks got closer to each other, and the lights on the bandstand, on the quartet, turned to a kind of indigo. Then they all looked different there. Creole looked about him for the last time, as though he were making certain that all his chickens were in the coop, and then he—jumped and struck the fiddle. And there they were.

All I know about music is that not many people ever really hear it. And even then, on the rare occasions when something opens within, and the music enters, what we mainly hear, or hear corroborated, are personal, private, vanishing evocations. But the man who creates the music is hearing something else, is dealing with the roar rising from the void and imposing order on it as it hits the air. What is evoked in him, then, is of another order, more terrible because it has no words, and triumphant, too, for that same reason. And his triumph, when he triumphs, is ours. I just watched Sonny's face. His face was troubled, he was working hard, but he wasn't with it. And I had the feeling that, in a way, everyone on the bandstand was waiting for him, both waiting for him and pushing him along. But as I began to watch Creole, I realized that it was Creole who held them all back. He had them on a short rein. Up there, keeping the beat with his whole body, wailing on the fiddle, with his eyes half closed, he was listening to everything, but he was listening to Sonny. He was having a dialogue with Sonny. He wanted Sonny to leave the shoreline and strike out for the deep water. He was Sonny's witness that deep water and drowning were not the same thing—he had been there, and he knew. And he wanted Sonny to know. He was waiting for Sonny to do the things on the keys which would let Creole know that Sonny was in the water.

And, while Creole listened, Sonny moved, deep within, exactly like someone in torment. I had never before thought of how awful the relationship must be between the musician and his instrument. He has to fill it, this instrument, with the breath of life, his own. He has to make it do what he wants it to do. And a piano is just a piano. It's made out of so much wood and wires and little hammers and big ones, and ivory. While there's only so much you can do with it, the only way to find this out is to try; to try and make it do everything.

And Sonny hadn't been near a piano for over a year. And he wasn't on much better terms with his life, not the life that stretched before him now. He and the piano stammered, started one way, got scared, stopped; started another way, panicked, marked time, started again; then seemed to have found a direction, panicked again, got stuck. And the face I saw on Sonny I'd never seen before. Everything had been burned out of it, and, at the same time, things usually hidden were being burned in, by the fire and fury of the battle which was occurring in him up there.

Yet, watching Creole's face as they neared the end of the first set, I had the feeling that something had happened, something I hadn't heard. Then they finished, there was scattered applause, and then, without an instant's warning, Creole started into something else, it was almost sardonic, it was *Am I Blue*.[8] And, as though he commanded, Sonny began to play. Something began to happen. And Creole let out the reins. The dry, low, black man said something awful on the drums, Creole answered, and the drums talked back. Then the horn insisted, sweet and high, slightly detached perhaps, and Creole listened, commenting now and then, dry, and driving, beautiful and calm and old. Then they all came together again, and Sonny was part of the family again. I could tell this from his face. He seemed to have found, right there beneath his fingers, a damn brand-new piano. It seemed that he couldn't get over it. Then, for a while, just being happy with Sonny, they seemed to be agreeing with him that brand-new pianos certainly were a gas.

Then Creole stepped forward to remind them that what they were playing was the blues. He hit something in all of them, he hit something in me, myself, and the music tightened and deepened, apprehension began to beat the air. Creole began to tell us what the blues were all about. They were not about anything very new. He and his boys up there were keeping it new, at the risk of ruin, destruction, madness, and death, in order to find new ways to make us listen. For, while the tale of how we suffer, and how we are delighted, and how we may triumph is never new, it always must be heard. There isn't any other tale to tell, it's the only light we've got in all this darkness.

And this tale, according to that face, that body, those strong hands on those strings, has another aspect in every country, and a new depth in every generation. Listen, Creole seemed to be saying, listen. Now these are Sonny's blues. He made the little black man on the drums know it, and the bright, brown man on the horn. Creole wasn't trying any longer to get Sonny in the water. He was wishing him Godspeed. Then he stepped back, very slowly, filling the air with the immense suggestion that Sonny speak for himself.

Then they all gathered around Sonny and Sonny played. Every now and again one of them seemed to say, amen. Sonny's fingers filled the air with life, his life. But that life contained so many others. And Sonny went all the way back, he really began with the spare, flat statement of the opening phrase of the song. Then he began to make it his. It was very beautiful because it wasn't hurried and it was no longer a lament. I seemed to hear with what burning he had made it his, with what burning we had yet to make it ours, how we could cease lamenting. Freedom lurked around us and I understood, at last, that he could help us to be free if we would listen, that he would never be free until we did. Yet, there was no battle in his face now, I heard what he had

8. By Grant Clark and Harry Akst, sung by Ethel Waters in 1929 film, "On with the Show," brilliantly recorded by Billy Holiday, and a favorite blues piece.

gone through, and would continue to go through until he came to rest in earth. He had made it his: that long line, of which we knew only Mama and Daddy. And he was giving it back, as everything must be given back, so that, passing through death, it can live forever. I saw my mother's face again, and felt, for the first time, how the stones of the road she had walked on must have bruised her feet. I saw the moonlit road where my father's brother died. And it brought something else back to me, and carried me past it, I saw my little girl again and felt Isabel's tears again, and I felt my own tears begin to rise. And I was yet aware that this was only a moment, that the world waited outside, as hungry as a tiger, and that trouble stretched above us, longer than the sky.

Then it was over. Creole and Sonny let out their breath, both soaking wet, and grinning. There was a lot of applause and some of it was real. In the dark, the girl came by and I asked her to take drinks to the bandstand. There was a long pause, while they talked up there in the indigo light and after awhile I saw the girl put a Scotch and milk on top of the piano for Sonny. He didn't seem to notice it, but just before they started playing again, he sipped from it and looked toward me, and nodded. Then he put it back on top of the piano. For me, then, as they began to play again, it glowed and shook above my brother's head like the very cup of trembling.[9]

1965

GABRIEL GARCÍA MÁRQUEZ

A Very Old Man with Enormous Wings[*]

A TALE FOR CHILDREN

On the third day of rain they had killed so many crabs inside the house that Pelayo had to cross his drenched courtyard and throw them into the sea, because the newborn child had a temperature all night and they thought it was due to the stench. The world had been sad since Tuesday. Sea and sky were a single ash-gray thing and the sands of the beach, which on March nights glimmered like powdered light, had become a stew of mud and rotten shellfish. The light was so weak at noon that when Pelayo was coming back to the house after throwing away the crabs, it was hard for him to see what it was that was moving and groaning in the rear of the courtyard.

---

9. See *Isaiah* 51:17, 22–23: "Awake, awake, stand up, O Jerusalem, which hast drunk at the hand of the Lord the cup of his fury; thou hast drunken the dregs of the cup of trembling, and wrung them out. . . . Behold, I have taken out of thine hand the cup of trembling, even the dregs of the cup of my fury; thou shalt no more drink it again: But I will put it into the hands of them that afflict thee; . . . ."

* Translated by Gregory Rabassa.

He had to go very close to see that it was an old man, a very old man, lying face down in the mud, who, in spite of his tremendous efforts, couldn't get up, impeded by his enormous wings.

Frightened by that nightmare, Pelayo ran to get Elisenda, his wife, who was putting compresses on the sick child, and he took her to the rear of the courtyard. They both looked at the fallen body with mute stupor. He was dressed like a ragpicker. There were only a few faded hairs left on his bald skull and very few teeth in his mouth, and his pitiful condition of a drenched great-grandfather had taken away any sense of grandeur he might have had. His huge buzzard wings, dirty and half-plucked, were forever entangled in the mud. They looked at him so long and so closely that Pelayo and Elisenda very soon overcame their surprise and in the end found him familiar. Then they dared speak to him, and he answered in an incomprehensible dialect with a strong sailor's voice. That was how they skipped over the inconvenience of the wings and quite intelligently concluded that he was a lonely castaway from some foreign ship wrecked by the storm. And yet, they called in a neighbor woman who knew everything about life and death to see him, and all she needed was one look to show them their mistake.

"He's an angel," she told them. "He must have been coming for the child, but the poor fellow is so old that the rain knocked him down."

On the following day everyone knew that a flesh-and-blood angel was held captive in Pelayo's house. Against the judgment of the wise neighbor woman, for whom angels in those times were the fugitive survivors of a celestial conspiracy, they did not have the heart to club him to death. Pelayo watched over him all afternoon from the kitchen, armed with his bailiff's club, and before going to bed he dragged him out of the mud and locked him up with the hens in the wire chicken coop. In the middle of the night, when the rain stopped, Pelayo and Elisenda were still killing crabs. A short time afterward the child woke up without a fever and with a desire to eat. Then they felt magnanimous and decided to put the angel on a raft with fresh water and provisions for three days and leave him to his fate on the high seas. But when they went out into the courtyard with the first light of dawn, they found the whole neighborhood in front of the chicken coop having fun with the angel, without the slightest reverence, tossing him things to eat through the openings in the wire as if he weren't a supernatural creature but a circus animal.

Father Gonzaga arrived before seven o'clock, alarmed at the strange news. By that time onlookers less frivolous than those at dawn had already arrived and they were making all kinds of conjectures concerning the captive's future. The simplest among them thought that he should be named mayor of the world. Others of sterner mind felt that he should be promoted to the rank of five-star general in order to win all wars. Some visionaries hoped that he could be put to stud in order to implant on earth a race of winged wise men who could take charge of the universe. But Father Gonzaga, before becoming a priest, had been a robust woodcutter. Standing by the wire, he reviewed his catechism in an instant and asked them to open the door so that he could take a close look at that pitiful man who looked more like a huge decrepit hen among the fascinated chickens. He was lying in a corner drying his open wings in the sunlight among the fruit peels and breakfast leftovers that the early risers had thrown him. Alien to the impertinences of the world, he only lifted his antiquarian eyes and murmured something in his dialect when Father Gonzaga went into the chicken coop and said good morning to him in Latin. The parish priest had his first suspicion of an imposter when he saw that he did not understand the language of God or know how to greet His ministers. Then he noticed that seen close up he was much too human: he had an unbearable smell of the outdoors, the back side of his wings was strewn with parasites and his main feathers had been mistreated by terrestrial winds, and nothing about him measured up to the proud dignity of angels. Then he came out of the chicken coop and in a brief sermon warned the curious against the risks of being ingenuous. He reminded them that the devil had the bad habit of making use of carnival tricks in order to confuse the unwary. He argued that if wings were not the essential element in determining the difference between a hawk and an airplane, they were even less so in the recognition of angels. Nevertheless, he promised to write a letter to his bishop so that the latter would write to his primate so that the latter would write to the Supreme Pontiff in order to get the final verdict from the highest courts.

His prudence fell on sterile hearts. The news of the captive angel spread with such rapidity that after a few hours the courtyard had the bustle of a marketplace and they had to call in troops with fixed bayonets to disperse the mob that was about to knock the house down. Elisenda, her spine all twisted from sweeping up so much marketplace trash, then got the idea of fencing in the yard and charging five cents admission to see the angel.

The curious came from far away. A traveling carnival arrived with a flying acrobat who buzzed over the crowd several times, but no one paid any attention to him because his wings were not those of an angel but, rather, those of a sidereal bat. The most unfortunate invalids on earth came in search of health: a poor woman who since childhood had been counting her heartbeats and had run out of numbers; a Portuguese man who couldn't sleep because the noise of the stars disturbed him; a sleepwalker who got up at night to undo the things he had done while awake; and many others with less serious ailments. In the midst of that shipwreck disorder that made the earth tremble, Pelayo and Elisenda were happy with fatigue, for in less than a week they had crammed their rooms with money and the line of pilgrims waiting their turn to enter still reached beyond the horizon.

The angel was the only one who took no part in his own act. He spent his time trying to get comfortable in his borrowed nest, befuddled by the hellish heat of the oil lamps and sacramental candles that had been placed along the wire. At first they tried to make him eat some mothballs, which, according to the wisdom of the wise

neighbor woman, were the food prescribed for angels. But he turned
them down, just as he turned down the papal lunches[1] that the peni-
tents brought him, and they never found out whether it was because
he was an angel or because he was an old man that in the end he
ate nothing but eggplant mush. His only supernatural virtue seemed
to be patience. Especially during the first days, when the hens pecked
at him, searching for the stellar parasites that proliferated in his
wings, and the cripples pulled out feathers to touch their defective
parts with, and even the most merciful threw stones at him, trying to
get him to rise so they could see him standing. The only time they
succeeded in arousing him was when they burned his side with an
iron for branding steers, for he had been motionless for so many hours
that they thought he was dead. He awoke with a start, ranting in his
hermetic language and with tears in his eyes, and he flapped his wings
a couple of times, which brought on a whirlwind of chicken dung and
lunar dust and a gale of panic that did not seem to be of this world.
Although many thought that his reaction had been one not of rage
but of pain, from then on they were careful not to annoy him, because
the majority understood that his passivity was not that of a hero
taking his ease but that of a cataclysm in repose.

Father Gonzaga held back the crowd's frivolity with formulas of
maidservant inspiration while awaiting the arrival of a final judgment on the nature of the captive. But the mail from Rome showed no
sense of urgency. They spent their time finding out if the prisoner had
a navel, if his dialect had any connection with Aramaic, how many
times he could fit on the head of a pin, or whether he wasn't just a
Norwegian with wings. Those meager letters might have come and
gone until the end of time if a providential event had not put an end
to the priest's tribulations.

It so happened that during those days, among so many other
carnival attractions, there arrived in town the traveling show of the
woman who had been changed into a spider for having disobeyed
her parents. The admission to see her was not only less than the admission to see the angel, but people were permitted to ask her all
manner of questions about her absurd state and to examine her up
and down so that no one would ever doubt the truth of her horror.
She was a frightful tarantula the size of a ram and with the head of a
sad maiden. What was most heart-rending, however, was not her out-
landish shape but the sincere affliction with which she recounted the
details of her misfortune. While still practically a child she had
sneaked out of her parents' house to go to a dance, and while she was
coming back through the woods after having danced all night without permission, a fearful thunderclap rent the sky in two and through
the crack came the lightning bolt of brimstone that changed her into
a spider. Her only nourishment came from the meatballs that
charitable souls chose to toss into her mouth. A spectacle like that, full
of so much human truth and with such a fearful lesson, was bound to
defeat without even trying that of a haughty angel who scarcely

1. Choice, extremely expensive meals.

deigned to look at mortals. Besides, the few miracles attributed to the angel showed a certain mental disorder, like the blind man who didn't recover his sight but grew three new teeth, or the paralytic who didn't get to walk but almost won the lottery, and the leper whose sores sprouted sunflowers. Those consolation miracles, which were more like mocking fun, had already ruined the angel's reputation when the woman who had been changed into a spider finally crushed him completely. That was how Father Gonzaga was cured forever of his insomnia and Pelayo's courtyard went back to being as empty as during the time it had rained for three days and crabs walked through the bedrooms.

The owners of the house had no reason to lament. With the money they saved they built a two-story mansion with balconies and gardens and high netting so that crabs wouldn't get in during the winter, and with iron bars on the windows so that angels wouldn't get in. Pelayo also set up a rabbit warren close to town and gave up his job as bailiff for good, and Elisenda bought some satin pumps with high heels and many dresses of iridescent silk, the kind worn on Sunday by the most desirable women in those times. The chicken coop was the only thing that didn't receive any attention. If they washed it down with creolin[2] and burned tears of myrrh inside it every so often, it was not in homage to the angel but to drive away the dungheap stench that still hung everywhere like a ghost and was turning the new house into an old one. At first, when the child learned to walk, they were careful that he not get too close to the chicken coop. But then they began to lose their fears and got used to the smell, and before the child got his second teeth he'd gone inside the chicken coop to play, where the wires were falling apart. The angel was no less standoffish with him than with other mortals, but he tolerated the most ingenious infamies with the patience of a dog who had no illusions. They both came down with chicken pox at the same time. The doctor who took care of the child couldn't resist the temptation to listen to the angel's heart, and he found so much whistling in the heart and so many sounds in his kidneys that it seemed impossible for him to be alive. What surprised him most, however, was the logic of his wings. They seemed so natural on that completely human organism that he couldn't understand why other men didn't have them too.

When the child began school it had been some time since the sun and rain had caused the collapse of the chicken coop. The angel went dragging himself about here and there like a stray dying man. They would drive him out of the bedroom with a broom and a moment later find him in the kitchen. He seemed to be in so many places at the same time that they grew to think that he'd been duplicated, that he was reproducing himself all through the house, and the exasperated and unhinged Elisenda shouted that it was awful living in that hell full of angels. He could scarcely eat and his antiquarian eyes had also become so foggy that he went about bumping

2. A disinfectant.

into posts. All he had left were the bare cannulae of his last feathers. Pelayo threw a blanket over him and extended him the charity of letting him sleep in the shed, and only then did they notice that he had a temperature at night, and was delirious with the tongue twisters of an old Norwegian. That was one of the few times they became alarmed, for they thought he was going to die and not even the wise neighbor woman had been able to tell them what to do with dead angels.

And yet he not only survived his worst winter, but seemed improved with the first sunny days. He remained motionless for several days in the farthest corner of the courtyard, where no one would see him, and at the beginning of December some large, stiff feathers began to grow on his wings, the feathers of a scarecrow, which looked more like another misfortune of decrepitude. But he must have known the reason for those changes, for he was quite careful that no one should notice them, that no one should hear the sea chanteys that he sometimes sang under the stars. One morning Elisenda was cutting some bunches of onions for lunch when a wind that seemed to come from the high seas blew into the kitchen. Then she went to the window and caught the angel in his first attempts at flight. They were so clumsy that his fingernails opened a furrow in the vegetable patch and he was on the point of knocking the shed down with the ungainly flapping that slipped on the light and couldn't get a grip on the air. But he did manage to gain altitude. Elisenda let out a sigh of relief, for herself and for him, when she saw him pass over the last houses, holding himself up in some way with the risky flapping of a senile vulture. She kept watching him even when she was through cutting the onions and she kept on watching until it was no longer possible for her to see him, because then he was no longer an annoyance in her life but an imaginary dot on the horizon of the sea.

1972

ALICE MUNRO

Boys and Girls

My father was a fox farmer. That is, he raised silver foxes, in pens; and in the fall and early winter, when their fur was prime, he killed them and skinned them and sold their pelts to the Hudson's Bay Company or the Montreal Fur Traders. These companies supplied us with heroic calendars to hang, one on each side of the kitchen door. Against a background of cold blue sky and black pine forests and treacherous northern rivers, plumed adventurers planted the flags of England or of France; magnificent savages bent their backs to the portage.

For several weeks before Christmas, my father worked after supper in the cellar of our house. The cellar was whitewashed, and lit by a hundred-watt bulb over the worktable. My brother Laird and I sat on the top step and watched. My father removed the pelt inside-out from the body of the fox, which looked surprisingly small, mean and rat-like, deprived of its arrogant weight of fur. The naked, slippery bodies were collected in a sack and buried at the dump. One time the hired man, Henry Bailey, had taken a swipe at me with this sack, saying, "Christmas present!" My mother thought that was not funny. In fact she disliked the whole pelting operation—that was what the killing, skinning, and preparation of the furs was called—and wished it did not have to take place in the house. There was the smell. After the pelt had been stretched inside-out on a long board my father scraped away delicately, removing the little clotted webs of blood vessels, the bubbles of fat; the smell of blood and animal fat, with the strong primitive odor of the fox itself, penetrated all parts of the house. I found it reassuringly seasonal, like the smell of oranges and pine needles.

Henry Bailey suffered from bronchial troubles. He would cough and cough until his narrow face turned scarlet, and his light blue, derisive eyes filled up with tears; then he took the lid off the stove, and, standing well back, shot out a great clot of phlegm—hsss—straight into the heart of the flames. We admired him for this performance and for his ability to make his stomach growl at will, and for his laughter, which was full of high whistlings and gurglings and involved the whole faulty machinery of his chest. It was sometimes hard to tell what he was laughing at, and always possible that it might be us.

After we had been sent to bed we could still smell fox and still hear Henry's laugh, but these things, reminders of the warm, safe, brightly lit downstairs world, seemed lost and diminished, floating on the stale cold air upstairs. We were afraid at night in the winter. We were not afraid of *outside* though this was the time of year when snowdrifts curled around our house like sleeping whales and the wind harassed us all night, coming up from the buried fields, the frozen swamp, with its old bugbear chorus of threats and misery. We were afraid of *inside*, the room where we slept. At this time the upstairs of our house was not finished. A brick chimney went up one wall. In the middle of the floor was a square hole, with a wooden railing around it; that was where the stairs came up. On the other side of the stairwell were the things that nobody had any use for any more—a soldiery roll of linoleum, standing on end, a wicker baby carriage, a fern basket, china jugs and basins with cracks in them, a picture of the Battle of Balaclava,[1] very sad to look at. I had told Laird, as soon as he was old enough to understand such things, that bats and skeletons lived over there; whenever a man escaped from the county jail, twenty miles away, I imagined that he had somehow let himself in the window and was hiding behind the linoleum. But we had rules to keep us safe. When the light was on, we were safe as long as we did not step off the square of worn carpet which

1. An indecisive Crimean War bàttle fought on October 25, 1854.

defined our bedroom-space; when the light was off no place was safe
but the beds themselves. I had to turn out the light kneeling on the
end of my bed, and stretching as far as I could to reach the cord.

In the dark we lay on our beds, our narrow life rafts, and fixed
our eyes on the faint light coming up the stairwell, and sang songs.
Laird sang "Jingle Bells," which he would sing any time, whether
it was Christmas or not, and I sang "Danny Boy." I loved the sound
of my own voice, frail and supplicating, rising in the dark. We could
make out the tall frosted shapes of the windows now, gloomy and
white. When I came to the part, *When I am dead, as dead I well
may be*—a fit of shivering caused not by the cold sheets but by
pleasurable emotion almost silenced me. *You'll kneel and say, an Ave
there above me*—What was an Ave? Every day I forgot to find out.

Laird went straight from singing to sleep. I could hear his long,
satisfied, bubbly breaths. Now for the time that remained to me, the
most perfectly private and perhaps the best time of the whole day,
I arranged myself tightly under the covers and went on with one
of the stories I was telling myself from night to night. These stories
were about myself, when I had grown a little older; they took place
in a world that was recognizably mine, yet one that presented oppor-
tunities for courage, boldness and self-sacrifice, as mine never did. I
rescued people from a bombed building (it discouraged me that the
real war had gone on so far away from Jubilee). I shot two rabid
wolves who were menacing the schoolyard (the teachers cowered
terrified at my back). I rode a fine horse spiritedly down the main
street of Jubilee, acknowledging the townspeople's gratitude for some
yet-to-be-worked-out piece of heroism (nobody ever rode a horse
there, except King Billy in the Orangemen's Day[2] parade). There
was always riding and shooting in these stories, though I had only
been on a horse twice—bareback because we did not own a saddle—
and the second time I had slid right around and dropped under the
horse's feet; it had stepped placidly over me. I really was learning
to shoot, but I could not hit anything yet, not even tin cans on
fence posts.

Alive, the foxes inhabited a world my father made for them. It was
surrounded by a high guard fence, like a medieval town, with a
gate that was padlocked at night. Along the streets of this town
were ranged large, sturdy pens. Each of them had a real door that
a man could go through, a wooden ramp along the wire, for the foxes
to run up and down on, and a kennel—something like a clothes chest
with airholes—where they slept and stayed in winter and had their
young. There were feeding and watering dishes attached to the wire
in such a way that they could be emptied and cleaned from the
outside. The dishes were made of old tin cans, and the ramps and
kennels of odds and ends of old lumber. Everything was tidy and
ingenious; my father was tirelessly inventive and his favorite book in

2. The Orange Society is an Irish Prot-
estant group named after William of
Orange, who, as King William III of Eng-
land, defeated the Catholic James II. The
Society sponsors an annual procession on
July 12 to commemorate the victory of
William III at the Battle of the Boyne.

the world was Robinson Crusoe.[3] He had fitted a tin drum on a wheelbarrow, for bringing water down to the pens. This was my job in summer, when the foxes had to have water twice a day. Between nine and ten o'clock in the morning, and again after supper, I filled the drum at the pump and trundled it down through the barnyard to the pens, where I parked it, and filled my watering can and went along the streets. Laird came too, with his little cream and green gardening can, filled too full and knocking against his legs and slopping water on his canvas shoes. I had the real watering can, my father's, though I could only carry it three-quarters full.

The foxes all had names, which were printed on a tin plate and hung beside their doors. They were not named when they were born, but when they survived the first year's pelting and were added to the breeding stock. Those my father had named were called names like Prince, Bob, Wally and Betty. Those I had named were called Star or Turk, or Maureen or Diana. Laird named one Maud after a hired girl we had when he was little, one Harold after a boy at school, and one Mexico, he did not say why.

Naming them did not make pets out of them, or anything like it. Nobody but my father ever went into the pens, and he had twice had blood-poisoning from bites. When I was bringing them their water they prowled up and down on the paths they had made inside their pens, barking seldom—they saved that for nighttime, when they might get up a chorus of community frenzy—but always watching me, their eyes burning, clear gold, in their pointed, malevolent faces. They were beautiful for their delicate legs and heavy, aristocratic tails and the bright fur sprinkled on dark down their backs—which gave them their name—but especially for their faces, drawn exquisitely sharp in pure hostility, and their golden eyes.

Besides carrying water I helped my father when he cut the long grass, and the lamb's quarter and flowering money-musk, that grew between the pens. He cut with the scythe and I raked into piles. Then he took a pitchfork and threw fresh-cut grass all over the top of the pens, to keep the foxes cooler and shade their coats, which were browned by two much sun. My father did not talk to me unless it was about the job we were doing. In this he was quite different from my mother, who, if she was feeling cheerful, would tell me all sorts of things—the name of a dog she had had when she was a little girl, the names of boys she had gone out with later on when she was grown up, and what certain dresses of hers had looked like—she could not imagine now what had become of them. Whatever thoughts and stories my father had were private, and I was shy of him and would never ask him questions. Nevertheless I worked willingly under his eyes, and with a feeling of pride. One time a feed salesman came down into the pens to talk to him and my father said, "Like to have you meet my new hired man." I turned away and raked furiously, red in the face with pleasure.

3. Novel (1719) by Daniel Defoe that is about a man shipwrecked on a desert   island and that goes into great detail about his ingenious contraptions.

"Could of fooled me," said the salesman. "I thought it was only a girl."

After the grass was cut, it seemed suddenly much later in the year. I walked on stubble in the earlier evening, aware of the reddening skies, the entering silences, of fall. When I wheeled the tank out of the gate and put the padlock on, it was almost dark. One night at this time I saw my mother and father standing talking on the little rise of ground we called the gangway, in front of the barn. My father had just come from the meathouse; he had his stiff bloody apron on, and a pail of cut-up meat in his hand.

It was an odd thing to see my mother down at the barn. She did not often come out of the house unless it was to do something—hang out the wash or dig potatoes in the garden. She looked out of place, with her bare lumpy legs, not touched by the sun, her apron still on and damp across the stomach from the supper dishes. Her hair was tied up in a kerchief, wisps of it falling out. She would tie her hair up like this in the morning, saying she did not have time to do it properly, and it would stay tied up all day. It was true, too; she really did not have time. These days our back porch was piled with baskets of peaches and grapes and pears, bought in town, and onions and tomatoes and cucumbers grown at home, all waiting to be made into jelly and jam and preserves, pickles and chili sauce. In the kitchen there was a fire in the stove all day, jars clinked in boiling water, sometimes a cheesecloth bag was strung on a pole between two chairs straining blue-black grape pulp for jelly. I was given jobs to do and I would sit at the table peeling peaches that had been soaked in the hot water, or cutting up onions, my eyes smarting and streaming. As soon as I was done I ran out of the house, trying to get out of earshot before my mother thought of what she wanted me to do next. I hated the hot dark kitchen in summer, the green blinds and the flypapers, the same old oilcloth table and wavy mirror and bumpy linoleum. My mother was too tired and preoccupied to talk to me, she had no heart to tell about the Normal School Graduation Dance; sweat trickled over her face and she was always counting under her breath, pointing at jars, dumping cups of sugar. It seemed to me that work in the house was endless, dreary and peculiarly depressing; work done out of doors, and in my father's service, was ritualistically important.

I wheeled the tank up to the barn, where it was kept, and I heard my mother saying, "Wait till Laird gets a little bigger, then you'll have a real help."

What my father said I did not hear. I was pleased by the way he stood listening, politely as he would to a salesman or a stranger, but with an air of wanting to get on with his real work. I felt my mother had no business down here and I wanted him to feel the same way. What did she mean about Laird? He was no help to anybody. Where was he now? Swinging himself sick on the swing, going around in circles, or trying to catch caterpillars. He never once stayed with me till I was finished.

"And then I can use her more in the house," I heard my mother say. She had a dead-quiet, regretful way of talking about me that always made me uneasy. "I just get my back turned and she runs off. It's not like I had a girl in the family at all."

I went and sat on a feed bag in the corner of the barn, not wanting to appear when this conversation was going on. My mother, I felt, was not to be trusted. She was kinder than my father and more easily fooled, but you could not depend on her, and the real reasons for the things she said and did were not to be known. She loved me, and she sat up late at night making a dress of the difficult style I wanted, for me to wear when school started, but she was also my enemy. She was always plotting. She was plotting now to get me to stay in the house more, although she knew I hated it (*because* she knew I hated it) and keep me from working for my father. It seemed to me she would do this simply out of perversity, and to try her power. It did not occur to me that she could be lonely, or jealous. No grown-up could be; they were too fortunate. I sat and kicked my heels monotonously against a feed bag, raising dust, and did not come out till she was gone.

At any rate, I did not expect my father to pay any attention to what she said. Who could imagine Laird doing my work—Laird remembering the padlock and cleaning out the watering dishes with a leaf on the end of a stick, or even wheeling the tank without it tumbling over? It showed how little my mother knew about the way things really were.

I have forgotten to say what the foxes were fed. My father's bloody apron reminded me. They were fed horsemeat. At this time most farmers still kept horses, and when a horse got too old to work, or broke a leg or got down and would not get up, as they sometimes did, the owner would call my father, and he and Henry went out to the farm in the truck. Usually they shot and butchered the horse there, paying the farmer from five to twelve dollars. If they had already too much meat on hand, they would bring the horse back alive, and keep it for a few days or weeks in our stable, until the meat was needed. After the war the farmers were buying tractors and gradually getting rid of horses altogether, so it sometimes happened that we got a good healthy horse, that there was just no use for any more. If this happened in the winter we might keep the horse in our stable till spring, for we had plenty of hay and if there was a lot of snow—and the plow did not always get our road cleared—it was convenient to be able to go to town with a horse and cutter.[4]

The winter I was eleven years old we had two horses in the stable. We did not know what names they had had before, so we called them Mack and Flora. Mack was an old black workhorse, sooty and indifferent. Flora was a sorrel mare, a driver. We took them both out in the cutter. Mack was slow and easy to handle. Flora was given to fits of violent alarm, veering at cars and even at other horses, but we loved her speed and high-stepping, her general air of gallantry and abandon. On Saturdays we went down to the stable and as soon as

4. A small, light, one-horse sleigh.

we opened the door on its cosy, animal-smelling darkness Flora threw up her head, rolled her eyes, whinnied despairingly and pulled herself through a crisis of nerves on the spot. It was not safe to go into her stall; she would kick.

This winter also I began to hear a great deal more on the theme my mother had sounded when she had been talking in front of the barn. I no longer felt safe. It seemed that in the minds of the people around me there was a steady undercurrent of thought, not to be deflected, on this one subject. The word *girl* had formerly seemed to me innocent and unburdened, like the word *child*; now it appeared that it was no such thing. A girl was not, as I had supposed, simply what I was; it was what I had to become. It was a definition, always touched with emphasis, with reproach and disappointment. Also it was a joke on me. Once Laird and I were fighting, and for the first time ever I had to use all my strength against him; even so, he caught and pinned my arm for a moment, really hurting me. Henry saw this, and laughed, saying, "Oh, that there Laird's gonna show you, one of these days!" Laird was getting a lot bigger. But I was getting bigger too.

My grandmother came to stay with us for a few weeks and I heard other things. "Girls don't slam doors like that." "Girls keep their knees together when they sit down." And worse still, when I asked some questions, "That's none of girls' business." I continued to slam the doors and sit as awkwardly as possible, thinking that by such measures I kept myself free.

When spring came, the horses were let out in the barnyard. Mack stood against the barn wall trying to scratch his neck and haunches, but Flora trotted up and down and reared at the fences, clattering her hooves against the rails. Snow drifts dwindled quickly, revealing the hard gray and brown earth, the familiar rise and fall of the ground, plain and bare after the fantastic landscape of winter. There was a great feeling of opening-out, of release. We just wore rubbers now, over our shoes; our feet felt ridiculously light. One Saturday we went out to the stable and found all the doors open, letting in the unaccustomed sunlight and fresh air. Henry was there, just idling around looking at his collection of calendars which were tacked up behind the stalls in a part of the stable my mother had probably never seen.

"Come to say goodbye to your old friend Mack?" Henry said. "Here, you give him a taste of oats." He poured some oats into Laird's cupped hands and Laird went to feed Mack. Mack's teeth were in bad shape. He ate very slowly, patiently shifting the oats around in his mouth, trying to find a stump of a molar to grind it on. "Poor old Mack," said Henry mournfully. "When a horse's teeth's gone, he's gone. That's about the way."

"Are you going to shoot him today?" I said. Mack and Flora had been in the stable so long I had almost forgotten they were going to be shot.

Henry didn't answer me. Instead he started to sing in a high, trembly, mocking-sorrowful voice, *Oh, there's no more work, for poor*

Uncle Ned, he's gone where the good darkies go.[5] Mack's thick, blackish tongue worked diligently at Laird's hand. I went out before the song was ended and sat down on the gangway.

I had never seen them shoot a horse, but I knew where it was done. Last summer Laird and I had come upon a horse's entrails before they were buried. We had thought it was a big black snake, coiled up in the sun. That was around in the field that ran up beside the barn. I thought that if we went inside the barn, and found a wide crack or a knothole to look through, we would be able to see them do it. It was not something I wanted to see; just the same, if a thing really happened, it was better to see it, and know.

My father came down from the house, carrying the gun.

"What are you doing here?" he said.

"Nothing."

"Go on up and play around the house."

He sent Laird out of the stable. I said to Laird, "Do you want to see them shoot Mack?" and without waiting for an answer led him around to the front door of the barn, opened it carefully, and went in. "Be quiet or they'll hear us," I said. We could hear Henry and my father talking in the stable, then the heavy, shuffling steps of Mack being backed out of his stall.

In the loft it was cold and dark. Thin, crisscrossed beams of sunlight fell through the cracks. The hay was low. It was a rolling country, hills and hollows, slipping under our feet. About four feet up was a beam going around the walls. We piled hay up in one corner and I boosted Laird up and hoisted myself. The beam was not very wide; we crept along it with our hands flat on the barn walls. There were plenty of knotholes, and I found one that gave me the view I wanted—a corner of the barnyard, the gate, part of the field. Laird did not have a knothole and began to complain.

I showed him a widened crack between two boards. "Be quiet and wait. If they hear you you'll get us in trouble."

My father came in sight carrying the gun. Henry was leading Mack by the halter. He dropped it and took out his cigarette papers and tobacco; he rolled cigarettes for my father and himself. While this was going on Mack nosed around in the old, dead grass along the fence. Then my father opened the gate and they took Mack through. Henry led Mack way from the path to a patch of ground and they talked together, not loud enough for us to hear. Mack again began searching for a mouthful of fresh grass, which was not to be found. My father walked away in a straight line, and stopped short at a distance which seemed to suit him. Henry was walking away from Mack too, but sideways, still negligently holding on to the halter. My father raised the gun and Mack looked up as if he had noticed something and my father shot him.

Mack did not collapse at once but swayed, lurched sideways and fell, first on his side; then he rolled over on his back and, amazingly, kicked his legs for a few seconds in the air. At this Henry laughed, as if Mack had done a trick for him. Laird, who had drawn a long, groaning breath of surprise when the shot was fired, said out loud, "He's not dead." And it seemed to me it might be true. But his legs stopped, he rolled on his side again, his muscles quivered and sank. The two men walked over and looked at him in a business-like way; they bent down and examined his forehead where the bullet had gone in, and now I saw his blood on the brown grass.

"Now they just skin him and cut him up," I said. "Let's go." My legs were a little shaky and I jumped gratefully down into the hay. "Now you've seen how they shoot a horse," I said in a congratulatory way, as if I had seen it many times before. "Let's see if any barn cat's had kittens in the hay." Laird jumped. He seemed young and obedient again. Suddenly I remembered how, when he was little, I had brought him into the barn and told him to climb the ladder to the top beam. That was in the spring, too, when the hay was low. I had done it out of a need for excitement, a desire for something to happen so that I could tell about it. He was wearing a little bulky brown and white checked coat, made down from one of mine. He went all the way up just as I told him, and sat down on the top beam with the hay far below him on one side, and the barn floor and some old machinery on the other. Then I ran screaming to my father, "Laird's up on the top beam!" My father came, my mother came, my father went up the ladder talking very quietly and brought Laird down under his arm, at which my mother leaned against the ladder and began to cry. They said to me, "Why weren't you watching him?" but nobody ever knew the truth. Laird did not know enough to tell. But whenever I saw the brown and white checked coat hanging in the closet, or at the bottom of the rag bag, which was where it ended up, I felt a weight in my stomach, the sadness of unexorcised guilt.

I looked at Laird, who did not even remember this, and I did not like the look on this thin, winter-pale face. His expression was not frightened or upset, but remote, concentrating. "Listen," I said, in an unusually bright and friendly voice, "you aren't going to tell, are you?"

"No," he said absently.

"Promise."

"Promise," he said. I grabbed the hand behind his back to make sure he was not crossing his fingers. Even so, he might have a night-mare; it might come out that way. I decided I had better work hard to get all thoughts of what he had seen out of his mind—which, it seemed to me, could not hold very many things at a time. I got some money I had saved and that afternoon we went into Jubilee and saw a show, with Judy Canova,[6] at which we both laughed a great deal. After that I thought it would be all right.

Two weeks later I knew they were going to shoot Flora. I knew from the night before, when I heard my mother ask if the hay was holding out all right, and my father said, "Well, after tomorrow there'll just be the cow, and we should be able to put her out to grass in

---

6. American comedian best known for her yodeling in hillbilly movies of the 1940s.

another week." So I knew it was Flora's turn in the morning.

This time I didn't think of watching it. That was something to see just one time. I had not thought about it very often since, but sometimes when I was busy, working at school, or standing in front of the mirror combing my hair and wondering if I would be pretty when I grew up, the whole scene would flash into my mind: I would see the easy, practiced way my father raised the gun, and hear Henry laughing when Mack kicked his legs in the air. I did not have any great feeling of horror and opposition, such as a city child might have had; I was too used to seeing the death of animals as a necessity by which we lived. Yet I felt a little ashamed, and there was a new wariness, a sense of holding-off, in my attitude to my father and his work.

It was a fine day, and we were going around the yard picking up tree branches that had been torn off in winter storms. This was something we had been told to do, and also we wanted to use them to make a teepee. We heard Flora whinny, and then my father's voice and Henry's shouting, and we ran down to the barnyard to see what was going on.

The stable door was open. Henry had just brought Flora out, and she had broken away from him. She was running free in the barnyard, from one end to the other. We climbed up on the fence. It was exciting to see her running, whinnying, going up on her hind legs, prancing and threatening like a horse in a Western movie, an unbroken ranch horse, though she was just an old driver, an old sorrel mare. My father and Henry ran after her and tried to grab the dangling halter. They tried to work her into a corner, and they had almost succeeded when she made a run between them, wild-eyed, and disappeared around the corner of the barn. We heard the rails clatter down as she got over the fence, and Henry yelled, "She's into the field now!"

That meant she was in the long L-shaped field that ran up by the house. If she got around the center, heading towards the lane, the gate was open; the truck had been driven into the field this morning. My father shouted to me, because I was on the other side of the fence, nearest the lane, "Go shut the gate!"

I could run very fast. I ran across the garden, past the tree where our swing was hung, and jumped across a ditch into the lane. There was the open gate. She had not got out, I could not see her up on the road; she must have run to the other end of the field. The gate was heavy. I lifted it out of the gravel and carried it across the roadway. I had it halfway across when she came in sight, galloping straight towards me. There was just time to get the chain on. Laird came scrambling through the ditch to help me.

Instead of shutting the gate, I opened it as wide as I could. I did not make any decision to do this, it was just what I did. Flora never slowed down; she galloped straight past me, and Laird jumped up and down, yelling, "Shut it, shut it!" even after it was too late. My father and Henry appeared in the field a moment too late to see what I had done. They only saw Flora heading for the township road.

They would think I had not got there in time.

They did not waste any time asking about it. They went back to the barn and got the gun and the knives they used, and put these in the truck; then they turned the truck around and came bouncing up the field toward us. Laird called to them, "Let me go too, let me go too!" and Henry stopped the truck and they took him in. I shut the gate after they were all gone.

I supposed Laird would tell. I wondered what would happen to me. I had never disobeyed my father before, and I could not understand why I had done it. Flora would not really get away. They would catch up with her in the truck. Or if they did not catch her this morning somebody would see her and telephone us this afternoon or tomorrow. There was no wild country here for her to run to, only farms. What was more, my father had paid for her, we needed the meat to feed the foxes, we needed the foxes to make our living. All I had done was make more work for my father who worked hard enough already. And when my father found out about it he was not going to trust me any more; he would know that I was not entirely on his side. I was on Flora's side, and that made me no use to anybody, not even to her. Just the same, I did not regret it; when she came running at me and I held the gate open, that was the only thing I could do.

I went back to the house, and my mother said, "What's all the commotion?" I told her that Flora had kicked down the fence and got away. "Your poor father," she said, "now he'll have to go chasing over the countryside. Well, there isn't any use planning dinner before one." She put up the ironing board. I wanted to tell her, but thought better of it and went upstairs and sat on my bed.

Lately I had been trying to make my part of the room fancy, spreading the bed with old lace curtains, and fixing myself a dressing table with some leftovers of cretonne for a skirt. I planned to put up some kind of barricade between my bed and Laird's, to keep my section separate from his. In the sunlight, the lace curtains were just dusty rags. We did not sing at night any more. One night when I was singing Laird said, "You sound silly," and I went right on but the next night I did not start. There was not so much need to anyway, we were no longer afraid. We knew it was just old furniture over there, old jumble and confusion. We did not keep to the rules. I still stayed awake after Laird was asleep and told myself stories, but even in these stories something different was happening, mysterious alterations took place. A story might start off in the old way, with a spectacular danger, a fire or wild animals, and for a while I might rescue people; then things would change around, and instead, somebody would be rescuing me. It might be a boy from our class at school, or even Mr. Campbell, our teacher, who tickled girls under the arms. And at this point the story concerned itself at great length with what I looked like—how long my hair was, and what kind of dress I had on; by the time I had these details worked out the real excitement of the story was lost.

It was later than one o'clock when the truck came back. The tarpaulin was over the back, which meant there was meat in it. My mother had to heat dinner up all over again. Henry and my father had changed from their bloody overalls into ordinary working overalls in the barn, and they washed their arms and necks and faces at the sink, and splashed water on their hair and combed it. Laird lifted his arm to show off a streak of blood. "We shot old Flora," he said, "and cut her up in fifty pieces."

"Well I don't want to hear about it," my mother said. "And don't come to my table like that."

My father made him go and wash the blood off.

We sat down and my father said grace and Henry pasted his chewing gum on the end of his fork, the way he always did; when he took it off he would have us admire the pattern. We began to pass the bowls of steaming, overcooked vegetables. Laird looked across the table at me and said proudly, distinctly, "Anyway it was her fault Flora got away."

"What?" my father said.

"She could of shut the gate and she didn't. She just open' it up and Flora run out."

"Is that right?" my father said.

Everybody at the table was looking at me. I nodded, swallowing food with great difficulty. To my shame, tears flooded my eyes.

My father made a curt sound of disgust. "What did you do that for?"

I did not answer. I put down my fork and waited to be sent from the table, still not looking up.

But this did not happen. For some time nobody said anything, then Laird said matter-of-factly, "She's crying."

"Never mind," my father said. He spoke with resignation, even good humor, the words which absolved and dismissed me for good. "She's only a girl," he said.

I didn't protest that, even in my heart. Maybe it was true.

1968

BOBBIE ANN MASON

Shiloh

Leroy Moffitt's wife, Norma Jean, is working on her pectorals. She lifts three-pound dumbbells to warm up, then progresses to a twenty-pound barbell. Standing with her legs apart, she reminds Leroy of Wonder Woman.

"I'd give anything if I could just get these muscles to where they're real hard," says Norma Jean. "Feel this arm. It's not as hard as the other one."

"That's 'cause you're right-handed," says Leroy, dodging as she swings the barbell in an arc.

"Do you think so?"

"Sure."

Leroy is a truckdriver. He injured his leg in a highway accident four months ago, and his physical therapy, which involves weights and a pulley, prompted Norma Jean to try building herself up. Now she is attending a body-building class. Leroy has been collecting temporary disability since his tractor-trailer jackknifed in Missouri, badly twisting his left leg in its socket. He has a steel pin in his hip. He will probably not be able to drive his rig again. It sits in the backyard, like a gigantic bird that has flown home to roost. Leroy has been home in Kentucky for three months, and his leg is almost healed but the accident frightened him and he does not want to drive any more long hauls. He is not sure what to do next. In the meantime, he makes things from craft kits. He started by building a miniature log cabin from notched Popsicle sticks. He varnished it and placed it on the TV set, where it remains. It reminds him of a rustic Nativity scene. Then he tried string art (sailing ships on black velvet), a macramé owl kit, a snap-together B-17 Flying Fortress,[1] and a lamp made out of a model truck, with a light fixture screwed in the top of the cab. At first the kits were diversions, something to kill time, but now he is thinking about building a full-scale log house from a kit. It would be considerably cheaper than building a regular house, and besides, Leroy has grown to appreciate how things are put together. He has begun to realize that in all the years he was on the road he never took time to examine anything. He was always flying past scenery.

"They won't let you build a log cabin in any of the new subdivisions," Norma Jean tells him.

"They will if I tell them it's for you," he says, teasing her. Ever since they were married, he has promised Norma Jean he would build her a new home one day. They have always rented, and the house they live in is small and nondescript. It does not even feel like a home, Leroy realizes now.

Norma Jean works at the Rexall drugstore, and she has acquired an amazing amount of information about cosmetics. When she explains to Leroy the three stages of complexion care, involving creams, toners, and moisturizers, he thinks happily of other petroleum products—axle grease, diesel fuel. This is a connection between him and Norma Jean. Since he has been home, he has felt unusually tender about his wife and guilty over his long absences. But he can't tell what she feels about him. Norma Jean has never complained about his traveling; she has never made hurt remarks, like calling his truck a "widow-maker." He is reasonably certain she has been faithful to him, but he wishes she would celebrate his permanent homecoming more happily. Norma Jean is often startled to find Leroy at home, and he thinks she seems a little disappointed about it. Perhaps he reminds her too much of the early days of their marriage, before he went on the road. They had a

---

1. World War II bomber.

child who died as an infant, years ago. They never speak about their memories of Randy, which have almost faded, but now that Leroy is home all the time, they sometimes feel awkward around each other, and Leroy wonders if one of them should mention the child. He has the feeling that they are waking up out of a dream together—that they must create a new marriage, start afresh. They are lucky they are still married. Leroy has read that for most people losing a child destroys the marriage—or else he heard this on *Donahue*. He can't always remember where he learns things anymore.

At Christmas, Leroy bought an electric organ for Norma Jean. She used to play the piano when she was in high school. "It don't leave you," she told him once. "It's like riding a bicycle."

The new instrument had so many keys and buttons that she was bewildered by it at first. She touched the keys tentatively, pushed some buttons, then pecked out "Chopsticks." It came out in an amplified fox-trot rhythm, with marimba sounds.

"It's an orchestra!" she cried.

The organ had a pecan-look finish and eighteen preset chords, with optional flute, violin, trumpet, clarinet, and banjo accompaniments. Norma Jean mastered the organ almost immediately. At first she played Christmas songs. Then she bought *The Sixties Songbook* and learned every tune in it, adding variations to each with the rows of brightly colored buttons.

"I didn't like these old songs back then," she said. "But I have this crazy feeling I missed something."

"You didn't miss a thing," said Leroy.

Leroy likes to lie on the couch and smoke a joint and listen to Norma Jean play "Can't Take My Eyes Off You"[2] and "I'll Be Back." He is back again. After fifteen years on the road, he is finally settling down with the woman he loves. She is still pretty. Her skin is flawless. Her frosted curls resemble pencil trimmings.

Now that Leroy has come home to stay, he notices how much the town has changed. Subdivisions are spreading across western Kentucky like an oil slick. The sign at the edge of town says "Pop: 11,500"—only seven hundred more than it said twenty years before. Leroy can't figure out who is living in all the new houses. The farmers who used to gather around the courthouse square on Saturday afternoons to play checkers and spit tobacco juice have gone. It has been years since Leroy has thought about the farmers, and they have disappeared without his noticing.

Leroy meets a kid named Stevie Hamilton in the parking lot at the new shopping center. While they pretend to be strangers meeting over a stalled car, Stevie tosses an ounce of marijuana under the front seat of Leroy's car. Stevie is wearing orange jogging shoes and a T-shirt that says CHATTAHOOCHEE SUPER-RAT. His father is a prominent doctor who lives in one of the expensive subdivisions in a new white-

---

2. A 1967 song by Bob Crewe and Bob Gaudio; best-selling records in 1967 by Frankie Valli, 1968 by The Lettermen, and 1969–70 by Nancy Wilson. *Below:*

"I'll Be Back," 1964, by John Lennon and Paul McCartney and recorded by the Beatles.

columned brick house that looks like a funeral parlor. In the phone book under his name there is a separate number, with the listing "Teenagers."

"Where do you get this stuff?" asks Leroy. "From your pappy?"

"That's for me to know and you to find out," Stevie says. He is slit-eyed and skinny.

"What else you got?"

"What you interested in?"

"Nothing special. Just wondered."

Leroy used to take speed on the road. Now he has to go slowly. He needs to be mellow. He leans back against the car and says, "I'm aiming to build me a log house, soon as I get time. My wife, though, I don't think she likes the idea."

"Well, let me know when you want me again," Stevie says. He has a cigarette in his cupped palm, as though sheltering it from the wind. He takes a long drag, then stomps it on the asphalt and slouches away.

Stevie's father was two years ahead of Leroy in high school. Leroy is thirty-four. He married Norma Jean when they were both eighteen, and their child Randy was born a few months later, but he died at the age of four months and three days. He would be about Stevie's age now. Norma Jean and Leroy were at the drive-in, watching a double feature (*Dr. Strangelove* and *Lover Come Back*),[3] and the baby was sleeping in the back seat. When the first movie ended, the baby was dead. It was the sudden infant death syndrome. Leroy remembers handing Randy to a nurse at the emergency room, as though he were offering her a large doll as a present. A dead baby feels like a sack of flour. "It just happens sometimes," said the doctor, in what Leroy always recalls as a nonchalant tone. Leroy can hardly remember the child anymore, but he still sees vividly a scene from *Dr. Strangelove* in which the President of the United States was talking in a folksy voice on the hot line to the Soviet premier about the bomber accidentally headed toward Russia. He was in the War Room, and the world map was lit up. Leroy remembers Norma Jean standing catatonically beside him in the hospital and himself thinking: Who is this strange girl? He had forgotten who she was. Now scientists are saying that crib death is caused by a virus. Nobody knows anything, Leroy thinks. The answers are always changing.

When Leroy gets home from the shopping center, Norma Jean's mother, Mabel Beasley, is there. Until this year, Leroy has not realized how much time she spends with Norma Jean. When she visits, she inspects the closets and then the plants, informing Norma Jean when a plant is droopy or yellow. Mabel calls the plants "flowers," although there are never any blooms. She always notices if Norma Jean's laundry is piling up. Mabel is a short, overweight woman whose tight, brown-dyed curls look more like a wig than the actual wig she sometimes wears. Today she has brought Norma Jean an off-white dust ruffle she made for the bed; Mabel works in a custom-upholstery shop.

3. A 1963 satire on nuclear war and a 1961 Rock Hudson–Doris Day romantic comedy satirizing the advertising business.

"This is the tenth one I made this year," Mabel says. "I got started and couldn't stop."

"It's real pretty," says Norma Jean.

"Now we can hide things under the bed," says Leroy, who gets along with his mother-in-law primarily by joking with her. Mabel has never really forgiven him for disgracing her by getting Norma Jean pregnant. When the baby died, she said that fate was mocking her.

"What's that thing?" Mabel says to Leroy in a loud voice, pointing to a tangle of yarn on a piece of canvas.

Leroy holds it up for Mabel to see. "It's my needlepoint," he explains. "This is a *Star Trek* pillow cover."

"That's what a woman would do," says Mabel. "Great day in the morning!"

"All the big football players on TV do it," he says.

"Why, Leroy, you're always trying to fool me. I don't believe you for one minute. You don't know what to do with yourself—that's the whole trouble. Sewing!"

"I'm aiming to build us a log house," says Leroy. "Soon as my plans come."

"Like *heck* you are," says Norma Jean. She takes Leroy's needlepoint and shoves it into a drawer. "You have to find a job first. Nobody can afford to build now anyway."

Mabel straightens her girdle and says, "I still think before you get tied down y'all ought to take a little run to Shiloh."

"One of these days, Mama," Norma Jean says impatiently.

Mabel is talking about Shiloh, Tennessee. For the past few years, she has been urging Leroy and Norma Jean to visit the Civil War battleground there.[4] Mabel went there on her honeymoon—the only real trip she ever took. Her husband died of a perforated ulcer when Norma Jean was ten, but Mabel, who was accepted into the United Daughters of the Confederacy in 1975, is still preoccupied with going back to Shiloh.

"I've been to kingdom come and back in that truck out yonder," Leroy says to Mabel, "but we never yet set foot in that battleground. Ain't that something? How did I miss it?"

"It's not even that far," Mabel says.

After Mabel leaves, Norma Jean reads to Leroy from a list she has made. "Things you could do," she announces. "You could get a job as a guard at Union Carbide, where they'd let you set on a stool. You could get on at the lumberyard. You could do a little carpenter work, if you want to build so bad. You could—"

"I can't do something where I'd have to stand up all day."

"You ought to try standing up all day behind a cosmetics counter. It's amazing that I have strong feet, coming from two parents that never had strong feet at all." At the moment Norma Jean is holding

---

4. Where, in April 1862, more than 23,000 troops of the North and South, one-quarter of those who fought there, died. This was the first real indication of how bitter and bloody the war was to be. General Ulysses S. Grant, when reinforcements arrived, drove the Confederate forces, which had gained an initial victory by a surprise attack, back to their base in Corinth, Mississippi.

on to the kitchen counter, raising her knees one at a time as she talks. She is wearing two-pound ankle weights.

"Don't worry," says Leroy. "I'll do something."

"You could truck calves to slaughter for somebody. You wouldn't have to drive any big old truck for that."

"I'm going to build you this house," says Leroy. "I want to make you a real home."

"I don't want to live in any log cabin."

"It's not a cabin. It's a house."

"I don't care. It looks like a cabin."

"You and me together could lift those logs. It's just like lifting weights."

Norma Jean doesn't answer. Under her breath, she is counting. Now she is marching through the kitchen. She is doing goose steps.

Before his accident, when Leroy came home he used to stay in the house with Norma Jean, watching TV in bed and playing cards. She would cook fried chicken, picnic ham, chocolate pie—all his favorites. Now he is home alone much of the time. In the mornings, Norma Jean disappears, leaving a cooling place in the bed. She eats a cereal called Body Buddies, and she leaves the bowl on the table, with the soggy tan balls floating in a milk puddle. He sees things about Norma Jean that he never realized before. When she chops onions, she stares off into a corner, as if she can't bear to look. She puts on her house slippers almost precisely at nine o'clock every evening and nudges her jogging shoes under the couch. She saves bread heels for the birds. Leroy watches the birds at the feeder. He notices the peculiar way goldfinches fly past the window. They close their wings, then fall, then spread their wings to catch and lift themselves. He wonders if they close their eyes when they fall. Norma Jean closes her eyes when they are in bed. She wants the lights turned out. Even then, he is sure she closes her eyes.

He goes for long drives around town. He tends to drive a car rather carelessly. Power steering and an automatic shift make a car feel so small and inconsequential that his body is hardly involved in the driving process. His injured leg stretches out comfortably. Once or twice he has almost hit something, but even the prospect of an accident seems minor in a car. He curses the new subdivisions, feeling like a criminal rehearsing for a robbery. Norma Jean is probably right about a log house being inappropriate here in the new subdivisions. All the houses look grand and complicated. They depress him.

One day when Leroy comes home from a drive he finds Norma Jean in tears. She is in the kitchen making a potato and mushroom-soup casserole, with grated-cheese topping. She is crying because her mother caught her smoking.

"I didn't hear her coming. I was standing here puffing away pretty as you please," Norma Jean says, wiping her eyes.

"I knew it would happen sooner or later," says Leroy, putting his arm around her.

"She don't know the meaning of the word 'knock,'" says Norma

Jean. "It's a wonder she hadn't caught me years ago."

"Think of it this way," Leroy says. "What if she caught me with a joint?"

"You better not let her!" Norma Jean shrieks. "I'm warning you, Leroy Moffitt!"

"I'm just kidding. Here, play me a tune. That'll help you relax."

Norma Jean puts the casserole in the oven and sets the timer. Then she plays a ragtime tune, with horns and banjo, as Leroy lights up a joint and lies on the couch, laughing to himself about Mabel's catching him at it. He thinks of Stevie Hamilton—a doctor's son pushing grass. Everything is funny. The whole town seems crazy and small. He is reminded of Virgil Mathis, a boastful policeman Leroy used to shoot pool with. Virgil recently led a drug bust in a back room at a bowling alley, where he seized ten thousand dollars' worth of marijuana. The newspaper had a picture of him holding up the bags of grass and grinning widely. Right now, Leroy can imagine Virgil breaking down the door and arresting him with a lungful of smoke. Virgil would probably have been alerted to the scene because of all the racket Norma Jean is making. Now she sounds like a hard-rock band. Norma Jean is terrific. When she switches to a Latin-rhythm version of "Sunshine Superman,"[5] Leroy hums along. Norma Jean's foot goes up and down, up and down.

"Well, what do you think?" Leroy says, when Norma Jean pauses to search through her music.

"What do I think about what?"

His mind has gone blank. Then he says, "I'll sell my rig and build us a house." That wasn't what he wanted to say. He wanted to know what she thought—what she *really* thought—about them.

"Don't start in on that again," says Norma Jean. She begins playing "Who'll Be the Next in Line?"

Leroy used to tell hitchhikers his whole life story—about his travels, his hometown, the baby. He would end with a question: "Well, what do you think?" It was just a rhetorical question. In time, he had the feeling that he'd been telling the same story over and over to the same hitchhikers. He quit talking to hitchhikers when he realized how his voice sounded—whining and self-pitying, like some teenage-tragedy song. Now Leroy has the sudden impulse to tell Norma Jean about himself, as if he had just met her. They have known each other so long they have forgotten a lot about each other. They could become reacquainted. But when the oven timer goes off and she runs to the kitchen, he forgets why he wants to do this.

The next day, Mabel drops by. It is Saturday and Norma Jean is cleaning. Leroy is studying the plans of his log house, which have finally come in the mail. He has them spread out on the table—big sheets of stiff blue paper, with diagrams and numbers printed in white. While Norma Jean runs the vacuum, Mabel drinks coffee. She sets her coffee cup on a blueprint.

5. A 1966 song by Donovan Leitch, best-selling record by "Donovan"; *below*: "Who'll Be Next in Line," also British, 1965, by Ray Davies, best-selling record by The Kinks.

"I'm just waiting for time to pass," she says to Leroy, drumming her fingers on the table.

As soon as Norma Jean switches off the vacuum, Mabel says in a loud voice, "Did you hear about the datsun dog that killed the baby?"

Norma Jean says, "The word is 'dachshund.'"

"They put the dog on trial. It chewed the baby's legs off. The mother was in the next room all the time." She raises her voice. "They thought it was neglect."

Norma Jean is holding her ears. Leroy manages to open the refrigerator and get some Diet Pepsi to offer Mabel. Mabel still has some coffee and she waves away the Pepsi.

"Datsuns are like that," Mabel says. "They're jealous dogs. They'll tear a place to pieces if you don't keep an eye on them."

"You better watch out what you're saying, Mabel," says Leroy.

"Well, facts is facts."

Leroy looks out the window at his rig. It is like a huge piece of furniture gathering dust in the backyard. Pretty soon it will be an antique. He hears the vacuum cleaner. Norma Jean seems to be cleaning the living room rug again.

Later, she says to Leroy, "She just said that about the baby because she caught me smoking. She's trying to pay me back."

"What are you talking about?" Leroy says, nervously shuffling blueprints.

"You know good and well," Norma Jean says. She is sitting in a kitchen chair with her feet up and her arms wrapped around her knees. She looks small and helpless. She says, "The very idea, her bringing up a subject like that! Saying it was neglect."

"She didn't mean that," Leroy says.

"She might not have *thought* she meant it. She always says things like that. You don't know how she goes on."

"But she didn't really mean it. She was just talking."

Leroy opens a king-sized bottle of beer and pours it into two glasses, dividing it carefully. He hands a glass to Norma Jean and she takes it from him mechanically. For a long time, they sit by the kitchen window watching the birds at the feeder.

Something is happening. Norma Jean is going to night school. She has graduated from her six-week body-building course and now she is taking an adult-education course in composition at Paducah Community College. She spends her evenings outlining paragraphs.

"First you have a topic sentence," she explains to Leroy. "Then you divide it up. Your secondary topic has to be connected to your primary topic."

To Leroy, this sounds intimidating. "I never was any good in English," he says.

"It makes a lot of sense."

"What are you doing this for, anyhow?"

She shrugs. "It's something to do." She stands up and lifts her dumbbells a few times.

"Driving a rig, nobody cared about my English."

"I'm not criticizing your English."

Norma Jean used to say, "If I lose ten minutes' sleep, I just drag all day." Now she stays up late, writing compositions. She got a B on her first paper—a how-to theme on soup-based casseroles. Recently Norma Jean has been cooking unusual foods—tacos, lasagna, Bombay chicken. She doesn't play the organ anymore, though her second paper was called "Why Music Is Important to Me." She sits at the kitchen table, concentrating on her outlines, while Leroy plays with his log house plans, practicing with a set of Lincoln Logs. The thought of getting a truckload of notched, numbered logs scares him, and he wants to be prepared. As he and Norma Jean work together at the kitchen table, Leroy has the hopeful thought that they are sharing something, but he knows he is a fool to think this. Norma Jean is miles away. He knows he is going to lose her. Like Mabel, he is just waiting for time to pass.

One day, Mabel is there before Norma Jean gets home from work, and Leroy finds himself confiding in her. Mabel, he realizes, must know Norma Jean better than he does.

"I don't know what's got into that girl," Mabel says. "She used to go to bed with the chickens. Now you say she's up all hours. Plus her a-smoking. I like to died."

"I want to make her this beautiful home," Leroy says, indicating the Lincoln logs. "I don't think she even wants it. Maybe she was happier with me gone."

"She don't know what to make of you, coming home like this."

"Is that it?"

Mabel takes the roof off his Lincoln Log cabin. "You couldn't get *me* in a log cabin," she says. "I was raised in one. It's no picnic, let me tell you."

"They're different now," says Leroy.

"I tell you what," Mabel says, smiling oddly at Leroy.

"What?"

"Take her on down to Shiloh. Y'all need to get out together, stir a little. Her brain's all balled up over them books."

Leroy can see traces of Norma Jean's features in her mother's face. Mabel's worn face has the texture of crinkled cotton, but suddenly she looks pretty. It occurs to Leroy that Mabel has been hinting all along that she wants them to take her with them to Shiloh.

"Let's all go to Shiloh," he says. "You and me and her. Come Sunday."

Mabel throws up her hands in protest. "Oh, no, not me. Young folks want to be by theirselves."

When Norma Jean comes in with groceries, Leroy says excitedly, "Your mama here's been dying to go to Shiloh for thirty-five years. It's about time we went, don't you think?"

"I'm not going to butt in on anybody's second honeymoon," Mabel says.

"Who's going on a honeymoon, for Christ's sake?" Norma Jean says loudly.

"I never raised no daughter of mine to talk that-a-way," Mabel says.

"You ain't seen nothing yet," says Norma Jean. She starts putting away boxes and cans, slamming cabinet doors.

"There's a log cabin at Shiloh," Mabel says. "It was there during the battle. There's bullet holes in it."

"When are you going to *shut up* about Shiloh, Mama?" asks Norma Jean.

"I always thought Shiloh was the prettiest place, so full of history," Mabel goes on. "I just hoped y'all could see it once before I die, so you could tell me about it." Later, she whispers to Leroy, "You do what I said. A little change is what she needs."

"Your name means 'the king,'" Norma Jean says to Leroy that evening. He is trying to get her to go to Shiloh, and she is reading a book about another century.

"Well, I reckon I ought to be right proud."

"I guess so."

"Am I still king around here?"

Norma Jean flexes her biceps and feels them for hardness. "I'm not fooling around with anybody, if that's what you mean," she says.

"Would you tell me if you were?"

"I don't know."

"What does *your* name mean?"

"It was Marilyn Monroe's real name."

"No kidding!"

"Norma comes from the Normans. They were invaders," she says. She closes her book and looks hard at Leroy. "I'll go to Shiloh with you if you'll stop staring at me."

On Sunday, Norma Jean packs a picnic and they go to Shiloh. To Leroy's relief, Mabel says she does not want to come with them. Norma Jean drives, and Leroy, sitting beside her, feels like some boring hitchhiker she has picked up. He tries some conversation, but she answers him in monosyllables. At Shiloh, she drives aimlessly through the park, past bluffs and trails and steep ravines. Shiloh is an immense place, and Leroy cannot see it as a battleground. It is not what he expected. He thought it would look like a golf course. Monuments are everywhere, showing through the thick clusters of trees. Norma Jean passes the log cabin Mabel mentioned. It is surrounded by tourists looking for bullet holes.

"That's not the kind of log house I've got in mind," says Leroy apologetically.

"I know *that*."

"This is a pretty place. Your mama was right."

"It's O.K.," says Norma Jean. "Well, we've seen it. I hope she's satisfied."

They burst out laughing together.

At the park museum, a movie on Shiloh is shown every half hour, but they decide that they don't want to see it. They buy a souvenir Confederate flag for Mabel, and then they find a picnic spot near the cemetery. Norma Jean has brought a picnic cooler, with pimiento sandwiches, soft drinks, and Yodels. Leroy eats a sandwich and then smokes a joint, hiding it behind the picnic cooler. Norma Jean has quit smoking altogether. She is picking cake crumbs from the cellophane wrapper, like a fussy bird.

Leroy says, "So the boys in gray ended up in Corinth. The Union soldiers zapped 'em finally. April 7, 1862."

They both know that he doesn't know any history. He is just talking about some of the historical plaques they have read. He feels awkward, like a boy on a date with an older girl. They are still just making conversation.

"Corinth is where Mama eloped to," says Norma Jean.

They sit in silence and stare at the cemetery for the Union dead and, beyond, at a tall cluster of trees. Campers are parked nearby, bumper to bumper, and small children in bright clothing are cavorting and squealing. Norma Jean wads up the cake wrapper and squeezes it tightly in her hand. Without looking at Leroy, she says, "I want to leave you."

Leroy takes a bottle of Coke out of the cooler and flips off the cap. He holds the bottle poised near his mouth but cannot remember to take a drink. Finally he says, "No, you don't."

"Yes, I do."

"I won't let you."

"You can't stop me."

"Don't do me that way."

Leroy knows Norma Jean will have her own way. "Didn't I promise to be home from now on?" he says.

"In some ways, a woman prefers a man who wanders," says Norma Jean. "That sounds crazy, I know."

"You're not crazy."

Leroy remembers to drink from his Coke. Then he says, "Yes, you *are* crazy. You and me could start all over again. Right back at the beginning."

"We *have* started all over again," says Norma Jean. "And this is how it turned out."

"What did I do wrong?"

"Nothing."

"Is this one of those women's lib things?" Leroy asks.

"Don't be funny."

The cemetery, a green slope dotted with white markers, looks like a subdivision site. Leroy is trying to comprehend that his marriage is breaking up, but for some reason he is wondering about white slabs in a graveyard.

"Everything was fine till Mama caught me smoking," says Norma Jean, standing up. "That set something off."

"What are you talking about?"

"She won't leave me alone—*you* won't leave me alone." Norma Jean seems to be crying, but she is looking away from him. "I feel eighteen again. I can't face that all over again." She starts walking away. "No, it *wasn't* fine. I don't know what I'm saying. Forget it."

Leroy takes a lungful of smoke and closes his eyes as Norma Jean's words sink in. He tries to focus on the fact that thirty-five hundred soldiers died on the grounds around him. He can only think of that war as a board game with plastic soldiers. Leroy almost smiles, as he compares the Confederates' daring attack on the Union camps and Virgil Mathis's raid on the bowling alley. General Grant, drunk and furious, shoved the Southerners back to Corinth, where Mabel and Jet Beasley were married years later, when Mabel was still thin and good-looking. The next day, Mabel and Jet visited the battleground, and then Norma Jean was born, and then she married Leroy and they had a baby, which they lost, and now Leroy and Norma Jean are here at the same battleground. Leroy knows he is leaving out a lot. He is leaving out the insides of history. History was always just names and dates to him. It occurs to him that building a house out of logs is similarly empty—too simple. And the real inner workings of a marriage, like most of history, have escaped him. Now he sees that building a log house is the dumbest idea he could have had. It was clumsy of him to think Norma Jean would want a log house. It was a crazy idea. He'll have to think of something else, quickly. He will wad the blueprints into tight balls and fling them into the lake. Then he'll get moving again. He opens his eyes. Norma Jean has moved away and is walking through the cemetery, following a serpentine brick path.

Leroy gets up to follow his wife, but his good leg is asleep and his bad leg still hurts him. Norma Jean is far away, walking rapidly toward the bluff by the river, and he tries to hobble toward her. Some children run past him, scr aming noisily. Norma Jean has reached the bluff, and she is looking out over the Tennessee River. Now she turns toward Leroy and waves her arms. Is she beckoning to him? She seems to be doing an exercise for her chest muscles. The sky is unusually pale—the color of the dust ruffle Mabel made for their bed.

1982

POETRY

POETRY

1 EXPERIENCING POETRY

People seldom feel neutral about poetry. Those who love it sometimes give the impression that it is an adequate substitute for food, shelter, and love. It isn't. It won't feed you or do your work for you or help you defeat your enemies, and, however satisfying words can be, they are never an equivalent for life itself and its human experiences. Those who dislike poetry on principle sometimes claim, on the other hand, that poetry is only words and good for nothing. That's not true either. It is easy to become frustrated by words—in poetry or in life—but when words represent, express, and recreate genuine human feelings, as they often do in poetry, they can be crucially important. Poetry is, in fact, more than just words. It is an *experience* of words, and those who know how to read poetry can easily extend their experience of life, their sense of what other people are like, and especially their awareness of personal feelings.

Feelings. One reason why poetry can be so important is that it is so intimately concerned with feelings. Poetry is often full of ideas, too, and sometimes poems can be powerful experiences of the mind, but most poems are primarily about how people feel rather than how people think. Poems provide, in fact, a language for feeling, and one of poetry's most insistent virtues involves its attempt to express the inexpressible. How can anyone, for example, put into words what it means to be in love? or what it feels like to lose to death someone one cares about? Poetry tries, and it often captures exactly the shade of emotion that feels just right to the reader. No one poem can be said to express all the things that love or death feels like, or means, but one of the joys of experiencing poetry occurs when we read a poem and want to say, "Yes, that is just what it is like; I know exactly what that line means but I've never been able to express it so well." Poetry can be the mouthpiece of our feelings even when our minds are speechless with grief or joy.

Here are two poems that talk about the sincerity and depth of love between two people. Each is written as if it were spoken or read by one person to his or her lover, and each is definite and powerful about the intensity and quality of love; but the poems work in quite different ways—the first one asserting the strength and depth of love, the second implying intense feeling by reminiscing about events in the relationship between the two people.

whole = more than sum of parts

ELIZABETH BARRETT BROWNING

How Do I Love Thee?

How do I love thee? Let me count the ways.
I love thee to the depth and breadth and height
My soul can reach, when feeling out of sight
For the ends of Being and ideal Grace.
I love thee to the level of every day's   5
Most quiet need, by sun and candlelight.
I love thee freely, as men strive for Right;
I love thee purely, as they turn from Praise;
I love thee with the passion put to use
In my old griefs, and with my childhood's faith.   10
I love thee with a love I seemed to lose
With my lost saints—I love thee with the breath,
Smiles, tears of all my life!—and, if God choose,
I shall but love thee better after death.

1850

JAROLD RAMSEY

The Tally Stick

Here from the start, from our first of days, look:
I have carved our lives in secret on this stick
of mountain mahogany the length of your arms
outstretched, the wood clear red, so hard and rare.
It is time to touch and handle what we know we share.   5

Near the butt, this intricate notch where the grains
converge and join: it is our wedding.
I can read it through with a thumb and tell you now
who danced, who made up the songs, who meant us joy.
These little arrowheads along the grain,   10
they are the births of our children. See,
they make a kind of design with these heavy crosses,
the deaths of our parents, the loss of friends.

Over it all as it goes, of course, I
have chiseled Events, History—random   15
hashmarks cut against the swirling grain.
See, here is the Year the World Went Wrong,
we thought, and here the days the Great Men fell.
The lengthening runes of our lives run through it all.

See, our tally stick is whittled nearly end to end;   20
delicate as scrimshaw, it would not bear you up.

Regrets have polished it, hand over hand.
Yet let us take it up, and as our fingers
like children leading on a trail cry back
our unforgotten wonders, sign after sign,   25
we will talk softly as of ordinary matters,
and in one another's blameless eyes go blind.

p. 1977

The first poem is direct, but fairly abstract. It lists several ways in which the poet feels love and connects them to some noble ideas of higher obligations—to justice (line 7), for example, and to spiritual aspiration (lines 2–4). It suggests a wide range of things that love can mean and notices a variety of emotions. It is an ardent statement of feeling and asserts a permanence that will extend even beyond death. It contains admirable thoughts and memorable phrases that many lovers would like to hear said to themselves. What it does not do is say very much about what the relationship between the two lovers is like on an everyday basis, what experiences they have had together, what distinguishes their relationship from that of other devoted or ideal lovers. Its appeal is to our general sense of what love is like and how intense feelings can be; it does not offer everyday details. Love may differ from person to person and even from moment to moment, and so can poems about love.

The Tally Stick is much more concrete. The whole poem concentrates on a single object that, like the poem above, "counts" or "tallies" the ways in which this couple love one another. The stick stands for their love and becomes a kind of physical reminder of it: its natural features—the notches and arrowheads and cross marks (lines 6, 10, and 12) along with the marks carved on it (lines 15–16, 20–21)—indicate events in the story of the relationship. (We could say that the stick *symbolizes* their love; later on, we will look at a number of terms like this that can be used to make it easier to talk about some aspects of poems, but for now it is enough to notice that the stick serves the lovers as a reminder of some specific details of their love.) It is a special kind of reminder to them because its language is "secret" (line 2), something they can share privately (except that we as readers of the poem are sort of looking over their shoulders, not intruding but sharing their secret). The poet interprets the particular features of the stick as standing for particular events—their wedding and the births of their children, for example—and carves marks into it as reminders of other events (lines 15ff.). The stick itself becomes a very personal object, and in the last stanza of the poem it is as if we watch the lovers touching the stick together and reminiscing over it, gradually dissolving into their emotions and each other as they recall the "unforgotten wonders" (line 25) of their lives together.

Both poems are powerful statements of feelings, each in its own way. Some readers will prefer one and some the other. Personal preference does not mean that objective standards for poetry cannot be found (some poems are better than others, and later we will look in detail at features which help us to evaluate poems), but we need have no preconceived standard that all poetry must be one thing or another or work in one particular way. Some good poems are quite abstract, others quite specific. Any poem that helps us to articulate and clarify human feelings and ideas has a legitimate claim on us as readers. We tend to like poems (or people) for what they do, what they are, and what they represent to us.

Both *How Do I Love Thee* and *The Tally Stick* are written as if they were addressed to the partner in the love relationship, and both talk directly about the intensity of the love. The next poem we will look at talks only indirectly about the quality and intensity of love. It is written as if it were a letter from a woman to her husband who has gone on a long journey on business, and it clearly expresses how much she misses him, but indirectly suggests how much she cares about him.

EZRA POUND

The River-Merchant's Wife: A Letter

(*after Rihaku*[1])

While my hair was still cut straight across my forehead
I played about the front gate, pulling flowers.
You came by on bamboo stilts, playing horse,
You walked about my seat, playing with blue plums.
And we went on living in the village of Chokan: 5
Two small people, without dislike or suspicion.

At fourteen I married My Lord you.
I never laughed, being bashful.
Lowering my head, I looked at the wall.
Called to, a thousand times, I never looked back.   10

At fifteen I stopped scowling,
I desired my dust to be mingled with yours
For ever and for ever and for ever.
Why should I climb the look out?

At sixteen you departed,   15
You went into far Ku-to-yen, by the river of swirling eddies,
And you have been gone five months.
The monkeys make sorrowful noise overhead.

You dragged your feet when you went out.
By the gate now, the moss is grown, the different mosses,   20

1. The Japanese name for Li Po, an 8th-century Chinese poet. Pound's poem is a loose paraphrase of Li Po's.

Too deep to clear them away!
The leaves fall early this autumn, in wind.
The paired butterflies are already yellow with August
Over the grass in the West garden;
They hurt me. I grow older.   25
If you are coming down through the narrows of the river Kiang,
Please let me know beforehand,
And I will come out to meet you
    As far as Cho-fu-Sa.

1915

The "letter" tells us only a few facts about the nameless merchant's wife: that she is about sixteen and a half years old, that she married at fourteen and fell in love with her husband a year later, that she is now very lonely. And about their relationship we know only that they were childhood playmates in a small Chinese village, that their marriage originally was not a matter of personal choice, and that the husband unwillingly went away on a long journey five months ago. But the words tell us a great deal about how the young wife feels, and the simplicity of her language suggests her sincere and deep longing. The daily noises she hears seem "sorrowful" (line 18), and she worries about the dangers of the far-away place where her husband is, thinking of it in terms of its perilous "river of swirling eddies" (line 16). She thinks of how moss has grown up over the unused gate, and more time seems to her to have passed than actually has (lines 22–25). She remembers nostalgically their innocent childhood, when they played together without deeper love or commitment (lines 1–6), and contrasts that with her later satisfaction in their love (lines 11–14) and with her present anxiety, loneliness, and desire. We do not need to know the details of the geography of the river Kiang or how far Cho-fu-Sa is to sense that her wish to see him is very strong, that her desire is powerful enough to make her venture beyond the ordinary geographical bounds of her existence so that their reunion will come sooner. The closest she comes to a direct statement about her love is her statement that she desired that her dust be mingled with his "For ever and for ever and for ever" (lines 12–13). But her single-minded vision of the world, her perception of even the beauty of nature as only a record of her husband's absence and the passage of time, and her plain, apparently uncalculated language about her rejection of other suitors and her shutting out of the rest of the world all show her to be committed, desirous, nearly desperate for his presence. In a different sense, she has also counted the ways that she loves her man.

Here is another poem that similarly expresses a woman's intense desire for her lover, but here the expression is much more openly physical and sexual.

DIANE WAKOSKI

Uneasy Rider[2]

Falling in love with a mustache
is like saying
you can fall in love with
the way a man polishes his shoes
         which,   5
         of course,
         is one of the things that turns on
         my tuned-up engine

         those trim buckled boots

         (I feel like an advertisement   10
           for men's fashions
           when I think of your ankles)

Yeats was hung up with a girl's beautiful face[3]

and I find myself

a bad moralist,   15

a failing aesthetician,

a sad poet,

wanting to touch your arms and feel the muscles
that make a man's body have so much substance,
that makes a woman   20
lean and yearn in that direction
that makes her melt/ she is a rainy day
in your presence
the pool of wax under a burning candle
the foam from a waterfall   25

You are more beautiful than any Harley-Davidson
She is the rain,
waits in it for you,
finds blood spotting her legs
from the long ride.   30

                                  1971

---

2. From Wakoski's volume, *The Motorcycle Betrayal Poems. Easy Rider* was one of the most popular motorcycle films of the late 1960s and early '70s.

3. See, for example, Yeats's "Among School Children," p. 550.

Physical details of the man's body and his clothing are plentiful here, and the woman is very direct about their effects—emotional and physical—upon her as she talks about what "turns on" her "tuned-up engine" (lines 7–8), and how his muscles make her "lean and yearn" and her body "melt" (lines 18–22). So vivid and intense are the various pictures of melting ("a rainy day," "a pool of wax," and "foam from a waterfall") that the poem pulls its focus back a bit from the couple near the end and talks of them as "a man" and "a woman": the woman who is speaking the poem adopts the third-person "she" to distance herself (and us) from the fire and energy of passion.

Poems can, of course, be about the meaning of a relationship or about disappointment just as easily as about sex or emotional fulfillment, and poets are often very good at suggesting the contradictions and uncertainties that tend to affect most relationships. Like other people, poets often find love and its complications quaint or downright funny, too, mainly because it involves human beings who, however serious their intentions and concerns, are often inept, uncertain, and self-contradictory—in short, human. Showing us ourselves as others see us is one of the more useful tasks that poems perform, but the poems that result can be just as entertaining and pleasurable as they are educational. Here is a poem which imagines a very strange scene, a kind of fantasy of what happens when we *think* too much about the implications of sex or love, and it is likely to leave us laughing, whether or not we take it seriously as a statement of human anxiety and of the tendency to intellectualize too much.

TOM WAYMAN

Wayman in Love

At last Wayman gets the girl into bed.
He is locked in one of those embraces
so passionate his left arm is asleep
when suddenly he is bumped in the back.
"Excuse me," a voice mutters, thick with German.   5
Wayman and the girl sit up astounded
as a furry gentleman in boots and a frock coat
climbs in under the covers.

"My name is Doktor Marx," the intruder announces
settling his neck comfortably on the pillow.   10
"I'm here to consider for you the cost of a kiss."
He pulls out a notepad. "Let's see now,
we have the price of the mattress, this room must be rented,
your time off work, groceries for two,
medical fees in case of accidents . . ."   15

"Look," Wayman says,
"couldn't we do this later?"
The philosopher sighs, and continues: "You are affected too,
    Miss.
If you are not working, you are going to resent   20
your dependent position. This will influence
I assure you, your most intimate moments . . ."

"Doctor, please," Wayman says. "All we want
is to be left alone."
But another beard, more nattily dressed,   25
is also getting into the bed.
There is a shifting and heaving of bodies
as everyone wriggles out room for themselves.
"I want you to meet a friend from Vienna,"
Marx says. "This is Doktor Freud."   30

The newcomer straightens his glasses,
peers at Wayman and the girl.
"I can see," he begins,
"that you two have problems . . ."

1973

Another traditional subject of poetry is death, and on this subject,
too, poets often describe frequent, recurrent human emotions in a
variety of ways. In the following poem, a father struggles to understand and control his grief.

BEN JONSON

On My First Son

Farewell, thou child of my right hand,[4] and joy;
My sin was too much hope of thee, loved boy:
Seven years thou'wert lent to me, and I thee pay,
Exacted by thy fate, on the just [5]day.
O could I lose all father now! for why   5
Will man lament the state he should envý,
To have so soon 'scaped world's and flesh's rage,
And, if no other misery, yet age?
Rest in soft peace, and asked, say, "Here doth lie

4. A literal translation of the son's name, Benjamin.
5. Exact; the son died on his seventh birthday, in 1603.

Ben Jonson his[6] best piece of poetry."
For whose sake henceforth all his vows be such
As what he loves may never like too much.

1616

The poem's attempts to rationalize the death are quite conventional, and although the father tries to be comforted by pious thoughts, his feelings keep showing through. The poem's beginning—with its formal "farewell" and the rather distant-sounding address to the dead boy ("child of my right hand")—cannot be sustained for long: both of the first two lines end with bursts of emotion. It is as if the father is trying to explain the death to himself and to keep his emotions under control, but cannot quite manage it. Even the punctuation suggests the way his feelings compete with conventional attempts to put the death into some sort of perspective that will soften the grief, and the comma near the end of each of the first two lines marks a pause that cannot quite hold back the overflowing emotion. But finally the only "idea" that the poem supports is that the father wishes he did not feel so intensely; in the fifth line he fairly blurts that he wishes he could lose his fatherly emotions, and in the final lines he resolves never again to "like" so much that he can be this deeply hurt. Philosophy and religion offer their useful counsels in this poem, but they prove far less powerful than feeling; and rather than drawing some kind of moral about what death means, the poem presents the actuality of feeling as inevitable and nearly all-consuming.

There is much more going on in the poems that we have glanced at than we have taken time to consider, but even the quickest look at these poems suggests something of the range of feelings that poems can offer—the depth of feeling, the clarity, the experience that may be articulately and precisely shared. Later we will look more carefully at *how* these things happen.

6. Ben Jonson's (a common Renaissance form of the possessive).

A Gathering of Poems about Love

THEODORE ROETHKE

I Knew a Woman

I knew a woman, lovely in her bones,
When small birds sighed, she would sigh back at them;
Ah, when she moved, she moved more ways than one:
The shapes a bright container can contain!
Of her choice virtues only gods should speak,   5
Or English poets who grew up on Greek
(I'd have them sing in chorus, cheek to cheek).

How well her wishes went! She stroked my chin,
She taught me Turn, and Counter-turn, and Stand;[1]
She taught me Touch, that undulant white skin;   10
I nibbled meekly from her proffered hand;
She was the sickle; I, poor I, the rake,
Coming behind her for her pretty sake
(But what prodigious mowing we did make).

Love likes a gander, and adores a goose: 15
Her full lips pursed, the errant note to seize;
She played it quick, she played it light and loose;
My eyes, they dazzled at her flowing knees;
Her several parts could keep a pure repose,
Or one hip quiver with a mobile nose   20
(She moved in circles, and those circles moved).

Let seed be grass, and grass turn into hay:
I'm martyr to a motion not my own;
What's freedom for? To know eternity.
I swear she cast a shadow white as stone.   25
But who would count eternity in days?
These old bones live to learn her wanton ways:
(I measure time by how a body sways).

1958

MARGARET ATWOOD

Variation on the Word *Sleep*

I would like to watch you sleeping,
which may not happen.

1. Literary terms for the parts of a Pindaric ode.

368

I would like to watch you,
sleeping. I would like to sleep
with you, to enter   5
your sleep as its smooth dark wave
slides over my head

and walk with you through that lucent
wavering forest of bluegreen leaves
with its watery sun & three moons   10
towards the cave where you must descend,
towards your worst fear

I would like to give you the silver
branch, the small white flower, the one
word that will protect you   15
from the grief at the center
of your dream, from the grief
at the center. I would like to follow
you up the long stairway
again & become   20
the boat that would row you back
carefully, a flame
in two cupped hands
to where your body lies
beside me, and you enter   25
it as easily as breathing in

I would like to be the air
that inhabits you for a moment
only. I would like to be that unnoticed   30
& that necessary.

1981

AUDRE LORDE

Recreation

Coming together
it is easier to work
after our bodies
meet
paper and pen   5
neither care nor profit
whether we write or not
but as your body moves
under my hands,
charged and waiting   10
we cut the leash.
you create me against your thighs

hilly with images
moving through our word countries
my body   15
writes into your flesh
the poem
you make of me.

Touching you I catch midnight
as moon fires set in my throat   20
I love you flesh into blossom
I made you
and take you made
into me.

                                                        1978

WILLIAM SHAKESPEARE

Let Me Not to the Marriage of True Minds

Let me not to the marriage of true minds
Admit impediments.[2] Love is not love
Which alters when it alteration finds,
Or bends with the remover to remove:
Oh, no! it is an ever-fixéd mark,   5
That looks on tempests and is never shaken;
It is the star to every wandering bark,
Whose worth's unknown, although his height be taken.[3]
Love's not Time's fool, though rosy lips and cheeks
Within his bending sickle's compass come;   10
Love alters not with his brief hours and weeks,
But bears it out even to the edge of doom.[4]
If this be error and upon me proved,
I never writ, nor no man ever loved.

                                                        1609

ANONYMOUS

Western Wind

Western wind, when wilt thou blow,
The small rain down can rain?
Christ, if my love were in my arms
And I in my bed again!

ca. 1300   15th century

2. The Marriage Service contained this address to the observers: "If any of you know cause or just impediments why these persons should not be joined together . . .".

3. I.e., measuring the altitude of stars (for purposes of navigation) is not a measurement of value.
4. End of the world.

MARGE PIERCY

To Have Without Holding

Learning to love differently is hard,
love with the hands wide open, love
with the doors banging on their hinges,
the cupboard unlocked, the wind
roaring and whimpering in the rooms   5
rustling the sheets and snapping the blinds
that thwack like rubber bands
in an open palm.

It hurts to love wide open
stretching the muscles that feel   10
as if they are made of wet plaster,
then of blunt knives, then
of sharp knives.

It hurts to thwart the reflexes
of grab, of clutch; to love and let   15
go again and again. It pesters to remember
the lover who is not in the bed,
to hold back what is owed to the work
that gutters like a candle in a cave
without air, to love consciously,   20
conscientiously, concretely, constructively.

I can't do it, you say it's killing
me, but you thrive, you glow
on the street like a neon raspberry,
You float and sail, a helium balloon   25
bright bachelor's button blue and bobbing
on the cold and hot winds of our breath,
as we make and unmake in passionate
diastole and systole the rhythm
of our unbound bonding, to have   30
and not to hold, to love
with minimized malice, hunger
and anger moment by moment balanced.

                                                           1980

SHARON OLDS

Sex Without Love

How do they do it, the ones who make love
without love? Beautiful as dancers,
gliding over each other like ice-skaters
over the ice, fingers hooked

inside each other's bodies, faces
red as steak, wine, wet as the
children at birth whose mothers are going to
give them away) How do they come to the
come to the   come to the   God   come to the
still waters, and not love   10
the one who came there with them, light
rising slowly as steam off their joined
skin? These are the true religious,
the purists, the pros, the ones who will not
accept a false Messiah,) love the   15
priest instead of the God. They do not
mistake the lover for their own pleasure,
they are like great runners: they know they are alone
with the road surface, the cold, the wind,
the fit of their shoes, their over-all cardio-   20
vascular health—just factors, like the partner
in the bed, and not the truth, which is the
single body alone in the universe
against its own best time.

                                                              1984

SIR THOMAS WYATT

They Flee from Me

They flee from me, that sometime did me seek,
With naked foot stalking in my chamber.
I have seen them, gentle, tame, and meek,
That now are wild, and do not remember
That sometime they put themselves in danger   5
To take bread at my hand; and now they range,
Busily seeking with a continual change.

Thankèd be Fortune it hath been otherwise,
Twenty times better; but once in special,
In thin array, after a pleasant guise,   10
When her loose gown from her shoulders did fall,
And she me caught in her arms long and small.[5]
And therewith all sweetly did me kiss
And softly said, "Dear heart, how like you this?"

5. Slender.

It was no dream, I lay broad waking.
But all is turned, thorough[6] my gentleness,
Into a strange fashion of forsaking;
And I have leave to go, of her goodness,
And she also to use newfangleness.[7]
But since that I so kindely[8] am servéd,   20
I fain[9] would know what she hath deservéd.

1557

A Gathering of Poems about Mothers and Fathers

ROBERT CREELEY

Mother's Voice

In these few years
since her death I hear
mother's voice say
under my own, I won't

want any more of that.   5
My cheekbones resonate
with her emphasis. Nothing
of not wanting only

but the distance there from
common fact of others   10
frightens me. I look out
at all this demanding world

and try to put it quietly back,
from me, say, thank you,
I've already had some   15
though I haven't

and would like to
but I've said no, she has,
it's not my own voice anymore.
It's higher as hers was   20

and accommodates too simply
its frustrations when
I at least think I want more
and must have it.

1983

---

6. Through.
7. Fondness for novelty.

8. In a way natural to women.
9. Eagerly.

ROBERT HAYDEN

Those Winter Sundays

in addition to workdays

Sundays too my father got up early
and put his clothes on in the blueblack cold,
then with cracked hands that ached
from labor in the weekday weather made
banked fires blaze. No one ever thanked him.   5

I'd wake and hear the cold splintering, breaking.
When the rooms were warm, he'd call,
and slowly I would rise and dress,
fearing the chronic angers of that house,

Speaking indifferently to him,   10
who had driven out the cold
and polished my good shoes as well. — *for church*
What did I know, what did I know
of love's austere and lonely offices?

1966

D. H. LAWRENCE

Piano

Softly, in the dusk, a woman is singing to me; *move*
Taking me back down the vista of years, till I see
A child sitting under the piano, in the boom of the tingling strings
And pressing the small, poised feet of a mother who smiles as she sings.

In spite of myself, the insidious mastery of song   5
Betrays me back, till the heart of me weeps to belong
To the old Sunday evenings at home, with winter outside
And hymns in the cozy parlor, the tinkling piano our guide.

So now it is vain for the singer to burst into clamor
With the great black piano appassionato. The glamour *appassionato power*   10
Of childish days is upon me, my manhood is cast
Down in the flood of remembrance, I weep like a child for the past.

1918

SYLVIA PLATH

Daddy

You do not do, you do not do
Any more, black shoe
In which I have lived like a foot
For thirty years, poor and white,
Barely daring to breathe or Achoo.   5

Daddy, I have had to kill you.
You died before I had time——
Marble-heavy, a bag full of God,
Ghastly statue with one gray toe
Big as a Frisco seal   10

And a head in the freakish Atlantic
Where it pours bean green over blue
In the waters off beautiful Nauset.[1]
I used to pray to recover you.
Ach, du.[2]   15

In the German tongue, in the Polish town
Scraped flat by the roller
Of wars, wars, wars.
But the name of the town is common.
My Polack friend   20

Says there are a dozen or two.
So I never could tell where you
Put your foot, your root,
I never could talk to you.
The tongue stuck in my jaw.   25

It stuck in a barb wire snare.
Ich, ich, ich, ich,
I could hardly speak.
I thought every German was you.
And the language obscene   30

An engine, an engine
Chuffing me off like a Jew.
A Jew to Dachau, Auschwitz, Belsen.[8]
I began to talk like a Jew.
I think I may well be a Jew.   35

---

1. An inlet on Cape Cod.
2. Literally, "Oh, you" in German.
Plath often portrays herself as Jewish and her oppressors as German.
3. Sites of World War II German death camps.

The snows of the Tyrol,[4] the clear beer of Vienna
Are not very pure or true.
With my gypsy-ancestress and my weird luck
And my Taroc[5] pack and my Taroc pack
I may be a bit of a Jew.   40

German pure race [handwritten]

I have always been scared of *you,*
With your Luftwaffe,[6] your gobbledygoo.
And your neat moustache
And your Aryan eye, bright blue.
Panzer-man, panzer-man, O You—   45

bag full of God [handwritten]

Not God but a swastika
So black no sky could squeak through.
Every woman adores a Fascist,
The boot in the face, the brute
Brute heart of a brute like you.   50

You stand at the blackboard, daddy,
In the picture I have of you,
A cleft in your chin instead of your foot   *devil* [handwritten]
But no less a devil for that, no not
Any less the black man who   55

Bit my pretty red heart in two.
I was ten when they buried you.
At twenty I tried to die
And get back, back, back to you.
I thought even the bones would do   60

imitation [handwritten]

But they pulled me out of the sack,
And they stuck me together with glue.
And then I knew what to do.
I made a model of you,
A man in black with a Meinkampf look   *Hitler — my struggle* [handwritten]   65

And a love of the rack and the screw.   *torture* [handwritten]
And I said I do, I do.   *marriage* [handwritten]
So daddy, I'm finally through.
The black telephone's off at the root,
The voices just can't worm through.   70

communication [handwritten]

If I've killed one man, I've killed two——
The vampire who said he was you   *did same things* [handwritten]
And drank my blood for a year,
Seven years, if you want to know.
Daddy, you can lie back now.   75

---

4. Alpine region in Austria and northern Italy. The snow there is, legendarily,
as pure as the beer is clear in Vienna.
5. A variant of Tarot, playing cards
used mainly for fortune-telling, said to
have been introduced into Europe by gyp-
sies in the 15th century.
6. German air force.

There's a stake in your fat black heart
And the villagers never like you.
They are dancing and stamping on you.
They always *knew* it was you.
Daddy, daddy, you bastard, I'm through.　　　　80

1966

GALWAY KINNELL

After Making Love We Hear Footsteps

For I can snore like a bullhorn
or play loud music
or sit up talking with any reasonably sober Irishman
and Fergus will only sink deeper
into his dreamless sleep, which goes by all in one flash,　　5
but let there be that heavy breathing
or a stifled come-cry anywhere in the house
and he will wrench himself awake
and make for it on the run—as now, we lie together,
after making love, quiet, touching along the length of our bodies,　　10
familiar touch of the long-married,
and he appears—in his baseball pajamas, it happens,
the neck opening so small
he has to screw them on, which one day may make him wonder
about the mental capacity of baseball players—　　15
and says, "Are you loving and snuggling? May I join?"
He flops down between us and hugs us and snuggles himself to sleep,
his face gleaming with satisfaction at being this very child.

In the half darkness we look at each other
and smile　　　　20
and touch arms across his little, startlingly muscled body—
this one whom habit of memory propels to the ground of his making,
sleeper only the mortal sounds can sing awake,
this blessing love gives again into our arms.

1980

2   EXPECTATION AND SURPRISE

Poetry is full of surprises. Poems express anger or outrage just as effectively as love or sadness, and good poems can be written about going to a rock concert or having lunch or cutting the lawn, as well as about making love or gazing at a cloudless sky or smelling flowers. Even poems on "predictable" subjects can surprise us with unpredicted attitudes, unusual events, or a sudden twist. Knowing that a poem is about some particular subject—love, for example, or death—may give us a general idea of what to expect, but it never tells us altogether what we will find in a particular poem. Experiencing a poem fully means being open to the poem and its surprises, being willing to let the poem guide us to its own attitudes, feelings, and ideas. The following two poems—one about death and one about love—are rather different from those we looked at in Chapter 1.

MARGE PIERCY

Barbie Doll

This girlchild was born as usual
and presented dolls that did pee-pee
and miniature GE stoves and irons
and wee lipsticks the color of cherry candy.
Then in the magic of puberty, a classmate said: 5
You have a great big nose and fat legs.

She was healthy, tested intelligent,
possessed strong arms and back,
abundant sexual drive and manual dexterity.
She went to and fro apologizing.   10
Everyone saw a fat nose on thick legs.

She was advised to play coy,
exhorted to come on hearty,
exercise, diet, smile and wheedle.
Her good nature wore out   15
like a fan belt.
So she cut off her nose and her legs
and offered them up.

In the casket displayed on satin she lay
with the undertaker's cosmetics painted on,   20
a turned-up putty nose,
dressed in a pink and white nightie.
Doesn't she look pretty? everyone said.
Consummation at last.
To every woman a happy ending.   25

1973

W. D. SNODGRASS

Leaving the Motel

Outside, the last kids holler
Near the pool: they'll stay the night.
Pick up the towels; fold your collar
Out of sight.

Check: is the second bed   5
Unrumpled, as agreed?
Landlords have to think ahead
In case of need,

Too. Keep things straight: don't take
The matches, the wrong keyrings—   10
We've nowhere we could keep a keepsake—
Ashtrays, combs, things

That sooner or later others
Would accidentally find.
Check: take nothing of one another's   15
And leave behind

Your license number only,
Which they won't care to trace;
We've paid. Still, should such things get lonely,
Leave in their vase   20

An aspirin to preserve
Our lilacs, the wayside flowers
We've gathered and must leave to serve
A few more hours;

That's all. We can't tell when   25
We'll come back, can't press claims;
We would no doubt have other rooms then,
Or other names.

1968

    The first poem has the strong note of sadness that characterizes
many death poems, but its emphasis is not on the response to the girl's
death but on the disappointments in her life. The only "scene" in the
poem (lines 19–23) portrays the unnamed girl at rest in her casket, but
the still body in the casket contrasts not with vitality but with frustration and anxiety: her life since puberty (lines 5–6) had been full of
apologies and attempts to change her physical appearance and emo-

tional makeup. The rest she achieves in death is not, however, a triumph, despite what people say (line 23). Although the poem's last two words are "happy ending" this girl without a name has died in embarrassment and without fulfillment, and the final lines are **ironic**, meaning the opposite of what they say. The cheerful comments at the end lack force and truth because of what we already know; we understand them as ironic because they emphasize how unhappy the girl was and how false her cosmeticized corpse is to the sad truth of her life.

The poem's concern is to suggest the falsity and destructiveness of those standards of beauty which have led to the tragedy of the girl's life. In an important sense, the poem is not really *about* death at all in spite of the fact that the girl's death and her repaired corpse are central to it. As the title suggests, the poem dramatizes how standardized, commercialized notions of femininity and prettiness can be painful and destructive to those whose bodies do not precisely fit the conformist models, and the poem attacks vigorously those conventional standards and the widespread, unthinking acceptance of them.

Leaving the Motel similarly goes in quite a different direction from many poems on the subject of love. Instead of expressing assurance about how love lasts and endures, or about the sincerity and depth of affection, this poem dramatizes a brief sexual encounter. But it does not emphasize sexuality or eroticism in the meeting of the nameless lovers (we see them only as they prepare to leave), nor does it suggest why or how they have found each other, or what either of them is like as a person. Its emphasis is on how careful they must be not to get caught, how exact and calculating they must be in their planning, how finite and limited their encounter must be, how sealed off this encounter is from the rest of their lives. The poem stresses the tiny details the lovers must think of, the agreements they must observe, and the ritual checklist of their duties ("Check . . . Keep things straight . . . Check . . ." lines 5, 9, 15). Affection and sentiment have their small place in the poem (notice the care for the flowers, lines 19–24, and the thought of "pressing claims," line 26), but the emphasis is on temporariness, uncertainty, and limits. The poem is about an illicit, perhaps adulterous sexual encounter, but there is no sex in the poem, only a kind of archeological record of lust.

Labeling a poem as a "love poem" or a "death poem" is primarily a matter of convenience, a grouping based on the **subject matter** in a poem or the event or **topic** it chooses to engage. But as the poems we have been looking at suggest, poems that may be loosely called love poems or death poems may differ widely from one another, express totally different attitudes or ideas, and concentrate on very different aspects of the subject. The main advantages of grouping poems in this way for study is that a reader can become conscious of individual differences: a reading of two poems side by side may suggest how each is distinctive in what it has to say and how it says it.

What a poem has to say is often called its **theme**, the kind of statement it makes about its subject. We could say, for example, that the theme of *Leaving the Motel* is that illicit love is secretive, careful, transitory, and short on emotion and sentiment, or that secret sexual encounters tend to be brief, calculated, and characterized by restrained and insecure feelings. The theme of a poem usually may be expressed in several different ways, and poems often have more than one theme. *Barbie Doll* suggests that commercialized standards destroy human values; that rigid and idealized notions of normalty cripple people who are different; that false standards of appearance and behavior can destroy human beings and lead to personal tragedy; that people are easily and tragically led to accept evaluations thrust upon them by others; that American consumers tend to be conformists, easily influenced in their outlook by advertising and by commercial products; that children who do not conform to middle-class standards and notions don't have a chance. Each of these statements could be demonstrated to be said or implied in the poem and rather central to it. But none of these statements individually nor all of them together would be an adequate substitute for the poem itself. To state the theme in such a brief and abstract way—while it may be helpful in clarifiying what the poem does and does not say—never does justice to the experience of the poem, the way it works on us as readers. Poems affect us in all sorts of ways—emotional and psychological as well as rational—and often a poem's dramatization of a story, an event, or a moment bypasses our rational responses and affects us far more deeply than a clear and logical argument would.

Poems, then, may differ widely from one another even when they share a common subject. And the subjects of poetry also vary widely. It isn't true that there are certain "poetic" subjects and that there are others which aren't appropriate to poetry. Any human activity, any thought or feeling can be the subject of poetry. Poetry often deals with beauty and the softer, more attractive human emotions, but it can deal with ugliness and less attractive human conduct as well, for poetry seeks to mirror human beings and human events, showing us ourselves not only as we'd like to be but as we are. Good poetry gets written about all kinds of topics, in all kinds of forms. This poem, for example, celebrates a famous rock concert.

JONI MITCHELL

Woodstock[1]

I came upon a child of God
He was walking along the road
And I asked him, where are you going
And this he told me
I'm going on down to Yasgur's farm   5
I'm going to join in a rock'n'roll band

---

1. Written after the rock festival there in 1969, celebrating not only the festival but what came to be called the "Woodstock Nation."

I'm going to camp out on the land
And try an' get my soul free
   We are stardust
   We are golden   10
   And we've got to get ourselves
   Back to the garden

Then can I walk beside you
I have come here to lose the smog
And I feel to be a cog in something turning   15
Well maybe it is just the time of year
Or maybe it's the time of man
I don't know who I am
But life is for learning
   We are stardust   20
   We are golden
   And we've got to get ourselves
   Back to the garden

By the time we got to Woodstock
We were half a million strong   25
And everywhere there was song and celebration
And I dreamed I saw the bombers
Riding shotgun in the sky
And they were turning into butterflies
Above our nation   30
   We are stardust
   We are golden
   And we've got to get ourselves
   Back to the garden

1969

This particular poem is also a song. (The lyrics to some songs "work" as poems; others don't because they aren't sufficiently verbal or because their particular effects depend too much on the music that goes with the words.) The account it gives of Woodstock may now seem rather dated in its optimism about transforming, through love and togetherness, the machines of war (lines 27–30), but its ideals of simplicity and peace are stated powerfully. The recurrent idea of returning somehow to an original ideal of innocence (the Garden of Eden) suggests the high aspirations ("stardust") and urgency ("got to") of the sixties' sense of things gone wrong. The mental pictures portray rural simplicity, freedom, the power of united efforts, and the joys of music as an alternative to urban crowding and pollution (line 14), political conflict (lines 27–28), and confusion over personal identity (lines 18–19). The poem's theme—that human beings can, through love and working together, recreate a perfect age of innocence and peace—represents human aspirations at a very high level and does so persuasively and highmindedly, despite the particular details of time and place that anchor the poem to a particular moment in history and a specific experience.

Much less flattering to human nature is this poem about a prison inmate.

ETHERIDGE KNIGHT

Hard Rock Returns to Prison from the Hospital for the Criminal Insane

Hard Rock was "known not to take no shit
From nobody," and he had the scars to prove it:
Split purple lips, lumped ears, welts above
His yellow eyes, and one long scar that cut
Across his temple and plowed through a thick   5
Canopy of kinky hair.

The WORD was that Hard Rock wasn't a mean nigger
Anymore, that the doctors had bored a hole in his head,
Cut out part of his brain, and shot electricity
Through the rest. When they brought Hard Rock back,   10
Handcuffed and chained, he was turned loose,
Like a freshly gelded stallion, to try his new status.
And we all waited and watched, like indians at a corral,
To see if the WORD was true.

As we waited we wrapped ourselves in the cloak   15
Of his exploits: "Man, the last time, it took eight
Screws[2] to put him in the Hole." "Yeah, remember when he
Smacked the captain with his dinner tray?" "He set
The record for time in the Hole—67 straight days!"
"Ol Hard Rock! man, that's one crazy nigger."   20
And then the jewel of a myth that Hard Rock had once bit
A screw on the thumb and poisoned him with syphilitic spit.

The testing came, to see if Hard Rock was really tame.
A hillbilly called him a black son of a bitch
And didn't lose his teeth, a screw who knew Hard Rock   25
From before shook him down and barked in his face.
And Hard Rock did *nothing*. Just grinned and looked silly,
His eyes empty like knot holes in a fence.

2. Guards. "Hole": solitary confinement.

And even after we discovered that it took Hard Rock
Exactly 3 minutes to tell you his first name,   30
We told ourselves that he had just wised up,
Was being cool; but we could not fool ourselves for long,
And we turned away, our eyes on the ground. Crushed.
He had been our Destroyer, the doer of things
We dreamed of doing but could not bring ourselves to do,   35
The fears of years, like a biting whip,
Had cut grooves too deeply across our backs.

1968

The picture of Hard Rock as a kind of hero to other prison in-
mates is established early in the poem through a retelling of the
legends circulated about him; the straightforward chronology of the
poem sets up the mystery of how he will react after his "treatment"
in the hospital. The poem identifies with those who wait; they are
hopeful that Hard Rock's spirit has not been broken by surgery or shock
treatments, and the lines crawl almost to a stop with disappointment
in stanza four. The "nothing" (line 27) of Hard Rock's response to
teasing and taunting and the emptiness of his eyes ("like knot holes
in a fence," line 28) reduce the heroic hopes and illusions to despair.
The final stanza recounts the observers' attempts to reinterpret, to hang
onto hope that their symbol of heroism could stand up against the
best efforts to tame him, but the spirit has gone out of the hero-
worshipers too, and the poem records them as beaten, conformed,
deprived of their spirit as Hard Rock has been of his. The poem
records the despair of the hopeless and it protests against the exercise
of power that can curb even as rebellious a figure as Hard Rock.

The following poem is equally full of anger and disappointment,
but it uses a kind of playfulness with words to make the seriousness of
the situation seem all the more relentless.

WILLIAM BLAKE

London

I wander through each chartered street,
Near where the chartered Thames does flow,
And mark in every face I meet
Marks of weakness, marks of woe.

In every cry of every man,   5
In every Infant's cry of fear,
In every voice, in every ban,
The mind-forged manacles I hear.

How the Chimney-sweeper's cry
Every black'ning Church appalls;   10
And the hapless Soldier's sigh
Runs in blood down Palace walls.

But most through midnight streets I hear
How the youthful Harlot's curse
Blasts the new-born Infant's tear,   15
And blights with plagues the Marriage hearse.

1794

The poem gives a strong sense of how London feels to this particular observer; it is cluttered, constricting, oppressive. The wordplay here articulates and connects the strong emotions he associates with London experiences. The repeated words—"every," for example, or "cry"—intensify the sense of total despair in the city and weld connections between things not necessarily related—the cries of street vendors, for example, with the cries for help. The word "chartered" implies strong feelings too, and the word gives a particularly rigid sense of streets. Instead of seeming alive with people or bustling with movement, they are rigidly, coldly determined, controlled, cramped. And the same word is used for the river, as if it too were planned, programed, laid out by an oppressor. In fact, the course of the Thames had been altered (slightly) by the government before Blake's time, but most important is the word's emotional force, the sense it projects of constriction and artificiality: the person speaking experiences London as if human artifice had totally altered nature. According to the poem, people are victimized too, "marked" by their confrontations with urbanness and the power of institutions: the "soldier's sigh" that "runs in blood down Palace walls" vividly suggests, through a metaphor that visually dramatizes the speaker's feelings, both the powerlessness of the individual and the callousness of power. The "description" of the city has clearly become, by now, a subjective, highly emotional, and vivid expression of how the speaker feels about London and what it represents to him.

One more thing about *London:* at first it looks like an account of a personal experience, as if the speaker is describing and interpreting as he goes along: "I wander through each chartered street." But soon it is clear that he is describing many wanderings, putting together impressions from many walks, recreating a generalized or typical walk—which shows him "every" person in the streets, allows him to generalize about the churches being "appalled" (literally, made white) by the cry of the representative Chimney-sweeper, and presents his conclusions about soldiers, prostitutes, and infants. What we are given is not a personal record of an event, but a re-presentation of it, as it seems in the mind in retrospect—not a story, not a narrative or chronological account of events, but a dramatization of self that compresses many experiences into one.

The **tone** of *London* is somber in spite of the poet's playfulness with words. Wordplay may be witty and funny if it calls attention to its own cleverness, but here it involves the discovery of unsuspected (but meaningful) connections between things. The term **tone** is used to describe the attitude the poem takes toward its subject and theme. If the theme of a poem is *what* the poem says, the tone involves *how* one says it. The "how" involves feelings, attitudes that are expressed by how one says the words. The tone of *London* is sad, despairing, and angry; reading *London* aloud, one would try to show in one's voice the strong feelings that the poem expresses, just as one would try to reproduce tenderness and caring in reading aloud *The Tally Stick* or *How Do I Love Thee*.

Subject, theme, and tone. Each of these categories gives us a way to begin considering poems and showing how one poem differs from another. Comparing poems on the same subject, or with a similar theme or tone, can lead to a clearer understanding of each individual poem and can refine our responses to the subtleties of individual differences. The title of a poem (*Leaving the Motel*, for example) or the way the poem first introduces its subject often can give us a sense of what to expect, but we need to be open to surprise too. No two poems are going to be exactly alike in their effect on us; the variety of possible poems multiplies when you think of all the possible themes and tones that can be explored within any single subject. Varieties of feeling often coincide with varieties of thinking, and readers open to the pleasures of the unexpected may find themselves learning, growing, becoming more sensitive to ideas and human issues as well as more articulate about feelings and thoughts they already have.

The following two poems might be said to be about animals, although both of them place their final emphasis on what human beings are like: the animal in each case is only the means to the end of exploring human nature. The poems share a common assumption that animals reflect human habits and conduct and may reveal much about ourselves, and in each case the woman central to the poem is revealed to be surprisingly unlike the way she thinks of herself. But the poems are very different from one another. As you read them, see if you can think of appropriate words to describe the main character and to indicate the right tone of voice to use in reading each poem.

MAXINE KUMIN

Woodchucks

Gassing the woodchucks didn't turn out right.
The knockout bomb from the Feed and Grain Exchange
was featured as merciful, quick at the bone
and the case we had against them was airtight,
both exits shoehorned shut with puddingstone,[3]   5
but they had a sub-sub-basement out of range.

3. A mixture of cement, pebbles, and gravel: a conglomerate.

Next morning they turned up again, no worse
for the cyanide than we for our cigarettes
and state-store Scotch, all of us up to scratch.
They brought down the marigolds as a matter of course   10
and then took over the vegetable patch
nipping the broccoli shoots, beheading the carrots.

The food from our mouths, I said, righteously thrilling
to the feel of the .22, the bullets' neat noses.
I, a lapsed pacifist fallen from grace   15
puffed with Darwinian pieties for killing,
now drew a bead on the littlest woodchuck's face.
He died down in the everbearing roses.

Ten minutes later I dropped the mother. She
flipflopped in the air and fell, her needle teeth   20
still hooked in a leaf of early Swiss chard.
Another baby next. O one-two-three
the murderer inside me rose up hard,
the hawkeye killer came on stage forthwith.

There's one chuck left. Old wily fellow, he keeps   25
me cocked and ready day after day after day.
All night I hunt his humped-up form. I dream
I sight along the barrel in my sleep.
If only they'd all consented to die unseen
gassed underground the quiet Nazi way.   30

1972

ADRIENNE RICH

Aunt Jennifer's Tigers

Aunt Jennifer's tigers prance across a screen,
Bright topaz denizens of a world of green.
They do not fear the men beneath the tree;
They pace in sleek chivalric certainty.

Aunt Jennifer's fingers fluttering through her wool   5
Find even the ivory needle hard to pull.
The massive weight of Uncle's wedding band
Sits heavily upon Aunt Jennifer's hand.

When Aunt is dead, her terrified hands will lie
Still ringed with ordeals she was mastered by.   10
The tigers in the panel that she made
Will go on prancing, proud and unafraid.

1951

How would your tone of voice change if you read *Woodchucks* aloud from beginning to end? What tone would you use to read the ending? How does the hunter feel about her increasing attraction to violence? Why does the poem begin by calling the gassing of the woodchucks "merciful" and end by describing it as "the quiet Nazi way"? What names does the hunter call herself? How does the name-calling affect your feelings about her? Exactly when does the hunter begin to *enjoy* the feel of the gun and the idea of killing? How does the poet make that clear?

Why are tigers a particularly appropriate contrast to the quiet and subdued manner of Aunt Jennifer? What words used to describe the tigers seem particularly significant? In what ways is the tiger an opposite of Aunt Jennifer? In what ways does it externalize her secrets? Why are Aunt Jennifer's hands described as "terrified"? What clues does the poem give about why Aunt Jennifer is so afraid? How does the poem make you feel about Aunt Jennifer? about her tigers? about her life? How would you describe the tone of the poem? How does the poet feel about Aunt Jennifer?

Twenty years after writing *Aunt Jennifer's Tigers*, Adrienne Rich said this about the poem:

> In writing this poem, composed and apparently cool as it is, I thought I was creating a portrait of an imaginary woman. But this woman suffers from the opposition of her imagination, worked out in tapestry, and her life style, "ringed with ordeals she was mastered by." It was important to me that Aunt Jennifer was a person as distinct from myself as possible—distanced by the formalism of the poem, by its objective, observant tone—even by putting the woman in a different generation. In those years formalism was part of the strategy—like asbestos gloves, it allowed me to handle materials I couldn't pick up bare-handed.[4]

Not often do we have such an explicit comment on a poem by its author, and we don't actually have to have it to understand and experience the force of the poem (although such a statement may clarify why the author chose particular modes of presentation and how the poem fits into the author's own patterns of thinking and growing). Most poems contain within them what we need to know in order to tap the human and artistic resources they offer us.

In the chapters that follow we will look at various technical aspects of poetry, considering how poems are put together and what sorts of things we need to know in order to read well, that is, how to experience sensitively and fully other poems you may want to read later. Not all poems are as accessible as those we've looked at so far, and even the ones that are accessible usually yield themselves to us more readily and more completely if we approach them systematically by developing specific reading habits and skills—just as someone learning to play tennis systematically learns the rules, the techniques, the things to

4. In *When We Dead Awaken: Writing as Re-Vision*, a talk given in December, 1971, at the Women's Forum of the Modern Language Association.

watch out for that are distinctive to the pleasures and hazards of that skill or craft. It helps if you know what to expect, and the chapters that follow will help you to an understanding of the things that poets can do—and thus to what poems can do for you.

But knowing what to expect isn't everything, and I have one bit of advice to offer every prospective reader of poetry before going any further: Be open. Be open to new experience, be open to new feelings, be open to new ideas. Every poem in the world is a potential new experience, and no matter how sophisticated you become, you can still be surprised (and delighted) by new poems—and by rereading old ones. Good poems bear many, many rereadings, and often one discovers something new with every new reading. Be willing to let poems surprise you when you come to them; let them come on their own terms, let them be themselves. If you are open to poetry, you are open to much that the world can offer you.

No one can give you a method that will offer you total experience of all poems. But because many characteristics of an individual poem are characteristics that one poem shares with other poems, there are guidelines which can prompt you to ask the right questions. The chapters that follow will help you in detail with a variety of problems, but meanwhile here is a checklist of some things to remember:

1. *Identify the poem's situation.* What is said is often conditioned by where it is said and by whom. Identifying the speaker and his or her place in the situation puts what he or she says in perspective.

2. *Read the syntax literally.* What the words say literally in normal sentences is only a starting point, but it is the place to start. Not all poems use normal prose syntax, but most of them do, and you can save yourself embarrassment by paraphrasing accurately (that is, rephrasing what the poem literally says, in plain prose) and not simply free-associating from an isolated word or phrase.

3. *Articulate for yourself what the title, subject, and situation make you expect.* Poets often use false leads and try to surprise you by doing shocking things, but defining expectation lets you be conscious of where you are when you begin.

4. *Be willing to be surprised.* Things often happen in poems that turn them around. A poem may seem to suggest one thing at first, then persuade you to its opposite, or at least to a significant qualification or variation.

5. *Find out what is implied by the traditions behind the poem.* Verse forms, poetic kinds, and metrical patterns all have a frame of reference, traditions of the way they are usually used and for what. For example, the anapest is usually used for comic poems, and if a poet uses it "straight" he is aware of his "departure" and is probably making a point by doing it.

6. *Remember that poems exist in time, and times change.* Not only the meanings of words, but whole ways of looking at the universe and man's role vary in different ages. Consciousness of time works two ways: your knowledge of history provides a context for reading the poem, and the poem's *use* of a word or idea may modify your notion of a particular age.

7. *Bother the reference librarian.* Look up anything you don't understand: an unfamiliar word (or an ordinary word used in an unfamiliar way), a place, a person, a myth, an idea—anything the poem uses. When you can't find what you need or don't know where to look, ask for help.

8. *Take a poem on its own terms.* Adjust to the poem; don't make the poem adjust to you. Be prepared to hear things you do not want to hear. Not all poems are about your ideas, nor will they always present emotions you want to feel. But be tolerant and listen to the poem's ideas, not only to your desire to revise them for yourself.

9. *Argue.* Discussion usually results in clarification and keeps you from being too dependent on personal biases and preoccupations which sometimes mislead even the best readers. Talking a poem over with someone else (especially someone very different) can expand the limits of a too narrow perspective.

10. *Assume there is a reason for everything.* Poets do make mistakes, but in poems that show some degree of verbal control it is usually safest to assume that the poet chose each word carefully; if the choice seems peculiar to us, it is usually *we* who are missing something. Craftsmanship obliges us to try to account for the specific choices and only settle for conclusions of ineptitude if no hypothetical explanation will make sense.

What *is* poetry? Let your definition be cumulative as you read the poems in this book. No dictionary definition will cover all that you find, and it is better to discover for yourself poetry's many ingredients, its many effects, its many ways of acting. What can it do for you? Wait and see. Begin to add up its effects after you have read carefully —after you have studied and reread—a hundred or so poems; that will be a beginning, and you will be able to add to that total as long as you continue to read new poems or reread old ones.

A Gathering of Poems about Animals

EMILY DICKINSON

A Narrow Fellow in the Grass

A narrow Fellow in the Grass
Occasionally rides—
You may have met Him—did you not
His notice sudden is—

The Grass divides as with a Comb— 5
A spotted shaft is seen—
And then it closes at your feet
And opens further on—

He likes a Boggy Acre
A Floor too cool for Corn— 10
Yet when a Boy, and Barefoot—
I more than once at Noon

Have passed, I thought, a Whip lash
Unbraiding in the Sun
When stooping to secure it 15
It wrinkled, and was gone—

Several of Nature's People
I know, and they know me—
I feel for them a transport
Of cordiality— 20

But never met this Fellow
Attended, or alone
Without a tighter breathing
And Zero at the Bone—

1866

EDWARD THOMAS

The Owl

Downhill I came, hungry, and yet not starved;
Cold, yet had heat within me that was proof
Against the North wind; tired, yet so that rest
Had seemed the sweetest thing under a roof.

Then at the inn I had food, fire, and rest, 5
Knowing how hungry, cold, and tired was I.
All of the night was quite barred out except
An owl's cry, a most melancholy cry

Shaken out long and clear upon the hill,
No merry note, nor cause of merriment, 10
But one telling me plain what I escaped
And others could not, that night, as in I went.

And salted was my food, and my repose,
Salted and sobered, too, by the bird's voice
Speaking for all who lay under the stars, 15
Soldiers and poor, unable to rejoice.

1917

OGDEN NASH

The Chipmunk

My friends all know that I am shy,
But the chipmunk is twice as shy as I.
He moves with flickering indecision
Like stripes across the television.
He's like the shadow of a cloud,   5
Or Emily Dickinson read aloud.
Yet his ultimate purpose is obvious, very:
To get back to his chipmonastery.

1953

WILLIAM STAFFORD

Traveling through the Dark

Traveling through the dark I found a deer
dead on the edge of the Wilson River road.
It is usually best to roll them into the canyon:
that road is narrow; to swerve might make more dead.

By glow of the tail-light I stumbled back of the car   5
and stood by the heap, a doe, a recent killing;
she had stiffened already, almost cold.
I dragged her off; she was large in the belly.

My fingers touching her side brought me the reason—
her side was warm; her fawn lay there waiting,   10
alive, still, never to be born.
Beside that mountain road I hesitated.

The car aimed ahead its lowered parking lights;
under the hood purred the steady engine.
I stood in the glare of the warm exhaust turning red;   15
around our group I could hear the wilderness listen.

I thought hard for us all—my only swerving—,
then pushed her over the edge into the river.

1962

ALAN DUGAN

Funeral Oration for a Mouse

This, Lord, was an anxious brother and
a living diagram of fear: full of health himself,
    he brought diseases like a gift
to give his hosts. Masked in a cat's moustache
    but sounding like a bird, he was a ghost   5
    of lesser noises and a kitchen pest
for whom some ladies stand on chairs. So,
Lord, accept our felt though minor guilt
    for an ignoble foe and ancient sin:
        the murder of a guest   10
    who shared our board: just once he ate
        too slowly, dying in our trap
from necessary hunger and a broken back.

Humors of love aside, the mousetrap was our own
    opinion of the mouse, but for the mouse   15
        it was the tree of knowledge with
        its consequential fruit, the true cross
    and the gate of hell. Even to approach
        it makes him like or better than
    its maker: his courage as a spoiler never once   20
impressed us, but to go out cautiously at night,
    into the dining room—what bravery, what
        hunger! Younger by far, in dying he
    was older than us all: his mobile tail and nose
    spasmed in the pinch of our annoyance. Why,   25
then, at that snapping sound, did we, victorious,
        begin to laugh without delight?

        Our stomachs, deep in an analysis
            of their own stolen baits
(and asking, "Lord, Host, to whom are we the pests?"),   30
    contracted and demanded a retreat
    from our machine and its effect of death,
        as if the mouse's fingers, skinnier
    than hairpins and as breakable as cheese,
        could grasp our grasping lives, and in   35
    their drowning movement pull us under too,
into the common death beyond the mousetrap.

                                            1961

GALWAY KINNELL

Saint Francis and the Sow

The bud
stands for all things,
even for those things that don't flower,
for everything flowers, from within, of self-blessing;
though sometimes it is necessary   5
to reteach a thing its loveliness,
to put a hand on its brow
of the flower
and retell it in words and in touch
it is lovely   10
until it flowers again from within, of self-blessing;
as Saint Francis[1]
put his hand on the creased forehead
of the sow, and told her in words and in touch
blessings of earth on the sow, and the sow   15
began remembering all down her thick length,
from the earthen snout all the way
through the fodder and slops to the spiritual curl of the tail,
from the hard spininess spiked out from the spine
down through the great broken heart   20
to the blue milken dreaminess spurting and shuddering
from the fourteen teats into the fourteen mouths sucking and blowing
        beneath them:
the long, perfect loveliness of sow.

                                                                     1980

---

1. St. Francis of Assisi, thirteenth-century founder of the Franciscan Order, was famous for his love of all living things, and, according to legend, sometimes preached to "congregations" of animals.

3   SPEAKER

Poems are personal. The thoughts and feelings they express belong to a specific person, and however "universal" or general their sentiments seem to be, poems come to us as the expression of a human voice—an individual voice. That voice is often the voice of the poet. But not always. Poets sometimes create a "character" just as writers of fiction or drama do—people who speak for them only indirectly. A character may, in fact, be very different from the poet, just as a character in a play or story is different from the author, and that person, the **speaker** of the poem, may express ideas or feelings very different from the poet's own. In the following poem, *two* individual voices in fact speak, and it is clear that, rather than himself speaking directly to us, the poet has chosen to create two speakers, each of whom has a distinctive voice.

THOMAS HARDY

The Ruined Maid

"O 'Melia,[1] my dear, this does everything crown!
Who could have supposed I should meet you in Town?
And whence such fair garments, such prosperi-ty?"—
"O didn't you know I'd been ruined?" said she.

—"You left us in tatters, without shoes or socks,   5
Tired of digging potatoes, and spudding up docks;[2]
And now you've gay bracelets and bright feathers three!"—
"Yes: that's how we dress when we're ruined," said she.

—"At home in the barton[3] you said 'thee' and 'thou,'
And 'thik oon,' and 'theäs oon,' and 't'other'; but now   10
Your talking quite fits 'ee for high compa-ny!"—
"Some polish is gained with one's ruin," said she.

—"Your hands were like paws then, your face blue and bleak
But now I'm bewitched by your delicate cheek,
And your little gloves fit as on any la-dy!"—   15
"We never do work when we're ruined," said she.

—"You used to call home-life a hag-ridden dream,
And you'd sigh, and you'd sock;[4] but at present you seem
To know not of megrims[5] or melancho-ly!"—
"True. One's pretty lively when ruined," said she.   20

1. Short for Amelia.
2. Spading up weeds.
3. Farmyard.

4. Deliver angry blows.
5. Migraine headaches.

—"I wish I had feathers, a fine sweeping gown,
And a delicate face, and could strut about Town!"—
"My dear—a raw country girl, such as you be,
Cannot quite expect that. You ain't ruined," said she.
1866

The first voice, that of the sister who has stayed home, is designated typographically (that is, by the way the poem is printed):
there are dashes at the beginning and end of each of her speeches.
The second sister regularly gets the last line in each stanza (and in
the last stanza, two lines), so it is easy to tell who is talking at every
point. Also, the two speakers are just as clearly distinguished by what
they say, how they say it, and what sort of person each proves to be.
The nameless stay-at-home shows little knowledge of the world, and
everything surprises her: seeing her sister at all, but especially seeing
her well clothed, cheerful, and polished; and as the poem develops
she shows increasing envy of her more worldly sister. She is the "raw
country girl" (line 23) that her sister says she is, and she still speaks
the country dialect ("fits 'ee," line 11, for example) that she notices
her sister has lost (lines 9–11). The "ruined" sister ('Melia), on the
other hand, says little except to keep repeating the refrain about
having been ruined, but even the slight variations she plays on that
theme suggest her sophistication and amusement at her countrified
sister, although she still uses a rural "ain't" at the end. We are not
told the full story of their lives (was the ruined sister thrown out?
did she run away from home?), but we know enough (that they've
been separated for some time, that the stay-at-home did not know
where her sister had gone) to allow the dialogue to articulate the
contrast between them. The style of speech of each speaker then does
the rest.

It is equally clear that there is a speaker (or, in this case, actually
a singer) in stanzas two through nine of this poem:

X. J. KENNEDY

In a Prominent Bar in Secaucus One Day

*To the tune of "The Old Orange Flute" or
the tune of "Sweet Betsy from Pike"*

In a prominent bar in Secaucus[6] one day
Rose a lady in skunk with a topheavy sway,
Raised a knobby red finger—all turned from their beer—
While with eyes bright as snowcrust she sang high and clear:

6. A small, smoggy town on the Hackensack River in New Jersey, a few miles west
of Manhattan.

"Now who of you'd think from an eyeload of me   5
That I once was a lady as proud as could be?
Oh I'd never sit down by a tumbledown drunk
If it wasn't, my dears, for the high cost of junk.

"All the gents used to swear that the white of my calf
Beat the down of a swan by a length and a half   10
In the kerchief of linen I caught to my nose
Ah, there never fell snot, but a little gold rose.

"I had seven gold teeth and a toothpick of gold,
My Virginia cheroot was a leaf of it rolled
And I'd light it each time with a thousand in cash—   15
Why the bums used to fight if I flicked them an ash.

"Once the toast of the Biltmore,[7] the belle of the Taft,
I would drink bottle beer at the Drake, never draft,
And dine at the Astor on Salisbury steak
With a clean tablecloth for each bite I did take.   20

"In a car like the Roxy[8] I'd roll to the track,
A steel-guitar trio, a bar in the back,
And the wheels made no noise, they turned over so fast,
Still it took you ten minutes to see me go past.

"When the horses bowed down to me that I might choose,   25
I bet on them all, for I hated to lose.
Now I'm saddled each night for my butter and eggs
And the broken threads race down the backs of my legs.

"Let you hold in mind, girls, that your beauty must pass
Like a lovely white clover that rusts with its grass.   30
Keep your bottoms off barstools and marry you young
Or be left—an old barrel with many a bung.

"For when time takes you out for a spin in his car
You'll be hard-pressed to stop him from going too far
And be left by the roadside, for all your good deeds,   35
Two toadstools for tits and a face full of weeds."

All the house raised a cheer, but the man at the bar
Made a phonecall and up pulled a red patrol car
And she blew us a kiss as they copped her away
From that prominent bar in Secaucus, N.J.   40

                                                           1961

Again, we learn about the character primarily through her own words, although we don't have to believe everything she tells us about her past. From her introduction in the first stanza we get some general notion of her appearance and condition, but it is she who tells us that she is a junkie (line 8), a prostitute (line 27), and that her face and figure are pretty well shot (lines 32, 36). That information could make her a sad case, and the poem might lament her state or allow her to lament it, but instead the poem presents her cheerfully. She is anxious to give advice and sound moralistic (line 31, for example), but she's also enormously cheerful about herself, and her spirit repeatedly bursts through her song. Her performance gives her a lot of pleasure as she exaggerates outrageously about her former luxury and prominence, and even her departure in a patrol car she chooses to treat as a grand exit, throwing a kiss to her audience. The comedy is bittersweet, perhaps, but she is allowed to present herself, through her own words and attitudes, as a likable character. The glorious fiction of her life, narrated with energy and polish in the manner of a practiced and accomplished liar, betrays some rather naive notions of good taste and luxurious living (lines 18–26). But this "lady in skunk" has a picturesque and engaging style, a refreshing sense of humor about herself, and (like the cheap fur she wears) her experiences in what she considers high life satisfy her sense of style and drama. The self-portrait accumulates, almost completely through how she talks about herself, and the poet develops our attitude toward her by allowing her to recount her story herself, in her own words—or rather in words chosen for her by the author.

It is, of course, equally possible to create a speaker who makes us dislike himself or herself, also because of what the poet makes him or her say, as the following poem does. Here the speaker, as the title implies, is a monk, but he shows himself to be most unmonklike: mean, self-righteous, and despicable.

ROBERT BROWNING

Soliloquy of the Spanish Cloister[9]

Gr-r-r—there go, my heart's abhorrence!
    Water your damned flower-pots, do!
If hate killed men, Brother Lawrence,
    God's blood, would not mine kill you!
What? your myrtle-bush wants trimming?   5
    Oh, that rose has prior claims—
Needs its leaden vase filled brimming?
    Hell dry you up with its flames!

---

9. Monastery.

At the meal we sit together:
 Salve tibi![1] I must hear   10
Wise talk of the kind of weather,
 Sort of season, time of year:
Not a plenteous cork-crop: scarcely
 Dare we hope oak-galls,[2] *I doubt:*
What's the Latin name for "parsley"? 15
 What's the Greek name for Swine's Snout?

Whew! We'll have our platter burnished,
 Laid with care on our own shelf!
With a fire-new spoon we're furnished,
 And a goblet for ourself,   20
Rinsed like something sacrificial
 Ere 'tis fit to touch our chaps[3]—
Marked with L. for our initial!
 (He-he! There his lily snaps!)

Saint, forsooth! While brown Dolores 25
 Squats outside the Convent bank
With Sanchicha, telling stories,
 Steeping tresses in the tank,
Blue-black, lustrous, thick like horsehairs,
 —Can't I see his dead eye glow,   30
Bright as 'twere a Barbary corsair's?[4]
 (That is, if he'd let it show!)

When he finishes refection,[5]
 Knife and fork he never lays
Cross-wise, to my recollection,   35
 As do I, in Jesu's praise.
I the Trinity illustrate,
 Drinking watered orange-pulp—
In three sips the Arian[6] frustrate;
 While he drains his at one gulp.   40

Oh, those melons? If he's able
 We're to have a feast! so nice!
One goes to the Abbot's table,
 All of us get each a slice.
How go on your flowers? None double? 45
 Not one fruit-sort can you spy?
Strange!—And I, too, at such trouble,
 Keep them close-nipped on the sly!

---

1. Hail to thee. Italics usually indicate the words of Brother Lawrence.
2. Abnormal growth on oak trees, used for tanning.
3. Jaws.
4. African pirate's.
5. A meal.
6. A heretical sect which denied the Trinity.

There's a great text in Galatians,[7]
  Once you trip on it, entails   50
Twenty-nine distinct damnations,
  One sure, if another fails:
If I trip him just a-dying,
  Sure of heaven as sure can be,
Spin him round and send him flying   55
  Off to hell, a Manichee?[8]

Or, my scrofulous French novel
  On gray paper with blunt type!
Simply glance at it, you grovel
  Hand and foot in Belial's gripe:[9]   60
If I double down its pages
  At the woeful sixteenth print,
When he gathers his greengages,
  Ope a sieve and slip it in't?

Or, there's Satan!—one might venture   65
  Pledge one's soul to him, yet leave
Such a flaw in the indenture
  As he'd miss till, past retrieve,
Blasted lay that rose-acacia
  We're so proud of! *Hy, Zy, Hine* . . .[1]   70
'St, there's Vespers! *Plena gratiâ*
  Ave, Virgo.[2] Gr-r-r—you swine!

                           1842

Not many poems begin with a growl, and in this one it turns out to be fair warning that we are about to get to know a real beast, even though he is in the clothing of a religious man. In line 1, he has already shown himself to hold a most uncharitable attitude toward his fellow monk, Brother Lawrence, and by line 4 he has uttered two profanities and admitted his intense feelings of hatred and vengefulness. His ranting and roaring is full of exclamation points (four in the first stanza), and he reveals his own personality and character when he imagines curses and unflattering nicknames for Brother Lawrence or plots malicious jokes on him. By the end, we have accumulated no knowledge of Brother Lawrence that makes him seem a fit target for such rage (except that he is pious, dutiful, and pleasant—perhaps enough to make this sort of speaker despise him), but we have discovered the speaker to be lecherous (stanza 4), full of false piety (stanza 5), malicious in trivial matters (stanza 6),

7. "Cursed is every one that continueth not in all things which are written in the book of law to do them," *Galatians* 3:10. *Galatians* 5:15–23 provides a long list of possible offenses, but they do not add up to 29.

8. A heretic. According to the Manichean heresy, the world was divided into the forces of good and evil, equally powerful.

9. In the clutches of Satan.

1. Possibly the beginning of an incantation or curse.

2. The opening words of the *Ave Maria,* here reversed: "Full of grace, Hail, Virgin."

ready to use his theological learning to sponsor damnation rather than salvation (stanza 7), a closet reader and viewer of pornography within the monastery (stanza 8)—even willing to risk his own soul in order to torment Brother Lawrence (last stanza). The speaker is made to characterize himself; the details accrue and accumulate into a fairly full portrait, and here we do not have even an opening and closing "objective" description (as in *In a Prominent Bar*) or another speaker (as in *The Ruined Maid*) to give us perspective. Except for the moments when the speaker mimics or parodies Brother Lawrence (usually in italic type), we have only the speaker's own words and thoughts. But that is enough; the poet has controlled them so carefully that we clearly know what he thinks of the speaker he has created—that he is a mean-spirited, vengeful hypocrite, a thoroughly disreputable and unlikable character. The whole poem has been about him and his attitudes; the point of the poem has been to characterize the speaker and develop in us a dislike of him and what he stands for—total hypocrisy. In reading a poem like this aloud, we would want our voice to suggest all the unlikable features of a hypocrite. We would also need to suggest, through the tone of voice we used, the author's contemptuous mocking of the rage and hypocrisy, and we would want, like an actor, to create strong disapproval in the hearer. The poem's words (the ones the author has given to the speaker) clearly imply those attitudes, and we would want our voice to express them. Usually there is much more to a poem than the identification and characterization of the speaker, but in many cases it is necessary to identify the speaker and determine his or her character before we can appreciate what else goes on in the poem. And sometimes, as here, in looking for the speaker of the poem, we come near to the center of the poem itself.

The speaker in the following poem is, from the first, clearly much more likable, but we do not get a very full sense of her until the poem is well along. As you read, try to imitate the tone of voice you think this kind of person would use. Exactly when do you begin to feel that you know what she is like?

DOROTHY PARKER

A Certain Lady

Oh, I can smile for you, and tilt my head,
    And drink your rushing words with eager lips,
And paint my mouth for you a fragrant red,
    And trace your brows with tutored finger-tips.
When you rehearse your list of loves to me,
    Oh, I can laugh and marvel, rapturous-eyed.
And you laugh back, nor can you ever see
    The thousand little deaths my heart has died.
And you believe, so well I know my part,
    That I am gay as morning, light as snow,   10

And all the straining things within my heart
    You'll never know.

Oh, I can laugh and listen, when we meet,
    And you bring tales of fresh adventurings—
Of ladies delicately indiscreet,   15
    Of lingering hands, and gently whispered things.
And you are pleased with me, and strive anew
    To sing me sagas of your late delights.
Thus do you want me—marveling, gay, and true—
    Nor do you see my staring eyes of nights.   20
And when, in search of novelty, you stray,
    Oh, I can kiss you blithely as you go . . .
And what goes on, my love, while you're away,
    You'll never know.

1937

To whom does the speaker seem to be talking? What sort of person is he? How do you feel about him? Which habits and attitudes of his do you like least? How soon can you tell that the speaker is not altogether happy about his conversation and conduct? In what tone of voice would you read the first 22 lines aloud? What attitude would you try to express toward the person spoken to? What tone would you use for the last two lines? How would you describe the speaker's personality? What aspects of her behavior are most crucial to the poem's effect?

It is easy to assume that the speaker in a poem is an extension of the poet. Is the speaker in this poem Dorothy Parker?—Maybe. A lot of Parker's poems present a similiar world-weary posture and a kind of cynicism about romantic love. But the poem is hardly an example of self-revelation, a giving away of personal secrets. If it were, it would be silly, not to say risky, to address her lover in a way that gives damaging facts about a pose she has been so careful to set up. We may be *tempted* to think of the speaker as Dorothy Parker, but it is best to resist the temptation and think of the character as an imagined person. Besides, the poem is called *A Certain Lady*, as if it were a speaking portrait of someone. Is the speaker based on any real person at all? Probably not; we are given no reason to think that the speaker is anyone in particular or that the poet has done anything but create a fictional character and situation. In any case, the poem's effect does not depend on our thinking that the speaker is someone specific and historical; it depends on our surprise at her honesty and openness in giving away a secret, something more likely in a fictional speaker than in real life. In poetry we can be overhearers of a conversation; in real life such a role could be dangerous to hearer as well as speaker—and seldom in real life do we get so quick and pointed a characterization as this poem develops in just a few well-organized and well-calculated lines.

In poems like *The Ruined Maid, In a Prominent Bar,* and *Soliloquy,* we are in no danger of mistaking the speaker for the poet, once we have recognized that poets may create speakers who participate in specific situations much as in fiction or drama. When there is a pointed discrepancy between the speaker and what we know of the poet—when the speaker is a woman, for example, and the poet is a man—we know we have a created speaker to contend with and that the point (or at least *one* point) in the poem is to observe the characterization carefully. In *A Certain Lady* we may be less sure, and in other poems the discrepancy between speaker and poet may be even more uncertain. What are we to make, for example, of the speaker in *Woodchucks* in the previous chapter (p. 571)? Is that speaker the real Maxine Kumin? At best (without knowing something quite specific about the author) we can only say "maybe" to that question. What we can be sure of is the sort of person the speaker is portrayed to be—someone (man? or woman?) surprised to discover feelings and attitudes that contradict values apparently held confidently. And that is exactly what we need to know for the poem to have its effect.

A similar kind of self-mocking of the speaker is present in the following poem, but here the mockery is put to less revelatory, more comic ends.

A. R. AMMONS

Needs

I want something suited to my special needs
I want chrome hubcaps, pin-on attachments
and year round use year after year
I want a workhorse with smooth uniform cut,
dozer blade and snow blade & deluxe steering   5
wheel
I want something to mow, throw snow, tow
and sow with
I want precision reel blades
I want a console styled dashboard   10
I want an easy spintype recoil starter
I want combination bevel and spur gears, 14
gauge stamped steel housing and
washable foam element air cleaner
I want a pivoting front axle and extrawide   15
turf tires
I want an inch of foam rubber inside a vinyl
covering
and especially if it's not too much, if I
can deserve it, even if I can't pay for it   20
I want to mow while riding.

1970

The poet here may be teasing himself about his desire for comfort and ease—and showing how readily advertisements and catalog descriptions manipulate us. But the speaker doesn't have to be the author for the teasing to work. In fact, the effect is to tease those attitudes no matter who holds them by teasing a speaker who illustrates the attitudes. It doesn't matter to the poem whether the speaker is the poet himself or some totally invented character. If the speaker is a version of the poet himself—perhaps a *side* of his personality that he is exploring—the portrait is still fictional in an important sense. The poem presents not a whole human being (*no* poem could do that) but only a version of him—a mood perhaps, an aspect, an attitude, a part of that person. Here, the poet presents someone with an obsession, in this case a small and not very damaging one, and allows him to spurt phrases as if he were reciting from an ad. Here the "portrait" is made more comic by a clear sense the poem projects that what we have is only a part of the person, an interest grown too intense, gone askew, gotten out of proportion, something that happens to most of us from time to time. The speaker may be a side of the poet, or maybe not. All we know about the speaker is that he has a one-track mind, that he is obsessed by his own luxurious comfort. He may not even be a "he": there is nothing in the poem that makes us certain that the speaker is male. It is customary to think of the speaker in a poem written by a man as "he" and in a poem written by a woman as "she" (as in Maxine Kumin's *Woodchucks*) unless the poem presents contrary evidence, but it is merely a convenience, a habit, nothing more.

Even when poets present themselves as if they were speaking directly to us in their own voices, their poems present only a partial portrait, something considerably less than the full personality of the poet. Even when there is not an obviously created character—someone with distinct characteristics which are different from those of the poet—strategies of characterization are used to present the person speaking in one way and not another. Even in a poem like the following one, it is still a good idea to talk of the speaker instead of the poet, although here it is probable that the poet is writing about a personal, actual experience.

WILLIAM WORDSWORTH

She Dwelt Among the Untrodden Ways

> She dwelt among the untrodden ways
>   Beside the springs of Dove,[3]
> A Maid whom there were none to praise
>   And very few to love:

3. A small stream in the Lake District in northern England, near where Wordsworth lived in Dove Cottage at Grasmere.

A violet by a mossy stone   5
  Half hidden from the eye!
—Fair as a star, when only one
  Is shining in the sky.

She lived unknown, and few could know
  When Lucy ceased to be;   10
But she is in her grave, and, oh,
  The difference to me!

1800

It is hard to say whether this poem is more about Lucy or about how the speaker feels about her death. Her simple life, far removed from fame and known only to a few, is said nevertheless to have been beautiful. We know little else about her beyond her name and where she lived, in a beautiful but then isolated section of northern England. We don't know if she was young or old, only that the speaker thinks of her as "fair" and compares her to a "violet by a mossy stone." What we do know is that the speaker feels her loss deeply, so deeply that he is almost inarticulate with grief, lapsing into simple exclamation ("oh," line 11) and unable to articulate the "difference" that her death makes.

Did Lucy actually live? Was she a friend of the poet? We don't know; the poem doesn't tell us, and even biographers of Wordsworth are unsure. What we do know is that Wordsworth was able to represent grief over the death very powerfully. Whether the speaker is the historical Wordsworth or not, that speaker is a major focus of the poem, and it is his feelings which the poem isolates and expresses. We need to recognize some characteristics of the speaker and be sensitive to his feelings for the poem to work. We may be tempted to identify the speaker with the poet—it seems to be a natural tendency for most readers to make that assumption unless there is overwhelming evidence to the contrary in the poem—but it is still best to think of the voice we hear in the poem as that of the speaker. We don't need to give him a name, but we do need to understand his values as the poem expresses them and to recognize his deep feelings.

The poems we have looked at in this chapter—and the group that follows at the end of the chapter—all suggest the value of beginning the reading of any poem with a simple question: Who is speaking and what do we know about him or her? Putting together the evidence that the poem presents in answer to this question can often take us a long way into the poem. For some poems, this question won't help a great deal because the speaking voice is too indistinct or the character behind the poem too scantily presented, but in many cases asking this question will lead you toward the central experience the poem offers.

HENRY REED

Lessons of the War

Judging Distances

Not only far away, but the way that you say it
Is very important. Perhaps you may never get
The knack of judging a distance, but at least you know
How to report on a landscape: the central sector,
The right of arc and that, which we had last Tuesday,   5
     And at least you know

That maps are of time, not place, so far as the army
Happens to be concerned—the reason being,
Is one which need not delay us. Again, you know
There are three kinds of tree, three only, the fir and the poplar,   10
And those which have bushy tops to; and lastly
     That things only seem to be things.

A barn is not called a barn, to put it more plainly,
Or a field in the distance, where sheep may be safely grazing.
You must never be over-sure. You must say, when reporting: 15
At five o'clock in the central sector is a dozen
Of what appear to be animals; whatever you do,
     Don't call the bleeders *sheep*.

I am sure that's quite clear; and suppose, for the sake of example,
The one at the end, asleep, endeavors to tell us   20
What he sees over there to the west, and how far away,
After first having come to attention. There to the west,
On the fields of summer the sun and the shadows bestow
     Vestments of purple and gold.

The still white dwellings are like a mirage in the heat,   25
And under the swaying elms a man and a woman
Lie gently together. Which is, perhaps, only to say
That there is a row of houses to the left of arc,
And that under some poplars a pair of what appear to be humans
     Appear to be loving.   30

Well that, for an answer, is what we might rightly call
Moderately satisfactory only, the reason being,
Is that two things have been omitted, and those are important.
The human beings, now: in what direction are they,
And how far away, would you say? And do not forget   35
     There may be dead ground in between.

There may be dead ground in between; and I may not have got
The knack of judging a distance; I will only venture
A guess that perhaps between me and the apparent lovers,
(Who, incidentally, appear by now to have finished,)   40
At seven o'clock from the houses, is roughly a distance
     Of about one year and a half.

1946

SEAMUS HEANEY

Mid-Term Break

I sat all morning in the college sick bay
Counting bells knelling classes to a close.
At two o'clock our neighbors drove me home.

In the porch I met my father crying—
He had always taken funerals in his stride—   5
And Big Jim Evans saying it was a hard blow.

The baby cooed and laughed and rocked the pram
When I came in, and I was embarrassed
By old men standing up to shake my hand

And tell me they were "sorry for my trouble,"   10
Whispers informed strangers I was the eldest,
Away at school, as my mother held my hand

In hers and coughed out angry tearless sighs.
At ten o'clock the ambulance arrived
With the corpse, stanched and bandaged by the nurses.   15

Next morning I went up into the room. Snowdrops
And candles soothed the bedside; I saw him
For the first time in six weeks. Paler now,

Wearing a poppy bruise on his left temple,
He lay in the four foot box as in his cot.   20
No gaudy scars, the bumper knocked him clear.

A four foot box, a foot for every year.

1966

JOHN BETJEMAN

In Westminster Abbey[4]

Let me take this other glove off
    As the *vox humana*[5] swells,
And the beauteous fields of Eden
    Bask beneath the Abbey bells.
Here, where England's statesmen lie,   5
Listen to a lady's cry.

4. The famous Gothic church in London
in which English monarchs are crowned
and famous Englishmen are buried (see

lines 5, 39–40).
5. Organ tones which resemble the human voice.

Gracious Lord, oh bomb the Germans.
　　Spare their women for Thy Sake,
And if that is not too easy
　　We will pardon Thy Mistake.   10
But, gracious Lord, whate'er shall be,
Don't let anyone bomb me.

Keep our Empire undismembered
　　Guide our Forces by Thy Hand,
Gallant blacks from far Jamaica,   15
　　Honduras and Togoland;
Protect them Lord in all their fights,
And, even more, protect the whites.

Think of what our Nation stands for,
　　Books from Boots[6] and country lanes,   20
Free speech, free passes, class distinction,
　　Democracy and proper drains.
Lord, put beneath Thy special care
One-eighty-nine Cadogan Square.[7]

Although dear Lord I am a sinner,   25
　　I have done no major crime;
Now I'll come to Evening Service
　　Whensoever I have the time.
So, Lord, reserve for me a crown,
And do not let my shares go down.   30

I will labor for Thy Kingdom,
　　Help our lads to win the war,
Send white feathers to the cowards[8]
　　Join the Women's Army Corps,[9]
Then wash the Steps around Thy Throne   35
In the Eternal Safety Zone.

Now I feel a little better,
　　What a treat to hear Thy Word
Where the bones of leading statesmen,
　　Have so often been interred.   40
And now, dear Lord, I cannot wait
Because I have a luncheon date.

                                        1940

---

6. A chain of London pharmacies.
7. Presumably where the speaker lives, in a fairly fashionable area.
8. White feathers were sometimes given, or sent, to men not in uniform, to suggest that they were cowards and should join the armed forces.
9. The speaker uses the old World War I name (Women's Army Auxiliary Corps) of the Auxiliary Territorial Service, an organization which performed domestic (and some foreign) defense duties.

TOM WAYMAN

Picketing Supermarkets

Because all this food is grown in the store
do not take the leaflet.
Cabbages, broccoli and tomatoes
are raised at night in the aisles.
Milk is brewed in the rear storage areas.   5
Beef produced in vats in the basement.
Do not take the leaflet.
Peanut butter and soft drinks
are made fresh each morning by store employees.
Our oranges and grapes   10
are so fine and round
that when held up to the lights they cast no shadow.
Do not take the leaflet.

And should you take one
do not believe it.   15
This chain of stores has no connection
with anyone growing food someplace else.
How could we have an effect on local farmers?
Do not believe it.

The sound here is Muzak, for your enjoyment.   20
It is not the sound of children crying.
There *is* a lady offering samples
to mark Canada Cheese Month.
There is no dark-skinned man with black hair beside her
wanting to show you the inside of a coffin.   25
You would not have to look if there was.
And there are no Nicaraguan heroes
in any way connected with the bananas.

Pay no attention to these people.
The manager is a citizen.   30
All this food is grown in the store.

1973

4   SITUATION AND SETTING

Questions about speaker ("Who?" questions) in a poem almost always lead to questions of "Where?" "When?" and "Why?" Identifying the speaker usually is, in fact, part of a larger process of defining the entire imagined **situation** in a poem: What is happening? Where is it happening? Who is the speaker speaking to? Who else is present? Why is this event occurring? In order to understand the dialogue in *The Ruined Maid,* for example, we need to become aware that the sisters are meeting again after a period of absence and that they are meeting in a town large enough to seem substantially different in setting from the rural area in which they grew up together. And we infer (from the opening lines) that the meeting is accidental, and that no other family members are present for the conversation. The poem's whole "story" depends upon the fact of their situation: after leading separate lives for some time they have some catching up to do. We don't know what specific town is involved, or what year, season, or time of day because those details are not important to the poem's effect. But crucial to the poem are the where and when questions that define the situation and relationship of the two speakers, and the answer to the why question—that the meeting is by chance—is important too. In another poem we looked at in the previous chapter, *A Certain Lady,* the specific moment and place are not important, but we do need to notice that the "lady" is talking to (or having an imaginary conversation with) her man and that they are talking about a relationship of some duration.

Sometimes a *specific* time and place (**setting**) may be important. The "lady in skunk" sings her life story "in a prominent bar in Secaucus, N.J.," a smelly and unfashionable town, but on no particular occasion ("One Day"). In *Soliloquy of the Spanish Cloister,* the setting (a monastery) adds to the irony because of the gross inappropriateness of such sentiments and attitudes in such a supposedly holy place, and the setting of *In Westminster Abbey* similarly helps us to judge the speaker's ideas, attitudes, and self-conception.

The title of the following poem suggests that place may be important, and it is, although you may be surprised to discover exactly what exists at this address and what uses the speaker makes of it.

JAMES DICKEY

Cherrylog Road

Off Highway 106[1]
At Cherrylog Road I entered
The '34 Ford without wheels,
Smothered in kudzu,[2]

---

1. The poem is set in the mountains of North Georgia.
2. A rapidly growing vine, introduced from Japan to combat erosion but now covering whole fields and groves of trees.

With a seat pulled out to run 5
Corn whiskey down from the hills,

And then from the other side
Crept into an Essex
With a rumble seat of red leather
And then out again, aboard 10
A blue Chevrolet, releasing
The rust from its other color,

Reared up on three building blocks.
None had the same body heat;
I changed with them inward, toward 15
The weedy heart of the junkyard
For I knew that Doris Holbrook
Would escape from her father at noon

And would come from the farm
To seek parts owned by the sun 20
Among the abandoned chassis,
Sitting in each in turn
As I did, leaning forward
As in a wild stock-car race

In the parking lot of the dead. 25
Time after time, I climbed in
And out the other side, like
An envoy or movie star
Met at the station by crickets.
A radiator cap raised its head, 30

Become a real toad or a kingsnake
As I neared the hub of the yard,
Passing through many states,
Many lives, to reach
Some grandmother's long Pierce-Arrow 35
Sending platters of blindness forth

From its nickel hubcaps
And spilling its tender upholstery
On sleepy roaches,
The glass panel in between 40
Lady and colored driver
Not all the way broken out,

The back-seat phone
Still on its hook.
I got in as though to exclaim, 45
"Let us go to the orphan asylum,
John; I have some old toys
For children who say their prayers."

I popped with sweat as I thought
I heard Doris Holbrook scrape   50
Like a mouse in the southern-state sun
That was eating the paint in blisters
From a hundred car tops and hoods.
She was tapping like code,   *secret message*

Loosening the screws,   55
Carrying off headlights,
Sparkplugs, bumpers,
Cracked mirrors and gear-knobs,
Getting ready, already,
To go back with something to show   60

Other than her lips' new trembling
I would hold to me soon, soon,
Where I sat in the ripped back seat
Talking over the interphone,
Praying for Doris Holbrook   65
To come from her father's farm

And to get back there
With no trace of me on her face
To be seen by her red-haired father
Who would change, in the squalling barn,   70
Her back's pale skin with a strop.
Then lay for me

In a bootlegger's roasting car
With a string-triggered 12-gauge shotgun
To blast the breath from the air.   75
Not cut by the jagged windshields,
Through the acres of wrecks she came
With a wrench in her hand,

Through dust where the blacksnake dies
Of boredom, and the beetle knows   80
The compost has no more life.
Someone outside would have seen
The oldest car's door inexplicably
Close from within:

I held her and held her and held her,   85
Convoyed at terrific speed
By the stalled, dreaming traffic around us,
So the blacksnake, stiff
With inaction, curved back
Into life, and hunted the mouse   90

With deadly overexcitement,
The beetles reclaimed their field
As we clung, glued together,
With the hooks of the seat springs
Working through to catch us red-handed   95
Amidst the gray breathless batting

That burst from the seat at our backs.
We left by separate doors
Into the changed, other bodies
Of cars, she down Cherrylog Road   100
And I to my motorcycle
Parked like the soul of the junkyard

Restored, a bicycle fleshed
With power, and tore off
Up Highway 106, continually   105
Drunk on the wind in my mouth,
Wringing the handlebar for speed,
Wild to be wreckage forever.

                                                     1964

The *exact* location of the junkyard is not important (there is no Highway 106 near the real Cherrylog Road in North Georgia), but we do need to know that the setting is rural, that the time is summer and that the summer is hot, and that moonshine whiskey is native to the area. Following the story is no problem once we have sorted out these few facts, and we are prepared to meet the cast of characters: Doris Holbrook, her red-haired father, and the speaker. About each we learn just enough to appreciate the sense of vitality, adventure, and power that constitute the major effects of the poem.

The situation of love-making in another setting than the junkyard would not produce the same effects, and the exotic sense of a forbidden meeting in this unlikely place helps to recreate the speaker's sense of the episode. For him, it is memorable (notice all the tiny details he remembers), powerful (notice his reaction when he gets back on his motorcycle), dreamlike (notice the sense of time standing still, especially in lines 85–89), and important (notice how the speaker perceives his environment as changed by their love-making, lines 88–91 and 98–100). The wealth of details about setting also helps us to raise other, related questions. Why does the speaker fantasize about being shot by the father (lines 72–75)? Why, in a poem so full of details, do we find out so little about what Doris Holbrook looks like? What gives us the sense that this incident is a composite of episodes, an event that was repeated many times? What gives us the impression that the events occurred long ago? What makes the speaker feel so powerful at the end? What does he mean when he talks of himself as being "wild to be wreckage forever"? All of the poem's attention to the speaker's reactions, reflections, and memories is intricately tied up with the particulars of setting. Making love in a junkyard is crucial to the speaker's sense of both power and wreckage, and Doris is merely a matter of excitement, adventure, and pretty skin, appreciated because she makes the world seem different and because she is willing to take risks and to suffer for meeting him like this. The more we probe the poem with questions about situation, the more likely we are to catch the poem's full effect.

Cherrylog Road is a fairly easy poem to read, but its effect is more complex than its simple story line suggests. The next poem we will look at is, at first glance, much more difficult to follow. Part of the difficulty is that the poem is from an earlier age, and its language is a little different, and part is because the action in the poem is so closely connected to what is being said. But its opening lines—addressed to someone who is resisting the speaker's suggestions—disclose the situation, and gradually we can figure out the scene: a man is trying to convince a woman that they should make love. When a flea happens by, the speaker uses it for an unlikely example as part of his argument. And once we recognize the situation, we can readily follow (and be amused by) the speaker's witty and intricate argument.

JOHN DONNE

The Flea

Mark but this flea, and mark in this[3]
How little that which thou deny'st me is;
It sucked me first, and now sucks thee,
And in this flea our two bloods mingled be;
Thou know'st that this cannot be said   5
A sin, nor shame, nor loss of maidenhead,
    Yet this enjoys before it woo,
    And pampered[4] swells with one blood made of two,
    And this, alas, is more than we would do.[5]

Oh stay, three lives in one flea spare,   10
Where we almost, yea more than, married are.
This flea is you and I, and this
Our marriage bed, and marriage temple is;
Though parents grudge, and you, we're met
And cloistered in these living walls of jet.   15
    Though use[6] make you apt to kill me,
    Let not to that, self-murder added be,
    And sacrilege, three sins in killing three.

Cruel and sudden, hast thou since
Purpled thy nail in blood of innocence?   20

---

3. Medieval preachers and rhetoricians asked their hearers to "mark" (look at) an object which illustrated a moral or philosophical lesson they wished to emphasize.
4. Fed luxuriously.

5. According to contemporary medical theory, conception involved the literal mingling of the lovers' blood.
6. Habit.

Wherein could this flea guilty be,
Except in that drop which it sucked from thee?
Yet thou triumph'st, and say'st that thou
Find'st not thyself, nor me, the weaker now;
    'Tis true; then learn how false, fears be;   25
    Just so much honor, when thou yield'st to me,
    Will waste, as this flea's death took life from thee.

                                    1633

The scene in *The Flea* develops almost as in a play. Action even occurs right along with the words. Between stanzas 1 and 2, the woman makes a move to kill the flea (as stanza 2 opens, the speaker is trying to stop her), and between stanzas 2 and 3 the woman has squished the flea with her fingernail. Once we try to make sense of what the speaker says, the action is just as clear from the words as if we had stage directions in the margin. All of the speaker's verbal cleverness and all of his specious arguments follow from the situation, and in this poem (as in *Soliloquy of the Spanish Cloister* or *In Westminster Abbey*) we watch as if we were observing a scene on the stage. The speaker is, in effect, giving a dramatic monologue for our benefit.

Neither time nor place is important to *The Flea*, except in the sense that the speaker and his friend have to be assumed to be in the same place and have the leisure for some playfulness. The situation could occur in any place where a man, a woman, and a flea could be together. Indoors, outdoors, morning, evening, city, country, it is all one; the situation could occur in cottage or palace, on a boat or in a bedroom. We do know, from the date of publication of the poem (1633), that the poet was writing about people of more than three centuries ago, but the conduct he describes might equally happen in later ages just as well. Only the habits of language (and perhaps the speaker's religious attitudes) date the poem; the situation could equally be set in any age or place.

Some poems, however, refer to a certain actual place and time. The following poem depends upon historical information (it also assumes that we know the terminology of children's games); if you don't know the history of atomic warfare, you may want to read the footnote before you read the poem.

ROBERT FROST

U. S. 1946 King's X[7]

Having invented a new Holocaust,
And been the first with it to win a war,
How they make haste to cry with fingers crossed,
King's X—no fairs to use it any more!

                                    p. 1946

7. Shortly after exploding the two atomic bombs that ended World War II, the United States proposed to share nuclear information with other countries in exchange for an agreement that the information would be used only for peaceful purposes. In children's games, time out is sometimes signaled by crossing fingers and saying "King's X."

Our knowledge of the relevant historical facts does not necessarily mean that we will agree with the poet's criticism of U. S. policy at the end of World War II, but we certainly can't understand or appreciate the poem's equation of nuclear policy with a child's fear of consequence unless we do know the facts. Often it is hard to place ourselves fully enough in another time or place to imagine sympathetically what a particular historical moment would have been like, and even the best poetic efforts do not necessarily transport us there. But poets sometimes record a particular moment or event in order to commemorate it or comment upon it. A poem written about a specific occasion is usually called an **occasional poem,** and such a poem is **referential;** that is, it refers to a specific historical moment or event. For such poems we need, at the least, specific historical information— plus a willingness on our part as readers to be transported imaginatively to that particular time, sometimes (as in *U. S. 1946 King's X*) by mentioning explicitly a particular time, sometimes by recreating that moment in a dramatic situation.

Time or place may, of course, be used much less specifically and still be important to a poem, and the most common uses of setting involve drawing upon common notions of a particular time or place. Setting a poem in a garden, for example, or writing about apples almost inevitably reminds us of the Garden of Eden because it is part of our common heritage of belief or knowledge. Even people who don't read at all or who lack Judaeo-Christian religious commitments are likely to know about Eden, and a poet writing in our culture can count on that. In Joni Mitchell's *Woodstock* (p.566), for example (as we noticed in Chapter 2) the idea of the innocence in Woodstock is drawn into the poem by an allusion to Eden; the final refrain in each stanza of the poem insists that "we've got to get ourselves / Back to the garden." An **allusion** is a reference to something outside the poem that carries a history of meaning and strong emotional associations. For example, gardens may carry suggestions of innocence and order, or temptation and the fall, or both, depending on how the poem handles the allusion. Well-known places from history or myth may be popularly associated with particular ideas or values or ways of life.

The place involved in a poem is its **spatial setting,** and the time is its **temporal setting.** The temporal setting may involve a specific date or an era, a season of the year or a time of day. We tend, for example, to think of spring as a time of discovery and growth, and poems set in spring are likely to draw upon that association; morning usually suggests discovery as well—beginnings, vitality, the world fresh and new—even to those of us who in reality take our waking slow. Temporal or spatial setting are often used to influence our expectation of theme and tone in a specific way, although the poet may then go on to surprise us by making something very different of our expectation. Setting is often an important factor in creating the mood in poems just as in stories, plays, or films. Often the details of setting have a lot to do with the way we ultimately respond to the poem's subject or theme, as in this poem:

SYLVIA PLATH

Point Shirley

From Water-Tower Hill to the brick prison
The shingle booms, bickering under
The sea's collapse.
Snowcakes break and welter. This year
The gritted wave leaps   5
The seawall and drops onto a bier
Of quahog chips,[8]
Leaving a salty mash of ice to whiten

In my grandmother's sand yard. She is dead,
Whose laundry snapped and froze here, who   10
Kept house against
What the sluttish, rutted sea could do.
Squall waves once danced
Ship timbers in through the cellar window;
A thresh-tailed, lanced   15
Shark littered in the geranium bed—

Such collusion of mulish elements
She wore her broom straws to the nub.
Twenty years out
Of her hand; the house still hugs in each drab   20
Stucco socket
The purple egg-stones: from Great Head's knob
To the filled-in Gut
The sea in its cold gizzard ground those rounds.

Nobody wintering now behind   25
The planked-up windows where she set
Her wheat loaves
And apple cakes to cool. What is it
Survives, grieves
So, over this battered, obstinate spit   30
Of gravel? The waves'
Spewed relics clicker masses in the wind,

Gray waves the stub-necked eiders ride.
A labor of love, and that labor lost.
Steadily the sea   35
Eats at Point Shirley. She died blessed,
And I come by
Bones, bones only, pawed and tossed,
A dog-faced sea.
The sun sinks under Boston, bloody red.   40

---

8. Chips from quahog clam shells, common on the New England coast.

I would get from these dry-papped stones
The milk your love instilled in them.
The black ducks dive.
And though your graciousness might stream,
And I contrive,   45
Grandmother, stones are nothing of home
To that spumiest dove.
Against both bar and tower the black sea runs.

1960

One does not have to know the New England coast by personal experience to have it vividly recalled by Plath's poem. A reader who knows that coast or another like it may have an advantage in being able to respond more quickly to the poem's precision of description, but the poem does not depend on such knowledge from outside the poem. The precise location of Point Shirley, near Boston, is not especially important, but visualization of the setting is. Crucial to the poem's tone and mood is the sense of the sea as aggressor, a force powerful enough to change the contours of the coast and invade the privacy of yards and homes. The energy, relentlessness, and impersonality of the sea met their match, though a temporary one, in the speaker's grandmother who "Kept house against / What the sluttish, rutted sea could do" (lines 11–12). The grandmother *belonged* in this setting, and it seemed hers, but twenty years of her absence (since her death) now begin to show. Still, the marks of her obstinacy and love are there, although ultimately doomed by the sea's more enduring power.

Details—and how they are amassed—are important here rather than historic particulars of time and place. The grays and whites and drab colors of the sea and its leavings provide both a visual sense of the scene and the mood for the poem. The stubbornness which the speaker admired in the grandmother comes to seem a part of that tenacious grayness. Nothing happens rapidly here; things wear down. Even the "bloody red" (line 40) of the sun's setting—an ominous sign that adds a vivid fright to the dullness rather than brightening it— makes promises that seem slow and long-term. The toughness of the boarded-up house is a monument to the grandmother's loving care and becomes a way for the speaker to touch her human spirit, but the poem's final emphasis is on the relentless black sea which continues to run against the landmarks and fortresses that had been identified with the setting in the very first line.

Questions about situation and setting begin as simple questions of identification but often become more complex when we sort out all the implications. Often it takes only a moment to determine a poem's situation, but it may take much longer to discover all of the things that time and place imply, for their meanings may depend upon visual details, or upon actual historical occurrences, or upon habitual ways of thinking about certain times and places—or all three at once. As you read the following poem, notice how the setting—another shore—prepares us for the speaker's moods and ideas, and then watch how the movement of his mind is affected by what he sees.

MATTHEW ARNOLD

Dover Beach[9]

The sea is calm tonight.
The tide is full, the moon lies fair
Upon the straits; on the French coast the light
Gleams and is gone; the cliffs of England stand,
Glimmering and vast, out in the tranquil bay.   5
Come to the window, sweet is the night-air!
Only, from the long line of spray
Where the sea meets the moon-blanched land,
Listen! you hear the grating roar
Of pebbles which the waves draw back, and fling,   10
At their return, up the high strand,
Begin, and cease, and then again begin,
With tremulous cadence slow, and bring
The eternal note of sadness in.

Sophocles long ago   15
Heard it on the Aegean, and it brought
Into his mind the turbid ebb and flow
Of human misery;[1] we
Find also in the sound a thought,
Hearing it by this distant northern sea.   20

The Sea of Faith
Was once, too, at the full, and round earth's shore
Lay like the folds of a bright girdle furled.
But now I only hear
Its melancholy, long, withdrawing roar,   25
Retreating, to the breath
Of the night-wind, down the vast edges drear
And naked shingles[2] of the world.

Ah, love, let us be true
To one another! for the world, which seems   30
To lie before us like a land of dreams,
So various, so beautiful, so new,

Hath really neither joy, nor love, nor light,
Nor certitude, nor peace, nor help for pain;
And we are here as on a darkling plain   35
Swept with confused alarms of struggle and flight,
Where ignorant armies clash by night.

ca. 1851

---

9. At the narrowest point on the English
Channel. The lights on the French coast
(lines 3–4) would be about 20 miles away.
1. In *Antigone*, lines 583–91, the chorus
compares the fate of the house of Oedipus
to the waves of the sea.
2. Pebble-strewn beaches.

Exactly what is the dramatic situation in *Dover Beach?* How soon
are you aware that someone is being spoken to? How much are we
told about the person spoken to? How would you describe the speaker's mood? What does the speaker's mood have to do with time and
place? Do any details of present place and time help to account for
his tendency to talk repeatedly of the past and the future? How
important is it to the poem's total effect that the beach here involves
an international border? What particulars of the Dover Beach seem
especially important to the poem's themes? to its emotional effects?

Not all poems have an identifiable situation or setting, just as not
all poems have a speaker that is distinct from the author. Poems that
simply present a series of thoughts and feelings directly, in a con-
templative, meditative, or reflective way, may not set up any kind of
action, plot, or situation at all, preferring to speak directly without the
intermediary of a dramatic device. But most poems depend crucially
upon a sense of place, a sense of time, and an understanding of human
interaction in scenes that resemble the strategies of drama or film.
And questions about these matters will often lead you to define not
only the "facts" but also the feelings central to a poem's design upon us.

ROBERT BROWNING

My Last Duchess

Ferrara[3]

That's my last Duchess painted on the wall,
Looking as if she were alive. I call
That piece a wonder, now: Frà Pandolf's hands[4]
Worked busily a day, and there she stands.
Will't please you sit and look at her? I said   5
"Frà Pandolf" by design, for never read
Strangers like you that pictured countenance,
The depth and passion of its earnest glance,
But to myself they turned (since none puts by
The curtain I have drawn for you, but I)   10
And seemed as they would ask me, if they durst,
How such a glance came there; so, not the first

---

3. Alfonso II, Duke of Ferrara in Italy
in the mid-16th century, is the presumed
speaker of the poem, which is loosely based
on historical events. The Duke's first wife
—whom he had married when she was 14
—died under suspicious circumstances at
17, and he then negotiated through an
agent (to whom the poem is spoken) for
the hand of the niece of the Count of
Tyrol in Austria.
4. Frà Pandolf is, like Claus (line 56),
fictitious.

Are you to turn and ask thus. Sir, 'twas not
Her husband's presence only, called that spot
Of joy into the Duchess' cheek: perhaps   15
Frà Pandolf chanced to say "Her mantle laps
Over my lady's wrist too much," or "Paint
Must never hope to reproduce the faint
Half-flush that dies along her throat": such stuff
Was courtesy, she thought, and cause enough   20
For calling up that spot of joy. She had
A heart—how shall I say?—too soon made glad,
Too easily impressed; she liked whate'er
She looked on, and her looks went everywhere.
Sir, 'twas all one! My favor at her breast,   25
The dropping of the daylight in the West,
The bough of cherries some officious fool
Broke in the orchard for her, the white mule
She rode with round the terrace—all and each
Would draw from her alike the approving speech,   30
Or blush, at least. She thanked men,—good! but thanked
Somehow—I know not how—as if she ranked
My gift of a nine-hundred-years-old name
With anybody's gift. Who'd stoop to blame
This sort of trifling? Even had you skill   35
In speech—which I have not—to make your will
Quite clear to such an one, and say, "Just this
Or that in you disgusts me; here you miss,
Or there exceed the mark"—and if she let
Herself be lessoned so, nor plainly set   40
Her wits to yours, forsooth, and made excuse,
—E'en then would be some stooping; and I choose
Never to stoop. Oh sir, she smiled, no doubt,
Whene'er I passed her; but who passed without
Much the same smile? This grew; I gave commands;   45
Then all smiles stopped together. There she stands
As if alive. Will't please you rise? We'll meet
The company below, then. I repeat,
The Count your master's known munificence
Is ample warrant that no just pretense   50
Of mine for dowry will be disallowed;
Though his fair daughter's self, as I avowed
At starting, is my object. Nay, we'll go
Together down, sir. Notice Neptune, though,
Taming a sea-horse, thought a rarity,   55
Which Claus of Innsbruck cast in bronze for me!

1842

W. H. AUDEN

Musée des Beaux Arts[5]

About suffering they were never wrong,
The Old Masters: how well they understood
Its human position; how it takes place
While someone else is eating or opening a window or just walking dully
    along;
How, when the aged are reverently, passionately waiting   5
For the miraculous birth, there always must be
Children who did not specially want it to happen, skating
On a pond at the edge of the wood:
They never forgot
That even the dreadful martyrdom must run its course   10
Anyhow in a corner, some untidy spot
Where the dogs go on with their doggy life and the torturer's horse
Scratches its innocent behind on a tree.

In Brueghel's *Icarus*,[6] for instance: how everything turns away
Quite leisurely from the disaster; the plowman may   15
Have heard the splash, the forsaken cry,
But for him it was not an important failure; the sun shone
As it had to on the white legs disappearing into the green
Water; and the expensive delicate ship that must have seen
Something amazing, a boy falling out of the sky,   20
Had somewhere to get to and sailed calmly on.

                                    1938

JOHN DONNE ✓

A Valediction: Forbidding Mourning

As virtuous men pass mildly away,
    And whisper to their souls to go,
Whilst some of their sad friends do say,
    "The breath goes now," and some say, "No,"

So let us melt, and make no noise,   5
    No tear-floods, nor sigh-tempests move;
'Twere profanation of our joys
    To tell the laity our love.

---

5. The Museum of the Fine Arts, in Brussels.

6. "Landscape with the Fall of Icarus," by Pieter Brueghel the elder, located in the Brussels Museum. According to Greek myth, Daedalus and his son Icarus escaped from imprisonment by using home-made wings of wax; but Icarus flew too near the sun, the wax melted, and he fell into the sea and drowned. In the Brueghel painting the central figure is a peasant plowing, and several other figures are more immediately noticeable than Icarus who, disappearing into the sea, is easy to miss in the lower right-hand corner. Equally ignored by the figures is a dead body in the woods.

Moving of the earth[7] brings harms and fears,
    Men reckon what it did and meant;   10
But trepidation of the spheres,[8]
    Though greater far, is innocent.

Dull sublunary[9] lovers' love
    (Whose soul is sense) cannot admit
Absence, because it doth remove   15
    Those things which elemented[1] it.

But we, by a love so much refined
    That our selves know not what it is,
Inter-assured of the mind,
    Care less, eyes, lips, and hands to miss.   20

Our two souls therefore, which are one,
    Though I must go, endure not yet
A breach, but an expansion,
    Like gold to airy thinness beat.

If they be two, they are two so   25
    As stiff twin compasses are two:
Thy soul, the fixed foot, makes no show
    To move, but doth, if the other do;

And though it in the center sit,
    Yet when the other far doth roam,   30
It leans, and hearkens after it,
    And grows erect, as that comes home.

Such wilt thou be to me, who must,
    Like the other foot, obliquely run;
Thy firmness makes my circle[2] just,   35
    And makes me end where I begun.

                        1611(?)

7. Earthquakes.
8. The Renaissance hypothesis that the celestial spheres trembled and thus caused unexpected variations in their orbits. Such movements are "innocent" because earthlings do not observe or fret about them.
9. Below the moon; i.e., changeable.

According to the traditional cosmology which Donne invokes here, the moon was considered the dividing line between the immutable celestial world and the earthly mortal one.
1. Comprised.
2. A traditional symbol of perfection.

5 WORDS

Fiction and drama depend upon language just as poetry does, but in a poem almost everything comes down to words. In stories and plays, we are likely to keep our attention primarily on narrative and plot—what is happening in front of us or in the action as we imagine it in our minds—and although words are crucial to how we imagine the characters and how we respond to what happens to them, we are less likely to pause over any one word as we may need to in a poem. Besides, poems often are short and use only a few words, so a lot depends on every single one. Poetry sometimes feels like prose that is distilled: only the most essential words are there, just barely enough so that we communicate in the most basic way, using the most elemental signs of meaning and feeling—and each one chosen for exactly the right shade of meaning. But elemental does not necessarily mean simple, and these signs may be very rich in their meanings and complex in their effects.

Let's look first at two poems, each of which depends heavily upon a single key word.

RICHARD ARMOUR

Hiding Place

A speaker at a meeting of the New York State Frozen Food Locker Association declared that the best hiding place in event of an atomic explosion is a frozen-food locker, where "radiation will not penetrate."[1]   NEWS ITEM.

> Move over, ham
>   And quartered cow,
> My Geiger[2] says
>   The time is now.
> Yes, now I lay me   5
>   Down to sleep,
> And if I die,
>   At least I'll keep.

1954

YVOR WINTERS

At the San Francisco Airport

To my daughter, 1954

This is the terminal: the light
Gives perfect vision, false and hard;

1. Before home freezers became popular, many Americans rented lockers in specially equipped commercial buildings.

2. Geiger counter: used to detect radiation.

The metal glitters, deep and bright.
Great planes are waiting in the yard—
They are already in the night.   5

And you are here beside me, small,
Contained and fragile, and intent
On things that I but half recall—
Yet going whither you are bent.
I am the past, and that is all.   10

But you and I in part are one:
The frightened brain, the nervous will,
The knowledge of what must be done,
The passion to acquire the skill
To face that which you dare not shun.   15

The rain of matter upon sense
Destroys me momently. The score:
There comes what will come. The expense
Is what one thought, and something more—
One's being and intelligence.   20

This is the terminal, the break.
Beyond this point, on lines of air,
You take the way that you must take;
And I remain in light and stare—
In light, and nothing else, awake.   25

1954

In *Hiding Place*, almost all the poem's comedy depends on the final
word, "keep." In the child's prayer which the poem echoes, to "pray
the Lord my soul to keep" does not exactly involve cold storage, and
so the poem depends upon an outrageous double meaning. The key
word is chosen because it can mean more than one thing; in this case,
the importance of the word involves its **ambiguity** (an ability to mean
more than one thing) rather than its **precision** (exactness).

In the second poem, the several possible meanings of a single word
are probed more soberly and thoughtfully. What does it *mean* to be in
a place called a "terminal"? the poem asks. As the parting of father
and daughter is explored, carefully, the place of parting and the
means of transportation begin to take on meanings larger than their
simple referential ones. The poem is full of contrasts—young and old,
light and dark, past and present, security and adventure—as the parting of generations is pondered. The father ("I am the past," line 10)
remains in the light, among known objects and experience familiar to
his many years; the daughter is about to depart into the night, the
unknown, the uncertain future. But they both share a sense of the
necessity of the parting, of the need for the daughter to mature, gain
knowledge, acquire experience. Is she going off to school? to college?

to her first job? The specifics are not given, but her plane ride clearly means a new departure and a clean break with childhood, dependency, the past.

So much depends upon the meanings of "terminal." It is the airport building, of course, but it also implies a boundary, an extremity, an end, something that is limited, a place where a connection is broken. The clear, crisp meanings of other words are important too. The words "break," "point," "lines," "way," and "remain" all express literally and sharply what the event means. The final stanza of the poem is full of words that state flatly and **denote** exactly, as if the speaker has recovered completely from the momentary confusion of stanza 4, when "being and intelligence" are lost in the emotion of the parting itself. The crisp articulation of the last stanza puts an almost total emphasis on the precise meaning of each word, its **denotation,** what it precisely denotes or refers to. The words "break," "point," "way," and "remain" are almost completely unemotional and colorless; they do not make value judgments or offer personal views, but rather define and describe. It is as if the speaker is trying to disengage himself from the emotion of the situation and just give the facts.

Words, however, are more than hard blocks of meaning on whose sense everyone agrees. They also have a more personal side, and they carry emotional force and shades of suggestion. The words we use indicate not only what we mean but how we feel about it, and we choose words that we hope will carry a persuasive emotional engagement with others, in conversation and daily usage as well as in poems. A person who holds office is, quite literally (and unemotionally), an "officeholder," a word that clearly denotes what he or she does. But if we want to convince someone that an officeholder is wise, trustworthy, and deserving of political support we may call that person a "political leader" or perhaps a "statesman"; whereas if we want to promote distrust or contempt of officeholders we might call them "politicians" or "bureaucrats" or "political hacks." These latter words have clear **connotations**—suggestions of emotional coloration that imply our attitude and invite a similar one on the part of our hearers. What words **connote** can be just as important to a poem as what they denote, although some poems depend primarily on denotation and some more on connotation.

At the San Francisco Airport seems to depend primarily on denotation; the speaker tries to *specify* the meanings and implications of the parting with his daughter, and his tendency to split categories neatly for the two of them at first contributes to the sense of clarity and certainty which the speaker wants to project. He is the past (line 10) and what remains (line 24); he has age and experience, his life is the known quantity, he stands in the light. She, on the other hand, is committed to the adventure of going into the night; she seems small, fragile, and her identity exists in the uncertain future. Yet the connotations of some words carry strong emotional force as well as clear definition: that the daughter seems "small" and "fragile" to the speaker suggests his fear for her, something quite different from her sense of adventure. The neat, clean categories keep breaking down, and the speaker's feelings keep showing through. In stanza 1, the speaker tells us that the light in the terminal gives "perfect vision" but he also notices, indirectly, its artificial quality: it is "false" and "hard," suggesting the limits of the rationalism he tries to maintain. That artificial light shines over most of the poem and honors the speaker's effort, but the whole poem represents his struggle, and in stanza 4 the signals of disturbance are very strong as, despite an insistence on a vocabulary of calculation, his rational facade collapses completely. If we have observed his verbal strategies carefully, we should not be surprised to find him at the end just *staring* in the artificial light, merely awake, although the poem has shown him to be unconsciously awake to much more than he will candidly admit.

At the San Francisco Airport is an unusually intricate and complicated poem, and it offers us, if we are willing to examine very precisely its carefully crafted fabric, an unusually rich insight into how complex a thing it is to be human and have human feelings and foibles when we think we must be rational machines. Connotations often work more simply. The following poem, for example, even though it describes the mixed feelings one person has about another, depends heavily on the common connotations of fairly common words.

WALTER DE LA MARE

Slim Cunning Hands

Slim cunning hands at rest, and cozening eyes—
Under this stone one loved too wildly lies;
How false she was, no granite could declare;
Nor all earth's flowers, how fair.

1950

What the speaker in *Slim Cunning Hands* remembers about the dead woman—her hands, her eyes—tells part of the story; her physical presence was clearly important to him, and the poem's other nouns—stone, granite, flowers—all remind us of her death and its finality. All these words denote objects having to do with rituals that memorialize a departed life. Granite and stone connote finality as well, and flowers connote fragility and suggest the shortness of life (which is why they have become the symbolic language of funerals). The way the speaker talks about the woman expresses, in just a few words, how complexly he feels about his love for her. She was loved, he says, too "wildly"—by him perhaps, and by others. The excitement she offered is suggested by the word, and also the lack of control. The words "cunning" and "cozening" help us interpret both her wildness and falsity; they suggest her calculation, cleverness, and untrustworthiness as well as her skill, persuasiveness, and ability to place. And the word "fair," a simple yet very inclusive word, suggests how totally attractive the speaker finds her: her beauty is just as incapable of being expressed by flowers as her fickleness is of being expressed in something as permanent as stone. Simple words here tell us perhaps all we need to know of a long story.

Words like "fair" and "cozening" are clearly loaded: they have strong, clear connotations and tell us what to think, what evaluation to make. The connotations may also suggest or imply the basis for the evaluation. In the two poems that follow we can readily see why the specific words are chosen because, although both poems express a preference for the same sort of feminine appearance, the grounds of appeal are vastly different.

BEN JONSON

Still to Be Neat[3]

Still[4] to be neat, still to be dressed,
As you were going to a feast;
Still to be powdered, still perfumed;
Lady, it is to be presumed,
Though art's hid causes are not found,   5
All is not sweet, all is not sound.

Give me a look, give me a face
That makes simplicity a grace;
Robes loosely flowing, hair as free;
Such sweet neglect more taketh me   10
Than all th' adulteries of art.
They strike mine eyes, but not my heart.

1609

ROBERT HERRICK

Delight in Disorder

A sweet disorder in the dress
Kindles in clothes a wantonness.
A lawn[5] about the shoulders thrown
Into a fine distractiön;
An erring lace, which here and there   5
Enthralls the crimson stomacher,[6]
A cuff neglectful, and thereby

---

3. A song from Jonson's play, *The Silent Woman.*
4. Continually.
5. Scarf of fine linen.
6. Ornamental covering for the breasts.

Ribbands[7] to flow confusedly;
A winning wave, deserving note,
In the tempestuous petticoat;   10
A careless shoestring, in whose tie
I see a wild civility;
Do more bewitch me than when art
Is too precise[8] in every part.

1648

The poem *Still to Be Neat* begins by describing a woman who looks
too neat and orderly; she seems too perfect to be believed, the speaker
says, and he has to assume that there is a reason for such overly
fastidious grooming, that she is covering up something. He worries
that something is wrong underneath—that not all is "sweet" and
"sound." "Sweet" could mean several possible things, and its meaning
becomes clearer when it is repeated in the next stanza in a more
specific context. But "sound" begins to suggest the speaker's moral
earnestness: it is a strong word, implying a suspicion that something
is deeply wrong.

When "sweet" is repeated in line 10, it has taken on specific attributes from what the speaker has said about things he likes in a less
calculated physical appearance. Now it appears to mean easy, attrac-
ive, unpremeditated. And when the speaker springs "adulteries" on
us in the next line as a description of the woman's cosmeticizing,
it is clear what he fears—that the appearance of the too neat, too
made-up woman covers serious flaws, things which try to make her
appear someone she is not. "Adulteries" suggests the addition of something foreign, something unlike her own nature, and it is a strong, dis-
approving word. The "soundness" he had worried about involves her
integrity; his objection is certainly moral, probably sexual. He wants
his women simple and chaste; he wants them to be just what they
seem to be.

The speaker in *Delight in Disorder* wants his women easy and simple too, but for different reasons. He finds disorder "sweet" too (line
1), and seems almost to be answering the first speaker, providing a
different rationale for artless appearance. His grounds of preference are
clear early: his support of "wantonness" (line 2) is close to the opposite in its moral suppositions of the first speaker's disapproval of "adulteries." This speaker wants a careless look because he thinks it's sexy,
and many of the words he chooses suggest sensuality and availability: "distraction" (line 4), "erring" (line 5), "tempestuous" (line 10),
"wild" (line 12). The speakers in the two poems read informality
of dress very differently and have very different expectations of the
person who dresses in a particular way. We find out quite a lot
about each speaker. Their common subject allows us to see clearly
how different they both are, and how what one sees is in the eye

7. Ribbons.
8. In the 16th and 17th centuries Puritans were often called Precisians because of
their fastidiousness.

of the beholder, how values and assumptions are built into the words one chooses even for description. Jonson has created a speaker who wants an informally clad woman who has a natural grace and ease of manner because she is confident of herself, dependable, and chaste. Herrick has created a speaker who finds informality of dress fetching and sexy and indicative of sensuality and availability.

It would be hard to exaggerate how important words are to poems. Poets who know their craft pick each word with care, so that each word will express exactly what needs to be expressed and suggest every emotional shade that the poem is calculated to evoke in us. Often individual words qualify and amplify one another—suggestions clarify other suggestions, and meanings grow upon meanings— and thus the way the words are put together can be important too. Notice, for example, that in *Slim Cunning Hands* the final emphasis is on how *fair* the speaker's woman was; that is his last word, the thing he can't forget in spite of his distrust of her, and that is where the poem chooses to leave the emphasis, on that one word which, even though it doesn't justify everything else, qualifies all the disappointment and hurt.

That word does not stand all by itself, however, any more than any other word in a poem can be considered all alone. Every word exists within larger units of meaning—sentences, patterns of comparisons and contrasts, the whole poem—and where the word is and how it is used often are very important. The final word or words may be especially emphatic (as in *Slim Cunning Hands*), and words that are repeated take on a special intensity, as "terminal" does in *At the San Francisco Airport* or as "chartered" and "cry" do in *London,* a poem we looked at in Chapter 2. Certain words often stand out, because they are used in an unusual way (like "chartered" in *London* or "adulteries" in *Still To Be Neat*) or because they are given an artificial prominence, through unusual sentence structure, for example, or because the title calls special attention to them. In the following poem, notice how the title calls upon us to wonder, from the beginning, how playful and how patterned the boy's bedtime romp with his father is. As you read it, try to be conscious of the emotional effects created by the choice of words that seem to be key ones. Which words establish the bond between the two males?

THEODORE ROETHKE

My Papa's Waltz

The whiskey on your breath
Could make a small boy dizzy;
But I hung on like death:
Such waltzing was not easy.

We romped until the pans   5
Slid from the kitchen shelf;
My mother's countenance
Could not unfrown itself.

The hand that held my wrist
Was battered on one knuckle;   10
At every step you missed
My right ear scraped a buckle.

You beat time on my head
With a palm caked hard by dirt,
Then waltzed me off to bed   15
Still clinging to your shirt.

                                                                1948

Exactly what is the situation in *My Papa's Waltz?* What are the
economic circumstances in the family? How can you tell? What indications are there of the family's social class? of the father's line of work?
How would you characterize the speaker? How does the poem indicate his pleasure in the bedtime ritual? Which words suggest the boy's
excitement? Which suggest his anxiety? How can you tell how the
speaker feels about his father? What clues are there about what the
mother is like? How can you tell that the experience is remembered at
some years' distance? What clues are there in the word choice that
an adult is remembering a childhood experience? In what sense is the
poem a tribute to memories of the father? How would you describe the
poem's tone?

The subtlety and force of word choice is sometimes very much
affected by **word order**, the way the sentences are put together.
Sometimes poems are driven to unusual word order because of the
demands of rhyme and meter, but ordinarily poets use word order
very much as prose writers do, to create a particular emphasis. When
an unusual word order is used, you can be pretty sure that something
worth noticing is going on. Notice, for example, the odd constructions
in the second and third stanzas of *My Papa's Waltz.* In the third
stanza, the way the speaker talks about the abrasion of buckle on ear
is very unusual. He does not say that the buckle scraped his ear, but
rather puts it the other way round—a big difference in the kind of
effect created, for it avoids placing blame and refuses to specify any
unpleasant effect. Had he said that the buckle scraped his ear—the
normal way of putting it—we would have to worry about the fragile
ear. The **syntax** (sentence structure) of the poem channels our feeling
and helps to control what we think of the waltz.

The most curious part of the poem is the second stanza, for it is
there that the silent mother appears, and the syntax there is peculiar
in two places. In lines 5–6, the connection between the romping and

the pans falling is stated oddly: "We romped *until* the pans / Slid from the kitchen shelf." The speaker does not say that they knocked down the pans or imply that there was awkwardness, but he does suggest energetic activity and duration. He implies intensity, almost design—as though the romping were not complete until the pans fell. And the sentence about the mother—odd but effective—makes her position clear. She is a silent bystander in this male ritual, and her frown seems molded on her face. It is not as if she is frightened or angry but as if she too is performing a ritual, holding a frown on her face as if it is part of her role in the ritual, as well as perhaps a facet of her stern character. The syntax implies that she *has to* maintain the frown, and the falling of the pans almost seems to be for her benefit. She disapproves, but she is still their audience.

Word order is not always as complicated or crucial as it is in *My Papa's Waltz*, but poets often manipulate the ordinary prose order of a sentence to make a specific point or create a specific emphasis or effect. The poems that follow suggest some of the ways in which poets use words and word order to create for us the various experiences they want us to have of their words.

GERARD MANLEY HOPKINS

Pied Beauty[9]

Glory be to God for dappled things—
   For skies of couple-color as a brinded[1] cow;
     For rose-moles all in stipple[2] upon trout that swim;
Fresh-firecoal chestnut-falls;[3] finches' wings;
     Landscape plotted and pieced—fold, fallow, and plow;   5
   And all trades, their gear and tackle and trim.

All things counter, original, spare, strange;
   Whatever is fickle, freckled (who knows how?)
     With swift, slow; sweet, sour; adazzle, dim;
He fathers-forth whose beauty is past change: 10
     Praise him.

1877

---

9. Particolored beauty: having patches or sections of more than one color.
1. Streaked or spotted.
2. Rose-colored dots or flecks.
3. Fallen chestnuts as red as burning coals.

EMILY DICKINSON

After Great Pain

After great pain, a formal feeling comes—
The Nerves sit ceremonious, like Tombs—
The stiff Heart questions was it He, that bore,
And Yesterday, or Centuries before?

The Feet, mechanical, go round—   5
Of Ground, or Air, or Ought—
A Wooden way
Regardless grown,
A Quartz contentment, like a stone—

This is the Hour of Lead—   10
Remembered, if outlived,
As Freezing Persons recollect tne Snow—
First—Chill—then Stupor—then the letting go—

ca. 1862

WILLIAM CARLOS WILLIAMS

The Red Wheelbarrow

so much depends
upon

a red wheel
barrow

glazed with rain   5
water

beside the white
chickens.

1923

6 FIGURATIVE LANGUAGE

Metaphor and Simile

The language of poetry is almost always picturesque. Rather than depending primarily on abstract ideas and elaborate reasoning, poems depend mainly upon the creation of pictures in our minds, helping us to see things fresh and new, or to feel them suggestively through our other physical senses, such as hearing or the sense of touch. Poetry is most often vital in the sense that it helps us form, in our minds, visual impressions. We "see" a corpse at a funeral, a child chasing geese in the garden, or two lovers sitting together on the bank of a stream, so that our response begins from a vivid impression of exactly what is happening. Some people think that those arts and media which challenge the imagination of a reader or hearer—radio drama, for example, or poetry—allow us to respond more fully than arts (such as film or theater) that actually show things more fully to our physical senses. Certainly they leave more to our imagination, to our mind's eye.

But being visual does not just mean describing, telling us facts, indicating shapes, colors, and specific details. Often the vividness of the picture in our minds depends upon comparisons. What we are trying to imagine is pictured in terms of something else familiar to us, and we are asked to think of one thing as if it were something else. Many such comparisons, or **figures of speech**, in which something is pictured or imaged or figured forth in terms of something already familiar to us, are taken for granted in daily life. Things we can't see or which aren't familiar to us are pictured as things we can; for example, God is said to be like a father, Italy is said to be shaped like a boot. Poems use figurative language much of the time. A speaker may tell us that his ladylove is like a red rose, or that the way to imagine how it feels to be spiritually secure is to think of the way a shepherd takes care of his sheep. The pictorialness of our imagination may *clarify* things for us—scenes, states of mind, ideas—but at the same time it stimulates us to think of how those pictures make us *feel.* Pictures, even when they are mental pictures or imagined visions, may be both denotative and connotative, just as individual words are: they may clarify and make precise, and they may channel our feelings. In this chapter, we will look at some of the ways that poets create pictures in our minds—images that help us think clearly about what they are saying and feel clearly the emotions they want us to feel. Most poetry depends, at least in part, on the pictorial quality of words and upon the notion that something becomes clearer when we compare it with something else that is more familiar. In the poem that follows, the poet helps us to visualize the old age and approaching death of the speaker by making comparisons with familiar things—the coming of winter, the approach of sunset, and the dying embers of a fire.

434

WILLIAM SHAKESPEARE

That Time of Year

*late
fall–winter*

That time of year thou mayst in me behold
When yellow leaves, or none, or few, do hang
Upon those boughs which shake against the cold,
Bare ruined choirs, where late the sweet birds sang.
In me thou see'st the twilight of such day   5
As after sunset fadeth in the west;
Which by and by[1] black night doth take away,
Death's second self,[2] that seals up all in rest.
In me thou see'st the glowing of such fire,
That on the ashes of his youth doth lie,   10
As the deathbed whereon it must expire,
Consumed with that which it was nourished by.
This thou perceiv'st, which makes thy love more strong,
To love that well which thou must leave ere long.

                                                    1609

The first four lines of *That Time of Year* make the comparison to
seasonal change; but notice that the poet does not have the speaker
say directly that his physical condition and age make him resemble
autumn. He draws the comparison without stating directly that it is
a comparison: you can see, he says, my own state in the coming of
winter in late autumn when the leaves are almost all off the trees.
The speaker portrays himself *indirectly* by talking about the passing
of the year. The poem uses metaphor; that is, one thing is pictured
as if it were something else. *That Time of Year* goes on to another
metaphor in lines 5–8 and still another in lines 9–12, and each of the
metaphors contributes to our understanding of the speaker's sense
of his old age and approaching death. Even more important, however,
is the way the metaphors give us feelings, an emotional sense of the
speaker's age and of his own attitude toward aging. Through the
metaphors we come to understand, appreciate, and to some extent
share the increasing sense of anxiety and urgency that the poem
expresses. Our emotional sense of the poem is largely influenced by
the way each metaphor is developed and by the way each metaphor
leads, with its own kind of internal logic, to another.

The images of late autumn in the first four lines all suggest loneliness, loss, and nostalgia for earlier times. As in the rest of the poem,

1. Shortly.   2. Sleep.

our eyes are imagined to be the main vehicle for noticing the speaker's age and condition; the phrase "thou mayst in me behold" (line 1) introduces what we are asked to see, and in both lines 5 and 9 we are similarly told "In me thou see'st. . . ." The picture of the trees shedding their leaves suggests that autumn is nearly over, and we can imagine trees either with yellow leaves, or without leaves, or with just a trace of foliage remaining—the latter perhaps most feelingly suggesting the bleakness and loneliness that characterize the change of seasons, the ending of the life cycle. But other senses are invoked too. The boughs shaking against the cold represent an appeal to our tactile sense, and the next line appeals to our sense of hearing, although only as a reminder that the birds no longer sing. (Notice how exact the visual representation is of the bare, or nearly bare, limbs, even as the cold and the lack of birds are noted; birds lined up like a choir on risers would have made a striking visual image on the barren limbs one above the other, but now there is only the *reminder* of what used to be. The present is quiet, bleak, trembly, and lonely.)

The next four lines are slightly different in tone, and the color changes. From a black-and-white landscape with a few yellow leaves, we come upon a rich and almost warm reminder of a faded sunset. But a somber note does enter the poem in these lines through another figure of speech, personification, which involves treating an abstraction, such as death or justice or beauty, as if it were a person. The poem is talking about the coming of night and of sleep, and Sleep is personified and identified as the "second self" of Death (that is, as a kind of reflection of death). The main emphasis is on how night and sleep close in on our sense of twilight, and only secondarily does a reminder of death enter the poem. But it does enter.

The third metaphor—that of the dying embers of a fire—begins in line 9 and continues to color and warm the bleak cold that the poem began with, but it also sharpens the reminder of death. The three main metaphors in the poem work in a way to make our sense of old age and approaching death more familiar, but also more immediate: moving from barren trees, to fading twilight, to dying embers suggests a sensuous increase of color and warmth, but also an increasing urgency. The first metaphor involves a whole season, or at least a segment of one, a matter of days or possibly weeks; the second involves the passing of a single day, reducing the time scale to a matter of minutes, and the third draws our attention to that split second when a glowing ember fades into a simple ash. The final part of the fire metaphor introduces the most explicit sense of death so far, as the metaphor of embers shifts into a direct reminder of death. Embers which had been a metaphor of the speaker's aging body now themselves become, metaphorically, a deathbed; the vitality that nourishes youth is used up just as a log in a fire is. The urgency of the reminder of coming death has now peaked. It is friendlier but now seems immediate and inevitable, a natural part of the life process, and the final two lines then make an explicit plea to make good and intense use of the remaining moments of human relationship.

That Time of Year represents an unusually intricate use of images to organize a poem and focus its emotional impact. Not all poems are so skillfully made, and not all depend on such a full and varied use of metaphor. But most poems use metaphors for at least part of their effect, and often a poem is based on a single metaphor which is fully developed as the major way of making the poem's statement and impact, as in this poem about the role of a mother and wife.

LINDA PASTAN

Marks

My husband gives me an A
for last night's supper,
an incomplete for my ironing,
a B plus in bed.
My son says I am average,   5
an average mother, but if
I put my mind to it
I could improve.
My daughter believes
in Pass/Fail and tells me   10
I pass. Wait 'til they learn
I'm dropping out.

1978

The speaker in *Marks* is obviously not thrilled with the idea of continually being judged, and the metaphor of marks (or grades) as a way of talking about her performance of roles in the family suggests her irritation. The list of the roles implies the many things expected of her, and the three different systems of marking (letter grades, categories to be checked off on a chart, and pass/fail) detail the difficulties of multiple standards. The poem retains the language of schooldays all the way to the end ("learn," line 11; "dropping out," line 12), and the major effect of the poem depends on the irony of the speaker's agreeing to surrender to the metaphor the family has thrust upon her; if she is to be judged as if she were a student, she retains the right to drop out. Ironically, she joins the system (adopts the metaphor for herself) in order to defeat it.

The difficulty of conveying what some experiences are like and how we feel about them sometimes leads poets to startling comparisons and figures of speech that may at first seem far-fetched but which, in one way or another, do in fact suggest the quality of the experience or the feelings associated with it. Sometimes a series of metaphors is used, as if no one kind of visualization will serve, but several together may suggest the full complexity of the experience or cumulatively define the feeling precisely. Metaphors open up virtually endless possibilities of comparison, giving words a chance to be more than words, offering our mind's eye a challenge to keep up with the fertile and articulate imagination of writers who make it their business to see things that ordinary people miss, noticing the most surprising likenesses.

Sometimes, in poetry as in prose, comparisons are made explicitly, as in the following poem.

ROBERT BURNS

A Red, Red Rose

O, my luve's like a red, red rose
That's newly sprung in June.
O, my luve is like the melodie
That's sweetly played in tune.

As fair art thou, my bonnie lass,   5
So deep in luve am I;
And I will luve thee still, my dear,
Till a' the seas gang³ dry.

Till a' the seas gang dry, my dear,
And the rocks melt wi' the sun;   10
And I will luve thee still, my dear,
While the sands o' life shall run.

And fare thee weel, my only luve,
And fare thee weel a while!
And I will come again, my luve,   15
Though it were ten thousand mile.

1796

The first four lines make two explicit comparisons: the speaker says that his love is "like a rose" and "like a melodie." Such *explicit* comparison is called a **simile,** and usually (as here) the comparison involves the words "like" or "as." Similes work much as do metaphors, except that they usually are used more passingly, more incidentally; they make a quick comparison and usually do not elaborate, whereas metaphors often extend over a long section of a poem (in which case they are called **extended metaphors**) or even over the whole poem as in Marks (in which case they are called **controlling metaphors**).

The two similes in *A Red, Red Rose* assume that we already have

3. Go.

a favorable opinion of roses and of melodies. Here the poet does not develop the comparison or even remind us of attractive details about roses or tunes. He pays the quick compliment and moves on. Similes sometimes develop more elaborate comparisons than this and occasionally even control long sections of a poem (in which case they are called **analogies**), but usually a simile is briefer and relies more fully on something we already know. The speaker in *My Papa's Waltz* says that he hung on "like death"; he doesn't have to explain or elaborate the comparison: we know the anxiety he refers to.

Like metaphors, similes may imply both meaning and feeling; they may both explain something and invoke feelings about it. All figurative language involves an attempt to clarify something *and* to help readers feel a certain way about it. Saying that one's love is like a rose implies a delicate and fragile beauty and invites our senses into play so that we can share sensuously a response to fragrant appeal and soft touch, just as the shivering boughs and dying embers in Shakespeare's poem explain separation and loss at the same time that they allow us to share the cold sense of loneliness and the warmth of old friendship. The poems that follow suggest some other varieties of figures of speech in poems. But you will also find metaphors and similes elsewhere, in fact nearly everywhere. Once you are alerted to look for them you will find figures in poem after poem; they are among the most common devices through which poets share their vision with us.

RANDALL JARRELL

The Death of the Ball Turret Gunner[4]

From my mother's sleep I fell into the State,
And I hunched in its belly till my wet fur froze.
Six miles from earth, loosed from its dream of life,
I woke to black flak and the nightmare fighters.
When I died they washed me out of the turret with a hose.   5

1945

JOHN DONNE

Batter My Heart

Batter my heart, three-personed God; for You
As yet but knock, breathe, shine, and seek to mend;
That I may rise and stand, o'erthrow me, and bend

---

4. "A ball turret was a plexiglass sphere set into the belly of a B-17 or B-24 and inhabited by two .50 caliber machine-guns and one man, a short, small man. When this gunner tracked with his machine-guns a fighter attacking his bomber from below, he revolved with the turret; hunched upside-down in his little sphere, he looked like the foetus in the womb. The fighters which attacked him were armed with cannon firing explosive shells. The hose was a steam hose." (Jarrell's note)

Your force, to break, blow, burn, and make me new.
I, like an usurped town, to another due,   5
Labor to admit You, but Oh, to no end!
Reason, Your viceroy[5] in me, me should defend,
But is captived, and proves weak or untrue.
Yet dearly I love You, and would be loved fain.[6]
But am betrothed unto Your enemy: 10
Divorce me, untie, or break that knot again,
Take me to You, imprison me, for I,
Except You enthrall me, never shall be free,
Nor ever chaste, except You ravish me.

1633

ANONYMOUS
(Traditionally attributed to King David)

The Twenty-Third Psalm

The Lord is my shepherd; I shall not want.

He maketh me to lie down in green pastures: he leadeth me beside
    the still waters.

He restoreth my soul: he leadeth me in the paths of righteousness
    for his name's sake.
Yea, though I walk through the valley of the shadow of death,
    I will fear no evil: for thou art with me;
    thy rod and thy staff they comfort me.
Thou preparest a table before me in the presence of mine enemies:
    thou anointest my head with oil; my cup runneth over.
Surely goodness and mercy shall follow me all the days of my life:
    and I will dwell in the house of the Lord for ever.

MARGE PIERCY

September Afternoon at Four O'clock

Full in the hand, heavy
with ripeness, perfume spreading
its fan: moments now resemble
sweet russet pears glowing
on the bough, peaches warm   5

5. One who rules as the representative   6. Gladly.
of a higher power.

from the afternoon sun, amber
and juicy, flesh that can
make you drunk.

There is a turn in things
that makes the heart catch.   10
We are ripening, all the hard
green grasping, the stony will
swelling into sweetness, the acid
and sugar in balance, the sun
stored as energy that is pleasure   15
and pleasure that is energy.

Whatever happens, whatever,
we say, and hold hard and let
go and go on. In the perfect
moment the future coils,   20
a tree inside a pit. Take,
eat, we are each other's
perfection, the wine of our
mouths is sweet and heavy.
Soon enough comes the vinegar.   25
The fruit is ripe for the taking
and we take. There is
no other wisdom.

1980

Symbol

One can get into a good argument with a literary critic, a philosopher,
or just about anybody else simply by mentioning the word symbol.
A symbol is many things to many people, and often it means no
more than that the person using the term is dealing with something
he doesn't know how to describe or think about precisely. The term
is difficult to be precise about, but it can be used quite sensibly. A
symbol is, put simply, something which stands for something else.
The everyday world is full of common examples; a flag, a logo, a
trademark, or a skull and crossbones all suggest things beyond themselves, and everyone is likely to understand what their display is
meant to signify, whether or not the viewer shares a commitment to
what the object represents. In common usage a prison is a symbol
of confinement, constriction, and loss of freedom, and in specialized
traditional usage a cross may symbolize oppression, cruelty, suffering,
death, resurrection, triumph, or the intersection of two separate
things, traditions, or ideas (as in crossroads and crosscurrents, for
example). The specific symbolic significance is controlled by the context; a reader may often decide by looking at contiguous details in
the poem and by examining the poem's attitude toward a particular

tradition or body of beliefs. A star means one kind of thing to a Jewish poet and something else to a Christian poet, still something else to a Nazi or to someone whose religion is surfing. In a very literal sense, words themselves are all symbols (they stand for an object, action, or quality, not just for letters or sounds), but symbols in poetry are said to be those words and groups of words which have a range of reference beyond their literal denotation.

Poems sometimes create a symbol out of a thing, action, or event which has no previously agreed upon symbolic significance. In the following poem, for example, a random gesture is given symbolic significance.

SHARON OLDS

Leningrad Cemetery, Winter of 1941[1]

That winter, the dead could not be buried.
The ground was frozen, the gravediggers weak from hunger,
the coffin wood used for fuel. So they were covered with
   something
and taken on a child's sled to the cemetery
in the sub-zero air. They lay on the soil,   5
some of them wrapped in dark cloth
bound with rope like the tree's ball of roots
when it waits to be planted; others wound in sheets,
their pale, gauze, tapered shapes
stiff as cocoons that will split down the center   10
when the new life inside is prepared;
but most lay like corpses, their coverings
coming undone, naked calves
hard as corded wood spilling
from under a cloak, a hand reaching out   15
with no sign of peace, wanting to come back
even to the bread made of glue and sawdust,
even to the icy winter, and the siege.

                                    p. 1979

All of the corpses—frozen, neglected, beginning to be in disarray— vividly stamp upon our minds a sense of the horrors of war, and the detailed picture of the random, uncounted clutter of bodies is likely to stick in our minds long after we have finished reading the poem. Several of the details are striking, and the poem's language heightens our sense of them. The corpses wound in sheets, for example, are

1. The 900-day siege of Leningrad during World War II began in September 1941.

described in "their pale, gauze, tapered shapes," and they are compared to cocoons that one day will split and emit new life; and the limbs that dangle loose when the coverings come undone are said to be "hard as corded wood spilling." But clearly the most memorable sight is the hand dangling from one corpse that is coming unwrapped, for the poet invests that hand with special significance, giving its gesture *meaning*. The hand is described as "reaching out . . . wanting to come back": it is as if the dead can still gesture even if they cannot speak, and the gesture seems to signify the desire of the dead to come back at any price. They would be glad to be alive, even under the grim conditions that attend the living in Leningrad during this grim war. Suddenly the grimness which we—living—have been witnessing pales by comparison with what the dead have lost simply by being dead. The hand has been made to symbolize the desire of the dead to return, to be alive, to be still among us, anywhere. The hand reaches out in the poem as a gesture that means; the poet has made it a symbol of desire.

The whole array of dead bodies in the poem might be said to be symbolic as well. As a group, they stand for the human waste that the war has produced, and their dramatic visual presence on the scene provides the poem with a dramatic visualization of how war and its requirements have no time for decency, not even the decency of burial. The bodies are a symbol in the sense that they stand for what the poem as a whole asserts.

This next poem also arises out of a historical moment, but this time the event is a personal one which the poet gives a significance by the interpretation he puts upon it.

JAMES DICKEY

The Leap

The only thing I have of Jane MacNaughton
Is one instant of a dancing-class dance.
She was the fastest runner in the seventh grade,
My scrapbook says, even when boys were beginning
To be as big as the girls,   5
But I do not have her running in my mind,
Though Frances Lane is there, Agnes Fraser,
Fat Betty Lou Black in the boys-against-girls
Relays we ran at recess: she must have run

Like the other girls, with her skirts tucked up   10
So they would be like bloomers,
But I cannot tell; that part of her is gone.
What I do have is when she came,
With the hem of her skirt where it should be

For a young lady, into the annual dance   15
Of the dancing-class we all hated, and with a light
Grave leap, jumped up and touched the end
Of one of the paper-ring decorations

To see if she could reach it. She could,
And reached me now as well, hanging in my mind   20
From a brown chain of brittle paper, thin
And muscular, wide-mouthed, eager to prove
Whatever it proves when you leap
In a new dress, a new womanhood, among the boys
Whom you easily left in the dust   25
Of the passionless playground. If I said I saw
In the paper where Jane MacNaughton Hill,

Mother of four, leapt to her death from a window
Of a downtown hotel, and that her body crushed-in
The top of a parked taxi, and that I held   30
Without trembling a picture of her lying cradled
In that papery steel as though lying in the grass,
One shoe idly off, arms folded across her breast,
I would not believe myself. I would say
The convenient thing, that it was a bad dream   35
Of maturity, to see that eternal process

Most obsessively wrong with the world
Come out of her light, earth-spurning feet
Grown heavy: would say that in the dusty heels
Of the playground some boy who did not depend   40
On speed of foot, caught and betrayed her.
Jane, stay where you are in my first mind:
It was odd in that school, at that dance.
I and the other slow-footed yokels sat in corners
Cutting rings out of drawing paper   45

Before you leapt in your new dress
And touched the end of something I began,
Above the couples struggling on the floor,
New men and women clutching at each other
And prancing foolishly as bears: hold on   50
To that ring I made for you, Jane—
My feet are nailed to the ground
By dust I swallowed thirty years ago—
While I examine my hands.

                                                                    1967

Memory is crucial to *The Leap*. The fact that Jane MacNaughton's graceful leap in dancing class has stuck in the speaker's mind for all these years means that this leap was important to him, meant something to him, stood for something in his mind. For the speaker, the leap is an "instant" and the "only thing" he has of Jane. Its grace and ease are what he remembers, and he struggles at several points to articulate its meaning (lines 15–26, 44–50), but even without articulation or explanation it is there in his head as a visual memory, a symbol for him of something beyond himself, something he cannot do, something he wanted to be. What that leap had stood for, or symbolized, was boldness, confidence, accomplishment, maturity, the ability to go beyond her fellow students in dancing class—the transcending of childhood by someone beginning to be a woman. Her feet now seem "earth-spurning" (line 38) in that original leap, and they separate her from everyone else. Jane MacNaughton was beyond the speaker's abilities and any attempt he could make to articulate his hopes, but not beyond his dreams. And even before articulation, she symbolized that dream.

The leap to her death seems cruelly ironic in the context of her earlier leap. In memory she is suspended in air, as if there were no gravity, no coming back to earth, as if life could exist as dream. And so the photograph, recreated in precise detail, is a cruel dashing of the speaker's dream—a detailed record of the ending of a leap, a denial of the suspension in which his memory had held her. His dream is grounded; her mortality is insistent. But what the speaker wants to hang on to (line 42) is still that symbolic moment which, although now confronted in more mature implications, wil never be altogether replaced or surrendered.

The leap is ultimately symbolic in the *poem*, too, not just in the speaker's mind. In the poem (and for us as readers) the symbolism of the leap is double: the first leap is aspiration, and the second is frustration of high hopes; the two are complementary, one unable to be imagined without the other. The poem is horrifying in some ways, a dramatic reminder that human beings don't ultimately transcend their mortality, their limits, no matter how heroic or unencumbered by gravity they may seem to an observer. But it is not altogether sad and despairing either, partly because it notices and affirms the validity of the original leap and partly because another symbol is created and elaborated in the poem. That symbol is the paper chain.

The chain connects Jane to the speaker both literally and figuratively. It is, in part, his paper chain which she had leaped to touch in dancing class (lines 18–19), and he thinks of her first leap as "touch[ing] the end of something I began" (line 47). He and the other "slow footed," earthbound "yokels" (line 44) were the makers of the chain, and thus they are connected to her original leap, just as a photograph glimpsed in a paper connects the speaker to her second leap. The paper in the chain is "brittle" (line 21), and its creators seem dull artisans compared to the artistic performer that Jane was. They are heavy and left in the dust (lines 25, 52–53), and she is "light" (line 16) and able to transcend them but even in transcendence touching their lives and what they are able to do. And so the paper chain becomes the poem's symbol of linkage, connecting lower accomplishment to higher possibility, the artisan to the artist, material substance to the act of imagination. And the speaker at the end examines the hands that made the chain because those hands certify his connection to her and the imaginative leap she had made for him. The chain thus symbolizes not only the lower capabilities of those who cannot leap like the budding Jane could, but (later) the connection with her leap as both transcendence and mortality. Like the leap itself, the chain has been elevated to special meaning, given symbolic significance, by the poet's treatment of it. A leap and a chain have no necessary significance in themselves to most of us—at least no significance that we have all agreed upon together.

But some objects and acts do have such significance. Over the years some things have acquired an agreed-upon significance, an accepted value in our minds. They already stand for something before the poet cites them; they are **traditional symbols.** Their uses in poetry have to do with the fact that poets can count on a recognition of their traditional suggestions and meanings outside the poem, and the poem does not have to propose or argue a particular symbolic value. Birds, for example, traditionally symbolize flight, freedom from confinement, detachment from earthbound limits, the ability to soar beyond rationality and transcend mortal limits. Traditionally, birds have also been linked with imagination, especially poetic imagination, and poets often identify with them as ideal singers of songs, as in Keats's *Ode to a Nightingale* (p. 506). One of the most traditional symbols is that of the rose. It may be a simple and fairly plentiful flower in its season, but it has been allowed to stand for particular qualities for so long that to name it raises predictable expectations. Its beauty, delicacy, fragility, shortness of life, and depth of color have made it a symbol of the transitoriness of beauty, and countless poets have counted on its accepted symbolism—sometimes to compliment a friend (as Burns does in *A Red, Red Rose*) or sometimes to make a point about the nature of symbolism. The following poem draws on, in a quite traditional way, the traditional meanings.

JOHN CLARE

Love's Emblem

Go, rose, my Chloe's[2] bosom grace:
    How happy should I prove,
Could I supply that envied place
    With never-fading love.

Accept, dear maid, now summer glows,   5
    This pure, unsullied gem,
Love's emblem in a full-blown rose,
    Just broken from the stem.

2. A standard "poetic" name for a woman in traditional love poetry.

Accept it as a favorite flower
   For thy soft breast to wear;   10
'Twill blossom there its transient hour,
   A favorite of the fair.

Upon thy cheek its blossom glows,
   As from a mirror clear,
Making thyself a living rose,   15
   In blossom all the year.

It is a sweet and favorite flower
   To grace a maiden's brow,
Emblem of love without its power—
   A sweeter rose art thou.   20

The rose, like hues of insect wing,
   May perish in an hour;
'Tis but at best a fading thing,
   But thou'rt a living flower.

The roses steeped in morning dews   25
   Would every eye enthrall,
But woman, she alone subdues;
   Her beauty conquers all.

                       1873

   The speaker in *Love's Emblem* sends the rose to Chloe to decorate her bosom (lines 1, 10) and reflect the blush of her cheek and brow (lines 13, 18), and he goes on to mention some of the standard meanings: the rose is pure (line 6), transitory (line 11), fragrant, beautiful, and always appreciated (line 17). The poet need not elaborate or argue these things; he can assume the reader's acquiescence. To say that the rose is an emblem of love is to say that it traditionally symbolizes love, and the speaker expects Chloe to accept his gift readily; she will understand it as a compliment, a pledge, and a bond. She will understand, too, that her admirer is being conventional and complimentary in going on to call her (and women in general) a rose (line 20), except that her qualities are said to be more lasting than those of a momentary flower.

   Several of the poems at the end of this chapter explore the traditional meanings of the rose as symbol, sometimes playing with the meanings and modifying them, sometimes consciously trying to create new and untraditional meanings, or suggesting the primacy of symbol over physical artifact *(Poem:* "The rose fades").

   Sometimes symbols—traditional or not—become so insistent in the world of a poem that the larger referential world is left almost totally behind. In such cases the symbol is everything, and the poem does not just *use* symbols but becomes a **symbolic poem.**

   Here is an example of such a poem:

WILLIAM BLAKE

The Sick Rose[3]

O rose, thou art sick.
The invisible worm
That flies in the night
In the howling storm

Has found out thy bed   5
Of crimson joy,
And his dark secret love
Does thy life destroy.

1794

The poem does not seem to be about a rose, but about what the
rose represents—not in this case something altogether understandable
through the traditional meanings of rose.

We know that the rose is usually associated with beauty and love,
often with sex; and here several key terms have sexual connotations:
"bed," "worm," and "crimson joy." The violation of the rose by the
worm is the poem's main concern; the violation seems to have involved
secrecy, deceit, and "dark" motives, and the result is sickness rather
than the joy of love. The poem is sad; it involves a sense of hurt
and tragedy, nearly of despair. The poem cries out against the misuse
of the rose, against its desecration, implying that instead of a healthy
joy in sensuality and sexuality, in this case, there has been destruction
and hurt because of misunderstanding and repression and lack of
sensitivity.

But to say so much about this poem I have had to extrapolate
from other poems by this poet, and have introduced information from
outside the poem. Fully symbolic poems often require that, and thus
they ask us to go beyond the normal procedures of reading which we
have discussed here. As presented in this poem, the rose is not part
of the normal world that we ordinarily see, and it is symbolic in a
special sense. The poet does not simply take an object from that
everyday world and give it special significance, making it a symbol
in the same sense that the leap is a symbol, or the corpse's hand.
Here the rose seems to belong to its own world, a world made entirely inside the poem. The rose is not referential. The whole poem
is symbolic; it is not paraphrasable; it lives in its own world. But
what is the rose here a symbol of? In general terms, we can say
from what the poem tells us; but we may not be as confident as we
can be in the more nearly everyday world of *The Leap* or *Leningrad
Cemetery, Winter of 1941*, poems that contain actions we recognize
from the world of probabilities in which we live. In *The Sick Rose*,
it seems inappropriate to ask the standard questions: What rose?

3. In Renaissance emblem books, the scarab beetle, worm, and rose are closely associated: The beetle feeds on dung, and the smell of the rose is fatal to it.

Where? Which worm? What are the particulars here? In the world of this poem worms can fly and may be invisible. We are altogether in a world of meanings.

Negotiation of meanings in symbolic poems can be very difficult indeed. The skill of reading symbolic poems is an advanced skill that depends on special knowledge of authors and of the traditions they work from, and these skills need to be developed carefully and cautiously under the tutelage of a skilled teacher. You will find in this book some examples of symbolic poems (*Sailing to Byzantium*, for example), but the symbols you will usually find in poems are referential, and these meanings are readily discoverable from the careful study of the poems themselves, as in poems like *The Leap* and *Love's Emblem*.

EMILY DICKINSON

Go Not Too Near a House of Rose

fragile

Go not too near a House of Rose—
The depredation of a Breeze
Or inundation of a Dew
Alarms its walls away—

Nor try to tie the Butterfly, *per Traumen* 5
Nor climb the Bars of Ecstasy,
In insecurity to lie.
Is Joy's insuring quality.

ca. 1878

WILLIAM CARLOS WILLIAMS

permanence d'art

Poem

life – death

The rose fades
and is renewed again
by its seed, naturally
but where

save in the poem 5
shall it go
to suffer no diminution
of its splendor

art deathless

1962

DOROTHY PARKER

One Perfect Rose

A single flow'r he sent me, since we met.
   All tenderly his messenger he chose;
Deep-hearted, pure, with scented dew still wet—
   One perfect rose.

I knew the language of the floweret;   5
   "My fragile leaves," it said, "his heart enclose."
Love long has taken for his amulet
   One perfect rose.

Why is it no one ever sent me yet
   One perfect limousine, do you suppose?   10
Ah no, it's always just my luck to get
   One perfect rose.

1937

7 SOUND AND SIGHT

The Sounds of Poetry

A lot of what happens in a poem happens in your mind's eye, but some of it happens in your voice. Poems are full of sounds and silences as well as words and sentences that are meaningful. Besides choosing words for their meanings, poets sometimes choose words because they involve certain sounds, and use sound effects to create a mood or establish a tone, just as films do. Sometimes the sounds of words are crucial to what is happening in the text of the poem.

The following poem explores the sounds of a particular word, tries them on, and analyzes them in relation to the word itself.

HELEN CHASIN

The Word *Plum*

The word *plum* is delicious

pout and push, luxury of
self-love, and savoring murmur

full in the mouth and falling
like fruit   5

taut skin
pierced, bitten, provoked into
juice, and tart flesh

question
and reply, lip and tongue   10
of pleasure.

1968

The poem savors the sounds of the word as well as the taste and feel of the fruit itself. It is almost as if the poem is tasting the sounds and rolling them carefully on the tongue. The second and third lines even replicate the "p," "l," "uh," and "m" sounds of the word while at the same time imitating the squishy sounds of eating the fruit. Words like "delicious" and "luxury" sound juicy, and other words imitate sounds of satisfaction and pleasure—"murmur," for example. Even the process of eating is in part recreated aurally. The tight, clipped sounds of "taut skin / pierced" suggest the sharp breaking of the skin and solid flesh, and as the tartness is described, the words ("provoked," "question") force the mouth to pucker as it would if it were savoring a tart fruit. The poet is having fun here recreating the various sense appeals of a plum, teasing the sounds and meanings out of available words. The words must mean something appropriate and describe something accurately first of all, of course, but when they can also imitate the sounds and feel of the process, they can do double duty. Not all poems manipulate sound as consciously or as fully as *The Word Plum*, but many poems at least contain passages in which the sounds of life are reproduced by the human voice reading the poem. To get the full effect of this poem—and of many others—reading aloud is essential; that way, one can pay attention to the vocal rhythms and can articulate the sounds as the poem calls for them to be reproduced by the human voice.

Almost always a poem's effect will be helped by reading it aloud, using your voice to pronounce the words so that the poem becomes a spoken communication. Historically, poetry began as an oral phenomenon, and often poems that seem very difficult when looked at silently come alive when they are turned into sound. Early bards chanted their verses, and the music of poetry—its cadences and rhythms—developed from this kind of performance. Often in primitive poetry (and sometimes in later ages) poetry performances have been accompanied by some kind of musical instrument. The rhythms of any poem become clearer when you say or hear them.

Poetry is, almost always, a vocal art, dependent on the human voice to become its full self (for some exceptions look at the shaped verse at the end of this chapter). In a sense, it begins to exist as a real phenomenon when a reader reads and actualizes it. Poems don't really achieve their full meaning when they merely exist on a page; a poem on a page is more a set of stage directions for a poem than a poem itself. Sometimes, in fact, it is hard to experience the poem at all unless you hear it. A good poetry reading might easily convince you of the importance of a good voice sensitive to the poem's requirements, but you can also persuade yourself by reading poems aloud in the privacy of your own room. An audience is even better, however, because then there is someone to share the pleasure in the sounds themselves and consider what they imply.

MONA VAN DUYN

What the Motorcycle Said

Br-r-r-am-m-m, rackety-am-m, OM, *Am:*
All—r-r-room, r-r-ram, ala-bas-ter—
Am, the world's my oyster.

I hate plastic, wear it black and slick,
hate hardhats, wear one on my head,
that's what the motorcycle said.   5

Passed phonies in Fords, knocked down billboards, landed
on the other side of The Gap, and Whee,
bypassed history.

When I was born (The Past), baby knew best. *Speech*   10
They shook when I bawled, took Freud's path,
threw away their wrath.

R-r-rackety-am-m, *Am.* War, rhyme,
soap, meat, marriage, the Phantom Jet
are shit, and like that.   15

Hate pompousness, punishment, patience, am into Love,
hate middle-class moneymakers, live on Dad,
that's what the motorcycle said.

Br-r-r-am-m-m. It's Nowsville, man. Passed Oldies, Uglies,
Straighties, Honkies. I'll never be *live forever*   20
mean, tired or unsexy.

Passed cigarette suckers, souses, mother-fuckers,
losers, went back to Nature and found
how to get VD, stoned.

Passed a cow, too fast to hear her moo, "I rolled *Coy Metres* 25
our leaves of grass into one ball.
I am the grassy All."

Br-r-r-am-m-m, rackety-am-m, OM, *Am:*
All—gr-r-rin, oooohgah, gl-l-utton—
Am, the world's my smilebutton.   30

                                                              1973

Saying this poem as if you were a motorcycle with the power of speech (sort of) is part of the poem's fun, and the rich, loud sounds of a motorcycle revving up concentrate and intensify the effect and enrich the pleasure. It's a shame not to hear a poem like this aloud; a lot of it is missed if you don't try to imitate the sounds or if you don't try to pick up the motor's rhythms in the poem. A performance here is clearly worth it: a human being as motorcycle, motorcycle as human being.

And it's a good poem, too, that does something interesting, important, and maybe a bit subversive. The speaking motorcycle seems to take on the values of some of its riders, the noisy and obtrusive ones that readers are most likely to associate with motorcycles in their minds. The riders made fun of here are themselves sort of mindless and mechanical; they are the sort who have cult feelings about their group, who travel in packs, and who live no life beyond their machines. The speaking motorcycle, like such riders, grooves on power and speed, lives for the moment, and has little respect for people, the past, for institutions, or for anything beyond its own small world. It is self-centered, modish, ignorant, and inarticulate; but proud, mighty proud, and feels important in its own sounds. That's what the motorcycle says.

The following poem uses sound effects efficiently, too.

KENNETH FEARING

Dirge

1-2-3 was the number he played but today the number came 3-2-1;
Bought his Carbide at 30, and it went to 29; had the favorite at Bowie
but the track was slow—

O executive type, would you like to drive a floating-power, knee-action,
silk-upholstered six? Wed a Hollywood star? Shoot the course in
58? Draw to the ace, king, jack?
O fellow with a will who won't take no, watch out for three cigarettes
on the same, single match; O democratic voter born in August
under Mars, beware of liquidated rails—

Denouement to denouement, he took a personal pride in the certain,
certain way he lived his own, private life,   5
But nevertheless, they shut off his gas; nevertheless, the bank foreclosed;
nevertheless, the landlord called; nevertheless, the radio broke,

And twelve o'clock arrived just once too often,
Just the same he wore one gray tweed suit, bought one straw hat, drank
one straight Scotch, walked one short step, took one long look,
drew one deep breath,
Just one too many,

And wow he died as wow he lived,   10
Going whop to the office and blooie home to sleep and biff got married
and bam had children and oof got fired,
Zowie did he live and zowie did he die,

With who the hell are you at the corner of his casket, and where the
hell're we going on the right-hand silver knob, and who the hell
cares walking second from the end with an American Beauty
wreath from why the hell not,

Very much missed by the circulation staff of the New York Evening
Post; deeply, deeply mourned by the B.M.T.[1]

1. A New York subway line.

Wham, Mr. Roosevelt; pow, Sears Roebuck; awk, big dipper; bop,
    summer rain;   15
Bong, Mr., bong, Mr., bong, Mr., bong.

                                           1935

As the title implies, this poem is a kind of musical lament, in this
case for a certain sort of businessman who took a lot of chances and
saw his investments and life go down the drain in the depression of
the early thirties. Reading this poem aloud is a big help partly because it contains expressive words which echo the action, words like
"oof" and "blooie" (which primarily carry their meaning in their sounds,
for they have no literal or referential meaning). Reading aloud also
helps us notice that the poem employs rhythms much as a song would
and that it frequently shifts its pace and mood. Notice how carefully
the first two lines are balanced, and then how quickly the rhythm
shifts as the "executive type" begins to be addressed directly in line
3. (Line 2 is long and dribbles over in the narrow pages of a book
like this; a lot of the lines here are especially long, and the irregu-
larity of the line lengths is one aspect of the special sound effects
the poem creates.) In the direct address, the poem first picks up a
series of advertising features which it recites in rapid-fire order rather
like the advertising phrases in *Needs* in Chapter 3 In stanza 3 here,
the rhythm shifts again, but the poem gives us helpful clues about
how to read. Line 5 sounds like prose and is long, drawn out, and
rather dull (rather like its subject), but line 6 sets up a regular
(and monotonous) rhythm with its repeated "nevertheless" which
punctuates the rhythm like a drumbeat: "But nevertheless *tuh-tuh-
tuh-tuh-tuh*; nevertheless *tuh-tuh-tuh-tuh*; nevertheless *tuh-tuh-tuh-
tuh*; nevertheless *tuh-tuh-tuh-tuh-tuh*." In the next stanza, the repetitive phrasing comes again, this time guided by the word "one" in
cooperation with other words of one syllable: "wore *one* gray tweed
suit, bought *one* straw hat, *tuh* one *tuh-tuh*; *tuh* one *tuh-tuh*; *tuh*
one *tuh-tuh*; *tuh* one *tuh-tuh*." And then a new rhythm and a new
technique in stanza 5 as the language of comic books is imitated
to describe in violent, exaggerated terms the routine of his life. You
have to say words like "whop" and "zowie" aloud and in the rhythm
of the whole sentence to get the full effect of how boring his life is,
no matter how he tries to jazz it up with exciting words. And so it
goes—repeated words, shifting rhythms, emphasis on routine and aver-
ageness—until the final bell ("Bong . . . bong . . . bong . . . bong")
tolls rhythmically for the dead man in the final clanging line.

    Sometimes sounds in poems just provide special effects, rather like
a musical score behind a film, setting mood and getting us into an
appropriate frame of mind. But often sound and meaning go hand in
hand, and the poet finds words that in their sounds echo the action.
A word which captures or approximates the sound of what it describes, such as "splash" or "squish" or "murmur" is called an **onomatopoeic** word, and the device itself is called **onomatopoeia**. And simi-

lar things can be done poetically with pacing and rhythm, sounds and pauses. The punctuation, the length of vowels, and the combination of consonant sounds help to control the way we read so that we imitate what is being described.

Here is a classic passage in which a skillful poet talks about the virtues of making the sound echo the sense—and shows at the same time how to do it:

ALEXANDER POPE

[Sound and Sense][2]

But most by numbers[3] judge a poet's song,	337
And smooth or rough, with them, is right or wrong;	
In the bright muse though thousand charms conspire,[4]	
Her voice is all these tuneful fools admire,	340
Who haunt Parnassus[5] but to please their ear,	
Not mend their minds; as some to church repair,	
Not for the doctrine, but the music there.	
These, equal syllables[6] alone require,	
Though oft the ear the open vowels tire,	345
While expletives[7] their feeble aid do join,	
And ten low words oft creep in one dull line,	
While they ring round the same unvaried chimes,	
With sure returns of still expected rhymes.	
Wheree'er you find "the cooling western breeze,"	350
In the next line, it "whispers through the trees";	
If crystal streams "with pleasing murmurs creep,"	
The reader's threatened (not in vain) with "sleep."	
Then, at the last and only couplet fraught	
With some unmeaning thing they call a thought,	355
A needless Alexandrine[8] ends the song,	
That, like a wounded snake, drags its slow length along.	
Leave such to tune their own dull rhymes, and know	
What's roundly smooth, or languishingly slow;	
And praise the easy vigor of a line,	360

---

2. From *An Essay on Criticism*, Pope's poem on the art of poetry and the problems of literary criticism. The passage excerpted here follows a discussion of several common weaknesses of critics: failure to regard an author's intention, for example, or over-emphasis on clever metaphors and ornate style.

3. Meter, rhythm, sound.

4. Unite.

5. A mountain in Greece, traditionally associated with the muses and considered the seat of poetry and music.

6. Regular accents.

7. Filler words, such as "do."

8. A six-foot line, sometimes used in pentameter poems to vary the pace mechanically. Line 357 is an alexandrine.

Where Denham's strength and Waller's[9] sweetness join.
True ease in writing comes from art, not chance,
As those move easiest who have learned to dance.
'Tis not enough no harshness gives offense,
The sound must seem an echo to the sense: 365
Soft is the strain when Zephyr[1] gently blows,
And the smooth stream in smoother numbers flows;
But when loud surges lash the sounding shore,
The hoarse, rough verse should like the torrent roar.
When Ajax[2] strives, some rock's vast weight to throw,   370
The line too labors, and the words move slow;
Not so, when swift Camilla[3] scours the plain,
Flies o'er th' unbending corn, and skims along the main.
Hear how Timotheus'[4] varied lays surprise,
And bid alternate passions fall and rise!   375
While, at each change, the son of Libyan Jove[5]
Now burns with glory, and then melts with love;
Now his fierce eyes with sparkling fury glow,
Now sighs steal out, and tears begin to flow:
Persians and Greeks like turns of nature[6] found,   380
And the world's victor stood subdued by sound!
The pow'r of music all our hearts allow,
And what Timotheus was, is DRYDEN now.

                                                              1711

A lot of things go on here simultaneously. The poem uses a number of echoic or onomatopoeic words, and pleasant and unpleasant consonant sounds are used in some lines to underline a particular point or add some mood music. When the poet talks about a particular weakness in poetry, he illustrates it at the same time—by using open vowels (line 345), expletives (line 346), monosyllabic words (line 347), predictable rhymes (lines 350–353), or long, slow lines (line 357). And the good qualities of poetry he talks about and illustrates as well (line 360, for example). But the main effects of the passage come from an interaction of several strategies at once. The effects are fairly simple and easy to spot, but their causes involve a lot of poetic ingenuity. In line 340, for example, a careful cacophonous effect is achieved by the repetition of the $\overline{oo}$ vowel sound and the repetition of the L consonant sound together with the interruption (twice) of the rough F sound in the middle; no one wants to be caught admiring that music when the poet gets through with us, but the careful harmony of the preceding sounds has set us up beautifully. And in lines 347, 357, and 359, the pace of the lines is carefully con-

9. Sir John Denham and Edmund Waller, 17th-century poets credited with perfecting the heroic couplet.
1. The west wind.
2. A Greek hero of the Trojan War, noted for his strength.
3. A woman warrior in *The Aeneid*.
4. The court-musician of Alexander the Great, celebrated in a famous poem by

Dryden (see line 383) for the power of his music over Alexander's emotions.
5. In Greek tradition, the chief god of any people was often given the name Zeus (Jove), and the chief god of Libya (the Greek name for all of Africa) was called Zeus Ammon. Alexander visited his oracle and was proclaimed son of the god.
6. Similar alternations of emotion.

trolled by consonant sounds as well as by the use of long vowels. Line 347 moves incredibly slowly and seems much longer than it is because almost all the one-syllable words end in a consonant which refuses to blend with the beginning of the next word, making the words hard to say without distinct, awkward pauses between them. And in lines 357 and 359, long vowels such as those in "wounded," "snake," "slow," "along," "roundly," and "smooth" help to slow down the pace, and the same trick of juxtaposing awkward, unpronounceable consonants is also employed. The commas also provide nearly a full stop in the midst of each line to slow us down still more. Similarly, the harsh lashing of the shore in lines 368–69 is partly accomplished by onomatopoeia, partly by a shift in the pattern of stress which creates irregular waves in line 368, and partly by the dominance of rough consonants in line 369. (In Pope's time, the English *r* was still trilled gruffly so that it could be made to sound extremely rough and harsh.) Almost every line in this passage could serve as a demonstration of how to make sound echo sense.

As the passage from Pope and the poem *Dirge* suggest, sound is most effectively manipulated in poetry when the rhythm of the voice is carefully controlled so that not only are the proper sounds heard, but they are heard at precisely the right moment. Pace and rhythm are nearly as important to a good poem as they are to a good piece of music. The human voice naturally develops certain rhythms in speech; some syllables and some words receive more stress than others, and a careful poet controls the flow of stresses to that, in many poems, a certain basic rhythm develops almost like a quiet percussion instrument in the background. The most common rhythm in English is the regular alternation of unstressed and stressed syllables, as in the passage from Pope. There, most lines have five sets of unstressed/stressed syllables, although plenty of lines have slight variations so that there is little danger (if you read sensitively) of falling into too expected a rhythm, a dull sing-song. The unstressed/stressed pattern (in that order) is called **iambic** rhythm. Other fairly common rhythms are the **trochaic** (a stressed syllable followed by an unstressed one), the **anapestic** (two unstressed syllables followed by a stressed one), and **dactylic** (a stressed syllable followed by two unstressed ones). Each unit of measurement is called a **foot**.

Here is a poem which names and illustrates many of the meters. If you read it aloud and chart the unstressed (∪) and stressed (—) syllables you should have a chart similar to that done by the poet himself in the text.

SAMUEL TAYLOR COLERIDGE

Metrical Feet

Lesson for a Boy

Trōchĕe trĭps frŏm lŏng tŏ shōrt;⁷
From long to long in solemn sort
Slōw Spōndēe stālks; strŏng fŏŏt! yet ill able
Ēvĕr tŏ cōme ŭp wĭth Dāctўl trĭsўllăblĕ.
Ĭambĭcs mārch frŏm shŏrt tŏ lōng—   5
Wĭth ă lēap ănd ă bōund thĕ swĭft Ānăpĕsts thrōng;
One syllable long, with one short at each side,
Ămphĭbrăchўs hāstes wĭth ă stātelў stride—
Fĭrst ănd lāst bēĭng lōng, mĭddlĕ shōrt, Ămphĭmācer
Strĭkes hĭs thūndĕrĭng hōŏfs lĭke ă prōud hĭgh-brĕd Rācer.   10
If Derwent⁸ be innocent, steady, and wise,
And delight in the things of earth, water, and skies;
Tender warmth at his heart, with these meters to show it,
With sound sense in his brains, may make Derwent a poet—
May crown him with fame, and must win him the love   15
Of his father on earth and his Father above.
              My dear, dear child!
Could you stand upon Skiddaw,⁹ you would not from its whole ridge
See a man who so loves you as your fond s. t. COLERIDGE.
1806

The following poem exemplifies **dactylic** rhythm, and the limericks that follow are written in **anapestic** meter.

ARTHUR W. MONKS

Twilight's Last Gleaming

Higgledy-piggledy
President Jefferson
Gave up the ghost on the
Fourth of July.

So did John Adams, which   5
Shows that such patriots
Propagandistically
Knew how to die.

1967

7. The long and short marks over syllables are Coleridge's the kinds of metrical feet named and exemplified here are defined in the glossary, p. 891.

8. Written originally for Coleridge's son Hartley, the poem was later adapted for his younger son, Derwent.

9. A mountain in the lake country of northern England (where Coleridge lived in his early years), near the town of Derwent.

ANONYMOUS

[A Staid Schizophrenic Named Struther]

A staid schizophrenic named Struther,
When told of the death of his brother,
　　Said: "Yes, I am sad;
　　It makes me feel bad,
But then, I still have each other."

ANONYMOUS

[There Once Was a Pious Young Priest]

There once was a pious young priest
Who lived almost wholly on yeast.
　　He said, "It's so plain
　　We must all rise again
That I'd like to get started at least."

ANONYMOUS

[There Once Was a Spinster of Ealing]

There once was a spinster of Ealing,
Endowed with such delicate feeling,
　　That she thought an armchair
　　Should not have its legs bare—
So she kept her eyes trained on the ceiling.

This poem is composed in the more common **trochaic** meter.

SIR JOHN SUCKLING

Song

Why so pale and wan, fond Lover?
　　Prithee why so pale?
Will, when looking well can't move her,
　　Looking ill prevail?
　　Prithee why so pale?   5

Why so dull and mute, young Sinner?
　Prithee why so mute?
Will, when speaking well can't win her,
　Saying nothing do 't?
　Prithee why so mute?　　　　　　　10

Quit, quit, for shame, this will not move,
　This cannot take her;
If of her self she will not love,
　Nothing can make her,
　The Devil take her.　　　　　　　15

　　　　　　　　　　　　　1646

　The basic meter in the following poem is the most common one in
English, **iambic**:

JOHN DRYDEN

To the Memory of Mr. Oldham[1]

Farewell, too little, and too lately known,
Whom I began to think and call my own;
For sure our souls were near allied, and thine
Cast in the same poetic mold with mine.
One common note on either lyre did strike,　　　5
And knaves and fools we both abhorred alike.
To the same goal did both our studies drive;
The last set out the soonest did arrive.
Thus Nisus fell upon the slippery place,
While his young friend performed and won the race.[2]　　10
O early ripe! to thy abundant store
What could advancing age have added more?
It might (what nature never gives the young)
Have taught the numbers[3] of thy native tongue.
But satire needs not those, and wit will shine　　　15
Through the harsh cadence of a rugged line.[4]
A noble error, and but seldom made,
When poets are by too much force betrayed.
Thy generous fruits, though gathered ere their prime,
Still showed a quickness; and maturing time　　　20
But mellows what we write to the dull sweets of rhyme.
Once more, hail and farewell; farewell, thou young,
But ah too short, Marcellus[5] of our tongue;

1. John Oldham (1653–83), who like
Dryden (see lines 3–6) wrote satiric poetry.
2. In Vergil's *Aeneid* (Book V), Nisus
(who is leading the race) falls and then
trips the second runner so that his friend
Euryalus can win.

3. Rhythms.
4. In Dryden's time, R's were pronounced with a harsh, trilling sound.
5. The nephew of the Roman emperor
Augustus; he died at 20, and Vergil celebrated him in *The Aeneid*, Book VI.

Thy brows with ivy, and with laurels bound;
But fate and gloomy night encompass thee around.   25

1684

Once you have figured out the basic rhythm of a poem, you can often find some interesting things by looking carefully at the departures from the pattern. Departures from the basic iambic meter of *To the Memory of Mr. Oldham*, for example, suggest some of the imaginative things that poets can do within the apparently very restrictive requirements of traditional meter. Try marking the stressed and unstressed syllables in *To the Memory of Mr. Oldham* and then look carefully at each of the places which vary from the basic iambic pattern. Which of these variations call special attention to a particular sound or action being talked about in the poem? Which ones specifically mimic or echo the sense? Which variations seem to exist primarily for emphasis? Which ones seem primarily intended to mark structural breaks in the poem?

DONALD JUSTICE

Counting the Mad

This one was put in a jacket,
This one was sent home,
This one was given bread and meat
But would eat none,
And this one cried No No No No   5
All day long.

This one looked at the window
As though it were a wall,
This one saw things that were not there,
This one things that were,   10
And this one cried No No No No
All day long.

This one thought himself a bird,
This one a dog,
And this one thought himself a man,   15
An ordinary man,
And cried and cried No No No No
All day long.

1960

JAMES MERRILL

Watching the Dance

1. BALANCHINE'S[6]

> Poor savage, doubting that a river flows
> But for the myriad eddies made
> By unseen powers twirling on their toes,
>
> Here in this darkness it would seem
> You had already died, and were afraid.   5
> Be still. Observe the powers. Infer the stream.

2. DISCOTHÈQUE.

> Having survived entirely your own youth,
> Last of your generation, purple gloom
> Investing you, sit, Jonah,[7] beyond speech,
>
> And let towards the brute volume VOOM whale mouth   10
> VAM pounding viscera VAM VOOM
> A teenage plankton luminously twitch.

1967

GERARD MANLEY HOPKINS

Spring and Fall:

To a Young Child

> Márgarét áre you gríeving
> Over Goldengrove unleaving?
> Leáves, líke the things of man, you
> With your fresh thoughts care for, can you?
> Áh! ás the heart grows older   5
> It will come to such sights colder
> By and by, nor spare a sigh
> Though worlds of wanwood[8] leafmeal lie;
> And yet you wíll weep and know why.
> Now no matter, child, the name: 10
> Sórrow's spríngs áre the same.
> Nor mouth had, no nor mind, expressed
> What heart heard of, ghost[9] guessed:
> It ís the blight man was born for,
> It is Margaret you mourn for.   15

1880

---

6. George Balanchine, Russian-born (1894) ballet choreographer and teacher.
7. According to *Jonah* 4, Jonah sat in gloom near Nineveh after its residents repented and God decided to spare the city from destruction.
8. Pale, gloomy woods. "leafmeal": broken up, leaf by leaf (analogous to "piecemeal").
9. Soul.

MICHAEL HARPER

Dear John, Dear Coltrane

> *a love supreme, a love supreme*[1]
> *a love supreme, a love supreme*

Sex fingers toes
in the marketplace
near your father's church
in Hamlet, North Carolina—[2]
witness to this love   5
in this calm fallow
of these minds,
there is no substitute for pain:
genitals gone or going,
seed burned out,   10
you tuck the roots in the earth,
turn back, and move
by river through the swamps,
singing: *a love supreme, a love supreme;*
what does it all mean?   15
Loss, so great each black
woman expects your failure
in mute change, the seed gone.
You plod up into the electric city—
your song now crystal and   20
the blues. You pick up the horn
with some will and blow
into the freezing night:
a love supreme, a love supreme—

Dawn comes and you cook   25
up the thick sin 'tween
impotence and death, fuel
the tenor sax cannibal
heart, genitals and sweat
that makes you clean—   30
a love supreme, a love supreme—

Why you so black?
cause I am
why you so funky?
cause I am   35
why you so black?
cause I am

1. Coltrane's record of "A Love Supreme," released in 1965, represents his moment of greatest public acclaim. The record was named Record of the Year and Coltrane was named jazz musician of the year in the *Downbeat* poll.

2. Coltrane's birthplace. His family shared a house with Coltrane's grandfather, who was the minister of St. Stephen's AME Zion Church there.

why you so sweet?
cause I am
why you so black?   40
cause I am
a love supreme, a love supreme:

So sick
you couldn't play **Naima**,[3]
so flat we ached   45
for song you'd concealed
with your own blood,
your diseased liver gave
out its purity,
the inflated heart   50
pumps out, the tenor kiss,
tenor love:
a love supreme, a love supreme—
a love supreme, a love supreme—

1970

The Way a Poem Looks

The way a poem looks is not nearly so important as the way it sounds—usually. But there are exceptions. A few poems are written to be seen rather than heard or read aloud, and their appearance on the page is crucial to their effect. The poem *l(a*, for example (p. 468), tries to visualize typographically what the poet asks you to see in your mind's eye. Occasionally, too, poems are composed in a specific shape so that the poem looks like a physical object. At the end of this chapter, several poems—some old, some new—illustrate some of the ways in which visual effects may be created. Even though poetry has traditionally been thought of as oral—words to be said, sung, or performed rather than looked at—the idea that poems can also be related to painting and the visual arts is also an old one. Theodoric in ancient Greece is credited with inventing **technopaegnia** —that is, constructing poems with visual appeal. Once, the shaping of words to resemble an object was thought to have mystical power, but more recent attempts at **shaped verse** (the general term that may be applied to any poem that uses visual appeal dramatically) are usually playful exercises (such as Robert Hollander's *You Too? Me Too—Why Not? Soda Pop*, which is shaped like a Coke bottle), attempting to supplement (or replace) verbal meanings with devices from painting and sculpture.

Reading a poem like *Easter Wings* aloud wouldn't make much sense. Our eyes are everything for a poem like that. A more frequent poetic device is to ask us to use our eyes as a guide to sound. The following poem depends upon recognition of some standard typographical symbols and knowledge of their names. We have to say those names to read the poem:

3. **Another standard Coltrane song, recorded in 1966 at the Village Vanguard.**

FRANKLIN P. ADAMS

Composed in the Composing Room

At stated .ic times
I love to sit and — off rhymes
Till ,tose at last I fall
Exclaiming "I don't ∧ all."

Though I'm an ° objection   5
By running this in this here §
This ☞ of the Fleeting Hour,
This lofty -ician Tower—

A ¶er's hope dispels   10
All fear of deadly ||.
You think these [ ] are a **pipe**?
Well, not on your †eotype.

1914

We create the right term here when we verbalize, putting the visual signs together with the words or letters printed in the poem, for example making the word "periodic" out of ".ic" or "high Phoenician" out of "-ician." This, too, involves an extreme instance and involves a game more than any serious emotional effect. More often poets give us—by the visual placement of sounds—a guide to reading, inviting us to regulate the pace of our reading, notice pauses or silences, pay attention both to the syntax of the poem and to the rhetoric of the voice, thus providing us a set of stage directions for reading.

e. e. cummings

portrait

Buffalo Bill's
defunct
          who used to
          ride a watersmooth-silver
                                        stallion   5
and break onetwothreefourfive pigeonsjustlikethat
                                                    Jesus
he was a handsome man
                          and what i want to know is
how do you like your blueeyed boy   10
Mister Death

1923

The unusual spacing of words here, with some run together and others widely separated, provides a guide to reading, regulating both speed and sense, so that the poem can capture aloud some of the excitement and wonder of a boy's enthusiasm for a theatrical act as spectacular as that of Buffalo Bill. A good reader-aloud, with only this typographical guidance, can capture some of the wide-eyed boy's responses, remembered now in retrospect long after Buffalo Bill's act is out of business and the man himself is dead.

In prose, syntax and punctuation are the main guides to the voice of a reader, providing indicators of emphasis, pace, and speed, and in poetry they are also more conventional and more common guides

GEORGE HERBERT

Easter Wings

Lord, who createdst man in wealth and store,[1]
Though foolishly he lost the same,
Decaying more and more,
Till he became
Most poor:
                    With thee
                O let me rise
            As larks,[2] harmoniously,
        And sing this day thy victories:
    Then shall the fall further the flight in me.

My tender age in sorrow did begin;
And still with sicknesses and shame
Thou didst so punish sin,
That I became
Most thin.
                    With thee
                Let me combine,
            And feel this day thy victory;
        For, if I imp[3] my wing on thine,
    Affliction shall advance the flight in me.

1633

1. In plenty.
2. Which herald the morning.
3. Engraft. In falconry, to engraft feathers in a damaged wing, so as to restore the powers of flight (OED).

e. e. cummings

l(a

l(a

le

af

fa

ll

s)

one

l

iness

5

1958

ROBERT HOLLANDER

You Too? Me Too—Why Not?
Soda Pop

I am
look
ing at
the Co
caCola
bottle
which is
green wi
th ridges
just like

c   c   c
o   o   o
l   l   l
u   u   u
m   m   m
n   n   n
s   s   s

and on itself it says

COCA-COLA
reg.u.s.pat.off.

exactly like an art pop
statue of that kind of
bottle but not so green
that the juice inside
gives other than the co
lor it has when I pour
it out in a clear glass
glass on this table top
(It's making me thirsty
all this winking and
beading of Hippocrene
please let me pause
drinking the fluid in)
ah! it is enticing how
each color is the same
brown in green bottle
brown in uplifted glass
making each utensil on
the table laid a brown
fork in a brown shade
making me long to watch
them harvesting the crop
which makes the deep-aged
rich brown wine of America
that is to say which makes
soda   pop

p. 1968

8 STANZAS AND VERSE FORMS

Most poems of more than a few lines are divided into **stanzas,** groups of lines divided from other groups by white space on the page. Putting some space between the groupings of lines has the effect of sectioning off the poem, giving its physical appearance a series of divisions that often mark breaks in thought in the poem, or changes of scenery or imagery, or other shifts in the direction of the poem. In *The Flea* (p. 414), for example, the stanza divisions mark distinctive stages in the action; between the first and second stanzas, the speaker stops his companion from killing the flea, and between the second and third stanzas, the companion follows through on her intention and kills the flea. Not all stanzas are quite so neatly patterned, but any poem divided into stanzas calls attention on the page to the fact of the divisions and invites some sort of response to what appear to be gaps or silences that may be structural indicators.

Historically, stanzas have most often been organized internally by patterns of rhyme, and thus stanza divisions have been a visual indicator of patterns in sound. In most traditional stanza forms, the pattern of rhyme is repeated in stanza after stanza throughout the poem, and the voice and ear become familiar with the pattern so that, in a sense, we come to depend on it. We can thus "hear" variations, just as we do in music. In a poem of more than a few stanzas, the accumulation of pattern may even mean that our ear comes to expect repetition and finds a kind of comfort in its increasing familiarity. The rhyme thus becomes an organizational device in the poem, and ordinarily the metrical patterns stay constant from stanza to stanza. In Shelley's *Ode to the West Wind,* for example, the first and third lines in each stanza rhyme, and the middle line then rhymes with the first and third lines of the next stanza. (In indicating rhyme, a different letter of the alphabet is conventionally used to represent each sound; in the following example, if we begin with "being" as *a* and "dead" as *b,* then "fleeing" is also *a,* and "red" and "bed" are *b.*)

O wild West Wind, thou breath of Autumn's being,	a
Thou, from whose unseen presence the leaves dead	b
Are driven, like ghosts from an enchanter fleeing,	a
Yellow, and black, and pale, and hectic red,	b
Pestilence-stricken multitudes: O thou,	c
Who chariotest to their dark wintry bed	b
The wingèd seeds, where they lie cold and low,	c
Each like a corpse within its grave, until	d
Thine azure sister of the Spring shall blow	c

In this stanza form, known as **terza rima,** the stanzas are thus linked to each other by a common sound: one rhyme sound from each stanza is picked up in the next stanza, and so on to the end of the group of stanzas. This stanza form is the one used by Dante in *The Divine Comedy*; its use is not all that common in English because it is a rhyme-rich stanza form—that is, it requires many, many rhymes, and English is, relatively speaking, a rhyme-poor language (that is, not so rich in rhyme possibilities as are languages such as Italian or French). One reason for this is that English words derive from so many different language families that we have fewer similar word endings than languages that have remained more "pure," more dependent for vocabulary on roots and patterns in their own language system.

Shortly, we will look at some other stanza forms, but first a brief Defense of Rhyme, or at least an explanation of its uses. Contemporary poets seldom use it, finding it neither necessary nor appealing, but until the last half century or so rhyme was central to most poems. Historically, there are good reasons for rhyme. Why have most recent poets avoided rhyme as vigorously as older poets pursued it? There is no single easy answer, but one can suggest why poetry traditionally found rhyme attractive and notice that some of those needs no longer exist. Because poetry was originally an oral art (and its texts not always written down) various kinds of **memory devices** (sometimes called **mnemonic devices**) were built into poems to help reciters remember them. Rhyme was one such device, and most people still find it easier to memorize poetry that rhymes. The simple pleasure of hearing the repetition of familiar sounds may also help to account for the traditional popularity of rhyme, and perhaps plain habit (for both poets and hearers) had a lot to do with why rhyme flourished for so many centuries as a standard expectation. No doubt, too, rhyme helped to give poetry a special quality that distinguished it from prose, a significant advantage in ages that worried about decorum and propriety and that were anxious to preserve a strong sense of poetic tradition. Some ages have been very concerned that poetry should not in any way be mistaken for prose or made to serve prosaic functions, and the literary critics and theorists in those ages made extraordinary efforts to emphasize the distinctions between poetry, which was thought to be artistically superior, and prose, which was thought to be primarily utilitarian. A pride in elitism and a fear that an expanded reading public could ultimately mean a dilution of the possibilities of traditional art forms have been powerful cultural forces in Western civilization, and if such forces were not themselves responsible for creating rhyme in poetry, they did help to preserve a sense of its necessity.

But there are at least two other reasons for rhyme. One is complex and hard to state justly without long explanations. It involves traditional ideas of the symmetrical relationship of different aspects of the world and ideas about the function of poetry to reflect the universe as human learning understood it. Most poets in earlier centuries assumed that rhyme was proper to verse, perhaps even essential. They would have felt themselves eccentric to compose poems any other way. Some poets did experiment—very successfully—with **blank verse** (that is, verse which did not rhyme but which nevertheless had strict metrical requirements), but the cultural pressure was almost constantly for rhyme. Why? Custom or habit may account for part of the assumption that rhyme was necessary, but probably not all of it. Rather, the poets' sense that poetry was an imitation of larger relationships in the universe made it seem natural to use rhyme to recreate a sense of harmony, correspondence, symmetry, and order. The sounds of poetry were thus faint reminders of the harmonious cosmos, of the music of the spheres that animated the planets, the processes of nature, the interrelationship of all created things and beings. Probably poets never said to themselves, "I shall now tunefully emulate the harmony of God's carefully ordered universe," but the tendency to use rhyme and other repetitions or re-echoings of sound nevertheless stems ultimately from basic assumptions about how the universe worked. In a modern world increasingly perceived as fragmented, rambling, and unrelated, there is of course a much lessened tendency to testify to a sense of harmony and symmetry. It would be too easy and too mechanical to think that rhyme in a poem specifically means that the poet has a firm sense of cosmic order, and that an unrhymed poem testifies to chaos, but cultural assumptions do affect the expectations of both poets and readers, and cultural tendencies create a kind of pressure upon the individual creator.

One other reason for using rhyme is that it provides a kind of discipline for the poet, a way of harnessing poetic talents and keeping a rein on the imagination, so that the results are ordered, controlled, put into some kind of meaningful and recognizable form. Robert Frost used to be fond of saying that writing poems without rhyme was like playing tennis without a net. Writing good poetry does require a lot of discipline, and Frost speaks for many (perhaps most) traditional poets in suggesting that rhyme can be a major source of that discipline. But it is not the only possible source, and more recent poets have usually felt they would rather play by new rules or invent their own as they go along, and have therefore sought their sources of discipline elsewhere, preferring the more spare tones that unrhymed poetry provides. It is not that contemporary poets cannot think of rhyme words or that they do not care about the sounds of their poetry; rather, recent poets have consciously decided not to work with rhyme and to use instead other aural devices and other strategies for organizing stanzas, just as they have chosen to work with experimental and variable rhythms instead of writing primarily in the traditional English meters. Some few modern poets, though, have protested the abandonment of rhyme and have continued to write rhymed verse successfully in a more or less traditional way.

The amount and density of rhyme varies widely in stanza and verse forms, some requiring elaborate and intricate patterns of rhyme, others more casual or spare sound repetitions. The **Spenserian stanza,** for example, is even more rhyme rich than terza rima, using only three rhyme sounds in nine rhymed lines.

Her falt'ring hand upon the balustrade,	a
Old Angela was feeling for the stair,	b
When Madeline, St. Agnes' charmèd maid,	a
Rose, like a missioned spirit, unaware:	b
With silver taper's light, and pious care,	b
She turned, and down the agèd gossip led	c
To a safe level matting. Now prepare,	b
Young Porphyro, for gazing on that bed;	c
She comes, she comes again, like ring dove frayed and fled.	c

On the other hand, the **ballad stanza** has only one rhyme in four lines; lines 1 and 3 in each stanza do not rhyme at all.

The king sits in Dumferling toune,	a
Drinking the blude-reid wine:	b
"O whar will I get guid sailor,	c
To sail this ship of mine?"	b

Most stanzas have a metrical pattern as well as a rhyme scheme. Terza rima, for example, involves five-beat lines (iambic pentameter), and most of the Spenserian stanza (the first 8 lines) is also in iambic pentameter, but the ninth line in each stanza has one extra foot (it is iambic hexameter). The ballad stanza, also iambic as are most English stanza and verse forms, alternates three-beat and four-beat lines; lines 1 and 3 are unrhymed iambic tetrameter, and lines 2 and 4 are rhymed iambic trimeter.

Several stanza forms are exemplified in this book, most of them based on rhyme schemes, but some (such as blank verse or syllabic verse) are based entirely on meter or other measures of sound, or on some more elaborate scheme such as the measured repetition of words, as in the **sestina,** or the repetition of whole lines, as in the **villanelle.** You can probably deduce the principles involved in each of the following stanza or verse forms by looking carefully at a poem which uses it

What are stanza forms good for? What use is it to recognize them? Why do poets bother? Matters discussed in this chapter so far have suggested two reasons: 1. Breaks between stanzas provide convenient pauses for reader and writer, something roughly equivalent to paragraphs in prose. The eye thus picks up the places where some kind of pause or break occurs. 2. Poets sometimes use stanza forms, as they do rhyme itself, as a discipline: writing in a certain kind of stanza form imposes a shape on their act of imagination. To suggest some other uses, we will look in more detail at one particular verse form, the **sonnet**. A sonnet has only a single stanza and offers several related possibilities for its rhyme scheme, but it is always fourteen lines long and usually written in iambic pentameter. The sonnet has remained a popular verse form in English for more than four centuries, and even in an age that largely rejects rhyme it continues to attract a variety of poets, including (curiously) radical and even revolutionary poets who find its firm structure very useful. Its uses, although quite varied, can be illustrated fairly precisely.

As a verse form, the sonnet is contained, compact, demanding; whatever it does, it must do concisely and quickly. To be effective, it must take advantage of the possibilities inherent in its shortness and its relative rigidity. It is best suited to intensity of feeling and concentration of expression. Not too surprisingly, one subject it frequently discusses is confinement itself.

WILLIAM WORDSWORTH

Nuns Fret Not

Nuns fret not at their convent's narrow room;
And hermits are contented with their cells;
And students with their pensive citadels;
Maids at the wheel, the weaver at his loom,
Sit blithe and happy; bees that soar for bloom,   5
High as the highest Peak of Furness-fells,[1]
Will murmur by the hour in foxglove bells:[2]
In truth the prison, unto which we doom
Ourselves, no prison is: and hence for me,
In sundry moods, 'twas pastime to be bound   10
Within the sonnet's scanty plot of ground;
Pleased if some souls (for such there needs must be)
Who have felt the weight of too much liberty,
Should find brief solace there, as I have found.

1807

1. Mountains in England's Lake District, where Wordsworth lived.

2. Flowers from which digitalis (a heart medicine) began to be made in 1799.

Most sonnets are structured according to one of two principles of division. On one principle, the sonnet divides into three units of four lines each and a final unit of two lines. On the other, the fundamental break is between the first eight lines (called an octave) and the last six (called a sestet). The 4-4-4-2 sonnet is usually called the **English** or **Shakespearean sonnet,** and ordinarily its rhyme scheme reflects the structure: the scheme of *abab cdcd efef gg* is the classic one, but many variations from that pattern still reflect the basic 4-4-4-2 division. The 8-6 sonnet is usually called the **Italian** or **Petrarchan sonnet** (the Italian poet Petrarch was an early master of this structure), and its "typical" rhyme scheme is *abbaabba cdecde,* although it too produces many variations that still reflect the basic division into two parts.

The two kinds of sonnet structures are useful for two different sorts of argument. The 4-4-4-2 structure works very well for constructing a poem that wants to make a three-step argument (with a quick summary at the end), or for setting up brief, cumulative images. *That Time of Year* (p. 435), for example, uses the 4-4-4-2 structure to mark the progressive steps toward death and the parting of friends by using three distinct images, then summarizing. Shakespeare's *Let Me Not to the Marriage of True Minds* (p. 370) works very similarly, following the kind of organization that in Chapter 7 I called the 1-2-3 structure—and doing it compactly and economically.

Here, on the other hand, is a poem which uses the 8-6 pattern:

HENRY CONSTABLE

My Lady's Presence Makes the Roses Red

My lady's presence makes the roses red
Because to see her lips they blush for shame.
The lily's leaves, for envy, pale became,
And her white hands in them this envy bred.
The marigold the leaves abroad doth spread   5
Because the sun's and her power is the same.
The violet of purple color came,
Dyed in the blood she made my heart to shed.
In brief, all flowers from her their virtue take;
From her sweet breath their sweet smells do proceed;   10
The living heat which her eyebeams doth make
Warmeth the ground and quickeneth the seed.
The rain wherewith she watereth the flowers
Falls from mine eyes, which she dissolves in showers.

1594

Here, the first eight lines argue that the lady's presence is responsible for the color of all of nature's flowers, and the final six lines summarize and extend that argument to smells and heat—and finally to the rain that the lady draws from the speaker's eyes. That kind of two-part structure, in which the octave states a proposition or gen-eralization and the sestet provides a particularization or application of it, has a variety of uses. The final lines may, for example, reverse the first eight and achieve a paradox or irony in the poem, or the poem may *nearly* balance two comparable arguments. Basically, the 8-6 structure lends itself to poems with two points to make, or to those which wish to make one fairly brief point and illustrate it.

Sometimes the neat and precise structure I have described is al-tered—either slightly, as in *Nuns Fret Not* above (where the 8-6 structure is more of an 8½-5½ structure) or more radically as par-ticular needs or effects may demand. And the two basic structures certainly do not define all the structural possibilities within a fourteen-line poem, even if they do suggest the most traditional ways of taking advantage of the sonnet's compact and well-kept container.

JOHN KEATS

On the Sonnet

If by dull rhymes our English must be chained,
And like Andromeda,[3] the sonnet sweet
Fettered, in spite of painéd loveliness,
Let us find, if we must be constrained,
Sandals more interwoven and complete   5
To fit the naked foot of Poesy:[4]
Let us inspect the lyre, and weigh the stress
Of every chord,[5] and see what may be gained
By ear industrious, and attention meet;
Misers of sound and syllable, no less   10
Than Midas[6] of his coinage, let us be
Jealous[7] of dead leaves in the bay-wreath crown;[8]
So, if we may not let the Muse be free,
She will be bound with garlands of her own.

1819

---

3. Who, according to Greek myth, was chained to a rock so that she would be devoured by a sea monster. She was res-cued by Perseus, who married her. When she died she was placed among the stars.

4. In a letter which contained this son-net, Keats expressed impatience with the traditional Petrarchan and Shakespearean sonnet forms: "I have been endeavoring to discover a better sonnet stanza than we have."

5. Lyre-string.

6. The legendary king of Phrygia who asked, and got, the power to turn all he touched to gold.

7. Suspiciously watchful.

8. The bay tree was sacred to Apollo, god of poetry, and bay wreaths came to symbolize true poetic achievement. The withering of the bay tree is sometimes con-sidered an omen of death.

PERCY BYSSHE SHELLEY

Ozymandias[9]

I met a traveler from an antique land
Who said: Two vast and trunkless legs of stone
Stand in the desert. . . . Near them, on the sand,
Half sunk, a shattered visage lies, whose frown,
And wrinkled lip, and sneer of cold command,   5
Tell that its sculptor well those passions read
Which yet survive, stamped on these lifeless things,
The hand that mocked them, and the heart that fed:
And on the pedestal these words appear:
"My name is Ozymandias, King of Kings: 10
Look on my works, ye Mighty, and despair!"
Nothing beside remains. Round the decay
Of that colossal wreck, boundless and bare
The lone and level sands stretch far away.

1818

WILLIAM WORDSWORTH

London, 1802

Milton! thou should'st be living at this hour:
England hath need of thee: she is a fen[1]
Of stagnant waters: altar, sword, and pen,
Fireside, the heroic wealth of hall and bower,
Have forfeited their ancient English dower[2]   5
Of inward happiness. We are selfish men;
Oh! raise us up, return to us again;
And give us manners, virtue, freedom, power.
Thy soul was like a star, and dwelt apart:
Thou hadst a voice whose sound was like the sea: 10
Pure as the naked heavens, majestic, free,
So didst thou travel on life's common way,
In cheerful godliness; and yet thy heart
The lowliest duties on herself did lay.

1802

---

9. The Greek name for Rameses II, 13th-century B.C. pharaoh of Egypt. According to a first century B.C. Greek historian, Diodorus Siculus, the largest statue in Egypt was inscribed: "I am Ozymandias, king of kings; if anyone wishes to know what I am and where I lie, let him surpass me in some of my exploits."
1. Marsh.
2. Inheritance.

GWENDOLYN BROOKS

First Fight. Then Fiddle.

First fight. Then fiddle. Ply the slipping string
With feathery sorcery; muzzle the note
With hurting love; the music that they wrote
Bewitch, bewilder. Qualify to sing
Threadwise. Devise no salt, no hempen thing   5
For the dear instrument to bear. Devote
The bow to silks and honey. Be remote
A while from malice and from murdering.
But first to arms, to armor. Carry hate
In front of you and harmony behind.   10
Be deaf to music and to beauty blind.
Win war. Rise bloody, maybe not too late
For having first to civilize a space
Wherein to play your violin with grace.

1949

Poems for Further Reading

MAYA ANGELOU

Africa

Thus she had lain
sugar cane sweet
deserts her hair
golden her feet
mountains her breasts   5
two Niles her tears
Thus she has lain
Black through the years.

Over the white seas
rime white and cold   10
brigands ungentled
icicle bold
took her young daughters
sold her strong sons
churched her with Jesus   15
bled her with guns.
Thus she has lain.

Now she is rising
remember her pain
remember the losses   20
her screams loud and vain
remember her riches
her history slain
now she is striding
although she had lain.   25

1975

ANONYMOUS

Sir Patrick Spens

The king sits in Dumferling toune,[1]
Drinking the blude-reid[2] wine:
"O whar will I get guid sailor,
To sail this ship of mine?"

1. Town.   2. Blood-red.

Up and spake an eldern knicht,   5
    Sat at the king's richt knee:
"Sir Patrick Spens is the best sailor
    That sails upon the sea."

The king has written a braid[3] letter
    And signed it wi' his hand,   10
And sent it to Sir Patrick Spens,
    Was walking on the sand.

The first line that Sir Patrick read,
    A loud lauch[4] lauched he;
The next line that Sir Patrick read,   15
    The tear blinded his ee.[5]

"O wha is this has done this deed,
    This il deed done to me,
To send me out this time o' the year,
    To sail upon the sea?   20

"Make haste, make haste, my merry men all,
    Our guid ship sails the morn."
"O say na sae,[6] my master dear,
    For I fear a deadly storm.

"Late, late yestre'en I saw the new moon   25
    Wi' the auld moon in her arm,
And I fear, I fear, my dear mastér,
    That we will come to harm."

O our Scots nobles were richt laith[7]
    To weet their cork-heeled shoon,[8]   30
But lang owre a'[9] the play were played
    Their hats they swam aboon.[1]

O lang, lang, may their ladies sit,
    Wi' their fans into their hand,
Or ere they see Sir Patrick Spens   35
    Come sailing to the land.

O lang, lang, may the ladies stand
    Wi' their gold kems[2] in their hair,
Waiting for their ain[3] dear lords,
    For they'll see them na mair.   40

3. Broad: explicit.
4. Laugh.
5. Eye.
6. Not so.
7. Right loath: very reluctant.
8. To wet their cork-heeled shoes. Cork
was expensive, and therefore such shoes
were a mark of wealth and status.
9. Before all.
1. Their hats swam above them.
2. Combs.
3. Own.

Half o'er, half o'er to Aberdour
  It's fifty fadom deep,
And there lies guid Sir Patrick Spens
  Wi' the Scots lords at his feet.

(probably 13th century)

MARGARET ATWOOD

Death of a Young Son by Drowning

He, who navigated with success
the dangerous river of his own birth
once more set forth

on a voyage of discovery
into the land I floated on   5
but could not touch to claim.

His feet slid on the bank,
the currents took him;
he swirled with ice and trees in the swollen water

and plunged into distant regions,   10
his head a bathysphere;
through his eyes' thin glass bubbles

he looked out, reckless adventurer
on a landscape stranger than Uranus
we have all been to and some remember.   15

There was an accident; the air locked,
he was hung in the river like a heart.
They retrieved the swamped body,

cairn of my plans and future charts,
with poles and hooks   20
from among the nudging logs.

It was spring, the sun kept shining, the new grass
leapt to solidity;
my hands glistened with details.

After the long trip I was tired of waves.   25
My foot hit rock. The dreamed sails
collapsed, ragged.

    I planted him in this country
    like a flag.

W. H. AUDEN

In Memory of W. B. Yeats

(*d. January, 1939*)

I

He disappeared in the dead of winter:
The brooks were frozen, the airports almost deserted,
And snow disfigured the public statues;
The mercury sank in the mouth of the dying day.
What instruments we have agree   5
The day of his death was a dark cold day.

Far from his illness
The wolves ran on through the evergreen forests,
The peasant river was untempted by the fashionable quays;
By mourning tongues   10
The death of the poet was kept from his poems.

But for him it was his last afternoon as himself,
An afternoon of nurses and rumors;
The provinces of his body revolted,
The squares of his mind were empty,   15
Silence invaded the suburbs,
The current of his feeling failed; he became his admirers.

Now he is scattered among a hundred cities
And wholly given over to unfamiliar affections,
To find his happiness in another kind of wood   20
And be punished under a foreign code of conscience.
The words of a dead man
Are modified in the guts of the living.

But in the importance and noise of tomorrow
When the brokers are roaring like beasts on the floor of the Bourse,[4]   25
And the poor have the sufferings to which they are fairly accustomed,
And each in the cell of himself is almost convinced of his freedom,
A few thousand will think of this day
As one thinks of a day when one did something slightly unusual.
What instruments we have agree   30
The day of his death was a dark cold day.

II

You were silly like us; your gift survived it all:
The parish of rich women, physical decay,
Yourself. Mad Ireland hurt you into poetry.
Now Ireland has her madness and her weather still,   35
For poetry makes nothing happen: it survives
In the valley of its making where executives

4. The Paris stock exchange.

Would never want to tamper, flows on south
From ranches of isolation and the busy griefs,
Raw towns that we believe and die in; it survives,   40
A way of happening, a mouth.

III

Earth, receive an honored guest:
William Yeats is laid to rest.
Let the Irish vessel lie
Emptied of its poetry.   45

In the nightmare of the dark
All the dogs of Europe bark,
And the living nations wait,
Each sequestered in its hate;

Intellectual disgrace   50
Stares from every human face,
And the seas of pity lie
Locked and frozen in each eye.

Follow, poet, follow right
To the bottom of the night,   55
With your unconstraining voice
Still persuade us to rejoice;

With the farming of a verse
Make a vineyard of the curse,
Sing of human unsuccess   60
In a rapture of distress;

In the deserts of the heart
Let the healing fountain start,
In the prison of his days
Teach the free man how to praise.   65

1939

WILLIAM BLAKE

The Lamb

Little Lamb, who made thee?
Dost thou know who made thee?
Gave thee life, and bid thee feed
By the stream and o'er the mead;
Gave thee clothing of delight,   5
Softest clothing woolly bright;
Gave thee such a tender voice,
Making all the vales rejoice?
Little Lamb, who made thee?
Dost thou know who made thee?   10

Little Lamb, I'll tell thee!
Little Lamb, I'll tell thee:
He is calléd by thy name,
For he calls himself a Lamb,
He is meek and he is mild;   15
He became a little child.
I a child and thou a lamb,
We are calléd by his name.
Little Lamb, God bless thee!
Little Lamb, God bless thee!   20

1789

WILLIAM BLAKE

The Tiger

Tiger, Tiger, burning bright
In the forests of the night,
What immortal hand or eye
Could frame thy fearful symmetry?

In what distant deeps or skies   5
Burnt the fire of thine eyes?
On what wings dare he aspire?
What the hand dare seize the fire?

And what shoulder and what art,
Could twist the sinews of thy heart?   10
And when thy heart began to beat,
What dread hand, and what dread feet?

What the hammer? What the chain?
In what furnace was thy brain?
What the anvil? What dread grasp   15
Dare its deadly terrors clasp?

When the stars threw down their spears
And watered heaven with their tears,
Did he smile his work to see?
Did he who made the Lamb make thee?

Tiger, Tiger, burning bright
In the forests of the night,
What immortal hand or eye
Dare frame thy fearful symmetry?

SAMUEL TAYLOR COLERIDGE

Kubla Khan: or, a Vision in a Dream [5]

In Xanadu did Kubla Khan
  A stately pleasure-dome decree:
Where Alph, the sacred river, ran
Through caverns measureless to man
  Down to a sunless sea.   5
So twice five miles of fertile ground
With walls and towers were girdled round:
And here were gardens bright with sinuous rills
Where blossomed many an incense-bearing tree;
And here were forests ancient as the hills,   10
Enfolding sunny spots of greenery.
But oh! that deep romantic chasm which slanted
Down the green hill athwart a cedarn cover! [6]
A savage place! as holy and enchanted
As e'er beneath a waning moon was haunted   15
By woman wailing for her demon-lover! [7]
And from this chasm, with ceaseless turmoil seething,
As if this earth in fast thick pants were breathing,
A mighty fountain momently was forced,
Amid whose swift half-intermitted burst   20
Huge fragments vaulted like rebounding hail,
Or chaffy grain beneath the thresher's flail:
And 'mid these dancing rocks at once and ever
It flung up momently the sacred river.
Five miles meandering with a mazy motion   25
Through wood and dale the sacred river ran,
Then reached the caverns measureless to man,
And sank in tumult to a lifeless ocean:
And 'mid this tumult Kubla heard from far
Ancestral voices prophesying war!   30

    The shadow of the dome of pleasure
    Floated midway on the waves;
    Where was heard the mingled measure
    From the fountain and the caves.
It was a miracle of rare device,   35
A sunny pleasure-dome with caves of ice!
    A damsel with a dulcimer [8]
    In a vision once I saw:
    It was an Abyssinian maid,
    And on her dulcimer she played,   40
    Singing of Mount Abora.

5. Coleridge said he wrote this fragment immediately after waking from an opium dream and that after he was interrupted by a caller he was unable to finish the poem.

6. From side to side of a cover of cedar trees.

7. In a famous and often imitated German ballad, the lady Lenore is carried off on horseback by the specter of her lover and married to him at his grave.

8. A stringed instrument, prototype of the piano.

Could I revive within me
Her symphony and song,
To such a deep delight 'twould win me,
That with music loud and long,   45
I would build that dome in air,
That sunny dome! those caves of ice!
And all who heard should see them there,
And all should cry, Beware! Beware!   *mystic*   50
His flashing eyes, his floating hair!
Weave a circle round him thrice,
And close your eyes with holy dread,
For he on honey-dew hath fed,
And drunk the milk of Paradise.   *food of gods*

supernatural

1798

e. e. cummings

chanson innocente

in Just-
spring   when the world is mud-
luscious the little
lame balloonman

whistles   far   and wee   5

and eddieandbill come
running from marbles and
piracies and it's
spring

when the world is puddle-wonderful   10

the queer
old balloonman whistles
far   and   wee
and bettyandisbel come dancing

from hop-scotch and jump-rope and   15

it's
spring
and
    the

goat-footed   20

balloonMan   whistles
far
and
wee [9]

1923

9. Pan, whose Greek name means "everything," is traditionally represented with a syrinx (or the pipes of Pan). The upper half of his body is human, the lower half goat, and as the father of Silenus he is associated with the spring rites of Dionysus.

EMILY DICKINSON

Because I Could Not Stop for Death

Because I could not stop for Death—
He kindly stopped for me—
The Carriage held but just Ourselves—
And Immortality.

We slowly drove—He knew no haste   5
And I had put away
My labor and my leisure too,
For His Civility—

We passed the School, where Children strove
At Recess—in the Ring—   10
We passed the Fields of Gazing Grain—
We passed the Setting Sun—

Or rather—He passed Us—
The Dews drew quivering and chill—
For only Gossamer,[1] my Gown—   15
My Tippet[2]—only Tulle[3]—

We paused before a House that seemed
A Swelling of the Ground—
The Roof was scarcely visible—
The Cornice—in the Ground—   20

Since then—'tis Centuries—and yet
Feels shorter than the Day
I first surmised the Horses' Heads
Were toward Eternity—

ca. 1863

EMILY DICKINSON

I Dwell in Possibility

I dwell in Possibility—
A fairer House than Prose—
More numerous of Windows—
Superior—for Doors—

1. A soft sheer fabric.   3. A fine net fabric.
2. Scarf.

Of Chambers as the Cedars—   5
Impregnable of Eye—
And for an Everlasting Roof
The Gambrels [4] of the Sky—

Of Visitors—the fairest—
For Occupation—This—   10
The spreading wide my narrow Hands
To gather Paradise—

ca. 1862

EMILY DICKINSON

Wild Nights! Wild Nights!

Wild Nights—Wild Nights!
Were I with thee
Wild Nights should be
Our luxury!

Futile—the Winds—   5
To a Heart in port—
Done with the Compass—
Done with the Chart!

Rowing in Eden—
Ah, the Sea!   10
Might I but moor—Tonight—
In Thee!

ca. 1861

JOHN DONNE

The Canonization

For God's sake hold your tongue and let me love!
    Or chide my palsy or my gout,
My five gray hairs or ruined fortune flout;
With wealth your state, your mind with arts improve,
    Take you a course, get you a place,   5
    Observe his Honor or his Grace,
Or the king's real or his stampéd face [5]
    Contemplate; what you will, approve,
        So you will let me love.

4. Roofs with double slopes.   5. On coins.

Alas, alas, who's injured by my love?   10
    What merchant's ships have my sighs drowned?
Who says my tears have overflowed his ground?
When did my colds a forward spring remove?
    When did the heats which my veins fill
    Add one man to the plaguy bill?[6]   15
Soldiers find wars, and lawyers find out still
    Litigious men which quarrels move,
        Though she and I do love.

Call us what you will, we are made such by love.
    Call her one, me another fly,   20
We're tapers[7] too, and at our own cost die;
And we in us find th' eagle and the dove.[8]
    The phoenix riddle[9] hath more wit[1]
    By us; we two, being one, are it.
So to one neutral thing both sexes fit,   25
    We die and rise the same, and prove
        Mysterious by this love.

We can die by it, if not live by love;
    And if unfit for tombs and hearse
Our legend be, it will be fit for verse;
And if no piece of chronicle we prove,[2]   30
    We'll build in sonnets[3] pretty rooms
    (As well a well-wrought urn becomes[4]
The greatest ashes, as half-acre tombs),
    And by these hymns all shall approve   35
        Us canonized for love.

And thus invoke us: "You whom reverent love
    Made one another's hermitage,
You to whom love was peace, that now is rage,
Who did the whole world's soul extract, and drove[5]   40
    Into the glasses of your eyes
    (So made such mirrors and such spies
That they did all to you epitomize)
    Countries, towns, courts; beg from above
        A pattern of your love!"   45

1633

---

6. List of plague victims.
7. Which consume themselves. To "die" is Renaissance slang for consummating the sexual act, which was popularly believed to shorten life by one day. "fly": a traditional symbol of transitory life.
8. Traditional symbols of strength and purity.
9. According to tradition, only one phoenix existed at a time, dying in a funeral pyre of its own making and being reborn from its own ashes. The bird's existence was thus a riddle akin to a religious mystery (line 27), and a symbol sometimes fused with Christian representations of immortality.
1. Meaning.
2. I.e., if we don't turn out to be an authenticated piece of historical narrative.
3. Love poems. In Italian, *stanza* means rooms.
4. Befits.
5. Compressed.

JOHN DONNE

Death Be Not Proud

Death be not proud, though some have calléd thee
Mighty and dreadful, for thou art not so;
For those whom thou think'st thou dost overthrow
Die not, poor Death, nor yet canst thou kill me.
From rest and sleep, which but thy pictures[6] be,   5
Much pleasure; then from thee much more must flow,
And soonest[7] our best men with thee do go,
Rest of their bones, and soul's delivery.[8]
Thou art slave to Fate, Chance, kings, and desperate men,
And dost with Poison, War, and Sickness dwell;   10
And poppy or charms can make us sleep as well,
And better than thy stroke; why swell'st[9] thou then?
One short sleep past, we wake eternally
And death shall be no more; Death, thou shalt die.

1633

T. S. ELIOT

Journey of the Magi[1]

"A cold coming we had of it,
Just the worst time of the year
For a journey, and such a long journey:
The ways deep and the weather sharp,
The very dead of winter."[2]   5
And the camels galled, sore-footed, refractory,
Lying down in the melting snow.
There were times we regretted
The summer palaces on slopes, the terraces,
And the silken girls bringing sherbet.   10
Then the camel men cursing and grumbling
And running away, and wanting their liquor and women,
And the night-fires going out, and the lack of shelters,
And the cities hostile and the towns unfriendly
And the villages dirty and charging high prices: 15
A hard time we had of it.
At the end we preferred to travel all night,
Sleeping in snatches,
With the voices singing in our ears, saying
That this was all folly.   20

---

6. Likenesses.
7. Most willingly.
8. Deliverance.
9. Puff with pride.

1. The wise men who followed the star of Bethlehem. See *Matthew* 2:1–12.
2. An adaptation of a passage from a 1622 sermon by Lancelot Andrewes.

Then at dawn we came down to a temperate valley,
Wet, below the snow line, smelling of vegetation;
With a running stream and a water-mill beating the darkness,
And three trees on the low sky,[3]
And an old white horse galloped away in the meadow.   25
Then we came to a tavern with vine-leaves over the lintel,
Six hands at an open door dicing for pieces of silver,
And feet kicking the empty wine-skins.
But there was no information, and so we continued
And arrived at evening, not a moment too soon   30
Finding the place; it was (you may say) satisfactory.

All this was a long time ago, I remember,
And I would do it again, but set down
This set down
This: were we led all that way for   35
Birth or Death? There was a Birth, certainly,
We had evidence and no doubt. I had seen birth and death,
But had thought they were different; this Birth was
Hard and bitter agony for us, like Death, our death.
We returned to our places, these Kingdoms,[4]   40
But no longer at ease here, in the old dispensation,
With an alien people clutching their gods.
I should be glad of another death.

1927

ROBERT FROST

Range-Finding

The battle rent a cobweb diamond-strung
And cut a flower beside a groundbird's nest
Before it stained a single human breast.
The stricken flower bent double and so hung.
And still the bird revisited her young.   5
A butterfly its fall had dispossessed,
A moment sought in air his flower of rest,
Then lightly stooped to it and fluttering clung.
On the bare upland pasture there had spread
O'ernight 'twixt mullein[5] stalks a wheel of thread   10
And straining cables wet with silver dew.
A sudden passing bullet shook it dry.
The indwelling spider ran to greet the fly,
But finding nothing, sullenly withdrew.

1916

3. Suggestive of the three crosses of the Crucifixion (*Luke* 23:32–33). The Magi see several objects which suggest later events in Christ's life: pieces of silver (see *Matthew* 26:14–16), the dicing (see *Matthew* 27:35), the white horse (see *Revelation* 6:2 and 19:11–16), and the empty wine-skins (see *Matthew* 9:14–17, possibly relevant also to lines 41–42).
4. The Bible only identifies the wise men as "from the East," and subsequent tradition has made them kings. In Persia, Magi were members of an ancient priestly caste.
5. Weed.

ROBERT FROST

The Road Not Taken

Two roads diverged in a yellow wood,
And sorry I could not travel both
And be one traveler, long I stood
And looked down one as far as I could
To where it bent in the undergrowth;   5

Then took the other, as just as fair,
And having perhaps the better claim,
Because it was grassy and wanted wear;
Though as for that the passing there
Had worn them really about the same,   10

And both that morning equally lay
In leaves no step had trodden black.
Oh, I kept the first for another day!
Yet knowing how way leads on to way,
I doubted if I should ever come back.   15

I shall be telling this with a sigh
Somewhere ages and ages hence:
Two roads diverged in a wood, and I—
I took the one less traveled by,
And that has made all the difference.   20

1916

ROBERT FROST

Stopping by Woods on a Snowy Evening

Whose woods these are I think I know.
His house is in the village, though;
He will not see me stopping here
To watch his woods fill up with snow.

My little horse must think it queer   5
To stop without a farmhouse near
Between the woods and frozen lake
The darkest evening of the year.

He gives his harness bells a shake
To ask if there is some mistake.   10
The only other sound's the sweep
Of easy wind and downy flake.

The woods are lovely, dark, and deep,
But I have promises to keep,
And miles to go before I sleep,   15
And miles to go before I sleep.

                                                    1923

THOMAS HARDY

Channel Firing [6]

That night your great guns, unawares,
Shook all our coffins as we lay,
And broke the chancel window squares,[7]
We thought it was the Judgment-day [8]

And sat upright. While drearisome   5
Arose the howl of wakened hounds:
The mouse let fall the altar-crumb,[9]
The worms drew back into the mounds,

The glebe cow[1] drooled. Till God called, "No;
It's gunnery practice out at sea   10
Just as before you went below;
The world is as it used to be:

"All nations striving strong to make
Red war yet redder. Mad as hatters
They do no more for Christés sake   15
Than you who are helpless in such matters.

"That this is not the judgment-hour
For some of them's a blessed thing,
For if it were they'd have to scour
Hell's floor for so much threatening . . .   20

"Ha, ha. It will be warmer when
I blow the trumpet (if indeed
I ever do; for you are men,
And rest eternal sorely need)."

So down we lay again. "I wonder,   25
Will the world ever saner be,"
Said one, "than when He sent us under
In our indifferent century!"

---

6. Naval practice on the English Channel preceded the outbreak of World War I
in the summer of 1914.
7. The windows near the altar in a
church.

8. When, according to tradition, the
dead will be awakened.
9. Breadcrumbs from the sacrament.
1. Parish cow pastured on the meadow
next to the churchyard.

And many a skeleton shook his head.
"Instead of preaching forty year,"   30
My neighbor Parson Thirdly said,
"I wish I had stuck to pipes and beer."

Again the guns disturbed the hour,
Roaring their readiness to avenge.
As far inland as Stourton Tower,   35
And Camelot, and starlit Stonehenge.[2]

April, 1914

THOMAS HARDY

The Darkling Thrush

I leant upon a coppice gate
   When Frost was specter gray,
And Winter's dregs made desolate
   The weakening eye of day.
The tangled bine-stems scored the sky   5
   Like strings of broken lyres,
And all mankind that haunted nigh
   Had sought their household fires.

The land's sharp features seemed to be
   The Century's corpse outleant,   10
His crypt the cloudy canopy,
   The wind his death-lament.
The ancient pulse of germ and birth
   Was shrunken hard and dry,
And every spirit upon earth   15
   Seemed fervorless as I.

At once a voice arose among
   The bleak twigs overhead
In a full-hearted evensong
   Of joy illimited;   20
An aged thrush, frail, gaunt, and small,
   In blast-beruffled plume,
Had chosen thus to fling his soul
   Upon the growing gloom.

So little cause for carolings   25
   Of such ecstatic sound
Was written on terrestrial things

2. Stourton Tower, built in the 18th century to commemorate King Alfred's ninth-century victory over the Danes, in Stourhead Park, Wiltshire. Camelot is the legendary site of King Arthur's court, said to have been in Cornwall or Somerset. Stonehenge, a circular formation of upright stones dating from about 1800 B.C., is on Salisbury Plain, Wiltshire; it is thought to have been a ceremonial site for political and religious occasions or an early scientific experiment in astronomy.

Afar or nigh around,
That I could think there trembled through
  His happy good-night air   30
Some blessed Hope, whereof he knew
  And I was unaware.
December 31, 1900

THOMAS HARDY

During Wind and Rain

They sing their dearest songs—
He, she, all of them—yea,
Treble and tenor and bass,
  And one to play;
With the candles mooning each face. . . .   5
  Ah, no; the years O!
How the sick leaves reel down in throngs!

They clear the creeping moss—
Elders and juniors—aye,
Making the pathway neat   10
  And the garden gay;
And they build a shady seat. . . .
  Ah, no; the years, the years;
See, the white stormbirds wing across!

They are blithely breakfasting all—   15
Men and maidens—yea,
Under the summer tree,
  With a glimpse of the bay,
While pet fowl come to the knee. . . .
  Ah, no; the years O!   20
And the rotten rose is ripped from the wall.

They change to a high new house,
He, she, all of them—aye,
Clocks and carpets, and chairs
  On the lawn all day,   25
And brightest things that are theirs. . . .
  Ah, no; the years, the years;
Down their carved names the rain drop ploughs.

1917

ROBERT HAYDEN

Frederick Douglass[3]

When it is finally ours, this freedom, this liberty, this beautiful
and terrible thing, needful to man as air,
usable as earth; when it belongs at last to all,
when it is truly instinct, brain matter, diastole, systole,
reflex action; when it is finally won; when it is more   5
than the gaudy mumbo jumbo of politicians:
this man, this Douglass, this former slave, this Negro
beaten to his knees, exiled, visioning a world
where none is lonely, none hunted, alien,
this man, superb in love and logic, this man   10
shall be remembered. Oh, not with statues' rhetoric,
not with legends and poems and wreaths of bronze alone,
but with the lives grown out of his life, the lives
fleshing his dream of the beautiful, needful thing.

1966

ROBERT HERRICK

To the Virgins, to Make Much of Time

Gather ye rosebuds while ye may,
    Old time is still a-flying;
And this same flower that smiles today
    Tomorow will be dying.

The glorious lamp of heaven, the sun,   5
    The higher he's a-getting,
The sooner will his race be run,
    And nearer he's to setting.

That age is best which is the first,
    When youth and blood are warmer;   10
But being spent, the worse, and worst
    Times still succeed the former.

Then be not coy, but use your time,
    And, while ye may, go marry;
For, having lost but once your prime,   15
    You may forever tarry.

1648

3. Frederick Douglass (1817–1895), escaped slave. Douglass was involved in the Underground Railroad, and became the publisher of the famous abolitionist newspaper the *North Star,* in Rochester, N.Y.

JOHN HOLLANDER

Adam's Task

"And Adam gave names to all cattle, and to the fowl of the air, and to every beast of the field . . ."—*Gen.* 2:20

Thou, paw-paw-paw; thou, glurd; thou, spotted
  Glurd; thou, whitestap, lurching through
The high-grown brush; thou, pliant-footed,
  Implex; thou, awagabu.

Every burrower, each flier   5
  Came for the name he had to give:
Gay, first work, ever to be prior,
  Not yet sunk to primitive.

Thou, verdle; thou, McFleery's pomma;
  Thou; thou; thou—three types of grawl;   10
Thou, flisket; thou, kabasch; thou, comma-
  Eared mashawk; thou, all; thou, all.

Were, in a fire of becoming,
  Laboring to be burned away,
Then work, half-measuring, half-humming,   15
  Would be as serious as play.

Thou, pambler; thou, rivarn; thou, greater
  Wherret, and thou, lesser one;
Thou, sproal; thou, zant; thou, lily-eater.
  Naming's over. Day is done.   20

1971

GERARD MANLEY HOPKINS

God's Grandeur

The world is charged with the grandeur of God.
  It will flame out, like shining from shook foil; [4]
  It gathers to a greatness, like the ooze of oil
Crushed. Why do men then now not reck his rod? [5]
Generations have trod, have trod, have trod;   5
  And all is seared with trade; bleared, smeared with toil;
  And wears man's smudge and shares man's smell: the soil
Is bare now, nor can foot feel, being shod.

4. "I mean foil in its sense of leaf or tinsel. . . . Shaken goldfoil gives off broad glares like sheet lightning and also, and this is true of nothing else, owing to its zig-zag dints and creasings and net-work of small many cornered facets, a sort of fork lightning too." *Letters of Gerard Manley Hopkins to Robert Bridges*, ed. C. C. Abbott, 1955, p. 169.
  5. Heed his authority.

And for all this, nature is never spent;
   There lives the dearest freshness deep down things;   10
And though the last lights off the black West went
   Oh, morning, at the brown brink eastward, springs—
Because the Holy Ghost over the bent
   World broods with warm breast and with ah! bright wings.

1918

GERARD MANLEY HOPKINS

The Windhover [6]

To Christ Our Lord

I caught this morning morning's minion,[7] king-
   dom of daylight's dauphin,[8] dapple-dawn-drawn Falcon, in his
     riding
   Of the rolling level underneath him steady air, and striding
High there, how he rung upon the rein of a wimpling[9] wing
In his ecstasy! then off, off forth on swing,   5
   As a skate's heel sweeps smooth on a bow-bend: the hurl and
     gliding
   Rebuffed the big wind. My heart in hiding
Stirred for a bird,—the achieve of, the mastery of the thing!

Brute beauty and valor and act, oh, air, pride, plume, here
   Buckle![1] AND the fire that breaks from thee then, a billion   10
Times told lovelier, more dangerous, O my chevalier![2]

   No wonder of it: sheér plód makes plow down sillion[3]
Shine, and blue-bleak embers, ah my dear,
   Fall, gall themselves, and gash gold-vermilion.
1877

A. E. HOUSMAN

Terence, This Is Stupid Stuff

   "Terence,[4] this is stupid stuff:
   You eat your victuals fast enough;
   There can't be much amiss, 'tis clear,
   To see the rate you drink your beer.
   But oh, good Lord, the verse you make,   5

6. A small hawk, the kestrel, which habitually hovers in the air, headed into the wind.
   7. Favorite, beloved.
   8. Heir to regal splendor.
   9. Rippling.
   1. Several meanings may apply: to join closely, to prepare for battle, to grapple with, to collapse.
   2. Horseman, knight.
   3. The narrow strip of land between furrows in an open field divided for separate cultivation.
   4. Housman originally titled the volume in which this poem appeared "The Poems of Terence Hearsay."

It gives a chap the belly-ache.
The cow, the old cow, she is dead;
It sleeps well, the horned head:
We poor lads, 'tis our turn now
To hear such tunes as killed the cow.　　　　　10
Pretty friendship 'tis to rhyme
Your friends to death before their time
Moping melancholy mad:
Come, pipe a tune to dance to, lad."

　　Why, if 'tis dancing you would be,　　　　15
There's brisker pipes than poetry.
Say, for what were hop-yards meant,
Or why was Burton built on Trent?[5]
Oh many a peer of England brews
Livelier liquor than the Muse,　　　　　　　20
And malt does more than Milton can
To justify God's ways to man.[6]
Ale, man, ale's the stuff to drink
For fellows whom it hurts to think:
Look into the pewter pot　　　　　　　　　　25
To see the world as the world's not.
And faith, 'tis pleasant till 'tis past:
The mischief is that 'twill not last.
Oh I have been to Ludlow fair[7]
And left my necktie God knows where,　　　30
And carried half-way home, or near,
Pints and quarts of Ludlow beer:
Then the world seemed none so bad,
And I myself a sterling lad;
And down in lovely muck I've lain,　　　　　35
Happy till I woke again.
Then I saw the morning sky:
Heigho, the tale was all a lie;
The world, it was the old world yet,
I was I, my things were wet,　　　　　　　　40
And nothing now remained to do
But begin the game anew.

　　Therefore, since the world has still
Much good, but much less good than ill,
And while the sun and moon endure　　　　45
Luck's a chance, but trouble's sure,
I'd face it as a wise man would,
And train for ill and not for good.
'Tis true, the stuff I bring for sale
Is not so brisk a brew as ale:　　　　　　　50

---

5. Burton was famous for its ales, originally brewed from special springs there.
6. Milton said his purpose in *Paradise Lost* was to "justify the ways of God to men."

7. Ludlow was a market town in Shropshire, and its town fair would be a social high point for a youth growing up in the county.

Out of a stem that scored the hand
I wrung it in a weary land.
But take it: if the smack is sour,
The better for the embittered hour;
It should do good to heart and head   55
When your soul is in my soul's stead;
And I will friend you, if I may,
In the dark and cloudy day.

There was a king reigned in the East:
There, when kings will sit to feast,   60
They get their fill before they think
With poisoned meat and poisoned drink.
He gathered all that springs to birth
From the many-venomed earth;
First a little, thence to more,   65
He sampled all her killing store;
And easy, smiling, seasoned sound,
Sate the king when healths went round.
They put arsenic in his meat
And stared aghast to watch him eat;   70
They poured strychnine in his cup
And shook to see him drink it up:
They shook, they stared as white's their shirt:
Them it was their poison hurt.
—I tell the tale that I heard told.   75
Mithridates,[8] he died old.

                                                                  1896

A. E. HOUSMAN

To an Athlete Dying Young

The time you won your town the race
We chaired[9] you through the marketplace;
Man and boy stood cheering by,
And home we brought you shoulder-high.

Today, the road all runners come,   5
Shoulder-high we bring you home,
And set you at your threshold down,
Townsman of a stiller town.

Smart lad, to slip betimes away
From fields where glory does not stay,   10
And early though the laurel[1] grows
It withers quicker than the rose.

8. The king of Pontus, he was said to
have developed a tolerance of poison by
taking gradually increasing quantities.

9. Carried aloft in triumph.
1. Wreath of honor.

Eyes the shady night has shut
Cannot see the record cut,
And silence sounds no worse than cheers   15
After earth has stopped the ears:

Now you will not swell the rout
Of lads that wore their honors out,
Runners whom renown outran
And the name died before the man.   20

So set, before its echoes fade,
The fleet foot on the sill of shade,
And hold to the low lintel[2] up
The still-defended challenge-cup.

And round that early-laureled head   25
Will flock to gaze the strengthless dead,
And find unwithered on its curls
The garland[3] briefer than a girl's.

                                                 1896

LANGSTON HUGHES

Harlem (A Dream Deferred)

What happens to a dream deferred?

> Does it dry up
> like a raisin in the sun?
> Or fester like a sore—
> And then run?   5
> Does it stink like rotten meat?
> Or crust and sugar over—
> like a syrupy sweet?

> Maybe it just sags
> like a heavy load.   10

> *Or does it explode?*

                                                 1951

2. Upper part of a door frame.   3. Wreath of flowers.

LANGSTON HUGHES

The Negro Speaks of Rivers

I've known rivers:
I've known rivers ancient as the world and older than the flow of human
    blood in human veins.

My soul has grown deep like the rivers.

I bathed in the Euphrates when dawns were young.
I built my hut near the Congo and it lulled me to sleep.   5
I looked upon the Nile and raised the pyramids above it.
I heard the singing of the Mississippi when Abe Lincoln went down
    to New Orleans, and I've seen its muddy bosom turn all golden in
    the sunset.

I've known rivers:
Ancient, dusky rivers.

My soul has grown deep like the rivers.   10

        1926

LANGSTON HUGHES

Theme for English B

The instructor said,

    Go home and write
    a page tonight.
    And let that page come out of you—
    Then, it will be true.   5

I wonder if it's that simple?
I am twenty-two, colored, born in Winston-Salem.
I went to school there, then Durham,[4] then here
to this college[5] on the hill above Harlem.
I am the only colored student in my class.   10
The steps from the hill lead down into Harlem,
through a park, then I cross St. Nicholas,[6]
Eighth Avenue, Seventh, and I come to the Y,
the Harlem Branch Y, where I take the elevator
up to my room, sit down, and write this page: 15

It's not easy to know what is true for you or me
at twenty-two, my age. But I guess I'm what
I feel and see and hear, Harlem, I hear you:

---

4. Cities in North Carolina.   6. An avenue east of Columbia Uni-
5. Columbia University.   versity.

hear you, hear me—we two—you, me, talk on this page.
(I hear New York, too.) Me—who?   20

Well, I like to eat, sleep, drink, and be in love.
I like to work, read, learn, and understand life.
I like a pipe for a Christmas present,
or records—Bessie,[7] bop, or Bach.
I guess being colored doesn't make me *not* like   25
the same things other folks like who are other races.
So will my page be colored that I write?

Being me, it will not be white.
But it will be
a part of you, instructor.   30
You are white—
yet a part of me, as I am a part of you.
That's American.
Sometimes perhaps you don't want to be a part of me.
Nor do I often want to be a part of you.   35
But we are, that's true!
As I learn from you,
I guess you learn from me—
although you're older—and white—
and somewhat more free.   40

This is my page for English B.

                                                                         1959

RICHARD HUGO

To Women

You start it all. You are lovely.
We look at you and we flow.
So a line begins, on the page, on air,
in the all of self. We have misused you,
invested you with primal sin. You bleed   5
for our regret we are not more.
The dragon wins. We come home and sob
and you hold us and say we are brave
and in the future will do better.
So far, so good.   10

Now some of you want out and I don't
blame you, not a tiny bit. You've caught on.
You have the right to veer off flaming
in a new direction, mud flat and diamond mine,
clavicord and dead drum. Whatever.   15

---

7. Bessie Smith (1898?–1937), famous blues singer.

Please know our need remains the same.
It's a new game every time, one on one.

In me today is less rage than ever, less hurt.
When I imagine some good woman young   20
I no longer imagine her cringing
in cornstalks, cruel father four rows away
beating corn leaves aside with a club.
That is release you never expected
from a past you never knew you had.   25
My horse is not sure he can make it
to the next star. You are free.

                                                                    1980

BEN JONSON

Epitaph on Elizabeth, L. H.

Wouldst thou hear what man can say
In a little? Reader, stay.
Underneath this stone doth lie
As much beauty as could die;
Which in life did harbor give   5
To more virtue than doth live.
If at all she had a fault,
Leave it buried in this vault.
One name was Elizabeth;
Th' other, let it sleep with death: 10
Fitter, where it died, to tell,
Than that it lived at all. Farewell.

                                                                    1616

JOHN KEATS

Ode on a Grecian Urn

I

Thou still unravished bride of quietness,
    Thou foster-child of silence and slow time,
Sylvan [8] historian, who canst thus express
    A flowery tale more sweetly than our rhyme:
What leaf-fringed legend haunts about thy shape   5
    Of deities or mortals, or of both,
        In Tempe or the dales of Arcady? [9]
What men or gods are these? What maidens loath?
    What mad pursuit? What struggle to escape?
        What pipes and timbrels? What wild ecstasy?   10

8. Rustic. The urn depicts a woodland scene.
9. Arcadia. Tempe is a beautiful valley near Mt. Olympus in Greece, and the valley ("dales") of Arcadia a picturesque section of the Peloponnesus; both came to be associated with the pastoral ideal.

II

Heard melodies are sweet, but those unheard
   Are sweeter; therefore, ye soft pipes, play on;
Not to the sensual[1] ear, but, more endeared,
   Pipe to the spirit ditties of no tone:
Fair youth, beneath the trees, thou canst not leave   15
   Thy song, nor ever can those trees be bare;
     Bold Lover, never, never canst thou kiss,
Though winning near the goal—yet, do not grieve;
     She cannot fade, though thou hast not thy bliss,
       For ever wilt thou love, and she be fair!   20

III

Ah, happy, happy boughs! that cannot shed
   Your leaves, nor ever bid the Spring adieu;
And, happy melodist, unweariéd,
   For ever piping songs for ever new;
More happy love! more happy, happy love!   25
   For ever warm and still to be enjoyed,
     For ever panting, and for ever young;
All breathing human passion far above,
     That leaves a heart high-sorrowful and cloyed,
      A burning forehead, and a parching tongue.   30

IV

Who are these coming to the sacrifice?
   To what green altar, O mysterious priest,
Lead'st thou that heifer lowing at the skies,
   And all her silken flanks with garlands dressed?
What little town by river or sea shore,   35
   Or mountain-built with peaceful citadel,
     Is emptied of this folk, this pious morn?
And, little town, thy streets for evermore
     Will silent be; and not a soul to tell
      Why thou art desolate, can e'er return.   40

V

O Attic[2] shape! Fair attitude! with brede[3]
   Of marble men and maidens overwrought,
With forest branches and the trodden weed;
   Thou, silent form, dost tease us out of thought
As doth eternity: Cold Pastoral!   45
   When old age shall this generation waste,
     Thou shalt remain, in midst of other woe
Than ours, a friend to man, to whom thou say'st,
     Beauty is truth, truth beauty[4]—that is all
      Ye know on earth, and all ye need to know.   50

May, 1819

1. Of the senses, as distinguished from the "ear" of the spirit or imagination.
2. Attica was the district of ancient Greece surrounding Athens.
3. Woven pattern. "overwrought": ornamented all over.

4. In some texts of the poem "Beauty is truth, truth beauty" is in quotation marks and in some texts it is not, leading to critical disagreements about whether the last line and a half are also inscribed on the urn or spoken by the poet.

JOHN KEATS

Ode to a Nightingale

I

My heart aches, and a drowsy numbness pains
  My sense, as though of hemlock[5] I had drunk,
Or emptied some dull opiate to the drains
  One minute past, and Lethe-wards[6] had sunk:
'Tis not through envy of thy happy lot,   5
  But being too happy in thine happiness,
    That thou, light-wingéd Dryad[7] of the trees,
      In some melodious plot
  Of beechen green, and shadows numberless,
    Singest of summer in full-throated ease.   10

II

O, for a draught of vintage! that hath been
  Cooled a long age in the deep-delvéd earth,
Tasting of Flora[8] and the country green,
  Dance, and Provençal song,[9] and sunburnt mirth!
O for a beaker full of the warm South,   15
  Full of the true, the blushful Hippocrene,[1]
    With beaded bubbles winking at the brim,
      And purple-stainéd mouth;
  That I might drink, and leave the world unseen,
    And with thee fade away into the forest dim: 20

III

Fade far away, dissolve, and quite forget
  What thou among the leaves hast never known,
The weariness, the fever, and the fret
  Here, where men sit and hear each other groan;
Where palsy shakes a few, sad, last gray hairs,   25
  Where youth grows pale, and specter-thin, and dies;
    Where but to think is to be full of sorrow
      And leaden-eyed despairs,
  Where Beauty cannot keep her lustrous eyes,
    Or new Love pine at them beyond tomorrow.   30

IV

Away! away! for I will fly to thee,
  Not charioted by Bacchus and his pards,[2]
But on the viewless wings of Poesy,
  Though the dull brain perplexes and retards:
Already with thee! tender is the night,   35
  And haply the Queen-Moon is on her throne,
    Clustered around by all her starry Fays;[3]

5. A poisonous drug.
6. Toward the river of forgetfulness (Lethe) in Hades.
7. Wood nymph.
8. Roman goddess of flowers.
9. The medieval troubadors of Provence (in southern France) were famous for their love songs.

1. The fountain of the Muses on Mt. Helicon, whose waters bring poetic inspiration.
2. The Roman god of wine was sometimes portrayed in a chariot drawn by leopards. "viewless": invisible.
3. Fairies.

But here there is no light,
　Save what from heaven is with the breezes blown
　　Through verdurous glooms and winding mossy ways.　　40

V

I cannot see what flowers are at my feet,
　Nor what soft incense hangs upon the boughs,
But, in embalméd[4] darkness, guess each sweet
　Wherewith the seasonable month endows
The grass, the thicket, and the fruit-tree wild;　　45
　White hawthorn, and the pastoral eglantine;[5]
　　Fast fading violets covered up in leaves;
　　　And mid-May's eldest child,
　The coming musk-rose, full of dewy wine,
　　The murmurous haunt of flies on summer eves.　　50

VI

Darkling[6] I listen; and, for many a time
　I have been half in love with easeful Death,
Called him soft names in many a muséd rhyme,
　To take into the air my quiet breath;
Now more than ever seems it rich to die,　　55
　To cease upon the midnight with no pain,
　　While thou art pouring forth thy soul abroad
　　　In such an ecstasy!
　Still wouldst thou sing, and I have ears in vain—
　　To thy high requiem become a sod.　　60

VII

Thou wast not born for death, immortal Bird!
　No hungry generations tread thee down;
The voice I hear this passing night was heard
　In ancient days by emperor and clown:
Perhaps the selfsame song that found a path　　65
　Through the sad heart of Ruth,[7] when, sick for home,
　　She stood in tears amid the alien corn;
　　　The same that ofttimes hath
　Charmed magic casements, opening on the foam
　　Of perilous seas, in faery lands forlorn.　　70

VIII

Forlorn! the very word is like a bell
　To toll me back from thee to my sole self!
Adieu! the fancy cannot cheat so well
　As she is famed to do, deceiving elf.
Adieu! adieu! thy plaintive anthem fades　　75
　Past the near meadows, over the still stream,

---

4. Fragrant, aromatic.
5. Sweetbriar or honeysuckle.
6. In the dark.
7. A virtuous Moabite widow who, ac-

cording to the Old Testament *Book of Ruth*, found a husband while gleaning in the wheat fields of Judah.

Up the hillside; and now 'tis buried deep
In the next valley-glades:
Was it a vision, or a waking dream?
Fled is that music:—Do I wake or sleep?   80

May, 1819

JOHN KEATS

On First Looking into Chapman's Homer [8]

Much have I traveled in the realms of gold,
And many goodly states and kingdoms seen;
Round many western islands have I been
Which bards in fealty[9] to Apollo hold.
Oft of one wide expanse had I been told   5
That deep-browed Homer ruled as his demesne;[1]
Yet did I never breathe its pure serene[2]
Till I heard Chapman speak out loud and bold:
Then felt I like some watcher of the skies
When a new planet swims into his ken;[3]   10
Or like stout Cortez[4] when with eagle eyes
He stared at the Pacific—and all his men
Looked at each other with a wild surmise—
Silent, upon a peak in Darien.

1816

JOHN KEATS

To Autumn

I

Season of mists and mellow fruitfulness,
    Close bosom-friend of the maturing sun;
Conspiring with him how to load and bless
    With fruit the vines that round the thatch-eves run;
To bend with apples the mossed cottage-trees,   5
    And fill all fruit with ripeness to the core;
        To swell the gourd, and plump the hazel shells
With a sweet kernel; to set budding more,
    And still more, later flowers for the bees,
    Until they think warm days will never cease,   10
        For Summer has o'er-brimmed their clammy cells.

---

8. Chapman's were among the most famous Renaissance translations; his *Iliad* was completed in 1611, *The Odyssey* in 1616. Keats wrote the sonnet after being led to Chapman by his former teacher and reading *The Iliad* all night long.
9. Literally, the loyalty owed by a vas-sal to his feudal lord. Apollo was the Greek and Roman god of poetry and music.
1. Estate, feudal possession.
2. Atmosphere.
3. Range of vision.
4. Actually, Balboa; he first viewed the Pacific from Darien, in Panama.

II

Who hath not seen thee oft amid thy store?
    Sometimes whoever seeks abroad may find
Thee sitting careless on a granary floor,
    Thy hair soft-lifted by the winnowing wind;[5]   15
Or on a half-reaped furrow sound asleep,
    Drowsed with the fume of poppies, while thy hook[6]
        Spares the next swath and all its twinéd flowers:
And sometimes like a gleaner thou dost keep
    Steady thy laden head across a brook;   20
    Or by a cider-press, with patient look,
        Thou watchest the last oozings hours by hours.

III

Where are the songs of Spring? Ay, where are they?
    Think not of them, thou hast thy music too—
While barréd clouds bloom the soft-dying day,   25
    And touch the stubble-plains with rosy hue;
Then in a wailful choir the small gnats mourn
    Among the river sallows,[7] borne aloft
        Or sinking as the light wind lives or dies;
And full-grown lambs loud bleat from hilly bourn;[8]   30
    Hedge-crickets sing; and now with treble soft
    The red-breast whistles from a garden-croft;[9]
        And gathering swallows twitter in the skies.
September 19, 1819

PHILIP LARKIN

Church Going

Once I am sure there's nothing going on
I step inside, letting the door thud shut.
Another church: matting, seats, and stone,
And little books; sprawlings of flowers, cut
For Sunday, brownish now; some brass and stuff   5
Up at the holy end; the small neat organ;
And a tense, musty, unignorable silence,
Brewed God knows how long. Hatless, I take off
My cycle-clips in awkward reverence,

5. Which sifts the grain from the chaff.
6. Scythe or sickle.
7. Willows.

8. Domain.
9. An enclosed garden near a house.

Move forward, run my hand around the font.[1]   10
From where I stand, the roof looks almost new—
Cleaned, or restored? Someone would know: I don't.
Mounting the lectern, I peruse a few
Hectoring[2] large-scale verses, and pronounce
"Here endeth" much more loudly than I'd meant.   15
The echoes snigger briefly. Back at the door
I sign the book, donate an Irish sixpence,
Reflect the place was not worth stopping for.

Yet stop I did: in fact I often do,
And always end much at a loss like this,   20
Wondering what to look for; wondering, too,
When churches fall completely out of use
What we shall turn them into, if we shall keep
A few cathedrals chronically on show,
Their parchment, plate and pyx[3] in locked cases,   25
And let the rest rent-free to rain and sheep.
Shall we avoid them as unlucky places?

Or, after dark, will dubious women come
To make their children touch a particular stone;
Pick simples[4] for a cancer; or on some   30
Advised night see walking a dead one?
Power of some sort or other will go on
In games, in riddles, seemingly at random;
But superstition, like belief, must die,
And what remains when disbelief has gone?   35
Grass, weedy pavement, brambles, buttress, sky,

A shape less recognizable each week,
A purpose more obscure. I wonder who
Will be the last, the very last, to seek
This place for what it was; one of the crew   40
That tap and jot and know what rood-lofts[5] were?
Some ruin-bibber,[6] randy for antique,
Or Christmas-addict, counting on a whiff
Of gown-and-bands and organ-pipes and myrrh?
Or will he be my representative,   45

Bored, uninformed, knowing the ghostly silt
Dispersed, yet tending to this cross of ground
Through suburb scrub because it held unspilt
So long and equally what since is found
Only in separation—marriage, and birth,   50
And death, and thoughts of these—for whom was built

---

1. A bowl for baptismal water, mounted on a stone pedestal.
2. Intimidating.
3. A container for the Eucharist.
4. Medicinal herbs.
5. Galleries atop the screens (on which crosses are mounted) which divide the naves or main bodies of churches from the choirs or chancels.
6. Literally, ruin-drinker: someone extremely attracted to antiquarian objects.

This special shell? For, though I've no idea
What this accoutered frowsty barn is worth,
It pleases me to stand in silence here;

A serious house on serious earth it is,   55
In whose blent air all our compulsions meet,
Are recognized, and robed as destinies.
And that much never can be obsolete,
Since someone will forever be surprising
A hunger in himself to be more serious,   60
And gravitating with it to this ground,
Which, he once heard, was proper to grow wise in,
If only that so many dead lie round.

         1955

CHRISTOPHER MARLOWE

The Passionate Shepherd to His Love

Come live with me and be my love,
And we will all the pleasures prove [7]
That valleys, groves, hills, and fields,
Woods, or steepy mountain yields.

And we will sit upon the rocks,   5
Seeing the shepherds feed their flocks,
By shallow rivers to whose falls
Melodious birds sing madrigals.

And I will make thee beds of roses
And a thousand fragrant posies,   10
A cap of flowers, and a kirtle [8]
Embroidered all with leaves of myrtle;

A gown made of the finest wool
Which from our pretty lambs we pull;
Fair lined slippers for the cold,   15
With buckles of the purest gold;

A belt of straw and ivy buds,
With coral clasps and amber studs:
And if these pleasures may thee move,
Come live with me, and be my love.   20

The shepherd swains [9] shall dance and sing
For thy delight each May morning:
If these delights thy mind may move,
Then live with me and be my love.

         1600

7. Try.
8. Gown.

9. Youths.

ANDREW MARVELL

To His Coy Mistress

Had we but world enough, and time,
This coyness,[1] lady, were no crime.
We would sit down, and think which way
To walk, and pass our long love's day.
Thou by the Indian Ganges' side   5
Shouldst rubies[2] find: I by the tide
Of Humber[3] would complain. I would
Love you ten years before the Flood,
And you should if you please refuse
Till the conversion of the Jews.[4]   10
My vegetable love[5] should grow
Vaster than empires, and more slow;
An hundred years should go to praise
Thine eyes, and on thy forehead gaze;
Two hundred to adore each breast,   15
But thirty thousand to the rest.
An age at least to every part,
And the last age should show your heart.
For, lady, you deserve this state;[6]
Nor would I love at lower rate.   20
But at my back I always hear
Time's wingéd chariot hurrying near;
And yonder all before us lie
Deserts of vast eternity.
Thy beauty shall no more be found,   25
Nor, in thy marble vault, shall sound
My echoing song; then worms shall try
That long preserved virginity,
And your quaint honor turn to dust,
And into ashes all my lust: 30
The grave's a fine and private place,
But none, I think, do there embrace.
Now therefore, while the youthful hue
Sits on thy skin like morning dew,[7]
And while thy willing soul transpires[8]   35
At every pore with instant fires,
Now let us sport us while we may,
And now, like am'rous birds of prey,
Rather at once our time devour

1. Hesitancy, modesty (not necessarily suggesting calculation).
2. Talismans which are supposed to preserve virginity.
3. A small river which flows through Marvell's home town, Hull. "complain": write love complaints, conventional songs lamenting the cruelty of love.
4. Which, according to popular Christian belief, will occur just before the end of the world.

5. Which is capable only of passive growth, not of consciousness. The "Vegetable Soul" is lower than the other two divisions of the Soul, "Animal" and "Rational."
6. Dignity.
7. The text reads "glew." "Lew" (warmth) has also been suggested as an emendation.
8. Breathes forth.

Than languish in his slow-chapped[9] pow'r.   40
Let us roll all our strength and all
Our sweetness up into one ball,
And tear our pleasures with rough strife
Thorough[1] the iron gates of life.
Thus, though we cannot make our sun   45
Stand still,[2] yet we will make him run.[3]

                                            1681

MARIANNE MOORE

Poetry

I, too, dislike it: there are things that are important beyond all this
        fiddle.
    Reading it, however, with a perfect contempt for it, one discovers in
    it after all, a place for the genuine.
        Hands that can grasp, eyes
        that can dilate, hair that can rise   5
            if it must, these things are important not because a

high-sounding interpretation can be put upon them but because they
        are
    useful. When they become so derivative as to become unintelligible,
    the same thing may be said for all of us, that we
        do not admire what   10
        we cannot understand: the bat
            holding on upside down or in quest of something to

eat, elephants pushing, a wild horse taking a roll, a tireless wolf under
    a tree, the immovable critic twitching his skin like a horse that feels
            a flea, the base-
        ball fan, the statistician—   15
            nor is it valid
                to discriminate against "business documents and

school-books"[4]; all these phenomena are important. One must make a
        distinction
    however: when dragged into prominence by half poets, the result is
        not poetry,

9. Slow-jawed. Chronos (Time), ruler of the world in early Greek myth, devoured all of his children except Zeus, who was hidden. Later, Zeus seized power (see line 46 and note).
  1. Through.
  2. To lengthen his night of love with Alcmene, Zeus made the sun stand still.
  3. Each sex act was believed to shorten life by one day.

4. *"Diary of Tolstoy,* p. 84: 'Where the boundary between prose and poetry lies, I shall never be able to understand. The question is raised in manuals of style, yet the answer to it lies beyond me. Poetry is verse: prose is not verse. Or else poetry is everything with the exception of business documents and school books.'" (Moore's note)

nor till the poets among us can be   20
　　"literalists of
　　the imagination"[5]—above
　　　　insolence and triviality and can present

for inspection, "imaginary gardens with real toads in them," shall we
　　have
it. In the meantime, if you demand on the one hand,   25
the raw material of poetry in
　　all its rawness and
　　that which is on the other hand
　　　　genuine, you are interested in poetry.

                                                                          1921

HOWARD NEMEROV

Life Cycle of Common Man

Roughly figured, this man of moderate habits,
This average consumer of the middle class,
Consumed in the course of his average life span
Just under half a million cigarettes,
Four thousand fifths of gin and about   5
A quarter as much vermouth; he drank
Maybe a hundred thousand cups of coffee,
And counting his parents' share it cost
Something like half a million dollars
To put him through life. How many beasts   10
Died to provide him with meat, belt and shoes
Cannot be certainly said.
　　　　　　　　But anyhow,
It is in this way that a man travels through time,
Leaving behind him a lengthening trail   15
Of empty bottles and bones, of broken shoes,
Frayed collars and worn out or outgrown
Diapers and dinnerjackets, silk ties and slickers.
Given the energy and security thus achieved,
He did . . . ? What? The usual things, of course,   20
The eating, dreaming, drinking and begetting,
And he worked for the money which was to pay
For the eating, et cetera, which were necessary
If he were to go on working for the money, et cetera,
But chiefly he talked. As the bottles and bones   25
Accumulated behind him, the words proceeded

---

5. " 'Literalists of the imagination.' Yeats, *Ideas of Good and Evil* (A. H. Bullen, 1903), p. 182. 'The limitation of his view was from the very intensity of his vision; he was a too literal realist of imagination, as others are of nature; and be- cause he believed that the figures seen by the mind's eye, when exalted by inspiration, were "eternal existences," symbols of divine essences, he hated every grace of style that might obscure their lineaments.' " (Moore's note)

Steadily from the front of his face as he
Advanced into the silence and made it verbal.
Who can tally the tale of his words? A lifetime
Would barely suffice for their repetition;   30
If you merely printed all his commas the result
Would be a very large volume, and the number of times
He said "thank you" or "very little sugar, please,"
Would stagger the imagination. There were also
Witticisms, platitudes, and statements beginning   35
"It seems to me" or "As I always say."

Consider the courage in all that, and behold the man
Walking into deep silence, with the ectoplastic
Cartoon's balloon of speech proceeding
Steadily out of the front of his face, the words   40
Borne along on the breath which is his spirit
Telling the numberless tale of his untold Word[6]
Which makes the world his apple, and forces him to eat.

                                                                              1960

GABRIEL OKARA

Piano and Drums

When at break of day at a riverside
I hear jungle drums telegraphing
the mystic rhythm, urgent, raw
like bleeding flesh, speaking of
primal youth and the beginning,   5
I see the panther ready to pounce,
the leopard snarling about to leap
and the hunters crouch with spears poised;

And my blood ripples, turns torrent,
topples the years and at once I'm   10
in my mother's lap a suckling;
at once I'm walking simple
paths with no innovations,
rugged, fashioned with the naked
warmth of hurrying feet and groping hearts   15
in green leaves and wild flowers pulsing.

Then I hear a wailing piano
solo speaking of complex ways
in tear-furrowed concerto;
of far-away lands   20

6. *Logos,* the principle of creation and order.

and new horizons with
coaxing diminuendo, counterpoint,
crescendo. But lost in the labyrinth
of its complexities, it ends in the middle
of a phrase at a daggerpoint.   25

And I lost in the morning mist
of an age at a riverside keep
wandering in the mystic rhythm
of jungle drums and the concerto.

                                                    1963

WILFRED OWEN

Dulce et Decorum Est[7]

Bent double, like old beggars under sacks,
Knock-kneed, coughing like hags, we cursed through sludge,
Till on the haunting flares we turned our backs
And towards our distant rest began to trudge.
Men marched asleep. Many had lost their boots   5
But limped on, blood-shod. All went lame; all blind;
Drunk with fatigue; deaf even to the hoots
Of disappointed shells that dropped behind.

Gas! Gas! Quick, boys!—An ecstasy of fumbling,
Fitting the clumsy helmets just in time;   10
But someone still was yelling out and stumbling
And floundering like a man in fire or lime.—
Dim, through the misty panes and thick green light
As under a green sea, I saw him drowning.

In all my dreams, before my helpless sight,   15
He plunges at me, guttering, choking, drowning.

If in some smothering dreams you too could pace
Behind the wagon that we flung him in,
And watch the white eyes writhing in his face,
His hanging face, like a devil's sick of sin;   20
If you could hear, at every jolt, the blood
Come gargling from the froth-corrupted lungs,
Obscene as cancer, bitter as the cud
Of vile, incurable sores on innocent tongues,—
My friend, you would not tell with such high zest   25
To children ardent for some desperate glory,
The old Lie: Dulce et decorum est
Pro patria mori.

1917

7. Part of a phrase from Horace, quoted in full in the last lines: "It is sweet and proper to die for one's country."

DOROTHY PARKER

The Little Old Lady in Lavender Silk

I was seventy-seven, come August,
    I shall shortly be losing my bloom;
I've experienced zephyr and raw gust
    And (symbolical) flood and simoom.

When you come to this time of abatement,   5
    To this passing from Summer to Fall,
It is manners to issue a statement
    As to what you got out of it all.

So I'll say, though reflection unnerves me
    And pronouncements I dodge as I can,   10
That I think (if my memory serves me)
    There was nothing more fun than a man!

In my youth, when the crescent was too wan
    To embarrass with beams from above,
By the aid of some local Don Juan   15
    I fell into the habit of love.

And I learned how to kiss and be merry—an
    Education left better unsung.
My neglect of the waters Pierian [8]
    Was a scandal, when Grandma was young.   20

Though the shabby unbalanced the splendid,
    And the bitter outmeasured the sweet,
I should certainly do as I then did,
    Were I given the chance to repeat.

For contrition is hollow and wraithful,   25
    And regret is no part of my plan,
And I think (if my memory's faithful)
    There was nothing more fun than a man!

                                          1937

MARGE PIERCY

What's That Smell in the Kitchen?

All over America women are burning dinners.
It's lambchops in Peoria; it's haddock
in Providence; it's steak in Chicago;

---

8. That is, poetry and learning. In classical mythology, the stream Hippocrene was associated with the Muses (the Pierides) and was sometimes called the Pierian spring.

tofu delight in Big Sur; red
rice and beans in Dallas.   5
All over America women are burning
food they're supposed to bring with calico
smile on platters glittering like wax.
Anger sputters in her brainpan, confined
but spewing out missiles of hot fat.   10
Carbonized despair presses like a clinker
from a barbecue against the back of her eyes.
If she wants to grill anything, it's
her husband spitted over a slow fire.
If she wants to serve him anything   15
it's a dead rat with a bomb in its belly
ticking like the heart of an insomniac.
Her life is cooked and digested,
nothing but leftovers in Tupperware.
Look, she says, once I was roast duck   20
on your platter with parsley but now I am Spam.
Burning dinner is not incompetence but war.

                                                        1983

SYLVIA PLATH

Black Rook in Rainy Weather

On the stiff twig up there
Hunches a wet black rook
Arranging and rearranging its feathers in the rain.
I do not expect miracle
Or an accident   5

To set the sight on fire
In my eye, nor seek
Any more in the desultory weather some design,
But let spotted leaves fall as they fall,
Without ceremony, or portent   10

Although, I admit, I desire,
Occasionally, some backtalk
From the mute sky, I can't honestly complain:
A certain minor light may still
Leap incandescent   15

Out of kitchen table or chair
As if a celestial burning took
Possession of the most obtuse objects now and then—
Thus hallowing an interval
Otherwise inconsequent   20

By bestowing largesse, honor,
One might say love. At any rate, I now walk
Wary (for it could happen
Even in this dull, ruinous landscape); skeptical,
Yet politic; ignorant   25

Of whatever angel may choose to flare
Suddenly at my elbow. I only know that a rook
Ordering its black feathers can so shine
As to seize my senses, haul
My eyelids up, and grant   30

A brief respite from fear
Of total neutrality. With luck,
Trekking stubborn through this season
Of fatigue, I shall
Patch together a content   35

Of sorts. Miracles occur,
If you care to call those spasmodic
Tricks of radiance miracles. The wait's begun again,
The long wait for the angel,
For that rare, random descent.[9]   40

1960

EZRA POUND

In a Station of the Metro[1]

The apparition of these faces in the crowd;
Petals on a wet, black bough.

p. 1913

EZRA POUND

A Virginal

No, no! Go from me. I have left her lately.
I will not spoil my sheath with lesser brightness,
For my surrounding air hath a new lightness;
Slight are her arms, yet they have bound me straitly
And left me cloaked as with a gauze of æther;   5
As with sweet leaves; as with a subtle clearness.
Oh, I have picked up magic in her nearness
To sheathe me half in half the things that sheathe her.
No, no! Go from me, I have still the flavor,
Soft as spring wind that's come from birchen bowers.   10

9. According to *Acts* 2, the Holy Ghost   Christ's disciples.
at Pentecost descended like a dove upon   1. The Paris subway.

Green come the shoots, aye April in the branches,
As winter's wound with her sleight hand she staunches,
Hath of the trees a likeness of the savor:
As white their bark, so white this lady's hours.

1912

DUDLEY RANDALL

Ballad of Birmingham

(On the bombing of a church in Birmingham, Alabama, 1963)

"Mother dear, may I go downtown
Instead of out to play,
And march the streets of Birmingham
In a Freedom March today?"

"No, baby, no, you may not go,   5
For the dogs are fierce and wild,
And clubs and hoses, guns and jails
Aren't good for a little child."

"But, mother, I won't be alone.
Other children will go with me,   10
And march the streets of Birmingham
To make our country free."

"No, baby, no, you may not go,
For I fear those guns will fire.
But you may go to church instead   15
And sing in the children's choir."

She has combed and brushed her night-dark hair,
And bathed rose petal sweet,
And drawn white gloves on her small brown hands,
And white shoes on her feet.   20

The mother smiled to know her child
Was in the sacred place,
But that smile was the last smile
To come upon her face.

For when she heard the explosion,   25
Her eyes grew wet and wild.
She raced through the streets of Birmingham
Calling for her child.

She clawed through bits of glass and brick,
Then lifted out a shoe.   30
"Oh, here's the shoe my baby wore,
But, baby, where are you?"

1969

ADRIENNE RICH

Diving into the Wreck

First having read the book of myths,
and loaded the camera,
and checked the edge of the knife-blade,
I put on
the body-armor of black rubber   5
the absurd flippers
the grave and awkward mask.
I am having to do this
not like Cousteau with his
assiduous team   10
aboard the sun-flooded schooner
but here alone.

There is a ladder.
The ladder is always there
hanging innocently   15
close to the side of the schooner.
We know what it is for,
we who have used it.
Otherwise
it's a piece of maritime floss   20
some sundry equipment.

I go down.
Rung after rung and still
the oxygen immerses me
the blue light   25
the clear atoms
of our human air.
I go down.
My flippers cripple me,
I crawl like an insect down the ladder   30
and there is no one
to tell me when the ocean
will begin.

First the air is blue and then
it is bluer and then green and then   35
black I am blacking out and yet
my mask is powerful
it pumps my blood with power
the sea is another story
the sea is not a question of power   40
I have to learn alone
to turn my body without force
in the deep element.

And now: it is easy to forget
what I came for   45
among so many who have always
lived here
swaying their crenellated fans
between the reefs
and besides   50
you breathe differently down here.

I came to explore the wreck.
The words are purposes.
The words are maps.
I came to see the damage that was done   55
and the treasures that prevail.
I stroke the beam of my lamp
slowly along the flank
of something more permanent
than fish or weed   60

the thing I came for:
the wreck and not the story of the wreck
the thing itself and not the myth
the drowned face always staring
toward the sun   65
the evidence of damage
worn by salt and sway into this threadbare beauty
the ribs of the disaster
curving their assertion
among the tentative haunters.   70

This is the place.
And I am here, the mermaid whose dark hair
streams black, the merman in his armored body
We circle silently
about the wreck   75
we dive into the hold.
I am she: I am he

whose drowned face sleeps with open eyes
whose breasts still bear the stress
whose silver, copper, vermeil cargo lies   80
obscurely inside barrels
half-wedged and left to rot
we are the half-destroyed instruments
that once held to a course
the water-eaten log   85
the fouled compass

We are, I am, you are
by cowardice or courage

the one who find our way
back to this scene   90
carrying a knife, a camera
a book of myths
in which
our names do not appear.

1972

ADRIENNE RICH

Planetarium

(*Thinking of Caroline Herschel, 1750–1848,
astronomer, sister of William; and others*)

A woman in the shape of a monster
a monster in the shape of a woman
the skies are full of them

a woman   "in the snow
among the Clocks and instruments   5
or measuring the ground with poles"

in her 98 years to discover
8 comets

she whom the moon ruled
like us   10
levitating into the night sky
riding the polished lenses

Galaxies of women, there
doing penance for impetuousness
ribs chilled   15
in those spaces   of the mind

An eye,
          "virile, precise and absolutely certain"
          from the mad webs of Uranisborg

                              encountering the NOVA

every impulse of light exploding   20
from the core
as life flies out of us

          Tycho[2] whispering at last
          "Let me not seem to have lived in vain"

2. Tycho Brahe (1546–1601), Danish astronomer whose cosmology tried to fuse the Ptolemaic and Copernican systems. He discovered and described (*"De Nova Stella,* 1573) a new star in what had previously been considered a fixed star-system. Uraniborg (line 19) was Tycho's famous and elaborate palace-laboratory-observatory.

What we see, we see   25
and seeing is changing

the light that shrivels a mountain
and leaves a man alive

Heartbeat of the pulsar
heart sweating through my body   30

The radio impulse
pouring in from Taurus
      I am bombarded yet   I stand

I have been standing all my life in the
direct path of a battery of signals   35
the most accurately transmitted most
untranslatable language in the universe
I am a galactic cloud so deep   so invo-
luted that a light wave could take 15
years to travel through me   And has   40
taken   I am an instrument in the shape
of a woman trying to translate pulsations
into images   for the relief of the body
and the reconstruction of the mind.

1968

EDWIN ARLINGTON ROBINSON

Richard Cory

Whenever Richard Cory went down town,
We people on the pavement looked at him:
He was a gentleman from sole to crown,
Clean favored, and imperially slim.

And he was always quietly arrayed,   5
And he was always human when he talked;
But still he fluttered pulses when he said,
"Good-morning," and he glittered when he walked.

And he was rich—yes, richer than a king—
And admirably schooled in every grace: 10
In fine, we thought that he was everything
To make us wish that we were in his place.

So on we worked, and waited for the light,
And went without the meat, and cursed the bread;
And Richard Cory, one calm summer night,   15
Went home and put a bullet through his head.

1897

THEODORE ROETHKE

The Dream

1

I met her as a blossom on a stem
Before she ever breathed, and in that dream
The mind remembers from a deeper sleep:
Eye learned from eye, cold lip from sensual lip.
My dream divided on a point of fire;   5
Light hardened on the water where we were;
A bird sang low; the moonlight sifted in;
The water rippled, and she rippled on.

2

She came toward me in the flowing air,
A shape of change, encircled by its fire.   10
I watched her there, between me and the moon;
The bushes and the stones danced on and on;
I touched her shadow when the light delayed;
I turned my face away, and yet she stayed.
A bird sang from the center of a tree;   15
She loved the wind because the wind loved me.

3

Love is not love until love's vulnerable.
She slowed to sigh, in that long interval.
A small bird flew in circles where we stood;
The deer came down, out of the dappled wood.   20
All who remember, doubt. Who calls that strange?
I tossed a stone, and listened to its plunge.
She knew the grammar of least motion, she
Lent me one virtue, and I live thereby.

4

She held her body steady in the wind;   25
Our shadows met, and slowly swung around;
She turned the field into a glittering sea;
I played in flame and water like a boy
And I swayed out beyond the white seafoam;
Like a wet log, I sang within a flame.   30
In that last while, eternity's confine,
I came to love, I came into my own.

1958

THEODORE ROETHKE

The Waking

I wake to sleep, and take my waking slow.
I feel my fate in what I cannot fear.
I learn by going where I have to go.

We think by feeling. What is there to know?
I hear my being dance from ear to ear.   5
I wake to sleep, and take my waking slow.

Of those so close beside me, which are you?
God bless the Ground! I shall walk softly there,
And learn by going where I have to go.

Light takes the Tree; but who can tell us how?   10
The lowly worm climbs up a winding stair;
I wake to sleep, and take my waking slow.

Great Nature has another thing to do
To you and me; so take the lively air,
And, lovely, learn by going where to go.   15

This shaking keeps me steady. I should know.
What falls away is always. And is near.
I wake to sleep, and take my waking slow.
I learn by going where I have to go.

1953

WILLIAM SHAKESPEARE

Hark, Hark! the Lark[3]

Hark, hark! the lark at heaven's gate sings,
   And Phoebus[4] 'gins arise,
His steeds to water at those springs
   On chaliced[5] flowers that lies;
And winking Mary-buds[6] begin   5
   To ope their golden eyes:
With every thing that pretty is,
   My lady sweet, arise!
   Arise, arise!

ca. 1610

---

3. From *Cymbeline*, Act II, sc. iii.
4. Apollo, the sun god.
5. Cup-shaped.
6. Buds of marigolds.

WILLIAM SHAKESPEARE

Not Marble, Nor the Gilded Monuments

Not marble, nor the gilded monuments
Of princes, shall outlive this powerful rhyme;
But you shall shine more bright in these conténts
Than unswept stone, besmeared with sluttish time.
When wasteful war shall statues overturn,   5
And broils root out the work of masonry,
Nor Mars his[7] sword nor war's quick fire shall burn
The living record of your memory.
'Gainst death and all-oblivious enmity
Shall you pace forth; your praise shall still find room   10
Even in the eyes of all posterity
That wear this world out to the ending doom.[8]
So, till the judgment that yourself arise,
You live in this, and dwell in lovers' eyes.

1609

PERCY BYSSHE SHELLEY

Ode to the West Wind

I

O wild West Wind, thou breath of Autumn's being,
Thou, from whose unseen presence the leaves dead
Are driven, like ghosts from an enchanter fleeing,

Yellow, and black, and pale, and hectic red,
Pestilence-stricken multitudes: O thou,   5
Who chariotest to their dark wintry bed

The wingéd seeds, where they lie cold and low,
Each like a corpse within its grave, until
Thine azure sister of the Spring shall blow

Her clarion[9] o'er the dreaming earth, and fill   10
(Driving sweet buds like flocks to feed in air)
With living hues and odors plain and hill:

Wild Spirit, which art moving everywhere;
Destroyer and preserver; hear, oh, hear!

II

Thou on whose stream, mid the steep sky's commotion,   15
Loose clouds like earth's decaying leaves are shed,
Shook from the tangled boughs of Heaven and Ocean,

---

7. Mars's (a common Renaissance form
of the possessive). "Nor . . . nor": neither
. . . nor.

8. Judgment Day.
9. Trumpet-call.

Angels[1] of rain and lightning: there are spread
On the blue surface of thine aëry surge,   20
Like the bright hair uplifted from the head

Of some fierce Maenad,[2] even from the dim verge
Of the horizon to the zenith's height,
The locks of the approaching storm. Thou dirge

Of the dying year, to which this closing night   25
Will be the dome of a vast sepulcher,
Vaulted with all thy congregated might

Of vapors, from whose solid atmosphere
Black rain, and fire, and hail will burst: oh, hear!

III

Thou who didst waken from his summer dreams
The blue Mediterranean, where he lay,   30
Lulled by the coil of his crystálline streams,

Beside a pumice isle in Baiae's bay,[3]
And saw in sleep old palaces and towers
Quivering within the wave's intenser day,

All overgrown with azure moss and flowers   35
So sweet, the sense faints picturing them! Thou
For whose path the Atlantic's level powers

Cleave themselves into chasms, while far below
The sea-blooms and the oozy woods which wear
The sapless foliage of the ocean, know   40

Thy voice, and suddenly grow gray with fear,
And tremble and despoil themselves:[4] oh, hear!

IV

If I were a dead leaf thou mightest bear;
If I were a swift cloud to fly with thee;
A wave to pant beneath thy power, and share   45

The impulse of thy strength, only less free
Than thou, O uncontrollable! If even
I were as in my boyhood, and could be

The comrade by thy wanderings over Heaven,
As then, when to outstrip thy skyey speed
Scarce seemed a vision; I would ne'er have striven

---

1. Messengers.
2. A frenzied female votary of Dionysus,
the Greek god of vegetation and fertility
who was supposed to die in the fall and
rise again each spring.
3. Where Roman emperors had erected
villas, west of Naples. "pumice": made of
porous lava turned to stone.
4. "The vegetation at the bottom of the
sea . . . sympathizes with that of the land
in the change of seasons." (Shelley's note)

As thus with thee in prayer in my sore need.
Oh, lift me as a wave, a leaf, a cloud!
I fall upon the thorns of life! I bleed!

A heavy weight of hours has chained and bowed   55
One too like thee: tameless, and swift, and proud.

V

Make me thy lyre,[5] even as the forest is:
What if my leaves are falling like its own!
The tumult of thy mighty harmonies

Will take from both a deep, autumnal tone,   60
Sweet though in sadness. Be thou, Spirit fierce,
My spirit! Be thou me, impetuous one!

Drive my dead thoughts over the universe
Like withered leaves to quicken a new birth!
And, by the incantation of this verse,   65

Scatter, as from an unextinguished hearth
Ashes and sparks, my words among mankind!
Be through my lips to unawakened earth

The trumpet of a prophecy! O Wind,
If Winter comes, can Spring be far behind?   70

1820

STEPHEN SPENDER

An Elementary School Classroom in a Slum

Far far from gusty waves these children's faces.
Like rootless weeds, the hair torn round their pallor.
The tall girl with her weighed-down head. The paper-
seeming boy, with rat's eyes. The stunted, unlucky heir
Of twisted bones, reciting a father's gnarled disease,   5
His lesson from his desk. At back of the dim class
One unnoted, sweet and young. His eyes live in a dream
Of squirrel's game, in tree room, other than this.

On sour cream walls, donations. Shakespeare's head,
Cloudless at dawn, civilized dome riding all cities.   10
Belled, flowery, Tyrolese valley.[6] Open-handed map
Awarding the world its world. And yet, for these
Children, these windows, not this world, are world,
Where all their future's painted with a fog,
A narrow street sealed in with a lead sky,   15
Far far from rivers, capes, and stars of words.

5. Aeolian lyre, a wind harp.
6. A rich and beautiful section of Austria with many scenes like those in typical
paintings of hamlets and picturesque coun-
trysides.

Surely, Shakespeare is wicked, the map a bad example
With ships and sun and love tempting them to steal—
For lives that slyly turn in their cramped holes
From fog to endless night? On their slag heap, these children   20
Wear skins peeped through by bones and spectacles of steel
With mended glass, like bottle bits on stones.
All of their time and space are foggy slum.
So blot their maps with slums as big as doom.

Unless, governor, teacher, inspector, visitor,   25
This map becomes their window and these windows
That shut upon their lives like catacombs,
Break O break open till they break the town
And show the children to green fields, and make their world
Run azure on gold sands, and let their tongues   30
Run naked into books, the white and green leaves open
History theirs whose language is the sun.

1939

WALLACE STEVENS

Anecdote of the Jar

I placed a jar in Tennessee,
And round it was, upon a hill.
It made the slovenly wilderness
Surround that hill.

The wilderness rose up to it,   5
And sprawled around, no longer wild.
The jar was round upon the ground
And tall and of a port in air.

It took dominion everywhere.
The jar was gray and bare.   10
It did not give of bird or bush,
Like nothing else in Tennessee.

1923

WALLACE STEVENS

The Emperor of Ice-Cream

Call the roller of big cigars,
The muscular one, and bid him whip
In kitchen cups concupiscent curds. [7]
Let the wenches dawdle in such dress
As they are used to wear, and let the boys   5
Bring flowers in last month's newspapers.
Let be be finale of seem. [8]
The only emperor is the emperor of ice-cream.

Take from the dresser of deal,
Lacking the three glass knobs, that sheet   10
On which she embroidered fantails [9] once
And spread it so as to cover her face.
If her horny feet protrude, they come
To show how cold she is, and dumb.
Let the lamp affix its beam.   15
The only emperor is the emperor of ice-cream.

1923

WALLACE STEVENS

Sunday Morning

I

Complacencies of the peignoir, and late
Coffee and oranges in a sunny chair,
And the green freedom of a cockatoo
Upon a rug mingle to dissipate
The holy hush of ancient sacrifice.   5
She dreams a little, and she feels the dark
Encroachment of that old catastrophe,[1]
As a calm darkens among water-lights.
The pungent oranges and bright, green wings
Seem things in some procession of the dead,   10
Winding across wide water, without sound.
The day is like wide water, without sound,
Stilled for the passing of her dreaming feet
Over the seas, to silent Palestine,
Dominion of the blood and sepulchre.   15

7. "The words 'concupiscent curds' have no genealogy; they are merely expressive: at least, I hope they are expressive. They express the concupiscence of life, but, by contrast with the things in relation in the poem, they express or accentuate life's destitution, and it is this that gives them something more than a cheap lustre" Wallace Stevens, *Letters* (New York: Knopf, 1960), p. 500.

8. ". . . the true sense of Let be be the finale of seem is let being become the conclusion or denouement of appearing to be: in short, ice cream is an absolute good. The poem is obviously not about ice cream, but about being as distinguished from seeming to be." *Letters*, p. 341.

9. Fantail pigeons.

1. The Crucifixion.

II

Why should she give her bounty to the dead?
What is divinity if it can come
Only in silent shadows and in dreams?
Shall she not find in comforts of the sun,
In pungent fruit and bright, green wings, or else   20
In any balm or beauty of the earth,
Things to be cherished like the thought of heaven?
Divinity must live within herself:
Passions of rain, or moods in falling snow;
Grievings in loneliness, or unsubdued   25
Elations when the forest blooms; gusty
Emotions on wet roads on autumn nights;
All pleasures and all pains, remembering
The bough of summer and the winter branch.
These are the measures destined for her soul.   30

III

Jove[2] in the clouds had his inhuman birth.
No mother suckled him, no sweet land gave
Large-mannered motions to his mythy mind
He moved among us, as a muttering king,
Magnificent, would move among his hinds,[3]   35
Until our blood, commingling, virginal,
With heaven, brought such requital to desire
The very hinds discerned it, in a star.[4]
Shall our blood fail? Or shall it come to be
The blood of paradise? And shall the earth   40
Seem all of paradise that we shall know?
The sky will be much friendlier then than now,
A part of labor and a part of pain,
And next in glory to enduring love,
Not this dividing and indifferent blue.   45

IV

She says, "I am content when wakened birds,
Before they fly, test the reality
Of misty fields, by their sweet questionings;
But when the birds are gone, and their warm fields
Return no more, where, then, is paradise?"   50
There is not any haunt of prophecy,
Nor any old chimera of the grave,
Neither the golden underground, nor isle
Melodious, where spirits gat[5] them home,
Nor visionary south, nor cloudy palm   55
Remote on heaven's hill, that has endured
As April's green endures, or will endure

---

2. Jupiter, the chief Roman god.   4. The star of Bethlehem.
3. Lowliest rural subjects.   5. Got.

Like her remembrance of awakened birds,
Or her desire for June and evening, tipped
By the consummation of the swallow's wings.   60

V

She says, "But in contentment I still feel
The need of some imperishable bliss."
Death is the mother of beauty; hence from her,
Alone, shall come fulfillment to our dreams
And our desires. Although she strews the leaves   65
Of sure obliteration on our paths,
The path sick sorrow took, the many paths
Where triumph rang its brassy phrase, or love
Whispered a little out of tenderness,
She makes the willow shiver in the sun   70
For maidens who were wont to sit and gaze
Upon the grass, relinquished to their feet.
She causes boys to pile new plums and pears
On disregarded plate.[6] The maidens taste
And stray impassioned in the littering leaves.   75

VI

Is there no change of death in paradise?
Does ripe fruit never fall? Or do the boughs
Hang always heavy in that perfect sky,
Unchanging, yet so like our perishing earth,
With rivers like our own that seek for seas   80
They never find, the same receding shores
That never touch with inarticulate pang?
Why set the pear upon those river-banks
Or spice the shores with odors of the plum?
Alas, that they should wear our colors there,   85
The silken weavings of our afternoons,
And pick the strings of our insipid lutes!
Death is the mother of beauty, mystical,
Within whose burning bosom we devise
Our earthly mothers waiting, sleeplessly.   90

VII

Supple and turbulent, a ring of men
Shall chant in orgy[7] on a summer morn
Their boisterous devotion to the sun,
Not as a god, but as a god might be,
Naked among them, like a savage source.   95
Their chant shall be a chant of paradise,
Out of their blood, returning to the sky;
And in their chant shall enter, voice by voice,

6. "Plate is used in the sense of so-
called family plate. Disregarded refers to
the disuse into which things fall that have
been possessed for a long time. I mean,
therefore, that death releases and renews.
What the old have come to disregard, the
young inherit and make use of" (*Letters
of Wallace Stevens* [1966], pp. 183–184).
7. Ceremonial revelry.

The windy lake wherein their lord delights,
The trees, like serafin,[8] and echoing hills,   100
That choir among themselves long afterward.
They shall know well the heavenly fellowship
Of men that perish and of summer morn.
And whence they came and whither they shall go
The dew upon their feet shall manifest.   105

VIII

She hears, upon that water without sound,
A voice that cries, "The tomb in Palestine
Is not the porch of spirits lingering.
It is the grave of Jesus, where he lay."
We live in an old chaos of the sun,   110
Or old dependency of day and night,
Or island solitude, unsponsored, free,
Of that wide water, inescapable.
Deer walk upon our mountains, and the quail
Whistle about us their spontaneous cries;   115
Sweet berries ripen in the wilderness;
And, in the isolation of the sky,
At evening, casual flocks of pigeons make
Ambiguous undulations as they sink,
Downward to darkness, on extended wings.   120

1915

ALFRED, LORD TENNYSON

Ulysses[9]

It little profits that an idle king,
By this still hearth, among these barren crags,
Matched with an agéd wife,[1] I mete and dole
Unequal laws unto a savage race,
That hoard, and sleep, and feed, and know not me.   5
   I cannot rest from travel; I will drink
Life to the lees.[2] All times I have enjoyed
Greatly, have suffered greatly, both with those
That loved me, and alone; on shore, and when
Through scudding drifts the rainy Hyades[3]   10
Vexed the dim sea. I am become a name;
For always roaming with a hungry heart

---

8. Seraphim, the highest of the nine orders of angels.

9. After the end of the Trojan War, Ulysses (or Odysseus), King of Ithaca and one of the Greek heroes of the war, returned to his island home (line 34). Homer's account of the situation is in the *Odyssey*, Book XI, but Dante's account of Ulysses in *The Inferno*, XXVI, is the more immediate background of the poem.

1. Penelope.

2. All the way down to the bottom of the cup.

3. A group of stars which were supposed to predict rain when they rose at the same time as the sun.

Much have I seen and known—cities of men
And manners, climates, councils, governments,
Myself not least, but honored of them all—   15
And drunk delight of battle with my peers,
Far on the ringing plains of windy Troy.
I am a part of all that I have met;
Yet all experience is an arch wherethrough
Gleams that untraveled world, whose margin fades   20
For ever and for ever when I move.
How dull it is to pause, to make an end,
To rust unburnished, not to shine in use!
As though to breathe were life. Life piled on life
Were all too little, and of one to me   25
Little remains; but every hour is saved
From that eternal silence, something more,
A bringer of new things; and vile it were
For some three suns to store and hoard myself,
And this gray spirit yearning in desire   30
To follow knowledge like a sinking star,
Beyond the utmost bound of human thought.

　　This is my son, mine own Telemachus,
To whom I leave the scepter and the isle—
Well-loved of me, discerning to fulfill   35
This labor by slow prudence to make mild
A rugged people, and through soft degrees
Subdue them to the useful and the good.
Most blameless is he, centered in the sphere
Of common duties, decent not to fail   40
In offices of tenderness, and pay
Meet adoration to my household gods,
When I am gone. He works his work, I mine.

　　There lies the port; the vessel puffs her sail:
There gloom the dark, broad seas. My mariners,   45
Souls that have toiled, and wrought, and thought with me—
That ever with a frolic welcome took
The thunder and the sunshine, and opposed
Free hearts, free foreheads—you and I are old;
Old age hath yet his honor and his toil.   50
Death closes all; but something ere the end,
Some work of noble note, may yet be done,
Not unbecoming men that strove with Gods.
The lights begin to twinkle from the rocks;
The long day wanes; the slow moon climbs; the deep 55
Moans round with many voices. Come, my friends.
'Tis not too late to seek a newer world.
Push off, and sitting well in order smite
The sounding furrows; for my purpose holds
To sail beyond the sunset, and the baths   60
Of all the western stars, until I die.

It may be that the gulfs will wash us down;[4]
It may be we shall touch the Happy Isles,[5]
And see the great Achilles, whom we knew.
Though much is taken, much abides; and though   65
We are not now that strength which in old days
Moved earth and heaven, that which we are, we are:
One equal temper of heroic hearts,
Made weak by time and fate, but strong in will
To strive, to seek, to find, and not to yield.   70

1833

DYLAN THOMAS

Do Not Go Gentle into That Good Night[6]

Do not go gentle into that good night,
Old age should burn and rave at close of day;
Rage, rage against the dying of the light.

Though wise men at their end know dark is right,
Because their words had forked no lightning they   5
Do not go gentle into that good night.

Good men, the last wave by, crying how bright
Their frail deeds might have danced in a green bay,
Rage, rage against the dying of the light.

Wild men who caught and sang the sun in flight,   10
And learn, too late, they grieved it on its way,
Do not go gentle into that good night.

Grave men, near death, who see with blinding sight
Blind eyes could blaze like meteors and be gay,
Rage, rage against the dying of the light.   15

And you, my father, there on the sad height,
Curse, bless, me now with your fierce tears, I pray.
Do not go gentle into that good night.
Rage, rage against the dying of the light.

1952

4. Beyond the Gulf of Gibraltar was
supposed to be a chasm that led to Hades.
5. Elysium, the Islands of the Blessed,
where heroes like Achilles (line 64) abide
after death.

6. Written during the final illness of
the poet's father.

DYLAN THOMAS

Fern Hill

Now as I was young and easy under the apple boughs
About the lilting house and happy as the grass was green,
    The night above the dingle starry,
      Time let me hail and climb
    Golden in the heydays of his eyes,   5
And honored among wagons I was prince of the apple towns
And once below a time I lordly had the trees and leaves
      Trail with daisies and barley
    Down the rivers of the windfall light.

And as I was green and carefree, famous among the barns   10
About the happy yard and singing as the farm was home,
    In the sun that is young once only,
      Time let me play and be
    Golden in the mercy of his means,
And green and golden I was huntsman and herdsman, the calves 15
Sang to my horn, the foxes on the hills barked clear and cold,
      And the sabbath rang slowly
    In the pebbles of the holy streams.

All the sun long it was running, it was lovely, the hay
Fields high as the house, the tunes from the chimneys, it was air 20
    And playing, lovely and watery
      And fire green as grass.
    And nightly under the simple stars
As I rode to sleep the owls were bearing the farm away,
All the moon long I heard, blessed among stables, the nightjars[7] 25
    Flying with the ricks,[8] and the horses
      Flashing into the dark.

And then to awake, and the farm, like a wanderer white
With the dew, come back, the cock on his shoulder: it was all
    Shining, it was Adam and maiden,   30
      The sky gathered again
    And the sun grew round that very day.
So it must have been after the birth of the simple light
In the first, spinning place, the spellbound horses walking warm
    Out of the whinnying green stable   35
      On to the fields of praise.

And honored among foxes and pheasants by the gay house
Under the new made clouds and happy as the heart was long,
    In the sun born over and over,
      I ran my heedless ways,   40
    My wishes raced through the house-high hay

---

7. Birds.   8. Haystacks.

And nothing I cared, at my sky-blue trades, that time allows
In all his tuneful turning so few and such morning songs
  Before the children green and golden
   Follow him out of grace,   45

Nothing I cared, in the lamb white days, that time would take me
Up to the swallow-thronged loft by the shadow of my hand,
  In the moon that is always rising,
   Nor that riding to sleep
  I should hear him fly with the high fields   50
And wake to the farm forever fled from the childless land.
Oh as I was young and easy in the mercy of his means,
  Time held me green and dying
  Though I sang in my chains like the sea.

            1946

DYLAN THOMAS

In My Craft or Sullen Art

  In my craft or sullen art
  Exercised in the still night
  When only the moon rages
  And the lovers lie abed
  With all their griefs in their arms,   5
  I labor by singing light
  Not for ambition or bread
  Or the strut and trade of charms
  On the ivory stages
  But for the common wages   10
  Of their most secret heart.

  Not for the proud man apart
  From the raging moon I write
  On these spindrift[9] pages
  Nor for the towering dead   15
  With their nightingales and psalms
  But for the lovers, their arms
  Round the griefs of the ages,
  Who pay no praise or wages
  Nor heed my craft or art.   20

            1946

EDMUND WALLER

Song

  Go, lovely rose!
  Tell her that wastes her time and me
   That now she knows,

9. Literally, wind-driven sea spray.

When I resemble[1] her to thee,
How sweet and fair she seems to be.   5

   Tell her that's young,
And shuns to have her graces spied,
   That hadst thou sprung
In deserts, where no men abide,
Thou must have uncommended died.   10

   Small is the worth
Of beauty from the light retired;
   Bid her come forth,
Suffer herself to be desired,
And not blush so to be admired.   15

   Then die! that she
The common fate of all things rare
   May read in thee;
How small a part of time they share
That are so wondrous sweet and fair!   20

                                     1645

WALT WHITMAN

When Lilacs Last in the Dooryard Bloomed[2]

1

When lilacs last in the dooryard bloomed,
And the great star early drooped in the western sky in the night,
I mourned, and yet shall mourn with ever-returning spring.

Ever-returning spring, trinity sure to me you bring,
Lilac blooming perennial and drooping star in the west,   5
And thought of him I love.

2

O powerful western fallen star!
O shades of night—O moody, tearful night!
O great star disappeared—O the black murk that hides the star!
O cruel hands that hold me powerless—O helpless soul of me!   10
O harsh surrounding cloud that will not free my soul.

3

In the dooryard fronting an old farm-house near the white-washed
    palings,
Stands the lilac-bush tall-growing with heart-shaped leaves of rich
    green,
With many a pointed blossom rising delicate, with the perfume strong
    I love,

---

1. Compare.
2. The "occasion" of the poem is the   assassination of Abraham Lincoln.

With every leaf a miracle—and from this bush in the dooryard,   15
With delicate-colored blossoms and heart-shaped leaves of rich green,
A sprig with its flower I break.

4

In the swamp in secluded recesses,
A shy and hidden bird is warbling a song.
Solitary the thrush,   20
The hermit withdrawn to himself, avoiding the settlements,
Sings by himself a song.

Song of the bleeding throat,
Death's outlet song of life (for well dear brother I know,
If thou wast not granted to sing thou would'st surely die).   25

5

Over the breast of the spring, the land, amid cities,
Amid lanes and through old woods, where lately the violets peeped
    from the ground, spotting the gray debris,
Amid the grass in the fields each side of the lanes, passing the endless
    grass,
Passing the yellow-speared wheat, every grain from its shroud in the
    dark-brown fields uprisen,
Passing the apple-tree blows of white and pink in the orchards,   30
Carrying a corpse to where it shall rest in the grave,
Night and day journeys a coffin.

6

Coffin that passes through lanes and streets, [3]
Through day and night with the great cloud darkening the land,
With the pomp of the inlooped flags with the cities draped in black,   35
With the show of the States themselves as of crepe-veiled women
    standing,
With processions long and winding and the flambeaus of the night,
With the countless torches lit, with the silent sea of faces and the un-
    bared heads,
With the waiting depot, the arriving coffin, and the somber faces,
With dirges through the night, with the thousand voices rising strong
    and solemn,   40
With all the mournful voices of the dirges poured around the coffin,
The dim-lit churches and the shuddering organs—where amid these
    you journey,
With the tolling tolling bells' perpetual clang,
Here, coffin that slowly passes,
I give you my sprig of lilac.   45

7

(Nor for you, for one alone,
Blossoms and branches green to coffins all I bring,
For fresh as the morning, thus would I chant a song for you O sane
    and sacred death.

---

3. The funeral cortege stopped at many towns between Washington and Springfield,
Illinois, where Lincoln was buried.

All over bouquets of roses,
O death, I cover you over with roses and early lilies,   50
But mostly and now the lilac that blooms the first,
Copious I break, I break the sprigs from the bushes,
With loaded arms I come, pouring for you,
For you and the coffins all of you O death.)

8

O western orb sailing the heaven,   55
Now I know what you must have meant as a month since I walked,
As I walked in silence the transparent shadowy night,
As I saw you had something to tell as you bent to me night after night,
As you drooped from the sky low down as if to my side (while the
    other stars all looked on),
As we wandered together the solemn night (for something I know
    not what kept me from sleep),   60
As the night advanced, and I saw on the rim of the west how full you
    were of woe,
As I stood on the rising ground in the breeze in the cool transparent
    night,
As I watched where you passed and was lost in the netherward black
    of the night,
As my soul in its trouble dissatisfied sank, as where you sad orb,
Concluded, dropped in the night, and was gone.   65

9

Sing on there in the swamp,
O singer bashful and tender, I hear your notes, I hear your call,
I hear, I come presently, I understand you,
But a moment I linger, for the lustrous star has detained me,
The star my departing comrade holds and detains me.   70

10

O how shall I warble myself for the dead one there I loved?
And how shall I deck my song for the large sweet soul that has gone?
And what shall my perfume be for the grave of him I love?
Sea-winds blown from east and west,
Blown from the Eastern sea and blown from the Western sea, till there
    on the prairies meeting,   75
These and with these and the breath of my chant,
I'll perfume the grave of him I love.

11

O what shall I hang on the chamber walls?
And what shall the pictures be that I hang on the walls,
To adorn the burial-house of him I love?   80

Pictures of growing spring and farms and homes,
With the Fourth-month eve at sundown, and the gray smoke lucid and
    bright,

With floods of the yellow gold of the gorgeous, indolent, sinking sun,
    burning, expanding the air,
With the fresh sweet herbage under foot, and the pale green leaves of
    the trees prolific,
In the distance the flowing glaze, the breast of the river, with a wind-
    dapple here and there,   85
With ranging hills on the banks, with many a line against the sky, and
    shadows,
And the city at hand with dwellings so dense, and stacks of chimneys,
And all the scenes of life and the workshops, and the workmen home-
    ward returning.

12

Lo, body and soul—this land,
My own Manhattan with spires, and the sparkling and hurrying tides,
    and the ships,   90
The varied and ample land, the South and the North in the light,
    Ohio's shores and flashing Missouri,
And ever the far-spreading prairies covered with grass and corn.

Lo, the most excellent sun so calm and haughty,
The violet and purple morn with just-felt breezes,
The gentle soft-born measureless light,   95
The miracle spreading bathing all, the fulfilled noon,
The coming eve delicious, the welcome night and the stars,
Over my cities shining all, enveloping man and land.

13

Sing on, sing on you gray-brown bird,
Sing from the swamps, the recesses, pour your chant from the bushes, 100
Limitless out of the dusk, out of the cedars and pines.

Sing on dearest brother, warble your reedy song,
Loud human song, with voice of uttermost woe.
O liquid and free and tender!
O wild and loose to my soul—O wondrous singer!   105
You only I hear—yet the star holds me (but will soon depart),
Yet the lilac with mastering odor holds me.

14

Now while I sat in the day and looked forth,
In the close of the day with its light and the fields of spring, and the
    farmers preparing their crops,
In the large unconscious scenery of my land with its lakes and forests, 110
In the heavenly aerial beauty (after the perturbed winds and the
    storms),
Under the arching heavens of the afternoon swift passing, and the
    voices of children and women.
The many-moving sea-tides, and I saw the ships how they sailed,
And the summer approaching with richness, and the fields all busy
    with labor,

And the infinite separate houses, how they all went on, each with its
    meals and minutia of daily usages,   115
And the streets how their throbbings throbbed, and the cities pent—lo,
    then and there,
Falling upon them all and among them all, enveloping me with the rest,
Appeared the cloud, appeared the long black trail,
And I knew death, its thought, and the sacred knowledge of death.

Then with the knowledge of death as walking one side of me,   120
And the thought of death close-walking the other side of me,
And I in the middle as with companions, and as holding the hands of
    companions,
I fled forth to the hiding receiving night that talks not,
Down to the shores of the water, the path by the swamp in the dim-
    ness,
To the solemn shadowy cedars and ghostly pines so still.   125

And the singer so shy to the rest received me,
The gray-brown bird I know received us comrades three,
And he sang the carol of death, and a verse for him I love.

From deep secluded recesses,
From the fragrant cedars and the ghostly pines so still,   130
Came the carol of the bird.

And the charm of the carol rapt me,
As I held as if by their hands my comrades in the night,
And the voice of my spirit tallied the song of the bird.

Come lovely and soothing death,   135
Undulate round the world, serenely arriving, arriving,
In the day, in the night, to all, to each,
Sooner or later delicate death.

Praised be the fathomless universe,
For life and joy, and for objects and knowledge curious,   140
And for love, sweet love—but praise! praise! praise!
For the sure-enwinding arms of cool-enfolding death.

Dark mother always gliding near with soft feet,
Have none chanted for thee a chant of fullest welcome?
Then I chant it for thee, I glorify thee above all,   145
I bring thee a song that when thou must indeed come, come unfalter-
    ingly.

Approach strong deliveress,
When it is so, when thou hast taken them I joyously sing the dead,
Lost in the loving floating ocean of thee,
Laved in the flood of thy bliss O death.   150

From me to thee glad serenades,
Dances for thee I propose saluting thee, adornments and feastings for
thee,
And the sights of the open landscape and the high-spread sky are
fitting,
And life and the fields, and the huge and thoughtful night.

The night in silence under many a star,   155
The ocean shore and the husky whispering wave whose voice I know,
And the soul turning to thee O vast and well-veiled death,
And the body gratefully nestling close to thee.

Over the tree-tops I float thee a song,
Over the rising and sinking waves, over the myriad fields and the
prairies wide,   160
Over the dense-packed cities all and the teeming wharves and ways,
I float this carol with joy, with joy to thee O death.

15

To the tally of my soul,
Loud and strong kept up the gray-brown bird,
With pure deliberate notes spreading filling the night.   165

Loud in the pines and cedars dim,
Clear in the freshness moist and the swamp-perfume,
And I with my comrades there in the night.

While my sight that was bound in my eyes unclosed,
As to long panoramas of visions.   170

And I saw askant the armies,
I saw as in noiseless dreams hundreds of battle-flags,
Borne through the smoke of the battles and pierced with missiles I saw
them,
And carried hither and yon through the smoke, and torn and bloody,
And at last but a few shreds left on the staffs (and all in silence),   175
And the staffs all splintered and broken.

I saw battle-corpses, myriads of them,
And the white skeletons of young men, I saw them,
I saw the debris and debris of all the slain soldiers of the war,   180
But I saw they were not as was thought,
They themselves were fully at rest, they suffered not,
The living remained and suffered, the mother suffered,
And the wife and the child and the musing comrade suffered,
And the armies that remained suffered.

4. Askance: sideways.

16

Passing the visions, passing the night,   185
Passing, unloosing the hold of my comrades' hands,
Passing the song of the hermit bird and the tallying song of my soul,
Victorious song, death's outlet song, yet varying ever-altering song,
As low and wailing, yet clear the notes, rising and falling, flooding the
    night,
Sadly sinking and fainting, as warning and warning, and yet again
    bursting with joy,   190
Covering the earth and filling the spread of the heaven,
As that powerful psalm in the night I heard from recesses,
Passing, I leave thee lilac with heart-shaped leaves,
I leave thee there in the door-yard, blooming, returning with spring.

I cease from my song for thee,   195
From my gaze on thee in the west, fronting the west, communing with
    thee,
O comrade lustrous with silver face in the night.

Yet each to keep and all, retrievements out of the night,
The song, the wondrous chant of the gray-brown bird,
And the tallying chant, the echo aroused in my soul,   200
With the lustrous and drooping star with the countenance full of woe,
With the holders holding my hand nearing the call of the bird,
Comrades mine and I in the midst, and their memory ever to keep, for
    the dead I loved so well,
For the sweetest, wisest soul of all my days and lands—and this for his
    dear sake,
Lilac and star and bird twined with the chant of my soul,   205
There in the fragrant pines and the cedars dusk and dim.
1865–66

RICHARD WILBUR

The Beautiful Changes

One wading a Fall meadow finds on all sides
The Queen Anne's Lace[5] lying like lilies
On water; it glides
So from the walker, it turns
Dry grass to a lake, as the slightest shade of you   5
Valleys my mind in fabulous blue Lucernes.[6]

---

5. A delicate-looking plant, with finely divided leaves and flat clusters of small white flowers, sometimes called "wild carrot."
6. Alfalfa, a plant resembling clover, with small purple flowers. Lake Lucerne is famed for deep blue color and its picturesque Swiss setting amid limestone mountains.

The beautiful changes as a forest is changed
By a chameleon's tuning his skin to it;
As a mantis, arranged
On a green leaf, grows   10
Into it, makes the leaf leafier, and proves
Any greenness is deeper than anyone knows.

Your hands hold roses always in a way that says
They are not only yours; the beautiful changes
In such kind ways,   15
Wishing ever to sunder
Things and things' selves for a second finding, to lose
For a moment all that it touches back to wonder.

                                                          1947

WILLIAM WORDSWORTH

Lines Composed a Few Miles above Tintern Abbey on Revisiting the Banks of the Wye During a Tour, July 13, 1798[7]

Five years have passed; five summers, with the length
Of five long winters! and again I hear
These waters, rolling from their mountain-springs
With a soft inland murmur. Once again
Do I behold these steep and lofty cliffs,   5
That on a wild secluded scene impress
Thoughts of more deep seclusion; and connect
The landscape with the quiet of the sky.
The day is come when I again repose
Here, under this dark sycamore, and view   10
These plots of cottage-ground, these orchard tufts,
Which at this season, with their unripe fruits,
Are clad in one green hue, and lose themselves
'Mid groves and copses.[8] Once again I see
These hedge-rows, hardly hedge-rows, little lines   15
Of sportive wood run wild: these pastoral farms,
Green to the very door; and wreaths of smoke
Sent up, in silence, from among the trees!
With some uncertain notice, as might seem
Of vagrant dwellers in the houseless woods,   20
Or of some hermit's cave, where by his fire
The hermit sits alone.   These beauteous forms,

7. Wordsworth had first visited the Wye
valley and the ruins of the medieval abbey
there in 1793, while on a solitary walking
tour. He was 23 then, 28 when he wrote
this poem.
8. Thickets.

Through a long absence, have not been to me
As is a landscape to a blind man's eye;
But oft, in lonely rooms, and 'mid the din   25
Of towns and cities, I have owed to them,
In hours of weariness, sensations sweet,
Felt in the blood, and felt along the heart;
And passing even into my purer mind,
With tranquil restoration—feelings too   30
Of unremembered pleasure: such, perhaps,
As have no slight or trivial influence
On that best portion of a good man's life,
His little, nameless, unremembered acts
Of kindness and of love. Nor less, I trust,   35
To them I may have owed another gift,
Of aspect more sublime; that blessèd mood,
In which the burthen[9] of the mystery,
In which the heavy and the weary weight
Of all this unintelligible world,   40
Is lightened—that serene and blessèd mood,
In which the affections gently lead us on—
Until, the breath of this corporeal frame
And even the motion of our human blood
Almost suspended, we are laid asleep   45
In body, and become a living soul;
While with an eye made quiet by the power
Of harmony, and the deep power of joy,
We see into the life of things.
                  If this
Be but a vain belief, yet, oh! how oft—   50
In darkness and amid the many shapes
Of joyless daylight; when the fretful stir
Unprofitable, and the fever of the world,
Have hung upon the beatings of my heart—
How oft, in spirit, have I turned to thee,   55
O sylvan Wye! thou wanderer through the woods,
How often has my spirit turned to thee!

   And now, with gleams of half-extinguished thought,
With many recognitions dim and faint,
And somewhat of a sad perplexity,   60
The picture of the mind revives again;
While here I stand, not only with the sense
Of present pleasure, but with pleasing thoughts
That in this moment there is life and food
For future years. And so I dare to hope,   65
Though changed, no doubt, from what I was when first
I came among these hills; when like a roe
I bounded o'er the mountains, by the sides
Of the deep rivers, and the lonely streams,

9. Burden.

Wherever nature led: more like a man   70
Flying from something that he dreads than one
Who sought the thing he loved. For nature then
(The coarser [1] pleasures of my boyish days,
And their glad animal movements all gone by)
To me was all in all—I cannot paint   75
What then I was. The sounding cataract
Haunted me like a passion; the tall rock,
The mountain, and the deep and gloomy wood,
Their colors and their forms, were then to me
An appetite; a feeling and a love,   80
That had no need of a remoter charm,
By thought supplied, nor any interest
Unborrowed from the eye. That time is past,
And all its aching joys are now no more,
And all its dizzy raptures. Not for this   85
Faint I,[2] nor mourn nor murmur; other gifts
Have followed; for such loss, I would believe,
Abundant recompense. For I have learned
To look on nature, not as in the hour
Of thoughtless youth; but hearing oftentimes   90
The still, sad music of humanity,
Nor harsh nor grating, though of ample power
To chasten and subdue. And I have felt
A presence that disturbs me with the joy
Of elevated thoughts; a sense sublime   95
Of something far more deeply interfused,
Whose dwelling is the light of setting suns,
And the round ocean and the living air,
And the blue sky, and in the mind of man:
A motion and a spirit, that impels   100
All thinking things, all objects of all thought,
And rolls through all things. Therefore am I still
A lover of the meadows and the woods
And mountains; and of all that we behold
From this green earth; of all the mighty world   105
Of eye, and ear—both what they half create,
And what perceive; well pleased to recognize
In nature and the language of the sense
The anchor of my purest thoughts, the nurse,
The guide, the guardian of my heart, and soul   110
Of all my moral being.
                    Nor perchance,
If I were not thus taught, should I the more
Suffer my genial spirits [3] to decay:
For thou art with me here upon the banks
Of this fair river; thou my dearest Friend, [4]   115

---

1. Physical.
2. Am I discouraged.
3. Natural disposition; i.e., the spirits

that are part of his individual genius.
4. His sister Dorothy.

My dear, dear Friend; and in thy voice I catch
The language of my former heart, and read
My former pleasures in the shooting lights
Of thy wild eyes. Oh! yet a little while
May I behold in thee what I was once,   120
My dear, dear Sister! and this prayer I make,
Knowing that Nature never did betray
The heart that loved her; 'tis her privilege,
Through all the years of this our life, to lead
From joy to joy: for she can so inform   125
The mind that is within us, so impress
With quietness and beauty, and so feed
With lofty thoughts, that neither evil tongues,
Rash judgments, nor the sneers of selfish men,
Nor greetings where no kindness is, nor all   130
The dreary intercourse of daily life,
Shall e'er prevail against us, or disturb
Our cheerful faith that all which we behold
Is full of blessings. Therefore let the moon
Shine on thee in thy solitary walk;   135
And let the misty mountain-winds be free
To blow against thee: and, in after years,
When these wild ecstasies shall be matured
Into a sober pleasure; when thy mind
Shall be a mansion for all lovely forms,   140
Thy memory be as a dwelling-place
For all sweet sounds and harmonies; oh! then,
If solitude, or fear, or pain, or grief,
Should be thy portion, with what healing thoughts
Of tender joy wilt thou remember me,   145
And these my exhortations! Nor, perchance—
If I should be where I no more can hear
Thy voice, nor catch from thy wild eyes these gleams
Of past existence—wilt thou then forget
That on the banks of this delightful stream   150
We stood together; and that I, so long
A worshiper of Nature, hither came
Unwearied in that service; rather say
With warmer love—oh! with far deeper zeal
Of holier love. Nor wilt thou then forget,   155
That after many wanderings, many years
Of absence, these steep woods and lofty cliffs,
And this green pastoral landscape, were to me
More dear, both for themselves and for thy sake!

1798

W. B. YEATS

Among School Children

I

I walk through the long schoolroom questioning;
A kind old nun in a white hood replies;
The children learn to cipher and to sing,
To study reading-books and history,
To cut and sew, be neat in everything   5
In the best modern way—the children's eyes
In momentary wonder stare upon
A sixty-year-old smiling public man.[5]

II

I dream of a Ledaean body,[6] bent
Above a sinking fire, a tale that she   10
Told of a harsh reproof, or trivial event
That changed some childish day to tragedy—
Told, and it seemed that our two natures blent
Into a sphere from youthful sympathy,
Or else, to alter Plato's parable,   15
Into the yolk and white of the one shell.[7]

III

And thinking of that fit of grief or rage
I look upon one child or t'other there
And wonder if she stood so at that age—
For even daughters of the swan can share   20
Something of every paddler's heritage—
And had that color upon cheek or hair,
And thereupon my heart is driven wild:
She stands before me as a living child.

IV

Her present image floats into the mind—   25
Did Quattrocento finger[8] fashion it
Hollow of cheek as though it drank the wind
And took a mess of shadows for its meat?
And I though never of Ledaean kind
Had pretty plumage once—enough of that,   30
Better to smile on all that smile, and show
There is a comfortable kind of old scarecrow.

---

5. At 60 (in 1925) Yeats had been a senator of the Irish Free State.

6. Like that of Helen of Troy, daughter of Leda. The memory dream is of Maud Gonne (see also lines 29–30), with whom Yeats had long been hopelessly in love.

7. In Plato's *Symposium*, the origin of human love is explained by parable: Human beings were once spheres, but Zeus was fearful of their power and cut them in half; now each half longs to be re-united with its missing half. Helen and Pollux were hatched from one of two eggs born to Leda after her union with Zeus in the form of a swan; the other contained Castor and Clytemnestra. According to Yeats in *A Vision*, "from one of [Leda's] eggs came Love and from the other War."

8. Fifteenth-century artists, who fall within the 15th Phase of the Christian cycle. Yeats especially admired Botticelli, and in *A Vision* praises his "deliberate strangeness everywhere [which] gives one an emotion of mystery which is new to painting." Botticelli is grouped with those who make "intellect and emotion, *primary* curiosity and the *antithetical* dream . . . for the moment one."

V

What youthful mother, a shape upon her lap
Honey of generation[9] had betrayed,
And that must sleep, shriek, struggle to escape   35
As recollection or the drug decide,
Would think her son, did she but see that shape
With sixty or more winters on its head,
A compensation for the pang of his birth,
Or the uncertainty of his setting forth?   40

VI

Plato thought nature but a spume that plays
Upon a ghostly paradigm of things; [1]
Solider Aristotle played the taws
Upon the bottom of a king of kings; [2]
World-famous golden-thighed Pythagoras [3]   45
Fingered upon a fiddle-stick or strings
What a star sang and careless Muses heard:
Old clothes upon old sticks to scare a bird.

VII

Both nuns and mothers worship images,
But those the candles light are not as those   50
That animate a mother's reveries,
But keep a marble or a bronze repose.
And yet they too break hearts—O Presences
That passion, piety or affection knows,
And that all heavenly glory symbolize—   55
O self-born mockers of man's enterprise;

VIII

Labor is blossoming or dancing where
The body is not bruised to pleasure soul,
Nor beauty born out of its own despair,
Nor blear-eyed wisdom out of midnight oil.   60
O chestnut-tree, great-rooted blossomer,
Are you the leaf, the blossom or the bole? [4]
O body swayed to music, O brightening glance,
How can we know the dancer from the dance?

1927

9. "I have taken the 'honey of generation' from Porphyry's essay on 'The Cave of the Nymphs' [*Odyssey*, Book XIII], but find no warrant in Porphyry for considering it the 'drug' that destroys the 'recollection' of prenatal freedom. He blamed a cup of oblivion given in the zodiacal sign of Cancer." (Yeats's note) Porphyry, a third-century Greek scholar and neoplatonic philosopher, says "honey of generation" means the "pleasure arising from copulation" which draws souls "downward" to generation.

1. Plato considered the world of nature an imperfect and illusory copy of the ideal world.

2. Aristotle, the teacher of Alexander the Great, disciplined him with a strap ("taw," line 43). His philosophy, insisting on the interdependence of form and matter, took the world of nature far more seriously than did Plato's.

3. Sixth-century B.C. Greek mathematician and philosopher, whose elaborate philosophical system included the doctrine of the harmony of the spheres. He was highly revered, and one legend describes his god-like golden thighs.

4. Trunk.

W. B. YEATS

Leda and the Swan [5]

A sudden blow: the great wings beating still
Above the staggering girl, her thighs caressed
By the dark webs, her nape caught in his bill,
He holds her helpless breast upon his breast.

How can those terrified vague fingers push   5
The feathered glory from her loosening thighs?
And how can body, laid in that white rush,
But feel the strange heart beating where it lies?

A shudder in the loins engenders there
The broken wall, the burning roof and tower   10
And Agamemnon dead.
                              Being so caught up,
So mastered by the brute blood of the air,
Did she put on his knowledge with his power
Before the indifferent beak could let her drop?

1923

W. B. YEATS

Sailing to Byzantium [6]

I

That [7] is no country for old men. The young
In one another's arms, birds in the trees
—Those dying generations—at their song,
The salmon-falls, the mackerel-crowded seas
Fish, flesh, or fowl, commend all summer long   5

5. According to Greek myth, Zeus took the form of a swan to seduce Leda, who became the mother of Helen of Troy and also of Clytemnestra, Agamemnon's wife and murderer. Helen's abduction by her husband, Menelaus, brother of Agamemnon, began the Trojan War (line 10). Yeats described the visit of Zeus to Leda as an annunciation like that to Mary (see *Luke* 1:26–38): "I imagine the annunciation that founded Greece as made to Leda. . . ." (*A Vision*).

6. The ancient name of Istanbul, the capital and holy city of Eastern Christendom from the late fourth century until 1453. It was famous for its stylized and formal mosaics, its symbolic, nonnaturalistic art, and its highly developed intellectual life. Yeats repeatedly uses it to symbolize a world of artifice and timelessness, free from the decay and death of the natural and sensual world. In *A Vision*, Yeats wrote: "I think if I could be given a month of Antiquity and leave to spend it where I chose, I would spend it in Byzantium a little before Justinian opened St. Sophia and closed the Academy of Plato [about

535 A.D.]. I think I could find in some little wineshop some philosophical worker in mosaic who could answer all my questions, the supernatural descending nearer to him than to Plotinus even, for the pride of his delicate skill would make what was an instrument of power to princes and clerics, a murderous madness in the mob, show as a lovely flexible presence like that of a perfect human body. I think that in early Byzantium, maybe never before or since in recorded history, religious, aesthetic and practical life were one, that architect and artificers . . . spoke to the multitude and the few alike. The painter, the mosaic worker, the worker in gold and silver, the illuminator of sacred books, were almost impersonal, almost perhaps without the consciousness of individual design, absorbed in their subject-matter and that the vision of the whole people. They could . . . weave all into a vast design, the work of many that seemed the work of one, that made building, picture, metal-work or rail and lamp, seem but a single image. . . ."

7. Ireland, as an instance of the natural, temporal world.

Whatever is begotten, born, and dies.
Caught in that sensual music all neglect
Monuments of unaging intellect.

II

An aged man is but a paltry thing,
A tattered coat upon a stick, unless   10
Soul clap its hands and sing, and louder sing
For every tatter in its mortal dress,
Nor is there singing school but studying
Monuments of its own magnificence;
And therefore I have sailed the seas and come   15
To the holy city of Byzantium.

III

O sages standing in God's holy fire
As in the gold mosaic of a wall,
Come from the holy fire, perne in a gyre, [8]
And be the singing-masters of my soul.   20
Consume my heart away; sick with desire
And fastened to a dying animal
It knows not what it is; and gather me
Into the artifice of eternity.

IV

Once out of nature I shall never take   25
My bodily form from any natural thing,
But such a form as Grecian goldsmiths make
Of hammered gold and gold enameling
To keep a drowsy Emperor awake; [9]
Or set upon a golden bough [1] to sing   30
To lords and ladies of Byzantium
Of what is past, or passing, or to come.

1927

8. I.e., whirl in a coiling motion, so that his soul may merge with its motion as the timeless world invades the cycles of history and nature. The gyre in "The Second Coming" moves in the opposite direction, up and out centripetally, so that "things fall apart." "Perne" is Yeats's coinage (from the noun "pirn"): to spin around in the kind of spiral pattern that thread makes as it comes off a bobbin or spool.

9. "I have read somewhere that in the Emperor's palace at Byzantium was a tree made of gold and silver, and artificial birds that sang." (Yeats's note)
1. In Book VI of *The Aeneid*, the sybil tells Aeneas that he must pluck a golden bough from a nearby tree in order to descend to Hades. There is only one such branch there, and when it is plucked an identical one takes its place.

W. B. YEATS

The Second Coming[2]

Turning and turning in the widening gyre[3]
The falcon cannot hear the falconer;
Things fall apart; the center cannot hold;
Mere anarchy is loosed upon the world,
The blood-dimmed tide is loosed, and everywhere   5
The ceremony of innocence is drowned;
The best lack all conviction, while the worst
Are full of passionate intensity.

Surely some revelation is at hand;
Surely the Second Coming is at hand.   10
The Second Coming! Hardly are those words out
When a vast image out of *Spiritus Mundi*[4]
Troubles my sight: somewhere in sands of the desert
A shape with lion body and the head of a man,
A gaze blank and pitiless as the sun,   15
Is moving its slow thighs, while all about it
Reel shadows of the indignant desert birds.[5]
The darkness drops again; but now I know
That twenty centuries of stony sleep
Were vexed to nightmare by a rocking cradle,   20
And what rough beast, its hour come round at last,
Slouches towards Bethlehem to be born?

p. 1920

2. The Second Coming of Christ, according to *Matthew* 24:29–44, will come after a time of "tribulation." Disillusioned by Ireland's continued civil strife, Yeats saw his time as the end of another historical cycle. In *A Vision* (1937) Yeats describes his view of history as dependent on cycles of about 2000 years: the birth of Christ had ended the cycle of Greco-Roman civilization, and now the Christian cycle seemed near an end, to be followed by an antithetical cycle, ominous in its portents.
3. Literally, the widening spiral of a falcon's flight. "Gyre" is Yeats's term for a cycle of history, which he diagramed in terms of a series of interpenetrating cones.
4. Or *Anima Mundi*, the spirit or soul of the world, a consciousness in which the individual participates. Yeats considered this universal consciousness or memory a fund from which poets drew their images and symbols. In *Per Amica Silentia Lunae* he wrote: "Before the mind's eye, whether in sleep or waking, came images that one was to discover presently in some book one had never read, and after looking in vain for explanation . . . , I came to believe in a great memory passing on from generation to generation."
5. Yeats later writes of the "brazen winged beast . . . described in my poem *The Second Coming*" as "associated with laughing, ecstatic destruction." "Our civilization was about to reverse itself, or some new civilization about to be born from all that our age had rejected . . . ; because we had worshipped a single god it would worship many."

DRAMA

DRAMA

1   EXPERIENCING DRAMA

Experiencing a play is very different from experiencing a story or a poem. Plays are written to be performed—by actors, on a stage, for an audience. To see and hear a play—to be a part of an audience responding to it—represents a different kind of experience from the usually solitary act of reading a story or a poem. Watching a performance is, for one thing, much more passive than the act of reading; the play comes to you rather than, as in the act of reading a story, your going to the text. There are, in fact, quite a few differences between performance and reading, and those differences are built into the nature of drama. Plays are written with a public performance in mind. Playwrights create plays in full consciousness of the possibilities that go beyond words and texts and extend to physical actions, stage effects, and other bits of theatricality that can create special effects on an audience.

All good literature tries to engage our imagination actively, inviting us to share feelings or think what it would be like to be a particular person in a particular place, time, or set of circumstances. But plays—when they are acted out on a stage—are more *concrete* than poems or stories: we see actions and hear words spoken through our physical senses; real live human beings stand for imaginary characters and actually say speeches and perform actions that we can hear and watch. Some of the imagination required is provided by the director and by actors who have made choices for us; they are interpreters of the play, and perform for a viewer part of the act of imagination that readers have to perform altogether for themselves. Seeing a play performed does involve an act of imagination, for the audience has to accept the illusion that the stage is actually a hotel room in New York, a meadow in the Midwest, or a court in Denmark, but that act of imagination is quite different from translating words on a page into people and actions.

Because plays are written with the explicit intention that they will be acted out upon a stage, *reading* a play requires an additional act of imagination. Readers of a play need to imagine not just feelings or a flow of action—as in poems and stories—but how the action and characters look in a theater, on a stage, before a live audience. We try to imagine how a character will look and move and talk; in effect, a reader casts a play as he or she reads it, putting actors into roles and making them move and speak in our imaginations. We imagine a whole layer of performance between the words on the page and the way we play out the plot in our minds.

The fact of a stage—physically limited in what it can contain and in what can be done within its confines—conditions the nature of drama, and a student of drama has to confront the particular limitations—and possibilities—that stages and staging are capable of to imagine fully how plays work. Experiencing drama is, thus, both more simple and more complex than experiencing poetry or fiction: more simple because the performance or imagined performance spells out for us far more detail in a far more vivid way than can words on a page, but more complex because as readers we have to construct in our imaginations the precise details our responses will ultimately depend on. In a sense, we become almost collaborators of the playwright as we go along—before we function fully as readers completing the potential of a text.

Drama on a stage often reflects the drama of everyday life, but (like other forms of literature and art) it concentrates life, focuses it, and holds it up to examination. Many scenes in plays could be slices of actual conversations, and sometimes playwrights make a special effort to have their dialogue take on the informality—or even the sloppiness and banality—of ordinary talk. Sometimes, too, the actions portrayed are everyday actions—drinking a cup of coffee, watching a bus go by, working out the subtleties of a relationship with a friend. Not all plays are about grand machinations of state or great loves or noble deeds (although some are), and not all artistic shapings of actuality into drama are formalized into traditional structures (although many are). Plays may be short, have only two or three characters, portray the routine matters of everyday life, and present conflicts that are personal or even trivial as well as great moments of national or cosmic significance. Sometimes it takes greater artistic control to make a very simple scene compelling than it does to portray grander actions that are more laden with deep conflict and greater in import. Here, for example, is a very brief contemporary piece of drama. Its author, Harold Pinter, does not call it a play but only a "sketch," a short piece suitable for staging and containing key elements of dramatic art.

HAROLD PINTER

The Black and White

The First Old Woman is sitting at a milk bar table. Small. A Second Old Woman approaches. Tall. She is carrying two bowls of soup, which are covered by two plates, on each of which is a slice of bread. She puts the bowls down on the table carefully.

SECOND   You see that one come up and speak to me at the counter? (*She takes the bread plates off the bowls, takes two spoons from her pocket, and places the bowls, plates and spoons.*)

FIRST   You got the bread, then?

SECOND   I didn't know how I was going to carry it. In the end I put the plates on top of the soup.

FIRST I like a bit of bread with my soup. (*They begin the soup. Pause.*)

SECOND Did you see that one come up and speak to me at the counter?

FIRST Who?

SECOND Comes up to me, he says, hullo, he says, what's the time by your clock? Bloody liberty. I was just standing there getting your soup.

FIRST It's tomato soup.

SECOND What's the time by your clock? he says.

FIRST I bet you answered him back.

SECOND I told him all right. Go on, I said, why don't you get back into your scraghole, I said, clear off out of it before I call a copper. (*Pause.*)

FIRST I not long got here.

SECOND Did you get the all-night bus?

FIRST I got the all-night bus straight here.

SECOND Where from?

FIRST Marble Arch.

SECOND Which one?

FIRST The two-nine-four, that takes me all the way to Fleet Street.

SECOND So does the two-nine-one. (*Pause.*) I see you talking to two strangers as I come in. You want to stop talking to strangers, old piece of boot like you, you mind who you talk to.

FIRST I wasn't talking to any strangers. (*Pause. The First Old Woman follows the progress of a bus through the window.*) That's another all-night bus gone down. (*Pause.*) Going up the other way. Fulham way. (*Pause.*) That was a two-nine-seven. (*Pause.*) I've never been up that way. (*Pause.*) I've been down to Liverpool Street.

SECOND That's up the other way.

FIRST I don't fancy going down there, down Fulham way, and all up there.

SECOND Uh-uh.

FIRST I've never fancied that direction much. (*Pause.*)

SECOND How's your bread? (*Pause.*)

FIRST Eh?

SECOND Your bread.

FIRST All right. How's yours? (*Pause.*)

SECOND They don't charge for the bread if you have soup.

FIRST They do if you have tea.

SECOND If you have tea they do. (*Pause.*) You talk to strangers they'll take you in. Mind my word. Coppers'll take you in.

FIRST I don't talk to strangers.

SECOND They took me away in the wagon once.

FIRST They didn't keep you though.

SECOND They didn't keep me, but that was only because they took a fancy to me. They took a fancy to me when they got me in the wagon.

FIRST Do you think they'd take a fancy to me?

SECOND   I wouldn't back on it. (*The First Old Woman gazes out of the window.*)

FIRST   You can see what goes on from this top table. (*Pause.*) It's better than going down to that place on the embankment, anyway.

SECOND   Yes, there's not too much noise.

FIRST   There's always a bit of noise.

SECOND   Yes, there's always a bit of life. (*Pause.*)

FIRST   They'll be closing down soon to give it a scrub-round.

SECOND   There's a wind out. (*Pause.*)

FIRST   I wouldn't mind staying.

SECOND   They won't let you.

FIRST   I know. (*Pause.*) Still, they only close hour and half, don't they? (*Pause.*) It's not long. (*Pause.*) You can go along, then come back.

SECOND   I'm going. I'm not coming back.

FIRST   When it's light I come back. Have my tea.

SECOND   I'm going. I'm going up to the Garden.

FIRST   I'm not going down there. (*Pause.*) I'm going up to Waterloo Bridge.

SECOND   You'll just about see the last two-nine-six come up over the river.

FIRST   I'll just catch a look of it. Time I get up there. (*Pause.*) It don't look like an all-night bus in daylight, do it?

1959

All the elements of drama are here in rather elementary form: there is a bit of story, mostly implied, about the lives of the two women; action on a modest scale, with a lot of emphasis on timing and relatively insignificant movements and props in order to emphasize the women's dependence on the everyday; characterization sufficient to give a quite clear idea of what the two women's lives are like; dialogue enough to suggest the characters' thoughts and feelings and to show how their lives intersect. Even a small element of conflict is present, just enough to make the scene interesting and lively and to highlight the quiet desperation of the women's lives.

What is such a sketch about? Why is it interesting? What makes it worth seeing, worth reading, worth studying, worth writing? What makes it "drama"?

It's easy enough to say what it's "about"—the essentially eventless lives of two elderly, lonely women who create a simple kind of sociality between each other and in relation to their rather mechanized, anonymous, modern environment. The order or structure of their lives is built on the predictable schedules of London's night buses and the odd opening and closing hours of an almost-all-night eatery. It reflects human routines in which not much—not even sleep —happens and in which little connection to other people exists. The women therefore create an artificial community with other riders and other patrons who are in fact unknown to them except by rituals, habits, and eccentricities. And with each other they develop some elemental sense of human relationship—a sort of parody of a conventional domestic relationship. One might say (although it sounds almost too pretentious and formal to describe the sketch) that the sketch is about loneliness, ritual, and a quest for meaning. But the point is less to prove or assert something profound or thematic than to present, poignantly, a sense of what life—or a brief slice of life— is like for two isolated people who at this point in their lives feel rather passed by.

The question of what makes the sketch interesting, memorable, and dramatic is more complicated. Once in a while we may witness, in life, a scene or vignette that seems to tell a story or offer a poignant sense of some aspect of human life. When we come upon such a moment, it is sort of art by accident, and in a way that is what Pinter manages to recreate here. We could just walk in on a scene like this, and the sketch goes out of its way to give that impression. The set is simple, the props are few and common, there is nothing especially complicated about the setting or about the way the action is set up. A production of the sketch is not likely to seem much like a production, and one can imagine the actors making it seem as little like a play—as untheatrical—as possible. They probably would not even seem to be actors. This is about as close to a segment of life as one can get, certainly far less portentous than a scene in *Oedipus* or *Hamlet*, far less organized and contrived than a carefully orchestrated confrontation in your favorite soap on television.

Yet the scene is very powerful. The action is efficient, there are no irrelevancies, except in the sense that the whole sketch depends on the conventional perceptions of two lives it presents as marginal. Its two main characters quickly reveal themselves. The setting gives them an opportunity to present, quickly and compactly, their situation and to imply their feelings. The action—almost a non-action—reflects that story of their lives and the theme of the sketch. And the setting and props—in their simplicity and spareness—not only set the stage for the dialogue but also reflect accurately the whole world of the women's lives. All things work together quickly and efficiently to create an impression, a vivid visual sense of the way some people (probably people most members of the audience wouldn't know much about) actually live, and a brief sense both of how those people feel about their lives and how we do.

The play at the end of this chapter—a short one-act play that also isolates quite quickly the lives and feelings of two people—somewhat more fully develops what is possible to do on a stage, in performance, with an audience looking on and responding as a group rather than reading and responding as a series of isolated individuals. In *The Black and White*, the themes of loneliness and isolation are especially touching and sad, in part because we watch the characters from a social perspective of our own, as part of a group that—while made up of individuals who may not know each other—watches together, shares the experience of the sketch, and (in effect) responds communally. If *The Black and White* were written as a story, it would have to use somewhat different strategies to achieve a similar impact. It would, in fact, be an interesting exercise to turn *The Black and White* into a story. How would you, in a narrative about the same two women, gain a similar effect? In *The Brute*, communal response is an equally important part of the play's effect, and in fact would probably be quite a bit more obvious if you were to see a performance of the play because the play is very funny and the audience would be likely to laugh together, creating a more tangible sense of commonality and community response. *The Brute* depends on some standard stereotypes of men and women, and the breaking down of those stereotypes involves some humorous surprises.

Plays are meant to be acted out by real people pretending to be someone else. In poems and stories, only the written text mediates between author and reader, but in plays all of the people involved in a particular production help to interpret the author's text for a specific audience. Not only actors, but directors, producers, even the people who build the sets, place an interpretation on the play, and every production of the play will differ somewhat from all the others. *How* words are spoken, *how* gestures are made, *how* the physical interaction takes place, *how* the set is designed and the place is made visual —all these things affect how an audience will respond to the play itself. Everyone involved in a play's performance is an interpreter— and in a sense a co-author—in a way that has no parallel in poems or stories. Being aware of the features of drama that make it more than a text, more than words on a page, makes the experience of plays take on dimentions that are beyond purely literary effects.

It is no accident that "creative" is one of the highest compliments we pay to performing artists, whether they are musicians, dancers, actors, or stand-up comedians, for no matter who is the author of their play, score, or routine, they bring it to life on the stage, and the original material becomes, in an important sense, theirs. Who gets the major credit for performed art varies considerably (and somewhat irrationally) from art to art. A comedian may sometimes have writers who get no credit at all, while performers of classical music usually take great pains to identify the composers whose music they perform. In drama, the credit is usually distributed fairly evenly between playwrights and leading actors (and sometimes directors). It is common to speak of Olivier's Hamlet (meaning the performance of the title role by Sir Laurence Olivier), of Maggie Smith's or Glenda Jackson's Hedda Gabler, or Zeffirelli's *Romeo and Juliet* (meaning the film interpretation of the play directed by Franco Zeffirelli) because in each case the hand of the actor or director leads to a distinctive interpretation of the play. A particular performance of a given play may well color our interpretation of a play forever after, especially if we see the play before we have read it, for it will influence how we respond to a later performance based on a different interpretation. The power of performance may well be more significant than the interpretive writing of critics which many people consider more abstract. Hamlet may be regarded as indecisive, melancholy, conniving, mad, vindictive, ambitious, or some combination of these things, and individual performances emphasize one attribute or another, always at some expense to other characteristics and interpretations. No play can be all things to an audience in any one performance, although it may be conceived richly enough to support a variety of different performances and different interpretations, so much so that it may appear to be almost a different play in the hands of different directors and actors.

Consciously or not, every director puts an interpretation on every scene by the way he or she stages the action; timing, the choice of actor, physical appearance of people and props, placement on the stage, physical interaction, and the phrasing and tone of every speech affect how the play will play. Every syllable uttered by every actor in some sense affects the outcome; tone of voice and the slightest body gesture are, for an actor, equivalent to the choices of words and sentence rhythm for a writer. Most directors and actors are, in fact, very self-conscious about their art and decide deliberately on a total view of the play. Most playwrights, in turn, leave a certain amount of latitude to performers, opening their plays to some range of interpretations, although they are obviously more pleased by some performances and interpretations than others. Directors and actors could, if they liked (and some historically have done so), undercut and pervert the clear intention of the playwright and meaning of a play, turning tragedy to farce. But most performances involve subtlety of interpretation, and the best of them are in some sense "true" to the written text, or at least to some reasonable interpretation of it. Written texts vary widely in how much direction they give to producers, directors, and actors, sometimes—as in the Pinter sketch—giving full details of what characters are to look like, how the stage is to be set, and how actions and gestures are to be performed.

The fact of a live audience also has an important impact on the way plays are created. The essential feature of an audience at a play involves the fact that they have, at a single instant, a common experience; they have assembled for the explicit purpose of seeing a play. Drama not only plays before a live audience of real people who respond directly and immediately to it (unlike a text that may lie silent and undisturbed in a book for days or even years at a time), but drama is also conceived of by the author in expectation of specific audience response. That is, authors write plays planning for the fact that they will be acted out in front of an audience; they calculate for the effect of a community of watchers rather than for the silent, or at least private, responses of single readers, and they know that the play's actual production may be affected by the way an audience reacts.

Especially in these days of home VCRs, people may watch a film in privacy, but to watch a play by oneself is a highly unusual experience. Drama is meant to be public—a form of collective behavior that persists in many forms in society. We go to football games or rock concerts as our primitive ancestors went to rain dances and fertility rites, to share an experience with others of similar interests or attitudes. When thousands of people gather at a rock concert, they expect something beyond the music. (A purer form of music is usually available more cheaply on records, and they could all be more comfortable and more purely receptive to the music at home.) What they seek is the *experience* of a concert; being there is what is important, and part of that is being there with each other. A live performance can hardly equal one achieved by the sophisticated techniques of the recording studio, but it *is* live and it is shared with thousands of other people. The individual feels the spirit and enthusiasm that makes collective experience meaningful.

Whatever the nature of a public performance, the individuals who make up the audience have made separate but common decisions to attend *Carmen* or *Cats*. They gather at the specified time and place, and in a sense they assume new identities as members of the group, partly expressed in their clothes—people dress one way for a football game and another for the opera—but also in such obvious ways as their new identities as seat numbers (Section 4, Row AA, Seat 103). These group identities strongly influence behavior, as anyone who has laughed at the wrong time in the theater or cheered for the visiting team while sitting among the home fans can testify. The group identity can become so strong that members of the group behave in ways they would not as individuals; cheering loudly, booing, and crying "Encore!" are simple examples. At its worst, the group can become a mob.

Plays are often more topical than poems or stories. They need to engage the audience in a group illusion, and one convenient and popular way to do so is to concentrate on a situation or a theme that broadly concerns the society and time. In recent years, for example, we have seen a number of plays dealing with aging. Arthur Kopit's *Wings* deals with the recovery of a stroke victim, an aging aviatrix. Such plays have more obvious relevance to a society like ours, in which the average age is rising, than to one in which it is falling. A play like *Wings* assumes an audience whose members are interested in a stroke because of either their own situation or that of aging relatives. Plays that aim primarily to entertain may avoid such an issue as aging in favor of examining the prevailing attitudes of the society toward the difference between marrying and living together. What is relevant will vary with the historical situation. Most of Shakespeare's great tragedies, for example, deal with succession to a throne or other positions of power. They were written when Elizabeth I was an aging queen, too old to produce a legitimate heir even if she had chosen to marry. For two centuries England had suffered war and destruction over issues of succession; not surprisingly, Shakespeare's audience was interested in the problems of transfer of power.

The audience also determines what can be seen onstage. In *Oedipus Tyrannus*, for example, Jocasta hangs herself offstage and Oedipus puts out his eyes offstage because the audience did not like to see violence onstage. Shakespeare's audience, on the other hand, seems to have loved onstage violence, if we are to believe the evidence of the last scene of *Hamlet* or the scene in Thomas Kyd's popular *Spanish Tragedy* in which the central character, Hieronimo, bites off his tongue and spits out the piece he has bitten off. In our own day we are witnessing the breakdown of audience taboos against nudity and sexual activity on stage, in films, and on television; audience approval of the mores of a society or a subgroup of that society is crucial for a production to exist.

A play on stage is different from a play on the page, not only because a stage production is transient, but also because every performance is a unique expression of a collaborative effort. Actors must remember hundreds of lines and perform movements on stage at certain times; the stagehands must change sets and install props between scenes; light and sound effects must occur on certain visual and aural cues. In any of these areas a single change or error—a new inflection at the end of a line or a misplaced prop—guarantees that a given performance will be unique. Nor are any two audiences the same, and the character of an audience inevitably affects the performance. A warm, responsive audience will bring out the best in the performers, as any actor will tell you, while a crowd's cold indifference often results in a tepid or stiff production. For these reasons, no staged realization of a play can ever duplicate another.

Not all this potential of dramatic experience is available when you read—rather than 'see—a play. But, in a way, reading plays draws even more fully on your imagination for as you read you become not only a critic, interpreter, and responder (as in stories and poems), but producer, director, actor, and set designer as well. You have to decide how you would cast the play; do you imagine Cloris Leachman playing the role of Mrs. Popov in *The Brute*? Meryl Streep? Joan Collins? Mia Farrow? How you would stage each scene, how you would coach the actors to walk, gesture, phrase and time their speeches. Those decisions can be difficult, but they are also challenging. And they help to clarify exactly what drama is about, how it differs from other, more purely verbal, forms of art. Ultimately, though, drama belongs in a theater, with actors performing under the supervision of a director in front of an audience. The real experience of drama involves being there.

ANTON CHEKHOV

The Brute[1]

CHARACTERS

MRS. POPOV, *widow and landowner, small, with dimpled cheeks.*
MR. GRIGORY S. SMIRNOV, *gentleman farmer, middle-aged.*
LUKA, *Mrs. Popov's footman, an old man.*
GARDENER, COACHMAN, HIRED MEN.

The drawing room of a country house. MRS. POPOV, *in deep mourning, is staring hard at a photograph.* LUKA *is with her.*

LUKA   It's not right, ma'am, you're killing yourself. The cook has gone off with the maid to pick berries. The cat's having a high old time in the yard catching birds. Every living thing is happy. But you stay moping here in the house like it was a convent, taking no pleasure in nothing. I mean it, ma'am! It must be a full year since you set foot out of doors.

MRS. POPOV   I must never set foot out of doors again, Luka. Never! I have nothing to set foot out of doors *for.* My life is done. *He* is in his grave. I have buried myself alive in this house. We are *both* in our graves.

LUKA   You're off again, ma'am. I just won't listen to you no more. Mr. Popov is dead, but what can we do about that? It's God's doing. God's will be done. You've cried over him, you've done your share of mourning, haven't you? There's a limit to everything. You can't go on weeping and wailing forever. My old lady died, for that matter, and I wept and wailed over her a whole month long. Well, that was it. I couldn't weep and wail all my life, she just wasn't worth it. [*He sighs*] As for the neighbours, you've forgotten all about them, ma'am. You don't visit them and you don't let them visit you. You and I are like a pair of spiders—excuse the expression, ma'am—here we are in this house like a pair of spiders, we never see the light of day. And it isn't like there was no nice people around either. The whole country's swarming with 'em. There's a regiment quartered at Riblov, and the officers are so good-looking! The girls can't take their eyes off them—There's a ball at the camp every Friday—The military band plays most every day of the week —What do you say, ma'am? You're young, you're pretty, you could enjoy yourself! Ten years from now you may want to strut and show your feathers to the officers, and it'll be too late.

MRS. POPOV   [*Firmly*]   You must never bring this subject up again, Luka. Since Popov died, life has been an empty dream to me, you know that. *You* may think I am alive. Poor ignorant Luka! You are wrong. I am dead. I'm in my grave. Never more shall I see the

1. Translated by Eric Bentley.

light of day, never strip from my body this . . . raiment of death! Are you listening, Luka? Let this ghost learn how I love him! Yes, *I* know, and *you* know, he was often unfair to me, he was cruel to me, and he was unfaithful to me. What of it? *I* shall be faithful to *him*, that's all. I will show him how *I* can love. Hereafter, in a better world than this, he will welcome me back, the same loyal girl I always was—

LUKA   Instead of carrying on this way, ma'am, you should go out in the garden and take a bit of a walk, ma'am. Or why not harness Toby and take a drive? Call on a couple of the neighbours, ma'am?

MRS. POPOV [*Breaking down*]   Oh, Luka!

LUKA   Yes, ma'am? What have I said, ma'am? Oh dear!

MRS. POPOV   Toby! You said Toby! He adored that horse. When he drove me out to the Korchagins and the Vlasovs, it was always with Toby! He was a wonderful driver, do you remember, Luka? So graceful! So strong! I can see him now, pulling at those reins with all his might and main! Toby! Luka, tell them to give Toby an extra portion of oats today.

LUKA   Yes, ma'am.

[*A BELL rings*]

MRS. POPOV   Who is that? Tell them I'm not at home.

LUKA   Very good, ma'am. [*Exit*]

MRS. POPOV [*Gazing again at the photograph*]   You shall see, my Popov, how a wife can love and forgive. Till death do us part. Longer than that. Till death re-unite us forever! [*Suddenly a titter breaks through her tears*]   Aren't you ashamed of yourself, Popov? Here's your little wife, being good, being faithful, so faithful she's locked up here waiting for her own funeral, while you—doesn't it make you ashamed, you naughty boy? You were terrible, you know. You were unfaithful, and you made those awful scenes about it, you stormed out and left me alone for weeks—

[*Enter* LUKA]

LUKA [*Upset*]   There's someone asking for you, ma'am. Says he must—

MRS. POPOV   I suppose you told him that since my husband's death I see no one?

LUKA   Yes, ma'am. I did, ma'am. But he wouldn't listen, ma'am. He says it's urgent.

MRS. POPOV [*Shrilly*]   I see no one!!

LUKA   He won't take no for an answer, ma'am. He just curses and swears and comes in anyway. He's a perfect monster, ma'am. He's in the dining room right now.

MRS. POPOV   In the dining room, is he? I'll give him his comeuppance. Bring him in here this minute.

[*Exit* LUKA]

[*Suddenly sad again*]   Why do they do this to me? Why? Insulting my grief, intruding on my solitude? [*She sighs*]   I'm afraid I'll have to enter a convent. I will, I *must* enter a convent!

[*Enter* MR. SMIRNOV *and* LUKA]

SMIRNOV [*To* LUKA]   Dolt! Idiot! You talk too much! [*Seeing* MRS. POPOV. *With dignity*]   May I have the honour of introducing myself, madam? Grigroy S. Smirnov, landowner and lieutenant of artillery, retired. Forgive me, madam, if I disturb your peace and quiet, but my business is both urgent and weighty.

MRS. POPOV [*Declining to offer him her hand*]   What is it you wish, sir?

SMIRNOV   At the time of his death, your late husband—with whom I had the honour to be acquainted, ma'am—was in my debt to the tune of twelve hundred rubles. I have two notes to prove it. Tomorrow, ma'am, I must pay the interest on a bank loan. I have therefore no alternative, ma'am, but to ask you to pay me the money today.

MRS. POPOV   Twelve hundred rubles? But what did my husband owe it to you for?

SMIRNOV   He used to buy his oats from me, madam.

MRS. POPOV [*To* LUKA, *with a sigh*]   Remember what I said. Luka: tell them to give Toby an extra portion of oats today!
    [*Exit* LUKA]
My dear Mr.—what was the name again?

SMIRNOV   Smirnov, ma'am.

MRS. POPOV   My dear Mr. Smirnov, if Mr. Popov owed you money, you shall be paid—to the last ruble, to the last kopeck. But today—you must excuse me, Mr.—what was it?

SMIRNOV   Smirnov, ma'am.

MRS. POPOV   Today, Mr. Smirnov, I have no ready cash in the house.
    [SMIRNOV *starts to speak*]
Tomorrow, Mr. Smirnov, no, the day after tomorrow, all will be well. My steward will be back from town. I shall see that he pays what is owing. Today, no. In any case, today is exactly seven months from Mr. Popov's death. On such a day you will understand that I am in no mood to think of money.

SMIRNOV   Madam, if you don't pay up now, you can carry me out feet foremost. They'll seize my estate.

MRS. POPOV   You can have your money.
    [*He starts to thank her*]
Tomorrow.
    [*He again starts to speak*]
That is: the day after tomorrow.

SMIRNOV   I don't need the money the day after tomorrow. I need it today.

MRS. POPOV   I'm sorry, Mr.—

SMIRNOV [*Shouting*]   Smirnov!

MRS. POPOV [*Sweetly*]   Yes, of course. But you can't have it today.

SMIRNOV   But I can't wait for it any longer!

MRS. POPOV   Be sensible, Mr. Smirnov. How can I pay you if I don't have it?

SMIRNOV   You don't have it?

MRS. POPOV   I don't have it.

SMIRNOV   Sure?

MRS. POPOV   Positive.

SMIRNOV   Very well. I'll make a note to that effect. [*Shrugging*] And then they want me to keep cool. I meet the tax commissioner on the street, and he says, 'Why are you always in such a bad humour, Smirnov?' Bad humour! How can I help it, in God's name? I need money, I need it desperately. Take yesterday: I leave home at the crack of dawn, I call on all my debtors. Not a one of them pays up. Footsore and weary, I creep at midnight into some little dive, and try to snatch a few winks of sleep on the floor by the vodka barrel. Then today, I come here, fifty miles from home, saying to myself, 'At last, at last, I can be sure of something,' and you're not in the mood! You give me a mood! Christ, how can I help getting all worked up?

MRS. POPOV   I thought I'd made it clear, Mr. Smirnov, that you'll get your money the minute my steward is back from town?

SMIRNOV   What the hell do I care about your steward? Pardon the expression, ma'am. But it was you I came to see.

MRS. POPOV   What language! What a tone to take to a lady! I refuse to hear another word. [*Quickly, exit*]

SMIRNOV   Not in the mood, huh? 'Exactly seven months since Popov's death,' huh? How about me? [*Shouting after her*] Is there this interest to pay, or isn't there? I'm asking you a question: is there this interest to pay, or isn't there? So your husband died, and you're not in the mood, and your steward's gone off some place, and so forth and so on, but what *I* can do about all that, huh? What do you think I should do? Take a running jump and shove my head through the wall? Take off in a balloon? You don't know my *other* debtors. I call on Gruzdeff. Not at home. I look for Yaroshevitch. He's hiding out. I find Kooritsin. He kicks up a row, and I have to throw him through the window. I work my way right down the list. Not a kopeck. Then I come to you, and God damn it to hell, if you'll pardon the expression, you're not in the mood! [*Quietly, as he realizes he's talking to air*] I've spoiled them all, that's what, I've let them play me for a sucker. Well, I'll show them. I'll show this one. I'll stay right her till she pays up. Ugh! [*He shudders with rage*] I'm in a rage! I'm in a positively towering rage! Every nerve in my body is trembling at forty to the dozen! I can't breathe, I feel ill, I think I'm going to faint, hey, you there!

[*Enter* LUKA]

LUKA   Yes, sir? Is there anything you wish, sir?

SMIRNOV   Water! Water! ! No, make it vodka.

[*Exit* LUKA]

Consider the logic of it. A fellow creature is desperately in need of cash, so desperately in need that he has to seriously contemplate hanging himself, and this woman, this mere chit of a girl, won't pay up, and why not? Because, forsooth, she isn't in the mood! Oh, the logic of women! Come to that, I never have liked them, I could do without the whole sex. Talk to a woman? I'd rather sit on a barrel of dynamite, the very thought gives me gooseflesh. Women! Creatures of poetry and romance! Just to see one in the distance gets me mad. My legs start twitching with rage. I feel like yelling for help.

[*Enter* LUKA, *handing* SMIRNOV *a glass of water*]

LUKA   Mrs. Popov is indisposed, sir. She is seeing no one.

SMIRNOV   Get out.

[*Exit* LUKA]

Indisposed, is she? Seeing no one, huh? Well, she can see me or not, but I'll be here, I'll be right here till she pays up. If you're sick for a week, I'll be here for a week. If you're sick for a year, I'll be here for a year. You won't get around *me* with your widow's weeds and your schoolgirl dimples. I know all about dimples. [*Shouting through the window*] Semyon, let the horses out of those shafts, we're not leaving, we're staying, and tell them to give the horses some oats, yes, oats, you fool, what do you think? [*Walking away from the window*] What a mess, what an unholy mess! I didn't sleep last night, the heat is terrific today, not a damn one of 'em has paid up, and here's this—this skirt in mourning that's not in the mood! My head aches, where's that— [*He drinks from the glass*] Water, ugh! You there!

[*Enter* LUKA]

LUKA   Yes, sir. You wish for something, sir?

SMIRNOV   Where's that confounded vodka I asked for?

[*Exit* LUKA]

[SMIRNOV *sits and looks himself over*] Oof! A fine figure of a man *I* am! Unwashed, uncombed, unshaven, straw on my vest, dust all over me. The little woman must've taken me for a highwayman. [*Yawns*] I suppose it wouldn't be considered polite to barge into a drawing room in this state, but who cares? I'm not a visitor, I'm a creditor—most unwelcome of guests, second only to Death.

[*Enter* LUKA]

LUKA   [*Handing him the vodka*]   If I may say so, sir, you take too many liberties, sir.

SMIRNOV   What?!

LUKA   Oh, nothing, sir, nothing.

SMIRNOV   Who in hell do you think you're talking to? Shut your mouth!

LUKA   [*Aside*]   There's an evil spirit abroad. The Devil must have sent him. Oh! [*Exit* LUKA]

SMIRNOV   What a rage I'm in! I'll grind the whole world to powder. Oh, I feel ill again. You there!

[*Enter* MRS. POPOV]

MRS. POPOV   [*Looking at the floor*]   In the solitude of my rural retreat, Mr. Smirnov, I've long since grown unaccustomed to the sound of the human voice. Above all, I cannot bear shouting. I must beg you not to break the silence.

SMIRNOV   Very well. Pay me my money and I'll go.

MRS. POPOV   I told you before, and I tell you again, Mr. Smirnov: I have no cash, you'll have to wait till the day after tomorrow. Can I express myself more plainly?

SMIRNOV   And *I* told *you* before, and I tell *you* again, that I need the money today, that the day after tomorrow is too late, and that if you don't pay, and pay now, I'll have to hang myself in the morning!

MRS. POPOV   But I have no cash. This is quite a puzzle.

SMIRNOV   You won't pay, huh?

MRS. POPOV I *can't* pay, Mr. Smirnov.

SMIRNOV In that case, I'm going to sit here and wait. [*Sits down.*] You'll pay up the day after tomorrow? Very good. Till the day after tomorrow, here I sit. [*Pause. He jumps up.*] Now look, do I have to pay that interest tomorrow, or don't I? Or do you think I'm joking?

MRS. POPOV I must ask you not to raise your voice, Mr. Smirnov. This is not a stable.

SMIRNOV Who said it was? Do I have to pay the interest tomorrow or not?

MRS. POPOV Mr. Smirnov, do you know how to behave in the presence of a lady?

SMIRNOV No, madam, I do not know how to behave in the presence of a lady.

MRS. POPOV Just what I thought. I look at you, and I say: ugh! I hear you talk, and I say to myself: 'That man doesn't know how to talk to a lady.'

SMIRNOV You'd like me to come simpering to you in French, I suppose. '*Enchanté, madame! Merci beaucoup* for not paying zee money, *madame! Pardonnez-moi* if I 'ave disturbed you, *madame!* How *charmante*[2] you look in mourning, *madame!*'

MRS. POPOV Now you're being silly, Mr. Smirnov.

SMIRNOV [*Mimicking*] 'Now you're being silly, Mr. Smirnov.' 'You don't know how to talk to a lady, Mr. Smirnov.' Look here, Mrs. Popov, I've known more women than you've known pussy cats. I've fought three duels on their account. I've jilted twelve, and been jilted by nine others. Oh, yes, Mrs. Popov, I've played the fool in my time, whispered sweet nothings, bowed and scraped and endeavoured to please. Don't tell me I don't know what it is to love, to pine away with longing, to have the blues, to melt like butter, to be weak as water. I was full of tender emotion. I was carried away with passion. I squandered half my fortune on the sex. I chattered about women's emancipation. But there's an end to everything, dear madam. Burning eyes, dark eyelashes, ripe, red lips, dimpled cheeks, heaving bosoms, soft whisperings, the moon above, the lake below —I don't give a rap for that sort of nonsense any more, Mrs. Popov. I've found out about women. Present company excepted, they're liars. Their behaviour is mere play acting; their conversation is sheer gossip. Yes, dear lady, women, young or old, are false, petty, vain, cruel, malicious unreasonable. As for intelligence, any sparrow could give them points. Appearances, I admit, can be deceptive. In appearance, a woman may be all poetry and romance, goddess and angel, muslin and fluff. To look at her exterior is to be transported to heaven. But I have looked at her interior, Mrs. Popov, and what did I find there—in her very soul? A crocodile. [*He has gripped the back of the chair so firmly that it snaps*] And, what is more revolting, a crocodile with an illusion, a crocodile that imagines tender sentiments are its own special province, a crocodile that

2. Enchanted (to meet you), madame. Thank you very much . . . . Pardon me . . . . How charming . . . .

thinks itself queen of the realm of love! Whereas, in sober fact, dear madam, if a woman can love anything except a lapdog you can hang me by the feet on that nail. For a man, love is suffering, love is sacrifice. A woman just swishes her train around and tightens her grip on your nose. Now, you're a woman, aren't you, Mrs. Popov? You must be an expert on some of this. Tell me, quite frankly, did you ever know a woman to be—faithful, for instance? Or even sincere? Only old hags, huh? Though some women are old hags from birth. But as for the others? You're right: a faithful woman is a freak of nature—like a cat with horns.

MRS. POPOV   Who *is* faithful, then? Who *have* you cast for the faithful lover? Not man?

SMIRNOV   Right first time, Mrs. Popov: man.

MRS. POPOV [*Going off into a peal of bitter laughter*]   Man! Man is faithful! That's a new one! [*Fiercely*] What right do you have to say this, Mr. Smirnov? Men faithful? Let me tell you something. Of all the men I have ever known my late husband Popov was the best. I loved him, and there are women who know how to love, Mr. Smirnov. I gave him my youth, my happiness, my life, my fortune. I worshipped the ground he trod on—and what happened? The best of men was unfaithful to me, Mr. Smirnov. Not once in a while. All the time. After he died, I found his desk drawer full of love letters. While he was alive, he was always going away for the week-end. He squandered my money. He made love to other women before my very eyes. But, in spite of all, Mr. Smirnov, *I* was faithful. Unto death. And beyond. I am *still* faithful, Mr. Smirnov! Buried alive in this house, I shall wear mourning till the day I, too, am called to my eternal rest.

SMIRNOV [*Laughing scornfully*]   Expect me to believe that? As if I couldn't see through all this hocus-pocus. Buried alive! Till you're called to your eternal rest! Till when? Till some little poet—or some little subaltern with his first moustache—comes riding by and asks: 'Can that be the house of the mysterious Tamara who for love of her late husband has buried herself alive, vowing to see no man?' Ha!

MRS. POPOV [*Flaring up*]   How dare you? How dare you insinuate—?

SMIRNOV   You may have buried yourself alive, Mrs. Popov, but you haven't forgotten to powder your nose.

MRS. POPOV [*Incoherent*]   How dare you? How—?

SMIRNOV   Who's raising his voice now? Just because I call a spade a spade. Because I shoot straight from the shoulder. Well, don't shout at me, I'm not your steward.

MRS. POPOV   I'm not shouting, you're shouting! Oh, leave me alone!

SMIRNOV   Pay me the money, and I will.

MRS. POPOV   You'll get no money out of me!

SMIRNOV   Oh, so that's it!

MRS. POPOV   Not a ruble, not a kopeck. Get out! Leave me alone!

SMIRNOV   Not being your husband, I must ask you not to make scenes with me. [*He sits*] I don't like scenes.

MRS. POPOV [*Choking with rage*]   You're sitting down?

SMIRNOV   Correct, I'm sitting down.

MRS. POPOV   I asked you to leave!

SMIRNOV   Then give me the money. [*Aside*] Oh, what a rage I'm in, what a rage!

MRS. POPOV   The impudence of the man! I won't talk to you a moment longer. Get out. [*Pause*] Are you going?

SMIRNOV   No.

MRS. POPOV   No?!

SMIRNOV   No.

MRS. POPOV   On your head be it. Luka!

[*Enter* LUKA]

Show the gentleman out, Luka.

LUKA [*Approaching*]   I'm afraid, sir, I'll have to ask you, um, to leave, sir, now, um—

SMIRNOV [*Jumping up*]   Shut your mouth, you old idiot! Who do you think you're talking to? I'll make mincemeat of you.

LUKA [*Clutching his heart*]   Mercy on us! Holy saints above! [*He falls into an armchair*] I'm taken sick! I can't breathe!!

MRS. POPOV   Then where's Dasha? Dasha! Dasha! Come here at once! [*She rings*]

LUKA   They gone picking berries, ma'am, I'm alone here—Water, water, I'm taken sick!

MRS. POPOV [*To* SMIRNOV]   Get out, you!

SMIRNOV   Can't you even be polite with me, Mrs. Popov?

MRS. POPOV [*Clenching her fists and stamping her feet*]   With you? You're a wild animal, you were never house-broken!

SMIRNOV   What? What did you say?

MRS. POPOV   I said you were a wild animal, you were never house-broken.

SMIRNOV [*Advancing upon her*]   And what right do you have to talk to me like that?

MRS. POPOV   Like what?

SMIRNOV   You have insulted me, madam.

MRS. POPOV   What of it? Do you think I'm scared of you?

SMIRNOV   So you think you can get away with it because you're a woman. A creature of poetry and romance, huh? Well, it doesn't go down with me. I hereby challenge you to a duel.

LUKA   Mercy on us! Holy saints alive! Water!

SMIRNOV   I propose we shoot it out.

MRS. POPOV   Trying to scare me again? Just because you have big fists and a voice like a bull? You're a brute.

SMIRNOV   No one insults Grigory S. Smirnov with impunity! And I don't care if you *are* a female.

MRS. POPOV [*Trying to outshout him*]   Brute, brute, brute!

SMIRNOV   The sexes are equal, are they? Fine: then it's just prejudice to expect men alone to pay for insults. I hereby challenge—

MRS. POPOV [*Screaming*]   All right! You want to shoot it out? All right! Let's shoot it out!

SMIRNOV   And let it be here and now!

MRS. POPOV   Here and now! All right! I'll have Popov's pistols here in one minute! [*Walks away, then turns*] Putting one of Popov's bullets through your silly head will be a pleasure! Au revoir. [*Exit*]

SMIRNOV   I'll bring her down like a duck, a sitting duck. I'm not one of your little poets, I'm no little subaltern with his first moustache. No, sir, there's no weaker sex where I'm concerned!

LUKA   Sir! Master! [*He goes down on his knees*] Take pity on a poor old man, and do me a favour: go away. It was bad enough before, you nearly scared me to death. But a duel—!

SMIRNOV   [*Ignoring him*] A duel! That's equality of the sexes for you! That's women's emancipation! Just as a matter of principle I'll bring her down like a duck. But what a woman! 'Putting one of Popov's bullets through your silly head . . .' Her cheeks were flushed, her eyes were gleaming! And, by God, she's accepted the challenge! I never knew a woman like this before!

LUKA   Sir! Master! Please go away! I'll always pray for you!

SMIRNOV   [*Again ignoring him*]   What a woman! Phew!! *She's* no sour puss, *she's* no cry baby. She's fire and brimstone. She's a human cannon ball. What a shame I have to kill her!

LUKA   [*Weeping*]   Please, kind sir, please, go away!

SMIRNOV   [*As before*]   I like her, isn't that funny? With those dimples and all? I like her. I'm even prepared to consider letting her off that debt. And where's my rage? It's gone. I never knew a woman like this before.

[*Enter* MRS. POPOV *with pistols*]

MRS. POPOV   [*Boldly*]   Pistols, Mr. Smirnov! [*Matter of fact*] But before we start, you'd better show me how it's done, I'm not too familiar with these things. In fact I never gave a pistol a second look.

LUKA   Lord, have mercy on us, I must go hunt up the gardener and the coachman. Why has this catastrophe fallen upon us, O Lord? [*Exit*]

SMIRNOV   [*Examining the pistols*]   Well, it's like this. There are several makes: one is the Mortimer, with capsules, especially constructed for duelling. What you have here are Smith and Wesson triple-action revolvers, with extractor, first-rate job, worth ninety rubles at the very least. You hold it this way. [*Aside*] My God, what eyes she has! They're setting me on fire.

MRS. POPOV   This way?

SMIRNOV   Yes, that's right. You cock the trigger, take aim like this, head up, arm out like this. Then you just press with this finger here, and it's all over. The main thing is, keep cool, take slow aim, and don't let your arm jump.

MRS. POPOV   I see. And if it's inconvenient to do the job here, we can go out in the garden.

SMIRNOV   Very good. Of course, I should warn you: I'll be firing in the air.

MRS. POPOV   What? This is the end. Why?

SMIRNOV   Oh, well—because—for private reasons.

MRS. POPOV   Scared, huh? [*She laughs heartily*] Now don't you try to get out of it, Mr. Smirnov. My blood is up. I won't be happy till I've drilled a hole through that skull of yours. Follow me. What's the matter? Scared?

SMIRNOV   That's right. I'm scared.

MRS. POPOV   Oh, come on, what's the matter with you?

SMIRNOV   Well, um, Mrs. Popov, I, um, I like you.

MRS. POPOV [*Laughing bitterly*]   Good God! He likes me, does he? The gall of the man. [*Showing him the door*] You may leave, Mr. Smirnov.

SMIRNOV [*Quietly puts the gun down, takes his hat, and walks to the door. Then he stops and the pair look at each other without a word. Then, approaching gingerly*]   Listen, Mrs. Popov. Are you still mad at me? I'm in the devil of a temper myself, of course. But then, you see—what I mean is—it's this way—the fact is—[*Roaring*] Well, is it my fault, damn it, if I like you. [*Clutches the back of a chair. It breaks*] Christ, what fragile furniture you have here. I like you. Know what I mean? I could fall in love with you.

MRS. POPOV   I hate you. Get out!

SMIRNOV   What a woman! I never saw anything like it. Oh, I'm lost, I'm done for, I'm a mouse in a trap.

MRS. POPOV   Leave this house, or I shoot!

SMIRNOV   Shoot away! What bliss to die of a shot that was fired by that little velvet hand! To die gazing into those enchanting eyes. I'm out of my mind. I know: you must decide at once. Think for one second, then decide. Because if I leave now, I'll never be back. Decide! I'm a pretty decent chap. Landed gentleman, I should say. Ten thousand a year. Good stable. Throw a kopeck up in the air, and I'll put a bullet through it. Will you marry me?

MRS. POPOV [*Indignant, brandishing the gun*]   We'll shoot it out! Get going! Take your pistol!

SMIRNOV   I'm out of my mind. I don't understand anything any more. [*Shouting*] You there! That vodka!

MRS. POPOV   No excuses! No delays! We'll shoot it out!

SMIRNOV   I'm out of my mind. I'm falling in love. I *have* fallen in love. [*He goes down on his knees*] I love you as I've never loved before. I jilted twelve, and was jilted by nine others. But I didn't love a one of them as I love you. I'm full of tender emotion. I'm melting like butter. I'm weak as water. I'm on my knees like a fool, and I offer you my hand. It's a shame, it's a disgrace. I haven't been in love in five years. I took a vow against it. And now, all of a sudden, to be swept off my feet, it's a scandal. I offer you my hand, dear lady. Will you or won't you? You won't? Then don't! [*He rises and walks toward the door*]

MRS. POPOV   I didn't say anything.

SMIRNOV [*Stopping*]   What?

MRS. POPOV   Oh, nothing, you can go. Well, no, just a minute. No, you can go. Go! I detest you! But, just a moment. Oh, if you knew how furious I feel! [*Throws the gun on the table*] My fingers have gone to sleep holding that horrid thing. [*She is tearing her handkerchief to shreds*] And what are you standing around for? Get out of here!

SMIRNOV   Goodbye.

MRS. POPOV   Go, go, go! [*Shouting*] Where are you going? Wait a minute! No, no, it's all right, just go. I'm fighting mad. Don't come near me, don't come near me!

smirnov [*Who is coming near her*]   I'm pretty disgusted with myself
—falling in love like a kid, going down on my knees like some
moongazing whippersnapper, the very thought gives me gooseflesh.
[*Rudely*] I love you. But it doesn't make sense. Tomorrow, I have
to pay that interest, and we've already started mowing. [*He puts
his arm about her waist*] I shall never forgive myself for this.

mrs. popov   Take your hands off me, I hate you! Let's shoot it out!

[*A long kiss. Enter* luka *with an axe, the* gardener *with a
rake, the* coachman *with a pitchwork,* hire men *with sticks*]

luka [*Seeing the kiss*]   Mercy on us! Holy saints above!

mrs. popov [*Dropping her eyes*]   Luka, tell them in the stable that
Toby is *not* to have any oats today.

CURTAIN

1888

2 STRUCTURE AND STAGE

An important part of the task of any storyteller, whether the story is to be narrative or dramatic, is the invention, selection, and arrangement of the action: in other words, the creation of the **plot**. Since dramatic plot usually involves **conflict**, dramatic structure centrally concerns the presentation—quite literally the embodiment or fleshing out—of that conflict.

A conflict whose outcome is never in doubt may have other kinds of interest, but it is not truly dramatic, so each of the opposing forces —whether character versus character, character versus society, nature, or whatever—should at some point or other have a chance to triumph. In *Hamlet*, for example, the effectiveness of the struggle between Hamlet and Claudius depends on their being evenly matched. Claudius has possession of the throne and the Queen, but Hamlet has his relation to the late king and his popularity with the people to balance his opponent's strengths. Early in the play Claudius has the upper hand, but he realizes that he has underestimated Hamlet and he overreacts. Until he stops the play-within-the-play, the king seems firmly in command; the odds seem to favor him. The play, however, does not end with Claudius's triumph.

The king's outburst in *Hamlet* is an example of the kind of dramatic event about which the typical structure of a play is built and which is called the **climax**. The typical dramatic structure of a play generally falls into five parts, which may or may not coincide with the division into acts and scenes. The first of these, the **exposition**, presents the situation as it exists at the opening of the play, introducing the characters and defining the relationships among them. In *The Brute* the bulk of the exposition is presented before Luka goes to answer the bell, and the rest of it—the introduction of Smirnov and his information about Popov's debt—is given immediately thereafter. The second part of the dramatic structure of a play, the **rising action**, consists in a series of events that complicate the original situation and create conflicts among the characters. During the rising action, the flow of the action is in a single direction, but at some crucial moment an event occurs that changes the direction of that flow, sometimes just by a sudden revelation: in *The Brute*, for example, the hostile Smirnov suddenly realizes he is falling in love with Mrs. Popov. This is the third part of the play, the **climax**, or **turning point**. The fourth part of a play is the **falling action**, the changes that characterize the unwinding or unknotting of the complication. Generally the falling action requires less time than the rising action. The final part of the play is its **conclusion** or **catastrophe**. The conclusion reestablishes a stable situation to end the drama.

Although this structure does not work the same way in every play, it may be helpful to see in detail how it works in a particular play. In *Hamlet* the exposition sets forth the established situation at the beginning of the play. We need to know about the death of the old king, the accession of Claudius rather than young Hamlet, the marriage of Claudius and Gertrude, Hamlet's return from Wittenberg, and the threat of invasion from Fortinbras. Shakespeare uses two devices to present this information: the recent return of Horatio from Wittenberg (and his need to be brought up to date) and Claudius's speech at the beginning of Act 1, Scene 2. In these and other ways we learn where things stand. At the same time we are witnessing the beginning of the rising action, the introduction of new elements that are to affect the action of the play: the appearance of the ghost, Claudius's refusal to allow Hamlet to return to Wittenberg, Hamlet's growing involvement with Ophelia, the return of Rosencrantz and Guildenstern, and so forth. These and other complications affect the action without changing its basic direction. They also set up events that are to happen later in the play, e.g., Laertes's departure for Paris sets up his return in Act 4. The climax, or turning point, occurs when the King loses control of himself at the play-within-the-play. He loses his advantage over Hamlet, who from then on is more or less in control of the situation. During the falling action the various strands of the plot begin to work themselves out. What happens to Ophelia? What is the result of Rosencrantz and Guildenstern's return? When such questions have been settled, we move to the conclusion of the play, the reestablishment of a new stable situation. In *Hamlet* the conclusion takes place in the final scene, where order is finally restored by the promise of Fortinbras as king.

Even a short play like *The Sacrifice of Isaac* contains all five of the parts: the exposition is presented concisely in Abraham's opening prayer, the action rises from there to the climax—the angel appearing to tell Abraham he need not kill his beloved son—and falls to the conclusion, when Isaac and Abraham head home, a new stability having been restored.

There are other devices by which a play can be made meaningful and effective. One such is called **dramatic irony**, the fulfillment of a plan, action, or expectation in a surprising way, often the opposite of what was intended. *Oedipus Tyrannus* offers a number of parallel instances of such dramatic irony, creating almost unbearable tension and frustration, a sense of powerlessness against the will of the gods. Oedipus opens the action by proclaiming that he will banish the criminal responsible for the plagues upon Thebes, only to discover at play's end that to do so means exiling himself. Oedipus further learns that by fleeing his adoptive parents in Corinth to avoid fulfilling a prophecy, he has in fact murdered his real father and married his mother as foreordained by the gods. And when Oedipus spurns the words of the blind seer Teiresias, Teiresias observes that his own blindness is only physical while Oedipus has eyes but cannot see his own destruction. When Oedipus finally does "see" the truth, he blinds himself. As in the investigation of a detective who discovers that he himself is the criminal he has been looking for, all of Oedipus's words and deeds are ironically reversed as the plot unfolds.

Such paralleled ironies are only one way of achieving thematic resonance through plotting. In *Death of a Salesman*, the unfolding story of Willy's life moves backward and forward through time so that Willy experiences the past as if it were the present, and we hear almost simultaneously conversations between friends inhabiting his grim present and those from an idealized past. These concurrent "plots"—the stories of Willy before and after the Depression—proceed chronologically as revealed to the reader and viewer through Willy's consciousness.

Besides structures like dramatic irony or theme that pull parts of the play together and the five dramatic structural divisions that shape the action, most plays also have formal divisions, such as **acts** and **scenes.** In the Greek theater scenes were separated by choral odes. In many French plays, a new scene begins with any significant entrance or exit. Many "classic" plays have five acts, because the poet Horace suggested that number, but modern plays tend to have two or three acts. Formal divisions are the result of the conventions of the period and the content of the individual play, and may vary from the one-act, one-scene play, such as *The Brute,* to such multi-act plays as O'Neill's *Mourning Becomes Electra.*

Dramatic structures and dramatic irony, even the formal divisions of a play are present to the reader as well as the viewer of the performance of a play, but of course in performance a play takes place on a **stage** or acting area rather than in the reader's mind. The design and significance of the acting area vary in different times and places. In the Greek theater, the audience was seated on a raised semicircle of seats (**amphitheater**) halfway around a circular area (**orchestra**) used primarily for dancing by the chorus. At the back of the orchestra was the **skene** or stage house, which represented the palace or temple before which the action took place. Shakespeare's stage, in contrast, basically involved a rectangular area built inside one end of a generally round enclosure, so that the audience was on three sides of the principal acting area. There were additional acting areas on either side of this stage, as well as a recessed area at the back of the stage, which could represent Gertrude's chamber in *Hamlet,* for example, or the cave in *The Tempest,* and an upper acting area, which could serve as Juliet's balcony, for example.

Modern stages are of three types. The **proscenium** stage evolved during the nineteenth century and is still the most common. For such a stage, the proscenium or proscenium arch is an architectural element that separates the auditorium from the stage and makes the action seem more real because the audience is viewing it through an invisible fourth wall. The proscenium stage lends itself to the use of a curtain, which can be lowered and raised—or closed and parted—between acts or scenes. Sometimes a part of the acting area is on the auditorium side of the proscenium. Such an area is an **apron** or forestage. The second type of modern stage is the **thrust stage,** in which the audience is seated around three-fourths of the major acting area. All of the action may take place on this projecting area, or some may occur in the extended area of the fourth side. In an **arena stage,** the third type, the audience is seated around the acting area. Entrances and exits are made through the auditorium, and restrictions on the sets are required to insure visibility.

At any given time and place the idea of what a stage is like is generally shared by audience and stage personnel, and most authors work with this generally understood notion of the kind of stage involved when they write a play. Of course, authors will sometimes innovate and they, the director, or set designer will work out new ways of using the stage, as in the flashbacks of *Death of a Salesman*. But even then Miller and his associates were working with the general understanding of the nature of one stage. Even greater differences are involved when we examine plays of different periods that have radically different conventions.

One such convention involves the notion of place. The audience knows that the stage is a stage, but they accept it for a public square or a room in a castle or an empty road. In *The Brute* we accept the stage as a drawing room in a Russian country house. There must be at least one door, leading to the entrance of the house, and the rest of the house and a window. There must be at least two (fragile) straight chairs and an armchair. The play is written for a proscenium stage. If the play is to work, the designer must make the audience aware of the objects, doors, windows, chairs, etc., required by the action. By contrast, *The Sacrifice of Isaac* was written to be performed outdoors on a wagon, probably with an elevated area to represent heaven and some indication that one part of the stage represents a field near Abraham's tent and another the place of sacrifice. There are no doors leading to specific places, and only a few objects are required.

The convention of place also involves how place is changed. In *The Sacrifice of Isaac* this was apparently accomplished by moving from one part of the wagon to another. In *The Brute* such a change would involve, if it had been required, lowering a curtain or darkening the stage while the sets and props were changed to produce the new place. In Greek drama, generally there was no change of place and the action was set up to involve only one place. If the presence of Teiresias was required, someone would be sent to bring him.

In *Hamlet* all the conventions are quite different. In Shakespeare's theater the acting area does not represent a specific place, but assumes a temporary identity from the characters who inhabit it, their costumes, and their speeches. At the opening of the play we know we are at a sentry station because a man dressed as a soldier challenges two others. By line 15 we know that we are in Denmark because the actors profess to be "liegemen to the Dane." At the end of the scene the actors leave the stage and in a sense take the sentry station with them. Shortly a group of people dressed in court costumes and a man and a woman wearing crowns appear. The audience knows that the acting area has now become a "chamber of state." As the play progresses, we learn more about the characters and the action, and identification of place become easier. Although the conventions differ, there is always some tacit agreement between playwright and actors on the one hand and the audience on the other about how place is represented as well.

A similar set of conventions governs the treatment of time on stage. Classical theories and practice suggest that in order to insure maximum dramatic impact the action of a play should be restricted to a very short time—sometimes as short as the actual performance (two or three hours), rarely longer than a single day. It is this concentration of time that impels a dramatist to select the moment when a stable situation is on the verge of change and to fill in the necessary prior details by exposition or even by some more elaborate device. In *Death of a Salesman,* you will remember, significant scenes from the past are enacted as dreams or memories on the stage (a device somewhat like the *flashback* in fiction). The action from the beginning to the end of the play thus can be concentrated in a very short period of represented time, rather than spread over fifteen years, moving toward the present crisis scene by scene, act by act. You might look back over the plays you have read so far and note how much time elapses from beginning to end and what devices, if any, preserve the restriction of represented time so as to concentrate the action and thus heighten the impact.

Even within the classical drama with its restricted time-span—or **unity of time**—there are conventions to mark the passing of represented time when it is supposed to pass at a greater rate than that of viewing or reading time. The choral odes in *Oedipus Tyrannus* are an example of one convention for representing the passage of time. The elapsed time between scenes may be that necessary to send for the shepherd from Mount Cithaeron and allow for his return or the much shorter time needed for Oedipus to enter his palace, discover Jocasta's suicide, blind himself, and return. The time covered by the ode is shorter or longer as necessary, without real reference to the length of the ode. In the Elizabethan theater the break between scenes covered whatever time was necessary without a formal device like the choral odes. Sometimes the time was short as the break between Hamlet's departure to see his mother at the end of Act 3, Scene 2, and the opening of the King's prayer at the beginning of the next scene; at other times the elapsed time between might be as long as that between Scenes 4 and 5 of Act 4, in which the news of Polonius's death reached Paris and Laertes returned to Denmark and there rallied his friends. The total elapsed time might be years as in *The Winter's Tale,* where the action begins before Perdita's birth and ends after her marriage. In *Hamlet* we cannot tell exactly what the time span is, but in a time of relatively primitive transportation Laertes goes to Paris, remains there for a time, and returns to Denmark; Fortinbras goes from Norway to Poland, fights a war, and returns to Denmark; and news of the deaths of Rosencrantz and Guildenstern, who left England between Acts 3 and 4, is brought back.

In reading fiction we recognize that what is going on in represented time is often supposed to be taking much longer than it takes us to read the words describing it. The time that is supposed to pass within one sentence can vary greatly from that which passes in another. All this does not bother us. In reading fiction, we are used to making such adjustments. In reading or watching a play, however, we expect the passage of time to be more clearly marked—by stage directions, scene or act endings. Otherwise we assume that the amount of time it takes an actor to walk across the stage or speak a line is exactly the time that has passed within the play while that action or talk has been going on (that is, represented time = reading/viewing time). The duration of a scene for reader or audience is just about the same as the time that is supposed to have passed during that scene.

Not so, necessarily, in Shakespeare. The first scene of *Hamlet*, for example, opens just on the stroke of midnight, yet in less than forty lines—with no obvious warning to the reader that so much time is passing—we learn it is one o'clock. And a hundred lines later the cock crows, and soon Horatio says that it is dawn. If we read this scene as if it were a story, we have no difficulty, perhaps, in adjusting represented time to reading time, but if we enact plays within our imagination while we read them we need to become very aware of this "undramatic handling of time. As a director, even a director of a play on the stage of our own imagination, we need to invent some sort of stage business to suggest the passing of represented time: those watching for the ghost may sit still for what seems to an audience a long time—a couple of minutes—or get up and stretch and walk about the stage, or lie down, toss and turn, perhaps sleep.

Drama is both a literary and performed art, and a play exists separately on page and stage. We must keep this dual nature in mind as we read, and indeed we need to do as much as we can to perform the play in our minds on the stage of our imagination.

ANONYMOUS

The Sacrifice of Isaac *

CHARACTERS

GOD   ISAAC, *his son*
AN ANGEL   A DOCTOR, *a learned man*
ABRAHAM, the patriarch

A field, near ABRAHAM'*s tent.*

ABRAHAM   Father of heaven omnipotent,
      With all my heart to thee I call.
  Thou hast given me both land and rent;
  And my livelihood thou hast me sent.
      I thank thee highly evermore of all.   5

  First of the earth thou madest Adam
      And Eve also to be his wife;
  All others creatures of them two came.
  And now thou hast grant to me, Abraham,
      Here in this land to lead my life.   10

  In my age thou hast granted me this,
      That this young child with me shall wone.[1]
  I love no thing so much, y-wis,[2]
  Except thine own self, dear Father of bliss,
      As Isaac here, my own sweet son.   15

  I have diverse children mo,[3]
      The which I love not half so well;
  This fair child he cheers me so
  In every place where that I go
      That no dis-ease here may I feel.   20

  And therefore, Father of heaven, I thee pray
      For his health and also for his grace.
  Now, Lord, keep him both night and day,
  That never disease nor no fray [4]
      Come to my child in no place.   25

  Now come, Isaac, my own sweet child
      Go we home and take our rest.

ISAAC   Abraham, mine own father so mild,
      To follow you I am full prest,[5]
        Both early and late.   30

---

* Often (and perhaps more accurately)
called "The Brome *Sacrifice of Isaac*"
(Brome was the name of the 19th-century
owner of the manuscript in which the
play appears). The events of the play are
based on *Genesis* 22.

1. Dwell.
2. Certainly.
3. More.
4. Fright.
5. Ready (Fr. *prêt*).

ABRAHAM   Come on, sweet child. I love thee best
    Of all the children that ever I begat.

  Heaven.

GOD Mine Angel, fast hie thee thy way
    And unto middle-earth[6] anon thou go;
Abram's heart now will I assay,   35
    Whether that he be steadfast or no.

Say I commanded him for to take
    Isaac, his young son, that he loves so well,
And with his blood sacrifice he make
    If any of my friendship he will feel.   40

Show him the way unto the hill
    Where that his sacrifice shall be.
I shall assay now his good will,
    Whether he loveth better his child or me.
All men shall take example by him   45
My commandments how they shall keep.

  The field, near ABRAHAM's *tent.*

ABRAHAM   Now, Father of heaven, that formed all things,
    My prayers I make to thee again,
For this day my tender offering[7]
    Here must I give to thee certain.   50
Ah! Lord God, almighty king,
    What manner beast will make thee most fain?
If I had thereof very[8] knowing,
    It should be done with all my main[9]
      Full soon anon.   55
To do thy pleasing on an hill,
Verily it is my will,
      Dear Father, God in Trinity.

ANGEL Abraham! Abraham! will thou rest!
    Our Lord commandeth thee for to take 60
Isaac, thy young son that thou lovest best,
    And with his blood sacrifice that thou make.
Into the Land of Vision[1] thou go,
    And offer thy child unto thy Lord;
I shall thee lead and show also.   65
    Unto God's hest,[2] Abraham, accord.

And follow me upon this green.

---

6. The earth.
7. Periodic sacrifice.
8. True.
9. Strength.
1. A translation of the phrase *in terram visionis* in *Genesis* 22:2 of the Vulgate,

the standard Latin Bible of the Middle Ages. Other versions, including the Authorized or King James Version, read "the land of Moriah."
2. Command.

ABRAHAM   Welcome to me be my Lord's sond,[3]
    And his hest I will not withstand.
    Yet Isaac, my young son in land,   70
A full dear child to me hath been.

I had liefer,[4] if God had been pleased,
    For to have forborne all the good that I have
Than Isaac my son should have been dis-eased,
    So God in heaven my soul might save!   75

I loved never thing so much in earth.
    And now I must the child go kill.
Ah! Lord God! My conscience is strongly stirred!
And yet, my dear Lord, I am sore a-feared
    To grudge anything against your will.   80

I love my child as my life;
    But yet I love my God much more.
For though my heart would make any strife,
Yet will I not spare for child nor wife,
    But do after my Lord's lore.[5]   85

Though I love my son never so well,
    Yet smite off his head soon I shall.
Ah! Father of heaven, to thee I kneel;
An hard death my son shall feel
    For to honor thee, Lord, withall.   90

ANGEL   Abraham! Abraham! This is well said!
    And all these commandments look that thou keep.
But in thy heart be nothing dismayed.
ABRAHAM   Nay, nay, forsooth[6] I hold me well appayed[7]
    To please my God to the best that I have.   95

For though my heart be heavily set
    To see the blood of mine own dear son,
Yet for all this I will not let,[8]
But Isaac, my son, I will go fetch,
    And come as fast as ever we can.   100

    Another part of the field.

Now, Isaac, my own son dear,
    Where art thou, child? Speak to me.
ISAAC   My father, sweet father, I am here,
    And make my prayers to the Trinity.

ABRAHAM   **Rise up, my child, and fast come hither,**   105
    My gentle bairn[9] that art so wise,

---

3. Messenger.   7. Pleased.
4. Rather.   8. Refrain.
5. Teaching.   9. Child.
6. In truth.

For we two, child, must go together
    And unto my Lord make sacrifice.

ISAAC   I am full ready, my father, lo!
    Even at your hands I stand right here;   110
And whatsoever ye bid me do,
    It shall be done with glad cheer,
        Full well and fine.
ABRAHAM   Ah! Isaac, my own son so dear,
    God's blessing I give thee and mine.   115

Hold this faggot upon thy back,
    And here myself fire shall bring.
ISAAC   Father, all this here will I pack;
    I am full fain to do your bidding.
ABRAHAM [*aside*]   Ah! Lord of heaven my hands I wring,   120
    This child's words all to-wound[1] my heart.

Now, Isaac, son, go we our way
    Unto yon mount, with all our main.[2]
ISAAC   Go we, my dear father, as fast as I may;
    To follow you I am full fain,   125
        Although I be slender.[3]
ABRAHAM [*aside*]   Ah! Lord, my heart breaketh in twain,
    This child's words they be so tender.

        ABRAHAM *and* ISAAC *arrive at the mountain.*

Ah! Isaac, son, anon lay it down;
    No longer upon thy back it hold.   130
For I must make ready bon[4]
    To honor my Lord God as I should.

ISAAC   Lo, my dear father, where it is!
    To cheer you alway I draw me near.
But, father, I marvel sore of this,   135
    Why that ye make this heavy cheer.[5]

And also, father, evermore dread I;
    Where is your quick[6] beast that ye should kill?
Both fire and wood we have ready,
    But quick beast have none on this hill.   140
A quick beast, I wot[7] well, must be dead
    Your sacrifice for to make.
ABRAHAM   Dread thee nought, my child, I thee rede,[8]
Our Lord will send me unto this stead[9]
    Some manner of beast for to take,   145
        Through his sweet sond.[1]

---

1. Wound severely.   6. Live.
2. Strength.   7. Know.
3. Weak.   8. Counsel.
4. Quite ready.   9. Place.
5. Countenance.   1. Messenger.

ISAAC   Yea, father, but my heart beginneth to quake
      To see that sharp sword in your hand.

  Why bear ye your sword drawn so?
      Of your countenance I have much wonder.   150
ABRAHAM [*aside*]   Ah! Father of heaven, so I am woe!
      This child here breaketh my heart asunder.

ISAAC   Tell me, dear father, ere that ye cease,
      Bear ye your sword drawn for me?
ABRAHAM   Ah! Isaac, sweet son, peace! peace!   155
      For, y-wis, thou break my heart in three.

ISAAC   Now, truly, somewhat, father, ye think
      That ye mourn thus more and more.
ABRAHAM [*aside*]   Ah! Lord of heaven, thy grace let sink,[2]
      For my heart was never half so sore.   160

ISAAC   I pray you, father, that ye will let me it wit[3]
      Whether shall I have any harm or no.
ABRAHAM   Y-wis, sweet son, I may not tell thee yet;
      My heart is now so full of woe.

ISAAC   Dear father, I pray you, hideth it not from me,   165
  But some of your thought that ye tell me.
ABRAHAM   Ah! Isaac, Isaac I must kill thee!
ISAAC   Kill me, father? Alas, what have I done?

  If I have trespassed against you aught,
      With a yard[4] ye may make me full mild;   170
  And with your sharp sword kill me nought,
      For, y-wis, father, I am but a child.

ABRAHAM   I am full sorry, son, thy blood for to spill
      But truly, my child, I may not choose.
ISAAC   Now I would to God my mother were here on his hill!   175
      She would kneel for me on both her knees
         To save my life.
  And sithen[5] that my mother is not here,
  I pray you, father, change your cheer,
         And kill me not with your knife.   180

ABRAHAM   Forsooth, son, but if[6] I thee kill,
      I should grieve God right sore, I dread.
  It is his commandment, and also his will,
      That I should do this same deed.

  He commanded me, son, for certain,   185
      To make my sacrifice with thy blood.
ISAAC   And is it God's will that I should be slain?
ABRAHAM   Aye, truly, Isaac, my son so good;
      And therefore my hands I wring.

         190

---

2. Descend.   5. Since.
3. Know.   6. Unless.
4. Rod.

ISAAC   Now, father, against my Lord's will
    I will never grudge, loud nor still.[7]
            He might have sent me a better destiny
            If it had have been his pleasure.

ABRAHAM   Forsooth, son, but if I did this deed,
            Grievously displeased our Lord will be.   195
ISAAC   Nay, nay, father, God forbid
            That ever you should grieve him for me.

    Ye have other children, one or two,
        The which ye should love well by kind.[8]
    I pray you, father, make ye no woe;   200
    For be I once dead, and from you go,
            I shall be soon out of your mind.

    Therefore do our Lord's bidding,
        And when I am dead, then pray for me.
    But, good father, tell ye my mother nothing;   205
    Say that I am in another country dwelling.
ABRAHAM   Ah! Isaac, Isaac, blessed might thou be!

    My heart beginneth strongly to rise,
        To see the blood of thy blessed body.
ISAAC   Father, since it may be no other wise.   210
        Let it pass over as well as I.

    But, father, ere I go unto my death,
        I pray you bless me with your hand.
ABRAHAM   Now, Isaac, with all my breath
        My blessing I give thee upon this land,   215
            And God's also thereto, y-wis.
        Isaac, Isaac, son, up thou stand,
            Thy fair sweet mouth that I may kiss.

ISAAC   Now farewell, my own father so fine;
        And greet well my mother in earth.   220
    But I pray you, father, to hide my eyen,[9]
        That I see not the stroke of your sharp sword,
            That my flesh shall defile.
ABRAHAM   Son, thy words make me weep full sore;
    Now, my dear son Isaac, speak no more.   225
ISAAC   Ah! my own dear father, wherefore?
        We shall speak together here but a while.
    And sithen[1] that I must needs be dead,
        Yet, my dear father, to you I pray,
    Smite but few strokes at my head,   230
        And make an end as soon as ye may,
            And tarry not too long.

---

7. In any way.   9. Eyes.
8. Natural affection.   1. Since.

ABRAHAM   Thy meek words, child, make me affray;[2]
       So "Well-a-way!"[3] may be my song,

Except all-only God's will.   235
    Ah! Isaac, my own sweet child,
Yet kiss me again upon this hill!
    In all this world is none so mild.

ISAAC   Now truly, father, all this tarrying
    It doth my heart but harm;   240
I pray you, father, make an ending.
ABRAHAM   Come up, sweet son, into my arm.

I must bind thy hands too,
    Although thou be never so mild.
ISAAC   Ah! mercy, father! Why should ye do so?   245
ABRAHAM   That thou shouldst not let[4] me, my child.

ISAAC   Nay, y-wis, father, I will not let you.
    Do on, for me, your will;
And on the purpose that ye have set you,
    For God's love keep it forth[5] still.   250

I am full sorry this day to die,
    But yet I keep[6] not my God to grieve.
Do on your list[7] for me hardly;
    My fair sweet father, I give you leave.

But, father, I pray you evermore,   255
    Tell ye my mother no deal;
If she wost[8] it, she would weep full sore,
    For y-wis, father, she loveth me full well.
        God's blessing might she have!

Now farewell, my mother so sweet!   260
We two be like no more to meet,
ABRAHAM   Ah! Isaac, Isaac! son, thou makest me to grate[9]
And with thy words thou distemperest me.

ISAAC   Y-wis, sweet father, I am sorry to grieve you.
    I cry you mercy of that I have done.   265
And of all trespass that ever I did move[1] you.
    Now, dear father, forgive me that I have done,
        God of heaven be with me!

ABRAHAM   Ah! dear child, leave off thy moans;
In all thy life thou grieved me never once.   270
Now blessed be thou, body and bones,
    That ever thou were bred and born!

---

2. Dread.
3. Alas.
4. Hinder.
5. Pursue it.
6. Wish.

7. Pleasure, will.
8. Knew.
9. Gnash my teeth.
1. Perform against.

Thou hast been to me child full good.
> But, y-wis, child, though I mourn never so fast
> Yet must I needs here at the last   275
In this place shed all thy blood.

Therefore, my dear son, here shall thou lie.
> Unto my work I must me stead.[2]
Y-wis, I had as lief[3] myself to die,
> If God will be pleased with my deed,   280
> And mine own body for to offer
ISAAC   Ah! mercy, father. Mourn ye no more!
> Your weeping maketh my heart sore,
> As my own death that I shall suffer.

Your kerchief, father, about my eyen[4] ye wind.   285
ABRAHAM   So I shall, my sweetest child in earth.
ISAAC   Now yet, good father, have this in mind
> And smite me not often with your sharp sword,
> But hastily that it be sped.
ABRAHAM   Now farewell, my child, so full of grace.   290
ISAAC   Ah! father, father. Turn downward my face,
> For of your sharp sword I am ever a-dread.

ABRAHAM [*aside*]   To do this deed I am full sorry,
> But, Lord, thine hest[5] I will not withstand.
ISAAC   Ah! Father of heaven, to thee I cry;   295
> Lord, receive me into thy hand.

ABRAHAM [*aside*]   Lo! now is the time come, certain,
> That my sword in his neck shall bite.
Ah! Lord, my heart raiseth there-again;[6]
> I may not findeth it in my heart to smite;   300
> My heart will not know thereto.
Yet fain I would work my Lord's will,
But this young innocent lieth so still,
I may not findeth it in my heart him to kill.
> Oh, Father of heaven, what shall I do?   305

ISAAC   Ah! mercy, father. Why tarry ye so,
> And let me lay thus long on this heath?
Now I would to God the stroke were do!
Father, I pray you heartily, short me out of my woe,
> And let me not look thus after my death.   310

ABRAHAM   Now, heart, why wouldest not thou break in three?
> Yet shall thou not make me to my God unmild.
I will no longer let[7] for thee,
For that my God a-grieved would be.
> Now hold[8] the stroke, my own dear child.   315

---

2. Steady myself.   6. Rises in protest against the act.
3. Gladly.   7. Refrain.
4. Eyes.   8. Receive.
5. Command.

ANGEL *appears*.

ANGEL   I am an angel, thou mayest see blithe,[9]
      That from heaven to thee is sent.
Our Lord thank thee an hundred sithe[1]
      For the keeping of his commandment.

He knowest thy will and also thy heart,   320
      That thou dreadest him above all thing;
And some of thy heaviness for to depart[2]
      A fair ram yonder I gan bring;[3]

He standeth tied, lo! among the briars.
      Now, Abraham, amend thy mood,   325
For Isaac, thy young son that here is,
      This day shall not shed his blood.

Go, make thy sacrifice with yon ram.
Now farewell, blessed Abraham,
      For unto Heaven I now go home;   330
      The way is full gain[4] that I must go.
        Take up thy son so free.[5]   *Exit.*
ABRAHAM   Ah! Lord, I thank thee of thy great grace,
Now am I yethed[6] in diverse wise.
Arise up, Isaac, my dear son, arise;   335
        Arise up, sweet child, and come to me.

ISAAC   Ah! mercy, father. Why smite ye nought?
      Ah! smite on, father, once with your knife.
ABRAHAM   Peace, my sweet son, and take no thought,
      For our Lord of heaven hath grant thy life   340
        By his angel now.

That thou shalt not die this day, son, truly.
ISAAC   Ah, father, full glad then were I,
      Y-wis, father, I say, y-wis,
If this tale were true.   345
ABRAHAM   An hundred times, my son fair of hue,
      For joy thy mouth now will I kiss.

ISAAC   Ah! my dear father Abraham,
      Will not God be wroth that we do thus?
ABRAHAM   No, no, hardly, my sweet son,   350
For yon same ram he hath us sent
      Hither down to us.

Yon beast shall die here in thy stead,
      In the worship of our Lord alone.
Go, fetch him hither, my child, indeed.   355

9. At once.   4. Straight.
1. Times.   5. Noble.
2. Remove.   6. Comforted.
3. Have brought.

ISAAC   Father, I will go hent[7] him by the head,
　　　　And bring yon beast with me anon.

Ah! sheep, sheep, blessed might thou be,
　　That ever thou were sent down hither!
Thou shall this day die for me   360
In the worship of the Holy Trinity.
　　　　Now come fast and go we together
　　　　　　To my Father of heaven.
Though thou be never so gentle and good,
Yet had I liefer[8] thou sheddest thy blood,   365
　　　　Y-wis, sheep, than I.

Lo! father, I have brought here full smart[9]
　　　This gentle sheep, and him to you I give.
But, Lord God, I thank thee with all my heart,
　　For I am glad that I shall live,   370
　　　　And kiss once my dear mother.
ABRAHAM   Now be right merry, my sweet child,
　For this quick[1] beast, that is so mild,
　　　Here I shall present before all other.
ISAAC   And I will fast begin to blow;   375
　　　This fire shall burn a full good speed.
But, father, will I stoop down low,
Ye will not kill me with your sword, I trow?[2]
ABRAHAM   No, hardly, sweet son, have no dread;
　　　My mourning is past.   380
ISAAC   Aye! but I would that sword were in a gled,[3]
　　　For, y-wis, father, it makes me full ill aghast.

ABRAHAM   Now, Lord God of heaven in Trinity,
　　　Almighty God omnipotent,
My offering I make in worship of thee,   385
　　　And with this quick beast I thee present.
　　　Lord, receive thou mine intent,
　　　　As thou art God and ground of our grace.

　　　GOD *appears above.*

GOD   Abraham, Abraham, well might thou speed,
　　　And Isaac, thy young son thee by!   390
Truly, Abraham, for this deed
I shall multiply your bothers[4] seed
　　　As thick as stars be in the sky,
　　　　Both more and less;
And as thick as gravel in the sea,   395
So thick multiplied your seed shall be.
　　　This grant I you for your goodness.

7. Seize.　　　　　　　2. Trust.
8. Rather.　　　　　　3. Fire.
9. Quickly.　　　　　　4. Both your.
1. Live.

Of you shall come fruit great won,[5]
    And ever be in bliss without end,
For ye dread me as God alone   400
And keep my commandments everyone;
    My blessing I give, wheresoever ye wend.[6]

ABRAHAM   Lo! Isaac, my son, how think ye
    By this work that we have wrought?
Full glad and blithe we may be,   405
    Against the will of God we grudged nought,
        Upon this fair heath.
ISAAC   Ah! father, I thank our Lord every deal,[7]
    That my wit served me so well
        For to dread God more than my death.   410

ABRAHAM   Why, dearworthy[8] son, were thou adread?[9]
    Hardly, my child, tell me thy lore.[1]
ISAAC   Aye! by my faith, father, now have I read,
    I was never so afraid before
        As I have been at yon hill.   415
But, by my faith, father, I swear,
I will nevermore come there
        But it be against my will.

ABRAHAM   Aye! come on with me, my own sweet son,
    And homeward fast now let us gone.   420
ISAAC   By my faith, father, thereto I grant;
    I had never so good will to go home,
        And to speak with my dear mother.
ABRAHAM   Ah! Lord of heaven, I thank thee,
    For now may I lead home with me   425
Isaac, my young son so free,
    The gentlest child above all other.

Now go we forth, my blessed son.
ISAAC   I grant, father, and let us gone;
    For, by my troth, were I at home,   430
    I would never go out under that form;
        This may I well avow.
        I pray God give us grace evermore,
        And all those we be holding to.[2]

      DOCTOR *comes forward and addresses the audience.*

DOCTOR   Lo! sovereigns and sires, now have we showed   435
    This solemn story to great and small.
It is good learning to learned and lewd,[3]
    And the wisest of us all,
        Withouten any barring

---

5. In great number.
6. Go.
7. In every way.
8. Beloved.

9. Afraid.
1. Knowledge.
2. To whom we are related.
3. Ignorant.

For this story shows you here   440
How we should keep to our power[4]
    God's commandment without grudging.

Trow ye,[5] sirs, and God sent an angel
    And commanded you your child to slain,
By my troth, is there any of you   445
    That either would grudge or strive thereagainst?

How think ye now, sirs, thereby?
    I trow there be three or four or more,
And these women that weep so sorrowfully
    Then that their children die them from,   450
        As nature will and kind;
It is but folly, I may well avow,
To grudge against God or to grieve you,
For ye shall never see them mischieved,[6] well I know,
    By land nor water, have this in mind.   455
And grudge not against our Lord God
In wealth or woe, whether[7] that he you send,
Though ye be never so hard bestead;
    For when he will, he may it amend,

His commandments truly if ye keep with good heart,   460
    As this story hath now showed you before,
And faithfully serve him while ye be quart,[8]
    That ye may please God both even and morn.
    Now Jesu, that weareth the crown of thorn,
        Bring us all to heaven's bliss.   465

Finis.[9]

Ms. 1470–1480

4. As best we can.
5. Trust.
6. In distress.

7. Whichever.
8. In good health.
9. The end.

WILLIAM SHAKESPEARE

Hamlet

CHARACTERS

CLAUDIUS, *King of Denmark*
HAMLET, *son of the former and nephew to the present King*
POLONIUS, *Lord Chamberlain*
HORATIO, *friend of Hamlet*
LAERTES, *son of Polonius*
VOLTEMAND
CORNELIUS
ROSENCRANTZ
GUILDENSTERN } *courtiers*
OSRIC
A GENTLEMAN
A PRIEST

MARCELLUS } *officers*
BERNARDO
FRANCISCO, *a soldier*
REYNALDO, *servant to Polonius*
PLAYERS
TWO CLOWNS, *gravediggers*
FORTINBRAS, *Prince of Norway*
A NORWEGIAN CAPTAIN
ENGLISH AMBASSADORS
GERTRUDE, *Queen of Denmark, and mother of Hamlet*
OPHELIA, *daughter of Polonius*
GHOST OF HAMLET'S FATHER

LORDS, LADIES, OFFICERS, SOLDIERS, SAILORS, MESSENGERS, *and* ATTENDANTS

SCENE: *The action takes place in or near the royal castle of Denmark at Elsinore.*

Act 1

SCENE 1: *A guard station atop the castle. Enter* BERNARDO *and* FRANCISCO, *two sentinels.*

BERNARDO   Who's there?
FRANCISCO   Nay, answer me. Stand and unfold yourself.
BERNARDO   Long live the king!
FRANCISCO   Bernardo?
BERNARDO   He.   5
FRANCISCO   You come most carefully upon your hour.
BERNARDO   'Tis now struck twelve. Get thee to bed, Francisco.
FRANCISCO   For this relief much thanks. 'Tis bitter cold,
And I am sick at heart.
BERNARDO   Have you had quiet guard?
FRANCISCO   Not a mouse stirring.   10
BERNARDO   Well, good night.
If you do meet Horatio and Marcellus,
The rivals[1] of my watch, bid them make haste.

Enter HORATIO *and* MARCELLUS.

FRANCISCO   I think I hear them. Stand, ho! Who is there?
HORATIO   Friends to this ground.

---

1. companions

595

MARCELLUS   And liegemen to the Dane.[2]   15
FRANCISCO   Give you good night.
MARCELLUS   O, farewell, honest soldier!
   Who hath relieved you?
FRANCISCO   Bernardo hath my place.
   Give you good night.   *Exit* FRANCISCO.
MARCELLUS   Holla, Bernardo!
BERNARDO   Say—
   What, is Horatio there?
HORATIO   A piece of him.
BERNARDO   Welcome, Horatio. Welcome, good Marcellus.   20
HORATIO   What, has this thing appeared again tonight?
BERNARDO   I have seen nothing.
MARCELLUS   Horatio says 'tis but our fantasy,
   And will not let belief take hold of him
   Touching this dreaded sight twice seen of us.   25
   Therefore I have entreated him along
   With us to watch the minutes of this night,
   That if again this apparition come,
   He may approve[3] our eyes and speak to it.
HORATIO   Tush, tush, 'twill not appear.
BERNARDO   Sit down awhile,   30
   And let us once again assail your ears,
   That are so fortified against our story,
   What we have two nights seen.
HORATIO   Well, sit we down,
   And let us hear Bernardo speak of this.
BERNARDO   Last night of all,   35
   When yond same star that's westward from the pole[4]
   Had made his course t' illume that part of heaven
   Where now it burns, Marcellus and myself,
   The bell then beating one—

       Enter GHOST.

MARCELLUS   Peace, break thee off. Look where it comes again.   40
BERNARDO   In the same figure like the king that's dead.
MARCELLUS   Thou art a scholar; speak to it, Horatio.
BERNARDO   Looks 'a[5] not like the king? Mark it, Horatio.
HORATIO   Most like. It harrows me with fear and wonder.
BERNARDO   It would be spoke to.
MARCELLUS   Speak to it, Horatio.   45
HORATIO   What art thou that usurp'st this time of night
   Together with that fair and warlike form
   In which the majesty of buried Denmark
   Did sometimes march? By heaven I charge thee, speak.
MARCELLUS   It is offended.
BERNARDO   See, it stalks away.   50

---

2. The "Dane" is the King of Denmark,   3. confirm the testimony of
who is also called "Denmark," as in line 48   4. polestar
of this scene. In line 61 the same figure is   5. he
used for the King of Norway.

HORATIO   Stay. Speak, speak. I charge thee, speak.   *Exit* GHOST.
MARCELLUS   'Tis gone and will not answer.
BERNARDO   How now, Horatio! You tremble and look pale.
   Is not this something more than fantasy?
   What think you on't?   55
HORATIO   Before my God, I might not this believe
   Without the sensible[6] and true avouch
   Of mine own eyes.
MARCELLUS   Is it not like the king?
HORATIO   As thou art to thyself.
   Such was the very armor he had on   60
   When he the ambitious Norway combated.
   So frowned he once when, in an angry parle,[7]
   He smote the sledded Polacks on the ice.
   'Tis strange.
MARCELLUS   Thus twice before, and jump[8] at this dead hour,   65
   With martial stalk hath he gone by our watch.
HORATIO   In what particular thought to work I know not,
   But in the gross and scope of mine opinion,
   This bodes some strange eruption to our state.
MARCELLUS   Good now, sit down, and tell me he that knows,   70
   Why this same strict and most observant watch
   So nightly toils the subject[9] of the land,
   And why such daily cast of brazen cannon
   And foreign mart for implements of war;
   Why such impress of shipwrights, whose sore task   75
   Does not divide the Sunday from the week.
   What might be toward that this sweaty haste
   Doth make the night joint-laborer with the day?
   Who is't that can inform me?
HORATIO   That can I.
   At least, the whisper goes so. Our last king,   80
   Whose image even but now appeared to us,
   Was as you know by Fortinbras of Norway,
   Thereto pricked on by a most emulate pride,
   Dared to the combat; in which our valiant Hamlet
   (For so this side of our known world esteemed him)   85
   Did slay this Fortinbras; who by a sealed compact
   Well ratified by law and heraldry,
   Did forfeit, with his life, all those his lands
   Which he stood seized of,[1] to the conqueror;
   Against the which a moiety competent[2]   90
   Was gagéd[3] by our king; which had returned
   To the inheritance of Fortinbras,
   Had he been vanquisher; as, by the same covenant
   And carriage of the article designed,
   His fell to Hamlet. Now, sir, young Fortinbras,   95

6. of the senses
7. parley
8. precisely
9. people

1. possessed
2. portion of similar value
3. pledged

Of unimprovéd mettle hot and full,
Hath in the skirts of Norway here and there
Sharked up a list of lawless resolutes
For food and diet to some enterprise
That hath a stomach in't; which is no other,   100
As it doth well appear unto our state,
But to recover of us by strong hand
And terms compulsatory, those foresaid lands
So by his father lost; and this, I take it,
Is the main motive of our preparations,   105
The source of this our watch, and the chief head
Of this post-haste and romage⁴ in the land.
BERNARDO   I think it be no other but e'en so.
Well may it sort⁵ that this portentous figure
Comes arméd through our watch so like the king   110
That was and is the question of these wars.
HORATIO   A mote⁶ it is to trouble the mind's eye.
In the most high and palmy state of Rome,
A little ere the mightiest Julius fell,
The graves stood tenantless, and the sheeted dead   115
Did squeak and gibber in the Roman streets;
As stars with trains of fire, and dews of blood,
Disasters in the sun; and the moist star,
Upon whose influence Neptune's empire stands,⁷
Was sick almost to doomsday with eclipse.   120
And even the like precurse⁸ of feared events,
As harbingers preceding still the fates
And prologue to the omen coming on,
Have heaven and earth together demonstrated
Unto our climatures⁹ and countrymen.   125

        Enter GHOST.

But soft, behold, lo where it comes again!
I'll cross it¹ though it blast me.—Stay, illusion.

                                    It spreads [its] arms.

If thou hast any-sound or use of voice,
Speak to me.
If there be any good thing to be done,   130
That may to thee do ease, and grace to me,
Speak to me.
If thou art privy to thy country's fate,
Which happily foreknowing may avoid,
O, speak!   135
Or if thou hast uphoarded in thy life

4. stir
5. chance
6. speck of dust
7. Neptune was the Roman sea god; the "moist star" is the moon.
8. precursor
9. regions
1. Horatio means either that he will move across the Ghost's path in order to stop him or that he will make the sign of the cross to gain power over him. The stage direction which follows is somewhat ambiguous. "It" seems to refer to the Ghost, but the movement would be appropriate to Horatio.

Extorted treasure in the womb of earth,
For which, they say, you spirits oft walk in death,

    The cock crows.

Speak of it. Stay, and speak. Stop it, Marcellus.
MARCELLUS   Shall I strike at it with my partisan[2]?   140
HORATIO   Do, if it will not stand.
BERNARDO   'Tis here.
HORATIO   'Tis here.
MARCELLUS   'Tis gone.   *Exit* GHOST.
    We do it wrong, being so majestical,
    To offer it the show of violence;
    For it is as the air, invulnerable,   145
    And our vain blows malicious mockery.
BERNARDO   It was about to speak when the cock crew.
HORATIO   And then it started like a guilty thing
    Upon a fearful summons. I have heard
    The cock, that is the trumpet to the morn,   150
    Doth with his lofty and shrill-sounding throat
    Awake the god of day, and at his warning,
    Whether in sea or fire, in earth or air,
    Th' extravagant and erring[3] spirit hies
    To his confine; and of the truth herein   155
    This present object made probation.[4]
MARCELLUS   It faded on the crowing of the cock.
    Some say that ever 'gainst that season comes
    Wherein our Savior's birth is celebrated,
    This bird of dawning singeth all night long,   160
    And then, they say, no spirit dare stir abroad,
    The nights are wholesome, then no planets strike,
    No fairy takes,[5] nor witch hath power to charm,
    So hallowed and so gracious is that time.
HORATIO   So have I heard and do in part believe it.   165
    But look, the morn in russet mantle clad
    Walks o'er the dew of yon high eastward hill.
    Break we our watch up, and by my advice
    Let us impart what we have seen tonight
    Unto young Hamlet, for upon my life   170
    This spirit, dumb to us, will speak to him.
    Do you consent we shall acquaint him with it,
    As needful in our loves, fitting our duty?
MARCELLUS   Let's do't, I pray, and I this morning know
    Where we shall find him most convenient.   *Exeunt.* 175

SCENE 2: *A chamber of state. Enter* KING CLAUDIUS, QUEEN GER-
TRUDE, HAMLET, POLONIUS, LAERTES, OPHELIA, VOLTEMAND, COR-
NELIUS *and other members of the court.*

2. halberd   4. proof
3. wandering out of bounds   5. enchants

KING   Though yet of Hamlet our dear brother's death
 The memory be green, and that it us befitted
 To bear our hearts in grief, and our whole kingdom
 To be contracted in one brow of woe,
 Yet so far hath discretion fought with nature   5
 That we with wisest sorrow think on him,
 Together with remembrance of ourselves.
 Therefore our sometime sister, now our queen,
 Th' imperial jointress[6] to this warlike state,
 Have we, as 'twere with a defeated joy,   10
 With an auspicious and a dropping eye,
 With mirth in funeral, and with dirge in marriage,
 In equal scale weighing delight and dole,
 Taken to wife; nor have we herein barred
 Your better wisdoms, which have freely gone   15
 With this affair along. For all, our thanks.
 Now follows that you know young Fortinbras,
 Holding a weak supposal of our worth,
 Or thinking by our late dear brother's death
 Our state to be disjoint and out of frame,   20
 Colleaguéd with this dream of his advantage,
 He hath not failed to pester us with message
 Importing the surrender of those lands
 Lost by his father, with all bands of law,
 To our most valiant brother. So much for him.   25
 Now for ourself, and for this time of meeting,
 Thus much the business is: we have here writ
 To Norway, uncle of young Fortinbras—
 Who, impotent and bedrid, scarcely hears
 Of this his nephew's purpose—to suppress   30
 His further gait[7] herein, in that the levies,
 The lists, and full proportions are all made
 Out of his subject; and we here dispatch
 You, good Cornelius, and you, Voltemand,
 For bearers of this greeting to old Norway,   35
 Giving to you no further personal power
 To business with the king, more than the scope
 Of these dilated[8] articles allow.
 Farewell, and let your haste commend your duty.
CORNELIUS ⎱
VOLTEMAND ⎰ In that, and all things will we show our duty. 40
KING   We doubt it nothing, heartily farewell.

          Exeunt VOLTEMAND *and* CORNELIUS.

 And now, Laertes, what's the news with you?
 You told us of some suit. What is't, Laertes?
 You cannot speak of reason to the Dane
 And lose your voice. What wouldst thou beg, Laertes, 45

---

6. A "jointress" is a widow who holds a
jointure or life interest in the estate of her
deceased husband.

7. progress
8. fully expressed

That shall not be my offer, not thy asking?
The head is not more native to the heart,
The hand more instrumental[9] to the mouth,
Than is the throne of Denmark to thy father.
What wouldst thou have, Laertes?
LAERTES   My dread lord,   50
  Your leave and favor to return to France,
  From whence, though willingly, I came to Denmark
  To show my duty in your coronation,
  Yet now I must confess, that duty done,
  My thoughts and wishes bend again toward France,   55
  And bow them to your gracious leave and pardon.
KING   Have you your father's leave? What says Polonius?
POLONIUS   He hath, my lord, wrung from me my slow leave
  By laborsome petition, and at last
  Upon his will I sealed my hard consent.   60
  I do beseech you give him leave to go.
KING   Take thy fair hour, Laertes. Time be thine,
  And thy best graces spend it at thy will.
  But now, my cousin[1] Hamlet, and my son—
HAMLET [*aside*]   A little more than kin, and less than kind.   65
KING   How is it that the clouds still hang on you?
HAMLET   Not so, my lord. I am too much in the sun.
QUEEN   Good Hamlet, cast thy nighted color off,
  And let thine eye look like a friend on Denmark.
  Do not for ever with thy vailéd lids[2]   70
  Seek for thy noble father in the dust.
  Thou know'st 'tis common—all that lives must die,
  Passing through nature to eternity.
HAMLET   Ay, madam, it is common.
QUEEN   If it be,
  Why seems it so particular with thee?   75
HAMLET   Seems, madam? Nay, it is. I know not "seems."
  'Tis not alone my inky cloak, good mother,
  Nor customary suits of solemn black,
  Nor windy suspiration of forced breath,
  No, nor the fruitful river in the eye,   80
  Nor the dejected havior[3] of the visage,
  Together with all forms, moods, shapes of grief,
  That can denote me truly. These indeed seem,
  For they are actions that a man might play,
  But I have that within which passes show—   85
  These but the trappings and the suits of woe.
KING   'Tis sweet and commendable in your nature, Hamlet,
  To give these mourning duties to your father,
  But you must know your father lost a father,
  That father lost, lost his, and the survivor bound 90
  In filial obligation for some term

9. serviceable   2. lowered eyes
1. "Cousin" is used here as a general   3. appearance
term of kinship.

To do obsequious[4] sorrow. But to persever
In obstinate condolement is a course
Of impious stubbornness. 'Tis unmanly grief.
It shows a will most incorrect to[5] heaven,   95
A heart unfortified, a mind impatient,
An understanding simple and unschooled.
For what we know must be, and is as common
As any the most vulgar thing to sense,
Why should we in our peevish opposition   100
Take it to heart? Fie, 'tis a fault to heaven,
A fault against the dead, a fault to nature,
To reason most absurd, whose common theme
Is death of fathers, and who still hath cried,
From the first corse[6] till he that died today,   105
"This must be so." We pray you throw to earth
This unprevailing woe, and think of us
As of a father, for let the world take note
You are the most immediate[7] to our throne,
And with no less nobility of love   110
Than that which dearest father bears his son
Do I impart toward you. For your intent
In going back to school in Wittenberg,
It is most retrograde[8] to our desire,
And we beseech you, bend you to remain   115
Here in the cheer and comfort of our eye,
Our chiefest courtier, cousin, and our son.
QUEEN   Let not thy mother lose her prayers, Hamlet.
I pray thee stay with us, go not to Wittenberg.
HAMLET   I shall in all my best obey you, madam.   120
KING   Why, 'tis a loving and a fair reply.
Be as ourself in Denmark. Madam, come.
This gentle and unforced accord of Hamlet
Sits smiling to my heart, in grace whereof,
No jocund health that Denmark drinks today   125
But the great cannon to the clouds shall tell,
And the king's rouse[9] the heaven shall bruit[1] again,
Respeaking earthly thunder. Come away.

Flourish. Exeunt all but HAMLET.

HAMLET   O, that this too too solid flesh would melt,
Thaw, and resolve itself into a dew,   130
Or that the Everlasting had not fixed
His canon[2] 'gainst self-slaughter. O God, God,
How weary, stale, flat, and unprofitable
Seem to me all the uses of this world!
Fie on't, ah, fie, 'tis an unweeded garden   135
That grows to seed. Things rank and gross in nature

---

4. suited for funeral obsequies
5. uncorrected toward
6. corpse
7. next in line

8. contrary
9. carousal
1. echo
2. law

Possess it merely.[3] That it should come to this,
But two months dead, nay, not so much, not two.
So excellent a king, that was to this
Hyperion to a satyr,[4] so loving to my mother,   140
That he might not beteem[5] the winds of heaven
Visit her face too roughly. Heaven and earth,
Must I remember? Why, she would hang on him
As if increase of appetite had grown
By what it fed on, and yet, within a month—   145
Let me not think on't. Frailty, thy name is woman—
A little month, or ere those shoes were old
With which she followed my poor father's body
Like Niobe,[6] all tears, why she, even she—
O God, a beast that wants discourse of reason   150
Would have mourned longer—married with my uncle,
My father's brother, but no more like my father
Than I to Hercules.[7] Within a month,
Ere yet the salt of most unrighteous tears
Had left the flushing in her gallèd eyes,   155
She married. O, most wicked speed, to post
With such dexterity to incestuous sheets!
It is not, nor it cannot come to good.
But break my heart, for I must hold my tongue.

Enter HORATIO, MARCELLUS, *and* BERNARDO.

HORATIO   Hail to your lordship!
HAMLET   I am glad to see you well.   160
    Horatio—or I do forget myself.
HORATIO   The same, my lord, and your poor servant ever.
HAMLET   Sir, my good friend, I'll change[8] that name with you.
    And what make you from Wittenberg, Horatio?
    Marcellus?   165
MARCELLUS   My good lord!
HAMLET   I am very glad to see you. [*To* BERNARDO.] Good even, sir.—
    But what, in faith, make you from Wittenberg?
HORATIO   A truant disposition, good my lord.
HAMLET   I would not hear your enemy say so,   170
    Nor shall you do my ear that violence
    To make it truster of your own report
    Against yourself. I know you are no truant.
    But what is your affair in Elsinore?
    We'll teach you to drink deep ere you depart.   175
HORATIO   My lord, I came to see your father's funeral.
HAMLET   I prithee do not mock me, fellow-student,
    I think it was to see my mother's wedding.

3. entirely
4. Hyperion, a sun god, stands here for
beauty in contrast to the monstrous satyr,
a lecherous creature, half man and half
goat.
5. permit
6. In Greek mythology Niobe was turned
to stone after a tremendous fit of weeping

over the death of her fourteen children, a
misfortune brought about by her boasting
over her fertility.
7. The demigod Hercules was noted for
his strength and the series of spectacular
labors which it allowed him to accomplish.
8. exchange

HORATIO   Indeed, my lord, it followed hard upon.
HAMLET   Thrift, thrift, Horatio. The funeral-baked meats   180
Did coldly furnish forth the marriage tables.
Would I had met my dearest[9] foe in heaven
Or ever I had seen that day, Horatio!
My father—methinks I see my father.
HORATIO   Where, my lord?
HAMLET   In my mind's eye, Horatio.   185
HORATIO   I saw him once, 'a was a goodly king.
HAMLET   'A was a man, take him for all in all,
I shall not look upon his like again.
HORATIO   My lord, I think I saw him yesternight.
HAMLET   Saw who?   190
HORATIO   My lord, the king your father.
HAMLET   The king my father?
HORATIO   Season[1] your admiration[2] for a while
With an attent[3] ear till I may deliver[4]
Upon the witness of these gentlemen
This marvel to you.
HAMLET   For God's love, let me hear!   195
HORATIO   Two nights together had these gentlemen,
Marcellus and Bernardo, on their watch
In the dead waste and middle of the night
Been thus encountered. A figure like your father,
Armed at point exactly,[5] cap-a-pe,[6]   200
Appears before them, and with solemn march
Goes slow and stately by them. Thrice he walked
By their oppressed and fear-surprisèd eyes
Within his truncheon's[7] length, whilst they, distilled
Almost to jelly with the act of fear,   205
Stand dumb and speak not to him. This to me
In dreadful secrecy impart they did,
And I with them the third night kept the watch,
Where, as they had delivered, both in time,
Form of the thing, each word made true and good,   210
The apparition comes. I knew your father.
These hands are not more like.
HAMLET   But where was this?
MARCELLUS   My lord, upon the platform where we watch.
HAMLET   Did you not speak to it?
HORATIO   My lord, I did,
But answer made it none. Yet once methought   215
It lifted up it head and did address
Itself to motion, like as it would speak;
But even then the morning cock crew loud,
And at the sound it shrunk in haste away
And vanished from our sight.

9. bitterest
1. moderate
2. wonder
3. attentive

4. relate
5. completely
6. from head to toe
7. baton of office

HAMLET   'Tis very strange.   220
HORATIO   As I do live, my honored lord, 'tis true,
    And we did think it writ down in our duty
    To let you know of it.
HAMLET   Indeed, sirs, but
    This troubles me. Hold you the watch tonight?
ALL   We do, my lord.
HAMLET   Armed, say you?
ALL   Armed, my lord.   225
HAMLET   From top to toe?
ALL   My lord, from head to foot.
HAMLET   Then saw you not his face?
HORATIO   O yes, my lord, he wore his beaver[8] up.
HAMLET   What, looked he frowningly?
HORATIO   A countenance more in sorrow than in anger.   230
HAMLET   Pale or red?
HORATIO   Nay, very pale.
HAMLET   And fixed his eyes upon you?
HORATIO   Most constantly.
HAMLET   I would I had been there.
HORATIO   It would have much amazed you.
HAMLET   Very like.   235
    Stayed it long?
HORATIO   While one with moderate haste might tell a hundred.
BOTH   Longer, longer.
HORATIO   Not when I saw't.
HAMLET   His beard was grizzled, no?
HORATIO   It was as I have seen it in his life,
    A sable silvered.
HAMLET   I will watch tonight.   240
    Perchance 'twill walk again.
HORATIO   I warr'nt it will.
HAMLET   If it assume my noble father's person,
    I'll speak to it though hell itself should gape[9]
    And bid me hold my peace. I pray you all,
    If you have hitherto concealed this sight,   245
    Let it be tenable[1] in your silence still,
    And whatsomever else shall hap tonight,
    Give it an understanding but no tongue.
    I will requite your loves. So fare you well.
    Upon the platform 'twixt eleven and twelve   250
    I'll visit you.
ALL   Our duty to your honor.
HAMLET   Your loves, as mine to you. Farewell.

                                        Exeunt all but HAMLET.

    My father's spirit in arms? All is not well.
    I doubt[2] some foul play. Would the night were come!

8. movable face protector   1. held
9. open (its mouth) wide   2. suspect

Till then sit still, my soul. Foul deeds will rise,   255
Though all the earth o'erwhelm them, to men's eyes.   *Exit.*

SCENE 3: *The dwelling of* POLONIUS. *Enter* LAERTES *and* OPHELIA.

LAERTES   My necessaries are embarked. Farewell.
  And, sister, as the winds give benefit
  And convoy³ is assistant,⁴ do not sleep,
  But let me hear from you.
OPHELIA   Do you doubt that?
LAERTES   For Hamlet, and the trifling of his favor,   5
  Hold it a fashion and a toy in blood,
  A violet in the youth of primy⁵ nature,
  Forward, not permanent, sweet, not lasting,
  The perfume and suppliance of a minute,
  No more.
OPHELIA   No more but so?
LAERTES   Think it no more.   10
  For nature crescent⁶ does not grow alone
  In thews and bulk, but as this temple⁷ waxes
  The inward service of the mind and soul
  Grows wide withal. Perhaps he loves you now,
  And now no soil nor cautel⁸ doth besmirch   15
  The virtue of his will, but you must fear,
  His greatness weighed,⁹ his will is not his own,
  For he himself is subject to his birth.
  He may not, as unvalued persons do,
  Carve for himself, for on his choice depends   20
  The safety and health of this whole state,
  And therefore must his choice be circumscribed
  Unto the voice¹ and yielding of that body
  Whereof he is the head. Then if he says he loves you,
  It fits your wisdom so far to believe it   25
  As he in his particular act and place
  May give his saying deed, which is no further
  Than the main voice of Denmark goes withal.
  Then weigh what loss your honor may sustain
  If with too credent² ear you list³ his songs,   30
  Or lose your heart, or your chaste treasure open
  To his unmastered importunity.
  Fear it, Ophelia, fear it, my dear sister,
  And keep you in the rear of your affection,
  Out of the shot and danger of desire.   35
  The chariest⁴ maid is prodigal enough
  If she unmask her beauty to the moon.
  Virtue itself scapes not calumnious strokes.

3. means of transport   9. rank considered
4. available   1. assent
5. of the spring   2. credulous
6. growing   3. listen to
7. body   4. most circumspect
8. deceit

The canker[5] galls the infants of the spring
Too oft before their buttons[6] be disclosed,   40
And in the morn and liquid dew of youth
Contagious blastments[7] are most imminent.
Be wary then; best safety lies in fear.
Youth to itself rebels, though none else near.

OPHELIA   I shall the effect of this good lesson keep   45
As watchman to my heart. But, good my brother,
Do not as some ungracious pastors do,
Show me the steep and thorny way to heaven,
Whiles like a puffed and reckless libertine
Himself the primrose path of dalliance treads   50
And recks[8] not his own rede.[9]

LAERTES   O, fear me not.

Enter POLONIUS.

I stay too long. But here my father comes.
A double blessing is a double grace;
Occasion smiles upon a second leave.

POLONIUS   Yet here, Laertes? Aboard, aboard, for shame!   55
The wind sits in the shoulder of your sail,
And you are stayed for. There—my blessing with thee,
And these few precepts in thy memory
Look thou character.[1] Give thy thoughts no tongue,
Nor any unproportioned thought his act.   60
Be thou familiar, but by no means vulgar.
Those friends thou hast, and their adoption tried,
Grapple them unto thy soul with hoops of steel;
But do not dull[2] thy palm with entertainment
Of each new-hatched, unfledged comrade. Beware   65
Of entrance to a quarrel, but being in,
Bear't[3] that th' opposéd[4] may beware of thee.
Give every man thy ear, but few thy voice;[5]
Take each man's censure, but reserve thy judgment.
Costly thy habit as thy purse can buy,   70
But not expressed in fancy; rich not gaudy,
For the apparel oft proclaims the man,
And they in France of the best rank and station
Are of a most select and generous chief[6] in that.
Neither a borrower nor a lender be,   75
For loan oft loses both itself and friend,
And borrowing dulls th' edge of husbandry.
This above all, to thine own self be true,
And it must follow as the night the day   80
Thou canst not then be false to any man.
Farewell. My blessing season this in thee!

5. rose caterpillar   2. make callous
6. buds   3. conduct it
7. blights   4. opponent
8. heeds   5. approval
9. advice   6. eminence
1. write

LAERTES   Most humbly do I take my leave, my lord.

POLONIUS   The time invites you. Go, your servants tend.[7]

LAERTES   Farewell, Ophelia, and remember well
What I have said to you.

OPHELIA   'Tis in my memory locked,   85
And you yourself shall keep the key of it.

LAERTES   Farewell.   *Exit* LAERTES.

POLONIUS   What is't, Ophelia, he hath said to you?

OPHELIA   So please you, something touching the Lord Hamlet.

POLONIUS   Marry, well bethought.   90
'Tis told me he hath very oft of late
Given private time to you, and you yourself
Have of your audience been most free and bounteous.
If it be so—as so 'tis put on me,
And that in way of caution—I must tell you,   95
You do not understand yourself so clearly
As it behooves my daughter and your honor.
What is between you? Give me up the truth.

OPHELIA   He hath, my lord, of late made many tenders
Of his affection to me.   100

POLONIUS   Affection? Pooh! You speak like a green girl,
Unsifted in such perilous circumstance.
Do you believe his tenders, as you call them?

OPHELIA   I do not know, my lord, what I should think.

POLONIUS   Marry, I will teach you. Think yourself a baby   105
That you have ta'en these tenders for true pay
Which are not sterling. Tender yourself more dearly,
Or (not to crack the wind of the poor phrase,
Running it thus) you'll tender me a fool.

OPHELIA   My lord, he hath importuned me with love   110
In honorable fashion.

POLONIUS   Ay, fashion you may call it. Go to, go to.

OPHELIA   And hath given countenance[8] to his speech, my lord,
With almost all the holy vows of heaven.

POLONIUS   Ay, springes[9] to catch woodcocks. I do know,   115
When the blood burns, how prodigal the soul
Lends the tongue vows. These blazes, daughter,
Giving more light than heat, extinct in both
Even in their promise, as it is a-making,
You must not take for fire. From this time   120
Be something scanter of your maiden presence.
Set your entreatments[1] at a higher rate
Than a command to parle. For Lord Hamlet,
Believe so much in him that he is young,
And with a larger tether may he walk   125
Than may be given you. In few, Ophelia,
Do not believe his vows, for they are brokers,[2]
Not of that dye which their investments[3] show,

7. await
8. confirmation
9. snares

1. negotiations before a surrender
2. panders
3. garments

But mere implorators[4] of unholy suits,
Breathing like sanctified and pious bawds,   130
The better to beguile. This is for all:
I would not, in plain terms, from this time forth
Have you so slander any moment leisure
As to give words or talk with the Lord Hamlet.
Look to't, I charge you. Come your ways.   135
OPHELIA   I shall obey, my lord.   *Exeunt.*

SCENE 4: *The guard station. Enter* HAMLET, HORATIO *and*
MARCELLUS.

HAMLET   The air bites shrewdly[5]; it is very cold.
HORATIO   It is a nipping and an eager[6] air.
HAMLET   What hour now?
HORATIO   I think it lacks of twelve.
MARCELLUS   No, it is struck.
HORATIO   Indeed? I heard it not. It then draws near the season   5
    Wherein the spirit held his wont to walk.
            A flourish of trumpets, and two pieces go off.
    What does this mean, my lord?
HAMLET   The king doth wake tonight and takes his rouse,
    Keeps wassail, and the swagg'ring up-spring[7] reels,
    And as he drains his draughts of Rhenish down,   10
    The kettledrum and trumpet thus bray out
    The triumph of his pledge.
HORATIO   Is it a custom?
HAMLET   Ay, marry, is't,
    But to my mind, though I am native here
    And to the manner born, it is a custom   15
    More honored in the breach than the observance.
    This heavy-headed revel east and west
    Makes us traduced and taxed of other nations.
    They clepe[8] us drunkards, and with swinish phrase
    Soil our addition,[9] and indeed it takes   20
    From our achievements, though performed at height,
    The pith and marrow of our attribute.[1]
    So oft it chances in particular men,
    That for some vicious mole of nature in them,
    As in their birth, wherein they are not guilty   25
    (Since nature cannot choose his origin),
    By the o'ergrowth of some complexion,
    Oft breaking down the pales[2] and forts of reason,
    Or by some habit that too much o'er-leavens
    The form of plausive[3] manners—that these men,   30
    Carrying, I say, the stamp of one defect,

4. solicitors
5. sharply
6. keen
7. a German dance
8. call

9. reputation
1. honor
2. barriers
3. pleasing

Being nature's livery or fortune's star,
His virtues else, be they as pure as grace,
As infinite as man may undergo,
 Shall in the general censure take corruption   35
From that particular fault. The dram of evil
Doth all the noble substance often doubt[4]
To his own scandal.

    Enter GHOST.

HORATIO   Look, my lord, it comes.
HAMLET   Angels and ministers of grace defend us!
 Be thou a spirit of health or goblin damned,   40
Bring with thee airs from heaven or blasts from hell,
Be thy intents wicked or charitable,
Thou com'st in such a questionable[5] shape
That I will speak to thee. I'll call thee Hamlet,
King, father, royal Dane. O, answer me!   45
Let me not burst in ignorance, but tell
Why thy canonized[6] bones, hearséd in death,
Have burst their cerements[7]; why the sepulchre
Wherein we saw thee quietly interred
Hath oped his ponderous and marble jaws   50
To cast thee up again. What may this mean
That thou, dead corse, again in complete steel[8]
Revisits thus the glimpses of the moon,
Making night hideous, and we fools of nature
So horridly to shake our disposition   55
With thoughts beyond the reaches of our souls?
Say, why is this? wherefore? What should we do?

    GHOST *beckons.*

HORATIO   It beckons you to go away it,
 As if it some impartment[9] did desire
To you alone.
MARCELLUS   Look with what courteous action   60
It waves[1] you to a more removéd[2] ground.
But do not go with it.
HORATIO   No, by no means.
HAMLET   It will not speak; then I will follow it.
HORATIO   Do not, my lord.
HAMLET   Why, what should be the fear?
 I do not set my life at a pin's fee,[3]   65
And for my soul, what can it do to that,
Being a thing immortal as itself?
It waves me forth again. I'll follow it.
HORATIO   What if it tempt you toward the flood, my lord,
 Or to the dreadful summit of the cliff   70

4. put out
5. prompting question
6. buried in accordance with church canons
   7. gravecloths
8. armor
9. communication
1. beckons
2. distant
3. price

That beetles[4] o'er his base into the sea,
And there assume some other horrible form,
Which might deprive[5] your sovereignty of reason[6]
And draw you into madness? Think of it.
The very place puts toys of desperation,[7]   75
Without more motive, into every brain
That looks so many fathoms to the sea
And hears it roar beneath.
HAMLET   It waves me still.
    Go on. I'll follow thee.
MARCELLUS   You shall not go, my lord.
HAMLET   Hold off your hands.   80
HORATIO   Be ruled. You shall not go.
HAMLET   My fate cries out
    And makes each petty artere in this body
    As hardy as the Nemean lion's nerve.[8]
    Still am I called. Unhand me, gentlemen.
    By heaven, I'll make a ghost of him that lets[9] me.   85
    I say, away! Go on. I'll follow thee.

                   Exeunt GHOST *and* HAMLET.

HORATIO   He waxes desperate with imagination.
MARCELLUS   Let's follow. 'Tis not fit thus to obey him.
HORATIO   Have after. To what issue will this come?
MARCELLUS   Something is rotten in the state of Denmark.   90
HORATIO   Heaven will direct it.
MARCELLUS   Nay, let's follow him.   *Exeunt.*

SCENE 5: *Near the guard station. Enter* GHOST *and* HAMLET.

HAMLET   Whither wilt thou lead me? Speak. I'll go no further.
GHOST   Mark me.
HAMLET   I will.
GHOST   My hour is almost come,
    When I to sulph'rous and tormenting flames
    Must render up myself.
HAMLET   Alas, poor ghost!
GHOST   Pity me not, but lend thy serious hearing   5
    To what I shall unfold.
HAMLET   Speak. I am bound to hear.
GHOST   So art thou to revenge, when thou shalt hear.
HAMLET   What?
GHOST   I am thy father's spirit,
    Doomed for a certain term to walk the night,   10
    And for the day confined to fast in fires,
    Till the foul crimes done in my days of nature[1]
    Are burnt and purged away. But that I am forbid

---

4. juts out
5. take away
6. rational power
7. desperate fancies
8. The Nemean lion was a mythological

monster slain by Hercules as one of his twelve labors.
9. hinders
1. i.e., while I was alive

To tell the secrets of my prison house,
I could a tale unfold whose lightest word   15
Would harrow up thy soul, freeze thy young blood,
Make thy two eyes like stars start from their spheres,
Thy knotted and combinéd[2] locks to part,
And each particular hair to stand an end,
Like quills upon the fretful porpentine.[3]   20
But this eternal blazon[4] must not be
To ears of flesh and blood. List, list, O, list!
If thou didst ever thy dear father love—

HAMLET   O God!

GHOST   Revenge his foul and most unnatural murder.   25

HAMLET   Murder!

GHOST   Murder most foul, as in the best it is,
But this most foul, strange, and unnatural.

HAMLET   Haste me to know't, that I, with wings as swift
As meditation or the thoughts of love,   30
May sweep to my revenge.

GHOST   I find thee apt,
And duller shouldst thou be than the fat weed
That rots itself in ease on Lethe[5] wharf,—
Wouldst thou not stir in this. Now, Hamlet, hear.
'Tis given out that, sleeping in my orchard,   35
A serpent stung me. So the whole ear of Denmark
Is by a forgéd process[6] of my death
Rankly abused. But know, thou noble youth,
The serpent that did sting thy father's life
Now wears his crown.

HAMLET   O my prophetic soul!   40
My uncle!

GHOST   Ay, that incestuous, that adulterate beast,
With witchcraft of his wits, with traitorous gifts—
O wicked wit and gifts that have the power
So to seduce!—won to his shameful lust   45
The will of my most seeming virtuous queen.
O Hamlet, what a falling off was there,
From me, whose love was of that dignity
That it went hand in hand even with the vow
I made to her in marriage, and to decline[7]   50
Upon a wretch whose natural gifts were poor
To those of mine!
But virtue, as it never will be moved,
Though lewdness court it in a shape of heaven,
So lust, though to a radiant angel linked,   55
Will sate itself in a celestial bed
And prey on garbage.
But soft, methinks I scent the morning air.

2. tangled
3. porcupine
4. description of eternity
5. The Lethe was one of the rivers of
the classical underworld. Its specific importance was that its waters when drunk
induced forgetfulness. The "fat weed" is
the asphodel which grew there.
6. false report
7. sink

Brief let me be. Sleeping within my orchard,
My custom always of the afternoon,   60
Upon my secure hour thy uncle stole,
With juice of cursed hebona[8] in a vial,
And in the porches of my ears did pour
The leperous distilment, whose effect
Holds such an enmity with blood of man   65
That swift as quicksilver it courses through
The natural gates and alleys of the body,
And with a sudden vigor it doth posset[9]
And curd,[1] like eager[2] droppings into milk,
The thin and wholesome blood. So did it mine,   70
And a most instant tetter[3] barked about[4]
Most lazar-like[5] with vile and loathsome crust
All my smooth body.
Thus was I sleeping by a brother's hand
Of life, of crown, of queen at once dispatched,   75
Cut off even in the blossoms of my sin,
Unhouseled, disappointed, unaneled,[6]
No reck'ning made, but sent to my account
With all my imperfections on my head.
O, horrible! O, horrible! most horrible!   80
If thou hast nature in thee, bear it not.
Let not the royal bed of Denmark be
A couch for luxury[7] and damnéd incest.
But howsomever thou pursues this act,
Taint not thy mind, nor let thy soul contrive   85
Against thy mother aught. Leave her to heaven,
And to those thorns that in her bosom lodge
To prick and sting her. Fare thee well at once.
The glowworm shows the matin[8] to be near,
And gins to pale his uneffectual fire.   90
Adieu, adieu, adieu. Remember me.   *Exit.*
HAMLET   O all you host of heaven! O earth! What else?
And shall I couple hell? O, fie! Hold, hold, my heart,
And you, my sinews, grow not instant old,
But bear me stiffly up. Remember thee?   95
Ay, thou poor ghost, whiles memory holds a seat
In this distracted globe.[9] Remember thee?
Yea, from the table[1] of my memory
I'll wipe away all trivial fond[2] records,
All saws of books, all forms, all pressures past   100
That youth and observation copied there,
And thy commandment all alone shall live
Within the book and volume of my brain,

8. a poison
9. coagulate
1. curdle
2. acid
3. a skin disease
4. covered like bark
5. leper-like
6. The Ghost means that he died with-

out the customary rites of the church, that
is, without receiving the sacrament, without
confession, and without extreme unction.
7. lust
8. morning
9. skull
1. writing tablet
2. foolish

Unmixed with baser matter. Yes, by heaven!
O most pernicious woman!   105
O villain, villain, smiling, damnéd villain!
My tables—meet it is I set it down
That one may smile, and smile, and be a villain.
At least I am sure it may be so in Denmark.
So, uncle, there you are. Now to my word[3]:   110
It is "Adieu, adieu. Remember me."
I have sworn't.

> *Enter* HORATIO *and* MARCELLUS.

HORATIO   My lord, my lord!
MARCELLUS   Lord Hamlet!
HORATIO   Heavens secure him!
HAMLET   So be it!
MARCELLUS   Illo, ho, ho, my lord!   115
HAMLET   Hillo, ho, ho, boy![4] Come, bird, come.
MARCELLUS   How is't, my noble lord?
HORATIO   What news, my lord?
HAMLET   O, wonderful!
HORATIO   Good my lord, tell it.
HAMLET   No, you will reveal it.
HORATIO   Not I, my lord, by heaven.
MARCELLUS   Nor I, my lord.   120
HAMLET   How say you then, would heart of man once think it?
   But you'll be secret?
BOTH   Ay, by heaven, my lord.
HAMLET   There's never a villain dwelling in all Denmark
   But he's an arrant knave.
HORATIO   There needs no ghost, my lord, come from the grave   125
   To tell us this.
HAMLET   Why, right, you are in the right,
   And so without more circumstance at all
   I hold it fit that we shake hands and part,
   You, as your business and desire shall point you,
   For every man hath business and desire   130
   Such as it is, and for my own poor part,
   I will go pray.
HORATIO   These are but wild and whirling words, my lord.
HAMLET   I am sorry they offend you, heartily;
   Yes, faith, heartily.
HORATIO   There's no offence, my lord.   135
HAMLET   Yes, by Saint Patrick, but there is, Horatio,
   And much offence too. Touching this vision here,
   It is an honest ghost, that let me tell you.
   For your desire to know what is between us,
   O'ermaster't as you may. And now, good friends,   140
   As you are friends, scholars, and soldiers,
   Give me one poor request.

_____

3. for my motto   4. a falconer's cry

HORATIO   What is't, my lord? We will.

HAMLET   Never make known what you have seen tonight.

BOTH   My lord, we will not.

HAMLET   Nay, but swear't.

HORATIO   In faith,   145
My lord, not I.

MARCELLUS   Nor I, my lord, in faith.

HAMLET   Upon my sword.

MARCELLUS   We have sworn, my lord, already.

HAMLET   Indeed, upon my sword, indeed.

      GHOST *cries under the stage.*

GHOST   Swear.

HAMLET   Ha, ha, boy, say'st thou so? Art thou there, truepenny[5]?
Come on. You hear this fellow in the cellarage.[6]   150
Consent to swear.

HORATIO   Propose the oath, my lord.

HAMLET   Never to speak of this that you have seen,
Swear by my sword.

GHOST [*beneath*]   Swear.

HAMLET   Hic et ubique?[7] Then we'll shift our ground.   155
Come hither, gentlemen,
And lay your hands again upon my sword.
Swear by my sword
Never to speak of this that you have heard.

GHOST [*beneath*]   Swear by his sword.   160

HAMLET   Well said, old mole! Canst work i' th' earth so fast?
A worthy pioneer![8] Once more remove, good friends.

HORATIO   O day and night, but this is wondrous strange!

HAMLET   And therefore as a stranger give it welcome.
There are more things in heaven and earth, Horatio,   165
Than are dreamt of in your philosophy.
But come.
Here as before, never, so help you mercy,
How strange or odd some'er I bear myself
(As I perchance hereafter shall think meet   170
To put an antic[9] disposition on),
That you, at such times, seeing me, never shall,
With arms encumbered[1] thus, or this head-shake,
Or by pronouncing of some doubtful phrase,
As "Well, well, we know," or "We could, and if we would"   175
Or "If we list to speak," or "There be, and if they might"
Or such ambiguous giving out, to note
That you know aught of me—this do swear,
So grace and mercy at your most need help you.

GHOST [*beneath*]   Swear.   *They swear.* 180

HAMLET   Rest, rest, perturbéd spirit! So, gentlemen,
With all my love I do commend me to you,

---

5. old fellow   8. soldier who digs trenches
6. below   9. grotesque
7. here and èverywhere   1. folded

And what so poor a man as Hamlet is
May do t'express his love and friending[2] to you,
God willing, shall not lack. Let us go in together,   185
And still your fingers on your lips, I pray.
The time is out of joint. O cursèd spite
That ever I was born to set it right!
Nay, come, let's go together.   *Exeunt.*

Act 2

SCENE 1: *The dwelling of* POLONIUS. *Enter* POLONIUS
and REYNALDO.

POLONIUS   Give him this money and these notes, Reynaldo.
REYNALDO   I will, my lord.
POLONIUS   You shall do marvellous wisely, good Reynaldo,
Before you visit him, to make inquire[3]
Of his behavior.
REYNALDO   My lord, I did intend it.   5
POLONIUS   Marry, well said, very well said. Look you, sir.
Enquire me first what Danskers[4] are in Paris,
And how, and who, what means, and where they keep,[5]
What company, at what expense; and finding
By this encompassment[6] and drift of question   10
That they do know my son, come you more nearer
Than your particular demands[7] will touch it.
Take you as 'twere some distant knowledge of him,
As thus, "I know his father and his friends,
And in part him." Do you mark this, Reynaldo?   15
REYNALDO   Ay, very well, my lord.
POLONIUS   "And in part him, but," you may say, "not well,
But if't be he I mean, he's very wild,
Addicted so and so." And there put on him
What forgeries[8] you please; marry, none so rank[9]   20
As may dishonor him. Take heed of that.
But, sir, such wanton, wild, and usual slips
As are companions noted and most known
To youth and liberty.
REYNALDO   As gaming, my lord.
POLONIUS   Ay, or drinking, fencing, swearing, quarrelling,   25
Drabbing[1]—you may go so far.
REYNALDO   My lord, that would dishonor him.
POLONIUS   Faith, no, as you may season it in the charge.[2]
You must not put another scandal on him,

That he is open to incontinency.[3]   30
That's not my meaning. But breathe his faults so quaintly[4]
That they may seem the taints of liberty,[5]
The flash and outbreak of a fiery mind,
A savageness in unreclaiméd[6] blood,
Of general assault.[7]

REYNALDO   But, my good lord—   35
POLONIUS   Wherefore should you do this?
REYNALDO   Ay, my lord,
   I would know that.
POLONIUS   Marry, sir, here's my drift,
   And I believe it is a fetch of warrant.[8]
   You laying these slight sullies on my son,
   As 'twere a thing a little soiled i' th' working,   40
   Mark you,
   Your party in converse,[9] him you would sound,
   Having ever seen in the prenominate[1] crimes
   The youth you breathe[2] of guilty, be assured
   He closes with you in this consequence,   45
   "Good sir," or so, or "friend," or "gentleman,"
   According to the phrase or the addition
   Of man and country.
REYNALDO   Very good, my lord.
POLONIUS   And then, sir, does 'a this—'a does—What was I about to
   say?   50
   By the mass, I was about to say something.
   Where did I leave?
REYNALDO   At "closes in the consequence."
POLONIUS   At "closes in the consequence"—ay, marry,
   He closes thus: "I know the gentleman.   55
   I saw him yesterday, or th' other day,
   Or then, or then, with such, or such, and as you say,
   There was 'a gaming, there o'ertook in's rouse,
   There falling out at tennis," or perchance
   "I saw him enter such a house of sale,"   60
   Videlicet,[3] a brothel, or so forth.
   See you, now—
   Your bait of falsehood takes this carp of truth,
   And thus do we of wisdom and of reach,[4]
   With windlasses and with assays of bias,[5]   65
   By indirections find directions out;
   So by my former lecture and advice
   Shall you my son. You have me, have you not?
REYNALDO   My lord, I have.
POLONIUS   God b'wi' ye; fare ye well.
REYNALDO   Good my lord.   70

---

3. sexual excess	9. conversation
4. with delicacy	1. already named
5. faults of freedom	2. speak
6. untamed	3. namely
7. touching everyone	4. ability
8. permissible trick	5. indirect tests

POLONIUS   Observe his inclination in yourself.
REYNALDO   I shall, my lord.
POLONIUS   And let him ply⁶ his music.
REYNALDO   Well, my lord.
POLONIUS   Farewell.   *Exit* REYNALDO.

       Enter OPHELIA.
                        How now, Ophelia, what's the matter?
OPHELIA   O my lord, my lord, I have been so affrighted!   75
POLONIUS   With what, i' th' name of God?
OPHELIA   My lord, as I was sewing in my closet,⁷
   Lord Hamlet with his doublet⁸ all unbraced,⁹
   No hat upon his head, his stockings fouled,
   Ungartered and down-gyvéd¹ to his ankle,   80
   Pale as his shirt, his knees knocking each other,
   And with a look so piteous in purport
   As if he had been looséd out of hell
   To speak of horrors—he comes before me.
POLONIUS   Mad for thy love?
OPHELIA   My lord, I do not know,   85
   But truly I do fear it.
POLONIUS   What said he?
OPHELIA   He took me by the wrist, and held me hard,
   Then goes he to the length of all his arm,
   And with his other hand thus o'er his brow,
   He falls to such perusal of my face   90
   As 'a would draw it. Long stayed he so.
   At last, a little shaking of mine arm,
   And thrice his head thus waving up and down,
   He raised a sigh so piteous and profound
   As it did seem to shatter all his bulk,²   95
   And end his being. That done, he lets me go,
   And with his head over his shoulder turned
   He seemed to find his way without his eyes,
   For out adoors he went without their helps,
   And to the last bended³ their light on me.   100
POLONIUS   Come, go with me. I will go seek the king.
   This is the very ecstasy of love,
   Whose violent property⁴ fordoes⁵ itself,
   And leads the will to desperate undertakings
   As oft as any passion under heaven   105
   That does afflict our natures. I am sorry.
   What, have you given him any hard words of late?
OPHELIA   No, my good lord, but as you did command
   I did repel⁶ his letters, and denied
   His access to me.

---

6. practice   2. body
7. chamber   3. directed
8. jacket   4. character
9. unlaced   5. destroys
1. fallen down like fetters   6. refuse

POLONIUS   That hath made him mad. 110
  I am sorry that with better heed and judgment
  I had not quoted[7] him. I feared he did but trifle,
  And meant to wrack[8] thee; but beshrew my jealousy.
  By heaven, it is as proper to our age
  To cast beyond ourselves in our opinions 115
  As it is common for the younger sort
  To lack discretion. Come, go we to the king.
  This must be known, which being kept close, might move
  More grief to hide than hate to utter love.
  Come.   *Exeunt.* 120

SCENE 2: *A public room. Enter* KING, QUEEN, ROSENCRANTZ
and GUILDENSTERN.

KING   Welcome, dear Rosencrantz and Guildenstern.
  Moreover that[9] we much did long to see you,
  The need we have to use you did provoke
  Our hasty sending. Something have you heard
  Of Hamlet's transformation—so call it, 5
  Sith[1] nor th' exterior nor the inward man
  Resembles that it was. What it should be,
  More than his father's death, that thus hath put him
  So much from th' understanding of himself,
  I cannot deem of. I entreat you both 10
  That, being of so young days[2] brought up with him,
  And sith so neighbored[3] to his youth and havior,
  That you vouchsafe your rest here in our court
  Some little time, so by your companies
  To draw him on to pleasures, and to gather 15
  So much as from occasion you may glean,
  Whether aught to us unknown afflicts him thus,
  That opened lies within our remedy.
QUEEN   Good gentlemen, he hath much talked of you,
  And sure I am two men there are not living 20
  To whom he more adheres. If it will please you
  To show us so much gentry[4] and good will
  As to expend your time with us awhile
  For the supply and profit of our hope,
  Your visitation shall receive such thanks 25
  As fits a king's remembrance.
ROSENCRANTZ   Both your majesties
  Might, by the sovereign power you have of us,
  Put your dread pleasures more into command
  Than to entreaty.
GUILDENSTERN   But we both obey,
  And here give up ourselves in the full bent[5] 30

7. observed
8. harm
9. in addition to the fact that
1. since

2. from childhood
3. closely allied
4. courtesy
5. completely

To lay our service freely at your feet,
To be commanded.
KING   Thanks, Rosencrantz and gentle Guildenstern.
QUEEN   Thanks, Guildenstern and gentle Rosencrantz.
And I beseech you instantly to visit   35
My too much changed son. Go, some of you,
And bring these gentlemen where Hamlet is.
GUILDENSTERN   Heavens make our presence and our practices
Pleasant and helpful to him!
QUEEN   Ay, amen!

Exeunt ROSENCRANTZ *and* GUILDENSTERN.

Enter POLONIUS.

POLONIUS   Th' ambassadors from Norway, my good lord,   40
Are joyfully returned.
KING   Thou still[6] hast been the father of good news.
POLONIUS   Have I, my lord? I assure you, my good liege,
I hold my duty as I hold my soul,
Both to my God and to my gracious king;   45
And I do think—or else this brain of mine
Hunts not the trail of policy[7] so sure
As it hath used to do—that I have found
The very cause of Hamlet's lunacy.
KING   O, speak of that, that do I long to hear.   50
POLONIUS   Give first admittance to th' ambassadors.
My news shall be the fruit[8] to that great feast.
KING   Thyself do grace to them, and bring them in.

Exit POLONIUS.

He tells me, my dear Gertrude, he hath found
The head and source of all your son's distemper.   55
QUEEN   I doubt it is no other but the main,
His father's death and our o'erhasty marriage.
KING   Well, we shall sift[9] him.

Enter Ambassadors (VOLTEMAND *and* CORNELIUS) *with*
POLONIUS.
                                    Welcome, my good friends,
Say, Voltemand, what from our brother Norway?
VOLTEMAND   Most fair return of greetings and desires.   60
Upon our first,[1] he sent out to suppress
His nephew's levies, which to him appeared
To be a preparation 'gainst the Polack,
But better looked into, he truly found
It was against your highness, whereat grieved,   65
That so his sickness, age, and impotence
Was falsely borne in hand,[2] sends out arrests[3]

6. ever
7. statecraft
8. dessert
9. examine

1. i.e., first appearance
2. deceived
3. orders to stop

On Fortinbras, which he in brief obeys,
Receives rebuke from Norway, and in fine,
Makes vow before his uncle never more   70
To give th' assay[4] of arms against your majesty.
Whereon old Norway, overcome with joy,
Gives him threescore thousand crowns in annual fee,
And his commission to employ those soldiers,
So levied as before, against the Polack,   75
With an entreaty, herein further shown,   *Gives* CLAUDIUS *a paper.*
That it might please you to give quiet pass[5]
Through your dominions for this enterprise,
On such regards of safety and allowance
As therein are set down.
KING   It likes[6] us well,   80
And at our more considered time[7] we'll read,
Answer, and think upon this business.
Meantime we thank you for your well-took[8] labor.
Go to your rest; at night we'll feast together.
Most welcome home!   *Exeunt* AMBASSADORS.
POLONIUS   This business is well ended.   85
My liege and madam, to expostulate[9]
What majesty should be, what duty is,
Why day is day, night night, and time is time,
Were nothing but to waste night, day, and time.
Therefore, since brevity is the soul of wit,   90
And tediousness the limbs and outward flourishes,[1]
I will be brief. Your noble son is mad.
Mad call I it, for to define true madness,
What is't but to be nothing else but mad?
But let that go.
QUEEN   More matter with less art.   95
POLONIUS   Madam, I swear I use no art at all.
That he is mad, 'tis true: 'tis true 'tis pity,
And pity 'tis 'tis true. A foolish figure,
But farewell it, for I will use no art.
Mad let us grant him, then, and now remains   100
That we find out the cause of this effect,
Or rather say the cause of this defect,
For this effect defective comes by cause.
Thus it remains, and the remainder thus.
Perpend.[2]   105
I have a daughter—have while she is mine—
Who in her duty and obedience, mark,
Hath given me this. Now gather, and surmise.
    "To the celestial, and my soul's idol, the most beautified
Ophelia."—That's an ill phrase, a vile phrase, "beautified" is a   110

4. trial   8. successful
5. safe conduct   9. discuss
6. pleases   1. adornments
7. time for more consideration   2. consider

vile phrase. But you shall hear. Thus:
"In her excellent white bosom, these, etc."
QUEEN   Came this from Hamlet to her?
POLONIUS   Good madam, stay awhile. I will be faithful.

"Doubt thou the stars are fire,   115
    Doubt that the sun doth move;
Doubt truth to be a liar;
    But never doubt I love.

O dear Ophelia, I am ill at these numbers.[3]
I have not art to reckon my groans, but that I love thee best, O   120
most best, believe it. Adieu.
                    Thine evermore, most dear lady, whilst
                        this machine[4] is to him, HAMLET."
This in obedience hath my daughter shown me,
And more above, hath his solicitings,   125
As they fell out by time, by means, and place,
All given to mine ear.
KING   But how hath she
Received his love?
POLONIUS   What do you think of me?
KING   As of a man faithful and honorable.
POLONIUS   I would fain prove so. But what might you think,   130
When I had seen this hot love on the wing,
(As I perceived it, I must tell you that,
Before my daughter told me), what might you,
Or my dear majesty your queen here, think,
If I had played the desk or table-book,   135
Or given my heart a winking, mute and dumb,
Or looked upon this love with idle sight,[5]
What might you think? No, I went round[6] to work,
And my young mistress thus I did bespeak:
"Lord Hamlet is a prince out of thy star.[7]   140
This must not be." And then I prescripts[8] gave her,
That she should lock herself from his resort,
Admit no messengers, receive no tokens.
Which done, she took[9] the fruits of my advice;
And he repelled, a short tale to make,   145
Fell into a sadness, then into a fast,
Thence to a watch, thence into a weakness,
Thence to a lightness, and by this declension,
Into the madness wherein now he raves,
And all we mourn for.
KING   Do you think 'tis this?   150
QUEEN   It may be, very like.

---

3. verses
4. body
5. Polonius means that he would have been at fault if, having seen Hamlet's attention to Ophelia, he had winked at it or not paid attention, an "idle sight," and if he had remained silent and kept the information to himself, as if it were written in a "desk" or "table-book."
6. directly
7. beyond your sphere
8. orders
9. followed

POLONIUS   Hath there been such a time—I would fain know that—
That I have positively said "Tis so,"
When it proved otherwise?

KING   Not that I know.

POLONIUS [*pointing to his head and shoulder*]   Take this from this, if
this be otherwise.   155
If circumstances lead me, I will find
Where truth is hid, though it were hid indeed
Within the centre.¹

KING   How may we try it further?

POLONIUS   You know sometimes he walks four hours together
Here in the lobby.

QUEEN   So he does, indeed.   160

POLONIUS   At such a time I'll loose² my daughter to him.
Be you and I behind an arras³ then.
Mark the encounter. If he love her not,
And be not from his reason fall'n thereon,
Let me be no assistant for a state,   165
But keep a farm and carters.

KING   We will try it.

Enter HAMLET *reading a book.*

QUEEN   But look where sadly the poor wretch comes reading.

POLONIUS   Away, I do beseech you both away,
I'll board⁴ him presently.

                                        Exeunt KING *and* QUEEN.

                              O, give me leave.
How does my good Lord Hamlet?   170

HAMLET   Well, God-a-mercy.

POLONIUS   Do you know me, my lord?

HAMLET   Excellent well, you are a fishmonger.

POLONIUS   Not I, my lord.

HAMLET   Then I would you were so honest a man.   175

POLONIUS   Honest, my lord?

HAMLET   Ay, sir, to be honest as this world goes, is to be one man
picked out of ten thousand.

POLONIUS   That's very true, my lord.

HAMLET   For if the sun breed maggots in a dead dog, being a god   180
kissing carrion⁵—Have you a daughter?

POLONIUS   I have, my lord.

HAMLET   Let her not walk i' th' sun. Conception is a blessing, but as
your daughter may conceive—friend, look to't.

POLONIUS   How say you by that? [*Aside.*] Still harping on my daughter. 185
Yet he knew me not at first. 'A said I was a fishmonger. 'A is far
gone. And truly in my youth I suffered much extremity for love.
Very near this. I'll speak to him again.—What do you read, my lord?

1. of the earth
2. let loose
3. tapestry
4. accost

5. A reference to the belief of the period
that maggots were produced spontaneously
by the action of sunshine on carrion.

HAMLET   Words, words, words.

POLONIUS   What is the matter, my lord?   190

HAMLET   Between who?

POLONIUS   I mean the matter that you read, my lord.

HAMLET   Slanders, sir; for the satirical rogue says here that old men
have grey beards, that their faces are wrinkled, their eyes purging
thick amber and plum-tree gum, and that they have a plentiful lack 195
of wit, together with most weak hams[6]—all which, sir, though I
most powerfully and potently believe, yet I hold it not honesty to
have it thus set down, for yourself, sir, shall grow old as I am, if like
a crab you could go backward.

POLONIUS [*aside*]   Though this be madness, yet there is method in't. 200
—Will you walk out of the air, my lord?

HAMLET   Into my grave?

POLONIUS [*aside*]   Indeed, that's out of the air. How pregnant sometime his replies are! a happiness that often madness hits on, which
reason and sanity could not so prosperously be delivered of. I will 205
leave him, and suddenly contrive the means of meeting between
him and my daughter.—My lord. I will take my leave of you.

HAMLET   You cannot take from me anything that I will more willingly
part withal—except my life, except my life, except my life.

Enter GUILDENSTERN *and* ROSENCRANTZ.

POLONIUS   Fare you well, my lord.   210

HAMLET   These tedious old fools!

POLONIUS   You go to seek the Lord Hamlet. There he is.

ROSENCRANTZ [*to* POLONIUS]   God save you, sir!   *Exit* POLONIUS.

GUILDENSTERN   My honored lord!

ROSENCRANTZ   My most dear lord!   215

HAMLET   My excellent good friends! How dost thou, Guildenstern?
Ah, Rosencrantz! Good lads, how do you both?

ROSENCRANTZ   As the indifferent[7] children of the earth.

GUILDENSTERN   Happy in that we are not over-happy;
On Fortune's cap we are not the very button.[8]   220

HAMLET   Nor the soles of her shoe?

ROSENCRANTZ   Neither, my lord.

HAMLET   Then you live about her waist, or in the middle of her favors.

GUILDENSTERN   Faith, her privates we.

HAMLET   In the secret parts of Fortune? O, most true, she is a 225
strumpet.[9] What news?

ROSENCRANTZ   None, my lord, but that the world's grown honest.

HAMLET   Then is doomsday near. But your news is not true. Let me
question more in particular. What have you, my good friends, deserved at the hands of Fortune, that she sends you to prison hither? 230

GUILDENSTERN   Prison, my lord?

HAMLET   Denmark's a prison.

---

6. limbs
7. ordinary
8. i.e., on top
9. Hamlet is indulging in characteristic
ribaldry. Guildenstern means that they are

"privates" = ordinary citizens, but Hamlet
takes him to mean "privates" = sexual organs and "middle of her favors" = waist =
sexual organs.

ROSENCRANTZ   Then is the world one.

HAMLET   A goodly one, in which there are many confines, wards,[1] and dungeons, Denmark being one o' th' worst.   235

ROSENCRANTZ   We think not so, my lord.

HAMLET   Why then 'tis none to you; for there is nothing either good or bad, but thinking makes it so. To me it is a prison.

ROSENCRANTZ   Why then your ambition makes it one. 'Tis too narrow for your mind.   240

HAMLET   O God, I could be bounded in a nutshell and count myself a king of infinite space, were it not that I have bad dreams.

GUILDENSTERN   Which dreams indeed are ambition; for the very substance of the ambitious is merely the shadow of a dream.

HAMLET   A dream itself is but a shadow.   245

ROSENCRANTZ   Truly, and I hold ambition of so airy and light a quality that it is but a shadow's shadow.

HAMLET   Then are our beggars bodies, and our monarchs and outstretched heroes the beggars' shadows. Shall we to th' court? for, by my fay,[2] I cannot reason.   250

BOTH   We'll wait upon you.

HAMLET   No such matter. I will not sort[3] you with the rest of my servants; for to speak to you like an honest man, I am most dreadfully attended. But in the beaten way of friendship, what make you at Elsinore?   255

ROSENCRANTZ   To visit you, my lord; no other occasion.

HAMLET   Beggar that I am, I am even poor in thanks, but I thank you; and sure, dear friends, my thanks are too dear a halfpenny.[4] Were you not sent for? Is it your own inclining? Is it a free visitation? Come, come, deal justly with me. Come, come, nay speak.   260

GUILDENSTERN   What should we say, my lord?

HAMLET   Why anything but to th' purpose. You were sent for, and there is a kind of confession in your looks, which your modesties have not craft enough to color. I know the good king and queen have sent for you.   265

ROSENCRANTZ   To what end, my lord?

HAMLET   That you must teach me. But let me conjure you by the rights of our fellowship, by the consonancy of our youth, by the obligation of our ever-preserved love, and by what more dear a better proposer can charge you withal, be even and direct[5] with me   270
whether you were sent for or no.

ROSENCRANTZ [*aside to* GUILDENSTERN]   What say you?

HAMLET [*aside*]   Nay, then, I have an eye of you.—If you love me, hold not off.

GUILDENSTERN   My lord, we were sent for.   275

HAMLET   I will tell you why; so shall my anticipation prevent your discovery,[6] and your secrecy to the king and queen moult no feather. I have of late—but wherefore I know not—lost all my mirth, forgone all custom of exercises; and indeed it goes so heavily with my disposition, that this goodly frame the earth seems to me   280

1. cells   4. not worth a halfpenny
2. faith   5. straightforward
3. include   6. disclosure

a sterile promontory, this most excellent canopy the air, look you, this brave o'er-hanging firmament, this majestical roof fretted[7] with golden fire, why it appeareth nothing to me but a foul and pestilent congregation of vapors. What a piece of work is a man, how noble in reason, how infinite in faculties, in form and moving, how express[8] 285 and admirable in action, how like an angel in apprehension, how like a god: the beauty of the world, the paragon of animals. And yet to me, what is this quintessence of dust? Man delights not me, nor woman neither, though by your smiling you seem to say so.

ROSENCRANTZ   My lord, there was no such stuff in my thoughts.   290

HAMLET   Why did ye laugh, then, when I said "Man delights not me"?

ROSENCRANTZ   To think, my lord, if you delight not in man, what lenten[9] entertainment the players shall receive from you. We coted[1] them on the way, and hither are they coming to offer you service.

HAMLET   He that plays the king shall be welcome—his majesty shall 295 have tribute on me; the adventurous knight shall use his foil and target[2]; the lover shall not sigh gratis; the humorous[3] man shall end his part in peace; the clown shall make those laugh whose lungs are tickle o' th' sere[4]; and the lady shall say her mind freely, or the blank verse shall halt for't. What players are they?   300

ROSENCRANTZ   Even those you were wont to take such delight in, the tragedians of the city.

HAMLET   How chances it they travel? Their residence, both in reputation and profit, was better both ways.

ROSENCRANTZ   I think their inhibition comes by the means of the late 305 innovation.

HAMLET   Do they hold the same estimation they did when I was in the city? Are they so followed?

ROSENCRANTZ   No, indeed, are they not.

HAMLET   How comes it? Do they grow rusty?   310

ROSENCRANTZ   Nay, their endeavor keeps in the wonted pace; but there is, sir, an eyrie of children, little eyases,[5] that cry out on the top of question,[6] and are most tyrannically clapped for't. These are now the fashion, and so berattle the common stages (so they call them) that many wearing rapiers are afraid of goose quills[7] and 315 dare scarce come thither.[8]

HAMLET   What, are they children? Who maintains 'em? How are they escoted[9]? Will they pursue the quality no longer than they can sing? Will they not say afterwards, if they should grow themselves to common players (as it is most like, if their means are no better), 320 their writers do them wrong to make them exclaim against their own succession[1]?

7. ornamented with fretwork
8. well built
9. scanty
1. passed
2. sword and shield
3. eccentric
4. easily set off
5. little hawks
6. with a loud, high delivery
7. pens of satirical writers
8. The passage refers to the emergence

at the time of the play of theatrical companies made up of children from London choir schools. Their performances became fashionable and hurt the business of the established companies. Hamlet says that if they continue to act, "pursue the quality," when they are grown, they will find that they have been damaging their own future careers.

9. supported
1. future careers

ROSENCRANTZ Faith, there has been much to do on both sides; and
the nation holds it no sin to tarre[2] them to controversy. There was
for a while no money bid for argument,[3] unless the poet and the 325
player went to cuffs[4] in the question.

HAMLET Is't possible?

GUILDENSTERN O, there has been much throwing about of brains.

HAMLET Do the boys carry it away?

ROSENCRANTZ Ay, that they do, my lord, Hercules and his load too.[5] 330

HAMLET It is not very strange, for my uncle is King of Denmark, and
those that would make mouths[6] at him while my father lived give
twenty, forty, fifty, a hundred ducats apiece for his picture in little.[7]
'Sblood, there is something in this more than natural, if philosophy
could find it out.   *A flourish.* 335

GUILDENSTERN There are the players.

HAMLET Gentlemen, you are welcome to Elsinore. Your hands. Come
then, th' appurtenance of welcome is fashion and ceremony. Let me
comply with[8] you in this garb, lest my extent[9] to the players, which
I tell you must show fairly outwards, should more appear like enter- 340
tainment[1] than yours. You are welcome. But my uncle-father and
aunt-mother are deceived.

GUILDENSTERN In what, my dear lord?

HAMLET I am but mad north-north-west; when the wind is southerly
I know a hawk from a handsaw.[2]   345

Enter POLONIUS.

POLONIUS Well be with you, gentlemen.

HAMLET Hark you, Guildenstern—and you too—at each ear a hearer.
That great baby you see there is not yet out of his swaddling clouts.[3]

ROSENCRANTZ Happily he is the second time come to them, for they
say an old man is twice a child.   350

HAMLET I will prophesy he comes to tell me of the players. Mark it.
—You say right, sir, a Monday morning, 'twas then indeed.

POLONIUS My lord, I have news to tell you.

HAMLET My lord, I have news to tell you.
When Roscius was an actor in Rome—[4]   355

POLONIUS The actors are come hither, my lord.

HAMLET Buzz, buzz.

POLONIUS Upon my honor—

HAMLET Then came each actor on his ass—

POLONIUS The best actors in the world, either for tragedy, comedy, 360
history, pastoral, pastoral-comical, historical-pastoral, tragical-
historical, tragical-comical-historical-pastoral, scene individable, or

2. urge
3. paid for a play plot
4. blows
5. During one of his labors Hercules assumed for a time the burden of the Titan
Atlas, who supported the heavens on his
shoulder. Also a reference to the effect on
business at Shakespeare's theater, the
Globe.
6. sneer

7. miniature
8. welcome
9. fashion
1. cordiality
2. A "hawk" is a plasterer's tool; Hamlet may also be using "handsaw" = hern-
shaw = heron.
3. wrappings for an infant
4. Roscius was the most famous actor of
classical Rome.

poem unlimited. Seneca cannot be too heavy nor Plautus too light.
For the law of writ and the liberty, these are the only men.[5]

HAMLET   O Jephtha, judge of Israel, what a treasure hadst thou![6] 365
POLONIUS   What a treasure had he, my lord?
HAMLET   Why—

> "One fair daughter, and no more,
> The which he loved passing well."

POLONIUS [*aside*]   Still on my daughter.   370
HAMLET   Am I not i' th' right, old Jephtha?
POLONIUS   If you call me Jephtha, my lord, I have a daughter that I
love passing well.
HAMLET   Nay, that follows not.
POLONIUS   What follows then, my lord?   375
HAMLET   Why—

> "As by lot, God wot"

and then, you know,

> "It came to pass, as most like it was."

The first row[7] of the pious chanson[8] will show you more, for look 380
where my abridgement[9] comes.

Enter the PLAYERS.

You are welcome, masters; welcome, all.—I am glad to see thee
well.—Welcome, good friends.—O, old friend! Why thy face is
valanced[1] since I saw thee last. Com'st thou to beard me in Denmark?—What, my young lady and mistress? By'r lady, your ladyship 385
is nearer to heaven than when I saw you last by the altitude of a
chopine.[2] Pray God your voice, like a piece of uncurrent gold, be not
cracked within the ring.—Masters, you are all welcome. We'll e'en
to't like French falconers, fly at anything we see. We'll have a speech
straight. Come give us a taste of your quality,[3] come a passionate 390
speech.
FIRST PLAYER   What speech, my good lord?
HAMLET   I heard thee speak me a speech once, but it was never acted,
or if it was, not above once, for the play, I remember, pleased not
the million; 'twas caviary[4] to the general.[5] But it was—as I received 395

5. Seneca and Plautus were Roman writers of tragedy and comedy, respectively.
The "law of writ" refers to plays written
according to such rules as the three unities;
the "liberty" to those written otherwise.
6. To insure victory, Jephtha promised
to sacrifice the first creature to meet him
on his return. Unfortunately, his only
daughter outstripped his dog and was the
victim of his vow. The Biblical story is told
in *Judges* 11.
7. stanza
8. song
9. that which cuts short by interrupting

1. fringed (with a beard)
2. A reference to the contemporary theatrical practice of using boys to play
women's parts. The company's "lady" has
grown in height by the size of a woman's
thick-soled shoe, "chopine," since Hamlet
saw him last. The next sentence refers to
the possibility, suggested by his growth,
that the young actor's voice may soon begin to change.
3. trade
4. caviar
5. masses

it, and others whose judgments in such matters cried in the top of[6] mine—an excellent play, well digested[7] in the scenes, set down with as much modesty as cunning. I remember one said there were no sallets[8] in the lines to make the matter savory, nor no matter in the phrase that might indict the author of affectation, but called it an honest method, as wholesome as sweet, and by very much more handsome than fine. One speech in't I chiefly loved. 'Twas Æneas' tale to Dido, and thereabout of it especially where he speaks of Priam's slaughter.[9] If it live in your memory, begin at this line—let me see, let me see:

"The rugged Pyrrhus, like th' Hyrcanian beast"[1]—

'tis not so; it begins with Pyrrhus—

"The rugged Pyrrhus, he whose sable arms,
Black as his purpose, did the night resemble
When he lay couchéd in th' ominous horse,[2]
Hath now this dread and black complexion smeared
With heraldry more dismal; head to foot
Now is he total gules,[3] horridly tricked[4]
With blood of fathers, mothers, daughters, sons,
Baked and impasted[5] with the parching[6] streets,
That lend a tyrannous and a damnéd light
To their lord's murder. Roasted in wrath and fire,
And thus o'er-sizéd[7] with coagulate[8] gore,
With eyes like carbuncles, the hellish Pyrrhus
Old grandsire Priam seeks."

So proceed you.

POLONIUS   Fore God, my lord, well spoken, with good accent and good discretion.

FIRST PLAYER   "Anon he[9] finds him[1]
Striking too short at Greeks. His antique[2] sword,
Rebellious[3] to his arm, lies where it falls,
Repugnant to command. Unequal matched,
Pyrrhus at Priam drives, in rage strikes wide.
But with the whiff and wind of his fell sword
Th' unnervéd father falls. Then senseless[4] Ilium,
Seeming to feel this blow, with flaming top
Stoops[5] to his base, and with a hideous crash

6. were weightier than
7. arranged
8. spicy passages
9. Aeneas, fleeing with his band from fallen Troy (Ilium), arrives in Carthage, where he tells Dido, the Queen of Carthage, of the fall of Troy. Here he is describing the death of Priam, the aged king of Troy, at the hands of Pyrrhus, the son of the slain Achilles.
1. tiger
2. i.e., the Trojan horse

3. completely red
4. adorned
5. crusted
6. burning
7. glued over
8. clotted,
9. Pyrrhus
1. Priam
2. which he used when young
3. refractory
4. without feeling
5. falls

Takes prisoner Pyrrhus' ear. For, lo! his sword,
Which was declining[6] on the milky head
Of reverend Priam, seemed i' th' air to stick.   435
So as a painted tyrant Pyrrhus stood,
And like a neutral to his will and matter,[7]
Did nothing.
But as we often see, against some storm,
A silence in the heavens, the rack[8] stand still,   440
The bold winds speechless, and the orb below
As hush as death, anon the dreadful thunder
Doth rend the region; so, after Pyrrhus' pause,
A roused vengeance sets him new awork,[9]
And never did the Cyclops' hammers fall   445
On Mars's armor, forged for proof eterne,[1]
With less remorse than Pyrrhus' bleeding sword
Now falls on Priam.
Out, out, thou strumpet, Fortune! All you gods,
In general synod take away her power,   450
Break all the spokes and fellies[2] from her wheel,
And bowl[3] the round nave[4] down the hill of heaven
As low as to the fiends."
POLONIUS   This is too long.
HAMLET   It shall to the barber's with your beard.—Prithee say on. 455
He's for a jig,[5] or a tale of bawdry, or he sleeps. Say on; come to
Hecuba.[6]
FIRST PLAYER   "But who, ah woe! had seen the mobled[7] queen—"
HAMLET   "The mobled queen"?
POLONIUS   That's good. "Mobled queen" is good.   460
FIRST PLAYER   "Run barefoot up and down, threat'ning the flames
With bisson rheum,[8] a clout[9] upon that head
Where late the diadem stood, and for a robe,
About her lank and all o'er-teeméd loins,
A blanket, in the alarm of fear caught up—   465
Who this had seen, with tongue in venom steeped,
'Gainst Fortune's state[1] would treason have pronounced.
But if the gods themselves did see her then,
When she saw Pyrrhus make malicious sport
In mincing[2] with his sword her husband's limbs,   470
The instant burst of clamor that she made,
Unless things mortal move them not at all,
Would have made milch[3] the burning eyes of heaven,
And passion in the gods."

6. about to fall
7. between his will and the fulfillment
of it
8. clouds
9. to work
1. Mars, as befits a Roman war god, had
armor made for him by the blacksmith god
Vulcan and his assistants, the Cyclops. It
was suitably impenetrable, of "proof
eterne."
2. parts of the rim
3. roll
4. hub

5. a comic act
6. Hecuba was the wife of Priam and
Queen of Troy. Her "loins" are described
below as "o'erteemed" because of her unusual fertility. The number of her children
varies in different accounts. but twenty is
a safe minimum.
7. muffled (in a hood)
8. blinding tears
9. cloth
1. government
2. cutting up
3. tearful (*lit.* milk-giving)

POLONIUS   Look whe'r[4] he has not turned his color, and has tears in's 475
eyes. Prithee no more.

HAMLET   'Tis well. I'll have thee speak out the rest of this soon.—
Good my lord, will you see the players well bestowed?[5] Do you
hear, let them be well used, for they are the abstract[6] and brief
chronicles of the time; after your death you were better have a bad 480
epitaph than their ill report while you live.

POLONIUS   My lord, I will use them according to their desert.

HAMLET   God's bodkin, man, much better. Use every man after his
desert, and who shall 'scape whipping? Use them after your own
honor and dignity. The less they deserve, the more merit is in your 485
bounty. Take them in.

POLONIUS   Come, sirs.

HAMLET   Follow him, friends. We'll hear a play tomorrow. [*Aside to*
FIRST PLAYER.] Dost thou hear me, old friend, can you play "The
Murder of Gonzago"?   490

FIRST PLAYER   Ay, my lord.

HAMLET   We'll ha't tomorrow night. You could for a need study a
speech of some dozen or sixteen lines which I would set down and
insert in't, could you not?

FIRST PLAYER   Ay, my lord.   495

HAMLET   Very well. Follow that lord, and look you mock him not.

Exeunt POLONIUS *and* PLAYERS.

My good friends, I'll leave you till night. You are welcome to
Elsinore.

ROSENCRANTZ   Good my lord.

Exeunt ROSENCRANTZ *and* GUILDENSTERN.

HAMLET   Ay, so God b'wi'ye. Now I am alone.   500
O, what a rogue and peasant slave am I!
Is it not monstrous that this player here,
But in a fiction, in a dream of passion,
Could force his soul so to his own conceit[7]
That from her working all his visage wanned;[8]   505
Tears in his eyes, distraction in his aspect,[9]
A broken voice, and his whole function suiting
With forms to his conceit? And all for nothing,
For Hecuba!
What's Hecuba to him or he to Hecuba,   510
That he should weep for her? What would he do
Had he the motive and the cue for passion
That I have? He would drown the stage with tears,
And cleave the general ear with horrid speech,
Make mad the guilty, and appal the free,   515
Confound the ignorant, and amaze indeed
The very faculties of eyes and ears.
Yet I,

4. whether   7. imagination
5. provided for   8. grew pale
6. summary   9. face

A dull and muddy-mettled[1] rascal, peak[2]
Like John-a-dreams,[3] unpregnant[4] of my cause,
And can say nothing; no, not for a king
Upon whose property and most dear life
A damned defeat was made. Am I a coward?
Who calls me villain, breaks my pate across,
Plucks off my beard and blows it in my face,
Tweaks me by the nose, gives me the lie i' th' throat
As deep as to the lungs? Who does me this?
Ha, 'swounds, I should take it; for it cannot be
But I am pigeon-livered and lack gall[5]
To make oppression bitter, or ere this
I should 'a fatted all the region kites[6]
With this slave's offal. Bloody, bawdy villain!
Remorseless, treacherous, lecherous, kindless[7] villain!
Why, what an ass am I! This is most brave,
That I, the son of a dear father murdered,
Prompted to my revenge by heaven and hell,
Must like a whore unpack[8] my heart with words,
And fall a-cursing like a very drab,
A scullion![9] Fie upon't! foh!
About, my brains. Hum—I have heard
That guilty creatures sitting at a play,
Have by the very cunning of the scene
Been struck so to the soul that presently
They have proclaimed[1] their malefactions;
For murder, though it have no tongue, will speak
With most miraculous organ. I'll have these players
Play something like the murder of my father
Before mine uncle. I'll observe his looks.
I'll tent[2] him to the quick. If 'a do blench,[3]
I know my course. The spirit that I have seen
May be a devil, and the devil hath power
T' assume a pleasing shape, yea, and perhaps
Out of my weakness and my melancholy,
As he is very potent with such spirits,
Abuses me to damn me. I'll have grounds
More relative[4] than this. The play's the thing
Wherein I'll catch the conscience of the king.   *Exit.*

520

525

530

535

540

545

550

555

---

1. dull-spirited
2. mope
3. a man dreaming
4. not quickened by
5. bitterness
6. birds of prey of the area
7. unnatural
8. relieve

9. In some versions of the play, the word "stallion," a slang term for a prostitute, appears in place of "scullion."
1. admitted
2. try
3. turn pale
4. conclusive

Act 3

SCENE 1: *A room in the castle. Enter* KING, QUEEN, POLONIUS, OPHELIA, ROSENCRANTZ *and* GUILDENSTERN.

KING   And can you by no drift of conference[5]
Get from him why he puts on this confusion,
Grating so harshly all his days of quiet
With turbulent[6] and dangerous lunacy?
ROSENCRANTZ   He does confess he feels himself distracted,   5
But from what cause 'a will by no means speak.
GUILDENSTERN   Nor do we find him forward[7] to be sounded,[8]
But with a crafty madness keeps aloof
When we would bring him on to some confession
Of his true state.
QUEEN   Did he receive you well?   10
ROSENCRANTZ   Most like a gentleman.
GUILDENSTERN   But with much forcing of his disposition.[9]
ROSENCRANTZ   Niggard of question, but of our demands[1]
Most free in his reply.
QUEEN   Did you assay[2] him
To any pastime?   15
ROSENCRANTZ   Madam, it so fell out that certain players
We o'er-raught[3] on the way. Of these we told him,
And there did seem in him a kind of joy
To hear of it. They are here about the court,
And as I think, they have already order   20
This night to play before him.
POLONIUS   'Tis most true,
And he beseeched me to entreat your majesties
To hear and see the matter.[4]
KING   With all my heart, and it doth much content me
To hear him so inclined.   25
Good gentlemen, give him a further edge,
And drive his purpose[5] into these delights.
ROSENCRANTZ   We shall, my lord.

Exeunt ROSENCRANTZ *and* GUILDENSTERN.

KING   Sweet Gertrude, leave us too,
For we have closely sent for Hamlet hither,
That he, as 'twere by accident, may here   30
Affront[6] Ophelia.
Her father and myself (lawful espials[7])
Will so bestow ourselves that, seeing unseen,
We may of their encounter frankly judge,

---

5. line of conversation
6. disturbing
7. eager
8. questioned
9. conversation
1. to our questions

2. tempt
3. passed
4. performance
5. sharpen his intention
6. confront
7. justified spies

And gather by him, as he is behaved,   35
If't be th' affliction of his love or no
That thus he suffers for.

QUEEN   I shall obey you.—
And for your part, Ophelia, I do wish
That your good beauties be the happy cause
Of Hamlet's wildness. So shall I hope your virtues   40
Will bring him to his wonted[8] way again,
To both your honors.

OPHELIA   Madam, I wish it may.   *Exit* QUEEN.

POLONIUS   Ophelia, walk you here.—Gracious,[9] so please you,
We will bestow ourselves.—[*To* OPHELIA.] Read on this book,
That show of such an exercise[1] may color[2]   45
Your loneliness.—We are oft to blame in this,
'Tis too much proved, that with devotion's visage
And pious action we do sugar o'er
The devil himself.

KING [*aside*]   O, 'tis too true.
How smart a lash that speech doth give my conscience!   50
The harlot's cheek, beautied with plast'ring[3] art,
Is not more ugly to the thing that helps it
Than is my deed to my most painted word.
O heavy burden!

POLONIUS   I hear him coming. Let's withdraw, my lord.   55

Exeunt KING *and* POLONIUS.

Enter HAMLET.

HAMLET   To be, or not to be, that is the question:
Whether 'tis nobler in the mind to suffer
The slings and arrows of outrageous fortune,
Or to take arms against a sea of troubles,
And by opposing end them. To die, to sleep—   60
No more; and by a sleep to say we end
The heartache, and the thousand natural shocks
That flesh is heir to. 'Tis a consummation
Devoutly to be wished—to die, to sleep—
To sleep, perchance to dream, ay there's the rub;   65
For in that sleep of death what dreams may come
When we have shuffled off this mortal coil[4]
Must give us pause—there's the respect[5]
That makes calamity of so long life.
For who would bear the whips and scorns of time,   70
Th' oppressor's wrong, the proud man's contumely,[6]
The pangs of despised love, the law's delay,
The insolence of office, and the spurns[7]
That patient merit of th' unworthy takes,

8. usual   3. thickly painted
9. Majesty   4. turmoil
1. act of devotion   5. consideration
2. explain   6. insulting behavior
                                   7. rejections

When he himself might his quietus[8] make   75
With a bare bodkin?[9] Who would fardels[1] bear,
To grunt and sweat under a weary life,
But that the dread of something after death,
The undiscovered country, from whose bourn[2]
No traveller returns, puzzles the will,   80
And makes us rather bear those ills we have
Than fly to others that we know not of?
Thus conscience does make cowards of us all;
And thus the native[3] hue of resolution
Is sicklied o'er with the pale cast of thought,   85
And enterprises of great pitch[4] and moment[5]
With this regard their currents turn awry
And lose the name of action.—Soft you now,
The fair Ophelia.—Nymph, in thy orisons[6]
Be all my sins remembered.

OPHELIA   Good my lord,   90
How does your honor for this many a day?

HAMLET   I humbly thank you, well, well, well.

OPHELIA   My lord, I have remembrances of yours
That I have longed long to re-deliver.
I pray you now receive them.

HAMLET   No, not I,   95
I never gave you aught.

OPHELIA   My honored lord, you know right well you did,
And with them words of so sweet breath composed
As made the things more rich. Their perfume lost,
Take these again, for to the noble mind   100
Rich gifts wax[7] poor when givers prove unkind.
There, my lord.

HAMLET   Ha, ha! are you honest?[8]

OPHELIA   My lord?

HAMLET   Are you fair?   105

OPHELIA   What means your lordship?

HAMLET   That if you be honest and fair, your honesty should admit
no discourse to your beauty.

OPHELIA   Could beauty, my lord, have better commerce[9] than with
honesty?   110

HAMLET   Ay, truly, for the power of beauty will sooner transform
honesty from what it is to a bawd than the force of honesty can
translate beauty into his likeness. This was sometime a paradox, but
now the time gives it proof. I did love you once.

OPHELIA   Indeed, my lord, you made me believe so.   115

HAMLET   You should not have believed me, for virtue cannot so in-
oculate[1] our old stock but we shall relish of it. I loved you not.

OPHELIA   I was the more deceived.

---

8. settlement
9. dagger
1. burdens
2. boundary
3. natural
4. height

5. importance
6. prayers
7. become
8. chaste
9. intercourse
1. change by grafting

HAMLET   Get thee to a nunnery.[2] Why wouldst thou be a breeder of
sinners? I am myself indifferent[3] honest, but yet I could accuse me   120
of such things that it were better my mother had not borne me: I
am very proud, revengeful, ambitious, with more offences at my
beck[4] than I have thoughts to put them in, imagination to give them
shape, or time to act them in. What should such fellows as I do
crawling between earth and heaven? We are arrant[5] knaves all; be-   125
lieve none of us. Go thy ways to a nunnery. Where's your father?
OPHELIA   At home, my lord.
HAMLET   Let the doors be shut upon him, that he may play the fool
nowhere but in's own house. Farewell.
OPHELIA   O, help him, you sweet heavens!   130
HAMLET   If thou dost marry, I'll give thee this plague for thy dowry:
be thou as chaste as ice, as pure as snow, thou shalt not escape
calumny. Get thee to a nunnery, farewell. Or if thou wilt needs
marry, marry a fool, for wise men know well enough what monsters[6]
you make of them. To a nunnery, go, and quickly too. Farewell.   135
OPHELIA   Heavenly powers, restore him!
HAMLET   I have heard of your paintings well enough. God hath given
you one face, and you make yourselves another. You jig, you amble,
and you lisp;[7] you nickname God's creatures, and make your wantonness your ignorance.[8] Go to, I'll no more on't, it hath made me mad.   140
I say we will have no more marriage. Those that are married already,
all but one, shall live. The rest shall keep as they are. To a nunnery,
go.   *Exit.*
OPHELIA   O, what a noble mind is here o'erthrown!
The courtier's, soldier's, scholar's, eye, tongue, sword,   145
Th' expectancy[9] and rose[1] of the fair state,
The glass[2] of fashion and the mould[3] of form,
Th' observed of all observers, quite quite down!
And I of ladies most deject and wretched,
That sucked the honey of his music[4] vows,   150
Now see that noble and most sovereign reason
Like sweet bells jangled, out of time and harsh;
That unmatched form and feature of blown[5] youth
Blasted with ecstasy. O, woe is me
T' have seen what I have seen, see what I see!   155

Enter KING *and* POLONIUS.

KING   Love! His affections do not that way tend,
Nor what he spake, though it lacked form a little,
Was not like madness. There's something in his soul
O'er which his melancholy sits on brood,[6]

2. With typical ribaldry Hamlet uses "nunnery" in two senses, the second as a slang term for brothel.
3. moderately
4. command
5. thorough
6. horned because cuckolded
7. walk and talk affectedly
8. Hamlet means that women call things by pet names and then blame the affectation on ignorance.
9. hope
1. ornament
2. mirror
3. model
4. musical
5. full-blown
6. i.e., like a hen

And I do doubt[7] the hatch and the disclose[8]   160
Will be some danger; which to prevent,
I have in quick determination
Thus set it down: he shall with speed to England
For the demand of our neglected tribute.
Haply the seas and countries different,   165
With variable objects, shall expel
This something-settled matter in his heart
Whereon his brains still beating puts him thus
From fashion of himself. What think you on't?
POLONIUS   It shall do well. But yet do I believe   170
The origin and commencement of his grief
Sprung from neglected love.—How now, Ophelia?
You need not tell us what Lord Hamlet said,
We heard it all.—My lord, do as you please,
But if you hold it fit, after the play   175
Let his queen-mother all alone entreat him
To show his grief. Let her be round[9] with him,
And I'll be placed, so please you, in the ear[1]
Of all their conference. If she find him not,[2]
To England send him; or confine him where   180
Your wisdom best shall think.
KING   It shall be so.
Madness in great ones must not unwatched go.   *Exeunt.*

SCENE 2: *A public room in the castle. Enter* HAMLET *and three of
the* PLAYERS.

HAMLET   Speak the speech, I pray you, as I pronounced it to you, trip-
pingly on the tongue; but if you mouth it as many of our players do,
I had as lief the town-crier spoke my lines. Nor do not saw the air
too much with your hand thus, but use all gently, for in the very torrent, tempest, and as I may say, whirlwind of your passion, you must   5
acquire and beget a temperance that may give it smoothness. O, it
offends me to the soul to hear a robustious[3] periwig-pated[4] fellow
tear a passion to tatters, to very rags, to split the ears of the ground-
lings,[5] who for the most part are capable of[6] nothing but inexplicable
dumb shows and noise. I would have such a fellow whipped for   10
o'erdoing Termagant. It out-herods Herod.[7] Pray you avoid it.
FIRST PLAYER   I warrant your honor.
HAMLET   Be not too tame neither, but let your own discretion be
your tutor. Suit the action to the word, the word to the action, with
this special observance, that you o'erstep not the modesty of nature;   15
for anything so o'erdone is from[8] the purpose of playing, whose end
both at the first, and now, was and is, to hold as 'twere the mirror up

7. fear
8. result
9. direct
1. hearing
2. discover his problem
3. noisy
4. bewigged

5. the spectators who paid least
6. i.e., capable of understanding
7. Termagant, a "Saracen" deity, and
the Biblical Herod were stock characters in
popular drama noted for the excesses of
sound and fury used by their interpreters.
8. contrary to

to nature, to show virtue her own feature, scorn her own image, and
the very age and body of the time his form and pressure.[9] Now this
overdone, or come tardy off, though it makes the unskilful[1] laugh,   20
cannot but make the judicious grieve, the censure[2] of the which one
must in your allowance o'erweigh a whole theatre of others. O, there
be players that I have seen play—and heard others praise, and that
highly—not to speak it profanely, that neither having th' accent of
Christians, nor the gait of Christian, pagan, nor man, have so strut-   25
ted and bellowed that I have thought some of nature's journeymen[3]
had made men, and not made them well, they imitated humanity so
abominably.

FIRST PLAYER   I hope we have reformed that indifferently[4] with us.

HAMLET   O, reform it altogether. And let those that play your clowns   30
speak no more than is set down for them, for there be of them that
will themselves laugh, to set on some quantity of barren[5] spectators
to laugh too, though in the meantime some necessary question of the
play be then to be considered. That's villainous, and shows a most
pitiful ambition in the fool that uses it. Go, make you ready.   35

Exeunt PLAYERS.

Enter POLONIUS, GUILDENSTERN, *and* ROSENCRANTZ.

How now, my lord? Will the king hear this piece of work?

POLONIUS   And the queen too, and that presently.

HAMLET   Bid the players make haste.   *Exit* POLONIUS.
Will you two help to hasten them?

ROSENCRANTZ   Ay, my lord.   *Exeunt they two.*   40

HAMLET   What, ho, Horatio!
Enter HORATIO.

HORATIO   Here, sweet lord, at your service.

HAMLET   Horatio, thou art e'en as just a man
As e'er my conversation coped[6] withal.

HORATIO   O my dear lord!

HAMLET   Nay, do not think I flatter,   45
For what advancement may I hope from thee,
That no revenue hast but thy good spirits
To feed and clothe thee? Why should the poor be flattered?
No, let the candied tongue lick absurd pomp,
And crook the pregnant[7] hinges of the knee   50
Where thrift[8] may follow fawning. Dost thou hear?
Since my dear soul was mistress of her choice
And could of men distinguish her election,
S'hath sealed thee for herself, for thou hast been
As one in suff'ring all that suffers nothing,   55
A man that Fortune's buffets and rewards

9. shape
1. ignorant
2. judgment
3. inferior craftsmen
4. somewhat

5. dull-witted
6. encountered
7. quick to bend
8. profit

Hast ta'en with equal thanks; and blest are those
Whose blood and judgment are so well commingled
That they are not a pipe⁹ for Fortune's finger
To sound¹ what stop² she please. Give me that man   60
That is not passion's slave, and I will wear him
In my heart's core, ay, in my heart of heart,
As I do thee. Something too much of this.
There is a play tonight before the king.
One scene of it comes near the circumstance   65
Which I have told thee of my father's death.
I prithee, when thou seest that act afoot,
Even with the very comment³ of thy soul
Observe my uncle. If his occulted⁴ guilt
Do not itself unkennel⁵ in one speech,   70
It is a damnéd ghost that we have seen,
And my imaginations are as foul
As Vulcan's stithy.⁶ Give him heedful note,⁷
For I mine eyes will rivet to his face,
And after we will both our judgments join   75
In censure of his seeming.⁸
HORATIO   Well, my lord.
If 'a steal aught the whilst this play is playing,
And 'scape detecting, I will pay⁹ the theft.

Enter Trumpets and Kettledrums, KING, QUEEN, POLONIUS,
OPHELIA, ROSENCRANTZ, GUILDENSTERN, *and other* LORDS *attendant.*

HAMLET   They are coming to the play. I must be idle.
Get you a place.   80
KING   How fares our cousin Hamlet?
HAMLET   Excellent, i' faith, of the chameleon's dish.¹ I eat the air,
promise-crammed. You cannot feed capons so.
KING   I have nothing with this answer, Hamlet. These words are not
mine.   85
HAMLET   No, nor mine now. [*To* POLONIUS.] My lord, you played once
i' th' university, you say?
POLONIUS   That did I, my lord, and was accounted a good actor.
HAMLET   What did you enact?
POLONIUS   I did enact Julius Cæsar. I was killed i' th' Capitol; Brutus 90
killed me.²
HAMLET   It was a brute part of him to kill so capital a calf there. Be
the players ready?

---

9. musical instrument
1. play
2. note
3. keenest observation
4. hidden
5. break loose
6. smithy
7. careful attention
8. manner

9. repay
1. A reference to a popular belief that
the chameleon subsisted on a diet of air.
Hamlet has deliberately misunderstood the
King's question.
2. The assassination of Julius Caesar by
Brutus and others is the subject of another
play by Shakespeare.

ROSENCRANTZ   Ay, my lord, they stay[3] upon your patience.[4]

QUEEN   Come hither, my dear Hamlet, sit by me.   95

HAMLET   No, good mother, here's metal more attractive.

POLONIUS [*to the* KING]   O, ho! do you mark that?

HAMLET   Lady, shall I lie in your lap?

Lying down at OPHELIA's *feet.*

OPHELIA   No, my lord.

HAMLET   I mean, my head upon your lap?   100

OPHELIA   Ay, my lord.

HAMLET   Do you think I meant country matters?[5]

OPHELIA   I think nothing, my lord.

HAMLET   That's a fair thought to lie between maids' legs.

OPHELIA   What is, my lord?   105

HAMLET   Nothing.

OPHELIA   You are merry, my lord.

HAMLET   Who, I?

OPHELIA   Ay, my lord.

HAMLET   O God, your only jig-maker![6] What should a man do but be 110
merry? For look you how cheerfully my mother looks, and my father
died within's two hours.

OPHELIA   Nay, 'tis twice two months, my lord.

HAMLET   So long? Nay then, let the devil wear black, for I'll have a
suit of sables. O heavens! die two months ago, and not forgotten   115
yet? Then there's hope a great man's memory may outlive his life
half a year, but by'r lady 'a must build churches then, or else shall
'a suffer not thinking on, with the hobby-horse, whose epitaph is
"For O, for O, the hobby-horse is forgot!"[7]

The trumpets sound. Dumb Show follows. Enter a KING *and a*
QUEEN *very lovingly; the* QUEEN *embracing him and he her.
She kneels, and makes show of protestation unto him. He takes
her up, and declines[8] his head upon her neck. He lies him down
upon a bank of flowers; she, seeing him asleep, leaves him.
Anon come in another man, takes off his crown, kisses it, pours
poison in the sleeper's ears, and leaves him. The* QUEEN *returns,
finds the* KING *dead, makes passionate action. The* POISONER
*with some three or four come in again, seem to condole with
her. The dead body is carried away. The* POISONER *woos the*
QUEEN *with gifts; she seems harsh awhile, but in the end accepts
love.*   *Exeunt.*

OPHELIA   What means this, my lord?   120

HAMLET   Marry, this is miching mallecho;[9] it means mischief.

OPHELIA   Belike this show imports[1] the argument[2] of the play.

---

3. wait
4. leisure
5. Presumably, rustic misbehavior, but
here and elsewhere in this exchange Hamlet treats Ophelia to some ribald double
meanings.
6. writer of comic scenes
7. In traditional games and dances one

of the characters was a man represented as
riding a horse. The horse was made of
something like cardboard and was worn
about the "rider's" waist.
8. lays
9. sneaking crime
1. explains
2. plot

Enter PROLOGUE.

HAMLET   We shall know by this fellow. The players cannot keep
counsel; they'll tell all.

OPHELIA   Will 'a tell us what this show meant?   125

HAMLET   Ay, or any show that you will show him. Be not you ashamed
to show, he'll not shame to tell you what it means.

OPHELIA   You are naught,[3] you are naught. I'll mark[4] the play.

PROLOGUE   *For us, and for our tragedy,*
Here stooping to your clemency,   130
We beg your hearing patiently.   *Exit.*

HAMLET   Is this a prologue, or the posy[5] of a ring?

OPHELIA   'Tis brief, my lord.

HAMLET   As woman's love.

Enter the PLAYER KING *and* QUEEN.

PLAYER KING   *Full thirty times hath Phœbus' cart gone round*   135
Neptune's salt wash and Tellus' orbéd ground,
And thirty dozen moons with borrowed sheen[6]
About the world have times twelve thirties been,
Since love our hearts and Hymen did our hands
Unite comutual[7] in most sacred bands.[8]   140

PLAYER QUEEN   *So many journeys may the sun and moon*
Make us again count o'er ere love be done!
But woe is me, you are so sick of late,
So far from cheer and from your former state,
That I distrust[9] you. Yet though I distrust,   145
Discomfort you, my lord, it nothing must.
For women's fear and love hold quantity,[1]
In neither aught, or in extremity.[2]
Now what my love is proof hath made you know,
And as my love is sized,[3] my fear is so.   150
Where love is great, the littlest doubts are fear;
Where little fears grow great, great love grows there.

PLAYER KING   *Faith, I must leave thee, love, and shortly too;*
My operant powers[4] their functions leave[5] to do.
And thou shalt live in this fair world behind,   155
Honored, beloved, and haply one as kind
For husband shalt thou—

PLAYER QUEEN   *O, confound the rest!*
Such love must needs be treason in my breast.

---

3. obscene
4. attend to
5. motto engraved inside
6. light
7. mutually
8. The speech contains several mythological references. "Phoebus" was a sun
god, and his chariot or "cart" the sun.
The "salt wash" of Neptune is the ocean;
"Tellus" was an earth goddess, and her

"orbed ground" is the earth, or globe.
Hymen was the god of marriage.
9. fear for
1. agree in weight
2. The lady means without regard to
too much or too little.
3. in size
4. active forces
5. cease

In second husband let me be accurst!
None wed the second but who killed the first.[6]   160
HAMLET   That's wormwood.
PLAYER QUEEN   *The instances*[7] *that second marriage move*
Are base respects[8] *of thrift, but none of love.*
A second time I kill my husband dead,
When second husband kisses me in bed.   165
PLAYER KING   *I do believe you think what now you speak,*
But what we do determine oft we break.
Purpose is but the slave to memory,
Of violent birth, but poor validity;
Which now, like fruit unripe, sticks on the tree,   170
But fall unshaken when they mellow be.
Most necessary 'tis that we forget
To pay ourselves what to ourselves is debt.
What to ourselves in passion we propose,
The passion ending, doth the purpose lose.   175
The violence of either grief or joy
Their own enactures[9] *with themselves destroy.*
Where joy most revels, grief doth most lament;
Grief joys, joy grieves, on slender accident.
This world is not for aye,[1] *nor 'tis not strange*   180
That even our loves should with our fortunes change;
For 'tis a question left us yet to prove,
Whether love lead fortune, or else fortune love.
The great man down, you mark his favorite flies;
The poor advanced makes friends of enemies;   185
And hitherto doth love on fortune tend,
For who not needs shall never lack a friend,
And who in want a hollow[2] *friend doth try,*
Directly seasons him[3] *his enemy.*
But orderly to end where I begun,   190
Our wills and fates do so contrary run
That our devices[4] *still are overthrown;*
Our thoughts are ours, their ends none of our own.
So think thou wilt no second husband wed,
But die thy thoughts when thy first lord is dead.   195
PLAYER QUEEN   *Nor earth to me give food, nor heaven light,*
Sport and repose lock from me day and night,
To desperation turn my trust and hope,
An anchor's cheer[5] *in prison be my scope,*
Each opposite that blanks[6] *the face of joy*   200
Meet what I would have well, and it destroy,
Both here and hence[7] *pursue me lasting strife,*
If once a widow, ever I be wife!

---

6. Though there is some ambiguity, she seems to mean that the only kind of woman who would remarry is one who has killed or would kill her first husband.
7. causes
8. concerns
9. actions

1. eternal
2. false
3. ripens him into
4. plans
5. anchorite's food
6. blanches
7. in the next world

HAMLET   If she should break it now!

PLAYER KING   *'Tis deeply sworn. Sweet, leave me here awhile.*   205
My spirits grow dull, and fain I would beguile
The tedious day with sleep.   *Sleeps.*

PLAYER QUEEN   *Sleep rock thy brain,*
And never come mischance between us twain!   *Exit.*

HAMLET   Madam, how like you this play?

QUEEN   The lady doth protest too much, methinks.   210

HAMLET   O, but she'll keep her word.

KING   Have you heard the argument? Is there no offence in't?

HAMLET   No, no, they do but jest, poison in jest; no offence i' th'
world.

KING   What do you call the play?   215

HAMLET   "The Mouse-trap." Marry, how? Tropically.[8] This play is the
image of a murder done in Vienna. Gonzago is the duke's name; his
wife, Baptista. You shall see anon. 'Tis a knavish piece of work, but
what of that? Your majesty, and we that have free souls, it touches
us not. Let the galled jade wince, our withers are unwrung.[9]   220

Enter LUCIANUS.

This is one Lucianus, nephew to the king.

OPHELIA   You are as good as a chorus, my lord.

HAMLET   I could interpret between you and your love, if I could see
the puppets dallying.

OPHELIA   You are keen, my lord, you are keen.   225

HAMLET   It would cost you a groaning to take off mine edge.

OPHELIA   Still better, and worse.

HAMLET   So you mis-take your husbands.—Begin, murderer. Leave
thy damnable faces and begin. Come, the croaking raven doth bel-
low for revenge.   230

LUCIANUS   *Thoughts black, hands apt, drugs fit, and time agreeing,*
Confederate season,[1] else no creature seeing,
Thou mixture rank, of midnight weeds collected,
With Hecate's ban thrice blasted, thrice infected,[2]
Thy natural magic[3] and dire property   235
On wholesome life usurps immediately.

Pours the poison in his ears.

HAMLET   'A poisons him i' th' garden for his estate. His name's Gonzago. The story is extant, and written in very choice Italian. You
shall see anon how the murderer gets the love of Gonzago's wife.

OPHELIA   The king rises.   240

HAMLET   What, frighted with false fire?

QUEEN   How fares my lord?

POLONIUS   Give o'er the play.

KING   Give me some light. Away!

POLONIUS   Lights, lights, lights!   245

---

8. figuratively
9. A "galled jade" is a horse, particularly one of poor quality, with a sore
back. The "withers" are the ridge between
a horse's shoulders; "unwrung withers" are
not chafed by the harness.

1. a helpful time for the crime
2. Hecate was a classical goddess of
witchcraft.
3. native power

Exeunt all but HAMLET *and* HORATIO.

HAMLET   Why, let the strucken deer go weep,
                        The hart ungallèd[4] play.
                   For some must watch while some must sleep;
                        Thus runs the world away.
            Would not this, sir, and a forest of feathers[5]—if the rest of my for- ²⁵⁰
            tunes turn Turk with me—with two Provincial roses on my razed
            shoes, get me a fellowship in a cry[6] of players?[7]

HORATIO   Half a share.

HAMLET   A whole one, I.

                   For thou dost know, O Damon dear,[8]   ²⁵⁵
                        This realm dismantled was
                   Of Jove himself, and now reigns here
                        A very, very—peacock.

HORATIO   You might have rhymed.

HAMLET   O good Horatio, I'll take the ghost's word for a thousand ²⁶⁰
            pound. Didst perceive?

HORATIO   Very well, my lord.

HAMLET   Upon the talk of the poisoning.

HORATIO   I did very well note[9] him.

HAMLET   Ah, ha! Come, some music. Come, the recorders.[1]   ²⁶⁵
            For if the king like not the comedy,
            Why then, belike he likes it not, perdy.[2]
            Come, some music.

            Enter ROSENCRANTZ *and* GUILDENSTERN.

GUILDENSTERN   Good my lord, vouchsafe me a word with you.

HAMLET   Sir, a whole history.   ²⁷⁰

GUILDENSTERN   The king, sir—

HAMLET   Ay, sir, what of him?

GUILDENSTERN   Is in his retirement[3] marvellous distempered.[4]

HAMLET   With drink, sir?

GUILDENSTERN   No, my lord, with choler.[5]   ²⁷⁵

HAMLET   Your wisdom should show itself more richer to signify this
            to the doctor, for for me to put him to his purgation[6] would perhaps
            plunge him into more choler.

GUILDENSTERN   Good my lord, put your discourse[7] into some frame,[8]
            and start not so wildly from my affair.   ²⁸⁰

HAMLET   I am tame, sir. Pronounce.

---

4. uninjured
5. plumes
6. company
7. Hamlet asks Horatio if "this" recitation, accompanied with a player's costume, including plumes and rosettes on shoes which have been slashed for decorative effect, might not entitle him to become a shareholder in a theatrical company in the event that Fortune goes against him, "turn Turk."
8. Damon was a common name for a young man or a shepherd in lyric, espe-

cially pastoral poetry. Jove was the chief god of the Romans. The Reader may supply for himself the rhyme referred to by Horatio.
9. observe
1. wooden end-blown flutes
2. *par Dieu* (by God)
3. place to which he has retired
4. vexed
5. bile
6. treatment with a laxative
7. speech
8. order

GUILDENSTERN   The queen your mother, in most great affliction of spirit, hath sent me to you.

HAMLET   You are welcome.

GUILDENSTERN   Nay, good my lord, this courtesy is not of the right 285 breed. If it shall please you to make me a wholesome[9] answer, I will do your mother's commandment. If not, your pardon and my return[1] shall be the end of my business.

HAMLET   Sir, I cannot.

ROSENCRANTZ   What, my lord?   290

HAMLET   Make you a wholesome answer; my wit's diseased. But, sir, such answer as I can make, you shall command, or rather, as you say, my mother. Therefore no more, but to the matter. My mother, you say—

ROSENCRANTZ   Then thus she says: your behavior hath struck her into 295 amazement and admiration.[2]

HAMLET   O wonderful son, that can so stonish a mother! But is there no sequel at the heels of this mother's admiration? Impart.[3]

ROSENCRANTZ   She desires to speak with you in her closet[4] ere you go to bed.   300

HAMLET   We shall obey, were she ten times our mother. Have you any further trade[5] with us?

ROSENCRANTZ   My lord, you once did love me.

HAMLET   And do still, by these pickers and stealers.[6]

ROSENCRANTZ   Good my lord, what is your cause of distemper? You 305 do surely bar the door upon your own liberty, if you deny your griefs to your friend.

HAMLET   Sir, I lack advancement.

ROSENCRANTZ   How can that be, when you have the voice of the king himself for your succession in Denmark?   310

HAMLET   Ay, sir, but "while the grass grows"—the proverb[7] is something musty.

Enter the PLAYERS *with recorders.*

O, the recorders! Let me see one. To withdraw with you[8]—why do you go about to recover the wind of me, as if you would drive me into a toil?[9]   315

GUILDENSTERN   O my lord, if my duty be too bold, my love is too unmannerly.

HAMLET   I do not well understand that. Will you play upon this pipe?[1]

GUILDENSTERN   My lord, I cannot.

HAMLET   I pray you.   320

GUILDENSTERN   Believe me, I cannot.

HAMLET   I do beseech you.

GUILDENSTERN   I know no touch of it,[2] my lord.

9. reasonable
1. i.e., to the Queen
2. wonder
3. tell me
4. bedroom
5. business
6. hands
7. The proverb ends "the horse starves."

8. let me step aside
9. The figure is from hunting. "You will approach me with the wind blowing from me toward you in order to drive me into the net."
1. recorder
2. have no ability

HAMLET   It is as easy as lying. Govern[3] these ventages[4] with your
fingers and thumb, give it breath with your mouth, and it will 325
discourse most eloquent music. Look you, these are the stops.[5]

GUILDENSTERN   But these cannot I command to any utt'rance of harmony. I have not the skill.

HAMLET   Why, look you now, how unworthy a thing you make of me!
You would play upon me, you would seem to know my stops, you 330
would pluck out the heart of my mystery, you would sound[6] me
from my lowest note to the top of my compass[7]; and there is much
music, excellent voice, in this little organ, yet cannot you make it
speak. 'Sblood, do you think I am easier to be played on than a pipe?
Call me what instrument you will, though you can fret[8] me, you 335
cannot play upon me.

Enter POLONIUS.

God bless you, sir!

POLONIUS   My lord, the queen would speak with you, and presently.[9]

HAMLET   Do you see yonder cloud that's almost in shape of a camel?

POLONIUS   By th' mass, and 'tis like a camel indeed.   340

HAMLET   Methinks it is like a weasel.

POLONIUS   It is backed like a weasel.

HAMLET   Or like a whale.

POLONIUS   Very like a whale.

HAMLET   Then I will come to my mother by and by. [*Aside.*] They 345
fool me to the top of my bent.[1]—I will come by and by.

POLONIUS   I will say so.   *Exit* POLONIUS.

HAMLET   "By and by" is easily said. Leave me, friends.

Exeunt all but HAMLET.

'Tis now the very witching time of night,
When churchyards yawn, and hell itself breathes out   350
Contagion to this world. Now could I drink hot blood,
And do such bitter business as the day
Would quake to look on. Soft, now to my mother.
O heart, lose not thy nature; let not ever
The soul of Nero[2] enter this firm bosom.   355
Let me be cruel, not unnatural;
I will speak daggers to her, but use none.
My tongue and soul in this be hypocrites—
How in my words somever she be shent,[3]
To give them seals[4] never, my soul, consent!   *Exit.* 360

SCENE 3: *A room in the castle. Enter* KING, ROSENCRANTZ
and GUILDENSTERN.

---

3. cover and uncover
4. holes
5. wind-holes
6. play
7. range
8. "Fret" is used in a double sense, to
annoy and to play a guitar or similar instrument using the "frets" or small bars on
the neck.

9. at once
1. treat me as an utter fool
2. The Emperor Nero, known for his
excesses, was believed to have been responsible for the death of his mother.
3. shamed
4. fulfillment in action

KING   I like him not,[5] nor stands it safe with us
　　　To let his madness range.[6] Therefore prepare you.
　　　I your commission will forthwith dispatch,
　　　And he to England shall along with you.
　　　The terms of our estate[7] may not endure   5
　　　Hazard so near's as doth hourly grow
　　　Out of his brows.
GUILDENSTERN   　　　We will ourselves provide.[8]
　　　Most holy and religious fear it is
　　　To keep those many many bodies safe
　　　That live and feed upon your majesty.   10
ROSENCRANTZ   The single and peculiar[9] life is bound
　　　With all the strength and armor of the mind
　　　To keep itself from noyance,[1] but much more
　　　That spirit upon whose weal[2] depends and rests
　　　The lives of many. The cess[3] of majesty   15
　　　Dies not alone, but like a gulf[4] doth draw
　　　What's near it with it. It is a massy[5] wheel
　　　Fixed on the summit of the highest mount,
　　　To whose huge spokes ten thousand lesser things
　　　Are mortised and adjoined,[6] which when it falls,   20
　　　Each small annexment, petty consequence,
　　　Attends[7] the boist'rous ruin. Never alone
　　　Did the king sigh, but with a general groan.
KING   Arm you, I pray you, to this speedy voyage,
　　　For we will fetters put about this fear,   25
　　　Which now goes too free-footed.
ROSENCRANTZ   　　　　　　　　We will haste us.

Exeunt ROSENCRANTZ *and* GUILDENSTERN.

Enter POLONIUS.

POLONIUS   My lord, he's going to his mother's closet.
　　　Behind the arras I'll convey[8] myself
　　　To hear the process.[9] I'll warrant she'll tax him home,[1]
　　　And as you said, and wisely was it said,   30
　　　'Tis meet that some more audience than a mother,
　　　Since nature makes them partial, should o'erhear
　　　The speech, of vantage.[2] Fare you well, my liege.
　　　I'll call upon you ere you go to bed,
　　　And tell you what I know.
KING   　　　　　　　　Thanks, dear my lord.   35

Exit POLONIUS.

5. distrust him
6. roam freely
7. condition of the state
8. equip (for the journey)
9. individual
1. harm
2. welfare
3. cessation
4. whirlpool
5. massive
6. attached
7. joins in
8. station
9. proceedings
1. sharply
2. from a position of vantage

O, my offence is rank, it smells to heaven;
It hath the primal eldest curse[3] upon't,
A brother's murder. Pray can I not,
Though inclination be as sharp as will.
My stronger guilt defeats my strong intent,   40
And like a man to double business[4] bound,
I stand in pause where I shall first begin,
And both neglect. What if this cursèd hand
Were thicker than itself with brothers' blood,
Is there not rain enough in the sweet heavens   45
To wash it white as snow? Whereto serves mercy
But to confront the visage of offence?
And what's in prayer but this twofold force,
To be forestallèd[5] ere we come to fall,
Or pardoned being down[6]? Then I'll look up.   50
My fault is past. But, O, what form of prayer
Can serve my turn? "Forgive me my foul murder"?
That cannot be, since I am still possessed
Of those effects[7] for which I did the murder—
My crown, mine own ambition, and my queen.   55
May one be pardoned and retain th' offence[8]?
In the corrupted currents of this world
Offence's gilded[9] hand may shove by justice,
And oft 'tis seen the wicked prize itself
Buys out the law. But 'tis not so above.   60
There is no shuffling; there the action[1] lies
In his true nature, and we ourselves compelled,
Even to the teeth and forehead of[2] our faults,
To give in evidence. What then? What rests[3]?
Try what repentance can. What can it not?   65
Yet what can it when one can not repent?
O wretched state! O bosom black as death!
O limèd[4] soul, that struggling to be free
Art more engaged! Help, angels! Make assay.
Bow, stubborn knees, and heart with strings of steel,   70
Be soft as sinews of the new-born babe.
All may be well.   *He kneels.*

   Enter HAMLET.

HAMLET   Now might I do it pat,[5] now 'a is a-praying,
And now I'll do't—and so 'a goes to heaven,
And so am I revenged. That would be scanned.[6]   75
A villain kills my father, and for that,
I, his sole son, do this same villain send
To heaven.

---

3. i.e., of Cain
4. two mutually opposed interests
5. prevented (from sin)
6. having sinned
7. gains
8. i.e., benefits of the offence
9. bearing gold as a bribe

1. case at law
2. face-to-face with
3. remains
4. caught as with bird-lime
5. easily
6. deserves consideration

Why, this is hire and salary, not revenge.
'A took my father grossly, full of bread,[7]   80
With all his crimes broad blown,[8] as flush[9] as May;
And how his audit stands who knows save heaven?
But in our circumstance and course of thought
'Tis heavy with him; and am I then revenged
To take him in the purging of his soul,   85
When he is fit and seasoned[1] for his passage?
No.
Up, sword, and know thou a more horrid hent.[2]
When he is drunk, asleep, or in his rage,
Or in th' incestuous pleasure of his bed   90
At game a-swearing, or about some act
That has no relish[3] of salvation in't—
Then trip him, that his heels may kick at heaven,
And that his soul may be as damned and black
As hell, whereto it goes. My mother stays.   95
This physic[4] but prolongs thy sickly days.   *Exit.*
KING [*rising*]   My words fly up, my thoughts remain below.
Words without thoughts never to heaven go.   *Exit.*

SCENE 4: *The Queen's chamber. Enter* QUEEN *and* POLONIUS.

POLONIUS   'A will come straight. Look you lay home to[5] him.
Tell him his pranks have been too broad[6] to bear with,
And that your grace hath screen'd[7] and stood between
Much heat and him. I'll silence me even here.
Pray you be round.
QUEEN   I'll warrant you. Fear[8] me not.   5
Withdraw, I hear him coming.

POLONIUS *goes behind the arras.*

Enter HAMLET.

HAMLET   Now, mother, what's the matter?
QUEEN   Hamlet, thou hast thy father much offended.
HAMLET   Mother, you have my father much offended.
QUEEN   Come, come, you answer with an idle tongue.   10
HAMLET   Go, go, you question with a wicked tongue.
QUEEN   Why, how now, Hamlet?
HAMLET   What's the matter now?
QUEEN   Have you forgot me?
HAMLET   No, by the rood,[9] not so.
You are the queen, your husband's brother's wife,
And would it were not so, you are my mother.   15
QUEEN   Nay, then I'll set those to you that can speak.

7. in a state of sin and without fasting
8. full-blown
9. vigorous
1. ready
2. opportunity
3. flavor

4. medicine
5. be sharp with
6. outrageous
7. acted as a fire screen
8. doubt
9. cross

HAMLET   Come, come, and sit you down. You shall not budge.
  You go not till I set you up a glass[1]
  Where you may see the inmost part of you.
QUEEN   What wilt thou do? Thou wilt not murder me?   20
  Help, ho!
POLONIUS [*behind*]   What, ho! help!
HAMLET [*draws*]   How now, a rat?
  Dead for a ducat, dead!

  Kills POLONIUS *with a pass through the arras.*

POLONIUS [*behind*]   O, I am slain!   25
QUEEN   O me, what hast thou done?
HAMLET   Nay, I know not.
  Is it the king?
QUEEN   O, what a rash and bloody deed is this!
HAMLET   A bloody deed!—almost as bad, good mother,
  As kill a king and marry with his brother.   30
QUEEN   As kill a king?
HAMLET   Ay, lady, it was my word.

  Parting the arras.

  Thou wretched, rash, intruding fool, farewell!
  I took thee for thy better. Take thy fortune.
  Thou find'st to be too busy[2] is some danger.—
  Leave wringing of your hands. Peace, sit you down   35
  And let me wring your heart, for so I shall
  If it be made of penetrable stuff,
  If damnéd custom have not brazed it[3] so
  That it be proof[4] and bulwark against sense.[5]
QUEEN   What have I done that thou dar'st wag thy tongue   40
  In noise so rude against me?
HAMLET   Such an act
  That blurs the grace and blush of modesty,
  Calls virtue hypocrite, takes off the rose
  From the fair forehead of an innocent love,
  And sets a blister[6] there, makes marriage-vows   45
  As false as dicers' oaths. O, such a deed
  As from the body of contraction[7] plucks
  The very soul, and sweet religion makes
  A rhapsody of words. Heaven's face does glow
  And this solidity and compound mass[8]   50
  With heated visage, as against the doom[9]—
  Is thought-sick at the act.
QUEEN   Ay me, what act,
  That roars so loud and thunders in the index[1]?
HAMLET   Look here upon this picture[2] and on this,

1. mirror
2. officious
3. plated it with brass
4. armor
5. feeling
6. brand

7. the marriage contract
8. meaningless mass (Earth)
9. Judgment Day
1. table of contents
2. portrait

The counterfeit presentment of two brothers.   55
See what a grace was seated on this brow:
Hyperion's curls, the front[3] of Jove himself,
An eye like Mars, to threaten and command,
A station[4] like the herald Mercury[5]
New lighted[6] on a heaven-kissing hill—   60
A combination and a form indeed
Where every god did seem to set his seal,[7]
To give the world assurance of a man.
This was your husband. Look you now what follows.
Here is your husband, like a mildewed ear   65
Blasting his wholesome brother. Have you eyes?
Could you on this fair mountain leave to feed,
And batten[8] on this moor? Ha! have you eyes?
You cannot call it love, for at your age
The heyday in the blood is tame, it's humble,   70
And waits upon the judgment, and what judgment
Would step from this to this? Sense sure you have,
Else could you not have motion, but sure that sense
Is apoplexed[9] for madness would not err,
Nor sense to ecstasy was ne'er so thralled   75
But it reserved some quantity[1] of choice
To serve in such a difference. What devil was't
That thus hath cozened[2] you at hoodman-blind[3]?
Eyes without feeling, feeling without sight,
Ears without hands or eyes, smelling sans[4] all,   80
Or but a sickly part of one true sense
Could not so mope.[5] O shame! where is thy blush?
Rebellious hell,
If thou canst mutine[6] in a matron's bones,
To flaming youth let virtue be as wax   85
And melt in her own fire. Proclaim no shame
When the compulsive ardor gives the charge,[7]
Since frost itself as actively doth burn,
And reason panders[8] will.
QUEEN   O Hamlet, speak no more!
Thou turn'st my eyes into my very soul;   90
And there I see such black and grainéd[9] spots
As will not leave their tinct.[1]
HAMLET   Nay, but to live
In the rank sweat of an enseaméd[2] bed,
Stewed in corruption, honeying and making love
Over the nasty sty—

3. forehead
4. bearing
5. Mercury was a Roman god who served as the messenger of the gods.
6. newly alighted
7. mark of approval
8. feed greedily
9. paralyzed
1. power
2. cheated

3. blindman's buff
4. without
5. be stupid
6. commit mutiny
7. attacks
8. pimps for
9. ingrained
1. lose their color
2. greasy

QUEEN   O, speak to me no more!   95
    These words like daggers enter in my ears;
    No more, sweet Hamlet.
HAMLET   A murderer and a villain,
    A slave that is not twentieth part the tithe[3]
    Of your precedent lord,[4] a vice of kings,[5]
    A cutpurse[6] of the empire and the rule,   100
    That from a shelf the precious diadem stole
    And put it in his pocket—
QUEEN   No more.

    Enter GHOST.

HAMLET   A king of shreds and patches—
    Save me and hover o'er me with your wings,   105
    You heavenly guards! What would your gracious figure?
QUEEN   Alas, he's mad.
HAMLET   Do you not come your tardy[7] son to chide,
    That lapsed in time and passion lets go by
    Th' important acting of your dread command?   110
    O, say!
GHOST   Do not forget. This visitation
    Is but to whet thy almost blunted purpose.
    But look, amazement on thy mother sits.
    O, step between her and her fighting soul!   115
    Conceit[8] in weakest bodies strongest works.
    Speak to her, Hamlet.
HAMLET   How is it with you, lady?
QUEEN   Alas, how is't with you,
    That you do bend[9] your eye on vacancy,
    And with th' incorporal air do hold discourse?   120
    Forth at your eyes your spirits wildly peep,
    And as the sleeping soldiers in th' alarm,
    Your bedded hairs like life in excrements[1]
    Start up and stand an end. O gentle son,
    Upon the heat and flame of thy distemper   125
    Sprinkle cool patience. Whereon do you look?
HAMLET   On him, on him! Look you how pale he glares.
    His form and cause conjoined,[2] preaching to stones,
    Would make them capable.[3]—Do not look upon me,
    Lest with piteous action you convert   130
    My stern effects.[4] Then what I have to do
    Will want true color—tears perchance for blood.
QUEEN   To whom do you speak this?
HAMLET   Do you see nothing there?
QUEEN   Nothing at all, yet all that is I see.   135
HAMLET   Nor did you nothing hear?

---

3. one-tenth
4. first husband
5. The "Vice," a common figure in the
popular drama, was a clown or buffoon.
  6. pickpocket
  7. slow to act

8. imagination
9. turn
1. nails and hair
2. working together
3. of responding
4. deeds

QUEEN   No, nothing but ourselves.

HAMLET   Why, look you there. Look how it steals away.
My father, in his habit[5] as he lived!
Look where he goes even now out at the portal.   *Exit* GHOST. 140

QUEEN   This is the very coinage[6] of your brain.
This bodiless creation ecstasy[7]
Is very cunning[8] in.

HAMLET   My pulse as yours doth temperately keep time,
And makes as healthful music. It is not madness   145
That I have uttered. Bring me to the test,
And I the matter will re-word, which madness
Would gambol[9] from. Mother, for love of grace,
Lay not that flattering unction[1] to your soul,
That not your trespass but my madness speaks.   150
It will but skin and film the ulcerous place
Whiles rank corruption, mining[2] all within,
Infects unseen. Confess yourself to heaven,
Repent what's past, avoid what is to come,
And do not spread the compost on the weeds,   155
To make them ranker. Forgive me this my virtue,
For in the fatness of these pursy[3] times
Virtue itself of vice must pardon beg,
Yea, curb[4] and woo for leave to do him good.

QUEEN   O Hamlet, thou hast cleft my heart in twain.   160

HAMLET   O, throw away the worser part of it,
And live the purer with the other half.
Good night—but go not to my uncle's bed.
Assume a virtue, if you have it not.
That monster custom[5] who all sense doth eat   165
Of habits evil, is angel yet in this,
That to the use of actions fair and good
He likewise gives a frock or livery
That aptly[6] is put on. Refrain tonight,
And that shall lend a kind of easiness   170
To the next abstinence; the next more easy;
For use almost can change the stamp of nature,
And either curb the devil, or throw him out
With wondrous potency. Once more, good night,
And when you are desirous to be blest,   175
I'll blessing beg of you. For this same lord
I do repent; but heaven hath pleased it so,
To punish me with this, and this with me,
That I must be their scourge and minister.
I will bestow[7] him and will answer well   180
The death I gave him. So, again, good night.
I must be cruel only to be kind.

---

5. costume	2. undermining
6. invention	3. bloated
7. madness	4. bow
8. skilled	5. habit
9. shy away	6. easily
1. ointment	7. dispose of

Thus bad begins and worse remains behind.
One word more, good lady.

QUEEN   What shall I do?

HAMLET   Not this, by no means, that I bid you do: 185
Let the bloat[8] king tempt you again to bed,
Pinch wanton[9] on your cheek, call you his mouse,
And let him, for a pair of reechy[1] kisses,
Or paddling in your neck with his damned fingers,
Make you to ravel[2] all this matter out,   190
That I essentially am not in madness,
But mad in craft. 'Twere good you let him know,
For who that's but a queen, fair, sober, wise,
Would from a paddock,[3] from a bat, a gib,[4]
Such dear concernings hide? Who would so do?   195
No, in despite of sense and secrecy,
Unpeg the basket on the house's top,
Let the birds fly, and like the famous ape,
To try conclusions, in the basket creep
And break your own neck down.[5]   200

QUEEN   Be thou assured, if words be made of breath
And breath of life, I have no life to breathe
What thou hast said to me.

HAMLET   I must to England; you know that?

QUEEN   Alack,
I had forgot. 'Tis so concluded on.   205

HAMLET   There's letters sealed, and my two school-fellows,
Whom I will trust as I will adders fanged,
They bear the mandate[6]; they must sweep[7] my way
And marshal me to knavery. Let it work,
For 'tis the sport to have the enginer   210
Hoist with his own petar; and't shall go hard
But I will delve[8] one yard below their mines
And blow them at the moon. O, 'tis most sweet
When in one line two crafts directly meet.[9]
This man shall set me packing.   215
I'll lug the guts into the neighbor room.
Mother, good night. Indeed, this counsellor
Is now most still, most secret, and most grave,
Who was in life a foolish prating knave.
Come sir, to draw toward an end with you.   220
Good night, mother.

Exit the QUEEN. *Then exit* HAMLET *tugging* POLONIUS.

---

8. bloated
9. lewdly
1. foul
2. reveal
3. toad
4. tomcat
5. Apparently a reference to a now lost fable in which an ape, finding a basket containing a cage of birds on a housetop, opens the cage. The birds fly away. The ape, thinking that if he were in the basket he too could fly, enters, jumps out, and breaks his neck.

6. command
7. prepare
8. dig
9. The "enginer" or engineer is a military man who is here described as being blown up by a bomb of his own construction, "hoist with his own petar." The military figure continues in the succeeding lines where Hamlet describes himself as digging a countermine or tunnel beneath the one Claudius is digging to defeat Hamlet. In line 214 the two tunnels unexpectedly meet.

Act 4

SCENE 1: *A room in tne castle. Enter* KING, QUEEN, ROSENCRANTZ *and* GUILDENSTERN.

KING   There's matter in these sighs, these profound heaves,
    You must translate[1]; 'tis fit we understand them.
    Where is your son?
QUEEN   Bestow this place on us a little while.

Exeunt ROSENCRANTZ *and* GUILDENSTERN.

    Ah, mine own lord, what have I seen tonight!   5
KING   What, Gertrude? How does Hamlet?
QUEEN   Mad as the sea and wind when both contend
    Which is the mightier. In his lawless fit,
    Behind the arras hearing something stir,
    Whips out his rapier, cries "A rat, a rat!"   10
    And in this brainish apprehension[2] kills
    The unseen good old man.
KING   O heavy deed!
    It had been so with us had we been there.
    His liberty is full of threats to all—
    To you yourself, to us, to every one.   15
    Alas, how shall this bloody deed be answered?
    It will be laid to us, whose providence[3]
    Should have kept short, restrained, and out of haunt,[4]
    This mad young man. But so much was our love,
    We would not understand what was most fit;   20
    But, like the owner of a foul disease,
    To keep it from divulging, let it feed
    Even on the pith of life. Where is he gone?
QUEEN   To draw apart the body he hath killed,
    O'er whom his very madness, like some ore   25
    Among a mineral of metals base,
    Shows itself pure: 'a weeps for what is done.
KING   O Gertrude, come away!
    The sun no sooner shall the mountains touch
    But we will ship him hence, and this vile deed   30
    We must with all our majesty and skill
    Both countenance and excuse. Ho, Guildenstern!

Enter ROSENCRANTZ *and* GUILDENSTERN.

    Friends both, go join you with some further aid.
    Hamlet in madness hath Polonius slain,
    And from his mother's closet hath he dragged him.   35
    Go seek him out; speak fair, and bring the body
    Into the chapel. I pray you haste in this.

1. explain   3. prudence
2. insane notion   4. away from court

Exeunt ROSENCRANTZ *and* GUILDENSTERN.

Come, Gertrude, we'll call up our wisest friends
And let them know both what we mean to do
And what's untimely done;   40
Whose whisper o'er the world's diameter,
As level[5] as the cannon to his blank,[6]
Transports his poisoned shot—may miss our name,
And hit the woundless air. O, come away!
My soul is full of discord and dismay.   *Exeunt.* 45

SCENE 2: *A passageway. Enter* HAMLET.

HAMLET   Safely stowed.—But soft, what noise? Who calls on Hamlet?
O, here they come.

Enter ROSENCRANTZ, GUILDENSTERN, *and* OTHERS.

ROSENCRANTZ   What have you done, my lord, with the dead body?
HAMLET   Compounded it with dust, whereto 'tis kin.
ROSENCRANTZ   Tell us where 'tis, that we may take it thence   5
And bear it to the chapel.
HAMLET   Do not believe it.
ROSENCRANTZ   Believe what?
HAMLET   That I can keep your counsel and not mine own. Besides, to
be demanded of[7] a sponge—what replication[8] should be made by   10
the son of a king?
ROSENCRANTZ   Take you me for a sponge, my lord?
HAMLET   Ay, sir, that soaks up the king's countenance,[9] his rewards,
his authorities. But such officers do the king best service in the end.
He keeps them like an apple in the corner of his jaw, first mouthed   15
to be last swallowed. When he needs what you have gleaned, it is
but squeezing you and, sponge, you shall be dry again.
ROSENCRANTZ   I understand you not, my lord.
HAMLET   I am glad of it. A knavish speech sleeps in a foolish ear.
ROSENCRANTZ   My lord, you must tell us where the body is, and go   20
with us to the king.
HAMLET   The body is with the king, but the king is not with the body.
The king is a thing—
GUILDENSTERN   A thing, my lord!
HAMLET   Of nothing. Bring me to him. Hide fox, and all after.[1]   25
                                                                Exeunt.

SCENE 3: *A room in the castle. Enter* KING.

KING   I have sent to seek him, and to find the body.
How dangerous is it that this man goes loose!
Yet must not we put the strong law on him.
He's loved of the distracted[2] multitude,

---

5. direct
6. mark
7. questioned by
8. answer

9. favor
1. Apparently a reference to a children's game like hide-and-seek.
2. confused

Who like not in their judgment but their eyes,   5
And where 'tis so, th' offender's scourge[3] is weighed,
But never the offence. To bear all smooth and even,
This sudden sending him away must seem
Deliberate pause.[4] Diseases desperate grown
By desperate appliance are relieved,   10
Or not at all.

> *Enter* ROSENCRANTZ, GUILDENSTERN, *and all the rest.*

           How now! what hath befall'n?
ROSENCRANTZ   Where the dead body is bestowed, my lord,
  We cannot get from him.
KING   But where is he?
ROSENCRANTZ   Without,[5] my lord; guarded, to know[6] your pleasure.
KING   Bring him before us.
ROSENCRANTZ   Ho! bring in the lord.   15

> *They enter with* HAMLET.

KING   Now, Hamlet, where's Polonius?
HAMLET   At supper.
KING   At supper? Where?
HAMLET   Not where he eats, but where 'a is eaten. A certain convoca-
tion[7] of politic[8] worms are e'en at him. Your worm is your only   20
emperor for diet. We fat all creatures else to fat us, and we fat
ourselves for maggots. Your fat king and your lean beggar is but
variable service—two dishes, but to one table. That's the end.
KING   Alas, alas!
HAMLET   A man may fish with the worm that hath eat of a king, and   25
eat of the fish that hath fed of that worm.
KING   What dost thou mean by this?
HAMLET   Nothing but to show you how a king may go a progress
through the guts of a beggar.
KING   Where is Polonius?   30
HAMLET   In heaven. Send thither to see. If your messenger find him
not there, seek him i' th' other place yourself. But if, indeed, you find
him not within this month, you shall nose[9] him as you go up the
stairs into the lobby.
KING [*to* ATTENDANTS]   Go seek him there.   35
HAMLET   'A will stay till you come.   *Exeunt* ATTENDANTS.
KING   Hamlet, this deed, for thine especial safety—
  Which we do tender,[1] as we dearly[2] grieve
  For that which thou hast done—must send thee hence
  With fiery quickness. Therefore prepare thyself.   40
  The bark is ready, and the wind at help,
  Th' associates tend, and everything is bent
  For England.

---

3. punishment
4. i.e., not an impulse
5. outside
6. await
7. gathering

8. statesmanlike
9. smell
1. consider
2. deeply

HAMLET   For England?
KING   Ay, Hamlet.
HAMLET   Good.
KING   So it is, if thou knew'st our purposes.
HAMLET   I see a cherub that sees them. But come, for England!   45
    Farewell, dear mother.
KING   Thy loving father, Hamlet.
HAMLET   My mother. Father and mother is man and wife, man and
    wife is one flesh. So, my mother. Come, for England.   *Exit.*
KING   Follow him at foot[3]; tempt him with speed aboard.   50
    Delay it not; I'll have him hence tonight.
    Away! for everything is sealed and done
    That else leans on th' affair. Pray you make haste.

                                      Exeunt all but the KING.

    And, England, if my love thou hold'st at aught—
    As my great power thereof may give thee sense,[4]   55
    Since yet thy cicatrice[5] looks raw and red
    After the Danish sword, and thy free awe
    Pays homage to us—thou mayst not coldly set[6]
    Our sovereign process,[7] which imports at full
    By letters congruing[8] to that effect   60
    The present death of Hamlet. Do it, England,
    For like the hectic[9] in my blood he rages,
    And thou must cure me. Till I know 'tis done,
    Howe'er my haps, my joys were ne'er begun.   *Exit.*

    SCENE 4: *Near Elsinore. Enter* FORTINBRAS *with his army.*

FORTINBRAS   Go, captain, from me greet the Danish king.
    Tell him that by his license Fortinbras
    Craves the conveyance[1] of a promised march
    Over his kingdom. You know the rendezvous.
    If that his majesty would aught with us,   5
    We shall express our duty in his eye,[2]
    And let him know so.
CAPTAIN   I will do't, my lord.
FORTINBRAS   Go softly on.   *Exeunt all but the* CAPTAIN.

    Enter HAMLET, ROSENCRANTZ, GUILDENSTERN, *and* OTHERS.

HAMLET   Good sir, whose powers are these?
CAPTAIN   They are of Norway, sir.   10
HAMLET   How purposed, sir, I pray you?
CAPTAIN   Against some part of Poland.
HAMLET   Who commands them, sir?
CAPTAIN   The nephew to old Norway, Fortinbras.

3. closely   8. agreeing
4. of its value   9. chronic fever
5. wound scar   1. escort
6. set aside   2. presence
7. mandate

HAMLET   Goes it against the main[3] of Poland, sir,   15
  Or for some frontier?
CAPTAIN   Truly to speak, and with no addition,[4]
  We go to gain a little patch of ground
  That hath in it no profit but the name.
  To pay five ducats,[5] five, I would not farm it;   20
  Nor will it yield to Norway or the Pole
  A ranker[6] rate should it be sold in fee.[7]
HAMLET   Why, then the Polack never will defend it.
CAPTAIN   Yes, it is already garrisoned.
HAMLET   Two thousand souls and twenty thousand ducats   25
  Will not debate the question of this straw.
  This is th' imposthume[8] of much wealth and peace,
  That inward breaks, and shows no cause without
  Why the man dies. I humbly thank you, sir.
CAPTAIN   God b'wi'ye, sir.   *Exit.*
ROSENCRANTZ   Will't please you go, my lord?   30
HAMLET   I'll be with you straight. Go a little before.

Exeunt all but HAMLET.

How all occasions do inform against me,
And spur my dull revenge! What is a man,
If his chief good and market[9] of his time
Be but to sleep and feed? A beast, no more.   35
Sure he that made us with such large discourse,[1]
Looking before and after, gave us not
That capability and godlike reason
To fust[2] in us unused. Now, whether it be
Bestial oblivion, or some craven scruple   40
Of thinking too precisely on th' event[3]—
A thought which, quartered, hath but one part wisdom
And ever three parts coward—I do not know
Why yet I live to say "This thing's to do,"
Sith[4] I have cause, and will, and strength, and means,   45
To do't. Examples gross as earth exhort me.
Witness this army of such mass and charge,[5]
Led by a delicate and tender prince,
Whose spirit, with divine ambition puffed,
Makes mouths at[6] the invisible event,   50
Exposing what is mortal and unsure
To all that fortune, death, and danger dare,
Even for an eggshell. Rightly to be great
Is not to stir without great argument,
But greatly to find quarrel in a straw   55

3. central part	1. ample reasoning power
4. exaggeration	2. grow musty
5. i.e., in rent	3. outcome
6. higher	4. since
7. outright	5. expense
8. abscess	6. scorns
9. occupation	

When honor's at the stake. How stand I then,
That have a father killed, a mother stained,
Excitements of my reason and my blood,
And let all sleep, while to my shame I see
The imminent death of twenty thousand men   60
That for a fantasy and trick of fame
Go to their graves like beds, fight for a plot
Whereon the numbers cannot try the cause,
Which is not tomb enough and continent
To hide the slain?[7] O, from this time forth,   65
My thoughts be bloody, or be nothing worth!   *Exit.*

SCENE 5: *A room in the castle. Enter* QUEEN, HORATIO *and a*
GENTLEMAN.

QUEEN   I will not speak with her.
GENTLEMAN   She is importunate, indeed distract.
  Her mood will needs be pitied.
QUEEN   What would she have?
GENTLEMAN   She speaks much of her father, says she hears
  There's tricks i' th' world, and hems, and beats her heart,   5
  Spurns enviously at straws,[8] speaks things in doubt
  That carry but half sense. Her speech is nothing,
  Yet the unshaped use of it doth move
  The hearers to collection[9]; they yawn at it,
  And botch the words up fit to their own thoughts,   10
  Which, as her winks and nods and gestures yield them,
  Indeed would make one think there might be thought,
  Though nothing sure, yet much unhappily.
HORATIO   'Twere good she were spoken with, for she may strew
  Dangerous conjectures in ill-breeding minds.   15
QUEEN   Let her come in.   *Exit* GENTLEMAN.
  [*Aside.*] To my sick soul, as sin's true nature is,
  Each toy[1] seems prologue to some great amiss.[2]
  So full of artless jealousy is guilt,
  It spills itself in fearing to be spilt.   20

         Enter OPHELIA *distracted.*

OPHELIA   Where is the beauteous majesty of Denmark?
QUEEN   How now, Ophelia!
OPHELIA   How should I your true love know   *She sings.*
                From another one?
                By his cockle hat and staff,[3]   25
                And his sandal shoon.[4]
QUEEN   Alas, sweet lady, what imports this song?

---

7. The plot of ground involved is so
small that it cannot contain the number of
men involved in fighting nor furnish burial
space for the number of those who will die.
8. takes offense at trifles
9. an attempt to order
1. trifle

2. catastrophe
3. A "cockle hat," one decorated with a
shell, indicated that the wearer had made a
pilgrimage to the shrine of St. James at
Compostela in Spain. The staff also marked
the carrier as a pilgrim.
4. shoes

OPHELIA Say you? Nay, pray you mark.

He is dead and gone, lady,
He is dead and gone;
At his head a grass-green turf,
At his heels a stone.

O, ho!

QUEEN Nay, but, Ophelia—

OPHELIA Pray you mark.
White his shroud as the mountain snow—

Enter KING.

QUEEN Alas, look here, my lord.

OPHELIA Larded all with sweet flowers;
Which bewept to the grave did not go
With true-love showers.

KING How do you, pretty lady?

OPHELIA Well, God dild[5] you! They say the owl was a baker's daughter. Lord, we know what we are, but know not what we may be. God be at your table!

KING Conceit[6] upon her father.

OPHELIA Pray let's have no words of this, but when they ask you what it means, say you this:

Tomorrow is Saint Valentine's day,
All in the morning betime,
And I a maid at your window,
To be your Valentine.
Then up he rose, and donn'd his clo'es,
And dupped[7] the chamber-door,
Let in the maid, that out a maid
Never departed more.

KING Pretty Ophelia!

OPHELIA Indeed, without an oath, I'll make an end on't.

By Gis[8] and by Saint Charity,
Alack, and fie for shame!
Young men will do't, if they come to't;
By Cock,[9] they are to blame.
Quoth she "Before you tumbled me,
You promised me to wed."

He answers:

"So would I 'a done, by yonder sun,
An thou hadst not come to my bed."

KING How long hath she been thus?

OPHELIA I hope all will be well. We must be patient, but I cannot choose but weep to think they would lay him i' th' cold ground. My brother shall know of it, and so I thank you for your good counsel.

5. yield
6. thought
7. opened
8. Jesus
9. God

Come, my coach! Good night, ladies, good night. Sweet ladies, good 70
night, good night.   *Exit.*
KING   Follow her close; give her good watch, I pray you.

Exeunt HORATIO *and* GENTLEMAN.

O, this is the poison of deep grief; it springs
All from her father's death, and now behold!
O Gertrude, Gertrude!   75
When sorrows come, they come not single spies,
But in battalions: first, her father slain;
Next, your son gone, and he most violent author
Of his own just remove; the people muddied,[1]
Thick and unwholesome in their thoughts and whispers   80
For good Polonius' death; and we have done but greenly[2]
In hugger-mugger[3] to inter him; poor Ophelia
Divided from herself and her fair judgment,
Without the which we are pictures, or mere beasts;
Last, and as much containing as all these,   85
Her brother is in secret come from France,
Feeds on his wonder, keeps himself in clouds,
And wants not buzzers to infect his ear
With pestilent speeches of his father's death,
Wherein necessity, of matter beggared,[4]   90
Will nothing stick[5] our person to arraign[6]
In ear and ear.[7] O my dear Gertrude, this,
Like to a murd'ring piece,[8] in many places
Gives me superfluous death. Attend,   *A noise within.*

Enter a MESSENGER.

Where are my Switzers[9]? Let them guard the door.   95
What is the matter?
MESSENGER   Save yourself, my lord.
The ocean, overpeering of his list,[1]
Eats not the flats with more impiteous[2] haste
Than young Laertes, in a riotous head,[3]
O'erbears your officers. The rabble call him lord,   100
And as the world were now but to begin,
Antiquity forgot, custom not known,
The ratifiers and props of every word,
They cry "Choose we, Laertes shall be king."
Caps, hands, and tongues, applaud it to the clouds,   105
"Laertes shall be king, Laertes king."
QUEEN   How cheerfully on the false trail they cry[4]!   *A noise within.*
O, this is counter,[5] you false Danish dogs!
KING   The doors are broke.

---

1. disturbed
2. without judgment
3. haste
4. short on facts
5. hesitate
6. accuse
7. from both sides

8. a weapon designed to scatter its shot
9. Swiss guards
1. towering above its limits
2. pitiless
3. with an armed band
4. as if following the scent
5. backward

Enter LAERTES, *with* OTHERS.

LAERTES   Where is this king?—Sirs, stand you all without.   110
ALL   No, let's come in.
LAERTES   I pray you give me leave.
ALL   We will, we will.   *Exeunt his followers.*
LAERTES   I thank you. Keep[6] the door.—O thou vile king,
  Give me my father!
QUEEN   Calmly, good Laertes.
LAERTES   That drop of blood that's calm proclaims me bastard,   115
  Cries cuckold to my father, brands the harlot
  Even here between the chaste unsmirchéd brow
  Of my true mother.
KING   What is the cause, Laertes,
  That thy rebellion looks so giant-like?
  Let him go, Gertrude. Do not fear[7] our person.   120
  There's such divinity doth hedge a king
  That treason can but peep to[8] what it would,
  Acts little of his will. Tell me, Laertes,
  Why thou art thus incensed. Let him go, Gertrude.
  Speak, man.
LAERTES   Where is my father?
KING   Dead.   125
QUEEN   But not by him.
KING   Let him demand[9] his fill.
LAERTES   How came he dead? I'll not be juggled with.
  To hell allegiance, vows to the blackest devil,
  Conscience and grace to the profoundest pit!
  I dare damnation. To this point I stand,   130
  That both the worlds[1] I give to negligence,[2]
  Let come what comes, only I'll be revenged
  Most throughly for my father.
KING   Who shall stay you?
LAERTES   My will, not all the world's.
  And for my means, I'll husband[3] them so well   135
  They shall go far with little.
KING   Good Laertes,
  If you desire to know the certainty
  Of your dear father, is't writ in your revenge
  That, swoopstake,[4] you will draw both friend and foe,
  Winner and loser?
LAERTES   None but his enemies.   140
KING   Will you know them, then?
LAERTES   To his good friends thus wide I'll ope my arms,
  And like the kind life-rend'ring pelican,[5]
  Repast them with my blood.

---

6. guard
7. fear for
8. look at over or through a barrier
9. question
1. i.e., this and the next

2. disregard
3. manage
4. sweeping the board
5. The pelican was believed to feed her
young with her own blood.

KING   Why, now you speak
Like a good child and a true gentleman.   145
That I am guiltless of your father's death,
And am most sensibly in grief for it,
It shall as level[6] to your judgment 'pear
As day does to your eye.

      A noise within: "Let her come in."

LAERTES   How now? What noise is that?   150

      Enter OPHELIA.

O, heat dry up my brains! tears seven times salt
Burn out the sense[7] and virtue[8] of mine eye!
By heaven, thy madness shall be paid with weight
Till our scale turn the beam. O rose of May,
Dear maid, kind sister, sweet Ophelia!   155
O heavens! is't possible a young maid's wits
Should be as mortal as an old man's life?
Nature is fine[9] in love, and where 'tis fine
It sends some precious instance of itself
After the thing it loves.[1]   160
OPHELIA   They bore him barefac'd on the bier;
             Hey non nonny, nonny, hey nonny;
             And in his grave rain'd many a tear—

Fare you well, my dove!
LAERTES   Hadst thou thy wits, and didst persuade revenge,   165
It could not move thus.
OPHELIA   You must sing "A-down, a-down, and you call him a-down-
a." O, how the wheel becomes it! It is the false steward, that stole his
master's daughter.[2]
LAERTES   This nothing's more than matter.   170
OPHELIA   There's rosemary, that's for remembrance. Pray you, love,
remember. And there is pansies, that's for thoughts.
LAERTES   A document[3] in madness, thoughts and remembrance fitted.
OPHELIA   There's fennel for you, and columbines. There's rue for you,
and here's some for me. We may call it herb of grace a Sundays. O,   175
you must wear your rue with a difference. There's a daisy. I would
give you some violets, but they withered all when my father died.
They say 'a made a good end.

      [*Sings.*]   For bonny sweet Robin is all my joy.

LAERTES   Thought and affliction, passion, hell itself,   180
She turns to favor[4] and to prettiness.

---

6. plain
7. feeling
8. function
9. refined
1. Laertes means that Ophelia, because of her love for her father, gave up her sanity as a token of grief at his death.
2. The "wheel" refers to the *burden* or refrain of a song, in this case "A-down, a-down, and you call him a-down-a." The

ballad to which she refers was about a false steward. Others have suggested that the "wheel" is the Wheel of Fortune, a spinning wheel to whose rhythm such a song might have been sung or a kind of dance movement performed by Ophelia as she sings.
3. lesson
4. beauty

OPHELIA   And will 'a not come again?
             And will 'a not come again?
                No, no, he is dead,
                   Go to thy death-bed,   185
             He never will come again.

             His beard was as white as snow,
             All flaxen was his poll[5];
                He is gone, he is gone,
                   And we cast away moan: 190
             God-a-mercy on his soul!

      And of all Christian souls, I pray God. God b'wi'you.   *Exit.*
LAERTES   Do you see this, O God?
KING   Laertes, I must commune with your grief,
      Or you deny me right. Go but apart,   195
      Make choice of whom your wisest friends you will,
      And they shall hear and judge 'twixt you and me.
      If by direct or by collateral[6] hand
      They find us touched,[7] we will our kingdom give,
      Our crown, our life, and all that we call ours,   200
      To you in satisfaction; but if not,
      Be you content to lend your patience to us,
      And we shall jointly labor with your soul
      To give it due content.
LAERTES   Let this be so.
      His means of death, his obscure funeral—   205
      No trophy, sword, nor hatchment,[8] o'er his bones,
      No noble rite nor formal ostentation[9]—
      Cry to be heard, as 'twere from heaven to earth,
      That I must call't in question.
KING   So you shall;
      And where th' offence is, let the great axe fall.   210
      I pray you go with me.   *Exeunt.*

      SCENE 6: *Another room in the castle. Enter* HORATIO *and*
      a GENTLEMAN.

HORATIO   What are they that would speak with me?
GENTLEMAN   Sea-faring men, sir. They say they have letters for you.
HORATIO   Let them come in.   *Exit* GENTLEMAN.
      I do not know from what part of the world
      I should be greeted, if not from Lord Hamlet.   5

         Enter SAILORS.

SAILOR   God bless you, sir.
HORATIO   Let him bless thee too.
SAILOR   'A shall, sir, an't please him. There's a letter for you, sir—it

---

5. head   8. coat of arms
6. indirect   9. pomp
7. by guilt

came from th' ambassador that was bound for England—if your
name be Horatio, as I am let to know[1] it is.   10
HORATIO   [*reads*]   "Horatio, when thou shalt have overlooked[2] this,
give these fellows some means[3] to the king. They have letters for
him. Ere we were two days old at sea, a pirate of very warlike appointment[4] gave us chase. Finding ourselves too slow of sail, we put
on a compelled valor, and in the grapple I boarded them. On the in-   15
stant they got clear of our ship, so I alone became their prisoner.
They have dealt with me like thieves of mercy, but they knew what
they did; I am to do a good turn for them. Let the king have the
letters I have sent, and repair thou to me with as much speed as thou
wouldest fly death. I have words to speak in thine ear will make   20
thee dumb; yet are they much too light for the bore of the matter.[5]
These good fellows will bring thee where I am. Rosencrantz and
Guildenstern hold their course for England. Of them I have much to
tell thee. Farewell.

> He that thou knowest thine, HAMLET."

Come, I will give you way[6] for these your letters,   25
And do't the speedier that you may direct me
To him from whom you brought them.   *Exeunt.*

SCENE 7: *Another room in the castle. Enter* KING *and* LAERTES.

KING   Now must your conscience my acquittance seal,[7]
And you must put me in your heart for friend,
Sith you have heard, and with a knowing ear,
That he which hath your noble father slain
Pursued my life.
LAERTES   It well appears. But tell me   5
Why you proceeded not against these feats,
So criminal and so capital in nature,
As by your safety, greatness, wisdom, all things else,
You mainly were stirred up.
KING   O, for two special reasons,
Which may to you, perhaps, seem much unsinewed,[8]   10
But yet to me th' are strong. The queen his mother
Lives almost by his looks, and for myself—
My virtue or my plague, be it either which—
She is so conjunctive[9] to my life and soul
That, as the star moves not but in his sphere,[1]   15
I could not but by her. The other motive,
Why to a public count[2] I might not go,
Is the great love the general gender[3] bear him,
Who, dipping all his faults in their affection,

---

1. informed
2. read through
3. access
4. equipment
5. A figure from gunnery, referring to
shot which is too small for the size of the
weapon to be fired.
6. means of delivery
7. grant me innocent

8. weak
9. closely joined
1. A reference to the Ptolemaic cosmology in which planets and stars were believed to revolve about the earth in crystal-
line spheres concentric with the earth.
2. reckoning
3. common people

Work like the spring that turneth wood to stone,[4]   20
Convert his gyves[5] to graces; so that my arrows,
Too slightly timbered[6] for so loud a wind,
Would have reverted to my bow again,
But not where I have aimed them.
LAERTES   And so have I a noble father lost,   25
A sister driven into desp'rate terms,
Whose worth, if praises may go back again,
Stood challenger on mount of all the age
For her perfections. But my revenge will come.
KING   Break not your sleeps for that. You must not think   30
That we are made of stuff so flat and dull
That we can let our beard be shook with danger,
And think it pastime. You shortly shall hear more.
I loved your father, and we love our self,
And that, I hope, will teach you to imagine—   35

Enter a MESSENGER *with letters.*

MESSENGER   These to your majesty; this to the queen.
KING   From Hamlet! Who brought them?
MESSENGER   Sailors, my lord, they say. I saw them not.
They were given me by Claudio; he received them
Of him that brought them.
KING   Laertes, you shall hear them.—   40
Leave us.   *Exit* MESSENGER.
    [*Reads.*] "High and mighty, you shall know I am set naked on
your kingdom. Tomorrow shall I beg leave to see your kingly eyes;
when I shall, first asking your pardon thereunto, recount the occasion
of my sudden and more strange return.   45
                                        HAMLET."
What should this mean? Are all the rest come back?
Or is it some abuse,[7] and no such thing?
LAERTES   Know you the hand?
KING   'Tis Hamlet's character.[8] "Naked"!   50
And in a postscript here, he says "alone."
Can you devise[9] me?
LAERTES   I am lost in it, my lord. But let him come.
It warms the very sickness in my heart
That I shall live and tell him to his teeth   55
"Thus didest thou."
KING   If it be so, Laertes—
As how should it be so, how otherwise?—
Will you be ruled by me?
LAERTES   Ay, my lord,
So you will not o'errule me to a peace.
KING   To thine own peace. If he be now returned,   60

4. Certain English springs contain so
much lime in the water that a lime covering will be deposited on a log placed in
one of them for a length of time.
    5. fetters

6. shafted
7. trick
8. handwriting
9. explain it to

As checking at[1] his voyage, and that he means
No more to undertake it, I will work him
To an exploit now ripe in my device,
Under the which he shall not choose but fall;
And for his death no wind of blame shall breathe   65
But even his mother shall uncharge[2] the practice
And call it accident.

LAERTES   My lord, I will be ruled;
  The rather if you could devise it so
  That I might be the organ.[3]

KING   It falls right.
  You have been talked of since your travel much,   70
  And that in Hamlet's hearing, for a quality
  Wherein they say you shine. Your sum of parts
  Did not together pluck such envy from him
  As did that one, and that, in my regard,
  Of the unworthiest siege.[4]

LAERTES   What part is that, my lord?   75

KING   A very riband in the cap of youth,
  Yet needful too, for youth no less becomes
  The light and careless livery that it wears
  Than settled age his sables and his weeds,[5]
  Importing health and graveness. Two months since   80
  Here was a gentleman of Normandy.
  I have seen myself, and served against, the French,
  And they can[6] well on horseback, but this gallant
  Had witchcraft in't. He grew unto his seat,
  And to such wondrous doing brought his horse,   85
  As had he been incorpsed and demi-natured
  With the brave beast. So far he topped my thought
  That I, in forgery[7] of shapes and tricks,
  Come short of what he did.[8]

LAERTES   A Norman was't?

KING   A Norman.   90

LAERTES   Upon my life, Lamord.

KING   The very same.

LAERTES   I know him well. He is the brooch indeed
  And gem of all the nation.

KING   He made confession[9] of you,
  And gave you such a masterly report   95
  For art and exercise in your defence,[1]
  And for your rapier most especial,
  That he cried out 'twould be a sight indeed
  If one could match you. The scrimers[2] of their nation

---

1. turning aside from
2. not accuse
3. instrument
4. rank
5. dignified clothing
6. perform
7. imagination
8. The gentleman referred to was so skilled in horsemanship that he seemed to share one body with the horse, "incorpsed." The King further extends the compliment by saying that he appeared like the mythical centaur, a creature who was man from the waist up and horse from the waist down, therefore "demi-natured."

9. gave a report
1. skill in fencing
2. fencers

He swore had neither motion, guard, nor eye, 100
If you opposed them. Sir, this report of his
Did Hamlet so envenom with his envy
That he could nothing do but wish and beg
Your sudden coming o'er, to play with you.
Now out of this—
LAERTES What out of this, my lord? 105
KING Laertes, was your father dear to you?
Or are you like the painting of a sorrow,
A face without a heart?
LAERTES Why ask you this?
KING Not that I think you did not love your father,
But that I know love is begun by time, 110
And that I see in passages of proof,[3]
Time qualifies the spark and fire of it.
There lives within the very flame of love
A kind of wick or snuff that will abate it,
And nothing is at a like goodness still, 115
For goodness, growing to a plurisy,[4]
Dies in his own too much.[5] That we would do,
We should do when we would; for this "would" changes,
And hath abatements and delays as many
As there are tongues, are hands, are accidents, 120
And then this "should" is like a spendthrift's sigh
That hurts by easing. But to the quick of th' ulcer—
Hamlet comes back; what would you undertake
To show yourself in deed your father's son
More than in words?
LAERTES To cut his throat i' th' church. 125
KING No place indeed should murder sanctuarize[6];
Revenge should have no bounds. But, good Laertes,
Will you do this? Keep close within your chamber.
Hamlet returned shall know you are come home.
We'll put on those shall praise your excellence, 130
And set a double varnish[7] on the fame
The Frenchman gave you, bring you in fine[8] together,
And wager on your heads. He, being remiss,[9]
Most generous, and free from all contriving,
Will not peruse[1] the foils, so that with ease, 135
Or with a little shuffling, you may choose
A sword unbated,[2] and in a pass of practice
Requite him for your father.
LAERTES I will do't,
And for that purpose I'll anoint my sword.
I bought an unction of a mountebank, 140
So mortal that but dip a knife in it,

---

3. tests of experience
4. fullness
5. excess
6. provide sanctuary for murder
7. gloss

8. in short
9. careless
1. examine
2. not blunted

Where it draws blood no cataplasm[3] so rare,
Collected from all simples[4] that have virtue
Under the moon, can save the thing from death
That is but scratched withal. I'll touch my point   145
With this contagion, that if I gall[5] him slightly,
It may be death.
KING   Let's further think of this,
Weigh what convenience both of time and means
May fit us to our shape. If this should fail,
And that our drift look[6] through our bad performance,   150
'Twere better not assayed. Therefore this project
Should have a back or second that might hold
If this did blast in proof.[7] Soft, let me see.
We'll make a solemn wager on your cunnings—
I ha't.   155
When in your motion you are hot and dry—
As make your bouts more violent to that end—
And that he calls for drink, I'll have preferred him
A chalice for the nonce, whereon but sipping,
If he by chance escape your venomed stuck,[8]   160
Our purpose may hold there.—But stay, what noise?

    Enter QUEEN.

QUEEN   One woe doth tread upon another's heel,
So fast they follow. Your sister's drowned, Laertes.
LAERTES   Drowned? O, where?
QUEEN   There is a willow grows aslant the brook   165
That shows his hoar leaves in the glassy stream.
Therewith fantastic garlands did she make
Of crowflowers, nettles, daisies, and long purples
That liberal[9] shepherds give a grosser[1] name,
But our cold[2] maids do dead men's fingers call them.   170
There on the pendent boughs her coronet weeds
Clamb'ring to hang, an envious[3] sliver broke,
When down her weedy trophies and herself
Fell in the weeping brook. Her clothes spread wide,
And mermaid-like awhile they bore her up,   175
Which time she chanted snatches of old tunes,
As one incapable[4] of her own distress,
Or like a creature native and indued[5]
Unto that element. But long it could not be
Till that her garments, heavy with their drink,   180
Pulled the poor wretch from her melodious lay
To muddy death.
LAERTES   Alas, then she is drowned?
QUEEN   Drowned, drowned.

---

3. poultice
4. herbs
5. scratch
6. intent become obvious
7. fail when tried
8. thrust

9. vulgar
1. coarser
2. chaste
3. malicious
4. unaware
5. habituated

LAERTES   Too much of water hast thou, poor Ophelia,
   And therefore I forbid my tears; but yet   185
   It is our trick; nature her custom holds,
   Let shame say what it will. When these are gone,
   The woman will be out. Adieu, my lord.
   I have a speech o' fire that fain would blaze
   But that this folly drowns it.   *Exit.*
KING   Let's follow, Gertrude.   190
   How much I had to do to calm his rage!
   Now fear I this will give it start again;
   Therefore let's follow.   *Exeunt.*

Act 5

SCENE 1: *A churchyard. Enter two* CLOWNS.[6]

CLOWN   Is she to be buried in Christian burial when she wilfully
   seeks her own salvation?

OTHER   I tell thee she is. Therefore make her grave straight. The
   crowner[7] hath sat on her,[8] and finds it Christian burial.

CLOWN   How can that be, unless she drowned herself in her own de-   5
   fence?

OTHER   Why, 'tis found so.

CLOWN   It must be "se offendendo";[9] it cannot be else. For here lies
   the point: if I drown myself wittingly, it argues an act, and an act
   hath three branches—it is to act, to do, to perform; argal,[1] she   10
   drowned herself wittingly.

OTHER   Nay, but hear you, Goodman Delver.

CLOWN   Give me leave. Here lies the water; good. Here stands the
   man; good. If the man go to this water and drown himself, it is, will
   he, nill he, he goes—mark you that. But if the water come to him   15
   and drown him, he drowns not himself. Argal, he that is not guilty
   of his own death shortens not his own life.

OTHER   But is this law?

CLOWN   Ay, marry, is't; crowner's quest[2] law.

OTHER   Will you ha' the truth on't? If this had not been a gentle-   20
   woman, she should have been buried out o' Christian burial.

CLOWN   Why, there thou say'st. And the more pity that great folk
   should have count'nance[3] in this world to drown or hang themselves
   more than their even-Christen.[4] Come, my spade. There is no ancient
   gentlemen but gard'ners, ditchers, and grave-makers. They hold up   25
   Adam's profession.

OTHER   Was he a gentleman?

CLOWN   'A was the first that ever bore arms.

OTHER   Why, he had none.

CLOWN   What, art a heathen? How dost thou understand the Scrip-   30

---

6. rustics
7. coroner
8. held an inquest
9. an error for *se defendendo,* in self-
defense

1. therefore
2. inquest
3. approval
4. fellow Christians

ture? The Scripture says Adam digged. Could he dig without arms?
I'll put another question to thee. If thou answerest me not to the
purpose, confess thyself—

OTHER   Go to.

CLOWN   What is he that builds stronger than either the mason, the 35
shipwright, or the carpenter?

OTHER   The gallows-maker, for that frame outlives a thousand tenants.

CLOWN   I like thy wit well, in good faith. The gallows does well. But
how does it well? It does well to those that do ill. Now thou dost ill
to say the gallows is built stronger than the church. Argal, the gal- 40
lows may do well to thee. To't again,[5] come.

OTHER   Who builds stronger than a mason, a shipwright, or a carpenter?

CLOWN   Ay tell me that, and unyoke.[6]

OTHER   Marry, now I can tell.   45

CLOWN   To't.

OTHER   Mass, I cannot tell.

CLOWN   Cudgel thy brains no more about it, for your dull ass will not
mend his pace with beating. And when you are asked this question
next, say "a grave-maker." The houses he makes lasts till doomsday. 50
Go, get thee in, and fetch me a stoup[7] of liquor. *Exit* OTHER CLOWN.

Enter HAMLET *and* HORATIO *as* CLOWN *digs and sings.*

   In youth, when I did love, did love,
      Methought it was very sweet,
   To contract[8] the time for-a my behove,[9]
      O, methought there-a was nothing-a meet.[1]   55

HAMLET   Has this fellow no feeling of his business, that 'a sings in
grave-making?

HORATIO   Custom hath made it in him a property of easiness.

HAMLET   'Tis e'en so. The hand of little employment hath the daintier
sense.   60

CLOWN   But age, with his stealing steps,
                     Hath clawed me in his clutch,
                  And hath shipped me into the land,
                     As if I had never been such.

Throws up a skull.

HAMLET   That skull had a tongue in it, and could sing once. How the 65
knave jowls[2] it to the ground, as if 'twere Cain's jawbone, that did
the first murder! This might be the pate of a politician, which this
ass now o'erreaches[3]; one that would circumvent God, might it not?

HORATIO   It might, my lord.

HAMLET   Or of a courtier, which could say "Good morrow, sweet lord! 70
How dost thou, sweet lord?" This might be my Lord Such-a-one,
that praised my Lord Such-a-one's horse, when 'a meant to beg it,
might it not?

5. guess again
6. finish the matter
7. mug
8. shorten
9. advantage
1. The gravedigger's song is a free ver-

sion of "The aged lover renounceth love"
by Thomas, Lord Vaux, published in *Tot-
tel's Miscellany*, 1557.
2. hurls
3. gets the better of

HORATIO   Ay, my lord.

HAMLET   Why, e'en so, and now my Lady Worm's, chapless,[4] and   75
knock'd abut the mazzard[5] with a sexton's spade. Here's fine revolution,[6] an we had the trick to see't. Did these bones cost no more the
breeding but to play at loggets with them?[7] Mine ache to think on't.

CLOWN   A pick-axe and a spade, a spade,
                   For and a shrouding sheet: 80
                   O, a pit of clay for to be made
                   For such a guest is meet.

Throws up another skull.

HAMLET   There's another. Why may not that be the skull of a lawyer?
Where be his quiddities now, his quillets, his cases, his tenures, and
his tricks? Why does he suffer this mad knave now to knock him   85
about the sconce[8] with a dirty shovel, and will not tell him of his
action of battery? Hum! This fellow might be in's time a great buyer
of land, with his statutes, his recognizances, his fines, his double
vouchers, his recoveries. Is this the fine[9] of his fines, and the recovery
of his recoveries, to have his fine pate full of fine dirt? Will his vouch-   90
ers vouch him no more of his purchases, and double ones too, than
the length and breadth of a pair of indentures[1]? The very convey-
ances of his lands will scarcely lie in this box, and must th' inheritor
himself have no more, ha?[2]

HORATIO   Not a jot more, my lord.   95

HAMLET   Is not parchment made of sheepskins?

HORATIO   Ay, my lord, and of calves' skins too.

HAMLET   They are sheep and calves which seek out assurance in that.
I will speak to this fellow. Whose grave's this, sirrah?

CLOWN   Mine, sir.   100

        [*Sings.*] O, a pit of clay for to be made—

HAMLET   I think it be thine indeed, for thou liest in't.

CLOWN   You lie out on't, sir, and therefore 'tis not yours. For my part,
I do not lie in't, yet it is mine.

HAMLET   Thou dost lie in't, to be in't and say it is thine. 'Tis for the [105]
dead, not for the quick[3]; therefore thou liest.

CLOWN   'Tis a quick lie, sir; 'twill away again from me to you.

HAMLET   What man dost thou dig it for?

CLOWN   For no man, sir.

HAMLET   What woman, then?   110

CLOWN   For none neither.

HAMLET   Who is to be buried in't?

CLOWN   One that was a woman, sir; but, rest her soul, she's dead.

HAMLET   How absolute[4] the knave is! We must speak by the card,[5] or
equivocation will undo us. By the Lord, Horatio, this three years I [115]

---

4. lacking a lower jaw
5. head
6. skill
7. "Loggets" were small pieces of wood
thrown as part of a game.
8. head
9. end

1. contracts
2. In this speech Hamlet reels off a list
of legal terms relating to property trans-
actions.
3. living
4. precise
5. exactly

have took note of it, the age is grown so picked[6] that the toe of the peasant comes so near the heel of the courtier, he galls his kibe.[7] How long hast thou been a grave-maker?

CLOWN   Of all the days i' th' year, I came to't that day that our last King Hamlet overcame Fortinbras.   120

HAMLET   How long is that since?

CLOWN   Cannot you tell that? Every fool can tell that. It was that very day that young Hamlet was born—he that is mad, and sent into England.

HAMLET   Ay, marry, why was he sent into England?   125

CLOWN   Why, because 'a was mad. 'A shall recover his wits there; or, if 'a do not, 'tis no great matter there.

HAMLET   Why?

CLOWN   'Twill not be seen in him there. There the men are as mad as he.   130

HAMLET   How came he mad?

CLOWN   Very strangely, they say.

HAMLET   How strangely?

CLOWN   Faith, e'en with losing his wits.

HAMLET   Upon what ground?   135

CLOWN   Why, here in Denmark. I have been sexton here, man and boy, thirty years.

HAMLET   How long will a man lie i' th' earth ere he rot?

CLOWN   Faith, if 'a be not rotten before 'a die—as we have many pocky[8] corses now-a-days that will scarce hold the laying in—'a will   140 last you some eight year or nine year. A tanner will last you nine year.

HAMLET   Why he more than another?

CLOWN   Why, sir, his hide is so tanned with his trade that 'a will keep out water a great while; and your water is a sore decayer of your   145 whoreson[9] dead body. Here's a skull now hath lien[1] you i' th' earth three and twenty years.

HAMLET   Whose was it?

CLOWN   A whoreson mad fellow's it was. Whose do you think it was?

HAMLET   Nay, I know not.   150

CLOWN   A pestilence on him for a mad rogue! 'A poured a flagon of Rhenish on my head once. This same skull, sir, was, sir, Yorick's skull, the king's jester.

HAMLET [*takes the skull*]   This?

CLOWN   E'en that.   155

HAMLET   Alas, poor Yorick! I knew him, Horatio—a fellow of infinite jest, of most excellent fancy. He hath bore me on his back a thousand times, and now how abhorred in my imagination it is! My gorge[2] rises at it. Here hung those lips that I have kissed I know not how oft. Where be your gibes now, your gambols, your songs, your flashes   160 of merriment that were wont to set the table on a roar? Not one now to mock your own grinning? Quite chap-fall'n[3]? Now get you to my

6. refined
7. rubs a blister on his heel
8. corrupted by syphilis
9. bastard (not literally)

1. lain
2. throat
3. lacking a lower jaw

lady's chamber, and tell her, let her paint an inch thick, to this favor[4] she must come. Make her laugh at that. Prithee, Horatio, tell me one thing.   165

HORATIO   What's that, my lord?

HAMLET   Dost thou think Alexander looked o' this fashion i' th' earth?

HORATIO   E'en so.

HAMLET   And smelt so? Pah!   *Throws down the skull.*

HORATIO   E'en so, my lord.   170

HAMLET   To what base uses we may return, Horatio! Why may not imagination trace the noble dust of Alexander till 'a find it stopping a bung-hole?

HORATIO   'Twere to consider too curiously[5] to consider so.

HAMLET   No, faith, not a jot, but to follow him thither with modesty[6]   175 enough, and likelihood to lead it. Alexander died, Alexander was buried, Alexander returneth to dust; the dust is earth; of earth we make loam; and why of that loam whereto he was converted might they not stop a beer-barrel?

> Imperious Cæsar, dead and turned to clay,   180
> Might stop a hole to keep the wind away.
> O, that that earth which kept the world in awe
> Should patch a wall t'expel the winter's flaw![7]

But soft, but soft awhile! Here comes the king,
The queen, the courtiers.

> *Enter* KING, QUEEN, LAERTES, *and the Corse with a* PRIEST *and*
> LORDS *attendant.*

                              Who is this they follow?   185
And with such maiméd[8] rites? This doth betoken
The corse they follow did with desperate hand
Fordo[9] it own life. 'Twas of some estate.[1]
Couch[2] we awhile and mark.   *Retires with* HORATIO.

LAERTES   What ceremony else[3]?   190

HAMLET   That is Laertes, a very noble youth. Mark.

LAERTES   What ceremony else?

PRIEST   Her obsequies have been as far enlarged[4]
As we have warranty. Her death was doubtful,
And but that great command o'ersways the order,[5]   195
She should in ground unsanctified been lodged
Till the last trumpet. For charitable prayers,
Shards, flints, and pebbles, should be thrown on her.
Yet here she is allowed her virgin crants,[6]
Her maiden strewments,[7] and the bringing home   200
Of bell and burial.

LAERTES   Must there no more be done?

4. appearance
5. precisely
6. moderation
7. gusty wind
8. cut short
9. destroy. *It*: its.
1. rank

2. conceal ourselves
3. more
4. extended
5. usual rules
6. wreaths
7. flowers strewn on the grave

PRIEST   No more be done.
We should profane the service of the dead
To sing a requiem and such rest to her
As to peace-parted souls.
LAERTES   Lay her i' th' earth,   205
And from her fair and unpolluted flesh
May violets spring! I tell thee, churlish priest,
A minist'ring angel shall my sister be
When thou liest howling.[8]
HAMLET   What, the fair Ophelia!
QUEEN   Sweets to the sweet. Farewell!   *Scatters flowers.* 210
I hoped thou shouldst have been my Hamlet's wife.
I thought thy bride-bed to have decked, sweet maid,
And not have strewed thy grave.
LAERTES   O, treble woe
Fall ten times treble on that curséd head
Whose wicked deed thy most ingenious sense[9]   215
Deprived thee of! Hold off the earth awhile,
Till I have caught her once more in mine arms.
                                   Leaps into the grave.
Now pile your dust upon the quick and dead,
Till of this flat a mountain you have made
T' o'er-top old Pelion or the skyish head   220
Of blue Olympus.[1]
HAMLET [*coming forward*]   What is he whose grief
Bears such an emphasis, whose phrase of sorrow
Conjures[2] the wand'ring stars, and makes them stand
Like wonder-wounded hearers? This is I,
Hamlet the Dane.   225

        HAMLET *leaps into the grave and they grapple.*

LAERTES   The devil take thy soul!
HAMLET   Thou pray'st not well.
I prithee take thy fingers from my throat,
For though I am not splenitive[3] and rash,
Yet have I in me something dangerous,
Which let thy wisdom fear. Hold off thy hand.   230
KING   Pluck them asunder.
QUEEN   Hamlet! Hamlet!
ALL   Gentlemen!
HORATIO   Good my lord, be quiet.

        The ATTENDANTS *part them, and they come out of the grave.*

HAMLET   Why, I will fight with him upon this theme   235
Until my eyelids will no longer wag.[4]

---

8. in Hell
9. lively mind
1. The rivalry between Laertes and
Hamlet in this scene extends even to their
rhetoric. Pelion and Olympus, mentioned
here by Laertes, and Ossa, mentioned below by Hamlet, were Greek mountains
noted in mythology for their height. Olym-

pus was the reputed home of the gods, and
the other two were piled one on top of the
other by the Giants in an attempt to reach
the top of Olympus and overthrow the gods.
2. casts a spell on
3. hot-tempered
4. move

QUEEN   O my son, what theme?

HAMLET   I loved Ophelia. Forty thousand brothers
  Could not with all their quantity of love
  Make up my sum. What wilt thou do for her?   240

KING   O, he is mad, Laertes.

QUEEN   For love of God, forbear[5] him.

HAMLET   'Swounds, show me what th'owt do.
  Woo't[6] weep, woo't fight, woo't fast, woo't tear thyself,
  Woo't drink up eisel,[7] eat a crocodile?   245
  I'll do't. Dost come here to whine?
  To outface[8] me with leaping in her grave?
  Be buried quick with her, and so will I.
  And if thou prate of mountains, let them throw
  Millions of acres on us, till our ground,   250
  Singeing his pate against the burning zone,[9]
  Make Ossa like a wart! Nay, an thou'lt mouth,
  I'll rant as well as thou.

QUEEN   This is mere madness;
  And thus awhile the fit will work on him.
  Anon, as patient as the female dove   255
  When that her golden couplets[1] are disclosed,
  His silence will sit drooping.

HAMLET   Hear you, sir.
  What is the reason that you use me thus?
  I loved you ever. But it is no matter.   260
  Let Hercules himself do what he may,
  The cat will mew, and dog will have his day.

KING   I pray thee, good Horatio, wait upon[2] him.
                        Exeunt HAMLET *and* HORATIO.
  [*To* LAERTES.] Strengthen your patience in our last night's speech.
  We'll put the matter to the present push.[3]—
  Good Gertrude, set some watch over your son.—   265
  This grave shall have a living monument.
  An hour of quiet shortly shall we see;
  Till then in patience our proceeding be.   *Exeunt.*

  SCENE 2: *A hall or public room. Enter* HAMLET *and* HORATIO.

HAMLET   So much for this, sir; now shall you see the other.
  You do remember all the circumstance?

HORATIO   Remember it, my lord!

HAMLET   Sir, in my heart there was a kind of fighting
  That would not let me sleep. Methought I lay   5
  Worse than the mutines[4] in the bilboes.[5] Rashly,
  And praised be rashness for it—let us know,
  Our indiscretion sometime serves us well,

---

5. bear with
6. will you
7. vinegar
8. get the best of
9. sky in the torrid zone

1. pair of eggs
2. attend
3. immediate trial
4. mutineers
5. stocks

When our deep plots do pall; and that should learn[6] us   10
There's a divinity that shapes our ends,
Rough-hew them how we will—
HORATIO   That is most certain.
HAMLET   Up from my cabin,
My sea-gown scarfed[7] about me, in the dark
Groped I to find out them, had my desire,
Fingered[8] their packet, and in fine[9] withdrew   15
To mine own room again, making so bold,
My fears forgetting manners, to unseal
Their grand commission; where I found, Horatio—
Ah, royal knavery!—an exact[1] command,
Larded[2] with many several sorts of reasons,   20
Importing Denmark's health, and England's too,
With, ho! such bugs and goblins in my life,[3]
That on the supervise,[4] no leisure bated,
No, not to stay the grinding of the axe,
My head should be struck off.
HORATIO   Is't possible?   25
HAMLET   Here's the commission; read it at more leisure.
But wilt thou hear now how I did proceed?
HORATIO   I beseech you.
HAMLET   Being thus benetted[5] round with villainies,
Or I could make a prologue to my brains,   30
They had begun the play. I sat me down,
Devised[6] a new commission, wrote it fair.[7]
I once did hold it, as our statists[8] do,
A baseness to write fair, and labored much
How to forget that learning; but sir, now   35
It did me yeoman's service. Wilt thou know
Th' effect[9] of what I wrote?
HORATIO   Ay, good my lord.
HAMLET   An earnest conjuration from the king,
As England was his faithful tributary,[1]
As love between them like the palm might flourish,   40
As peace should still her wheaten garland wear
And stand a comma 'tween their amities,[2]
And many such like as's of great charge,[3]
That on the view and knowing of these contents,
Without debatement[4] further more or less,   45
He should those bearers put to sudden death,
Not shriving-time allowed.[5]
HORATIO   How was this sealed?

6. teach
7. wrapped
8. stole
9. quickly
1. precisely stated
2. garnished
3. such dangers if I remained alive
4. as soon as the commission was read
5. caught in a net

6. made
7. legibly
8. politicians
9. contents
1. vassal
2. link friendships
3. import
4. consideration
5. without time for confession

HAMLET   Why, even in that was heaven ordinant,[6]
 I had my father's signet in my purse,
 Which was the model of that Danish seal,   50
 Folded the writ up in the form of th' other,
 Subscribed it, gave't th' impression,[7] placed it safely,
 The changeling[8] never known. Now, the next day
 Was our sea-fight, and what to this was sequent[9]
 Thou knowest already.   55
HORATIO   So Guildenstern and Rosencrantz go to't.
HAMLET   Why, man, they did make love to this employment.
 They are not near[1] my conscience; their defeat[2]
 Does by their own insinuation grow.
 'Tis dangerous when the baser nature comes   60
 Between the pass[3] and fell[4] incensèd points
 Of mighty opposites.
HORATIO   Why, what a king is this!
HAMLET   Does it not, think thee, stand me now upon—
 He that hath killed my king and whored my mother,
 Popped in between th' election and my hopes,   65
 Thrown out his angle[5] for my proper life,
 And with such coz'nage[6]—is't not perfect conscience
 To quit[7] him with this arm? And is't not to be damned
 To let this canker of our nature come
 In further evil?   70
HORATIO   It must be shortly known to him from England
 What is the issue[8] of the business there.
HAMLET   It will be short[9]; the interim is mine.
 And a man's life's no more than to say "one."
 But I am very sorry, good Horatio,   75
 That to Laertes I forgot myself;
 For by the image of my cause I see
 The portraiture of his. I'll court his favors.
 But sure the bravery[1] of his grief did put me
 Into a tow'ring passion.
HORATIO   Peace; who comes here?   80

  Enter OSRIC.

OSRIC   Your lordship is right welcome back to Denmark.
HAMLET   I humbly thank you, sir. [*Aside to* HORATIO.] Dost know
 this water-fly?
HORATIO [*aside to* HAMLET]   No, my good lord.
HAMLET [*aside to* HORATIO]   Thy state is the more gracious, for 'tis a 85
 vice to know him. He hath much land, and fertile. Let a beast be
 lord of beasts, and his crib shall stand at the king's mess. 'Tis a
 chough,[2] but as I say, spacious in the possession of dirt.

6. operative
7. of the seal
8. alteration
9. followed
1. do not touch
2. death
3. thrust
4. cruel

5. fishhook
6. trickery
7. repay
8. outcome
9. soon
1. exaggerated display
2. jackdaw

OSRIC   Sweet lord, if your lordship were at leisure, I should impart a thing to you from his majesty.   90

HAMLET   I will receive it, sir, with all diligence of spirit. Put your bonnet to his right use. 'Tis for the head.

OSRIC   I thank your lordship, it is very hot.

HAMLET   No, believe me, 'tis very cold; the wind is northerly.

OSRIC   It is indifferent[3] cold, my lord, indeed.   95

HAMLET   But yet methinks it is very sultry and hot for my complexion.[4]

OSRIC   Exceedingly, my lord; it is very sultry, as 'twere—I cannot tell how. My lord, his majesty bade me signify to you that 'a has laid a great wager on your head. Sir, this is the matter—   100

HAMLET   I beseech you, remember.

> HAMLET *moves him to put on his hat.*

OSRIC   Nay, good my lord; for my ease, in good faith. Sir, here is newly come to court Laertes; believe me, an absolute[5] gentleman, full of most excellent differences,[6] of very soft society and great showing.[7] Indeed, to speak feelingly of him, he is the card or calendar[8] of gentry, for you shall find in him the continent[9] of what part a gentleman would see.   105

HAMLET   Sir, his definement[1] suffers no perdition in you, though I know to divide him inventorially[2] would dozy[3] th' arithmetic of memory, and yet but yaw[4] neither in respect of his quick sail. But in the verity of extolment, I take him to be a soul of great article,[5] and his infusion[6] of such dearth and rareness as, to make true diction[7] of him, his semblage[8] is his mirror, and who else would trace[9] him, his umbrage,[1] nothing more.   110

OSRIC   Your lordship speaks most infallibly of him.   115

HAMLET   The concernancy,[2] sir? Why do we wrap the gentleman in our more rawer breath?[3]

OSRIC   Sir?

HORATIO   Is't not possible to understand in another tongue? You will to't, sir, really.   120

HAMLET   What imports the nomination[4] of this gentleman?

OSRIC   Of Laertes?

HORATIO   [*aside*]   His purse is empty already. All's golden words are spent.

HAMLET   Of him, sir.   125

OSRIC   I know you are not ignorant—

HAMLET   I would you did, sir; yet, in faith, if you did, it would not much approve me. Well, sir.

OSRIC   You are not ignorant of what excellence Laertes is—

---

3. moderately
4. temperament
5. perfect
6. qualities
7. good manners
8. measure
9. sum total
1. description
2. examine bit by bit
3. daze

4. steer wildly
5. scope
6. nature
7. telling
8. rival
9. keep pace with
1. shadow
2. meaning
3. cruder words
4. naming

HAMLET   I dare not confess that, lest I should compare[5] with him in 130
excellence; but to know a man well were to know himself.

OSRIC   I mean, sir, for his weapon; but in the imputation[6] laid on him
by them, in his meed he's unfellowed.[7]

HAMLET   What's his weapon?

OSRIC   Rapier and dagger.   135

HAMLET   That's two of his weapons—but well.

OSRIC   The king, sir, hath wagered with him six Barbary horses,
against the which he has impawned,[8] as I take it, six French rapiers
and poniards, with their assigns,[9] as girdle, hangers, and so. Three
of the carriages, in faith, are very dear to fancy,[1] very responsive to 140
the hilts, most delicate[2] carriages, and of very liberal conceit.[3]

HAMLET   What call you the carriages?

HORATIO   [*aside to* HAMLET]   I knew you must be edified by the
margent[4] ere you had done.

OSRIC   The carriages, sir, are the hangers.   145

HAMLET   The phrase would be more germane to the matter if we
could carry a cannon by our sides. I would it might be hangers till
then. But on! Six Barbary horses against six French swords, their
assigns, and three liberal conceited carriages; that's the French bet
against the Danish. Why is this all impawned, as you call it?   150

OSRIC   The king, sir, hath laid, sir, that in a dozen passes between
yourself and him he shall not exceed you three hits; he hath laid on
twelve for nine, and it would come to immediate trial if your lordship would vouchsafe the answer.

HAMLET   How if I answer no?   155

OSRIC   I mean, my lord, the opposition of your person in trial.

HAMLET   Sir, I will walk here in the hall. If it please his majesty, it is
the breathing time[5] of day with me. Let the foils be brought, the
gentleman willing, and the king hold his purpose; I will win for
him an I can. If not, I will gain nothing but my shame and the 160
odd hits.

OSRIC   Shall I deliver you so?

HAMLET   To this effect, sir, after what flourish your nature will.

OSRIC   I commend my duty to your lordship.

HAMLET   Yours, yours. [*Exit* OSRIC.] He does well to commend it 165
himself; there are no tongues else for's turn.

HORATIO   This lapwing runs away with the shell on his head.[6]

HAMLET   'A did comply,[7] sir, with his dug[8] before 'a sucked it. Thus
has he, and many more of the same bevy that I know the drossy age
dotes on, only got the tune of the time; and out of an habit of en- 170
counter, a kind of yesty[9] collection which carries them through and
through the most fanned and winnowed opinions; and do but blow
them to their trial, the bubbles are out.

5. i.e., compare myself
6. reputation
7. unequaled in his excellence
8. staked
9. appurtenances
1. finely designed
2. well adjusted
3. elegant design
4. marginal gloss

5. time for exercise
6. The lapwing was thought to be so
precocious that it could run immediately
after being hatched, even as here with bits
of the shell still on its head.
7. deal formally
8. mother's breast
9. yeasty

Enter a LORD.

LORD   My lord, his majesty commended him to you by young Osric, who brings back to him that you attend[1] him in the hall. He sends to know if your pleasure hold to play with Laertes, or that you will take longer time. 175

HAMLET   I am constant to my purposes; they follow the king's pleasure. If his fitness speaks, mine is ready; now or whensoever, provided I be so able as now. 180

LORD   The king and queen and all are coming down.

HAMLET   In happy time.

LORD   The queen desires you to use some gentle entertainment[2] to Laertes before you fall to play.

HAMLET   She well instructs me.   *Exit* LORD. 185

HORATIO   You will lose this wager, my lord.

HAMLET   I do not think so. Since he went into France I have been in continual practice. I shall win at the odds. But thou wouldst not think how ill[3] all's here about my heart. But it is no matter.

HORATIO   Nay, good my lord— 190

HAMLET   It is but foolery, but it is such a kind of gaingiving[4] as would perhaps trouble a woman.

HORATIO   If your mind dislike anything, obey it. I will forestall their repair[5] hither, and say you are not fit.

HAMLET   Not a whit, we defy augury. There is special providence in 195 the fall of a sparrow. If it be now, 'tis not to come; if it be not to come, it will be now; if it be not now, yet it will come. The readiness is all. Since no man of aught he leaves knows, what is't to leave betimes? Let be.

A table prepared. Enter TRUMPETS, DRUMS, *and* OFFICERS *with cushions;* KING, QUEEN, OSRIC *and* ATTENDANTS *with foils, daggers, and* LAERTES.

KING   Come, Hamlet, come and take this hand from me.   200

The KING *puts* LAERTES' *hand into* HAMLET'*s.*

HAMLET   Give me your pardon, sir. I have done you wrong,
But pardon 't as you are a gentleman.
This presence[6] knows, and you must needs have heard,
How I am punished with a sore distraction.
What I have done 205
That might your nature, honor, and exception,[7]
Roughly awake, I here proclaim was madness.
Was 't Hamlet wronged Laertes? Never Hamlet.
If Hamlet from himself be ta'en away,
And when he's not himself does wrong Laertes, 210
Then Hamlet does it not, Hamlet denies it.
Who does it then? His madness. If't be so,

1. await
2. cordiality
3. uneasy
4. misgiving

5. coming
6. company
7. resentment

Hamlet is of the faction that is wronged;
His madness is poor Hamlet's enemy.
Sir, in this audience,   215
Let my disclaiming from[8] a purposed evil
Free[9] me so far in your most generous thoughts
That I have shot my arrow o'er the house
And hurt my brother.
LAERTES   I am satisfied in nature,
Whose motive in this case should stir me most   220
To my revenge. But in my terms of honor
I stand aloof, and will no reconcilement
Till by some elder masters of known honor
I have a voice[1] and precedent of peace
To keep my name ungored.[2] But till that time   225
I do receive your offered love like love,
And will not wrong it.
HAMLET   I embrace it freely,
And will this brother's wager frankly[3] play.
Give us the foils.
LAERTES   Come, one for me.
HAMLET   I'll be your foil, Laertes. In mine ignorance   230
Your skill shall, like a star i' th' darkest night,
Stick fiery off[4] indeed.
LAERTES   You mock me, sir.
HAMLET   No, by this hand.
KING   Give them the foils, young Osric. Cousin **Hamlet**,
You know the wager?
HAMLET   Very well, my lord;   235
Your Grace has laid the odds o' th' weaker side.
KING   I do not fear it, I have seen you both;
But since he is bettered,[5] we have therefore odds.
LAERTES   This is too heavy; let me see another.
HAMLET   This likes[6] me well. These foils have all a[7] length?   240

They prepare to play.

OSRIC   Ay, my good lord.
KING   Set me the stoups of wine upon that table.
If Hamlet give the first or second hit,
Or quit in answer of[8] the third exchange,
Let all the battlements their ordnance fire.   245
The king shall drink to Hamlet's better breath,
And in the cup an union[9] shall he throw,
Richer than that which four successive kings
In Denmark's crown have worn. Give me the cups,
And let the kettle[1] to the trumpet speak,   250
The trumpet to the cannoneer without,

8. denying of
9. absolve
1. authority
2. unshamed
3. without rancor
4. shine brightly

5. reported better
6. suits
7. the same
8. repay
9. pearl
1. kettledrum

The cannons to the heavens, the heaven to earth,
"Now the king drinks to Hamlet." Come, begin—

Trumpets the while.

And you, the judges, bear a wary eye.
HAMLET   Come on, sir.
LAERTES   Come, my lord.   *They play.*
HAMLET   One.
LAERTES   No.
HAMLET   Judgment?   255
OSRIC   A hit, a very palpable hit.

Drums, trumpets, and shot. Flourish; a piece goes off.

LAERTES   Well, again.
KING   Stay, give me drink. Hamlet, this pearl is thine.
Here's to thy health. Give him the cup.
HAMLET   I'll play this bout first; set it by awhile.   260
Come.   *They play.*
Another hit; what say you?
LAERTES   I do confess't.
KING   Our son shall win.
QUEEN   He's fat,[2] and scant of breath.
Here, Hamlet, take my napkin, rub thy brows.   265
The queen carouses to thy fortune, Hamlet.
HAMLET   Good madam!
KING   Gertrude, do not drink.
QUEEN   I will, my lord; I pray you pardon me.
KING [*aside*]   It is the poisoned cup; it is too late.   270
HAMLET   I dare not drink yet, madam; by and by.
QUEEN   Come, let me wipe thy face.
LAERTES   My lord, I'll hit him now.
KING   I do not think't.
LAERTES [*aside*]   And yet it is almost against my conscience.
HAMLET   Come, for the third, Laertes. You do but dally.   275
I pray you pass[3] with your best violence;
I am afeard you make a wanton of me.[4]
LAERTES   Say you so? Come on.   *They play.*
OSRIC   Nothing, neither way.
LAERTES   Have at you now!   280

LAERTES *wounds* HAMLET: *then, in scuffling, they change rapiers, and* HAMLET *wounds* LAERTES.

KING   Part them. They are incensed.
HAMLET   Nay, come again.   *The* QUEEN *falls.*
OSRIC   Look to the queen there, ho!
HORATIO   They bleed on both sides. How is it, my lord?

2. out of shape
3. attack
4. trifle with me

OSRIC   How is't, Laertes?   285
LAERTES   Why, as a woodcock to mine own springe,[5] Osric.
   I am justly killed with mine own treachery.
HAMLET   How does the queen?
KING   She swoons to see them bleed.
QUEEN   No, no, the drink, the drink! O my dear Hamlet!
   The drink, the drink! I am poisoned.   *Dies.* 290
HAMLET   O, villainy! Ho! let the door be locked.
   Treachery! seek it out.
LAERTES   It is here, Hamlet. Hamlet, thou art slain;
   No med'cine in the world can do thee good.
   In thee there is not half an hour's life.   295
   The treacherous instrument is in thy hand,
   Unbated[6] and envenomed. The foul practice
   Hath turned itself on me. Lo, here I lie,
   Never to rise again. Thy mother's poisoned.
   I can no more. The king, the king's to blame.   300
HAMLET   The point envenomed too?
   Then, venom, to thy work.   *Hurts the* KING.
ALL   Treason! treason!
KING   O, yet defend me, friends. I am but hurt.[7]
HAMLET   Here, thou incestuous, murd'rous, damnéd Dane,   305
   Drink off this potion. Is thy union here?
   Follow my mother.   *The* KING *dies.*
LAERTES   He is justly served.
   It is a poison tempered[8] by himself.
   Exchange forgiveness with me, noble Hamlet.
   Mine and my father's death come not upon thee,   310
   Nor thine on me!   *Dies.*
HAMLET   Heaven make thee free of[9] it! I follow thee.
   I am dead, Horatio. Wretched queen, adieu!
   You that look pale and tremble at this chance,[1]
   That are but mutes or audience to this act,   315
   Had I but time, as this fell sergeant Death
   Is strict in his arrest,[2] O, I could tell you—
   But let it be. Horatio, I am dead:
   Thou livest; report me and my cause aright
   To the unsatisfied.[3]
HORATIO   Never believe it.   320
   I am more an antique Roman than a Dane.
   Here's yet some liquor left.
HAMLET   As th'art a man,
   Give me the cup. Let go. By heaven, I'll ha't.
   O God, Horatio, what a wounded name,
   Things standing thus unknown, shall live behind me!   325
   If thou didst ever hold me in thy heart,
   Absent thee from felicity awhile,

5. snare   9. forgive
6. unblunted   1. circumstance
7. wounded   2. summons to court
8. mixed   3. uninformed

And in this harsh world draw thy breath in pain,
To tell my story.   *A march afar off.*
            What warlike noise is this?
OSRIC   Young Fortinbras, with conquest come from Poland,   330
  To th' ambassadors of England gives
  This warlike volley.[4]
HAMLET   O, I die, Horatio!
  The potent poison quite o'er-crows[5] my spirit.
  I cannot live to hear the news from England,
  But I do prophesy th' election lights   335
  On Fortinbras. He has my dying voice.[6]
  So tell him, with th' occurrents,[7] more and less,
  Which have solicited[8]—the rest is silence.   *Dies.*
HORATIO   Now cracks a noble heart. Good night, sweet prince,
  And flights of angels sing thee to thy rest!   *March within.* 340
  Why does the drum come hither?

        Enter FORTINBRAS, *with the* AMBASSADORS *and with drum,*
        colors, and ATTENDANTS.

FORTINBRAS   Where is this sight?
HORATIO   What is it you would see?
  If aught of woe or wonder, cease your search.
FORTINBRAS   This quarry cries on havoc.[9] O proud death,
  What feast is toward[1] in thine eternal cell   345
  That thou so many princes at a shot
  So bloodily hast struck?
AMBASSADORS   The sight is dismal;
  And our affairs from England come too late.
  The ears are senseless[2] that should give us hearing
  To tell him his commandment is fulfilled,   350
  That Rosencrantz and Guildenstern are dead.
  Where should we have our thanks?
HORATIO   Not from his mouth,
  Had it th' ability of life to thank you.
  He never gave commandment for their death.
  But since, so jump[3] upon this bloody question,   355
  You from the Polack wars, and you from England,
  Are here arrived, give orders that these bodies
  High on a stage be placéd to the view,
  And let me speak to th' yet unknowing world
  How these things came about. So shall you hear   360
  Of carnal, bloody, and unnatural acts;

---

4. The staging presents some difficulties
here. If Osric is not clairvoyant, he must
have left the stage at some point and returned. One possibility is that he might
have left to carry out Hamlet's order to
lock the door (line 291) and returned
when the sound of the distant march is
heard.
5. overcomes

6. support
7. circumstances
8. brought about this scene
9. The game killed in the hunt proclaims a slaughter.
1. in preparation
2. without sense of hearing
3. exactly

Of accidental judgments, casual[4] slaughters;
Of deaths put on by cunning and forced cause;
And, in this upshot,[5] purposes mistook
Fall'n on th' inventors' heads. All this can I   365
Truly deliver.
FORTINBRAS   Let us haste to hear it,
And call the noblest to the audience.[6]
For me, with sorrow I embrace my fortune.
I have some rights of memory[7] in this kingdom,
Which now to claim my vantage[8] doth invite me.   370
HORATIO   Of that I shall have also cause to speak,
And from his mouth whose voice will draw on more.
But let this same be presently performed,
Even while men's minds are wild, lest more mischance
On plots and errors happen.
FORTINBRAS   Let four captains   375
Bear Hamlet like a soldier to the stage,
For he was likely, had he been put on,[9]
To have proved most royal; and for his passage
The soldier's music and the rite of war
Speak loudly for him.   380
Take up the bodies. Such a sight as this
Becomes the field, but here shows much amiss.
Go, bid the soldiers shoot.

Exeunt marching. A peal of ordnance shot off.

ca. 1600

---

4. brought about by apparent accident   7. succession
5. result   8. position
6. hearing   9. elected king

3   CHARACTER AND ACTOR

Human beings are ultimately the subject of almost all literature, and individual works of art—especially narrative works such as novels and short stories, but sometimes poems as well—often explore the lives of individuals in some detail. Most literature tends to be rather analytical about human nature, often suggesting both the great complexity of individual people and the great variety of kinds of people who live in the world that literature reflects. People—their activities, habits, eccentricities, and personalities—are ultimately the center of almost all the stories that literature tells. Just as literature is written for human eyes—and has no meaningful existence as text unless people read it and respond—literature always has people at the center of attention within the text. It is the human fascination with **character**— that is, those qualities of mind, spirit, and behavior that make one individual different from every other—that is the basis for literature and the human interest in it, for literature analyzes, describes, portrays, helps us to understand just what it is about ourselves and others that makes us interesting, or sometimes infuriating, to observe and deal with.

Almost all literature depends for its central interest on the portrayal of character; in fact, we regularly call the people presented in literature "characters," signifying that they are imaginary creatures structured according to some carefully defined idea of individual distinctiveness. The primary act of imagination for writers, prior to verbal and aesthetic considerations, prior even to questions of organization and structure, involves the invention of character. That starting point is basic to any literature that tells a story: novels, short stories, films, narrative or dramatic poems, sometimes even lyric poems that explore an integrated set of feelings. But plays have a special engagement with character because of the visual and concrete manner in which they portray people on the stage. The very process of acting calls extraordinary attention to character—for actors, audience, and even playwrights—simply because actors have to take on, quite specifically, characteristics that are not their own and that therefore have to be defined, studied, and specifically imitated. They have to achieve a specific identity; they try "to get *in* character." Actors quite literally try, for a short while, to *be* someone else, and in that process have to define exactly what about the person (or character) they are playing is distinctive, individual, *character*istic.

Some say that there are Dramas of Plot and Dramas of Character, and it is true that some plays emphasize external action while others place more emphasis on what happens in characters' minds and perceptions. But the difference is really one of degree: all plays tell some sort of story and feature actions that are interesting or significant in themselves. And all depend heavily on the portrayal of people and an understanding of how their individual differences contribute to the action, conflict, and resolution of the plot. Often, an important part of a play's effect depends upon our understanding of the inner life of one or more characters. Always, the first task of a play is to introduce the people with whose lives we are to be concerned and establish the central facts of their characters.

The first page of text of most plays contains a complete list of the *dramatis personae*, that is, the persons whose lives are to be presented dramatically. Often the printed program for a particular performance also contains the list (together with the names of the actors playing each part), sometimes with a brief description of each character and an indication of the relationships among characters. Still, whatever textual aids may be provided for curious readers, the play has to *present* characters on the stage as if from scratch, as if the audience has no notion, until instructed, of what to expect. Stories or poems may comment on a character or editorialize rather directly, but plays have to *reveal* character—that is, let the character dramatize the kind of person he or she is by his or her own words and actions. Other characters may, of course, express opinions about a particular character, and our feelings as members of the audience may be influenced by rumor and innuendo. But all characters who appear on the stage ultimately have to be credible in their own terms, and what they appear to be, through their own appearance, actions, and words, is what they are likely to *be* in the minds of an audience.

Establishing character is one of the first tasks of any play, and the opening minutes of exposition contain an explanation to the audience of who the main characters are as well as what the situation is. One way to handle exposition is to have someone appear before the audience and recite a *prologue* which explains directly what the audience needs to know about plot and character. Most modern plays, however, present the exposition more indirectly. In *The Brute*, for example, the opening conversation between Mrs. Popov and her servant Luka tells us essentially what we need to know about her as well as her situation —not only that her husband has recently died but that she has decided that she will pine away in "grief" at his passing, that her grief is more anger at her dead husband than anything else, and that her notion of her behavior is based on some abstract romantic principle of what is honorable, proper, and likely to gain her the reputation of being a noble, self-sacrificing, and unappreciated widow rather than on personal feelings and desires. The attempts by Luka to talk her out of her silly resolution are primarily a pretense to get the play off the ground; within the first two or three minutes the play is fully set up, and we know what we need to know about Mrs. Popov's character.

The other major character, Smirnov, has not yet been heard of, but the main action of the play has been prepared for because the character of Mrs. Popov—romantic, unfulfilled, long-suffering, unhappy, self-deluded, lonely, adamant but needing to be talked out of her hopelessness—has been sufficiently established to make the subsequent events believable. Then Smirnov reveals himself, without any preparation or exposition, by the way he speaks, rants, and storms about the stage in his desperation and rage. The characters "fit": the resolution, although cleverly arranged and carefully drawn out to maximize the effect, makes sense.

Similarly, in *Hamlet* the opening scenes tell us the situation and set an expectation of the major characters. The hero or heroine of a play seldom appears on stage until he or she has been "prepared for," and some specific expectation has been built up in the audience. As in *Hamlet,* it is often minor (or even inconsequential) characters who provide the initial information, sometimes hardly appearing again after performing their expository function. In *Hamlet,* the exposition is handled with extreme subtlety, and (besides crucial information) an appropriate atmosphere for the play is provided at once: things are misty, dark, mysterious, and the talk of uncertain beings (forces that go beyond individual will or possibly even human power) plunge us at once into a complex world where it is difficult to sort truth from fantasy or fear. The character of Hamlet, like everything else in the play, is terribly complicated, and new wrinkles and revelations are continually occurring. The early exposition of Hamlet's character—through Claudius's patronizing address to him, through his mother's loving but specious concern, and through his own language: the bold expressions of anger, doubt, and self-loathing in his soliloquy and his frank and friendly bantering with Horatio—by no means tells us all we need to know, as might happen in a shorter or simpler play, but it sets us on the right track of expectation.

Titles sometimes give away at once that a play is going to focus on a single individual. *Hamlet, King Lear, Auntie Mame, Evita, Hedda Gabler, Death of a Salesman, The Country Wife, The Brute*—such titles imply that a single character gets the primary stage attention, and in most cases the expectations of titles are fulfilled in the play itself, and the main character (or **protagonist**) is not only at the center of the action but also is the primary object of the playwright's (and the audience's) concern. Defining the character of that protagonist (sometimes by comparison and contrast with a competitor, or **antagonist**) often becomes the consuming interest of the play, and the action seems designed to illustrate, or clarify, or develop that character. Occasionally, of course, a title may be a mere convenience (in which case it means nothing about the play's focus) or it may set up misleading expectations so that our attention can be diverted and responses manipulated. (Does the title of *The Brute* refer to Smirnov or to the absent Popov? Is either the real center of attention?) But in plays that genuinely do follow, relentlessly, the inner life as well as the fortunes of one main character, the revelation of that person's attributes, eccentricities, and effects upon other people continues to occupy center stage throughout the play. In such plays, characters are not just introduced so that their characteristics can play themselves out in the plot; characterization continues throughout the play and new complications and subtleties in the character are revealed in the last act as well as the first.

In *Hedda Gabler,* for example, the protagonist's self-centeredness and cruelty are not fully clear until the play is well along. Our first, indirect impressions of Hedda are rather positive. We hear about what a beauty she is, how sought-after she was and how prominent her family. She has just returned from her honeymoon, and it is from her new husband and his Aunt Juju that we hear about Hedda and learn how lucky they feel that she has—rather inexplicably—chosen to marry the unprepossessing Tesman.

There are cautionary hints that Hedda is less than perfect, however. Tesman says she insisted on having all her baggage with her on the journey. Aunt Juliana is a bit shocked by Hedda's having removed the chintz covers from the furniture and the pretension of using the drawing-room as parlor. When Hedda enters she is a bit snappy with both her husband and his aunt. It is quite possible, however, that the audience shares Hedda's low opinion of her new groom and his family, that we are on her side and are trying to figure out how she was trapped into marrying a rather unattractive, thick-skulled, bloodless oaf like Tesman. (Whether this is a fair estimate of his character remains to be seen.)

We may interpret on the page and an actress portray on the stage the pathetic entrapment of a beautiful but vulnerable aristocrat by a crass, if well-meaning, social-climbing member of the bourgeoisie. Read or acted this way the episode in which Hedda mistakes Aunt Juliana's new hat for an old one that must belong to the maid may well tickle our snobbish sense of ourselves and our superiority to the Tesmans. Later in the play, when Hedda's spoiled, unstable, cruel character has been more and more clearly revealed, we learn that this "mistake" was deliberate, that Hedda was trying to put down Tesman's flighty, doting aunt. First impressions are difficult to overcome, and it may take us much of the play to erase our initial admiration of and pity for Hedda. Indeed, we may never erase it, and the tug of the trapped aristocratic beauty and that of the spoiled bitch may alternate or blend. It is this complexity that makes Hedda such a challenging role for an actress and one that all actresses seem to want to try.

Plays contain all kinds of characters, and the characters may be categorized in a variety of ways. They may be labeled by their importance to the plot: protagonist and antagonist, for example, or hero and heroine; they may be called supporting characters, minor characters, or enclitic characters (that is, who are not important in themselves but merely perform a structural function). They may be categorized by the talents they require in actors—there are demanding and challenging roles, juicy parts and dull or routine ones, roles for stars, character-actors, comedians, straight men, and novices—or by their ethnic, religious, or social identities (Jewish mothers, Roumanian ravenhaired beauties, pious frauds, social climbers), by their body types, personality roles or clichéd behaviors (stringbeans, klutzes, dumb blondes, jocks), etc. However individualized characters ultimately turn out to be, they usually begin as some identifiable "type" of person that the audience will recognize and have certain expectations about. Gangsters, flirts, lawyers, Irishmen, pennypinchers, know-it-alls, and drunks are all common examples (from drama and from life) of character-types who have predictable habits and who evoke stock responses.

The range of characters portrayed in any single play may be limited by the kind of play it is or by particular thematic, ideological, and artistic intentions of the playwright. Most good plays do not set out specifically to include a variety of types, but playwrights often find it convenient to use some stereotypes—stereotypes of a nation, an occupation, or body- or personality-type—for special effects, even in serious plays where the emphasis on complexities of character may be significant elsewhere in the play. Rosencrantz and Guildenstern in *Hamlet,* for example, are stereotypical courtiers of Shakespeare's time: they flatter, dissemble, smile, and double cross. Similarly, Polonius is a foolish old man, given to providing advice that no one wants; he is pompous and ultimately silly, and can readily be played as a comic subtype even though he performs a fairly significant role in the play. Secondary characters in even the best plays are often recognizable "types." And even major characters are sometimes portrayed at first as types—before they are complicated, differentiated, and individualized as the play develops and shows them more fully. Hedda Gabler, for example, at first is a Great Beauty who is beginning to age and panic; she is also rich, spoiled, ambitious, used to having her own way. Less and less attractive as she reveals herself more and more, yet more and more helpless in a trap only in part of her own making, Hedda becomes more and more complex, but she begins as a quite predictable (and at first rather harmless-seeming) stereotype.

Ibsen makes no apparent attempt to determine why Hedda has become the way she is. Plausible contexts exist in her social background and family upbringing, but Ibsen does not seem to explore them. His portrait is starkly realistic, purely dramatic in that no narrator or mediator or interpreter stands between us and Hedda, so we are on our own in attempting to understand her fully. To what degree is Hedda more sinned against than sinning? Should she be played for sympathy, a beautiful, fine lady trapped in an ugly bourgeois world and reduced by frustration and abhorrence to deliberate, almost vicious cruelty? Or should she be played as the thoroughly spoiled brat, used to primacy and getting her own way, who lashes out at the weak and innocent, and uses everyone to satisfy her need and greed? Probably neither, but some subtle mix of the two. No wonder actresses clamor for the part.

Tesman similarly begins almost as a comic type—the otherworldly and somewhat absent-minded professor who doesn't really understand veiled allusions to pregnancy, who has little sense of money, who is affectionate without suspicion, who is generally unsophisticated about the ways of the world and very trusting of human nature. He, too, becomes complicated as the play develops (although he is always more simple and straightforward than Hedda), but his annoying mannerisms (his habit of ending most of his sentences with "what," for example) continue to categorize him.

Most plays offer a related pattern of rising complication in character portrayal, and almost all start out from recognizable "types": types are something to build expectations on, and playwrights use the device as a quick introduction to the audience. Good plays almost never—except in melodrama or farce—settle ultimately for character types in the main roles, but the departure from type is almost always a matter of time and degree. Ultimately a character like Hamlet cannot be meaningfully pigeonholed as any of the types he is associated with—he is not simply a revenger, or a hesitator, or a son in love with his mother—but he has elements of several recognizable types in his personality, and it is part of Shakespeare's skill to build a full human being so carefully from audience expectations ready at hand.

Characterization in plays involves four separate processes. The first involves the **conception** of the character in the playwright's mind, at the moment when the play begins to be an idea, when the playwright first begins to construct—or even dream about—a plot, structure, or theme that will ultimately become drama. Characters may develop or change radically in this process of conception, and nothing in this process is really complete or final until the other three processes are also complete. The second process involves **presentation** of the character by the playwright through the words and actions specified in the text. The artistic decision about how much to present and when to present it (structural decisions, really) can have an important effect on how the audience responds to a character and what sort of character ultimately is realized in the play. But the full effect of characterization in a play ultimately comes only when the play is fleshed out on the stage with a live actor playing the part and adding the final personal touches to the character with body gestures, facial expressions and tones of voice. In **casting** a play—that is, in deciding what actors are to play the parts—a director takes a major step in determining how a character will seem to the audience, for the choice of actor determines not only the physical appearance, quality of voice, and degree of presence that a character will present on stage, but also more subtle details of presentation. The acting talents of each individual actor—the ranges of emotion that he or she can project, the subtleties of facial expression and body language, the quality of intelligence and understanding of the role that the actor is capable of—determine how a character will ultimately *seem* to an audience. The final process, that of **acting** itself, is the last logical step in characterization, for in the actual production the actor makes something distinctive of her or his talents in relation to the author's original conception. The embodying of a character onstage in a fully realized production is the ultimate fulfillment of an art that goes beyond words and stage directions and is ultimately an exercise in impersonation—when one person steps out of him- or herself and becomes for a brief while someone different, someone with different character, someone who is a character, wholly created in the imagination of playwright, director, and actor as collaborators.

HENRIK IBSEN

Hedda Gabler*

CHARACTERS

GEORGE TESMAN, *research gradu-*
ate in cultural history
HEDDA, *his wife*
MISS JULIANA TESMAN, *his aunt*

MRS. ELVSTED
JUDGE BRACK
EILERT LOEVBORG
BERTHA, *a maid*

The action takes place in Tesman's villa, in the fashionable quarter of town.

Act 1

A large drawing room, handsomely and tastefully furnished; deco-rated in dark colors. In the rear wall is a broad open doorway, with curtains drawn back to either side. It leads to a smaller room, deco-rated in the same style as the drawing room. In the right-hand wall of the drawing room, a folding door leads out to the hall. The opposite wall, on the left, contains french windows, also with curtains drawn back on either side. Through the glass we can see part of a verandah, and trees in autumn colors. Downstage stands an oval table, covered by a cloth and surrounded by chairs. Down-stage right, against the wall, is a broad stove tiled with dark porce-lain; in front of it stand a high-backed armchair, a cushioned foot-rest, and two footstools. Upstage right, in an alcove, is a corner sofa, with a small, round table. Downstage left, a little away from the wall, is another sofa. Upstage of the french windows, a piano. On either side of the open doorway in the rear wall stand what-nots holding ornaments of terra cotta and majolica. Against the rear wall of the smaller room can be seen a sofa, a table, and a couple of chairs. Above this sofa hangs the portrait of a handsome old man in general's uniform. Above the table a lamp hangs from the ceiling, with a shade of opalescent, milky glass. All round the drawing room bunches of flowers stand in vases and glasses. More bunches lie on the tables. The floors of both rooms are covered with thick carpets. Morning light. The sun shines in through the french windows.

MISS JULIANA TESMAN, *wearing a hat and carrying a parasol, enters from the hall, followed by* BERTHA, *who is carrying a bunch of flowers wrapped in paper.* MISS TESMAN *is about sixty-five, of pleasant and kindly appearance. She is neatly but simply dressed in gray outdoor clothes.* BERTHA, *the maid, is rather simple and rustic-looking. She is getting on in years.*

MISS TESMAN [*stops just inside the door, listens, and says in a hushed voice*] No, bless my soul! They're not up yet.
BERTHA [*also in hushed tones*] What did I tell you, miss? The boat

° Translated by Michael Meyer.

didn't get in till midnight. And when they did turn up—Jesus, miss, you should have seen all the things Madam made me unpack before she'd go to bed!

MISS TESMAN   Ah, well. Let them have a good lie in. But let's have some nice fresh air waiting for them when they do come down.

Goes to the french windows and throws them wide open.

BERTHA [*bewildered at the table, the bunch of flowers in her hand*] I'm blessed if there's a square inch left to put anything. I'll have to let it lie here, miss.

Puts it on the piano.

MISS TESMAN   Well, Bertha dear, so now you have a new mistress. Heaven knows it nearly broke my heart to have to part with you.

BERTHA [*snivels*]   What about me, Miss Juju? How do you suppose I felt? After all the happy years I've spent with you and Miss Rena?

MISS TESMAN   We must accept it bravely, Bertha. It was the only way. George needs you to take care of him. He could never manage without you. You've looked after him ever since he was a tiny boy.

BERTHA   Oh, but, Miss Juju, I can't help thinking about Miss Rena, lying there all helpless, poor dear. And that new girl! She'll never learn the proper way to handle an invalid.

MISS TESMAN   Oh, I'll manage to train her. I'll do most of the work myself, you know. You needn't worry about my poor sister, Bertha dear.

BERTHA   But Miss Juju, there's another thing. I'm frightened Madam may not find me suitable.

MISS TESMAN   Oh, nonsense, Bertha. There may be one or two little things to begin with—

BERTHA   She's a real lady. Wants everything just so.

MISS TESMAN   But of course she does! General Gabler's daughter! Think of what she was accustomed to when the General was alive. You remember how we used to see her out riding with her father? In that long black skirt? With the feather in her hat?

BERTHA   Oh, yes, miss. As if I could forget! But, Lord! I never dreamed I'd live to see a match between her and Master Georgie.

MISS TESMAN   Neither did I. By the way, Bertha, from now on you must stop calling him Master Georgie. You must say: Dr. Tesman.

BERTHA   Yes, Madam said something about that too. Last night—the moment they'd set foot inside the door. Is it true, then, miss?

MISS TESMAN   Indeed it is. Just imagine, Bertha, some foreigners have made him a doctor.[1] It happened while they were away. I had no idea till he told me when they got off the boat.

BERTHA   Well, I suppose there's no limit to what he won't become. He's that clever. I never thought he'd go in for hospital work, though.

MISS TESMAN   No, he's not that kind of doctor.

1. Awarded him a doctoral degree.

Nods impressively.

In any case, you may soon have to address him by an even grander title.

BERTHA   You don't say! What might that be, miss?

MISS TESMAN [*smiles*]   Ah! If you only knew!

Moved.

Dear God, if only poor dear Joachim could rise out of his grave and see what his little son has grown into!

Looks round.

But, Bertha, why have you done this? Taken the chintz covers off all the furniture!

BERTHA   Madam said I was to. Can't stand chintz covers on chairs, she said.

MISS TESMAN   But surely they're not going to use this room as a parlor?

BERTHA   So I gathered, miss. From what Madam said. He didn't say anything. The Doctor.

GEORGE TESMAN *comes into the rear room, from the right, humming, with an open, empty traveling bag in his hand. He is about thirty-three, of medium height and youthful appearance, rather plump, with an open, round, contented face, and fair hair and beard. He wears spectacles, and is dressed in comfortable, indoor clothes.*

MISS TESMAN   Good morning! Good morning, George!

TESMAN [*in open doorway*]   Auntie Juju! Dear Auntie Juju!

Comes forward and shakes her hand.

You've come all the way out here! And so early! What?

MISS TESMAN   Well, I had to make sure you'd settled in comfortably.

TESMAN   But you can't have had a proper night's sleep.

MISS TESMAN   Oh, never mind that.

TESMAN   We were so sorry we couldn't give you a lift. But you saw how it was—Hedda had so much luggage—and she insisted on having it all with her.

MISS TESMAN   Yes, I've never seen so much luggage.

BERTHA [*to* TESMAN]   Shall I go and ask Madam if there's anything I can lend her a hand with?

TESMAN   Er—thank you, Bertha; no, you needn't bother. She says if she wants you for anything she'll ring.

BERTHA [*over to right*]   Oh. Very good.

TESMAN   Oh, Bertha—take this bag, will you?

BERTHA [*takes it*]   I'll put it in the attic.

Goes out into the hall.

TESMAN   Just fancy, Auntie Juju, I filled that whole bag with notes for my book. You know, it's really incredible what I've managed to find rooting through those archives. By Jove! Wonderful old things no one even knew existed—

MISS TESMAN   I'm sure you didn't waste a single moment of your honeymoon, George dear.

TESMAN   No, I think I can truthfully claim that. But, Auntie Juju, do take your hat off. Here. Let me untie it for you.

MISS TESMAN   [*as he does so*]   Oh dear, oh dear! It's just as if you were still living at home with us.

TESMAN   [*turns the hat in his hand and looks at it*]   I say! What a splendid new hat!

MISS TESMAN   I bought it for Hedda's sake.

TESMAN   For Hedda's sake? What?

MISS TESMAN   So that Hedda needn't be ashamed of me, in case we ever go for a walk together.

TESMAN   [*pats her cheek*]   You still think of everything, don't you, Auntie Juju?

Puts the hat down on a chair by the table.

Come on, let's sit down here on the sofa. And have a little chat while we wait for Hedda.

They sit. She puts her parasol in the corner of the sofa.

MISS TESMAN   [*clasps both his hands and looks at him*]   Oh, George, it's so wonderful to have you back, and be able to see you with my own eyes again! Poor dear Joachim's own son!

TESMAN   What about me! It's wonderful for me to see you again, Auntie Juju. You've been a mother to me. And a father, too.

MISS TESMAN   You'll always keep a soft spot in your heart for your old aunties, won't you, George dear?

TESMAN   I suppose Auntie Rena's no better? What?

MISS TESMAN   Alas, no. I'm afraid she'll never get better, poor dear. She's lying there just as she has all these years. Please God I may be allowed to keep her for a little longer. If I lose her I don't know what I'd do. Especially now I haven't you to look after.

TESMAN   [*pats her on the back*]   There, there, there!

MISS TESMAN   [*with a sudden change of mood*]   Oh but George, fancy you being a married man! And to think it's you who've won Hedda Gabler! The beautiful Hedda Gabler! Fancy! She was always so surrounded by admirers.

TESMAN   [*hums a little and smiles contentedly*]   Yes, I suppose there are quite a few people in this town who wouldn't mind being in my shoes. What?

MISS TESMAN   And what a honeymoon! Five months! Nearly six.

TESMAN   Well, I've done a lot of work, you know. All those archives to go through. And I've had to read lots of books.

MISS TESMAN   Yes, dear, of course.

Lowers her voice confidentially.

But tell me, George—haven't you any—any extra little piece of news to give me?

TESMAN   You mean, arising out of the honeymoon?

MISS TESMAN   Yes.

TESMAN   No, I don't think there's anything I didn't tell you in my letters. My doctorate, of course—but I told you about that last night, didn't I?

MISS TESMAN   Yes, yes, I didn't mean that kind of thing. I was just wondering—are you—are you expecting—?

TESMAN   Expecting what?

MISS TESMAN   Oh, come on George, I'm your old aunt!

TESMAN   Well actually—yes, I am expecting something.

MISS TESMAN   I knew it!

TESMAN   You'll be happy to hear that before very long I expect to become a professor.

MISS TESMAN   Professor?

TESMAN   I think I may say that the matter has been decided. But, Auntie Juju, you know about this.

MISS TESMAN [*gives a little laugh*]   Yes, of course. I'd forgotten.

Changes her tone.

But we were talking about your honeymoon. It must have cost a dreadful amount of money, George?

TESMAN   Oh well, you know, that big research grant I got helped a good deal.

MISS TESMAN   But how on earth did you manage to make it do for two?

TESMAN   Well, to tell the truth it was a bit tricky. What?

MISS TESMAN   Especially when one's traveling with a lady. A little bird tells me that makes things very much more expensive.

TESMAN   Well, yes, of course it does make things a little more expensive. But Hedda has to do things in style, Auntie Juju. I mean, she has to. Anything less grand wouldn't have suited her.

MISS TESMAN   No, no, I suppose not. A honeymoon abroad seems to be the vogue nowadays. But tell me, have you had time to look round the house?

TESMAN   You bet. I've been up since the crack of dawn.

MISS TESMAN   Well, what do you think of it?

TESMAN   Splendid. Absolutely splendid. I'm only wondering what we're going to do with those two empty rooms between that little one and Hedda's bedroom.

MISS TESMAN [*laughs slyly*]   Ah, George dear, I'm sure you'll manage to find some use for them—in time.

TESMAN   Yes, of course, Auntie Juju, how stupid of me. You're thinking of my books. What?

MISS TESMAN   Yes, yes, dear boy. I was thinking of your books.

TESMAN   You know, I'm so happy for Hedda's sake that we've managed to get this house. Before we became engaged she often used to say this was the only house in town she felt she could really bear to live in. It used to belong to Mrs. Falk—you know, the Prime Minister's widow.

MISS TESMAN   Fancy that! And what a stroke of luck it happened to come into the market. Just as you'd left on your honeymoon.

TESMAN   Yes, Auntie Juju, we've certainly had all the luck with us. What?

MISS TESMAN   But, George dear, the expense! It's going to make a dreadful hole in your pocket, all this.

TESMAN [*a little downcast*]   Yes, I—I suppose it will, won't it?

MISS TESMAN   Oh, George, really!

TESMAN   How much do you think it'll cost? Roughly, I mean? What?

MISS TESMAN   I can't possibly say till I see the bills.

TESMAN   Well, luckily Judge Brack's managed to get it on very favorable terms. He wrote and told Hedda so.

MISS TESMAN   Don't you worry, George dear. Anyway I've stood security for all the furniture and carpets.

TESMAN   Security? But dear, sweet Auntie Juju, how could you possibly stand security?

MISS TESMAN   I've arranged a mortgage on our annuity.

TESMAN [*jumps up*]   What? On your annuity? And—Auntie Rena's?

MISS TESMAN   Yes. Well, I couldn't think of any other way.

TESMAN [*stands in front of her*]   Auntie Juju, have you gone completely out of your mind? That annuity's all you and Auntie Rena have.

MISS TESMAN   All right, there's no need to get so excited about it. It's a pure formality, you know. Judge Brack told me so. He was so kind as to arrange it all for me. A pure formality; those were his very words.

TESMAN   I dare say. All the same—

MISS TESMAN   Anyway, you'll have a salary of your own now. And, good heavens, even if we did have to fork out a little—tighten our belts for a week or two—why, we'd be happy to do so for your sake.

TESMAN   Oh, Auntie Juju! Will you never stop sacrificing yourself for me?

MISS TESMAN [*gets up and puts her hands on his shoulders*]   What else have I to live for but to smooth your road a little, my dear boy? You've never had any mother or father to turn to. And now at last we've achieved our goal. I won't deny we've had our little difficulties now and then. But now, thank the good Lord, George dear, all your worries are past.

TESMAN   Yes, it's wonderful really how everything's gone just right for me.

MISS TESMAN   Yes! And the enemies who tried to bar your way have been struck down. They have been made to bite the dust. The man who was your most dangerous rival has had the mightiest fall. And now he's lying there in the pit he dug for himself, poor misguided creature.

TESMAN   Have you heard any news of Eilert? Since I went away?

MISS TESMAN   Only that he's said to have published a new book.

TESMAN   What! Eilert Loevborg? You mean—just recently? What?

MISS TESMAN   So they say. I don't imagine it can be of any value,
do you? When your new book comes out, that'll be another story.
What's it going to be about?

TESMAN   The domestic industries of Brabant[2] in the Middle Ages.

MISS TESMAN   Oh, George! The things you know about!

TESMAN   Mind you, it may be some time before I actually get down
to writing it. I've made these very extensive notes, and I've got to
file and index them first.

MISS TESMAN   Ah, yes! Making notes; filing and indexing; you've always been wonderful at that. Poor dear Joachim was just the same.

TESMAN   I'm looking forward so much to getting down to that. Especially now I've a home of my own to work in.

MISS TESMAN   And above all, now that you have the girl you set your
heart on, George dear.

TESMAN [*embraces her*]   Oh, yes, Auntie Juju, yes! Hedda's the loveli-
est thing of all!

Looks towards the doorway.

I think I hear her coming. What?

> HEDDA *enters the rear room from the left, and comes into the
> drawing room. She is a woman of twenty-nine. Distinguished,
> aristocratic face and figure. Her complexion is pale and opales-
> cent. Her eyes are steel-gray, with an expression of cold, calm
> serenity. Her hair is of a handsome auburn color, but is not
> especially abundant. She is dressed in an elegant, somewhat
> loose-fitting morning gown.*

MISS TESMAN [*goes to greet her*]   Good morning, Hedda dear! Good
morning!

HEDDA [*holds out her hand*]   Good morning, dear Miss Tesman. What
an early hour to call. So kind of you.

MISS TESMAN [*seems somewhat embarrassed*]   And has the young
bride slept well in her new home?

HEDDA   Oh—thank you, yes. Passably well.

TESMAN [*laughs*]   Passably. I say, Hedda, that's good! When I
jumped out of bed, you were sleeping like a top.

HEDDA   Yes. Fortunately. One has to accustom oneself to anything
new, Miss Tesman. It takes time.

Looks left.

Oh, that maid's left the french windows open. This room's flooded
with sun.

MISS TESMAN [*goes towards the windows*]   Oh—let me close them.

---

2. Prosperous duchy (1190–1477), now divided between Belgium and the Netherlands.

HEDDA   No, no, don't do that. Tesman dear, draw the curtains. This light's blinding me.

TESMAN [*at the windows*]   Yes, yes, dear. There, Hedda, now you've got shade and fresh air.

HEDDA   This room needs fresh air. All these flowers— But my dear Miss Tesman, won't you take a seat?

MISS TESMAN   No, really not, thank you. I just wanted to make sure you have everything you need. I must see about getting back home. My poor dear sister will be waiting for me.

TESMAN   Be sure to give her my love, won't you? Tell her I'll run over and see her later today.

MISS TESMAN   Oh yes, I'll tell her that. Oh, George—

Fumbles in the pocket of her skirt.

I almost forgot. I've brought something for you.

TESMAN   What's that, Auntie Juju? What?

MISS TESMAN [*pulls out a flat package wrapped in newspaper and gives it to him*]   Open and see, dear boy.

TESMAN [*opens the package*]   Good heavens! Auntie Juju, you've kept them! Hedda, this is really very touching. What?

HEDDA [*by the what-nots, on the right*]   What is it, Tesman?

TESMAN   My old shoes! My slippers, Hedda!

HEDDA   Oh, them. I remember you kept talking about them on our honeymoon.

TESMAN   Yes, I missed them dreadfully.

Goes over to her.

Here, Hedda, take a look.

HEDDA [*goes away towards the stove*]   Thanks, I won't bother.

TESMAN [*follows her*]   Fancy, Hedda, Auntie Rena's embroidered them for me. Despite her being so ill. Oh, you can't imagine what memories they have for me.

HEDDA [*by the table*]   Not for me.

MISS TESMAN   No, Hedda's right there, George.

TESMAN   Yes, but I thought since she's one of the family now—

HEDDA [*interrupts*]   Tesman, we really can't go on keeping this maid.

MISS TESMAN   Not keep Bertha?

TESMAN   What makes you say that, dear? What?

HEDDA [*points*]   Look at that! She's left her old hat lying on the chair.

TESMAN [*appalled, drops his slippers on the floor*]   But, Hedda—!

HEDDA   Suppose someone came in and saw it?

TESMAN   But, Hedda—that's Auntie Juju's hat.

HEDDA   Oh?

MISS TESMAN [*picks up the hat*]   Indeed it's mine. And it doesn't happen to be old, Hedda dear.

HEDDA   I didn't look at it very closely, Miss Tesman.

MISS TESMAN [*tying on the hat*]   As a matter of fact, it's the first time I've worn it. As the good Lord is my witness.

TESMAN   It's very pretty, too. Really smart.

MISS TESMAN   Oh, I'm afraid it's nothing much really.

Looks round.

My parasol? Ah, here it is.

Takes it.

This is mine, too.

Murmurs.

Not Bertha's.

TESMAN   A new hat and a new parasol! I say, Hedda, fancy that!

HEDDA   Very pretty and charming

TESMAN   Yes, isn't it? What? But Auntie Juju, take a good look at Hedda before you go. Isn't she pretty and charming?

MISS TESMAN   Dear boy, there's nothing new in that. Hedda's been a beauty ever since the day she was born.

Nods and goes right.

TESMAN [*follows her*]   Yes, but have you noticed how strong and healthy she's looking? And how she's filled out since we went away?

MISS TESMAN [*stops and turns*]   Filled out?

HEDDA [*walks across the room*]   Oh, can't we forget it?

TESMAN   Yes, Auntie Juju—you can't see it so clearly with that dress on. But I've good reason to know—

HEDDA [*by the french windows, impatiently*]   You haven't good reason to know anything.

TESMAN   It must have been the mountain air up there in the Tyrol—

HEDDA [*curtly, interrupts him*]   I'm exactly the same as when I went away.

TESMAN   You keep on saying so. But you're not. I'm right, aren't I, Auntie Juju?

MISS TESMAN [*has folded her hands and is gazing at her*]   She's beautiful—beautiful. Hedda is beautiful.

Goes over to HEDDA, *takes her head between her hands, draws it down and kisses her hair.*

God bless and keep you, Hedda Tesman. For George's sake.

HEDDA [*frees herself politely*]   Oh—let me go, please.

MISS TEMAN [*quietly, emotionally*]   I shall come and see you both every day.

TESMAN   Yes, Auntie Juju, please do. What?

MISS TESMAN   Good-bye! Good-bye!

She goes out into the hall. TESMAN *follows her. The door remains open.* TESMAN *is heard sending his love to Aunt Rena and thanking* MISS TESMAN *for his slippers. Meanwhile* HEDDA *walks up and down the room raising her arms and clenching her fists as though in desperation. Then she throws aside the curtains from the french windows and stands there, looking out. A few moments later,* TESMAN *returns and closes the door behind him.*

TESMAN [*picks up his slippers from the floor*]   What are you looking at, Hedda?

HEDDA [*calm and controlled again*]   Only the leaves. They're so golden. And withered.

TESMAN [*wraps up the slippers and lays them on the table*]   Well, we're into September now.

HEDDA [*restless again*]   Yes. We're already into September.

TESMAN   Auntie Juju was behaving rather oddly, I thought, didn't you? Almost as though she was in church or something. I wonder what came over her. Any idea?

HEDDA   I hardly know her. Does she often act like that?

TESMAN   Not to the extent she did today.

HEDDA [*goes away from the french windows*]   Do you think she was hurt by what I said about the hat?

TESMAN   Oh, I don't think so. A little at first, perhaps—

HEDDA   But what a thing to do, throw her hat down in someone's drawing room. People don't do such things.

TESMAN   I'm sure Auntie Juju doesn't do it very often.

HEDDA   Oh well, I'll make it up with her.

TESMAN   Oh Hedda, would you?

HEDDA   When you see them this afternoon invite her to come out here this evening.

TESMAN   You bet I will! I say, there's another thing which would please her enormously.

HEDDA   Oh?

TESMAN   If you could bring yourself to call her Auntie Juju. For my sake, Hedda? What?

HEDDA   Oh no, really, Tesman, you mustn't ask me to do that. I've told you so once before. I'll try to call her Aunt Juliana. That's as far as I'll go.

TESMAN [*after a moment*]   I say, Hedda, is anything wrong? What?

HEDDA   I'm just looking at my old piano. It doesn't really go with all this.

TESMAN   As soon as I start getting my salary we'll see about changing it.

HEDDA   No, no, don't let's change it. I don't want to part with it. We can move it into that little room and get another one to put in here.

TESMAN [*a little downcast*]   Yes, we—might do that.

HEDDA [*picks up the bunch of flowers from the piano*]   These flowers weren't here when we arrived last night.

TESMAN   I expect Auntie Juju brought them.

HEDDA   Here's a card.

Takes it out and reads.

"Will come back later today." Guess who it's from?

TESMAN   No idea. Who? What?

HEDDA   It says: "Mrs. Elvsted."

TESMAN   No, really? Mrs. Elvsted! She used to be Miss Rysing, didn't she?

HEDDA   Yes. She was the one with that irritating hair she was always showing off. I hear she used to be an old flame of yours.

TESMAN   [*laughs*]   That didn't last long. Anyway, that was before I got to know you, Hedda. By Jove, fancy her being in town!

HEDDA   Strange she should call. I only knew her at school.

TESMAN   Yes, I haven't seen her for—oh, heaven knows how long. I don't know how she manages to stick it out up there in the north. What?

HEDDA   [*thinks for a moment, then says suddenly*]   Tell me, Tesman, doesn't he live somewhere up in those parts? You know—Eilert Loevborg?

TESMAN   Yes, that's right. So he does.

BERTHA *enters from the hall.*

BERTHA   She's here again, madam. The lady who came and left the flowers.

Points.

The ones you're holding.

HEDDA   Oh, is she? Well, show her in.

BERTHA *opens the door for* MRS. ELVSTED *and goes out.* MRS. ELVSTED *is a delicately built woman with gentle, attractive features. Her eyes are light blue, large, and somewhat prominent, with a frightened, questioning expression. Her hair is extremely fair, almost flaxen, and is exceptionally wavy and abundant. She is two or three years younger than* HEDDA. *She is wearing a dark visiting dress, in good taste but not quite in the latest fashion.*

HEDDA   [*goes cordially to greet her*]   Dear Mrs. Elvsted, good morning. How delightful to see you again after all this time.

MRS. ELVSTED   [*nervously, trying to control herself*]   Yes, it's many years since we met.

TESMAN   And since *we* met. What?

HEDDA   Thank you for your lovely flowers.

MRS. ELVSTED   Oh, please—I wanted to come yesterday afternoon. But they told me you were away—

TESMAN   You've only just arrived in town, then? What?

MRS. ELVSTED   I got here yesterday, around midday. Oh, I became almost desperate when I heard you weren't here.

HEDDA   Desperate? Why?

TESMAN   My dear Mrs. Rysing—Elvsted—

HEDDA   There's nothing wrong, I hope?

MRS. ELVSTED   Yes, there is. And I don't know anyone else here whom I can turn to.

HEDDA   [*puts the flowers down on the table*]   Come and sit with me on the sofa—

MRS. ELVSTED   Oh, I feel too restless to sit down.

HEDDA   You must. Come along, now.

She pulls MRS. ELVSTED *down on to the sofa and sits beside her.*

TESMAN   Well? Tell us, Mrs.—er—

HEDDA   Has something happened at home?

MRS. ELVSTED   Yes—that is, yes and no. Oh, I do hope you won't misunderstand me—

HEDDA   Then you'd better tell us the whole story, Mrs. Elvsted.

TESMAN   That's why you've come. What?

MRS. ELVSTED   Yes—yes, it is. Well, then—in case you don't already know—Eilert Loevborg is in town.

HEDDA   Loevborg here?

TESMAN   Eilert back in town? By Jove, Hedda, did you hear that?

HEDDA   Yes, of course I heard.

MRS. ELVSTED   He's been here a week. A whole week! In this city. Alone. With all those dreadful people—

HEDDA   But my dear Mrs. Elvsted, what concern is he of yours?

MRS. ELVSTED   [*gives her a frightened look and says quickly*]   He's been tutoring the children.

HEDDA   Your children?

MRS. ELVSTED   My husband's. I have none.

HEDDA   Oh, you mean your stepchildren.

MRS. ELVSTED   Yes.

TESMAN   [*gropingly*]   But was he sufficien.ly—I don't know how to put it—sufficiently regular in his habits to be suited to such a post? What?

MRS. ELVSTED   For the past two to three years he has been living irreproachably.

TESMAN   You don't say! By Jove, Hedda, hear that?

HEDDA   I hear.

MRS. ELVSTED   Quite irreproachably, I assure you. In every respect. All the same—in this big city—with money in his pockets—I'm so dreadfully frightened something may happen to him.

TESMAN   But why didn't he stay up there with you and your husband?

MRS. ELVSTED   Once his book had come out, he became restless.

TESMAN   Oh, yes—Auntie Juju said he'd brought out a new book.

MRS. ELVSTED   Yes, a big new book about the history of civilization. A kind of general survey. It came out a fortnight ago. Everyone's been buying it and reading it—it's created a tremendous stir—

TESMAN   Has it really? It must be something he's dug up, then.

MRS. ELVSTED   You mean from the old days?

TESMAN   Yes.

MRS. ELVSTED   No, he's written it all since he came to live with us.

TESMAN   Well, that's splendid news, Hedda. Fancy that!

MRS. ELVSTED   Oh, yes! If only he can go on like this!

HEDDA   Have you met him since you came here?

MRS. ELVSTED   No, not yet. I had such dreadful difficulty finding his address. But this morning I managed to track him down at last.

HEDDA [*looks searchingly at her*]   I must say I find it a little strange that your husband—hm—

MRS. ELVSTED [*starts nervously*]   My husband! What do you mean?

HEDDA   That he should send you all the way here on an errand of this kind. I'm surprised he didn't come himself to keep an eye on his friend.

MRS. ELVSTED   Oh, no, no—my husband hasn't the time. Besides. I—er—wanted to do some shopping here.

HEDDA [*with a slight smile*]   Ah. Well, that's different.

MRS. ELVSTED [*gets up quickly, restlessly*]   Please, Mr. Tesman, I beg you—be kind to Eilert Loevborg if he comes here. I'm sure he will. I mean, you used to be such good friends in the old days. And you're both studying the same subject, as far as I can understand. You're in the same field, aren't you?

TESMAN   Well, we used to be, anyway.

MRS. ELVSTED   Yes—so I beg you earnestly, do please, please, keep an eye on him. Oh, Mr. Tesman, do promise me you will.

TESMAN   I shall be only too happy to do so, Mrs. Rysing.

HEDDA   Elvsted.

TESMAN   I'll do everything for Eilert that lies in my power. You can rely on that.

MRS. ELVSTED   Oh, how good and kind you are!

Presses his hands.

Thank you, thank you, thank you.

Frightened.

My husband's so fond of him, you see.

HEDDA [*gets up*]   You'd better send him a note, Tesman. He may not come to you of his own accord.

TESMAN   Yes, that'd probably be the best plan, Hedda. What?

HEDDA   The sooner the better. Why not do it now?

MRS. ELVSTED [*pleadingly*]   Oh yes, if only you would!

TESMAN   I'll do it this very moment. Do you have his address, Mrs.—er—Elvsted?

MRS. ELVSTED   Yes.

Takes a small piece of paper from her pocket and gives it to him.

TESMAN   Good, good. Right, well I'll go inside and—

Looks round.

Where are my slippers? Oh yes, here.

Picks up the package and is about to go.

HEDDA   Try to sound friendly. Make it a nice long letter.
TESMAN   Right, I will.
MRS. ELVSTED   Please don't say anything about my having seen you.
TESMAN   Good heavens no, of course not. What?

Goes out through the rear room to the right.

HEDDA [*goes over to* MRS. ELVSTED, *smiles, and says softly*]   Well!
Now we've killed two birds with one stone.
MRS. ELVSTED   What do you mean?
HEDDA   Didn't you realize I wanted to get him out of the room?
MRS. ELVSTED   So that he could write the letter?
HEDDA   And so that I could talk to you alone.
MRS. ELVSTED [*confused*]   About this?
HEDDA   Yes, about this.
MRS. ELVSTED [*in alarm*]   But there's nothing more to tell, Mrs. Tes-
man. Really there isn't.
HEDDA   Oh, yes there is. There's a lot more. I can see that. Come
along, let's sit down and have a little chat.

She pushes MRS. ELVSTED *down into the armchair by the stove
and seats herself on one of the footstools.*

MRS. ELVSTED [*looks anxiously at her watch*]   Really, Mrs. Tesman,
I think I ought to be going now.
HEDDA   There's no hurry. Well? How are things at home?
MRS. ELVSTED   I'd rather not speak about that.
HEDDA   But my dear, you can tell me. Good heavens, we were at
school together.
MRS. ELVSTED   Yes, but you were a year senior to me. Oh, I used to
be terribly frightened of you in those days.
HEDDA   Frightened of me?
MRS. ELVSTED   Yes, terribly frightened. Whenever you met me on the
staircase you used to pull my hair.
HEDDA   No, did I?
MRS. ELVSTED   Yes. And once you said you'd burn it all off.
HEDDA   Oh, that was only in fun.
MRS. ELVSTED   Yes, but I was so silly in those days. And then after-
wards—I mean, we've drifted so far apart. Our backgrounds were so
different.
HEDDA   Well, now we must try to drift together again. Now listen.
When we were at school we used to call each other by our Christian
names—
MRS. ELVSTED   No, I'm sure you're mistaken.
HEDDA   I'm sure I'm not. I remember it quite clearly. Let's tell each
other our secrets, as we used to in the old days.

Moves closer on her footstool.

There, now.

Kisses her on the cheek.

You must call me Hedda.

MRS. ELVSTED [*squeezes her hands and pats them*] Oh you're so kind. I'm not used to people being so nice to me.

HEDDA Now, now, now. And I shall call you Tora, the way I used to.

MRS. ELVSTED My name is Thea.

HEDDA Yes, of course. Of course. I meant Thea.

Looks at her sympathetically.

So you're not used to kindness, Thea? In your own home?

MRS. ELVSTED Oh, if only I had a home! But I haven't. I've never had one.

HEDDA [*looks at her for a moment*] I thought that was it.

MRS. ELVSTED [*stares blankly and helplessly*] Yes—yes—yes.

HEDDA I can't remember exactly now, but didn't you first go to Mr. Elvsted as a housekeeper?

MRS. ELVSTED Governess, actually. But his wife—at the time, I mean —she was an invalid, and had to spend most of her time in bed. So I had to look after the house too.

HEDDA But in the end, you became mistress of the house.

MRS. ELVSTED [*sadly*] Yes, I did.

HEDDA Let me see. Roughly how long ago was that?

MRS. ELVSTED When I got married, you mean?

HEDDA Yes.

MRS. ELVSTED About five years.

HEDDA Yes; it must be about that.

MRS. ELVSTED Oh, those five years! Especially the last two or three, Oh, Mrs. Tesman, if you only knew—!

HEDDA [*slaps her hand gently*] Mrs. Tesman? Oh, Thea!

MRS. ELVSTED I'm sorry, I'll try to remember. Yes—if you had any idea—

HEDDA [*casually*] Eilert Loevborg's been up there too, for about three years, hasn't he?

MRS. ELVSTED [*looks at her uncertainly*] Eilert Loevborg? Yes, he has.

HEDDA Did you know him before? When you were here?

MRS. ELVSTED No, not really. That is—I knew him by name, of course.

HEDDA But up there, he used to visit you?

MRS. ELVSTED Yes, he used to come and see us every day. To give the children lessons. I found I couldn't do that as well as manage the house.

HEDDA I'm sure you couldn't. And your husband—? I suppose being a magistrate he has to be away from home a good deal?

MRS. ELVSTED Yes. You see, Mrs.—you see, Hedda, he has to cover the whole district.

HEDDA [*leans against the arm of* MRS. ELVSTED's *chair*]   Poor, pretty
little Thea! Now you must tell me the whole story. From beginning
to end.

MRS. ELVSTED   Well—what do you want to know?

HEDDA   What kind of a man is your husband, Thea? I mean, as a
person. Is he kind to you?

MRS. ELVSTED [*evasively*]   I'm sure he does his best to be.

HEDDA   I only wonder if he isn't too old for you. There's more than
twenty years between you, isn't there?

MRS. ELVSTED [*irritably*]   Yes, there's that too. Oh, there are so many
things. We're different in every way. We've nothing in common.
Nothing whatever.

HEDDA   But he loves you, surely? In his own way?

MRS. ELVSTED   Oh, I don't know. I think he just finds me useful. And
then I don't cost much to keep. I'm cheap.

HEDDA   Now you're being stupid.

MRS. ELVSTED [*shakes her head*]   It can't be any different. With him.
He doesn't love anyone except himself. And perhaps the children—
a little.

HEDDA   He must be fond of Eilert Loevborg, Thea.

MRS. ELVSTED [*looks at her*]   Eilert Loevborg? What makes you think
that?

HEDDA   Well, if he sends you all the way down here to look for him—

Smiles almost imperceptibly.

Besides, you said so yourself to Tesman.

MRS. ELVSTED [*with a nervous twitch*]   Did I? Oh yes, I suppose I
did.

Impulsively, but keeping her voice low.

Well, I might as well tell you the whole story. It's bound to come
out sooner or later.

HEDDA   But my dear Thea—?

MRS. ELVSTED   My husband had no idea I was coming here.

HEDDA   What? Your husband didn't know?

MRS. ELVSTED   No, of course not. As a matter of fact, he wasn't even
there. He was away at the assizes. Oh, I couldn't stand it any longer,
Hedda! I just couldn't. I'd be so dreadfully lonely up there now.

HEDDA   Go on.

MRS. ELVSTED   So I packed a few things. Secretly. And went.

HEDDA   Without telling anyone?

MRS. ELVSTED   Yes. I caught the train and came straight here.

HEDDA   But my dear Thea! How brave of you!

MRS. ELVSTED [*gets up and walks across the room*]   Well, what else
could I do?

HEDDA   But what do you suppose your husband will say when you
get back?

MRS. ELVSTED [*by the table, looks at her*]   Back there? To him?

HEDDA   Yes. Surely—?

MRS. ELVSTED   I shall never go back to him.

HEDDA [*gets up and goes closer*]   You mean you've left your home for good?

MRS. ELVSTED   Yes. I didn't see what else I could do.

HEDDA   But to do it so openly!

MRS. ELVSTED   Oh, it's no use trying to keep a thing like that secret.

HEDDA   But what do you suppose people will say?

MRS. ELVSTED   They can say what they like.

Sits sadly, wearily on the sofa.

I had to do it.

HEDDA [*after a short silence*]   What do you intend to do now? How are you going to live?

MRS. ELVSTED   I don't know. I only know that I must live wherever Eilert Loevborg is. If I am to go on living.

HEDDA [*moves a chair from the table, sits on it near* MRS. ELVSTED *and strokes her hands*]   Tell me, Thea, how did this—friendship between you and Eilert Loevborg begin?

MRS. ELVSTED   Oh, it came about gradually. I developed a kind of—power over him.

HEDDA   Oh?

MRS. ELVSTED   He gave up his old habits. Not because I asked him to. I'd never have dared to do that. I suppose he just noticed I didn't like that kind of thing. So he gave it up.

HEDDA [*hides a smile*]   So you've made a new man of him. Clever little Thea!

MRS. ELVSTED   Yes—anyway, he says I have. And he's made a—sort of—real person of me. Taught me to think—and to understand all kinds of things.

HEDDA   Did he give you lessons too?

MRS. ELVSTED   Not exactly lessons. But he talked to me. About—oh, you've no idea—so many things! And then he let me work with him. Oh, it was wonderful. I was so happy to be allowed to help him.

HEDDA   Did he allow you to help him!

MRS. ELVSTED   Yes. Whenever he wrote anything we always—did it together.

HEDDA   Like good pals?

MRS. ELVSTED [*eagerly*]   Pals! Yes—why, Hedda, that's exactly the word he used! Oh, I ought to feel so happy. But I can't. I don't know if it will last.

HEDDA   You don't seem very sure of him.

MRS. ELVSTED [*sadly*]   Something stands between Eilert Loevborg and me. The shadow of another woman.

HEDDA   Who can that be?

MRS. ELVSTED   I don't know. Someone he used to be friendly with in—in the old days. Someone he's never been able to forget.

HEDDA   What has he told you about her?

MRS. ELVSTED   Oh, he only mentioned her once, casually.

HEDDA   Well! What did he say?

MRS. ELVSTED   He said when he left her she tried to shoot him with a pistol.

HEDDA [*cold, controlled*]   What nonsense. People don't do such things. The kind of people we know.

MRS. ELVSTED   No. I think it must have been that red-haired singer he used to—

HEDDA   Ah yes, very probably.

MRS. ELVSTED   I remember they used to say she always carried a loaded pistol.

HEDDA   Well then, it must be her.

MRS. ELVSTED   But, Hedda, I hear she's come back, and is living here. Oh, I'm so desperate—!

HEDDA [*glances towards the rear room*]   Ssh! Tesman's coming.

Gets up and whispers.

Thea, we mustn't breathe a word about this to anyone.

MRS. ELVSTED [*jumps up*]   Oh, no, no! Please don't!

GEORGE TESMAN *appears from the right in the rear room with a letter in his hand, and comes into the drawing room.*

TESMAN   Well, here's my little epistle all signed and sealed.

HEDDA   Good. I think Mrs. Elvsted wants to go now. Wait a moment —I'll see you as far as the garden gate.

TESMAN   Er—Hedda, do you think Bertha could deal with this?

HEDDA [*takes the letter*]   I'll give her instructions.

BERTHA *enters from the hall.*

BERTHA   Judge Brack is here and asks if he may pay his respects to Madam and the Doctor.

HEDDA   Yes, ask him to be so good as to come in. And—wait a moment —drop this letter in the post box.

BERTHA [*takes the letter*] Very good, madam.

She opens the door for JUDGE BRACK, *and goes out.* JUDGE BRACK *is forty-five; rather short, but well-built, and elastic in his movements. He has a roundish face with an aristocratic profile. His hair, cut short, is still almost black, and is carefully barbered. Eyes lively and humorous. Thick eyebrows. His moustache is also thick, and is trimmed square at the ends. He is wearing outdoor clothes which are elegant but a little too youthful for him. He has a monocle in one eye; now and then he lets it drop.*

BRACK [*hat in hand, bows*]   May one presume to call so early?

HEDDA   One may presume.

TESMAN [*shakes his hand*]   You're welcome here any time. Judge Brack—Mrs. Rysing.

HEDDA *sighs.*

BRACK [*bows*]   Ah—charmed—

HEDDA [*looks at him and laughs*]   What fun to be able to see you by daylight for once, Judge.

BRACK   Do I look—different?

HEDDA   Yes. A little younger, I think.

BRACK   Obliged.

TESMAN   Well, what do you think of Hedda? What? Doesn't she look well? Hasn't she filled out—?

HEDDA   Oh, do stop it. You ought to be thanking Judge Brack for all the inconvenience he's put himself to—

BRACK   Nonsense, it was a pleasure—

HEDDA   You're a loyal friend. But my other friend is pining to get away. Au revoir, Judge. I won't be a minute.

> *Mutual salutations.* MRS. ELVSTED *and* HEDDA *go out through the hall.*

BRACK   Well, is your wife satisfied with everything?

TESMAN   Yes, we can't thank you enough. That is—we may have to shift one or two things around, she tells me. And we're short of one or two little items we'll have to purchase.

BRACK   Oh? Really?

TESMAN   But you mustn't worry your head about that. Hedda says she'll get what's needed. I say, why don't we sit down? What?

BRACK   Thanks, just for a moment.

> *Sits at the table.*

There's something I'd like to talk to you about, my dear Tesman.

TESMAN   Oh? Ah yes, of course.

> *Sits.*

After the feast comes the reckoning. What?

BRACK   Oh, never mind about the financial side—there's no hurry about that. Though I could wish we'd arranged things a little less palatially.

TESMAN   Good heavens, that'd never have done. Think of Hedda, my dear chap. You know her. I couldn't possibly ask her to live like a suburban housewife.

BRACK   No, no—that's just the problem.

TESMAN   Anyway, it can't be long now before my nomination[3] comes through.

BRACK   Well, you know, these things often take time.

TESMAN   Have you heard any more news? What?

BRACK   Nothing definite.

> *Changing the subject.*

3. To a professorship at the university.

Oh, by the way, I have one piece of news for you.

TESMAN   What?

BRACK   Your old friend Eilert Loevborg is back in town.

TESMAN   I know that already.

BRACK   Oh? How did you hear that?

TESMAN   She told me. That lady who went out with Hedda.

BRACK   I see. What was her name? I didn't catch it.

TESMAN   Mrs. Elvsted.

BRACK   Oh, the magistrate's wife. Yes, Loevborg's been living up near them, hasn't he?

TESMAN   I'm delighted to hear he's become a decent human being again.

BRACK   Yes, so they say.

TESMAN   I gather he's published a new book, too. What?

BRACK   Indeed he has.

TESMAN   I hear it's created rather a stir.

BRACK   Quite an unusual stir.

TESMAN   I say, isn't that splendid news! He's such a gifted chap— and I was afraid he'd gone to the dogs for good.

BRACK   Most people thought he had.

TESMAN   But I can't think what he'll do now. How on earth will he manage to make ends meet? What?

As he speaks his last words, HEDDA *enters from the hall.*

HEDDA   [*to* BRACK, *laughs slightly scornfully*]   Tesman is always worrying about making ends meet.

TESMAN   We were talking about poor Eilert Loevborg, Hedda dear.

HEDDA   [*gives him a quick look*]   Oh, were you?

Sits in the armchair by the stove and asks casually.

Is he in trouble?

TESMAN   Well, he must have run through his inheritance long ago by now. And he can't write a new book every year. What? So I'm wondering what's going to become of him.

BRACK   I may be able to enlighten you there.

TESMAN   Oh?

BRACK   You mustn't forget he has relatives who wield a good deal of influence.

TESMAN   Relatives? Oh, they've quite washed their hands of him, I'm afraid.

BRACK   They used to regard him as the hope of the family.

TESMAN   Used to, yes. But he's put an end to that.

HEDDA   Who knows?

With a little smile.

I hear the Elvsteds have made a new man of him.

BRACK   And then this book he's just published—

TESMAN   Well, let's hope they find something for him. I've just writ-

ten him a note. Oh, by the way, Hedda, I asked him to come over
and see us this evening.

BRACK   But my dear chap, you're coming to me this evening. My
bachelor party. You promised me last night when I met you at the
boat.

HEDDA   Had you forgotten, Tesman?

TESMAN   Good heavens, yes, I'd quite forgotten.

BRACK   Anyway, you can be quite sure he won't turn up here.

TESMAN   Why do you think that? What?

BRACK   [*a little unwillingly, gets up and rests his hands on the back
of his chair*]   My dear Tesman—and you, too, Mrs. Tesman—
there's something I feel you ought to know.

TESMAN   Concerning Eilert?

BRACK   Concerning him and you.

TESMAN   Well, my dear Judge, tell us, please!

BRACK   You must be prepared for your nomination not to come
through quite as quickly as you hope and expect.

TESMAN   [*jumps up uneasily*]   Is anything wrong? What?

BRACK   There's a possibility that the appointment may be decided by
competition—

TESMAN   Competition! By Jove, Hedda, fancy that!

HEDDA   [*leans further back in her chair*]   Ah! How interesting!

TESMAN   But who else—? I say, you don't mean—?

BRACK   Exactly. By competition with Eilert Loevborg.

TESMAN   [*clasps his hands in alarm*]   No, no, but this is inconceivable!
It's absolutely impossible! What?

BRACK   Hm. We may find it'll happen, all the same.

TESMAN   No, but—Judge Brack, they couldn't be so inconsiderate
towards me!

Waves his arms.

I mean, by Jove, I—I'm a married man! It was on the strength of
this that Hedda and I *got* married! We ran up some pretty hefty
debts. And borrowed money from Auntie Juju! I mean, good
heavens, they practically promised me the appointment. What?

BRACK   Well, well, I'm sure you'll get it. But you'll have to go through
a competition.

HEDDA   [*motionless in her armchair*]   How exciting, Tesman. It'll be a
kind of duel, by Jove.

TESMAN   My dear Hedda, how can you take it so lightly?

HEDDA   [*as before*]   I'm not. I can't wait to see who's going to win.

BRACK   In any case, Mrs. Tesman, it's best you should know how
things stand. I mean before you commit yourself to these little items
I hear you're threatening to purchase.

HEDDA   I can't allow this to alter my plans.

BRACK   Indeed? Well, that's your business. Good-bye.

To TESMAN.

I'll come and collect you on the way home from my afternoon walk.

TESMAN   Oh, yes, yes. I'm sorry, I'm all upside down just now.

HEDDA [*lying in her chair, holds out her hand*]   Good-bye, Judge. See you this afternoon.

BRACK   Thank you. Good-bye, good-bye.

TESMAN [*sees him to the door*]   Good-bye, my dear Judge. You will excuse me, won't you?

JUDGE BRACK *goes out through the hall.*

TESMAN [*pacing up and down*]   Oh, Hedda! One oughtn't to go plunging off on wild adventures. What?

HEDDA [*looks at him and smiles*]   Like you're doing?

TESMAN   Yes. I mean, there's no denying it, it was a pretty big adventure to go off and get married and set up house merely on expectation.

HEDDA   Perhaps you're right.

TESMAN   Well, anyway, we have our home, Hedda. By Jove, yes. The home we dreamed of. And set our hearts on. What?

HEDDA [*gets up slowly, wearily*]   You agreed that we should enter society. And keep open house. That was the bargain.

TESMAN   Yes. Good heavens, I was looking forward to it all so much. To seeing you play hostess to a select circle. By Jove! What? Ah, well, for the time being we shall have to make do with each other's company, Hedda. Perhaps have Auntie Juju in now and then. Oh dear, this wasn't at all what you had in mind—

HEDDA   I won't be able to have a liveried footman. For a start.

TESMAN   Oh no, we couldn't possibly afford a footman.

HEDDA   And that thoroughbred horse you promised me—

TESMAN [*fearfully*]   Thoroughbred horse!

HEDDA   I mustn't even think of that now.

TESMAN   Heaven forbid!

HEDDA [*walks across the room*]   Ah, well. I still have one thing left to amuse myself with.

TESMAN [*joyfully*]   Thank goodness for that. What's that, Hedda? What?

HEDDA [*in the open doorway, looks at him with concealed scorn*]   My pistols, George darling.

TESMAN [*alarmed*]   Pistols!

HEDDA [*her eyes cold*]   General Gabler's pistols.

She goes into the rear room and disappears.

TESMAN [*runs to the doorway and calls after her*]   For heaven's sake, Hedda dear, don't touch those things. They're dangerous. Hedda— please—for my sake! What?

Act 2

The same as in Act One, except that the piano has been removed and an elegant little writing table, with a bookcase, stands in its place. By the sofa on the left a smaller table has been placed. Most of the flowers have been removed. MRS. ELVSTED'S *bouquet stands on the larger table, downstage. It is afternoon.*

HEDDA, *dressed to receive callers, is alone in the room. She is standing by the open french windows, loading a revolver. The pair to it is lying in an open pistol case on the writing table.*

HEDDA [*looks down into the garden and calls*]   Good afternoon, Judge.
BRACK [*in the distance, below*]   Afternoon, Mrs. Tesman.
HEDDA [*raises the pistol and takes aim*]   I'm going to shoot you, Judge Brack.
BRACK [*shouts from below*]   No, no, no! Don't aim that thing at me!
HEDDA   This'll teach you to enter houses by the back door.

> *Fires.*

BRACK [*below*]   Have you gone completely out of your mind?
HEDDA   Oh dear! Did I hit you?
BRACK [*still outside*]   Stop playing these silly tricks.
HEDDA   All right, Judge. Come along in.

> JUDGE BRACK, *dressed for a bachelor party, enters through the french windows. He has a light overcoat on his arm.*

BRACK   For God's sake! Haven't you stopped fooling around with those things yet? What are you trying to hit?
HEDDA   Oh, I was just shooting at the sky.
BRACK [*takes the pistol gently from her hand*]   By your leave, ma'am.

> *Looks at it.*

Ah, yes—I know this old friend well.

> *Looks around.*

Where's the case? Oh, yes.

> *Puts the pistol in the case and closes it.*

That's enough of that little game for today.
HEDDA   Well, what on earth *am* I to do?
BRACK   You haven't had any visitors?
HEDDA [*closes the french windows*]   Not one. I suppose the best people are all still in the country.
BRACK   Your husband isn't home yet?
HEDDA [*locks the pistol away in a drawer of the writing table*]   No. The moment he'd finished eating he ran off to his aunties. He wasn't expecting you so early.
BRACK   Ah, why didn't I think of that? How stupid of me.
HEDDA [*turns her head and looks at him*]   Why stupid?
BRACK   I'd have come a little sooner.

HEDDA [*walks across the room*]   There'd have been no one to receive you. I've been in my room since lunch, dressing.

BRACK   You haven't a tiny crack in the door through which we might have negotiated?

HEDDA   You forgot to arrange one.

BRACK   Another stupidity.

HEDDA   Well, we'll have to sit down here. And wait. Tesman won't be back for some time.

BRACK   Sad. Well, I'll be patient.

> HEDDA *sits on the corner of the sofa.* BRACK *puts his coat over the back of the nearest chair and seats himself, keeping his hat in his hand. Short pause. They look at each other.*

HEDDA   Well?

BRACK [*in the same tone of voice*]   Well?

HEDDA   I asked first.

BRACK [*leans forward slightly*]   Yes, well, now we can enjoy a nice, cozy little chat—Mrs. Hedda.

HEDDA [*leans further back in her chair*]   It seems such ages since we had a talk. I don't count last night or this morning.

BRACK   You mean: *à deux*?

HEDDA   Mm—yes. That's roughly what I meant.

BRACK   I've been longing so much for you to come home.

HEDDA   So have I.

BRACK   You? Really, Mrs. Hedda? And I thought you were having such a wonderful honeymoon.

HEDDA   Oh, yes. Wonderful!

BRACK   But your husband wrote such ecstatic letters.

HEDDA   He! Oh, yes! He thinks life has nothing better to offer than rooting around in libraries and copying old pieces of parchment, or whatever it is he does.

BRACK [*a little maliciously*]   Well, that *is* his life. Most of it, anyway.

HEDDA   Yes, I know. Well, it's all right for him. But for me! Oh no, my dear Judge. I've been bored to death.

BRACK [*sympathetically*]   Do you mean that? Seriously?

HEDDA   Yes. Can you imagine? Six whole months without ever meeting a single person who was one of us, and to whom I could talk about the kind of things we talk about.

BRACK   Yes, I can understand. I'd miss that, too.

HEDDA   That wasn't the worst, though.

BRACK   What was?

HEDDA   Having to spend every minute of one's life with—with the same person.

BRACK [*nods*]   Yes. What a thought! Morning; noon; and—

HEDDA [*coldly*]   As I said: every minute of one's life.

BRACK   I stand corrected. But dear Tesman is such a clever fellow, I should have thought one ought to be able—

HEDDA   Tesman is only interested in one thing, my dear Judge. His special subject.

BRACK   True.

HEDDA   And people who are only interested in one thing don't make the most amusing company. Not for long, anyway.

BRACK   Not even when they happen to be the person one loves?

HEDDA   Oh, don't use that sickly, stupid word.

BRACK [*starts*]   But, Mrs. Hedda—!

HEDDA [*half laughing, half annoyed*]   You just try it, Judge. Listening to the history of civilization morning, noon and—

BRACK [*corrects her*]   Every minute of one's life.

HEDDA   All right. Oh, and those domestic industries of Brabant in the Middle Ages! That really is beyond the limit.

BRACK [*looks at her searchingly*]   But, tell me—if you feel like this why on earth did you—? Ha—

HEDDA   Why on earth did I marry George Tesman?

BRACK   If you like to put it that way.

HEDDA   Do you think it so very strange?

BRACK   Yes—and no, Mrs. Hedda.

HEDDA   I'd danced myself tired, Judge. I felt my time was up—

Gives a slight shudder.

No, I mustn't say that. Or even think it.

BRACK   You've no rational cause to think it.

HEDDA   Oh—cause, cause—

Looks searchingly at him.

After all, George Tesman—well, I mean, he's a very respectable man.

BRACK   Very respectable, sound as a rock. No denying that.

HEDDA   And there's nothing exactly ridiculous about him. Is there?

BRACK   Ridiculous? N-no, I wouldn't say that.

HEDDA   Mm. He's very clever at collecting material and all that, isn't he? I mean, he may go quite far in time.

BRACK [*looks at her a little uncertainly*]   I thought you believed, like everyone else, that he would become a very prominent man.

HEDDA [*looks tired*]   Yes, I did. And when he came and begged me on his bended knees to be allowed to love and to cherish me, I didn't see why I shouldn't let him.

BRACK   No, well—if one looks at it like that—

HEDDA   It was more than my other admirers were prepared to do, Judge dear.

BRACK [*laughs*]   Well, I can't answer for the others. As far as I myself am concerned, you know I've always had a considerable respect for the institution of marriage. As an institution.

HEDDA [*lightly*]   Oh, I've never entertained any hopes of you.

BRACK   All I want is to have a circle of friends whom I can trust, whom I can help with advice or—or by any other means, and into whose houses I may come and go as a—trusted friend.

HEDDA   Of the husband?

BRACK [*bows*]   Preferably, to be frank, of the wife. And of the hus-

band too, of course. Yes, you know, this kind of—triangle is a delightful arrangement for all parties concerned.

HEDDA   Yes, I often longed for a third person while I was away. Oh,
those hours we spent alone in railway compartments—

BRACK   Fortunately your honeymoon is now over.

HEDDA [*shakes her head*]   There's a long, long way still to go. I've
only reached a stop on the line.

BRACK   Why not jump out and stretch your legs a little, Mrs. Hedda?

HEDDA   I'm not the jumping sort.

BRACK   Aren't you?

HEDDA   No. There's always someone around who—

BRACK [*laughs*]   Who looks at one's legs?

HEDDA   Yes. Exactly.

BRACK   Well, but surely—

HEDDA [*with a gesture of rejection*]   I don't like it. I'd rather stay
where I am. Sitting in the compartment. *À deux.*

BRACK   But suppose a third person were to step into the compartment?

HEDDA   That would be different.

BRACK   A trusted friend—someone who understood—

HEDDA   And was lively and amusing—

BRACK   And interested in—more subjects than one—

HEDDA [*sighs audibly*]   Yes, that'd be a relief.

BRACK [*hears the front door open and shut*]   The triangle is completed.

HEDDA [*half under breath*]   And the train goes on.

> GEORGE TESMAN, *in gray walking dress with a soft felt hat,
> enters from the hall. He has a number of paper-covered books
> under his arm and in his pockets.*

TESMAN [*goes over to the table by the corner sofa*]   Phew! It's too
hot to be lugging all this around.

> *Puts the books down.*

I'm positively sweating, Hedda. Why, hullo, hullo! You here already, Judge? What? Bertha didn't tell me.

BRACK [*gets up*]   I came in through the garden.

HEDDA   What are all those books you've got there?

TESMAN [*stands glancing through them*]   Oh, some new publications
dealing with my special subject. I had to buy them.

HEDDA   Your special subject?

BRACK   His special subject, Mrs. Tesman.

> BRACK *and* HEDDA *exchange a smile.*

HEDDA   Haven't you collected enough material on your special
subject?

TESMAN   My dear Hedda, one can never have too much. One must
keep abreast of what other people are writing.

HEDDA   Yes. Of course.

TESMAN   [*rooting among the books*]   Look—I bought a copy of Eilert Loevborg's new book, too.

> *Holds it out to her.*

Perhaps you'd like to have a look at it, Hedda? What?

HEDDA   No, thank you. Er—yes, perhaps I will, later.

TESMAN   I glanced through it on my way home.

BRACK   What's your opinion—as a specialist on the subject?

TESMAN   I'm amazed how sound and balanced it is. He never used to write like that.

> *Gathers his books together.*

Well, I must get down to these at once. I can hardly wait to cut the pages. Oh, I've got to change, too.

> *To* BRACK.

We don't have to be off just yet, do we? What?

BRACK   Heavens, no. We've plenty of time yet.

TESMAN   Good, I needn't hurry, then.

> *Goes with his books, but stops and turns in the doorway.*

Oh, by the way, Hedda, Auntie Juju won't be coming to see you this evening.

HEDDA   Won't she? Oh—the hat, I suppose.

TESMAN   Good heavens, no. How could you think such a thing of Auntie Juju? Fancy—! No, Auntie Rena's very ill.

HEDDA   She always is.

TESMAN   Yes, but today she's been taken really bad.

HEDDA   Oh, then it's quite understandable that the other one should want to stay with her. Well, I shall have to swallow my disappointment.

TESMAN   You can't imagine how happy Auntie Juju was in spite of everything. At your looking so well after the honeymoon!

HEDDA   [*half beneath her breath, as she rises*]   Oh, these everlasting aunts!

TESMAN   What?

HEDDA   [*goes over to the french windows*]   Nothing.

TESMAN   Oh. All right.

> *Goes into the rear room and out of sight.*

BRACK   What was that about the hat?

HEDDA   Oh, something that happened with Miss Tesman this morning. She'd put her hat down on a chair.

Looks at him and smiles.

And I pretended to think it was the servant's.

BRACK [*shakes his head*] But my dear Mrs. Hedda, how could you do such a thing? To that poor old lady?

HEDDA [*nervously, walking across the room*] Sometimes a mood like that hits me. And I can't stop myself.

Throws herself down in the armchair by the stove.

Oh, I don't know how to explain it.

BRACK [*behind her chair*] You're not really happy. That's the answer.

HEDDA [*stares ahead of her*] Why on earth should I be happy? Can you give me a reason?

BRACK Yes. For one thing you've got the home you always wanted.

HEDDA [*looks at him*] You really believe that story?

BRACK You mean it isn't true?

HEDDA Oh, yes, it's partly true.

BRACK Well?

HEDDA It's true I got Tesman to see me home from parties last summer—

BRACK It was a pity my home lay in another direction.

HEDDA Yes. Your interests lay in another direction, too.

BRACK [*laughs*] That's naughty of you, Mrs. Hedda. But to return to you and Tesman—

HEDDA Well, we walked past this house one evening. And poor Tesman was fidgeting in his boots trying to find something to talk about. I felt sorry for the great scholar—

BRACK [*smiles incredulously*] Did you? Hm.

HEDDA Yes, honestly I did. Well, to help him out of his misery, I happened to say quite frivolously how much I'd love to live in this house.

BRACK Was that all?

HEDDA That evening, yes.

BRACK But—afterwards?

HEDDA Yes. My little frivolity had its consequences, my dear Judge.

BRACK Our little frivolities do. Much too often, unfortunately.

HEDDA Thank you. Well, it was our mutual admiration for the late Prime Minister's house that brought George Tesman and me together on common ground. So we got engaged, and we got married, and we went on our honeymoon, and— Ah well, Judge, I've —made my bed and I must lie in it, I was about to say.

BRACK How utterly fantastic! And you didn't really care in the least about the house?

HEDDA God knows I didn't.

BRACK Yes, but now that we've furnished it so beautifully for you?

HEDDA Ugh—all the rooms smell of lavender and dried roses. But perhaps Auntie Juju brought that in.

BRACK [*laughs*] More likely the Prime Minister's widow, rest her soul.

HEDDA   Yes, it's got the odor of death about it. It reminds me of the flowers one has worn at a ball—the morning after.

Clasps her hands behind her neck, leans back in the chair and looks up at him.

Oh, my dear Judge, you've no idea how hideously bored I'm going to be out here.

BRACK   Couldn't you find some kind of occupation, Mrs. Hedda? Like your husband?

HEDDA   Occupation? That'd interest me?

BRACK   Well—preferably.

HEDDA   God knows what. I've often thought—

Breaks off.

No, that wouldn't work either.

BRACK   Who knows? Tell me about it.

HEDDA   I was thinking—if I could persuade Tesman to go into politics, for example.

BRACK [*laughs*]   Tesman! No, honestly, I don't think he's quite cut out to be a politician.

HEDDA   Perhaps not. But if I could persuade him to have a go at it?

BRACK   What satisfaction would that give you? If he turned out to be no good? Why do you want to make him do that?

HEDDA   Because I'm bored.

After a moment.

You feel there's absolutely no possibility of Tesman becoming Prime Minister, then?

BRACK   Well, you know, Mrs. Hedda, for one thing he'd have to be pretty well off before he could become that.

HEDDA [*gets up impatiently*]   There you are!

Walks across the room.

It's this wretched poverty that makes life so hateful. And ludicrous. Well, it is!

BRACK   I don't think that's the real cause.

HEDDA   What is, then?

BRACK   Nothing really exciting has ever happened to you.

HEDDA   Nothing serious, you mean?

BRACK   Call it that if you like. But now perhaps it may.

HEDDA [*tosses her head*]   Oh, you're thinking of this competition for that wretched professorship? That's Tesman's affair. I'm not going to waste my time worrying about that.

BRACK   Very well, let's forget about that then. But suppose you were to find yourself faced with what people call—to use the conventional phrase—the most solemn of human responsibilities?

Smiles.

A new responsibility, little Mrs. Hedda.

HEDDA [*angrily*]   Be quiet! Nothing like that's going to happen.

BRACK [*warily*]   We'll talk about it again in a year's time. If not earlier.

HEDDA [*curtly*]   I've no leanings in that direction, Judge. I don't want any—responsibilities.

BRACK   But surely you must feel some inclination to make use of that —natural talent which every woman—

HEDDA [*over by the french windows*]   Oh, be quiet, I say! I often think there's only one thing for which I have any natural talent.

BRACK [*goes closer*]   And what is that, if I may be so bold as to ask?

HEDDA [*stands looking out*]   For boring myself to death. Now you know.

> *Turns, looks toward the rear room and laughs.*

Talking of boring, here comes the Professor.

BRACK [*quietly, warningly*]   Now, now, now, Mrs. Hedda!

> GEORGE TESMAN, *in evening dress, with gloves and hat in his hand, enters through the rear room from the right.*

TESMAN   Hedda, hasn't any message come from Eilert? What?

HEDDA   No.

TESMAN   Ah, then we'll have him here presently. You wait and see.

BRACK   You really think he'll come?

TESMAN   Yes, I'm almost sure he will. What you were saying about him this morning is just gossip.

BRACK   Oh?

TESMAN   Yes. Auntie Juju said she didn't believe he'd ever dare to stand in my way again. Fancy that!

BRACK   Then everything in the garden's lovely.

TESMAN [*puts his hat, with his gloves in it, on a chair, right*]   Yes, but you really must let me wait for him as long as possible.

BRACK   We've plenty of time. No one'll be turning up at my place before seven or half past.

TESMAN   Ah, then we can keep Hedda company a little longer. And see if he turns up. What?

HEDDA [*picks up* BRACK's *coat and hat and carries them over to the corner sofa*]   And if the worst comes to the worst, Mr. Loevborg can sit here and talk to me.

BRACK [*offering to take his things from her*]   No, please. What do you mean by "if worst comes to worst"?

HEDDA   If he doesn't want to go with you and Tesman.

TESMAN [*looks doubtfully at her*]   I say, Hedda, do you think it'll be all right for him to stay here with you? What? Remember Auntie Juju isn't coming.

HEDDA   Yes, but Mrs. Elvsted is. The three of us can have a cup of tea together.

TESMAN   Ah, that'll be all right then.

BRACK [*smiles*]   It's probably the safest solution as far as he's concerned.

HEDDA Why?

BRACK My dear Mrs. Tesman, you always say of my little bachelor parties that they should be attended only by men of the strongest principles.

HEDDA But Mr. Loevborg is a man of principle now. You know what they say about a reformed sinner—

BERTHA *enters from the hall.*

BERTHA Madam, there's a gentleman here who wants to see you—

HEDDA Ask him to come in.

TESMAN [*quietly*] I'm sure it's him. By Jove. Fancy that!

EILERT LOEVBORG *enters from the hall. He is slim and lean, of the same age as* TESMAN, *but looks older and somewhat haggard. His hair and beard are of a blackish-brown; his face is long and pale, but with a couple of reddish patches on his cheekbones. He is dressed in an elegant and fairly new black suit, and carries black gloves and a top hat in his hand. He stops just inside the door and bows abruptly. He seems somewhat embarrassed.*

TESMAN [*goes over and shakes his hand*] My dear Eilert! How grand to see you again after all these years!

EILERT LOEVBORG [*speaks softly*] It was good of you to write, George.

Goes nearer to HEDDA.

May I shake hands with you, too, Mrs. Tesman?

HEDDA [*accepts his hand*] Delighted to see you, Mr. Loevborg.

With a gesture.

I don't know if you two gentlemen—

LOEVBORG [*bows slightly*] Judge Brack, I believe.

BRACK [*also with a slight bow*] Correct. We—met some years ago—

TESMAN [*puts his hands on* LOEVBORG's *shoulders*] Now you're to treat this house just as though it were your own home, Eilert. Isn't that right, Hedda? I hear you've decided to settle here again? What?

LOEVBORG Yes, I have.

TESMAN Quite understandable. Oh, by the bye—I've just bought your new book. Though to tell the truth I haven't found time to read it yet.

LOEVBORG You needn't bother.

TESMAN Oh? Why?

LOEVBORG There's nothing much in it.

TESMAN By Jove, fancy hearing that from you!

BRACK But everyone's praising it.

LOEVBORG That was exactly what I wanted to happen. So I only wrote what I knew everyone would agree with.

BRACK   Very sensible.

TESMAN   Yes, but my dear Eilert—

LOEVBORG   I want to try to re-establish myself. To begin again—from the beginning.

TESMAN [*a little embarrassed*]   Yes, I—er—suppose you do. What?

LOEVBORG [*smiles, puts down his hat and takes a package wrapped in paper from his coat pocket*]   But when this gets published—George Tesman—read it. This is my real book. The one in which I have spoken with my own voice.

TESMAN   Oh, really? What's it about?

LOEVBORG   It's the sequel.

TESMAN   Sequel? To what?

LOEVBORG   To the other book.

TESMAN   The one that's just come out?

LOEVBORG   Yes.

TESMAN   But my dear Eilert, that covers the subject right up to the present day.

LOEVBORG   It does. But this is about the future.

TESMAN   The future! But, I say, we don't know anything about that.

LOEVBORG   No. But there are one or two things that need to be said about it.

Opens the package.

Here, have a look.

TESMAN   Surely that's not your handwriting?

LOEVBORG   I dictated it.

Turns the pages.

It's in two parts. The first deals with the forces that will shape our civilization.

Turns further on towards the end.

And the second indicates the direction in which that civilization may develop.

TESMAN   Amazing! I'd never think of writing about anything like that.

HEDDA [*by the french windows, drumming on the pane*]   No. You wouldn't.

LOEVBORG [*puts the pages back into their cover and lays the package on the table*]   I brought it because I thought I might possibly read you a few pages this evening.

TESMAN   I say, what a kind idea! Oh, but this evening—?

Glances at BRACK.

I'm not quite sure whether—

LOEVBORG   Well, some other time, then. There's no hurry.

BRACK   The truth is, Mr. Loevborg, I'm giving a little dinner this evening. In Tesman's honor, you know.

LOEVBORG [*looks round for his hat*]   Oh—then I mustn't—

BRACK   No, wait a minute. Won't you do me the honor of joining us?

LOEVBORG [*curtly, with decision*]   No I can't. Thank you so much.

BRACK   Oh, nonsense. Do—please. There'll only be a few of us. And I can promise you we shall have some good sport, as Mrs. Hed—as Mrs. Tesman puts it.

LOEVBORG   I've no doubt. Nevertheless—

BRACK   You could bring your manuscript along and read it to Tesman at my place. I could lend you a room.

TESMAN   By Jove, Eilert, that's an idea. What?

HEDDA [*interposes*]   But, Tesman, Mr. Loevborg doesn't want to go. I'm sure Mr. Loevborg would much rather sit here and have supper with me.

LOEVBORG [*looks at her*]   With you, Mrs. Tesman?

HEDDA   And Mrs. Elvsted.

LOEVBORG   Oh.

> *Casually.*

I ran into her this afternoon.

HEDDA   Did you? Well, she's coming here this evening. So you really must stay, Mr. Loevborg. Otherwise she'll have no one to see her home.

LOEVBORG   That's true. Well—thank you, Mrs. Tesman, I'll stay then.

HEDDA   I'll just tell the servant.

> *She goes to the door which leads into the hall, and rings.* BERTHA *enters.* HEDDA *talks softly to her and points towards the rear room.* BERTHA *nods and goes out.*

TESMAN [*to* LOEVBORG, *as* HEDDA *does this*]   I say, Eilert. This new subject of yours—the—er—future—is that the one you're going to lecture about?

LOEVBORG   Yes.

TESMAN   They told me down at the bookshop that you're going to hold a series of lectures here during the autumn.

LOEVBORG   Yes, I am. I—hope you don't mind, Tesman.

TESMAN   Good heavens, no! But—?

LOEVBORG   I can quite understand it might queer your pitch a little.

TESMAN [*dejectedly*]   Oh well, I can't expect you to put them off for my sake.

LOEVBORG   I'll wait till your appointment's been announced.

TESMAN   You'll wait! But—but—aren't you going to compete with me for the post? What?

LOEVBORG   No. I only want to defeat you in the eyes of the world.

TESMAN   Good heavens! Then Auntie Juju was right after all! Oh, I knew it, I knew it! Hear that, Hedda? Fancy! Eilert *doesn't* want to stand in our way.

HEDDA [*curtly*]   Our? Leave me out of it, please.

She goes towards the rear room, where BERTHA *is setting a tray with decanters and glasses on the table.* HEDDA *nods approval, and comes back into the drawing room.* BERTHA *goes out.*

TESMAN [*while this is happening*]   Judge Brack, what do you think about all this? What?

BRACK   Oh, I think honor and victory can be very splendid things—

TESMAN   Of course they can. Still—

HEDDA [*looks at* TESMAN *with a cold smile*]   You look as if you'd been hit by a thunderbolt.

TESMAN   Yes, I feel rather like it.

BRACK   There was a black cloud looming up, Mrs. Tesman. But it seems to have passed over.

HEDDA [*points towards the rear room*]   Well, gentlemen, won't you go in and take a glass of cold punch?

BRACK [*glances at his watch*]   A stirrup cup? Yes, why not?

TESMAN   An admirable suggestion, Hedda. Admirable! Oh, I feel so relieved!

HEDDA   Won't you have one, too, Mr. Loevborg?

LOEVBORG   No, thank you. I'd rather not.

BRACK   Great heavens, man, cold punch isn't poison. Take my word for it.

LOEVBORG   Not for everyone, perhaps.

HEDDA   I'll keep Mr. Loevborg company while you drink.

TESMAN   Yes, Hedda dear, would you?

He and BRACK *go into the rear room, sit down, drink punch, smoke cigarettes and talk cheerfully during the following scene.* EILERT LOEVBORG *remains standing by the stove.* HEDDA *goes to the writing table.*

HEDDA [*raising her voice slightly*]   I've some photographs I'd like to show you, if you'd care to see them. Tesman and I visited the Tyrol[4] on our way home.

She comes back with an album, places it on the table by the sofa and sits in the upstage corner of the sofa. EILERT LOEVBORG *comes towards her, stops and looks at her. Then he takes a chair and sits down on her left, with his back towards the rear room.*

HEDDA [*opens the album*]   You see these mountains, Mr. Loevborg? That's the Ortler group. Tesman has written the name underneath. You see: "The Ortler Group near Meran."

LOEVBORG [*has not taken his eyes from her; says softly, slowly*]   Hedda—Gabler!

HEDDA [*gives him a quick glance*]   Ssh!

LOEVBORG [*repeats softly*]   Hedda Gabler!

---

4. Region in the Alps, now primarily in Austria.

HEDDA [*looks at the album*] Yes, that used to be my name. When we first knew each other.

LOEVBORG And from now on—for the rest of my life—I must teach myself never to say: Hedda Gabler.

HEDDA [*still turning the pages*] Yes, you must. You'd better start getting into practice. The sooner the better.

LOEVBORG [*bitterly*] Hedda Gabler married? And to George Tesman?

HEDDA Yes. Well—that's life.

LOEVBORG Oh, Hedda, Hedda! How could you throw yourself away like that?

HEDDA [*looks sharply at him*] Stop it.

LOEVBORG What do you mean?

TESMAN comes in and goes towards the sofa.

HEDDA [*hears him coming and says casually*] And this, Mr. Loevborg, is the view from the Ampezzo valley. Look at those mountains.

Glances affectionately up at TESMAN.

What did you say those curious mountains were called, dear?

TESMAN Let me have a look. Oh, those are the Dolomites.

HEDDA Of course. Those are the Dolomites, Mr. Loevborg.

TESMAN Hedda, I just wanted to ask you, can't we bring some punch in here? A glass for you, anyway. What?

HEDDA Thank you, yes. And a biscuit or two, perhaps.

TESMAN You wouldn't like a cigarette?

HEDDA No.

TESMAN Right.

He goes into the rear room and over to the right. BRACK is sitting there, glancing occasionally at HEDDA and LOEVBORG.

LOEVBORG [*softly, as before*] Answer me, Hedda. How could you do it?

HEDDA [*apparently absorbed in the album*] If you go on calling me Hedda I won't talk to you any more.

LOEVBORG Mayn't I even when we're alone?

HEDDA No. You can think it. But you mustn't say it.

LOEVBORG Oh, I see. Because you love George Tesman.

HEDDA [*glances at him and smiles*] Love? Don't be funny.

LOEVBORG You don't love him?

HEDDA I don't intend to be unfaithful to him. That's not what I want.

LOEVBORG Hedda—just tell me one thing—

HEDDA Ssh!

TESMAN enters from the rear room, carrying a tray.

TESMAN Here we are! Here come the goodies!

Puts the tray down on the table.

HEDDA   Why didn't you ask the servant to bring it in?

TESMAN [*fills the glasses*]   I like waiting on you, Hedda.

HEDDA   But you've filled both glasses. Mr. Loevborg doesn't want to drink.

TESMAN   Yes, but Mrs. Elvsted'll be here soon.

HEDDA   Oh, yes, that's true. Mrs. Elvsted—

TESMAN   Had you forgotten her? What?

HEDDA   We're so absorbed with these photographs.

Shows him one.

You remember this little village?

TESMAN   Oh, that one down by the Brenner Pass. We spent a night there—

HEDDA   Yes, and met all those amusing people.

TESMAN   Oh yes, it was there, wasn't it? By Jove, if only we could have had you with us, Eilert! Ah, well.

Goes back into the other room and sits down with BRACK.

LOEVBORG   Tell me one thing, Hedda.

HEDDA   Yes?

LOEVBORG   Didn't you love me either? Not—just a little?

HEDDA   Well now, I wonder? No, I think we were just good pals— Really good pals who could tell each other anything.

Smiles.

You certainly poured your heart out to me.

LOEVBORG   You begged me to.

HEDDA   Looking back on it, there was something beautiful and fascinating—and brave—about the way we told each other everything. That secret friendship no one else knew about.

LOEVBORG   Yes, Hedda, yes! Do you remember? How I used to come up to your father's house in the afternoon—and the General sat by the window and read his newspaper—with his back towards us—

HEDDA   And we sat on the sofa in the corner—

LOEVBORG   Always reading the same illustrated magazine—

HEDDA   We hadn't any photograph album.

LOEVBORG   Yes, Hedda. I regarded you as a kind of confessor. Told you things about myself which no one else knew about—then. Those days and nights of drinking and— Oh, Hedda, what power did you have to make me confess such things?

HEDDA   Power? You think I had some power over you?

LOEVBORG   Yes—I don't know how else to explain it. And all those— oblique questions you asked me—

HEDDA   You knew what they meant.

LOEVBORG   But that you could sit there and ask me such questions! So unashamedly—

HEDDA   I thought you said they were oblique.

LOEVBORG   Yes, but you asked them so unashamedly. That you could question me about—about that kind of thing!

HEDDA   You answered willingly enough.

LOEVBORG   Yes—that's what I can't understand—looking back on it. But tell me, Hedda—what you felt for me—wasn't that—love? When you asked me those questions and made me confess my sins to you, wasn't it because you wanted to wash me clean?

HEDDA   No, not exactly.

LOEVBORG   Why did you do it, then?

HEDDA   Do you find it so incredible that a young girl, given the chance to do so without anyone knowing, should want to be allowed a glimpse into a forbidden world of whose existence she is supposed to be ignorant?

LOEVBORG   So that was it?

HEDDA   One reason. One reason—I think.

LOEVBORG   You didn't love me, then. You just wanted—knowledge. But if that was so, why did you break it off?

HEDDA   That was your fault.

LOEVBORG   It was you who put an end to it.

HEDDA   Yes, when I realized that our friendship was threatening to develop into something—something else. Shame on you, Eilert Loevborg! How could you abuse the trust of your dearest friend?

LOEVBORG   [*clenches his fists*]   Oh, why didn't you do it? Why didn't you shoot me dead? As you threatened to?

HEDDA   I was afraid. Of the scandal.

LOEVBORG   Yes, Hedda. You're a coward at heart.

HEDDA   A dreadful coward.

Changes her tone.

Luckily for you. Well, now you've found consolation with the Elvsteds.

LOEVBORG   I know what Thea's been telling you.

HEDDA   I dare say you told her about us.

LOEVBORG   Not a word. She's too silly to understand that kind of thing.

HEDDA   Silly?

LOEVBORG   She's silly about that kind of thing.

HEDDA   And I am a coward.

Leans closer to him, without looking him in the eyes, and says quietly.

But let me tell you something. Something you don't know.

LOEVBORG   [*tensely*]   Yes?

HEDDA   My failure to shoot you wasn't my worst act of cowardice that evening.

LOEVBORG   [*looks at her for a moment, realizes her meaning and whispers passionately*]   Oh, Hedda! Hedda Gabler! Now I see what was behind those questions. Yes! It wasn't knowledge you wanted! It was life!

HEDDA [*flashes a look at him and says quietly*]   Take care! Don't you delude yourself!

> It has begun to grow dark. BERTHA, *from outside, opens the door leading into the hall.*

HEDDA [*closes the album with a snap and cries, smiling*]   Ah, at last! Come in, Thea dear!

> MRS. ELVSTED *enters from the hall, in evening dress. The door is closed behind her.*

HEDDA [*on the sofa, stretches out her arms towards her*]   Thea darling, I thought you were never coming!

> MRS. ELVSTED *makes a slight bow to the gentlemen in the rear room as she passes the open doorway, and they to her. Then she goes to the table and holds out her hand to* HEDDA. EILERT LOEVBORG *has risen from his chair. He and* MRS. ELVSTED *nod silently to each other.*

MRS. ELVSTED   Perhaps I ought to go in and say a few words to your husband?

HEDDA   Oh, there's no need. They're happy by themselves. They'll be going soon.

MRS. ELVSTED   Going?

HEDDA   Yes, they're off on a spree this evening.

MRS. ELVSTED [*quickly, to* LOEVBORG]   You're not going with them?

LOEVBORG   No.

HEDDA   Mr. Loevborg is staying here with us.

MRS. ELVSTED [*takes a chair and is about to sit down beside him*]   Oh, how nice it is to be here!

HEDDA   No, Thea darling, not there. Come over here and sit beside me. I want to be in the middle.

MRS. ELVSTED   Yes, just as you wish.

> She goes round the table and sits on the sofa, on HEDDA's right. LOEVBORG sits down again in his chair.

LOEVBORG [*after a short pause, to* HEDDA]   Isn't she lovely to look at?

HEDDA [*strokes her hair gently*]   Only to look at?

LOEVBORG   Yes. We're just good pals. We trust each other implicitly. We can talk to each other quite unashamedly.

HEDDA   No need to be oblique?

MRS. ELVSTED [*nestles close to* HEDDA *and says quietly*]   Oh, Hedda, I'm so happy. Imagine—he says I've inspired him!

HEDDA [*looks at her with a smile*]   Dear Thea! Does he really?

LOEVBORG   She has the courage of her convictions, Mrs. Tesman.

MRS. ELVSTED   I? Courage?

LOEVBORG   Absolute courage. Where friendship is concerned.

HEDDA   Yes. Courage. Yes. If only one had that—

LOEVBORG   Yes?

HEDDA   One might be able to live. In spite of everything.

Changes her tone suddenly.

Well, Thea darling, now you're going to drink a nice glass of cold punch.

MRS. ELVSTED   No, thank you. I never drink anything like that.

HEDDA   Oh. You, Mr. Loevborg?

LOEVBORG   Thank you, I don't either.

MRS. ELVSTED   No, he doesn't either.

HEDDA [*looks into his eyes*]   But if I want you to?

LOEVBORG   That doesn't make any difference.

HEDDA [*laughs*]   Have I no power over you at all? Poor me!

LOEVBORG   Not where this is concerned.

HEDDA   Seriously, I think you should. For your own sake.

MRS. ELVSTED   Hedda!

LOEVBORG   Why?

HEDDA   Or perhaps I should say for other people's sake.

LOEVBORG   What do you mean?

HEDDA   People might think you didn't feel absolutely and unashamedly sure of yourself. In your heart of hearts.

MRS. ELVSTED [*quietly*]   Oh, Hedda, no!

LOEVBORG   People can think what they like. For the present.

MRS. ELVSTED [*happily*]   Yes, that's true.

HEDDA   I saw it so clearly in Judge Brack a few minutes ago.

LOEVBORG   Oh. What did you see?

HEDDA   He smiled so scornfully when he saw you were afraid to go in there and drink with them.

LOEVBORG   Afraid! I wanted to stay here and talk to you.

MRS. ELVSTED   That was only natural, Hedda.

HEDDA   But the Judge wasn't to know that. I saw him wink at Tesman when you showed you didn't dare to join their wretched little party.

LOEVBORG   Didn't dare! Are you saying I didn't dare?

HEDDA   I'm not saying so. But that was what Judge Brack thought.

LOEVBORG   Well, let him.

HEDDA   You're not going, then?

LOEVBORG   I'm staying here with you and Thea.

MRS. ELVSTED   Yes, Hedda, of course he is.

HEDDA [*smiles, and nods approvingly to* LOEVBORG]   Firm as a rock! A man of principle! That's how a man should be!

Turns to MRS. ELVSTED *and strokes her cheek.*

Didn't I tell you so this morning when you came here in such a panic—

LOEVBORG [*starts*]   Panic?

MRS. ELVSTED [*frightened*]   Hedda! But—Hedda!

HEDDA   Well, now you can see for yourself. There's no earthly need for you to get scared to death just because—

Stops.

Well! Let's all three cheer up and enjoy ourselves.

LOEVBORG   Mrs. Tesman, would you mind explaining to me what this is all about?

MRS. ELVSTED   Oh, my God, my God, Hedda, what are you saying? What are you doing?

HEDDA   Keep calm. That horrid Judge has his eye on you.

LOEVBORG   Scared to death, were you? For my sake?

MRS. ELVSTED   [*quietly, trembling*]   Oh, Hedda! You've made me so unhappy!

LOEVBORG   [*looks coldly at her for a moment. His face is distorted*] So that was how much you trusted me.

MRS. ELVSTED   Eilert dear, please listen to me—

LOEVBORG   [*takes one of the glasses of punch, raises it and says quietly, hoarsely*]   Skoal, Thea!

Empties the glass, puts it down and picks up one of the others.

MRS. ELVSTED   [*quietly*]   Hedda, Hedda! Why did you want this to happen?

HEDDA   *I*—want it? Are you mad?

LOEVBORG   Skoal to you too, Mrs. Tesman. Thanks for telling me the truth. Here's to the truth!

Empties his glass and refills it.

HEDDA   [*puts her hand on his arm*]   Steady. That's enough for now. Don't forget the party.

MRS. ELVSTED   No, no, no!

HEDDA   Ssh! They're looking at you.

LOEVBORG   [*puts down his glass*]   Thea, tell me the truth—

MRS. ELVSTED   Yes!

LOEVBORG   Did your husband know you were following me?

MRS. ELVSTED   Oh, Hedda!

LOEVBORG   Did you and he have an agreement that you should come here and keep an eye on me? Perhaps he gave you the idea? After all, he's a magistrate. I suppose he needed me back in his office. Or did he miss my companionship at the card table?

MRS. ELVSTED   [*quietly, sobbing*]   Eilert, Eilert!

LOEVBORG   [*seizes a glass and is about to fill it*]   Let's drink to him, too.

HEDDA   No more now. Remember you're going to read your book to Tesman.

LOEVBORG   [*calm again, puts down his glass*]   That was silly of me, Thea. To take it like that, I mean. Don't be angry with me, my dear. You'll see—yes, and they'll see, too—that though I fell, I— I have raised myself up again. With your help, Thea.

MRS. ELVSTED   [*happily*]   Oh, thank God!

BRACK *has meanwhile glanced at his watch. He and* TESMAN *get up and come into the drawing room.*

BRACK [*takes his hat and overcoat*]   Well, Mrs. Tesman, it's time for us to go.

HEDDA   Yes, I suppose it must be.

LOEVBORG [*gets up*]   Time for me too, Judge.

MRS. ELVSTED [*quietly, pleadingly*]   Eilert, please don't!

HEDDA [*pinches her arm*]   They can hear you.

MRS. ELVSTED [*gives a little cry*]   Oh!

LOEVBORG [*to* BRACK]   You were kind enough to ask me to join you.

BRACK   Are you coming?

LOEVBORG   If I may.

BRACK   Delighted.

LOEVBORG [*puts the paper package in his pocket and says to* TESMAN]   I'd like to show you one or two things before I send it off to the printer.

TESMAN   I say, that'll be fun. Fancy—! Oh, but, Hedda, how'll Mrs. Elvsted get home? What?

HEDDA   Oh, we'll manage somehow.

LOEVBORG [*glances over towards the ladies*]   Mrs. Elvsted? I shall come back and collect her, naturally.

> *Goes closer.*

About ten o'clock, Mrs. Tesman? Will that suit you?

HEDDA   Yes. That'll suit me admirably.

TESMAN   Good, that's settled. But you mustn't expect me back so early, Hedda.

HEDDA   Stay as long as you c— as long as you like, dear.

MRS. ELVSTED [*trying to hide her anxiety*]   Well then, Mr. Loevborg, I'll wait here till you come.

LOEVBORG [*his hat in his hand*]   Pray do, Mrs. Elvsted.

BRACK   Well, gentlemen, now the party begins. I trust that, in the words of a certain fair lady, we shall enjoy good sport.

HEDDA   What a pity the fair lady can't be there, invisible.

BRACK   Why invisible?

HEDDA   So as to be able to hear some of your uncensored witticisms, your honor.

BRACK [*laughs*]   Oh, I shouldn't advise the fair lady to do that.

TESMAN [*laughs too*]   I say, Hedda, that's good. By Jove! Fancy that!

BRACK   Well, good night, ladies, good night!

LOEVBORG [*bows farewell*]   About ten o'clock, then.

> BRACK, LOEVBORG *and* TESMAN *go out through the hall. As they do so,* BERTHA *enters from the rear room with a lighted lamp. She puts it on the drawing-room table, then goes out the way she came.*

MRS. ELVSTED [*has got up and is walking uneasily to and fro*]   Oh, Hedda, Hedda! How is all this going to end?

HEDDA   At ten o'clock, then. He'll be here. I can see him. With a crown of vine-leaves[5] in his hair. Burning and unashamed!

---

5. Worshippers of Dionysus, Greek god of vegetation and wine, wore garlands of vine leaves as a sign of divine intoxication.

MRS. ELVSTED   Oh, I do hope so!

HEDDA   Can't you see? Then he'll be himself again! He'll be a free man for the rest of his days!

MRS. ELVSTED   Please God you're right.

HEDDA   That's how he'll come!

Gets up and goes closer.

You can doubt him as much as you like. I believe in him! Now we'll see which of us—

MRS. ELVSTED   You're after something, Hedda.

HEDDA   Yes, I am. For once in my life I want to have the power to shape a man's destiny.

MRS. ELVSTED   Haven't you that power already?

HEDDA   No, I haven't. I've never had it.

MRS. ELVSTED   What about your husband?

HEDDA   Him! Oh, if you could only understand how poor I am. And you're allowed to be so rich, so rich!

Clasps her passionately.

I think I'll burn your hair off after all!

MRS. ELVSTED   Let me go! Let me go! You frighten me, Hedda!

BERTHA   [*in the open doorway*]   I've laid tea in the dining room, madam.

HEDDA   Good, we're coming.

MRS. ELVSTED   No, no, no! I'd rather go home alone! Now—at once!

HEDDA   Rubbish! First you're going to have some tea, you little idiot. And then—at ten o'clock—Eilert Loevborg will come. With a crown of vine-leaves in his hair!

She drags MRS. ELVSTED *almost forcibly towards the open doorway.*

Act 3

The same. The curtains are drawn across the open doorway, and also across the french windows. The lamp, half turned down, with a shade over it, is burning on the table. In the stove, the door of which is open, a fire has been burning, but it is now almost out.

MRS. ELVSTED, wrapped in a large shawl and with her feet resting on a footstool, is sitting near the stove, huddled in the armchair. HEDDA is lying asleep on the sofa, fully dressed, with a blanket over her.

MRS. ELVSTED   [*after a pause, suddenly sits up in her chair and listens tensely. Then she sinks wearily back again and sighs*]   Not back yet! Oh, God! Oh, God! Not back yet!

BERTHA *tiptoes cautiously in from the hall. She has a letter in her hand.*

MRS. ELVSTED [*turns and whispers*]   What is it? Has someone come?
BERTHA [*quietly*]   Yes, a servant's just called with this letter.
MRS. ELVSTED [*quickly, holding out her hand*]   A letter! Give it to me!
BERTHA   But it's for the Doctor, madam.
MRS. ELVSTED   Oh. I see.
BERTHA   Miss Tesman's maid brought it. I'll leave it here on the table.
MRS. ELVSTED   Yes, do.
BERTHA [*puts down the letter*]   I'd better put the lamp out. It's starting to smoke.
MRS. ELVSTED   Yes, put it out. It'll soon be daylight.
BERTHA [*puts out the lamp*]   It's daylight already, madam.
MRS. ELVSTED   Yes. Broad day. And not home yet.
BERTHA   Oh dear, I was afraid this would happen.
MRS. ELVSTED   Were you?
BERTHA   Yes. When I heard that a certain gentleman had returned to town, and saw him go off with them. I've heard all about him.
MRS. ELVSTED   Don't talk so loud. You'll wake your mistress.
BERTHA [*looks at the sofa and sighs*]   Yes. Let her go on sleeping, poor dear. Shall I put some more wood on the fire?
MRS. ELVSTED   Thank you, don't bother on my account.
BERTHA   Very good.

Goes quietly out through the hall.

HEDDA [*wakes as the door closes and looks up*]   What's that?
MRS. ELVSTED   It was only the maid.
HEDDA [*looks round*]   What am I doing here? Oh, now I remember.

Sits up on the sofa, stretches herself and rubs her eyes.

What time is it, Thea?
MRS. ELVSTED   It's gone seven.
HEDDA   When did Tesman get back?
ELVSTED   He's not back yet.
HEDDA   Not home yet?
MRS. ELVSTED [*gets up*]   No one's come.
HEDDA   And we sat up waiting for them till four o'clock.
MRS. ELVSTED   God! How I waited for him!
HEDDA [*yawns and says with her hand in front of her mouth*]   Oh, dear. We might have saved ourselves the trouble.
MRS. ELVSTED   Did you manage to sleep?
HEDDA   Oh, yes. Quite well, I think. Didn't you get any?
MRS. ELVSTED   Not a wink. I couldn't, Hedda. I just couldn't.
HEDDA [*gets up and comes over to her*]   Now, now, now. There's nothing to worry about. I know what's happened.
MRS. ELVSTED   What? Please tell me.

HEDDA   Well, obviously the party went on very late—
MRS. ELVSTED   Oh dear, I suppose it must have. But—
HEDDA   And Tesman didn't want to come home and wake us all up in the middle of the night.

> *Laughs.*

Probably wasn't too keen to show his face either, after a spree like that.
MRS. ELVSTED   But where could he have gone?
HEDDA   I should think he's probably slept at his aunts'. They keep his old room for him.
MRS. ELVSTED   No, he can't be with them. A letter came for him just now from Miss Tesman. It's over there.
HEDDA   Oh?

> *Looks at the envelope.*

Yes, it's Auntie Juju's handwriting. Well, he must still be at Judge Brack's, then. And Eilert Loevborg is sitting there, reading to him. With a crown of vine-leaves in his hair.
MRS. ELVSTED   Hedda, you're only saying that. You don't believe it.
HEDDA   Thea, you really are a little fool.
MRS. ELVSTED   Perhaps I am.
HEDDA   You look tired to death.
MRS. ELVSTED   Yes. I am tired to death.
HEDDA   Go to my room and lie down for a little. Do as I say, now; don't argue.
MRS. ELVSTED   No, no. I couldn't possibly sleep.
HEDDA   Of course you can.
MRS. ELVSTED   But your husband'll be home soon. And I must know at once—
HEDDA   I'll tell you when he comes.
MRS. ELVSTED   Promise me, Hedda?
HEDDA   Yes, don't worry. Go and get some sleep.
MRS. ELVSTED   Thank you. All right, I'll try.

> *She goes out through the rear room.* HEDDA *goes to the french windows and draws the curtains. Broad daylight floods into the room. She goes to the writing table, takes a small hand mirror from it and arranges her hair. Then she goes to the door leading into the hall and presses the bell. After a few moments,* BERTHA *enters.*

BERTHA   Did you want anything, madam?
HEDDA   Yes, put some more wood on the fire. I'm freezing.
BERTHA   Bless you, I'll soon have this room warmed up.

> *She rakes the embers together and puts a fresh piece of wood on them. Suddenly she stops and listens.*

There's someone at the front door, madam.

HEDDA   Well, go and open it. I'll see to the fire.

BERTHA   It'll burn up in a moment.

She goes out through the hall. HEDDA *kneels on the footstool and puts more wood in the stove. After a few seconds,* GEORGE TESMAN *enters from the hall. He looks tired, and rather worried. He tiptoes towards the open doorway and is about to slip through the curtains.*

HEDDA [*at the stove, without looking up*]   Good morning.

TESMAN [*turns*]   Hedda!

Comes nearer.

Good heavens, are you up already? What?

HEDDA   Yes, I got up very early this morning.

TESMAN   I was sure you'd still be sleeping. Fancy that!

HEDDA   Don't talk so loud. Mrs. Elvsted's asleep in my room.

TESMAN   Mrs. Elvsted? Has she stayed the night here?

HEDDA   Yes. No one came to escort her home.

TESMAN   Oh. No, I suppose not.

HEDDA [*closes the door of the stove and gets up*]   Well. Was it fun?

TESMAN   Have you been anxious about me? What?

HEDDA   Not in the least. I asked if you'd had fun.

TESMAN   Oh yes, rather! Well, I thought, for once in a while— The first part was the best; when Eilert read his book to me. We arrived over an hour too early—what about that, eh? By Jove! Brack had a lot of things to see to, so Eilert read to me.

HEDDA [*sits at the right-hand side of the table*]   Well? Tell me about it.

TESMAN [*sits on a footstool by the stove*]   Honestly, Hedda, you've no idea what a book that's going to be. It's really one of the most remarkable things that's ever been written. By Jove!

HEDDA   Oh, never mind about the book—

TESMAN   I'm going to make a confession to you, Hedda. When he'd finished reading a sort of beastly feeling came over me.

HEDDA   Beastly feeling?

TESMAN   I found myself envying Eilert for being able to write like that. Imagine that, Hedda!

HEDDA   Yes. I can imagine.

TESMAN   What a tragedy that with all those gifts he should be so incorrigible.

HEDDA   You mean he's less afraid of life than most men?

TESMAN   Good heavens, no. He just doesn't know the meaning of the word moderation.

HEDDA   What happened afterwards?

TESMAN   Well, looking back on it I suppose you might almost call it an orgy, Hedda.

HEDDA   Had he vine-leaves in his hair?

TESMAN   Vine-leaves? No, I didn't see any of them. He made a long, rambling oration in honor of the woman who'd inspired him to write this book. Yes, those were the words he used.

HEDDA   Did he name her?

TESMAN   No. But I suppose it must be Mrs. Elvsted. You wait and see!

HEDDA   Where did you leave him?

TESMAN   On the way home. We left in a bunch—the last of us, that is—and Brack came with us to get a little fresh air. Well, then, you see, we agreed we ought to see Eilert home. He'd had a drop too much.

HEDDA   You don't say?

TESMAN   But now comes the funny part, Hedda. Or I should really say the tragic part. Oh, I'm almost ashamed to tell you. For Eilert's sake, I mean—

HEDDA   Why, what happened?

TESMAN   Well, you see, as we were walking towards town I happened to drop behind for a minute. Only for a minute—er—you understand—

HEDDA   Yes, yes—?

TESMAN   Well then, when I ran on to catch them up, what do you think I found by the roadside. What?

HEDDA   How on earth should I know?

TESMAN   You mustn't tell anyone, Hedda. What? Promise me that—for Eilert's sake.

Takes a package wrapped in paper from his coat pocket.

Just fancy! I found this.

HEDDA   Isn't this the one he brought here yesterday?

TESMAN   Yes! The whole of that precious, irreplaceable manuscript! And he went and lost it! Didn't even notice! What about that? By Jove! Tragic.

HEDDA   But why didn't you give it back to him?

TESMAN   I didn't dare to, in the state he was in.

HEDDA   Didn't you tell any of the others?

TESMAN   Good heavens, no. I didn't want to do that. For Eilert's sake, you understand.

HEDDA   Then no one else knows you have his manuscript?

TESMAN   No. And no one must be allowed to know.

HEDDA   Didn't it come up in the conversation later?

TESMAN   I didn't get a chance to talk to him any more. As soon as we got into the outskirts of town, he and one or two of the others gave us the slip. Disappeared, by Jove!

HEDDA   Oh? I suppose they took him home.

TESMAN   Yes, I imagine that was the idea. Brack left us, too.

HEDDA   And what have you been up to since then?

TESMAN   Well, I and one or two of the others—awfully jolly chaps, they were—went back to where one of them lived, and had a cup of morning coffee. Morning-after coffee—what? Ah, well. I'll just lie down for a bit and give Eilert time to sleep it off, poor chap, then I'll run over and give this back to him.

HEDDA [*holds out her hand for the package*]   No, don't do that. Not just yet. Let me read it first.

TESMAN   Oh no, really, Hedda dear, honestly, I daren't do that.

HEDDA   Daren't?

TESMAN   No—imagine how desperate he'll be when he wakes up and finds his manuscript's missing. He hasn't any copy, you see. He told me so himself.

HEDDA   Can't a thing like that be rewritten?

TESMAN   Oh no, not possibly, I shouldn't think. I mean, the inspiration, you know—

HEDDA   Oh, yes. I'd forgotten that.

Casually.

By the way, there's a letter for you.

TESMAN   Is there? Fancy that!

HEDDA [*holds it out to him*]   It came early this morning.

TESMAN   I say, it's from Auntie Juju! What on earth can it be?

Puts the package on the other footstool, opens the letter, reads it and jumps up.

Oh, Hedda! She says poor Auntie Rena's dying.

HEDDA   Well, we've been expecting that.

TESMAN   She says if I want to see her I must go quickly. I'll run over at once.

HEDDA [*hides a smile*]   Run?

TESMAN   Hedda dear, I suppose you wouldn't like to come with me? What about that, eh?

HEDDA [*gets up and says wearily and with repulsion*]   No, no, don't ask me to do anything like that. I can't bear illness or death. I loathe anything ugly.

TESMAN   Yes, yes. Of course.

In a dither.

My hat? My overcoat? Oh yes, in the hall. I do hope I won't get there too late, Hedda? What?

BERTHA *enters from the hall.*

HEDDA   You'll be all right if you run.

BERTHA   Judge Brack's outside and wants to know if he can come in.

TESMAN   At this hour? No, I can't possibly receive him now.

HEDDA   I can.

To BERTHA.

Ask his honor to come in.

BERTHA *goes.*

HEDDA [*whispers quickly*]   The manuscript, Tesman.

She snatches it from the footstool.

TESMAN   Yes, give it to me.
HEDDA   No, I'll look after it for now.

She goes over to the writing table and puts it in the bookcase.
TESMAN *stands dithering, unable to get his gloves on.* JUDGE
BRACK *enters from the hall.*

HEDDA [*nods to him*]   Well, you're an early bird.
BRACK   Yes, aren't I?

To TESMAN.

Are you up and about, too?
TESMAN   Yes, I've got to go and see my aunts. Poor Auntie Rena's
dying.
BRACK   Oh dear, is she? Then you mustn't let me detain you. At so
tragic a—
TESMAN   Yes, I really must run. Good-bye! Good-bye!

Runs out through the hall.

HEDDA [*goes nearer*]   You seem to have had excellent sport last night
—Judge.
BRACK   Indeed yes, Mrs. Hedda. I haven't even had time to take my
clothes off.
HEDDA   *You* haven't either?
BRACK   As you see. What's Tesman told you about last night's
escapades?
HEDDA   Oh, only some boring story about having gone and drunk
coffee somewhere.
BRACK   Yes, I've heard about that coffee party. Eilert Loevborg wasn't
with them, I gather?
HEDDA   No, they took him home first.
BRACK   Did Tesman go with him?
HEDDA   No, one or two of the others, he said.
BRACK [*smiles*]   George Tesman is a credulous man, Mrs. Hedda.
HEDDA   God knows. But—has something happened?
BRACK   Well, yes, I'm afraid it has.
HEDDA   I see. Sit down and tell me.

She sits on the left of the table, BRACK *at the long side of it,
near her.*

HEDDA   Well?
BRACK   I had a special reason for keeping track of my guests last
night. Or perhaps I should say some of my guests.
HEDDA   Including Eilert Loevborg?

BRACK   I must confess—yes.

HEDDA   You're beginning to make me curious.

BRACK   Do you know where he and some of my other guests spent the latter half of last night, Mrs. Hedda?

HEDDA   Tell me. If it won't shock me.

BRACK   Oh, I don't think it'll shock you. They found themselves participating in an exceedingly animated *soirée*.

HEDDA   Of a sporting character?

BRACK   Of a highly sporting character.

HEDDA   Tell me more.

BRACK   Loevborg had received an invitation in advance—as had the others. I knew all about that. But he had refused. As you know, he's become a new man.

HEDDA   Up at the Elvsteds', yes. But he went?

BRACK   Well, you see, Mrs. Hedda, last night at my house, unhappily, the spirit moved him.

HEDDA   Yes, I hear he became inspired.

BRACK   Somewhat violently inspired. And as a result, I suppose, his thoughts strayed. We men, alas, don't always stick to our principles as firmly as we should.

HEDDA   I'm sure you're an exception, Judge Brack. But go on about Loevborg.

BRACK   Well, to cut a long story short, he ended up in the establishment of a certain Mademoiselle Danielle.

HEDDA   Mademoiselle Danielle?

BRACK   She was holding the *soirée*. For a selected circle of friends and admirers.

HEDDA   Has she got red hair?

BRACK   She has.

HEDDA   A singer of some kind?

BRACK   Yes—among other accomplishments. She's also a celebrated huntress—of men, Mrs. Hedda. I'm sure you've heard about her. Eilert Loevborg used to be one of her most ardent patrons. In his salad days.

HEDDA   And how did all this end?

BRACK   Not entirely amicably, from all accounts. Mademoiselle Danielle began by receiving him with the utmost tenderness and ended by resorting to her fists.

HEDDA   Againt Loevborg?

BRACK   Yes. He accused her, or her friends, of having robbed him. He claimed his pocketbook had been stolen. Among other things. In short, he seems to have made a bloodthirsty scene.

HEDDA   And what did this lead to?

BRACK   It led to a general free-for-all, in which both sexes participated. Fortunately, in the end the police arrived.

HEDDA   The police too?

BRACK   Yes. I'm afraid it may turn out to be rather an expensive joke for Master Eilert. Crazy fool!

HEDDA   Oh?

BRACK   Apparently he put up a very violent resistance. Hit one of the constables on the ear and tore his uniform. He had to accompany them to the police station.

HEDDA   Where did you learn all this?

BRACK   From the police.

HEDDA [*to herself*]   So that's what happened. He didn't have a crown of vine-leaves in his hair.

BRACK   Vine-leaves, Mrs. Hedda?

HEDDA [*in her normal voice again*]   But, tell me, Judge, why do you take such a close interest in Eilert Loevborg?

BRACK   For one thing it'll hardly be a matter of complete indifference to me if it's revealed in court that he came there straight from my house.

HEDDA   Will it come to court?

BRACK   Of course. Well, I don't regard that as particularly serious. Still, I thought it my duty, as a friend of the family, to give you and your husband a full account of his nocturnal adventures.

HEDDA   Why?

BRACK   Because I've a shrewd suspicion that he's hoping to use you as a kind of screen.

HEDDA   What makes you think that?

BRACK   Oh, for heaven's sake, Mrs. Hedda, we're not blind. You wait and see. This Mrs. Elvsted won't be going back to her husband just yet.

HEDDA   Well, if there were anything between those two there are plenty of other places where they could meet.

BRACK   Not in anyone's home. From now on every respectable house will once again be closed to Eilert Loevborg.

HEDDA   And mine should be too, you mean?

BRACK   Yes. I confess I should find it more than irksome if this gentleman were to be granted unrestricted access to this house. If he were superfluously to intrude into—

HEDDA   The triangle?

BRACK   Precisely. For me it would be like losing a home.

HEDDA [*looks at him and smiles*]   I see. You want to be the cock of the walk.

BRACK [*nods slowly and lowers his voice*]   Yes, that is my aim. And I shall fight for it with—every weapon at my disposal.

HEDDA [*as her smile fades*]   You're a dangerous man, aren't you? When you really want something.

BRACK   You think so?

HEDDA   Yes, I'm beginning to think so. I'm deeply thankful you haven't any kind of hold over me.

BRACK [*laughs equivocally*]   Well, well, Mrs. Hedda—perhaps you're right. If I had, who knows what I might not think up?

HEDDA   Come, Judge Brack. That sounds almost like a threat.

BRACK [*gets up*]   Heaven forbid! In the creation of a triangle—and its continuance—the question of compulsion should never arise.

HEDDA   Exactly what I was thinking.

BRACK   Well, I've said what I came to say. I must be getting back. Good-bye, Mrs. Hedda.

Goes towards the french windows.

HEDDA [*gets up*]   Are you going out through the garden?

BRACK   Yes, it's shorter.

HEDDA   Yes. And it's the back door, isn't it?

BRACK   I've nothing against back doors. They can be quite intriguing
—sometimes.

HEDDA   When people fire pistols out of them, for example?

BRACK [*in the doorway, laughs*]   Oh, people don't shoot tame cocks.

HEDDA [*laughs too*]   I suppose not. When they've only got one.

> *They nod good-bye, laughing. He goes. She closes the french
> windows behind him, and stands for a moment, looking out
> pensively. Then she walks across the room and glances through
> the curtains in the open doorway. Goes to the writing table,
> takes* LOEVBORG's *package from the bookcase and is about to
> leaf through the pages when* BERTHA *is heard remonstrating
> loudly in the hall.* HEDDA *turns and listens. She hastily puts the
> package back in the drawer, locks it and puts the key on the
> inkstand.* EILERT LOEVBORG, *with his overcoat on and his hat in
> his hand, throws the door open. He looks somewhat confused
> and excited.*

LOEVBORG [*shouts as he enters*]   I must come in, I tell you! Let me
pass!

> *He closes the door, turns, sees* HEDDA, *controls himself imme-
> diately and bows.*

HEDDA [*at the writing table*]   Well, Mr. Loevborg, this is rather a late
hour to be collecting Thea.

LOEVBORG   And an early hour to call on you. Please forgive me.

HEDDA   How do you know she's still here?

LOEVBORG   They told me at her lodgings that she has been out all
night.

HEDDA [*goes to the table*]   Did you notice anything about their behavior when they told you?

LOEVBORG [*looks at her, puzzled*]   Notice anything?

HEDDA   Did they sound as if they thought it—strange?

LOEVBORG [*suddenly understands*]   Oh, I see what you mean. I'm
dragging her down with me. No, as a matter of fact I didn't notice
anything. I suppose Tesman isn't up yet?

HEDDA   No, I don't think so.

LOEVBORG   When did he get home?

HEDDA   Very late.

LOEVBORG   Did he tell you anything?

HEDDA   Yes. I gather you had a merry party at Judge Brack's last
night.

LOEVBORG   He didn't tell you anything else?

HEDDA   I don't think so. I was so terribly sleepy—

MRS. ELVSTED *comes through the curtains in the open doorway.*

MRS. ELVSTED [*runs towards him*]   Oh, Eilert! At last!

LOEVBORG   Yes—at last. And too late.

MRS. ELVSTED   What is too late?

LOEVBORG   Everything—now. I'm finished, Thea.

MRS. ELVSTED   Oh, no, no! Don't say that!

LOEVBORG   You'll say it yourself, when you've heard what I—

MRS. ELVSTED   I don't want to hear anything!

HEDDA   Perhaps you'd rather speak to her alone? I'd better go.

LOEVBORG   No, stay.

MRS. ELVSTED   But I don't want to hear anything, I tell you!

LOEVBORG   It's not about last night.

MRS. ELVSTED   Then what—?

LOEVBORG   I want to tell you that from now on we must stop seeing each other.

MRS. ELVSTED   Stop seeing each other!

HEDDA [*involuntarily*]   I knew it!

LOEVBORG   I have no further use for you, Thea.

MRS. ELVSTED   You can stand there and say that! No further use for me! Surely I can go on helping you? We'll go on working together, won't we?

LOEVBORG   I don't intend to do any more work from now on.

MRS. ELVSTED [*desperately*]   Then what use have I for my life?

LOEVBORG   You must try to live as if you had never known me.

MRS. ELVSTED   But I can't!

LOEVBORG   Try to, Thea. Go back home—

MRS. ELVSTED   Never! I want to be wherever you are! I won't let myself be driven away like this! I want to stay here—and be with you when the book comes out.

HEDDA [*whispers*]   Ah, yes! The book!

LOEVBORG [*looks at her*]   Our book; Thea's and mine. It belongs to both of us.

MRS. ELVSTED   Oh, yes! I feel that, too! And I've a right to be with you when it comes into the world. I want to see people respect and honor you again. And the joy! The joy! I want to share it with you!

LOEVBORG   Thea—our book will never come into the world.

HEDDA   Ah!

MRS. ELVSTED   Not—?

LOEVBORG   It cannot. Ever.

MRS. ELVSTED   Eilert—what have you done with the manuscript? Where is it?

LOEVBORG   Oh Thea, please don't ask me that!

MRS. ELVSTED   Yes, yes—I must know. I've a right to know. Now!

LOEVBORG   The manuscript. I've torn it up.

MRS. ELVSTED [*screams*]   No, no!

HEDDA [*involuntarily*]   But that's not—!

LOEVBORG [*looks at her*]   Not true, you think?

HEDDA [*controls herself*]   Why—yes, of course it is, if you say so. It just sounded so incredible—

LOEVBORG   It's true, nevertheless.

MRS. ELVSTED   Oh, my God, my God, Hedda—he's destroyed his own book!

LOEVBORG   I have destroyed my life. Why not my life's work, too?

MRS. ELVSTED   And you—did this last night?

LOEVBORG   Yes, Thea. I tore it into a thousand pieces. And scattered them out across the fjord. It's good, clean, salt water. Let it carry them away; let them drift in the current and the wind. And in a little while, they will sink. Deeper and deeper. As I shall, Thea.

MRS. ELVSTED   Do you know, Eilert—this book—all my life I shall feel as though you'd killed a little child?

LOEVBORG   You're right. It is like killing a child.

MRS. ELVSTED   But how could you? It was my child, too!

HEDDA [*almost inaudibly*]   Oh—the child—!

MRS. ELVSTED [*breathes heavily*]   It's all over, then. Well—I'll go now, Hedda.

HEDDA   You're not leaving town?

MRS. ELVSTED   I don't know what I'm going to do. I can't see anything except—darkness.

> *She goes out through the hall.*

HEDDA [*waits a moment*]   Aren't you going to escort her home, Mr. Loevborg?

LOEVBORG   I? Through the streets? Do you want me to let people see her with me?

HEDDA   Of course I don't know what else may have happened last night. But is it so utterly beyond redress?

LOEVBORG   It isn't just last night. It'll go on happening. I know it. But the curse of it is, I don't want to live that kind of life. I don't want to start all that again. She's broken my courage. I can't spit in the eyes of the world any longer.

HEDDA [*as though to herself*]   That pretty little fool's been trying to shape a man's destiny.

> *Looks at him.*

But how could you be so heartless towards her?

LOEVBORG   Don't call me heartless!

HEDDA   To go and destroy the one thing that's made her life worth living? You don't call that heartless?

LOEVBORG   Do you want to know the truth, Hedda?

HEDDA   The truth?

LOEVBORG   Promise me first—give me your word—that you'll never let Thea know about this.

HEDDA   I give you my word.

LOEVBORG   Good. Well; what I told her just now was a lie.

HEDDA   About the manuscript?

LOEVBORG   Yes. I didn't tear it up. Or throw it in the fjord.

HEDDA   You didn't? But where is it, then?

LOEVBORG   I destroyed it, all the same. I destroyed it, Hedda!

HEDDA　I don't understand.

LOEVBORG　Thea said that what I had done was like killing a child.

HEDDA　Yes. That's what she said.

LOEVBORG　But to kill a child isn't the worst thing a father can do to it.

HEDDA　What could be worse than that?

LOEVBORG　Hedda—suppose a man came home one morning, after a night of debauchery, and said to the mother of his child: "Look here. I've been wandering round all night. I've been to—such-and-such a place and such-and-such a place. And I had our child with me. I took him to—these places. And I've lost him. Just—lost him. God knows where he is or whose hands he's fallen into."

HEDDA　I see. But when all's said and done, this was only a book—

LOEVBORG　Thea's heart and soul were in that book. It was her whole life.

HEDDA　Yes. I understand.

LOEVBORG　Well, then you must also understand that she and I cannot possibly ever see each other again.

HEDDA　Where will you go?

LOEVBORG　Nowhere. I just want to put an end to it all. As soon as possible.

HEDDA　[*takes a step towards him*]　Eilert Loevborg, listen to me. Do it—beautifully!

LOEVBORG　Beautifully?

　　　Smiles.

With a crown of vine-leaves in my hair? The way you used to dream of me—in the old days?

HEDDA　No. I don't believe in that crown any longer. But—do it beautifully, all the same. Just this once. Good-bye. You must go now. And don't come back.

LOEVBORG　Adieu, madam. Give my love to George Tesman.

　　　Turns to go.

HEDDA　Wait. I want to give you a souvenir to take with you.

　　　She goes over to the writing table, opens the drawer and the pistol-case, and comes back to LOEVBORG *with one of the pistols.*

LOEVBORG　[*looks at her*]　This? Is this the souvenir?

HEDDA　[*nods slowly*]　You recognize it? You looked down its barrel once.

LOEVBORG　You should have used it then.

HEDDA　Here! Use it now!

LOEVBORG　[*puts the pistol in his breast pocket*]　Thank you.

HEDDA　Do it beautifully, Eilert Loevborg. Only promise me that!

LOEVBORG　Good-bye, Hedda Gabler.

He goes out through the hall. HEDDA *stands by the door for a moment, listening. Then she goes over to the writing table, takes out the package containing the manuscript, glances inside it, pulls some of the pages half out and looks at them. Then she takes it to the armchair by the stove and sits down with the package in her lap. After a moment, she opens the door of the stove; then she opens the packet.*

HEDDA [*throws one of the pages into the stove and whispers to herself*] I'm burning your child, Thea! You with your beautiful wavy hair!

She throws a few more pages into the stove.

The child Eilert Loevborg gave you.

Throws the rest of the manuscript in.

I'm burning it! I'm burning your child!

Act 4

The same. It is evening. The drawing room is in darkness. The small room is illuminated by the hanging lamp over the table. The curtains are drawn across the french windows. HEDDA, *dressed in black, is walking up and down in the darkened room. Then she goes into the small room and crosses to the left. A few chords are heard from the piano. She comes back into the drawing room.*

BERTHA *comes through the small room from the right with a lighted lamp, which she places on the table in front of the corner sofa in the drawing room. Her eyes are red with crying, and she has black ribbons on her cap. She goes quietly out, right.* HEDDA *goes over to the french windows, draws the curtains slightly to one side and looks out into the darkness.*

A few moments later, MISS TESMAN *enters from the hall. She is dressed in mourning, with a black hat and veil.* HEDDA *goes to meet her and holds out her hand.*

MISS TESMAN Well, Hedda, here I am in the weeds of sorrow. My poor sister has ended her struggles at last.

HEDDA I've already heard. Tesman sent me a card.

MISS TESMAN Yes, he promised me he would. But I thought, no, I must go and break the news of death to Hedda myself—here, in the house of life.

HEDDA It's very kind of you.

MISS TESMAN Ah, Rena shouldn't have chosen a time like this to pass away. This is no moment for Hedda's house to be a place of mourning.

HEDDA [*changing the subject*] She died peacefully, Miss Tesman?

MISS TESMAN Oh, it was quite beautiful! The end came so calmly.

And she was so happy at being able to see George once again. And say good-bye to him. Hasn't he come home yet?

HEDDA   No. He wrote that I mustn't expect him too soon. But please sit down.

MISS TESMAN   No, thank you, Hedda dear—bless you. I'd like to. But I've so little time. I must dress her and lay her out as well as I can. She shall go to her grave looking really beautiful.

HEDDA   Can't I help with anything?

MISS TESMAN   Why, you mustn't think of such a thing! Hedda Tesman mustn't let her hands be soiled by contact with death. Or her thoughts. Not at this time.

HEDDA   One can't always control one's thoughts.

MISS TESMAN [*continues*]   Ah, well, that's life. Now we must start to sew poor Rena's shroud. There'll be sewing to be done in this house too before long, I shouldn't wonder. But not for a shroud, praise God.

> GEORGE TESMAN *enters from the hall.*

HEDDA   You've come at last! Thank heavens!

TESMAN   Are you here, Auntie Juju? With Hedda? Fancy that!

MISS TESMAN   I was just on the point of leaving, dear boy. Well, have you done everything you promised me?

TESMAN   No, I'm afraid I forgot half of it. I'll have to run over again tomorrow. My head's in a complete whirl today. I can't collect my thoughts.

MISS TESMAN   But George dear, you mustn't take it like this.

TESMAN   Oh? Well—er—how should I?

MISS TESMAN   You must be happy in your grief. Happy for what's happened. As I am.

TESMAN   Oh, yes, yes. You're thinking of Aunt Rena.

HEDDA   It'll be lonely for you now, Miss Tesman.

MISS TESMAN   For the first few days, yes. But it won't last long, I hope. Poor dear Rena's little room isn't going to stay empty.

TESMAN   Oh? Whom are you going to move in there? What?

MISS TESMAN   Oh, there's always some poor invalid who needs care and attention.

HEDDA   Do you really want another cross like that to bear?

MISS TESMAN   Cross! God forgive you, child. It's been no cross for me.

HEDDA   But now—if a complete stranger comes to live with you—?

MISS TESMAN   Oh, one soon makes friends with invalids. And I need so much to have someone to live for. Like you, my dear. Well, I expect there'll soon be work in this house too for an old aunt, praise God!

HEDDA   Oh—please!

TESMAN   By Jove, yes! What a splendid time the three of us could have together if—

HEDDA   If?

TESMAN [*uneasily*]   Oh, never mind. It'll all work out. Let's hope so—what?

MISS TESMAN   Yes, yes. Well, I'm sure you two would like to be alone.

Smiles.

Perhaps Hedda may have something to tell you, George. Good-bye.
I must go home to Rena.

Turns to the door.

Dear God, how strange! Now Rena is with me and with poor dear
Joachim.

TESMAN   Fancy that. Yes, Auntie Juju! What?

MISS TESMAN *goes out through the hall.*

HEDDA [*follows* TESMAN *coldly and searchingly with her eyes*]   I
really believe this death distresses you more than it does her.

TESMAN   Oh, it isn't just Auntie Rena. It's Eilert I'm so worried about.

HEDDA [*quickly*]   Is there any news of him?

TESMAN   I ran over to see him this afternoon. I wanted to tell him his
manuscript was in safe hands.

HEDDA   Oh? You didn't find him?

TESMAN   No. He wasn't at home. But later I met Mrs. Elvsted and
she told me he'd been here early this morning.

HEDDA   Yes, just after you'd left.

TESMAN   It seems he said he'd torn the manuscript up. What?

HEDDA   Yes, he claimed to have done so.

TESMAN   You told him we had it, of course?

HEDDA   No.

Quickly.

Did you tell Mrs. Elvsted?

TESMAN   No, I didn't like to. But you ought to have told him. Think
if he should go home and do something desperate! Give me the
manuscript, Hedda. I'll run over to him with it right away. Where
did you put it?

HEDDA [*cold and motionless, leaning against the armchair*]   I haven't
got it any longer.

TESMAN   Haven't got it? What on earth do you mean?

HEDDA   I've burned it.

TESMAN [*starts, terrified*]   Burned it! Burned Eilert's manuscript!

HEDDA   Don't shout. The servant will hear you.

TESMAN   Burned it! But in heaven's name—! Oh, no, no, no! This is
impossible!

HEDDA   Well, it's true.

TESMAN   But, Hedda, do you realize what you've done? That's
appropriating lost property! It's against the law! By Jove! You ask
Judge Brack and see if I'm not right.

HEDDA   You'd be well advised not to talk about it to Judge Brack or
anyone else.

TESMAN   But how could you go and do such a dreadful thing? What on earth put the idea into your head? What came over you? Answer me! What?

HEDDA [*represses an almost imperceptible smile*]   I did it for your sake, George.

TESMAN   For my sake?

HEDDA   When you came home this morning and described how he'd read his book to you—

TESMAN   Yes, yes?

HEDDA   You admitted you were jealous of him.

TESMAN   But, good heavens, I didn't mean it literally!

HEDDA   No matter. I couldn't bear the thought that anyone else should push you into the background.

TESMAN [*torn between doubt and joy*]   Hedda—is this true? But—but—but I never realized you loved me like that! Fancy—

HEDDA   Well, I suppose you'd better know. I'm going to have—

Breaks off and says violently.

No, no—you'd better ask your Auntie Juju. She'll tell you.

TESMAN   Hedda! I think I understand what you mean.

Clasps his hands.

Good heavens, can it really be true! What?

HEDDA   Don't shout. The servant will hear you.

TESMAN [*laughing with joy*]   The servant! I say, that's good! The servant! Why, that's Bertha! I'll run out and tell her at once!

HEDDA [*clenches her hands in despair*]   Oh, it's destroying me, all this —it's destroying me!

TESMAN   I say, Hedda, what's up? What?

HEDDA [*cold, controlled*]   Oh, it's all so—absurd—George.

TESMAN   Absurd? That I'm so happy? But surely—? Ah, well—perhaps I won't say anything to Bertha.

HEDDA   No, do. She might as well know too.

TESMAN   No, no, I won't tell her yet. But Auntie Juju—I must let her know! And you—you called me George! For the first time! Fancy that! Oh, it'll make Auntie Juju so happy, all this! So very happy!

HEDDA   Will she be happy when she hears I've burned Eilert Loevborg's manuscript—for your sake?

TESMAN   No, I'd forgotten about that. Of course no one must be allowed to know about the manuscript. But that you're burning with love for me, Hedda, I must certainly let Auntie Juju know that. I say, I wonder if young wives often feel like that towards their husbands? What?

HEDDA   You might ask Auntie Juju about that too.

TESMAN   I will, as soon as I get the chance.

Looks uneasy and thoughtful again.

But I say, you know, that manuscript. Dreadful business. Poor Eilert!

MRS. ELVSTED, *dressed as on her first visit, with hat and over-coat, enters from the hall.*

MRS. ELVSTED [*greets them hastily and tremulously*] Oh, Hedda dear, do please forgive me for coming here again.

HEDDA   Why, Thea, what's happened?

TESMAN   Is it anything to do with Eilert Loevborg? What?

MRS. ELVSTED   Yes—I'm so dreadfully afraid he may have met with an accident.

HEDDA [*grips her arm*] You think so?

TESMAN   But, good heavens, Mrs. Elvsted, what makes you think that?

MRS. ELVSTED   I heard them talking about him at the boarding-house, as I went in. Oh, there are the most terrible rumors being spread about him in town today.

TESMAN   Fancy. Yes, I heard about them too. But I can testify that he went straight home to bed. Fancy that!

HEDDA   Well—what did they say in the boarding-house?

MRS. ELVSTED   Oh, I couldn't find out anything. Either they didn't know, or else— They stopped talking when they saw me. And I didn't dare to ask.

TESMAN [*fidgets uneasily*] We must hope—we must hope you misheard them, Mrs. Elvsted.

MRS. ELVSTED   No, no, I'm sure it was he they were talking about. I heard them say something about a hospital—

TESMAN   Hospital!

HEDDA   Oh no, surely that's impossible!

MRS. ELVSTED   Oh, I became so afraid. So I went up to his rooms and asked to see him.

HEDDA   Do you think that was wise, Thea?

MRS. ELVSTED   Well, what else could I do? I couldn't bear the uncertainty any longer.

TESMAN   But *you* didn't manage to find him either? What?

MRS. ELVSTED   No. And they had no idea where he was. They said he hadn't been home since yesterday afternoon.

TESMAN   Since yesterday? Fancy that!

MRS. ELVSTED   I'm sure he must have met with an accident.

TESMAN   Hedda, I wonder if I ought to go into town and make one or two inquiries?

HEDDA   No, no, don't you get mixed up in this.

JUDGE BRACK *enters from the hall, hat in hand.* BERTHA, *who has opened the door for him, closes it. He looks serious and greets them silently.*

TESMAN   Hullo, my dear Judge. Fancy seeing you!

BRACK   I had to come and talk to you.

TESMAN   I can see Auntie Juju's told you the news.

BRACK   Yes, I've heard about that too.

TESMAN   Tragic, isn't it?

BRACK   Well, my dear chap, that depends how you look at it.

TESMAN [*looks uncertainly at him*]   Has something else happened?

BRACK   Yes.

HEDDA   Another tragedy?

BRACK   That also depends on how you look at it, Mrs. Tesman.

MRS. ELVSTED   Oh, it's something to do with Eilert Loevborg!

BRACK [*looks at her for a moment*]   How did you guess? Perhaps you've heard already—?

MRS. ELVSTED [*confused*]   No, no, not at all—I—

TESMAN   For heaven's sake, tell us!

BRACK [*shrugs his shoulders*]   Well, I'm afraid they've taken him to the hospital. He's dying.

MRS. ELVSTED [*screams*]   Oh God, God!

TESMAN   The hospital! Dying!

HEDDA [*involuntarily*]   So quickly!

MRS. ELVSTED [*weeping*]   Oh, Hedda! And we parted enemies!

HEDDA [*whispers*]   Thea—Thea!

MRS. ELVSTED [*ignoring her*]   I must see him! I must see him before he dies!

BRACK   It's no use, Mrs. Elvsted. No one's allowed to see him now.

MRS. ELVSTED   But what's happened to him? You must tell me!

TESMAN   He hasn't tried to do anything to himself? What?

HEDDA   Yes, he has. I'm sure of it.

TESMAN   Hedda, how can you—?

BRACK [*who has not taken his eyes from her*]   I'm afraid you've guessed correctly, Mrs. Tesman.

MRS. ELVSTED   How dreadful!

TESMAN   Attempted suicide! Fancy that!

HEDDA   Shot himself!

BRACK   Right again, Mrs. Tesman.

MRS. ELVSTED [*tries to compose herself*]   When did this happen, Judge Brack?

BRACK   This afternoon. Between three and four.

TESMAN   But, good heavens—where? What?

BRACK [*a little hesitantly*]   Where? Why, my dear chap, in his rooms of course.

MRS. ELVSTED   No, that's impossible. I was there soon after six.

BRACK   Well, it must have been somewhere else, then. I don't know exactly. I only know that they found him. He'd shot himself— through the breast.

MRS. ELVSTED   Oh, how horrible! That he should end like that!

HEDDA [*to* BRACK]   Through the breast, you said?

BRACK   That is what I said.

HEDDA   Not through the head?

BRACK   Through the breast, Mrs. Tesman.

HEDDA   The breast. Yes; yes. That's good, too.

BRACK   Why, Mrs. Tesman?

HEDDA   Oh—no, I didn't mean anything.

TESMAN   And the wound's dangerous, you say? What?

BRACK   Mortal. He's probably already dead.

MRS. ELVSTED   Yes, yes—I feel it! It's all over. All over. Oh Hedda—!

TESMAN   But, tell me, how did you manage to learn all this?

BRACK [*curtly*]   From the police. I spoke to one of them.

HEDDA [*loudly, clearly*]   At last! Oh, thank God!

TESMAN [*appalled*]   For God's sake, Hedda, what are you saying?

HEDDA   I am saying there's beauty in what he has done.

BRACK   Hm—Mrs. Tesman—

TESMAN   Beauty! Oh, but I say!

MRS. ELVSTED   Hedda, how can you talk of beauty in connection with a thing like this?

HEDDA   Eilert Loevborg has settled his account with life. He's had the courage to do what—what he had to do.

MRS. ELVSTED   No, that's not why it happened. He did it because he was mad.

TESMAN   He did it because he was desperate.

HEDDA   You're wrong! I know!

MRS. ELVSTED   He must have been mad. The same as when he tore up the manuscript.

BRACK [*starts*]   Manuscript? Did he tear it up?

MRS. ELVSTED   Yes. Last night.

TESMAN [*whispers*]   Oh, Hedda, we shall never be able to escape from this.

BRACK   Hm. Strange.

TESMAN [*wanders round the room*]   To think of Eilert dying like that. And not leaving behind him the thing that would have made his name endure.

MRS. ELVSTED   If only it could be pieced together again!

TESMAN   Yes, fancy! If only it could! I'd give anything—

MRS. ELVSTED   Perhaps it can, Mr. Tesman.

TESMAN   What do you mean?

MRS. ELVSTED [*searches in the pocket of her dress*]   Look! I kept the notes he dictated it from.

HEDDA [*takes a step nearer*]   Ah!

TESMAN   You kept them, Mrs. Elvsted! What?

MRS. ELVSTED   Yes, here they are. I brought them with me when I left home. They've been in my pocket ever since.

TESMAN   Let me have a look.

MRS. ELVSTED [*hands him a wad of small sheets of paper*]   They're in a terrible muddle. All mixed up.

TESMAN   I say, just fancy if we can sort them out! Perhaps if we work on them together—?

MRS. ELVSTED   Oh, yes! Let's try, anyway!

TESMAN   We'll manage it. We must! I shall dedicate my life to this.

HEDDA   *You*, George? Your life?

TESMAN   Yes—well, all the time I can spare. My book'll have to wait. Hedda, you do understand? What? I owe it to Eilert's memory.

HEDDA   Perhaps.

TESMAN   Well, my dear Mrs. Elvsted, you and I'll have to pool our brains. No use crying over spilt milk, what? We must try to approach this matter calmly.

MRS. ELVSTED   Yes, yes, Mr. Tesman. I'll do my best.

TESMAN   Well, come over here and let's start looking at these notes right away. Where shall we sit? Here? No, the other room. You'll excuse us, won't you, Judge? Come along with me Mrs. Elvsted.

MRS. ELVSTED   Oh, God! If only we can manage to do it!

> TESMAN *and* MRS. ELVSTED *go into the rear room. He takes off his hat and overcoat. They sit at the table beneath the hanging lamp and absorb themselves in the notes.* HEDDA *walks across to the stove and sits in the armchair. After a moment,* BRACK *goes over to her.*

HEDDA [*half aloud*]   Oh, Judge! This act of Eilert Loevborg's—doesn't it give one a sense of release!

BRACK   Release, Mrs. Hedda? Well, it's a release for him, of course—

HEDDA   Oh, I don't mean him—I mean me! The release of knowing that someone can do something really brave! Something beautiful!

BRACK [*smiles*]   Hm—my dear Mrs. Hedda—

HEDDA   Oh, I know what you're going to say. You're a bourgeois at heart too, just like—ah, well!

BRACK [*looks at her*]   Eilert Loevborg has meant more to you than you're willing to admit to yourself. Or am I wrong?

HEDDA   I'm not answering questions like that from you. I only know that Eilert Loevborg has had the courage to live according to his own principles. And now, at last, he's done something big! Something beautiful! To have the courage and the will to rise from the feast of life so early!

BRACK   It distresses me deeply, Mrs. Hedda, but I'm afraid I must rob you of that charming illusion.

HEDDA   Illusion?

BRACK   You wouldn't have been allowed to keep it for long, anyway.

HEDDA   What do you mean?

BRACK   He didn't shoot himself on purpose.

HEDDA   Not on purpose?

BRACK   No. It didn't happen quite the way I told you.

HEDDA   Have you been hiding something? What is it?

BRACK   In order to spare poor Mrs. Elvsted's feelings, I permitted myself one or two small—equivocations.

HEDDA   What?

BRACK   To begin with, he is already dead.

HEDDA   He died at the hospital?

BRACK   Yes. Without regaining consciousness.

HEDDA   What else haven't you told us?

BRACK   The incident didn't take place at his lodgings.

HEDDA   Well, that's utterly unimportant.

BRACK   Not utterly. The fact is, you see, that Eilbert Loevborg was found shot in Mademoiselle Danielle's boudoir.

HEDDA [*almost jumps up, but instead sinks back in her chair*]   That's impossible. He can't have been there today.

BRACK   He was there this afternoon. He went to ask for something he claimed they'd taken from him. Talked some crazy nonsense about a child which had got lost—

HEDDA   Oh! So that was the reason!

BRACK   I thought at first he might have been referring to his manuscript. But I hear he destroyed that himself. So he must have
meant his pocketbook—I suppose.

HEDDA   Yes, I suppose so. So they found him there?

BRACK   Yes; there. With a discharged pistol in his breast pocket. The
shot had wounded him mortally.

HEDDA   Yes. In the breast.

BRACK   No. In the—hm—stomach. The—lower part—

HEDDA   [*looks at him with an expression of repulsion*]   That too! Oh,
why does everything I touch become mean and ludicrous? It's like
a curse!

BRACK   There's something else, Mrs. Hedda. It's rather disagreeable,
too.

HEDDA   What?

BRACK   The pistol he had on him—

HEDDA   Yes? What about it?

BRACK   He must have stolen it.

HEDDA   [*jumps up*]   Stolen it! That isn't true! He didn't.

BRACK   It's the only explanation. He must have stolen it. Ssh!

> TESMAN *and* MRS. ELVSTED *have got up from the table in the
> rear room and come into the drawing room.*

TESMAN   [*his hands full of papers*]   Hedda, I can't see properly under
that lamp. Think!

HEDDA   I am thinking.

TESMAN   Do you think we could possibly use your writing table for
a little? What?

HEDDA   Yes, of course.

> *Quickly.*

No, wait! Let me tidy it up first.

TESMAN   Oh, don't you trouble about that. There's plenty of room.

HEDDA   No, no, let me tidy it up first, I say. I'll take this in and put
them on the piano. Here.

> *She pulls an object, covered with sheets of music, out from
> under the bookcase, puts some more sheets on top and carries
> it all into the rear room and away to the left.* TESMAN *puts his
> papers on the writing table and moves the lamp over from the
> corner table. He and* MRS. ELVSTED *sit down and begin work-
> ing again.* HEDDA *comes back.*

HEDDA   [*behind* MRS. ELVSTED's *chair, ruffles her hair gently*]   Well, my
pretty Thea! And how is work progressing on Eilert Loevborg's
memorial?

MRS. ELVSTED   [*looks up at her, dejectedly*]   Oh, it's going to be terribly difficult to get these into any order.

TESMAN   We've got to do it. We must! After all, putting other people's papers into order is rather my specialty, what?

>   HEDDA *goes over to the stove and sits on one of the footstools.* BRACK *stands over her, leaning against the armchair.*

HEDDA [*whispers*]   What was that you were saying about the pistol?
BRACK [*softly*]   I said he must have stolen it.
HEDDA   Why do you think that?
BRACK   Because any other explanation is unthinkable, Mrs. Hedda, or ought to be.
HEDDA   I see.
BRACK [*looks at her for a moment*]   Eilert Loevborg was here this morning. Wasn't he?
HEDDA   Yes.
BRACK   Were you alone with him?
HEDDA   For a few moments.
BRACK   You didn't leave the room while he was here?
HEDDA   No.
BRACK   Think again. Are you sure you didn't go out for a moment?
HEDDA   Oh—yes, I might have gone into the hall. Just for a few seconds.
BRACK   And where was your pistol-case during this time?
HEDDA   I'd locked it in that—
BRACK   Er—Mrs. Hedda?
HEDDA   It was lying over there on my writing table.
BRACK   Have you looked to see if both the pistols are still there?
HEDDA   No.
BRACK   You needn't bother. I saw the pistol Loevborg had when they found him. I recognized it at once. From yesterday. And other occasions.
HEDDA   Have you got it?
BRACK   No. The police have it.
HEDDA   What will the police do with this pistol?
BRACK   Try to trace the owner.
HEDDA   Do you think they'll succeed?
BRACK [*leans down and whispers*]   No, Hedda Gabler. Not as long as I hold my tongue.
HEDDA [*looks nervously at him*]   And if you don't?
BRACK [*shrugs his shoulders*]   You could always say he'd stolen it.
HEDDA   I'd rather die!
BRACK [*smiles*]   People say that. They never do it.
HEDDA [*not replying*]   And suppose the pistol wasn't stolen? And they trace the owner? What then?
BRACK   There'll be a scandal, Hedda.
HEDDA   A scandal!
BRACK   Yes, a scandal. The thing you're so frightened of. You'll have to appear in court. Together with Mademoiselle Danielle. She'll have to explain how it all happened. Was it an accident, or was it—homicide? Was he about to take the pistol from his pocket to

threaten her? And did it go off? Or did she snatch the pistol from his hand, shoot him and then put it back in his pocket? She might quite easily have done it. She's a resourceful lady, is Mademoiselle Danielle.

HEDDA   But I had nothing to do with this repulsive business.

BRACK   No. But you'll have to answer one question. Why did you give Eilert Loevborg this pistol? And what conclusions will people draw when it is proved you did give it to him?

HEDDA [*bows her head*]   That's true. I hadn't thought of that.

BRACK   Well, luckily there's no danger as long as I hold my tongue.

HEDDA [*looks up at him*]   In other words, I'm in your power, Judge. From now on, you've got your hold over me.

BRACK [*whispers, more slowly*]   Hedda, my dearest—believe me—I will not abuse my position.

HEDDA   Nevertheless, I'm in your power. Dependent on your will, and your demands. Not free. Still not free!

> *Rises passionately.*

No. I couldn't bear that. No.

BRACK [*looks half-derisively at her*]   Most people resign themselves to the inevitable, sooner or later.

HEDDA [*returns his gaze*]   Possibly they do.

> *She goes across to the writing table.*

HEDDA [*represses an involuntary smile and says in* TESMAN's *voice*] Well, George. Think you'll be able to manage? What?

TESMAN   Heaven knows, dear. This is going to take months and months.

HEDDA [*in the same tone as before*]   Fancy that, by Jove!

> *Runs her hands gently through* MRS. ELVSTED's *hair.*

Doesn't it feel strange, Thea? Here you are working away with Tesman just the way you used to work with Eilert Loevborg.

MRS. ELVSTED   Oh—if only I can inspire your husband too!

HEDDA   Oh, it'll come. In time.

TESMAN   Yes—do you know, Hedda, I really think I'm beginning to feel a bit—well—that way. But you go back and talk to Judge Brack.

HEDDA   Can't I be of use to you two in any way?

TESMAN   No, none at all.

> *Turns his head.*

You'll have to keep Hedda company from now on, Judge, and see she doesn't get bored. If you don't mind.

BRACK [*glances at* HEDDA]   It'll be a pleasure.

HEDDA   Thank you. But I'm tired this evening. I think I'll lie down on the sofa in there for a little while.

TESMAN   Yes, dear—do. What?

HEDDA *goes into the rear room and draws the curtains behind her. Short pause. Suddenly she begins to play a frenzied dance melody on the piano.*

MRS. ELVSTED [*starts up from her chair*]   Oh, what's that?

TESMAN [*runs to the doorway*]   Hedda dear, please! Don't play dance music tonight! Think of Auntie Rena. And Eilert.

HEDDA [*puts her head out through the curtains*]   And Auntie Juju. And all the rest of them. From now on I'll be quiet.

Closes the curtains behind her.

TESMAN [*at the writing table*]   It distresses her to watch us doing this. I say, Mrs. Elvsted, I've an idea. Why don't you move in with Auntie Juju? I'll run over each evening, and we can sit and work there. What?

MRS. ELVSTED   Yes, that might be the best plan.

HEDDA [*from the rear room*]   I can hear what you're saying, Tesman. But how shall I spend the evenings out here?

TESMAN [*looking through his papers*]   Oh, I'm sure Judge Brack'll be kind enough to come over and keep you company. You won't mind my not being here, Judge?

BRACK [*in the armchair, calls gaily*]   I'll be delighted, Mrs. Tesman. I'll be here every evening. We'll have great fun together, you and I.

HEDDA [*loud and clear*]   Yes, that'll suit you, won't it, Judge? The only cock on the dunghill—!

A shot is heard from the rear room. TESMAN, MRS. ELVSTED *and* JUDGE BRACK *start from their chairs.*

TESMAN   Oh, she's playing with those pistols again.

He pulls the curtains aside and runs in. MRS. ELVSTED *follows him.* HEDDA *is lying dead on the sofa. Confusion and shouting.* BERTHA *enters in alarm from the right.*

TESMAN [*screams to* BRACK]   She's shot herself! Shot herself in the head! By Jove! Fancy that!

BRACK [*half paralyzed in the armchair*]   But, good God! People don't do such things!

1890

4 LANGUAGE AND PERFORMANCE

The audience at a play sees the stage, the sets, the props, the costumes, the actors, their movements and gestures, their facial expressions. An audience hears sounds and sound effects, voices, spoken words. The reader of a play has only printed words. Even with stage directions for assembling a set on the stage of the imagination, for visualizing the characters and their actions, but it is all in printed words. For a reader of plays, language is everything, but even for the audience, despite all the visual effects, the medium of the play is language.

Sometimes that language is distinctly different from ordinary speech. Not many of us would say, "Look, the sun's coming up," this way:

> But look, the morn in russet mantle clad
> Walks o'er the dew of yon high eastward hill.

It is no doubt fitting that the high art of traditional tragedy—plays whose characters are kings and queens, princes and princesses, nobles and courtiers—should be embodied in elevated language, even, like *Hamlet*, in highly figurative and metrical language:

> Mother, for love of grace,
> Lay not that flattering unction to your soul,
> That not your trespass but my madness speaks.
> It will but skin and film the ulcerous place
> Whiles rank corruption, mining all within,
> Infects unseen. Confess yourself to heaven,
> Repent what's past, avoid what is to come,
> And do not spread the compost on the weeds,
> To make them ranker.

Much of the play is in verse like this, with five "beats," or emphasized syllables, to the line (and typically five less accented syllables). This rhythm sets up expectations, and one of the pleasures of poetic drama as in traditional poetry is the delight in fulfilled expectations of sound and pleasure in modified, modulated, or syncopated, rhythms. To some extent the meter dictates how an actor reads the lines and, perhaps, how we sound them on our inner ear as we read. An actor, however, must make a choice whether to emphasize the poetic or the prose aspect of each line: how much stress or emphasis do you give the "to" in the second line above or the "on" in the eighth? The text for a performer is like the score for a musical performer: all the notes are there but each performance differs. If you can, listen to recordings of John Barrymore and of Maurice Evans, or Richard Burton and Sir Laurence Olivier, reading this passage and you will hear how differently the same words can be read. How do you yourself read the lines? Do you actually sound them out in your mind, choosing one possibility or the other? Are you, or can you become, aware of the tug of the meter and meaning simultaneously? Marking the end of Hamlet's **soliloquy** (speech to oneself) is a beautifully balanced line in which *break* and *heart* in the first half line balance *hold* and *tongue* in the second half, pivoting around the *I*—"But break my heart, for I must hold my tongue." It is doubtful whether this line would have quite the finality and effect were it not for expectations of rhythm built up by the earlier verse.

But isn't poetic drama very artificial, somewhat like opera in which people are singing in each others' faces things like, "Who's at the door?" and "My name is Mimi"? While "artificial" means "unnatural" or "unrealistic," it also means "made by art," and it is possible both to be deeply moved by the human passion and truth of a play like *Hamlet* and thrilled by the skill in structure and language. Indeed, it is possible that our response is fullest and greatest when we are moved by both, conscious of both, even though the two—significance and structure, or meaning and language—are inseparable. Is it the spitting out of the sibilant sounds or the "idea" of his mother's racing into bed with his uncle that makes Hamlet's "O most wicked speed, to post / With such dexterity to incestuous sheets!" so clearly and dramatically reveal his disgust at his mother's marrying Claudius so soon after her husband's death?

The rhythms and sounds, the unseen images called up by the words —russet mantle, flattering unction—are available to reader and audience, as are the statements and implications of the dialogue creating the effects, themes, and significance of the play. The language creates all these things while remaining language, and reader and audience are conscious of the beauty or appropriateness of the sounds and of the precise words, the verbal artistry, even while enthralled by the characters and actions, drawn into the world of the play, and stirred by the resonances of the play's image of man in the world.

The actor's physical presence, the gestures, the intonation and emphasis in the delivery of the lines (as well as sets, costumes, and so on), while they evoke specific emotions and clarify *a* meaning of the play, restrict the audience to the interpretation of the play by director and actor in a way that the words do not. There is no question, for example, that Hamlet is, to put it mildly, upset at his mother's precipitously marrying Claudius, his father's brother, as his language makes clear in the "incestuous sheets" passage and in many others (for example, "to live / In the rank sweat of an enseaméd bed, / Stewed in corruption, honeying, and making love / Over the nasty sty—" 3:4:93–95). But is this the central motivation and meaning of the play? At times an actor and director will play it as if it is, as Sir Laurence Olivier virtually does in his film version. The political and other themes are muted if not cut entirely from the play. The reader, however, though lacking the neatness and clarity of an interpretation, has all the words and so all the themes and possibilities present in the text. In reading, you can perform it one way, unperform it, and reperform it in another, even perform it two ways at once, perhaps, in your imagination as you read. Charles Lamb was so upset by how much the performed play limited his imagination, he vowed not ever again to see Shakespeare on the stage.

Even plays in very prosaic prose frequently call attention to their language, both its use and its limits. At times the characters in Harold Pinter's *The Black and White* converse, that is, they respond to each other:

FIRST   I not long got here.
SECOND   Did you get the all-night bus?
FIRST   I got the all-night bus straight here.
SECOND   Where from?
FIRST   Marble Arch.
SECOND   Which one?
FIRST   The two-nine-four, that takes me all the way to Fleet Street.
SECOND   So does the two-nine-one.

The impression is that the conversation is entirely banal, and, while Pinter may be telling us something about the banality of the characters, and the kind of conversation that one hears in an all-night milk bar in central London, there is something uncomfortably familiar about it. So the language calls attention to the way language is used and perhaps to the way we ourselves converse. (The way everyone converses? Is Pinter's dialogue natural or artificial? Is it what two vagrant old dears from London's East End might say, or is it an exaggeration, a stylization? Or is it both? And in either case doesn't its repetition show us something about the nature of our conversation, something very different from the usual representation of speech? And don't its non sequiturs show us that dialogue is often not communication but independent monologues occasionally intersecting?

Notice how each of Pinter's two characters carries on her own half of the conversation without immediately paying much attention to what the other is saying. The sketch opens just that way:

SECOND   You see that one come up and speak to me at the counter?
FIRST   You got the bread, then?

A few lines later:

SECOND   Comes up to me, he says, hullo, he says, what's the time by your clock? Bloody liberty. I was just standing there getting your soup.
FIRST   It's tomato soup.
SECOND   What's the time by your clock? he says.

The first woman finally responds. One of the reasons for so much repetition is that people—only such people? all people?—do not listen very carefully, are too wrapped up in their own thoughts and feelings, so that it takes repetition to get their attention.

Pinter's language may seem as stylized and artificial as Shakespeare's blank verse. It certainly is not the language of "realist" drama like that of Ibsen or Miller. There, as in real life, language is a practical tool. We are probably not—and not meant to be—so conscious of the language as language. Tesman's repeated "By Jove" and "what?" (in the translation) do not call attention to themselves as language, even as banal language, but as indication of the kind of conventional character Tesman is: the words are more important for what they point to than they are in themselves as words.

The language in *Death of a Salesman* is frequently of that order. Happy says, "you're the tops," and Willy warns about "counting your chickens," and the waiter Stanley calls it a "dog's life." The clichés in the mouths of the characters are not evidence of poor writing on Miller's part but characterize the ordinariness of the characters (which ordinariness contributes to the pathos of the play: here is no Hamlet, no great matter in the history of the human race, but still a human in moral agony). When they strive to express their emotions, reach for poetry, the very poverty of their language generates a moving pathos, as when Willy is remembering Biff's triumphant day on the football field:

> Like a young god. Hercules—something like that. And the sun, the sun all around him. Remember how he waved to me? Right up from the field, with the representatives of three colleges standing by? And the buyers I brought, and the cheers when he came out—Loman, Loman, Loman! God Almighty, he'll be great yet. A star like that, magnificent, can never really fade away!

Sometimes language, even the very ordinary language that *that* person would use at *that* time in *that* situation, calls attention to itself by its very appropriateness. There are expressions, some sentimental— "he's only a little boat looking for a harbor"—and some more harsh —"spewing out the vomit from his mind"—that reach above the banality of the rest, though they perhaps do not call too much attention to themselves as noticeably expressive language despite their figurativeness. Linda, who can be banal as any in expressing her love for Willy—"He's the dearest man in the world to me"—can also have moments in which the rhythm of her language and the repetitions of words and structure achieve a certain impressive eloquence:

> I don't say he is a great man. Willy Loman never made a lot of money. His name was never in the paper. He's not the finest character that ever lived. But he's a human being, and a terrible thing is happening to him. So attention must be paid. He's not to be allowed to fall into his grave like an old dog. Attention, attention must be finally paid to such a person.

Here the language rises above the merely useful.

There is one scene, in act two, when Willy goes to see Howard Wagner, the son of his late friend and boss, to ask for a non-traveling job with the company, that is a little reminiscent of the Pinter: Willy is down and desperate, Howard is excited with his new toy, a wire-recorder (i.e., early tape recorder). The two men are so entangled in their own affairs they cannot listen to the other (though our sympathies are with Willy, who tries to respond and whose need for dialogue is great). There is also an ironic and wrenching contrast between the emotions of Willy and the mechanically reproduced sounds: the whistling of a popular bar-room song, "Roll Out the Barrel" and the rote repetition by Wagner's five-year-old of the capitals of the states in alphabetical order. When Howard leaves the room there is a macabre incident. The distraught Willy addresses Howard's dead father but accidentally activates the recorder:

> HOWARD'S SON . . . of New York is Albany. The capital of Ohio is Cincinnati, the capital of Rhode Island is . . . *The recitation continues.*

The little boy's voice is no more unresponsive to Willy's plight than Howard was: language is emptied of meaning and feeling.

So even a realistic play can raise our awareness of its language. *Death of a Salesman* is in the flat and empty, inexpressive "real" language of the artificial world of business and the ambition to be wealthy and "number one." The very inexpressiveness of its language helps to define the emptiness of that world, and it is, ironically, through that language that the powerful poignancy of emotions that cannot be articulated is expressed.

Language, then, even in realistic drama is not "merely" realistic: it is crafted to give the illusion of reality, and in its own way embodies and interprets a view of the world seen from a particular vantage point, even as does the language of poetic drama. Consciousness of the language, what it says and what it suggests, how it relates to "real" language and how it differs, how it embodies its world, is essential to understanding and intensifying the experience of reading drama.

ARTHUR MILLER

Death of a Salesman

CHARACTERS

WILLY LOMAN
LINDA
BIFF
HAPPY
BERNARD
THE WOMAN
CHARLEY

UNCLE BEN
HOWARD WAGNER
JENNY
STANLEY
MISS FORSYTHE (GIRL)
LETTA

Act 1

A melody is heard, played upon a flute. It is small and fine, telling of grass and trees and the horizon. The curtain rises

Before us is the Salesman's house. We are aware of towering, angular shapes behind it, surrounding it on all sides. Only the blue light of the sky falls upon the house and forestage; the surrounding area shows an angry glow of orange. As more light appears, we see a solid vault of apartment houses around the small, fragile-seeming home. An air of the dream clings to the place, a dream rising out of reality. The kitchen at center seems actual enough, for there is a kitchen table with three chairs, and a refrigerator. But no other fixtures are seen. At the back of the kitchen there is a draped entrance, which leads to the living room. To the right of the kitchen, on a level raised two feet, is a bedroom furnished only with a brass bedstead and a straight chair. On a shelf over the bed a silver athletic trophy stands. A window opens onto the apartment house at the side.

Behind the kitchen, on a level raised six and a half feet, is the boys' bedroom, at present barely visible. Two beds are dimly seen, and at the back of the room a dormer window. (This bedroom is above the unseen living room.) At the left a stairway curves up to it from the kitchen.

The entire setting is wholly or, in some places, partially transparent. The roof-line of the house is one-dimensional; under and over it we see the apartment buildings. Before the house lies an apron, curving beyond the forestage into the orchestra. This forward area serves as the back yard as well as the locale of all WILLY's *imaginings and of his city scenes. Whenever the action is in the present the actors observe the imaginary wall-lines, entering the house only through its door at the left. But in the scenes of the past these boundaries are broken, and characters enter or leave a room by stepping "through" a wall onto the forestage.*

From the right, WILLY LOMAN, *the Salesman, enters, carrying two large sample cases. The flute plays on. He hears but is not aware of it. He is past sixty years of age, dressed quietly. Even as he crosses the stage to the doorway of the house, his exhaustion is apparent. He unlocks the door, comes into the kitchen, and thankfully lets his burden down, feeling the soreness of his palms. A word-sigh escapes his lips—it might be "Oh, boy, oh, boy." He closes the door, then carries his cases out into the living-room, through the draped kitchen doorway.*

LINDA, *his wife, has stirred in her bed at the right. She gets out and puts on a robe, listening. Most often jovial, she has developed an iron repression of her exceptions to* WILLY'S *behavior—she more than loves him, she admires him, as though his mercurial nature, his temper, his massive dreams and little cruelties, served her only as sharp reminders of the turbulent longings within him, longings which she shares but lacks the temperament to utter and follow to their end.*

LINDA [*hearing* WILLY *outside the bedroom, calls with some trepidation*]   Willy!

WILLY   It's all right. I came back.

LINDA   Why? What happened? [*Slight pause*]. Did something happen, Willy?

WILLY   No, nothing happened.

LINDA   You didn't smash the car, did you?

WILLY [*with casual irritation*]   I said nothing happened. Didn't you hear me?

LINDA   Don't you feel well?

WILLY   I'm tired to the death. [*The flute has faded away. He sits on the bed beside her, a little numb.*] I couldn't make it. I just couldn't make it, Linda.

LINDA [*very carefully, delicately*]   Where were you all day? You look terrible.

WILLY   I got as far as a little above Yonkers. I stopped for a cup of coffee. Maybe it was the coffee.

LINDA   What?

WILLY [*after a pause*]   I suddenly couldn't drive any more. The car kept going off onto the shoulder, y'know?

LINDA [*helpfully*]   Oh. Maybe it was the steering again. I don't think Angelo knows the Studebaker.

WILLY   No, it's me, it's me. Suddenly I realize I'm goin' sixty miles an hour and I don't remember the last five minutes. I'm—I can't seem to—keep my mind to it.

LINDA   Maybe it's your glasses. You never went for your new glasses.

WILLY   No, I see everything. I came back ten miles an hour. It took me nearly four hours from Yonkers.

LINDA [*resigned*]   Well, you'll just have to take a rest, Willy, you can't continue this way.

WILLY   I just got back from Florida.

LINDA   But you didn't rest your mind. Your mind is overactive, and the mind is what counts, dear.

WILLY I'll start out in the morning. Maybe I'll feel better in the morning. [*She is taking off his shoes.*] These goddam arch supports are killing me.

LINDA Take an aspirin. Should I get you an aspirin? It'll soothe you.

WILLY [*with wonder*] I was driving along, you understand? And I was fine. I was even observing the scenery. You can imagine, me looking at scenery, on the road every week of my life. But it's so beautiful up there, Linda, the trees are so thick, and the sun is warm. I opened the windshield and just let the warm air bathe over me. And then all of a sudden I'm goin' off the road! I'm tellin' ya, I absolutely forgot I was driving. If I'd've gone the other way over the white line I might've killed somebody. So I went on again—and five minutes later I'm dreamin' again, and I nearly—[*He presses two fingers against his eyes.*] I have such thoughts, I have such strange thoughts.

LINDA Willy, dear. Talk to them again. There's no reason why you can't work in New York.

WILLY They don't need me in New York. I'm the New England man. I'm vital in New England.

LINDA But you're sixty years old. They can't expect you to keep traveling every week.

WILLY I'll have to send a wire to Portland. I'm supposed to see Brown and Morrison tomorrow morning at ten o'clock to show the line. Goddammit, I could sell them! [*He starts putting on his jacket.*]

LINDA [*taking the jacket from him*] Why don't you go down to the place tomorrow and tell Howard you've simply got to work in New York? You're too accommodating, dear.

WILLY If old man Wagner was alive I'd a been in charge of New York now! That man was a prince, he was a masterful man. But that boy of his, that Howard, he don't appreciate. When I went north the first time, the Wagner Company didn't know where New England was!

LINDA Why don't you tell those things to Howard, dear?

WILLY [*encouraged*] I will, I definitely will. Is there any cheese?

LINDA I'll make you a sandwich.

WILLY No, go to sleep. I'll take some milk. I'll be up right away. The boys in?

LINDA They're sleeping. Happy took Biff on a date tonight.

WILLY [*interested*] That so?

LINDA It was so nice to see them shaving together, one behind the other, in the bathroom. And going out together. You notice? The whole house smells of shaving lotion.

WILLY Figure it out. Work a lifetime to pay off a house. You finally own it, and there's nobody to live in it.

LINDA Well, dear, life is a casting off. It's always that way.

WILLY No, no, some people—some people accomplish something. Did Biff say anything after I went this morning?

LINDA You shouldn't have criticized him, Willy, especially after he just got off the train. You mustn't lose your temper with him.

WILLY When the hell did I lose my temper? I simply asked him if he was making any money. Is that a criticism?

LINDA   But, dear, how could he make any money?

WILLY [*worried and angered*]   There's such an undercurrent in him. He became a moody man. Did he apologize when I left this morning?

LINDA   He was crestfallen, Willy. You know how he admires you. I think if he finds himself, then you'll both be happier and not fight any more.

WILLY   How can he find himself on a farm? Is that a life? A farm-hand? In the beginning, when he was young, I thought, well, a young man, it's good for him to tramp around, take a lot of different jobs. But it's more than ten years now and he has yet to make thirty-five dollars a week!

LINDA   He's finding himself, Willy.

WILLY   Not finding yourself at the age of thirty-four is a disgrace!

LINDA   Shh!

WILLY   The trouble is he's lazy, goddammit!

LINDA   Willy, please!

WILLY   Biff is a lazy bum!

LINDA   They're sleeping. Get something to eat. Go on down.

WILLY   Why did he come home? I would like to know what brought him home.

LINDA   I don't know. I think he's still lost, Willy. I think he's very lost.

WILLY   Biff Loman is lost. In the greatest country in the world a young man with such—personal attractiveness, gets lost. And such a hard worker. There's one thing about Biff—he's not lazy.

LINDA   Never.

WILLY [*with pity and resolve*]   I'll see him in the morning; I'll have a nice talk with him. I'll get him a job selling. He could be big in no time. My God! Remember how they used to follow him around in high school? When he smiled at one of them their faces lit up. When he walked down the street . . . [*He loses himself in reminiscences.*]

LINDA [*trying to bring him out of it*]   Willy, dear, I got a new kind of American-type cheese today. It's whipped.

WILLY   Why do you get American when I like Swiss?

LINDA   I just thought you'd like a change—

WILLY   I don't want a change! I want Swiss cheese. Why am I always being contradicted?

LINDA [*with a covering laugh*]   I thought it would be a surprise.

WILLY   Why don't you open a window in here, for God's sake?

LINDA [*with infinite patience*]   They're all open, dear.

WILLY   The way they boxed us in here. Bricks and windows, windows and bricks.

LINDA   We should've bought the land next door.

WILLY   The street is lined with cars. There's not a breath of fresh air in the neighborhood. The grass don't grow any more, you can't raise a carrot in the back yard. They should've had a law against apartment houses. Remember those two beautiful elm trees out there? When I and Biff hung the swing between them?

LINDA   Yeah, like being a million miles from the city.

WILLY   They should've arrested the builder for cutting those down.

They massacred the neighborhood. [*Lost*] More and more I think of those days, Linda. This time of year it was lilac and wisteria. And then the peonies would come out, and the daffodils. What fragrance in this room!

LINDA   Well, after all, people had to move somewhere.

WILLY   No, there's more people now.

LINDA   I don't think there's more people. I think—

WILLY   There's more people! That's what's ruining this country! Population is getting out of control. The competition is maddening! Smell the stink from that apartment house! And another one on the other side . . . How can they whip cheese?

> *On* WILLY'S *last line,* BIFF *and* HAPPY *raise themselves up in their beds, listening.*

LINDA   Go down, try it. And be quiet.

WILLY   [*turning to Linda, guilty*]   You're not worried about me, are you, sweetheart?

BIFF   What's the matter?

HAPPY   Listen!

LINDA   You've got too much on the ball to worry about.

WILLY   You're my foundation and my support, Linda.

LINDA   Just try to relax, dear. You make mountains out of molehills.

WILLY   I won't fight with him any more. If he wants to go back to Texas, let him go.

LINDA   He'll find his way.

WILLY   Sure. Certain men just don't get started till later in life. Like Thomas Edison, I think. Or B. F. Goodrich. One of them was deaf. [*He starts for the bedroom doorway.*] I'll put my money on Biff.

LINDA   And Willy—if it's warm Sunday we'll drive in the country. And we'll open the windshield, and take lunch.

WILLY   No, the windshields don't open on the new cars.

LINDA   But you opened it today.

WILLY   Me? I didn't. [*He stops.*] Now isn't that peculiar! Isn't that a remarkable—[*He breaks off in amazement and fright as the flute is heard distantly.*]

LINDA   What, darling?

WILLY   That is the most remarkable thing.

LINDA   What, dear?

WILLY   I was thinking of the Chevvy. [*Slight pause.*] Nineteen twenty-eight . . . when I had that red Chevvy— [*Breaks off.*] That funny? I coulda sworn I was driving that Chevvy today.

LINDA   Well, that's nothing. Something must've reminded you.

WILLY   Remarkable. Ts. Remember those days? The way Biff used to simonize that car? The dealer refused to believe there was eighty thousand miles on it. [*He shakes his head.*] Heh! [*To Linda*] Close your eyes, I'll be right up. [*He walks out of the bedroom.*]

HAPPY   [*to Biff*]   Jesus, maybe he smashed up the car again!

LINDA   [*calling after Willy*]   Be careful on the stairs, dear! The cheese is on the middle shelf! [*She turns, goes over to the bed, takes his jacket, and goes out of the bedroom.*]

Light has risen on the boys' room. Unseen, WILLY *is heard talking to himself, "Eighty thousand miles," and a little laugh.* BIFF *gets out of bed, comes downstage a bit, and stands attentively.* BIFF *is two years older than his brother* HAPPY, *well built, but in these days bears a worn air and seems less self-assured. He has succeeded less, and his dreams are stronger and less acceptable than* HAPPY'S. HAPPY *is tall, powerfully made. Sexuality is like a visible color on him, or a scent that many women have discovered. He, like his brother, is lost, but in a different way, for he has never allowed himself to turn his face toward defeat and is thus more confused and hard-skinned, although seemingly more content.*

HAPPY [*getting out of bed*]   He's going to get his license taken away if he keeps that up. I'm getting nervous about him, y'know, Biff?

BIFF   His eyes are going.

HAPPY   No, I've driven with him. He sees all right. He just doesn't keep his mind on it. I drove into the city with him last week. He stops at a green light and then it turns red and he goes. [*He laughs.*]

BIFF   Maybe he's color-blind.

HAPPY   Pop? Why he's got the finest eye for color in the business. You know that.

BIFF [*sitting down on his bed*]   I'm going to sleep.

HAPPY   You're not still sour on Dad, are you, Biff?

BIFF   He's all right, I guess.

WILLY [*underneath them, in the living room*]   Yes, sir, eighty thousand miles—eighty-two thousand!

BIFF   You smoking?

HAPPY [*holding out a pack of cigarettes*]   Want one?

BIFF [*taking a cigarette*]   I can never sleep when I smell it.

WILLY   What a simonizing job, heh!

HAPPY [*with deep sentiment*]   Funny, Biff, y'know? Us sleeping in here again? The old beds. [*He pats his bed affectionately.*] All the talk that went across those two beds, huh? Our whole lives.

BIFF   Yeah. Lotta dreams and plans.

HAPPY [*with a deep and masculine laugh*]   About five hundred women would like to know what was said in this room.

They share a soft laugh.

BIFF   Remember that big Betsy something—what the hell was her name—over on Bushwick Avenue?

HAPPY [*combing his hair*]   With the collie dog!

BIFF   That's the one. I got you in there, remember?

HAPPY   Yeah, that was my first time—I think. Boy, there was a pig! [*They laugh, almost crudely.*] You taught me everything I know about women. Don't forget that.

BIFF   I bet you forgot how bashful you used to be. Especially with girls.

HAPPY Oh, I still am, Biff.

BIFF Oh, go on.

HAPPY I just control it, that's all. I think I got less bashful and you got more so. What happened, Biff? Where's the old humor, the old confidence? [*He shakes* BIFF's *knee.* BIFF *gets up and moves restlessly about the room.*] What's the matter?

BIFF Why does Dad mock me all the time?

HAPPY He's not mocking you, he—

BIFF Everything I say there's a twist of mockery on his face. I can't get near him.

HAPPY He just wants you to make good, that's all. I wanted to talk to you about Dad for a long time, Biff. Something's—happening to him. He—talks to himself.

BIFF I noticed that this morning. But he always mumbled.

HAPPY But not so noticeable. It got so embarrassing I sent him to Florida. And you know something? Most of the time he's talking to you.

BIFF What's he say about me?

HAPPY I can't make it out.

BIFF What's he say about me?

HAPPY I think the fact that you're not settled, that you're still kind of up in the air . . .

BIFF There's one or two other things depressing him, Happy.

HAPPY What do you mean?

BIFF Never mind. Just don't lay it all to me.

HAPPY But I think if you just got started—I mean—is there any future for you out there?

BIFF I tell ya, Hap, I don't know what the future is. I don't know—what I'm supposed to want.

HAPPY What do you mean?

BIFF Well, I spent six or seven years after high school trying to work myself up. Shipping clerk, salesman, business of one kind or another. And it's a measly manner of existence. To get on that subway on the hot mornings in summer. To devote your whole life to keeping stock, or making phone calls, or selling or buying. To suffer fifty weeks of the year for the sake of a two-week vacation, when all you really desire is to be outdoors, with your shirt off. And always to have to get ahead of the next fella. And still—that's how you build a future.

HAPPY Well, you really enjoy it on a farm? Are you content out there?

BIFF [*with rising agitation*] Hap, I've had twenty or thirty different kinds of jobs since I left home before the war, and it always turns out the same. I just realized it lately. In Nebraska when I herded cattle, and the Dakotas, and Arizona, and now in Texas. It's why I came home now, I guess, because I realized it. This farm I work on, it's spring there now, see? And they've got about fifteen new colts. There's nothing more inspiring or—beautiful than the sight of a mare and a new colt. And it's cool there now, see? Texas is cool now, and it's spring. And whenever spring comes to where I am, I suddenly get the feeling, my God, I'm not gettin' anywhere! What the hell am I doing, playing around with horses, twenty-eight dollars a week! I'm thirty-four years old, I oughta be makin' my future. That's when I come running home. And now, I get here, and I don't know what to do with myself. [*After a pause*] I've always made a point of not wasting my life, and every time I come back here I know that all I've done is to waste my life.

HAPPY   You're a poet, you know that, Biff? You're a—you're an idealist!

BIFF   No, I'm mixed up very bad. Maybe I oughta get married. Maybe I oughta get stuck into something. Maybe that's my trouble. I'm like a boy. I'm not married, I'm not in business, I just—I'm like a boy. Are you content, Hap? You're a success, aren't you? Are you content?

HAPPY   Hell, no!

BIFF   Why? You're making money, aren't you?

HAPPY   [*moving about with energy, expressiveness*]   All I can do now is wait for the merchandise manager to die. And suppose I get to be merchandise manager? He's a good friend of mine, and he just built a terrific estate on Long Island. And he lived there about two months and sold it, and now he's building another one. He can't enjoy it once it's finished. And I know that's just what I would do. I don't know what the hell I'm workin' for. Sometimes I sit in my apartment—all alone. And I think of the rent I'm paying. And it's crazy. But then, it's what I always wanted. My own apartment, a car, and plenty of women. And still, goddammit, I'm lonely.

BIFF   [*with enthusiasm*]   Listen, why don't you come out West with me?

HAPPY   You and I, heh?

BIFF   Sure, maybe we could buy a ranch. Raise cattle, use our muscles. Men built like we are should be working out in the open.

HAPPY   [*avidly*]   The Loman Brothers, heh?

BIFF   [*with vast affection*]   Sure, we'd be known all over the counties!

HAPPY   [*enthralled*]   That's what I dream about, Biff. Sometimes I want to just rip my clothes off in the middle of the store and outbox that goddam merchandise manager. I mean I can outbox, outrun, and outlift anybody in that store, and I have to take orders from those common, petty sons-of-bitches till I can't stand it any more.

BIFF   I'm tellin' you, kid, if you were with me I'd be happy out there.

HAPPY   [*enthused*]   See, Biff, everybody around me is so false that I'm constantly lowering my ideals . . .

BIFF   Baby, together we'd stand up for one another, we'd have someone to trust.

HAPPY   If I were around you—

BIFF   Hap, the trouble is we weren't brought up to grub for money. I don't know how to do it.

HAPPY   Neither can I!

BIFF   Then let's go!

HAPPY   The only thing is—what can you make out there?

BIFF   But look at your friend. Builds an estate and then hasn't the peace of mind to live in it.

HAPPY Yeah, but when he walks into the store the waves part in front of him. That's fifty-two thousand dollars a year coming through the revolving door, and I got more in my pinky finger than he's got in his head.

BIFF Yeah, but you just said—

HAPPY I gotta show some of those pompous, self-important executives over there that Hap Loman can make the grade. I want to walk into the store the way he walks in. Then I'll go with you, Biff. We'll be together yet, I swear. But take those two we had tonight. Now weren't they gorgeous creatures?

BIFF Yeah, yeah, most gorgeous I've had in years.

HAPPY I get that any time I want, Biff. Whenever I feel disgusted. The only trouble is, it gets like bowling or something. I just keep knockin' them over and it doesn't mean anything. You still run around a lot?

BIFF Naa. I'd like to find a girl—steady, somebody with substance.

HAPPY That's what I long for.

BIFF Go on! You'd never come home.

HAPPY I would! Somebody with character, with resistance! Like Mom, y'know? You're gonna call me a bastard when I tell you this. That girl Charlotte I was with tonight is engaged to be married in five weeks. [*He tries on his new hat.*]

BIFF No kiddin'!

HAPPY Sure, the guy's in line for the vice-presidency of the store. I don't know what gets into me, maybe I just have an overdeveloped sense of competition or something, but I went and ruined her, and furthermore I can't get rid of her. And he's the third executive I've done that to. Isn't that a crummy characteristic? And to top it all, I go to their weddings! [*Indignantly, but laughing*] Like I'm not supposed to take bribes. Manufacturers offer me a hundred-dollar bill now and then to throw an order their way. You know how honest I am, but it's like this girl, see. I hate myself for it. Because I don't want the girl, and, still, I take it and—I love it!

BIFF Let's go to sleep.

HAPPY I guess we didn't settle anything, heh?

BIFF I just got one idea that I think I'm going to try.

HAPPY What's that?

BIFF Remember Bill Oliver?

HAPPY Sure, Oliver is very big now. You want to work for him again?

BIFF No, but when I quit he said something to me. He put his arm on my shoulder, and he said, "Biff, if you ever need anything, come to me."

HAPPY I remember that. That sounds good.

BIFF I think I'll go to see him. If I could get ten thousand or even seven or eight thousand dollars I could buy a beautiful ranch.

HAPPY I bet he'd back you. 'Cause he thought highly of you, Biff. I mean, they all do. You're well liked, Biff. That's why I say to come back here, and we both have the apartment. And I'm tellin' you, Biff, any babe you want . . .

BIFF No, with a ranch I could do the work I like and still be something. I just wonder though. I wonder if Oliver still thinks I stole that carton of basketballs.

HAPPY   Oh, he probably forgot that long ago. It's almost ten years. You're too sensitive. Anyway, he didn't really fire you.

BIFF   Well, I think he was going to. I think that's why I quit. I was never sure whether he knew or not. I know he thought the world of me, though. I was the only one he'd let lock up the place.

WILLY [*below*]   You gonna wash the engine, Biff?

HAPPY   Shh!

BIFF *looks at* HAPPY, *who is gazing down, listening.* WILLY *is mumbling in the parlor.*

HAPPY   You hear that?

They listen. WILLY *laughs warmly.*

BIFF [*growing angry*]   Doesn't he know Mom can hear that?

WILLY   Don't get your sweater dirty, Biff!

A look of pain crosses BIFF's *face.*

HAPPY   Isn't that terrible? Don't leave again, will you? You'll find a job here. You gotta stick around. I don't know what to do about him, it's getting embarrassing.

WILLY   What a simonizing job!

BIFF   Mom's hearing that!

WILLY   No kiddin', Biff, you got a date? Wonderful!

HAPPY   Go on to sleep. But talk to him in the morning, will you?

BIFF [*reluctantly getting into bed*]   With her in the house. Brother!

HAPPY [*getting into bed*]   I wish you'd have a good talk with him.

The light on their room begins to fade.

BIFF [*to himself in bed*]   That selfish, stupid . . .

HAPPY   Sh . . . Sleep, Biff.

Their light is out. Well before they have finished speaking, WILLY's *form is dimly seen below in the darkened kitchen. He opens the refrigerator, searches in there, and takes out a bottle of milk. The apartment houses are fading out, and the entire house and surroundings become covered with leaves. Music insinuates itself as the leaves appear.*

WILLY   Just wanna be careful with those girls, Biff, that's all. Don't make any promises. No promises of any kind. Because a girl, y'know, they always believe what you tell 'em, and you're very young, Biff, you're too young to be talking seriously to girls.

Light rises on the kitchen. WILLY, *talking, shuts the refrigerator*

*door and comes downstage to the kitchen table. He pours milk
into a glass. He is totally immersed in himself, smiling faintly.*

WILLY   Too young entirely, Biff. You want to watch your schooling
first. Then when you're all set, there'll be plenty of girls for a
boy like you. [*He smiles broadly at a kitchen chair.*] That so? The
girls pay for you? [*He laughs.*] Boy, you must really be makin' a
hit.

> WILLY *is gradually addressing—physically—a point offstage,
> speaking through the wall of the kitchen, and his voice has
> been rising in volume to that of a normal conversation.*

WILLY   I been wondering why you polish the car so careful. Ha!
Don't leave the hubcaps, boys. Get the chamois to the hubcaps.
Happy, use newspaper on the windows, it's the easiest thing. Show
him how to do it, Biff! You see, Happy? Pad it up, use it like a pad.
That's it, that's it, good work. You're doin' all right, Hap. [*He
pauses, then nods in approbation for a few seconds, then looks upward.*] Biff, first thing we gotta do when we get time is clip that
big branch over the house. Afraid it's gonna fall in a storm and hit
the roof. Tell you what. We get a rope and sling her around, and
then we climb up there with a couple of saws and take her down.
Soon as you finish the car, boys, I wanna see ya. I got a surprise
for you, boys.

BIFF [*offstage*]   Whatta ya got, Dad?

WILLY   No, you finish first. Never leave a job till you're finished—remember that. [*Looking toward the "big trees"*] Biff, up in Albany
I saw a beautiful hammock. I think I'll buy it next trip, and we'll
hang it right between those two elms. Wouldn't that be something?
Just swingin' there under those branches. Boy, that would be . . .

> YOUNG BIFF *and* YOUNG HAPPY *appear from the direction* WILLY
> *was addressing.* HAPPY *carries rags and a pail of water.* BIFF,
> *wearing a sweater with a block "S," carries a football.*

BIFF [*pointing in the direction of the car offstage*]   How's that, Pop,
professional?

WILLY   Terrific. Terrific job, boys. Good work, Biff.

HAPPY   Where's the surprise, Pop?

WILLY   In the back seat of the car.

HAPPY   Boy! [*He runs off.*]

BIFF   What is it, Dad? Tell me, what'd you buy?

WILLY [*laughing, cuffs him*]   Never mind, something I want you to
have.

BIFF [*turns and starts off*]   What is it, Hap?

HAPPY [*offstage*]   It's a punching bag!

BIFF   Oh, Pop!

WILLY   It's got Gene Tunney's[1] signature on it!

---

1. Tunney (b. 1897) was world heavy-weight boxing champion from 1926 to 1928.

HAPPY *runs onstage with a punching bag.*

BIFF   Gee, how'd you know we wanted a punching bag?

WILLY   Well, it's the finest thing for the timing.

HAPPY [*lies down on his back and pedals with his feet*]   I'm losing weight, you notice, Pop?

WILLY [*to Happy*]   Jumping rope is good too.

BIFF   Did you see the new football I got?

WILLY [*examining the ball*]   Where'd you get a new ball?

BIFF   The coach told me to practice my passing.

WILLY   That so? And he gave you the ball, heh?

BIFF   Well, I borrowed it from the locker room. [*He laughs confidentially.*]

WILLY [*laughing with him at the theft*]   I want you to return that.

HAPPY   I told you he wouldn't like it!

BIFF [*angrily*]   Well, I'm bringing it back!

WILLY [*stopping the incipient argument, to* HAPPY]   Sure, he's gotta practice with a regulation ball, doesn't he? [*To* BIFF] Coach'll probably congratulate you on your initiative!

BIFF   Oh, he keeps congratulating my initiative all the time, Pop.

WILLY   That's because he likes you. If somebody else took that ball there'd be an uproar. So what's the report, boys, what's the report?

BIFF   Where'd you go this time, Dad? Gee we were lonesome for you.

WILLY [*pleased, puts an arm around each boy and they come down to the apron*]   Lonesome, heh?

BIFF   Missed you every minute.

WILLY   Don't say? Tell you a secret, boys. Don't breathe it to a soul. Someday I'll have my own business, and I'll never have to leave home any more.

HAPPY   Like Uncle Charley, heh?

WILLY   Bigger than Uncle Charley! Because Charley is not—liked. He's liked, but he's not—well liked.

BIFF   Where'd you go this time, Dad?

WILLY   Well, I got on the road, and I went north to Providence. Met the Mayor.

BIFF   The Mayor of Providence!

WILLY   He was sitting in the hotel lobby.

BIFF   What'd he say?

WILLY   He said, "Morning!" And I said, "You got a fine city here, Mayor." And then he had coffee with me. And then I went to Waterbury. Waterbury is a fine city. Big clock city, the famous Waterbury clock. Sold a nice bill there. And then Boston—Boston is the cradle of the Revolution. A fine city. And a couple of other towns in Mass., and on to Portland and Bangor and straight home!

BIFF   Gee, I'd love to go with you sometime, Dad.

WILLY   Soon as summer comes.

HAPPY   Promise?

WILLY   You and Hap and I, and I'll show you all the towns. America is full of beautiful towns and fine, upstanding people. And they know me, boys, they know me up and down New England. The

finest people. And when I bring you fellas up, there'll be open
sesame for all of us, 'cause one thing, boys: I have friends. I can
park my car in any street in New England, and the cops protect
it like their own. This summer, heh?

BIFF and HAPPY [*together*]   Yeah! You bet!

WILLY   We'll take our bathing suits.

HAPPY   We'll carry your bags, Pop!

WILLY   Oh, won't that be something! Me comin' into the Boston stores
with you boys carryin' my bags. What a sensation!

> BIFF *is prancing around, practicing passing the ball.*

WILLY   You nervous, Biff, about the game?

BIFF   Not if you're gonna be there.

WILLY   What do they say about you in school, now that they made
you captain?

HAPPY   There's a crowd of girls behind him everytime the classes
change.

BIFF [*taking* WILLY's *hand*]   This Saturday, Pop, this Saturday—just
for you, I'm going to break through for a touchdown.

HAPPY   You're supposed to pass.

BIFF   I'm takin' one play for Pop. You watch me, Pop, and when I
take off my helmet, that means I'm breakin' out. Then you watch
me crash through that line!

WILLY [*kisses* BIFF]   Oh, wait'll I tell this in Boston!

> BERNARD *enters in knickers. He is younger than* BIFF, *earnest
> and loyal, a worried boy.*

BERNARD   Biff, where are you? You're supposed to study with me
today.

WILLY   Hey, looka Bernard. What're you lookin' so anemic about,
Bernard?

BERNARD   He's gotta study, Uncle Willy. He's got Regents[2] next week.

HAPPY [*tauntingly, spinning* BERNARD *around*]   Let's box, Bernard!

BERNARD   Biff! [*He gets away from* HAPPY.] Listen, Biff, I heard Mr.
Birnbaum say that if you don't start studyin' math he's gonna flunk
you, and you won't graduate. I heard him!

WILLY   You better study with him, Biff. Go ahead now.

BERNARD   I heard him!

BIFF   Oh, Pop, you didn't see my sneakers! [*He holds up a foot for*
WILLY *to look at.*]

WILLY   Hey, that's a beautiful job of printing!

BERNARD [*wiping his glasses*]   Just because he printed University of
Virginia on his sneakers doesn't mean they've got to graduate him,
Uncle Willy!

WILLY [*angrily*]   What're you talking about? With scholarships to
three universities they're gonna flunk him?

---

2. A statewide examination administered to New York high school students.

BERNARD   But I heard Mr. Birnbaum say—
WILLY   Don't be a pest, Bernard! [*To his boys*] What an anemic!
BERNARD   Okay, I'm waiting for you in my house, Biff.

BERNARD *goes off. The Lomans laugh.*

WILLY   Bernard is not well liked, is he?
BIFF   He's liked, but he's not well liked.
HAPPY   That's right, Pop.
WILLY   That's just what I mean. Bernard can get the best marks in school, y'understand, but when he gets out in the business world, y'understand, you are going to be five times ahead of him. That's why I thank Almighty God you're both built like Adonises.[3] Because the man who makes an appearance in the business world, the man who creates personal interest, is the man who gets ahead. Be liked and you will never want. You take me, for instance. I never have to wait in line to see a buyer. "Willy Loman is here!" That's all they have to know, and I go right through.
BIFF   Did you knock them dead, Pop?
WILLY   Knocked 'em cold in Providence, slaughtered 'em in Boston.
HAPPY   [*on his back, pedaling again*]   I'm losing weight, you notice, Pop?

LINDA *enters, as of old, a ribbon in her hair, carrying a basket of washing.*

LINDA   [*with youthful energy*]   Hello, dear!
WILLY   Sweetheart!
LINDA   How'd the Chevvy run?
WILLY   Chevrolet, Linda, is the greatest car ever built. [*To the boys*] Since when do you let your mother carry wash up the stairs?
BIFF   Grab hold there, boy!
HAPPY   Where to, Mom?
LINDA   Hang them up on the line. And you better go down to your friends, Biff. The cellar is full of boys. They don't know what to do with themselves.
BIFF   Ah, when Pop comes home they can wait!
WILLY   [*laughs appreciatively*]   You better go down and tell them what to do, Biff.
BIFF   I think I'll have them sweep out the furnace room.
WILLY   Good work, Biff.
BIFF   [*goes through wall-line of kitchen to doorway at back and calls down*]   Fellas! Everybody sweep out the furnace room! I'll be right down!
VOICES   All right! Okay, Biff.
BIFF   George and Sam and Frank, come out back! We're hangin' up the wash! Come on, Hap, on the double! [*He and* HAPPY *carry out the basket.*]

---

3. In Greek mythology Adonis was a beautiful youth, the favorite of Aphrodite, Goddess of Love.

LINDA   The way they obey him!

WILLY   Well, that's training, the training. I'm tellin' you, I was sellin' thousands and thousands, but I had to come home.

LINDA   Oh, the whole block'll be at that game. Did you sell anything?

WILLY   I did five hundred gross in Providence and seven hundred gross in Boston.

LINDA   No! Wait a minute, I've got a pencil. [*She pulls pencil and paper out of her apron pocket.*] That makes your commission . . . Two hundred—my God! Two hundred and twelve dollars!

WILLY   Well, I didn't figure it yet, but . . .

LINDA   How much did you do?

WILLY   Well, I—I did—about a hundred and eighty gross in Providence. Well, no—it came to—roughly two hundred gross on the whole trip.

LINDA   [*without hesitation*] Two hundred gross. That's . . . [*She figures.*]

WILLY   The trouble was that three of the stores were half closed for inventory in Boston. Otherwise I woulda broke records.

LINDA   Well, it makes seventy dollars and some pennies. That's very good.

WILLY   What do we owe?

LINDA   Well, on the first there's sixteen dollars on the refrigerator—

WILLY   Why sixteen?

LINDA   Well, the fan belt broke, so it was a dollar eighty.

WILLY   But it's brand new.

LINDA   Well, the man said that's the way it is. Till they work themselves in, y'know.

They move through the wall-line into the kitchen.

WILLY   I hope we didn't get stuck on that machine.

LINDA   They got the biggest ads of any of them!

WILLY   I know, it's a fine machine. What else?

LINDA   Well, there's nine-sixty for the washing machine. And for the vacuum cleaner there's three and a half due on the fifteenth. Then the roof, you got twenty-one dollars remaining.

WILLY   It don't leak, does it?

LINDA   No, they did a wonderful job. Then you owe Frank for the carburetor.

WILLY   I'm not going to pay that man! That goddam Chevrolet, they ought to prohibit the manufacture of that car!

LINDA   Well, you owe him three and a half. And odds and ends, comes to around a hundred and twenty dollars by the fifteenth.

WILLY   A hundred and twenty dollars! My God, if business don't pick up I don't know what I'm gonna do!

LINDA   Well, next week you'll do better.

WILLY   Oh, I'll knock 'em dead next week. I'll go to Hartford. I'm very well liked in Hartford. You know, the trouble is, Linda, people don't seem to take to me.

They move onto the forestage.

LINDA   Oh, don't be foolish.

WILLY   I know it when I walk in. They seem to laugh at me.

LINDA   Why? Why would they laugh at you? Don't talk that way, Willy.

> WILLY *moves to the edge of the stage.* LINDA *goes into the kitchen and starts to darn stockings.*

WILLY   I don't know the reason for it, but they just pass me by. I'm not noticed.

LINDA   But you're doing wonderful, dear. You're making seventy to a hundred dollars a week.

WILLY   But I gotta be at it ten, twelve hours a day. Other men—I don't know—they do it easier. I don't know why—I can't stop myself—I talk too much. A man oughta come in with a few words. One thing about Charley. He's a man of few words, and they respect him.

LINDA   You don't talk too much, you're just lively.

WILLY   [*smiling*]   Well, I figure, what the hell, life is short, a couple of jokes. [*To himself*] I joke too much! [*The smile goes.*]

LINDA   Why? You're—

WILLY   I'm fat. I'm very—foolish to look at, Linda. I didn't tell you, but Christmas time I happened to be calling on F. H. Stewarts, and a salesman I know, as I was going in to see the buyer I heard him say something about—walrus. And I—I cracked him right across the face. I won't take that. I simply will not take that. But they do laugh at me. I know that.

LINDA   Darling . . .

WILLY   I gotta overcome it. I know I gotta overcome it. I'm not dressing to advantage, maybe.

LINDA   Willy, darling, you're the handsomest man in the world—

WILLY   Oh, no, Linda.

LINDA   To me you are. [*Slight pause.*] The handsomest.

> *From the darkness is heard the laughter of a woman.* WILLY *doesn't turn to it, but it continues through* LINDA's *lines.*

LINDA   And the boys, Willy. Few men are idolized by their children the way you are.

> *Music is heard as behind a scrim, to the left of the house,* THE WOMAN, *dimly seen, is dressing.*

WILLY   [*with great feeling*]   You're the best there is, Linda, you're a pal, you know that? On the road—on the road I want to grab you sometimes and just kiss the life outa you.

> *The laughter is loud now, and he moves into a brightening area at the left, where* THE WOMAN *has come from behind the scrim and is standing, putting on her hat, looking into a "mirror" and laughing.*

WILLY   'Cause I get so lonely—especially when business is bad and there's nobody to talk to. I get the feeling that I'll never sell anything again, that I won't make a living for you, or a business, a business for the boys. [*He talks through* THE WOMAN'*s subsiding laughter;* THE WOMAN *primps at the "mirror."*] There's so much I want to make for—

THE WOMAN   Me? You didn't make me, Willy. I picked you.

WILLY [*pleased*]   You picked me?

THE WOMAN [*who is quite proper-looking,* WILLY'*s age*]   I did. I've been sitting at that desk watching all the salesmen go by, day in, day out. But you've got such a sense of humor, and we do have a good time together, don't we?

WILLY   Sure, sure. [*He takes her in his arms.*] Why do you have to go now?

THE WOMAN   It's two o'clock . . .

WILLY   No, come on in! [*He pulls her.*]

THE WOMAN   . . . my sisters'll be scandalized. When'll you be back?

WILLY   Oh, two weeks about. Will you come up again?

THE WOMAN   Sure thing. You do make me laugh. It's good for me. [*She squeezes his arm, kisses him.*] And I think you're a wonderful man.

WILLY   You picked me, heh?

THE WOMAN   Sure. Because you're so sweet. And such a kidder.

WILLY   Well, I'll see you next time I'm in Boston.

THE WOMAN   I'll put you right through to the buyers.

WILLY [*slapping her bottom*]   Right. Well, bottoms up!

THE WOMAN [*slaps him gently and laughs*]   You just kill me, Willy. [*He suddenly grabs her and kisses her roughly.*] You kill me. And thanks for the stockings. I love a lot of stockings. Well, good night.

WILLY   Good night. And keep your pores open!

THE WOMAN   Oh, Willy!

> THE WOMAN *bursts out laughing, and* LINDA'*s laughter blends in.* THE WOMAN *disappears into the dark. Now the area at the kitchen table brightens.* LINDA *is sitting where she was at the kitchen table, but now is mending a pair of her silk stockings.*

LINDA   You are, Willy. The handsomest man. You've got no reason to feel that—

WILLY [*coming out of* THE WOMAN'*s dimming area and going over to* LINDA]   I'll make it all up to you, Linda, I'll—

LINDA   There's nothing to make up, dear. You're doing fine, better than—

WILLY [*noticing her mending*]   What's that?

LINDA   Just mending my stockings. They're so expensive—

WILLY [*angrily, taking them from her*]   I won't have you mending stockings in this house! Now throw them out!

> LINDA *puts the stockings in her pocket.*

BERNARD [*entering on the run*]   Where is he? If he doesn't study!

WILLY [*moving to the forestage, with great agitation*]   You'll give
   him the answers!
BERNARD   I do, but I can't on a Regents! That's a state exam! They're
   liable to arrest me!
WILLY   Where is he? I'll whip him, I'll whip him!
LINDA   And he'd better give back that football, Willy, it's not nice.
WILLY   Biff! Where is he? Why is he taking everything?
LINDA   He's too rough with the girls, Willy. All the mothers are
   afraid of him!
WILLY   I'll whip him!
BERNARD   He's driving the car without a license!

   THE WOMAN'*s laugh is heard.*

WILLY   Shut up!
LINDA   All the mothers—
WILLY   Shut up!
BERNARD [*backing quietly away and out*]   Mr. Birnbaum says he's
   stuck up.
WILLY   Get outa here!
BERNARD   If he doesn't buckle down he'll flunk math! [*He goes off.*]
LINDA   He's right, Willy, you've gotta—
WILLY [*exploding at her*]   There's nothing the matter with him!
   You want him to be a worm like Bernard? He's got spirit, per-
   sonality . . .

   As he speaks, LINDA, *almost in tears, exits into the living room.*
   WILLY *is alone in the kitchen, wilting and staring. The leaves
   are gone. It is night again, and the apartment houses look
   down from behind.*

WILLY   Loaded with it. Loaded! What is he stealing? He's giving it
   back, isn't he? Why is he stealing? What did I tell him? I never in
   my life told him anything but decent things.

   HAPPY *in pajamas has come down the stairs;* WILLY *suddenly
   becomes aware of* HAPPY'*s presence.*

HAPPY   Let's go now, come on.
WILLY [*sitting down at the kitchen table*]   Huh! Why did she have
   to wax the floors herself? Every time she waxes the floors she keels
   over. She knows that!
HAPPY   Shh! Take it easy. What brought you back tonight?
WILLY   I got an awful scare. Nearly hit a kid in Yonkers. God! Why
   didn't I go to Alaska with my brother Ben that time! Ben! That
   man was a genius, that man was success incarnate! What a mistake!
   He begged me to go.
HAPPY   Well, there's no use in—
WILLY   You guys! There was a man started with the clothes on his
   back and ended up with diamond mines!
HAPPY   Boy, someday I'd like to know how he did it.

WILLY   What's the mystery? The man knew what he wanted and went out and got it! Walked into a jungle, and comes out, the age of twenty-one, and he's rich! The world is an oyster, but you don't crack it open on a mattress!

HAPPY   Pop, I told you I'm gonna retire you for life.

WILLY   You'll retire me for life on seventy goddam dollars a week? And your women and your car and your apartment, and you'll retire me for life! Christ's sake, I couldn't get past Yonkers today! Where are you guys, where are you? The woods are burning! I can't drive a car!

> CHARLEY *has appeared in the doorway. He is a large man, slow of speech, laconic, immovable. In all he says, despite what he says, there is pity, and, now, trepidation. He has a robe over pajamas, slippers on his feet. He enters the kitchen.*

CHARLEY   Everything all right?

HAPPY   Yeah, Charley, everything's . . .

WILLY   What's the matter?

CHARLEY   I heard some noise. I thought something happened. Can't we do something about the walls? You sneeze in here, and in my house hats blow off.

HAPPY   Let's go to bed, Dad. Come on.

> CHARLEY *signals to* HAPPY *to go.*

WILLY   You go ahead, I'm not tired at the moment.

HAPPY   [*to* WILLY]   Take it easy, huh? [*He exits.*]

WILLY   What're you doin' up?

CHARLEY   [*sitting down at the kitchen table opposite Willy*]   Couldn't sleep good. I had a heartburn.

WILLY   Well, you don't know how to eat.

CHARLEY   I eat with my mouth.

WILLY   No, you're ignorant. You gotta know about vitamins and things like that.

CHARLEY   Come on, let's shoot. Tire you out a little.

WILLY   [*hesitantly*]   All right. You got cards?

CHARLEY   [*taking a deck from his pocket*]   Yeah, I got them. Someplace. What is it with those vitamins?

WILLY   [*dealing*]   They build up your bones. Chemistry.

CHARLEY   Yeah, but there's no bones in a heartburn.

WILLY   What are you talkin' about? Do you know the first thing about it?

CHARLEY   Don't get insulted.

WILLY   Don't talk about something you don't know anything about.

> *They are playing. Pause.*

CHARLEY   What're you doin' home?

WILLY   A little trouble with the car.

CHARLEY   Oh. [*Pause.*] I'd like to take a trip to California.

WILLY   Don't say.

CHARLEY   You want a job?

WILLY   I got a job, I told you that. [*After a slight pause*] What the hell are you offering me a job for?

CHARLEY   Don't get insulted.

WILLY   Don't insult me.

CHARLEY   I don't see no sense in it. You don't have to go on this way.

WILLY   I got a good job. [*Slight pause.*] What do you keep comin' in here for?

CHARLEY   You want me to go?

WILLY   [*after a pause, withering*]   I can't understand it. He's going back to Texas again. What the hell is that?

CHARLEY   Let him go.

WILLY   I got nothin' to give him, Charley, I'm clean, I'm clean.

CHARLEY   He won't starve. None a them starve. Forget about him.

WILLY   Then what have I got to remember?

CHARLEY   You take it too hard. To hell with it. When a deposit bottle is broken you don't get your nickel back.

WILLY   That's easy enough for you to say.

CHARLEY   That ain't easy for me to say.

WILLY   Did you see the ceiling I put up in the living room?

CHARLEY   Yeah, that's a piece of work. To put up a ceiling is a mystery to me. How do you do it?

WILLY   What's the difference?

CHARLEY   Well, talk about it.

WILLY   You gonna put up a ceiling?

CHARLEY   How could I put up a ceiling?

WILLY   Then what the hell are you bothering me for?

CHARLEY   You're insulted again.

WILLY   A man who can't handle tools is not a man. You're disgusting.

CHARLEY   Don't call me disgusting, Willy.

> UNCLE BEN, *carrying a valise and an umbrella, enters the forestage from around the right corner of the house. He is a stolid man, in his sixties, with a mustache and an authoritative air. He is utterly certain of his destiny, and there is an aura of far places about him. He enters exactly as* WILLY *speaks.*

WILLY   I'm getting awfully tired, Ben.

> BEN'*s music is heard.* BEN *looks around at everything.*

CHARLEY   Good, keep playing; you'll sleep better. Did you call me Ben?

> BEN *looks at his watch.*

WILLY   That's funny. For a second there you reminded me of my brother Ben.

BEN   I only have a few minutes. [*He strolls, inspecting the place.*

WILLY *and* CHARLEY *continue playing.*]

CHARLEY   You never heard from him again, heh? Since that time?

WILLY   Didn't Linda tell you? Couple of weeks ago we got a letter from his wife in Africa. He died.

CHARLEY   That so.

BEN [*chuckling*]   So this is Brooklyn, eh?

CHARLEY   Maybe you're in for some of his money.

WILLY   Naa, he had seven sons. There's just one opportunity I had with that man . . .

BEN   I must make a train, William. There are several properties I'm looking at in Alaska.

WILLY   Sure, sure! If I'd gone with him to Alaska that time, everything would've been totally different.

CHARLEY   Go on, you'd froze to death up there.

WILLY   What're you talking about?

BEN   Opportunity is tremendous in Alaska, William. Surprised you're not up there.

WILLY   Sure, tremendous.

CHARLEY   Heh?

WILLY   There was the only man I ever met who knew the answers.

CHARLEY   Who?

BEN   How are you all?

WILLY [*taking a pot, smiling*]   Fine, fine.

CHARLEY   Pretty sharp tonight.

BEN   Is Mother living with you?

WILLY   No, she died a long time ago.

CHARLEY   Who?

BEN   That's too bad. Fine specimen of a lady, Mother.

WILLY [*to* CHARLEY]   Heh?

BEN   I'd hoped to see the old girl.

CHARLEY   Who died?

BEN   Heard anything from Father, have you?

WILLY [*unnerved*]   What do you mean, who died?

CHARLEY [*taking a pot*]   What're you talkin' about?

BEN [*looking at his watch*]   William, it's half-past eight!

WILLY [*as though to dispel his confusion he angrily stops* CHARLEY'S *hand*]   That's my build!

CHARLEY   I put the ace—

WILLY   If you don't know how to play the game I'm not gonna throw my money away on you!

CHARLEY [*rising*]   It was my ace, for God's sake!

WILLY   I'm through, I'm through!

BEN   When did Mother die?

WILLY   Long ago. Since the beginning you never knew how to play cards.

CHARLEY [*picks up the cards and goes to the door*]   All right! Next time I'll bring a deck with five aces.

WILLY   I don't play that kind of game!

CHARLEY [*turning to him*].   You ought to be ashamed of yourself!

WILLY   Yeah?

CHARLEY   Yeah! [*He goes out.*]

WILLY [*slamming the door after him*]   Ignoramus!

BEN [*as* WILLY *comes toward him through the wall-line of the kitchen*]
So you're William.

WILLY [*shaking* BEN'*s hand*]   Ben! I've been waiting for you so long!
What's the answer? How did you do it?

BEN   Oh, there's a story in that.

LINDA *enters the forestage, as of old, carrying the wash basket.*

LINDA   Is this Ben?

BEN [*gallantly*]   How do you do, my dear.

LINDA   Where've you been all these years. Willy's always wondered
why you—

WILLY [*pulling* BEN *away from her impatiently*]   Where is Dad?
Didn't you follow him? How did you get started?

BEN   Well, I don't know how much you remember.

WILLY   Well, I was just a baby, of course, only three or four years
old—

BEN   Three years and eleven months.

WILLY   What a memory, Ben!

BEN   I have many enterprises, William, and I have never kept books.

WILLY   I remember I was sitting under the wagon in—was it
Nebraska?

BEN   It was South Dakota, and I gave you a bunch of wild flowers.

WILLY   I remember you walking away down some open road.

BEN [*laughing*]   I was going to find Father in Alaska.

WILLY   Where is he?

BEN   At that age I had a very faulty view of geography, William. I
discovered after a few days that I was heading due south, so instead of Alaska, I ended up in Africa.

LINDA   Africa!

WILLY   The Gold Coast!

BEN   Principally diamond mines.

LINDA   Diamond mines!

BEN   Yes, my dear. But I've only a few minutes—

WILLY   No! Boys! Boys! [YOUNG BIFF *and* HAPPY *appear.*] Listen to
this. This is your Uncle Ben, a great man! Tell my boys, Ben!

BEN   Why, boys, when I was seventeen I walked into the jungle,
and when I was twenty-one I walked out. [*He laughs.*] And by
God I was rich.

WILLY [*to the boys*]   You see what I been talking about? The greatest
things can happen!

BEN [*glancing at his watch*]   I have an appointment in Ketchikan
Tuesday week.

WILLY   No, Ben! Please tell about Dad. I want my boys to hear. I
want them to know the kind of stock they spring from. All I remember is a man with a big beard, and I was in Mamma's lap,
sitting around a fire, and some kind of high music.

BEN   His flute. He played the flute.

WILLY   Sure, the flute, that's right!

New music is heard, a high, rollicking tune.

BEN   Father was a very great and a very wild-hearted man. We would start in Boston, and he'd toss the whole family into the wagon, and then he'd drive the team right across the country; through Ohio, and Indiana, Michigan, Illinois, and all the Western states. And we'd stop in the towns and sell the flutes that he'd made on the way. Great inventor, Father. With one gadget he made more in a week than a man like you could make in a lifetime.

WILLY   That's just the way I'm bringing them up, Ben—rugged, well liked, all-around.

BEN   Yeah? [*To* BIFF] Hit that, boy—hard as you can. [*He pounds his stomach.*]

BIFF   Oh, no, sir!

BEN   [*taking boxing stance*]   Come on, get to me! [*He laughs.*]

WILLY   Go to it, Biff! Go ahead, show him!

BIFF   Okay! [*He cocks his fists and starts in.*]

LINDA   [*to* WILLY]   Why must he fight, dear?

BEN   [*sparring with* BIFF]   Good boy! Good boy!

WILLY   How's that, Ben, heh?

HAPPY   Give him a left, Biff!

LINDA   Why are you fighting?

BEN   Good boy! [*Suddenly comes in, trips* BIFF, *and stands over him, the point of his umbrella poised over* BIFF'*s eye.*]

LINDA   Look out, Biff!

BIFF   Gee!

BEN   [*patting* BIFF'*s knee*]   Never fight fair with a stranger, boy. You'll never get out of the jungle that way. [*Taking* LINDA'*s hand and bowing*] It was an honor and a pleasure to meet you, Linda.

LINDA   [*withdrawing her hand coldly, frightened*]   Have a nice—trip.

BEN   [*to* WILLY]   And good luck with your—what do you do?

WILLY   Selling.

BEN   Yes. Well . . . [*He raises his hand in farewell to all.*]

WILLY   No, Ben, I don't want you to think . . . [*He takes* BEN'*s arm to show him.*] It's Brooklyn, I know, but we hunt too.

BEN   Really, now.

WILLY   Oh, sure, there's snakes and rabbits and—that's why I moved out here. Why, Biff can fell any one of these trees in no time! Boys! Go right over to where they're building the apartment house and get some sand. We're gonna rebuild the entire front stoop right now! Watch this, Ben!

BIFF   Yes, sir! On the double, Hap!

HAPPY   [*as he and* BIFF *run off*]   I lost weight, Pop, you notice?

CHARLEY *enters in knickers, even before the boys are gone.*

CHARLEY   Listen, if they steal any more from that building the watch-man'll put the cops on them!

LINDA   [*to* WILLY]   Don't let Biff . . .

BEN *laughs lustily.*

WILLY   You shoulda seen the lumber they brought home last week. At least a dozen six-by-tens worth all kinds of money.

CHARLEY   Listen, if that watchman—

WILLY   I gave them hell, understand. But I got a couple of fearless characters there.

CHARLEY   Willy, the jails are full of fearless characters.

BEN [*clapping* WILLY *on the back, with a laugh at* CHARLEY]   And the stock exchange, friend!

WILLY [*joining in* BEN's *laughter*]   Where are the rest of your pants?

CHARLEY   My wife bought them.

WILLY   Now all you need is a golf club and you can go upstairs and go to sleep. [*To* BEN] Great athlete! Between him and his son Bernard they can't hammer a nail!

BERNARD [*rushing in*]   The watchman's chasing Biff!

WILLY [*angrily*]   Shut up! He's not stealing anything!

LINDA [*alarmed, hurrying off left*]   Where is he? Biff, dear! [*She exits.*]

WILLY [*moving toward the left, away from* BEN]   There's nothing wrong. What's the matter with you?

BEN   Nervy boy. Good!

WILLY [*laughing*]   Oh, nerves of iron, that Biff!

CHARLEY   Don't know what it is. My New England man comes back and he's bleedin', they murdered him up there.

WILLY   It's contacts, Charley, I got important contacts!

CHARLEY [*sarcastically*]   Glad to hear it, Willy. Come in later, we'll shoot a little casino. I'll take some of your Portland money. [*He laughs at* WILLY *and exits.*]

WILLY [*turning to* BEN]   Business is bad, it's murderous. But not for me, of course.

BEN   I'll stop by on my way back to Africa.

WILLY [*longingly*]   Can't you stay a few days? You're just what I need, Ben, because I—I have a fine position here, but I—well, Dad left when I was such a baby and I never had a chance to talk to him and I still feel—kind of temporary about myself.

BEN   I'll be late for my train.

They are at opposite ends of the stage.

WILLY   Ben, my boys—can't we talk? They'd go into the jaws of hell for me, see, but I—

BEN   William, you're being first-rate with your boys. Outstanding, manly chaps!

WILLY [*hanging on to his words*]   Oh, Ben, that's good to hear! Because sometimes I'm afraid that I'm not teaching them the right kind of—Ben, how should I teach them?

BEN [*giving great weight to each word, and with a certain vicious audacity*]   William, when I walked into the jungle, I was seventeen. When I walked out I was twenty-one. And, by God, I was rich! [*He goes off into darkness around the right corner of the house.*]

WILLY   . . . was rich! That's just the spirit I want to imbue them with! To walk into a jungle! I was right! I was right! I was right!

> BEN *is gone, but* WILLY *is still speaking to him as* LINDA, *in nightgown and robe, enters the kitchen, glances around for* WILLY, *then goes to the door of the house, looks out and sees him. Comes down to his left. He looks at her.*

LINDA   Willy, dear? Willy?

WILLY   I was right!

LINDA   Did you have some cheese? [*He can't answer.*] It's very late, darling. Come to bed, heh?

WILLY [*looking straight up*]   Gotta break your neck to see a star in this yard.

LINDA   You coming in?

WILLY   Whatever happened to that diamond watch fob? Remember? When Ben came from Africa that time? Didn't he give me a watch fob with a diamond in it?

LINDA   You pawned it, dear. Twelve, thirteen years ago. For Biff's radio correspondence course.

WILLY   Gee, that was a beautiful thing. I'll take a walk.

LINDA   But you're in your slippers.

WILLY [*starting to go around the house at the left*]   I was right! I was! [*Half to* LINDA, *as he goes, shaking his head*] What a man! There was a man worth talking to. I was right!

LINDA [*calling after* WILLY]   But in your slippers, Willy!

> WILLY *is almost gone when* BIFF, *in his pajamas, comes down the stairs and enters the kitchen.*

BIFF   What is he doing out there?

LINDA   Sh!

BIFF   God Almighty, Mom, how long has he been doing this?

LINDA   Don't, he'll hear you.

BIFF   What the hell is the matter with him?

LINDA   It'll pass by morning.

BIFF   Shouldn't we do anything?

LINDA   Oh, my dear, you should do a lot of things, but there's nothing to do, so go to sleep.

> HAPPY *comes down the stair and sits on the steps.*

HAPPY   I never heard him so loud, Mom.

LINDA   Well, come around more often; you'll hear him. [*She sits down at the table and mends the lining of* WILLY'S *jacket.*]

BIFF   Why didn't you ever write me about this, Mom?

LINDA   How would I write to you? For over three months you had no address.

BIFF   I was on the move. But you know I thought of you all the time. You know that, don't you, pal?

LINDA   I know, dear, I know. But he likes to have a letter. Just to know that there's still a possibility for better things.

BIFF   He's not like this all the time, is he?

LINDA   It's when you come home he's always the worst.

BIFF   When I come home?

LINDA   When you write you're coming, he's all smiles, and talks about the future, and—he's just wonderful. And then the closer you seem to come, the more shaky he gets, and then, by the time you get here, he's arguing, and he seems angry at you. I think it's just that maybe he can't bring himself to—to open up to you. Why are you so hateful to each other? Why is that?

BIFF [*evasively*]   I'm not hateful, Mom.

LINDA   But you no sooner come in the door than you're fighting!

BIFF   I don't know why. I mean to change. I'm tryin', Mom, you understand?

LINDA   Are you home to stay now?

BIFF   I don't know. I want to look around, see what's doin'.

LINDA   Biff, you can't look around all your life, can you?

BIFF   I just can't take hold, Mom. I can't take hold of some kind of a life.

LINDA   Biff, a man is not a bird, to come and go with the springtime.

BIFF   Your hair . . . [*He touches her hair*]. Your hair got so gray.

LINDA   Oh, it's been gray since you were in high school. I just stopped dyeing it, that's all.

BIFF   Dye it again, will ya? I don't want my pal looking old. [*He smiles.*]

LINDA   You're such a boy! You think you can go away for a year and . . . You've got to get it into your head now that one day you'll knock on this door and there'll be strange people here—

BIFF   What are you talking about? You're not even sixty, Mom.

LINDA   But what about your father?

BIFF [*lamely*]   Well, I meant him too.

HAPPY   He admires Pop.

LINDA   Biff, dear, if you don't have any feeling for him, then you can't have any feeling for me.

BIFF   Sure I can, Mom.

LINDA   No. You can't just come to see me, because I love him. [*With a threat, but only a threat, of tears*] He's the dearest man in the world to me, and I won't have anyone making him feel unwanted and low and blue. You've got to make up your mind now, darling, there's no leeway any more. Either he's your father and you pay him that respect, or else you're not to come here. I know he's not easy to get along with—nobody knows that better than me—but . . .

WILLY [*from the left, with a laugh*]   Hey, hey, Biffo!

BIFF [*starting to go out after* WILLY]   What the hell is the matter with him? [HAPPY *stops him.*]

LINDA   Don't—don't go near him!

BIFF   Stop making excuses for him! He always, always wiped the floor with you. Never had an ounce of respect for you.

HAPPY   He's always had respect for—

BIFF   What the hell do you know about it?

HAPPY [*surlily*]   Just don't call him crazy!

BIFF   He's got no character— Charley wouldn't do this. Not in his own house—spewing out that vomit from his mind.

HAPPY   Charley never had to cope with what he's got to.

BIFF   People are worse off than Willy Loman. Believe me, I've seen them!

LINDA   Then make Charley your father, Biff. You can't do that, can you? I don't say he's a great man. Willy Loman never made a lot of money. His name was never in the paper. He's not the finest character that ever lived. But he's a human being, and a terrible thing is happening to him. So attention must be paid. He's not to be allowed to fall into his grave like an old dog. Attention, attention must be finally paid to such a person. You called him crazy—

BIFF   I didn't mean—

LINDA   No, a lot of people think he's lost his—balance. But you don't have to be very smart to know what his trouble is. The man is exhausted.

HAPPY   Sure!

LINDA   A small man can be just as exhausted as a great man. He works for a company thirty-six years this March, opens up un-heard-of territories to their trademark, and now in his old age they take his salary away.

HAPPY [*indignantly*]   I didn't know that, Mom.

LINDA   You never asked, my dear! Now that you get your spending money someplace else you don't trouble your mind with him.

HAPPY   But I gave you money last—

LINDA   Christmas time, fifty dollars! To fix the hot water it cost ninety-seven fifty! For five weeks he's been on straight commission, like a beginner, an unknown!

BIFF   Those ungrateful bastards!

LINDA   Are they any worse than his sons? When he brought them business, when he was young, they were glad to see him. But now his old friends, the old buyers that loved him so and always found some order to hand him in a pinch—they're all dead, retired. He used to be able to make six, seven calls a day in Boston. Now he takes his valises out of the car and puts them back and takes them out again and he's exhausted. Instead of walking he talks now. He drives seven hundred miles, and when he gets there no one knows him any more, no one welcomes him. And what goes through a man's mind, driving seven hundred miles home without having earned a cent? Why shouldn't he talk to himself? Why? When he has to go to Charley and borrow fifty dollars a week and pretend to me that it's his pay? How long can that go on? How long? You see what I'm sitting here and waiting for? And you tell me he has no character? The man who never worked a day but for your benefit? When does he get the medal for that? Is this his reward— to turn around at the age of sixty-three and find his sons, who he loved better than his life, one a philandering bum—

HAPPY   Mom!

LINDA   That's what you are, my baby! [*To* BIFF] And you! What hap-pened to the love you had for him? You were such pals! How you used to talk to him on the phone every night! How lonely he was till he could come home to you!

BIFF   All right, Mom. I'll live here in my room, and I'll get a job. I'll keep away from him, that's all.

LINDA   No, Biff. You can't stay here and fight all the time.

BIFF   He threw me out of this house, remember that.

LINDA   Why did he do that? I never knew why.

BIFF   Because I know he's a fake and he doesn't like anybody around who knows!

LINDA   Why a fake? In what way? What do you mean?

BIFF   Just don't lay it all at my feet. It's between me and him—that's all I have to say. I'll chip in from now on. He'll settle for half my pay check. He'll be all right. I'm going to bed. [*He starts for the stairs.*]

LINDA   He won't be all right.

BIFF   [*turning on the stairs, furiously*]   I hate this city and I'll stay here. Now what do you want?

LINDA   He's dying, Biff.

HAPPY *turns quickly to her, shocked.*

BIFF   [*after a pause*]   Why is he dying?

LINDA   He's been trying to kill himself.

BIFF   [*with great horror*]   How?

LINDA   I live from day to day.

BIFF   What're you talking about?

LINDA   Remember I wrote you that he smashed up the car again? In February?

BIFF   Well?

LINDA   The insurance inspector came. He said that they have evidence. That all these accidents in the last year—weren't—weren't—accidents.

HAPPY   How can they tell that? That's a lie.

LINDA   It seems there's a woman . . . [*She takes a breath as*

(BIFF, *sharply but contained*]   What woman?

(LINDA, *simultaneously*] . . . and this woman . . .

LINDA   What?

BIFF   Nothing. Go ahead.

LINDA   What did you say?

BIFF   Nothing. I just said what woman?

HAPPY   What about her?

LINDA   Well, it seems she was walking down the road and saw his car. She says that he wasn't driving fast at all, and that he didn't skid. She says he came to that little bridge, and then deliberately smashed into the railing, and it was only the shallowness of the water that saved him.

BIFF   Oh, no, he probably just fell asleep again.

LINDA   I don't think he fell asleep.

BIFF   Why not?

LINDA   Last month . . . [*With great difficulty*]   Oh, boys, it's so hard to say a thing like this! He's just a big stupid man to you, but I tell you there's more good in him than in many other people. [*She chokes, wipes her eyes.*] I was looking for a fuse. The lights blew out, and I went down the cellar. And behind the fuse box—it happened to fall out—was a length of rubber pipe—just short.

HAPPY   No kidding?

LINDA   There's a little attachment on the end of it. I knew right away. And sure enough, on the bottom of the water heater there's a new little nipple on the gas pipe.

HAPPY [*angrily*]   That—jerk.

BIFF   Did you have it taken off?

LINDA   I'm—I'm ashamed to. How can I mention it to him? Every day I go down and take away that little rubber pipe. But, when he comes home, I put it back where it was. How can I insult him that way? I don't know what to do. I live from day to day, boys. I tell you, I know every thought in his mind. It sounds so old-fashioned and silly, but I tell you he put his whole life into you and you've turned your backs on him. [*She is bent over in the chair, weeping, her face in her hands.*] Biff, I swear to God! Biff, his life is in your hands!

HAPPY [*to* BIFF]   How do you like that damned fool!

BIFF [*kissing her*]   All right, pal, all right. It's all settled now. I've been remiss. I know that, Mom. But now I'll stay, and I swear to you, I'll apply myself. [*Kneeling in front of her, in a fever of self-reproach.*] It's just—you see, Mom, I don't fit in business. Not that I won't try. I'll try, and I'll make good.

HAPPY   Sure you will. The trouble with you in business was you never tried to please people.

BIFF   I know, I—

HAPPY   Like when you worked for Harrison's. Bob Harrison said you were tops, and then you go and do some damn fool thing like whistling whole songs in the elevator like a comedian.

BIFF [*against* HAPPY]   So what? I like to whistle sometimes.

HAPPY   You don't raise a guy to a responsible job who whistles in the elevator!

LINDA   Well, don't argue about it now.

HAPPY   Like when you'd go off and swim in the middle of the day instead of taking the line around.

BIFF [*his resentment rising*]   Well, don't you run off? You take off sometimes, don't you? On a nice summer day?

HAPPY   Yeah, but I cover myself!

LINDA   Boys!

HAPPY   If I'm going to take a fade the boss can call any number where I'm supposed to be and they'll swear to him that I just left. I'll tell you something that I hate to say, Biff, but in the business world some of them think you're crazy.

BIFF [*angered*]   Screw the business world!

HAPPY   All right, screw it! Great, but cover yourself!

LINDA   Hap, Hap!

BIFF   I don't care what they think! They've laughed at Dad for

years, and you know why? Because we don't belong in this nut-
house of a city! We should be mixing cement on some open plain,
or—or carpenters. A carpenter is allowed to whistle!

WILLY *walks in from the entrance of the house, at left.*

WILLY   Even your grandfather was better than a carpenter. [*Pause.
They watch him.*] You never grew up. Bernard does not whistle in
the elevator, I assure you.
BIFF [*as though to laugh* WILLY *out of it*]   Yeah, but you do, Pop.
WILLY   I never in my life whistled in an elevator! And who in the
business world thinks I'm crazy?
BIFF   I didn't mean it like that, Pop. Now don't make a whole thing
out of it, will ya?
WILLY   Go back to the West! Be a carpenter, a cowboy, enjoy
yourself!
LINDA   Willy, he was just saying—
WILLY   I heard what he said!
HAPPY [*trying to quiet* WILLY]   Hey, Pop, come on now . . .
WILLY [*continuing over* HAPPY's *line*]   They laugh at me, heh? Go to
Filene's, go to the Hub, go to Slattery's, Boston. Call out the name
Willy Loman and see what happens! Big shot!
BIFF   All right, Pop.
WILLY   Big!
BIFF   All right!
WILLY   Why do you always insult me?
BIFF   I didn't say a word. [*To* LINDA]   Did I say a word?
LINDA   He didn't say anything, Willy.
WILLY [*going to the doorway of the living room*]   All right, good
night, good night.
LINDA   Willy, dear, he just decided . . .
WILLY [*to* BIFF]   If you get tired hanging around tomorrow, paint the
ceiling I put up in the living room.
BIFF   I'm leaving early tomorrow.
HAPPY   He's going to see Bill Oliver, Pop.
WILLY [*interestedly*]   Oliver? For what?
BIFF [*with reserve, but trying, trying*]   He always said he'd stake me.
I'd like to go into business, so maybe I can take him up on it.
LINDA   Isn't that wonderful?
WILLY   Don't interrupt. What's wonderful about it? There's fifty men
in the City of New York who'd stake him. [*To* BIFF] Sporting goods?
BIFF   I guess so. I know something about it and—
WILLY   He knows something about it! You know sporting goods
better than Spalding, for God's sake! How much is he giving you?
BIFF   I don't know, I didn't even see him yet, but—
WILLY   Then what're you talkin' about?
BIFF [*getting angry*]   Well, all I said was I'm gonna see him, that's
all!
WILLY [*turning away*]   Ah, you're counting your chickens again.
BIFF [*starting left for the stairs*]   Oh, Jesus, I'm going to sleep!
WILLY [*calling after him*]   Don't curse in this house!

BIFF [*turning*]   Since when did you get so clean?

HAPPY [*trying to stop them*]   Wait a . . .

WILLY   Don't use that language to me! I won't have it!

HAPPY [*grabbing* BIFF, *shouts*]   Wait a minute! I got an idea. I got a feasible idea. Come here, Biff, let's talk this over now, let's talk some sense here. When I was down in Florida last time, I thought of a great idea to sell sporting goods. It just came back to me. You and I, Biff—we have a line, the Loman Line. We train a couple of weeks, and put on a couple of exhibitions, see?

WILLY   That's an idea!

HAPPY   Wait! We form two basketball teams, see? Two water polo teams. We play each other. It's a million dollars' worth of publicity. Two brothers, see? The Loman Brothers. Displays in the Royal Palms—all the hotels. And banners over the ring and the basketball court: "Loman Brothers." Baby, we could sell sporting goods!

WILLY   That is a one-million-dollar idea!

LINDA   Marvelous!

BIFF   I'm in great shape as far as that's concerned.

HAPPY   And the beauty of it is, Biff, it wouldn't be like a business. We'd be out playin' ball again . . .

BIFF [*enthused*]   Yeah, that's . . .

WILLY   Million-dollar . . .

HAPPY   And you wouldn't get fed up with it, Biff. It'd be the family again. There'd be the old honor, and comradeship, and if you wanted to go off for a swim or somethin'—well, you'd do it! Without some smart cooky gettin' up ahead of you!

WILLY   Lick the world! You guys together could absolutely lick the civilized world.

BIFF   I'll see Oliver tomorrow. Hap, if we could work that out . . .

LINDA   Maybe things are beginning to—

WILLY [*wildly enthused, to* LINDA]   Stop interrupting! [*To* BIFF] But don't wear sport jacket and slacks when you see Oliver.

BIFF   No, I'll—

WILLY   A business suit, and talk as little as possible, and don't crack any jokes.

BIFF   He did like me. Always liked me.

LINDA   He loved you!

WILLY [*to* LINDA]   Will you stop! [*To* BIFF] Walk in very serious. You are not applying for a boy's job. Money is to pass. Be quiet, fine, and serious. Everybody likes a kidder, but nobody lends him money.

HAPPY   I'll try to get some myself, Biff. I'm sure I can.

WILLY   I see great things for you kids, I think your troubles are over. But remember, start big and you'll end big. Ask for fifteen. How much you gonna ask for?

BIFF   Gee, I don't know—

WILLY   And don't say "Gee." "Gee" is a boy's word. A man walking in for fifteen thousand dollars does not say "Gee!"

BIFF   Ten, I think, would be top though.

WILLY   Don't be so modest. You always started too low. Walk in with a big laugh. Don't look worried. Start off with a couple of your good stories to lighten things up. It's not what you say, it's how you say it—because personality always wins the day.

LINDA   Oliver always thought the highest of him—

WILLY   Will you let me talk?

BIFF   Don't yell at her, Pop, will ya?

WILLY [*angrily*]   I was talking, wasn't I?

BIFF   I don't like you yelling at her all the time, and I'm tellin' you, that's all.

WILLY   What're you, takin' over this house?

LINDA   Willy—

WILLY [*turning on her*]   Don't take his side all the time, goddammit!

BIFF [*furiously*]   Stop yelling at her!

WILLY [*suddenly pulling on his cheek, beaten down, guilt ridden*] Give my best to Bill Oliver—he may remember me. [*He exits through the living room doorway.*]

LINDA [*her voice subdued*]   What'd you have to start that for? [BIFF *turns away.*] You see how sweet he was as soon as you talked hopefully? [*She goes over to* BIFF.] Come up and say good night to him. Don't let him go to bed that way.

HAPPY   Come on, Biff, let's buck him up.

LINDA   Please, dear. Just say good night. It takes so little to make him happy. Come. [*She goes through the living room doorway, calling upstairs from within the living room*] Your pajamas are hanging in the bathroom, Willy!

HAPPY [*looking toward where* LINDA *went out*]   What a woman! They broke the mold when they made her. You know that, Biff?

BIFF   He's off salary. My God, working on commission!

HAPPY   Well, let's face it: he's no hot-shot selling man. Except that sometimes, you have to admit, he's a sweet personality.

BIFF [*deciding*]   Lend me ten bucks, will ya? I want to buy some new ties.

HAPPY   I'll take you to a place I know. Beautiful stuff. Wear one of my striped shirts tomorrow.

BIFF   She got gray. Mom got awful old. Gee, I'm gonna go in to Oliver tomorrow and knock him for a—

HAPPY   Come on up. Tell that to Dad. Let's give him a whirl. Come on.

BIFF [*steamed up*]   You know, with ten thousand bucks, boy!

HAPPY [*as they go into the living room*]   That's the talk, Biff, that's the first time I've heard the old confidence out of you! [*From within the living room, fading off*] You're gonna live with me, kid, and any babe you want just say the word . . . [*The last lines are hardly heard. They are mounting the stairs to their parents' bedroom.*]

LINDA [*entering her bedroom and addressing* WILLY, *who is in the bathroom. She is straightening the bed for him*]   Can you do anything about the shower? It drips.

WILLY [*from the bathroom*]   All of a sudden everything falls to pieces! Goddam plumbing, oughta be sued, those people. I hardly finished putting it in and the thing . . . [*His words rumble off.*]

LINDA   I'm just wondering if Oliver will remember him. You think he might?

WILLY [*coming out of the bathroom in his pajamas*]   Remember him? What's the matter with you, you crazy? If he'd've stayed with Oliver he'd be on top by now! Wait'll Oliver gets a look at him. You don't know the average caliber any more. The average young man today—[*he is getting into bed*]—is got a caliber of zero. Greatest thing in the world for him was to bum around.

> BIFF *and* HAPPY *enter the bedroom. Slight pause.*

WILLY [*stops short, looking at* BIFF]   Glad to hear it, boy.

HAPPY   He wanted to say good night to you, sport.

WILLY [*to* BIFF]   Yeah. Knock him dead, boy. What'd you want to tell me?

BIFF   Just take it easy, Pop. Good night. [*He turns to go.*]

WILLY [*unable to resist*]   And if anything falls off the desk while you're talking to him—like a package or something—don't you pick it up. They have office boys for that.

LINDA   I'll make a big breakfast—

WILLY   Will you let me finish? [*To* BIFF]   Tell him you were in the business in the West. Not farm work.

BIFF   All right, Dad.

LINDA   I think everything—

WILLY [*going right through her speech*]   And don't undersell yourself. No less than fifteen thousand dollars.

BIFF [*unable to bear him*]   Okay. Good night, Mom. [*He starts moving.*]

WILLY   Because you got a greatness in you, Biff, remember that. You got all kinds a greatness . . . [*He lies back, exhausted.* BIFF *walks out.*]

LINDA [*calling after* BIFF]   Sleep well, darling!

HAPPY   I'm gonna get married, Mom. I wanted to tell you.

LINDA   Go to sleep, dear.

HAPPY [*going*]   I just wanted to tell you.

WILLY   Keep up the good work. [HAPPY *exits.*] God . . . remember that Ebbets Field[4] game? The championship of the city?

LINDA   Just rest. Should I sing to you?

WILLY   Yeah. Sing to me. [LINDA *hums a soft lullaby.*] When that team came out—he was the tallest, remember?

LINDA   Oh, yes. And in gold.

> BIFF *enters the darkened kitchen, takes a cigarette, and leaves the house. He comes downstage into a golden pool of light. He smokes, staring at the night.*

WILLY   Like a young god. Hercules—something like that. And the sun all around him. Remember how he waved to me? Right up from the field, with the representatives of three colleges standing by? And the buyers I brought, and the cheers when he came out— Loman, Loman, Loman! God Almighty, he'll be great yet. A star like that, magnificent, can never really fade away!

4. A Brooklyn sports stadium named after Charles H. Ebbets (1859–1925) and torn down in 1960.

The light on WILLY *is fading. The gas heater begins to glow through the kitchen wall, near the stairs, a blue flame beneath red coils.*

LINDA [*timidly*]   Willy dear, what has he got against you?
WILLY   I'm so tired. Don't talk any more.

BIFF *slowly returns to the kitchen. He stops, stares toward the heater.*

LINDA   Will you ask Howard to let you work in New York?
WILLY   First thing in the morning. Everything'll be all right.

BIFF *reaches behind the heater and draws out a length of rubber tubing. He is horrified and turns his head toward* WILLY'S *room, still dimly lit, from which the strains of* LINDA'S *desperate but monotonous humming rise.*

WILLY [*staring through the window into the moonlight*]   Gee, look at the moon moving between the buildings!

BIFF *wraps the tubing around his hand and quickly goes up the stairs.*

CURTAIN

Act 2

Music is heard, gay and bright. The curtain rises as the music fades away. WILLY, *in shirt sleeves, is sitting at the kitchen table, sipping coffee, his hat in his lap.* LINDA *is filling his cup when she can.*

WILLY   Wonderful coffee. Meal in itself.
LINDA   Can I make you some eggs?
WILLY   No. Take a breath.
LINDA   You look so rested, dear.
WILLY   I slept like a dead one. First time in months. Imagine, sleeping till ten on a Tuesday morning. Boys left nice and early, heh?
LINDA   They were out of here by eight o'clock.
WILLY   Good work!
LINDA   It was so thrilling to see them leaving together. I can't get over the shaving lotion in this house!
WILLY [*smiling*]   Mmm—
LINDA   Biff was very changed this morning. His whole attitude seemed to be hopeful. He couldn't wait to get downtown to see Oliver.
WILLY   He's heading for a change. There's no question, there simply are certain men that take longer to get—solidified. How did he dress?

LINDA   His blue suit. He's so handsome in that suit. He could be a—anything in that suit!

WILLY *gets up from the table.* LINDA *holds his jacket for him.*

WILLY   There's no question, no question at all. Gee, on the way home tonight I'd like to buy some seeds.

LINDA   [*laughing*]   That'd be wonderful. But not enough sun gets back there. Nothing'll grow any more.

WILLY   You wait, kid, before it's all over we're gonna get a little place out in the country, and I'll raise some vegetables, a couple of chickens . . .

LINDA   You'll do it yet, dear.

WILLY *walks out of his jacket.* LINDA *follows him.*

WILLY   And they'll get married, and come for a weekend. I'd build a little guest house. 'Cause I got so many fine tools, all I'd need would be a little lumber and some peace of mind.

LINDA   [*joyfully*]   I sewed the lining . . .

WILLY   I could build two guest houses, so they'd both come. Did he decide how much he's going to ask Oliver for?

LINDA   [*getting him into the jacket*]   He didn't mention it, but I imagine ten or fifteen thousand. You going to talk to Howard today?

WILLY   Yeah. I'll put it to him straight and simple. He'll just have to take me off the road.

LINDA   And Willy, don't forget to ask for a little advance, because we've got the insurance premium. It's the grace period now.

WILLY   That's a hundred . . . ?

LINDA   A hundred and eight, sixty-eight. Because we're a little short again.

WILLY   Why are we short?

LINDA   Well, you had the motor job on the car . . .

WILLY   That goddam Studebaker!

LINDA   And you got one more payment on the refrigerator . . .

WILLY   But it just broke again!

LINDA   Well, it's old, dear.

WILLY   I told you we should've bought a well-advertised machine. Charley bought a General Electric and it's twenty years old and it's still good, that son-of-a-bitch.

LINDA   But, Willy—

WILLY   Whoever heard of a Hastings refrigerator? Once in my life I would like to own something outright before it's broken! I'm always in a race with the junkyard! I just finished paying for the car and it's on its last legs. The refrigerator consumes belts like a goddam maniac. They time those things. They time them so when you finally paid for them, they're used up.

LINDA   [*buttoning up his jacket as he unbuttons it*]   All told, about two hundred dollars would carry us, dear. But that includes the last payment on the mortgage. After this payment, Willy, the house belongs to us.

WILLY   It's twenty-five years!

LINDA   Biff was nine years old when we bought it.

WILLY   Well, that's a great thing. To weather a twenty-five-year mortgage is—

LINDA   It's an accomplishment.

WILLY   All the cement, the lumber, the reconstruction I put in this house! There ain't a crack to be found in it any more.

LINDA   Well, it served its purpose.

WILLY   What purpose? Some stranger'll come along, move in, and that's that. If only Biff would take this house, and raise a family . . . [*He starts to go.*] Good-by, I'm late.

LINDA   [*suddenly remembering*] Oh, I forgot! You're supposed to meet them for dinner.

WILLY   Me?

LINDA   At Frank's Chop House on Forty-eighth near Sixth Avenue.

WILLY   Is that so! How about you?

LINDA   No, just the three of you. They're gonna blow you to a big meal!

WILLY   Don't say! Who thought of that?

LINDA   Biff came to me this morning, Willy, and he said, "Tell Dad, we want to blow him to a big meal." Be there six o'clock. You and your two boys are going to have dinner.

WILLY   Gee whiz! That's really somethin'. I'm gonna knock Howard for a loop, kid. I'll get an advance, and I'll come home with a New York job. Goddammit, now I'm gonna do it!

LINDA   Oh, that's the spirit, Willy!

WILLY   I will never get behind a wheel the rest of my life!

LINDA   It's changing, Willy, I can feel it changing!

WILLY   Beyond a question. G'by, I'm late. [*He starts to go again.*]

LINDA   [*calling after him as she runs to the kitchen table for a handkerchief*] You got your glasses?

WILLY   [*feels for them, then comes back in*] Yeah, yeah, got my glasses.

LINDA   [*giving him the handkerchief*] And a handkerchief.

WILLY   Yeah, handkerchief.

LINDA   And your saccharin?

WILLY   Yeah, my saccharin.

LINDA   Be careful on the subway stairs.

She kisses him, and a silk stocking is seen hanging from her hand. WILLY *notices it.*

WILLY   Will you stop mending stockings? At least while I'm in the house. It gets me nervous. I can't tell you. Please.

LINDA *hides the stocking in her hand as she follows* WILLY *across the forestage in front of the house.*

LINDA   Remember, Frank's Chop House.

WILLY   [*passing the apron*] Maybe beets would grow out there.

LINDA   [*laughing*] But you tried so many times.

WILLY   Yeah. Well, don't work hard today. [*He disappears around the right corner of the house.*]

LINDA   Be careful!

As WILLY *vanishes,* LINDA *waves to him. Suddenly the phone rings. She runs across the stage and into the kitchen and lifts it.*

LINDA   Hello? Oh, Biff! I'm so glad you called, I just . . . Yes, sure, I just told him. Yes, he'll be there for dinner at six o'clock, I didn't forget. Listen, I was just dying to tell you. You know that little rubber pipe I told you about? That he connected to the gas heater? I finally decided to go down the cellar this morning and take it away and destroy it. But it's gone! Imagine? He took it away himself, it isn't there! [*She listens.*] When? Oh, then you took it. Oh—nothing, it's just that I'd hoped he'd taken it away himself. Oh, I'm not worried, darling, because this morning he left in such high spirits, it was like the old days! I'm not afraid any more. Did Mr. Oliver see you? . . . Well, you wait there then. And make a nice impression on him, darling. Just don't perspire too much before you see him. And have a nice time with Dad. He may have big news too! . . . That's right, a New York job. And be sweet to him tonight, dear. Be loving to him. Because he's only a little boat looking for a harbor. [*She is trembling with sorrow and joy.*] Oh, that's wonderful, Biff, you'll save his life. Thanks, darling. Just put your arm around him when he comes into the restaurant. Give him a smile. That's the boy . . . Good-by, dear. . . . You got your comb? . . . That's fine. Good-by, Biff dear.

In the middle of her speech, HOWARD WAGNER, *thirty-six, wheels on a small typewriter table on which is a wire-recording machine and proceeds to plug it in. This is on the left forestage. Light slowly fades on* LINDA *as it rises on* HOWARD. HOWARD *is intent on threading the machine and only glances over his shoulder as* WILLY *appears.*

WILLY   Pst! Pst!

HOWARD   Hello, Willy, come in.

WILLY   Like to have a little talk with you, Howard.

HOWARD   Sorry to keep you waiting. I'll be with you in a minute.

WILLY   What's that, Howard?

HOWARD   Didn't you ever see one of these? Wire recorder.

WILLY   Oh. Can we talk a minute?

HOWARD   Records things. Just got delivery yesterday. Been driving me crazy, the most terrific machine I ever saw in my life. I was up all night with it.

WILLY   What do you do with it?

HOWARD   I bought it for dictation, but you can do anything with it. Listen to this. I had it home last night. Listen to what I picked up. The first one is my daughter. Get this. [*He flicks the switch and "Roll out the Barrel" is heard being whistled.*] Listen to that kid whistle.

WILLY   That is lifelike, isn't it?

HOWARD   Seven years old. Get that tone.

WILLY   Ts, ts. Like to ask a little favor if you . . .

The whistling breaks off, and the voice of HOWARD's *daughter is heard.*

HIS DAUGHTER   "Now you, Daddy."

HOWARD   She's crazy for me! [*Again the same song is whistled.*] That's me! Ha! [*He winks.*]

WILLY   You're very good!

The whistling breaks off again. The machine runs silent for a moment.

HOWARD   Sh! Get this now, this is my son.

HIS SON   "The capital of Alabama is Montgomery; the capital of Arizona is Phoenix; the capital of Arkansas is Little Rock; the capital of California is Sacramento . . ." [*and on, and on.*]

HOWARD   [*holding up five fingers*]   Five years old. Willy!

WILLY   He'll make an announcer some day!

HIS SON   [*continuing*]   "The capital . . ."

HOWARD   Get that—alphabetical order! [*The machine breaks off suddenly.*] Wait a minute. The maid kicked the plug out.

WILLY   It certainly is a—

HOWARD   Sh, for God's sake!

HIS SON   "It's nine o'clock, Bulova watch time. So I have to go to sleep."

WILLY   That really is—

HOWARD   Wait a minute! The next is my wife.

They wait.

HOWARD'S VOICE   "Go on, say something." [*Pause.*] "Well, you gonna talk?"

HIS WIFE   "I can't think of anything."

HOWARD'S VOICE   "Well, talk—it's turning."

HIS WIFE   [*shyly, beaten*]   "Hello." [*Silence.*] "Oh, Howard, I can't talk into this . . ."

HOWARD   [*snapping the machine off*]   That was my wife.

WILLY   That is a wonderful machine. Can we—

HOWARD   I tell you, Willy, I'm gonna take my camera, and my bandsaw, and all my hobbies, and out they go. This is the most fascinating relaxation I ever found.

WILLY   I think I'll get one myself.

HOWARD   Sure, they're only a hundred and a half. You can't do without it. Supposing you wanna hear Jack Benny,[5] see? But you can't be at home at that hour. So you tell the maid to turn the radio on

5. Jack Benny (1894–1974), a vaudeville, radio, television, and motion picture star, hosted America's most popular radio show from 1932 to 1955.

when Jack Benny comes on, and this automatically goes on with the radio . . .

WILLY   And when you come home you . . .

HOWARD   You can come home twelve o'clock, one o'clock, any time you like, and you get yourself a Coke and sit yourself down, throw the switch, and there's Jack Benny's program in the middle of the night!

WILLY   I'm definitely going to get one. Because lots of time I'm on the road, and I think to myself, what I must be missing on the radio!

HOWARD   Don't you have a radio in the car?

WILLY   Well, yeah, but who ever thinks of turning it on?

HOWARD   Say, aren't you supposed to be in Boston?

WILLY   That's what I want to talk to you about, Howard. You got a minute? [*He draws a chair in from the wing.*]

HOWARD   What happened? What're you doing here?

WILLY   Well . . .

HOWARD   You didn't crack up again, did you?

WILLY   Oh, no. No . . .

HOWARD   Geez, you had me worried there for a minute. What's the trouble?

WILLY   Well, tell you the truth, Howard. I've come to the decision that I'd rather not travel any more.

HOWARD   Not travel! Well, what'll you do?

WILLY   Remember, Christmas time, when you had the party here? You said you'd try to think of some spot for me here in town.

HOWARD   With us?

WILLY   Well, sure.

HOWARD   Oh, yeah, yeah. I remember. Well, I couldn't think of anything for you, Willy.

WILLY   I tell ya, Howard. The kids are all grown up, y'know. I don't need much any more. If I could take home—well, sixty-five dollars a week, I could swing it.

HOWARD   Yeah, but Willy, see I—

WILLY   I tell ya why, Howard. Speaking frankly and between the two of us, y'know—I'm just a little tired.

HOWARD   Oh, I could understand that, Willy. But you're a road man, Willy, and we do a road business. We've only got a half-dozen salesmen on the floor here.

WILLY   God knows, Howard, I never asked a favor of any man. But I was with the firm when your father used to carry you in here in his arms.

HOWARD   I know that, Willy, but—

WILLY   Your father came to me the day you were born and asked me what I thought of the name of Howard, may he rest in peace.

HOWARD   I appreciate that, Willy, but there just is no spot here for you. If I had a spot I'd slam you right in, but I just don't have a single solitary spot.

He looks for his lighter. WILLY *has picked it up and gives it to him. Pause.*

WILLY [*with increasing anger*]   Howard, all I need to set my table is fifty dollars a week.

HOWARD   But where am I going to put you, kid?

WILLY   Look, it isn't a question of whether I can sell merchandise, is it?

HOWARD   No, but it's a business, kid, and everybody's gotta pull his own weight.

WILLY [*desperately*]   Just let me tell you a story, Howard—

HOWARD   'Cause you gotta admit, business is business.

WILLY [*angrily*]   Business is definitely business, but just listen for a minute. You don't understand this. When I was a boy—eighteen, nineteen—I was already on the road. And there was a question in my mind as to whether selling had a future for me. Because in those days I had a yearning to go to Alaska. See, there were three gold strikes in one month in Alaska, and I felt like going out. Just for the ride, you might say.

HOWARD [*barely interested*]   Don't say.

WILLY   Oh, yeah, my father lived many years in Alaska. He was an adventurous man. We've got quite a little streak of self-reliance in our family. I thought I'd go out with my older brother and try to locate him, and maybe settle in the North with the old man. And I was almost decided to go when I met a salesman in the Parker House. His name was Dave Singleman. And he was eighty-four years old, and he'd drummed merchandise in thirty-one states. And old Dave, he'd go up to his room, y'understand, put on his green velvet slippers—I'll never forget—and pick up his phone and call the buyers, and without ever leaving his room, at the age of eighty-four, he made his living. And when I saw that, I realized that selling was the greatest career a man could want. 'Cause what could be more satisfying than to be able to go, at the age of eighty-four, into twenty or thirty different cities, and pick up a phone, and be remembered and loved and helped by so many different people? Do you know? when he died—and by the way he died the death of a salesman, in his green velvet slippers in the smoker of the New York, New Haven and Hartford, going into Boston—when he died, hundreds of salesmen and buyers were at his funeral. Things were sad on a lotta trains for months after that. [*He stands up.* HOWARD *has not looked at him.*] In those days there was personality in it, Howard. There was respect, and comradeship, and gratitude in it. Today, it's all cut and dried, and there's no chance for bringing friendship to bear—or personality. You see what I mean? They don't know me any more.

HOWARD [*moving away, to the right*]   That's just the thing, Willy.

WILLY   If I had forty dollars a week—that's all I'd need. Forty dollars, Howard.

HOWARD   Kid, I can't take blood from a stone, I—

WILLY [*desperation is on him now*]   Howard, the year Al Smith[6] was nominated, your father came to me and—

HOWARD [*starting to go off*]   I've got to see some people, kid.

---

6. Alfred E. Smith (1873–1944) was the Democratic presidential nominee who lost to Herbert Hoover in 1928.

WILLY [*stopping him*] I'm talking about your father! There were promises made across this desk! You mustn't tell me you've got people to see—I put thirty-four years into this firm, Howard, and now I can't pay my insurance! You can't eat the orange and throw the peel away—a man is not a piece of fruit! [*After a pause*] Now pay attention. Your father—in 1928 I had a big year. I averaged a hundred and seventy dollars a week in commissions.

HOWARD [*impatiently*] Now, Willy, you never averaged—

WILLY [*banging his hand on the desk*] I averaged a hundred and seventy dollars a week in the year of 1928! And your father came to me—or rather, I was in the office here—it was right over this desk—and he put his hand on my shoulder—

HOWARD [*getting up*] You'll have to excuse me, Willy, I gotta see some people. Pull yourself together. [*Going out*] I'll be back in a little while.

> On HOWARD's *exit, the light on his chair grows very bright and strange.*

WILLY Pull myself together! What the hell did I say to him? My God, I was yelling at him! How could I! [WILLY *breaks off, staring at the light, which occupies the chair, animating it. He approaches this chair, standing across the desk from it.*] Frank, Frank, don't you remember what you told me that time? How you put your hand on my shoulder, and Frank . . . [*He leans on the desk and as he speaks the dead man's name he accidentally switches on the recorder, and instantly:*]

HOWARD'S SON ". . . of New York is Albany. The capital of Ohio is Cincinnati, the capital of Rhode Island is . . ." [*The recitation continues.*]

WILLY [*leaping away with fright, shouting*] Ha! Howard! Howard! Howard!

HOWARD [*rushing in*] What happened?

WILLY [*pointing at the machine, which continues nasally, childishly, with the capital cities*] Shut it off! Shut it off!

HOWARD [*pulling the plug out*] Look, Willy . . .

WILLY [*pressing his hands to his eyes*] I gotta get myself some coffee. I'll get some coffee . . .

> WILLY *starts to walk out.* HOWARD *stops him.*

HOWARD [*rolling up the cord*] Willy, look . . .

WILLY I'll go to Boston.

HOWARD Willy, you can't go to Boston for us.

WILLY Why can't I go?

HOWARD I don't want you to represent us. I've been meaning to tell you for a long time now.

WILLY Howard, are you firing me?

HOWARD I think you need a good long rest, Willy.

WILLY Howard—

HOWARD And when you feel better, come back, and we'll see if we can work something out.

WILLY   But I gotta earn money, Howard. I'm in no position to—
HOWARD   Where are your sons? Why don't your sons give you a hand?
WILLY   They're working on a very big deal.
HOWARD   This is no time for false pride, Willy. You go to your sons
and you tell them that you're tired. You've got two great boys,
haven't you?
WILLY   Oh, no question, no question, but in the meantime . . .
HOWARD   Then that's that, heh?
WILLY   All right, I'll go to Boston tomorrow.
HOWARD   No, no.
WILLY   I can't throw myself on my sons. I'm not a cripple!
HOWARD   Look, kid, I'm busy this morning.
WILLY [*grasping* HOWARD's *arm*]   Howard, you've got to let me go to
Boston!
HOWARD [*hard, keeping himself under control*]   I've got a line of
people to see this morning. Sit down, take five minutes, and pull
yourself together, and then go home, will ya? I need the office,
Willy. [*He starts to go; turns, remembering the recorder, starts to
push off the table holding the recorder.*] Oh, yeah. Whenever you
can this week, stop by and drop off the samples. You'll feel better,
Willy, and then come back and we'll talk. Pull yourself together,
kid, there's people outside.

> HOWARD *exits, pushing the table off left.* WILLY *stares into
> space, exhausted. Now the music is heard—*BEN's *music—first
> distantly, then closer, closer. As* WILLY *speaks,* BEN *enters from
> the right. He carries valise and umbrella.*

WILLY   Oh, Ben, how did you do it? What is the answer? Did you
wind up the Alaska deal already?
BEN   Doesn't take much time if you know what you're doing. Just a
short business trip. Boarding ship in an hour. Wanted to say
good-by.
WILLY   Ben, I've got to talk to you.
BEN [*glancing at his watch*]   Haven't the time, William.
WILLY [*crossing the apron to* BEN]   Ben, nothing's working out. I
don't know what to do.
BEN   Now, look here, William. I've bought timberland in Alaska and
I need a man to look after things for me.
WILLY   God, timberland! Me and my boys in those grand outdoors!
BEN   You've a new continent at your doorstep, William. Get out of
these cities, they're full of talk and time payments and courts of
law. Screw on your fists and you can fight for a fortune up there.
WILLY   Yes, yes! Linda, Linda!

> LINDA *enters as of old, with the wash.*

LINDA   Oh, you're back?
BEN   I haven't much time.
WILLY   No, wait! Linda, he's got a proposition for me in Alaska.
LINDA   But you've got— [*To* BEN]He's got a beautiful job here.

WILLY   But in Alaska, kid, I could—

LINDA   You're doing well enough, Willy!

BEN [*to* LINDA]   Enough for what, my dear?

LINDA [*frightened of* BEN *and angry at him*]   Don't say those things
to him! Enough to be happy right here, right now. [*To* WILLY,
while BEN *laughs*] Why must everybody conquer the world? You're
well liked, and the boys love you, and someday—[*to* BEN]—why,
old man Wagner told him just the other day that if he keeps it up
he'll be a member of the firm, didn't he, Willy?

WILLY   Sure, sure. I am building something with this firm, Ben, and
if a man is building something he must be on the right track,
mustn't he?

BEN   What are you building? Lay your hand on it. Where is it?

WILLY [*hesitantly*]   That's true, Linda, there's nothing.

LINDA   Why? [*To* BEN] There's a man eighty-four years old—

WILLY   That's right, Ben, that's right. When I look at that man I say,
what is there to worry about?

BEN   Bah!

WILLY   It's true, Ben. All he has to do is go into any city, pick up the
phone, and he's making his living and you know why?

BEN [*picking up his valise*]   I've got to go.

WILLY [*holding* BEN *back*]   Look at this boy!

> *Biff, in his high school sweater, enters carrying suitcase.*
> HAPPY *carries* BIFF's *shoulder guards, gold helmet, and football
> pants.*

WILLY   Without a penny to his name, three great universities are
begging for him, and from there the sky's the limit, because it's not
what you do, Ben. It's who you know and the smile on your face!
It's contacts, Ben, contacts! The whole wealth of Alaska passes over
the lunch table at the Commodore Hotel, and that's the wonder,
the wonder of this country, that a man can end with diamonds
here on the basis of being liked! [*He turns to* BIFF.] And that's why
when you get out on that field today it's important. Because thousands of people will be rooting for you and loving you. [*To* BEN,
who has again begun to leave] And Ben! when he walks into a
business office his name will sound out like a bell and all the doors
will open to him! I've seen it, Ben, I've seen it a thousand times!
You can't feel it with your hand like timber, but it's there!

BEN   Good-by, William.

WILLY   Ben, am I right? Don't you think I'm right? I value your
advice.

BEN   There's a new continent at your doorstep, William. You could
walk out rich. Rich! [*He is gone.*]

WILLY   We'll do it here, Ben! You hear me? We're gonna do it here!

> YOUNG BERNARD *rushes in. The gay music of the Boys is heard.*

BERNARD   Oh, gee, I was afraid you left already!

WILLY   Why? What time is it?

BERNARD   It's half-past one!

WILLY   Well, come on, everybody! Ebbets Field next stop! Where's the pennants? [*He rushes through the wall-line of the kitchen and out into the living room.*]

LINDA [*to* BIFF]   Did you pack fresh underwear?

BIFF [*who has been limbering up*]   I want to go!

BERNARD   Biff, I'm carrying your helmet, ain't I?

HAPPY   No, I'm carrying the helmet.

BERNARD   Oh, Biff, you promised me.

HAPPY   I'm carrying the helmet.

BERNARD   How am I going to get in the locker room?

LINDA   Let him carry the shoulder guards. [*She puts her coat and hat on in the kitchen.*]

BERNARD   Can I, Biff? 'Cause I told everybody I'm going to be in the locker room.

HAPPY   In Ebbets Field it's the clubhouse.

BERNARD   I meant the clubhouse. Biff!

HAPPY   Biff!

BIFF [*grandly, after a slight pause*]   Let him carry the shoulder guards.

HAPPY [*as he gives* BERNARD *the shoulder guards*]   Stay close to us now.

WILLY *rushes in with the pennants.*

WILLY [*handing them out*]   Everybody wave when Biff comes out on the field. [HAPPY *and* BERNARD *run off.*] You set now, boy?

The music has died away.

BIFF   Ready to go, Pop. Every muscle is ready.

WILLY [*at the edge of the apron*]   You realize what this means?

BIFF   That's right, Pop.

WILLY [*feeling* BIFF'*s muscles*]   You're comin' home this afternoon captain of the All-Scholastic Championship Team of the City of New York.

BIFF   I got it, Pop. And remember, pal, when I take off my helmet, that touchdown is for you.

WILLY   Let's go! [*He is starting out, with his arm around* BIFF, *when* CHARLEY *enters, as of old, in knickers*] I got no room for you, Charley.

CHARLEY   Room? For what?

WILLY   In the car.

CHARLEY   You goin' for a ride? I wanted to shoot some casino.

WILLY [*furiously*]   Casino! [*Incredulously*] Don't you realize what today is?

LINDA   Oh, he knows, Willy. He's just kidding you.

WILLY   That's nothing to kid about!

CHARLEY   No, Linda, what's goin' on?

LINDA   He's playing in Ebbets Field.

CHARLEY   Baseball in this weather?

WILLY   Don't talk to him. Come on, come on! [*He is pushing them out.*]

CHARLEY   Wait a minute, didn't you hear the news?

WILLY   What?

CHARLEY   Don't you listen to the radio? Ebbets Field just blew up.

WILLY   You go to hell! [CHARLEY *laughs. Pushing them out*] Come on, come on! We're late.

CHARLEY [*as they go*]   Knock a homer, Biff, knock a homer!

WILLY [*the last to leave, turning to* CHARLEY]   I don't think that was funny, Charley. This is the greatest day of his life.

CHARLEY   Willy, when are you going to grow up?

WILLY   Yeah, heh? When this game is over, Charley, you'll be laughing out the other side of your face. They'll be calling him another Red Grange.[7] Twenty-five thousand a year.

CHARLEY [*kidding*]   Is that so?

WILLY   Yeah, that's so.

CHARLEY   Well, then, I'm sorry, Willy. But tell me something.

WILLY   What?

CHARLEY   Who is Red Grange?

WILLY   Put up your hands. Goddam you, put up your hands!

> CHARLEY, *chuckling, shakes his head and walks away, around the left corner of the stage.* WILLY *follows him. The music rises to a mocking frenzy.*

WILLY   Who the hell do you think you are, better than everybody else? You don't know everything, you big, ignorant, stupid . . . Put up your hands!

> *Light rises, on the right side of the forestage, on a small table in the reception room of* CHARLEY's *office. Traffic sounds are heard.* BERNARD, *now mature, sits whistling to himself. A pair of tennis rackets and an overnight bag are on the floor beside him.*

WILLY [*offstage*]   What are you walking away for? Don't walk away! If you're going to say something say it to my face! I know you laugh at me behind my back. You'll laugh out of the other side of your goddam face after this game. Touchdown! Touchdown! Eighty thousand people! Touchdown! Right between the goal posts.

> BERNARD *is a quiet, but self-assured young man.* WILLY's *voice is coming from right upstage now.* BERNARD *lowers his feet off the table and listens.* JENNY, *his father's secretary, enters.*

JENNY [*distressed*]   Say, Bernard, will you go out in the hall?

BERNARD   What is that noise? Who is it?

JENNY   Mr. Loman. He just got off the elevator.

BERNARD [*getting up*]   Who's he arguing with?

---

7. Harold Edward Grange, All-American halfback at the University of Illinois (1923–1925) who played professionally with the Chicago Bears.

JENNY   Nobody. There's nobody with him. I can't deal with him any more, and your father gets all upset everytime he comes. I've got a lot of typing to do, and your father's waiting to sign it. Will you see him?

WILLY   [*entering*] Touchdown! Touch— [*He sees* JENNY.] Jenny, Jenny, good to see you. How're ya? Workin'? Or still honest?

JENNY   Fine. How've you been feeling?

WILLY   Not much any more, Jenny. Ha, ha! [*He is surprised to see the rackets.*]

BERNARD   Hello, Uncle Willy.

WILLY   [*almost shocked*] Bernard! Well, look who's here! [*He comes quickly, guiltily, to* BERNARD *and warmly shakes his hand.*]

BERNARD   How are you? Good to see you.

WILLY   What are you doing here?

BERNARD   Oh, just stopped by to see Pop. Get off my feet till my train leaves. I'm going to Washington in a few minutes.

WILLY   Is he in?

BERNARD   Yes, he's in his office with the accountant. Sit down.

WILLY   [*sitting down*] What're you going to do in Washington?

BERNARD   Oh, just a case I've got there, Willy.

WILLY   That so? [*Indicating the rackets*] You going to play tennis there?

BERNARD   I'm staying with a friend who's got a court.

WILLY   Don't say. His own tennis court. Must be fine people, I bet.

BERNARD   They are, very nice. Dad tells me Biff's in town.

WILLY   [*with a big smile*] Yeah, Biff's in. Working on a very big deal, Bernard.

BERNARD   What's Biff doing?

WILLY   Well, he's been doing very big things in the West. But he decided to establish himself here. Very big. We're having dinner. Did I hear your wife had a boy?

BERNARD   That's right. Our second.

WILLY   Two boys! What do you know!

BERNARD   What kind of a deal has Biff got?

WILLY   Well, Bill Oliver—very big sporting-goods man—he wants Biff very badly. Called him from the West. Long distance, carte blanche, special deliveries. Your friends have their own private tennis court?

BERNARD   You still with the old firm, Willy?

WILLY   [*after a pause*] I'm—I'm overjoyed to see how you made the grade, Bernard, overjoyed. It's an encouraging thing to see a young man really—really— Looks very good for Biff—very— [*He breaks off, then*] Bernard— [*He is so full of emotion, he breaks off again.*]

BERNARD   What is it, Willy?

WILLY   [*small and alone*] What—what's the secret?

BERNARD   What secret?

WILLY   How—how did you? Why didn't he ever catch on?

BERNARD   I wouldn't know that, Willy.

WILLY   [*confidentially, desperately*] You were his friend, his boy-hood friend. There's something I don't understand about it. His life ended after that Ebbets Field game. From the age of seventeen nothing good ever happened to him.

BERNARD   He never trained himself for anything.

WILLY   But he did, he did. After high school he took so many correspondence courses. Radio mechanics; television; God knows what, and never made the slightest mark.

BERNARD [*taking off his glasses*]   Willy, do you want to talk candidly?

WILLY [*rising, faces* BERNARD]   I regard you as a very brilliant man, Bernard. I value your advice.

BERNARD   Oh, the hell with the advice, Willy. I couldn't advise you. There's just one thing I've always wanted to ask you. When he was supposed to graduate, and the math teacher flunked him—

WILLY   Oh, that son-of-a-bitch ruined his life.

BERNARD   Yeah, but, Willy, all he had to do was go to summer school and make up that subject.

WILLY   That's right, that's right.

BERNARD   Did you tell him not to go to summer school?

WILLY   Me? I begged him to go. I ordered him to go!

BERNARD   Then why wouldn't he go?

WILLY   Why? Why! Bernard, that question has been trailing me like a ghost for the last fifteen years. He flunked the subject, and laid down and died like a hammer hit him!

BERNARD   Take it easy, kid.

WILLY   Let me talk to you—I got nobody to talk to. Bernard, Bernard, was it my fault? Y'see? It keeps going around in my mind, maybe I did something to him. I got nothing to give him.

BERNARD   Don't take it so hard.

WILLY   Why did he lay down? What is the story there? You were his friend!

BERNARD   Willy, I remember, it was June, and our grades came out. And he's flunked math.

WILLY   That son-of-a-bitch!

BERNARD   No, it wasn't right then. Biff just got very angry, I remember, and he was ready to enroll in summer school.

WILLY [*surprised*]   He was?

BERNARD   He wasn't beaten by it·at all. But then, Willy, he disappeared from the block for almost a month. And I got the idea that he'd gone up to New England to see you. Did he have a talk with you then?

WILLY *stares in silence.*

BERNARD   Willy?

WILLY [*with a strong edge of resentment in his voice*]   Yeah, he came to Boston. What about it?

BERNARD   Well, just that when he came back—I'll never forget this, it always mystifies me. Because I'd thought so well of Biff, even though he'd always taken advantage of me. I loved him, Willy, y'know? And he came back after that month and took his sneakers—remember those sneakers with "University of Virginia" printed on them? He was so proud of those, wore them every day. And he took them down in the cellar, and burned them up in the furnace. We had a fist fight. It lasted at least half an hour. Just the two of us, punching each other down the cellar, and crying right through it. I've often thought how strange it was that I knew he'd given up his life. What happened in Boston, Willy?

WILLY *looks at him as at an intruder.*

BERNARD   I just bring it up because you asked me.
WILLY [*angrily*]   Nothing. What do you mean, "What happened?" What's that got to do with anything?
BERNARD   Well, don't get sore.
WILLY   What are you trying to do, blame it on me? If a boy lays down is that my fault?
BERNARD   Now, Willy, don't get—
WILLY   Well, don't—don't talk to me that way! What does that mean, "What happened?"

CHARLEY *enters. He is in his vest, and he carries a bottle of bourbon.*

CHARLEY   Hey, you're going to miss that train. [*He waves the bottle.*]
BERNARD   Yeah, I'm going. [*He takes the bottle.*] Thanks, Pop. [*He picks up his rackets and bag.*] Good-by, Willy, and don't worry about it. You know, "If at first you don't succeed . . ."
WILLY   Yes, I believe in that.
BERNARD   But sometimes, Willy, it's better for a man just to walk away.
WILLY   Walk away?
BERNARD   That's right.
WILLY   But if you can't walk away?
BERNARD [*after a slight pause*]   I guess that's when it's tough. [*Extending his hand*] Good-by, Willy.
WILLY [*shaking* BERNARD'S *hand*]   Good-by, boy.
CHARLEY [*an arm on* BERNARD'S *shoulder*]   How do you like this kid? Gonna argue a case in front of the Supreme Court.
BERNARD [*protesting*]   Pop!
WILLY [*genuinely shocked, pained, and happy*]   No! The Supreme Court!
BERNARD   I gotta run. 'By, Dad!
CHARLEY   Knock 'em dead, Bernard!

BERNARD *goes off.*

WILLY [*as* CHARLEY *takes out his wallet*]   The Supreme Court! And he didn't even mention it!
CHARLEY [*counting out money on the desk*]   He don't have to—he's gonna do it.
WILLY   And you never told him what to do, did you? You never took any interest in him.

CHARLEY   My salvation is that I never took any interest in anything. There's some money—fifty dollars. I got an accountant inside.

WILLY   Charley, look . . . [*With difficulty*] I got my insurance to pay. If you can manage it—I need a hundred and ten dollars.

CHARLEY *doesn't reply for a moment; merely stops moving.*

WILLY   I'd draw it from my bank but Linda would know, and I . . .

CHARLEY   Sit down, Willy.

WILLY [*moving toward the chair*]   I'm keeping an account of everything, remember. I'll pay every penny back. [*He sits.*]

CHARLEY   Now listen to me, Willy.

WILLY   I want you to know I appreciate . . .

CHARLEY [*sitting down on the table*]   Willy, what're you doin? What the hell is goin' on in your head?

WILLY   Why? I'm simply . . .

CHARLEY   I offered you a job. You can make fifty dollars a week. And I won't send you on the road.

WILLY   I've got a job.

CHARLEY   Without pay? What kind of a job is a job without pay? [*He rises.*] Now, look, kid, enough is enough. I'm no genius but I know when I'm being insulted.

WILLY   Insulted!

CHARLEY   Why don't you want to work for me?

WILLY   What's the matter with you? I've got a job.

CHARLEY   Then what're you walkin' in here every week for?

WILLY [*getting up*]   Well, if you don't want me to walk in here—

CHARLEY   I am offering you a job.

WILLY   I don't want your goddam job!

CHARLEY   When the hell are you going to grow up?

WILLY [*furiously*]   You big ignoramus, if you say that to me again I'll rap you one! I don't care how big you are! [*He's ready to fight.*]

Pause.

CHARLEY [*kindly, going to him*]   How much do you need, Willy?

WILLY   Charley, I'm strapped. I'm strapped. I don't know what to do. I was just fired.

CHARLEY   Howard fired you?

WILLY   That snotnose. Imagine that? I named him. I named him Howard.

CHARLEY   Willy, when're you gonna realize that them things don't mean anything? You named him Howard, but you can't sell that. The only thing you got in this world is what you can sell. And the funny thing is that you're a salesman, and you don't know that.

WILLY   I've always tried to think otherwise, I guess. I always felt that if a man was impressive, and well liked, that nothing—

CHARLEY   Why must everybody like you? Who liked J. P. Morgan?[8] Was he impressive? In a Turkish bath he'd look like a butcher.

8. John Pierpont Morgan (1887–1943), famous New York banker and financier.

But with his pockets on he was very well liked. Now listen, Willy, I know you don't like me, and nobody can say I'm in love with you, but I'll give you a job because—just for the hell of it, put it that way. Now what do you say?

WILLY   I—I just can't work for you, Charley.

CHARLEY   What're you, jealous of me?

WILLY   I can't work for you, that's all, don't ask me why.

CHARLEY [*angered, takes out more bills*] You been jealous of me all your life, you damned fool! Here, pay your insurance. [*He puts the money in* WILLY's *hand.*]

WILLY   I'm keeping strict accounts.

CHARLEY   I've got some work to do. Take care of yourself. And pay your insurance.

WILLY [*moving to the right*] Funny, y'know? After all the highways, and the trains, and the appointments, and the years, you end up worth more dead than alive.

CHARLEY   Willy, nobody's worth nothin' dead. [*After a slight pause*] Did you hear what I said?

> WILLY *stands still, dreaming.*

CHARLEY   Willy!

WILLY   Apologize to Bernard for me when you see him. I didn't mean to argue with him. He's a fine boy. They're all fine boys, and they'll end up big—all of them. Someday they'll all play tennis together. Wish me luck, Charley. He saw Bill Oliver today.

CHARLEY   Good luck.

WILLY [*on the verge of tears*] Charley, you're the only friend I got. Isn't that a remarkable thing? [*He goes out.*]

CHARLEY   Jesus!

> CHARLEY *stares after him a moment and follows. All light blacks out. Suddenly raucous music is heard, and a red glow rises behind the screen at right.* STANLEY, *a young waiter, appears, carrying a table, followed by* HAPPY, *who is carrying two chairs.*

STANLEY [*putting the table down*] That's all right, Mr. Loman, I can handle it myself. [*He turns and takes the chairs from* HAPPY *and places them at the table.*]

HAPPY [*glancing around*] Oh, this is better.

STANLEY   Sure, in the front there you're in the middle of all kinds a noise. Whenever you got a party, Mr. Loman, you just tell me and I'll put you back here. Y'know, there's a lotta people they don't like it private, because when they go out they like to see a lotta action around them because they're sick and tired to stay in the house by theirself. But I know you, you ain't from Hackensack. You know what I mean?

HAPPY [*sitting down*] So how's it coming, Stanley?

STANLEY   Ah, it's a dog's life. I only wish during the war they'd a took me in the Army. I coulda been dead by now.

HAPPY   My brother's back, Stanley.

STANLEY   Oh, he come back, heh? From the Far West.

HAPPY   Yeah, big cattle man, my brother, so treat him right. And my father's coming too.

STANLEY   Oh, your father too!

HAPPY   You got a couple of nice lobsters?

STANLEY   Hundred per cent, big.

HAPPY   I want them with the claws.

STANLEY   Don't worry, I don't give you no mice. [HAPPY *laughs.*] How about some wine? It'll put a head on the meal.

HAPPY   No. You remember, Stanley, that recipe I brought you from overseas? With the champagne in it?

STANLEY   Oh, yeah, sure. I still got it tacked up yet in the kitchen. But that'll have to cost a buck apiece anyways.

HAPPY   That's all right.

STANLEY   What'd you, hit a number or somethin'?

HAPPY   No, it's a little celebration. My brother is—I think he pulled off a big deal today. I think we're going into business together.

STANLEY   Great! That's the best for you. Because a family business, you know what I mean?—that's the best.

HAPPY   That's what I think.

STANLEY   'Cause what's the difference? Somebody steals? It's in the family. Know what I mean? [*Sotto voce*] Like this bartender here. The boss is goin' crazy what kinda leak he's got in the cash register. You put it in but it don't come out.

HAPPY [*raising his head*]   Sh!

STANLEY   What?

HAPPY   You notice I wasn't lookin' right or left, was I?

STANLEY   No.

HAPPY   And my eyes are closed.

STANLEY   So what's the—?

HAPPY   Strudel's comin'.

STANLEY [*catching on, looks around*]   Ah, no, there's no—

He breaks off as a furred, lavishly dressed GIRL *enters and sits at the next table. Both follow her with their eyes.*

STANLEY   Geez, how'd ya know?

HAPPY   I got radar or something. [*Staring directly at her profile*] Oooooooo . . . Stanley.

STANLEY   I think that's for you, Mr. Loman.

HAPPY   Look at that mouth. Oh, God. And the binoculars.

STANLEY   Geez, you got a life, Mr. Loman.

HAPPY   Wait on her.

STANLEY [*going to the* GIRL'S *table*]   Would you like a menu, ma'am?

GIRL   I'm expecting someone, but I'd like a—

HAPPY   Why don't you bring her—excuse me, miss, do you mind? I sell champagne, and I'd like you to try my brand. Bring her a champagne, Stanley.

GIRL   That's awfully nice of you.

HAPPY   Don't mention it. It's all company money. [*He laughs.*]

GIRL   That's a charming product to be selling, isn't it?

HAPPY   Oh, gets to be like everything else. Selling is selling, y'know.

GIRL   I suppose.

HAPPY   You don't happen to sell, do you?

GIRL   No, I don't sell.

HAPPY   Would you object to a compliment from a stranger? You ought to be on a magazine cover.

GIRL   [*looking at him a little archly*]   I have been.

STANLEY *comes in with a glass of champagne.*

HAPPY   What'd I say before, Stanley? You see? She's a cover girl.

STANLEY   Oh, I could see, I could see.

HAPPY [*to the* GIRL]   What magazine?

GIRL   Oh, a lot of them. [*She takes the drink.*] Thank you.

HAPPY   You know what they say in France, don't you? "Champagne is the drink of the complexion"—Hya, Biff!

BIFF *has entered and sits with* HAPPY.

BIFF   Hello, kid. Sorry I'm late.

HAPPY   I just got here. Uh, Miss—?

GIRL   Forsythe.

HAPPY   Miss Forsythe, this is my brother.

BIFF   Is Dad here?

HAPPY   His name is Biff. You might've heard of him. Great football player.

GIRL   Really? What team?

HAPPY   Are you familiar with football?

GIRL   No, I'm afraid I'm not.

HAPPY   Biff is quarterback with the New York Giants.

GIRL   Well, that is nice, isn't it? [*She drinks.*]

HAPPY   Good health.

GIRL   I'm happy to meet you.

HAPPY   That's my name. Hap. It's really Harold, but at West Point they called me Happy.

GIRL [*now really impressed*]   Oh, I see. How do you do? [*She turns her profile.*]

BIFF   Isn't Dad coming?

HAPPY   You want her?

BIFF   Oh, I could never make that.

HAPPY   I remember the time that idea would never come into your head. Where's the old confidence, Biff?

BIFF   I just saw Oliver—

HAPPY   Wait a minute. I've got to see that old confidence again. Do you want her? She's on call.

BIFF   Oh, no. [*He turns to look at the* GIRL.]

HAPPY   I'm telling you. Watch this. [*Turning to the* GIRL] Honey? [*She turns to him.*] Are you busy?

GIRL   Well, I am . . . but I could make a phone call.

HAPPY   Do that, will you, honey? And see if you can get a friend.

We'll be here for a while. Biff is one of the greatest football players in the country.

GIRL [*standing up*]   Well, I'm certainly happy to meet you.

HAPPY   Come back soon.

GIRL   I'll try.

HAPPY   Don't try, honey, try hard.

The GIRL *exits.* STANLEY *follows, shaking his head in bewildered admiration.*

HAPPY   Isn't that a shame now? A beautiful girl like that? That's why I can't get married. There's not a good woman in a thousand. New York is loaded with them, kid!

BIFF   Hap, look—

HAPPY   I told you she was on call!

BIFF [*strangely unnerved*]   Cut it out, will ya? I want to say something to you.

HAPPY   Did you see Oliver?

BIFF   I saw him all right. Now look, I want to tell Dad a couple of things and I want you to help me.

HAPPY   What? Is he going to back you?

BIFF   Are you crazy? You're out of your goddam head, you know that?

HAPPY   Why? What happened?

BIFF [*breathlessly*]   I did a terrible thing today, Hap. It's been the strangest day I ever went through. I'm all numb, I swear.

HAPPY   You mean he wouldn't see you?

BIFF   Well, I waited six hours for him, see? All day. Kept sending my name in. Even tried to date his secretary so she'd get me to him, but no soap.

HAPPY   Because you're not showin' the old confidence, Biff. He remembered you, didn't he?

BIFF [*stopping* HAPPY *with a gesture*]   Finally, about five o'clock, he comes out. Didn't remember who I was or anything. I felt like such an idiot, Hap.

HAPPY   Did you tell him my Florida idea?

BIFF   He walked away. I saw him for one minute. I got so mad I could've torn the walls down! How the hell did I ever get the idea I was a salesman there? I even believed myself that I'd been a salesman for him! And then he gave me one look and—I realized what a ridiculous lie my whole life has been! We've been talking in a dream for fifteen years. I was a shipping clerk.

HAPPY   What'd you do?

BIFF [*with great tension and wonder*]   Well, he left, see. And the secretary went out. I was all alone in the waiting room. I don't know what came over me, Hap. The next thing I know I'm in his office—paneled walls, everything. I can't explain it. I—Hap, I took his fountain pen.

HAPPY   Geez, did he catch you?

BIFF   I ran out. I ran down all eleven flights. I ran and ran and ran.

HAPPY   That was an awful dumb—what'd you do that for?

BIFF [*agonized*]   I don't know, I just—wanted to take something, I don't know. You gotta help me, Hap, I'm gonna tell Pop.

HAPPY   You crazy? What for?

BIFF   Hap, he's got to understand that I'm not the man somebody lends that kind of money to. He thinks I've been spiting him all these years and it's eating him up.

HAPPY   That's just it. You tell him something nice.

BIFF   I can't.

HAPPY   Say you got a lunch date with Oliver tomorrow.

BIFF   So what do I do tomorrow?

HAPPY   You leave the house tomorrow and come back at night and say Oliver is thinking it over. And he thinks it over for a couple of weeks, and gradually it fades away and nobody's the worse.

BIFF   But it'll go on forever!

HAPPY   Dad is never so happy as when he's looking forward to something!

WILLY *enters.*

HAPPY   Hello, scout!

WILLY   Gee, I haven't been here in years!

STANLEY *has followed* WILLY *in and sets a chair for him.* STANLEY *starts off but* HAPPY *stops him.*

HAPPY   Stanley!

STANLEY *stands by, waiting for an order.*

BIFF [*going to* WILLY *with guilt, as to an invalid*]   Sit down, Pop. You want a drink?

WILLY   Sure, I don't mind.

BIFF   Let's get a load on.

WILLY   You look worried.

BIFF   N-no. [*To* STANLEY]   Scotch all around. Make it doubles.

STANLEY   Doubles, right. [*He goes.*]

WILLY   You had a couple already, didn't you?

BIFF   Just a couple, yeah.

WILLY   Well, what happened, boy? [*Nodding affirmatively, with a smile*]   Everything go all right?

BIFF [*takes a breath, then reaches out and grasps* WILLY's *hand*]   Pal . . . [*He is smiling bravely, and* WILLY *is smiling too.*]   I had an experience today.

HAPPY   Terrific, Pop.

WILLY   That so? What happened?

BIFF [*high, slightly alcoholic, above the earth*]   I'm going to tell you everything from first to last. It's been a strange day. [*Silence. He looks around, composes himself as best he can, but his breath keeps breaking the rhythm of his voice.*]   I had to wait quite a while for him, and—

WILLY   Oliver?

BIFF   Yeah, Oliver. All day, as a matter of cold fact. And a lot of— instances—facts, Pop, facts about my life came back to me. Who was it, Pop? Who ever said I was a salesman with Oliver?

WILLY   Well, you were.

BIFF   No, Dad, I was a shipping clerk.

WILLY   But you were practically—

BIFF   [*with determination*]   Dad, I don't know who said it first, but I was never a salesman for Bill Oliver.

WILLY   What're you talking about?

BIFF   Let's hold on to the facts tonight, Pop. We're not going to get anywhere bullin' around. I was a shipping clerk.

WILLY   [*angrily*]   All right, now listen to me—

BIFF   Why don't you let me finish?

WILLY   I'm not interested in stories about the past or any crap of that kind because the woods are burning, boys, you understand? There's a big blaze going on all around. I was fired today.

BIFF   [*shocked*]   How could you be?

WILLY   I was fired, and I'm looking for a little good news to tell your mother, because the woman has waited and the woman has suffered. The gist of it is that I haven't got a story left in my head, Biff. So don't give me a lecture about facts and aspects. I am not interested. Now what've you got to say to me?

STANLEY *enters with three drinks. They wait until he leaves.*

WILLY   Did you see Oliver?

BIFF   Jesus, Dad!

WILLY   You mean you didn't go up there?

HAPPY   Sure he went up there.

BIFF   I did. I—saw him. How could they fire you?

WILLY   [*on the edge of his chair*]   What kind of a welcome did he give you?

BIFF   He won't even let you work on commission?

WILLY   I'm out! [*Driving*]   So tell me, he gave you a warm welcome?

HAPPY   Sure, Pop, sure!

BIFF   [*driven*]   Well, it was kind of—

WILLY   I was wondering if he'd remember you. [*To* HAPPY]   Imagine, man doesn't see him for ten, twelve years and gives him that kind of a welcome!

HAPPY   Damn right!

BIFF   [*trying to return to the offensive*]   Pop, look—

WILLY   You know why he remembered you, don't you? Because you impressed him in those days.

BIFF   Let's talk quietly and get this down to the facts, huh?

WILLY   [*as though* BIFF *had been interrupting*]   Well, what happened? It's great news, Biff. Did he take you into his office or'd you talk in the waiting room?

BIFF   Well, he came in, see, and—

WILLY   [*with a big smile*]   What'd he say? Betcha he threw his arm around you.

BIFF   Well, he kinda—

WILLY   He's a fine man. [*To* HAPPY] Very hard man to see, y'know.
HAPPY [*agreeing*]   Oh, I know.
WILLY [*to* BIFF]   Is that where you had the drinks?
BIFF   Yeah, he gave me a couple of—no, no!
HAPPY [*cutting in*]   He told him my Florida idea.
WILLY   Don't interrupt. [*To* BIFF] How'd he react to the Florida idea?
BIFF   Dad, will you give me a minute to explain?
WILLY   I've been waiting for you to explain since I sat down here!
   What happened? He took you into his office and what?
BIFF   Well—I talked. And—and he listened, see.
WILLY   Famous for the way he listens, y'know. What was his answer?
BIFF   His answer was— [*He breaks off, suddenly angry.*] Dad, you're
   not letting me tell you what I want to tell you!
WILLY [*accusing, angered*]   You didn't see him, did you?
BIFF   I did see him!
WILLY   What'd you insult him or something? You insulted him,
   didn't you?
BIFF   Listen, will you let me out of it, will you just let me out of it!
HAPPY   What the hell!
WILLY   Tell me what happened!
BIFF [*to* HAPPY]   I can't talk to him!

> *A single trumpet note jars the ear. The light of green leaves
> stains the house, which holds the air of night and a dream.*
> YOUNG BERNARD *enters and knocks on the door of the house.*

YOUNG BERNARD [*frantically*]   Mrs. Loman, Mrs. Loman!
HAPPY   Tell him what happened!
BIFF [*to* HAPPY]   Shut up and leave me alone!
WILLY   No, no! You had to go and flunk math!
BIFF   What math? What're you talking about?
YOUNG BERNARD   Mrs. Loman, Mrs. Loman!

> LINDA *appears in the house, as of old.*

WILLY [*wildly*]   Math, math, math!
BIFF   Take it easy, Pop!
YOUNG BERNARD   Mrs. Loman!
WILLY [*furiously*]   If you hadn't flunked you'd've been set by now!
BIFF   Now, look, I'm gonna tell you what happened, and you're going
   to listen to me.
YOUNG BERNARD   Mrs. Loman!
BIFF   I waited six hours—
HAPPY   What the hell are you saying?
BIFF   I kept sending in my name but he wouldn't see me. So finally
   he . . . [*He continues unheard as light fades low on the restaurant.*]
YOUNG BERNARD   Biff flunked math!
LINDA   No!
YOUNG BERNARD   Birnbaum flunked him! They won't graduate him!
LINDA   But they have to. He's gotta go to the university. Where is he?
   Biff! Biff!

YOUNG BERNARD   No, he left. He went to Grand Central.

LINDA   Grand— You mean he went to Boston!

YOUNG BERNARD   Is Uncle Willy in Boston?

LINDA   Oh, maybe Willy can talk to the teacher. Oh, the poor, poor boy!

Light on house area snaps out.

BIFF [*at the table, now audible, holding up a gold fountain pen*] . . . so I'm washed up with Oliver, you understand? Are you listening to me?

WILLY [*at a loss*]   Yeah, sure. If you hadn't flunked—

BIFF   Flunked what? What're you talking about?

WILLY   Don't blame everything on me! I didn't flunk math—you did! What pen?

HAPPY   That was awful dumb, Biff, a pen like that is worth—

WILLY [*seeing the pen for the first time*]   You took Oliver's pen?

BIFF [*weakening*]   Dad, I just explained it to you.

WILLY   You stole Bill Oliver's fountain pen!

BIFF   I didn't exactly steal it! That's just what I've been explaining to you!

HAPPY   He had it in his hand and just then Oliver walked in, so he got nervous and stuck it in his pocket!

WILLY   My God, Biff!

BIFF   I never intended to do it, Dad!

OPERATOR'S VOICE   Standish Arms, good evening!

WILLY [*shouting*]   I'm not in my room!

BIFF [*frightened*]   Dad, what's the matter? [*He and* HAPPY *stand up.*]

OPERATOR   Ringing Mr. Loman for you!

WILLY   I'm not there, stop it!

BIFF [*horrified, gets down on one knee before* WILLY]   Dad, I'll make good, I'll make good. [WILLY *tries to get to his feet.* BIFF *holds him down.*] Sit down now.

WILLY   No, you're no good, you're no good for anything.

BIFF   I am, Dad, I'll find something else, you understand? Now don't worry about anything. [*He holds up* WILLY'S *face*] Talk to me, Dad.

OPERATOR   Mr. Loman does not answer. Shall I page him?

WILLY [*attempting to stand, as though to rush and silence the Operator*]   No, no, no!

HAPPY   He'll strike something, Pop.

WILLY   No, no . . .

BIFF [*desperately, standing over* WILLY]   Pop listen! Listen to me! I'm telling you something good. Oliver talked to his partner about the Florida idea. You listening? He—he talked to his partner, and he came to me . . . I'm going to be all right, you hear? Dad, listen to me, he said it was just a question of the amount!

WILLY   Then you . . . got it?

HAPPY   He's gonna be terrific, Pop!

WILLY [*trying to stand*]   Then you got it, haven't you? You got it! You got it!

BIFF [*agonized, holds* WILLY *down*]   No, no. Look, Pop. I'm supposed to have lunch with them tomorrow. I'm just telling you this so you'll know that I can still make an impression, Pop. And I'll make good somewhere, but I can't go tomorrow, see?

WILLY   Why not? You simply—

BIFF   But the pen, Pop!

WILLY   You give it to him and tell him it was an oversight!

HAPPY   Sure, have lunch tomorrow!

BIFF   I can't say that—

WILLY   You were doing a crossword puzzle and accidentally used his pen!

BIFF   Listen, kid, I took those balls years ago, now I walk in with his fountain pen? That clinches it, don't you see? I can't face him like that! I'll try elsewhere.

PAGE'S VOICE   Paging Mr. Loman!

WILLY   Don't you want to be anything?

BIFF   Pop, how can I go back?

WILLY   You don't want to be anything, is that what's behind it?

BIFF   [*now angry at* WILLY *for not crediting his sympathy*]   Don't take it that way! You think it was easy walking into that office after what I'd done to him? A team of horses couldn't have dragged me back to Bill Oliver!

WILLY   Then why'd you go?

BIFF   Why did I go? Why did I go! Look at you! Look at what's become of you!

Off left, THE WOMAN *laughs.*

WILLY   Biff, you're going to go to that lunch tomorrow, or—

BIFF   I can't go. I've got no appointment!

HAPPY   Biff, for . . . !

WILLY   Are you spiting me?

BIFF   Don't take it that way! Goddammit!

WILLY   [*strikes* BIFF *and falters away from the table*]   You rotten little louse! Are you spiting me?

THE WOMAN   Someone's at the door, Willy!

BIFF   I'm no good, can't you see what I am?

HAPPY   [*separating them*]   Hey, you're in a restaurant! Now cut it out, both of you! [*The girls enter.*] Hello, girls, sit down.

THE WOMAN *laughs, off left.*

MISS FORSYTHE   I guess we might as well. This is Letta.

THE WOMAN   Willy, are you going to wake up?

BIFF   [*ignoring* WILLY]   How're ya, miss, sit down. What do you drink?

MISS FORSYTHE   Letta might not be able to stay long.

LETTA   I gotta get up very early tomorrow. I got jury duty. I'm so excited! Were you fellows ever on a jury?

BIFF   No, but I been in front of them! [*The girls laugh.*] This is my father.

LETTA   Isn't he cute? Sit down with us, Pop.

HAPPY   Sit him down, Biff!

BIFF [*going to him*]   Come on, slugger, drink us under the table. To hell with it! Come on, sit down, pal.

On BIFF's *last insistence,* WILLY *is about to sit.*

THE WOMAN [*now urgently*]   Willy, are you going to answer the door!

THE WOMAN's *call pulls* WILLY *back. He starts right, befuddled.*

BIFF   Hey, where are you going?

WILLY   Open the door.

BIFF   The door?

WILLY   The washroom . . . the door . . . where's the door?

BIFF [*leading* WILLY *to the left*]   Just go straight down.

WILLY *moves left.*

THE WOMAN   Willy, Willy, are you going to get up, get up, get up, get up?

WILLY *exits left.*

LETTA   I think it's sweet you bring your daddy along.

MISS FORSYTHE   Oh, he isn't really your father!

BIFF [*at left, turning to her resentfully*]   Miss Forsythe, you've just seen a prince walk by. A fine, troubled prince. A hard-working, unappreciated prince. A pal, you understand? A good companion. Always for his boys.

LETTA   That's so sweet.

HAPPY   Well, girls, what's the program? We're wasting time. Come on, Biff. Gather round. Where would you like to go?

BIFF   Why don't you do something for him?

HAPPY   Me!

BIFF   Don't you give a damn for him, Hap?

HAPPY   What're you talking about? I'm the one who—

BIFF   I sense it, you don't give a good goddam about him. [*He takes the rolled-up hose from his pocket and puts it on the table in front of* HAPPY.] Look what I found in the cellar, for Christ's sake. How can you bear to let it go on?

HAPPY   Me? Who goes away? Who runs off and—

BIFF   Yeah, but he doesn't mean anything to you. You could help him—I can't! Don't you understand what I'm talking about? He's going to kill himself, don't you know that?

HAPPY   Don't I know it! Me!

BIFF   Hap, help him! Jesus . . . help him . . . Help me, help me, I can't bear to look at his face! [*Ready to weep, he hurries out, up right.*]

HAPPY [*starting after him*]   Where are you going?

MISS FORSYTHE   What's he so mad about?

HAPPY   Come on, girls, we'll catch up with him.

MISS FORSYTHE   [*as* HAPPY *pushes her out*]   Say, I don't like that temper of his!

HAPPY   He's just a little overstrung, he'll be all right!

WILLY   [*off left, as* THE WOMAN *laughs*]   Don't answer! Don't answer!

LETTA   Don't you want to tell your father—

HAPPY   No, that's not my father. He's just a guy. Come on, we'll catch Biff, and, honey, we're going to paint this town! Stanley, where's the check! Hey, Stanley!

They exit. STANLEY *looks toward left.*

STANLEY   [*calling to* HAPPY *indignantly*]   Mr. Loman! Mr. Loman!

> STANLEY *picks up a chair and follows them off. Knocking is heard off left.* THE WOMAN *enters, laughing.* WILLY *follows her. She is in a black slip; he is buttoning his shirt. Raw, sensuous music accompanies their speech.*

WILLY   Will you stop laughing? Will you stop?

THE WOMAN   Aren't you going to answer the door? He'll wake the whole hotel.

WILLY   I'm not expecting anybody.

THE WOMAN   Whyn't you have another drink, honey, and stop being so damn self-centered?

WILLY   I'm so lonely.

THE WOMAN   You know you ruined me, Willy? From now on, whenever you come to the office, I'll see that you go right through to the buyers. No waiting at my desk any more, Willy. You ruined me.

WILLY   That's nice of you to say that.

THE WOMAN   Gee, you are self-centered! Why so sad? You are the saddest, self-centeredest soul I ever did see-saw. [*She laughs. He kisses her.*] Come on inside, drummer boy. It's silly to be dressing in the middle of the night. [*As knocking is heard*] Aren't you going to answer the door?

WILLY   They're knocking on the wrong door.

THE WOMAN   But I felt the knocking. And he heard us talking in here. Maybe the hotel's on fire!

WILLY   [*his terror rising*]   It's a mistake.

THE WOMAN   Then tell him to go away!

WILLY   There's nobody there.

THE WOMAN   It's getting on my nerves, Willy. There's somebody standing out there and it's getting on my nerves!

WILLY   [*pushing her away from him*]   All right, stay in the bathroom here, and don't come out. I think there's a law in Massachusetts about it, so don't come out. It may be that new room clerk. He looked very mean. So don't come out. It's a mistake, there's no fire.

The knocking is heard again. He takes a few steps away from her, and she vanishes into the wing. The light follows him, and now he is facing YOUNG BIFF, *who carries a suitcase.* BIFF *steps toward him. The music is gone.*

BIFF   Why didn't you answer?

WILLY   Biff! What are you doing in Boston?

BIFF   Why didn't you answer? I've been knocking for five minutes, I called you on the phone—

WILLY   I just heard you. I was in the bathroom and had the door shut. Did anything happen home?

BIFF   Dad—I let you down.

WILLY   What do you mean?

BIFF   Dad . . .

WILLY   Biffo, what's this about? [*Putting his arm around* BIFF] Come on, let's go downstairs and get you a malted.

BIFF   Dad, I flunked math.

WILLY   Not for the term?

BIFF   The term. I haven't got enough credits to graduate.

WILLY   You mean to say Bernard wouldn't give you the answers?

BIFF   He did, he tried, but I only got a sixty-one.

WILLY   And they wouldn't give you four points?

BIFF   Birnbaum refused absolutely. I begged him, Pop, but he won't give me those points. You gotta talk to him before they close the school. Because if he saw the kind of man you are, and you just talked to him in your way, I'm sure he'd come through for me. The class came right before practice, see, and I didn't go enough. Would you talk to him? He'd like you, Pop. You know the way you could talk.

WILLY   You're on. We'll drive right back.

BIFF   Oh, Dad, good work! I'm sure he'll change it for you!

WILLY   Go downstairs and tell the clerk I'm checkin' out. Go right down.

BIFF   Yes, sir! See, the reason he hates me, Pop—one day he was late for class so I got up at the blackboard and imitated him. I crossed my eyes and talked with a lithp.

WILLY [*laughing*]   You did? The kids like it?

BIFF   They nearly died laughing!

WILLY   Yeah? What'd you do?

BIFF   The thquare root of thixthy twee is . . . [WILLY *bursts out laughing;* BIFF *joins him.*] And in the middle of it he walked in!

WILLY *laughs and* THE WOMAN *joins in offstage.*

WILLY [*without hesitation*]   Hurry downstairs and—

BIFF   Somebody in there?

WILLY   No, that was next door.

THE WOMAN *laughs offstage.*

BIFF   Somebody got in your bathroom!

WILLY   No, it's the next room, there's a party—

THE WOMAN [*enters, laughing. She lisps this*]   Can I come in? There's something in the bathtub, Willy, and it's moving!

> WILLY *looks at* BIFF, *who is staring open-mouthed and horrified at* THE WOMAN.

WILLY   Ah—you better go back to your room. They must be finished painting by now. They're painting her room so I let her take a shower here. Go back, go back . . . [*He pushes her.*]

THE WOMAN [*resisting*]   But I've got to get dressed, Willy, I can't—

WILLY   Get out of here! Go back, go back . . . [*Suddenly striving for the ordinary*] This is Miss Francis, Biff, she's a buyer. They're painting her room. Go back, Miss Francis, go back . . .

THE WOMAN   But my clothes, I can't go out naked in the hall!

WILLY [*pushing her offstage*]   Get outa here! Go back, go back!

> BIFF *slowly sits down on his suitcase as the argument continues offstage.*

THE WOMAN   Where's my stockings? You promised me stockings, Willy!

WILLY   I have no stockings here!

THE WOMAN   You had two boxes of size nine sheers for me, and I want them!

WILLY   Here, for God's sake, will you get outa here!

THE WOMAN [*enters holding a box of stockings*]   I just hope there's nobody in the hall. That's all I hope. [*To* BIFF] Are you football or baseball?

BIFF   Football.

THE WOMAN [*angry, humiliated*]   That's me too. G'night. [*She snatches her clothes from* WILLY, *and walks out.*]

WILLY [*after a pause*]   Well, better get going. I want to get to the school first thing in the morning. Get my suits out of the closet. I'll get my valise. [BIFF *doesn't move.*] What's the matter? [BIFF *remains motionless, tears falling.*] She's a buyer. Buys for J. H. Simmons. She lives down the hall—they're painting. You don't imagine— [*He breaks off. After a pause*] Now listen, pal, she's just a buyer. She sees merchandise in her room and they have to keep it looking just so . . . [*Pause. Assuming command*] All right, get my suits. [BIFF *doesn't move.*] Now stop crying and do as I say. I gave you an order. Biff, I gave you an order! Is that what you do when I give you an order? How dare you cry! [*Putting his arm around* BIFF] Now look, Biff, when you grow up you'll understand about these things. You mustn't—you mustn't overemphasize a thing like this. I'll see Birnbaum first thing in the morning.

BIFF   Never mind.

WILLY [*getting down beside* BIFF]   Never mind! He's going to give you those points. I'll see to it.

BIFF   He wouldn't listen to you.

WILLY   He certainly will listen to me. You need those points for the U. of Virginia.

BIFF   I'm not going there.

WILLY   Heh? If I can't get him to change that mark you'll make it up in summer school. You've got all summer to—

BIFF [*his weeping breaking from him*]   Dad . . .

WILLY [*infected by it*]   Oh, my boy . . .

BIFF   Dad . . .

WILLY   She's nothing to me, Biff. I was lonely, I was terribly lonely.

BIFF   You—you gave her Mama's stockings! [*His tears break through and he rises to go.*]

WILLY [*grabbing for* BIFF]   I gave you an order!

BIFF   Don't touch me, you—liar!

WILLY   Apologize for that!

BIFF   You fake! You phony little fake! You fake! [*overcome, he turns quickly and weeping fully goes out with his suitcase,* WILLY *is left on the floor on his knees.*]

WILLY   I gave you an order! Biff, come back here or I'll beat you! Come back here! I'll whip you!

STANLEY *comes quickly in from the right and stands in front of* WILLY.

WILLY [*shouts at* STANLEY]   I gave you an order . . .

STANLEY   Hey, let's pick it up, pick it up, Mr. Loman. [*He helps* WILLY *to his feet.*] Your boys left with the chippies. They said they'll see you home.

A second waiter watches some distance away.

WILLY   But we were supposed to have dinner together.

Music is heard, WILLY's *theme.*

STANLEY   Can you make it?

WILLY   I'll—sure, I can make it. [*Suddenly concerned about his clothes*] Do I—I look all right?

STANLEY   Sure, you look all right. [*He flicks a speck off* WILLY's *lapel.*]

WILLY   Here—here's a dollar.

STANLEY   Oh, your son paid me. It's all right.

WILLY [*putting it in* STANLEY's *hand*]   No, take it. You're a good boy.

STANLEY   Oh, no, you don't have to . . .

WILLY   Here—here's some more, I don't need it any more. [*After a slight pause*] Tell me—is there a seed store in the neighborhood?

STANLEY   Seeds? You mean like to plant?

As WILLY *turns,* STANLEY *slips the money back into his jacket pocket.*

WILLY   Yes. Carrots, peas . . .

STANLEY   Well, there's hardware stores on Sixth Avenue, but it may be too late now.

WILLY [*anxiously*]   Oh, I'd better hurry. I've got to get some seeds. [*He starts off to the right.*] I've got to get some seeds, right away. Nothing's planted. I don't have a thing in the ground.

> WILLY *hurries out as the light goes down.* STANLEY *moves over to the right after him, watches him off. The other waiter has been staring at* WILLY.

STANLEY [*to the waiter*]   Well, whatta you looking at?

> *The waiter picks up the chairs and moves off right.* STANLEY *takes the table and follows him. The light fades on this area. There is a long pause, the sound of the flute coming over. The light gradually rises on the kitchen, which is empty.* HAPPY *appears at the door of the house, followed by* BIFF. HAPPY *is carrying a large bunch of long-stemmed roses. He enters the kitchen, looks around for* LINDA. *Not seeing her, he turns to* BIFF, *who is just outside the house door, and makes a gesture with his hands, indicating "Not here, I guess." He looks into the living room and freezes. Inside,* LINDA, *unseen, is seated,* WILLY's *coat on her lap. She rises ominously and quietly and moves toward* HAPPY, *who backs up into the kitchen, afraid.*

HAPPY   Hey, what're you doing up? [LINDA *says nothing but moves toward him implacably.*] Where's Pop? [*He keeps backing to the right, and now* LINDA *is in full view in the doorway to the living room.*] Is he sleeping?

LINDA   Where were you?

HAPPY [*trying to laugh it off*]   We met two girls, Mom, very fine types. Here, we brought you some flowers. [*Offering them to her*] Put them in your room, Ma.

> *She knocks them to the floor at* BIFF's *feet. He has now come inside and closed the door behind him. She stares at* BIFF, *silent.*

HAPPY   Now what'd you do that for? Mom, I want you to have some flowers—

LINDA [*cutting* HAPPY *off, violently to* BIFF]   Don't you care whether he lives or dies?

HAPPY [*going to the stairs*]   Come upstairs, Biff.

BIFF [*with a flare of disgust, to* HAPPY]   Go away from me! [*To* LINDA]   What do you mean, lives or dies? Nobody's dying around here, pal.

LINDA   Get out of my sight! Get out of here!

BIFF   I wanna see the boss.

LINDA   You're not going near him!

BIFF   Where is he? [*He moves to the living room and* LINDA *follows.*]

LINDA   [*shouting at* BIFF]   You invite him for dinner. He looks forward to it all day—[BIFF *appears in his parents' bedroom, looks around, and exits*]—and then you desert him there. There's no stranger you'd do that to!

HAPPY   Why? He had a swell time with us. Listen, when I—[LINDA *comes back into the kitchen*]—desert him I hope I don't outlive the day!

LINDA   Get out of here!

HAPPY   Now look, Mom . . .

LINDA   Did you have to go to women tonight? You and your lousy rotten whores!

BIFF *re-enters the kitchen.*

HAPPY   Mom, all we did was follow Biff around trying to cheer him up! [*To* BIFF] Boy, what a night you gave me!

LINDA   Get out of here, both of you, and don't come back! I don't want you tormenting him any more. Go on now, get your things together! [*To* BIFF] You can sleep in his apartment. [*She starts to pick up the flowers and stops herself.*] Pick up this stuff, I'm not your maid any more. Pick it up, you bum, you!

HAPPY *turns his back on her in refusal.* BIFF *slowly moves over and gets down on his knees, picking up the flowers.*

LINDA   You're a pair of animals! Not one, not another living soul would have had the cruelty to walk out on that man in a restaurant!

BIFF [*not looking at her*]   Is that what he said?

LINDA   He didn't have to say anything. He was so humiliated he nearly limped when he came in.

HAPPY   But, Mom, he had a great time with us—

BIFF [*cutting him off violently*]   Shut up!

Without another word, HAPPY *goes upstairs.*

LINDA   You! You didn't even go in to see if he was all right!

BIFF [*still on the floor in front of* LINDA, *the flowers in his hand; with self-loathing*]   No. Didn't. Didn't do a damned thing. How do you like that, heh? Left him babbling in a toilet.

LINDA   You louse. You . . .

BIFF   Now you hit it on the nose! [*He gets up, throws the flowers in the wastebasket.*] The scum of the earth, and you're looking at him!

LINDA   Get out of here!

BIFF   I gotta talk to the boss, Mom. Where is he?

LINDA   You're not going near him. Get out of this house!

BIFF [*with absolute assurance, determination*]   No. We're gonna have an abrupt conversation, him and me.

LINDA   You're not talking to him!

Hammering is heard from outside the house, off right. BIFF *turns toward the noise.*

LINDA [*suddenly pleading*]   Will you please leave him alone?

BIFF   What's he doing out there?

LINDA   He's planting the garden!

BIFF [*quietly*]   Now? Oh, my God!

BIFF *moves outside,* LINDA *following. The light dies down on them and comes up on the center of the apron as* WILLY *walks into it. He is carrying a flashlight, a hoe, and a handful of seed packets. He raps the top of the hoe sharply to fix it firmly, and then moves to the left, measuring off the distance with his foot. He holds the flashlight to look at the seed packets, reading off the instructions. He is in the blue of night.*

WILLY   Carrots . . . quarter-inch apart. Rows . . . one-foot rows. [*He measures it off.*] One foot. [*He puts down a package and measures off.*] Beets [*He puts down another package and measures again.*] Lettuce. [*He reads the package, puts it down.*] One foot— [*He breaks off as* BEN *appears at the right and moves slowly down to him.*] What a proposition, ts, ts. Terrific, terrific. 'Cause she's suffered, Ben, the woman has suffered. You understand me? A man can't go out the way he came in, Ben, a man has got to add up to something. You can't, you can't— [BEN *moves toward him as though to interrupt.*] You gotta consider, now. Don't answer so quick. Remember, it's a guaranteed twenty-thousand-dollar proposition. Now look, Ben, I want you to go through the ins and outs of this thing with me. I've got nobody to talk to, Ben, and the woman has suffered, you hear me?

BEN [*standing still, considering*]   What's the proposition?

WILLY   It's twenty thousand dollars on the barrelhead. Guaranteed, gilt-edged, you understand?

BEN   You don't want to make a fool of yourself. They might not honor the policy.

WILLY   How can they dare refuse? Didn't I work like a coolie to meet every premium on the nose? And now they don't pay off? Impossible!

BEN   It's called a cowardly thing, William.

WILLY   Why? Does it take more guts to stand here the rest of my life ringing up a zero?

BEN [*yielding*]   That's a point, William. [*He moves, thinking, turns.*] And twenty thousand—that *is* something one can feel with the hand, it is there.

WILLY [*now assured, with rising power*]   Oh, Ben, that's the whole beauty of it! I see it like a diamond, shining in the dark, hard and rough, that I can pick up and touch in my hand. Not like—like an appointment! This would not be another damn-fool appointment, Ben, and it changes all the aspects. Because he thinks I'm nothing, see, and so he spites me. But the funeral— [*Straightening up*] Ben, that funeral will be massive! They'll come from Maine, Massachusetts, Vermont, New Hampshire! All the old-timers with the strange license plates—that boy will be thunder-struck, Ben, because he never realized—I am known! Rhode Island, New York, New Jersey—I am known, Ben, and he'll see it with his eyes once and for all. He'll see what I am, Ben! He's in for a shock, that boy!

BEN [*coming down to the edge of the garden*]   He'll call you a coward.

WILLY [*suddenly fearful*]   No, that would be terrible.

BEN   Yes. And a damned fool.

WILLY   No, no, he mustn't, I won't have that! [*He is broken and desperate.*]

BEN   He'll hate you, William.

> *The gay music of the Boys is heard.*

WILLY   Oh, Ben, how do we get back to all the great times? Used to be so full of light, and comradeship, the sleigh-riding in winter, and the ruddiness on his cheeks. And always some kind of good news coming up, always something nice coming up ahead. And never even let me carry the valises in the house, and simonizing, simonizing that little red car! Why, why can't I give him something and not have him hate me?

BEN   Let me think about it. [*He glances at his watch.*] I still have a little time. Remarkable proposition, but you've got to be sure you're not making a fool of yourself.

> BEN *drifts off upstage and goes out of sight.* BIFF *comes down from the left.*

WILLY [*suddenly conscious of* BIFF, *turns and looks up at him, then begins picking up the packages of seeds in confusion*]   Where the hell is that seed? [*Indignantly*] You can't see nothing out here! They boxed in the whole goddam neighborhood!

BIFF   There are people all around here. Don't you realize that?

WILLY   I'm busy. Don't bother me.

BIFF [*taking the hoe from* WILLY]   I'm saying good-by to you, Pop. [WILLY *looks at him, silent, unable to move.*] I'm not coming back any more.

WILLY   You're not going to see Oliver tomorrow?

BIFF   I've got no appointment, Dad.

WILLY   He put his arm around you, and you've got no appointment?

BIFF   Pop, get this now, will you? Every time I've left it's been a fight that sent me out of here. Today I realized something about myself and I tried to explain it to you and I—I think I'm just not smart enough to make any sense out of it for you. To hell with whose fault it is or anything like that. [*He takes* WILLY's *arm.*] Let's just wrap it up, heh? Come on in, we'll tell Mom. [*He gently tries to pull* WILLY *to left.*]

WILLY [*frozen, immobile, with guilt in his voice*]   No, I don't want to see her.

BIFF   Come on! [*He pulls again, and* WILLY *tries to pull away.*]

WILLY [*highly nervous*]   No, no, I don't want to see her.

BIFF [*tries to look into* WILLY's *face, as if to find the answer there*]   Why don't you want to see her?

WILLY [*more harshly now*]   Don't bother me, will you?

BIFF   What do you mean, you don't want to see her? You don't want them calling you yellow, do you? This isn't your fault; it's me, I'm a bum. Now come inside! [WILLY *strains to get away.*] Did you hear what I said to you?

> WILLY *pulls away and quickly goes by himself into the house.*
> BIFF *follows.*

LINDA [*to* WILLY]   Did you plant, dear?

BIFF [*at the door, to* LINDA]   All right, we had it out. I'm going and I'm not writing any more.

LINDA [*going to* WILLY *in the kitchen*]   I think that's the best way, dear. 'Cause there's no use drawing it out, you'll just never get along.

> WILLY *doesn't respond.*

BIFF   People ask where I am and what I'm doing, you don't know, and you don't care. That way it'll be off your mind and you can start brightening up again. All right? That clears it, doesn't it? [WILLY *is silent, and* BIFF *goes to him.*] You gonna wish me luck, scout? [*He extends his hand.*] What do you say?

LINDA   Shake his hand, Willy.

WILLY [*turning to her, seething with hurt*]   There's no necessity to mention the pen at all, y'know.

BIFF [*gently*]   I've got no appointment, Dad.

WILLY [*erupting fiercely*]   He put his arm around . . . ?

BIFF   Dad, you're never going to see what I am, so what's the use of arguing? If I strike oil I'll send you a check. Meantime forget I'm alive.

WILLY [*to* LINDA]   Spite, see?

BIFF   Shake hands, Dad.

WILLY   Not my hand.

BIFF   I was hoping not to go this way.

WILLY   Well, this is the way you're going. Good-by.

> BIFF *looks at him a moment, then turns sharply and goes to the stairs.*

WILLY [*stops him with*]   May you rot in hell if you leave this house!

BIFF [*turning*]   Exactly what is it that you want from me?

WILLY   I want you to know, on the train, in the mountains, in the valleys, wherever you go, that you cut down your life for spite!

BIFF   No, no.

WILLY   Spite, spite, is the word of your undoing! And when you're down and out, remember what did it. When you're rotting somewhere beside the railroad tracks, remember, and don't you dare blame it on me!

BIFF   I'm not blaming it on you!

WILLY   I won't take the rap for this, you hear?

HAPPY *comes down the stairs and stands on the bottom step, watching.*

BIFF   That's just what I'm telling you!

WILLY [*sinking into a chair at the table with full accusation*]   You're trying to put a knife in me—don't think I don't know what you're doing!

BIFF   All right, phony! Then let's lay it on the line. [*He whips the rubber tube out of his pocket and puts it on the table.*]

HAPPY   You crazy—

LINDA   Biff! [*She moves to grab the hose, but* BIFF *holds it down with his hand.*]

BIFF   Leave it there! Don't move it!

WILLY [*not looking at it*]   What is that?

BIFF   You know goddam well what that is.

WILLY [*caged, wanting to escape*]   I never saw that.

BIFF   You saw it. The mice didn't bring it into the cellar! What is this supposed to do, make a hero out of you? This supposed to make me sorry for you?

WILLY   Never heard of it.

BIFF   There'll be no pity for you, you hear it? No pity!

WILLY [*to* LINDA]   You hear the spite!

BIFF   No, you're going to hear the truth—what you are and what I am!

LINDA   Stop it!

WILLY   Spite!

HAPPY [*coming down toward* BIFF]   You cut it now!

BIFF [*to* HAPPY]   The man don't know who we are! The man is gonna know! [*To* WILLY] We never told the truth for ten minutes in this house!

HAPPY   We always told the truth!

BIFF [*turning on him*]   You big blow, are you the assistant buyer? You're one of the two assistants to the assistant, aren't you?

HAPPY   Well, I'm practically—

BIFF   You're practically full of it! We all are! And I'm through with it. [*To* WILLY] Now hear this, Willy, this is me.

WILLY   I know you!

BIFF   You know why I had no address for three months? I stole a suit in Kansas City and I was in jail. [*To* LINDA, *who is sobbing*] Stop crying. I'm through with it.

LINDA *turns away from them, her hands covering her face.*

WILLY   I suppose that's my fault!

BIFF   I stole myself out of every good job since high school!

WILLY   And whose fault is that?

BIFF   And I never got anywhere because you blew me so full of hot air I could never stand taking orders from anybody! That's whose fault it is!

WILLY   I hear that!

LINDA   Don't, Biff!

BIFF   It's goddam time you heard that! I had to be boss big shot in two weeks, and I'm through with it!

WILLY   Then hang yourself! For spite, hang yourself!

BIFF   No! Nobody's hanging himself, Willy! I ran down eleven flights with a pen in my hand today. And suddenly I stopped, you hear me? And in the middle of that office building, do you hear this? I stopped in the middle of that building and I saw—the sky. I saw the things that I love in this world. The work and the food and time to sit and smoke. And I looked at the pen and said to myself, what the hell am I grabbing this for? Why am I trying to become what I don't want to be? What am I doing in an office, making a contemptuous, begging fool of myself, when all I want is out there, waiting for me the minute I say I know who I am! Why can't I say that, Willy? [*He tries to make* WILLY *face him, but* WILLY *pulls away and moves to the left.*]

WILLY   [*with hatred, threateningly*]   The door to your life is wide open!

BIFF   Pop! I'm a dime a dozen, and so are you!

WILLY   [*turning on him now in an uncontrolled outburst*]   I am not a dime a dozen! I am Willy Loman, and you are Biff Loman!

BIFF *starts for* WILLY, *but is blocked by* HAPPY. *In his fury,* BIFF *seems on the verge of attacking his father.*

BIFF   I am not a leader of men, Willy, and neither are you. You were never anything but a hard-working drummer who landed in the ash can like all the rest of them! I'm one dollar an hour, Willy! I tried seven states and couldn't raise it. A buck an hour! Do you gather my meaning? I'm not bringing home any prizes any more, and you're going to stop waiting for me to bring them home!

WILLY   [*directly to* BIFF]   You vengeful, spiteful mut!

BIFF *breaks from* HAPPY. WILLY, *in fright, starts up the stairs.* BIFF *grabs him.*

BIFF [*at the peak of his fury*] Pop, I'm nothing! I'm nothing, Pop. Can't you understand that? There's no spite in it any more. I'm just what I am, that's all.

> BIFF's *fury has spent itself, and he breaks down, sobbing, holding on to* WILLY, *who dumbly fumbles for* BIFF's *face.*

WILLY [*astonished.*] What're you doing? What're you doing? [*To* LINDA] Why is he crying?

BIFF [*crying, broken*] Will you let me go, for Christ's sake? Will you take that phony dream and burn it before something happens? [*Struggling to contain himself, he pulls away and moves to the stairs.*] I'll go in the morning. Put him—put him to bed. [*Exhausted,* BIFF *moves up the stairs to his room.*]

WILLY [*after a long pause, astonished, elevated*] Isn't that—isn't that remarkable? Biff—he likes me!

LINDA He loves you, Willy!

HAPPY [*deeply moved*] Always did, Pop.

WILLY Oh, Biff! [*Staring wildly*] He cried! Cried to me. [*He is choking with his love, and now cries out his promise*] That boy— that boy is going to be magnificent!

> BEN *appears in the light just outside the kitchen.*

BEN Yes, outstanding, with twenty thousand behind him.

LINDA [*sensing the racing of his mind, fearfully, carefully*] Now come to bed, Willy. It's all settled now.

WILLY [*finding it difficult not to rush out of the house*] Yes, we'll sleep. Come on. Go to sleep, Hap.

BEN And it does take a great kind of a man to crack the jungle.

> *In accents of dread,* BEN's *idyllic music starts up.*

HAPPY [*his arm around* LINDA] I'm getting married, Pop, don't forget it. I'm changing everything. I'm gonna run that department before the year is up. You'll see, Mom. [*He kisses her.*]

BEN The jungle is dark but full of diamonds, Willy.

> WILLY *turns, moves, listening to* BEN.

LINDA Be good. You're both good boys, just act that way, that's all.

HAPPY 'Night, Pop. [*He goes upstairs.*]

LINDA [*to* WILLY] Come, dear.

BEN [*with greater force*] One must go in to fetch a diamond out.

WILLY [*to* LINDA, *as he moves slowly along the edge of the kitchen, toward the door*] I just want to get settled down, Linda. Let me sit alone for a little.

LINDA [*almost uttering her fear*] I want you upstairs.

WILLY [*taking her in his arms*]   In a few minutes, Linda. I couldn't sleep right now. Go on, you look awful tired. [*He kisses her.*]

BEN   Not like an appointment at all. A diamond is rough and hard to the touch.

WILLY   Go on now. I'll be right up.

LINDA   I think this is the only way, Willy.

WILLY   Sure, it's the best thing.

BEN   Best thing!

WILLY   The only way. Everything is gonna be—go on, kid, get to bed. You look so tired.

LINDA   Come right up.

WILLY   Two minutes.

> LINDA *goes into the living room, then reappears in her bedroom.* WILLY *moves just outside the kitchen door.*

WILLY   Loves me. [*Wonderingly*] Always loved me. Isn't that a remarkable thing? Ben, he'll worship me for it!

BEN [*with promise*]   It's dark there, but full of diamonds.

WILLY   Can you imagine that magnificence with twenty thousand dollars in his pocket?

LINDA [*calling from her room*]   Willy! Come up!

WILLY [*calling into the kitchen*]   Yes! Coming! It's very smart, you realize that, don't you, sweetheart? Even Ben sees it. I gotta go, baby. 'By! 'By! [*Going over to* BEN, *almost dancing*] Imagine? When the mail comes he'll be ahead of Bernard again!

BEN   A perfect proposition all around.

WILLY   Did you see how he cried to me? Oh, if I could kiss him, Ben!

BEN   Time, William, time!

WILLY   Oh, Ben, I always knew one way or another we were gonna make it, Biff and I!

BEN [*looking at his watch*]   The boat. We'll be late [*He moves slowly off into the darkness.*]

WILLY [*elegiacally, turning to the house*]   Now when you kick off, boy, I want a seventy-yard boot, and get right down the field under the ball, and when you hit, hit low and hit hard, because it's important, boy. [*He swings around and faces the audience.*] There's all kinds of important people in the stands, and the first thing you know . . . [*Suddenly realizing he is alone*] Ben! Ben, where do I . . . [*He makes a sudden movement of search.*] Ben, how do I . . . . ?

LINDA [*calling*]   Willy, you coming up?

WILLY [*uttering a gasp of fear, whirling about as if to quiet her*]   Sh! [*He turns around as if to find his way; sounds, faces, voices, seem to be swarming in upon him and he flicks at them, crying*] Sh! Sh! [*Suddenly music, faint and high, stops him. It rises in intensity, almost to an unbearable scream. He goes up and down on his toes, and rushes off around the house.*] Shhh!

LINDA   Willy?

There is no answer. Linda waits. BIFF *gets up off his bed. He is still in his clothes.* HAPPY *sits up.* BIFF *stands listening.*

LINDA [*with real fear*]   Willy, answer me! Willy!

There is the sound of a car starting and moving away at full speed.

LINDA   No!
BIFF [*rushing down the stairs*]   Pop!

As the car speeds off, the music crashes down in a frenzy of sound, which becomes the soft pulsation of a single cello string. BIFF *slowly returns to his bedroom. He and* HAPPY *gravely don their jackets.* LINDA *slowly walks out of her room. The music has developed into a dead march. The leaves of day are appearing over everything.* CHARLEY *and* BERNARD, *somberly dressed, appear and knock on the kitchen door.* BIFF *and* HAPPY *slowly descend the stairs to the kitchen as* CHARLEY *and* BERNARD *enter. All stop a moment when* LINDA, *in clothes of mourning, bearing a little bunch of roses, comes through the draped doorway into the kitchen. She goes to* CHARLEY *and takes his arm. Now all move toward the audience, through the wall-line of the kitchen. At the limit of the apron,* LINDA *lays down the flowers, kneels, and sits back on her heels. All stare down at the grave.*

Requiem

CHARLEY   It's getting dark, Linda.

LINDA *doesn't react. She stares at the grave.*

BIFF   How about it, Mom? Better get some rest, heh? They'll be closing the gate soon.

LINDA *makes no move. Pause.*

HAPPY [*deeply angered*]   He had no right to do that. There was no necessity for it. We would've helped him.
CHARLEY [*grunting*]   Hmmm.
BIFF   Come along, Mom.
LINDA   Why didn't anybody come?
CHARLEY   It was a very nice funeral.
LINDA   But where are all the people he knew? Maybe they blame him.
CHARLEY   Naa. It's a rough world, Linda. They wouldn't blame him.

LINDA   I can't understand it. At this time especially. First time in thirty-five years we were just about free and clear. He only needed a little salary. He was even finished with the dentist.

CHARLEY   No man only needs a little salary.

LINDA   I can't understand it.

BIFF   There were a lot of nice days. When he'd come home from a trip; or on Sundays, making the stoop; finishing the cellar; putting on the new porch; when he built the extra bathroom; and put up the garage. You know something, Charley, there's more of him in that front stoop than in all the sales he ever made.

CHARLEY   Yeah. He was a happy man with a batch of cement.

LINDA   He was so wonderful with his hands.

BIFF   He had the wrong dreams. All, all, wrong.

HAPPY [*almost ready to fight* BIFF]   Don't say that!

BIFF   He never knew who he was.

CHARLEY [*stopping* HAPPY's *movement and reply. To* BIFF]   Nobody dast blame this man. You don't understand: Willy was a salesman. And for a salesman, there is no rock bottom to the life. He don't put a bolt to a nut, he don't tell you the law or give you medicine. He's a man way out there in the blue, riding on a smile and a shoeshine. And when they start not smiling back—that's an earthquake. And then you get yourself a couple of spots on your hat, and you're finished. Nobody dast blame this man. A salesman is got to dream, boy. It comes with the territory.

BIFF   Charley, the man didn't know who he was.

HAPPY [*infuriated*]   Don't say that!

BIFF   Why don't you come with me, Happy?

HAPPY   I'm not licked that easily. I'm staying right in this city, and I'm gonna beat this racket! [*He looks at* BIFF, *his chin set.*] The Loman Brothers!

BIFF   I know who I am, kid.

HAPPY   All right, boy. I'm gonna show you and everybody else that Willy Loman did not die in vain. He had a good dream. It's the only dream you can have—to come out number-one man. He fought it out here, and this is where I'm gonna win it for him.

BIFF [*with a hopeless glance at* HAPPY, *bends toward his mother*] Let's go, Mom.

LINDA   I'll be with you in a minute. Go on, Charley. [*He hesitates.*] I want to, just for a minute. I never had a chance to say good-by.

> CHARLEY *moves away, followed by* HAPPY. BIFF *remains a slight distance up and left of* LINDA. *She sits there, summoning herself. The flute begins, not far away, playing behind her speech.*

LINDA   Forgive me, dear. I can't cry. I don't know what it is, but I can't cry. I don't understand it. Why did you ever do that? Help me, Willy, I can't cry. It seems to me that you're just on another trip. I keep expecting you. Willy, dear, I can't cry. Why did you do it? I search and search and search, and I can't understand it, Willy. I made the last payment on the house today. Today, dear. And there'll be nobody home. [*A sob rises in her throat.*] We're free and clear. [*Sobbing more fully, released*] We're free. [BIFF *comes slowly toward her.*] We're free . . . We're free . . .

BIFF *lifts her to her feet and moves out up right with her in his arms.* LINDA *sobs quietly.* BERNARD *and* CHARLEY *come together and follow them, followed by* HAPPY. *Only the music of the flute is left on the darkening stage as over the house the hard towers of the apartment buildings rise into sharp focus, and*

THE CURTAIN FALLS

1949

Plays for Further Reading

SOPHOCLES

Oedipus Tyrannus[*]

CHARACTERS

OEDIPUS, *Ruler of Thebes*[1]
JOCASTA, *Wife of* OEDIPUS
CREON, *Brother of* JOCASTA
TEIRESIAS, *A Blind Prophet*
A PRIEST
MESSENGER 1
MESSENGER 2

A SHEPHERD
AN ATTENDANT
ANTIGONE } *Daughters of* OEDIPUS *and* JOCASTA
ISMENE
CHORUS OF THEBAN ELDERS

OEDIPUS   What is it, children, sons of the ancient house of Cadmus? Why do you sit as suppliants crowned with laurel branches? What is the meaning of the incense which fills the city? The pleas to end pain? The cries of sorrow? I chose not to hear it from my messengers, but came myself—I came, Oedipus, Oedipus, whose name is known to all. You, old one—age gives you the right to speak for all of them —you tell me why they sit before my altar. Has something frightened you? What brings you here? Some need? Some want? I'll help you all I can. I would be cruel did I not greet you with compassion when you are gathered here before me.

PRIEST   My Lord and King, we represent the young and old; some are priests and some the best of Theban youth. And I—I am a priest of Zeus. There are many more who carry laurel boughs like these— in the market-places, at the twin altars of Pallas, by the sacred ashes of Ismenus' oracle.[2] You see yourself how torn our city is, how she craves relief from the waves of death which now crash over her. Death is everywhere—in the harvests of the land, in the flocks that roam the pastures, in the unborn children of our mothers' wombs. A fiery plague is ravaging the city, festering, spreading its pestilence, wasting the house of Cadmus, filling the house of Hades with screams of pain and of fear. This is the reason why we come to you, these children and I. No, we do not think you a god. But we deem you a mortal set apart to face life's common issues and the trials which the gods dispense to men. It was you who once before came to Thebes and freed us from the spell that hypnotized our lives. You did this, and yet you knew no more than we—less even. You had no help from us. God aided you. Yes, you restored our life. And now a second time, great Oedipus, we turn to you for help. Find some relief for us, whether with god or man to guide your way. You helped us then. Yes. And we believe that you will help us now. O Lord, revive our city; restore her life. Think of your fame, your own repute. The

[*] Translated by Luci Berkowitz and Theodore F. Brunner.
1. See the note on Thebes and the House of Cadmus, p. 868.
2. Zeus was the king of the Greek gods. His daughter Pallas, or Athena, was spe- cifically a goddess of wisdom, but she had played an important part in the founding of Thebes. Apollo (or Phoebus), the sun god, had a shrine near Thebes, close to the river Ismenus.

people know you saved us from our past despair. Let no one say you raised us up to let us fall. Save us and keep us safe. You found good omens once to aid you and brought us fortune then. Find them again. If you will rule this land as king and lord, rule over men and not a wall encircling emptiness. No city wall, no ship can justify its claim to strength if it is stripped of men who give it life.

OEDIPUS   O my children, I know well the pain you suffer and under-stand what brings you here. You suffer—and yet not one among you suffers more than I. Each of you grieves for himself alone, while my heart must bear the strain of sorrow for all—myself and you and all our city's people. No, I am not blind to it. I have wept and in my weeping set my thoughts on countless paths, searching for an answer. I have sent my own wife's brother Creon, son of Menoeceus, to Apollo's Pythian shrine[3] to learn what I might say or do to ease our city's suffering. I am concerned that he is not yet here—he left many days ago. But this I promise: whenever he returns, whatever news he brings, whatever course the god reveals—*that* is the course that I shall take.

PRIEST   Well spoken. Look! They are giving signs that Creon is re-turning.

OEDIPUS   O God! If only he brings news as welcome as his smiling face.

PRIEST   I think he does. His head is crowned with laurel leaves.

OEDIPUS   We shall know soon enough. There. My Lord Creon, what word do you bring from the god?

Enter CREON.

CREON   Good news. I tell you this: if all goes well, our troubles will be past.

OEDIPUS   But what was the oracle? Right now I'm swaying between hope and fear.

CREON   If you want to hear it in the presence of these people, I shall tell you. If not, let's go inside.

OEDIPUS   Say it before all of us. I sorrow more for them than for my-self.

CREON   Then I shall tell you exactly what the god Apollo answered. These are his words: Pollution. A hidden sore is festering in our land. We are to stop its growth before it is too late.

OEDIPUS   Pollution? How are we to save ourselves?

CREON   Blood for blood. To save ourselves we are to banish a man or pay for blood with blood. It is a murder which has led to this despair.

OEDIPUS   Murder? Whose? Did the god say whose . . . ?

CREON   My Lord, before you came to rule our city, we had a king. His name was Laius . . .

OEDIPUS   I know, although I never saw him.

CREON   He was murdered. And the god's command is clear: we must find the assassin and destroy him.

OEDIPUS   But where? Where is he to be found? How can we find the traces of a crime committed long ago?

---

3. The oracle at Delphi was the principal shrine of Apollo and was called "Pythian" because it celebrated his victory over the monster Python.

CREON   He lives among us. If we seek, we will find; what we do not seek cannot be found.

OEDIPUS   Where was it that Laius met his death? At home? The country? In some foreign land?

CREON   One day he left and told us he would go to Delphi. That was the last we saw of him.

OEDIPUS   And there was no one who could tell what happened? No one who traveled with him? Did no one see? Is there no evidence?

CREON   All perished. All—except one who ran in panic from the scene and could not tell us anything for certain, except . . .

OEDIPUS   Except? What? What was it? One clue might lead to many. We have to grasp the smallest shred of hope.

CREON   He said that robbers—many of them—fell upon Laius and his men and murdered them.

OEDIPUS   Robbers? Who committed *murder?* Why? Unless they were paid assassins?

CREON   We considered that. But the king was dead and we were plagued with trouble. No one came forth as an avenger.

OEDIPUS   Trouble? What could have kept you from investigating the death of your king?

CREON   The Sphinx.[4] The Sphinx was confounding us with her riddles, forcing us to abandon our search for the unknown and to tend to what was then before us.

OEDIPUS   Then I—I shall begin again. I shall not cease until I bring the truth to light. Apollo has shown, and you have shown, the duty which we owe the dead. You have my gratitude. You will find me a firm ally, and together we shall exact vengeance for our land and for the god. I shall not rest till I dispel this defilement—not just for another man's sake, but for my own as well. For whoever the assassin—he might turn his hand against me too. Yes, I shall be serving Laius and myself. Now go, my children. Leave the steps of my altar. Go. Take away your laurel branches. Go to the people of Cadmus. Summon them. Tell them that I, their king, will leave nothing untried. And with the help of God, we shall find success—or ruin.

Exit OEDIPUS.

PRIEST   Come, children. We have learned what we came to learn. Come, Apollo, come yourself, who sent these oracles!
Come as our savior! Come! Deliver us from this plague!

CHORUS

O prophecy of Zeus, sweet is the sound of your words
as they come to our glorious city of Thebes
from Apollo's glittering shrine.
Yet I quake and I dread and I tremble at those words.
Io, Delian Lord![5]

4. The Sphinx was a winged monster with the head of a woman and the body of a lion who had terrorized Thebes, demanding the answer to her riddle, "What walks on four feet in the morning, two at noon, and three in the evening?" When the young Oedipus appeared at Thebes, he saved the city by answering her riddle, "Man," thus bringing about her death.

5. "Io" was a cry of generalized meaning used by worshippers in praise or supplication. Apollo was called "Delian Lord" because he had been born on the island of Delos.

What will you bring to pass? Disaster unknown,
or familiar to us, as the ever recurring seasons?
Tell me, O oracle,
heavenly daughter of blessèd hope.

Foremost I call on you, daughter of Zeus,
Athena, goddess supreme;
and on Artemis[6] shielding the world,
shielding this land from her circular shrine
graced with renown.
And on you I call, Phoebus, Lord of the unerring bow.

Come to my aid, you averters of doom!
Come to my aid if ever you came!
Come to my aid as once you did, when you quenched
the fires of doom that fell on our soil!
Hear me, and come to my aid!

Boundless the pain, boundless the grief I bear;
sickness pervades this land,
affliction without reprieve.
Barren the soil, barren of fruit;
children are born no longer to light;
all of us flutter in agony
winging our way into darkness and death.

Countless the number of dead in the land;
corpses of children cover the plain,
children dying before they have lived,
no one to pity them,
reeking, and spreading diseases and death.

Moaning and wailing our wives,
moaning and wailing our mothers
stream to the altars this way and that,
scream to the air with helpless cries.
Hear us, golden daughter of Zeus,
hear us! Send us release!

Ares[7] now rages in our midst
brandishing in his hands
the firebrands of disease,
raving, consuming, rousing the screams of death.
Hear us, O goddess!
Help us, and still his rage!
Turn back his assault!
Help us! Banish him from our land!

---

6. Artemis (called Diana by the Romans) was the twin sister of Apollo. She was primarily a moon goddess.
7. Ares (Roman Mars) was the war god.

Drive him into the angry sea,
to the wave-swept border of Thrace![8]

We who escape him tonight
will be struck down at dawn.
Help us, O father Zeus,
Lord of the thunderbolt,
crush him! Destroy him!
Burn him with fires of lightning!

Help us, Apollo, Lycean Lord!
Stand at our side with your golden bow!
Artemis, help us!
Come from the Lycian[9] hills!
Come with your torches aflame!
Dionysus,[1] protector, come to our aid,
come with your revelers' band!
Burn with your torch the god
hated among the gods!

Enter OEDIPUS.

OEDIPUS   I have heard your prayers and answer with relief and help,
if you will heed my words and tend the sickness with the cure it
cries for. My words are uttered as a stranger to the act, a stranger to
its tale. I cannot trace its path alone, without a sign. As a citizen
newer to Thebes than you, I make this proclamation: If one among
you knows who murdered Laius, the son of Labdacus, let him tell us
now. If he fears for his life, let him confess and know a milder pen-
alty. He will be banished from this land. Nothing more. Or if you
know the assassin to be an alien, do not protect him with your silence. You will be rewarded. But if in fear you protect yourself or
any other man and keep your silence, then hear what I say now:
Whoever he is, this assassin must be denied entrance to your homes.
Any man where I rule is forbidden to receive him or speak to him or
share with him his prayers and sacrifice or offer him the holy rites of
purification. I command you to drive this hideous curse out of your
homes; I command you to obey the will of Pythian Apollo. I will
serve the god and the dead. On the assassin or assassins, I call down
the most vile damnation—for this vicious act, may the brand of
shame be theirs to wear forever. And if I knowingly harbor their
guilt within my own walls, I shall not exempt myself from the curse
that I have called upon them. It is for me, for God, and for this city
that staggers toward ruin that you must fulfill these injunctions. Even
if Heaven gave you no sign, you had the sacred duty to insure that
this act did not go unexamined, unavenged! It was the assassination

of a noble man—your king! Now that I hold the powers that he once held, his bed, his wife—had fate been unopposed, his children would have bound us closer yet—and now on him has this disaster fallen. I will avenge him as I would avenge my own father. I will leave nothing untried to expose the murderer of Laius, the son of Labdacus, heir to the house of Cadmus and Agenor. On those who deny me obedience, I utter this curse: May the gods visit them with barrenness in their harvests, barrenness in their women, barrenness in their fate. Worse still—may they be haunted and tormented and never know the peace that comes with death. But for you, my people, in sympathy with me—I pray that Justice and all the gods attend you forever.

CHORUS   You have made me swear an oath, my Lord, and under oath I speak. I did not kill the king and cannot name the man who did. The question was Apollo's. He could name the man you seek.

OEDIPUS   I know. And yet no mortal can compel a god to speak.

CHORUS   The next-best thing, it seems to me . . .

OEDIPUS   Tell me. Tell me all your thoughts. We must consider everything.

CHORUS   There is one man, second only to Apollo, who can see the truth, who can clearly help us in our search—Teiresias.

OEDIPUS   I thought of this. On Creon's advice, I sent for him. Twice. He should be here.

CHORUS   There were some rumors once, but no one hears them now.

OEDIPUS   What rumors? I want to look at every tale that is told.

CHORUS   They said that travelers murdered Laius.

OEDIPUS   I have heard that too. And yet there's no one to be found who saw the murderer in the act.

CHORUS   He will come forth himself, once he has heard your curse, if he knows what it means to be afraid.

OEDIPUS   Why? Why should a man now fear words if then he did not fear to kill?

CHORUS   But there is one man who can point him out—the man in whom the truth resides, the god-inspired prophet. And there—they are bringing him now.

Enter TEIRESIAS, *guided by a servant.*

OEDIPUS   Teiresias, all things are known to you—the secrets of heaven and earth, the sacred and profane. Though you are blind, you surely see the plague that rakes our city. My Lord Teiresias, we turn to you as our only hope. My messengers may have told you—we have sent to Apollo and he has answered us. We must find Laius' murderers and deal with them. Or drive them out. Then—only then will we find release from our suffering. I ask you not to spare your gifts of prophecy. Look to the voices of prophetic birds or the answers written in the flames. Spare nothing. Save all of us—yourself, your city, your king, and all that is touched by this deathly pollution. We turn to you. My Lord, it is man's most noble role to help his fellow man the best his talents will allow.

TEIRESIAS   O God! How horrible wisdom is! How horrible when it

does not help the wise! How could I have forgotten? I should not
have come.

OEDIPUS   Why? What's wrong?

TEIRESIAS   Let me go. It will be better if you bear your own distress
and I bear mine. It will be better this way.

OEDIPUS   This city gave you life and yet you refuse her an answer! You
speak as if you were her enemy.

TEIRESIAS   No! No! It is because I see the danger in your words. And
mine would add still more.

OEDIPUS   For God's sake, if you know, don't turn away from us! We
are pleading. We are begging you.

TEIRESIAS   Because you are blind! No! I shall not reveal my secrets.
I shall not reveal yours.

OEDIPUS   What? You know, and yet you refuse to speak? Would you
betray us and watch our city fall helplessly to her death?

TEIRESIAS   I will not cause you further grief. I will not grieve myself.
Stop asking me to tell; I will tell you nothing.

OEDIPUS   You will not tell? You monster! You could stir the stones of
earth to a burning rage! You will never tell? What will it take?

TEIRESIAS   Know yourself, Oedipus. You denounce me, but you do
not yet know yourself.

OEDIPUS   Yes! You disgrace your city. And then you expect us to control our rage!

TEIRESIAS   It does not matter if I speak; the future has already been
determined.

OEDIPUS   And if it has, then it is for you to tell me, *prophet!*

TEIRESIAS   I shall say no more. Rage, if you wish.

OEDIPUS   I *am* enraged. And now I will tell you what *I* think. I think
this was *your* doing. *You* plotted the crime, *you* saw it carried out.
It was *your* doing. All but the actual killing. And had you not been
blind, you would have done *that*, too!

TEIRESIAS   Do you believe what you have said? Then accept your own
decree! From this day on, deny yourself the right to speak to anyone.
You, Oedipus, are the desecrator, the polluter of this land!

OEDIPUS   You traitor! Do you think that you can get away with this?

TEIRESIAS   The truth is my protection.

OEDIPUS   Who taught you this? It did not come from prophecy!

TEIRESIAS   *You* taught me. *You* drove me, *you* forced me to say it
against my will.

OEDIPUS   Say it again. I want to make sure that I understand you.

TEIRESIAS   Understand me? Or are you trying to provoke me?

OEDIPUS   No, I want to be sure, I want to know. Say it again.

TEIRESIAS   I say that you, Oedipus Tyrannus, are the murderer you
seek.

OEDIPUS   So! A second time! Now twice you will regret what you have
said!

TEIRESIAS   Shall I tell you more? Shall I fan your flames of anger?

OEDIPUS   Yes. Tell me more. Tell me more—whatever suits you. It will
be in vain.

TEIRESIAS   I say you live in shame with the woman you love, blind
to your own calamity.

OEDIPUS   Do you think you can speak like this forever?

TEIRESIAS   I do, if there is any strength in truth.

OEDIPUS   There is—for everyone but you. You—you cripple! Your ears are deaf, your eyes are blind, your mind—your *mind* is crippled!

TEIRESIAS   You fool! You slander me when one day you will hear the same . . .

OEDIPUS   You live in night, Teiresias, in night that never turns to day. And so, you cannot hurt me—or any man who sees the light.

TEIRESIAS   No—it is not I who will cause your fall. That is Apollo's office—and he will discharge it.

OEDIPUS   Was this *your* trick—or Creon's?

TEIRESIAS   No, not Creon's. No, Oedipus. You are destroying yourself!

OEDIPUS   Ah, wealth and sovereignty and skill surpassing skill in life's contentions, why must envy always attend them? This city *gave* me power; I did not ask for it. And Creon, my friend, my trusted friend, would plot to overthrow me—with this charlatan, this impostor, who auctions off his magic wares! His eyes see profit clearly, but they are blind in prophecy. Tell me, Teiresias, what makes you a prophet? Where were you when the monster was here weaving her spells and taunts? What words of relief did Thebes hear from you? Her riddle would stagger the simple mind; it demanded the mind of a seer. Yet, put to the test, all your birds and god-craft proved useless; you had no answer. Then *I* came—ignorant Oedipus—*I* came and smothered her, using only my wit. There were no birds to tell me what to do. I am the man you would overthrow so you can stand near Creon's throne. You will regret—you and your conspirator—you will regret your attempt to purify this land. If you were not an old man, I would make you suffer the pain which you deserve for your audacity.

CHORUS   Both of you, my Lord, have spoken in bitter rage. No more —not when we must direct our every thought to obey the god's command.

TEIRESIAS   Though you are king, the right to speak does not belong to you alone. It is *my* right as well and I shall claim it. I am not your servant and Creon is not my patron. I serve only Loxian Apollo.[2] And I tell you this, since you mock my blindness. You have eyes, Oedipus, and do not see your own destruction. You have eyes and do not see what lives with you. Do you know whose son you are? I say that you have sinned and do not know it; you have sinned against your own—the living and the dead. A double scourge, your mother's and your father's curse, will drive you from this land. Then darkness will shroud those eyes that now can see the light. Cithaeron—the whole earth will resound with your mournful cries when you discover the meaning of the wedding-song that brought you to this place you falsely thought a haven. More sorrow still awaits you—more than you can know—to show you what you are and what our children are. Damn Creon, if you will; damn the words I say. No man on earth will ever know the doom that waits for you.

OEDIPUS   How much of this am I to bear? Leave! Now! Leave my house!

2. Apollo was called "Loxian" because the answer given by his oracles at Delphi and elsewhere were frequently ambiguous.

TEIRESIAS   I would not be here had you not sent for me.

OEDIPUS   I never would have sent for you had I known the madness I would hear.

TEIRESIAS   To you, I am mad; but not to your parents . . .

OEDIPUS   Wait! My parents? Who are my parents?

TEIRESIAS   This day shall bring you birth *and* death.

OEDIPUS   Why must you persist with riddles?

TEIRESIAS   Are you not the best of men when it comes to riddles?

OEDIPUS   You mock the very skill that proves me great.

TEIRESIAS   A great misfortune—which will destroy you.

OEDIPUS   I don't care. If I have saved this land, I do not care.

TEIRESIAS   Then I shall go. [*To his servant.*] Come, take me home.

OEDIPUS   Yes, go home. You won't be missed.

TEIRESIAS   I will go when I've said all that I came to say. I am not afraid of you. You cannot hurt me. And I tell you this: The man you seek—the man whose death or banishment you ordered, the man who murdered Laius—that man is here, passing as an alien, living in our midst. Soon it will be known to all of you—he is a native Theban. And he will find no joy in that discovery. His eyes now see, but soon they will be blind: rich now, but soon a beggar. Holding a scepter now, but soon a cane, he will grope for the earth beneath him—in a foreign land. Both brother and father to the children that he loves. Both son and husband to the woman who bore him. Both heir and spoiler of his father's bed and the one who took his life. Go, think on this. And if you find the words I speak are lies, *then* say that I am blind.

Exeunt OEDIPUS, TEIRESIAS.

CHORUS

Who is he? Who is the man?
Who is the man whom the voice of the Delphian shrine
denounced as the killer, the murderer,
the man who committed the terrible crime?
Where is he? Where is he now?
Let him run, let him flee!
Let him rush with the speed of the wind on his flight!
For with fire and lightning the god will attack,
and relentlessy fate will pursue him and haunt him
and drive him to doom.

Do you hear? Do you hear the command of the god?
From Parnassus[3] he orders the hunt.
In vain will the murderer hide,
in vain will he run,
in vain will he lurk in the forests and caves
like an animal roaming the desolate hills.
Let him flee to the edge of the world:
On his heels he will find
the command of the god!

3. Parnassus was a mountain near Delphi, sacred to Apollo and the Muses, minor goddesses associated with the arts.

Confusion and fear
have been spread by the prophet's words.
For I cannot affirm, yet I cannot refute
what he spoke. And I'm lost, I am lost—
What am I to believe?
Now foreboding is gripping my heart.
Was there ever a strife between Laius and Polybus' house?[4]
Can I test? Can I prove?
Can I ever believe that the name of my king
has been soiled by a murder unknown?

It is Zeus and Apollo who know,
who can see the affairs of men.
But the seer and I,
we are mortal, and blind.
Who is right? Who can judge?
We are mortal, our wisdom assigned in degrees.
Does the seer know? Do I?
No, I will not believe in the prophet's charge
till the charge has been proved to my mind.
For I saw how the king
in the test with the Sphinx
proved his wisdom and worth
when he saved this city from doom.
No! I can *never* condemn the king!

> *Enter* CREON.

CREON   My fellow citizens, anger has impelled me to come because
I have heard the accusation which Oedipus has brought against me
—and I will not tolerate it. If he thinks that I—in the midst of this
torment—*I* have thought to harm him in any way, I will not spend
the rest of my life branded by his charge. Doesn't he see the implications of such slander? To you, to my friends, to my city—I would be
a traitor!

CHORUS   He spoke in anger—without thinking.

CREON   Yes—and who was it who said that the prophet lied on my
advice?

CHORUS   It was said, but I don't know how it was meant.

CREON   And was this a charge leveled by one whose eyes were clear?
Whose head was clear?

CHORUS   I don't know. I do not judge my master's actions. But here he
comes.

> *Enter* OEDIPUS.

OEDIPUS   Why have you come, Creon? Do you have the audacity to
show your face in my presence? Assassin! And now you would steal
my throne! What drove you to this plot? Did you see cowardice in
me? Stupidity? Did you imagine that I would not see your treachery? Did you expect that I wouldn't act to stop you? You fool! Your

---

4. Polybus, the King of Corinth, and his wife Merope were the reputed parents of
Oedipus.

plot was mad! You go after a throne without money, without friends! How do you think thrones are won?

CREON   You listen to me! And when you have heard me out, when you have heard the truth, *then* judge for yourself.

OEDIPUS   Ah yes, your oratory! I can learn nothing from that. This is what I have learned—you are my enemy!

CREON   Just let me say . . .

OEDIPUS   Say one thing—say that you are not a traitor.

CREON   If you think that senseless stubbornness is a precious gift, you are a fool.

OEDIPUS   If you think that you can threaten the house of Cadmus— your own house—and not pay for it, you are mad.

CREON   I grant you that. But tell me: just what is this terrible thing you say I have done to you?

OEDIPUS   Did you or did you not tell me to send for that—that— prophet?

CREON   I did. And I would again.

OEDIPUS   Then, how long since Laius . . . ?

CREON   What? I do not follow . . .

OEDIPUS   . . . Disappeared?

CREON   A long time ago.

OEDIPUS   Your Teiresias—was he—was he a prophet then?

CREON   Yes—and just as honored and just as wise.

OEDIPUS   Did he ever mention me—then?

CREON   Not in my presence.

OEDIPUS   But didn't you investigate the murder?

CREON   Of course we did—

OEDIPUS   And why didn't the prophet say anything *then?*

CREON   I do not know. It's not for me to try to understand.

OEDIPUS   You know this much which you will try to tell me . . .

CREON   What is it? I will tell you if I can.

OEDIPUS   Just this: Had he not acted under your instructions, he would not have named *me* killer of Laius.

CREON   If this is what he said, you ought to know. You heard him. But now I claim the right to question you, as you have me.

OEDIPUS   Ask what you wish. I am not the murderer.

CREON   Then answer me. Did you marry my sister?

OEDIPUS   Of course I did.

CREON   And do you rule on equal terms with her?

OEDIPUS   She has all that she wants from me.

CREON   And am I not the third and equal partner?

OEDIPUS   You are—and that is where you have proved yourself a traitor.

CREON   Not true. Consider rationally, as I have done. First ask your- self—would any man prefer a life of fear to one in which the self- same rank, the self-same rights are guaranteed untroubled peace? I have no wish to be a king when I can act as one without a throne. And any man would feel the same, if he were wise. I share with you a king's prerogatives, yet you alone must face the danger lurking around the throne. If *I* were king, I would have to act in many ways against my pleasure. What added benefit could kingship hold when

I have rank and rule without the threat of pain? I am not deluded
—no, I would not look for honors beyond the ones which profit me.
I have the favor of every man; each greets me first when he would
hope to have *your* favor. Why should I exchange this for a throne?
Only a fool would. No, I am not a traitor nor would I aid an act of
treason. You want proof? Go to Delphi; ask if I have brought you
the truth. Then, if you find me guilty of conspiracy with the prophet,
command my death. I will face that. But do not condemn me without
proof. You are wrong to judge the guilty innocent, the innocent guilty
—without proof. Casting off a true friend is like casting off your
greatest prize—your life. You will know in time that this is true.
Time alone reveals the just; a single day condemns the guilty.

CHORUS   He is right, my Lord. Respect his words. A man who plans in
haste will gamble the result.

OEDIPUS   This is a plot conceived in rashness. It must be met with
quick response. I cannot sit and wait until the plot succeeds.

CREON   What will you do then? Do you intend to banish me?

OEDIPUS   No. No, not banish you. I want to see you *dead*—to make
you an example for all aspiring to my throne.

CREON   Then you won't do as I suggest? You won't believe me?

OEDIPUS   You have not shown that you deserve belief.

CREON   No, because I see that you are mad.

OEDIPUS   In my own eyes, I am sane.

CREON   You should be sane in mine as well.

OEDIPUS   No. You are a traitor!

CREON   And what if you are wrong?

OEDIPUS   Still—*I* will rule.

CREON   Not when you rule treacherously.

OEDIPUS   O Thebes! My city! Listen to him!

CREON   *My* city too!

CHORUS   My Lords, no more. Here comes Jocasta. Perhaps the queen
can end this bitter clash.

Enter JOCASTA.

JOCASTA   Why do you behave like senseless fools and quarrel without
reason? Are you not ashamed to add trouble of your own when your
city is sick and dying? Go, Creon. Go and leave us alone. Forget
those petty grievances which you exaggerate. How important can
they be?

CREON   This important, sister: Oedipus, your husband, in his insanity,
has threatened me with banishment or death.

OEDIPUS   Yes, for I have realized his plot—a plot against my person.

CREON   May the gods haunt me forever, if that is true—if I am guilty
of that charge.

JOCASTA   In the name of God, believe him, Oedipus! Believe him for
the sake of his oath, for my own sake, and for theirs!

CHORUS   Listen to her, my Lord. I beg you to consider and comply.

OEDIPUS   What would you have me do?

CHORUS   Respect the oath that Creon gave you. Respect his past integrity.

OEDIPUS   Do you know what you are asking?

CHORUS   Yes, I know.

OEDIPUS   Then, tell me what you mean.

CHORUS   I mean that you are wrong to charge a friend who has invoked a curse upon his head. You are wrong to slander without proof
and be the cause for his dishonor.

OEDIPUS   Then you must know that when you ask for this, you ask for
banishment or doom—for *me*.

CHORUS

O God, no!
O Helios,[5] no!
May Heaven and Earth exact my doom
if that is what I thought!
When our city is torn by sickness
and my heart is torn with pain—
do not compound the troubles
that beset us!

OEDIPUS   Then, let him go, although it surely means my death—or
banishment with dishonor. *Your* words—not his—have touched my
heart. But Creon—wherever he may be—I will hate him.

CREON   You are hard when you should yield, cruel when you should
pity. Such natures deserve the pain they bear.

OEDIPUS   Just go—and leave me in peace.

CREON   I will go—my guilt pronounced by you alone. Behold my
judge and jury—Oedipus Tyrannus!

Exit CREON.

CHORUS   My queen, persuade your husband to rest awhile.

JOCASTA   I will—when I have learned the truth.

CHORUS   Blind suspicion has consumed the king. And Creon's passions flared beneath the sting of unjust accusations.

JOCASTA   Are *both* at fault?

CHORUS   Yes, both of them.

JOCASTA   But what is the reason for their rage?

CHORUS   Don't ask again. Our city is weary enough from suffering.
Enough. Let the matter rest where it now stands.

OEDIPUS   Do you see what you have done? Do you see where you
have come—with your good intentions, your noble efforts to dull
the sharpness of my anger?

CHORUS

My Lord, I have said before
and now I say again:
I would be mad,
a reckless fool
to turn away my king,
who saved us from a sea of troubles
and set us on a fairer course,
and who will lead us once again
to peace, a haven from our pain.

5. Helios was the name of a sun god, hence Apollo.

JOCASTA   In the name of Heaven, my Lord, tell me the reason for your bitterness.

OEDIPUS   I will—because you mean more to me than anyone. The reason is Creon and his plot against my throne.

JOCASTA   But can you *prove* a plot?

OEDIPUS   He says that I—Oedipus—bear the guilt of Laius' death.

JOCASTA   How does he justify this charge?

OEDIPUS   He does not stain his own lips by saying it. No. He uses that false prophet to speak for him.

JOCASTA   Then, you can exonerate yourself because no mortal has the power of divination. And I can prove it. An oracle came to Laius once from the Pythian priests—I'll not say from Apollo himself— that he would die at the hands of his own child, his child and mine. Yet the story, which *we* heard was that robbers murdered Laius in a place where three roads meet. As for the child—when he was three days old, Laius drove pins into his ankles and handed him to someone to cast upon a deserted mountain path—to die. And so, Apollo's prophecy was unfulfilled—the child did not kill his father. And Laius' fears were unfulfilled—he did not die by the hand of his child. Yet, these had been the prophecies. You need not give them any credence. For the god will reveal what he wants.

OEDIPUS   Jocasta—my heart is troubled at your words. Suddenly, my thoughts are wandering, disturbed . . .

JOCASTA   What is it? What makes you so frightened?

OEDIPUS   Your statement—that Laius was murdered in a place where three roads meet. Isn't that what you said?

JOCASTA   Yes. That was the story then; that is the story now.

OEDIPUS   Where is this place where three roads meet?

JOCASTA   In the land called Phocis where the roads from Delphi and from Daulia converge.[6]

OEDIPUS   How long a time has passed since then?

JOCASTA   We heard it shortly before you came.

OEDIPUS   O God, what have you planned for me?

JOCASTA   What is it, Oedipus? What frightens you?

OEDIPUS   Do not ask me. Do not ask. Just tell me—what was Laius like? How old was he?

JOCASTA   He was tall and his hair was lightly cast with silver tones, the contour of his body much like yours.

OEDIPUS   O God! Am I cursed and cannot see it?

JOCASTA   What is it, Oedipus? You frighten me.

OEDIPUS   It cannot be—that the prophet sees! Tell me one more thing.

JOCASTA   You frighten me, my Lord, but I will try to tell you what I know.

OEDIPUS   Who traveled with the king? Was he alone? Was there a guide? An escort? A few? Many?

JOCASTA   There were five—one of them a herald—and a carriage in which Laius rode.

OEDIPUS   O God! O God! I see it all now! Jocasta, who told you this?

JOCASTA   A servant—the only one who returned alive.

---

6. The Oracle at Delphi was located in the region of central Greece called Phocis. Daulia was a city to the east of Delphi.

OEDIPUS   Is he here now? In our house?

JOCASTA   No. When he came back and saw you ruling where once his master was, he pleaded with me—begged me—to send him to the fields to tend the flocks, far from the city. And so I did. He was a good servant and I would have granted him more than that, if he had asked.

OEDIPUS   Could we arrange to have him here—now?

JOCASTA   Yes, but what do you want with him?

OEDIPUS   I am afraid, Jocasta. I have said too much and now I have to see him.

JOCASTA   Then he shall be brought. But I, too, must know the cause of your distress. I have the right to know.

OEDIPUS   Yes, you have that right. And I must tell you—now. You, more than anyone, will have to know what I am going through. My father was Polybus of Corinth, my mother a Dorian—Merope. I was held in high regard in Corinth until—until something strange occurred—something uncanny and strange, although I might have given it too much concern. There was a man dining with us one day who had had far too much wine and shouted at me—half-drunk and shouting that I was not rightly called my father's son. I could barely endure the rest of that day and on the next I went to my parents and questioned them. They were enraged at the remark. I felt relieved at their response. But still, this—this thing—kept gnawing at my heart. And it was spread about in vulgar whispers. And then, without my parents' knowledge, I went to Delphi, but Apollo did not say what I had gone to hear. Instead, he answered questions I had not asked and told of horror and misery beyond belief—how I would know my mother's bed and bring to the world a race of children too terrible for men to see and cause the death of my own father. I trembled at those words and fled from Corinth—as far as I could—to where no star could ever guide me back, where I could never see that infamous prophecy fulfilled. And as I traveled, I came to that place where you say the king was murdered. This is the truth, Jocasta—I was in that place where the three roads meet. There was a herald leading a carriage drawn by horses and a man riding in the carriage—just as you described. The man in front, and the old one, ordered me out of the path. I refused. The driver pushed. In anger, I struck him. The old man saw it, reached for his lash and waited till I had passed. Then he struck me on the head. But he paid—oh yes, he paid. He lost his balance and fell from the carriage and as he lay there helpless—on his back—I killed him. I killed them all. But if this stranger had any tie with Laius—O God —who could be more hated in the eyes of Heaven and Earth? *I* am the one whom strangers and citizens are forbidden to receive! *I* am the one to whom all are forbidden to speak! *I* am the one who must be driven out! *I* am the one for whom my curse was meant! I have touched his bed with the very hands that killed him! O God! The sin! The horror! *I* am to be banished, never to see my people, never to walk in my fatherland. Or else I must take my mother for a bride and kill my father Polybus, who gave me life and cared for me. What cruel god has sent this torture? Hear me, you gods, you holy gods—I will never see that day! I will die before I ever see the stain of this abominable act!

CHORUS   Your words frighten us, my Lord. But you must have hope until you hear the story from the man who saw.

OEDIPUS   Yes—hope. My only hope is waiting for this shepherd.

JOCASTA   Why? What do you hope to find with him?

OEDIPUS   This—if his story agrees with what you say, then I am safe.

JOCASTA   What did I say that makes you sure of this?

OEDIPUS   You said he told of *robbers*—that *robbers* killed the king. If he still *says robbers*, then I am not the guilty one—because no man can talk of many when he means a single one. But if he names a *single* traveler, there will be no doubt—the guilt is mine.

JOCASTA   You can be sure that this was what he said—and he cannot deny it. The whole city heard him—not I alone. But even if he alters what he said before, he cannot prove that Laius met his death as it was prophesied. For Apollo said that he would die at the hand of a child—of mine. And as it happens, the child is dead. So prophecy is worthless. I wouldn't dignify it with a moment's thought.

OEDIPUS   You are right. But still—send someone for the shepherd. Now.

JOCASTA   I shall—immediately. I shall do what you ask. But now— let us go inside.

Exeunt OEDIPUS, JOCASTA.

CHORUS
I pray, may destiny permit
that honestly I live my life
in word and deed.
That I obey the laws
the heavens have begotten
and prescribed.
Those laws created by Olympus,[7]
laws pure, immortal,
forever lasting, essence of the god
who lives in them.
On arrogance and pride
a tyrant feeds.
The goad of insolence,
of senseless overbearing, blind conceit,
of seeking things unseasonable,
unreasonable,
will prick a man to climb to heights
where he must lose his footing
and tumble to his doom.
Ambition must be used
to benefit the state;
else it is wrong, and God
must strike it from this earth.
Forever, God, I pray,
may you stand at my side!

7. The highest mountain of the Greek peninsula and the reputed home of the gods.

A man who goes through life
with insolence in word and deed,
who lacks respect for law and right,
and scorns the shrines and temples of the gods,
may he find evil fate and doom
as his reward for wantonness,
for seeking ill-begotten gains
and reaching after sacred things
with sacrilegious hands.
No! Surely no such man
escapes the wrath, the vengeance of the god!
For if he did, if he could find reward
in actions which are wrong,
why should I trouble to acclaim,
to honor you, God, in my song?

No longer shall my feet
take me to Delphi's sacred shrine;
no longer shall they Abae or Olympia's altars[8] seek
unless the oracles are shown to tell the truth
to mortals without fail!
Where are you, Zeus, all-powerful, all-ruling?
You must be told,
you must know in your all-pervading power:
Apollo's oracles now fall into dishonor,
and what the god has spoken about Laius
finds disregard.
Could God be dead?

Enter JOCASTA.

JOCASTA   My Lords, I want to lay these laurel wreaths and incense
offerings at the shrines of Thebes—for Oedipus is torturing himself,
tearing his heart with grief. His vision to weigh the present against
the past is blurred by fear and terror. He devours every word of
dread, drinks in every thought of pain, destruction, death. And I
no longer have the power to ease his suffering. Now I turn to you,
Apollo, since you are nearest, with prayer and suppliant offerings.
Find some way to free us, end our agony! O God of Light, release
us! You see the fear that grips us—like sailors who watch their captain paralyzed by some unknown terror on the seas.

Enter MESSENGER 1.

MESSENGER 1   Strangers, would you direct me to the house of Oedipus?
Or if you know where I might find the king himself, please tell me.
CHORUS   This is his house, stranger. He is inside. But this is the queen
—his wife, and mother of his children.
MESSENGER 1   Then, blessings on the house of Oedipus—his house,
his children, and his wife.
JOCASTA   Blessings on you as well, stranger. Your words are kind. But
why have you come? What is it?

8. Important oracles were located at Abae and Olympia in ancient times.

MESSENGER 1   Good news, my lady—for your husband and your house.

JOCASTA   What news? Where do you come from?

MESSENGER 1   From Corinth, my lady. My news will surely bring you joy—but sorrow, too.

JOCASTA   What? How can that be?

MESSENGER 1   Your husband now is ruler of the Isthmus!

JOCASTA   Do you mean that Polybus of Corinth has been deposed?

MESSENGER 1   Deposed by death, my lady. He has passed away.

JOCASTA   What! Polybus dead?

MESSENGER 1   I swear on my life that this is true.

JOCASTA   [*to a servant*] Go! Quickly! Tell your master. [*To the heavens.*] You prophecies—you divinely-uttered prophecies! Where do you stand now? The man that Oedipus feared, the man he dared not face lest he should be his killer—that man is dead! Time claimed his life—not Oedipus!

Enter OEDIPUS.

OEDIPUS   Why, Jocasta? Why have you sent for me again?

JOCASTA   I want you to listen to this man. Listen to him and judge for yourself the worth of those holy prophecies.

OEDIPUS   Who is he? What news could he have for me?

JOCASTA   He comes from Corinth with the news that—that Polybus—is dead.

OEDIPUS   What! Tell me.

MESSENGER 1   If you must know this first, then I shall tell you—plainly. Polybus has died.

OEDIPUS   How? An act of treason? Sickness? How?

MESSENGER 1   My Lord, only a slight shift in the scales is required to bring the agèd to their rest.

OEDIPUS   Then it was sickness. Poor old man.

MESSENGER 1   Sickness—yes. And the weight of years.

OEDIPUS   Oh, Jocasta! Why? Why should we even look to oracles, the prophetic words delivered at their shrines or the birds that scream above us? They led me to believe that I would kill my father. But he is dead and in his grave, while I stand here—never having touched a weapon. Unless he died of longing for his son. If that is so, then I *was* the instrument of his death. And those oracles! Where are they now? Polybus has taken them to his grave. What worth have they now?

JOCASTA   Have I not been saying this all along?

OEDIPUS   Yes, you have. But I was misled by fear.

JOCASTA   Now you will no longer have to think of it.

OEDIPUS   But—my mother's bed. I still have *that* to fear.

JOCASTA   No. No, mortals have no need to fear when chance reigns supreme. The knowledge of the future is denied to us. It is better to live as you will, live as you can. You need not fear a union with your mother. Men often, in their dreams, approach their mothers' beds, lie with them, possess them. But the man who sees that this is meaningless can live without the threat of fear.

OEDIPUS   You would be right, Jocasta, if my mother were not alive. But she *is* alive. And no matter what you say, I have reason to fear.

JOCASTA   At least your father's death has brought some comfort.

OEDIPUS   Yes—some comfort. But my fear is of *her* as long as she lives.

MESSENGER 1   Who is *she?* The woman you fear?

OEDIPUS   Queen Merope, old man, the wife of Polybus.

MESSENGER 1   But why does *she* instill fear in you?

OEDIPUS   There was an oracle—a dreadful oracle sent by the gods.

MESSENGER 1   Can you tell me—a stranger—what it is?

OEDIPUS   Yes, it is all right to tell. Once Loxian Apollo said that I would take my mother for my bride and murder my father with my own hands. This is the reason that I left Corinth long ago. Fortunately. And yet, I have often longed to see my parents.

MESSENGER 1   Is this the fear that drove you away from Corinth?

OEDIPUS   Yes. I did not want to kill my father.

MESSENGER 1   But I can free you from this fear, my Lord. My purpose for coming was a good one.

OEDIPUS   And I shall see that you receive a fitting reward.

MESSENGER 1   Yes—that's why I came. To fare well myself by your returning home.

OEDIPUS   Home? To Corinth? To my parents? Never.

MESSENGER 1   My son, you do not realize what you are doing.

OEDIPUS   What do you mean, old man? For God's sake, tell me what you mean.

MESSENGER 1   I mean—the reasons why you dread returning home.

OEDIPUS   I dread Apollo's prophecy—and its fulfillment.

MESSENGER 1   You mean the curse—the stain they say lies with your parents?

OEDIPUS   Yes, old man. That is the fear that lives with me.

MESSENGER 1   Then you must realize that this fear is groundless.

OEDIPUS   How can that be—if I am their son?

MESSENGER 1   Because Polybus was no relative of yours.

OEDIPUS   What are you saying! Polybus was *not* my father?

MESSENGER 1   No more than I.

OEDIPUS   No more than you? But you are nothing to me.

MESSENGER 1   He was not your father any more than I.

OEDIPUS   Then why did he call me his son?

MESSENGER 1   You were a gift to him—from me.

OEDIPUS   A gift? From you? And yet he loved me as his son?

MESSENGER 1   Yes, my Lord. He had been childless.

OEDIPUS   And when you gave me to him—had you bought me? Or found me?

MESSENGER 1   I found you—in the hills of Cithaeron.

OEDIPUS   What were you doing there?

MESSENGER 1   Tending sheep along the mountain side.

OEDIPUS   Then you were a—hired shepherd?

MESSENGER 1   Yes, my son—a hired shepherd who saved you at that time.

OEDIPUS   Saved me? Was I in pain when you found me? Was I in trouble?

MESSENGER 1   Yes, your ankles are the proof of that.

OEDIPUS   Ah, you mean this old trouble. What has that to do with it?

MESSENGER 1   When I found you, your ankles were pierced with rivets. And I freed you.

OEDIPUS   Yes, I have had this horrible stigma since infancy.

MESSENGER 1   And so it was the swelling in your ankles that caused your name: Oedipus—"Clubfoot."

OEDIPUS   Oh! Who did this to me? My father? Or my mother?

MESSENGER 1   I don't know. You will have to ask the man who handed you to me.

OEDIPUS   You mean—you did not find me? It was someone else?

MESSENGER 1   Another shepherd.

OEDIPUS   Who? Do you remember who he was?

MESSENGER 1   I think—he was of the house of Laius.

OEDIPUS   The king who ruled this city?

MESSENGER 1   Yes. He was a shepherd in the service of the king.

OEDIPUS   Is he still alive? Can I see him?

MESSENGER 1   [*addressing the* CHORUS] You—you people here—could answer that.

OEDIPUS   Do any of you know this shepherd? Have you seen him in the fields? Here in Thebes? Tell me now! Now is the time to unravel this mystery—once and for all.

CHORUS   I think it is the shepherd you asked to see before. But the queen will know.

OEDIPUS   Jocasta, is that the man he means? Is it the shepherd we have sent for? Is *he* the one?

JOCASTA   Why? What difference does it make? Don't think about it. Pay no attention to what he said. It makes no difference.

OEDIPUS   No difference? When I must have every clue to untangle the line of mystery surrounding my birth?

JOCASTA   In the name of God, if you care at all for your own life, you must not go on with this. I cannot bear it any longer.

OEDIPUS   Do not worry, Jocasta. Even if I am a slave—a third-generation slave, it is no stain on your nobility.

JOCASTA   Oedipus! I beg you—don't do this!

OEDIPUS   I can't grant you that. I cannot leave the truth unknown.

JOCASTA   It is for *your* sake that I beg you to stop. For your own good.

OEDIPUS   My own good has brought me pain too long.

JOCASTA   God help you! May you never know what you are!

OEDIPUS   Go, someone, and bring the shepherd to me. Leave the queen to exult in her noble birth.

JOCASTA   God help you! This is all that I can say to you—now or ever.

Exit JOCASTA.

CHORUS   Why has the queen left like this—grief-stricken and tortured with pain? My Lord, I fear—I fear that from her silence some horror will burst forth.

OEDIPUS   Let it explode! I will still want to uncover the secret of my birth—no matter how horrible. She—she is a woman with a woman's pride—and she feels shame for my humble birth. But I am the child of Fortune—beneficent Fortune—and I shall not be shamed! She is my mother. My sisters are the months and they have seen me rise and fall. This is my family. I will never deny my birth—and I will learn its secret!

Exit OEDIPUS.

CHORUS
Ah Cithaeron,
if in my judgment I am right,
if I interpret what I hear correctly,
then—by Olympus' boundless majesty!—
tomorrow's full moon will not pass
before, Cithaeron, you will find
that Oedipus will honor you
as mother and as nurse!
That we will praise you in our song,
benevolent and friendly to our king.
Apollo, our Lord, may you find joy in this!

Who bore you, Oedipus? A nymph?
Did Pan beget you in the hills?
Were you begotten by Apollo?
Perhaps so, for he likes the mountain glens.
Could Hermes be your father?[9]
Or Dionysus? Could it be
that he received you as a gift
high in the mountains from a nymph
with whom he lay?

Enter OEDIPUS.

OEDIPUS   My Lords, I have never met him, but could that be the shepherd we have been waiting for? He seems to be of the same age as the stranger from Corinth. And I can see now—those are my servants who are bringing him here. But, perhaps you know— if you have seen him before. Is he the shepherd?

Enter SHEPHERD.

CHORUS   Yes. I recognize him. He was a shepherd in the service of Laius—as loyal as any man could be.
OEDIPUS   Corinthian, I ask you—is this the man you mean?
MESSENGER 1   Yes, my Lord. This is the man.
OEDIPUS   And you, old man, look at me and answer what I ask. Were you in the service of Laius?
SHEPHERD   I was. But not bought. I was reared in his house.
OEDIPUS   What occupation? What way of life?
SHEPHERD   Tending flocks—for most of my life.
OEDIPUS   And where did you tend those flocks?
SHEPHERD   Sometimes Cithaeron, sometimes the neighboring places.
OEDIPUS   Have you ever seen this man before?
SHEPHERD   What man do you mean? Doing what?

9. Pan was a woodland god and a protector of herds. Hermes (Roman Mercury) was the messenger of the gods.

OEDIPUS   This man. Have you ever met him before?

SHEPHERD   Not that I recall, my Lord.

MESSENGER 1   No wonder, my Lord. But I shall help him to recall. I am sure that he'll remember the time we spent on Cithaeron— he with his two flocks and I with one. Six months—spring to autumn —every year—for three years. In the winter I would drive my flocks to my fold in Corinth, and he to the fold of Laius. Isn't that right, sir?

SHEPHERD   That is what happened. But it was a long time ago.

MESSENGER 1   Then tell me this. Do you remember a child you gave me to bring up as my own?

SHEPHERD   What are you saying? Why are you asking me this?

MESSENGER 1   This, my friend, this—is that child.

SHEPHERD   Damn you! Will you keep your mouth shut!

OEDIPUS   Save your reproaches, old man. It is you who deserve them— your words deserve them.

SHEPHERD   But master—how have I offended?

OEDIPUS   By refusing to answer his question about the child.

SHEPHERD   He doesn't know what he's saying. He's crazy.

OEDIPUS   If you don't answer of your own accord, we'll make you talk.

SHEPHERD   No! My Lord, please! Don't hurt an old man.

OEDIPUS   [*to the* CHORUS]   One of you—twist his hands behind his back!

SHEPHERD   Why? Why? What do you want to know?

OEDIPUS   Did you or did you not give him that child?

SHEPHERD   I did. I gave it to him—and I wish that I had died that day.

OEDIPUS   You tell the truth, or you'll have your wish now.

SHEPHERD   If I tell, it will be worse.

OEDIPUS   Still he puts it off!

SHEPHERD   I said that I gave him the child!

OEDIPUS   Where did you get it? Your house? Someone else's? Where?

SHEPHERD   Not mine. Someone else's.

OEDIPUS   Whose? One of the citizens'? Whose house?

SHEPHERD   O God, master! Don't ask me any more.

OEDIPUS   This is the last time that I ask you.

SHEPHERD   It was a child—of the house of Laius.

OEDIPUS   A slave? Or of his own line?

SHEPHERD   Ah master, do I *have* to speak?

OEDIPUS   You have to. And I *have* to hear.

SHEPHERD   They said—it was his child. But the queen could tell you best.

OEDIPUS   Why? Did *she* give you the child?

SHEPHERD   Yes, my Lord.

OEDIPUS   Why?

SHEPHERD   To—kill!

OEDIPUS   Her own child!

SHEPHERD   Yes. Because she was terrified of some dreadful prophecy.

OEDIPUS   What prophecy?

SHEPHERD   The child would kill his father.

OEDIPUS   Then why did you give him to this man?

SHEPHERD   I felt sorry for him, master. And I thought that he would take him to his own home. But he saved him from his suffering—

for worse suffering yet. My Lord, if you are the man he says you are
—O God—you were born to suffering!

OEDIPUS   O God! O no! I see it all now! All clear! O Light! I will never
look on you again! Sin! Sin in my birth! Sin in my marriage! Sin in
blood!

Exit OEDIPUS.

CHORUS
O generations of men, you are nothing!
You are nothing!
And I count you as not having lived at all!
Was there ever a man,
was there ever a man on this earth
who could say he was happy,
who knew happiness, true happiness,
not an image, a dream,
an illusion, a vision, which would disappear?
Your example, Oedipus,
your example, your fate, your disaster,
show that none of us mortals
ever knew, ever felt what happiness truly is.

Here is Oedipus,
fortune and fame and bliss
leading him by the hand,
prodding him on to heights
mortals had never attained.
Zeus, it was he who removed
the scourge of the riddling maid,
of the sharp-clawed, murderous Sphinx!
He restored me to life from the brink
of disaster, of doom and of death.
It was he who was honored and hailed,
who was crowned and acclaimed as our king.

Here is Oedipus:
Who on this earth has been
struck by a harder blow
or stung by a fate more perverse?
Wretched Oedipus!
Father and son alike,
pleasures you took from where
once you were given life.
Furrows your father ploughed
bore you in silence. How, how, oh how could it be?

Time found you out,
all-seeing, irrepressible time.
Time sits in judgment on
the union that never could be;
judges you, father and son,

begot and begetter alike.
Would that I never had
laid eyes on Laius' child!
Now I wail and I weep,
and my lips are drenched in lament.
It was you, who offered me life;
it is you, who now bring me death.

Enter MESSENGER 2.

MESSENGER 2   O you most honored citizens of Thebes, you will mourn
for the things you will hear, you will mourn for the things you will
see, and you will ache from the burden of sorrow—if you are true
sons of the house of Labdacus, if you care, if you feel. The waters
of Ister and Phasis[1] can never cleanse this house of the horrors
hidden within it and soon to be revealed—horrors willfully done!
Worst of the sorrows we know are those that are willfully done!

CHORUS   We have mourned enough for sorrows we have known. What
more is there that you can add?

MESSENGER 2   One more and only one—Jocasta, the queen, is dead.

CHORUS   O God—no! How!

MESSENGER 2   By her own hand. But the most dreadful pain you have
not seen. You have not seen the worst. I have seen it and I shall tell
you what I can of her terrible suffering. She ran in frenzied despair
through the palace halls and rushed straight to her bridal bed—her
fingers clutching and tearing at her hair. Then, inside the bedroom,
she flung the doors closed and cried out to Laius, long since dead.
She cried out to him, remembering the son that she had borne long
ago, the son who killed his father, the son who left her to bear a
dread curse—the children of her own son! She wept pitifully for that
bridal bed which she had twice defiled—husband born of husband,
child born of child. I didn't see what happened then. I didn't see her
die. At that moment the king rushed in and shrieked in horror. All
eyes turned to him as he paced in frantic passion and confusion. He
sprang at each of us and begged to have a sword. He begged to
know where he could find the wife that was no wife to him, the
woman who had been mother to him and to his children. Some
power beyond the scope of man held him in its sway and guided
him to her. It was none of us. Then—as if somebody had beckoned
to him and bade him follow—he screamed in terror and threw himself against the doors that she had locked. His body's weight and
force shattered the bolts and thrust them from their sockets and he
rushed into the room. There we saw the queen hanging from a noose
of twisted cords. And when the king saw her, he cried out and
moaned in deep, sorrowful misery. Then he untied the rope that
hung about her neck and laid her body on the ground. But what
happened then was even worse. Her gold brooches, her pins—he
tore them from her gown and plunged them into his eyes again and
again and again and screamed, "No longer shall you see the suffering

1. The Ister was a name for the lower Danube. The Phasis flowed from the Caucasus
to the Black Sea. They are invoked here together as examples of large rivers.

you have known and caused! You saw what was forbidden to be seen, yet failed to recognize those whom you longed to see! Now you shall see only darkness!" And as he cried out in such desperate misery, he struck his eyes over and over—until a shower of blood and tears splattered down his beard, like a torrent of crimson rain and hail. And now suffering is mingled with pain for man and wife for the sins that both have done. Not one alone. Once—long ago—this house was happy—and rightly so. But now—today—sorrow, destruction, death, shame—all torments that have a name—all, all are theirs to endure.

CHORUS   But the king—does he have any relief from his suffering now?

MESSENGER 2   He calls for someone to unlock the gates and reveal to Thebes his father's killer, his mother's—I can't say it. I cannot say this unholy word. He cries out that he will banish himself from the land to free this house of the curse that he has uttered. But he is weak, drained. There is no one to guide his way. The pain is more than he can bear. You will see for yourselves. The palace gates are opening. You will see a sight so hideous that even his most bitter enemy would pity him.

Enter OEDIPUS.

CHORUS
Ah!
Dread horror for men to see!
Most dreadful of all that I have seen!
Ah!
Wretched one,
what madness has possessed you?
What demon has descended upon you
and bound you to this dire fate?
Ah!
Wretched one,
I cannot bear to look at you.
I want to ask you more
and learn still more
and understand—
but I shudder at the sight of you!

OEDIPUS   Ah! Ah! Where has this misery brought me? Is this my own voice I hear—carried on the wings of the air? O Fate! What have you done to me?

CHORUS   Terrible! Too terrible to hear! Too terrible to see!

OEDIPUS   O cloud of darkness! Cruel! Driven by the winds of fate! Assaulting me! With no defense to hold you back! O God! The pain! The pain! My flesh aches from its wounds! My soul aches from the memory of its horrors!

CHORUS   Body and soul—each suffers and mourns.

OEDIPUS   Ah! You still remain with me—a constant friend. You still remain to care for me—a blind man now. Now there is darkness and I cannot see your face. But I can hear your voice and I know that you are near.

CHORUS O my Lord, how could you have done this? How could you blind yourself? What demon drove you?

OEDIPUS Apollo! It was Apollo! *He* brought this pain, this suffering to me. But it was my own hand that struck the blow. Not his. O God! Why should I have sight when all that I would see is ugliness?

CHORUS It is as you say.

OEDIPUS What is there for me to see and love? What sight would give me joy? What sound? Take me away! Take me out of this land! I am cursed! Doomed! I am the man most hated by the gods!

CHORUS You have suffered equally for your fortune and for your disaster. I wish that you had never come to Thebes.

OEDIPUS Damn the man who set me free! Who loosed the fetters from my feet and let me live! I never will forgive him. If he had let me die, I would never have become the cause—the grief . . .

CHORUS I wish that it had been this way.

OEDIPUS If it had been, I would not have come to this—killer of my father, bridegroom of the woman who gave me birth, despised by the gods, child of shame, father and brother to my children. Is there any horror worse than these—any horror that has not fallen upon Oedipus.

CHORUS My Lord, I cannot condone what you have done. You would have been better dead than alive and blind.

OEDIPUS I did what I had to. You know I did. No more advice. Could these eyes have looked upon my father in the house of Hades? Could these eyes have faced my mother in her agony? I sinned against them both—a sin no suicide could purge. Could I have joy at the sight of my children—born as they were born? With these eyes? Never! Could I look upon the city of Thebes? The turrets that grace her walls? The sacred statues of her gods? Never! Damned! I—the noblest of the sons of Thebes—I have damned myself. It was I who commanded that Thebes must cast out the one who is guilty, unholy, cursed by the heavenly gods. *I* was the curse of Thebes! Could these eyes look upon the people? Never! And if I could raise a wall to channel the fountain of my hearing, I would spare nothing to build a prison for this defiled body where sight and sound would never penetrate. Then only would I have peace—where grief could not reach my mind. O Cithaeron! Why did you receive me? Why did you not let me die then? Why did you let me live to show the world how I was born? O Polybus! O Corinth! My home that was no home! You raised me, thinking I was fair and never knowing the evil that festered beneath. Now—now see the evil from which I was born, the evil I have become. O God! The three roads! The hidden glen! The thickets! The pathway where three roads meet! The blood you drank from my hands—do you not know—it was the blood of my father! Do you remember? Do you remember what I did then and what I did for Thebes? Wedding-rites! You gave me birth and gave my children birth! Born of the same womb that bore my children! Father! Brother! Child! Incestuous sin! Bride! Wife! Mother! All of one union! All the most heinous sins that man can know! The most horrible shame—I can no longer speak of it. For the love of God, hide me somewhere. Hide me away from this land! Kill me! Cast me into the sea where you will never have to look at me again! I beg you—touch me—in my misery. Touch me. Do not be afraid. My sins are mine alone to bear and touch no other man.

Enter CREON.

CHORUS   My Lord, Creon is here to act or counsel in what you ask. In your stead—he is now our sole protector.

OEDIPUS   What can I say to him? How can I ask for his trust? I have wronged him. I know that now.

CREON   I have not come to mock you, Oedipus, nor to reproach you for the past. But you—if you have no respect for men, at least respect the lord of the sun whose fires give life to men. Hide your naked guilt from his sight. No earth or sacred rain or light can endure its presence. [*To a servant.*] Take him inside. It is impious for any but his own family to see and hear his suffering.

OEDIPUS   I ask you in the name of God to grant me one favor. You have been kinder to me than I deserved. But one favor. I ask it for you—not for myself.

CREON   What do you ask of me?

OEDIPUS   Cast me out of this land. Cast me out to where no man can see me. Cast me out now.

CREON   I would have done so, you can be sure. But I must wait and do the will of the god.

OEDIPUS   He has signified his will—with clarity. Destroy the parricide! Destroy the unholy one! Destroy Oedipus!

CREON   That was the god's command, I know. But now—with what has happened—I think it better to wait and learn what we must do.

OEDIPUS   You mean that you would ask for guidance for a man so sorrowful as I?

CREON   Surely, you are ready to put your trust in the god—now.

OEDIPUS   Yes, I am ready now. But I ask this of you. Inside—she is lying inside—give her whatever funeral rites you wish. You will do the right thing for her. She is your sister. But for me—do not condemn this city—my father's city—to suffer any longer from my presence as long as I live. Let me go and live upon Cithaeron—O Cithaeron, your name is ever linked with mine! Where my parents chose a grave for me. Where they would have had me die. Where I shall die in answer to their wish. And yet, I know, neither sickness nor anything else will ever bring me death. For I would not have been saved from death that once. No—I was saved for a more dreadful fate. Let it be. Creon, do not worry about my sons. They are boys and will have all they need, no matter where they go. But my daughters—poor creatures! They never ate a single meal without their father. We shared everything together. Creon, take care of them. Creon, let me touch them one last time. And let me weep— one last time. Please, my Lord, please, allow it—you're generous, you're kind. If I could only touch them and feel that they are with me—as I used to—when I could see them. [*Enter* ANTIGONE *and* ISMENE.] What is that crying? Is it my daughters? Has Creon taken pity on me? Has he sent my daughters to me? Are they here?

CREON Yes, Oedipus, they are here. I had them brought to you. I know how much you love them, how much you have always loved them.

OEDIPUS Bless you for this, Creon. Heaven bless you and grant you greater kindness than it has granted me. Ah, children, where are you? Come—come, touch my hands, the hands of your father, the hands of your brother, the hands that blinded these eyes which once were bright—these eyes—your father's eyes which neither saw nor knew what he had done when he became your father. I weep for you, my children. I cannot see you now. But when I think of the bitterness that waits for you in life, what you will have to suffer— the festivals, the holidays—the sadness you will know when you should share in gaiety! And when you are old enough to marry— who will there be, who will be the man strong enough to bear the slander that will haunt you—because you are *my* children? What disgrace will you not know? Your father killed his father. And lay with the woman that bore him and his children. These are the taunts that will follow you. And what man will marry you? No man, my children. You will spend your lives unwed—without children of your own—barren and wasted. Ah, Creon, you are the only father left to them. We—their parents—are lost. We gave them life. And we are lost to them. Take care of them. See that they do not wander poor and lonely. Do not let them suffer for what I have done. Pity them. They are so young. So lost. They have no one but you. Take my hand and promise me. And oh, my children, if you were older, I could make you understand. But now, make this your prayer—to find some place where you can live and have a better life than what your father knew.

CREON Enough, my Lord. Go inside now.

OEDIPUS Yes. I do not want to, but I will go.

CREON All things have their time and their place.

OEDIPUS I shall go—on this condition.

CREON What condition? I am listening.

OEDIPUS That you will send me away.

CREON That is the god's decision, not mine.

OEDIPUS The gods will not care where I go.

CREON Then you shall have your wish.

OEDIPUS Then—you consent?

CREON It has nothing to do with my consent.

OEDIPUS Let me go away from here.

CREON Go then—but leave the children.

OEDIPUS No! Do not take them away from me!

CREON Do not presume that you are still in power. Your power has not survived with you.

CHORUS

There goes Oedipus—
he was the man who was able
to answer the riddle proposed by the Sphinx.
Mighty Oedipus—
he was an object of envy
to all for his fortune and fame.

There goes Oedipus—
now he is drowning in waves of dread and despair.
Look at Oedipus—
proof that none of us mortals
can truly be thought of as happy
until he is granted deliverance from life,
until he is dead
and must suffer no more.

ca. 429 B.C.

THEBES AND THE HOUSE OF CADMUS

Many of the principal myths of the Greeks centered about royal families who seemed particularly susceptible to sensational crimes and punishments. Few families had more lurid histories than that of Cadmus, the founder of Thebes.

When Cadmus' sister Europa was stolen by Zeus, in the form of a white bull, his father, Agenor of Sidon, sent Cadmus and his brothers forth to search for her. After various adventures, Cadmus, led by Athena, set out to establish a city. Led by a cow chosen by the goddess, he came to a spring where he was to establish the city. When most of his men were killed by a serpent who lived there, Cadmus killed the serpent and, again following the instructions of the goddess, sowed its teeth. From the teeth sprang up armed men who began fighting among themselves until Cadmus stopped them by throwing a stone into their midst. These "Sown Men" and their descendants were the great families of Thebes. Among them were Echion, the father of Pentheus, and an ancestor of Menoeceus, the father of Jocasta and Creon.

The chart below shows the relations of the members of the house of Cadmus who are mentioned in *Oedipus Tyrannus* and *The Bacchae.* A number of their relatives with equally spectacular destinies are omitted to make the chart more useful to readers of these two plays.

Although *Oedipus Tyrannus* and *The Bacchae* occur in different generations, the figure of Teiresias, the blind prophet, occurs in both. The name may have designated an office rather than an individual.

Thebes was the principal city of Boeotia, a district to the northwest of Attica in which Athens was located. This may help to explain its prominence in the Athenian drama. The two plays here considered make frequent reference to some of the features of the city, including its seven gates (where *The Seven Against Thebes* fought), the great mountain Cithaeron, which was nearby, the streams Ismenus, Dirce, and Asopus, and the neighboring villages of Hysiae and Erythrae.

OSCAR WILDE

The Importance of Being Earnest

JOHN WORTHING, J.P.   LADY BRACKNELL
ALGERNON MONCRIEFF   HON. GWENDOLEN FAIRFAX
REV. CANON CHASUBLE D. D. CECILY CARDEW
LANE, *Manservant*   MISS PRISM, *Governess*
MERRIMAN, *Butler*   A FOOTMAN

The first act takes place in ALGERNON's *flat in Half-Moon Street, London. The remaining acts take place at the Manor House, Woolton, Hertfordshire, the second in the garden and the third in the drawing-room.*

Act 1

Morning-room in ALGERNON's *flat in Half-Moon Street.*[1] *The room is luxuriously and artistically furnished. The sound of a piano is heard in the adjoining room.*

LANE is arranging afternoon tea on the table, and after the music has ceased, ALGERNON *enters.*

ALGERNON Did you hear what I was playing, Lane?
LANE I didn't think it polite to listen, sir.
ALGERNON I'm sorry for that, for your sake. I don't play accurately—any one can play accurately—but I play with wonderful expression. As far as the piano is concerned, sentiment is my forte. I keep science for Life.
LANE Yes, sir.
ALGERNON And, speaking of the science of Life, have you got the cucumber sandwiches cut for Lady Bracknell?
LANE Yes, sir. [*Hands them on a salver.*]
ALGERNON [*inspects them, takes two, and sits down on the sofa*] Oh! . . . by the way, Lane, I see from your book that on Thursday night, when Lord Shoreman and Mr. Worthing were dining with me, eight bottles of champagne are entered as having been consumed.
LANE Yes, sir; eight bottles and a pint.
ALGERNON Why is it that at a bachelor's establishment the servants invariably drink the champagne? I ask merely for information.
LANE I attribute it to the superior quality of the wine, sir. I have often observed that in married households the champagne is rarely of a first-rate brand.

---

1. Half-Moon Street runs north from Piccadilly near Hyde Park. Like many of the addresses in the play, it is in Mayfair, a very fashionable section of London.

ALGERNON   Good heavens! Is marriage so demoralizing as that?

LANE   I believe it is a very pleasant state, sir. I have had very little experience of it myself up to the present. I have only been married once. That was in consequence of a misunderstanding between myself and a young person.

ALGERNON [*languidly*]   I don't know that I am much interested in your family life, Lane.

LANE   No, sir; it is not a very interesting subject. I never think of it myself.

ALGERNON   Very natural, I am sure. That will do, Lane, thank you.

LANE   Thank you, sir. [*Goes out.*]

ALGERNON   Lane's views on marriage seem somewhat lax. Really, if the lower orders don't set us a good example, what on earth is the use of them? They seem, as a class, to have absolutely no sense of moral responsiblity.

Enter LANE.

LANE   Mr. Ernest Worthing.

Enter JACK. LANE *goes out.*

ALGERNON   How are you, my dear Ernest? What brings you up to town?

JACK   Oh, pleasure, pleasure! What else should bring one anywhere? Eating as usual, I see, Algy!

ALGERNON [*stiffly*]   I believe it is customary in good society to take some slight refreshment at five o'clock. Where have you been since last Thursday?

JACK [*sitting down on the sofa*]   In the country.

ALGERNON   What on earth do you do there?

JACK [*pulling off his gloves*]   When one is in town one amuses oneself. When one is in the country one amuses other people. It is excessively boring.

ALGERNON   And who are the people you amuse?

JACK [*airily*]   Oh, neighbors, neighbors.

ALGERNON   Got nice neighbors in your part of Shropshire?

JACK   Perfectly horrid! Never speak to one of them.

ALGERNON   How immensely you must amuse them! [*Goes over and takes sandwich.*] By the way, Shropshire is your county, is it not?

JACK   Eh? Shropshire? Yes, of course.[2] Hallo! Why all these cups? Why cucumber sandwiches? Why such reckless extravagance in one so young? Who is coming to tea?

ALGERNON   Oh! merely Aunt Augusta and Gwendolen.

JACK   How perfectly delightful!

ALGERNON   Yes, that is all very well; but I am afraid Aunt Augusta won't quite approve of your being here.

JACK   May I ask why?

2. As we learn later, Jack's country place is in Hertfordshire, to the north of London. He is attempting to deceive Algernon by giving a false location to the west, on the Welsh border.

ALGERNON   My dear fellow, the way you flirt with Gwendolen is perfectly disgraceful. It is almost as bad as the way Gwendolen flirts with you.

JACK   I am in love with Gwendolen. I have come up to town expressly to propose to her.

ALGERNON   I thought you had come up for pleasure? . . . I call that business.

JACK   How utterly unromantic you are!

ALGERNON   I really don't see anything romantic in proposing. It is very romantic to be in love. But there is nothing romantic about a definite proposal. Why, one may be accepted. One usually is, I believe. Then the excitement is all over. The very essence of romance is uncertainty. If ever I get married, I'll certainly try to forget the fact.

JACK   I have no doubt about that, dear Algy. The Divorce Court was specially invented for people whose memories are so curiously constituted.

ALGERNON   Oh! there is no use speculating on that subject. Divorces are made in Heaven—

> JACK *puts out his hand to take a sandwich.* ALGERNON *at once interferes.*

Please don't touch the cucumber sandwiches. They are ordered specially for Aunt Augusta. [*Takes one and eats it.*]

JACK   Well, you have been eating them all the time.

ALGERNON   That is quite a different matter. She is my aunt. [*Takes plate from below.*] Have some bread and butter. The bread and butter is for Gwendolen. Gwendolen is devoted to bread and butter.

JACK [*advancing to table and helping himself*]   And very good bread and butter it is too.

ALGERNON   Well, my dear fellow, you need not eat as if you were going to eat it all. You behave as if you were married to her already. You are not married to her already, and I don't think you ever will be.

JACK   Why on earth do you say that?

ALGERNON   Well, in the first place, girls never marry the men they flirt with. Girls don't think it right.

JACK   Oh, that is nonsense!

ALGERNON   It isn't. It is a great truth. It accounts for the extraordinary number of bachelors that one sees all over the place. In the second place, I don't give my consent.

JACK   Your consent!

ALGERNON   My dear fellow, Gwendolen is my first cousin. And before I allow you to marry her, you will have to clear up the whole question of Cecily. [*Rings bell.*]

JACK   Cecily! What on earth do you mean? What do you mean, Algy, by Cecily? I don't know any one of the name of Cecily.

> *Enter* LANE.

ALGERNON   Bring me that cigarette case Mr. Worthing left in the smoking-room the last time he dined here.

LANE   Yes, sir. [*Goes out.*]

JACK   Do you mean to say you have had my cigarette case all this time? I wish to goodness you had let me know. I have been writing frantic letters to Scotland Yard[3] about it. I was very nearly offering a large reward.

ALGERNON   Well, I wish you would offer one. I happen to be more then usually hard up.

JACK   There is no good offering a large reward now that the thing is found.

Enter LANE *with the cigarette case on a salver.* ALGERNON *takes it at once.* LANE *goes out.*

ALGERNON   I think that is rather mean of you. Ernest, I must say. [*Opens case and examines it.*] However, it makes no matter, for now that I look at the inscription inside, I find that the thing isn't yours after all.

JACK   Of course it's mine. [*Moving to him.*] You have seen me with it a hundred times, and you have no right whatsoever to read what is written inside. It is a very ungentlemanly thing to read a private cigarette case.

ALGERNON   Oh! it is absurd to have a hard and fast rule about what one should read and what one shouldn't. More than half of modern culture depends on what one shouldn't read.

JACK   I am quite aware of the fact, and I don't propose to discuss modern culture. It isn't the sort of thing one should talk of in private. I simply want my cigarette case back.

ALGERNON   Yes; but this isn't your cigarette case. This cigarette case is a present from someone of the name of Cecily, and you said you didn't know anyone of that name.

JACK   Well, if you want to know, Cecily happens to be my aunt.

ALGERNON   Your aunt!

JACK   Yes. Charming old lady she is, too. Lives at Tunbridge Wells.[4] Just give it back to me, Algy.

ALGERNON [*retreating to back of sofa*]   But why does she call herself little Cecily if she is your aunt and lives at Tunbridge Wells. [*Reading.*] "From little Cecily with her fondest love."

JACK [*moving to sofa and kneeling upon it*]   My dear fellow, what on earth is there in that? Some aunts are tall, some aunts are not tall. That is a matter that surely an aunt may be allowed to decide for herself. You seem to think that every aunt should be exactly like your aunt! That is absurd. For Heaven's sake give me back my cigarette case. [*Follows* ALGERNON *round the room.*]

ALGERNON   Yes. But why does your aunt call you her uncle? "From little Cecily, with her fondest love to her dear Uncle Jack." There is no objection. I admit, to an aunt being a small aunt, but why an

---

3. The headquarters of the London Metropolitan Police are in Scotland Yard, near the Houses of Parliament.

4. Tunbridge Wells is a resort town in Kent, to the southeast of London.

aunt, no matter what her size may be, should call her own nephew her uncle, I can't quite make out. Beside, your name isn't Jack at all; it is Ernest.

JACK   It isn't Ernest; it's Jack.

ALGERNON   You have always told me it was Ernest. I have introduced you to everyone as Ernest. You answer to the name of Ernest. You look as if your name was Ernest. You are the most earnest-looking person I ever saw in my life. It is perfectly absurd your saying that your name isn't Ernest. It's on your cards. Here is one of them. [*Taking it from case.*] "Mr. Ernest Worthing, B.4, The Albany."[5] I'll keep this as a proof that your name is Ernest if ever you attempt to deny it to me, or to Gwendolen, or to any one else. [*Puts the card in his pocket.*]

JACK   Well, my name is Ernest in town and Jack in the country, and the cigarette case was given to me in the country.

ALGERNON   Yes, but that does not account for the fact that your small Aunt Cecily, who lives at Tunbridge Wells, calls you her dear uncle. Come, old boy, you had much better have the thing out at once.

JACK   My dear Algy, you talk exactly as if you were a dentist. It is very vulgar to talk like a dentist when one isn't a dentist. It produces a false impression.

ALGERNON   Well, that is exactly what dentists always do. Now, go on! Tell me the whole thing. I may mention that I have always suspected you of being a confirmed and secret Bunburyist, and I am quite sure of it now.

JACK   Bunburyist? What on earth do you mean by a Bunburyist?

ALGERNON   I'll reveal to you the meaning of that incomparable expression as soon as you are kind enough to inform me why you are Ernest in town and Jack in the country.

JACK   Well, produce my cigarette case first.

ALGERNON   Here it is. [*Hands cigarette case.*] Now produce your explanation, and pray make it improbable. [*Sits on sofa.*]

JACK   My dear fellow, there is nothing improbable about my explanation at all. In fact it's perfectly ordinary. Old Mr. Thomas Cardew, who adopted me when I was a little boy, made me in his will guardian to his granddaughter, Miss Cecily Cardew. Cecily, who addresses me as her uncle from motives of respect that you could not possibly appreciate, lives at my place in the country under the charge of her admirable governess, Miss Prism.

ALGERNON   Where is that place in the country, by the way?

JACK   That is nothing to you, dear boy. You are not going to be invited. . . . I may tell you candidly that the place is not in Shropshire.

ALGERNON   I suspected that, my dear fellow! I have Bunburyed all over Shropshire on two separate occasions. Now, go on. Why are you Ernest in town and Jack in the country?

JACK   My dear Algy, I don't know whether you will be able to understand my real motives. You are hardly serious enough. When

---

5. An apartment building for single gentlemen on Piccadilly, to the east of Algernon's flat.

one is placed in the position of guardian, one has to adopt a very high moral tone on all subjects. It's one's duty to do so. And as a high moral tone can hardly be said to conduce very much to either one's health or one's happiness, in order to get up to town I have always pretended to have a younger brother of the name of Ernest, who lives in the Albany, and gets into the most dreadful scrapes. That, my dear Algy, is the whole truth pure and simple.

ALGERNON   The truth is rarely pure and never simple. Modern life would be very tedious if it were either, and modern literature a complete impossibility!

JACK   That wouldn't be at all a bad thing.

ALGERNON   Literary criticism is not your forte, my dear fellow. Don't try it. You should leave that to people who haven't been at a University. They do it so well in the daily papers. What you really are is a Bunburyist. I was quite right in saying you were a Bunburyist. You are one of the most advanced Bunburyists I know.

JACK   What on earth do you mean?

ALGERNON   You have invented a very useful young brother called Ernest, in order that you may be able to come up to town as often as you like. I have invented an invaluable permanent invalid called Bunbury, in order that I may be able to go down into the country whenever I choose. Bunbury is perfectly invaluable. If it wasn't for Bunbury's extraordinary bad health, for instance, I wouldn't be able to dine with you at Willis's[6] tonight, for I have been really engaged to Aunt Augusta for more than a week.

JACK   I haven't asked you to dine with me anywhere tonight.

ALGERNON   I know. You are absurdly careless about sending out invitations. It is very foolish of you. Nothing annoys people so much as not receiving invitations.

JACK   You had much better dine with your Aunt Augusta.

ALGERNON   I haven't the smallest intention of doing anything of the kind. To begin with, I dined there on Monday, and once a week is quite enough to dine with one's own relations. In the second place, whenever I do dine there I am always treated as a member of the family, and sent down with either no woman at all, or two. In the third place, I know perfectly well whom she will place me next to, tonight. She will place me next to Mary Farquhar, who always flirts with her own husband across the dinner table. That is not very pleasant. Indeed, it is not even decent . . . and that sort of thing is enormously on the increase. The amount of women in London who flirt with their own husbands is perfectly scandalous. It looks so bad. It is simply washing one's clean linen in public. Besides, now that I know you to be a confirmed Bunburyist I naturally want to talk to you about Bunburying. I want to tell you the rules.

JACK   I'm not a Bunburyist at all. If Gwendolen accepts me, I am going to kill my brother, indeed I think I'll kill him in any case. Cecily is a little too much interested in him. It is rather a bore. So I am going to get rid of Ernest. And I strongly advise you to

6. A well-known establishment for dining on King Street, off St. James's Street and quite near Piccadilly.

do the same with Mr. . . . with your invalid friend who has the absurd name.

ALGERNON Nothing will induce me to part with Bunbury, and if you ever get married, which seems to me extremely problematic, you will be very glad to know Bunbury. A man who marries without knowing Bunbury has a very tedious time of it.

JACK That is nonsense. If I marry a charming girl like Gwendolen, and she is the only girl I every saw in my life that I would marry, I certainly won't want to know Bunbury.

ALGERNON Then your wife will. You don't seem to realize, that in married life three is company and two is none.

JACK [*sententiously*] That, my dear young friend, is the theory that the corrupt French Drama has been propounding for the last fifty years.[7]

ALGERNON Yes! and that the happy English home has proved in half the time.

JACK For heaven's sake, don't try to be cynical. It's perfectly easy to be cynical.

ALGERNON My dear fellow, it isn't easy to be anything nowadays. There's such a lot of beastly competition about.

The sound of an electric bell is heard.

Ah! that must be Aunt Augusta, Only relatives, or creditors, ever ring in that Wagnerian manner.[8] Now, if I get her out of the way for ten minutes, so that you can have an opportunity for proposing to Gwendolen, may I dine with you tonight at Willis's?

JACK I suppose so, if you want to.

ALGERNON Yes, but you must be serious about it. I hate people who are not serious about meals. It is so shallow of them.

Enter LANE.

LANE Lady Bracknell and Miss Fairfax.

ALGERNON *goes forward to meet them. Enter* LADY BRACKNELL *and* GWENDOLEN.

LADY BRACKNELL Good afternoon, dear Algernon, I hope you are behaving very well.

ALGERNON I'm feeling very well, Aunt Augusta.

LADY BRACKNELL That's not quite the same thing. In fact the two things rarely go together. [*Sees* JACK *and bows to him with icy coldness.*]

ALGERNON [*to* GWENDOLEN] Dear me, you are smart!

7. Beginning in the middle of the 19th century, such diverse forces as the theatrical sensationalism of Eugene Scribe (1791–1861) and Victorien Sardou (1832–1908) and the movement toward realism in Alexandre Dumas *fils* (1824–1895) and Emil Augier (1820–1889) produced plays dealing with subjects such as adultery, prostitution, and illegitimacy. The heavily censored English theater either avoided such subjects or dealt with them more circumspectly.

8. Many earlier hearers of the music of Richard Wagner found it extremely loud and, consequently, peremptory in demanding attention.

GWENDOLEN   I am always smart! Am I not, Mr. Worthing?

JACK   You're quite perfect, Miss Fairfax.

GWENDOLEN   Oh! I hope I am not that. I would leave no room for developments, and I intend to develop in many directions.

GWENDOLEN *and* JACK *sit down together in the corner.*

LADY BRACKNELL   I'm sorry if we are a little late, Algernon, but I was obliged to call on dear Lady Harbury. I hadn't been there since her poor husband's death. I never saw a woman so altered; she looks quite twenty years younger. And now I'll have a cup of tea and one of those nice cucumber sandwiches you promised me.

ALGERNON   Certainly, Aunt Augusta. [*Goes over to tea-table.*]

LADY BRACKNELL   Won't you come and sit here, Gwendolen?

GWENDOLEN   Thanks, mamma, I'm quite comfortable where I am.

ALGERNON   [*picking up empty plate in horror*]   Good heavens! Lane! Why are there no cucumber sandwiches? I ordered them specially.

LANE   [*gravely*]   There were no cucumbers in the market this morning, sir. I went down twice.

ALGERNON.   No cucumbers!

LANE   No, sir. Not even for ready money.

ALGERNON   That will do, Lane, thank you.

LANE   Thank you, sir. [*Goes out.*]

ALGERNON   I am greatly distressed, Aunt Augusta, about there being no cucumbers, not even for ready money.

LADY BRACKNELL   It really makes no matter, Algernon. I had some crumpets with Lady Harbury, who seems to me to be living entirely for pleasure now.

ALGERNON   I hear her hair has turned quite gold from grief.

LADY BRACKNELL   It certainly has changed its color. From what cause I, of course, cannot say.

ALGERNON *crosses and hands tea.*

Thank you. I've quite a treat for you tonight, Algernon. I am going to send you down with Mary Farquhar. She is such a nice woman, and so attentive to her husband. It's delightful to watch them.

ALGERNON   I am afraid, Aunt Augusta, I shall have to give up the pleasure of dining with you tonight after all.

LADY BRACKNELL   [*frowning*]   I hope not, Algernon. It would put my table completely out. Your uncle would have to dine upstairs. Fortunately he is accustomed to that.

ALGERNON   It is a great bore, and, I need hardly say, a terrible disappointment to me, but the fact is I have just had a telegram to say that my poor friend Bunbury is very ill again. [*Exchanges glances with* JACK.] They seem to think I should be with him.

LADY BRACKNELL   It is very strange. This Mr. Bunbury seems to suffer from curiously bad health.

ALGERNON   Yes; poor Bunbury is a dreadful invalid.

LADY BRACNELL   Well, I must say, Algernon, that I think it is high time that Mr. Bunbury made up his mind whether he was going to live or to die. This shilly-shallying with the question is absurd. Nor do I in any way approve of the modern sympathy with invalids. I consider it morbid. Illness of any kind is hardly a thing to be encouraged in others. Health is the primary duty of life. I am always telling that to your poor uncle, but he never seems to take much notice . . . as far as any improvement in his ailments goes. I should be much obliged if you would ask Mr. Bunbury, from me, to be kind enough not to have a relapse on Saturday, for I rely on you to arrange my music for me. It is my last reception, and one wants something that will encourage conversation, particularly at the end of the season when everyone has practically said whatever they had to say, which, in most cases, was probably not much.

ALGERNON I'll speak to Bunbury, Aunt Augusta, if he is still conscious, and I think I can promise you he'll be all right by Saturday. Of course the music is a great difficulty. You see, if one plays good music, people don't listen, and if one plays bad music, people don't talk. But I'll run over the program I've drawn out, if you will kindly come into the next room for a moment.

LADY BRACKNELL Thank you, Algernon. It is very thoughtful of you. [*Rising, and following* ALGERNON.] I'm sure the program will be delightful, after a few expurgations. French songs I cannot possibly allow. People always seem to think that they are improper, and either look shocked, which is vulgar, or laugh, which is worse. But German sounds a thoroughly respectable language, and, indeed I believe is so. Gwendolen, you will accompany me.

GWENDOLEN Certainly, mamma.

LADY BRACKNELL *and* ALGERNON *go into the music-room;* GWENDOLEN *remains behind.*

JACK Charming day it has been, Miss Fairfax.

GWENDOLEN Pray don't talk to me about weather, Mr. Worthing. Whenever people talk to me about the weather, I always feel quite certain that they mean something else. And that makes me so nervous.

JACK I do mean something else.

GWENDOLEN I thought so. In fact, I am never wrong.

JACK And I would like to be allowed to take advantage of Lady Bracknell's temporary absence . . .

GWENDOLEN I would certainly advise you to do so. Mamma has a way of coming back suddenly into a room that I have often had to speak to her about.

JACK [*nervously*] Miss Fairfax, ever since I met you I have admired you more than any girl . . . I have ever met since . . . I met you.

GWENDOLEN Yes, I am quite aware of the fact. And I often wish that in public, at any rate, you had been more demonstrative. For me you have always had an irresistible fascination. Even before I met you I was far from indifferent to you.

JACK *looks at her in amazement.*

We live, as I hope you know, Mr. Worthing, in an age of ideals. The fact is constantly mentioned in the more expensive monthly magazines, and has reached the provincial pulpits, I am told; and my ideal has always been to love some one of the name of Ernest. There is something in that name that inspires absolute confidence. The moment Algernon first mentioned to me that he had a friend called Ernest, I knew I was destined to love you.

JACK   You really love me, Gwendolen?

GWENDOLEN   Passionately!

JACK   Darling! You don't know how happy you've made me.

GWENDOLEN   My own Ernest!

JACK   But you don't really mean to say that you couldn't love me if my name wasn't Ernest?

GWENDOLEN   But your name is Ernest.

JACK   Yes, I know it is. But supposing it was something else? Do you mean to say you couldn't love me then?

GWENDOLEN   [*glibly*] Ah! that is clearly a metaphysical speculation, and like most metaphysical speculations has very little reference at all to the actual facts of real life, as we know them.

JACK   Personally, darling, to speak quite candidly, I don't much care about the name of Ernest. . . . I don't think the name suits me at all.

GWENDOLEN   It suits you perfectly. It is a divine name. It has a music of its own. It produces vibrations.

JACK   Well, really, Gwendolen, I must say that I think there are lots of other much nicer names. I think Jack, for instance, a charming name.

GWENDOLEN   Jack? . . . No, there is very little music in the name Jack, if any at all, indeed. It does not thrill. It produces absolutely no vibrations. . . . I have known several Jacks, and they all, without exception, were more than usually plain. Besides, Jack is a notorious domesticity for John! And I pity any woman who is married to a man called John. She would probably never be allowed to know the entrancing pleasure of a single moment's solitude. The only really safe name is Ernest.

JACK   Gwendolen, I must get christened at once—I mean we must get married at once. There is no time to be lost.

GWENDOLEN   Married, Mr. Worthing?

JACK   [*astounded*] Well . . . surely. You know that I love you, and you led me to believe, Miss Fairfax, that you were not absolutely indifferent to me.

GWENDOLEN   I adore you. But you haven't proposed to me yet. Nothing has been said at all about marriage. The subject has not even been touched on.

JACK   Well . . . may I propose to you now?

GWENDOLEN   I think it would be an admirable opportunity. And to spare you any possible disappointment, Mr. Worthing, I think it only fair to tell you quite frankly beforehand that I am fully determined to accept you.

JACK   Gwendolen!

GWENDOLEN   Yes, Mr. Worthing, what have you got to say to me?

JACK   You know what I have got to say to you.

GWENDOLEN   Yes, but you don't say it.

JACK   Gwendolen, will you marry me? [*Goes on his knees.*]

GWENDOLEN   Of course I will, darling. How long you have been about it! I am afraid you have had very little experience in how to propose.

JACK   My own one, I have never loved any one in the world but you.

GWENDOLEN   Yes, but men often propose for practice. I know my brother Gerald does. All my girl-friends tell me so. What wonderfully blue eyes you have, Ernest! They are quite, quite blue. I hope you will always look at me just like that, especially when there are other people present.

    Enter LADY BRACKNELL.

LADY BRACKNELL   Mr. Worthing! Rise, sir, from this semi-recumbent posture. It is most indecorous.

GWENDOLEN   Mamma! [*He tries to rise; she restrains him.*] I must beg you to retire. This is no place for you. Besides, Mr. Worthing has not quite finished yet.

LADY BRACKNELL   Finished what, may I ask?

GWENDOLEN   I am engaged to Mr. Worthing, mamma.

    They rise together.

LADY BRACKNELL   Pardon me, you are not engaged to anyone. When you do become engaged to some one, I, or your father, should his health permit him, will inform you of the fact. An engagement should come on a young girl as a surprise, pleasant or unpleasant, as the case may be. It is hardly a matter that she could be allowed to arrange for herself. . . . And now I have a few questions to put to you, Mr. Worthing. While I am making these inquiries, you, Gwendolen, will wait for me below in the carriage.

GWENDOLEN [*reproachfully*]   Mamma!

LADY BRACKNELL   In the carriage, Gwendolen!

    GWENDOLEN *goes to the door. She and* JACK *blow kisses to each other behind* LADY BRACKNELL'*s back.* LADY BRACKNELL *looks vaguely about as if she could not understand what the noise was. Finally turns around.*

Gwendolen, the carriage!

GWENDOLEN   Yes, mamma. [*Goes out, looking back at* JACK.]

LADY BRACKNELL [*sitting down*]   You can take a seat, Mr. Worthing. [*Looks in her pocket for notebook and pencil.*]

JACK   Thank you, Lady Bracknell, I prefer standing.

LADY BRACKNELL [*pencil and notebook in hand*]   I feel bound to tell you that you are not down on my list of eligible young men, although I have the same list as the dear Duchess of Bolton has. We work together, in fact. However, I am quite ready to enter your name, should your answers be what a really affectionate mother requires. Do you smoke?

JACK   Well, yes, I must admit I smoke.

LADY BRACKNELL   I am glad to hear it. A man should always have an occupation of some kind. There are far too many idle men in London as it is. How old are you?

JACK   Twenty-nine.

LADY BRACKNELL   A very good age to be married at. I have always been of the opinion that a man who desires to get married should know either everything or nothing. Which do you know?

JACK [*after some hestitation*]   I know nothing, Lady Bracknell.

LADY BRACKNELL   I am pleased to hear it. I do not approve of anything that tampers with natural ignorance. Ignorance is like a delicate exotic fruit; touch it and the bloom is gone. The whole theory of modern education is radically unsound. Fortunately in England, at any rate, education produces no effect whatsoever. If it did, it would prove a serious danger to the upper classes, and probably lead to acts of violence in Grosvenor Square.[9] What is your income?

JACK   Between seven and eight thousand a year.[1]

LADY BRACKNELL [*makes a note in her book*]   In land, or in investments?

JACK   In investments, chiefly.

LADY BRACKNELL   That is satisfactory. What between the duties expected of one during one's lifetime, and the duties exacted from one after one's death, land has ceased to be either a profit or a pleasure. It gives one position, and prevents one from keeping it up. That's all that can be said about land.

JACK   I have a country house with some land, of course, attached to it, about fifteen hundred acres, I believe; but I don't depend on that for my real income. In fact, as far as I can make out, the poachers are the only people who make anything out of it.

LADY BRACKNELL   A country house! How many bedrooms? Well, that point can be cleared up afterwards. You have a town house, I hope? A girl with a simple, unspoiled nature, like Gwendolen, could hardly be expected to reside in the country.

JACK   Well, I own a house in Belgrave Square,[2] but it is let by the year to Lady Bloxham. Of course, I can get it back whenever I like, at six months' notice.

LADY BRACKNELL   Lady Bloxham? I don't know her.

JACK   Oh, she goes about very little. She is a lady considerably advanced in years.

LADY BRACKNELL   Ah, nowadays that is no guarantee of respectability of character. What number in Belgrave Square?

JACK   149.

9. A fashionable location in Mayfair.
1. At the time of the play, the pound was worth about $4.87. Jack's income was thus about thirty thousand dollars a year, a not inconsiderable figure when the New York *Times* was three cents daily and five cents on Sundays, when a can of corn was on sale at nine cents, and when $45 would purchase first-class passage from New York to Amsterdam.
2. Belgrave Square is near the southeast corner of Hyde Park in Belgravia, another fashionable section of London.

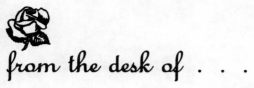

from the desk of . . .

Bea Flint

Jerome Hennigan

3rd gear

Emery Lane School

LADY BRACKNELL [*shaking her head*]   The unfashionable side. I thought there was something. However, that could easily be altered.

JACK   Do you mean the fashion, or the side?

LADY BRACKNELL [*sternly*]   Both, if necessary, I presume. What are your politics?

JACK   Well, I am afraid I really have none. I am a Liberal Unionist.

LADY BRACKNELL   Oh, they count as Tories.[3] They dine with us. Or come in the evening, at any rate. Now to minor matters. Are your parents living?

JACK   I have lost both my parents.

LADY BRACKNELL   To lose one parent, Mr. Worthing, may be regarded as a misfortune; to lose both looks like carelessness. Who was your father? He was evidently a man of some wealth. Was he born in what the Radical papers call the purple of commerce, or did he rise from the ranks of the aristocracy?

JACK   I am afraid I really don't know. That fact is, Lady Bracknell, I said I had lost my parents. It would be nearer the truth to say that my parents seem to have lost me. . . . I don't actually know who I am by birth. I was . . . well, I was found.

LADY BRACKNELL   Found!

JACK   The late Mr. Thomas Cardew, an old gentleman of a very charitable and kindly disposition, found me, and gave me the name of Worthing, because he happened to have a first-class ticket for Worthing in his pocket at the time. Worthing is a place in Sussex. It is a seaside resort.

LADY BRACKNELL   Where did the charitable gentleman who had a first-class ticket for this seaside resort find you?

JACK [*gravely*]   In a handbag.

LADY BRACKNELL   A handbag?

JACK [*very seriously*]   Yes, Lady Bracknell. I was in a handbag—a somewhat large, black leather handbag, with handles to it—an ordinary handbag in fact.

LADY BRACKNELL   In what locality did this Mr. James, or Thomas, Cardew come across this ordinary handbag?

JACK   In the cloakroom at Victoria Station.[4] It was given to him in mistake for his own.

LADY BRACKNELL   The cloakroom at Victoria Station?

JACK   Yes. The Brighton line.

LADY BRACKNELL   The line is immaterial. Mr. Worthing, I confess I feel somewhat bewildered by what you have just told me. To be born, or at any rate bred, in a handbag, whether it had handles or not, seems to me to display a contempt for the ordinary decencies of family life that reminds one of the worst excesses of the French Revolution. And I presume you know what the unfortunate movement led to? As for the particular locality in which the handbag was found, a cloakroom at a railway station might serve to conceal a

---

3. Liberal Unionists were a late 19th-century political group which had split from the Liberal Party over home rule for Ireland. "Tories" were members of the Conservative Party—the latter was the more customary designation after the First Reform Bill of 1832.

4. Victoria Station is a major railroad terminus in London, particularly for trains to the south of England, including those going to the popular seaside resort of Brighton.

social indiscretion—has probably, indeed, been used for that purpose before now—but it could hardly be regarded as an assured basis for a recognized position in good society.

JACK   May I ask you then what you would advise me to do? I need
hardly say I would do anything in the world to ensure Gwendolen's
happiness.

LADY BRACKNELL   I would strongly advise you, Mr. Worthing, to try
and acquire some relations as soon as possible, and to make a
definite effort to produce at any rate one parent, of either sex, before the season is quite over.

JACK   Well, I don't see how I could possibly manage to do that. I
can produce the handbag at any moment. It is in my dressing-room
at home. I really think that should satisfy you, Lady Bracknell.

LADY BRACKNELL   Me, sir! What has it to do with me? You can
hardly imagine that I and Lord Bracknell would dream of allowing
our only daughter—a girl brought up with the utmost care—to marry
into a cloakroom, and form an alliance with a parcel. Good morning,
Mr. Worthing!

LADY BRACKNELL *sweeps out in majestic indignation.*

JACK   Good morning!

ALGERNON, *from the other room, strikes up the Wedding March.*
JACK *looks perfectly furious, and goes to the door.*

For goodness' sake don't play that ghastly tune, Algy! How idiotic
you are!

The music stops and ALGERNON *enters cheerily.*

ALGERNON   Didn't it go off all right, old boy? You don't mean to say
Gwendolen refused you? I know it is a way she has. She is always
refusing people. I think it is most ill-natured of her.

JACK   Oh, Gwendolen is as right as a trivet.[5] As far as she is concerned, we are engaged. Her mother is perfectly unbearable.
Never met such a Gorgon.[6] . . . I don't really know what a Gorgon
is like, but I am quite sure that Lady Bracknell is one. In any
case, she is a monster, without being a myth, which is rather unfair. . . . I beg your pardon, Algy, I suppose I shouldn't talk about
your own aunt in that way before you.

ALGERNON   My dear boy, I love hearing my relations abused. It is
the only thing that makes me put up with them at all. Relations
are simply a tedious pack of people, who haven't got the remotest
knowledge of how to live, nor the smallest instinct about when to
die.

JACK   Oh, that is nonsense!

---

5. A proverbial expression, referring to
the solidity of a tripod on its three legs.
6. A mythological creature of horrible
aspect, particularly because the Gorgon
had snakes in place of hair. According to
myth, those who looked on a Gorgon were
turned to stone by the experience.

ALGERNON   It isn't!

JACK   Well, I won't argue about the matter. You always want to argue about things.

ALGERNON   That is exactly what things were originally made for.

JACK   Upon my word, if I thought that, I'd shoot myself. . . . [*A pause.*] You don't think there is any chance of Gwendolen becoming like her mother in about a hundred and fifty years, do you, Algy?

ALGERNON   All women become like their mothers. That is their tragedy. No man does. That's his.

JACK   Is that clever?

ALGERNON   It is perfectly phrased! and quite as true as any observation in civilized life should be.

JACK   I am sick to death of cleverness. Everybody is clever nowadays. You can't go anywhere without meeting clever people. The thing has become an absolute public nuisance. I wish to goodness we had a few fools left.

ALGERNON   We have.

JACK   I should extremely like to meet them. What do they talk about?

ALGERNON   The fools? Oh! about the clever people, of course.

JACK   What fools.

ALGERNON   By the way, did you tell Gwendolen the truth about your being Ernest in town, and Jack in the country?

JACK   [*in a very patronizing manner*]   My dear fellow, the truth isn't quite the sort of thing one tells to a nice, sweet, refined girl. What extraordinary ideas you have about the way to behave to a woman!

ALGERNON   The only way to behave to a woman is to make love to her, if she is pretty, and to someone else, if she is plain.

JACK   Oh, that is nonsense.

ALGERNON   What about your brother? What about the profligate Ernest?

JACK   Oh, before the end of the week I shall have got rid of him. I'll say he died in Paris of apoplexy. Lots of people die of apoplexy, quite suddenly, don't they?

ALGERNON   Yes, but it's hereditary, my dear fellow. It's a sort of thing that runs in families. You had much better say a severe chill.

JACK   You are sure a severe chill isn't hereditary, or anything of that kind?

ALGERNON   Of course it isn't!

JACK   Very well, then. My poor brother Ernest is carried off suddenly, in Paris, by a severe chill. That gets rid of him.

ALGERNON   But I thought you said that . . . Miss Cardew was a little too much interested in your poor brother Ernest? Won't she feel his loss a good deal?

JACK   Oh, that is all right. Cecily is not a silly romantic girl, I am glad to say. She has got a capital appetite, goes on long walks, and pays no attention at all to her lessons.

ALGERNON   I would rather like to see Cecily.

JACK   I will take very good care you never do. She is excessively pretty, and she is only just eighteen.

ALGERNON   Have you told Gwendolen yet that you have an excessively pretty ward who is only just eighteen?

JACK   Oh! one doesn't blurt these things out to people. Cecily and Gwendolen are perfectly certain to be extremely great friends. I'll bet you anything you like that half an hour after they have met, they will be calling each other sister.

ALGERNON   Women only do that when they have called each other a lot of other things first. Now, my dear boy, if we want to get a good table at Willis's, we really must go and dress. Do you know it is nearly seven?

JACK [*irritably*]   Oh! it always is nearly seven.

ALGERNON   Well, I'm hungry.

JACK   I never knew you when you weren't. . . .

ALGERNON   What shall we do after dinner? Go to a theatre?

JACK   Oh no! I loathe listening.

ALGERNON   Well, let us go to the Club?

JACK   Oh, no! I hate talking.

ALGERNON   Well, we might trot round to the Empire[7] at ten?

JACK   Oh, no! I can't bear looking at things. It is so silly.

ALGERNON   Well, what shall we do?

JACK   Nothing!

ALGERNON   It is awfully hard work doing nothing. However, I don't mind hard work where there is no definite object of any kind.

Enter LANE.

LANE   Miss Fairfax.

Enter GWENDOLEN. LANE *goes out.*

ALGERNON   Gwendolen, upon my word!

GWENDOLEN   Algy, kindly turn your back. I have something very particular to say to Mr. Worthing.

ALGERNON   Really, Gwendolen, I don't think I can allow this at all.

GWENDOLEN   Algy, you always adopt a strictly immoral attitude towards life. You are not quite old enough to do that.

ALGERNON *retires to the fireplace.*

JACK   My own darling!

GWENDOLEN   Ernest, we may never be married. From the expression on mamma's face I fear we never shall. Few parents nowadays pay any regard to what their children say to them. The old-fashioned respect for the young is fast dying out. Whatever influence I ever had over mamma, I lost at the age of three. But although she may prevent us from becoming man and wife, and I may marry someone else, and marry often, nothing that she can possibly do can alter my eternal devotion to you.

7. The Empire Theatre of Varieties, a music hall on Leicester Square.

JACK   Dear Gwendolen!

GWENDOLEN   The story of your romantic origin, as related to me by mamma, with unpleasing comments, has naturally stirred the deeper fibres of my nature. Your Christian name has an irresistible fascination. The simplicity of your character makes you exquisitely incomprehensible to me. Your town address at the Albany I have. What is your address in the country?

JACK   The Manor House, Woolton, Hertfordshire.

> ALGERNON, *who has been carefully listening, smiles to himself, and writes the address on his shirt-cuff. Then picks up the Railway Guide.*

GWENDOLEN   There is a good postal service, I suppose? It may be necessary to do something desperate. That of course will require serious consideration. I will communicate with you daily.

JACK   My own one!

GWENDOLEN   How long do you remain in town?

JACK   Till Monday.

GWENDOLEN   Good! Algy, you may turn round now.

ALGERNON   Thanks, I've turned round already.

GWENDOLEN   You may also ring the bell.

JACK   You will let me see you to your carriage, my own darling?

GWENDOLEN   Certainly.

JACK [*to* LANE, *who now enters*]   I will see Miss Fairfax out.

LANE   Yes, sir.

> JACK *and* GWENDOLEN *go off.* LANE *presents several letters on a salver to* ALGERNON. *It is to be surmised that they are bills, as* ALGERNON, *after looking at the envelopes, tears them up.*

ALGERNON   A glass of sherry, Lane.

LANE   Yes, sir.

ALGERNON   Tomorrow, Lane, I'm going Bunburying.

LANE   Yes, sir.

ALGERNON   I shall probably not be back till Monday. You can put up my dress clothes, my smoking jacket, and all the Bunbury suits . . .

LANE   Yes, sir. [*Handing sherry.*]

ALGERNON   I hope tomorrow will be a fine day, Lane.

LANE   It never is, sir.

ALGERNON   Lane, you're a perfect pessimist.

LANE   I do my best to give satisfaction, sir.

> *Enter* JACK. LANE *goes off.*

JACK   There's a sensible, intellectual girl; the only girl I ever cared for in my life.

> ALGERNON *is laughing immoderately.*

What on earth are you so amused at?

ALGERNON   Oh, I'm a little anxious about poor Bunbury, that is all.

JACK   If you don't take care, your friend Bunbury will get you into a serious scrape some day.

ALGERNON   I love scrapes. They are the only things that are never serious.

JACK   Oh, that's nonsense, Algy. You never talk anything but nonsense.

ALGERNON   Nobody ever does.

> JACK *looks indignantly at him, and leaves the room.* ALGERNON *lights a cigarette, reads his shirt-cuff, and smiles.*

Act 2

> *Garden at the Manor House. A flight of gray stone steps leads up to the house. The garden, an old-fashioned one, full of roses. Time of year, July. Basket chairs, and a table covered with books, are set under a large yew-tree.*
>
> MISS PRISM *discovered seated at the table.* CECILY *is at the back, watering flowers.*

MISS PRISM [*calling*]   Cecily, Cecily! Surely such a utilitarian occupation as the watering of flowers is rather Moulton's duty than yours? Especially at a moment when intellectual pleasures await you. Your German grammar is on the table. Pray open it at page fifteen. We will repeat yesterday's lesson.

CECILY [*coming over very slowly*]   But I don't like German. It isn't at all a becoming language. I know perfectly well that I look quite plain after my German lesson.

MISS PRISM   Child, you know how anxious your guardian is that you should improve yourself in every way. He laid particular stress on your German, as he was leaving for town yesterday. Indeed, he always lays stress on your German when he is leaving for town.

CECILY   Dear Uncle Jack is so very serious! Sometimes he is so serious that I think he cannot be quite well.

MISS PRISM [*drawing herself up*]   Your guardian enjoys the best of health, and his gravity of demeanor is especially to be commended in one so comparatively young as he is. I know no one who has a higher sense of duty and responsibility.

CECILY   I suppose that is why he often looks a little bored when we three are together.

MISS PRISM   Cecily! I am surprised at you. Mr. Worthing has many troubles in his life. Idle merriment and triviality would be out of place in his conversation. You must remember his constant anxiety about that unfortunate young man, his brother.

CECILY   I wish Uncle Jack would allow that unfortunate young man, his brother, to come down here sometimes. We might have a good influence over him, Miss Prism. I am sure you certainly would. You know German, and geology, and things of that kind influence a man very much. [CECILY *begins to write in her diary.*]

MISS PRISM [*shaking her head*]   I do not think that even I could produce any effect on a character that according to his own brother's admission is irretrievably weak and vacillating. Indeed I am not sure that I would desire to reclaim him. I am not in favor of this modern mania for turning bad people into good people at a moment's notice. As a man sows so let him reap. You must put away your diary, Cecily. I really don't see why you should keep a diary at all.

CECILY   I keep a diary in order to enter the wonderful secrets of my life. If I didn't write them down, I should probably forget all about them.

MISS PRISM   Memory, my dear Cecily, is the diary that we all carry about with us.

CECILY   Yes, but it usually chronicles the things that have never happened, and couldn't possibly have happened. I believe that Memory is responsible for nearly all the three-volume novels that Mudie sends us.[8]

MISS PRISM   Do not speak slightingly of the three-volume novel, Cecily. I wrote one myself in earlier days.

CECILY   Did you really, Miss Prism? How wonderfully clever you are! I hope it did not end happily! I don't like novels that end happily. They depress me so much.

MISS PRISM   The good ended happily, and the bad unhappily. That is what Fiction means.

CECILY   I suppose so. But it seems very unfair. And was your novel ever published?

MISS PRISM   Alas! no. The manuscript unfortunately was abandoned.

CECILY *starts.*

I used the word in the sense of lost or mislaid. To your work, child, these speculations are profitless.

CECILY [*smiling*]   But I see dear Dr. Chasuble coming up through the garden.

MISS PRISM [*rising and advancing*]   Dr. Chasuble! This is indeed a pleasure.

Enter CANON CHASUBLE.

CHASUBLE   And how are we this morning? Miss Prism, you are, I trust, well?

CECILY   Miss Prism has just been complaining of a slight headache. I think it would do her so much good to have a short stroll with you in the Park, Dr. Chasuble.

MISS PRISM   Cecily, I have not mentioned anything about a headache.

CECILY   No, dear Miss Prism, I know that, but I felt instinctively that you had a headache. Indeed I was thinking about that, and not about my German lesson, when the Rector came in.

8. From the 1860s to the 1880s most novels were published in three volumes. Because of the resultant price, most readers could not afford to buy copies and obtained them by subscription from lending libraries, of which Mudie's in London was by far the largest.

CHASUBLE   I hope, Cecily, you are not inattentive.

CECILY   Oh, I am afraid I am.

CHASUBLE   That is strange. Were I fortunate enough to be Miss Prism's pupil, I would hang upon her lips.

MISS PRISM *glares.*

I spoke metaphorically.—My metaphor was drawn from bees. Ahem! Mr. Worthing, I suppose, has not returned from town yet?

MISS PRISM   We do not expect him till Monday afternoon.

CHASUBLE   Ah yes, he usually likes to spend his Sunday in London. He is not one of those whose sole aim is enjoyment, as, by all accounts, that unfortunate young man his brother seems to be. But I must not disturb Egeria[9] and her pupil any longer.

MISS PRISM   Egeria? My name is Laetitia, Doctor.

CHASUBLE [*bowing*]   A classical allusion merely, drawn from the Pagan authors. I shall see you both no doubt at Evensong?

MISS PRISM   I think, dear, Doctor, I will have a stroll with you. I find I have a headache after all, and a walk might do it good.

CHASUBLE   With pleasure, Miss Prism, with pleasure. We might go as far as the schools and back.

MISS PRISM   That would be delightful. Cecily, you will read your Political Economy in my absence.[1] The chapter on the Fall of the Rupee you may omit. It is somewhat too sensational. Even these metallic problems have their melodramatic side. [*Goes down the garden with* DR. CHASUBLE.]

CECILY [*picks up books and throws them back on table*]   Horrid Political Economy! Horrid Geography! Horrid, horrid German!

Enter MERRIMAN *with a card on a salver.*

MERRIMAN   Mr. Ernest Worthing has just driven over from the station. He has brought his luggage with him.

CECILY [*takes the card and reads it*]   "Mr. Ernest Worthing, B.4, The Albany, W." Uncle Jack's brother! Did you tell him Mr. Worthing was in town?

MERRIMAN   Yes, Miss. He seemed very much disappointed. I mentioned that you and Miss Prism were in the garden. He said he was anxious to speak to you privately for a moment.

CECILY   Ask Mr. Ernest Worthing to come here. I suppose you had better talk to the housekeeper about a room for him.

MERRIMAN   Yes, Miss. [*Goes off.*]

CECILY   I have never met any really wicked person before. I feel rather frightened. I am so afraid he will look just like every one else.

Enter ALGERNON, *very gay and debonair.*

---

9. A nymph in classical mythology, famous as the wise counselor of Numa Pompilius, the second of the legendary kings of Rome.

1. Political Economy was a branch of social science which dealt with the reve-
nues and general financial resources of nations. The term came into use at the beginning of the 17th century. In this century it has developed into the study we call Economics. The rupee is the currency unit of India.

He does!

ALGERNON [*raising his hat*] You are my little cousin Cecily, I'm sure.

CECILY You are under some strange mistake. I am not little. In fact, I believe I am more than usually tall for my age.

      ALGERNON *is rather taken aback.*

But I am your cousin Cecily. You, I see from your card, are Uncle Jack's brother, my cousin Ernest, my wicked cousin Ernest.

ALGERNON Oh! I am not really wicked at all, Cousin Cecily. You mustn't think that I am wicked.

CECILY If you are not, then you have certainly been deceiving us all in a very inexcusable manner. I hope you have not been leading a double life, pretending to be wicked and being really good all the time. That would be hypocrisy.

ALGERNON [*looks at her in amazement*] Oh! Of course I have been rather reckless.

CECILY I am glad to hear it.

ALGERNON In fact, now you mention the subject, I have been very bad in my own small way.

CECILY I don't think you should be so proud of that, though I am sure it must have been very pleasant.

ALGERNON It is much pleasanter being here with you.

CECILY I can't understand how you are here at all. Uncle Jack won't be back till Monday afternoon.

ALGERNON That is a great disappointment. I am obliged to go up by the first train on Monday morning. I have a business appointment that I am anxious . . . to miss!

CECILY Couldn't you miss it anywhere but in London?

ALGERNON No: the appointment is in London.

CECILY Well, I know, of course, how important it is not to keep a business engagement, if one wants to retain any sense of the beauty of life, but still I think you had better wait till Uncle Jack arrives. I know he wants to speak to you about your emigrating.

ALGERNON About my what?

CECILY Your emigrating. He has gone up to buy your outfit.

ALGERNON I certainly wouldn't let Jack buy my outfit. He has no taste in neckties at all.

CECILY I don't think you will require neckties. Uncle Jack is sending you to Australia.

ALGERNON Australia! I'd sooner die.

CECILY Well, he said at dinner on Wednesday night, that you would have to choose between this world, the next world, and Australia.

ALGERNON Oh, well! The accounts I have received of Australia and the next world are not particularly encouraging. This world is good enough for me, Cousin Cecily.

CECILY Yes, but are you good enough for it?

ALGERNON I'm afraid I'm not that. That is why I want you to reform me. You might make that your mission, if you don't mind, Cousin Cecily.

CECILY I'm afraid I've no time, this afternoon.

ALGERNON   Well, would you mind my reforming myself this afternoon?

CECILY   It is rather Quixotic of you. But I think you should try.

ALGERNON   I will. I feel better already.

CECILY   You are looking a little worse.

ALGERNON   That is because I am hungry.

CECILY   How thoughtless of me. I should have remembered that
when one is going to lead an entirely new life, one requires regular
and wholesome meals. Won't you come in?

ALGERNON   Thank you. Might I have a buttonhole first?[2] I never have
any appetite unless I have a buttonhole first.

CECILY   A Maréchal Niel? [*Picks up scissors.*]

ALGERNON   No, I'd sooner have a pink rose.

CECILY   Why? [*Cuts a flower.*]

ALGERNON   Because you are like a pink rose, Cousin Cecily.

CECILY   I don't think it can be right for you to talk to me like that.
Miss Prism never says such things to me.

ALGERNON   Then Miss Prism is a shortsighted old lady.

CECILY *puts the rose in his buttonhole.*

You are the prettiest girl I ever saw.

CECILY   Miss Prism says that all good looks are a snare.

ALGERNON   They are a snare that every sensible man would like to be
caught in.

CECILY   Oh, I don't think I would care to catch a sensible man. I
shouldn't know what to talk to him about.

They pass into the house. MISS PRISM *and* DR. CHASUBLE
return.

MISS PRISM   You are too much alone, dear Dr. Chasuble. You should
get married. A misanthrope I can understand—a womanthrope,
never!

CHASUBLE [*with a scholar's shudder*]   Believe me, I do not deserve
so neologistic a phrase. The precept as well as the practice of the
Primitive Church was distinctly against matrimony.

MISS PRISM [*sententiously*]   That is obviously the reason why the
Primitive Church has not lasted up to the present day. And you do
not seem to realize, dear Doctor, that by persistently remaining
single, a man converts himself into a permanent public temptation.
Men should be more careful; this very celibacy leads weaker vessels
astray.

CHASUBLE   But is a man not equally attractive when married?

MISS PRISM   No married man is ever attractive except to his wife.

CHASUBLE   And often, I've been told, not even to her.

MISS PRISM   That depends on the intellectual sympathies of the
woman. Maturity can always be depended on. Ripeness can be
trusted. Young women are green.

---

2. A "buttonhole" is a flower to be
worn on the lapel of a man's coat, in this
case a popular yellow rose of the period.
Hardier varieties are available now, and
the Maréchal Niel is seldom grown.

DR. CHASUBLE *starts.*

I spoke horticulturally. My metaphor was drawn from fruits. But where is Cecily?
CHASUBLE   Perhaps she followed us to the schools.

Enter JACK *slowly from the back of the garden. He is dressed in the deepest mourning, with crepe hatband and black gloves.*

MISS PRISM   Mr. Worthing!
CHASUBLE   Mr. Worthing?
MISS PRISM   This is indeed a surprise. We did not look for you till Monday afternoon.
JACK [*shakes* MISS PRISM's *hand in a tragic manner*]   I have returned sooner than I expected. Dr. Chasuble, I hope you are well?
CHASUBLE   Dear Mr. Worthing, I trust this garb of woe does not betoken some terrible calamity?
JACK   My brother.
MISS PRISM   More shameful debts and extravagance?
CHASUBLE   Still leading his life of pleasure?
JACK [*shaking his head*]   Dead!
CHASUBLE   Your brother Ernest dead?
JACK   Quite dead.
MISS PRISM   What a lesson for him! I trust he will profit by it.
CHASUBLE   Mr. Worthing, I offer you my sincere condolence. You have at least the consolation of knowing that you were always the most generous and forgiving of brothers.
JACK   Poor Ernest! He had many faults, but it is a sad, sad blow.
CHASUBLE   Very sad indeed. Were you with him at the end?
JACK   No. He died abroad; in Paris, in fact. I had a telegram last night from the manager of the Grand Hotel.
CHASUBLE   Was the cause of death mentioned?
JACK   A severe chill, it seems.
MISS PRISM   As a man sows, so shall he reap.
CHASUBLE [*raising his hand*]   Charity, dear Miss Prism, charity! None of us is perfect. I myself am peculiarly susceptible to drafts. Will the interment take place here?
JACK   No. He seems to have expressed a desire to be buried in Paris.
CHASUBLE   In Paris! [*Shakes his head.*] I fear that hardly points to any very serious state of mind at the last. You would no doubt wish me to make some slight allusion to this tragic domestic affliction next Sunday.

JACK *presses his hand convulsively.*

My sermon on the meaning of the manna in the wilderness can be adapted to almost any occasion, joyful, or, as in the present case, distressing.

All sigh.

I have preached it at harvest celebrations, christenings, confirmations, on days of humiliation and festal days. The last time I delivered it was in the Cathedral, as a charity sermon on behalf of the Society for the Prevention of Discontent among the Upper Orders. The Bishop, who was present, was much struck by some of the analogies I drew.

JACK   Ah! that reminds me, you mentioned christenings, I think, Dr. Chasuble? I suppose you know how to christen all right?

DR. CHASUBLE *looks astounded.*

I mean, of course, you are continually christening, aren't you?

MISS PRISM   It is, I regret to say, one of the Rector's most constant duties in this parish. I have often spoken to the poorer classes on the subject. But they don't seem to know what thrift is.

CHASUBLE   But is there any particular infant in whom you are interested, Mr. Worthing? Your brother was, I believe, unmarried, was he not?

JACK   Oh yes.

MISS PRISM [*bitterly*]   People who live entirely for pleasure usually are.

JACK   But it is not for any child, dear Doctor. I am very fond of children. No! the fact is, I would like to be christened myself, this afternoon, if you have nothing better to do.

CHASUBLE   But surely, Mr. Worthing, you have been christened already?

JACK   I don't remember anything about it.

CHASUBLE   But have you any grave doubts on the subject?

JACK   I certainly intend to have. Of course I don't know if the thing would bother you in any way, or if you think I am a little too old now.

CHASUBLE   Not at all. The sprinkling, and, indeed, the immersion of adults is a perfectly canonical practice.

JACK   Immersion!

CHASUBLE   You need have no apprehensions. Sprinkling is all that is necessary, or indeed I think advisable. Our weather is so changeable. At what hour would you wish the ceremony performed?

JACK   Oh, I might trot round about five if that would suit you.

CHASUBLE   Perfectly, perfectly! In fact I have two similar ceremonies to perform at that time. A case of twins that occurred recently in one of the outlying cottages on your own estate. Poor Jenkins the carter, a most hard-working man.

JACK   Oh! I don't see much fun in being christened along with other babies. It would be childish. Would half-past five do?

CHASUBLE   Admirably! Admirably! [*Takes out watch.*] And now, dear Mr. Worthing, I will not intrude any longer into a house of sorrow. I would merely beg you not to be too much bowed down by grief. What seem to us bitter trials are often blessings in disguise.

MISS PRISM   This seems to me a blessing of an extremely obvious kind.

Enter CECILY *from the house.*

CECILY Uncle Jack! Oh, I am pleased to see you back. But what horrid clothes you have got on. Do go and change them.
MISS PRISM Cecily!
CHASUBLE My child! My child!

> CECILY *goes towards* JACK; *he kisses her brow in a melancholy manner.*

CECILY What is the matter, Uncle Jack? Do look happy! You look as if you had toothache, and I have got such a surprise for you. Who do you think is in the dining-room? Your brother!
JACK Who?
CECILY Your brother Ernest. He arrived about half an hour ago.
JACK What nonsense! I haven't got a brother.
CECILY Oh, don't say that. However badly he may have behaved to you in the past he is still your brother. You couldn't be so heartless as to disown him. I'll tell him to come out. And you will shake hands with him, won't you, Uncle Jack? [*Runs back into the house.*]
CHASUBLE These are very joyful tidings.
MISS PRISM After we had all been resigned to his loss, his sudden return seems to me peculiarly distressing.
JACK My brother is in the dining-room? I don't know what it all means. I think it is perfectly absurd.

> Enter ALGERNON *and* CECILY *hand in hand. They come slowly up to* JACK.

JACK Good heavens! [*Motions* ALGERNON *away.*]
ALGERNON Brother John, I have come down from town to tell you that I am very sorry for all the trouble I have given you, and that I intend to lead a better life in the future.

> JACK *glares at him and does not take his hand.*

CECILY Uncle Jack, you are not going to refuse your own brother's hand?
JACK Nothing will induce me to take his hand. I think his coming down here disgraceful. He knows perfectly well why.
CECILY Uncle Jack, do be nice. There is some good in everyone. Ernest has just been telling me about his poor invalid friend Mr. Bunbury whom he goes to visit so often. And surely there must be much good in one who is kind to an invalid, and leaves the pleasures of London to sit by a bed of pain.
JACK Oh! he has been talking about Bunbury, has he?
CECILY Yes, he has told me all about poor Mr. Bunbury, and his terrible state of health.
JACK Bunbury! Well, I won't have him to talk to you about Bunbury or about anything else. It is enough to drive one perfectly frantic.
ALGERNON Of course I admit that the faults were all on my side. But I must say that I think that Brother John's coldness to me is peculiarly painful. I expected a more enthusiastic welcome, espe-

cially considering it is the first time I have come here.

CECILY   Uncle Jack, if you don't shake hands with Ernest I will never forgive you.

JACK   Never forgive me?

CECILY   Never, never, never!

JACK   Well, this is the last time I shall ever do it. [*Shakes hands with* ALGERNON *and glares.*]

CHASUBLE   It's pleasant, is it not, to see so perfect a reconciliation? I think we might leave the two brothers together.

MISS PRISM   Cecily, you will come with us.

CECILY   Certainly, Miss Prism. My little task of reconciliation is over.

CHASUBLE   You have done a beautiful action today, dear child.

MISS PRISM   We must not be premature in our judgments.

CECILY   I feel very happy.

They all go off except JACK *and* ALGERNON.

JACK   You young scoundrel, Algy, you must get out of this place as soon as possible. I don't allow any Bunburying here.

Enter MERRIMAN.

MERRIMAN   I have put Mr. Ernest's things in the room next to yours, sir. I suppose that is all right?

JACK   What?

MERRIMAN   Mr. Ernest's luggage, sir. I have unpacked it and put it in the room next to your own.

JACK   His luggage?

MERRIMAN   Yes sir. Three portmanteaus, a dressing-case, two hat-boxes, and a large luncheon-basket.

ALGERNON   I am afraid I can't stay more than a week this time.

JACK   Merriman, order the dogcart³ at once. Mr. Ernest has been suddenly called back to town.

MERRIMAN   Yes, sir. [*Goes back into the house.*]

ALGERNON   What a fearful liar you are, Jack. I have not been called back to town at all.

JACK   Yes, you have.

ALGERNON   I haven't heard any one call me.

JACK   Your duty as a gentleman calls you back.

ALGERNON   My duty as a gentleman has never interfered with my pleasures in the smallest degree.

JACK   I can quite understand that.

ALGERNON   Well, Cecily is a darling.

JACK   You are not to talk of Miss Cardew like that. I don't like it.

ALGERNON   Well, I don't like your clothes. You look perfectly ridiculous in them. Why on earth don't you go up and change? It is perfectly childish to be in deep mourning for a man who is actually staying for a whole week with you in your house as a guest. I call it grotesque.

---

3. A light, two-wheeled carriage, usually drawn by one horse; it has two transverse seats positioned back to back.

JACK   You are certainly not staying with me for a whole week as a guest or anything else. You have got to leave . . . by the four-five train.

ALGERNON   I certainly won't leave you so long as you are in mourning. It would be most unfriendly. If I were in mourning you would stay with me, I suppose. I should think it very unkind if you didn't.

JACK   Well, will you go if I change my clothes?

ALGERNON   Yes, if you are not too long. I never saw anybody take so long to dress, and with such little result.

JACK   Well, at any rate, that is better than being always overdressed as you are.

ALGERNON   If I am occasionally a little overdressed, I make up for it by being always immensely overeducated.

JACK   Your vanity is ridiculous, your conduct an outrage, and your presence in my garden utterly absurd. However, you have got to catch the four-five, and I hope you will have a pleasant journey back to town. This Bunburying, as you call it, has not been a great success for you. [*Goes into the house.*]

ALGERNON   I think it has been a great success. I'm in love with Cecily, and that is everything.

> *Enter* CECILY *at the back of the garden. She picks up the can and begins to water the flowers.*

But I must see her before I go, and make arrangements for another Bunbury. Ah, there she is.

CECILY   Oh, I merely came back to water the roses. I thought you were with Uncle Jack.

ALGERNON   He's gone to order the dogcart for me.

CECILY   Oh, is he going to take you for a nice drive?

ALGERNON   He's going to send me away.

CECILY   Then have we got to part?

ALGERNON   I am afraid so. It's a very painful parting.

CECILY   It is always painful to part from people whom one has known for a very brief space of time. The absence of old friends one can endure with equanimity. But even a momentary separation from anyone to whom one has just been introduced is almost unbearable.

ALGERNON   Thank you.

> *Enter* MERRIMAN.

MERRIMAN   The dogcart is at the door, sir.

> ALGERNON *looks appealingly at* CECILY.

CECILY   It can wait, Merriman . . . for . . . five minutes.

MERRIMAN   Yes, miss. [*Exit.*]

ALGERNON   I hope, Cecily, I shall not offend you if I state quite frankly and openly that you seem to me to be in every way the visible personification of absolute perfection.

CECILY   I think your frankness does you great credit, Ernest. If you will allow me, I will copy your remarks into my diary. [*Goes over to table and begins writing in diary.*]

ALGERNON   Do you really keep a diary? I'd give anything to look at it. May I?

CECILY   Oh no. [*Puts her hand over it.*] You see, it is simply a very young girl's record of her own thoughts and impressions, and consequently meant for publication. When it appears in volume form I hope you will order a copy. But pray, Ernest, don't stop. I delight in taking down from dictation. I have reached "absolute perfection." You can go on. I am quite ready for more.

ALGERNON [*somewhat taken aback*]   Ahem! Ahem!

CECILY   Oh, don't cough, Ernest. When one is dictating one should speak fluently and not cough. Besides, I don't know how to spell a cough. [*Writes as* ALGERNON *speaks.*]

ALGERNON [*speaking very rapidly*]   Cecily, ever since I first looked upon your wonderful and incomparable beauty, I have dared to love you wildly, passionately, devotedly, hopelessly.

CECILY   I don't think that you should tell me that you love me wildly, passionately, devotedly, hopelessly. Hopelessly doesn't seem to make much sense, does it?

ALGERNON   Cecily.

Enter MERRIMAN.

MERRIMAN   The dogcart is waiting, sir.

ALGERNON   Tell it to come round next week, at the same hour.

MERRIMAN [*looks at* CECILY, *who makes no sign*].   Yes, sir. [MERRIMAN *retires.*]

CECILY   Uncle Jack would be very much annoyed if he knew you were staying on till next week, at the same hour.

ALGERNON   Oh, I don't care about Jack. I don't care for anybody in the whole world but you. I love you, Cecily. You will marry me, won't you?

CECILY   You silly boy! Of course. Why, we have been engaged for the last three months.

ALGERNON   For the last three months?

CECILY   Yes, it will be exactly three months on Thursday.

ALGERNON   But how did we become engaged?

CECILY   Well, ever since dear Uncle Jack first confessed to us that he had a younger brother who was very wicked and bad, you of course have formed the chief topic of conversation between myself and Miss Prism. And of course a man who is much talked about is always very attractive. One feels there must be something in him, after all. I daresay it was foolish of me, but I fell in love with you, Ernest.

ALGERNON   Darling. And when was the engagement actually settled?

CECILY   On the 14th of February last. Worn out by your entire ignorance of my existence, I determined to end the matter one way or the other, and after a long struggle with myself I accepted you under this dear old tree here. The next day I bought this little ring in your name, and this is the little bangle with the true lovers' knot I promised you always to wear.

ALGERNON   Did I give you this? It's very pretty, isn't it?

CECILY   Yes, you've wonderfully good taste, Ernest. It's the excuse I've always given for your leading such a bad life. And this is the box in which I keep all your dear letters. [*Kneels at table, opens box, and produces letters tied up with blue ribbon.*]

ALGERNON   My letters! But, my own sweet Cecily, I have never written you any letters.

CECILY   You need hardly remind me of that, Ernest. I remember only too well that I was forced to write your letters for you. I wrote always three times a week, and sometimes oftener.

ALGERNON   Oh, do let me read them, Cecily?

CECILY   Oh, I couldn't possibly. They would make you far too conceited. [*Replaces box.*] The three you wrote me after I had broken off the engagement are so beautiful, and so badly spelled, that even now I can hardly read them without crying a little.

ALGERNON   But was our engagement ever broken off?

CECILY   Of course it was. On the 22nd of last March. You can see the entry if you like. [*Shows diary.*] "Today I broke off my engagement with Ernest. I feel it is better to do so. The weather still continues charming."

ALGERNON   But why on earth did you break it off? What had I done? I had done nothing at all. Cecily, I am very much hurt indeed to hear you broke it off. Particularly when the weather was so charming.

CECILY   It would hardly have been a really serious engagement if it hadn't been broken off at least once. But I forgave you before the week was out.

ALGERNON [*crossing to her, and kneeling*]   What a perfect angel you are, Cecily.

CECILY   You dear romantic boy. [*He kisses her, she puts her fingers through his hair.*]   I hope your hair curls naturally, does it?

ALGERNON   Yes darling, with a little help from others.

CECILY   I am so glad.

ALGERNON   You'll never break off our engagement again, Cecily?

CECILY   I don't think I could break it off now that I have actually met you. Besides, of course, there is the question of your name.

ALGERNON   Yes, of course. [*Nervously.*]

CECILY   You must not laugh at me, darling, but it had always been a girlish dream of mine to love some one whose name was Ernest.

ALGERNON *rises,* CECILY *also.*

There is something in that name that seems to inspire absolute confidence. I pity any poor married woman whose husband is not called Ernest.

ALGERNON   But, my dear child, do you mean to say you could not love me if I had some other name?

CECILY   But what name?

ALGERNON   Oh, any name you like—Algernon—for instance . . .

CECILY   But I don't like the name of Algernon.

ALGERNON   Well, my own dear sweet, loving little darling, I really can't see why you should object to the name of Algernon. It is not at all a bad name. In fact, it is rather an aristocratic name. Half of the chaps who get into the Bankruptcy Court are called Algernon. But seriously, Cecily . . . [*Moving to her.*] if my name was Algy, couldn't you love me?

CECILY   [*rising*]   I might respect you, Ernest, I might admire your character, but I fear that I should not be able to give you my undivided attention.

ALGERNON   Ahem! Cecily! [*Picking up hat.*] Your Rector here is, I suppose, thoroughly experienced in the practice of all the rites and ceremonials of the Church?

CECILY   Oh, yes. Dr. Chasuble is a most learned man. He has never written a single book, so you can imagine how much he knows.

ALGERNON   I must see him at once on a most important christening—I mean on most important business.

CECILY   Oh!

ALGERNON   I shan't be away more than half an hour.

CECILY   Considering that we have been engaged since February the 14th, and that I only met you today for the first time, I think it is rather hard that you should leave me for so long a period as half an hour. Couldn't you make it twenty minutes?

ALGERNON   I'll be back in no time. [*Kisses her and rushes down the garden.*]

CECILY   What an impetuous boy he is! I like his hair so much. I must enter his proposal in my diary.

Enter MERRIMAN.

MERRIMAN   A Miss Fairfax just called to see Mr. Worthing. On very important business, Miss Fairfax states.

CECILY   Isn't Mr. Worthing in his library?

MERRIMAN   Mr. Worthing went over in the direction of the Rectory some time ago.

CECILY   Pray ask the lady to come out here; Mr. Worthing is sure to be back soon. And you can bring tea.

MERRIMAN   Yes. Miss. [*Goes out.*]

CECILY   Miss Fairfax! I suppose one of the many good elderly women who are associated with Uncle Jack in some of his philanthropic work in London. I don't quite like women who are interested in philanthropic work. I think it is so forward of them.

Enter MERRIMAN.

MERRIMAN   Miss Fairfax.

Enter GWENDOLEN. *Exit* MERRIMAN.

CECILY [*advancing to meet her*]   Pray let me introduce myself to you. My name is Cecily Cardew.

GWENDOLEN   Cecily Cardew? [*Moving to her and shaking hands.*] What a very sweet name! Something tells me that we are going to be great friends. I like you already more than I can say. My first impressions of people are never wrong.

CECILY   How nice of you to like me so much after we have known each other such a comparatively short time. Pray sit down.

GWENDOLEN [*still standing up*]   I may call you Cecily, may I not?

CECILY   With pleasure!

GWENDOLEN   And you will always call me Gwendolen, won't you?

CECILY   If you wish.

GWENDOLEN   Then that is all quite settled, is it not?

CECILY   I hope so. [*A pause. They both sit down together.*]

GWENDOLEN   Perhaps this might be a favorable opportunity for my mentioning who I am. My father is Lord Bracknell. You have never heard of papa, I suppose?

CECILY   I don't think so.

GWENDOLEN   Outside the family circle, papa, I am glad to say, is entirely unknown. I think that is quite as it should be. The home seems to me to be the proper sphere for the man. And certainly once a man begins to neglect his domestic duties he becomes painfully effeminate, does he not? And I don't like that. It makes men so very attractive. Cecily, mamma, whose views on education are remarkably strict, has brought me up to be extremely short-sighted; it is part of her system; so do you mind my looking at you through my glasses?

CECILY   Oh! not at all, Gwendolen. I am very fond of being looked at.

GWENDOLEN [*after examining* CECILY *carefully through a lorgnette*] You are here on a short visit, I suppose.

CECILY   Oh no! I live here.

GWENDOLEN [*severely*]   Really? Your mother, no doubt, or some female relative of advanced years, resides here also?

CECILY   Oh no! I have no mother, nor, in fact, any relations.

GWENDOLEN   Indeed?

CECILY   My dear guardian, with the assistance of Miss Prism, has the arduous task of looking after me.

GWENDOLEN   Your guardian?

CECILY   Yes, I am Mr. Worthing's ward.

GWENDOLEN   Oh! It is strange he never mentioned to me that he had a ward. How secretive of him! He grows more interesting hourly. I am not sure, however, that the news inspires me with feelings of unmixed delight. [*Rising and going to her.*] I am very fond of you, Cecily; I have liked you ever since I met you! But I am bound to state that now I know that you are Mr. Worthing's ward, I cannot help expressing a wish you were—well, just a little older than you seem to be—and not quite so very alluring in appearance. In fact, if I may speak candidly—

CECILY   Pray do! I think that whenever one has anything unpleasant to say, one should always be quite candid.

GWENDOLEN   Well, to speak with perfect candor, Cecily, I wish that you were fully forty-two, and more than usually plain for your age. Ernest has a strong upright nature. He is the very soul of truth and honor. Disloyalty would be as impossible to him as deception. But even men of the noblest possible moral character are extremely susceptible to the influence of the physical charms of others. Modern, no less than Ancient History, supplies us with many most painful examples of what I refer to. If it were not so, indeed, History would be quite unreadable.

CECILY   I beg your pardon, Gwendolen, did you say Ernest?

GWENDOLEN   Yes.

CECILY   Oh, but it is not Mr. Ernest Worthing who is my guardian. It is his brother—his elder brother.

GWENDOLEN   [*sitting down again*]   Ernest never mentioned to me that he had a brother.

CECILY   I am sorry to say they have not been on good terms for a long time.

GWENDOLEN   Ah! that accounts for it. And now that I think of it I have never heard any man mention his brother. The subject seems distasteful to most men. Cecily, you have lifted a load from my mind. I was growing almost anxious. It would have been terrible if any cloud had come across a friendship like ours, would it not? Of course you are quite, quite sure that it is not Mr. Worthing who is your guardian?

CECILY   Quite sure. [*A pause.*] In fact, I am going to be his.

GWENDOLEN   [*inquiringly*]   I beg your pardon?

CECILY   [*rather shy and confidingly*]   Dearest Gwendolen, there is no reason why I should make a secret of it to you. Our little country newspaper is sure to chronicle the fact next week. Mr. Ernest Worthing and I are engaged to be married.

GWENDOLEN   [*quite politely, rising*]   My darling Cecily, I think there must be some slight error. Mr. Ernest Worthing is engaged to me. The announcement will appear in the *Morning Post* on Saturday at the latest.

CECILY   [*very politely, rising*]   I am afraid you must be under some misconception. Ernest proposed to me exactly ten minutes ago. [*Shows diary.*]

GWENDOLEN   [*examines diary through her lorgnette carefully*]   It is very curious, for he asked me to be his wife yesterday afternoon at 5:30. If you would care to verify the incident, pray do so. [*Produces diary of her own.*] I never travel without my diary. One should always have something sensational to read in the train. I am so sorry, dear Cecily, if it is any disappointment to you, but I am afraid I have the prior claim.

CECILY   It would distress me more than I can tell you, dear Gwendolen, if it caused you any mental or physical anguish, but I feel bound to point out that since Ernest proposed to you he clearly has changed his mind.

GWENDOLEN   [*meditatively*]   If the poor fellow has been entrapped into any foolish promise I shall consider it my duty to rescue him at once, and with a firm hand.

CECILY [*thoughtfully and sadly*]   Whatever unfortunate entanglement my dear boy may have got into, I will never reproach him with it after we are married.

GWENDOLEN   Do you allude to me, Miss Cardew, as an entanglement? You are presumptuous. On an occasion of this kind it becomes more than a moral duty to speak one's mind. It becomes a pleasure.

CECILY   Do you suggest, Miss Fairfax, that I entrapped Ernest into an engagement? How dare you? This is no time for wearing the shallow mask of manners. When I see a spade I call it a spade.

GWENDOLEN [*satirically*]   I am glad to say that I have never seen a spade. It is obvious that our social spheres have been widely different.

> *Enter* MERRIMAN, *followed by the* FOOTMAN. *He carries a salver, table cloth, and plate stand.* CECILY *is about to retort. The presence of the servants exercises a restraining influence, under which both girls chafe.*

MERRIMAN   Shall I lay tea here as usual, Miss?

CECILY [*sternly, in a calm voice*]   Yes, as usual.

> MERRIMAN *begins to clear table and lay cloth. A long pause.* CECILY *and* GWENDOLEN *glare at each other.*

GWENDOLEN   Are there many interesting walks in the vicinity, Miss Cardew?

CECILY   Oh! yes! a great many. From the top of one of the hills quite close one can see five counties.

GWENDOLEN   Five counties! I don't think I should like that; I hate crowds.

CECILY [*sweetly*]   I suppose that is why you live in town?

> GWENDOLEN *bites her lip, and beats her foot nervously with her parasol.*

GWENDOLEN [*looking around*]   Quite a well-kept garden this is, Miss Cardew.

CECILY   So glad you like it, Miss Fairfax.

GWENDOLEN   I had no idea there were any flowers in the country.

CECILY   Oh, flowers are as common here, Miss Fairfax, as people are in London.

GWENDOLEN   Personally I cannot understand how anybody manages to exist in the country, if anybody who is anybody does. The country always bores me to death.

CECILY   Ah! This is what the newspapers call agricultural depression, is it not? I believe the aristocracy are suffering very much from it just at present. It is almost an epidemic amongst them, I have been told. May I offer you some tea, Miss Fairfax?

GWENDOLEN [*with elaborate politeness*]   Thank you. [*Aside.*] Detestable girl! But I require tea!

CECILY [*sweetly*]   Sugar?
GWENDOLEN [*superciliously*]   No, thank you. Sugar is not fashionable any more.

> CECILY *looks angrily at her, takes up the tongs and puts four lumps of sugar into the cup.*

CECILY [*severely*]   Cake or bread and butter?
GWENDOLEN [*in a bored manner*]   Bread and butter, please. Cake is rarely seen at the best houses nowadays.
CECILY [*cuts a very large slice of cake and puts it on the tray*]   Hand that to Miss Fairfax.

> MERRIMAN *does so, and goes out with* FOOTMAN. GWENDOLEN *drinks the tea and makes a grimace. Puts down cup at once, reaches out her hand to the bread and butter, looks at it, and finds it is cake. Rises in indignation.*

GWENDOLEN   You have filled my tea with lumps of sugar, and though I asked most distinctly for bread and butter, you have given me cake. I am known for the gentleness of my disposition, and the extraordinary sweetness of my nature, but I warn you, Miss Cardew, you may go too far.
CECILY [*rising*]   To save my poor, innocent, trusting boy from the machinations of any other girl there are no lengths to which I would not go.
GWENDOLEN   From the moment I saw you I distrusted you. I felt that you were false and deceitful. I am never deceived in such matters. My first impressions of people are invariably right.
CECILY   It seems to me, Miss Fairfax, that I am trespassing on your valuable time. No doubt you have many other calls of a similar character to make in the neighbourhood.

> *Enter* JACK.

GWENDOLEN [*catching sight of him*]   Ernest! My own Ernest!
JACK   Gwendolen! Darling! [*Offers to kiss her.*]
GWENDOLEN [*drawing back*]   A moment! May I ask if you are engaged to be married to this young lady? [*Points to* CECILY.]
JACK [*laughing*]   To dear little Cecily! Of course not! What could have put such an idea into your pretty little head?
GWENDOLEN   Thank you. You may! [*Offers her cheek.*]
CECILY [*very sweetly*]   I knew there must be some misunderstanding, Miss Fairfax. The gentleman whose arm is at present round your waist is my dear guardian, Mr. John Worthing.
GWENDOLEN   I beg your pardon?
CECILY   This is Uncle Jack.
GWENDOLEN [*receding*]   Jack! Oh!

> *Enter* ALGERNON.

CECILY   Here is Ernest.

ALGERNON [*goes straight over to* CECILY *without noticing anyone else*]   My own love! [*Offers to kiss her.*]

CECILY [*drawing back*]   A moment, Ernest! May I ask you—are you engaged to be married to this young lady?

ALGERNON [*looking around*]   To what young lady? Good heavens! Gwendolen!

CECILY   Yes: to good heavens, Gwendolen, I mean to Gwendolen.

ALGERNON [*laughing*]   Of course not! What could have put such an idea into your pretty little head?

CECILY   Thank you. [*Presenting her cheek to be kissed.*] You may.

> ALGERNON *kisses her.*

GWENDOLEN   I felt there was some slight error, Miss Cardew. The gentleman who is now embracing you is my cousin, Mr. Algernon Moncrieff.

CECILY [*breaking away from* ALGERNON]   Algernon Moncrieff! Oh!

> *The two girls move towards each other and put their arms round each other's waists as if for protection.*

CECILY   Are you called Algernon?

ALGERNON   I cannot deny it.

CECILY   Oh!

GWENDOLEN   Is your name really John?

JACK [*standing rather proudly*]   I could deny it if I liked. I could deny anything if I liked. But my name certainly is John. It has been John for years.

CECILY [*to* GWENDOLEN]   A gross deception has been practiced on both of us.

GWENDOLEN   My poor wounded Cecily!

CECILY   My sweet wronged Gwendolen!

GWENDOLEN [*slowly and seriously*]   You will call me sister, will you not?

> *They embrace.* JACK *and* ALGERNON *groan and walk up and down.*

CECILY [*rather brightly*]   There is just one question I would like to be allowed to ask my guardian.

GWENDOLEN   An admirable idea! Mr. Worthing, there is just one question I would like to be permitted to put to you. Where is your brother Ernest? We are both engaged to be married to your brother Ernest, so it is a matter of some importance to us to know where your brother Ernest is at present.

JACK [*slowly and hesitatingly*]   Gwendolen—Cecily—it is very painful for me to be forced to speak the truth. It is the first time in my life that I have ever been reduced to such a painful position, and I am really quite inexperienced in doing anything of the kind. However, I will tell you quite frankly that I have no brother Ernest. I have no brother at all. I never had a brother in my life, and I certainly have not the smallest intention of ever having one in the future.

CECILY [*surprised*]   No brother at all?

JACK [*cheerily*]   None!

GWENDOLEN [*severely*]   Had you never a brother of any kind?

JACK [*pleasantly*]   Never. Not even of any kind.

GWENDOLEN   I am afraid it is quite clear, Cecily, that neither of us is engaged to be married to anyone.

CECILY....It is not a very pleasant position for a young girl suddenly to find herself in. Is it?

GWENDOLEN   Let us go into the house. They will hardly venture to come after us there.

CECILY   No, men are so cowardly, aren't they?

They retire into the house with scornful looks.

JACK   This ghastly state of things is what you call Bunburying, I suppose?

ALGERNON   Yes, and a perfectly wonderful Bunbury it is. The most wonderful Bunbury I have ever had in my life.

JACK   Well, you've no right whatsoever to Bunbury here.

ALGERNON   That is absurd. One has a right to Bunbury anywhere one chooses. Every serious Bunburyist knows that.

JACK   Serious Bunburyist? Good heavens!

ALGERNON   Well, one must be serious about something, if one wants to have any amusement in life. I happen to be serious about Bunburying. What on earth you are serious about I haven't got the remotest idea. About everything, I should fancy. You have such an absolutely trivial nature.

JACK   Well, the only small satisfaction I have in the whole of this wretched business is that your friend Bunbury is quite exploded. You won't be able to run down to the country quite so often as you used to do, dear Algy. And a very good thing too.

ALGERNON   Your brother is a little off color, isn't he, dear Jack? You won't be able to disappear to London quite so frequently as your wicked custom was. And not a bad thing either.

JACK   As for your conduct towards Miss Cardew, I must say that you taking in a sweet, simple, innocent girl like that is quite inexcusable. To say nothing of the fact that she is my ward.

ALGERNON   I can see no possible defense at all for your deceiving a brilliant, clever, thoroughly experienced young lady like Miss Fairfax. To say nothing of the fact that she is my cousin.

JACK   I wanted to be engaged to Gwendolen, that is all. I love her.

ALGERNON   Well, I simply wanted to be engaged to Cecily. I adore her.

JACK   There is certainly no chance of your marrying Miss Cardew.

ALGERNON   I don't think there is much likelihood, Jack, of you and Miss Fairfax being united.

JACK   Well, that is no business of yours.

ALGERNON   If it was my business, I wouldn't talk about it. [*Begins to eat muffins.*] It is very vulgar to talk about one's business. Only people like stockbrokers do that, and then merely at dinner parties.

JACK   How you can sit there, calmly eating muffins, when we are in this horrible trouble, I can't make out. You seem to me to be perfectly heartless.

ALGERNON   Well, I can't eat muffins in an agitated manner. The butter would probably get on my cuffs. One should always eat muffins quite calmly. It is the only way to eat them.

JACK   I say it's perfectly heartless your eating muffins at all, under the circumstances.

ALGERNON   When I am in trouble, eating is the only thing that consoles me. Indeed, when I am in really great trouble, as any one who knows me intimately will tell you, I refuse everything except food and drink. At the present moment I am eating muffins because I am unhappy. Besides, I am particularly fond of muffins. [*Rising.*]

JACK [*rising*]....Well, there is no reason why you should eat them all in that greedy way. [*Takes muffins from* ALGERNON.]

ALGERNON [*offering tea-cake*]   I wish you would have tea-cake instead. I don't like tea-cake.

JACK   Good heavens! I suppose a man may eat his own muffins in his own garden.

ALGERNON   But you have just said it was perfectly heartless to eat muffins.

JACK   I said it was perfectly heartless of you, under the circumstances. That is a very different thing.

ALGERNON   That may be. But the muffins are the same. [*He seizes the muffin-dish from* JACK.]

JACK   Algy, I wish to goodness you would go.

ALGERNON   You can't possibly ask me to go without having some dinner. It's absurd. I never go without my dinner. No one ever does, except vegetarians and people like that. Besides I have just made arrangements with Dr. Chasuble to be christened at a quarter to six under the name of Ernest.

JACK   My dear fellow, the sooner you give up that nonsense the better. I made arrangements this morning with Dr. Chasuble to be christened myself at 5:30, and I naturally will take the name of Ernest. Gwendolen would wish it. We can't both be christened Ernest. It's absurd. Besides, I have a perfect right to be christened if I like. There is no evidence at all that I have ever been christened by anybody. I should think it extremely probable I never was, and so does Dr. Chasuble. It is entirely different in your case. You have been christened already.

ALGERNON   Yes, but I have not been christened for years.

JACK   Yes, but you have been christened. That is the important thing.

ALGERNON   Quite so. So I know my constitution can stand it. If you are not quite sure about your ever having been christened, I must say I think it rather dangerous your venturing on it now. It might make you very unwell. You can hardly have forgotten that someone very closely connected with you was very nearly carried off this week in Paris by a severe chill.

JACK   Yes, but you said yourself that a severe chill was not hereditary.

ALGERNON   It usen't to be, I know—but I daresay it is now. Science is always making wonderful improvements in things.

JACK [*picking up the muffin-dish*]   Oh, that is nonsense; you are always talking nonsense.

ALGERNON   Jack, you are at the muffins again! I wish you wouldn't. There are only two left. [*Takes them.*] I told you I was particularly fond of muffins.

JACK   But I hate tea-cake.

ALGERNON   Why on earth then do you allow tea-cake to be served up for your guests? What ideas you have of hospitality!

JACK   Algernon! I have already told you to go. I don't want you here. Why don't you go?

ALGERNON   I haven't quite finished my tea yet! and there is still one muffin left.

> JACK *groans, and sinks into a chair.* ALGERNON *still continues eating.*

Act 3

> *Drawing room at the Manor House.* GWENDOLEN *and* CECILY *are at the window, looking out into the garden.*

GWENDOLEN   The fact that they did not follow us at once into the house, as any one else would have done, seems to me to show that they have some sense of shame left.

CECILY   They have been eating muffins. That looks like repentance.

GWENDOLEN [*after a pause*]   They don't seem to notice us at all. Couldn't you cough?

CECILY   But I haven't got a cough.

GWENDOLEN   They're looking at us. What effrontery!

CECILY   They're approaching. That's very forward of them.

GWENDOLEN   Let us preserve a dignified silence.

CECILY   Certainly. It's the only thing to do now.

> *Enter* JACK *followed by* ALGERNON. *They whistle some dreadful popular air from a British opera.*

GWENDOLEN   This dignified silence seems to produce an unpleasant effect.

CECILY   A most distasteful one.

GWENDOLEN   But we will not be the first to speak.

CECILY   Certainly not.

GWENDOLEN   Mr. Worthing, I have something very particular to ask you. Much depends on your reply.

CECILY   Gwendolen, your common sense is invaluable. Mr. Moncrieff, kindly answer me the following question. Why did you pretend to be my guardian's brother?

ALGERNON   In order that I might have an opportunity of meeting you.

CECILY [*to* GWENDOLEN]   That certainly seems a satisfactory explanation, does it not?

GWENDOLEN   Yes, dear, if you can believe him.

CECILY   I don't. But that does not affect the wonderful beauty of his answer.

GWENDOLEN   True. In matters of grave importance, style, not sincerity, is the vital thing. Mr. Worthing, what explanation can you offer to me for pretending to have a brother? Was it in order that you might have an opportunity of coming up to town to see me as often as possible?

JACK   Can you doubt it, Miss Fairfax?

GWENDOLEN   I have the gravest doubts about the subject. But I intend to crush them. This is not the moment for German skepticism.[4] [*Moving to* CECILY.] Their explanations appear to be quite satisfactory, especially Mr. Worthing's. That seems to me to have the stamp of truth upon it.

CECILY   I am more than content with what Mr. Moncrieff said. His voice alone inspires one with absolute credulity.

GWENDOLEN   Then you think we should forgive them?

CECILY   Yes. I mean no.

GWENDOLEN   True! I had forgotten. There are principles at stake that one cannot surrender. Which of us should tell them? The task is not a pleasant one.

CECILY   Could we not both speak at the same time?

GWENDOLEN   An excellent idea! I nearly always speak at the same time as other people. Will you take the time from me?

CECILY   Certainly.

GWENDOLEN *beats time with uplifted finger.*

GWENDOLEN *and* CECILY [*speaking together*]   Your Christian names are still an insuperable barrier. That is all!

JACK *and* ALGERNON [*speaking together*]   Our Christian names! Is that all? But we are going to be christened this afternoon.

GWENDOLEN [*to* JACK]   For my sake you are prepared to do this terrible thing?

JACK   I am.

CECILY [*to* ALGERNON]   To please me you are ready to face this fearful ordeal?

ALGERNON   I am!

GWENDOLEN   How absurd to talk of the equality of the sexes! Where questions of self-sacrifice are concerned, men are infinitely beyond us.

JACK   We are. [*Clasps hands with* ALGERNON.]

CECILY   They have moments of physical courage of which we women know absolutely nothing.

GWENDOLEN [*to* JACK]   Darling!

ALGERNON [*to* CECILY]   Darling!

4. A reference to such philosophical movements as the Materialism of Ludwig Feuerbach (1804–1872) and such theological movements as the "Higher Criticism," a movement which subjected the Bible to the same kind of study as that accorded other books.

They fall into each other's arms. Enter MERRIMAN. *When he enters he coughs loudly, seeing the situation.*

MERRIMAN   Ahem! Ahem! Lady Bracknell.

JACK   Good heavens!

Enter LADY BRACKNELL. *The couples separate in alarm. Exit* MERRIMAN.

LADY BRACKNELL   Gwendolen! What does this mean?

GWENDOLEN   Merely that I am engaged to be married to Mr. Worthing, mamma.

LADY BRACKNELL   Come here. Sit down. Sit down immediately. Hesitation of any kind is a sign of mental decay in the young, of physical weakness in the old. [*Turns to* JACK.] Apprised, sir, of my daughter's sudden flight by her trusty maid, whose confidence I purchased by means of a small coin, I followed her at once by a luggage train. Her unhappy father is, I am glad to say, under the impression that she is attending a more than usually lengthy lecture by the University Extension Scheme on the Influence of a Permanent Income on Thought. I do not propose to undeceive him. Indeed I have never undeceived him on any question. I would consider it wrong. But, of course, you will clearly understand that all communication between yourself and my daughter must cease immediately from this moment. On this point, as indeed on all points, I am firm.

JACK   I am engaged to be married to Gwendolen, Lady Bracknell!

LADY BRACKNELL   You are nothing of the kind, sir. And now as regards Algernon! . . . Algernon!

ALGERNON   Yes, Aunt Augusta.

LADY BRACKNELL   May I ask if it is in this house that your invalid friend Mr. Bunbury resides?

ALGERNON [*stammering*]   Oh! no! Bunbury doesn't live here. Bunbury is somewhere else at present. In fact, Bunbury is dead.

LADY BRACKNELL   Dead! When did Mr. Bunbury die? His death must have been extremely sudden.

ALGERNON [*airily*]   Oh! I killed Bunbury this afternoon. I mean poor Bunbury died this afternoon.

LADY BRACKNELL   What did he die of?

ALGERNON   Bunbury? Oh, he was quite exploded.

LADY BRACKNELL   Exploded! Was he the victim of a revolutionary outrage? I was not aware that Mr. Bunbury was interested in social legislation. If so, he is well punished for his morbidity.

ALGERNON   My dear Aunt Augusta, I mean he was found out! The doctors found out that Bunbury could not live, that is what I mean —so Bunbury died.

LADY BRACKNELL   He seems to have had great confidence in the opinion of his physicians. I am glad, however, that he made up his mind at the last to some definite course of action, and acted under proper medical advice. And now that we have finally got rid of this Mr. Bunbury, may I ask, Mr. Worthing, who is that young person whose hand my nephew Algernon is now holding in what seems to me a peculiarly unnecessary manner?

JACK   That lady is Miss Cecily Cardew, my ward.

LADY BRACKNELL *bows coldly to* CECILY.

ALGERNON   I am engaged to be married to Cecily, Aunt Augusta.

LADY BRACKNELL   I beg your pardon?

CECILY   Mr. Moncrieff and I are engaged to be married, Lady Bracknell.

LADY BRACKNELL [*with a shiver, crossing to the sofa and sitting down*] I do not know whether there is anything peculiarly exciting in the air of this particular part of Hertfordshire, but the number of engagements that go on seems to me considerably above the proper average that statistics have laid down for our guidance. I think some preliminary inquiry on my part would not be out of place. Mr. Worthing, is Miss Cardew at all connected with any of the larger railway stations in London? I merely desire information. Until yesterday I had no idea that there were any families or persons whose origin was a Terminus.

JACK *looks perfectly furious, but restrains himself.*

JACK [*in a cold, clear voice*] Miss Cardew is the granddaughter of the late Mr. Thomas Cardew of 149 Belgrave Square, S.W.; Gervase Park, Dorking, Surrey; and the Sporran, Fifeshire, N.B.[5]

LADY BRACKNELL   That sounds not unsatisfactory. Three addresses always inspire confidence, even in tradesmen. But what proof have I of their authenticity?

JACK   I have carefully preserved the Court Guides of the period. They are open to your inspection, Lady Bracknell.

LADY BRACKNELL [*grimly*] I have known strange errors in that publication.

JACK   Miss Cardew's family solicitors are Messrs. Markby, Markby, and Markby.

LADY BRACKNELL   Markby, Markby, and Markby? A firm of the very highest position in their profession. Indeed I am told that one of the Mr. Markbys is occasionally to be seen at dinner parties. So far I am satisfied.

JACK [*very irritably*] How extremely kind of you, Lady Bracknell! I have also in my possession, you will be pleased to hear, certificates of Miss Cardew's birth, baptism, whooping cough, registration, vaccination, confirmation, and the measles; both the German and the English variety.

LADY BRACKNELL   Ah! A life crowded with incident, I see; though perhaps somewhat too exciting for a young girl. I am not myself in favor of premature experiences. [*Rises, looks at her watch.*] Gwen-

5. In addition to his London residence in Belgrave Square (already referred to in Act 1), Mr. Cardew maintained establishments in the south of England (Dorking, Surrey) and in Scotland (Fifeshire).

dolen! the time approaches for our departure. We have not a moment to lose. As a matter of form, Mr. Worthing, I had better ask you if Miss Cardew has any little fortune?

JACK   Oh! about a hundred and thirty thousand pounds in the Funds.[6] That is all. Good-bye, Lady Bracknell. So pleased to have seen you.

LADY BRACKNELL [*sitting down again*]   A moment, Mr. Worthing. A hundred and thirty thousand pounds! And in the Funds! Miss Cardew seems to me a most attractive young lady, now that I look at her. Few girls of the present day have any really solid qualities, any of the qualities that last, and improve with time. We live, I regret to say, in an age of surfaces. [*To* CECILY.] Come over here, dear.

       CECILY *goes across.*

Pretty child! your dress is sadly simple, and your hair seems almost as Nature might have left it. But we can soon alter all that. A thoroughly experienced French maid produces a really marvellous result in a very brief space of time. I remember recommending one to young Lady Lancing, and after three months her own husband did not know her.

JACK   And after six months nobody knew her.

LADY BRACKNELL [*glares at* JACK *for a few moments. Then bends, with a practiced smile, to* CECILY]   Kindly turn round, sweet child.

       CECILY *turns completely round.*

No, the side view is what I want.

       CECILY *presents her profile.*

Yes, quite as I expected. There are distinct social possibilities in your profile. The two weak points in our age are its want of principle and its want of profile. The chin a little higher, dear. Style largely depends on the way the chin is worn. They are worn very high, just at present. Algernon!

ALGERNON   Yes, Aunt Augusta!

LADY BRACKNELL   There are distinct social possibilities in Miss Cardew's profile.

ALGERNON   Cecily is the sweetest, dearest, prettiest girl in the whole world. And I don't care twopence about social possibilities.

LADY BRACKNELL   Never speak disrespectfully of Society, Algernon. Only people who can't get into it do that. [*To* CECILY.] Dear child, of course you know that Algernon has nothing but his debts to depend upon. But I do not approve of mercenary marriages. When I married Lord Bracknell I had no fortune of any kind. But I never dreamed for a moment of allowing that to stand in my way. Well, I suppose I must give my consent.

6. Stock of the British National Debt.

ALGERNON   Thank you, Aunt Augusta.

LADY BRACKNELL   Cecily, you may kiss me!

CECILY [*kisses her*]   Thank you, Lady Bracknell.

LADY BRACKNELL   You may also address me as Aunt Augusta for the future.

CECILY   Thank you, Aunt Augusta.

LADY BRACKNELL   The marriage, I think, had better take place quite soon.

ALGERNON   Thank you, Aunt Augusta.

CECILY   Thank you, Aunt Augusta.

LADY BRACKNELL   To speak frankly, I am not in favor of long engagements. They give people the opportunity of finding out each other's character before marriage, which I think is never advisable.

JACK   I beg your pardon for interrupting you, Lady Bracknell, but this engagement is out of the question. I am Miss Cardew's guardian, and she cannot marry without my consent until she comes of age. That consent I absolutely decline to give.

LADY BRACKNELL   Upon what grounds, may I ask? Algernon is an extremely, I may almost say an ostentatiously, eligible young man. He has nothing, but he looks everything. What more can one desire?

JACK   It pains me very much to have to speak frankly to you, Lady Bracknell, about your nephew, but the fact is that I do not approve at all of his moral character. I suspect him of being untruthful.

ALGERNON *and* CECILY *look at him in indignant amazement.*

LADY BRACKNELL   Untruthful! My nephew Algernon? Impossible! He is an Oxonian.[7]

JACK   I fear there can be no possible doubt about the matter. This afternoon during my temporary absence in London on an important question of romance, he obtained admission to my house by means of the false pretense of being my brother. Under an assumed name he drank, I've just been informed by my butler, an entire pint bottle of my Perrier-Jouet, Brut, '89;[8] wine I was specially reserving for myself. Continuing his disgraceful deception, he succeeded in the course of the afternoon in alienating the affections of my only ward. He subsequently stayed to tea, and devoured every single muffin. And what makes his conduct all the more heartless is, that he was perfectly well aware from the first that I have no brother, that I never had a brother, and that I don't intend to have a brother, not even of any kind. I distinctly told him so myself yesterday afternoon.

LADY BRACKNELL   Ahem! Mr. Worthing, after careful consideration I have decided entirely to overlook my nephew's conduct to you.

JACK   That is very generous of you, Lady Bracknell. My own decision, however, is unalterable. I decline to give my consent.

LADY BRACKNELL [*to* CECILY]   Come here, sweet child.

CECILY *goes over.*

---

7. A graduate of Oxford University.   8. A very dry champagne.

How old are you, dear?

CECILY   Well, I am really only eighteen, but I always admit to twenty when I go to evening parties.

LADY BRACKNELL   You are perfectly right in making some slight alteration. Indeed, no woman should ever be quite accurate about her age. It looks so calculating. . . . [*In a meditative manner.*] Eighteen, but admitting to twenty at evening parties. Well, it will not be very long before you are of age and free from the restraints of tutelage. So I don't think your guardian's consent is, after all, a matter of any importance.

JACK   Pray excuse me, Lady Bracknell, for interrupting you again, but it is only fair to tell you that according to the terms of her grandfather's will Miss Cardew does not come legally of age till she is thirty-five.

LADY BRACKNELL   That does not seem to me to be a grave objection. Thirty-five is a very attractive age. London society is full of women of the very highest birth who have, of their own free choice, remained thirty-five for years. Lady Dumbleton is an instance in point. To my own knowledge she has been thirty-five ever since she arrived at the age of forty, which was many years ago now. I see no reason why our dear Cecily should not be even still more attractive at the age you mention than she is at present. There will be a large accumulation of property.

CECILY   Algy, could you wait for me till I was thirty-five?

ALGERNON   Of course I could, Cecily. You know I could.

CECILY   Yes, I felt it instinctively, but I couldn't wait all that time. I hate waiting even five minutes for anybody. It always makes me rather cross. I am not punctual myself, I know, but I do like punctuality in others, and waiting, even to be married, is quite out of the question.

ALGERNON   Then what is to be done, Cecily?

CECILY   I don't know, Mr. Moncrieff.

LADY BRACKNELL   My dear Mr. Worthing, as Miss Cardew states positively that she cannot wait till she is thirty-five—a remark which I am bound to say seems to me to show a somewhat impatient nature—I would beg of you to reconsider your decision.

JACK   But my dear Lady Bracknell, the matter is entirely in your own hands. The moment you consent to my marriage with Gwendolen, I will most gladly allow your nephew to form an alliance with my ward.

LADY BRACKNELL   [*rising and drawing herself up*]   You must be quite aware that what you propose is out of the question.

JACK   Then a passionate celibacy is all that any of us can look forward to.

LADY BRACKNELL   That is not the destiny I propose for Gwendolen. Algernon, of course, can choose for himself. [*Pulls out her watch.*] Come, dear [GWENDOLEN *rises.*], we have already missed five, if not six, trains. To miss any more might expose us to comment on the platform.

Enter DR. CHASUBLE.

CHASUBLE   Everything is quite ready for the christenings.

LADY BRACKNELL   The christenings, sir! Is not that somewhat premature?

CHASUBLE [*looking rather puzzled, and pointing to* JACK *and* ALGER-
NON]   Both these gentlemen have expressed a desire for immediate
baptism.

LADY BRACKNELL   At their age? The idea is grotesque and irreligious!
Algernon, I forbid you to be baptized. I will not hear of such excesses. Lord Bracknell would be highly displeased if he learned
that that was the way in which you wasted your time and money.

CHASUBLE   Am I to understand then that there are to be no christenings at all this afternoon?

JACK   I don't think that, as things are now, it would be of much
practical value to either of us, Dr. Chasuble.

CHASUBLE   I am grieved to hear such sentiments from you, Mr.
Worthing. They savour of the heretical views of the Anbaptists,[9]
views that I have completely refuted in four of my unpublished
sermons. However, as your present mood seems to be one peculiarly
secular, I will return to the church at once. Indeed, I have just
been informed by the pew-opener[1] that for the last hour and a
half Miss Prism has been waiting for me in the vestry.

LADY BRACKNELL [*starting*]   Miss Prism! Did I hear you mention a
Miss Prism?

CHASUBLE   Yes, Lady Bracknell. I am on my way to join her.

LADY BRACKNELL   Pray allow me to detain you for a moment. This
matter may prove to be one of vital importance to Lord Bracknell
and myself. Is this Miss Prism a female of repellent aspect, remotely
connected with education?

CHASUBLE [*somewhat indignantly*]   She is the most cultivated of
ladies, and the very picture of respectability.

LADY BRACKNELL   It is obviously the same person. May I ask what
position she holds in your household?

CHASUBLE [*severely*]   I am a celibate, madam.

JACK [*interposing*]   Miss Prism, Lady Bracknell, has been for the last
three years Miss Cardew's esteemed governess and valued companion.

LADY BRACKNELL   In spite of what I hear of her, I must see her at
once. Let her be sent for.

CHASUBLE [*looking off*]   She approaches; she is nigh.

Enter MISS PRISM *hurriedly.*

MISS PRISM   I was told you expected me in the vestry, dear Canon. I
have been waiting for you there for an hour and three-quarters.
[*Catches sight of* LADY BRACKNELL, *who has fixed her with a stony*

9. A 16th-century religious group, most
nearly like contemporary Mennonites. Dr.
Chasuble, however, is probably using the
term loosely to apply to a group more like
contemporary Baptists.
1. An usher. Since most pews were
completely enclosed, his duties would have
included opening the gate that provided
entrance for the worshipers. In addition,
since most pews were rented for the use
of specific persons, he would have been
responsible for seeing that worshipers were
seated in the correct pews.

glare. MISS PRISM *grows pale and quails. She looks anxiously round as if desirous to escape.*]

LADY BRACKNELL [*in a severe, judicial voice*]   Prism!

MISS PRISM *bows her head in shame.*

Come here, Prism!

MISS PRISM *approaches in a humble manner.*

Prism! Where is that baby?

General consternation. The CANON *starts back in horror.* ALGERNON *and* JACK *pretend to be anxious to shield* CECILY *and* GWENDOLEN *from hearing the details of terrible public scandal.*

Twenty-eight years ago, Prism, you left Lord Bracknell's house, Number 104, Upper Grosvenor Square, in charge of a perambulator that contained a baby of the male sex. You never returned. A few weeks later, through the elaborate investigations of the Metropolitan police, the perambulator was discovered at midnight standing by itself in a remote corner of Bayswater.[2] It contained the manuscript of a three-volume novel of more than usually revolting sentimentality.

MISS PRISM *starts in involuntary indignation.*

But the baby was not there.

Everyone looks at MISS PRISM.

Prism! Where is that baby?

A pause.

MISS PRISM   Lady Bracknell, I admit with shame that I do not know. I only wish I did. The plain facts of the case are these. On the morning of the day you mention, a day that is for ever branded on my memory, I prepared as usual to take the baby out in its perambulator. I had also with me a somewhat old, but capacious handbag in which I had intended to place the manuscript of a work of fiction that I had written during my few unoccupied hours. In a moment of mental abstraction, for which I can never forgive myself, I deposited the manuscript in the bassinette and placed the baby in the handbag.

JACK [*who has been listening attentively*]   But where did you deposit the handbag?

2. Bayswater is a residential section to the north of Hyde Park and Kensington Gardens.

MISS PRISM   Do not ask me, Mr. Worthing.

JACK   Miss Prism, this is a matter of no small importance to me. I insist on knowing where you deposited the handbag that contained that infant.

MISS PRISM   I left it in the cloakroom of one of the larger railway stations in London.

JACK   What railway station?

MISS PRISM [*quite crushed*]   Victoria. The Brighton line. [*Sinks into a chair.*]

JACK   I must retire to my room for a moment. Gwendolen, wait here for me.

GWENDOLEN   If you are not too long, I will wait here for you all my life.

    Exit JACK *in great excitement.*

CHASUBLE   What do you think this means, Lady Bracknell?

LADY BRACKNELL   I dare not even suspect, Dr. Chasuble. I need hardly tell you that in families of high position strange coincidences are not supposed to occur. They are hardly considered the thing.

    Noises heard overhead as if some one was throwing trunks about. Everyone looks up.

CECILY   Uncle Jack seems strangely agitated.

CHASUBLE   Your guardian has a very emotional nature.

LADY BRACKNELL   This noise is extremely unpleasant. It sounds as if he was having an argument. I dislike arguments of any kind. They are always vulgar, and often convincing.

CHASUBLE [*looking up*]   It has stopped now.

    The noise is redoubled.

LADY BRACKNELL   I wish he would arrive at some conclusion.

GWENDOLEN   This suspense is terrible. I hope it will last.

    Enter JACK *with a handbag of black leather in his hand.*

JACK [*rushing over to* MISS PRISM]   Is this the handbag, Miss Prism? Examine is carefully before you speak. The happiness of more than one life depends on your answer.

MISS PRISM [*calmly*]   It seems to be mine. Yes, here is the injury it received through the upsetting of a Gower Street omnibus in younger and happier days. Here is the stain on the lining caused by the explosion of a temperance beverage, an incident that occurred at Leamington. And here, on the lock, are my initials. I had forgotten that in an extravagant mood I had had them placed there. The bag is undoubtedly mine. I am delighted to have it so unexpectedly restored to me. It has been a great inconvenience being without it all these years.

JACK [*in a pathetic voice*]   Miss Prism, more is restored to you than this handbag. I was the baby you placed in it.

MISS PRISM [*amazed*]   You?

JACK [*embracing her*]   Yes . . . mother!

MISS PRISM [*recoiling in indignant astonishment*]   Mr. Worthing, I am unmarried!

JACK   Unmarried! I do not deny that is a serious blow. But after all, who has the right to cast a stone against one who has suffered? Cannot repentance wipe out an act of folly? Why should there be one law for men, and another for women? Mother. I forgive you. [*Tries to embrace her again.*]

MISS PRISM [*still more indignant*]   Mr. Worthing, there is some error. [*Pointing to* LADY BRACKNELL.] There is the lady who can tell you who you really are.

JACK [*after a pause*]   Lady Bracknell, I hate to seem inquisitive, but would you kindly inform me who I am?

LADY BRACKNELL   I am afraid that the news I have to give you will not altogether please you. You are the son of my poor sister, Mrs. Moncrieff, and consequently Algernon's elder brother.

JACK   Algy's elder brother! Then I have a brother after all. I knew I had a brother! I always said I had a brother! Cecily—how could you have ever doubted that I had a brother? [*Seizes hold of* ALGERNON.] Dr. Chasuble, my unfortunate brother. Miss Prism, my unfortunate brother. Gwendolen, my unfortunate brother. Algy, you young scoundrel, you will have to treat me with more respect in the future. You have never behaved to me like a brother in all your life.

ALGERNON   Well, not till today, old boy, I admit. I did my best, however, though I was out of practice. [*Shakes hands.*]

GWENDOLEN [*to* JACK]   My own! But what own are you? What is your Christian name, now that you have become someone else?

JACK   Good heavens! . . . I had quite forgotten that point. Your decision on the subject of my name is irrevocable, I suppose?

GWENDOLEN   I never change, except in my affections.

CECILY   What a noble nature you have, Gwendolen!

JACK   Then the question had better be cleared up at once. Aunt Augusta, a moment. At the time when Miss Prism left me in the handbag, had I been christened already?

LADY BRACKNELL   Every luxury that money could buy, including christening, had been lavished on you by your fond and doting parents.

JACK   Then I was christened! That is settled. Now, what name was I given? Let me know the worst.

LADY BRACKNELL   Being the eldest son you were naturally christened after your father.

JACK [*irritably*]   Yes, but what was my father's Christian name?

LADY BRACKNELL [*meditatively*]   I cannot at the present moment recall what the General's Christian name was. But I have no doubt he had one. He was eccentric, I admit. But only in later years. And that was the result of the Indian climate, and marriage, and indigestion, and other things of that kind.

JACK   Algy! Can't you recollect what our father's Christian name was?

ALGERNON   My dear boy, we were never even on speaking terms. He died before I was a year old.

JACK   His name would appear in the Army Lists of the period, I suppose, Aunt Augusta?

LADY BRACKNELL   The General was essentially a man of peace, except in his domestic life. But I have no doubt his name would appear in any military directory.

JACK   The Army Lists of the last forty years are here. These delightful records should have been my constant study. [*Rushes to bookcase and tears the books out.*] M. Generals . . . Mallam, Maxbohm, Magley—what ghastly names they have—Markby, Migsby, Mobbs, Moncrieff! Lieutenant 1840, Captain, Lieutenant-Colonel, Colonel, General 1869, Christian names, Ernest John. [*Puts book very quietly down and speaks quite calmly.*] I always told you, Gwendolen, my name was Ernest, didn't I? Well, it is Ernest after all. I mean it naturally is Ernest.

LADY BRACKNELL   Yes, I remember now that the General was called Ernest. I knew I had some particular reason for disliking the name.

GWENDOLEN   Ernest! My own Ernest! I felt from the first that you could have no other name!

JACK   Gwendolen, it is a terrible thing for a man to find out suddenly that all his life he has been speaking nothing but the truth. Can you forgive me?

GWENDOLEN   I can. For I feel that you are sure to change.

JACK   My own one!

CHASUBLE [*to* MISS PRISM]   Laetitia! [*Embraces her.*]

MISS PRISM [*enthusiastically*]   Frederick! At last!

ALGERNON   Cecily! [*Embraces her.*] At last!

JACK   Gwendolen! [*Embraces her.*] At last!

LADY BRACKNELL   My nephew, you seem to be displaying signs of triviality.

JACK   On the contrary, Aunt Augusta, I've now realized for the first time in my life the vital Importance of Being Earnest.

1895

Krapp's Last Tape

A late evening in the future.

KRAPP's *den.*

Front centre a small table, the two drawers of which open towards audience.

Sitting at the table, facing front, i.e., across from the drawers, a wearish old man: KRAPP.

Rusty black narrow trousers too short for him. Rusty black sleeveless waistcoat, four capacious pockets. Heavy silver watch and chain. Grimy white shirt open at neck, no collar. Surprising pair of dirty white boots, size ten at least, very narrow and pointed.

White face. Purple nose. Disordered grey hair. Unshaven.

Very near-sighted (but unspectacled). Hard of hearing.

Cracked voice. Distinctive intonation.

Laborious walk.

On the table a tape-recorder with microphone and a number of cardboard boxes containing reels of recorded tapes.

Table and immediately adjacent area in strong white light. Rest of stage in darkness.

KRAPP *remains a moment motionless, heaves a great sigh, looks at his watch, fumbles in his pockets, takes out an envelope, puts it back, fumbles, takes out a small bunch of keys, raises it to his eyes, chooses a key, gets up and moves to front of table. He stoops, unlocks first drawer, peers into it, feels about inside it, takes out a reel of tape, peers at it, puts it back, locks drawer, unlocks second drawer, peers into it, feels about inside it, takes out a large banana, peers at it, locks drawer, puts keys back in his pocket. He turns, advances to edge of stage, halts, strokes banana, peels it, drops skin at his feet, puts end of banana in his mouth and remains motionless, staring vacuously before him. Finally he bites off the end, turns aside and begins pacing to and fro at edge of stage, in the light, i.e. not more than four or five paces either way, meditatively eating banana. He treads on skin, slips, nearly falls, recovers himself, stoops and peers at skin and finally pushes it, still stooping, with his foot over the edge of stage into pit. He resumes his pacing, finishes banana, returns to table, sits down, remains a moment*

*motionless, heaves a great sigh, takes keys from his pockets, raises
them to his eyes, chooses key, gets up and moves to front of table,
unlocks second drawer, takes out a second large banana, peers at
it, locks drawer, puts back keys in his pocket, turns, advances to
edge of stage, halts, strokes banana, peels it, tosses skin into pit,
puts end of banana in his mouth and remains motionless, staring
vacuously before him. Finally he has an idea, puts banana in his
waistcoat pocket, the end emerging, and goes with all the speed he
can muster backstage into darkness. Ten seconds. Loud pop of
cork. Fifteen seconds. He comes back into light carrying an old
ledger and sits down at table. He lays ledger on table, wipes his
mouth, wipes his hands on the front of his waistcoat, brings them
smartly together and rubs them.*

KRAPP [*briskly*]   Ah! [*He bends over ledger, turns the pages, finds the
entry he wants, reads.*] Box . . . thrree . . . spool . . . five. [*He raises
his head and stares front. With relish.*] Spool! [*Pause.*] Spool!
[*Happy smile. Pause. He bends over table, starts peering and poking at the boxes.*] Box . . . thrree . . . thrree . . . four . . . two . . .
[*with surprise*] nine! good God! . . . seven . . . ah! the little rascal!
[*He takes up box, peers at it.*] Box thrree. [*He lays it on table,
opens it and peers at spools inside.*] Spool . . . [*he peers at ledger*]
. . . five . . . [*he peers at spools*] . . . five . . . five . . . ah! the little
scoundrel! [*He takes out a spool, peers at it.*] Spool five. [*He lays
it on table, closes box three, puts it back with the others, takes up
the spool.*] Box thrree, spool five. [*He bends over the machine,
looks up. With relish.*] Spooool! [*Happy smile. He bends, loads
spool on machine, rubs his hands.*] Ah! [*He peers at ledger, reads
entry at foot of page.*] Mother at rest at last . . . Hm . . . The black
ball . . . [*He raises his head, stares blankly front. Puzzled.*] Black
ball? . . . [*He peers again at ledger, reads.*] The dark nurse . . . [*He
raises his head, broods, peers again at ledger, reads.*] Slight
improvement in bowel condition . . . Hm . . . Memorable . . .
what? [*He peers closer.*] Equinox, memorable equinox. [*He raises
his head, stares blankly front. Puzzled.*] Memorable equinox? . . .
[*Pause. He shrugs his shoulders, peers again at ledger, reads.*]
Farewell to—[*He turns the page*]—love.

> *He raises his head, broods, bends over machine, switches on
> and assumes listening posture, i.e. leaning forward, elbows on
> table, hand cupping ear towards machine, face front.*

TAPE [*strong voice, rather pompous, clearly* KRAPP's *at a much earlier
time.*]   Thirty-nine today, sound as a—[*Settling himself more
comfortably he knocks one of the boxes off thte table, curses,
switches off, sweeps boxes and ledger violently to the ground, winds
tape back to beginning, switches on, resumes posture.*] Thirty-nine
today, sound as a bell, apart from my old weakness, and intellectually I have now every reason to suspect at the . . . [*hesitates*] . . .
crest of the wave—or thereabouts. Celebrated the awful occasion,
as in recent years, quietly at the Winehouse. Not a soul. Sat before

the fire with closed eyes, separating the grain from the husks. Jotted down a few notes, on the back of an envelope. Good to be back in my den, in my old rags. Have just eaten I regret to say three bananas and only with difficulty refrained from a fourth. Fatal things for a man with my condition. [*Vehemently.*] Cut 'em out! [*Pause.*] The new light above my table is a great improvement. With all this darkness round me I feel less alone. [*Pause.*] In a way. [*Pause.*] I love to get up and move about in it, then back here to . . . [*hesitates*] . . . me. [*Pause.*] Krapp.

Pause.

The grain, now what I wonder do I mean by that, I mean . . . [*hesitates*] . . . I suppose I mean those things worth having when all the dust has—when all *my* dust has settled. I close my eyes and try and imagine them.

Pause. KRAPP *closes his eyes briefly.*

Extraordinary silence this evening, I strain my ears and do not hear a sound. Old Miss McGlome always sings at this hour. But not tonight. Songs of her girlhood, she says. Hard to think of her as a girl. Wonderful woman though. Connaught, I fancy. [*Pause.*] Shall I sing when I am her age, if I ever am? No. [*Pause.*] Did I sing as a boy? No. [*Pause.*] Did I ever sing? No.

Pause.

Just been listening to an old year, passages at random. I did not check in the book, but it must be at least ten or twelve years ago. At that time I think I was still living on and off with Bianca in Kedar Street. Well out of that, Jesus yes! Hopeless business. [*Pause.*] Not much about her, apart from a tribute to her eyes. Very warm. I suddenly saw them again. [*Pause.*] Incomparable! [*Pause.*] Ah well . . . [*Pause.*] These old P.M.s are gruesome, but I often find them—[KRAPP *switches off, broods, switches on*]—a help before embarking on a new . . . [*hesitates*] . . . retrospect. Hard to believe I was ever that young whelp. The voice! Jesus! And the aspirations! [*Brief laugh in which Krapp joins.*] And the resolutions! [*Brief laugh in which* KRAPP *joins.*] To drink less, in particular. [*Brief laugh of* KRAPP *alone.*] Statistics. Seventeen hundred hours, out of the preceding eight thousand odd, consumed on licensed premises alone. More than 20%, say 40% of his waking life. [*Pause.*] Plans for a less . . . [*hesitates*] . . . engrossing sexual life. Last illness of his father. Flagging pursuit of happiness. Unattainable laxation. Sneers at what he calls his youth and thanks to God that it's over. [*Pause.*] False ring there. [*Pause.*] Shadows of the opus . . . magnum. Closing with a—[*brief laugh*]—yelp to Providence. [*Prolonged laugh in which* KRAPP *joins.*] What remains of all that misery? A girl in a shabby green coat, on a railway-station platform? No?

Pause.

When I look—

> KRAPP *switches off, broods, looks at his watch, gets up, goes backstage into darkness. Ten seconds. Pop of cork. Ten seconds. Second cork. Ten seconds. Third cork. Ten seconds. Brief burst of quavering song.*

KRAPP [*sings*]   Now the days is over,
                  Night is drawing nigh-igh,
                  Shadows—

> *Fit of coughing. He comes back into light, sits down, wipes his mouth, switches on, resumes his listening posture.*

TAPE   —back on the year that is gone, with what I hope is perhaps a glint of the old eye to come, there is of course the house on the canal where mother lay a-dying, in the late autumn, after her long viduity [*Krapp gives a start*], and the—[*Krapp switches off, winds back tape a little, bends his ear closer to machine, switches on*]— a-dying, after her long viduity, and the—

> KRAPP *switches off, raises his head, stares blankly before him. His lips move in the syllables of "viduity." No sound. He gets up, goes backstage into darkness, comes back with an enormous dictionary, lays it on table, sits down and looks up the word.*

KRAPP [*reading from dictionary*]   State—or condition of being—or remaining—a widow—or widower. [*Looks up. Puzzled.*] Being— or remaining? . . . [*Pause. He peers again at dictionary. Reading.*] "Deep weeds of viduity" . . . Also of an animal, especially a bird . . . the vidua or weaver-bird . . . Black plumage of male . . . [*He looks up. With relish.*] The vidua-bird!

> *Pause. He closes dictionary, switches on, resumes listening posture.*

TAPE   —bench by the weir from where I could see her window. There I sat, in the biting wind, wishing she were gone. [*Pause.*] Hardly a soul, just a few regulars, nursemaids, infants, old men, dogs. I got to know them quite well—oh by appearance of course I mean! One dark young beauty I recollect particularly, all white and starch, incomparable bosom, with a big black hooded perambulator, most funereal thing. Whenever I looked in her direction she had her eyes on me. And yet when I was bold enough to speak to her—not having been introduced—she threatened to call a policeman. As if I had designs on her virtue! [*Laugh. Pause.*] The face she had! The eyes! Like . . . [*hesitates*] . . . chrysolite! [*Pause.*] Ah well . . . [*Pause.*] I was there when—[KRAPP *switches off, broods, switches on again*]—the blind went down, one of those dirty brown roller affairs, throwing a ball for a little white dog, as chance would have it. I happened to look up and there it was. All over and done with, at last. I sat on for a few moments with the ball in my hand and the dog yelping and pawing at me. [*Pause.*] Moments. Her moments, my moments. [*Pause.*] The dog's moments. [*Pause.*] In the end I held it out to him and he took it in his mouth, gently, gently. A small, old, black, hard, solid rubber ball. [*Pause.*] I shall feel it, in my hand, until my dying day. [*Pause.*] I might have kept it. [*Pause.*] But I gave it to the dog.

Pause.

Ah well . . .

Pause.

Spiritually a year of profound gloom and indigence until that memorable night in March, at the end of the jetty, in the howling wind, never to be forgotten, when suddenly I saw the whole thing. The vision, at last. This I fancy is what I have chiefly to record this evening, against the day when my work will be done and perhaps no place left in my memory, warm or cold, for the miracle that . . . [*hesitates*] . . . for the fire that set it alight. What I suddenly saw then was this, that the belief I had been going on all my life, namely—[KRAPP *switches off impatiently, winds tape forward, switches on again*]—great granite rocks the foam flying up in the light of the lighthouse and the wind-gauge spinning like a propellor, clear to me at last that the dark I have always struggled to keep under is in reality my most—[KRAPP *curses, switches off, winds tape forward, switches on again*]—unshatterable association until my dissolution of storm and night with the light of the understanding and the fire—[KRAPP *curses louder, switches off, winds tape forward, switches on again*]—my face in her breasts and my hand on her. We lay there without moving. But under us all moved, and moved us, gently, up and down, and from side to side.

Pause.

Past midnight. Never knew such silence. The earth might be uninhabited.

Pause.

Here I end—

KRAPP switches off, winds tape back, switches on again.

—upper lake, with punt, bathed off the bank, then pushed out into the stream and drifted. She lay stretched out on the floorboards with her hands under her head and her eyes closed. Sun blazing down, bit of a breeze, water nice and lively. I noticed a scratch on her thigh and asked her how she came by it. Picking gooseberries, she said. I said again I thought it was hopeless and no good going on, and she agreed, without opening her eyes. [*Pause.*] I asked her to look at me and after a few moments—[*pause*]—*after a few* moments she did, but the eyes just slits, because of the glare. I bent over her to get them in the shadow and they opened. [*Pause. Low.*] Let me in. [*Pause.*] We drifted in among the flags and stuck. The way they went down, sighing, before the stem! [*Pause.*] I lay down, sighing, before the stem! [*Pause.*] I lay down across her with my face in her breasts and my hand on her. We lay there without moving. But under us all moved, and moved us, gently, up and down, and from side to side.

Pause.

Past midnight. Never knew—

> KRAPP *switches off, broods. Finally he fumbles in his pockets, encounters the banana, takes it out, peers at it, puts it back, fumbles, brings out the envelope, fumbles, puts back envelope, looks at his watch, gets up and goes backstage into darkness. Ten seconds. Sound of bottle against glass, then brief siphon. Ten seconds. Bottle against glass alone. Ten seconds. He comes back a little unsteadily into light, goes to front of table, takes out keys, raises them to his eyes, chooses key, unlocks first drawer, peers into it, feels about inside, takes out reel, peers at it, locks drawer, puts keys back in his pocket, goes and sits down, takes reel off machine, lays it on dictionary, loads virgin reel on machine, takes envelope from his pocket, consults back of it, lays it on table, switches on, clears his throat and begins to record.*

KRAPP   Just been listening to that stupid bastard I took myself for thirty years ago, hard to believe I was ever as bad as that. Thank God that's all done with anyway. [*Pause.*] The eyes she had! [*Broods, realizes he is recording silence, switches off, broods. Finally.*] Everything there, everything, all the—[*Realizes this is not being recorded, switches on.*] Everything there, everything on this old muckball, all the light and dark and famine and feasting of . . . [*hesitates*] . . . the ages! [*In a shout.*] Yes! [*Pause.*] Let that go! Jesus! Take his mind off his homework! Jesus! [*Pause. Weary.*] Ah well, maybe he was right. [*Pause.*] Maybe he was right. [*Broods. Realizes. Switches off. Consults envelope.*] Pah! [*Crumples it and throws it away. Broods. Switches on.*] Nothing to say, not a squeak. What's a year now? The sour cud and the iron stool. [*Pause.*] Revelled in the word spool. [*With relish.*] Spooool! Happiest moment of the past half million. [*Pause.*] Seventeen copies sold, of which eleven at trade price to free circulating libraries beyond the seas. Getting known. [*Pause.*] One pound six and something, eight I have little doubt. [*Pause.*] Crawled out once or twice, before the summer was cold. Sat shivering in the park, drowned in dreams and burning to be gone. Not a soul. [*Pause.*] Last fancies. [*Vehemently.*] Keep 'em under! [*Pause.*] Scalded the eyes out of me reading *Effie* again, a page a day, with tears again. Effie . . . [*Pause.*] Could have been happy with her, up there on the Baltic, and the pines, and the dunes. [*Pause.*] Could I? [*Pause.*] And she? [*Pause.*] Pah! [*Pause.*] Fanny came in a couple of times. Bony old ghost of a whore. Couldn't do much, but I suppose better than a kick in the crutch. The last time wasn't so bad. How do you manage it, she said, at your age? I told her I'd been saving up for her all my life. [*Pause.*] Went to Vespers once, like when I was in short trousers. [*Pause. Sings.*]

> Now the day is over,
> Night is drawing nigh-igh,
> Shadows—[*coughing, then almost
>   inaudible*]—of the evening
> Steal across the sky.

[*Gasping.*] Went to sleep and fell off the pew. [*Pause.*] Sometimes wondered in the night if a last effort mightn't—[*Pause.*] Ah finish your booze now and get to your bed. Go on with this drivel in the morning. Or leave it at that. [*Pause.*] Leave it at that. [*Pause.*] Lie propped up in the dark—and wander. Be again in the dingle on a Christmas Eve, gathering holly, the red-berried. [*Pause.*] Be again on Croghan[1] on a Sunday morning, in the haze, with the bitch, stop and listen to the bells. [*Pause.*] Be again, be again. [*Pause.*] All that old misery. [*Pause.*] Once wasn't enough for you. [*Pause.*] Lie down across her.

Long pause. He suddenly bends over machine, switches off, wrenches off tape, throws it away, puts on the other, winds it forward to the passage he wants, switches on, listens staring front.

TAPE   —gooseberries, she said. I said again I thought it was hopeless and no good going on, and she agreed, without opening her eyes. [*Pause.*] I asked her to look at me and after a few moments— [*Pause*]—after a few moments she did, but the eyes just slits, because of the glare. I bent over her to get them in the shadow and they opened. [*Pause. Low.*] Let me in. [*Pause.*] We drifted in among the flags and stuck. They way they went down, sighing, before the stem! [*Pause.*] I lay down across her with my face in her breasts and my hand on her. We lay there without moving. But under us all moved, and moved us, gently, up and down, and from side to side.

Pause. KRAPP's *lips moved.* No sound.

---

1. Mountain in southeastern Ireland.

Past midnight. Never knew such silence. The earth might be uninhabited.

Pause.

Here I end this reel. Box—[*pause.*]—three, spool—[*pause*]—five. [*Pause.*] Perhaps my best years are gone. When there was a chance of happiness. But I wouldn't want them back. Not with the fire in me now. No, I wouldn't want them back.

KRAPP *motionless staring before him. The tape runs on in silence.*

CURTAIN

1958

MARSHA NORMAN

Third and Oak: The Laundromat[1]

CHARACTERS

ALBERTA—a woman who values her education, who cares what she looks like, even at three o'clock in the morning. Alberta listens quietly, and is quite opinionated, but generally expresses her opinions so as to protect the feelings of the other person. She is in her mid to late forties and has spent her life as a teacher. Alberta believes that there is a right way to do things, and that is how she does them. Alberta is a careful woman, verging on being picky, but she is harder on herself than on others in this regard.

DEEDEE—a nineteen year old, chatty and constantly in motion. She eats too much sugar and watches too much TV. She once had a job in an all-night grocery, but she was fired for talking too much. She is attractive, but no matter how long she spends getting dressed, she always looks thrown together.

SHOOTER—a handsome black disc jockey, whose late night radio show has been first in the local ratings for years. He is as smooth as they come.

SET: The play takes place in a standard, dreary laundromat. There are tile floors, washers, dryers, coin-op vending machines for soaps, soft drinks and candy bars. There is a bulletin board on which various notices are posted. There is a table for folding clothes as well as a low table and ugly chair littered with magazines. There is a coffee can ash tray on the table. A clock on the wall reads 3:00 o'clock and should continue to run during the show. One side of The Laundromat will be used as a window looking out into the street.

> *As the lights come up, the song "Stand By Your Man" is playing on the radio. The door to the Attendant's room is slightly ajar.*
SHOOTER'S VOICE [*over the final chords of the song*]   And that's all for tonight, night owls. This is your A-Number-One Night Owl saying it's 3 o'clock, all right, and time to rock your daddy to dreams of delight. And Mama, I'm comin' home. And the rest of you night owls gonna have to make it through the rest of this night by yourself, or with the help of your friends, if you know what I mean. And you know what I mean.
> *The radio station goes dead, music replaced by an irritating static.*
> ALBERTA *opens the door tentatively, looks around and walks in. She has dressed carefully and her laundry basket exhibits the same care. She checks the top of a washer for dust or water before putting down her purse and basket. She walks back to the open Attendant door and is startled briefly when she looks in.*

---

1. As originally performed, *The Laundromat* is the first act of *Third and Oak. The Laundromat* is published separately by Dramatists Play Service, and does not include the Shooter character. This version is the original first act, which includes the Shooter character. [Author's note.]

ALBERTA   Hello! [*steps back, seeing that he is asleep*] Sleep? Is that how you do your job? Sleep?

> *She leans in and turns off the radio. We hear the click and the static stops. She walks back toward the basket talking to herself.*

ALBERTA   Now just be quiet, Alberta. I mean, you don't want him out here talking to you, do you? [*turning back quickly*] Maybe you should take his cigar out of his . . . [*changing her mind*] It wasn't burning, was it. It's not your cigar, is it? Mind your own business. Do your wash. [*procrastinating*] No, first. . . .

> ALBERTA *takes an index card out of her purse, on which is printed a message. She tacks it up on the bulletin board. We must see that it is very important to her.*

> ALBERTA *opens a washer lid and runs her fingers around the soap tray. She takes out the lint and deposits it in one of the coffee cans. As she does this, she accidentally knocks over her purse.*

ALBERTA   [*trying to calm down*]   It's all right. Everything is all right.

> *She bends down and begins to put the things back in her purse. She cannot see as* DEEDEE *backs in the door of The Laundromat.* DEEDEE *is a wreck. She carries her clothes tied up in a man's shirt. She trips over a wastebasket on the floor and falls on her laundry as it spills out of the shirt.*

DEEDEE   Well, poo-rats!

ALBERTA   [*stands up, startled, then walks over to* DEEDEE]   Are you all right?

DEEDEE   [*grudgingly*]   Cute, huh?

ALBERTA   [*moves the wastebasket out of the way*]   Probably a wet spot on the floor. [*goes back to her laundry*]

DEEDEE   I already picked these clothes off the floor once tonight. [*no response from* ALBERTA] We been in our apartment two years and Joe still ain't found the closets. He thinks hangers are for when you lock your keys in your car. [*still no response*] I mean, he's got this coat made outta sheep's fur or something and my Mom came over one day and asked where did we git that fuzzy little rug. [*no response from* ALBERTA] He works at the Ford plant. [*getting up and gathering her clothes*] I asked him why they call it that. I said, "How often do you have to water a Ford plant?" [DEEDEE *is very nervous*] It was just a little joke, but he didn't think it was very funny.

ALBERTA   They probably do have a sprinkler system.

DEEDEE   Huh?

ALBERTA   Nothing.

DEEDEE   [*doesn't understand, but keeps talking*]   Shoulda saved my breath and just tripped over the coffee table. He'd a' laughed at that. [*no response from* ALBERTA] Well, I guess it's just you and me.

ALBERTA   Yes.

DEEDEE   Guess not too many people suds their duds in the middle of the night.

ALBERTA   Suds their duds?

DEEDEE   I do mine at Mom's. [DEEDEE *begins to put her clothes in two washers, imitating* ALBERTA] I mean, I take our stuff over to Mom's. She's got matching Maytags. She buys giant size Cheer and we sit around and watch the soaps 'til the clothes come out. Suds the duds, that's what she says. Well, more than that. She wrote it on a little card and sent it in to Cheer so they could use it on their TV ads.

ALBERTA   Gives you a chance to talk, I guess. Visit.

DEEDEE   She says "Just leave em, I'll do em," but that wouldn't be right, so I stay. Course she don't ever say how she likes seein' me, but she holds back, you know. I mean, there's stuff you don't have to say when it's family.

ALBERTA   So, she's not home tonight?

DEEDEE   No, probably just asleep. [ALBERTA *nods.* DEEDEE *reads the washer instructions*] Five Cycle Turbomatic Deluxe. [*punches the buttons on the machine*] Hot wash—warm rinse, warm wash— warm rinse, warm wash—cold rinse, cold wash—cold rinse, cold wash—delicate cycle. Is that like on TV?

ALBERTA   Is what like on TV?

DEEDEE   That hot-cold-warm, thing. Wait, I remember. Whites in hot water, perma press in cold, colors and special fabrics in warm.

ALBERTA   It's the other way around. Perma press in warm, colors and special fabrics in cold.

DEEDEE   What's this? "Add Laundry Aids."

ALBERTA   Your mother does your laundry.

DEEDEE   You don't have a washer either, huh?

ALBERTA   It's broken.

DEEDEE   Get your husband to fix it. [*now looks at* ALBERTA's *wash*] Got a heap o' shirts, don't he?

ALBERTA   It can't be fixed.

DEEDEE   Where are *your* clothes?

ALBERTA   Mine are mostly hand wash.

DEEDEE   We just dump all our stuff in together.

ALBERTA   That's nice.

DEEDEE   Joe can fix just about anything. He's real good with his hands. [*laughs*] I been sayin' that since high school. [*no response from* ALBERTA] He makes trucks. God, I'd hate to see the truck I'd put together. [*nervous laugh*] Had to work the double shift tonight. [*going on quickly.*] They do all kinds out there. Pick-ups, dump trucks . . . they got this joke, him and his buddies, about what rhymes with pickle truck, but I don't know the end of it, you know, the punch line. Goes like . . . "I'll come to get you baby in a pickle truck. I'll tell you what I'm wanting is a . . . [*stops*] See, that's the part I don't know. The end. [*shrugs her shoulders*]

ALBERTA   Does he do this often? Have to work late?

DEEDEE   A whole lot, here lately. He says people are buyin' more trucks cause farmers have to raise more cows cause we got a population explosion goin' on. Really crummy, you know, people I don't even know having babies means Joe can't come home at the right time. Don't seem fair.

ALBERTA   Or true.

DEEDEE   Huh?

ALBERTA   The population explosion is over. The birthrate is declining now.

DEEDEE   Oh.

ALBERTA   You don't like to be in the house by yourself?

DEEDEE   See, we live over there, on top of the Mexican restaurant. [*goes over to the window*] That window with the blue light in it, that's ours. It's a bunch of blueberries on a stalk, only it's a light. Joe gave it to me. He thinks blue is my favorite color.

ALBERTA   And the restaurant noise was bothering you.

DEEDEE   I guess. They got this bar stays open til 4. That's how Joe picked the apartment. He hates to run out for beer late. Runnin' *down* ain't so bad. [*brightly*] Ole Mexico Taco Tavern. Except Joe says it's sposed to be Olé Mexico, like what they say in bullfights.

ALBERTA   Bullfights are disgusting.

DEEDEE   You've seen a real bullfight?

ALBERTA   We used to travel quite a bit.

DEEDEE   Well, tell me about it!

ALBERTA   There's not much to tell. The bull comes out and they kill it.

DEEDEE   I bet a man thought that up.

ALBERTA   [*a little laugh*]   I'll bet you're right.

DEEDEE   Your husband works nights, too?

ALBERTA   Herb is out of town. [*now seeing what* DEEDEE *is doing*] Did you mean to put that in there?

DEEDEE   [*peering into her washer*]   Huh?

ALBERTA   Your whites will come out green.

DEEDEE   [*retrieving the shirt*]   Joe wouldn't like that. No sir. Be like when Mom's washer chewed this hole in his bowling shirt. Whoo-ee! Was he hot. Kicked the chest of drawers, broke his toe. [*a pause*] Broke the chest of drawers too. [*a pause*] Is Herb picky like that?

ALBERTA   [*reaching for her soap*]   Herb likes to look nice.

DEEDEE   Hey! You forgot one. [*picking the remaining shirt out of* ALBERTA's *basket*] See? [*opens it out, showing an awful stain*] Yuck. Looks like vomit.

ALBERTA   [*reluctantly*]   It's my cabbage soup.

DEEDEE   Well . . . [*helpfully*] in it goes! [*opening one of* ALBERTA's *washers*]

ALBERTA   [*suddenly*]   No!

DEEDEE   [*reaching for the other washer*]   The other one?

ALBERTA   [*taking it away from her*]   I don't want to . . . it's too . . . that stain will never . . . [*enforcing a calm now*] It needs to presoak. I forgot the Woolite.

DEEDEE   Sorry.

ALBERTA   [*putting the shirt back in the basket*]   That's quite all right.

DEEDEE   One of those machines give soap? [ALBERTA *points to one,* DEEDEE *walks to it*] It takes nickels. I only got quarters.

ALBERTA   [*putting her quarters in the washer*]   The attendant will give you change.

DEEDEE   [*looking in his doorway*]   He's asleep. [ALBERTA *nods*] Be terrible to wake him up just for some ol' nickels. Do you have any change?

ALBERTA   No.

DEEDEE   Looks like he's got a pocket full of money. Think it would
wake him up if I stuck my hand in there?

ALBERTA   [*feeling bad about not wanting to help*]   Twenty years ago,
maybe. [DEEDEE *laughs*] Here, I found some. [DEEDEE *walks back*,
gives ALBERTA *the quarters*, ALBERT *counts out the nickels*.] That's
ten, twenty, thirty, forty, fifty.

DEEDEE   [*putting the nickles in the soap machine*]   He shouldn't be
sleeping like that. Somebody could come in and rob him. You don't
thing he's dead, do you? I mean, I probably wouldn't know it if I
saw somebody dead.

ALBERTA   [*starting her washer*]   You'd know.

DEEDEE   [*pushing in the coin tray, starting the washers*]   O.K. Cheer
up! [*laughs*] That's what Mom always says, "Cheer up!" [*looks over
at* ALBERTA *now*] Hey, my name is Deedee. Deedee Johnson.

ALBERTA   [*picking up a magazine*]   Nice to meet you.

DEEDEE   What's yours?

ALBERTA   Alberta.

DEEDEE   Alberta what?

ALBERTA   [*reluctantly*]   Alberta Johnson.

DEEDEE   Hey! We might be related. I mean, Herb and Joe could be
cousins or something.

ALBERTA   I don't think so.

DEEDEE   Yeah. Guess there's lots of Johnsons.

ALBERTA   Yes.

DEEDEE   I'm botherin' you, aren't I? [ALBERTA *smiles*] I'd talk to
somebody else, but there ain't anybody else. 'Cept Sleepy back there.

ALBERTA   Would you like a magazine?

DEEDEE   No thanks. I brought a Dr. Pepper. You can have it if you
want.

ALBERTA   No thank you.

DEEDEE   Sleepy was one of the seven dwarfs. I can still name them
all. I couldn't tell you seven presidents of the United States, but I
can say the dwarfs. Sleepy, Grumpy, Sneezy, Dopey, Doc and
Bashful. [*very proud, doesn't notice she's only named six*]

ALBERTA   You could name seven presidents.

DEEDEE   Oh no.

ALBERTA   Try it.

DEEDEE   O.K. [*takes a big breath*] There's Carter, Nixon, Kennedy,
Lincoln, Ben Franklin, George Washington . . . uh . . .

ALBERTA   Think of Mount Rushmore.

DEEDEE   Who?

ALBERTA   How about Eleanor Roosevelt's husband.

DEEDEE   Mr. Roosevelt?

ALBERTA   Mr. Roosevelt. That's seven. Except Benjamin Franklin
was never president.

DEEDEE   You're a teacher or something, aren't you.

ALBERTA   I was. Say Mr. Roosevelt again.

DEEDEE   Mr. Roosevelt.

ALBERTA   There. Teddy makes seven.

DEEDEE   Around here? Or in the county schools?

ALBERTA   Ohio. Columbus.

DEEDEE   Great!

ALBERTA   Do you know Columbus?

DEEDEE   Not personally.

ALBERTA   Ah.

DEEDEE   I better be careful, huh? No ain'ts or nuthin.

ALBERTA   You can't say anything I haven't heard before.

DEEDEE   Want me to try?

ALBERTA   No.

DEEDEE   What does Herb do?

ALBERTA   Is Deedee short for something? Deidre, Deborah?

DEEDEE   No, just Deedee. The guys in high school always kidded me about my name. [*affecting a boy's voice*] Hey, Deedee. Is Deedee your name or your bra size?

ALBERTA   That wasn't very nice of them.

DEEDEE   That ain't even the worst. Wanna hear the worst? [ALBERTA *doesn't respond*] Ricky Baker, Icky Ricky Baker and David Duvall said this one. They'd come up to the locker bank, David's locker was right next to mine and Ricky'd say "Hey, you have a good time last night?" and David would say, "Yes, in Deedee." Then they'd slap each other and laugh like idiots.

ALBERTA   You could have had your locker moved.

DEEDEE   I guess. But, see, the basketball players always came down that hall at the end of school. Going to practice, you know.

ALBERTA   One of the basketball players I taught . . . [*begins to chuckle*]

DEEDEE   Yeah?

ALBERTA   . . . thought Herbert Hoover invented the vacuum cleaner. [ALBERTA *laughs at her joke.* DEEDEE *doesn't get it.* ALBERTA *steps back a little.* DEEDEE *tries to laugh*]

DEEDEE   Why did you quit . . . teaching.

ALBERTA   Age.

DEEDEE   You don't look old enough to retire.

ALBERTA   No, not my age. Theirs.

DEEDEE   Mine.

ALBERTA   Actually, mother was very sick then.

DEEDEE   Is she still alive?

ALBERTA   No.

DEEDEE   I'm sorry.

ALBERTA   There was quite a lot of pain at the end. It was a blessing, really.

DEEDEE   For her maybe, but what about you?

ALBERT   She was the one with the pain.

DEEDEE   Sounds like she was lucky to have you there, nursing her and all.

ALBERTA   I read her *Wuthering Heights* five times that year. I kept checking different ones out of the library, you know, *Little Women, Jane Eyre*, but each time she'd say, "No, I think I'd like to hear *Wuthering Heights*" like she hadn't heard it in 50 years. But each time, I'd read the last page and look up, and she'd say the same thing.

DEEDEE   What thing?

ALBERTA   She'd say, "I still don't understand it. They didn't have to have all that trouble. All they had to do was find him someplace to go every day. All Heathcliff needed was a job. [*pause*] But maybe I missed something. Read it again."

DEEDEE   My mother thinks Joe's a bum. [*somehow* DEEDEE *thinks this is an appropriate response, and* ALBERTA *is jolted back to the present*] No really, she kept paying this guy that worked at Walgreens to come over and strip our wallpaper. She said, "Deedee, he's gonna be manager of that drugstore someday." Hell, the only reason he worked there was getting a discount on his pimple cream. She thought that would get me off Joe. No way. We've been married two years last month. Mom says this is the itch year.

ALBERTA   The itch year?

DEEDEE   When guys get the itch, you know, to fool around with other women. Stayin' out late, comin' in with stories about goin' drinkin' with the boys or workin' overtime or . . . somethin'. Is that clock right?

ALBERTA   I think so.

DEEDEE   Bet Herb never did that, huh?

ALBERTA   Be unfaithful, you mean? [DEEDEE *nods*]   No.

DEEDEE   How can you be so sure like that? You keep him in the refrigerator?

ALBERTA   Well, I suppose he could have . . . [*doesn't believe this for a minute*]

DEEDEE   Like right now, while he's up in wherever he is . . .

ALBERTA   Akron.

DEEDEE   Akron, he could be sittin' at the bar in some all-night bowling alley polishin' some big blonde's ball.

ALBERTA   No.

DEEDEE   That's real nice to trust him like that.

ALBERTA   Aren't you afraid Joe will call you on his break and be worried about where you are?

DEEDEE   You got any kids?

ALBERTA   No.

DEEDEE   Didn't you want some?

ALBERTA   Oh yes.

DEEDEE   Me too. Lots of 'em. But Joe says he's not ready. Wants to be earning lots of money before we start our family.

ALBERTA   That's why he works this double-shift.

DEEDEE   Yeah. Only now he's fixin' up this '64 Chevy he bought to drag race. Then when the race money starts comin' in, we can have them kids. He's really lookin' forward to that—winnin' a big race and havin' me and the kids run out on the track and him smilin' and grabbin' up the baby and pourin' beer all over us while the crowd is yellin' and screamin' . . .

ALBERTA   So all his money goes into this car.

DEEDEE   Hey. I love it too. Sundays we go to the garage and work on it. [*gets a picture out of her wallet*] That devil painted there on the door, that cost 200 dollars!

ALBERTA   You help him?

DEEDEE   He says it's a real big help just havin' me there watchin'.

ALBERTA   I never understood that, men wanting you to watch them do whatever it . . . I mean . . . Well . . . [*deciding to tell this story*] Every year at Thanksgiving, Herb would watch over me washing the turkey, making the stuffing, stuffing the turkey. Made me nervous.

DEEDEE   You coulda told him to get lost.

ALBERTA   Actually, the last ten years or so, I sent him out for sage. For the dressing. He'd come in and sit down saying, "Mmmm boy, was this ever going to be the best turkey yet," and rubbing his hands together and I'd push jars around in the cabinet and look all worried and say, "Herb, I don't think I have enough sage." And he'd say, "Well, Bertie, my girl, I'll just run out for some."

DEEDEE   Bet you got a lot of that sage by now.

ALBERTA   I could open a store.

DEEDEE   I saw white pepper at the store last week. How do they do that?

ALBERTA   I don't know.

DEEDEE   Is Dr. Pepper made out of pepper?

ALBERTA   I don't know.

DEEDEE   What did Herb do, that you have to watch, I mean.

ALBERTA   He gardened. I didn't have to watch him plant the seeds or weed the plants or spray for pests or pick okra. But when the day came to turn over the soil, that was the day. Herb would rent a roto-tiller and bring out a lawn chair from the garage. He'd wipe it off and call in the kitchen window, "Alberta, it's so pleasant out here in the sunshine."

DEEDEE   And you watched.

ALBERTA   When he finished he'd bring out this little wooden sign and drive it into the ground.

DEEDEE   What'd it say?

ALBERTA   Herb Garden. [*pauses*] He thought that was funny.

DEEDEE   Did you laugh?

ALBERTA   Every year.

DEEDEE [*walking to the window*]   He's not doing one this year?

ALBERTA   No.

DEEDEE [*still staring out the window*]   Why not?

ALBERTA   What's out there?

DEEDEE   Oh nothing.

ALBERTA   You looked like . . .

DEEDEE   Joe should be home soon. I turned all the lights out except the blueberries so I could tell if he comes in, you know, when he turns the lights on.

ALBERTA   When is the shift over?

DEEDEE   Oh . . . [*with enforced cheer*] not for a long time yet. I just thought . . . He might get through early, he said. And we could go have a beer. Course, he might stop off and bowl a few games first.
        [ALBERTA *gets up to check on her wash.* DEEDEE *walks to the bulletin board on the wall.*]

DEEDEE [*reading*]   "Typing done. Hourly or by the page. Cheer." What on earth?

ALBERTA Must be "cheap." Better be cheap.

DEEDEE Most of this stuff is over already. [*taking some notices down*] Hey! Here's one for Herb. "Gardening Tools, never used. Rake, hoe, spade and towel."

ALBERTA Trowel.

DEEDEE [*irritated by the correction*]   You got great eyes, Alberta. [*continues to read*] 459-4734. A. Johnson. You think this A. Johnson is related to us? [*laughs*] No, that's right, you said Herb wasn't doing a garden any more. No, I got it! This A. Johnson is you. And the reason Herb ain't doin' a garden is you're selling his rakes. But this says "never used." Alberta, you shouldn't try to fool people like that. Washin' up Herb's hoe and selling it like it was new. Bad girl.

ALBERTA Actually, that is me. I bought Herb some new tools for his birthday and then he . . . gave it up . . . gardening.

DEEDEE Before his birthday?

ALBERTA What?

DEEDEE Did you have time to go buy him another present?

ALBERTA Yes . . . well, no. I mean, he told me before his birthday, but I didn't get a chance to get him anything else.

DEEDEE He's probably got everything anyhow.

ALBERTA Just about.

DEEDEE Didn't he get his feelings hurt?

ALBERTA No.

DEEDEE Joe never likes the stuff I give him.

ALBERTA Oh, I'm sure he does. He just doesn't know how to tell you.

DEEDEE No. He doesn't. For our anniversary, I planned real far ahead for this one, I'm tellin' you. I sent off my picture, not a whole body picture, just my face real close up, to this place in Massachusetts, and they painted, well I don't know if they really painted, but somehow or other, they *put* my face on this doll. It was unbelievable how it really looked like me. 'Bout this tall . . . [*indicates about two feet*] with overalls and a checked shirt. I thought it was real cute, and I wrote this card sayin' "From one livin' doll to another. Let's keep playin' house till the day we die."

ALBERTA Wasn't he surprised?

DEEDEE He laughed so hard he fell over backward out of the chair and cracked his head open on the radiator. We had to take him to the emergency room.

ALBERTA Was he hurt very badly?

DEEDEE We were sittin' there waitin' for him to get sewed up and this little kid comes in real sick and I brought the doll along, see, I don't know why, anyway, Joe says to me, [*getting a candy bar out of her purse*] "Deedee, that little girl is so much sicker than me. Let's give her this doll to make her feel better." And they were takin' her right on in to the doctors 'cause she looked pretty bad, and Joe rushes up and puts this doll in her arms.

ALBERTA They let her keep it?

DEEDEE   Her mother said, "Thanks a lot." Real sweet like they didn't
have much money to buy the kid dolls or something. It made Joe
feel real good.

ALBERTA   But it was your present to him. It was your face on the doll.

DEEDEE   Yeah. [*pause*] But I figure it was his present as soon as I
gave it to him, so if he wanted to give it away, that's his business.
But . . . [*and she stops*] . . . he didn't like it. I could tell. [*walks to
the window again*] They need to wash the window here.

ALBERTA   I gave Herb a fishing pole one year.

DEEDEE [*not interested*]   He fishes?

ALBERTA   No, but I thought he wanted to. He'd cut out a picture
of this husky man standing in water practically up to his waist,
fishing. I thought he left it out so I'd get the hint.

DEEDEE   But he didn't.

ALBERTA   Oh, it was a hint all right. He wanted the hat.

DEEDEE [*not listening*]   Right.

ALBERTA [*seeing that* DEEDEE *is increasingly upset*]   Do you like the
things Joe gives you?

DEEDEE   I'd like it if he came home, that's what I'd like.

ALBERTA   He'll be back soon. You'll probably see those lights go on
as soon as your clothes are dry.

DEEDEE   Sure.

ALBERTA   People can't always be where we want them to be, when
we want them to be there.

DEEDEE   Well, I don't like it.

ALBERTA   You don't have to like it. You just have to know it.

DEEDEE [*defensive*]   Wouldn't you like for Herb to be home right
now?

ALBERTA [*a small forced laugh*]   I made a lemon meringue pie tonight. But I forgot, he's the one who likes lemon meringue.

DEEDEE   'Cause if they were both home where they should be, we
wouldn't have to be here in this crappy laundromat washin' fuckin'
shirts in the middle of the night. [*kicks a dryer*] I'm sorry. You
probably don't use language like that, well, neither do I very often,
but I'm . . . [*now doing it on purpose*] pissed as hell at that
sunuvabitch.

> ALBERTA *picks up a magazine, trying to withdraw completely.*
> *She is offended, but wants to try not to appear self-righteous.*
> *The door has opened sometime during* DEEDEE's *fury. Now,*
> SHOOTER *pushes open the door.* DEEDEE *turns sharply and sees*
> *him. She storms back and sits down beside* ALBERTA. *Both*
> *women are somewhat alarmed at a black man entering this*
> *preserve so late at night.*

> SHOOTER *is poised and handsome. He is dressed neatly, but*
> *casually. He is carrying an army duffel bag full of clothes and*
> *a sack of tacos. He has a can of beer in one pocket. He moves*
> *toward a washer, sets down the duffel bag, pops the cap on the*
> *beer. He is aware that he has frightened them. This amuses*

him, but he understands it. Besides, he is so goddamned charming.

SHOOTER [*holding the taco sack so they can see it*]   Would either of you two ladies care to join me in a taco?

ALBERTA [*finally*]   No thank you.

SHOOTER [*as though in an ad*]   Freshly chopped lettuce, firm vine-ripened New Jersey beefsteak tomatoes, a-ged, shred-ded, ched-dar cheese, sweet slivers of Bermunda onion and Ole Mexico's very own, very hot taco sauce.

DEEDEE   That's just what they say on the radio.

SHOOTER   That's because I'm the "they" who says it on the radio.

DEEDEE   You are?

SHOOTER [*walking over*]   Shooter Stevens. [*shakes her hand*]

ALBERTA [*as he shakes her hand*]   Nice to meet you.

DEEDEE   You're the Number One Nightowl?

SHOOTER [*as he said it at the beginning of the act*]   . . . sayin' it's three o'clock, all right, and time to rock your daddy to dreams of de-light.

DEEDEE   You are! You really are! That's fantastic! I always listen to you!

SHOOTER [*walking back to his laundry*]   Yeah?

DEEDEE   Always. Except when . . . I mean, when I get to pick, I pick you. I mean, your station. You're on late.

SHOOTER   You got it.

DEEDEE [*to* ALBERTA]   Terrific. [*disgusted with herself*] I'm telling him he's on late. He knows he's on late. He's the one who's on late. Big news, huh?

SHOOTER   You a reporter?

DEEDEE [*pleased with the question*]   Oh no. [*stands up, stretches*] Gotten so stiff sitting there. [*walks over*] Don't you know what they put in those things?

SHOOTER   The tacos?

DEEDEE   Dog food.

SHOOTER [*laughing*]   Have to eat 'em anyway. Good business. I keep stopping in over there, they keep running the ad. Gonna kill me.

DEEDEE   No kidding. We take our . . . [*quickly*] My garbage cans are right next to theirs and whatta theirs got in em all the time? Dog food cans.

SHOOTER [*he smiles*]   Maybe they have a dog.

ALBERTA   It could be someone else in the building.

SHOOTER   See?

DEEDEE   She didn't mean they have a dog. She meant some old person in the building's eatin' dog food. It happens. A lot around here.

SHOOTER [*to* ALBERTA]   You her Mom?

ALBERTA   No.

DEEDEE   We just met in here. She's Alberta Johnson. I'm Deedee Johnson.

ALBERTA   Shooter is an unusual name.

SHOOTER [*nodding toward the pool hall next door*]   I play some pool.

DEEDEE [*pointing to the cue case*]   What's that?

SHOOTER   My cue.

DEEDEE   You any good?

SHOOTER   At what?

DEEDEE   At pool, dummy.

SHOOTER [*putting his clothes in the washer*]   I do O.K.

DEEDEE   You must do better than O.K. or else why would you have your own cue?

SHOOTER   Willie says, Willie's the guy who owns the place, Willie says pool cues are like women. You gotta have your own and you gotta treat her right.

DEEDEE [*seeing a piece of clothing he's dropped in*]   Did you mean to put that in here?

SHOOTER [*pulling it back out*]   This?

DEEDEE   Your whites will come out green.

SHOOTER [*dropping it back in the washer*]   Uh-uh. It's nylon.

ALBERTA   Your work sounds very interesting.

SHOOTER   Yes, it does.

DEEDEE   What's your real name?

SHOOTER   G.W.

DEEDEE   That's not a real name.

SHOOTER   I don't like my real name.

DEEDEE   Come on . . .

SHOOTER [*disgusted*]   It's Gary Wayne. Now do I look like Gary Wayne to you?

DEEDEE [*laughs*]   No.

SHOOTER   Mom's from Indiana.

ALBERTA   From Gary or Fort Wayne?

DEEDEE   Alberta used to be a teacher.

SHOOTER   It coulda been worse. She coulda named me Clarksville. [DEEDEE *laughs.*]

SHOOTER   Hey! Now why don't the two of you come over and join us for a beer.

ALBERTA   No thank you.

SHOOTER [*pouring in the soap*]   It's just Willie and me this time of night.

ALBERTA   No.

DEEDEE [*with a knowing look at* ALBERTA]   And watch you play pool?

SHOOTER   Actually, what we were planning to do tonight was whip us up a big devil's food cake and pour it in one of the pool tables to bake. Turn up the heat real high . . . watch it rise and then pour on the creamy fudge icing with lots of nuts.

DEEDEE   *You're* nuts.

SHOOTER   Get real sick if we have to eat it all ourselves.

DEEDEE   I've never seen anybody play pool.

SHOOTER   The key to pool's a . . . [*directly seductive now*] real smooth stroke . . . the feel of that stick in your hand . . .

DEEDEE   Feels good?

SHOOTER   You come on over, I'll show you just how it's done.

DEEDEE   Pool.

SHOOTER   Sure. [*smiles, then turns sharply and walks back to* ALBERTA, *depositing an empty soap box in the trash can*]   Willie always keeps hot water. You could have a nice cup of tea.

ALBERTA [*a pointed look at* DEEDEE] No.

DEEDEE Our wash is almost done. We have to . . .

SHOOTER We'll be there quite a while. Gets lonesome this late, you know.

DEEDEE We know. [*and suddenly, everybody feels quite uncomfortable*]

SHOOTER [*to* ALBERTA] It was nice meeting you. Hope I didn't interrupt your reading or anything.

DEEDEE She used to be a teacher.

SHOOTER That's what you said. [*walking toward the door*] Right next door, now. Can't miss it. [*to* DEEDEE] Give you a piece of that fudge cake.

DEEDEE Yeah, I'll bet you would.

SHOOTER Big piece. [*closing the door*]

> ALBERTA *watches* DEEDEE *watch to see which direction* SHOOTER *takes*

DEEDEE [*after a moment*] I thought we'd had it there for a minute, didn't you? [*visibly cheered*] Coulda been a murderer, or a robber or a rapist, just as easy! [*increasingly excited*] We coulda been hostages by now!

ALBERTA To have hostages you have to commit a hijacking. You do not hijack a laundromat.

DEEDEE Depends how bad you need clean clothes.

ALBERTA I didn't like the things he said to you.

DEEDEE He was just playin'.

ALBERTA He was not playing.

DEEDEE Well, what does it hurt? Just words.

ALBERTA Not those words.

DEEDEE You don't miss a thing, do you?

ALBERTA I'm not deaf.

DEEDEE Just prejudiced.

ALBERTA That's not true.

DEEDEE If that was a white DJ comin' in here, you'd still be talkin' to him, I bet. Seein' if he knows your "old" favorites.

ALBERTA If you don't want to know what I think, you can stop talking to me.

DEEDEE What you think is what's wrong with the world. People don't trust each other just because they're some other color from them.

ALBERTA And who was it that said he could be a murderer? That was you, Deedee. Would you have said that if he'd been white?

DEEDEE It just makes you sick, doesn't it. The thought of me and Shooter over there after you go home.

ALBERTA It's not my business.

DEEDEE That's for sure.

> ALBERTA *goes back to reading her magazine.* DEEDEE *wanders around.*

DEEDEE   You don't listen to him on the radio, but I do. And you know what he says after "rock your daddy to dreams of de-light?" He says, "And Mama, I'm comin' home." Now, if he has a "Mama" to go home to, what's he doing washing his own clothes? So he don't have a "Mama," and that means lonely. And he's loaded, too. So if he's got a wife, she's got a washer, so don't say maybe they don't have a washer. Lonely.

ALBERTA   All right. He's a nice young man who washes his own clothes and is "friendly" without regard to race, creed or national origin.

DEEDEE   I mean, we're both in here in the middle of the night and it don't mean we're on the make, does it?

ALBERTA   It's perfectly respectable.

DEEDEE   You always do this when Herb is out of town?

ALBERTA   No.

DEEDEE   You don't live in this neighborhood, do you?

ALBERTA   No.

DEEDEE   Know how I knew that? That garden. There ain't a garden for miles around here.

ALBERTA   You've been reading Sherlock Holmes.

DEEDEE   [*knows she's just been insulted*]   So why did you come here?

ALBERTA   [*knows she's made a mistake*]   I came for the same reason you did. To do my wash.

DEEDEE   In the middle of the night! Hah! It's a big mystery, isn't it, and you don't want to tell me. Is some man meetin' you here? Yeah, and you can't have your meetin' out where you live cause your friends might see you and give the word to ol' Herb when he gets back.

ALBERTA   No. [*pauses*] I'm sorry I said what I did. Go on over to the pool hall. I'll put your clothes in the dryer. They're almost finished.

DEEDEE   [*easily thrown off the track*]   And let him think I'm all hot for him? No sir. Besides, Joe might come home.

ALBERTA   That's right.

DEEDEE   Might just serve him right, though. Come in and see me drinkin' beer and eatin' fudge cake with Willie and Shooter. Joe hates black people. He says even when they're dancin' or playin' ball, they're thinking about killin'. Yeah, that would teach him to run out on me. A little dose of his own medicine. Watch him gag on it.

ALBERTA   He's run out on you?

DEEDEE   I told you he was working the double shift.

ALBERTA   I know you did.

DEEDEE   And you don't believe me. You think he just didn't come home, is that it? You think I was over there waitin' and waitin' in in my new nightgown and when the late show went off I turned on the radio and ate a whole pint of chocolate ice cream, and when the radio went off I couldn't stand it any more so I grabbed up all these clothes, dirty or not, and got outta there so he wouldn't come in and find me crying . . . Well . . . [*firmly*] I wasn't cryin'.

ALBERTA   [*after a considerable pause*]   I haven't cried in forty years.

DEEDEE   Just happy I guess.

ALBERTA   I had an aunt, Dora, who had a rabbit, Puffer, who died. I cried then. I cried for weeks.

DEEDEE   And it wasn't even your rabbit.

ALBERTA   I loved Aunt Dora. And she loved that rabbit. She had a high chair for it—at the table. I'd go visit and she'd tell me stories—what Puffer'd been up to that day—looking through seed catalogues, fingerpainting, telling her stories—Goldilocks and the Three Hares, Sleeping Bunny, The Rabbit Who Ate New York. Then we'd go outside and drink lemonade while Puffer ate lettuce and she'd say, "Now, what has my Bertie been up to today." She grew lettuce just for him. A whole back yard of it.

DEEDEE   [*glad to be on some other subject*]   You're kidding.

ALBERTA   I helped her bury him. Tears were streaming down my face. "Bertie," she said, "tears will not bring Puffer back to us. He didn't mean to go and leave us all alone and he'd feel bad if he knew he made us so miserable." But in the next few weeks, Aunt Dora got quieter and quieter till finally she wasn't talking at all and Mother put her in a nursing home.

DEEDEE   Where she died.

ALBERTA   Yes.

DEEDEE   Little cracked, huh?

ALBERTA   I suppose so, yes.

DEEDEE   Well, you better start cryin', Alberta, or you'll go just like she did. [*a bit too casual*] Hey! Our wash is done. [ALBERTA *doesn't seem to hear her.*] Look, I'll do it. You go sit.

ALBERTA   [*worried*]   No, I . . .

DEEDEE   Let me, really. I know this part. Mom says you can't blow this part, so I do it. She still checks, though, finds some reason to go downstairs and checks the heat I set. I don't mind, really. Can't be too careful.

> DEEDEE *begins to unload the washers and carry the clothes to the dryers.* ALBERTA *walks over to the bulletin board, takes down her notice, reads it, then decides to put it back up again.*

DEEDEE   [*setting the heat*]   Regular for you guys, warm for permos and undies. Now, Herb's shirts and shorts get hot. Pants and socks get . . .

ALBERTA   [*goes to the window*]   Warm.

DEEDEE   What's Herb got left to wear anyhow?

ALBERTA   His gray suit.

DEEDEE   [*laughs at how positive* ALBERTA *is about this*]   What color tie?

ALBERTA   Red with a silver stripe through it.

DEEDEE   [*still merry*]   Shirt?

ALBERTA   White.

DEEDEE   Shoes?

ALBERTA   [*quiet astonishment*]   I don't know.

DEEDEE   Whew! I thought for a minute you were seein' him out the window, telling me all that stuff he had on. Alberta . . .

ALBERTA [*worried, turns to face her*]   Yes?

DEEDEE   You got any dimes?

ALBERTA [*relieved*]   Sure. [*Walks to her purse, starts to check the dryer settings as she goes by them, then changes her mind and doesn't look.* DEEDEE *notices.*] How many do we need?

DEEDEE   Two each, I guess. 4 dryers makes 8. [*as* ALBERTA *is getting them out of her wallet*]   I don't know what I'd have done if you hadn't been here.

ALBERTA   You'd have done fine. Don't forget Sleepy back there.

DEEDEE   Men need so much sleep, don't they? Dad was always asleep. Joe can fall asleep right in the middle of what I'm saying. I know he's gotta have his rest, but it makes me feel like I'm the TV and he just changed channels.

ALBERTA   He could try to stay awake.

DEEDEE   Sometimes he does, try, you know. And sometimes I just go on talking. I mean, if he's already asleep, there's no reason not to.

ALBERTA   Sure. People put tape recorders under their pillows to learn foreign languages.

DEEDEE [*doesn't understand*]   They do?

ALBERTA   They do. So he hears you anyway.

DEEDEE   And he doesn't interrupt me or want something to eat.

ALBERTA   Exactly.

DEEDEE   I wish Mom were more like you.

ALBERTA   Stuck up?

DEEDEE   Smart. Nice to talk to.

ALBERTA   Thank you, but . . .

DEEDEE   No, really. You've been to Mexico and you've got a good man.

ALBERTA   I'm not much fun though.

DEEDEE   Mom's just got me and giant size Cheer. And she don't say two words while I'm there. Ever. I don't blame her, I guess.

ALBERTA   Well . . . [*feels a response is called for, but can't figure one out*]

DEEDEE   Yeah.

ALBERTA   But you're young and pretty. You have a wonderful sense of humor.

DEEDEE   Uh-huh.

ALBERTA   And you'll have those children some day.

DEEDEE   Yeah, I know. [*gloomily*] I have my whole life in front of me.

ALBERTA   You could get a job.

DEEDEE   Oh, I got one. This company in New Jersey, they send me envelopes and letters and lists of names and I write on the names and addresses and Dear Mr. Wilson or whatever at the top of the letter. I do have nice handwriting. I had to send them a sample first.

ALBERTA   I see.

DEEDEE   I get so bored doing it. Sometimes I want to take a fat orange crayon and scribble [*making letters in the air*] EAT BEANS, FATSO, and then draw funny faces all over the letter.

ALBERTA   I'm sure the extra money comes in handy.

DEEDEE   Well, Joe don't know I do it. I hide all the stuff before he comes home. And I keep the money at Mom's. She borrows from it sometimes. She says that makes us even for the water for the washing machine. See, I can't spend it or Joe will know I got it.

ALBERTA   He doesn't want you to work?

DEEDEE [*imitating Joe's voice*]   I'm the head of his house.

ALBERTA   He expects you to sit around all day?

DEEDEE   I guess. [*with good-humored rage*] Oh, I can wash the floor if I want.

ALBERTA   You should tell him how you feel.

DEEDEE   He'd leave me.

ALBERTA   Maybe.

DEEDEE [*getting what she thinks is* ALBERTA's *message*]   So what? Right?

ALBERTA   I just meant, if you give him the chance to understand . . .

DEEDEE   But what would I say?

ALBERTA   You'd figure something out, I'm sure.

DEEDEE   But I can't ever talk to him and just say one thing, you know? Like I keep, well, all this other stuff comes out. See, I'll start out saying we're having tuna casserole for dinner and end up telling him about this girl at the grocery that told me how to cook minute steaks. But by then, he's walked into the bathroom and shut the door, all because I got off the track only I don't know how it happened.

ALBERTA   Then you'll just have to . . .

DEEDEE   Then I'll just have to say, "Joe, I want to get a real job cause I can't just sit around here all day cause I gotta have something to think about besides when are you coming home and how long's it gonna be before you don't come home at all because you're lying to me all the time and I know it. Even tonight, you're not out bowling or working that double shift and I know it and I'm sick of pretending that I don't know it because I do know it!

ALBERTA [*cautioning her against suspicion*]   Now . . .

DEEDEE   No, really. I called the bowling alley and asked for him and the bartender said, "This Patsy? He's on his way, honey!" I hope he falls in the sewer.

ALBERTA   Deedee . . .

DEEDEE   I hope he gets his shirt caught in his zipper. I hope he wore socks with holes in 'em. I hope his baseball cap falls in the toilet. I hope she kills him. [*knocking over one of the carts*]

ALBERTA   Deedee!

DEEDEE   I do. Last night, I thought I'd surprise him and maybe we'd bowl a few . . . well, I was gettin' my shoes and I saw them down at lane 12, laughin' an all. He had one of his hands rubbin' her hair and the other one rubbin' his bowling ball. Boy did I get outta there quick. I've seen her there before. She teaches at the Weight Control upstairs, so she's probably not very strong but maybe she could poison him or something. She wears those pink leotards and I hate him.

ALBERTA   I'm sure you don't really . . .

DEEDEE   I do. He's mean and stupid. I thought he'd get over it, but he didn't. Mean and stupid. And I'm not all that smart, so if I know he's dumb, he must really be dumb. I used to think he just acted mean and stupid. Now I know he really *is* . . .

ALBERTA [*finishing her sentence for her*]   . . . mean and stupid.

DEEDEE   Why am I tellin' you this? You don't know nuthin about bein' dumped.

ALBERTA   At least you have some money saved.

DEEDEE   For what?

ALBERTA   And your mother would let you stay with her till you got your own place.

DEEDEE   She's the *last* person I'm tellin'.

ALBERTA   I'll bet you'd like being a telephone operator.

DEEDEE   But how's he gonna eat? The only time he ever even fried an egg, he flipped it over and it landed in the sink. It was the last egg, so he grabbed it up and ate it in one bite. [*indicating, however strangely, her perception of his need for her*]

ALBERTA   One bite?

DEEDEE [*ready to cry*]   Where is he?

ALBERTA   He stuffed a whole egg in his mouth?

DEEDEE   You're worse than Mom. [*angrily*] He's gonna be a famous race car driver someday and I want to be there.

ALBERTA   To have him pour beer all over you.

DEEDEE [*hostile*]   Yes. To have him pour beer all over me.

> ALBERTA *knows she has said too much. She checks the clothes in one of her dryers.*

ALBERTA   He could've come in without turning on the lights. If you want to go check, I'll watch your things here.

DEEDEE   You want to get rid of me, don't you? You want to be here all by yourself. Cause you want to take out all those shirts and shorts and fold them up real nice and take them home and put them away cause Herb, good ol' Herb, old herb-garden Herb, he ain't up in Akron at all. Herb is dead. Isn't he? You want me to run off and leave my husband so I'll be all alone too. Like you. And Mom after Dad left. And like your crazy old aunt after her stupid rabbit died. That's what you want, A. Johnson. And you didn't want nobody botherin' you, did you? So you came down to a crummy part of town in the middle of the night so none of your friends would find out Herb didn't even leave you enough money to get your washer fixed. Ain't that right.

ALBERTA [*calmly*]   What do I have to do to get you to leave me alone.

DEEDEE [*proud*]   I was right.

ALBERTA   You were right.

DEEDEE [*feels bad now*]   I'm so stupid.

ALBERTA   You . . .

DEEDEE   What? Tell me. Say something horrible.

ALBERTA [*slowly but now mean*]   You just don't know when to shut up.

DEEDEE   Worse than that. I don't know how.

ALBERTA   But you are not dumb, child. And don't let anybody tell you you are, O.K.? [*takes off her glasses and rubs her eyes*]

DEEDEE   I'm sorry, Mrs. Johnson. I really am sorry. You've probably been plannin' this night for a long time. Washin' his things up. And I barged in and spoiled it all.

ALBERTA   I've been avoiding it for a long time.

> DEEDEE *feels terrible. She wants to ask questions, but is trying very hard, for once, to control herself.*

ALBERTA   Herb died last winter, the day before his birthday.

DEEDEE   When you got him the rakes. [*pointing to the bulletin board*]

ALBERTA   He was being nosy, like I told you before, in the kitchen. I was making his cake. So I asked him to take out the garbage.

DEEDEE   How . . .

ALBERTA   I didn't miss him til I put the cake in the oven. Guess I thought he was checking his seed beds in the garage. [*pause*] I yelled out, "Herb, do you want butter cream or chocolate?" and then I saw him. Lying in the alley, covered in my cabbage soup. Paper towels everywhere. I ran out. A cat was watching.

DEEDEE   Did you . . .

ALBERTA   First, I threw a coffee can at that cat. Then I picked up his head in my hand and held it while I cleaned up as much of the stuff as I could. A tuna can, coffee grounds, egg shells, a bologna package . . .

DEEDEE [*carefully*]   You knew he was dead, not just knocked out?

ALBERTA   Yes.

DEEDEE   And you didn't cry?

ALBERTA   No.

DEEDEE   I'm sorry.

ALBERTA   I don't want you to be alone, that's not what I meant before.

DEEDEE   Looks like I'm alone anyway.

ALBERTA   That's what I meant.

DEEDEE   Sometimes I bring in a little stand-up mirror to the coffee table while I'm watchin TV. It's my face over there when I look, but it's a face just the same.

ALBERTA   Being alone isn't so awful. I mean, it's awful, but it's not that awful. There are hard things. [*the dryers stop*]

DEEDEE [*watches* ALBERTA *take a load of clothes from the dryer, holding them up to smell them*]   I'd probably eat pork and beans for weeks.

ALBERTA [*her back to* DEEDEE]   I found our beachball when I cleaned out the basement. I can't let the air out of it. [*turning around to face her now*] It's . . . his breath in there.

> ALBERTA *sees that* DEEDEE *is upset. She takes the rest of her clothes out of the dryer.*

ALBERTA   Get your clothes out. They'll wrinkle. [*starting to fold the clothes*]   That's amazing about the shoes.

DEEDEE   The shoes?

ALBERTA   Remember before, I was telling you what Herb was wearing?

DEEDEE   Gray suit, red tie . . . [*slowing down, understanding*] with a silver stripe . . .

ALBERTA   I hang onto this shirt he died in, and I don't even know if he's got shoes on in his coffin.

DEEDEE   [*trying to help*]   If he's flying around Heaven, he don't need 'em.

ALBERTA   I hope they speak English in Heaven. Herb never was much good at languages.

DEEDEE   You bought him all black socks.

ALBERTA   It was his idea. He thought it would be easier to match them up if they were all the same color.

DEEDEE   Is it?

ALBERTA   No. Now I have to match by length. Just because they're all black doesn't mean they all shrink the same. I guess I don't really have to match them now, though, do I? [*but she continues to pair the socks*]

DEEDEE   I'd like to lose all Joe's white ones.

> *She holds them up over the trash can, but then decides it's not such a good idea.*

ALBERTA   [*going back for a sock that must still be in the dryer*]   Your lights are on. [*looking toward the window*]

DEEDEE   You sure?

ALBERTA   Come see. [DEEDEE *walks over to the window*]

DEEDEE   You're right.

ALBERTA   Yes.

DEEDEE   So what do I do now?

ALBERTA   I don't know.

> *They look at each other quietly, then* DEEDEE *breaks the gaze to see that* SHOOTER's *washer has stopped.*

DEEDEE   [*walking over to the washer*]   Shooter's clothes are done.

ALBERTA   It won't hurt them to rest a while in there.

DEEDEE   [*picking up the dimes*]   Well, look at this. He left dimes on the washer.

ALBERTA   Very clever.

DEEDEE   Look. What will it hurt to dry his clothes for him?

ALBERTA   [*doesn't want to get into this again*]   Not a thing.

DEEDEE   You're going to tell me I'm making a big mistake taking his clothes back to him.

ALBERTA   You seem to know it already.

DEEDEE   So, should I rush right home? Ask Joe did he have a good time bowling a few games after his double shift? Listen to him brag about his score? His score he didn't make in the games he didn't bowl after the double shift he didn't work?

ALBERTA   It will be hard, but it's not more trouble. I think if you go see Shooter, you'll just be getting even with Joe for hurting you.

DEEDEE   And what's wrong with that?

ALBERTA   What's wrong with that is you'll forget how mad you are.
You don't have to put up with what he's doing. You can if you want
to, if you think you can't make it without him, but you don't have
to.

DEEDEE   But what should I say? Joe, if you don't stop going out on
me, I'm never speaking to you again? That's exactly what he wants.

ALBERTA   I don't know what you should say. But there is something
you must remember.

DEEDEE   What is it?

ALBERTA   Your own face in a mirror is better company than a man
who would eat a whole fried egg in one bite. [DEEDEE *laughs*] But
it won't be easy.

DEEDEE [*cautiously*]   Are you going to wash that other shirt ever?

ALBERTA   The cabbage soup shirt? No, I don't think so.

DEEDEE   Yeah.

ALBERTA   Maybe, in a few months or next year sometime, I'll be able
to give these away. They're nice things.

DEEDEE   People do need them. Hey! [*leaving her laundry and going
to the bulletin board.* ALBERTA *is loading up her basket.*] I told you
there ain't a garden for miles around here. [*takes* ALBERTA's *notice
down and walks back to the folding table*] You better hang onto
these hoes. You might get some carrots spring up all by themselves.

ALBERTA   I might at that. [*puts the note in her purse and is ready to
go*] Green beans growing out of sheer habit.

DEEDEE   Yeah.

ALBERTA [*looking around the room*]   Well, that's everything. I'll just
get my soap and . . .

DEEDEE [*hesitantly*]   Mrs. Johnson?

ALBERTA   Alberta.

DEEDEE   Alberta?

ALBERTA   Yes.

DEEDEE   I'm really lonely.

ALBERTA   I know.

DEEDEE   How can you stand it?

ALBERTA   I can't. [*pause*] But I have to, just the same.

DEEDEE   How do I . . . [*quickly*] How do you do that?

ALBERTA   I don't know. You call me if you think of something.

ALBERTA *gives her a small kiss on the forehead.*

DEEDEE [*asking for it*]   I don't have your number.

ALBERTA [*backing away to get her laundry*]   I really wanted to be
alone tonight.

DEEDEE   I know.

ALBERTA   I'm glad you talked me out of it.

DEEDEE   Boy, you can count on me for that. Hey! Don't go yet! I
owe you some money.

ALBERTA [*fondly*]   No, everybody deserves a free load now and then.

DEEDEE   Thank you.

ALBERTA　Now, I suggest you go wake up Sleepy back there and see
　　if there's something he needs to talk about. [*opening the door*]
DEEDEE　Tell you the truth, I'm ready for a little peace and quiet.
ALBERTA　Good night. [*leaves*]
DEEDEE [*going back to her clothes*]　Peace and quiet. [*picking up her
　　Dr. Pepper*] Too bad it don't come in cans.

　　　　And DEEDEE *continues to fold her laundry as the lights go
　　　　down and we have*

THE END

1978

WRITING
ABOUT LITERATURE

INTRODUCTION

Writing about literature ought to be easier than writing about anything else. When you write about painting, for example, you have to translate shapes and colors and textures into words. When you write about music, you have to translate various aspects and combinations of sounds into words. When you write about that complex, mysterious, fleeting thing called "reality" or "life," you have an even more difficult task. Worst of all, perhaps, is trying to put into words all that is going on at any given moment inside your particular and unique self. So you ought to be relieved to know that you are going to write—that is, use words—about literature—again, words. How much easier it is going to be than writing about how you spent your summer vacation or what you think and feel about Van Gogh's sunflowers, capital punishment, or your parents. Or it should be.

But writing about literature will not be easy if you haven't learned to *read* literature, for in order to write about anything you have to know that something rather well. Helping you to learn to read literature is what the rest of this book is about; this chapter is about the writing. (But, as you will see, you cannot fully separate the writing from the reading.)

Another thing keeps writing about literature from being easy: writing itself is not easy. Writing well requires a variety of language skills —a good working vocabulary, for example—and a sense of ordering your ideas, of how to link one idea or statement to another, of what to put in and what to leave out. Worse, writing is not a finite or definite skill or art; you never really "know how to write," you just learn how to write a little better about a little more. It's like maturity: you're always getting there but never quite make it. You no doubt write better than you did in the first grade or in the fifth grade, and perhaps even better than you did last year. If you work at it in this course, you will be able to write a lot better next year. But even then, you will still be able to improve your writing; and even then it may not come easily. These very words you are reading have been written and revised several times, even though your editors have had a good many years in which to practice.

REPRESENTING THE LITERARY TEXT

Copying

If writing about literature is using words about words, what words should you use? Since most writers work very hard to get each word exactly right and in exactly the right order, there are no better words to use in discussing what the literature is about than those of the literary work itself. Faced with writing about a poem, then, you could just write the poem over again, word for word:

> Once upon a midnight dreary, while I pondered weak and weary,
> Over many a quaint and curious volume of forgotten lore. . . .

and so on until the end. Copying texts was useful in medieval monasteries, but nowadays, what with printing and Xerox, it would not seem to be very useful. Besides, if you try to copy a text, you will probably find that spelling or punctuation errors, reversed word order, missing or added or just different words seem mysteriously to appear. Still, it's a good exercise for teaching yourself accuracy and attention to detail, and you will probably discover things about the text you are copying that you would be unlikely to notice otherwise. Early in a literature course, particularly, copying can serve as a useful step in the direction of learning how to read and write about literature; later, being able to copy a passage accurately will help when you want to quote a passage to illustrate or prove a point you are making. But copying is not, in itself, writing *about* literature.

Reading aloud, a variation of copying, may be a more original and interpretive exercise than copying itself, since by tone, emphasis, and pace you are clarifying the text or indicating the way you understand the text. But it, too, is not *writing* about literature, and you will not long be satisfied with merely repeating someone else's words. You will have perceptions, responses, and ideas that you will want to express for yourself about what you are reading. And having something to say, and wanting to say or write it, is the first and most significant step in learning to write about literature.

Paraphrase

If you look away from the text for a while and then write the same material but in your own words, you are writing a **paraphrase.**

For example, let's try to paraphrase the first sentence of Jane Austen's *Pride and Prejudice*: "It is a truth universally acknowledged that a single man in possession of a good fortune, must be in want of a wife." We can start by making "It is a truth" a little less formal: *It's true that*, perhaps. Now "universally acknowledged": *everybody acknowledges*, or, a little more loosely, *everybody agrees*. Now we may choose to drop the whole first clause and begin, *Everybody agrees that* "a single man"—*a bachelor*—" in possession of a good fortune"—*rich* —"must be in want of a wife"—*wants a wife*. Or is it *needs a wife*? Okay, *Everybody agrees that a rich bachelor needs* (or *wants*) *a wife*. You can see that the process of paraphrase is something like that of translation. We are translating Austen's nineteenth-century formal English prose into twentieth-century informal American prose.

But what good is that? First of all, it enables us to test whether we really understand what we are reading. Second, certain elements of the text become clearer: we may see now that Austen's sentence is meant to be ironic or humorous, and we now understand the two possible meanings of "in want of." Third, we can check our paraphrase with those of others, our classmates' versions, for example, to compare our understanding of the passage with theirs. Finally, we have learned how dependent literature is upon words. A paraphrase, no matter how precise, can render only an approximate equivalent of the meaning of a text—how *good* Austen's sentence is, how *flat* our paraphrase.

Paraphrasing, like copying, is not in itself an entirely satisfactory way of writing about literature, but, like copying, it can be a useful tool when you write about literature in other ways. In trying to explain or clarify a literary text for someone, to illustrate a point you are making about that text, or to remind your readers of or to acquaint them with a text or passage you will at times want to paraphrase. Unlike an exact copy, a paraphrase, being in your own words, adds something of yours to the text or passage—your emphasis, your perspective, your understanding.

Summary

Paraphrase follows faithfully the outlines of the text. But if you stand back far enough from the text so as not to see its specific words or smaller details and put down briefly in your own words what you believe the work is about, you will have a **summary.** How briefly? Well, you could summarize the 108 lines of Poe's *The Raven* in about 180 words or so, like this, for example:

> The speaker of Poe's *The Raven* is sitting in his room late at night reading in order to forget the death of his beloved Lenore. There's a tap at the door; after some hesitation he opens it and calls Lenore's name, but there is only an echo. When he goes back into his room he hears the rapping again, this time at his window, and when he opens it a raven enters. He asks the raven its name, and it answers very clearly, "Nevermore." When the speaker says that the bird, like his friends, will leave, the raven again says, "Nevermore." As the speaker's thoughts run back to Lenore, he realizes the aptness of the raven's word: she shall sit there nevermore. But, he says, sooner or later he will forget her and the grief will lessen. "Nevermore," the raven says again, too aptly. Now the speaker wants the bird to leave, but "Nevermore," the raven says once again. At the end, the speaker knows he'll never escape the raven or his dark message.

You could be very brief, summarizing *Hamlet*, for example, in a single sentence: "A young man, seeking to avenge the murder of his father by his uncle, kills his uncle, but he himself and others die in the process." Has *too* much been left out? What do you feel it essential to add? Let's try again: "In Denmark, many centuries ago, a young prince avenged the murder of his father, the king, by his uncle, who had usurped the throne, but the prince himself was killed as were others, and a well-led foreign army had no trouble successfully invading the decayed and troubled state." A classmate may have written this summary: "From the ghost of his murdered father a young prince learns that his uncle, who has married the prince's mother, much to the young man's shame and disgust, is the father's murderer, and he plots revenge, feigning madness, acting erratically—even to insulting the woman he loves—and, though gaining his revenge, causes the suicide of his beloved and the deaths of others and, finally, of himself."

The last two, though accurate enough, sound like two different plays, don't they? To summarize means to select and emphasize and so to interpret: that is, not to replicate the text in miniature, as a reduced photograph might replicate the original, but while reducing it to change the angle of vision and even the filter, to represent the essentials as the reader or summarizer sees them. When you write a summary you should try to be as objective as possible; nevertheless, your summary will reflect not only the literary text but also your own understanding and attitudes. There's nothing wrong with your fingerprints or "mindprints" appearing on the summary, so long as you recognize that in summarizing you are doing more than copying, paraphrasing, or merely reflecting the literary text. You might learn something about both literature and yourself by comparing your summaries of, say, three or four poems, a couple of short stories, or a play with summaries of the same works by several of your classmates. Try to measure the refraction of the text as it passes through the lens of each student's mind. You might then write a composite summary that would include all that any one reader felt important. You might try the same exercise again on different texts. Has the practice made you more careful? More inclusive? Is there a greater degree of uniformity in your summaries?

A good summary can be a form of literary criticism, and learning—largely by practice—how to summarize is an essential part of writing about literature; though you will seldom be called upon merely to summarize a work, a good deal of writing about literature requires that at some point or other you do summarize—a whole work, a particular incident or aspect, a stanza, chapter, or scene. But beware: a summary is not a do-it-yourself critical-essay-kit. A mere summary, no matter how accurate, will seldom satisfy the demand for a critical essay. Furthermore, summary is not, in itself, the answer to any question you may be asked about a text nor the evidence and conclusion for any topic you may be asked to write about.

REPLYING TO THE TEXT

Imitation and Parody

While paraphrase is something like translation—a faithful following of the original text but in different words—and summary is the faithful reduction of the matter, there is another kind of writing about literature that faithfully follows the manner or matter or both of a literary text, but that does so for different ends. It's called **imitation.**

Art students learn to paint by copying the Old Masters, and imitation, especially the variety of imitation that used to be called "writing from models," was for many generations the way students were taught to write. Many poets, novelists, and playwrights have learned to write by imitating literary works. Indeed, many serious works are, in one way or another, imitations: *The Aeneid,* for example, may be said to be an imitation of *The Odyssey,* and, in a very different way, so might James Joyce's *Ulysses.* You too may be able to learn a good deal about writing—and reading—by trying your hand at an imitation.

Some imitations, such as *The Aeneid,* may be the sincerest form of flattery, but not all are entirely flattering. Alexander Pope no doubt meant to pay tribute to John Donne's *Satires* by writing his imitation of them. What he says he is doing, however, is "versifying" them; since Donne's satires are already in verse, this has the effect of saying you are going to write a comic version of *Gilligan's Island.* Pope was not poking fun, good-natured or not, at Donne or his poetry; he was merely "regularizing" Donne's meter and syntax, converting or "translating" the works into the kind of verse admired in Pope's own day.

Sometimes you can poke fun at a work by imitating it—but at the same time exaggerating its style or prominent characteristics, or placing it in an inappropriate context; that kind of imitation, a kind that is still popular, is called a **parody.** T. S. Eliot's *The Love Song of J. Alfred Prufrock* begins,

> Let us go then, you and I,
> When the evening is spread out against the sky
> Like a patient etherized upon a table; . . .

John Abbott Clark's parody of *Prufrock* keeps the same form and some of the same words; it begins,

> Let us go then, you and I,
> When Dartmouth is spread out against the sky
> Like a student cracked-up on a ski run . . .

Eliot's unheroic protagonist, hesitating to ask an "overwhelming question," says,

> I should have been a pair of ragged claws
> Scuttling across the floors of silent seas. . . .

In Clark's parody the passage appears as

> I should have been a pair of shoulder pads
> Scatting across the gridiron, beating Yale. . . .

The title of the parody indicates that the target of the parody is not only T. S. Eliot's poem but also a famous novelist's infamous nostalgia for youth, especially his college days; Clark's poem is called *The Love Song of F. Scott Fitzgerald.*

But how would *you* go about writing an imitation? You first analyze the original—that is, break it down into its characteristics or qualities —and decide just what you want to preserve in your version. The list of qualities and the model might be much the same for a serious imitation and for a parody, only in a parody you can exaggerate a little—or a lot—just as a cartoonist selects Nixon's nose or Carter's teeth as identifying qualities and exaggerates them. To parody Poe's *The Raven*, we may decide to stick closely to Poe's rhythms, his use of repetitive mood words or of several words that mean almost the same thing, and his frequent use of alliteration (words that begin with the same sound). We might want to exaggerate the characteristic stylistic devices as C. L. Edson does in his parody; it begins,

> Once upon a midnight dreary, eerie, scary,
> I was wary, I was weary, full of worry, thinking of my lost Lenore,
> Of my cheery, airy, faerie, fierie Dearie—(Nothing more).

We may choose another kind of parody, keeping the form as close as possible to the original but applying it to a ludicrously unsuitable subject, as Pope does in his mock epic *The Rape of the Lock*, where he uses all the grand epic machinery in a poem about cutting off a lock of a lady's hair. In writing such a parody of *The Raven*, we will keep the rhythm closer to Poe's and the subject matter less close. How about this?

> Once upon a midday murky, crunching on a Christmas turkey,
> And guzzling giant Jereboams of gin . . .

And maybe we could use the "Nevermore" refrain as if it were an antacid commercial.

You will have noticed that in order to write a good imitation or parody you must read and re-read the original very carefully, examine it, and identify just those elements and qualities that go to make it up and be itself. Since you admire works you wish to imitate, such close study should be a pleasure. You may or may not greatly admire a work you wish to parody, but parody itself is fun to do and fun to read. In either case, you are having fun while gaining a deeper, more intimate knowledge of the nature and details of a work of literature. Moreover, such close attention to how a professional piece of writing is put together and how its parts function together to do what it does along with your effort to reproduce the effects in your own imitation or parody are sure to help you understand the process of writing and so help you improve your own ability to write about literature knowledgeably.

Re-creation and Reply

Sometimes a poem, story, or play will seem so partial, biased, or unrealistic that it will stimulate a response that is neither an imitation nor a parody but a retort. While Christopher Marlowe's "shepherd" in *The Passionate Shepherd to His Love* paints an idyllic scene of love in the country for his beloved and pleads, "Come live with me and be my love," Sir Walter Ralegh apparently feels obliged to reply in the name of the beloved "nymph": it won't always be spring, she says in *The Nymph's Reply to the Shepherd*; we won't always be young, and, besides, I can scarcely trust myself to someone who offers me such a phony view of reality.

Ralegh's nymph confronts the invitation and the words of Marlowe's shepherd directly and almost detail for detail. In fiction the reply is less likely to be so directly verbal a retort and is more likely to involve a shift in perspective. It may tell the same story as the original but from a different angle, may not only give a different view of the same events and people but also add details that the original focus ignored or could not perceive. In *Jane Eyre*, for example, Bertha Mason Rochester is the hero's bestial, mad wife, whom he has locked away upstairs and whose existence, when it comes to light, prevents our heroine, our Jane, from marrying her heart's desire; Bertha is, in effect, the villainess. In *The Wide Sargasso Sea*, Jean Rhys not only gives Bertha's side of Charlotte Brontë's story but tells us more details about Bertha's earlier life: poor Bertha was more sinned against than sinning, it turns out. How do you think Margaret Macomber would describe the macho world of the safari, and how did she get involved with Francis and that world in the first place?

We may respond to a work whose view seems partial or distorted by shifting the perspective in time as well as in space. Are Francis Weed's marital and other problems solved by his recognition, at the end of *The Country Husband*, that life in the suburbs can be, in its own way, as adventurous as more romantic kinds of existence? What will happen to him next spring? On his fortieth birthday? As he lies dying? What will the speaker of *My Papa's Waltz* be thinking about as he plays or dances with *his* son or daughter?

You may have noticed that while retorts can often be witty, they are also serious. Usually they say not merely, "That's not how the story went," but "That's not what life is really like," and the latter statement is what a great deal of literature seems to testify to—"It has been written that life is like this, but I say unto you. . . ." Though we must always read literature initially with the aim of understanding it and taking it at its highest value (rather than reducing it and quibbling), and though we must try to "hear" what it is saying and not impose our own notions of reality prematurely upon a work but if possible learn from it and broaden our own views, we must finally read it critically as well, asking, "Is this the way things *really* are?" or, more generously, "If I were standing over there, where the story, poem, play (author, character) is, would things really look that way?"

Works responding to other works need not be negative. Tom Stoppard's *Rosencrantz and Guildenstern Are Dead* views *Hamlet* through two of the play's minor characters (even incorporating pieces of the original play from time to time), not so as to diminish Shakespeare's great tragedy, but to add a humble dimension. And, by writing his play in a manner closer to that of Samuel Beckett's *Waiting for Godot* than Shakespeare's *Hamlet*, Stoppard reveals how universal, how adaptable to other worlds and times *Hamlet* is.

Perhaps the most familiar kind of literary re-creation or reply is the **adaptation,** especially that of fiction into film. (Among the stories in this anthology that have been made into feature-length films are *The Most Dangerous Game, The Short Happy Life of Francis Macomber, An Occurrence at Owl Creek Bridge, The Lady with the Dog,* and *The Rocking-Horse Winner.*) In adaptation, the rather contradictory demands of faithfulness to the original and appropriateness to the new medium can teach us a great deal both about the content and the medium of the original. It is unlikely you will have the opportunity to make a film based on a poem, play, or story in this course, but you can still try your hand at adapting a work or piece of a work to a new medium. You might want to turn *The Cask of Amontillado* into verse (probably as a dramatic monologue) or write a short story called *The Dumb Waiter* or a one-act play called *Young Goodman Brown.* It is quite likely that you will learn not only about the nature of the original work but also something of the nature of the medium in which you are trying to work.

EXPLAINING THE TEXT

Description

To give an account of the form of a work or passage rather than merely a brief version of its content or plot (and a plot summary, even of a poem, is usually what we mean by "summary") you may wish to write a **description.** We have given a summary of Poe's *The Raven* earlier, concentrating there, as summaries tend to do, on subject and plot. A description, on the other hand, may concentrate on the form of the stanzas, the lines, the rhyme scheme, perhaps like this:

> Poe's *The Raven* is a poem of 108 lines divided into eighteen 6-line stanzas. If in describing the rhyme scheme you were to look just at the ends of the lines, you would notice only one or two unusual features: not only is there only one rhyme sound per stanza, lines 2, 4, 5, and 6 rhyming, but that one rhyme sound is the same in all eighteen stanzas, so that there are 72 lines ending with the sound "ore"; in addition, the fourth and fifth lines of each stanza end with the identical word, and in six of the stanzas that word is "door" and in four others "Lenore." There is even more repetition: the last line of six of the first seven stanzas ends with the words "nothing more," and the last eleven

stanzas end with the word "Nevermore." The rhyming lines—other than the last, which is very short—in each stanza are fifteen syllables long, the unrhymed lines sixteen. The longer lines give the effect of shorter ones, however, and add still further to the frequency of repeated sounds, for the first half of each opening line rhymes with the second half of the line, and so do the halves of line three. There is still more: the first half of line 4 rhymes with the halves of line 3 (in the first stanza the rhymes are "dreary"/"weary" and "napping"/ "tapping"/"rapping"). So at least nine words in each eight-line stanza are involved in the regular rhyme scheme, and in many stanzas there are added instances of rhyme or repetition. As if this were not enough, all the half-line rhymes are rich feminine rhymes, where both the accented and the following unaccented syllables rhyme—"drēarӳ"/ "wēarӳ."

This is a detailed and complicated description of a complex and unusual pattern of rhymes. Though there are many other elements of the poem we could describe—images and symbols, for example—the unusual and dominant element in this poem is clearly the intricate and insistent pattern of rhyme and repetition. Moreover, this paragraph shows how you can describe at length, in depth, and with considerable complexity, certain aspects of a work without mentioning the content at all. You can describe a play in comparable terms—acts, scenes, settings, time lapses perhaps—and you might describe a novel in terms of chapters, books, summary narration, dramatized scenes. Frequently, however, descriptions of elements involve content, as in this description of the structure of a short story:

> *The Short Happy Life of Francis Macomber* is made up of two major hunting scenes and a scene at the camp. The story opens with the camp scene though the first hunting episode has actually occurred earlier and is told in the form of a "flashback," through the memory of Macomber. We are not always in Macomber's mind, however: the story moves freely in and out of the minds of the other two main characters—Mrs. Macomber and the hunting guide. And there are bits of exposition: who Macomber is, where he lives when he's not on safari, and so forth—told by an omniscient narrator.

In addition to describing the structure of a short story, you might also describe the diction (word-choice), the sentence structure, the amount of description of the characters or landscape, and so on.

Analysis

Like copying, paraphrase, and summary, a description of a work or passage rarely stands alone as a piece of writing about literature. It is, instead, a tool, a means of supporting a point or opinion. Even the descriptions we have given above border on **analysis**. To analyze is to break something down into its parts to discover what they are and, usually, how they function in or relate to the whole. The description of the rhyme scheme of *The Raven* tells you what that scheme or pattern is but says nothing about how it functions in the poem. If you were to add such an account to the description, then, you would have analyzed one aspect of the poem. In order to do so, however, you would first have to decide what, in a general way, the poem is about: what its *theme* is. If you defined the theme of *The Raven* as "inconsolable grief," you could then write an analytical paper suggesting how the rhyme scheme reinforces that theme. You might begin something like this:

Obsessive Rhyme in *The Raven*

We all know that gloomy poem with that gloomy bird, Edgar Allan Poe's *The Raven*. The time is midnight, the room is dark, the bird is black, and the poem is full of words like "dreary," "sad," "mystery," and "ghastly." We all know too it has a rather sing-song rhythm and repeated rhymes, but we do not often stop to think how the rhymes contribute to the mood or meaning. Before we do so here, perhaps it would be a good idea to describe in detail just what that rhyme scheme is.

—Then follow with the description of the rhyme scheme, and go on like this:

Of course the most obvious way in which the rhyme scheme reinforces the theme of inconsolable loss is through the emphatic repetition of "Nevermore." Since this refrain comes at the very end of each of the last stanzas it is even more powerful in its effect.

What is not so obvious as the effect of repeating "Nevermore" is the purpose of the over-all abundance and richness of rhyme. Some might say it is not abundant and rich but excessive and cloying. These harsh critics cynically add that in a way the rhymes and repetitions are appropriate to this poem because the whole poem is excessive and cloying: grief over loss, even intense grief, does, human experience tells us, pass away. This criticism is just, however, only if we have accurately defined the theme of the poem as "inconsolable sorrow." The very insistence of the rhyme and repetition, however, suggests we may need to adjust slightly our definition of that theme. Perhaps the poem is not about "inconsolable sorrow" in so neutral a way; maybe it would be better to say it is about obsessive grief. Then the insistent, pounding rhyme and repetition make sense (just as the closed-in dark chamber does). Obsessive repetition of words and sounds thus helps to create the meaning of the poem almost as much as the words themselves do.

Interpretation

Principles and Procedures

If you have been reading carefully, you may have noticed what looks like a catch: to turn description into analysis, you must relate what you are describing to the theme, the over-all effect and meaning of the work of literature. But how do you know what the theme is? If analysis relates the part to the whole, how can you know the "whole" before you have analyzed each part? But then, how can you analyze each part—relating it to the whole—if you don't know what that whole is?

Perhaps if you have been reading *very* carefully, you may have spotted a clue here and there, especially in the last paragraph of the short paper on *The Raven*. There the reader's initial sense of the theme of the poem was "inconsolable sorrow," an assumption good enough to permit an analysis of the rhyme scheme, showing how that element functioned in the poem and supported the theme or meaning of the whole. But that analysis, itself, modified the reader's initial perception of the theme, so that "obsessive grief" now seemed a better rendering. Further analysis—of rhyme scheme or other aspects of the poem—may generate further modifications or "fine tuning" of your understanding of the work.

From this example, several principles and procedures may emerge. **Interpretation,** or the expression of your conception of a literary work and its meaning, involves an initial general impression that is then supported and, often, modified by analysis of the particulars. It involves looking at the whole, the part, the whole, the part, the whole, the part in a series of approximations and adjustments. (Note, too, how you must keep your mind open for modifications or changes rather than forcing your analysis to confirm your first impressions.)

This procedure should in turn suggest something of the nature and even the form of the critical essay, or essay of interpretation. The essay should present the over-all theme and support that generalization with close analyses of the major elements of the text (or, in some essays, an analysis of one significant element)—showing how one or more of such elements as rhyme or speaker, plot or setting reinforce, define, or modify the theme of the poem, story, or play. Often the conclusion of such an essay will be a fuller, refined statement of the theme. If we were to continue the essay on *The Raven* beyond its last sentence—"Obsessive repetition of words and sounds thus helps to create the meaning of the poem almost as much as the words themselves do"—and were to discuss how the kinds of words used, the images, and perhaps other elements reinforce or modify the theme, we would be writing a full-fledged interpretation.

You will have noticed that both the definition of and the procedures for interpreting a work suggest that a literary text is unified, probably around a theme, a meaning and effect. In interpreting, you therefore keep asking of each element or detail, "How does it fit? How does it contribute to *the* theme or whole?" In most instances, especially when you are writing on shorter works, if you dig hard and deep enough, you will find a satisfactory interpretation or central theme. Even after you have done your best, however, you must hold your "reading" or interpretation as a hypothesis rather than a final truth. Your experience of reading criticism has probably already shown you that more than one reading of a literary work is possible and that no reading exhausts the meaning and totality of a work. Essays on *Hamlet*, for example, may offer several convincing but different interpretations of the work, all of which are satisfactory and all of which are incapable of fully "explaining" the play. You may, then, want to settle for description, describing the play in terms of several possible meanings, or you may want to use the fact that a work like *Hamlet* does offer these different meanings or perspectives to make some other point about literature and human experience and understanding. Nonetheless, you must begin reading a literary text, including, no doubt, *Hamlet*, as if it were going to make a central statement and create a single effect, no matter how complex. You must try as conscientiously as you can to "make sense" of the work, to analyze it, show how its elements work together. In analyzing elements, you kept your initial sense of the whole as hypothesis and did not try to force evidence to fit your first impression. So, too, you must hold your interpretation as a hypothesis even in its final stages, even at the end. It is, you must be sure, the fullest and best "reading" of the text you are capable of at this time, with the evidence and knowledge you have at this moment; but only that. In other words, an interpretation is "only an opinion." But just as your political and other opinions are not lightly held but are what you really feel and believe based on all you know and have experienced and all you have thought and felt, so your opinion or interpretation of a literary work should be as responsible as you can make it. Your opinions are a measure of your knowledge, intelligence, and sensibility. They should not be lightly changed but neither should they be obstinately and inflexibly held.

Reading and Theme Making

Because you need a sense of the whole text before you can analyze it—you don't, after all, know or believe that *The Raven* is about "inconsolable loss" until you've read some or all of the poem—analysis and interpretation would seem to be possible only after repeated readings. Though obvious, logical, and partially true, this may not be *entirely* true. In reading, we actually anticipate theme or meaning much as we anticipate what will happen next. Often this anticipation or expectation of theme or effect begins with our first opening a book—or even before, in reading the title. If you were to read *Hamlet* in an edition that gives its full title—*The Tragedy of Hamlet, Prince of Denmark*—even if, as unlikely as it may seem, you had never heard of the play or its author before—you would have some idea or hypothesis about who the protagonist is, where the action will more than likely be set, how the play will end, and even some of the feelings it will arouse.

Such anticipation of theme and effect, projecting and modifying understanding and response, continues as you read. When you read the first four words of *The Zebra Storyteller*—"Once upon a time . . ." —the strange title is to some extent explained and the kind of story you are about to read and its relation to everyday reality has been established. We have already seen in the chapter on plot in fiction (pp. 14–62) how the title and the first short section of *The Most Dangerous Game* arouse expectations of the supernatural, the frightening, the adventurous, creating suspense: "What will happen next?" we ask as we read the first few paragraphs. The brief conversation about hunting, toward the end of that section, not only educates our expectations but also generates a moral and thematic question: "Are there really two animal classes—the hunters and the hunted—and does being lucky enough to be among the hunters justify insensitivity toward the feelings of the hunted?" While the question may recede from the foreground of our attention for a while, it has nonetheless been raised. It is, in addition, reinforced by the break on the page, which forces us to pause and, even if but momentarily, reflect. It comes forward again when General Zaroff introduces the subject of hunting. At these two points, at least, a thematic hypothesis based on hunters and hunted begins forming, however faintly, in our minds. That is enough to give us grounds—even as we read the story for the first time—for an analysis of elements and their relationship to our very tentatively formulated theme, and perhaps for beginning to modify or modulate our articulation of that theme. Many details in the story indicate that there is a political coloring to the theme: Zaroff is a Cossack—a people noted for fierceness—and is, or was, a czarist general; he keeps a giant Cossack servant who was an official flogger under the czar; he refers to the Revolution of 1917 in Russia as a "debacle"; he is clearly a racist. We may want to alter "hunter" and "hunted" in our first version of the anticipated theme to something broader—"strong" and "weak," perhaps, or "privileged" and "underprivileged," or we may need fuller definitions of the implications of the terms "hunter" and "hunted."

Just as we have more than one expectation of what may happen next as we read a poem, play, or story, so we may have more than one expectation of what it is going to be "about" in the more general sense: as we read along we have expectations or hypotheses of meaning, and so we consciously or unconsciously try to fit together the pieces or elements of what we are reading into a pattern of significance. By the end of our first reading we should have a fairly well-defined sense of what the story, poem, or play is "about," what it means, even how some of the elements have worked together to produce that meaning and effect. Indeed, isn't this the way we read when we are not reading for a class or performance? Don't most people read most stories, poems, plays only once? And don't we usually think we have understood what we have read? Shouldn't we be able to read a sonnet or a very short story in class just once and immediately write an interpretive paper based on that first reading?

This is not to say that we cannot understand more about a work by repeated re-readings, or that there is some virtue or purity of response in the naïve first reading that is lost in closer study. Our first "reading" —"reading" both in the sense of "casting our eye over" and "interpretation"—is almost certain to be modified or refined by re-reading: if nothing else, we know from the beginning of our second reading why it is important to be Earnest, know what Keats's urn has to say, what the most dangerous game is, why Macomber's life is short and perhaps why it is happy. This time, then, we can concentrate on such aspects or details as how Lady Bracknell's attitudes toward Algernon function in defining the theme; how the images on the urn relate to what it "says," and so on. The theme or meaning is likely to be modulated by later readings, the way the elements function in defining or embodying meaning is likely to be clearer; the effect of the second reading is certain to be different from that of the first. It may be instructive to re-read several times the short work we interpreted in class after a single reading, write a new interpretive essay, and see how our understanding has been changed and enriched by subsequent readings.

Opinions, Right and Wrong

Just as each of our own separate readings is different, so naturally one reader's fullest and "final" reading, interpretation, or opinion will differ somewhat from another's. Seldom will readers agree entirely with any full statement of the theme of a literary text. Nor is one of these interpretations entirely "right" and all the others necessarily "wrong." For no thematic summary, no analysis or interpretation, no matter how full, can exhaust the affective or intellectual significance of a major literary text. There are various approximate readings of varying degrees of acceptability, various competent or "good" readings, not just one single "right" reading. Anyone who has heard two accomplished musicians faithfully perform the same work, playing all the "same" notes, or anyone who has seen two performances of *Hamlet*, will recognize how "interpretations" can be both correct and different. You might try to get hold of several recordings of one or more of Hamlet's soliloquies—by John Barrymore, Sir John Gielgud, Richard Burton, Sir Lawrence Olivier, for example—and notice how each of these actors lends to identical passages his own emphasis, pacing, tone, color, his own effect, and so, ultimately, his own meaning. These actors reading the identical words are, in effect, "copying," not paraphrasing or putting Shakespeare's Elizabethan poetry into modern American prose, not "interpreting," or putting his play into their own words. If merely performing or reading the words aloud generates significant differences in interpretation, it is no wonder that when you write an interpretive essay about literature, when you give your conception of the meaning and effect of the literary text in your own words, your interpretation will differ from other interpretations, even when each of the different interpretations is competent and "correct."

That quite different interpretations may be "correct" is not to say, with Alice's Humpty-Dumpty, that a word or a work "means just what I choose it to mean." Though there may not be one "right" reading, some readings are more appropriate and convincing than others and some readings are demonstrably wrong. In grammar, "It is I," "It's me," and "It be me" may all be used by native speakers of the English language in certain groups and circumstances. We are used to calling the last two "wrong," but they are not "wrong," merely ineffective or inappropriate when used outside the community in which they are the "standard" and "accepted." (Just as the "correct" form may be inappropriate in some circumstances or for certain purposes.) It is unlikely, however, that any native speaker of the English language would say in any group or under any circumstances, "It are me." That, then, is clearly wrong—anywhere, any time.

What would you say about this reading of *Hamlet*?

> The play is about the hero's sexual love for his mother. He sees his father's "ghost" because he feels guilty, somehow responsible for his father's death, more than likely because he had often wished his father dead. To free himself from this feeling of guilt, he imagines that he sees his father's ghost and that the ghost tells him that his uncle murdered his father. He focuses upon his uncle because he is fiercely jealous that it is his uncle not himself who has replaced his father in his mother's bed. He so resents his mother's choice of so unworthy a mate, he attributes it not to love but to mere lust, clearly a projection of his own lust for his mother, which he calls love. His mother's lust so disgusts him that he hates all women now, even Ophelia. When his father was alive he could be fond of Ophelia, for his sexual feeling for his mother was deflected by his father-the-king's powerful presence. Now, however, he must alienate Ophelia not only because of his new hatred of women but because he has a chance of winning his mother, especially if he can get rid of Claudius, his uncle.

Such a reading explains more or less convincingly certain details in the play, but it wrenches some out of context and it leaves a good deal out and a good deal unexplained: why, for example, do others see the ghost of Hamlet's father if it is just a figment of his imagination? What are Horatio and Fortinbras and the political elements doing in the play? *If* you accept certain Freudian premises about human psychology and see life in Freudian terms; if you see literary texts as the *author's* psychic fantasy stimulating your own psychic fantasies and believe that interpretation of *Hamlet* is not merely a reading of the play itself but an analysis of Shakespeare's psyche, you will find this reading convincing. You will perhaps explain away some of the details of the play that do not seem to fit your Freudian reading as a cover-up, an attempt by Shakespeare to disguise the true but hidden meaning of his dramatic fantasy from others—and from himself. Such a reading is probably neither right nor wrong but only a way of interpreting *Hamlet* based on certain assumptions about psychology and about the way literature *means*. In Scots law there is a legal verdict other than "guilty" or "innocent"—"not proved." Perhaps that is what we should say of such competent but not wholly or universally acceptable interpretations.

Suppose one of your ingenious classmates were to argue that the real subject of *Hamlet* is that the hero has tuberculosis. This would explain, your classmate would say, the hero's moodiness, his pretended madness that sometimes seems real, his rejection of Ophelia (he wouldn't want their children to suffer from the disease), his father's ghost (he, too, died of consumption), his anger at his uncle (who carries the disease, of course) for marrying Hamlet's mother, and so on. Your classmate might even argue that the text of the play is flawed, that it was just copied down during a performance by someone in the audience or was printed from an actor's imperfect copy. Therefore, "O that this too too *solid flesh*" should read "*sullied flesh*," as many scholars have argued (and might not "sullied flesh" suggest tuberculosis?). And, therefore, isn't it quite possible that the most famous soliloquy in the play really began or was meant to begin, "TB or not TB"? "No way!" we'd say. We would be reasonably sure that this is not just "not proved" but just plain *wrong*. It might be interesting and illuminating to rebut that reading in a paper of your own and to notice what kinds of evidence you bring to bear on an interpretive argument.

But if a piece of literature does not *say* something specific, does not *mean* something specific, then what good is it anyway? Why should we bother to read it at all? Isn't the author trying to say something? And if he or she cannot say it, say it so we or our professors or anybody can understand it, then what good is it?

Reader and Text

If it is difficult sometimes to say exactly what a piece of literature *says*, it is usually not because it is vague or meaningless but because it is too specific and meaning*ful* to paraphrase satisfactorily in any language other than its own. Since no two human beings are identical and no two people can inhabit the same space at the same time, no two people can see exactly the same reality from the same angle and vantage point. Most of us get around this awkward truth by saying that we see—or by only actually seeing—what we are "supposed" to see, a generalized, common-sense approximation of reality. We "know" a table is rectangular and so we think we see it that way, whereas if we really looked we might see it as a diamond or a trapezoid or some other quadrilateral figure. We are all, in effect, like Polonius in the third act of *Hamlet*, who sees in a cloud a camel, a weasel, a whale—whatever Hamlet tells him he sees.

Some individuals resist the communal pressure to accept the generalized version and struggle to see things as fully and clearly as possible from their own unique vantage point in space and time. Those who try to communicate to others their particular—even peculiar—vision in our common language are or seek to be writers of literature.

There is for these authors a constant tug-of-war between the uniqueness and therefore ultimate inexpressibility of their individual visions and the generalizing and therefore reductive or distorting nature of language. The battle does not always result in sheer loss, however. Often, in the very struggle to get their own perceptions into language writers sharpen those perceptions or discover in the process what they themselves did not know they knew when they began to write. You have probably made similar discoveries some time or other in the process of writing an assigned paper, or perhaps in writing a letter. Very often too, however, perhaps always, writers find that what they have written does not perfectly embody what they meant it to, just as you perhaps have found that your finished papers have been not quite so brilliant as your original idea.

The first task of the reader, therefore, is to get not to the author's intention, but to the general statement that the work itself makes— that is, its theme or thesis. After a few readings we can usually make a stab at articulating the theme of most works. We have already seen, in the case of *The Raven*, that further reading and analysis can sharpen or modify our rendering of the theme. What a work says in the way of a general theme, however, is not necessarily its full or ultimate meaning; otherwise we would read theme summaries and not stories, poems, or plays. The theme is the meaning accessible to all through close reading of the text and common to all, but a literary text is not all statement. There are often cloudy areas in the text where we cannot be sure what is *implication*, the suggestion of the text, and what is our *inference*, or interpretation, of the text. What is the speaker of *The Raven* doing, for example, in the opening lines of that poem? He is reading, or, rather, pondering over "many a quaint and curious volume of forgotten lore." Now why should a man so stricken by the death of a loved one be reading? The poem does not say, but we might infer from our own experience that he is trying to forget, to distract his attention from his loss, and indeed the final "message" of the raven is that he shall nevermore be able to escape his grief. But why is he reading quaint old educational or instructional books instead of entertaining ones, if he is merely seeking to distract himself? No wonder he's weary. Words like "quaint," "curious," "forgotten," and "lore" in the context of his obsessive grief may suggest to you, especially if other macabre works of Poe's are part of your past reading experience, that he has been studying black magic, some way of raising or communicating with the dead Lenore. The black carrion-eating bird enters then to tell him there is no way, not even by magic; he will see Lenore nevermore. Poe's poem does not *say* what the volumes are about. Many readers, however, will find this inference convincing. If accepted, this changes the theme of the poem to some degree. Still, it need not be accepted; the poem does not, will never say what those volumes contain. The meaning of the poem for the reader who is convinced will differ from the meaning for the reader who is not convinced.

The full meaning of a work for you the reader is not only in its stated theme, one that everyone can agree on, but in the meaning you derive by bringing together that generalized theme, the precise language of the text, and your own applicable experiences—including reading experience—and imagination. That "meaning" is not the total meaning of the work, not what the author originally perceived and "meant to say"; it is the vision of the author as embodied in the work and re-viewed from your own angle of vision.

Your role in producing a meaning from the text does not free you, please note, from paying very close attention to the precise language of the text, the words and their meanings, their order, the syntax of the sentences, and even such mundane details as punctuation. You cannot impose a meaning on the text, no matter how sincerely and intensely you feel it, in defiance of the rules of grammar and the nature of the language.

Or, you should not. Yet we feel this may have happened to one of our favorite poems, William Butler Yeats's *The Second Coming* (p. 554). The poem ends, as you see, with a question mark where the structure of the final sentence leads us to expect a period. Readers have generally (we could say *always*) read the sentence as a question, as the final punctuation gives them the right to do, but they have rarely if ever acknowledged the possibility of reading it as a simple declarative statement, which the sentence structure would seem to dictate. We can choose to read the ending as a query, but we must recognize that such a reading is an interpretation that goes beyond the facts of the text. The reader's license to produce a meaning from the author's text does not give the reader the right to ignore the details of the text that the author has created.

Still, the reader must be an artist too, trying to experience the reality of the work as the author experienced reality, and with the same reverence and sense of responsibility for the original. To write about literature you must try to embody your reading experience—or interpretation—of the work in language. Alas, writing about literature, using words about words, is not as easy as it sounded at first. But it is more exciting, giving you a chance to see with another's eyes, to explore another's perceptions or experiences, and to explore and more fully understand your own in the process, thus expanding the horizon of your experience, perception, consciousness.

When some rich works, like *Hamlet*, then, seem to have more than one meaning or no entirely satisfactory meaning or universally agreed upon single theme, it is not that they are not saying something, and saying something very specific, but that what they are saying is too specific, and complex, and profound, and true, perhaps, to be generalized or paraphrased in a few dozen words. The literary work is meaning*ful*—that is, full of meaning or meanings; but it is the reader who produces each particular meaning from the work, using the work itself, the language of the community and of the work, and his or her own experience and imagination.

As readers trying to understand the unique perception of the author, we must translate the text as best we can into terms we can understand for ourselves. We try not to reduce the text to our own earlier, limited understanding but to stretch our minds and feelings toward its vision.

An interpretation, then, is not a clarification of what the writer "was trying to say"; it is a process that itself says, in effect, "The way I am trying to understand *Hamlet* is. . . ."

WRITING ABOUT STORIES, POEMS, PLAYS

So far we have been discussing writing about literature in general, rather than writing about a story, a poem, or a play in particular, though we have used specific works as examples. There are topics, such as a study of imagery, symbol, or theme, that are equally applicable to all three genres: you can write a paper on the images or symbols in or the theme of a story, a poem, or a play. Indeed, you can write an essay comparing imagery, say, in a story, poem, and play— comparing the water imagery in James Baldwin's story *Sonny's Blues,* for example, with the air or wind imagery in Shelley's *Ode to the West Wind,* and the fire or burning imagery in Ibsen's *Hedda Gabler.* Fiction and drama also have action and character in common, so that you can not only choose to write on the plot of a story or play or on characters or characterization in a particular story or play, but you can compare, for example, a character in a story with a character in a play—Hemingway's Margaret Macomber with Ibsen's Hedda Gabler perhaps.

Narrative

A story has not only elements common to all three genres, such as plot and character, however; it also has something special—a narrator, someone who tells the story. Everything in fiction—action, character, theme, structure, even the language—is mediated: everything comes to us through an intervening mind or voice; we often see the story from a particular vantage point or several vantage points *(focus)* and always are told the story by someone, whether that someone is identified or is merely a disembodied *voice.* We must be aware of the narration, the means by which the story comes to us. We must be aware that the action, characters, all the elements in a story, are always mediated (there is someone between us and the story), and that the mediation contributes greatly to the meaning, structure, and effect of the story. Who is telling us the story of *The Lottery*? What is the physical and emotional relationship of the narrator of that story to its characters? How would you describe the language or voice of the narration? These are essential questions to ask about Shirley Jackson's superb story, and in answering them you may want to write a paper called *The Narrator in "The Lottery"* (or, if you want to be more dramatic, *The Ghostly Reporter of "The Lottery"*). A story is told *to* someone as well as by someone, and you might want to ask yourself what the relationship is supposed to be between us—the audience—, the narrator, and the characters. Would Mr. Head and his grandson, the chief characters of Flannery O'Connor's *The Artificial Nigger,* understand the language and the literary and religious allusions in that story? What kind of reader is the narrator speaking to? How do the answers to these two questions define where we are in relation to the characters, the attitude we are supposed to take toward them, and the effect of the story? Such questions might lead to an analysis of the tone of that story—and a paper we might jazzily call *The Artificial Reader of "The Artificial Nigger."* These are the kinds of questions raised by the simple but central fact that stories do not come to us directly but are narrated; these are therefore the kinds of questions of special importance to readers of fiction and the kinds of questions writing about fiction frequently centers upon.

Even the conventional past tense in fiction that we take for granted implies a narrator. Since the story is not happening "now," in the present, is not being enacted before us but is over with, having already happened in the past, it is being recalled, and someone must be recalling it, someone who knows what happened and how it all came out. That someone is the narrator. Knowing the end, the narrator has been able to select and shape the events and details. For that reason everything in a well-constructed story is relevant and significant.

Even narrative time is purposefully structured. Stories, unlike actual time as we know it, have beginnings and endings, but they do not have to begin at the beginning and proceed in a uniform direction at a uniform pace toward the end. They can be told from end to beginning, or even from middle to beginning to end, as in *Macomber*. In a story an hour, day, or decade can be skipped or condensed into a narrative moment (a phrase or sentence), or a moment can be expanded to fill pages. Since this manipulation of time affects the meaning and effect of the story, we must pay close attention to it and question its significance. For example, the beginning of the third chapter of *An Occurrence at Owl Creek Bridge* follows immediately from the end of the first chapter, so why is the second chapter there at all? Why does the first chapter cover only a few minutes of action but the third chapter, only a little longer, cover what seems to be a whole day? Can you explain why—in terms of meaning and effect—each of the lengthy scenes in *The Lady with the Dog* is dwelled upon? Why other, longer periods are briefly summarized or skipped? Why do some stories, such as *Her First Ball*, cover only a very short period of time, while others, such as *A Rose for Emily*, cover years and years? Why are stories such as *Her First Ball* presented largely through dialogue, while others, such as *A Rose for Emily*, are "told" rather than presented, with few dramatized scenes and little dialogue?

Dramatization

Scenes presented more or less immediately (that is, without mediation) through dialogue and action, taking place over a short period of time, are said to be *dramatized*. Though there may be gaps of time *between* the scenes or acts of a play, once the action begins it takes exactly as much time on the stage as it would in actuality: the actors speak and move in "real" time. Though there is, of course, a play-wright who knew how it would all come out and has shaped the play accordingly, the language of the play that we respond to is in the present tense, the dialogue and action are happening in the present, right before our eyes. And though the playwright has written all the lines, his or her voice is not directly heard: only the characters speak. Neither the playwright nor a surrogate in the form of a narrator stands at your elbow to tell you who are the good guys and who the bad, what each character is like or whether what is being said is true, distorted, false. Only very rarely—as in the Shakespearean soliloquy or aside—do we know what a character is thinking. In plays such as *The Sacrifice of Isaac, Oedipus Tyrannus,* and even *Hamlet,* there are only very brief indications of setting, costume, movement of charac-ters, tone of voice, if they are present at all. Such stage directions—which may be as elaborate as the detailed description of setting and costumes and the instructions for action and tone in *Hedda Gabler*—are not, in a sense, purely dramatic. Watching a play being performed on a stage, we do not see or hear these words at all. On the page, they are usually distinguished from the text of the play by italics or some other typographical device, so as we read we register—or are supposed to register—them as separate from "the play itself." They seem to belong to some other dimension and clearly belong to a voice other than that of any character.

When we read a play we tend to imagine it—in the literal sense of putting it into images—in our minds as if it were being performed on a stage. We act, as it were, as our own directors; if we were to put into words all that would be necessary to stage the play as we see it in our minds, we would be writing the stage directions, or narrative, of the play. The relative absence of such narrative in drama makes our part in the imagining or staging of a play as we read more crucial than it is in reading fiction. How you would stage a play or a scene in order to bring out its full meaning and effect as you imagined it can serve as a significant topic for writing about drama. You might ask yourself such questions as, What instructions would I give the actors for speaking the apparently banal lines of *The Black and White* and what effect would I strive for? What scene or passage would I use as the best ex-ample of how the play should be read? How would I costume Oedipus in the first and last scenes in order to bring out the main movement and theme of the play? How can I, in the early scenes, subtly reveal that Oedipus has an injured ankle without detracting from the power and majesty of his presence at that time? . . . In the middle of his stage directions describing the set for *Hedda Gabler,* Ibsen specifies that on the rear wall of the smaller room there "hangs the portrait of a handsome old man in general's uniform." What, precisely, should this portrait look like? What expression should be on the general's face? How prominent should the picture be in the set as a whole?

Though you may wish to write on the theme, characters, action, imagery, or language of a play from time to time, one central element you will certainly want to write about sooner or later is the staging, or dramatization—the set, costumes, acting, moving of characters about on the stage, even lighting—and how this can enhance the effect and meaning of the play on the page.

Words

Some plays, like *Hamlet*, are written partly or entirely in verse. Though we may be able to make a distinction between poetry and verse, it is reasonable to say that as the term is generally used, poetry itself is not so much a literary genre as it is a medium. It might be more logical to break literature down into "prose" and "poetry" rather than into "fiction," "drama," and "poetry." For besides poetic dramas like *Hamlet*, there are also dramatic poems, such as Browning's *My Last Duchess* and John Donne's *The Flea*, poems in which a distinguishable character speaks in a definable, almost "stageable" situation. There are also narrative poems, those that tell a story through a narrator, such as *Sir Patrick Spens* or *Paradise Lost*. What these and other poems, lyrics, for example, have in common is rhythmical language (and, some people would add, highly figurative language).

All literature is embodied in words, of course, but poetry uses words most intensely, most fully. It uses not only the statements words make, what they signify or *denote*, using them with great precision; not only what words suggest or *connote*, usually with wide-ranging sensitivity and inclusiveness; but the very sounds of the words themselves. Not all poems have highly patterned or very regular meter, but almost all poetry is more highly patterned than almost any prose. Not all poems rhyme, but it seems safe to say that all extensively rhymed works are poems. So much writing about poetry concentrates on the words themselves: some treats the patterns of sounds, the rhythms or rhymes, some the precision or suggestiveness of the language, and some the relation of sounds to shades of meaning. This is not to say that excellent papers may not be written on the themes, characters, settings of poems. There are many excellent topics as well for comparative papers; the themes of a poem and a story may be compared—*Dover Beach* and *The Lady with the Dog*, for example—or of a poem and a play—*The Love Song of J. Alfred Prufrock* and *Hamlet*, perhaps. But in writing about poetry, even when discussing theme or other elements, at some point one usually comes to concentrate on the medium itself, the sound, precision, suggestiveness of the language. The sample paper on Dryden's *To the Memory of Mr. Oldham* (p. 461) are examples of how one writes about this central element of poetry, words.

Sample Topics and Titles

We have been stressing, on the one hand, writing about the most characteristic elements of stories, plays, and poems—narration, dramatization, and words—and on the other hand, writing about the elements common to all three genres, like theme or symbols. For further hints about likely topics you might look at the chapter headings in the table of contents of this volume and read the introductory material to the chapter, or chapters, that looks most interesting or most promising for your immediate purpose. You might look, too, at the list of sample topics that follows, not so much for the topic that you will actually come to write on but as a trigger for your own imagination and ideas.

Fiction

1. A Plotless Story about Plot: Grace Paley's *A Conversation with My Father*?

2. The Selection and Ordering of the Scenes in *A Rose for Emily*

3. What does the voice in *My Man Bovanne* contribute to the story's structure, tone, and effect?

4. Who Am I? The Nature of the Narrator in *Our Friend Judith*

5. The Self-Characterization of Montresor in *The Cask of Amontillado*

6. Sonny's Brother's Character

7. Beyond the Literal: Symbolism in *Beyond the Pale*

8. The Image and Import of the Sea in *The Lady with the Dog*

9. "Only a Girl": The Theme of *Boys and Girls*

10 What is the theme of *The Rocking-Horse Winner,* and how does it relate to the title of the story?

Poetry

1. Attitudes toward Authority in *Sir Patrick Spens*

2. Scene, Sequence, and Time in *Sir Patrick Spens*

3. Sir Patrick Spens as a Tragic Hero

4. Why "Facts" Are Missing in *Western Wind*

5. Birth and Death Imagery in *The Death of the Ball Turret Gunner*

6. Varieties of Violence in Frost's *Range-Finding*

7. The Characterization of God in *Channel Firing*

8. The Idea of Flight in *Ode to a Nightingale*

9. Attitudes toward the Past in *They Flee from Me, Those Winter Sundays,* and *The Leap*

10. Satire of Distinctive American Traits in *The Unknown Citizen, Dirge,* and *What the Motorcycle Said*

Drama

1. What is the conflict and what is the reversal (peripety) in *The Brute*?

2. What is the effect on the reader or audience of having so much of the major actions of *Hedda Gabler* (or *Oedipus*) happen offstage?

3. Rosencrantz and Guildenstern as Half-Men in *Hamlet*

4. The Past Recaptured: What We Know (or can Infer) about Alberta's (and/or Deedee's) life in *Third and Oak: The Laundromat*

5. Varieties of Verbal Wit as a Device of Characterization in *The Importance of Being Earnest*

6. Realistic Drama versus Comedy: Love and Marriage in *Hedda Gabler* and *The Importance of Being Earnest*

7. Write stage directions—including stage sets, costumes, instructions to actors for delivery of lines and gestures—for *The Sacrific of Isaac*.

8. Staging Polonius: Language and Cliché as Guides to Gestures, Facial Expression, and Character in *Hamlet*

9. How important is the visual impression that Hedda makes in *Hedda Gabler*? How would you stage her appearance? How would you clothe her? What gestures would you give her? How would you instruct the actress playing her to speak? What textual clues lead you to your decisions?

Intergeneric Topics

1. Motivation in *Hedda Gabler* and *Richard Cory*

2. The Functions of Spare Language in *The Short Happy Life of Francis Macomber* and *On My First Son*

3. The Uses of Fantasy in *Araby* and *Wild Nights! Wild Nights!*

4. The Disillusioned Lovers in Joyce's *Araby* and Wyatt's *They Flee from Me*

5. The Loyalty of the Survivor: de Maupassant's *The Jewelry* and Chekhov's *The Brute*

6. Hedda Gabler and Margaret Macomber: A Comparison

7. The Murderer Confesses: Browning's Duke of Ferrara and Poe's Montresor

8. Under Society's Veneer: Wilfred Owen's "Dulce et Decorum Est" and William Trevor's *Beyond the Pale*

9. Love in Elizabeth Barrett Browning's "How Do I Love Thee?" and Chekhov's *The Lady with the Dog*

10. A Death in the Family: Sylvia Plath's "Daddy" and Mordecai Richler's *The Summer My Grandmother Was Supposed to Die*

Creative Topics

1. The speaker in *My Last Duchess* has been charged with the murder of his last duchess. On the basis on his words in the poem, prepare a case for the prosecution.

2. Write a "reply" to the speaker of *To His Coy Mistress*, declining his invitation and picking out the flaws in his argument.

3. Write a soliloquy for Gertrude (*Hamlet*) in which she defends herself against the most serious charges made against her motives and conduct.

4. Reconstruct the events and sentiments in *Dover Beach* as a short mood play by writing dialogue and stage directions for a scene between the speaker and the woman.

5. Retell (in poetry or prose) the story in *Cherrylog Road* from the point of view of the woman who is looking back on the experience twenty years later.

6. Using *Fern Hill* as a model, write the kind of imaginary reverie Hedda Gabler might have written about her childhood.

7. What would happen in your neighborhood (town) if one morning there appeared a very old man with enormous wings?

8. Elo's (Joe Lee's) Version of the Dance in *My Man Bovanne*

9. Select three scenes for a one-act play called *The Rocking-Horse Winner*.

10. Choose one of the *Stories for Further Reading* that you have not read before (perhaps *The Secret Sharer*?), read to a crucial point or a pause marked by the author, and describe your expectations of how the story will develop and conclude.

DECIDING WHAT TO WRITE ABOUT

Having Something to Say

Deciding what to write about—what approach to use, which questions to ask—seems like the first step in the process of writing a paper about a work of literature. It isn't. Before that, you have to have confidence that you have something to say. If you are a beginner at this kind of writing, you are likely to have deep doubts about that. Developing confidence is not, at the beginning, easy. Confidence comes with experience and success, and you may feel that you do not yet know what you are doing. That feeling is common. You may feel as if you can *never* begin and want to put off the paper forever. Or you may want to plunge in fast and get it over with. Either of these approaches, though common and tempting, is a mistake. Blustering ahead won't give you confidence, and delay will make you less confident. The best way is to begin preparing for the paper as soon as possible—the moment you know you have one to write—but not to hurry into the writing itself.

The first step in building your confidence is to get close enough to the work to feel comfortable with it. Before you can tell anyone else about what you have read—and writing about literature is just another form of talking about literature, although a more formal and organized one—you need to "know" the work, to have a sure sense of what the work itself is like, how its parts function, what ideas it expresses, how it creates particular effects, how it makes you feel. And the only way you will get to know the work is to spend time with it, reading it carefully and thoughtfully and turning it over in your mind. "Read, read, read, read, my unlearned Reader" is the advice that the author of *Tristram Shandy* gives to those who want to know what his book is about. There is no substitute for reading, several times and with care, the work you are going to write about *before* you pick up a pen and prepare to write. Read carefully, read thoughtfully, read intensely, read in as many different paces and moods as you can. Read sympathetically, taking the work on its own terms; read critically, judging it in terms of your own thought, values, and experience. And then read it again. And let your reading be the *work itself*, not something *about* that work, at least at first. Later, your instructor may steer you to background materials or to critical readings about the work. But at first you should encounter the work alone and become aware, as fully as possible, of your own private responses to the work before you take the next step. Your writing about literature must, after all, come from your experience of reading. You have to trust yourself so that you will have the confidence to begin.

Begin, then, by reading, several times, the work you are going to write about. The first time, read it straight through at one sitting: read slowly, pausing at its natural divisions—between paragraphs, or stanzas, or at the ends of scenes—to consider how you are responding to the work. Trust your instincts, even if they may not always be right. Later, when your knowledge of the work is more nearly complete and when you have the "feel" of the whole, you can compare your early responses with your more considered thoughts about the work, in effect "correcting" your first impressions in whatever way seems necessary on the basis of new and better knowledge. But if you are noncommittal at first, refusing to notice what you think and feel, you will have nothing to correct, and you may cut yourself off from the most direct routes of response. Feelings are not always reliable—about literature any more than about people—but they are always the first point of contact with a literary work: You feel before you think. Try to start with your mind open, as if it were a blank sheet of paper ready to receive an impression from what you read.

When you have finished a first reading, think about your first impressions. If the assignment is a story, think about how it began, how it gained your interest, how its conflicts and issues were resolved, how it ended, how it made you feel from beginning to end. Write down any phrases or events that you remember especially vividly, anything you are afraid you might forget. Look back at any parts that puzzled you at first. Write down in one sentence what you think the story is about.

Then read the story again, this time much more slowly, making notes as you go on any passages that seem especially significant and pausing over any features or passages that puzzle you. Then write a longer statement—three or four sentences—summarizing the story and suggesting more fully what it seems to be about. Try to write the kind of summary described above on pages **953-954.**

Stop. Do something else for a while, something as different as possible—see a movie, do math problems, ride a bicycle, listen to music, have a meal, take a nap, mow the lawn, build a loft. Do NOT do some other reading you have been meaning to do. When you go back to the story and finish reading it for the third time—rapidly and straight through—write down in a sentence the most important thing you would want to tell someone else who was about to read the story for the first time: not just whether you liked it or not, but what exactly you liked, how the whole story seems to have worked. If your reading is a poem or a play, follow the same basic procedure: read the work, consider what it made you think and how it made you feel; read it again, make notes, and write a summary; then read it once more and make a single significant statement about it, articulating what seems to you most interesting or important about the way it "works."

Now you are ready to choose a topic.

Choosing a Topic

Once you are ready to choose a topic, the chances are that you have already—quietly and unconsciously—chosen one. The clue is in the last statement you wrote. The desire to tell someone about a work of literature is a wonderful place to begin. Good papers almost always grow out of a desire to communicate. Desire is not enough, of course; the substance (and most of the work, sentence by sentence) is still ahead of you. But desire will get you started. Chances are that what you wrote down as the one thing you most wanted to say is close to the heart of the central issue in the work you are going to write about. Your statement will become, perhaps, in somewhat revised form, your *thesis*.

The next step is to convert your personal feelings and desire to communicate into something communicable—into an "objective" statement about the work, a statement that will mean something to someone else. Again, you may already be further along than you realize. Look at the "summary" you wrote after your second reading. The summary will probably sound factual, objective, and general about the work; the personal statement you wrote after the third reading will be more emotional, subjective, and particular about some aspect of the work. In combining the two successfully lies the key to a good paper: what you need to do is to write persuasively an elaboration and explanation of the last statement so that your reader comes to share the "objective" view of the whole work that your summary expresses. The summary you have written will, in short, be implicit in the whole essay; your total essay will suggest to your reader the wholeness of the work you are writing about, but it will do so by focusing its attention on some particular aspect of the work—on a part that leads to, or suggests, or represents the whole. What you want to do is build an essay on the basis of your first statement, taking a firm hold on the handle you have found. The summary is your limit and guide: it reminds you of where you will come out, the bottom line. Any good topic ultimately leads back to the crucial perceptions involved in a summary. Ultimately, any good writing about literature leads to a full and resonant sense of the central thrust of the work, but the most effective way to find that center is by discovering a pathway that particularly interests you. The best writing about literature presents a clear—and well-argued—thesis about a work or works of literature and presents it from the perspective of personal, individual perception. But the thesis should clarify the central thrust of the work, helping the literary work to open itself up to readers more completely and more satisfyingly.

Topics often suggest themselves after a second or third reading, simply because one feature or problem stands out so prominently that it almost demands to be talked about. In *Western Wind*, for example, you almost have to account for what is not said, for the lack of narrative information, and in *My Papa's Waltz* you need to suggest how the boy's strong affections for his father and his pleasure in the "waltz" are expressed. Sometimes you may be lucky: your instructor may *assign* a topic instead of asking you to choose your own. At first glance, that may not seem like a good break: it often feels confining to follow specific directions or to have to operate within limits and rules prescribed by someone else. The advantage is that it may save a lot of time and prevent floundering around. If your instructor assigns a topic, it is almost certain to be one that will work, one that has a payoff if you approach it creatively and without too much resentment at being directed so closely and precisely. It is time consuming, even when you have tentatively picked a topic, to think through its implications and be sure it works. And an instructor's directions, especially if they are detailed and call attention to particular questions or passages, may aid greatly in helping you focus on particular issues or in leading you to evidence crucial to the topic.

If your instructor does *not* give you a topic and if no topic suggests itself to you after you have read a particular work three or four times, you may sometimes have to settle for the kind of topic that will—more or less—be safe for any literary work. Some topics are almost all-purpose. You can always analyze devices of characterization in a story, showing how descriptive detail, dialogue, and the reactions of other people in the story combine to present a particular character and evoke the reader's response to him or her; with a poem you can almost always write an adequate paper analyzing rhythm, or verse form, or imagery, or the connotations of key words. Such "fall-back" topics are, however, best used only as last resorts, when your instincts have failed you in a particular instance. When choice is free, a more lively and committed paper is likely to begin from a particular insight or question, something that grabs you and makes you want to say something, or solve a problem, or formulate a thesis. The best papers are usually very personal in origin; even when a topic is set by the assignment, the best papers come from a sense of having personally found an answer to a significant question. To turn a promising idea into a good paper, however, personal responses usually need to be supported by a considerable mass of evidence; the process often resembles the testing of "evidence" in a laboratory or the formulation of hypotheses and arguments in a law case—and they will usually need to go through repeated written revisions that will sharpen and refine them.

Considering Your Audience

Thinking of your paper as an argument or an explanation will also help with one of the most sensitive issues in writing about literature. The issue is: Who are you writing for? Who is your audience? The obvious answer is, your instructor, but in an important sense, that is the wrong answer. It is wrong because, although it could literally be true that your instructor will be the only person (besides you) who will ever read your paper, your object in writing about literature is to learn to write for an audience of peers, people a lot like yourself who are sensible, pretty well educated, and need to have something (in this case a literary work) explained to them so that they will be able to understand it more fully. Picture your ideal reader as someone about your own age and with about the same educational background. Assume that that person is intelligent and has some idea of what literature is like and how it works, but that he or she has just read this particular literary work for the first time and has not yet had a chance to think about it carefully. Don't be insulting and explain the obvious, but don't assume either that your reader has noticed and correctly interpreted every detail. The object is to inform and convince your reader, not try to impress.

Should you, then, altogether ignore the obvious fact that it is an instructor—probably with a master's degree or Ph.D. in literature—who is your actual reader? Not altogether: you don't want to get so carried away with speaking to people of your own age and interests that you slip into slang, or feel the need to explain what a stanza is, or leave an allusion to a rock star unexplained, and you do want to learn from the kind of advice your instructor has given in class or from comments he or she may have made on other papers you have written. But don't become preoccupied with the idea that you are writing for someone in "authority" or someone you need to please. Most of all, don't think of yourself as writing for a captive audience, for a reader who *has* to read what you write. It is not always easy to know exactly who your audience is or how interested your readers may be, so you have to pull out all the stops, do the best you can, make the most of every single word. Your roommate or your best friend or your instructor may feel obliged to listen and fake an interest in what you have read—or may even *be* interested—and thus put up with poor sentences and inexact details, with thoughts not fully formulated, or a monologue full of vocal pauses, and "you know's" and "I don't know how to express it." But a stranger—and the person at the other end of what you write is a stranger even if you can pretty well figure out what he or she will want to know—may not be charitable, patient, or interested. It is your job to get his or her attention. And you will have to do it subtly, making conscious assumptions about what your reader already knows and what he or she can readily understand. You cannot, as in a conversation, watch the facial expressions, the eyes, the gestures of your audience and improvise. Writing commits you to assumptions about your audience. Writing is more formal than speech, and a paper about a poem or a play or a story should be "respectable" enough that your grandmother could read it if she ever felt inclined: its tone should be serious and straightforward and its attitude respectful toward the reader, as well as toward the literary work. But its approach and vocabulary, while formal enough for academic writing, should be readily understandable by someone with your own background and reading experience. And it should be lively enough to interest someone like you. Try to imagine, as your ideal reader, the person in your class whom you most respect. Write to get, and hold, that person's serious attention. Try to communicate, try to teach.

FROM TOPIC TO ROUGH DRAFT

Writing about literature is very much like talking about literature. But there is one important difference. When we talk, we organize as we go—trying to get a handle, experimenting, working toward an understanding. And the early stages of preparing a paper—the notetaking, the outlining, the rough drafts—are much like that. A "finished" paper, however, has the uncertainties and tentativeness worked out and presents a smooth argument that moves carefully toward a conclusion. How does one get from here to there?

Once you have decided on a topic, the process of planning is fairly straightforward, but it can be time consuming and (often) frustrating. There are three basic steps in the planning process: first you gather the evidence, then you sort it into order, and (finally) you develop it into a convincing argument. The easiest way is to take these steps one by one.

Gathering Evidence

The first step involves accumulating evidence to support the statement you have decided to make about your topic (that is, your thesis), and (yet once more) it takes you back to the text. But before you read the text again, look over the notes you have already made, in the margin of that text or on separate pieces of paper. Which ones of them have something to do with the topic you have now defined? Which of them will be useful to you in making your main point? Which ones can you now set aside as irrelevant to the topic you have decided on?

Reading over the notes you have already made is a good preparation for re-reading the work again, for this time as you read it (at least the fourth time you will have read it) you will be looking at it in a new and quite specific way, looking for all the things in it that relate to the topic you have decided on. This time you will, in effect, be flagging everything—words, phrases, structural devices, changes of tone, anything—that bears upon your topic. As you read—very slowly and single-mindedly, with your topic always in mind—keep your pen constantly poised to mark useful points. Be ready to say something about the points as you come upon them; it's a good idea to write down, immediately, any sentences that occur to you as you re-read this time. Some of these sentences will turn out to be useful when you actually begin to write your paper. Some will be incorporated in your paper. But some will not; you will find that a lot of the notes you take, like a lot of the footage shot in making a film, will end up on the cutting room floor. Writing, properly done, is not an efficient process and a lot of the thoughts that will occur to you as you get ready to write will not end up being central to your argument. Don't get retentive about your notes.

No one can tell you exactly how to take notes. Good notetaking is a highly individualized skill; precisely what notes you will need to take and how will depend on the particulars of the paper you are about to write. Ultimately, you will develop a style that is right for you, but some general guidelines may be useful. Here are five hints toward successful notetaking:

1. Keep your topic and your thesis about your topic constantly in mind as you re-read and take notes. Mark all passages in the work that bear on your topic, and for each one write on a note card a single sentence that describes how the passage relates to your topic and thesis. Indicate, for each passage, the specific location in the text—by line number if you are writing about a poem; by page number (and location on the page) if you are working on a story; by act, scene, and line number if you are writing about a play.

2. Keep re-reading and taking notes until one of five things happens:
   (a) You get too tired and lose your concentration. (If that happens, stop and then start again when you are rested, preferably the next day.)
   (b) You stop finding relevant passages or perceive a noticeable

drying up of your ideas. (Again, time to pause; give the work at least one more reading later when your mind is fresh and see whether the juices start anew. If they don't, you may be ready to outline and write.)

(c) You begin to find yourself annotating every single sentence or line, and the evidence all begins to run together into a single blob. (Stop and sort out your thesis again, simplifying and narrowing it so that you don't try to include everything. Then go back to your notetaking and discriminate more carefully between what actually is important to your thesis and what only relates at some distance.)

(d) You become impatient with your notetaking and can't wait to get started writing. (Start writing. Use scrap paper, and be prepared to go back to systematic notetaking if your ideas or your energy fade. The chances are that the prose passages you write this way will find a place in your paper, but they may not belong exactly where you think they do when you first write them down.)

(e) You find that there is insufficient evidence for your thesis, that the evidence points in another direction, or that the evidence contradicts your thesis. (Revise your topic to reflect the evidence, and begin re-reading once more.)

3. When you think you have finished your notetaking, read all your note cards over slowly, one by one, and jot down any further ideas as they occur to you, each one on a separate note card. (Sometimes it will seem as if note cards beget note cards. Too much is better than too little at the notetaking stage: you can always discard them before the final draft. Don't worry if you seem to have too many notes and too much material. But later, when you boil down to essentials, you will have to be ruthless with yourself and omit some of your favorite ideas.)

4. Transfer all of your notes to pieces of paper—or note cards— that are all the same size, one note on each. It is easier to sort them this way when you get ready to organize and outline. If you like to write notes in the margin of your text (or on the backs of envelopes, or on dinner napkins, or on shirtsleeves), systematically transfer every note to uniform sheets of paper or cards before you begin to outline. Having everything easily recorded on sortable cards that can be moved from one pile to another makes organizing easier later, especially when you change your mind (as you will) and decide to move a point from one part of your paper to another. Index cards—either 3×5, if you write small and make economical notes, or 4×6, if you need more space— are ideal for notetaking and sorting (perhaps why they are called note cards, or index cards.)

5. When you think you are done taking notes (because you are out of ideas, or out of time, or getting beyond a manageable number of pieces of evidence), read through the whole pile one more time, again letting any new ideas—or ideas that take on a fresh look because you combine them in a new way—spawn new sentences for new note cards.

How many times should you read a story or play before you stop taking notes? There is no right answer. If you have read the work three times before settling on a topic, two more readings may do. But it could take several more. Common sense, endurance, and deadlines will all have an effect on how many re-readings you do. Almost certainly you will read a 20-line poem many more times than you will a 30-page story, not just because it takes less time per reading, but because in short compact works you will find the evidence more tightly interwoven and more in need of a careful unraveling. Let your conscience, your judgment, and your clock be your guide.

Organizing Your Notes

The notes you have taken will become, in the next few hours, almost the whole content of your paper. The task remaining is to give that content the form and shape that will make it appealing and persuasive. But it is not an easy task: the best content in the world isn't worth much if it isn't effectively presented. The key to the task is getting all your ideas into the right order, that is, into a sequence that will allow them to argue your thesis most persuasively. It is worth the trouble: the difference between ideas and evidence scattered randomly and a carefully ordered presentation is the same as the difference between winning and losing an argument or battle when the best resources are clearly on your side—or between failing a paper and writing a respectable one. As in most things, you may have to put a lot of effort into making your prose seem easy and effortless.

In order to put your notes into a proper order, you will need (ironically) to get a little distance from your notes. (The key to good planning and writing—and to many other pursuits—is in knowing when to back away and get some perspective.) Set your notes aside, but not too far away. On a fresh sheet of paper, write down all the major points you want to be sure to make. Write them down randomly, as they occur to you. Now read quickly through your pack of note cards and add to your list any important points you have left out. Then decide which ideas should go first, which should go second, and so on.

Putting your points in order is something of a guess at this point. You may well want to re-order them before you begin to write—or later when you are writing a first (or even later) draft. But make your best guess. The easiest way to try out an order is to take your random list and put a **1** in front of the point you will probably begin with, a **2** before the probable second point, and so on. Then copy the list, in numerical order, onto a clean sheet of paper, revising (if you need to) as you go. Do not be surprised if later you have to revise your list further. Your next task is to match up your note cards (and the examples they contain) with the points on your outline.

Putting things in a particular order is a spatial problem, and by having your notes on cards or pieces of paper of a uniform size you can do much of your organizing physically. Do your sorting on a large table or sit in the middle of the floor. Prepare a title card for each point in your outline, writing on it the point and its probable place in your paper. Then line them up in order, like this:

Point 1	Point 2	Point 3	Point 4
———		———	———
	———		

Point 5	Point 6	Point 7	Point 8
———	———	———	———
———		———	

Point 9	Point 10	Point 11	Point 12
———	———	———	———
		———	

Etcetera. You may have only three or four points, not twelve, but the principle is the same for a short or a long paper. Now go through your whole pack of cards; the object is to line up each note with its appropriate point by putting all your cards in the appropriate pile. If you have too few piles, you may need to subdivide the piles into subpoints before you begin writing.

Two-thirds of this exercise is quite easy: most examples and ideas you have written down will match quite easily with a particular point. But some cards will resist classification. Some cards will seem to belong in two or more places; others will not seem to belong at all. If a card seems to belong to more than one point, put it in the pile with the lowest number (but write on it the number or numbers of other possible locations). If, for example, a card may belong in point **2**, but could also belong in point **6** or **9**, put it in the pile of **2**s and write "maybe **6** or **9**" on the card; if you don't use it in writing about point **2**, move it to pile **6**; if you don't then use it in **6**, move it to **9**. Remember that you will work your way through the piles in numerical order, so that you have a safety system for notes that don't seem to belong where you first thought but that still belong somewhere in your paper. Move them to a possible later point, or put them in a special pile (marked "?" or "use in revised draft") and, once you have completed a first draft on your paper, go through this pile, carefully looking for places in your paper where these ideas may belong. Almost never will everything fit neatly into your first draft. If everything does seem to fit exactly as you had originally planned, you have either done an incredible job of planning and guessing about the organization of your paper, or you are forcing things into inappropriate places.

Don't be surprised if you have a large number of left-over note cards, that is, cards whose ideas you haven't yet used, after you have written your first draft. You will probably find places for many of these ideas later, but some just won't fit or won't be needed for the paper you ultimately write, no matter how good the ideas are. No paper will do everything it could do. Writing a paper is a *human* project; it has limits.

Before you actually start writing, you may want to develop a more elaborate outline, incorporating your examples and including topic sentences for each paragraph, or you may wish to work from your sketchy outline and the accompanying packs of cards. Do the more detailed outline if it seems right to you, but don't delay the writing too long. You are probably ready right now, and any exercises you invent to delay writing are probably just excuses.

Developing an Argument

Once you have decided on your major points and assembled your evidence, you have to decide how you are going to present your argument and how you are going to present *yourself*. What you say is, of course, more important than how you say it, but your manner of presentation can make a world of difference. Putting your evidence together effectively—in a coherent and logical order so that your readers' curiosities and questions are answered systematically and fully —is half the task in developing a persuasive argument. The other half involves your choice of a voice and tone that will make your readers want to read on—and make them favorably disposed toward what you say.

Your tone in your paper is just as important in its way as is the tone of the work of literature you are writing about. It is the basis of your relationship with your reader. If you have not done a lot of formal writing, you may feel that you have no *choice* of tone or of how you are going to present yourself. "I will just be *me*," you may say, "and write naturally." But writing is not a "natural" act, any more than swinging a tennis racket, carrying a football, or dancing a pirouette. The "me" you choose to present is only one of several possible me's; you will project a certain mood, a certain attitude toward your subject, a certain confidence. Will you choose to be cocky and arrogant? Tentative and uncertain? Rigid, difficult, and dogmatic? Insecure, bewildered, and hesitant? The question is, how do you want your readers to feel about you and your argument? Being too positive can make your readers feel stupid and inadequate and can turn them into defensive, resistant readers who will rebel at your every point. Friendship with your reader is better than an adversary relationship. Sounding like a nice person who is talking reasonably and sensibly is not enough if in fact you don't make sense or have nothing to say, but the purpose of the tone you choose is to make your reader receptive to your content, not hostile. The rest of the job depends on the argument itself.

It has been said that all good papers should be organized in the same way:

1. Tell 'em what you're going to tell 'em.
2. Tell 'em.
3. Tell 'em what you told 'em.

That description fits—in pretty general terms—the most common kind of organization, which includes an introduction, a body of argument, and a conclusion, but if it is followed too simplistically it can lead to a paper that sounds kind of simple minded. You don't want to say "Dear Reader, what I am going to do is . . ." or "Dear Reader, what I have done is. . . ." The beginning does need to introduce the subject, sort out the essential issues, and suggest what your perspective will be, and the conclusion does need to sum up what you have said in the main part of your paper, but the first paragraph shouldn't give *every-thing* away, nor should the final one simply repeat what is already clear. Lead into your subject clearly but with a little subtlety and finesse; arrange your main points in the most effective manner you can think of, building a logical argument and supporting your general points with clear textual evidence, concisely phrased and presented, and at the end show *how* your argument has added up—don't just *say* that it did.

There are, of course, other ways to organize than the basic Tell[3] method. Some writers, for example, can develop an argument on the analogy of a mystery story—building suspense in a dramatic way and pulling all the parts of the argument together only at the end. But it is awfully easy to sound precious and cute that way, and such sophisti-cated devices of organizing are usually best left to more experienced writers.

Experiment with such methods later when you feel more confident, when you have succeeded repeatedly with a more simple structure. The imagination and originality that can be exercised in a straight-forward Tell[3] paper are practically unlimited. The challenge is to hold to the basic plan and subtly work enough variation on it that your readers are constantly surprised without ever feeling that they have been tricked or made fools of.

Writing the First Draft

It is now time to set pen to paper. No one can help you much now for a while: you are on your own. The main thing is to get started right with a clear first sentence that expresses your sense of direction and arrests the attention of your readers. (If you can't think of a good first sentence, don't pause over it too long. Write down a paraphrase of what you want it to say—something like the statement you wrote down after your third reading—and go on to start writing about your main points. Your "first" sentence may sometimes be the last one you will write.) And then you inch along, word by word and sentence by sentence, as you follow your outline from one paragraph to an-other. Keep at it. Struggle. Stare into space. Bite your pen when you feel like it. Get up and stride about the room. Scratch your head. Sharpen a pencil. Run your fingers through your hair. Groan. Snap your fingers. Pray. But keep writing.

It is often frustrating as you search for the right word or struggle to decide how the next sentence begins, but it is satisfying when you get it right. Stay with it until you complete a draft you think you can live with. Write "The End" at the bottom and set it aside. Put your favorite book on it so it won't leap up and fly away from its own excitement. Breathe a sigh of relief and try not to think about the revisions you will do tomorrow.

Welcome to the fellowship of writers.

FROM ROUGH DRAFT TO COMPLETED PAPER

Revising

This final stage of the process is the most important of all, and it is the easiest one to mismanage. The effort that raises a *C* paper to an *A* paper most often takes place here; there is a world of difference between a bunch of ideas that present a decent interpretation of a work of literature and a cogent, coherent, persuasive essay that will stir your readers to a nod of agreement and shared pleasure in a moment of insight—or that will prompt your instructor toward praise and generosity. If you haven't done good literary analysis and sorted out your insights earlier, nothing you do at this stage will help much, but if what you have done so far is satisfactory, this is the stage that can turn your paper into something special.

The important thing is not to allow yourself to be too easily satisfied. If you have struggled with earlier stages (and students who are honest with themselves will all admit that the early stages of writing a paper *are* a struggle), it may be tempting to think you are Finished when you have put a period to the last sentence in your first draft. It will often feel as if you are done: you may feel drained, tired of the subject, anxious to get on to other things, such as sleep or food or friends or another project. And it *is* a good idea to take a break once you've finished a draft and let what you have done settle for a few hours, preferably over night. (The Roman poet and critic Horace suggested putting a draft aside for nine years, but most instructors won't wait that long to grade an assignment.) Re-reading it "cold" may be discouraging, though: all those sentences that felt so good when you wrote them often seem flat and stale, or even worthless, when a little time has elapsed. The biggest battle, in moving from a first draft to a second one, is to keep from throwing what you have written into a wastebasket—or to keep from throwing up on top of it. Resist. It will get better, but not without your help.

It may take *several* more drafts to produce your best work. Often it is tempting to cut corners—to smooth out a troublesome paragraph by obscuring the issue or by omitting the difficult point altogether instead of confronting it, or to ask a roommate or friend for help in figuring out what is wrong with a particular passage. But you will learn more in the long run—and probably do better in the short run as well—if you make yourself struggle a bit. When a particular word or phrase you have used turns out to be imprecise, or misleading, or ambiguous, search until you find the *right* word or phrase. (At the least put a big X in the margin so that you will come back and fix it later; thoughtful revision does not all come at once, and you may sometimes profit from pondering one problem while you go on to something else.) If a paragraph is incomplete or poorly organized, fill it out or reorganize it. If a transition from one point to another does not work, look again at your outline and see if another way of ordering your points would help. *Never* decide that the problem can best be solved by hoping that your reader will not notice. The satisfaction of finally solving the problem will give you confidence, and if you get in the habit of overlooking or covering up little problems, you will build yourself a big long-range problem.

Reviewing Your Work and Revising Again

Precisely how you move from one draft to another is up to you and will properly depend on the ways you work best; the key is to find all the things that bother you (and that *should* bother you) and then gradually correct them, moving toward a better paper with each succeeding draft. Here are some things to watch for.

Thesis and central thrust: It is clear what your main point is? Do you state it clearly, effectively, and early? Do you make clear what the work is about? Are you fair to the spirit and the emphasis of the work? Do you make clear the relationship between your thesis and the central thrust of the work? Do you explain *how* the work creates its effect rather than just asserting it?

Organization: Does your paper move logically from beginning to end? Does your first paragraph set up the main issue you are going to discuss and suggest the direction of your discussion? Do your paragraphs follow each other in a coherent and logical order? Does the first sentence of each paragraph accurately suggest what that paragraph will contain? Does your final paragraph draw a conclusion that follows from the body of your paper? Do you resolve the issues you say you resolve?

Use of evidence: Do you use enough examples? Too many? Does each example prove what you say it does? Do you explain each example fully enough? Are the examples sufficiently varied? Are any of them labored, or over explained, or made to bear more weight than they can stand? Have you left out any examples useful to your thesis? Do you include any gratuitous ones just because you like them? Have you achieved a good balance between examples and generalizations?

Tone: How does your voice sound in the paper? Confident? Arrogant? Boastful? Does it show off too much? Is it too timid or self-effacing? Do you ever sound smug? Scared? Too tentative? Too dogmatic? Would a neutral reader be persuaded by the way you explain? Would such a reader be put off by any of your assertions? By your way of arguing? By your choice of examples? By the language you use?

Sentences: Does each sentence read clearly and crisply? Have you rethought and rewritten any sentences you can't explain? Is the first sentence of your paper a strong, clear one likely to gain the interest of a neutral reader? Is the first sentence of each paragraph an especially vigorous one? Are your sentences varied enough? Do you avoid the passive voice and "there is/there are" sentences?

Word choice: Have you used any words whose meaning you are not sure of? In any cases in which you were not sure of what word to use, did you stay with the problem until you found the exact word? Do your metaphors and figures of speech make literal sense? Are all the idioms used correctly? Is your terminology correct? Are your key words always used to mean *exactly* the same thing? Have you avoided sounding repetitive by varying your sentences rather than using several different terms to mean precisely the same thing?

Conciseness: Have you eliminated all the padding you put in when you didn't think your paper would be long enough? Have you gone through your paper, sentence by sentence, to eliminate all the unnecessary words and phrases? Have you looked for sentences (or even paragraphs) that essentially repeat what you have already said—and eliminated all repetition? Have you checked for multiple examples and pared down to the best and most vivid ones? Have you gotten rid of all inflated phrasing calculated to impress readers? Have you eliminated all roundabout phrases and rewritten long, complicated, or confusing sentences into shorter, clearer ones? Are you convinced that you have trimmed every possible bit of excess and that you cannot say what you have to say any more economically?

Mechanics: Have you checked the syntax in each *separate* sentence? Have you checked the spelling of any words that you are not sure of or that look funny? Have you examined each sentence separately for punctuation? Have you checked every quotation word by word against the original? Have you given proper credit for all material—written or oral—that you have borrowed from others? Have you followed the directions your instructor gave you for citations, footnotes, and form?

The most effective way to revise in the final stages is to read through your paper looking for one problem at a time, that is, to go through it once looking at paragraphing, another time looking at individual sentences, still another for word choice or problems of grammar. It is almost impossible to check too many things too often—although you can get so absorbed with little things that you overlook larger matters. With practice, you will learn to watch carefully for the kinds of mistakes you are most prone to. Everyone has individual weaknesses and flaws. Here are some of the most common temptations that beginning writers fall for:

    1. Haste. (Don't start too late, or finish too soon after you begin.)

    2. Pretentiousness. (Don't use words you don't understand, tackle problems that are too big for you, or write sentences you can't ex-

plain: it is more important to make sense than to make a big, empty impression.)

3. Boredom. (The quickest way to bore others is to be bored yourself. If you think your paper will be a drag, you are probably right. It is hard to fake interest in something you can't get excited about; keep at it until you find a spark.)

4. Randomness. (Don't try to string together half a dozen unrelated ideas or insights and con yourself into thinking that you have written a paper.)

5. Imprecision. (Don't settle for approximation, either in words or ideas; something that is 50 percent right is also 50 percent wrong.)

6. Universalism. (Don't try to be a philosopher and make grand statements about life; stick to what is in the story, poem, or play you are writing about.)

7. Vagueness. (Don't settle for a general "sense" of the work you are talking about; get it detailed, get it right.)

8. Wandering. (Don't lose track of your subject or the work that you are talking about.)

9. Sloppiness. (Don't sabotage all your hard work on analysis and writing by failing to notice misspelled words, grammatical mistakes, misquotations, incorrect citations or references, or typographical errors. Little oversights make readers suspicious.)

10. Impatience. (Don't be too anxious to get done. Enjoy the experience; savor the process. Have fun watching yourself learn.)

Being flexible—being willing to rethink your ideas and reorder your argument as you go—is crucial to success in writing, especially in writing about literature. You will find different (and better) ways to express your ideas and feelings as you struggle with revisions, and you will also find that—in the course of analyzing the work, preparing to write, writing, and rewriting—your response to the work itself will have grown and shifted somewhat. Part of the reason is that you will have gotten more knowledgeable—maybe even smarter—as a result of the time and effort you have spent, and you will have, by the time you finish, a more subtle understanding of the work. But part of the reason will also be that the work itself will not be exactly the same. Just as a work is a little different for every reader, it is also a little different with every successive reading by the *same* reader, and what you will be capturing in your words is some of the subtlety of the work in its capability of producing effects that are alive and therefore always changing just slightly. You need not, therefore, feel that you must say the final word about the work you are writing about—but you do want to say whatever word you have to say in the best possible way.

You can turn all this into a full-time job, of course, but you needn't. It is hard work, and at first the learning seems slow and the payoff questionable. A basketball novice watching the magic of a Julius Erving may find it hard to see the point of practicing layups, but even creative geniuses have to go through those awful moments of sitting down and putting pen to paper (and then crossing out and rewriting again and again). But that's the way you learn to make it seem easy. Art is mostly craft, and craft means methodical work. As one of our most accomplished poets once put it:

> True ease in writing comes from art, not chance,
> As those move easiest who have learned to dance.

It *will* come more easily with practice. But you needn't aspire to professional writing to take pleasure in what you accomplish. Learning to write well about literature will help you with all sorts of tasks, some of them having little to do with writing. Writing, like most other meaningful exercises in the educational process, trains the mind, creates habits, teaches you procedures that will have all kinds of long-range payoffs that you may not immediately recognize or be able to predict. And ultimately it is very satisfying, even if it is not easy, to be able to stand back and say, "That is mine. Those are my words. I did it. I have gotten it right. I know what I'm talking about. I understand, and I can make someone else understand." Communication through words is one of the activities that make us distinctively human.

One final bit of advice: do not follow, too rigidly or too closely, anyone's advice, including ours. We have suggested some general strategies and listed some common pitfalls. But writing is a very personal experience, and you will have talents (and faults) that are a little different from anyone else's. Learn to play to your own strengths and avoid the weaknesses that you are especially prone to. Pay attention to your instructor's comments; learn from your own mistakes.

A SUMMARY OF THE PROCESS

Here, briefly, is a summary, step by step, of the stages we have suggested you move through in preparing a paper about literature.

Stage One: Deciding what to write about.
- Read the work straight through, thoughtfully. Make notes at the end on any points that caught your special attention.
- Read the work again more slowly, pausing to think through all the parts you don't understand. When you finish, write a three- or four-sentence summary.
- Read the work again, carefully but quite quickly. Decide what you feel most strongly about in the work, and write down the one thing you would most want to explain to a friend about how the story (or poem or play) works, or (if the work still puzzles you) the one question you would most like to be able to answer.
- Decide how the statement you made at the end of your third reading relates to the summary you wrote down after the second reading.
- Write a one-paragraph "promise" of what your paper is going to argue.

Stage Two: Planning your paper
- Read the work at least twice more and make notes on anything that relates to your thesis.

- Read through all your notes so far, and for each write a sentence articulating how it relates to your thesis.
- Transfer all your notes to note cards of uniform size.
- Read through all your notes again and record any new observations or ideas on additional note cards.
- Set aside your note cards for the moment, and make a brief outline of the major points you intend to make.
- Sort the note cards into piles corresponding to the major points in your outline. Sort the cards in each separate pile into the most likely order of their use in the paper.
- Make a more detailed outline (including the most significant examples) from your pile of note cards on each point.
- Reconsider your order of presentation and make any necessary adjustments.
- Begin writing.

Stage Three: Rewriting.
- Go over your writing, word by word, sentence by sentence, and paragraph by paragraph, in draft after draft until your writing is worthy of the ideas you want to express.

SOME FINAL THOUGHTS

Why write about literature? There are two kinds of answers to this question in a literature course. One is that your instructor will probably insist on it. In fact, your college probably insists on it, one way or another, as a requirement for graduation. But there's a larger reason that lies behind your instructor's (and your college's) insistence. That is because writing is a way of knowing, or of coming to know. In a very real sense, you do not actually know whether you know a particular thing until you can explain it to someone else. Are you ever tempted to say: "I know what that poem means but I just can't explain it"? That's a clear sign that you need to read it again, maybe several more times, and try to figure out how to talk about the meaning, or the effect, or the total intellectual and emotional experience of the poem. No interpretation will *be* the poem, of course, or the perfect equivalent of the poem, but as you learn to interpret more precisely and more readily, you will discover that your experience itself is richer. You will get not just vague sensations of pleasure or pain, but more clearly defined responses that will let you know that you know. The old adage that the way to learn something thoroughly and permanently is to teach it to someone else is especially applicable to attempts to interpret literature by writing about it. Years from now you will remember very well the stories, poems, and plays that you write about, while others will have slipped away from you. But even more important, you will have exercised and refined your skills of knowing by applying them in a concentrated way; doing a good paper on one poem or one story or one play will make you a better reader of the next work of literature you read, of whatever kind.

Reading literature, even for students who begin with indifference, usually turns out to be a pleasure; writing about literature sometimes does not. We will not try to kid you: writing about literature is not easy, even though it does use words to describe other words. And even for people who get very good at it, it is hard work. But it can also be very satisfying work if you take the time and trouble to do it well and endure the frustration of confronting your weaknesses and mistakes. You can learn to do it, but it may take a lot of effort and some unsuccessful attempts along the way. You will soon develop your own habits and learn to play to your own strengths and capabilities. Meanwhile, here is a checklist of some things to keep in mind.

1. Begin early. Last minute means last resort.

2. Complete your analysis before you begin to write. It is easier to write when you know what you think.

3. Plan. Don't wait for divine inspiration or trust to luck.

4. Outline. Be sure you know where all your thoughts go and how they fit together.

5. Limit your subject. A paper that is about everything is about nothing.

6. Think clearly all the way to the end. Do not let your sentences or paragraphs trail off into uncertainty, vague attempts to sound impressive, or a hope for supernatural intervention.

7. Argue. A discussion with a friend or roommate will normally clarify what you think. Strong feelings are not enough to make a paper work, but vigor reinforces clarity.

8. Prove. Assertions are for headlines; an essay has to give evidence and convince its audience.

9. Be clear. Fog enlarges objects but does not enhance prose. "Partly cloudy" is not a favorable forecast for your paper.

10. Be varied. Do not write the same paper every week of the term. Once you know what you *can* do well, experiment with other possibilities. You will learn more by taking risks, even if sometimes you do not succeed, than you will by repeated success in the same rut. And most teachers will respect your attempt to improve yourself rather than basking in repeated reflection of past glories.

11. Be hard on yourself. Never settle for a sentence that almost makes sense or a word that is almost right.

12. Rewrite. Getting something right in words takes time and patience. Most papers take several drafts before they begin to seem smooth. It takes a lot of work to sound effortless. Let your prose "cool" between drafts whenever possible; you will find trouble spots more easily when you are a bit removed from the thoughts behind the writing. Sleeping on a paper is not always a good thing (it depends on what you do when you wake up), but it can help provide the distance that can lead to good critical judgment. It is better to find your own problems and correct them than to read about them in your instructor's comments.

13. Type. The chances are that your instructor does not have a

degree in hieroglyphics and did not work as a decoder in World War II.

14. Proofread. Who wants to read a paper you did not care enough about to read yourself?

15. Proofread again. Find your mistakes before someone else does. It is less expensive.

16. Read it one more time.

TWO SAMPLE PAPERS

The two essays that follow were written by students in their freshman
year at Emory University. We are grateful to Geoffrey Clement and
Christine Woodside for their kind permission to reprint their papers
here.

The Struggle to Surface

in the Water of <u>Sonny's Blues</u>

Geoffrey Clement

In <u>Sonny's Blues</u>, James Baldwin employs
water as a symbol that enables him to concentrate more clearly on the lack of and the
crucial need for a real sense of communication
among members of society. As Baldwin captures
the intensity of Sonny's and his brother's
struggles to understand their situation, he
vividly depicts a society that seeks to swallow
up the souls of its inhabitants and gradually
to drown them spiritually. Thus, Baldwin illus-

trates quite clearly his sense of the hopelessness in man's plight. In portraying the
struggle of street life in Harlem, he uses
water in its opposite forms—frozen water and
boiling water—and toward the end of the story,
as Sonny's and his brother's revelations help
to resolve the conflict, the water becomes calm.

Initially, and as a result of Sonny's
arrest, Sonny's brother gradually realizes that
he has not fulfilled his promise and that his
feelings of love for his brother have certainly
gone unexpressed, if indeed they exist. As a
result, he feels physically the coldness that
has permeated his emotional life: "It was a
special kind of ice. It kept melting, sending
trickles of ice water all up and down my veins,
but it never got less. Sometimes it hardened
and seemed to expand . . ." (p.305). So the ice
represents his guilt and his fears, both of
which will lessen little. Although he learns to
adapt to these feelings, they occasionally re-

surface. Upon Sonny's return from prison, for example, his brother thinks, "And thank God she [his wife] was there, for I was filled with that icy dread again. Everything I did seemed awkward to me, and everything I said sounded freighted with hidden meaning. . . . I was dying to hear him tell me he was safe." (p. 311) In addition to this guilt, Sonny's brother experiences much of the same emotional turmoil that Sonny has endured. In this passage in particular, he is seeking reassurance that there is a way to survive their imprisonment without having to feel the pain Sonny felt. Baldwin not only uses ice to show the brother's disappointment in his failures as a brother but also to point to the brother's own struggle for security, identity, and communication.

As Sonny's brother begins to realize that within him there has grown a heart hardened and haunted by the cold darkness of Harlem's streets, he also begins to recognize many of

the realities that his brother has faced and
that he too must eventually face. Sonny's
brother is spiritually walking through "the
vivid, killing steets of our childhood. These
steets hadn't changed, though housing projects
jutted up out of them now like rocks in the
middle of a boiling sea." (p. 310) Here, Baldwin paints an almost hellish picture of pain and
suffering, of emotional torment and fears, and
of spiritual drowning and isolation, all of
which slowly become real in the mind of Sonny's
brother. He begins to feel for the first time
in his life the depth of his denial of his
brother. Tragically, he finds that when he is
ready to reach out to help Sonny, he cannot, for
he is even more lost and confused than Sonny
himself. Sonny's brother wants desperately to
save Sonny from the inevitable struggle, yet he
learns from Sonny that "the storm inside" (p.
323) will pass over only with the constant expression of love. Clearly, the process of reve-

lation is a very dramatic one, since Sonny's
brother comes to understand Sonny's need for a
giving, communicating, responsible relationship,
a commitment filled with careful listening,
compassion, and understanding. Sonny does not
believe he can make his brother understand his
experiences with drugs: "I can never tell you.
I was all by myself at the bottom of something,
and I thought I'd die if I couldn't get away
from it and yet, all the same, I knew that
everything I was doing was just locking me in
with it" (p. 324). Once his brother grasps the
importance of listening with love and understanding, however, Sonny is finally able to
reach out.

Toward the end of the story, the ice and
the boiling sea come together, and there is
peace; Sonny is able to reach out, and he starts
to swim in the calmer water. Now, he finds
freedom in expressing his struggles through his
music, while at the same time alerting his

audience to the lessons he has learned. Creole "wanted Sonny to leave the shoreline and strike out for the deep water. He was Sonny's witness that deep water and drowning were not the same thing" (p. 326). As Sonny ventures further and further into his own understanding of life's struggles, he tries, his brother tells us, "to find new ways to make us listen. For while the tale of how we suffer, and how we are delighted, and how we triumph is never new, it always must be heard. . . . it's the only light we've got in all this darkness" (p. 327). In a powerful way, Sonny taught the audience to listen: "Freedom lurked around us and I understood, at last, that he could help us be free if we would listen, that we would never be free until we did" (p. 327). The boiling rage of the streets and the coldness within his heart are reconciled as the brother finally witnesses "Sonny's world" (p. 325). Finally, he recognizes that Sonny has found the strength of knowing that he has discovered in music the outlet through which he can express himself and warn others of his mistakes. He sends up to the bandstand not water, not ice, but Scotch and milk. Sonny sips it in a sort of communion and puts it back on top of the piano, where "it glowed and shook about . . . [his] head like the very cup of trembling" (p. 328).

Throughout his story, Baldwin stresses the lack of companionship to try to manipulate the reader's emotions. Playing on the contrasts between forms of water, he draws parallels to the theme of emotional conflict within the minds of Sonny and his brother. While the sea is calmer toward the end, there is still a sense of rage, because only in the expression, of his struggle is Sonny able to find meaning, satisfaction, and forgiveness for his brother. The streets, society's common ground, still try to isolate its members as each person individually struggles to reach the surface. But if the

struggler can find a listening helper, which
Sonny finds in his brother, then he will reach
the surface and breathe the fulfilling breath
of love. The cup of trembling will be taken out
of the struggler's hands, the Bible tells us,
and will be put "into the hands of them that
afflict thee" (p. 328 n.). Light gracefully
touches and penetrates the surface of the water,
and the cup of trembling is still.

Metrical Variation and Meaning
in "To the Memory of Mr. Oldham"

Christine Woodside

In his poem "To the Memory of Mr. Oldham,"
John Dryden rationalizes the death of a fellow
satirist by comparing himself to the dead man.
He begins by saying they were "cast in the same
poetic mold," then considers the fact that
Oldham's youth did not prevent him from reaching
the "same goal" before the older speaker.
Dryden also notes that while age—and thus experience—would have given Oldham a smoother
command of the English language, satire and wit
do not need such polishing and will "shine"
through a less-experienced poet's "rugged line."
He points out the possible stagnant quality
that experience can nurture and seems to imply
both that experience is unnecessary to produce

good satire and that Oldham's death was timely,
since he had already succeeded. Still, the poem
ends in a tired, labored farewell, suggesting
that Oldham's death was <u>not</u> timely, and that
"fate and gloomy night" surround him. Since this
poem is a single stanza, the shifts in thought
and tone are subtle. The occasional exceptions
to the iambic pentameter emphasize the different
themes Dryden addresses. Although the variations
in meter do not drastically alter the poem's
significance, they do clarify some of the main
<u>ideas</u> in the poem.

The first notable idea is the alliance
Dryden feels with Oldham, which is emphasized
by four separate metrical variations. The word
"allied" in the third line is accented on the
first syllable, which disturbs the metrical
flow that requires a stress on the second. In
the next line, "cast in the same" throws off the
iambic rhythm with an unexpected stress on the
word "cast." (This also highlights the word

"same," since two small words are unaccented between the two.) A third metrical surprise is in the fifth line, where the first three words, "One common note," receive accents. These accents not only emphasize the words, but actually slow down the reader. Another emphasis on unity is in the seventh line, where the first two words yield to stresses on the third and fourth in "To the same goal." All of these unsettling accent changes illustrate Dryden's conviction that both he and Oldham had the same goals in their poetry.

There are two variances in meter that emphasize youth. The first of these occurs when Dryden mentions that Oldham has surpassed his older and more experienced ally in a short amount of time: "While his young friend performed and won the race." Here the word "young" receives the unexpected accent. Not surprisingly, Dryden goes on to discuss Oldham's youth and youth's lack of control over the language.

The second metrical variation deals with this inexperience with language, saying that a young poet's work must show "Through the harsh cadence of a rugged line." By position, neither "harsh" nor "cadence" would normally receive the accent, but both stand out noticeably. Interestingly, Dryden chooses to emphasize, metrically, youthful inexperience while at the same time saying that satire does <u>not</u> need an experienced control of the language. By doing this, he is contending that youth is <u>not</u> a handicap, at least not in satire. Still, he does choose to emphasize the "harsh cadence" (the consonants are hard to pronounce) of inexperienced work.

The next three metrical variations shift the attention to experience, which, he says, only "mellows what we write to the dull sweets of rhyme." The word "dull" receives an unexpected accent and, together with "sweets," gives the line a tired, heavy quality. This mirrors

Dryden's thought that "maturing time" will only
make his work "dull." (Also, as he mentions that
rhyme can become stagnant, he has just completed three consecutive rhyming lines; the
pattern calls for two.) The second "dull"
metrical difference appears in line 22. "Once
more, hail" is also slow and heavy because all
three words need an accent. Finally, the last
line contains six iambic feet instead of five,
and the last word is redundant: "But fate and
gloomy night encompass thee around." To say
"encompass thee" would imply the word "around";
the last word does not change or clarify anything. It merely shows that Dryden allows the
"dull sweets of rhyme" to control his choice of
words! In the three metrical variations above,
Dryden generates the very dullness he criticizes
as characteristic of an older, experienced poet
such as himself.

    This poem discusses the "one common note"
Dryden shares with Oldham; it then considers

Oldham's youth; then deals with Dryden's age
and experience in relation to the dead man's
youth. All three of these ideas are reflected in
the variations of the iambic pentameter, and the
variations strengthen their impact.

Acknowledgments

James Baldwin: "Sonny's Blues" excerpted from the book *Going to Meet the Man* by James Baldwin. Copyright © 1948, 1951, 1957, 1958, 1960, 1965 by James Baldwin. Permission granted by The Dial Press.

Toni Cade Bambara: "My Man Bovanne" copyright © 1971 by Toni Cade Bambara. Reprinted from *Gorilla, My Love*, by Toni Cade Bambara, by permission of Random House, Inc.

Richard Connell: "The Most Dangerous Game" by Richard Connell, copyright 1924 by Richard Connell. Copyright renewed 1952 by Louise Fox Connell. Reprinted by permission of Brandt & Brandt Literary Agents, Inc.

William Faulkner: "A Rose for Emily" copyright 1930 and renewed 1958 by William Faulkner. "Barn Burning" copyright 1939 and renewed 1967 by Estelle Faulkner and Jill Faulkner Summers. Both stories are reprinted from *Collected Stories of William Faulkner* by permission.

Gabriel Garcia Marquez: "A Very Old Man with Enormous Wings" from *Leaf Storm and Other Stories* by Gabriel Garcia Marquez. Copyright © 1971 by Gabriel Garcia Marquez. Reprinted by permission of Harper & Row, Publishers, Inc.

Ernest Hemingway: "The Short Happy Life of Francis Macomber" (copyright 1936 by Ernest Hemingway; copyright renewed), from *The Short Stories of Ernest Hemingway*. Copyright 1938 by Ernest Hemingway; copyright renewed. Reprinted with the permission of Charles Scribner's Sons.

Spenver Holst: "The Zebra Storyteller" from *The Language of Cats and Other Stories* by Spencer Holst. Copyright © 1971 by Spencer Holst. Reprinted by permission of the publisher, E. P. Dutton, Inc.

Shirley Jackson: "The Lottery" from *The Lottery* by Shirley Jackson. Copyright 1948, 1949 by Shirley Jackson. Copyright renewed © 1976, 1977 by Laurence Hyman, Barry Hyman, Mrs. Sarah Webster, and Mrs. Joanne Schnurer. First published in *The New Yorker*. Reprinted by permission of Farrar, Strauss & Giroux, Inc.

James Joyce: "Araby" from *Dubliners* by James Joyce. Copyright © 1967 by the Estate of James Joyce. Reprinted by permission of Viking Penguin, Inc.

Franz Kafka: "A Hunger Artist" reprinted by permission of Schocken Books Inc. from *The Penal Colony* by Franz Kafka, trans. by Willa and Edwin Muir. Copyright © 1948, 1976 by Schocken Books Inc.

D. H. Lawrence: "The Rocking Horse Winner" from *The Complete Short Stories of D. H. Lawrence, Vol. III*, copyright 1934 by Frieda Lawrence; copyright © renewed 1962 by Angelo Ravagli and C. M. Weekly, Executors of the Estate of Frieda Lawrence Ravagli. Reprinted by permission of Viking Penguin, Inc.

Doris Lessing: "Our Friend Judith" from *A Man and Two Women* by Doris Lessing. Copyright © 1958, 1962, 1963 by Doris Lessing. Reprinted by permission of Simon & Schuster, Inc. and Jonathan Clowes Ltd., London, on behalf of Doris Lessing.

Katherine Mansfield: "Her First Ball," copyright 1922 by Alfred A. Knopf, Inc., and renewed 1950 by John Middleton Murry. Reprinted from *The Short Stories of Katherine Mansfield*, by Katherine Mansfield, by permission of Alfred A. Knopf, Inc.

Bobbie Ann Mason: "Shiloh" from *Shiloh and Other Stories* by Bobbie Ann Mason. Originally appeared in *The New Yorker*. Copyright © 1982 by Bobbie Ann Mason. Reprinted by permission of Harper & Row, Publishers, Inc.

Alice Munro: "Boys and Girls" from *The Dance of the Happy Shades* by Alice Munro. Copyright © Alice Munro, 1968. Reprinted by permission of McGraw-Hill Ryerson Limited, Toronto.

Flannery O'Connor: "The Artificial Nigger" copyright © 1955 by Flannery O'Connor. Reprinted from her volume *A Good Man is Hard to Find* by permission of Harcourt Brace Jovanovich, Inc.

Grace Paley: "A Conversation With My Father" from *Enormous Changes at the Last Minute* by Grace Paley. Copyright © 1972, 1974 by Grace Paley. Reprinted with the permission of Farrar, Straus & Giroux, Inc.

Katherine Anne Porter: "Flowering Judas" from *Flowering Judas and Other Stories*, copyright 1930, 1958 by Katherine Anne Porter. Reprinted by permission of Harcourt Brace Jovanovich, Inc.

Mordecai Richler: "The Summer My Grandmother Was Supposed to Die" from *The Street* by Mordecai Richler. Copyright © 1975 by Mordecai Richler. Reprinted by permission of Monica McCall, International Creative Management.

Leo Tolstoy: "How Much Land Does a Man Need?" reprinted from *Twenty-Three Tales* by Leo Tolstoy, translated by Louise and Aylmer Maude (1906), by permission of Oxford University Press.

William Trevor: "Beyond the Pale" from *Beyond the Pale and Other Stories* by William Trevor. Copyright © 1981 by William Trevor. Originally published in *The New Yorker*. Reprinted by permission of Viking Penguin, Inc. and A. D. Peters & Co. Ltd.

Franklin P. Adams: "Composed in the Composing Room" from *By and Large* by Franklin P. Adams. Copyright 1914 by Doubleday & Company, Inc. Reprinted by permission of the publisher.

A. R. Ammosn: "Needs" is reprinted from *Collected Poems, 1951–1971*, by A. R. Ammons, by permission of W. W. Norton & Company, Inc. Copyright © 1972 by A. R. Ammons.

Maya Angelou: "Africa" from *Oh Pray My Wings Are Gonna Fit Me Well*, by Maya Angelou. Copyright © 1975 by Maya Angelou. Reprinted by permission of Random House, Inc.

Richard Armour: "Hiding Place" from *Light Armour* by Richard Armour. Copyright © 1954 Richard Armour. Reprinted by permission of McGraw-Hill.

Margaret Atwood: "Death of a Young Son by Drowning" from *The Journals of Susanna Moodie*, copyright Oxford University Press Canada 1970. "Variation on the Word *Sleep*" from *True Stories* copyright © 1981 by Margaret Atwood. Reprinted by permission of

Simon & Schuster, Inc. and Oxford University Press Canada.

W. H. Auden: "In Memory of W. B. Yeats" and "Museé des Beaux Arts" copyright 1940 and renewed 1968 by W. H. Auden. Reprinted from *W. H. Auden: Collected Poems,* by W. H. Auden, edited by Edward Mendelson, by permission of Alfred A. Knopf, Inc. and Faber and Faber Ltd.

John Betjeman: "In Westminster Abbey" from *Collected Poems* by John Betjeman. Reprinted by permission of John Murray (Publishers) Ltd.

Gwendolyn Brooks: "First Fight. Then Fiddle" from *The World of Gwendolyn Brooks.* Copyright 1949 by Gwendolyn Brooks Blakely. Reprinted by permission of Harper & Row, Publishers.

Helen Chasin: "The Word *Plum*" from *Coming Close and Other Poems* reprinted by permission of Yale University Press. Copyright © 1968 by Yale University.

Robert Creeley: "Mother's Voice" from *Mirrors* by Robert Creeley. Copyright © 1983 by Robert Creeley. Reprinted by permission of New Directions Publishing Corporation.

e. e. cummings: "chanson innocente" and "portrait" reprinted from *Tulips and Chimneys* by e. e. cummings, by permission of Liveright Publishing Corporation. Copyright 1923, 1925 and renewed 1951, 1953 by e. e. cummings. Copyright © 1973, 1976 by the Trustees for the e. e. cummings Trust. Copyright © 1973, 1976 by George James Firmage. "l(a" © 1958 by e. e. cummings, renewed 1968 by Marion Morehouse Cummings. Reprinted from his volume *Complete Poems 1913–1962* by permission of Harcourt Brace Jovanovich, Inc.

Walter de la Mare: "Slim Cunning Hands" from *The Complete Poems of Walter de la Mare* is reprinted by permission of the Literary Executors of Walter de la Mare and The Society of Authors as their representative.

James Dickey: "Cherrylog Road" and "The Leap" from *Poems 1957–1967,* by James Dickey. Copyright © 1963, 1964 by James Dickey. Reprinted by permission of Wesleyan University Press. "Cherrylog Road" first appeared in *The New Yorker.*

Emily Dickinson: #s 341, 657, 712 and 986 are reprinted by permission of the Publishers and the Trustees of Amherst College from *The Poems of Emily Dickinson,* edited by Thomas H. Johnson, Cambridge, Mass.: The Belknap Press of Harvard University, Copyright 1951, © 1955, 1979, 1983 by The President and Fellows of Harvard College. #s 341 and 657 are also reprinted by permission of Little, Brown and Company from *The Complete Poems of Emily Dickinson* edited by Thomas H. Johnson copyright 1929 by Martha Dickinson Bianchi; copyright © renewed 1957 by Mary L. Hampson.

Alan Dugan: "Funeral Oration for a Mouse" copyright © 1961, 1962, 1968, 1972, 1973, 1974, 1983 by Alan Dugan. From *New and Collected Poems, 1961–1983* by Alan Dugan, published by The Ecco Press in 1983. Reprinted by permission.

T. S. Eliot: "The Journey of the Magi" from *Collected Poems 1909–1962* by T. S. Eliot, copyright 1936 by Harcourt Brace Jovanovich, Inc.; copyright © 1963, 1964 by T. S. Eliot. Reprinted by permission of Harcourt Brace Jovanovich, Inc. and Faber and Faber Ltd.

Kenneth Fearing: "Dirge" from *New and Selected Poems* by Kenneth Fearing. Reprinted by permission of the publisher, Indiana University Press.

Robert Frost: "Range-Finding," "The Road Not Taken," "Stopping by Woods on a Snowy Evening," and "U. S. 1946 King's X" from *The Poetry of Robert Frost* edited by Edward Connery Lathem. Copyright 1916, 1923, © 1969 by Holt, Rinehart and Winston. Copyright 1944, 1951 by Robert Frost. Copyright © 1975 by Leslie Frost Ballantine. Reprinted by permission of Henry Holt and Company, Inc.

Michael Harper: "Dear John, Dear Coltrane" copyright © 1970, 1985 by Michael S. Harper. Reprinted by permission of the author.

Robert Hayden: "Those Winter Sundays" and "Frederick Douglass" are reprinted from *Angel of Ascent: New and Selected Poems* by Robert Hayden, by permission by Liveright Publishing Corporation. Copyright © 1975, 1972, 1970, 1966 by Robert Hayden.

Seamus Heaney: "Mid-Term Break" from *Poems 1965–1975* by Seamus Heaney. Copyright © 1966, 1969, 1972, 1975, 1980 by Seamus Heaney. Reprinted by permission of Farrar, Straus & Giroux, Inc. Reprinted by permission of Faber and Faber Ltd. from *Death of a Naturalist* by Seamus Heaney.

John Hollander: "Adam's Task" from *The Night Mirror.* Copyright © 1971 John Hollander. Reprinted with the permission of Atheneum Publishers, Inc.

Robert Hollander: "You Too? Me Too—Why Not? Soda Pop" is reprinted from *The Massachusetts Review* © 1968 by The Massachusetts Review, Inc. by permission of the publisher.

A. E. Housman: "Terence, This is Stupid Stuff" and "To an Athlete Dying Young" from "A Shropshire Lad"—authorized edition—from *The Collected Poems of A. E. Housman.* Copyright 1939, 1940, © 1965 by Holt, Rinehart and Winston. Copyright © 1967, 1968 by Robert E. Symons. Reprinted by permission of Henry Holt and Company, Inc., The Society of Authors as the literary representative of the Estate of A. E. Housman, and Jonathan Cape Ltd., publishers of A. E. Housman's *Collected Poems.*

Langston Hughes: "The Negro Speaks of Rivers" copyright 1926 by Alfred A. Knopf, Inc. and renewed 1954 by Langston Hughes. Reprinted from *Selected Poems of Langston Hughes,* by permission of the publisher. "Harlem (A Dream Deferred)" copyright 1959 by Langston Hughes. Reprinted from *The Panther and the Lash,* by Langston Hughes, by permission of Alfred A. Knopf, Inc. "Theme for English B" from *Montage of a Dream Deferred* reprinted by permission of Harold Ober Associates Incorporated. Copyright 1951 by Langston Hughes. Copyright renewed 1979 by George Houston Bass.

Richard Hugo: "To Women" is reprinted from *Making Certain it Goes On: The Collected Poems of Richard Hugo,* by permission of W. W. Norton & Company, Inc. Copyright © 1984 by The Estate of Richard Hugo.

Randall Jarrell: "The Death of the Ball Turret Gunner" from *Randall Jarrell: The Complete Poems.* Copyright © 1945, 1947, 1969 by Mrs. Randall Jarrell. Copyright renewed © 1973 by Mrs. Randall Jarrell. Reprinted by permission of Farrar, Straus and Giroux, Inc.

Donald Justice: "Counting the Mad" from *The Summer Anniversaries,* copyright ©

1957, 1958 by Donald Justice. Reprinted by permission of Wesleyan University Press.
X. J. Kennedy: "In a Prominent Bar in Secaucus One Day" reprinted from *Cross Ties,*
© 1985 X. J. Kennedy. Reprinted by permission of the University of Georgia Press.
Galway Kinnell: "After Making Love We Hear Footsteps" and "St. Francis and the
Sow" from *Mortal Acts, Mortal Words* by Galway Kinnell. Copyright © 1980 by Galway
Kinnell. Reprinted by permission of Houghton Mifflin Company.
Etheridge Knight: "Hard Rock Returns to Prison from the Hospital for the Criminal
Insane" from *Poems from Prison* by Etheridge Knight, © 1968 by Etheridge Knight. Re-
printed by permission of Broadside/Crummel Press, Detroit, Michigan.
Maxine Kumin: "Woodchucks" from *Our Ground Time Here Will Be Brief* by Maxine
Kumin. Copyright © 1971 by Maxine Kumin. Reprinted by permission of Viking Pen-
guin Inc.
Philip Larkin: "Church Going" is reprinted from *The Less Deceived* by permission of
The Marvell Press, England.
D. H. Lawrence: "Piano" from *The Complete Poems of D. H. Lawrence.* Copyright ©
1964, 1971 by Angelo Ravagli and C. M. Weekley, Executors of the Estate of Frieda
Lawrence Ravagli. Reprinted by permission of Viking Penguin, Inc.
Audre Lorde: "Recreation" is reprinted from *The Black Unicorn, Poems* by Audre
Lorde, by permission of W. W. Norton & Company, Inc. Copyright © 1978 by Audre
Lorde.
James Merrill: "Watching the Dance" from *Nights and Days.* Copyright © 1966 James
Merrill. Reprinted with the permission of Atheneum Publishers, Inc.
Joni Mitchell: "Woodstock" © 1969 & 1974 Siquomb Publishing Corp. All Rights Re-
served. Used by permission of Warner Bros. Music.
Arthur W. Monks: "Twilight's Last Gleaming" by Arthur Monks from *Jiggery-Pokery:
A Compendium of Double Dactyls* edited by Anthony Hecht and John Hollander. Copy-
right © 1966 by Anthony Hecht and John Hollander. Reprinted with the permission of
Atheneum Publishers.
Marianne Moore: "Poetry" reprinted with the permission of Macmillan Publishing
Company from *Collected Poems* by Marianne Moore, copyright 1935 by Marianne Moore,
renewed 1963 by Marianne Moore and T. S. Eliot.
Ogden Nash: "The Chipmunk" from *Verses from 1929 On* by Ogden Nash. Copyright
1952 by Ogden Nash. First appeared in the Saturday Evening Post. By permission of
Little, Brown and Company.
Howard Nemerov: "Life Cycle of Common Man" from *The Collected Poems of Howard
Nemerov,* University of Chicago Press 1977. Reprinted by permission of the author.
Gabriel Okara: "Piano and Drums," which originally appeared in *Black Orpheus,* is
reprinted by permission of the author.
Sharon Olds: "Leningrad Cemetery: Winter of 1941" reprinted by permission; © 1979
The New Yorker Magazine, Inc. "Sex without Love" from *The Dead and the Living,* by
Sharon Olds. Copyright © 1983 by Sharon Olds. Reprinted by permission of Alfred A.
Knopf, Inc.
Wilfred Owen: "Dulce et Decorum Est" from *The Collected Poems of Wilfred Owen.*
Copyright © 1963 by Chatto and Windus, Ltd. Reprinted by permission of New Directions,
the author's estate, and Chatto and Windus.
Dorothy Parker: "A Certain Lady," "The Little Old Lady in Lavender Silk," and "One
Perfect Rose" from *The Portable Dorothy Parker* copyright 1931, renewed © 1959 by
Dorothy Parker. Reprinted by permission of Viking Penguin Inc.
Linda Pastan: "Marks" is reprinted from *PM/AM, New and Selected Poems* by Linda
Pastan, by permission of W. W. Norton & Company, Inc. Copyright © 1982 by Linda
Pastan.
Marge Piercy: "Barbie Doll" from *Circles on the Water,* by Marge Piercy. Copyright ©
1982 by Marge Piercy. Reprinted by permission of Alfred A. Knopf, Inc. "To Have With-
out Holding" and "September Afternoon at Four O'Clock" from *The Moon is Always
Female* by Marge Piercy. Copyright © 1980 by Marge Piercy. Reprinted by permission of
Alfred A. Knopf, Inc. "What's That Smell in the Kitchen?" copyright © 1980 by Marge
Piercy. Reprinted from *Stone, Paper, Knife,* by Marge Piercy, by permission of Alfred A.
Knopf, Inc.
Sylvia Plath: "Black Rook in Rainy Weather" (first published in somewhat different
form by William Heinemann Ltd.) from *Crossing the Water* by Sylvia Plath, copyright ©
1971 by Ted Hughes; and "Daddy" from *The Collected Poems of Sylvia Plath* edited by
Ted Hughes, copyright © 1963 by Ted Hughes, are reprinted by permission of Harper &
Row, Publishers, Inc. and Olwyn Hughes. "Point Shirley," copyright © 1959 by Sylvia
Plath, is reprinted from *The Colossus and Other Stories* by Sylvia Plath by permission of
Alfred A. Knopf, Inc. and Olwyn Hughes.
Ezra Pound: "In a Station of the Metro," "The River-Merchant's Wife: A Letter," and
"A Virginal" from *Personae* by Ezra Pound. Copyright 1926 by Ezra Pound. Reprinted by
permission of New Directions Publishing Corporation.
Jarold Ramsey: "The Tally Stick" is reprinted by permission of the author.
Dudley Randall: "Ballad of Birmingham" from *Poem Counter Poem,* © 1969 by
Margaret Danner and Dudley Randall. Reprinted by permission of Broadside/Crummel
Press, Detroit, Michigan.
Henry Reed: "Lessons of the War: Judging Distances" from *A Map of Verona* by
Henry Reed. Reprinted by permission of the author and Jonathan Cape Ltd.
Adrienne Rich: "Aunt Jennifer's Tigers," "Diving Into the Wreck," and "Planetarium"
are reprinted from *The Fact of a Doorframe: Poems Selected and New, 1950–1984* by
Adrienne Rich, by permission of W. W. Norton & Company, Inc. Copyright © 1984 by
Adrienne Rich. Copyright © 1975, 1978 by W. W. Norton & Company, Inc. Copyright ©
1981 by Adrienne Rich.
Edward Arlington Robinson: "Richard Cory" from *The Children of the Night* by Edward
Arlington Robinson is reprinted by permission of Charles Scribner's Sons and is fully pro-
tected by copyright.
Theodore Roethke: "The Dream" copyright 1955 by Theodore Roethke, "I Know a

Woman" copyright 1954 by Theodore Roethke, "My Papa's Waltz" copyright 1942 by Hearst Magazines Inc., and "The Waking" copyright 1953 by Theodore Roethke, are reprinted from the book *The Collected Poems of Theodore Roethke* by permission of Doubleday & Company, Inc.

W. D. Snodgrass: "Leaving the Motel" from *After Experience* by W. D. Snodgrass. Copyright © 1966 by W. D. Snodgrass. Reprinted by permission of Harper & Row, Publishers, Inc.

Stephen Spender: "An Elementary School Classroom in a Slum" copyright 1942 and renewed 1970 by Stephen Spender. Reprinted from *Collected Poems 1928–1953* by Stephen Spender, by permission of Random House, Inc. and Faber and Faber Ltd.

William Stafford: "Traveling Through the Dark" from *Stories That Could Be True* by William Stafford. Copyright © 1960 by William Stafford. Reprinted by permission of Harper & Row, Publishers, Inc.

Wallace Stevens: "The Emperor of Ice-Cream," "Anecdote of the Jar" and "Sunday Morning" copyright 1923 and renewed 1951 by Wallace Stevens. Reprinted from *The Collected Poems of Wallace Stevens*, by permission of Alfred A. Knopf, Inc.

Dylan Thomas: "Do Not Go Gentle Into That Good Night," "Fern Hill," and "In My Craft or Sullen Art," from *The Poems* by Dylan Thomas, copyright 1939, 1946. Reprinted by permission of New Directions Publishing Corporation, the Trustees for the Copyrights of the late Dylan Thomas, and David Higham Associates Ltd.

Mona Van Duyn: "What the Motorcycle Said" from *Merciful Disguises* by Mona Van Duyn. Copyright © 1973 by Mona Van Duyn. Used by permission of Atheneum Publishers.

Diane Wakoski: "Uneasy Rider," copyright © Diane Wakoski, is reprinted by permission of the author.

Tom Wayman: "Picketing Supermarkets" and "Wayman in Love," from *Waiting for Wayman* by Tom Wayman, are reprinted by permission of the author.

Richard Wilbur: "The Beautiful Changes" from *The Beautiful Changes and Other Poems*, copyright 1947, 1975 by Richard Wilbur. Reprinted by permission of Harcourt Brace Jovanovich, Inc.

William Carlos Williams: "Poem (The rose fades)" from *Pictures from Brueghel*, copyright © 1962 by William Carlos Williams. "The Red Wheelbarrow" from *Collected Earlier Poems* of William Carlos Williams, copyright 1938 by New Directions Publishing Corporation. Reprinted by permission of New Directions Publishing Corporation.

Yvor Winters: "At the San Francisco Airport" from *The Collected Poems of Yvor Winters*, 1978, Swallow Press. Reprinted with the permission of Ohio University Press.

William Butler Yeats: "Among School Children," "Leda and the Swan," and "Sailing to Byzantium" copyright 1928 by Macmillan Publishing Co., Inc., renewed 1956 by Georgie Yeats; "The Second Coming" copyright 1924 by Macmillan Publishing Co., Inc., renewed 1952 by Bertha Georgie Yeats. Reprinted by permission of Macmillan Publishing Co., Inc., Michael and Anne Yeats, Macmillan London Ltd., and A. P. Watt Ltd.

Samuel Beckett: *Krapp's Last Tape* reprinted by permission of Grove Press, Inc. and Faber and Faber Ltd. Copyright © 1957 by Samuel Beckett. Copyright 1958, 1959, 1960 by Grove Press, Inc.

Anton Chekhov: "The Brute" from *The Brute and Other Farces*, ed. Eric Bentley. Copyright © 1958 by Eric Bentley. *The Brute and Other Farces* is available from Applause Theatre Book Publishers, 211 West 71st Street, New York, N.Y. 10023. Reprinted by permission of Applause Theatre Book Publishers.

Henrik Ibsen: *Hedda Gabler* from *Hedda Gabler and Three Other Plays* by Henrik Ibsen, translator Michael Meyer. Copyright © 1961 by Michael Meyer. Reprinted by permission of Harold Ober Associates Incorporated.

Arthur Miller: *Death of a Salesman* copyright 1949 by Arthur Miller. © renewed 1967 by Arthur Miller. Reprinted by permission of Viking Penguin, Inc. This play in its printed form is designed for the reading public only. All dramatic rights in it are fully protected by copyright, and no public or private performance—professional or amateur—may be given without the written permission of the author and the payment of a royalty. As the courts have also ruled that the public reading of a play constitutes a public performance, no such reading may be given except under the conditions stated above. Communication should be addressed to the author's representative. International Creative Management, Inc., 40 W. 57th St., New York, N.Y. 10019.

Marsha Norman: *Third and Oak: The Laundromat* reprinted by permission of William Morris Agency, Inc. on behalf of the author. Copyright © 1978 by Marsha Norman.

Harold Pinter: "The Black and White" Copyright © 1961, 1966 Harold Pinter. Reprinted by permission of Grove Press, Inc. and Methuen London.

Sophocles: *Oedipus Tyrannus* is reprinted from the Norton Critical Edition, translated and edited by Luci Berkowitz and Theodore F. Brunner. By permission of W. W. Norton & Company, Inc.

INDEX OF AUTHORS

INDEX OF TITLES AND FIRST LINES